ECONOMICS

E C O N O M I C S

UNDERSTANDING THE CANADIAN ECONOMY
FOURTH EDITION

ROY VOGT
University of Manitoba

BEVERLY J. CAMERON
University of Manitoba

EDWIN G. DOLAN
George Mason University

DRYDEN

A Division of Holt, Rinehart and Winston of Canada, Limited

Toronto Montreal Orlando Fort Worth San Diego
Philadelphia London Sydney Tokyo

Canadian Cataloguing in Publication Data
Vogt, Roy.
  Economics : understanding the Canadian economy

4th ed.
Chapters 1–16 also issued under title: Microeconomics : understanding the Canadian economy, and chapts. 1–3, 15–29 also issued under title: Macroeconomics : understanding the Canadian economy.
Includes index
ISBN 0-03-922880-0

1. Economics. 2. Canada – Economic conditions – 1971– .* I. Cameron, Beverly J. II. Dolan, Edwin G. III. Title.

HB171.5.V6 1993   330   C92-093638-5

Editorial Director	Scott Duncan
Developmental Editor	Sarah J. Duncan
Editorial Manager	Marcel Chiera
Editorial Co-ordinator	Sandra L. Meadow
Production Manager	Sue-Ann Becker
Production Co-ordinator	Denise Wake
Copy Editor	Darlene Zeleney
Interior Design	Robert Garbutt Productions
Cover Design	Dave Peters
Typesetting and Assembly	Compeer Typographic Services Limited
Printing and Binding	Arcata Graphics Company

The stamps that appear on the cover have been selected because of the important economic issues they depict. The 20-cent Trade and Development stamp © 1983, United Nations, is reproduced with the permission of the United Nations Postal Administration. The publisher wishes to thank the Stamp Marketing office of Canada Post Corporation and the United Nations Postal Administration for their assistance in obtaining these stamps.

This book was printed in the United States of America on acid-free paper.

1 2 3 4 5   97 96 95 94 93

To Ruth and Norman, for their unfailing support and encouragement — the kind of contribution the economics profession has found no way to measure.

The Dryden Canada Series in Economics

Anderson   *Regional Economic Analysis: A Canadian Perspective*

Baker   *An Introduction to International Economics*

Baumol, Blinder, Scarth   *Economics: Principles and Policy*   Third Canadian Edition

Boreham and Bodkin   *Money, Banking and Finance: The Canadian Context*   Fourth Edition

Brodie   *The Political Economy of Canadian Regionalism*

Clower, Graves, and Sexton   *Intermediate Microeconomics*

Eastman   *Labour Market Theory and the Canadian Experience*

Eckert and Leftwich   *The Price System and Resource Allocation*   Tenth Edition

Gardner   *Comparative Economic Systems*

Glahe and Lee   *Microeconomics: Theory and Applications*   Second Edition

Griffin and Steele   *Energy Economics and Policy*   Second Edition

Hirsch and Rufolo   *Public Finance and Expenditure in a Federal System*

Hirschey and Pappas   *Fundamentals of Managerial Economics*   Fourth Edition

Hyman   *Public Finance: A Contemporary Application of Theory to Policy*   Third Edition

Keating and Wilson   *Managerial Economics*   Fourth Edition

Kreinin   *International Economics: A Policy Approach*   Sixth Edition

Landsburg   *Price Theory and Applications*   Second Edition

Nicholson   *Intermediate Microeconomics and Its Application*   Fifth Edition

Nicholson   *Microeconomic Theory: Basic Principles and Extensions*   Fifth Edition

Norrie and Owram   *A History of the Canadian Economy*

Ormiston   *Intermediate Microeconomics*

Oser and Brue   *The Evolution of Economic Thought*   Fourth Edition

Pappas and Hirschey   *Managerial Economics*   Sixth Edition

Ramanathan   *Introductory Econometrics with Applications*   Second Edition

Rukstad   *Corporate Decision Making in the World Economy: Company Case Studies*

Rukstad   *Macroeconomic Decision Making in the World Economy: Text and Cases*
   Third Edition

Samuelson and Marks   *Managerial Economics*

Scarth   *Macroeconomics: An Introduction to Advanced Methods*

Smith and Spudeck   *Interest Rates: Principles and Applications*

Strick   *Canadian Public Finance*   Fourth Edition

Yarbrough and Yarbrough   *The World Economy: Trade and Finance*   Second Edition

Zimbalist, Sherman, and Brown   *Comparing Economic Systems: A Political Economic
   Approach*   Second Edition

Preface

New developments in the field of economics, as well as dramatic changes in national and international affairs, make it imperative to revise and update economics textbooks. The persistence of high levels of unemployment in Canada in recent years — not less than the apparent willingness of policy makers to risk such high levels in an attempt to combat inflation — challenges the economics profession to develop new tools of understanding and a more incisive critique of economic policy. Similar challenges arise with the development of new trading arrangements with the United States and, farther afield, with the integration of Western European economies — on the heels of the virtual disintegration of several Eastern European economies.

This fourth Canadian edition of *Economics: Understanding the Canadian Economy* has been thoroughly revised to reflect these and other changes. Before outlining the major revisions to the text, we note the basic objectives that guided us in the revision:

1. To teach students how to think as economists. This means familiarizing them with the basic principles and tools of analysis developed by the economics profession over the last several centuries. This textbook explains economic principles, and the ways in which economists think and work, in the clearest possible language.

2. To promote among students a better understanding of the operation of an actual economy.

The underlying purpose of this textbook, then, is to equip students with the tools of effective economic thinking, so that they can make sense of the workings of a modern economy. (Professional economists — particularly academics — sometimes become so engrossed in the methodological processes and demands of their craft that the ultimate goal of understanding something as concrete as a real economy seems to become secondary.) To be more precise, this textbook aims to improve the student's understanding of a particular modern economy — the *Canadian* economy. In other words, in writing this book, we have taken very seriously the lament of the great American economist Robert Solow, that "you could drop a modern economist from a time machine . . . at any time, in any place, along with his or her personal computer; he or she could set up in business without even bothering to ask what time and which place."[1] The time that we observe in *Economics* is usually the last decade (or the future), and the place is Canada.

Unique Features of the Textbook

This book explores the elements of the Canadian economy that help explain its past development and its current problems. In the process, it offers a brief survey of Canadian economic history, as well as detailed treatment of recent economic policies — some of which are altering our economy profoundly. In short, this is a textbook deeply rooted in Canada's economic experience.

The brevity and clarity of the text continue to recommend it to thousands of students and instructors. The exposition of central points of theory is not only rigorous and clear, it is also concise: No attempt is made to offer encyclopedic coverage. We believe that students become discouraged when large parts of a textbook cannot be covered in classroom discussion for lack of time.

Effective critical thinking is encouraged in the text through the use of specially designed problems based on case studies. Indeed, effective thinking is emphasized in this edition more than ever before.

New Features and Organizational Changes

- Major developments in the Canadian economy, including the high rates of unemployment of recent years, growing ecological concerns, the perceived conflict between economic efficiency and social responsibility, the new trading relationship with the United States (and possibly Mexico), and the growing concentration of industry, receive new, fuller treatment in this edition.

- The book focusses more closely on international trade (Chapter 15), and devotes an entire chapter to economic continentalism (Chapter 16).

- The concept of sustainable development, along with the controversial proposals currently under discussion for selling pollution rights, is treated for the first time in this edition (Chapter 11).

- The chapter on Third World development (Chapter 29) has been completely rewritten to include a more detailed description and more thorough critical analysis of recent development strategies.

- In Chapter 2, discussion of comparative advantage has been greatly simplified, while a more rigorous examination of the concept, together with empirical demonstrations, is contained in the chapter on international trade (Chapter 15).

- The Keynesian income–expenditure model is retained throughout much of the macroeconomic analysis, but its presentation is clarified in this edition. For example, the basic model is now cast in real terms, showing more clearly the effects of changes in prices and taxes. The 45° line is no longer referred to as

---

[1]Robert Solow, "Economic History and Economics," *American Economic Review Proceedings* (May 1985): 328–31.

a supply curve but simply as a line of reference — an equilibrium line. The aggregate-demand–aggregate-supply model has been reworked and integrated more effectively with the income–expenditure model in the examination of current macroeconomic problems (Chapters 19–21 and 27).

• The rapid and unexpected shift of the Eastern and Central European countries away from socialism and central planning means that a simple textbook treatment of specific socialist countries is no longer needed. For this reason, Chapter 30 of the third edition of this textbook has been dropped for this new edition. However, the attempt on the part of these countries to make a quick transition to a market economy — a process that turns out to be much more difficult than was perhaps anticipated — calls for a more careful treatment of the basic nature of market systems. Chapter 1 has been thoroughly revised to reflect this new situation.

• *Microeconomics now precedes macroeconomics*, in response to requests from several instructors and in accordance with the authors' own predilections.

• This textbook appears in three versions. The full text, *Economics: Understanding the Canadian Economy*, contains all 29 chapters. The text is also available in two split editions, *Microeconomics: Understanding the Canadian Economy* and *Macroeconomics: Understanding the Canadian Economy*. In response to the needs of instructors and students, however, certain chapters appear in both split editions: Chapters 1, 2, and 3, which lay the essential groundwork, and which are relevant for students of both microeconomics and macroeconomics, and Chapters 15 and 16, which cover the topics of international trade and free trade. These trade issues are often considered in both macroeconomics and microeconomics courses, so instructors using the split editions are given the flexibility to teach these topics in either course.

    Users of the split editions will have no difficulty locating material in the textbook's ancillaries, as the chapter and page numbers in the split editions are exactly the same as in the combined text.

Pedagogy

Perhaps the most important single change in this edition is the new emphasis on *effective thinking*. In today's large classes, the temptation is to test students' *knowledge*, through multiple-choice questions, but to leave their ability to *think* largely unchallenged. The authors of this fourth edition have worked hard to remedy this defect. While considerable reliance is still placed on straightforward problem-solving questions — indeed, hundreds of new questions have been added to the textbook and the test bank — the really new feature is the addition, in the text, of six *effective-thinking questions*. These questions have been scattered evenly throughout the book (three in the macro section and three in the micro), each following textual material that lends itself particularly well to this learning approach. Specifically, the questions are found at the end of Chapters 4, 9, 11, 18, 21, and 26. Suggested solutions to the problems are given at the back of the book, while an explanation of the basic approach to effective thinking, along with a sample problem, is provided in the appendix to Chapter 3. Problems such as these have undergone successful classroom trials, and represent, in the authors' opinion, a minimal but essential effort to improve students' economic thinking. The appointment of Beverly Cameron as a co-author of this edition of *Economics* reflects our increased commitment to a more effective pedagogy.

As noted, many new questions have also been added in the Review Questions section at the end of most chapters. A new feature of this edition is the inclusion, at the back of the book, of the answers to about half of these new questions, a feature that increases the value of the textbook as a learning tool. (The answers to the remaining questions are provided in the instructor's manual.)

Another pedagogical improvement featured in this edition is the use of colour in the graphs: Red is used consistently for supply curves and blue for demand curves. (Please refer to the section called "About the Colours," on page xix, which describes how and why the colours are used.) In addition, we have incorporated a logo into the design of the book, which not only signals the start of each new part and chapter, but is also used to highlight "key boxes" throughout the text, in order to assist students in determining the most important graphs and tables in a chapter. (Key boxes are also listed at the end of each chapter.)

The authors and publishers feel confident that instructors and students will find this fourth edition a valuable teaching and learning tool.

ACKNOWLEDGEMENTS

We have been extremely fortunate in receiving assistance from many quarters in the preparation of this fourth Canadian edition. It is a pleasure to acknowledge that assistance here.

First, we thank Edwin G. Dolan for his past contributions to this textbook. Although the Canadian authors are solely responsible for this edition, much of the theoretical framework still owes its shape and simplicity to Edwin Dolan.

Next, we want to thank the reviewers who commented on various drafts of the manuscript and suggested countless improvements. We were able to respond positively to a large number of them, and we hope they will recognize their contribution in the final version of this edition. These reviewers are P.L. Arya, St. Mary's University; Emanuel Carvalho, University of Waterloo; George J. De Benedetti, Mount Allison University; Byron Eastman, Laurentian University; Peter Fortura, Algonquin College; Donald Garrie, Georgian College of Applied Arts and Technology; Brenda Gayle-Anyiwe, Seneca College of Applied Arts and Technology; Cyril Grant, St. Francis Xavier University; Ibrahim Hayani, Seneca College of Applied Arts and Technology; Ron McDonald, Mohawk College of Applied Arts and Technology; Rohinton Medhora, University of Toronto; Ian Parker, University of Toronto; Dagmar Rajagopal, Ryerson Polytechnical Institute; Stephen Rakoczy, Humber College of Applied Arts and Technology; Vivienne Saverimuttu, University of Manitoba; Marlyce Searcy, SIAST; M.S. Shedd, University of Calgary; Peter W. Sinclair, Wilfrid Laurier University.

A special debt of thanks is owed to Charles E. Wales of West Virginia University for his advice and for permission to use the guided-design (effective-thinking) problem-solving technique featured in this text.

We would also like to thank the excellent staff of HBJ-Holt, particularly the following: Scott Duncan, who set the plans for the fourth edition in motion; Sarah Duncan, who oversaw its development and patiently accommodated our numerous rounds of revision; and Sandy Meadow, Darlene Zeleney, Sue-Ann Becker, and Denise Wake, who carefully guided the book through production to publication. All their help and encouragement is greatly appreciated.

Finally, we thank the thousands of students we have taught over the course of the last few decades, who have shown us both the possibilities and the limitations of introductory economic analysis.

Roy Vogt and Beverly Cameron

PUBLISHER'S NOTE TO STUDENTS AND INSTRUCTORS

This textbook is a key component of your course. If you are the instructor of this course, you undoubtedly considered a number of texts carefully before choosing this as the one that would work best for your students and you. The authors and publishers spent considerable time and money to ensure its high quality, and we appreciate your recognition of this effort and accomplishment. Please note the copyright statement.

If you are a student, we are confident that this textbook will help you meet the objectives of your course. It will also become a valuable addition to your personal library.

Since we want to hear what you think about this book, please be sure to send us the stamped reply card at the end of the book. Your input will help us to continue to publish high-quality textbooks for your courses.

About the Colours

Graphing is an important element in the study of economics. Graphs are used to illustrate many essential and often complex points, and students may find them a difficult component to grasp. We have addressed this difficulty by adopting a deliberate and consistent approach to the use of colour throughout the graphic material in the book. The significance of each of the colours as they are used in the graphs is outlined below. (These colours have also been used in other elements throughout the book, without special significance, but to enhance the book's appearance and functionality.)

BLUE

- demand
- all generally downward-sloping curves
- marginal revenue

RED

- supply
- all generally upward-sloping curves
- marginal costs

PURPLE

- average curves

GREEN

- this colour is not used to illustrate particular economic concepts, but simply to differentiate visual elements

Contents in Brief

Contents

This textbook appears in three versions. The full text, Economics: Understanding the Canadian Economy, *contains all 29 chapters, as listed below. The split edition entitled* Microeconomics: Understanding the Canadian Economy *contains Chapters 1–16. The split edition entitled* Macroeconomics: Understanding the Canadian Economy *contains Chapters 1–3 and 15–29.*

PART TWO · THE THEORY OF PRICE AND OUTPUT DETERMINATION

PART THREE • MARKET FAILURE

PART FOUR • FACTOR MARKETS AND INCOME DISTRIBUTION

PART FIVE • CANADA IN THE INTERNATIONAL MARKET

PART SIX • UNDERSTANDING A NATIONAL ECONOMY: MACROECONOMICS

PART SEVEN • STABILIZATION PROBLEMS AND STRATEGIES

PART EIGHT • THE GLOBAL ECONOMY

ECONOMICS

Overview of Economics and the Canadian Economy

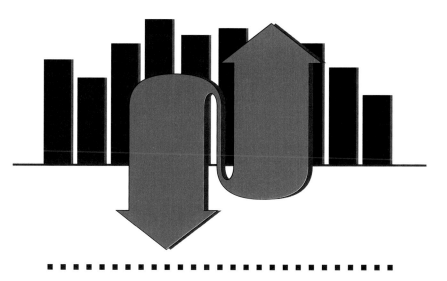

What Economics Is All About

After studying this chapter, you will be able to

1. Describe the basic features of an economy.
2. Define the terms *scarcity* and *economics*.
3. Discuss the functions of markets and economic planning.
4. Define the terms *socialism* and *capitalism*.
5. Define the terms *microeconomics* and *macroeconomics*.
6. Explain the use of theories and models in economics.
7. Distinguish between positive and normative economics and explain why this distinction is important.

A Preview   *What Went Wrong with Socialism?*

The restructuring of the Eastern European socialist economies may be the greatest economic experiment of our generation. Where did socialism go wrong? A Soviet economist suggested that the problem began with a faulty understanding of human nature.

Soviet Theorist Faults Karl Marx for Poor Reading of Human Nature

According to Aleksandr Tsipko, a consultant in the International Department of the Soviet Central Committee, "We [the USSR] have paid dearly for our neglect of man's true nature." Tsipko blames Karl Marx for misinterpreting human nature and as a result failing to understand the sources of human behaviour. Moreover, he attributes the current economic and social crisis in the Soviet Union to the application of Marx's mistaken ideas. The recognition that the Soviet approach was wrong, he wrote in *Politicheskoe obrazovanie* (no. 4, 1989), "is forcing us to rethink what is man and what is society."

The subject is timely. It is widely recognized that the Soviet economic system has failed to find a way of motivating the population to think creatively and work conscientiously. Mikhail Gorbachev has repeatedly said that the country's malaise can be cured only by "activating the human factor" — that is, by enhancing the role of the individual in the economy and the political process.

"Faulty Blueprint"

Soviet ideologists long ago warned against exaggerating the role of the individual in Soviet society and recoiled with horror from the idea that people should be motivated to work by financial reward and self-interest. The Bolsheviks' concept of what socialism should be like, Tsipko wrote, led to the construction of Soviet society according to "a faulty blueprint." Instead of liberating human energies, the Soviet system strangled them at birth. The result, he said, has been "a crisis of labour motivation such as the world has never before seen." Human beings think and work creatively, Tsipko wrote, only when they are free, independent, and motivated by self-interest.

SOURCE: From Radio Free Europe/ Radio Liberty, *Soviet/East European Report* 6, no. 36 (September 10, 1989).

ECONOMICS: A STUDY OF HUMAN BEHAVIOUR

Economist Aleksandr Tsipko's comments attributing the former Soviet Union's economic problems to socialism's failure to understand human nature point to the basic definition of economics as *a study of human behaviour*. The study of economics rests on two fundamental assumptions about human beings:

1. All human beings need some of the earth's resources in order to survive.

2. The supply of these resources is limited. This is known in economics as the problem of **scarcity**. Because of this problem, human beings have to make choices, and economies have to find ways to ration resources among the competing claims of different individuals and groups. If all the things people need were available in unlimited amounts, there would be no economic problem.

Scarcity
A situation in which there is not enough of a resource to meet all of people's wants and needs.

Economics can thus be defined as the study of the choices people make and the actions they take as they attempt to match up scarce resources with their virtually unlimited wants and needs.

People create economies to help them meet their needs. An **economy** consists of the ideas, institutions, rules, and factors of production by means of which a society attempts to satisfy the needs of its members. One may compare different *types* of economies, such as socialism and capitalism, or different national or regional economies, such as those of Canada and the United States or of Ontario and Quebec. Our purpose in this textbook is to study the ways in which people attempt to solve the problem of scarcity, both in theory and in the context of particular economies — especially our own.

Economics
The study of the choices people make and the actions they take in order to make the best use of scarce resources in meeting their wants and needs.

An economy
The set of ideas, institutions, rules, and factors of production by means of which a society attempts to satisfy the needs of its members.

THE BASIC ELEMENTS OF AN ECONOMY
Ideas

People tend to form their societies around a core of shared ideas, which usually include some definition of acceptable behaviour, theories about the ownership and distribution of society's resources, criteria defining "success," and beliefs about the role of the individual versus the group. These fundamental ideas of a society are often referred to as its **ideology**.

A society's ideology has a profound impact on the organization and performance of its economy. Should property be owned by the state or by private individuals? Should individuals be encouraged to compete or to co-operate with one another? The way a society answers such questions will have much to do with the way in which its economy develops.

In the Preview, Aleksandr Tsipko argues that the failure of the former Soviet economy to satisfy the needs of Soviet citizens can be traced back to the ideas of nineteenth-century economist Karl Marx. As we have already noted, economics is a study of human behaviour, and the ideas it produces about human nature may determine how people are expected to behave in a society. The case of the socialist economies illustrates that these ideas can also determine how people are *allowed* to behave.

Ideology
The shared ideas about acceptable forms of behaviour and goals around which a society is formed.

PROFILE   Karl Marx, Economist and Socialist

Karl Marx
(1818–1883)

Karl Marx — German philosopher, revolutionary, and patron saint of socialism — was also a well-known economist. From the age of 31, he lived and worked in London. His thinking was strongly influenced by the British classical school of economics, and especially by the writings of David Ricardo, a follower of Adam Smith. But whereas economists of the classical school were, for the most part, sympathetic to the capitalist system, Marx took the tools of classical economics and turned them against capitalism.

In his massive work *Das Kapital*, Marx tried to show that capitalism was headed for collapse and that it would be followed by a socialist revolution. All his life he worked with revolutionary groups to prepare for that day. He believed the revolution would make way for an economy based on collective ownership and economic planning. He gave the name *communism* to the highest form of socialism, toward which the revolution would strive. In this century, the terms *communism* and *socialism* have been used to describe the economic systems of the Soviet Union, most Eastern and Central European countries, China, and other countries that followed Marxist principles.

Marx was not the first socialist, and not all socialists are followers of Marx. Still, he must be regarded as the most influential thinker in the history of socialism and one of the most influential economists of all time.

With the success of the Russian Revolution in 1917, the ideas of Karl Marx came to play a central role in the design and establishment of a new Soviet economy (see the accompanying Profile on Marx). From Marx, the Soviet leaders (first Lenin, then Stalin) took ideas promoting, for example, state ownership of real property and the means of production, the elimination of profit, and the control of production and distribution through central planning. Like many social scientists in the West, Marx also taught that the behaviour of human beings is largely determined by their environment. A competitive society promoting individual accomplishment will, according to this view, produce competitive, industrious people. By contrast, a society in which competition is discouraged in favour of co-operation, and personal achievement is considered secondary to the advancement of society, should, in time, produce equally industrious but co-operative individuals concerned primarily with the collective good.

Marx's ideas strongly influenced not only the Soviet Union but a large number of other socialist countries. In contrast, most Western countries, including Canada, shaped their economies according to a very different ideology, founded on the teachings of an eighteenth-century economist, Adam Smith (see the accompanying Profile). Smith argued that human nature is such that individuals will be more industrious and creative when they are free to pursue their own interests in competition with others.

Who was right about human nature, Marx or Smith? Since the socialist economies that relied heavily on Marxist principles now appear to have failed rather dismally, and since Smith's ideas provided the ideology for the more successful capitalist economies, it would seem that the question has been settled in favour of Adam Smith. This is the conclusion of the Soviet economist quoted in the Preview, and it is supported by the majority of citizens of the formerly Communist countries of Eastern Europe, who feel that their economies can be revived only by means of a rapid transition to a system of free enterprise, based on private ownership and the pursuit of economic gain.

There are some individuals, however, in both the East and the West, who find this conclusion disturbing. Does economic success, they wonder, really depend on

Adam Smith on Human Nature

Adam Smith is the founder of economics as a distinct field of study. He wrote only one book on the subject, *The Wealth of Nations*, published in 1776 when Smith was 53 years old. His friend David Hume found the book such hard going that he doubted many people would read it. But Hume was wrong.

    The wealth of nations, in Smith's view, comes not from gold or silver, as many people supposed at the time, but rather from ordinary people's working and trading in free markets. Furthermore, the remarkable thing about the wealth produced by a market economy is that it is the result not of any organized plan, but of the actions of many people, each pursuing the incentives offered by the market with his or her own interests in mind. In Smith's words,

> It is not from the benevolence of the butcher, the brewer, or the baker that we expect our dinner, but from their regard to their own interest. . . . Every individual is continually exerting himself to find out the most advantageous employment for whatever capital he can command. . . . By directing that industry in such a manner as its produce may be of greatest value, he intends only his own gain, and he is in this, as in many other cases, led by an invisible hand to promote an end which was no part of his intention.

SOURCE: Adam Smith, *The Wealth of Nations*, 1776, Book 1, Chap. 2.

Adam Smith
(1723–1790)

the encouragement of human selfishness? Is it true that people are incapable of being responsible and productive for other than selfish reasons? Although the recent collapse of the major socialist economies has been interpreted by many as a sufficient answer to such questions, all the evidence may not, in fact, be in. To what extent did the socialist countries, in their brief history and under the iron rule of strong dictators, really have a chance to teach and practise an ideology of co-operation? Adam Smith may indeed have been right, but history so far has not proven it conclusively: the failure of people to be highly productive and creative while being cowed into submission by brutal dictators seems hardly to be a satis-factory test of the alternative theories of Karl Marx.

Institutions

A society's ideas about organizing its economy must be realized through appropri-ate institutions. Several types of institutions are important to most economies. They include the following:

1. *Households:* Individuals or families living as separate units.

2. *Production Organizations:* Business firms, farms, schools, hospitals, and so on, that produce a product or provide a service.

3. *Promoters of Ideology:* Schools, religious organizations, and special-interest groups (such as political parties and chambers of commerce) that develop and spread the ideas that constitute a society's ideology.

4. *Rule Setters and Enforcers:* Governments, courts, and professional associa-tions that use their power to translate a society's ideology into effective rules of behaviour.

The market
The network of business dealings through which a society's production and distribution decisions are co-ordinated.

5. ***Co-ordinators of Economic Activity:*** In a free-market economy, the thousands of individuals and business units who, in their daily commercial transactions, decide which goods and services to produce and how to distribute them. The arena in which they interact is the whole economy: it embraces all the decisions made about production and distribution and is referred to simply as **the market**.

The market is not a particular place but the entire network of business dealings through which, in an economy such as Canada's, decisions about what will be produced and how it will be distributed are co-ordinated. Adam Smith wrote that this unplanned co-ordination of production and distribution was guided by an "invisible hand." Visitors from another planet observing an economy such as Canada's for the first time might very well ask, "Who is in charge of this economy? Who decides how many houses will be built so that there will be neither too many nor too few, or how much food will be shipped to Toronto on a given morning?" The answer is that no single person or business firm makes such decisions. All the firms in a particular industry make guesses — some more thoroughly researched than others — in response to signals they have received from the market as to what and how much of their product or service are demanded. Through the workings of the "invisible hand" of the market, these thousands of individual, self-interested decisions succeed in meeting the needs of society through the efficient allocation of scarce resources.

A market is any arrangement people have for trading with one another. Some markets, like the Toronto Stock Exchange, are highly visible and organized. Others, like the word-of-mouth networks that put teenage baby-sitters in touch with people who need their services, do their work informally, out of sight. Whether visible or not, markets play a key role in putting scarce resources to their best uses in meeting people's wants and needs. Markets accomplish this by fulfilling three essential tasks.

The first task is *transmitting information*. In order to put resources to their best possible uses, the people who make decisions must know which resources are scarcest and which uses for them are best. Markets transmit information about scarcity and resource values in the form of prices. If a good becomes scarcer, its price is bid up. The rising price signals buyers to cut back on the amount of that good they buy, and it signals producers to find new sources of supply or substitute less costly resources. If a good becomes more abundant, its price tends to fall. The falling price signals users to favour that good over more costly ones.

The second task that markets perform is *providing incentives*. It is not enough to know the best use for scarce resources; people must have an incentive to use them in the best way. Markets offer many kinds of incentives. Consumers who are well informed and spend their money wisely achieve a higher standard of living with their limited budgets. Workers who stay alert to job opportunities and work where they can be most productive earn the highest income they can. And profits provide an incentive for business managers to improve production methods and to tailor their goods to the needs of consumers. The importance of the market as a source of incentives led Adam Smith to call it an "invisible hand" that nudges people into the roles they can play best in the economy. (See the accompanying Profile.)

The third task of markets is *distributing income*. People who have useful skills or own scarce resources receive high incomes if they put those skills and resources to the best possible use. People who have fewer skills or resources to sell receive lower incomes, even if they make just as great an effort to use wisely what they have. Businesspeople who take risks and guess right make large profits; those who take risks and guess wrong suffer losses. In short, the market distributes income according to the value of each person's contribution to the production process — and not always in proportion to the effort required to make that contribution.

Markets reward those who understand them and know how to use them. Unfortunately, as we shall see in later chapters, they can sometimes be manipulated and controlled by powerful individuals or institutions who in pursuit of their own self-interest may hinder others in the pursuit of theirs. The same Adam Smith who praised the virtues of markets lamented the tendency of businesspeople to control markets in their favour. He observed: "When, by an increase in demand, the market price of some particular commodity happens to rise a good deal, those who employ their stocks [resources] in supplying that market are generally careful to conceal this change [because] the market price would soon be reduced."[1] When the market is not free to provide correct information it will also fail to reward people appropriately.

In socialist economies, production and distribution decisions are most often co-ordinated in a different way — through **economic planning**. Instead of relying on the private decisions of hundreds of thousands of firms to meet society's needs for particular products, socialist countries, following the ideas of Marx, Lenin, and others, decided to put these decisions into the hands of government planning agencies. In all countries, including Canada, governments are involved in the economy to some extent and have some say in the production, regulation, and pricing of certain products and services. Economic planning, however, refers to comprehensive and systematic efforts by government to determine the output and distribution of society's resources. It represents a distinct alternative to market co-ordination and has historically signalled one of the most important differences between so-called capitalist and socialist economies: Capitalist economies have relied mostly on the market to co-ordinate economic activity, while socialist countries have relied mainly on economic planning.

> **Economic planning**
> Systematic intervention in the economy by government with the goal of improving co-ordination.

Rules

Rules include the laws and codes of behaviour that support certain rights and duties essential to the proper functioning of an economy. The duty to fulfil contracts and the right to own property are two important features of the Canadian economy that require the support of enforceable rules.

Factors of Production

The three basic inputs required to produce goods and services are called **factors of production**. They include labour, capital, and natural resources. **Labour** consists of the productive contributions made by people working with their minds

> **Factors of production**
> The three basic inputs used in producing all goods and services — labour, capital, and natural resources.

> **Labour**
> The contributions to production made by people working with their minds and their bodies.

---

[1]Adam Smith, *The Wealth of Nations*, Book 1, Chap. 7.

Capital
All means of production created by people, including tools, industrial equipment, and structures.

Natural resources
Anything that can be used as a productive input in its natural state, such as farmland, building sites, forests, and mineral deposits.

and their bodies. **Capital** consists of all the productive inputs created by people, including tools, machinery, structures, and such intangible items as computer programs. **Natural resources** include everything that can be used as a productive input in its natural state, such as farmland, building sites, forests, and mineral deposits. For example, the factors of production used in producing this book included the labour of the authors and the editors; capital in the form of word processors and printing presses; and natural resources in the form of energy to run the printing presses and pulpwood to make the paper.

HOW ECONOMIES DIFFER

All economies combine the three factors of production — labour, capital, and natural resources — in the production of the goods and services required by their populations. In this respect, all economies are fundamentally the same.

Economic system
A type of economy characterized by a particular ideology and particular institutions and rules.

Socialism
An economic system based on co-operation and the advancement of the society as a whole, centrally planned co-ordination of production and distribution, and communal ownership of capital and land.

Capitalism
An economic system based on competition and individual achievement, market co-ordination of production and distribution, and private ownership of capital and land.

Economies that follow different ideologies, develop different institutions, and formulate different rules of economic behaviour are said to differ *systematically.* Conversely, different national economies, such as those of Canada and the United States, may be said to belong to the same **economic system** if they follow the same ideology and develop similar institutions and rules. Based on these three distinguishing marks — ideology, institutions, and rules — it is possible to define more precisely terms such as *socialism* and *capitalism*, which we have used rather loosely thus far.

We can now define **socialism** as an economic system in which co-operation and the advancement of the society as a whole are stressed; planning institutions exist to co-ordinate centrally the production and distribution of goods; and two of the factors of production, capital and land (natural resources), are owned communally, either by the government or by associations of workers supported by the government.

Capitalism is an economic system in which competition and individual achievement are stressed, the market is relied upon to co-ordinate most production and distribution decisions, and capital and land are owned largely by private individuals or firms. (Labour is privately "owned" under both capitalism and socialism, meaning that workers in both systems have considerable freedom in choosing a vocation and perhaps even a particular type of job.)

There are, of course, more elements that distinguish these two economic systems from each other, but even this short list of fundamental differences provides some clues as to why it is so difficult to change from one system to the other, as the former Soviet republics and several other Eastern European countries are in the process of doing. It is necessary to change not only laws and institutions but deeply ingrained ways of thinking and modes of behaviour as well.

BASIC ECONOMIC DECISIONS AND THE CANADIAN ECONOMY

Economists have identified three basic decisions that every economy must make. They are as follows:

1. *What to produce*

2. *How to produce*

3. *For whom to produce*

Chapter 2 describes in greater detail how, and how successfully, these decisions are being made in Canada. The preceding discussion tells us that the way these decisions are made in Canada must be consistent with the type of economic system that has developed in this country. As we know, Canada is, in most important respects, a capitalist country, similar to the United States and Western European countries. In Canada, the promoters of ideology encourage competition and individual achievement; privately owned institutions determine what to produce and how to produce it, co-ordinating their decisions through the market; and goods and services are produced for those who can pay. This, however, is only the broad picture; it will be modified — sometimes significantly — by the details that we introduce in subsequent chapters. What is often most interesting and most important about the Canadian economy is the ways in which it departs from the basic model: Governments in this country in fact play a crucial role at many points in the economic process, and citizens welcome various types of government intervention. In other words, Canadians have historically found it to be desirable and necessary to place various restrictions on the operation of the market.

WHAT ECONOMISTS DO

A well-known member of the profession once jokingly defined economics as "what economists do." Just what is it that economists do? In the broadest sense, they study the ways in which people deal with the problem of scarcity. But as a preview of the contents of this book, let's take a more detailed look at what economists do. We begin with the distinction between *microeconomics* and *macroeconomics*.

Microeconomics

The prefix *micro* comes from the Greek word meaning "small." **Microeconomics** is the branch of economics that deals with the choices made by small economic units — that is, households, business firms, and units of government.

> **Microeconomics**
> The branch of economics that deals with the choices and actions of small economic units — that is, households, business firms, and units of government.

In economics, a *household* is a group of people who pool their incomes, own property in common, and make economic decisions jointly. People who do not belong to such a group are counted as one-person households.

Households play two major roles in the economy: They supply inputs that are used to produce goods and services, and they consume the goods and services that are produced.

Business firms are the second basic unit of microeconomic analysis. Firms buy factors of production from households and use them to produce goods and services. Firms come in many shapes and sizes. There are now more than one million business firms in Canada. These range from small stores and family farms to huge corporations. Chapter 3 will discuss the role of business firms in more detail.

Microeconomics also studies the actions of such units of government as federal and provincial agencies. As we will see throughout this book, units of government have a major impact on the economic life of firms and households.

Jobs held by microeconomists

To say that they study households, firms, and markets is one way to answer the question of what microeconomists do, but the question can be answered in another way as well. We can also look at what microeconomists do for a living — that is, at the kinds of jobs they hold.

Many microeconomists hold jobs in private firms. For example, an insurance company might employ economists to study the impact of economic trends on the insurance industry and to design new kinds of insurance policies to meet changing customer needs. An electric utility might employ economists to prepare proposals for rate changes. A trade association that represents the natural-gas industry might employ economists to analyze the impact of changes in government regulations. In these examples, the economist is employed by business as a specialist. In other cases, people trained in microeconomics rise to positions in the firm's general management.

Thousands of microeconomists are employed by government. Government regulation of business is the source of many of these jobs. The economists who work for insurance companies, electric utilities, gas pipelines, and the like find government economists working on the other side of every issue. Government economists often work closely with lawyers in cases that have to do with issues such as regulation, equal opportunity, and international trade disputes. While the lawyer interprets the laws that apply to the case, the economist analyzes the effects on prices, markets, incomes, and jobs.

Finally, many economists work for colleges, universities, and research institutes. Many divide their time between teaching and research into problems of economic theory. Academic economists do quite a bit of applied research as well. Business and law firms and government agencies often hire them as consultants, rather than employing full-time economists of their own.

Macroeconomics

Macroeconomics
The branch of economics that deals with large-scale economic phenomena, especially inflation, unemployment, and economic growth.

The prefix *macro* comes from the Greek work meaning "large." Thus, **macroeconomics** refers to the study of large-scale economic phenomena, especially inflation, unemployment, and economic growth. These phenomena result from the combined effects of millions of microeconomic choices made by households, firms, and units of government. Definitions and measurements of inflation, unemployment, and growth are provided in Chapter 2. The economic theories that explain the behaviour of these macroeconomic phenomena are explored in the second half of the textbook.

Jobs held by macroeconomists

Like microeconomists, macroeconomists hold jobs in business, government, and universities.

Business macroeconomists are hired to advise managers on potential changes in the national economy. Such knowledge is often crucial to the survival of the firm. As just one example, take the case of the residential construction industry. People's ability to buy houses depends on their income and on the interest rates at which they can obtain mortgage loans. Firms in every part of the home-building industry — construction, lumber, other building supplies, and so on — can benefit from knowledge about economic trends and policies. We will see shortly that it is not easy to forecast economic trends. But even when reliable forecasts are impossible, economists can help managers make plans based on a set of "what if" projections. What is true of the housing industry is true of other industries as well — consumer goods, banking, transportation, and so on.

Government agencies also employ macroeconomists to aid in planning and forecasting. In addition, thousands of economists are employed by the units of government responsible for macroeconomic policy. The Bank of Canada, which guides monetary policy, is a major employer of macroeconomists. The departments of finance of the federal and provincial governments also employ numerous economists.

Finally, many macroeconomists are employed by colleges, universities, and research institutes. Like academic microeconomists, they divide their time among teaching, research, and consulting.

Specialized Fields in Economics

As the discipline of economics has developed over the years, it has spawned several areas of specialization. There are economists who utilize the insights of micro- and macroeconomics, as well as ideas and techniques from other disciplines, to examine specific sets of problems. *Development economists*, for example, are concerned with the special problems of the less-developed countries of the world; *labour economists* examine the functions of labour unions and the complex bargaining relationships between labour and management; and *resource economists* are hired by government and private agencies to deal with the special problems associated with resources such as oil, gas, electricity, and timber.

Economic historians — one more of a large variety of specialists in economics — are, in a sense, development economists trying to understand the growth process of economies in the past. The Canadian economy, as will be noted more fully in Chapter 3, has emerged in its present form as the result of a wide range of social, political, geographical, *and* economic forces. Canadian economic historians such as Harold Adams Innis, whose work is highlighted in the accompanying Profile, have helped to shed some light on Canada's current economic problems (such as our dependence on foreign trade and investment and our regional disparities and economic instability) through their analyses of the early stages of Canadian economic development.

WHY ECONOMISTS SOMETIMES DISAGREE

Economists have borne the brunt of many jokes for their tendency to disagree with one another. George Bernard Shaw complained that if you took all the economists in the world and laid them end to end, they wouldn't reach a conclusion. Harry Truman begged for a one-armed economist — he was tired of those with two arms, because all they could tell him was, "On the one hand, . . . and then on the other hand, . . ." The noted economist Frank H. Knight, addressing the American Economics Association, once remarked, "I have been increasingly moved to wonder whether economists . . . should cover their faces or burst into laughter when they meet on the street."

One could say that economists are no worse than members of other professions. Physicists disagree about the origin of the universe. Doctors disagree about how to treat heart disease and breast cancer. Teachers disagree about the merits of new math versus old math. So why all the economist jokes?

The idea that economists can't agree has sprung, in part, from the simple fact that disagreements make the news and agreements don't. (In fact, economists agree on many things — perhaps even too many. Critics within the profession often complain about the widespread acceptance of certain "orthodox" views.) But the jokes about disagreements among economists have deeper roots than the fact that controversy is news. In the rest of this chapter, we will discuss some of the main causes of disagreements among economists under the headings of theory and reality, forecasting, and positive versus normative economics.

Theory and Reality

One reason economists are said to be unable to agree is that they do not deal with "reality." Another old joke makes this point: A physicist, a chemist, and an economist are shipwrecked on an island, with nothing to eat but a case of canned beans. How to open the cans? The physicist suggests using a mirror to focus the sun's rays on the cans, thereby expanding the contents and bursting the cans. The chemist suggests dipping the cans in seawater until they rust through. When the economist is asked for an idea, he says, "First, let's assume that we have a can opener."

Yes, economic theory is full of "unrealistic" assumptions. It has to be, for the simple reason that economic reality is extremely complex. To take just one example, suppose an economist is asked what effect a tax cut will have on total spending by consumers. There are hundreds of millions of consumers. Their spending depends on their moods, their hopes, their fears, their health, and the weather; on interest rates, bank regulations, and what new products are on the market; on wages, fringe benefits, lottery winnings, and — the list could go on, but we've probably made our point.

PROFILE   *Harold Adams Innis and Canadian Economic History*

Harold Adams Innis
(1894–1952)

Many Canadian scholars regard Harold Adams Innis as the most original and influential economist this country has produced. He brought to the study of Canadian economic history a restless and original mind, and the theories he expounded were supported by thorough empirical research. He influenced a wide range of social scientists through his prolific writings and his teaching and leadership at the University of Toronto.

His three major works were published at ten-year intervals: *The Fur Trade in Canada: An Introduction to Canadian Economic History* in 1930; *The Cod Fisheries: The History of an International Economy* in 1940; and *Empire and Communications* in 1950. He wrote dozens of other books and articles, but these three works illustrate most clearly the development of his approach to economic history, and the wealth of his ideas.

In his book on the fur trade, Innis examined the factors that shaped the growth of one of Canada's earliest industries and, in turn, the ways in which that industry influenced the creation of a unique Canadian nation. He emphasized the role of geography and technology in the rapid westward expansion of the fur trade, the importance of foreign markets, the high overhead costs involved in creating an effective transportation system, and the effects of the physical characteristics of the furs traded on the organization and stability of the economy. For example, because the beaver was easily caught, the supply of beaver skins in eastern Canada was quickly depleted, forcing hunters to move farther and farther westward. This resulted in a far-flung trading network, vulnerable to attacks from rivals and requiring substantial transportation outlays.

Innis applied a similar approach to the analysis of economic and social change in his other major works. In his study of another staple industry, the cod fisheries, he again focussed on the dependence of the industry on foreign markets; the impact of new technology (in this case, of iron, steam, and refrigeration); and the search for protection after periods of vigorous competition.

Following his work on the fisheries, Innis planned to make a similar study of another major industry, pulp and paper. But the more he examined this industry, the more impressed he became with the profound impact that communications media (such as newspapers) had on society, and the less able he felt to deal with the industry from a purely economic perspective. During the 1940s, he plunged into an intensive, far-ranging study of the ways in which communications media have influenced the growth and decline of civilizations. For example, in media such as stone and parchment, he detected what he called a "time bias." Societies using such media tended to restrict the enlargement of their boundaries and to foster traditions and political organizations that favoured stability over time. Eventually, such groups might be successfully invaded from outside by societies that favoured media with a "spatial bias," such as papyrus, paper, and printing. The latter societies, which would include the Roman Empire and modern Europe, were characterized by the tendency to move quickly over space, conquering territories devoted to stability and "time." However, these more aggressive societies made themselves vulnerable to new forces emerging at the boundaries of their far-flung empires. Internally, their neglect of time and tradition forced them to adopt measures favouring greater social cohesion, political centralization, and monopoly.

Innis recorded these ideas in his last major work, *Empire and Communications*. After his death in 1952, his ideas continued to influence scholars in numerous disciplines. In particular, they formed the basis for the famous work of Marshall McLuhan. McLuhan's well-known statement "The medium is the message" is closely linked to Innis's observation that the physical nature of a staple product or communications medium profoundly affects the economic, social, and political life of society.

In answering the question, the economist would not try to make a complete list of the things that influence consumer spending. Instead, he or she would try to identify the factors that have the greatest influence and to use them as the basis for a *theory*. In economics, as in other fields, a **theory** is an explanation of how facts are related. A mathematical or graphic rendition of an economic theory is called a **model**.

Theory
An explanation of how facts are related.

There is, in fact, a theory about the effects of tax cuts on consumer spending. It says that the change in consumer spending will depend on the amount by which the tax cut raises consumers' after-tax income and on the length of time consumers expect the tax cut to remain in effect. In proposing such a theory, economists don't deny that other things affect consumer spending; they simply suggest that of all the things that matter, it is most useful to focus on these two.

Model
A mathematical or graphic version of an economic theory.

It is clear, though, that this approach contains the seeds of many disagreements. One economist's model of consumer spending might take only the two factors just mentioned into account. Another's model might also take into account whether the tax cut has a greater effect on upper-income or middle-income consumers. Which theory is better? Economists try to test competing theories by seeing which one does a better job of explaining the phenomenon in question. But the tests are not always conclusive. Data on past events may not be reliable. One model may explain the events of one period very well, whereas another may be better suited to the events of a different period. Before the dispute is resolved, someone else may propose a third theory that challenges both models.

In addition to a large core of "mainstream" economists who try to understand economic reality by reducing its complexity to a few simple assumptions, there are other economists — economic historians among them — who attempt to deal with this reality in a more comprehensive way. They too build models by focussing on some causal factors and not others, but they consider a much broader range of data, including speculations about the possible influences of the particular political and social institutions of the economy in question. Because of the broader data base and the inclusion of social and political factors, the models used by such economists are difficult to formulate in mathematical terms, and are therefore usually expressed in words. For this reason, they may seem to lack the scientific character of the other models. Nevertheless, the work of these economists may be considered a legitimate way of trying to explain the complex reality that faces all economists. There are hundreds of economists in North America today (in addition to economic historians) who are committed to this type of economic analysis. Some call themselves **institutionalists**, because they are particularly interested in the impact of social and political institutions on economic behaviour. Others refer to themselves as **Marxists**, because their model of economic change is based at least partly on the insights of Karl Marx. These various groups of scholars publish their own journals and carry on their own agenda of economic research.

Institutionalists and Marxists
Economists who work with models that use a wide range of data, including the effects of the prevailing social and political institutions, to explain economic behaviour.

Forecasting

An economic theory is a good one if it correctly explains the relationships among two or more key facts. Such theories often help us understand past economic events. For example, in later chapters, we will present theories that provide useful insights into the causes of the high inflation rates of the late 1970s. But even the best economic theories are limited in their ability to help us foretell the future.

Economic theory does allow us to make statements that take the form, "If A, then B, other things being equal." Most economists would agree with the statement "If income taxes are lowered, consumers will spend more, provided that the many other factors that affect spending don't change in the meantime." It is a short step from this sort of statement to a **conditional forecast**, which is simply an if–then statement about the future. For example, an economist might say that if income tax rates are cut by 10 percent in July 1996, total consumer spending will rise by $10 billion in 1996, $12 billion 1997, and $14 billion in 1998, other things being equal.

Conditional forecast
A prediction of future economic events, stated in the form, "If A, then B, other things being equal."

Why are economic forecasts such a source of controversy? One reason, clearly, is that forecasters are often wrong.

Forecasters must always assume some things about government economic policy and even the performance of other economies, and when these things change unexpectedly, their forecasts can go seriously wrong. Forecasters also often disagree among themselves; it is not uncommon for one forecaster to be predicting recession while another predicts continued expansion.

But not all of the problem lies with the forecasters. Part of it lies with the way forecasts are reported to the public. On television and in the newspapers, forecasts are often reported in the form "This is how it will be," rather than in the form "If A, then B, other things being equal." In addition, it is not always made clear that, even when forecasts are reported as simple numbers, they are really statements about probabilities. For example, it may be reported that a certain economist has forecast that a tax cut will add $10 billion to consumer spending, when the proper way of putting it may be that there is a 90 percent probability that the tax cut will add between $8 billion and $12 billion to spending.

Most economists take the view that conditional forecasts, for all their faults, are a better basis for making business decisions and public policy than whims and guesswork. For example, a maker of building supplies might ask a forecaster, "If the economy grows as much in the second half of the year as it did in the first, how will the demand for new houses be affected?" The answer might be, "A

3 percent rate of economic growth will cause housing demand to rise by somewhat more than 3 percent, if interest rates remain the same. However, each percentage-point rise in the mortgage interest rate will cause about a 5 percent drop in the demand for housing." Getting an answer like this isn't as good as having a crystal ball, but it may be helpful.

At the same time, economists caution against relying too much on forecasts. In the 1970s, many forecasters projected higher oil prices throughout the 1980s. Many oil companies, banks, and even national governments got in trouble when they relied too much on these forecasts, which turned out to be wrong. This issue of how much government policy makers should rely on forecasts is especially controversial, because so much is at stake when major policy decisions are made.

Positive versus Normative Economics

Economists, as we have seen, sometimes disagree over issues of theory. They disagree even more often when they try their hand at forecasting. But nothing produces as much disagreement as issues of economic policy. Should price controls on natural gas be lifted? Should import quotas on cars be extended? Should taxes be raised in order to cut the federal budget deficit? Questions such as these tend to bring economists out of their corners, ready for a real fight.

Before the sparks start to fly, however, it is worth thinking about the chain of reasoning on which policy decisions are based. It is a three-step chain that goes like this:

1. If policy X is followed, outcome Y will result.

2. Outcome Y is a good (or bad) thing.

3. Therefore, hurrah (or boo) for policy X.

The first step in this chain of reasoning is a forecast, stated in the proper if–then form. Forecasts are examples of **positive economics** — the part of economics that is limited to making statements about facts and the relationships among them.

Disputes are common in positive economics. Economists may disagree about the accuracy of facts, the relationships among them, and the way they are likely to unfold in the future. But these disputes can usually be resolved by scientific methods. Repeated measurement, statistical tests of theories, and comparisons of forecasts with actual events are some of the ways to narrow the room for disagreement on matters of positive economics.

But positive statements of the type "If policy X, then outcome Y" do not tell us whether policy X is desirable. To make a policy decision, one must also decide whether outcome Y is good or bad. Statements of the type "Outcome Y is good" are examples of **normative economics** — the part of economics that makes judgements about which economic policies or outcomes are good and which are bad.

Most economists do not think of themselves as experts in philosophy or ethics. Yet economists are in a better position to influence policy if their views are based on general principles. Economists who base their assessment of a policy on whim or prejudice are less likely to be listened to than those who speak in terms of well-thought-out values. Calling your opponent a racist or a fascist may win cheers from those who already agree with you and boos from those who are

Positive economics
The part of economics that is limited to making statements about facts and the relationships among them.

Normative economics
The part of economics that makes judgements about economic policies or outcomes.

already against you, but it is not likely to win uncommitted people to your side. An articulate explanation of your reasons for thinking that your opponent's policies will have undesirable outcomes has far more promise in that regard. With this in mind, it is worth looking at some basic principles of normative economics.

Efficiency and fairness

One standard by which economic policies can be judged is *efficiency*. In economics, as elsewhere, this means doing something with a minimum of waste, effort, and expense. (A more precise definition of economic efficiency will be given in Chapter 2.) But a policy that is efficient is not necessarily a good one. It must meet other standards as well. Among the most important of these is fairness.

Fairness can play two roles in relation to efficiency. First, it may be viewed as an additional criterion to efficiency when the choice is between two or more policies that are equally efficient — policies, for example, that differ only in terms of which groups of people bear costs or receive benefits. In such a case, we might reason as follows:

1. Policies X and Y are equally efficient, but they will distribute benefits to different groups.

2. The distribution of benefits under policy X is more fair.

3. Therefore, we should follow policy X.

The second role of the standard of fairness is to override that of efficiency. Many people believe efficiency should not be pursued at the expense of fairness. If both goals cannot be reached at once, efficiency should be sacrificed in the name of fairness. In such cases, our reasoning might run as follows:

1. Policy X would be inefficient, but it would be more fair than policy Y.

2. Efficiency is desirable, but fairness is more important.

3. Therefore, if there is no policy that is both efficient and fair, choose policy X.

However it is used, the standard of fairness plays a major role in policy analysis. But the standard of fairness raises a problem that the standard of efficiency does not. This problem is that fairness means different things to different people. Rational debate on matters of economic policy is difficult when people attach different meanings to the same term and when they fail to make those meanings clear. With this problem in mind, let's look at two concepts of fairness that often arise in discussions of economic policy.

The egalitarian concept of fairness

One widely held view equates fairness with equitable distribution of income. The phrase "from each according to ability, to each according to need" reflects this point of view. This concept of fairness is based on the idea that all people, by virtue of their shared humanity, deserve a portion of the goods and services turned out by the economy.

There are many versions of this concept. Some people believe that all income and wealth should be distributed equally. Others think that people have a right to a "safety net" level of income, but that any surplus above this level may be distributed according to other standards. Some think there are certain "merit goods," such as health care, food, and education, that should be distributed equally, but that it is all right for other goods to be distributed unequally.

In policy debates, the egalitarian view of fairness is often expressed in the question "What effect will this policy have on the poor?" Consider the debate over price controls on natural gas. Some people favour ending these controls on the grounds that they discourage production and encourage wasteful use of this valuable resource. But others oppose ending price controls because they believe higher prices would cause hardship for consumers in low-income groups.

The libertarian concept of fairness

A second widely held view links fairness to the right of people to live their lives according to their own values, free from threats and coercion. This concept of fairness stems from a long tradition in Western political thought. In particular, it is linked closely to the concept of liberty as stated by such thinkers as John Locke and Thomas Jefferson.

The libertarian view of fairness puts economic rights, such as the right to own property and the right to make exchanges with others, on a par with the basic rights of free speech, a free press, and free worship. From the libertarian point of view, efforts to promote fairness should stress equality of opportunity. Attempts to redistribute income by placing a penalty on economic success or giving people unequal access to markets are seen as unfair, whether or not they lead to equality of income.

In policy debates, the libertarian point of view is often expressed in the argument that competition and economic freedom lead to a general prosperity that is good for everyone. For example, libertarian economists have been leaders in the fight to end regulations that protect business firms from competition. They have argued that when small, new airlines are allowed to compete with larger, more established ones, when trust companies are allowed to compete with banks, and when natural-gas producers are allowed to compete with oil producers in an open market, the firms that serve the consumer best will be the ones that prosper.

Why distinguish?

Distinguishing between positive and normative economics and among different meanings of normative terms such as *fairness* will not settle policy disputes. Still, viewing policy analysis as a three-step process in which positive and normative elements both play a role makes policy debates more rational in two ways.

First, the distinction between positive and normative analysis makes it clear that there are two kinds of disagreement on policy questions. We can disagree as to whether policy X is good or bad because we disagree on the positive issue of whether it will cause outcome Y, which we both desire. Or we can agree that policy X will cause outcome Y, but disagree on the normative issue of whether Y is a good thing. When the source of the disagreement is clear, the argument will be more focussed.

Second, when positive statements are mixed with normative ones, they may not be judged on their merits. Reactions to value judgements tend to be much stronger than reactions to statements of fact or theory. Consider the case of tax policy. There has been much debate in recent years about the effects of tax cuts and tax increases on the federal budget deficit, on interest rates, and on economic growth. Many issues of fact and theory need to be resolved. But positive economists often find it hard to focus the attention of policy makers on such issues, because they are distracted by charges and countercharges of "soaking the rich" or being "unfair to the poor."

This book will raise many controversial issues as it takes its tour of the subject matter of economics. For the most part, our discussion will focus on the positive economic theories that bear on these issues, although normative considerations will also be noted. It should be remembered, however, that a textbook can provide only a framework for thinking about public issues and policies. You, the reader, will have the job of blending positive theories and normative judgements within this framework to reach conclusions of your own.

SUMMARY

1. Economics is a study of human behaviour. It focusses in particular on the ways in which people cope with the problem of *scarcity*.

2. Resources are said to be scarce when people do not have enough of them to meet all their wants and needs. Everyone, at all times and in all societies, faces the problem of scarcity in one form or another. For many people, the problem takes the simple form of finding enough to eat. Even the wealthiest people face scarcity in such forms as limits on their time. Scarcity means that people cannot have everything or do everything they would like; they must make choices. The choices people make and the actions they take in their attempt to make the best possible use of scarce resources in meeting their wants and needs is the subject matter of *economics*.

3. An *economy* consists of ideas, institutions, rules, and factors of production. Institutions include households, production organizations, promoters of *ideology*, rule setters and enforcers, and the mechanisms that co-ordinate economic activity. *Markets* and *economic planning* represent two different mechanisms for co-ordinating economic activity. A market does so informally, through the interactions of numerous individuals and business firms, while economic planning is carried out by governments in a deliberate attempt to control production and distribution. The *factors of production* include *labour*, *capital*, and *natural resources*.

4. Economies that share the same ideology and have similar rules and institutions are said to belong to the same *economic system*. Canada, on the basis of its system of private ownership of property, its reliance on market forces to co-ordinate production and distribution, and its ideology of competition and individual achievement, may be called a *capitalist* country. *Socialist* countries endorse communal ownership of property, economic planning, and an ideology of co-operation and collective gain.

5. *Microeconomics* is the branch of economics that deals with the choices made by small economic units — households, business firms, and units of government. Households supply the basic factors of production — labour, capital, and natural resources. Business firms buy the factors of production from households and transform them into goods and services. Units of government, as will be noted throughout in this textbook, influence the economic choices made by households and firms. Those choices are also influenced by events in the economy.

6. *Macroeconomics* is the study of large-scale economic phenomena, especially unemployment, inflation, and economic growth.

7. A *theory* is an explanation of the ways in which given facts are related. In economics, a mathematical rendition of a theory is called a *model*. Theories often simplify economic reality, but if they are well conceived, this does not detract from their usefulness. Broader models of economic behaviour, which cannot be expressed easily in mathematical formulas, are used by such economists as economic historians, *institutionalists*, and *Marxists*.

8. The part of economics that is limited to *conditional forecasts* and statements of fact is known as *positive economics*. The part that makes judgements about whether economic policies or events are good or bad is called *normative economics*. Making a judgement about the value of an economic policy requires both a positive analysis of the policy's likely effects and a normative judgement of the desirability of those effects.

KEY TERMS

scarcity	capital	model
economics	natural resources	institutionalists
an economy	economic system	Marxists
ideology	socialism	conditional forecast
the market	capitalism	positive economics
economic planning	microeconomics	normative economics
factors of production	macroeconomics	
labour	theory	

REVIEW QUESTIONS

1. What system of allocation of goods do you actually prefer? To test your preferences, consider the following example: On the first day of classes at your university, it is discovered that 40 more students than can possibly be accommodated have registered in the only existing section of a course in criminology. In fact, when all resources have been checked, room for 10 more students is made available. How would you decide which of the 40 students should get those 10 places? Would you auction the places to the highest bidder? Offer them to those who registered first? Determine by detailed questioning who seems to need the course most? After you have determined your preference, ask yourself whether it is a "market" solution that you have chosen or a different type of solution. Were there special conditions in this example that influenced your choice?

2. Which of the following are microeconomic issues? Which are macroeconomic issues?
   a. How will an increase in the tax on cigarettes affect smoking habits?
   b. What caused the rate of inflation to fall so fast between 1980 and 1984?
   c. Does a high federal budget deficit tend to slow the rate of real economic growth?
   d. How would quotas on steel imports affect profits and jobs in industries that use steel as an input, such as the automobile and construction industries?

3. Minimum-wage laws have been passed in many provinces to provide higher incomes for workers. On the level of positive economics,

some people think that a high minimum wage increases the incomes of low-skilled workers, while others think that it reduces the number of jobs available to such workers. On a normative level, people disagree about the distribution of incomes that is appropriate. Using the three-step chain of reasoning discussed in this chapter, outline in paragraph form several analyses of the minimum-wage issue.

4. Assume that, in Country A, incomes range from $1000 to $3000 a year, and that the median income (the income level that half the households fall below and half exceed) is $1600. In Country B, incomes range from $800 to $6000, and the median income is $3000. Which of these economies do you think is "fairer" to its citizens? Examine carefully the grounds for your opinion.

Tools for Learning: Working with Graphs

How Economists Use Graphs

At a well-known college, the students have their own names for all the courses. They call the astronomy course "stars," the geology course "rocks," and the biology course "frogs." Their name for the economics course is "graphs and laughs." This choice of names indicates two things. First, it shows that the students think the professor has a sense of humour. Second, it shows that in the minds of students, economics is a matter of learning about graphs in the same sense that astronomy is a matter of learning about stars or geology a matter of learning about rocks.

Economics is not about graphs; it is about people. It is about the way people make choices, use resources, and co-operate with one another in an effort to overcome the universal problem of scarcity. Economics is a social science, not an offshoot of analytic geometry.

But if economics is not about graphs, why are there so many of them in this book? The answer is that economists use graphs to illustrate the theories they develop about people's economic behaviour in order to make them vivid, eye-catching, and easy to remember. Everything that can be said in the form of a graph can also be said in words or equations, but saying something in two different ways is a proven aid to learning. The purpose of this appendix is to show how to make maximum use of an important learning aid by explaining how to work with graphs.

Pairs of Numbers and Points

The first thing to learn is how to use points on a graph to represent pairs of numbers. Consider Box 1A.1. The small table presents five pairs of numbers. The two columns are labelled *x* and *y*. The first number in each pair is called the **x value**, and the second is called the **y value**. Each pair of numbers is labelled with a capital letter, *A* through *E*. Pair *A* has an *x* value of 2 and a *y* value of 3; pair *B* has an *x* value of 4 and a *y* value of 4, and so on.

Next to the table is a diagram. The two lines placed at right angles to each other along the bottom and the left-hand side of the diagram are called **co-ordinate axes**. Both axes are marked off into units, but the horizontal axis is used for measuring the *x* value, while the vertical axis is used for measuring the *y* value. In the space between these axes, each lettered pair of numbers from the table can be represented as a lettered point. For example, to put point *A* in place, begin at zero — which is called the point of origin — and go two units to the right along the horizontal axis to represent the *x* value of 2 and then three units straight up, parallel to the vertical axis, to represent the *y* value of 3. The other points are placed in the same way.

Usually, the visual effect of a graph is improved by connecting the points with a smooth line or curve. When this is done (as shown in the diagram), it can be

x value
Corresponds to a point's horizontal distance from the vertical axis.

y value
Corresponds to a point's vertical distance from the horizontal axis.

Co-ordinate axes
The horizontal and vertical axes used to measure the *x* value and *y* value.

BOX 1A.1   ## Pairs of Numbers and Points

Each lettered pair of numbers in the table corresponds to a lettered point on the graph. The *x* value of each point corresponds to the horizontal distance of the point from the vertical axis, and the *y* value corresponds to the vertical distance from the horizontal axis.

	x	*y*
A	2	3
B	4	4
C	6	5
D	8	6
E	10	7

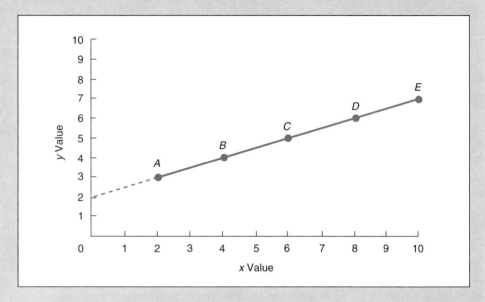

seen at a glance that as the *x* value increases, the *y* value also increases. The line in our graph can, in turn, be expressed in the form of an equation. In this example, which involves a straight line, the equation is of the form $y = a + bx$, in which *a* represents the point where the line, when extended leftwards, would cross the vertical axis, and *b* is the number by which *x* is multiplied to produce the changes in *y* associated with changes in *x*. For example, the equation for the line shown in Box 1A.1 would be $y = 2 + \frac{1}{2}x$. The line starts at 2 (indicating that *y* is 2 when *x* is zero), and then rises by $\frac{1}{2}$ unit for every 1-unit movement along the horizontal axis (indicating that *y* increases by $\frac{1}{2}$ unit for every 1-unit increase in *x*).

Common Economic Graphs

Economics is interested not in abstract relationships between *x*'s and *y*'s but in relationships that have to do with people and the way they behave under various conditions. This means that graphs in economics are labelled in terms of the ideas used in putting together economic theories. Box 1A.2 shows three types of relationships commonly graphed in economics, and the corresponding ways of labelling the co-ordinate axis. You will encounter each of these types of graphs many times throughout this book.

Box 1A.2(a) represents the relationship between the price of subway tokens in a city and the number of people who choose to ride the subway each day at any given price. The table shows that as the price of token goes up, the number

Three Typical Economic Graphs

This exhibit shows three graphs typical of those used in economics. Part (a) shows the relationship between the price of tokens and the number of riders per day on a city subway system. When a graph shows the relationship between a price and a quantity, it is conventional to put the price on the vertical axis. Part (b) shows the possible choices open to a person who has $2.50 to spend on lunch and can buy hamburgers at $0.50 each or milkshakes at $0.50 each. Part (c) shows how a graph can be used to represent change over time.

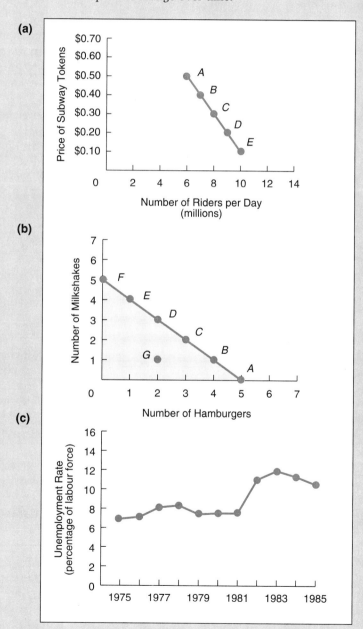

(a)

	Price of Subway Tokens	Number of Riders per Day (millions)
A	$0.50	6
B	$0.40	7
C	$0.30	8
D	$0.20	9
E	$0.10	10

(b)

	Number of Hamburgers	Number of Milkshakes
A	5	0
B	4	1
C	3	2
D	2	3
E	1	4
F	0	5

(c)

Year	Unemployment Rate
1975	6.9
1976	7.1
1977	8.1
1978	8.3
1979	7.4
1980	7.5
1981	7.5
1982	11.0
1983	11.9
1984	11.3
1985	10.5

SOURCE: Data for part (c) are from the Department of Finance, *Economic Review*, April 1986.

of people choosing to ride the subway goes down. The graph shows the same thing. As a matter of convention in economics, whenever a graph involves both money values and quantity units, the vertical axis is used to measure the money value (in this case, the price of subway tokens) and the horizontal axis to measure the quantity units (in this case, the number of riders per day). The graph clearly demonstrates how subway use declines at higher prices.

Box 1A.2(b) uses quantity units on both axes. Here, the problem is to represent the various combinations of milkshakes and hamburgers that can be bought when milkshakes cost $0.50 each, hamburgers cost $0.50 each, and the buyer has $2.50 to spend on lunch. The table shows that the possibilities are 5 burgers and no shakes, 4 burgers and 1 shake, 3 burgers and 2 shakes, and so on.

The graph offers a picture of the "menu" to choose from, given limited money to spend. The points from the table are drawn in and labelled, and any one of them can be chosen. A diagonal line has been sketched in to connect these points. If the purchase of parts of hamburgers and milkshakes were allowed, the buyer could choose from among all the points along this line (for example, 2.5 burgers and 2.5 shakes). The buyer who wanted to have some money left over could purchase a lunch represented by a point within the shaded area, such as point *G* (which stands for 2 burgers and 1 shake and costs just $1.50). But unless the buyer gets more money, she cannot choose points outside the shaded area.

Box 1A.2(c) illustrates still another kind of graph frequently used in economics — one that shows how some magnitude varies over time. This graph indicates what happened to the unemployment rate over the years 1975–85. The horizontal axis is used to represent the passage of time and the vertical axis to measure the percentage of the labour force officially classified as unemployed. Graphs like this are good for getting a quick idea of trends over time. For several years (1979–81), the unemployment rate was steady, at around 7.5 percent. Then it rose sharply, to 11 percent, in 1982, and showed significant decline only in 1985.

Slopes

Slope of a straight line
The ratio of the change in the *y* value to the change in the *x* value between any two points in the line.

When talking about graphs, it is frequently convenient to describe lines or curves in terms of their *slopes*. The **slope of a straight line** drawn between two points is defined as the ratio of the change in the *y* value to the change in the *x* value between any two points in that line. In Box 1A.3, for example, the slope of the line drawn between points *A* and *B* is 2. The *y* value changes by 6 units between these two points, while the *x* value changes by only 3 units. The slope is therefore the ratio 6/3, or 2.

When a line slants downward, as does the line between points *C* and *D* in Box 1A.3, the *x* value and the *y* value change in opposite directions. Going from point *C* to point *D*, the *y* value changes by −2 (that is, it decreases by 2 units), while the *x* value changes by +4 (that is, it increases by 4 units). The slope of this line is the ratio −2/4, or −1/2. A downward-sloping line such as this one is said to have a negative slope.

Slope of a curved line
At any given point, the slope of a straight line drawn tangent to the curve at that point.

The **slope of a curved line**, unlike that of a straight line, varies from point to point. The slope of a curve at any given point is defined as the slope of a straight line drawn tangent to the curve at that point. (A tangent line is one that just touches the curve, without crossing it.) Consider the curve in Box 1A.4. Applying the definition, the slope of this line at point *A* is 1, and the slope at point *B* is −2. When a straight line is described in equation form, such as

Slopes of Lines

The slope of a straight line drawn between two points is defined as the ratio of the change in the *y* value to the change in the *x* value between any two points in the line. For example, the line drawn between points *A* and *B* in this exhibit has a slope of +2, whereas the line drawn between points *C* and *D* has a slope of −¹/₂.

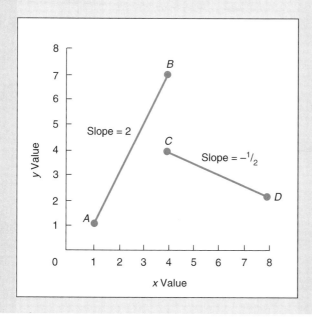

$y = a + bx$, the slope of the line is given by b, because b indicates the rate at which y changes in relation to changes in x. Thus, as you will recall, the equation for the line in Box 1A.1 was $y = 2 + \frac{1}{2}x$, where $b = \frac{1}{2}$, meaning that the slope of the line was $\frac{1}{2}$.

Abstract Graphs

In all the examples so far, we have had specific numbers to work with for the *x* and *y* values. Sometimes, though, we know only the general nature of the relationship between two economic magnitudes. For example, we might know that when people's incomes rise, they tend to increase their consumption of meat rapidly at first. But then, as they reach very high incomes, their meat consumption levels off. If we want to represent this sort of a relationship without specifying the numbers involved, we can draw a graph like the one shown in Box 1A.5. The vertical axis is labelled "quantity of meat consumed per month," without any indication of specific units. The horizontal axis is labelled "income," again without showing specific units. The curve, which rises rapidly at first and then levels off, tells us the general nature of the relationship between income and meat consumption: when income rises, meat consumption increases, but not in proportion to the change in income. We will use abstract graphs like this one very frequently in this book. Abstract graphs express general principles, whereas graphs with numbers on the axes summarize specific information.

BOX 1A.4 Slopes of Curves

The slope of a curve at any given point is defined as the slope of a straight line drawn tangent to the curve at that point. A tangent line is one that just touches the curve without crossing it. In this exhibit, the slope of the curve at point A is 1, and the slope of the curve at point B is -2. (Note: Between points A and B, the y value increases by 6 units — from 1 to 7 — while the x value changes by 3 units, from 1 to 4. Therefore the slope $= \dfrac{\text{change in } y}{\text{change in } x} = +\dfrac{6}{3} = 2$.)

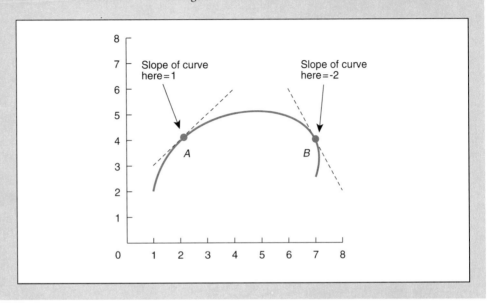

BOX 1A.5 An Abstract Graph

When we know the general form of an economic relationship but do not know the exact numbers involved, we can draw an abstract graph. Here, we know that as people's incomes rise, their consumption of meat increases rapidly at first, then levels off. Because we do not know the exact numbers for meat consumption or income, we have not marked any units on the axes.

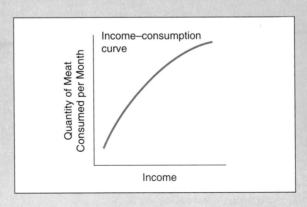

Tips for Studying Graphs

When you come to a chapter in the book that is full of graphs, what approach should you take to studying it? The first and most important rule is to understand the graphs. Every teacher of economics has had at least one student complain after failing an exam: "But I learned every one of those graphs! What happened?" The problem is that students often try to memorize graph lines rather than learning the economics contained in the graphs.

Here are some specific study hints for working with graphs: After reading carefully through a chapter that contains numerous graphs, go back through the graphs one at a time. Cover the explanatory note that appears beside each graph and try putting what the graph says into words. If you cannot say at least as much about the graph as the explanatory note does, read the text over again.

If you do well going from graphs to words, half the battle has been won. Next, try the exercise in reverse: Cover the graph and, using the explanatory note as a guide, sketch the graph on a piece of scratch paper. If you understand what the words mean and can comfortably go back and forth between the words and the graphs, you will find out that the two together make the principles involved much easier to remember and apply. If you "learn the graphs" as meaningless patterns of lines, you are lost.

Constructing Your Own Graphs

For some students, the most difficult kind of question on an exam is the kind that requires construction of an original graph as part of an essay answer. Here are some hints for constructing your own graphs:

1. Put down the answer to the question in words. Try to underline the most important quantities in what you have written. The result might be something like this: "The larger the *number of students* who attend a university, the lower the *cost per student* of providing them with an education." Only after you have put your ideas clearly into words should you begin to plan your graph.

2. Decide how you are going to label the co-ordinate axes of your graph. In our example, because it is conventional to put the money values on the vertical axis, we label the vertical axis "cost per student" and the horizontal axis "number of students."

3. Do you have exact numbers to work with? If you do, your next step should be to organize what you know into a table, from which you can plot your co-ordinates on the graph and sketch in the resulting line or curve. If you do not have numbers, you will be drawing an abstract graph. In this case, all you know is that the cost per student goes down when the number of students goes up. Sketch in any convenient downward-sloping line (as in Box 1A.6), and you will have done all that can be expected.

4. If your graph involves more than one relationship between pairs of economic quantities, repeat steps 1 to 3 for each relationship that you want to represent by a line or curve.

5. After your graph is completed, try translating it back into words. Does it really say what you wanted to say?

BOX 1A.6   Constructing a Graph

To construct a graph, first put down in words what you want to say: "The larger the *number of students* who attend a university, the lower the *cost per student* of providing them with an education." Next, label the co-ordinate axes. Then, if you have exact numbers to work with, construct a table and use it as a guide in sketching your graph. Here we have no exact numbers, so we draw an abstract graph that slopes downward to show that cost goes down as the number of students goes up. For graphs with more than one curve, repeat these steps.

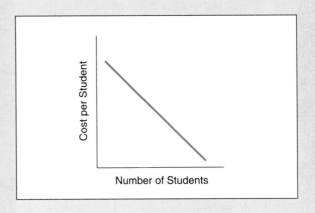

A Reminder

As you work through this book and are introduced to various kinds of graphs, turn back to this appendix now and then. Do not commit the fatal error of memorizing graphs as meaningless pictures. Remember that if you can go back and forth between graphs and words, the underlying theory that both are meant to express will stay with you more vividly than it would if you tried to rely on either graphs or words alone. Remember that economics is about *people*, not graphs.

KEY TERMS

x value
y value

co-ordinate axes
slope of a straight line

slope of a curved line

KEY BOXES

Box 1A.2 Three Typical Economic Graphs

Box 1A.3 Slopes of Lines

REVIEW QUESTIONS

1. Plot each of the following straight lines on a grid, with the x values on the horizontal axis and the y values on the vertical axis. Calculate the slopes of each line.

Line A	Line B
$x = 2, y = 1$	$x = 4, y = 8$
$x = 2, y = 2$	$x = 5, y = 7$
$x = 2, y = 3$	$x = 6, y = 6$
$x = 2, y = 4$	$x = 7, y = 5$

Line C	Line D
$x = 4, y = 3$	$x = 1, y = 4$
$x = 5, y = 3$	$x = 2, y = 6$
$x = 6, y = 3$	$x = 3, y = 8$
$x = 7, y = 3$	$x = 4, y = 10$

2. Plot each of the points identified below on a grid, then draw a line joining the points. What is the slope of the line between points A and B, between points C and D, and between points E and F?

Points on Graph	Co-ordinates
A	$x = 2, y = 4$
B	$x = 4, y = 6$
C	$x = 6, y = 7$
D	$x = 7, y = 5$
E	$x = 8, y = 4$
F	$x = 9, y = 5$

3. Plot the following relationship between a family's desired consumption pattern and their level of disposable income. Plot desired consumption in dollars on the vertical axis, and disposable income in dollars on the horizontal axis. Take a minute or two to think about the values you want to put on your x and y axes, but make the numerical scale values on both axes identical. When you have plotted this line (which is known as a consumption function), add a straight line to the graph, starting at zero and with a slope of $+1$ (this is known as a 45° line). At what value of disposable income does this new line cut the consumption function?

a. Below what level of disposable income is desired consumption greater than disposable income for this family? Above what level of income is disposable income greater than desired consumption for this family?

b. What purpose do you think the 45° line serves in this graph?

Points on Graph	Desired Consumption (dollars)	Disposable Income (dollars)
A	400	0
B	500	400
C	675	1000
D	800	1400
E	1000	2200

The Canadian Economy: Goals and Performance

WHAT YOU WILL LEARN IN THIS CHAPTER

After studying this chapter, you will be able to

1. Define the central choices faced by all economies.

2. Use the production possibilities frontier and the concept of opportunity cost to discuss the constraints on what an economy can produce.

3. Give examples of ways in which factors of production can be substituted for one another.

4. Explain comparative advantage and how it applies to the question Who will produce which goods and services?

5. Show how positive and normative economics bear on the question For whom should goods be produced?

6. Discuss efficiency and fairness as applied to production and to the mix and distribution of outputs.

7. Explain the role of entrepreneurship in economic decision making.

8. Describe and evaluate Canada's economic performance as measured by such yardsticks as unemployment, inflation, and growth.

A Preview   *Scarcity and Choice: Good Jobs, Bad Jobs, and No Jobs*

If the Canadian economy performed the way everyone would like it to, everyone who wanted to work would have a decent, well-paying job, and incomes would rise steadily. Instead, the job situation is such that many people seem destined to be without jobs or to remain in poor ones. Why can't the Canadian economy do better? The following article describes one trend that exemplifies the problem.

Big Growth in Service Jobs Will Widen Disparities

Canada's overall unemployment will grow through 1991, employment statistics indicate. And a massive long-term shift to service sector jobs will widen the economic gulf between the country's weak and strong regions.

"Our sense is that over the next five to ten years you'll see something of a worsening of regional disparities," said Tim Whitehead, regional economist at Canadian Imperial Bank of Commerce. Good jobs will, he added, "tend to locate in large urban areas to the detriment of weaker areas."

Over the past ten years, new jobs in services accounted for 93.7 percent of all jobs created. Manufacturing and processing jobs accounted for the 6.3 percent balance. Last year, service jobs accounted for 71.1 percent of all jobs, up from 66.6 percent in 1979.

And a recent study by the Economic Council of Canada found that middle-level service jobs are disappearing as work becomes polarized into so-called good jobs and bad jobs.

Good jobs are well-paid, stable, highly skilled work. Bad jobs require fewer skills and offer low pay, poor hours, and little stability.

Good service jobs tend to locate in or near big cities, leaving outlying areas and small towns with the bad jobs, the council warned.

Whitehead said about half of all service jobs created since the 1981–82 recession are in Ontario. Service jobs that require greater skills tend to concentrate in provinces with high populations, he said.

The council study said good jobs tend to be in dynamic services, such as transportation, communications, wholesale trade, business services, finance, insurance, and real estate. Bad jobs tend to be in traditional services, such as retail trade, personal services, food, and accommodation.

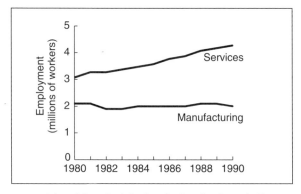

SOURCE: Adapted from Statistics Canada, *Canadian Economic Observer, Historical Statistical Supplement 1989/90*, p. 33, Catalogue no. 11-210, and *Canadian Economic Observer*, September 1991, p. 6.26, Catalogue no. 11-010. Reproduced with permission of the Minister of Supply and Services Canada, 1992.

Many jobs fall into the category of bad because they are nonstandard: part-time, self-employed, or temporary work. Nonstandard work accounted for about 50 percent of all jobs created between 1980 and 1988, and now represents about 30 percent of the country's total employment.

Part-time work, which accounts for an overwhelming portion of jobs in traditional services, fuelled much of that increase.

While the number of people holding full-time jobs rose by 16.5 percent over the past ten years, the number holding part-time jobs shot up 45.1 percent.

The growth in part-time jobs has been moderating over the past five years, however, and increased by just 0.3 percent last year, compared with 2.3 percent growth of full-time jobs.

SOURCE: Jennifer Lanthier, "Big Growth in Service Jobs Will Widen Disparities," *Financial Post*, March 5, 1990, p. 7. Reproduced with permission.

GOALS AND PERFORMANCE IN A MARKET ECONOMY

The Preview focusses on a problem faced by all market economies: how to provide enough good jobs for everyone. Jobs are created in response to consumer demand for various types of goods and services. If there is a growing demand for computers and a declining demand for farm products, people with computer training will find it easier to get jobs, while farm labourers will face increasing unemployment. Even at the best of times, it is difficult for any economy to match workers with jobs in a completely satisfactory way.

As we noted in Chapter 1, every economy, in the course of trying to meet such goals as full employment and adequate incomes for workers, must make the following three basic decisions:

1. **What** should be produced, in view of the needs of the people, the employment potential afforded by different types of goods, and the scarcity of labour, capital, and land? How many cars should Canada produce? How much bread? How many services?

2. **How** should goods and services be produced? Should cars continue to be produced by workers in mass assembly lines or should newer methods that make workers feel more involved in the production process be introduced?

3. **For whom** should goods and services be produced? For those who have the most money or for those who have the greatest need?

This chapter first considers each of these questions in turn, then evaluates the degree to which the Canadian economy seems to be making the right choices.

What to Produce?

The native people who first settled this country had to make economic decisions that were similar in nature, though perhaps not in scope and complexity, to the decisions that must be made in our modern economy. Within the limited time of each day, and with the resources and techniques available to them, they had to decide what they would eat, what they would use to clothe themselves, and what kinds of shelters they would construct. Would they fish on a given day, or would they hunt for buffalo? They might, of course, try to do both, but doing more of one meant giving up some of the other.

The decisions could be quite complex. Native tribes often traded with one another. Each tribe had to decide what it could best produce for its own needs and what it might produce to trade with others. Trade also permitted reduced production of goods that were easily obtained from others. At times, intertribal fighting occurred, and in anticipation of this, each tribe had to set aside a certain portion of its resources for the production of military goods. The coming of Europeans to Canada made the decisions even more complex.

In Canada today, millions of such output decisions are made every day. They are made by households, self-employed individuals, business firms, government agencies, and other organizations.

To illustrate the kinds of choices made, we will use the economist's technique of developing a simple model of an economy. We will assume an economy in which the citizens have to choose between two types of goods, *civilian goods*, represented in our model by beef production, and *military goods*, represented by the production of tanks. Let us call this hypothetical economy Adanac — a simplified mirror-image of Canada. Box 2.1 shows the choices open to Adanac, assuming that labour is the only input and that 1200 hours of it are available for the production of either good. Look first at the table. It shows that if Adanac spends all 1200 hours of its labour time on the production of beef, and none on the production of tanks, the output of beef will be eleven tonnes. On the other hand, if all labour resources are spent on the production of tanks, with no beef output (don't worry about the possibility of starvation — this is a hypothetical economy), fourteen tanks and no beef will be produced.

The production possibilities frontier

Box 2.1 also shows Adanac's production possibilities in the form of a graph. Point *A* in the graph represents all beef production and no manufacture of tanks. Point *G* represents all tank production and no output of beef. The other points represent the other combinations shown in the table.

Production possibilities frontier (PPF)
A graph showing the possible combinations of goods that can be produced by an economy, given the available resources and technology.

A graph such as this is called a **production possibilities frontier (PPF)**. It defines the choices open to an economy in terms of the different combinations of goods it can produce, in a given period of time, given the resources and technology available to it. We have defined labour as the only resource in Adanac, and have limited its availability to 1200 hours, meaning that citizens of Adanac can spend no more than 1200 hours on the production of goods. If they spend the full 1200 hours at work, they have the choice of producing any combination of goods represented by any point situated *on* the production possibilities frontier. If they want to spend fewer than 1200 hours working, they will have to be content with a combination of beef and tanks such as the one represented by point *H*, which lies *inside* the frontier. Since they have no more than 1200 labour hours to devote to the production of goods, however, they can choose no point — that is, no combination of goods — that lies *outside* the frontier.

Efficiency
A state of affairs in which, given the available knowledge and resources, no change can be made that would make one person better off without making another worse off.

A point on the production possibilities frontier represents a point of **efficiency** for the economy. Efficiency is defined by economists as a state of affairs in which, given the available knowledge and resources, no change can be made that would make one person better off without making another worse off. At point *H*, which is to the left and below the production possibilities frontier, it is possible to produce more of one good without producing less of another. That means that it is possible to make at least one person better off without making anyone else worse off. Therefore, point *H* is a point of *inefficiency* (if production actually occurs there, the resources of the economy are being underutilized). Only points that are *on* the production possibilities frontier are points of efficiency.[1]

The position and shape of the frontier in our example depend on Adanac's resources, its technology, and the skills of its labour force. A change in any of these conditions would change the frontier. For instance, a more efficient method of producing certain tank parts would allow more tanks to be built per hour. This would stretch the frontier outward to the right. This process will be examined later in the chapter.

---

[1]Efficiency, in this sense, is often called *Pareto optimality*, after the Italian economist Vilfredo Pareto, who proposed this definition. However, while production on the possibilities frontier is efficient, it isn't necessarily "optimal" for society. In addition to producing efficiently, an economy must produce the "right" mix of output in terms of people's preferences. As will be seen later in this chapter, the mix of goods and services produced and distributed in a given economy might not be chosen by a majority of consumers if all consumers had similar purchasing power.

Adanac's Production Possibilities Frontier   BOX 2.1

Adanac, the economy in our hypothetical example, spends 1200 labour hours each period to produce civilian goods (beef) or military goods (tanks). The table shows the number of tonnes of beef and the number of tanks that it can obtain by dividing its labour time in various ways. The same information is also displayed in the form of a graph called a production possibilities frontier. Points such as *H*, which require fewer than 1200 labour hours, are also possible, but any point outside the frontier is beyond Adanac's reach, requiring more labour time than is available to the economy.

(a)

Point on Graph	Hours Spent on Beef Production	Hours Spent on Tank Production	Tonnes of Beef Produced	Number of Tanks Produced
A	1200	0	11	0
B	1000	200	10	4
C	800	400	9	7
D	600	600	8	9
E	400	800	6	11
F	200	1000	3	13
G	0	1200	0	14

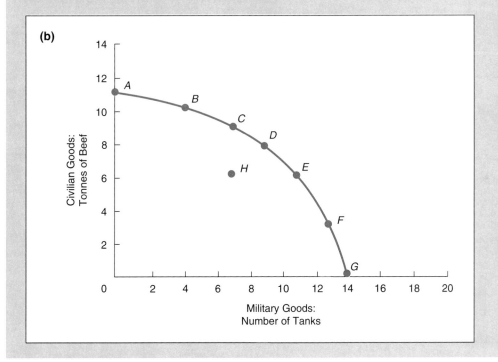

Opportunity cost

At any point along the production possibilities frontier, taking the time to produce more beef means giving up a chance to manufacture more tanks. Suppose we begin at point *G* (all tank production and no beef output) and then switch 200 hours to beef output. This will give us three tonnes of beef at the cost of just one tank. The cost of a good measured in terms of the lost opportunity to

Opportunity cost
The cost of a good measured in terms of the lost opportunity to pursue the best alternative activity with the same time and resources.

do something else with the same time and resources is known as the **opportunity cost** of that good. In the range between point *G* and point *F* on the graph, the opportunity cost of each tonne of beef is one-third of a tank.

Notice that, as Adanac moves upward and to the left along the production possibilities frontier, the trade-off between tanks and beef changes. This can happen (indeed, it is likely to happen) because the labour used in this economy will not be of the same quality or type, and will not be suited equally well to the production of each good. For example, in moving from point *G* to point *F* in our diagram, some workers would have to be transferred from the production of tanks to the production of beef — in other words, metal workers would have to learn how to farm. The opportunity cost of getting the first few new farmers might be low: Workers who were not particularly skilled at tank production but who were eager to get into farming would likely be the first ones recruited into beef production. The production of beef could rise appreciably, without a sharp drop in tank output. Gradually, however, people and resources better suited to tank production than to farming might begin to be shifted to farming. For example, if the economy moved from point *F* to point *E*, increasing the time devoted to beef production to 400 hours and decreasing the time for tank production to 800 hours, beef production would rise by another three tonnes, to six tonnes, but this time tank output would fall by two units (to eleven tanks) rather than only by one. An economist would therefore say that in the range between points *F* and *E*, the opportunity cost of producing each tonne of beef is two-thirds of a tank. Clearly, the opportunity cost of producing beef rises as the economy moves leftward along the production possibilities frontier and shifts more and more production out of tanks and into beef.

The concept of opportunity cost helps us understand more clearly the true cost of many of the choices we make. Getting more of something we want requires paying an opportunity cost in terms of something else.

For a person living on a limited budget, buying a car may mean giving up a chance to move to a better apartment. Getting a university education may mean giving up several years' income from a job (see the For Example . . . box). Working full-time while going to school may mean giving up sleep, vacations, and, possibly, good grades.

As we will see at many points in this book, the concept of opportunity cost applies to national economic policy as well as to individual decisions. The opportunity cost of an increased national-defence budget may be cutbacks in social services. The opportunity cost of a clean environment may be higher prices and smaller amounts of electricity, steel, and chemicals. Opportunity cost is a basic fact of economic life that must be faced whenever decisions are made about what to produce.

FOR EXAMPLE...
The Opportunity Cost of a University or College Education

How much does it cost you to go to university? If you are a resident student at a typical university or college in Canada, you could answer this question by making up a budget like the one shown in Table A. This can be called a budget of *out-of-*

pocket costs, because it includes all the items, and only those items, that you or your parents actually have to pay for in a year.

Your own out-of-pocket costs may be much higher or much lower than these average figures. Nonetheless, these are probably the items that come to mind when you think about the costs of university. As you begin to think like an economist, however, you may find yourself recasting your budget in terms of *opportunity costs*. Which of the items in Table A represent opportunities that you have forgone in order to go to university? Are any forgone opportunities missing from the table? To answer these questions, compare Table A with Table B, which is a budget of opportunity costs.

The first three items in the out-of-pocket budget show up again in the opportunity-cost budget. When you spend $2000 on tuition and fees and $325 on books and supplies, you are giving up the opportunity to spend that money on other goods and services — say, on a used car or the rental of a ski condo. When you spend $350 getting to and from school, you are passing up the opportunity to travel somewhere else or to spend that money on something other than travel. But the last two items in the out-of-pocket budget are not opportunity costs. By spending $5200 a year on room, board, and personal expenses during the year, you're not really giving up the opportunity to do something else. Whether you had gone to university or not, you would have to eat, to live somewhere, and to buy clothes. Because these are expenses that you would have in any case, they do not count as opportunity costs of going to university.

Thinking about what you would have done if you had not gone to university suggests a major item that needs to be added to the opportunity-cost budget — one that does not show up at all in the out-of-pocket budget. If you had not gone to university, you probably would have taken a job and started earning money soon after leaving high school. The average earnings for a high school graduate would be about $7500 during the nine months of the school year. (You can work in the summer even if you do go to university.) This potential income is something that you have to forgo for a postsecondary education, so it is a true opportunity cost.

The budget you use will depend on the kind of decision you are making. If you have already decided to go to university and are doing your financial planning, the out-of-pocket budget will tell you how much you have to raise from savings, parents' contributions, loans, and scholarships in order to make ends meet. But if you are making the more basic decision of whether to go to university or take up some career that does not require a postsecondary education, then it will be the opportunity cost of university that counts.

Table A. Budget of Out-of-Pocket Costs

Tuition and fees	$ 2 000
Books and supplies	325
Transportation to and from home	350
Room and board	4 500
Personal expenses	700
Total out-of-pocket costs	$ 7 875

Table B. Budget of Opportunity Costs

Tuition and fees	$ 2 000
Books and supplies	325
Transportation to and from home	350
Forgone income	7 500
Total opportunity costs	$10 175

Comparative advantage and opportunity cost

Division of labour, or specialization
The division of the production process into numerous specialized functions for purposes of greater productivity.

No country is capable of producing *all* the goods and services required to meet its people's needs. The history of many countries, however, demonstrates that economies can increase their output through **division of labour, or specialization**. Such specialization can occur within a single country, when people are motivated to pursue those occupations to which their talents are best suited. It can also take place between countries, with one country specializing in the production of certain goods and services to which it is best suited, while another country specializes in other goods and services more appropriate to it. Through both domestic and international specialization, countries can, in effect, push their production possibilities frontiers outward.

It can be shown quite easily that individuals and nations will benefit by specializing in, and trading, those goods and services that they produce most efficiently. If you are a better statistician than your friend, but she is a better lawyer than you, you should stick to statistics and get her to do your legal work, and vice versa. However, economic theory can also show that even if you are a better statistician *and* a better lawyer than your friend, it might still pay you to specialize in statistics and let her do your legal work.

Assume that you graduate with an A+ average in statistics and a B+ average in law, while your friend graduates with a B average in both subjects. The economist would say that you have an **absolute advantage** in both fields (because you are superior in both), but you have a **comparative advantage** in statistics, where your superiority is greatest. Your friend, by contrast, has an absolute *dis*advantage in both subjects (because she is inferior in both), but she has a *comparative advantage* in law, where her inferiority is least. The economist would recommend that you both choose the field of work in which you have a comparative advantage.

Absolute advantage
The ability to produce a good or service at absolutely lower cost, measured in terms of factor inputs used per unit of output.

Comparative advantage
The ability to produce a good or service at comparatively less cost than someone else.

Comparative and absolute advantage are commonly measured in terms of efficiency. The following example illustrates this. Assume that Farmer A can pick 15 kg of peas or 15 kg of strawberries in one hour, while Farmer B can pick only 7.5 kg of peas or 10 kg of strawberries in the same amount of time. Farmer A is more efficient than Farmer B in picking both peas and strawberries. It would cost Farmer A less than one hour of labour time to pick either 7.5 kg of peas or 10 kg of strawberries. Should Farmer A therefore pick both strawberries and peas, and Farmer B pick nothing?

An economist would observe that while Farmer A has an absolute advantage in both goods (it takes him less time to pick both), his efficiency in relation to Farmer B is greatest in the picking of peas. Farmer A picks twice as many peas in an hour as Farmer B, but only 50 percent more strawberries. In the economist's language, Farmer A has a comparative advantage in the picking of peas. Conversely, although Farmer B has an absolute *dis*advantage in picking both peas and strawberries, he is considered to have a *comparative advantage* in the picking of strawberries, where his disadvantage or inefficiency is least. Both farmers, then, should specialize on the basis of their comparative advantage: Farmer A should pick peas, and Farmer B, strawberries.

Comparative advantage can also be expressed in terms of opportunity cost. In our example, if Farmer A were to switch one hour of labour time from peas to strawberries, he would be sacrificing 15 kg of peas for 15 kg of strawberries. The opportunity cost for Farmer A of 1 kg of strawberries is therefore 1 kg of peas (15/15). If Farmer B were to switch one hour of labour time from peas to strawberries, he would be giving up 7.5 kg of peas for 10 kg of strawberries. The opportunity cost for Farmer B of a kilogram of strawberries is therefore only 0.75 kg of peas (7.5/10). The opportunity cost of a kilogram of strawberries is thus lower for Farmer B than for Farmer A.

Conversely, it can be shown that the opportunity cost of picking peas is lower for Farmer A than for Farmer B. If Farmer A switches one hour of labour time from strawberries to peas, he must give up 15 kg of strawberries for 15 kg of peas. The opportunity cost of each kilogram of peas, therefore, is a kilogram of strawberries (15/15). However, if Farmer B switches one hour of labour time from strawberries to peas, he must give up 10 kg of strawberries for 7.5 kg of peas. The opportunity cost of each kilogram of peas for Farmer B is therefore 1.33⅓ kg of strawberries (10/7.5) — which is one-third higher than Farmer A's opportunity cost of picking peas.

Farmer A is said to have a comparative advantage in picking peas, where his opportunity cost is lower than Farmer B's, while Farmer B has a comparative advantage in picking strawberries, where his opportunity cost is lower than Farmer A's.

On the basis of comparative advantage, measured either in terms of a perceived comparative superiority or in terms of opportunity cost, Farmers A and B can be guided in choosing *what* to produce. As Chapter 15 will show, the same principles can be used by entire nations to decide what they ought to produce.

How to Produce?

The second major decision facing every economy is *how* to produce the mix of goods and services it has chosen to produce. There is more than one way to produce almost anything. One of the basic choices to be made by the owners of business in any economy is how much capital and how much labour to use in the production process. To substitute more capital for labour, for example, may require a very substantial outlay of money, but in the long run, the resulting increase in production efficiency may justify that outlay.

Substitution of factors is possible in every line of production. In Canada, crops are grown on large farms employing relatively little labour. In some other countries, such as Indonesia, large amounts of labour are used to grow crops on small fields. Electricity can be generated by burning coal, a process that uses large quantities of natural resources, or it can be generated with the aid of solar collectors, which use fewer resources but require large capital investments. Coal can be strip-mined, using huge machines and relatively little labour, or it can be mined underground, using relatively more labour. The choices are endless.

As these examples suggest, there is no one way of producing a good that is right at all times and in all places. The optimal method depends on the relative scarcities of the various factors of production. In a country such as China, which is poor but has a large population, it makes sense to use huge pick-and-shovel gangs to build roads. It makes just as much sense to use bulldozers and small work crews to build roads in Australia, where capital is abundant and labour less so. But making the right choices is important. If the wrong choices are made, scarce factors of production are wasted and the total amount of goods and services produced is less than it might otherwise be.

For Whom Should Goods Be Produced?

The third fundamental economic question — For whom should goods and services be produced? — raises complex normative issues. In economies that impose few restrictions on the operation of the market, goods are produced for those who bring the most purchasing power to the market — in other words, for those who have the highest incomes. This practice may be considered fair in the sense that, if the income differences in the society accurately reflect the differences in individuals' and households' contributions to the economy, then people are simply being rewarded according to their output. This may also be considered a beneficial result for society: If goods are distributed in a way that rewards hard work and careful use of resources, there will ultimately be more goods for distribution. (Conversely, if goods are distributed in a way that is unrelated to people's efforts and choices, less will be produced.)

However, even in an economy where incomes are distributed in such a "fair" and efficient manner (and in any real-life market system, people are often rewarded for many things *other* than hard work or ability — as happens, for example, with the luck of a good inheritance), the distribution of goods might not be considered fair from another point of view. To examine this problem, think of the purchasing power that citizens bring to a market as the *votes* they cast for the types of goods and services that are to be produced. Obviously, richer people have more votes than poorer people, and, unless one attributes greater altruism to the rich than to people in general, it is likely that they will cast their votes for goods and services that meet their own needs and desires and not necessarily those of the population at large.

Visitors to certain market economies in South America and the Near East are struck by the extreme wealth of some members of those economies — in the form of luxury villas and shops — and the extreme poverty of many others. Although there is much wealth in evidence, the basic housing, health, and educational needs of large segments of the population seem badly neglected. But one doesn't have to go so far afield. In some of the larger cities of North America, extreme poverty coexists with considerable luxury (Harlem is only a few blocks from Park Avenue). Similarly, blighted rural areas struggle alongside burgeoning new industrial centres. Would we consider this to be a fair outcome of the operation of the market?

Although many market economies may be operating efficiently, on or close to their production possibilities frontiers, the mix of goods they have chosen to produce may leave something to be desired. To use the tools of analysis developed in this chapter, look back at the graph in Box 2.1 (page 37). Let us assume that a certain market economy is operating on the production possibilities frontier depicted there, and, more specifically, that a few very affluent people — those with most of the purchasing power in the economy — have opted for the mix of products represented by point *F*. They have, in other words, chosen to build a substantial military complex, with little emphasis on civilian goods. Presumably, most of the relatively small amount of beef being produced will go to them as well. If "votes" (in the form of purchasing power) were distributed more equally in this society, the people might opt for point *B* or *C* on the production possibilities frontier. All of those points — *B*, *C*, and *F* — are equally efficient, but the ways in which they satisfy the needs of the population are very different.

Because of this problem, most modern market economies have chosen to "interfere" with the market, at least to some extent. Through their taxation and spending powers, governments at various levels have profoundly altered the distribution of goods.

In later chapters of this book, we will examine the actual behaviour of our market system much more closely. We will discover that the distribution of goods is still determined to a large extent by the purchasing power of individuals and households, but we will also note the extensive role of government and the power of producers themselves to influence the purchasing decisions of consumers.

Economic Growth and Entrepreneurship

We have now examined, all too briefly, the three main problems of all economies. In this discussion, we have used what economists call a static model — that is, we have assumed that the economy is given certain resources in certain amounts, including a skilled labour force of a certain size and ability. A production possibilities frontier was developed for such an economy, illustrating the most output that could be realized with the given factors of production. In the real world, however, knowledge and factors of production don't remain the same for long. Knowledge is always increasing. Population growth expands the amount of labour available, and education improves its quality. The supply of capital grows as people set aside part of their income as savings and invest what they save in new machinery, buildings, and so on. And in many cases, though not all, new natural resources become available faster than old ones are used up.

As these things happen, the production possibilities frontier expands, as shown in Box 2.2. The economy breaks through its former limits. New production techniques are developed. New consumption opportunities are opened up. If productive efficiency means operating on a fixed production possibilities frontier, what do we call the force that allows the economy to keep up with the frontier as it expands over time? Economists call it **entrepreneurship**. Entrepreneurship is the process of seeking out new possibilities: making use of new ways of doing things, being alert to new opportunities, and helping to expand existing limits.

> **Entrepreneurship**
> The process of seeking out new possibilities: making use of new ways of doing things, being alert to new opportunities, and helping to expand existing limits.

In the world of business, entrepreneurship is often linked with the founding of new firms. When a Henry Ford sets out to establish a whole new industry, there are few givens to deal with. New production processes have to be invented. The constraints of existing sources of supply have to be overcome. Consumers are encouraged to satisfy wants and needs to which they gave little thought before, because there were no products that could satisfy them. This kind of exploring and experimenting is the essence of entrepreneurship.

But entrepreneurship is not limited to the founding of new firms. The manager of a Ford plant may be less of an entrepreneur than the founder, but the manager's work is not entirely routine. Unexpected problems arise that must be solved somehow — often by figuring out a new way of doing things.

Consumers and workers can be entrepreneurs, too. They do not simply repeat the same patterns of work and leisure every day. They seek variety — new jobs, new foods, new places to visit. Each time you try something new, you are taking a step into the unknown. In a small way, you are playing the role of entrepreneur.

THE PERFORMANCE OF THE CANADIAN ECONOMY

The preceding analysis prompts us to consider the questions How close is the Canadian economy to its production possibilities frontier? and How rapidly is that frontier shifting to the right? Such questions take us into the area of eco-

BOX 2.2   Expansion of the Production Possibilities Frontier

Production possibilities frontiers assume given supplies of factors of production and a given state of knowledge. As new factors of production become available and as scientific discoveries are made, entrepreneurs become aware of new opportunities and break through existing constraints. The production possibilities frontier then expands. Points that were once unattainable come within reach.

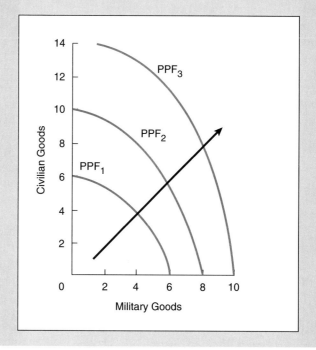

nomic performance. The first question can be addressed with the aid of such measures as the unemployment rate (How much of the country's labour supply is actually being used?) and the rate of inflation. The second question calls for a way of measuring economic growth.

Unemployment

One of the key indicators of the health of an economy is its ability to provide a job for anyone who wants to work. The economy's performance in this area is measured by the **unemployment rate** — the percentage of people in the labour force who are not working but are actively looking for work. People who are not actively looking for work — such as full-time students and retired people, as well as so-called discouraged workers (those who have given up their search for employment) — are not counted as members of the labour force and thus are not included in the unemployment rate.

Even in the best of times, the unemployment rate does not fall to zero. In a healthy, changing economy, it is normal for a certain number of people to be out of work for a short time when they first enter the labour force, or when they have quit a job in order to look for a better one. There is some disagreement as to what the "normal" level of unemployment is.

Unemployment rate
The percentage of people in the labour force who are not working but are actively looking for work.

Box 2.3 shows Canada's unemployment record since 1950. During the 1950s and 1960s, with only a few exceptions, the rate stayed between 4 and 6.5 percent. Then, in 1975, this "normal" rate started to climb considerably higher, reaching a post-Depression peak of 11.9 percent in 1983. Though it declined for a few years after that, it started to rise again in the late 1980s and remains at levels that are quite a bit higher than "normal."

Inflation

Inflation is a sustained increase in the average level of prices of all goods and services. The most widely used measure of inflation in Canada is the Consumer Price Index (CPI). The Consumer Price Index works as follows: the average level of prices of consumer goods and services in a base period (e.g., the year 1991) is given an index number of 100. If prices of those goods and services increase by 100 percent in, say, four years, the index increases to 200. If the index should

Inflation
A sustained increase in the average price of all goods and services.

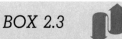

Unemployment in Canada since 1950   *BOX 2.3*

Economists do not agree on the "normal" level of unemployment for the Canadian economy, or whether it is even useful to think in such terms. However, many believe that an acceptable rate is somewhere in the range of 4 to 6.5 percent of the labour force. Rates lower than 4 percent are seldom reached because there are always people who are out of work while changing jobs or looking for a first job. As the graph shows, unemployment rates were considerably higher in the 1970s and 1980s than in the 1950s and 1960s.

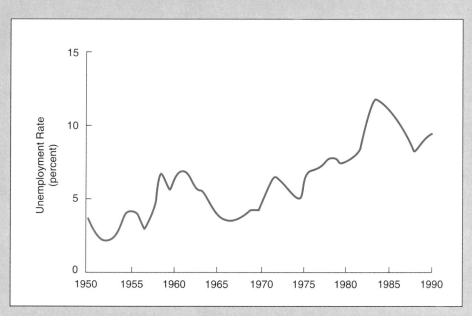

SOURCE: Adapted from Statistics Canada, *Canadian Economic Observer, Historical Statistical Supplement 1989/90*, p. 34, Catalogue no. 11-210. Reproduced with permission of the Minister of Supply and Services Canada, 1992.

increase to 250, it would mean that prices had risen by 150 percent since the base period. Price stability — that is, the absence of inflation — is a second major sign of the health of an economy. True price stability means no increase at all in the average level of prices from year to year. However, many economists and policy makers would settle for any rate of increase below 3 percent per year.

Box 2.4 shows trends in inflation in Canada since 1950. During the 1950s and 1960s, inflation stayed, for the most part, within the safe range. The high inflation of the early 1950s was related to the Korean War. The rate of inflation began to climb in 1971, dipped slightly in the mid-1970s, then rose sharply once again, peaking at 12.5 percent in 1981. The rate began to fall after that; indeed, the last few years provide some hope that we have reached a new era of lower rates of inflation (around 4 percent).

BOX 2.4 *Inflation in Canada since 1950*

True price stability means no increase at all in the average level of prices from year to year. However, many economists consider an inflation rate of less than 3 percent, as measured by the rate of increase of the Consumer Price Index, to be acceptable. As the graph shows, such low rates of inflation were the rule during much of the 1950s and 1960s, but in the 1970s, inflation soared, reaching a high of 12.5 percent in 1981. Since 1984, inflation rates have declined to more acceptable levels of about 4 percent a year.

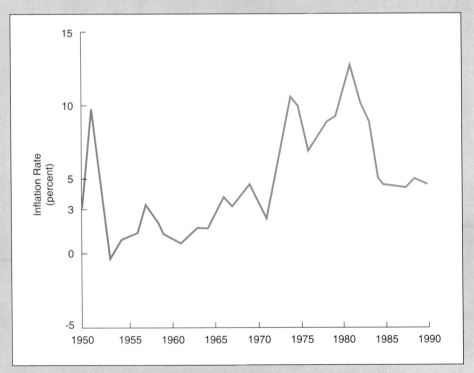

SOURCE: Adapted from Statistics Canada, *Canadian Economic Observer, Historical Statistical Supplement 1989/90*, p. 23, Catalogue no. 11-210. Reproduced with permission of the Minister of Supply and Services Canada, 1992.

Economic Growth

Economic growth is a third major sign of economic health. The economy must grow to provide jobs for new workers and to provide everyone with a rising standard of living.

Canada measures its total output in terms of **gross domestic product (GDP)**, which represents the value of all final goods and services produced within a country in a given year.

To be meaningful as a measure of economic growth, changes in GDP over time must be adjusted for the effects of inflation. Economists use the term **nominal** in reference to data that have not been adjusted for the effects of inflation, and

Gross domestic product (GDP)
The dollar value of all final goods and services produced within a country in a given year.

Nominal
In economics, a term used in reference to data that have not been adjusted for the effects of inflation.

The Growth of GDP in Canada, 1965–1990   BOX 2.5

This graph shows annual growth rates of real GDP for Canada between 1965 and 1990. There are tremendous variations around a "healthy" rate of 3 percent. In 18 of the 26 years depicted, the rate of growth was greater than or equal to 3 percent.

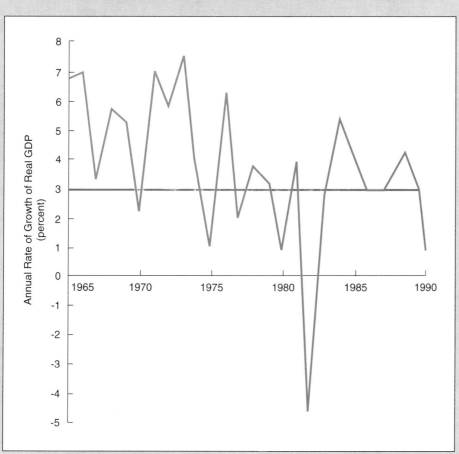

SOURCE: Adapted from Statistics Canada, *Canadian Economic Observer, Historical Statistical Supplement 1989/90*, p. 7, Catalogue no. 11-210. Reproduced with permission of the Minister of Supply and Services Canada, 1992.

Real
In economics, a term used in reference to data that have been adjusted for the effects of inflation.

Business cycle
A cycle in which periods of growth of real output (which may be accompanied by inflation) alternate with periods of falling output (which tend to be accompanied by high unemployment).

Recession
A period in which real output falls for six months or more.

the term **real** in reference to data that have been adjusted for inflation. In economics, we are interested in measuring changes in *real* GDP, or *real* output.

The growth process is not a steady one, and economists are particularly interested in variations in the growth rate from year to year. An annual growth rate in the GDP of about 3 percent is considered healthy and, indeed, quite attainable. Box 2.5 shows the annual growth rate of real GDP in Canada for each year from 1965 to 1990. (Compare the graph's jagged line with the straight line representing a steady annual rate of 3 percent.) What is most striking about this diagram is the tremendous fluctuation in the rate of growth from one year to another. The rates ranged from a high of 7.4 percent in 1973 to a low of −4.3 percent in 1982, with numerous sharp swings in between. A poor performance one year, as in 1982, is seldom followed by a poor performance the next year; unfortunately, good performances are also seldom sustained for more than a year or two.

The business cycle

The constant fluctuations of GDP just noted are referred to as the **business cycle**. As Box 2.6 shows, a typical business cycle consists of four parts. The first part, during which real GDP falls, is known as a **recession**. (Very short business downturns are usually ignored; normally, a downturn has to last six months or more

BOX 2.6 *The Business Cycle*

Over time, real output tends to grow at a rate of about 3 percent per year. However, the growth is not even. The economy tends to move in a cyclical pattern, with output sometimes falling below the level of the long-term trend and sometimes rising above it. This figure shows the phases of a typical business cycle. The first phase, in which real output falls for six months or more, is known as a recession. Once the recession has bottomed out — at the so-called trough of the cycle — real output begins to grow again. This phase is called the recovery. After the recovery reaches its peak, a new recession begins.

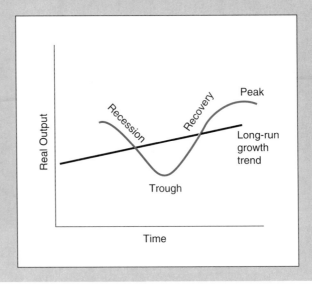

before economists count it as a recession.) The low point reached at the end of a recession is known as the *trough* of the business cycle. This is followed by the upturn, or **recovery**. At the end of the recovery, the business cycle reaches a *peak*, after which output turns down again and a new cycle begins.

Recovery
A period of renewed growth of real output following a recession.

The goals of full employment, price stability, and economic growth are closely linked. During a recession, when real output falls, the unemployment rate tends to rise. During a recovery, when real output is rising, the rate of inflation sometimes, but not always, tends to speed up. These are two of many linkages among economic phenomena. Macroeconomists have investigated these linkages in detail, along with others that involve interest rates, the supply of money, levels of consumption and investment, and the international value of the dollar.

CONCLUSION

This chapter began with a Preview describing the difficulties some Canadians are currently encountering in finding a good job. Part of the problem is created by the transition being experienced in the economy from resource-based and manufacturing industries to the service sector — now the fastest-growing sector of the economy. Furthermore, because this sector is strongest in metropolitan areas, the residents of large cities are now at a great advantage in finding new jobs. While Canadians once found their comparative advantage in resource-based industries, which are scattered across the country, most good jobs are now found in the largest cities, which means relocation for people living elsewhere. It is difficult adjustments such as these that make the attainment of the economy's basic goals a complex and difficult endeavour.

SUMMARY

1. The central economic problem is how to deal with scarcity. Deciding what should be produced, how it should be produced, and for whom it should be produced are all part of this problem. These questions must be addressed by every economy.

2. A range of production choices can be presented in graphic form as a *production possibilities frontier*. The frontier is the boundary between the mixes of goods that can be produced with available resources and know-how and those that cannot. Movement along the frontier represents a trade-off of one good for another.

3. An economy operating efficiently is operating at a point *on* its production possibilities frontier. *Efficiency*, as economists use the term, means a state of affairs in which, with the available knowledge and resources, no change can be made that would make one person better off without making someone else worse off. If an economy could produce more of one good without producing less of another, at least one person could be made better off; this would mean that the economy was operating inefficiently, underutilizing its resources.

4. The *opportunity cost* of a good is its cost in terms of lost opportunity to do something else with the same time and resources.

5. No two people are alike in terms of skills and abilities. Output and satisfaction can be increased by means of a *division of labour* based on *comparative advantage*. According to this principle, each person should specialize in the goods or services that he or she can produce at the least opportunity cost. Comparative advantage applies to the division of labour among countries as well.

6. There are many different ways to produce any good or service. Differences in production techniques often reflect substitutions of one factor of production for another. Techniques should be chosen that use scarce factors sparingly and less scarce ones more generously.

7. An economy must find a way not only to produce efficiently, but to produce the "right" mix of output and to distribute that output according to people's preferences. The normative issue of fairness plays a major role in determining for whom goods and services should be produced.

8. *Entrepreneurship* is the process of seeking out new possibilities — thinking of new ways of doing things, being alert to new opportunities, and overcoming constraints. It is a dynamic process that can be thought of as constantly bringing new knowledge and factors of production to bear as the economy's production possibilities frontier expands.

9. The performance of an economy is measured by several yardsticks, including the unemployment rate (which gives us an indication of how close to its PPF an economy is operating), inflation, and rates of economic growth (which tell us whether the economy's PPF is shifting to the right). The *unemployment rate* is the percentage of people in the labour force who are actively looking for work but are unable to find it. *Inflation* is a sustained increase in the average price level of all goods and services. It is often measured by the Consumer Price Index. Economic growth is measured by the rate of increase in real *gross domestic product*. (The term *real* is used in reference to economic quantities that have been adjusted for inflation. Quantities that have not been adjusted for inflation are referred to as *nominal*.)

KEY TERMS

production possibilities frontier
  (PPF)
efficiency
opportunity cost
division of labour, or
  specialization

absolute advantage
comparative advantage
entrepreneurship
unemployment rate
inflation
gross domestic product (GDP)

nominal
real
business cycle
recession
recovery

KEY BOXES

Box 2.1 Adanac's Production Possibilities Frontier
Box 2.3 Unemployment in Canada since 1950

Box 2.4 Inflation in Canada since 1950
Box 2.5 The Growth of GDP in Canada, 1965–1990

REVIEW QUESTIONS

1. A farmer has four fields spread out over a hillside. She can grow either wheat or potatoes on any of the fields, but the low fields are better for potatoes and the high ones are better for wheat. Here are some combinations of wheat and potatoes that she can produce:

Number of Fields Used for Potatoes	Tonnes of Potatoes	Tonnes of Wheat
4	1000	0
3	900	400
2	600	700
1	300	900
0	0	1000

Use these data to draw a production possibilities frontier for wheat and potatoes. What is the opportunity cost of wheat, stated in terms of potatoes, when the farmer switches the highest field into wheat production (leaving three fields for potatoes)? What happens to the opportunity cost of wheat as more and more fields are switched to wheat?

2. Because of changing consumer tastes and choices, the type of goods produced in an economy can change radically over time. Using library sources, examine how the number of employees in such industries as farming, manufacturing, and service industries has changed in Canada from, say, 1971 to 1991.

3. In Canada, it takes 100 labour hours to produce a tractor and 2 labour hours to produce a pair of shoes. In China, it takes 500 labour hours to build a tractor and 2.5 labour hours to make a pair of shoes. Which country has a comparative advantage in shoes? In tractors? How can the two countries gain from trade, even though both tractors and shoes can be produced with fewer labour hours in Canada?

4. "Any increase in an economy's output represents an increase in consumers' welfare." Discuss.

5. Farmer A can pick 15 kg of peas or 15 kg of strawberries in 1 hour. It takes Farmer B 2 hours to pick 15 kg of peas and 1.5 hours to pick 15 kg of strawberries. Calculate the opportunity cost for each farmer of picking peas and strawberries. (*Note*: The opportunity cost of picking 15 kg of peas is the amount of strawberries "given up" during the picking of the peas.)

6. In its *Twenty-Seventh Annual Review*, published in 1990, the Economic Council of Canada forecast that, in 1992, real GDP would increase by 4.0 percent, inflation (measured by the Consumer Price Index) would be 4.3 percent, and the unemployment rate would be 7.9 percent. Compare these projections with actual results. Consult your library.

7. Prof. Jim MacIntosh began teaching at a Canadian university in 1967 at a salary of $9500. By 1991, that salary had risen to $78 000. Assuming that the Consumer Price Index had risen from 100 to 535 during this period, how much did Professor MacIntosh's real income grow or shrink?

A Profile of the Canadian Economy

WHAT YOU WILL LEARN IN THIS CHAPTER

After studying this chapter, you will be able to

1. Identify Canada's leading industries by numbers of people employed.

2. Outline the broad features of Canada's economic development.

3. Describe the historical forces that led to the considerable degree of government involvement that is characteristic of the Canadian economy today.

4. Explain the meaning and significance of a staple product.

5. Distinguish between a "promotional" and a "regulatory" government.

6. Discuss the growth of government in Canada in terms of government purchases and transfer payments.

7. List four economic functions of government.

8. Compare the extent to which public enterprises are involved in the economies of different countries.

9. Explain the role of business in co-ordinating economic activity.

10. Discuss the advantages and disadvantages of various forms of business organization.

11. Explain why most large firms are organized as corporations.

A Preview   *Survival of the Fittest*

Economic institutions and practices are in a constant state of flux. In the transportation industry, the horse and buggy gave way to the automobile, and railways have lost much of their former market to airplanes and trucks. In Canada, the trucking industry, in turn, faces stiff competition from its American rivals. A market economy is a "dog-eat-dog" world, in which the participants must certainly depend on their own wits — but also, as the following article suggests, on the protection of governments.

Trucking in Canada: Downhill from Here

The shake-out continues in the Canadian trucking industry as sleek, cost-efficient U.S. carriers roll across our border. Once the dust settles, the industry won't look the same.

By the year 2000, says Ontario Trucking Association president Ray Cope, only three supercarriers will dominate the Canadian general freight industry. Last year, bankruptcies rose 74 percent in Canada. And in Ontario, where 40 percent of the industry draws a paycheque, 5000 trucking jobs were lost between June 1989 and December 1990.

The changing face of Canada's trucking industry is largely the result of the 1989 deregulation that threw open the doors to U.S. truckers by doing away with difficult licence requirements. The cost of doing business for Canadian carriers, meanwhile, has remained much higher than in the U.S. With cheaper fuel, lower taxes, and faster depreciation of equipment, U.S. carriers have enjoyed an 18-percent-per-kilometre operating advantage.

Canadian carriers have struggled to cope. For one thing, they've been beating a path south. In all, about twenty firms relocated in the U.S. last year. Mergers, too, have soared. Of the twenty largest Canadian trucking concerns operating ten years ago, only eight remain. Intercity Truck Lines, for instance, merged with Reimer Express Lines Ltd., and Kingsway Transports Ltd. joined Motorways Ltd. The trend, says Cope, won't soon ease up: "A lot of companies that were household names will be gone."

To give Canadian carriers a fighting chance, Cope is seeking tax relief from provincial and federal governments to bring back the level playing field that deregulation tilted in favour of U.S. truckers.

It may not be enough. "The industry is rationalizing," says Adil Cubukgil, president of Transmode Consultants Inc. "Only the fittest will survive."

SOURCE: Andrew Trimble, "Trucking in Canada: Downhill from Here," *Canadian Business*, April 1991, p. 15. Reproduced with permission.

CONSTANT CHANGE: A BASIC TRAIT OF MARKET ECONOMIES

A market economy such as Canada's is characterized by constant change. Some industries grow while others decline, and, within particular industries, new companies emerge as long-established companies fade from the scene. One noted economist, Joseph Schumpeter, called this process **creative destruction**. New companies are created by entrepreneurs producing new products or services in response to changing consumer demands. Their success depends on their ability to anticipate correctly what consumers want or, through effective marketing strategies, to persuade consumers to buy what is offered to them. This dynamic process results in the success of some companies and the failure of others — hence, the combination of creativity and destruction.

The failure of a company produces severe hardships for both owners and employees, as well as for many others who have come to depend on the firm. The closure of a small grocery store in a well-established neighbourhood, for example, may be a personal tragedy for its owners, but it is also a considerable inconvenience for local residents, some of whom may have chosen their home because it was near the store. However, while economists acknowledge the serious problems caused by business failure, they also argue that, in most cases, the simultaneous creation of new businesses and new products is beneficial to society as a whole. If new companies could not replace existing ones through competition, there would be little incentive for entrepreneurship — for the development of new products and new techniques. Formerly socialist countries, such as Poland and the Soviet Union, tried hard, and quite successfully, to shield workers and managers from the destructive effects of competition. Workers had job security because the government would not permit their company to fail and to be replaced by a new one. However, it is now acknowledged even by socialist economists that too high a price was paid for such security in terms of efficiency, quality of products, and standard of living. In capitalist countries, the pain associated with change has been accepted as an unfortunate but necessary condition of economic progress. This is not to say that all change is a mark of progress or that the destruction of a business is always compensated for by the substitution of something better. As Chapters 8, 9, and 10 will amply demonstrate, the immense power that some businesses have accumulated over time allows them to resist the normal pressures of competition and may enable them to "destroy" rival businesses that may have better ideas but less economic power. This is clearly not the *creative* destruction Schumpeter spoke of.

Creative destruction
The process within market economies whereby new firms or industries emerge to replace those that are in decline.

THE STRUCTURE OF THE CANADIAN ECONOMY

Despite such problems, the Canadian economy has indeed progressed, changing considerably in the course of one-and-a-quarter centuries. The profile of the Canadian economy sketched in Box 3.1 shows us how industries have changed in importance over time, as measured by the number of persons employed in them. It reveals, first of all, that slightly more than half the people in Canada in 1990 (13 681 000) were part of the labour force — that is, held a job or were actively looking for one. In 1950, only 5 198 000 people, or 38 percent of the population, were counted as part of the labour force. This increase between 1950 and 1990 in the proportion of the population that took part in the labour force

BOX 3.1 Employment in the Canadian Economy, 1950 and 1990

This table shows the number of Canadians in the labour force in the years 1950 and 1990, the number actually employed, and the types of jobs they had. While Canada's population did not quite double between 1950 and 1990, its labour force more than doubled, largely because the number of women in the labour force increased roughly fivefold. Employment in agriculture declined sharply, while most of the increase in the labour force was reflected in the growth of the service industries.

	1950	1990
Canada's Population	13 712 000	26 440 000
Number in the Labour Force*	5 198 000	13 681 000
Number Employed	5 056 000	12 572 000
Males employed	3 844 000	6 948 000
Females employed	1 112 000	5 624 000
Employment by Occupation		
Agriculture	1 066 000	429 000
Other primary industries (mining, fishing, forestry)	182 000	283 000
Manufacturing	1 321 000	2 001 000
Construction	335 000	778 000
Services	2 138 000	9 081 000

Note: Totals do not always add up, due to rounding.
*The labour force includes people who are gainfully employed and people fifteen years of age and older who do not have a job but are looking for one.

SOURCE: Data for 1950 are taken from M.C. Urquhart and K.A.H. Buckley, *Historical Statistics of Canada* (Toronto: Macmillan, 1965), pp. 14, 64; data for 1990 are from Statistics Canada, *Canadian Economic Observer*, May 1991, p. 5.26, and July 1991, p. 6.26, Catalogue no. 11-010. Reproduced with permission of the Minister of Supply and Services Canada, 1992.

is attributable in large measure to the growing number of women entering its ranks. Box 3.1 also tells us that almost all the new jobs created in recent years are in the service sector, including such fields as teaching, health care, wholesale and retail trade, finance and insurance, and other activities that do not result in a tangible, physical product. The agricultural labour force decreased during this 40-year period by more than 50 percent, while the number of people employed in manufacturing rose relatively little.

Is Canada a Post-Industrial Society?

Economic historians often look for universal patterns of economic development in the evolution of different societies. Many scholars maintain that advanced economies — those with a high standard of living and a significant industrial sector — have, in the last few centuries, passed through the following phases:

Phase 1: Traditional society, based on agriculture.

Phase 2: Modern society, based on industry.

Phase 3: Post-industrial society, based on services.

These three phases suggest that advanced economies have experienced two major turning points in their development: (1) when industry, including manufacturing, construction, and mining, supplanted agriculture as the major sector of the economy; and (2) when the **service sector** replaced industry as the leading sector. In many Western European economies, the first turning point occurred in the late nineteenth and early twentieth centuries, and the second, after World War II. This second turning point ushered in what is known as the **post-industrial society**.

As we have seen, Canada's service sector is much larger than its industrial sector. This does not mean, however, that it is accurate to speak of Canada as a post-industrial society, because, unlike most Western European nations, Canada never experienced an industrial phase — that is, a period during which industry was more important than services. Instead, Canada, as well as the United States and a few other countries, made a direct transition from a traditional agrarian economy — mixed with other natural-resource industries such as fishing and lumbering — to a service economy.

This somewhat unique pattern of development is illustrated in Box 3.2. The graph for Canada indicates that, in the period before 1920, employment levels were almost as high in industry as in services (but never higher), and that after 1920, the service sector grew much more rapidly than industry. This Canadian pattern is similar to that of the United States, but very different from that of Western Europe, where employment levels were higher in industry than in services until about 1960.

The Choice between Services and Goods

The trend toward services and away from industrial goods (as measured by employment levels) may be disturbing to some Canadians. There is a tendency to equate the success of an economy with the output of tangible, physical goods, partly because such goods meet what appear to be our most basic needs — for food, clothing, and shelter — and partly because they can be seen and measured. By contrast, we cannot "see" what a teacher produces, or a stockbroker, and we find it difficult to assess how vital these services are. In addition, there is a widespread inclination to think that economic growth in general — the raising of the standard of living of an entire society — depends much more on the growth of industry than on the growth of services. To use current terminology, industry is thought of as a "pro-active" force, stimulating activity in other sectors and thereby promoting economic development, while services are considered "reactive," responding to the stimulus created by industry but producing no spin-offs of their own. Town and city planners often seem especially pleased to announce the opening of a new industrial plant, promising that a lot of additional economic activity will follow in its wake, but they express fewer hopes and expectations with the opening of a new service facility, such as a dental clinic or a counselling centre.

Are such attitudes and opinions borne out by the facts? Not really. People obviously need industrial goods such as clothing and various kinds of equipment, and producing such goods can certainly mean employment for many workers. However, as Chapter 15 will show (and as we noted in the previous chapter), a country can obtain many of the things it needs by trading with other countries. (Japan is a notable example of this.) The jobs created in the service sector produce income that can be used to purchase goods produced virtually anywhere in the

Service sector
The sector of an economy consisting of service industries, such as health and education services; communication and transportation services; and financial, legal, and trading services.

Post-industrial society
The third phase of a society's economic evolution, following the traditional, agrarian phase and the modern, industrial phase. The post-industrial society is based on services.

BOX 3.2   *Industrial and Service Employment in Canada, the United States, and Western Europe, 1880–1980*

The graphs below show that, in both Canada and the United States, employment levels have never been as high in industry as in services. Thus, neither country has experienced a true industrial phase in its development, and the term "post-industrial society" is inaccurate for both countries. By contrast, in Western European countries, industry played a much more important role than services (in terms of employment levels) for many years, and the shift away from the industrial base that began only a few decades ago has been dramatic.

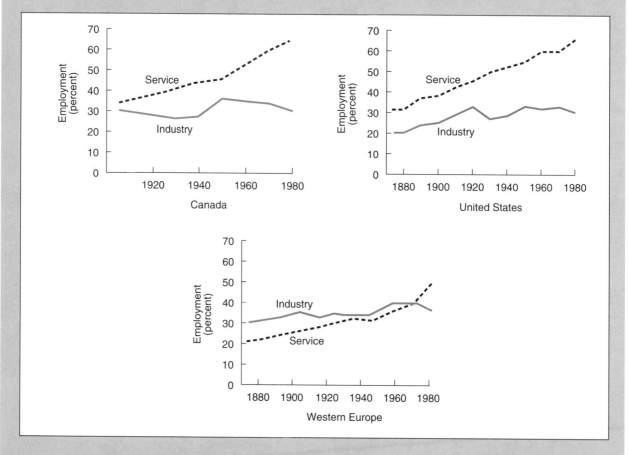

SOURCE: Hartmut Kaelble, "Was Prometheus Most Unbound in Europe? The Labour Force in Europe During the Late XIXth and XXth Centuries," *Journal of European Economic History* 18, no. 1 (Spring 1989): 72. Used with permission.

world. Furthermore, service industries are indeed pro-active, generating spin-off activities just as goods industries do. The building of a hospital, for example, stimulates activity in the construction industry, and the purchase of hospital equipment supports the machine industry. (Making a similar point, the Economic Council of Canada recently observed that "the goods sector and the service sector are tending to converge. . . . Business, financial, communication and other services increasingly form an integral component of the final product produced by the manufacturing industries.")[1] Moreover, as noted above, the income earned by those employed in the service industries goes into expenditures that support a wide range of other economic activity, just as the earnings of people in the goods industry do. And there is no reason to consider the "products" of the service sector any less legitimate than "real" products — that is, tangible, physical, and measurable goods. Both sectors provide something that is "consumed" by the population. Indeed, in a market economy, consumers basically determine what is produced — and Canadian consumers have clearly decided over the years that, in addition to such basic necessities as food, clothing, and shelter, they also want high-quality health services and good schooling; well-developed communication and transportation systems; and the numerous financial, legal, and trading services that help to organize and ease the flow of the other goods and services produced within the economy.

The Canadian economy developed later than the economies of the Western European countries and of the United States, and was therefore able to rely to a significant extent on the industrial goods and technology of those countries. Specializing in goods in the production of which it had a comparative advantage, Canada was able to achieve rapid economic growth following a pattern quite different from the one that European countries had experienced.

Canada has, in fact, developed a fairly substantial industrial base, while simultaneously creating a service sector that, especially in the areas of medicine and education, is the envy of many other countries. It must also be noted that while employment has either declined or grown relatively little in such sectors as farming, manufacturing, mining, and construction, the *output* of most of these sectors has continued to grow impressively, even in the last decade. By shifting its production possibilities frontier to the right, Canada has avoided having to choose *between* goods and services; instead, it has been able to increase its production and consumption of both. It is not clear, however, that the economy will be able to sustain this accomplishment through the 1990s.

CANADIAN ECONOMIC INSTITUTIONS
The Interplay of Government and Business

Our market economy consists of almost two million business enterprises, both small and large, bringing together the factors of land, labour, and capital in order to produce goods or services and to make a profit. The success of these firms depends on their ability to read the minds of consumers accurately.

However, markets never rely on the operation of private business organizations alone: In order to function, markets need governments. Governments provide the framework of law and regulation without which business activity would be impossible. It is this framework that receives our attention first in this discussion of Canada's economic institutions.

The mix of government and business that characterizes the Canadian economy is the result of forces that developed very early in our history. The European-based traders and settlers who began to create small commercial centres in the

---

[1] Economic Council of Canada, *Au Courant* 12, no. 1 (1991): 4. Reprinted with permission of the Chairman of the Economic Council of Canada.

Maritimes and along the shores of the St. Lawrence River and Lake Ontario in the seventeenth and eighteenth centuries developed business operations that profoundly affected the future course of this country.

As we noted in Chapter 1, economic historians such as Harold Adams Innis have identified some unique features of this early economic development. Given the abundance of land and the relative scarcity of labour and capital, early Canadian settlements concentrated on obtaining and exporting natural resources. The commodity, or resource, on which the economy of a settlement or region is based is called a **staple product**. Much of the energy of the early settlements was devoted to the exploitation of a succession of natural resources, from fish to fur to timber. This set a pattern for Canadian economic strategy for centuries to come.

Staple product
A commodity on which the economy of a settlement or region concentrates much of its labour and capital.

The very nature of its staple products affected Canada's development. When furs were in great demand in Europe, the ease with which fur-bearing animals could be caught led to rapid depletion of local supplies and consequently to rapid penetration of the Canadian hinterland by traders seeking more pelts. A vast but fragile economic system thus evolved, linking the eastern trading headquarters to native traders in the West. Increased amounts of capital were required to overcome the transportation problems created by the great distances that were involved. This requirement favoured organizations such as the Hudson's Bay Company, and led to the growth of monopoly in what had previously been an extremely competitive industry.

Ultimately, the need for capital to unite this fragile, far-flung economic system, and to protect it from the potential encroachment of the rapidly growing economy to the south, led to the formation of a national state and to the intertwining of private business and government in the creation of that state.

By the mid-nineteenth century, there were strong regional economies in the Maritimes and in central Canada, but it was far from clear whether, and how, these economies would co-operate with each other and how they should relate to the countries with which they did most of their trading.

Until the 1840s, the colonies of central Canada and the Maritimes benefited immensely from their trading connections with Great Britain, because the latter placed lower tariffs on goods from these regions than on goods from most other countries. However, in the 1840s, Great Britain lowered tariffs on almost all of its imports, and central Canadian and Maritime colonies lost their preferential position in the British market. They soon found that they could not compete effectively with some other countries in the export of timber to Britain. In frustration, these regions turned to the United States, hoping to find a more favourable market there. For twelve years, beginning in 1854, the British North American colonies participated in free trade with the United States in most nonmanufactured goods under the terms of a *reciprocity treaty* signed in that year. However, in 1866, after the conclusion of the U.S. Civil War, the northern states decided to impose tariffs on goods entering their markets from central Canada and the Maritimes. These events provided a powerful stimulus for the creation of a new east–west economic and political system, resulting finally, in 1867, in a confederation of provinces called Canada.

Manitoba and British Columbia entered Confederation in 1870 and 1873, respectively. British Columbia's entry was conditional on the promise that a national railway system would be built within ten years. The federal government thereby committed itself to a huge public investment project. The governments of central and eastern Canada had subsidized railway construction in the 1850s and 1860s with guarantees of bonded debt. Such guarantees had proved to be crippling financial burdens, so when the transcontinental railway system was first proposed in the early 1870s, the federal government decided to assist by means of cash and land grants. The Liberal government was prepared to build a government railway in stages, keeping pace with the westward expansion of settlement, but the Conservative government of John A. Macdonald opted for a full-scale effort in the construction of a transcontinental system, supported by both private enterprise and government grants.

In 1880, a group of private investors took up the government offer and, with $25 million in government cash grants and 25 million acres (10 million hectares) of free land, proceeded to build the Canadian Pacific Railway — a feat that has become a legend of Canadian history.

During this time of nation building, and even into the first decades of the twentieth century, government was expected to play a useful but limited role in its support of business and in pursuit of its own ends. As one Canadian scholar has observed, "Victorian businessmen had no objection to their government friends transferring public funds to their private projects, but they saw little need for further state intervention in their affairs."[2]

At this time, governments tended to assume what has been called a *promotional* role in the economy. The purpose of government was to promote business and nation building through such measures as subsidies and tariff protection, not to intervene in business affairs or to regulate them.

Government-supported construction of a transcontinental railway was part of a Conservative government development program that has been called the National Policy. It also included the establishment of protective tariffs in 1878 and a policy of land grants to encourage settlement of the West, thereby assuring both the growth of a market for consumer goods (and hence a stimulus for business) and a stronger nation.

Later, in the twentieth century, particularly as a result of the Great Depression of the 1930s and World War II, governments in Canada began to play a much larger role in the economy. During this time, organizations of groups such as farmers and labourers began to compete with business interests in obtaining government support and subsidization. There was increased pressure on government to use its powers of taxation, spending, and regulation to mobilize some of the country's resources in aid of those least able to function successfully in a market system. Such developments led to the creation of what has been called a *regulatory* or *interventionist* government.

As we shall see later in this chapter, the role of government continued to expand in the following decades. There is a broad base of concern about this development in Canada. The Macdonald Royal Commission suggested that one of the country's most urgent problems is to determine "the appropriate division of labour between the state and the economy." This, of course, is what democratic states are designed to do: to let citizens determine both what they want done by governments on their behalf and what they don't want governments to do. As Canadian economist Sylvia Ostry observes, "The mark of a democracy is that the 'big' choices that allocate scarce resources between public and private activities are ultimately made at the ballot box."[3] In other words, in our mixed-enterprise

---

[2]Tom Travis, "Business–Government Relations in Canadian History," in *Government and Enterprise in Canada*, ed. K.J. Ross and Nelson Wiseman (Toronto: Methuen, 1985), p. 9.

[3]Sylvia Ostry, "Government Intervention: Canada and the United States Compared," in *Government and Enterprise*, ed. Ross and Wiseman, p. 21.

system, based on democratic political institutions and a fairly open market, citizens make economic decisions not only when they make purchases from private businesses but also when they elect representatives to Parliament. In the last decade, Canadians elected a federal government that favoured less government control of the economy. Some Crown corporations, such as Air Canada, have been sold to private citizens; others, such as Canada Post, remain government owned, but are no longer subject to direct government control, and are expected to make a profit. Government-regulated industries, such as the airline industry, are also operating with much less government intervention.

The Distribution of Government Powers in Canada

One of the main purposes of a federal constitution is to reconcile the conflicting demands of various regional interests with one another and with the interests of the nation as a whole by creating different levels of government and assigning specific jurisdictions to each. Canada's Constitution, the British North America Act, sought to do this, but found no completely satisfactory way of assigning specific powers and responsibilities to the federal and provincial levels of government. Government action in the economic sphere was consequently made more difficult because of frequent disputes over divisions of power. The BNA Act gave the most far-reaching powers to the federal government in an effort to produce a strong nation that would withstand the powerful influence of the United States and avoid the type of civil war that had just occurred there.

Section 91 of the act listed 29 specific matters that belonged in the federal sphere, including the regulation of trade and commerce, taxation, the postal service, defence, banking and currency, and transportation and communication systems that serve two or more provinces. Later amendments gave the federal government jurisdiction over unemployment insurance and the old age pension (the latter jurisdiction shared with the provinces). Most important, the federal government was assigned residual powers (powers not explicitly granted to the provinces) and the general power to engage in any work deemed to be for the advantage of Canada.

In Section 92, the provincial legislatures were given general powers over local concerns and were assigned sixteen specific matters, including the power of direct taxation,[4] jurisdiction over municipal institutions, and most important, all property and civil rights in the province, which gave them control over land and resources. Section 93 placed education under their jurisdiction.

Agriculture and immigration were assigned to both the federal and the provincial governments in Section 95, with the federal government taking precedence in case of a conflict.

The federal government was intentionally placed in a much stronger financial position than the provincial governments. It could levy all kinds of taxes, while the provincial governments were restricted to direct taxes (for example, income and property taxes), which were quite unimportant at the time of Confederation.

---

[4]A direct tax is a tax applied to the person who is intended to pay it. An indirect tax may be shifted from the person to whom it is applied to another person. For example, the excise tax on cigarettes is an indirect tax because it is applied to the manufacturer but is actually added to the price of cigarettes and eventually paid by the consumer. Income taxes are direct taxes, whereas sales taxes are indirect taxes.

During the Great Depression of the 1930s, provincial and municipal governments found it impossible to cope with the social and economic problems that came under their jurisdiction. The Report of the Royal Commission on Dominion–Provincial Relations (the Rowell-Sirois Report) in 1940 called for the redistribution of some tax revenues from the federal to the provincial governments. The latter, in turn, were urged to transfer more of their revenues to the municipalities.

The growth of both the federal and the provincial levels of government in this century, reflecting the increased demands placed on governments by Canadian citizens, has brought the two levels into increasing conflict with each other. No royal commissions or constitutional changes are likely to resolve this problem. The difficulties between Quebec and the rest of Canada arise from the same conflict, compounded by Quebec's special cultural and linguistic aspirations.

WHAT DOES GOVERNMENT DO?

Governments do many things. They run military bases and prisons, pay benefits to farmers and poor city dwellers, build dams, print money, and run transit systems and hydro-electric plants. There are many debates about whether governments do too much or too little or the right mix of things. But while people may not agree on what governments should do, they can agree that the economic role of government has grown.

The Growth of Government

Box 3.3 gives us an indication of the growth of government over time. The graph shows what has happened to federal, provincial, and municipal **government purchases** of goods and services since 1947. Government purchases include all the finished products purchased by government (everything from submarines to computer disks), plus the cost of hiring the services of all government employees (everyone from the prime minister to the courthouse janitor). These purchases are shown as a percentage of gross domestic product (GDP). By this measure, government has clearly grown over time. Until the end of World War II, government purchases averaged less than 10 percent of GDP. Then, from about 1947 until 1970, they followed a steady trend upward. During the 1970s, total government purchases appear to have levelled off at about 20 percent of GDP, climbing slightly higher through the 1980s. Government purchases have followed almost precisely the same trend in the United States.

Box 3.4 provides a different kind of comparison. This table shows total government expenditures as a percentage of GDP for several countries. Total government expenditures include both government purchases and **transfer payments**, which are all payments made by government to individuals that are not in return for goods or services currently supplied. They include family allowance benefits, welfare payments, and unemployment insurance benefits. Using total expenditures rather than government purchases alone as a measure of government involvement in the economy naturally makes the public sector look larger. Government purchases plus transfer payments now approximate 45 percent of GDP in Canada. Compared with that of most leading market economies, government involvement in Canada is just slightly above average.

Government purchases
Expenditures made by federal, provincial, and municipal governments to purchase goods from private firms and to hire the services of government employees.

Transfer payments
All payments made by government to individuals that are not made in return for goods or services currently supplied. Social insurance benefits, welfare payments, and unemployment insurance benefits are major forms of transfer payments.

BOX 3.3 Government Purchases of Goods and Services as a Percentage of GDP, 1947–1990

Total government purchases as a percentage of GDP have grown substantially over time. Prior to World War II, government purchases averaged less than 10 percent of GDP. Now, however, government expenditures have grown to a peacetime average of slightly more than 20 percent of GDP.

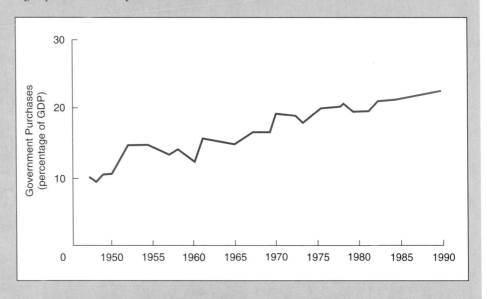

SOURCE: Adapted from Statistics Canada, *Canadian Economic Observer, Historical Statistical Supplement, 1989/90*, pp. 1, 2, Catalogue no. 11-210. Reproduced with permission of the Minister of Supply and Services Canada, 1992.

It should be noted, however, that the measurements of government activity in Canada shown in Boxes 3.3 and 3.4 do not include the expenditures of a wide variety of government-owned enterprises, or Crown corporations, such as provincial hydro utilities, Air Canada, Canadian National Railways, and Petro-Canada. If their activities were included, the figures for Canada would be higher.

The Functions of Government

Governments use a significant percentage of the GDP that passes through their hands to perform a wide variety of functions. These functions can be classified under four general headings: provision of public goods, transfer of income, economic stabilization, and regulation of private business firms.

Provision of public goods

The first function of government is to provide what economists call **public goods** — goods or services that (1) cannot be provided to one citizen without also being supplied to that citizen's neighbours, and (2) once provided for one citizen, cost

Public goods
Goods or services that (1) cannot be provided to one citizen without also being supplied to that person's neighbours, and (2) once provided for one citizen, cost no more to be provided to others.

Total Government Expenditures as a Percentage of GDP for Selected Countries BOX 3.4

The data in this table refer to total expenditures of central and local government units, including both government purchases of goods and services and transfer payments. By this measure, the size of government relative to the rest of the economy is larger than when only government purchases are taken into account. Government expenditures in Canada are growing and remain above average for six leading industrial nations.

Country	Average 1974–79	1989
Canada	39.2	44.3
France	43.7	49.7
Germany	47.5	45.1
Japan	28.4	32.9*
United Kingdom	44.4	40.9
United States	32.6	36.1
Average of 6 Largest Market Economies	39.3	48.3

*The figure for Japan is for 1988.

SOURCE: Organization for Economic Co-operation and Development, *Economic Outlook, Historical Statistics, 1960–1985*, p. 64, and OECD, *Economic Outlook*, July 1991, p. 189. Reproduced with permission.

no more to be provided to others. Perhaps the best example of a public good is national defence. One citizen cannot very well be protected against foreign invasion or nuclear holocaust without having the protection "spill over" onto others. Also, it costs no more to protect an entire city than to protect a single resident of a given area.

Box 3.5 compares government involvement in the provision of various types of goods and services in eighteen countries. It shows that, on the whole, Canada has adopted practices that are very similar to those of other countries. In every country, telecommunications, postal services, electricity, and railways are run largely by governments. In Canada, there is actually more private participation in telecommunications and railways than in most other countries. The chart indicates that among these eighteen nations, Canada, the United States, and Japan have the fewest industries dominated by government enterprises. Major "industries" not included in the chart, but in which governments in most countries provide most of the output, are education and hospital care.

In Canada, government businesses are organized in various forms. The postal service, for example, was run as a regular government department until it was changed into a Crown corporation — the Canada Post Corporation — in 1981. Crown corporations are uniquely Canadian government businesses. They have the legal status of independent entities, but all or most of their assets are owned by the government and they are ultimately accountable to the federal or provincial legislatures. In 1988, there were 236 provincial and federal Crown corporations in Canada.

BOX 3.5 *Extent of Public Enterprise in Eighteen Countries*

The chart below indicates the extent to which government enterprises are involved in eleven selected industries in eighteen countries. In the areas of postal services and electricity, Canadian governments participate to the same extent as the governments of the other countries, but in most of the other industries, Canadian government participation is less than the average.

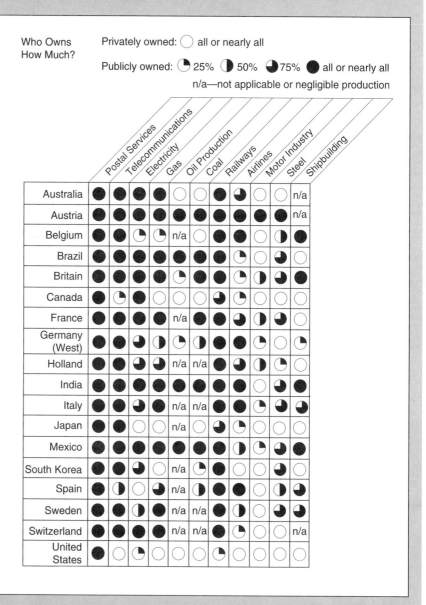

SOURCE: Donald G. McFetridge, *Economics of Industrial Policy and Strategy*, Royal Commission on the Economic Union and Development Prospects for Canada, Collected Research Studies 5 (Toronto: University of Toronto Press, 1985), p. 198. Based on J.R.W. Pritchard, ed., *Crown Corporation in Canada* (Toronto: Butterworths, 1983), p. 106; reprinted from *The Economist*, December 30, 1978, p. 39.

Some Crown corporations, such as Canadian National Railways and Canada Post (which ranked 28th and 30th in asset value, respectively, among all Canadian corporations in 1990), have special provisions that allow them to finance their operations independently of the government. Others, such as Atomic Energy of Canada Limited, are tied more closely to government and are called *agency* Crown corporations.

Transfer of income

The second function of government consists of making transfers of income and wealth from one citizen to another. Income is usually taken from citizens by means of taxation. Benefits are distributed in the form of either direct cash payments or free or below-cost provision of goods and services. Among the more familiar types of cash transfers are family allowance payments, welfare benefits, and unemployment insurance benefits. Goods and services provided as transfers include public education, public broadcasting (the CBC), public housing, fire protection, and medical care. They are provided at low or zero cost (rather than at market prices, on the basis of ability to pay) as a result of political decisions. Some of these goods and services can also be considered public goods. In the 1980s, government transfer payments accounted on average for about 11 percent of the income of all individuals and 60 percent of the income of the lowest fifth of the population (in terms of income share).

Economic stabilization

Stabilization is a third economic function of government. Particularly since World War II, in an effort to prevent the recurrence of a depression as severe as that of the Dirty Thirties, governments have tried to control the rates of economic growth, inflation, and unemployment. Such efforts are a part of **stabilization policy**, which refers to government's use of taxation and expenditure as tools to smooth out the ups and downs of the business cycle.

Stabilization policy
Efforts by government to control the level of national income and the related conditions of inflation, unemployment, and the balance of payments, using taxation and expenditure as its tools.

Regulation of private business firms

A fourth major function of government is the regulation of private business firms. Regulatory control is exercised through a network of specialized agencies and takes a variety of specific forms. The Food and Drug Services Directorate and the Health Protection Branch of Health and Welfare Canada exercise considerable control over what can be produced by the firms they regulate. The Canadian Transport Commission sets basic operating conditions for airlines and railways. Regulatory boards have come to influence a wide range of economic behaviour, and regulation is a subject of widespread research and controversy.

Today, governments regulate the prices of goods representing 23 percent of average consumer purchases; they include alcohol and tobacco; cable television; dairy products, eggs, and poultry; home heating charges (oil, gas, and electricity); transit, bus, rail, and air fares; postage; telephone charges; and water.

Criticism of Government Growth

Criticism of government growth may be linked to a perception that government enterprises are inherently less efficient than private enterprises. Is this perception accurate? Within economics, several schools of thought have addressed this question. One school, whose work is based on what is known as *property rights theory*, argues that government enterprises will inevitably be less efficient than private enterprises because poor management performance in a publicly owned firm cannot readily be halted by means of "shareholder" action. Citizens can terminate their ownership stakes only by leaving the country or by attempting to have the public firm abolished. Both are high-cost strategies, unlikely to be undertaken. Another school, espousing what is known as *political market theory*, argues quite the opposite: that public corporations are *constantly* subject to pressure from coalitions of voters or from special-interest groups. The problem is not that government enterprises are immune to external control, but rather that they are compelled to respond to the concerns of particular groups for political reasons and without due regard for long-term efficiency or the altruistic pursuit of the "public interest." A third school, identified with what is known as *managerial research*, incorporates some of the insights of the first two schools, but stresses the independent role that managers of public corporations play. According to this view, executives play a pivotal role even in public corporations, and may indeed behave very much the way executives in private corporations do. Thus, proponents of managerial research do not necessarily assume that public corporations will be less efficient than their private counterparts.

Research studies indicate that commercially oriented public corporations are essentially as efficient as private corporations.[5] It is difficult to compare other types of public agencies with private firms, because they usually have no counterpart in the private sector (as is the case, for example, with Atomic Energy of Canada). The same studies indicate that the *environment* in which an organization operates is a stronger determinant of efficiency than the nature of its ownership. For example, highly regulated private railways in the United States are less efficient than Canada's public railway line, because regulation has created an unfavourable environment.

When citizens criticize the spending programs of government, they may also be opposed to what they perceive as an unfair allocation of government expenditures. Even in political democracies based on the principle of "one person, one vote," people perceive some persons and groups to be more equal than others in their ability to influence government decision making. Many people in the business community, for example, seem to feel that governments in Canada have responded unduly to the appeals for help of those who are not working or whose incomes, for various reasons, are considerably below the average. Those with high, steady incomes may question the growth in government expenditures on such social programs as unemployment insurance and social assistance and may feel that they are taxed unfairly to provide these benefits. Other groups feel, on the contrary, that it is the wealthier citizens who benefit disproportionately from government programs. They point to the government subsidies that many businesses receive, and to government "bail-outs" of large firms and banks. They are also reminded, even by the business press, that large enterprises making considerable profits often pay little or no tax because of tax loopholes.

Concerns of this type are based on notions of fairness involving values that, however legitimate and important, will never be settled by rational argument. However, underlying such concerns are questions that scholars are attempting to explore. It would be important to know, for example, whether governments are

[5]These studies are summarized in Sanford F. Borins and Barry E.C. Bootham, "Crown Corporations and Economic Efficiency," in *Canadian Industrial Policy in Action*, ed. Donald G. McFetridge, Royal Commission on the Economic Union and Development Prospects for Canada, Collected Research Studies 4 (Toronto: University of Toronto Press, 1985), pp. 75–130. The summary of the various schools of thought is also derived from this source.

more influenced in their policy making by the lobbying of pressure groups between elections than by the general concerns of voters at election time. If so, a rational case might be made that highly organized groups benefit unduly from government activity. These are important questions that deserve careful examination.

People's concerns about the growth of government are often linked to worries about the growing *government debt*. Economists share this concern, not so much because they perceive current debt levels to be unmanageable, but because large government debts can interfere with the application of appropriate government stabilization policies.

PRIVATE BUSINESS ORGANIZATIONS IN CANADA

Though government has come to play an increasingly important role in the Canadian economy, private business organizations continue to use most of society's resources and produce most of its goods and services. Canadian business firms vary widely in terms of their size and the scope of their operations. They also differ in terms of their form of organization. In this section, we will discuss the four most common types of firms — sole proprietorships, partnerships, corporations, and co-operatives.

Sole Proprietorships

A **sole proprietorship** is a firm that is owned and usually managed by one person. In most cases, this person is also an operative employee. Responsibility for the success or failure of the firm rests solely on the proprietor's shoulders. From a legal point of view, he or she owns all the assets and owes all the debts of the organization.

The sole proprietorship is popular because it is easy to establish, the proprietor is entitled to 100 percent of any rewards, and, if things don't work out, it is easy to dissolve. But there are significant drawbacks as well: All the risk is borne by one person, who has unlimited financial liability, and it may be difficult to expand the operation, because capital expansion depends on the sole proprietor's own assets and ability to borrow.

Sole proprietorship
A firm owned and usually managed by one person, who receives all profits of the firm and who personally bears all the firm's liabilities.

Partnerships

A **partnership** is an association of two or more persons for the purpose of operating a business as co-owners by voluntary legal agreement. This means that at least two people own all the assets, owe all the liabilities, and have an equity in the business.

Many partnerships are formed to take advantage of the potential for greater managerial ability: the different partners' diverse talents complement one another. However, even a partnership will find it difficult to expand beyond a certain financial base, and each partner bears the risk of unlimited liability. The dissolution of a partnership can be difficult, requiring the co-operation of all the partners. However, any change in the combination of partners automatically causes the partnership's dissolution; thus, this form of enterprise has limited life. Like marriage, the strength of a partnership depends ultimately on the ability of the partners to work together harmoniously.

Partnership
A firm jointly owned and operated by two or more persons. Each partner bears full legal liability for the debts of the firm.

Corporations

Corporation
A firm organized as an independent legal entity, with ownership divided into equal parts called "shares." Each shareholder's liability is limited to the amount of his or her investment in the firm.

Corporations are the third major form of business organization. A **corporation** is a firm organized as an independent legal entity, with ownership divided into equal-value shares. The corporation is the predominant form of organization in the manufacturing sector. About three-quarters of all manufacturing firms in Canada are corporations, and they employ more than 95 percent of all workers in the manufacturing field. Box 3.6, which lists the 25 largest industrial corporations in Canada, contains many familiar names. A major feature of the corporation is that it can be dealt with legally just as if it were an individual. This means that the corporation serves as a buffer between the firm's owners and the government and community.

BOX 3.6   *The 25 Largest Canadian Industrial Corporations, 1990*

Each year, the *Financial Post* publishes a list of the 500 largest industrial corporations in Canada, ranked by sales. This box gives the top 25, based on sales for 1990.

Rank by Revenue			1990 Sales or Operating Revenue
1990	1989	Company	($ thousands)
1	1	General Motors of Canada Ltd., Oshawa	18 458 171
2	2	BCE Inc., Montreal	18 373 000
3	3	Ford Motor Co. of Canada, Oakville, Ont.	13 706 200
4	6	George Weston Ltd., Toronto	10 856 000
5	4	Canadian Pacific Ltd., Montreal	10 499 700
6	7	Imperial Oil Ltd., Toronto	10 223 000
7	5	Alcan Aluminium Ltd., Montreal	10 217 000
8	8	Noranda Inc., Toronto	9 565 000
9	10	Brascan Ltd., Toronto	7 163 000
10	9	Chrysler Canada Ltd., Windsor	7 067 000
11	12	Provigo Inc., Montreal (Jan. 1991)	6 525 700
12	11	Ontario Hydro, Toronto	6 484 000
13	13	Thomson Corp., Toronto	6 259 000
14	15	Seagram Co., Montreal (Jan. 1991)	5 865 000
15	14	Hydro-Québec, Montreal	5 822 988
16	17	Shell Canada Ltd., Calgary	5 508 000
17	23	Petro-Canada, Calgary	5 317 000
18	20	Hudson's Bay Co., Toronto (Jan. 1991)	5 041 733
19	19	Nova Corp. of Alberta, Calgary	4 736 000
20	18	John Labatt Ltd., London, Ont. (April 1990)	4 681 000
21	16	Oshawa Group Ltd., Toronto (Jan. 1991)	4 598 798
22	28	IBM Canada Ltd., Markham, Ont.	4 578 000
23	22	Sears Canada Inc., Toronto	4 571 100
24	32	Amoco Canada Petroleum Co., Calgary	4 444 000
25	27	Canada Safeway Ltd., Calgary	4 317 951

SOURCE: Adapted from *The Financial Post 500*, June 1991, p. 94. Reproduced with permission.

Persons who own shares in a corporation are called shareholders (or stock-holders). They elect officers to manage the business. Of course, if they own the majority of voting shares, they can, and often do, elect themselves as managers. Shares can be either "common" or "preferred." **Common shares** give their owners the right to vote in the selection of management and to share in any dividend payments. **Preferred shares** confer voting rights as well as a fixed return on investment, payable before any payment of dividends is made to owners of common shares.

Advantages

The main advantage of having the firm as a separate entity is that the owners carry only limited financial liability. This means that creditors can look only to the assets of the corporation for settlement of their claims; they cannot hold the owners liable for the debts of the corporation. If the corporation fails, the shareholders lose only the amount of their investment; their personal assets cannot be taken to pay the corporate debts. This is not the case for a sole proprietorship or a partnership, where the owners are held liable for all the debts and are forced, when necessary, to pay them out of their personal assets.

A corporation can grow to a larger size than a sole proprietorship or a partnership because it can attract capital from thousands of individuals. It can expand or increase its size because the advantage of limited financial liability makes investors more willing to purchase additional shares of stock. A corporation can raise $1 million by having a thousand people invest $1000 each, while in a sole proprietorship, one person would have to invest $1 million.

The transfer of ownership in a corporation is easily accomplished, especially for those corporations whose capital stock is listed and traded on the major stock exchanges and in the over-the-counter market. Thousands of shares of capital stock change hands daily. As a general rule, corporations allow shareholders to transfer their ownership to anyone at any time (assuming that the price is agreeable to both buyer and seller), without the approval of the other shareholders.

The transferability of ownership of corporate shares contributes to the continuity of the firm. Shareholders can withdraw by selling their shares or they can leave their shares to their heirs when they die without disturbing the legal existence of the corporation.

A further advantage may be the relatively low income tax rates that apply to the earnings of some corporations. Canadian-controlled corporations can pay as little as about 25 percent tax on the first $150 000 of income, while an individual earning that much might have to pay twice as much.

Disadvantages

The first disadvantage of the corporate form of business organization is the cost of chartering a corporation. The chartering can be done on either the provincial or the federal level and can cost from about five hundred dollars to several thousands of dollars in legal fees.

Most corporations issue shares held by the public and are obligated to report sales and profits (or losses) to their shareholders. Only a small number of large corporations, such as Eaton's, whose shares are privately held, escape this loss of privacy.

A further disadvantage is the "double" taxation of corporate income. Corporate profits are taxed first before they are paid out as dividends, and dividend income is subsequently taxed when it reaches the shareholders. However, dividend income is subject to "dividend tax credits" that reduce the effective tax rate considerably.

Concerns about corporate size and influence

A striking feature of the Canadian corporate scene is the very small number of large corporations that controls most of the assets in the industrial sector. For example, in 1987, in all industries combined, the largest 0.01 percent of enterprises controlled 54.6 percent of all assets.[6] (The term **enterprise** in this context refers to a group of corporations under common control.) To put it another way, the combined assets of the 447 726 small corporations in Canada (each with assets of less than $25 million) were less than half of the assets of the 2393 large corporations (those with assets of $25 million or more). The economic power wielded by these large corporations, and the influence they may have on government policy, is of concern to many Canadians. This question is dealt with at length in Chapters 9 and 10.

The growth of **transnational (or multinational) corporations** — corporations that have branch operations in more than one country — is also receiving increasing attention in the economics profession. Canada has often welcomed foreign corporations for the purpose of speeding up its own economic development. And, in recent years, a number of Canadian corporations, particularly some of the giants in real estate development, have established sizable operations in other countries. Transnational corporations are of particular concern to those who feel that businesses should serve a national purpose and should therefore be subject to national regulations. However, transnational corporations are difficult to control, as will become more evident in Chapter 16.

Co-operatives

The co-operative form of organization is quite important in the Canadian economy, much more so than in the United States. A **co-operative** is an organization that pools the resources of its members, just as a corporation does, but grants only one vote to each member regardless of the member's investment. Furthermore, earnings not retained are paid out according to the amount of business conducted by the member with the firm. Co-operatives may incorporate in order to obtain the benefits of limited liability and continuous existence. Co-operatives are of several types: consumers' co-operatives, which engage in retail trade; producer co-operatives, which manufacture goods; marketing co-operatives, which sell members' agricultural products; financial co-operatives (for example, credit unions and — in French Canada — *caisses populaires*); and insurance and service co-operatives (for example, funeral co-operatives).

The chief advantages of the co-operative are the one-member, one-vote form of democracy, the possibility of buying goods and services more cheaply, and the special tax privileges enjoyed under Canadian law. Patronage dividends are not taxable because they are considered to be either volume rebates for goods purchased by members or additional payments for members' goods received by the co-operative.

Enterprise
In one sense of the term, a group of corporations under common control.

Transnational (or multinational) corporation
A corporation that has branch operations in more than one country.

Co-operative
A firm that pools the resources of its members, as a corporation does, but grants only one vote to each member, regardless of the member's investment.

---

[6]Minister of Industry, Science and Technology, *Corporations and Labour Unions Returns Act*, 1987, p. 64, Catalogue no. 61-210. Reproduced with permission of the Minister of Supply and Services Canada, 1992.

The chief disadvantages of the co-operative are that it may be difficult to raise funds (because increased investment by members does not lead to increased control), and that radical democratic control may lead to inefficient management.

Some co-operatives rank high in the list of industrial corporations in Canada. Among producer co-operatives, the highest ranking in 1990 was the Saskatchewan Wheat Pool: Its sales of about $2 billion placed it sixty-first among all industrial corporations in Canada. Among financial institutions, credit unions such as the Vancouver City Savings Credit Union and Quebec's Confédération des caisses populaires are only two of a number of credit unions that easily rank among the top 50 financial institutions in the country.

Despite their different purposes and different legal forms of organization, all firms — whether "mom and pop" corner stores or giant steel corporations or powerful law partnerships or credit unions — have many things in common. The basic task that they collectively perform is to co-ordinate and carry out the basic decisions of an economy about what to produce and how and for whom to produce it.

CONCLUSIONS

This chapter has offered just a glimpse of some of the complexities underlying the operation of governments and business firms in our economy. It has examined the services government performs and has looked briefly at the rising cost of providing these services. But despite considerable criticism of government activities, it is not clear that Canadians would really like to make significant changes. In a democratic market system, governments respond to consumers in much the same way that private businesses do. However, the efficiency and fairness with which public goods are provided by government are issues that deserve careful scrutiny.

This chapter has also explored the nature of private business organizations in Canada. In many branches of economic theory, firms are treated as simple, homogeneous building blocks. In reality, they are neither simple nor homogeneous. Except for the smallest one-person operations, each firm is an organization of separate individuals united for a common purpose — to carry out the division of labour effectively. Depending on circumstances, this purpose may best be served by the legal form of a sole proprietorship, a partnership, a corporation, or a co-operative.

SUMMARY

1. As in most market economies, there is constant change in the industries and firms that play a leading role in the Canadian economy. Economic progress seems possible only in a society that supports *creative destruction* — that is, the emergence of new firms or industries to replace those that are in decline.

2. While Canada has a significant manufacturing industry, other industries — first agriculture and natural resources, and then services — have always employed the greatest proportion of the country's labour force. Thus, Canada did not move from an industrial to a *post-industrial* society, as Western European countries did, but made a direct transition from an agrarian and resource-based society to one based on *services*.

3. People need both goods and services, and, despite widespread opinion to the contrary, a society that favours services can grow as quickly and as successfully as one that favours industry.

4. Unique historical forces in Canada, including an early dependence on *staple products* and the development of a fragile, far-flung east–west economic system, have contributed to the development of an alliance between business and government in this country.

5. After Confederation, government policies pertaining to business were promotional, offering subsidies and protection in an effort to create a strong nation state. Later, in the twentieth century, governments assumed a more regulatory, interventionist strategy, responding to such new interest groups as those formed by farmers and workers.

6. The federal and provincial governments' jurisdictions were originally defined by the British North America Act. The two levels of government have been forced to resolve ongoing disputes about respective areas of responsibility and revenue and expenditure difficulties through negotiations and various types of tax-sharing arrangements.

7. Four major economic functions of government are the provision of *public goods*, the transfer of income, the *stabilization* of the economy, and the regulation of private business firms. The federal, provincial, and municipal levels of government combined now spend almost 50 percent of GDP, about half of which goes to the public in the form of *transfer payments*.

8. There is considerable concern in Canada and in other countries about the growth of government. There is a perception, for example, that government enterprises are inherently less efficient than private enterprises. Such empirical tests as have been possible in this area do not support this perception. However, several schools of thought, based on property rights theory, political market theory, and managerial research, have made significant hypotheses about the likely behaviour of government firms. Another concern of many Canadians is that government services may be unfair. Some feel that too much is being spent on lower-income groups, while others feel that it is higher-income groups that take unfair advantage of the system. Because these concerns are based on value judgements, it is difficult to assess their validity.

9. Private business firms perform an important co-ordinating function in society. They may be organized as *sole proprietorships, partnerships, corporations*, or *co-operatives*. Sole proprietorships are very common among small firms. They are easy to set up and have the advantage of giving the proprietor rights to all of the firm's profits. They have the disadvantage of unlimited liability. Partnerships share that disadvantage, but they benefit from the ability to combine the diverse skills and the capital of two or more partners. Corporations protect the investments of their shareholders through limited liability and permit huge sums of capital to be raised. They suffer the disadvantages of "double" taxation and closer regulation than other kinds of businesses are subject to. Co-operatives operate according to the principle of "one-member, one-vote," are able to buy goods and services more cheaply than individuals can, and enjoy tax privileges. They may have difficulty, however, in raising funds, and their democratic approach to management may prove to be inefficient.

KEY TERMS

creative destruction
service sector
post-industrial society
staple product
government purchases
transfer payments

public goods
stabilization policy
sole proprietorship
partnership
corporation
common share (or stock)

preferred share (or stock)
enterprise
transnational (or multinational)
  corporation
co-operative

KEY BOXES

Box 3.1 Employment in the Canadian Economy,
        1950 and 1990
Box 3.3 Government Purchases of Goods and
        Services as a Percentage of GDP,
        1947–1990

Box 3.5 Extent of Public Enterprise in
        Eighteen Countries

REVIEW QUESTIONS

1. Look for data to use in updating Boxes 3.1, 3.3, and 3.4. The source notes in the boxes will tell you where to start looking. Examine the most recent data that you find.

2. How can the size of the government sector in the Canadian economy be measured? By what measure, if any, has it grown in the past decade or more? Is government in Canada large or small compared with government in other advanced industrial countries?

3. On graduation, a classmate whom you barely know suggests that you go into business together selling sports equipment to the students in your university town. He wants to make the business a partnership. "You supply the brains; I'll put up the money," he says.

Would you agree to this arrangement, or do you think you might be better off if he set the business up as a sole proprietorship, with you as his employee, or as a corporation, with the two of you holding some of the shares? What would be the advantages and disadvantages to you of each alternative?

4. Suppose that there is only one supermarket in your town and you think its prices are too high. You decide to organize a food co-operative to compete with it. How would you persuade members to join? Would you limit shopping privileges to members only? If not, how would you keep nonmember "free riders" from reaping all the benefits of your hard work?

Tools for Learning: Effective Thinking and Problem Solving

Many students taking the principles of economics course approach their first test or assignment with trepidation and uncertainty — "Should I memorize definitions, formulas, and numbers from the text?" "Will I have to make calculations?" "If I have to use formulas, how will I be able to tell which ones to use?" "Is just a solution adequate, or do I have to show my calculations?" "What does my instructor want from me?" The answers to these questions can usually be summarized by the following: Your instructor wants you to understand the material by being an effective thinker. But what does this really mean?

Thinking: What Is It?

Understanding and thinking effectively are not easy; they require work and practice. Understanding and thinking are more than writing down what your professor says in lectures, more than memorizing definitions and formulas, and more than regurgitating something you read or were told. Understanding and thinking require you to apply your knowledge. They require analysis, synthesis, and evaluation of situations. In other words, understanding and thinking are an *active process*, one that requires you to *use* knowledge.

Thinking can involve finding more than one correct solution. In fact, in economics, you will find that thinking often doesn't lead to one correct answer, but rather to the *best* answer from among many possibilities.

Effective thinking occurs "when an individual not only knows, but is also able to interpret, understand, and use words, concepts, and symbols to facilitate his or her own thought processes and judgements."[7] All this requires the thinker to be *actively involved*, and not just passively absorbing information.

Levels of Thinking

Thinking can be divided into six levels of difficulty that fall into two sections called lower- and higher-order thinking skills.[8] The lower-order thinking skills are *knowledge*, which involves recall and recognition, and *comprehension*. Higher-order skills are *application, analysis, synthesis,* and *evaluation*. A discussion of levels of thinking may sound unnecessarily academic, but a basic understanding will help you study and prepare for problem sets and tests in economics. When you understand what is required of you and how to go about doing what is required, economics — and other courses — usually become easier.

---

[7] P.L. Dressel and D. Marcus, *On Teaching and Learning in College* (San Francisco: Jossey-Bass, 1982), p. 25.

[8] B.S. Bloom, ed., *Taxonomy of Educational Objectives. Handbook I: Cognitive Domain* (New York: Longmans, Green, 1956).

Lower-order thinking skills

Knowledge requires you to recall or recognize material or ideas. An example would be repeating the definition of the supply equation that you will learn about in Chapter 4. You don't necessarily have to understand the definition, you just have to recall it. To avoid confusion with a broader meaning of the word *knowledge*, we'll refer to the knowledge skill as *recall and recognition*.

Comprehension requires you to interpret meaning, translate a concept into your own words, and make inferences based on an understanding of the material. An example would be giving an explanation of a production possibilities frontier in your own words. Producing your own definition or explanation requires greater understanding than does just repeating a definition you have memorized.

Higher-order thinking skills

Higher-order thinking skills are more difficult to master than lower-order skills, but they are usually more useful and more interesting. *Application* requires you to select and apply appropriate content knowledge when you are faced with a new situation. For instance, as you will see in Chapter 4, you might be given data and expected to determine the quantity demanded at the equilibrium price. *Analysis* requires you to break material down into its component parts and to detect relationships among the parts. You might be asked to examine a market situation and to predict the likely economic consequences of a government-set maximum price for the good being sold. Analysis may require the use of formulas and data or a written or verbal analysis of an outcome. *Synthesis* requires you to integrate and use information from many sources. You must sort through possible sources of information and use those that are most relevant. Synthesis allows room for your own creativity. You might be asked for solutions to, and probable economic and social consequences of, a rental housing problem in a large metropolitan area.

Evaluation requires you to do even more. It asks you to make judgements about the value of an idea, a solution, or a method, for example, for some specified purpose. You may be given the criteria on which to base your evaluation or you may have to construct your own criteria. An example would be asking an economist to evaluate the appropriateness of a province's taxation and spending policy when the government's goal is to avoid a recession.

It is the use of higher-order thinking skills that earns the highest grades in most economics courses and that will be required to ever greater extent as you progress to more advanced courses. Using higher-order effective-thinking skills will be asked of you not only in economics, but in other fields, and on the job, as well. When you graduate and are hired as a professional, it is unlikely that you will be asked to repeat definitions you've learned in college and university courses. Your employer will want you to *use* the knowledge you have acquired. *You will be presented with problems and expected to solve them. You will be expected to be an effective thinker.*

The better your thinking skills, the more likely you are to be given challenging assignments, interesting jobs, and promotions. Honing your thinking skills in principles of economics can have benefits well beyond getting a good grade.

An Effective-Thinking Process

Effective thinking is often equated with problem solving. Both involve a process with a series of identifiable steps. Expert thinkers may appear to reach brilliant conclusions and solutions almost instantly, but this generally means they've had so much practice that they can go through the effective-thinking process very quickly. The essential point, however, is that effective thinkers do follow a process — one that they had to learn and that they have practised many times. Expert thinkers may not be able to describe the thinking process their minds go through to reach a solution or conclusion, but researchers have identified the steps that they do follow — whether knowingly or unknowingly.

Different researchers describe the effective-thinking steps with slight variations, but basically, the steps involve the following:

I. defining the situation;

II. stating the problem(s) and the exact goal(s) to be achieved;

III. generating ideas that could be used to reach the goal(s) and selecting the one(s) judged to be the best;

IV. defining the new situation that would result if the selected idea(s) were realized;

V. preparing a detailed plan to reach the goal based on the best idea(s) generated;

VI. implementing the plan and evaluating its success or failure.

Notice that the thinker must be actively involved in the thinking process to go through these steps. The effective thinker must define, state, generate, select, prepare, implement, and evaluate. Effective thinkers must *use* what they know.

Steps in an effective-thinking process

Experience shows that students become more effective thinkers when the process of effective thinking is made explicit to them, and when they can see examples of these steps being used.[9] To help you develop your effective-thinking skills, the explicit steps from a successful problem-solving process called Guided Design are listed below,[10] followed by a sample problem based on material that you will be studying in Chapter 4. This sample problem is intended only as a *model* of the effective-thinking process, as applied by one economist (other economists might generate slightly different responses to each step). You might find it interesting to read through the sample problem now, then return to it after you have studied Chapter 4 to compare your ideas with those of our "sample" economist.

Before we start, it should be mentioned that the effective-thinking steps that follow have been used by many students in principles courses as well as in higher-level economics courses. Effective thinking has also proved useful in teaching thinking skills to engineering students (for whom the Guided Design process was first developed), nursing students, and natural and social science students in a variety of disciplines. In research with engineering students, effec-

---

[9]W.J. McKeachie, R.R. Pintrich, Y.G. Lin, and D. Smith, *Teaching and Learning in the College Classroom: A Review of the Literature* (Ann Arbor, Mich.: University of Michigan, National Center for Research to Improve Postsecondary Teaching and Learning, 1986), p. 37.

[10]C.E. Wales, A.H. Nardi, and R.A. Stager, *Thinking Skills: Making a Choice* (Morgantown, W.V.: West Virginia University Center for Guided Design, 1987).

tive thinking helped raise students' averages in all four years of their program.[11] The steps that follow are tried and true!

I. Define the situation

Who is involved? What happened? What is involved? When and where did it happen? Why did it happen? How serious are the consequences? (You don't have to answer all of these questions for each situation. Pick the ones that help you define the particular situation you face.)

II. State the problem and the goal

Analysis   1 *What might be the problem(s)?*

This is the hardest step for most students. It's worth spending time on this step because it is very difficult to reach a good solution or conclusion if you don't know exactly what the problem is that you are attempting to solve. The statement of a problem comes from examining the Why and How statements in the Define the Situation step.

Synthesis   2 *What could be the goal(s) you want to achieve?*

This step requires creativity. Think of all the possible goals that *could* be generated in relation to the problem(s) in Step 1. Devise a goal for each one of the possible problems you have listed.

Evaluation   3 *Of all the possible goals in Step 2, decide which one(s) you could achieve.*

This step requires you to specify musts, wants, constraints, and assumptions. Evaluate all the possible goals in Step 2 and select the one(s) you think are best. Do not select too many goals; narrow them down to the best one or two.

III. Generate ideas for meeting your goal(s) in Step 3

Analysis   4 *What problems might be involved in meeting the goal(s) in Step 3?*

Look carefully at all aspects of your goal(s) from Step 3. What *might* cause problems in meeting your goal(s)?

Synthesis   5 *What could be done to solve the goal problems in Step 4?*

Again, creativity is called for. Imagine what *could* be done to solve each one of the goal problems in Step 4. Integrate ideas and synthesize to suggest possible solutions.

Evaluation   6 *Of all the possible solutions to your goal problems in Step 5, what should be done to solve those problems?*

This means that you have to evaluate all the possible solutions in Step 5 to find the best one(s). To do this, consider your goal(s) in Step 3 again, specify condi-

---

[11]C.E. Wales, "Does How You Teach Make a Difference?" *Engineering Education*, February 1979, pp. 394–98.

tional constraints, anticipate future consequences, and select the best combination of ideas. Then select the best solution, the one you think you *should* try.

IV. Define the new situation

The new situation is the old situation list of who, what, when, where, why, and how with the addition of the solutions you selected in Step 6. Include various costs and benefits of implementing your Step 6 solution(s) in your description of the new situation.

V. Prepare a plan

Analysis 7 *What might be a problem with the new situation?*

Look at all parts of the new situation to determine what *might* cause, contribute to, or be a problem.

Synthesis 8 *What could be part of a plan to solve the new-situation problems identified in Step 7?*

Use your imagination to determine possible plan options for solving the problems in Step 7. Generate plan options that *could* solve each problem. Integrate your ideas to produce a synthesis of new plans.

Evaluation 9 *Which of the possible plans in Step 8 should be used to solve the new-situation problems?*

Consider your goal(s) (Step 3), your selected solution(s) (Step 6), constraints, assumptions, and any anticipated future consequences in deciding which plan(s) from Step 8 you *should* choose. Evaluate the possible plans and select the best.

VI. Take action

Analysis 10 *What might be a problem with the plan you selected in Step 9?*

Rehearse and visualize the plan from Step 9 in your mind. Separate it into its component parts to determine what might possibly be, contribute to, or cause a problem when the plan is implemented.

Synthesis 11 *What could be becomes reality as you implement the plan.*

Actually implement the plan you selected in Step 9. As you do so, generate options for action that solve every problem that *could* occur.

Evaluation 12 *What should be the next action, once you see the results of the implemented plan?*

Compare the actual results of your plan with your goal(s) in Step 3, the ideas you selected in Step 6, and the plan you developed in Step 9. Specify any constraints and assumptions you've made, anticipate future consequences, evaluate the situation, and select the best future action.

Notice the different levels of thinking skills that are required as the thinker progresses through these steps. The higher-order skills of analysis, synthesis, and evaluation are specifically required in each of the four sections of this problem-solving process.

Is All This Necessary?

These twelve effective-thinking steps may seem a little rigid, nitpicking, and unnecessary. After all, you've been thinking all your life and you've done it well enough to get you into college or university. True enough, but the goal of this process is to make you a truly expert thinker, not just an average one. Becoming an expert thinker can sometimes seem to be a painstaking process, in the same way that becoming an expert in any skill or field of endeavour can. It takes time, there are a lot of steps involved — some of which may seem unnecessary — and your enthusiasm may flag at times.

Becoming an expert thinker can be likened to learning how to ride a bicycle. When you are first learning, it helps if you put your feet and hands in specified places each time you get on the bicycle. After a while, getting on the bike becomes second nature, and you become an expert cyclist. Even though you might still be putting your feet and hands in roughly the same places as when you first learned how to ride, the process is so automatic that you don't have to think about it. Becoming an expert thinker is much the same. If you start as a novice, learning and practising all the correct steps, you will eventually become an expert who doesn't need to think consciously about each step. Thinking is no longer a series of rigid steps. It becomes a fluid process that flows naturally from defining the situation and determining the problems to implementing a well-evaluated plan of action. The concepts involved in the following sample problem are discussed in detail in Chapter 4. You may want to refer to that material in working through the sample problem.

SAMPLE PROBLEM

The Rutabaga Problem

You are an economist employed by your province's Department of Agriculture. You are asked to suggest a solution to the problems currently faced by the province's influential and vocal Rutabaga Growers' Association. The rutabaga growers are complaining that prices for their crops — and, consequently, their incomes — have been falling over the last few years. It's your job to suggest a solution agreeable to both the Rutabaga Growers' Association and the government that provides for the efficient use of scarce resources.

You have also been given the following background information: Rutabagas have long been a popular agricultural crop in your province, and have provided a good steady income for several generations of farmers. Demand for rutabagas by consumers in your province, across Canada, and for export has been steady or slightly increasing for the last 40 or 50 years.

However, as a result of declining agricultural prices for other crops, more and more farmers in your province and across Canada have started to grow rutabagas. Rutabaga farmers in your province are strenuously objecting to this "invasion" by new producers.

In current dollars, rutabaga farmers in your province received an average price of $350 per tonne for all rutabagas delivered to the market over the last ten years. The current market price of rutabagas is $280 per tonne. The total current market for rutabagas can be graphed as shown in Box 3A.1.

I. Define the situation

Who is involved? Rutabaga Growers' Association; the provincial government; buyers and sellers in provincial, national, and international rutabaga markets.

What is involved? Low rutabaga prices relative to the last ten years; pressure on the provincial government to help ensure good incomes for rutabaga growers.

When did the situation happen? Over the last few years.

Why did the situation arise? Demands by the Rutabaga Growers' Association to ensure good prices for rutabagas and good incomes for growers.

How serious is the situation? Financial distress for rutabaga farmers in your province.

II. State the problem and the goal

Analysis 1 *What* might *be the problem(s)?*

- predicting future supply, demand, and equilibrium market prices for rutabagas
- predicting future incomes for rutabaga growers in your province
- finding an agreeable solution that allows for the efficient allocation of scarce resources

---

BOX 3A.1 *Current Market for Rutabagas*

This graph depicts the total current market for rutabagas. During the past ten years, rutabaga farmers received an average price of $350 per tonne, but the price has now fallen to $280 per tonne. Note that it isn't necessary to know exact quantities of rutabagas supplied and demanded to use the problem-solving process.

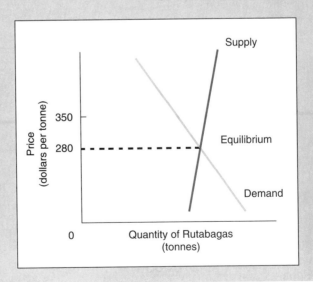

Synthesis 2 *What could be the goal(s) you want to achieve?*

- estimating future supply, demand, and equilibrium market prices for rutabagas
- estimating future incomes for rutabaga growers in your province
- convincing the Rutabaga Growers' Association and the government to consider the efficient allocation of scarce resources in reaching a solution

Evaluation 3 *Of all the possible goals in Step 2, which one(s) should you achieve?*

- estimating future supply, demand, and equilibrium market prices for rutabagas
- convincing the Rutabaga Growers' Association and the government to consider the efficient allocation of scarce resources in reaching a solution

III. Generate ideas for meeting your goals in Step 3

Analysis 4 *What problems might be involved in meeting the goals in Step 3?*

- lack of information about future production plans of Canadian rutabaga farmers in and outside your province
- lack of information about future production plans of non-Canadian rutabaga farmers
- lack of information about future demand for rutabagas in your province, in Canada, and in the world
- suggesting a solution that will encourage efficient use of scarce governmental and agricultural resources

Synthesis 5 *What could be done to solve the goal problems in Step 4?*

- exert some control over your province's rutabaga market by limiting the number of out-of-province rutabagas that come into your province
- take action to create a provincial (or Canada-wide) rutabaga marketing board that involves some control over prices and supplies of rutabagas
- set up a provincial or Canada-wide price-support program that guarantees a minimum price to rutabaga farmers by having government buy up, at a preset support price, any surplus that they can't sell
- encourage rutabaga farmers to produce other crops or agricultural products when rutabaga prices decline, thus allowing the rutabaga market to operate with little or no government involvement
- use government funds to support research to increase rutabaga yields so farmers can take more crops to the market at any equilibrium price
- attempt to increase the demand for rutabagas in the provincial, national, and international markets

Evaluation 6 *Of all the possible solutions to your goal problems in Step 5, what should be done to solve those problems?*

- encourage rutabaga farmers to produce other crops or agricultural products when rutabaga prices decline, thus allowing the rutabaga market to operate with little or no government involvement
- attempt to increase the demand for rutabagas in the provincial, national, and international markets

IV. Define the new situation

What is involved? The market for rutabagas operates largely free of government interference in your province; your provincial government engages in advertising and marketing efforts to increase demand for rutabagas provincially, nationally, and internationally.

Who is involved? Rutabaga Growers' Association; the provincial government; buyers and sellers in provincial, national, and international rutabaga markets.

When did the situation happen? Over the last few years.

Why did the situation arise? Demands by the Rutabaga Growers' Association to ensure good prices for rutabagas and good incomes for growers.

How serious is the problem? Rutabaga farmers in your province may find themselves in financial distress if prices remain low.

V. Prepare a plan

Analysis   7 *What might be a problem with the new situation?*

- the Rutabaga Growers' Association may not be satisfied with the proposed solutions
- your provincial government may not be satisfied with the proposed solutions
- costs to the government of proposed policies to increase rutabaga demand may not be acceptable to taxpayers
- if farmers diversify, starting to grow crops other than rutabagas, they may cause problems for established growers of those other crops
- a number of rutabaga farmers in your province may go bankrupt
- farmers who decide not to produce rutabagas when market prices are low may need help or retraining to produce other crops or find other jobs

Synthesis   8 *What could be part of a plan to solve the new-situation problems identified in Step 7?*

- consult with and get input from the Rutabaga Growers' Association and the government as your solution develops
- calculate costs to your provincial government, to provincial consumers and taxpayers, to rutabaga farmers, and so on, for all parts of your proposed solution
- provide rutabaga farmers with information on alternative crops or agricultural products they could produce
- provide all provincial farmers with estimates of future market supply, demand, and prices for all agricultural crops and output
- make low-cost loans available from your provincial government for farmers who need funds to make the switch from rutabagas to some other crop or agricultural output
- make low-cost loans and retraining programs available from your provincial government for all farmers who decide to leave farming for other types of jobs

Evaluation   9 *Which of the possible plans in Step 8 should be used to solve the new-situation problems?*

- consult with and get input from the Rutabaga Growers' Association and the government as your solution develops
- calculate costs to your provincial government, to provincial consumers and taxpayers, to rutabaga farmers, and so on, for all parts of your proposed solution

- make low-cost loans available from your provincial government for farmers who need funds to make the switch from rutabagas to some other crop or agricultural output
- make low-cost loans and retraining programs available from your provincial government for all farmers who decide to leave farming for other types of jobs

VI. Take action

Analysis   10 *What* might *be a problem with the plan you selected in Step 9?*

- policy-implementation costs may exceed budget projections
- the Rutabaga Growers' Association and government officials may not be satisfied with the proposed solution
- other provinces or nations (or both) may increase their rutabaga production, throwing off your supply, demand, and price predictions as well as your estimates of the loans and retraining that will be needed by farmers

Synthesis   11 *What* could be *becomes reality as you implement the plan.*

- implement your plan
- be prepared to change or adapt aspects of your solution in future years if market conditions change drastically

Evaluation   12 *What* should *be the next action, once you see the results of the implemented plan?*

- evaluate the results of the implemented solutions at the end of the first and succeeding crop years

A Comment on the Effective-Thinking Process

It may not be possible to take action and implement a plan in Section VI for all problems and situations. Although in some situations your plan may call, for example, for changing an estimate of an economic measurement and you may be able to incorporate the new estimate into a formula or a computer program and see the resulting changes, there will be other occasions on which you will have to be satisfied simply at having generated a plausible and well-thought-out solution to an economic problem. Professional economists are not always able to carry out the solutions they suggest: Sometimes, they just generate possible solutions based on economic theory and logic. However, economists who are involved in policy making for governments and those who develop investment strategies for firms — to name only two jobs performed by economists — often do get to see their proposed solutions implemented. Their task involves careful analysis, synthesis, and evaluation of solutions in action.

What Now?

There are six economic problems throughout this textbook (with possible solutions given at the back of the book) to help you practise the effective-thinking process that we have outlined in this appendix. Before looking at the suggested answers, you might find it useful to try working through the problem-solving steps on your own. If you want more problems or situations with which to practise the effective-thinking process, look through the Review Questions section at the end of each chapter. You should be able to find several questions in most chapters that lend themselves to the effective-thinking technique. Newspaper articles, as well as radio and television stories, are also good sources of current economic problems and situations for which you can think out solutions. Since media reports often contain economic analysis by professional economists, they give you the added benefit of an opportunity to compare your thought processes and solutions with those of professionals.

Remember that expert thinking is a skill that is developed with practice. Your economics course, your other courses, and life in general provide a wealth of problems and situations that can be better understood with the aid of effective-thinking techniques. Effective thinking isn't easy, but many students find it fun once they gain some experience and skill.

The Theory
of Price
and Output
Determination

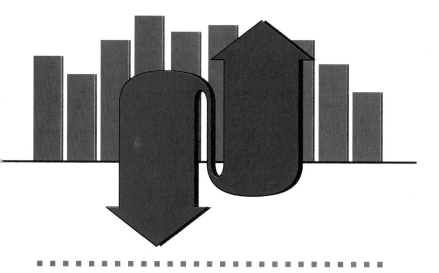

CHAPTER 4

Supply and Demand

WHAT YOU WILL LEARN IN THIS CHAPTER

After studying this chapter, you will be able to

1. Explain the behaviour of supply and demand.
2. Describe how the price of a good or service affects the quantity demanded by buyers.
3. Explain what causes a demand curve to shift.
4. Describe how the price of a good or service affects the quantity supplied by producers.
5. Explain what causes a supply curve to shift.
6. Define equilibrium in the market.
7. Explain how equilibrium changes as demand and supply change.
8. Apply supply-and-demand analysis to situations in which governments interfere with the operation of the market.

A Preview   *Identifying or Creating Market Demand*

In a market economy, business firms are successful only if they produce what consumers want. The trick is to be quick to identify consumer demand for different products. But consumers do not always know precisely what they want, so business often sets itself the task of "creating" a demand for a particular product. This is especially true of new products, as illustrated in the following newspaper article about in-line roller skates.

Roller Boom Hits the Road

In-line roller skates are taking over the roads and sidewalks of the nation.

These new-fangled, high-tech skates — which retail for $100 to $400 a pair — have become one of the fastest-selling sporting goods of the 1990s. Insiders expect the $114 million wholesale industry in Canada and the U.S. will double or triple this year.

Canstar Sports Inc., of Montreal, which owns the Bauer skate company, Canada's only in-line manufacturer, has seen skate sales jump from just 3–5 percent of 1990 revenue of $143.8 million to a projected 10–15 percent of this year's revenue. That represents more than 200 000 pairs in 1991.

In-lines are a cross between traditional roller skates and regular ice-hockey skates. The wheels are "in line" with one another, giving the manoeuvrability of ice skates with the fresh air and freedom of regular roller skates. Rollerblade Inc., of Minneapolis, is North America's biggest maker of in-line skates, originally developed in the 1700s by a Dutchman who nailed wooden spools to strips of wood that he attached to his shoes to simulate ice skating.

But for in-line makers such as Rollerblade and Canstar, the trick to sustaining demand is to create a market that does not see the skates simply as a fad. Retail consultant John Winter believes the only way to do that is to "ingrain [in-lines] as a way of life."

And that's what the industry is doing. The companies have designed marketing campaigns to persuade would-be buyers to keep in-lines on their feet, not in a box at the back of a cupboard.

Both major companies have adopted an aggressive, grass-roots approach to marketing. Rollerblade, for example, will have four vans, each with about 50 pairs of skates, tour different Canadian sporting events this summer to offer trial runs.

And Canstar estimates it will spend about $2 million on North American promotion, which includes joining forces with Pepsico's Mountain Dew division in the U.S. to help sponsor a series of road races.

Canstar executive vice-president Phil Chiarella believes the demographics of in-line buyers will ensure the skates are around for a while.

A recent survey of buyers of Canstar's Bauer in-lines found 40 percent were women, with another significant portion coming from people over 50 years old. Chiarella thinks the wide range of appeal will keep in-lines around for a while because they seem to offer something different to every age group and gender.

"We all feel it has tremendous potential to be around for a long time and it's definitely not a fad," he says.

SOURCE: Michael McHugh, "Roller Boom Hits the Road," *Financial Post* June 24, 1991, p. 2. Reproduced with permission.

Alfred Marshall on Supply and Demand

The work of Alfred Marshall represents a watershed between the classical economics of Adam Smith and the modern or neoclassical school that dominates the field today. Unlike Smith, who came to economics from philosophy, Marshall came to it from mathematics. Although historians sometimes refer to the "Marshallian revolution" in economic thought, Marshall did not see himself as a revolutionary. Instead, he viewed his work as strengthening classical economics through the use of mathematics.

Marshall is best known for his emphasis on supply and demand. In the second edition of his *Principles of Economics*, he wrote the following:

> In spite of a great variety in detail, nearly all the chief problems of economics agree in that they have a kernel of the same kind. This kernel is an inquiry as to the balancing of two opposed classes of motives, the one consisting of desires to acquire certain new goods, and thus satisfy wants; while the other consists of desires to avoid certain efforts or retain certain immediate enjoyment. . . . In other words, it is an inquiry into the balancing of the forces of supply and demand.

Alfred Marshall
(1842–1924)

ENTERING THE MARKET

Why did high-tech, in-line roller skates retail for $100 to $400 a pair in 1991? Why is Canstar, a Canadian skate producer, required to organize a massive marketing scheme in order to persuade Canadians to buy its skates? If skate sales do take off, what is likely to happen to their price?

The Preview article raises these questions, and more. It describes the manufacturer of a new product trying to break into the market. In order to succeed, this company must meet two basic requirements: It must organize supply, and it must ensure — to the extent that it can — that there is demand for its product. Presumably, this company has solved the problem of supply. It is not quite so sure that it will be able to solve the problem of demand, though great confidence is expressed.

Prices and markets play a key role in deciding what gets produced, how it is produced, who produces it, and who consumes it. In this chapter, we look more closely at the way markets work — at how supply and demand affect the prices of wheat, milk, dental services, air travel, diamonds, roller skates, and just about everything else.

The concepts of supply and demand are nothing new. For as long as there have been markets, sellers have known that one way to get people to buy more of a product is to offer it at a lower price. At the same time, buyers have long known that one way to get more of the things they want is to offer more for them. It is only in the past hundred years, though, that economists have used these concepts in a systematic way. In the English-speaking world, much of the credit for showing how useful the concepts of supply and demand can be goes to Alfred Marshall (see the accompanying Profile). This chapter builds on Marshall's work.

DEMAND

We can begin with a formal statement of the **law of demand**: In any market, other things being equal, the quantity of a good demanded by buyers tends to rise as the price of the good falls, and to fall as the price rises.

Law of demand
The principle that, other things being equal, the quantity of a good demanded by buyers tends to rise as the price of the good falls, and to fall as the price of the good rises.

We expect this to happen for two reasons. First, if the price of one good falls while the prices of other goods stay the same, people are likely to substitute the cheaper goods for goods that they would otherwise have bought instead. (When chicken is on sale and beef is not, people have chicken for dinner more often.) Second, when the price of one good falls while incomes and other prices stay the same, people feel a littler richer. They use their added buying power to buy a little more of many things, including a little more of the good whose price went down. In many cases, as we will see, these two factors act together to boost the sales of goods whose prices fall and to cut sales of goods whose prices rise.

Behind the Law of Demand

The main difference between the common-sense version of the law of demand and the economist's version is the care with which it is stated. Three points that underlie the economist's version are worth noting.

Quantity demanded

First, it is important to understand what is meant by *quantity demanded*. This is the quantity that buyers plan to buy and are able to buy over a given period, such as a month or a year. Quantity demanded is not the same thing as want or need. I might *want* a Porsche, but the sticker price, last time I checked, was more than $80 000. At that price, I do not plan to buy one. The quantity I demand at the going price is zero. I might *need* dental surgery to avoid losing my teeth, but suppose I am poor. If I cannot pay for the surgery, and if no one is willing to pay in my place, I am out of luck. The quantity of dental surgery I demand is zero, however great my need.

Other things being equal (ceteris paribus)

Ceteris paribus
A Latin expression often used in economics to express the condition "other things being equal."

Second, why is the phrase *other things being equal* (**ceteris paribus**) part of the law of demand? The reason is that a change in the price of a product is only one of a number of things that affect the quantity people plan to buy. If real incomes go up, people are likely to buy more of many goods even though their prices do not go down. If tastes change, people will buy more of some goods and less of others, even if prices do not change. Other factors, such as the price paid for our currency on the foreign-exchange market, can alter demand for our goods without a change in the domestic price of those goods.

Relative prices

Above all, "other things being equal" means that the prices of other goods are assumed to remain the same as buyers respond to a change in the price of a good. As economists put it, *relative prices* are what count.

It is important to distinguish between changes in relative prices and changes in nominal prices — the number of dollars actually paid per unit — during periods of inflation. If the price of eggs goes up 10 percent at the same time that consumers' nominal incomes and the prices of all other goods also go up 10 percent, we should not expect any change in the quantity of eggs demanded. The law of demand does not apply to this situation because other things are *not* equal as the price of eggs climbs.

The Demand Curve

The law of demand associates a quantity of a good or service demanded per unit of time with each possible price for that good or service. This systematic association between prices and quantities demanded for any particular good can be summarized in a table, such as the one in Box 4.1(a).

A Demand Schedule and a Demand Curve for Wheat   BOX 4.1

Both the demand schedule and the demand curve show the quantity of wheat demanded at various possible prices. Both show, for example, that when the price is $2 per bushel, the quantity demanded is 2 billion bushels per year.

(a) Demand Schedule

	Price of Wheat (dollars per bushel)	Quantity of Wheat Demanded (billions of bushels per year)
	3.20	1.4
	3.00	1.5
	2.80	1.6
	2.60	1.7
	2.40	1.8
	2.20	1.9
A	2.00	2.0
	1.80	2.1
	1.60	2.2
	1.40	2.3
	1.20	2.4
B	1.00	2.5
	0.80	2.6

(b) Demand Curve

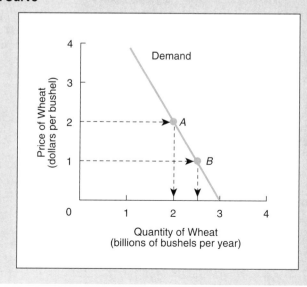

From the first line of the table, we learn that when the price of wheat is $3.20, the quantity demanded per year will be 1.4 billion bushels. Reading further, we see that as the price decreases, the quantity demanded increases. At $3 per bushel, buyers are willing and able to purchase 1.5 billion bushels per year; at $2.80, the quantity demanded is 1.6 billion bushels. The complete table is called the **demand schedule** for wheat.

The information given by the demand schedule can be expressed just as easily in graphical form. This is done in Box 4.1(b). The diagonal line of the graph is called the **demand curve** for wheat. Suppose that we want to use the demand curve to determine what quantity will be demanded when the price is $2.00 per bushel. With few exceptions, demand curves slope downward to the right. Beginning at $2 on the vertical axis, we follow across as shown by the arrow until we reach the demand curve. We then go down from that point to the horizontal axis, where we read the answer 2 billion bushels per year. This, of course, is the same answer given in the tabular demand schedule. The demand curve can also be expressed in equation form. The **demand equation** reads: Qd = f(P), or Qd = $a − b$P, meaning that the Quantity demanded (Qd) will be a certain amount (a) when the price is zero, and will decline at a certain rate (b) as price (P) rises. (In equations of this type, f stands for "a function of" or "related to.") In Box 4.1, Qd = 3 − $^{1}/_{2}$P, or P = 6 − 2Qd. This type of equation holds only for linear demand curves.

Movements along the demand curve

The effect of a change in the price of wheat, other things being equal, can be shown as a movement along the demand curve for wheat. Suppose the price drops from $2 per bushel to $1 per bushel. As the price falls, the quantity that buyers plan to buy rises. This moves the quantity demanded along the demand curve to point *B*, which corresponds to line *B* in the schedule.

Economists speak of a movement along a demand curve as a **change in quantity demanded**. This refers to the effect of a change in the price of the good in question, other things being equal.

Shifts in the demand curve

Demand curves like the one in Box 4.1 are always drawn on a *ceteris paribus* basis. They assume that as the price of wheat changes, other factors, such as the incomes of consumers, consumer tastes, and the prices of other goods, do not change. If any of these other factors changes, we have to draw a new demand curve. The new curve, like the old one, will slope downward, following the law of demand, but it will have shifted to the right or the left.

Economists speak of a shift in the demand curve that is produced by a change in an economic factor other than the price of the good as a **change in demand**. Several sources of changes in demand are worth looking at.

Four types of changes that can cause the demand curve to shift will be examined here: changes in (1) consumer income, (2) the prices of other goods, (3) consumer tastes, and (4) population.

Changes in Consumer Income

One of the key factors affecting the demand for a good is consumer income. If income rises, people tend to buy larger quantities of many goods (assuming that their prices do not change).

Demand schedule
A table showing the quantity of a good demanded at various prices.

Demand curve
A graphical representation of the relationship between the price of a good and the quantity of it demanded.

Demand equation
This equation can be written as Qd = $a − b$P, where Qd = quantity demanded, a = quantity demanded when the price (P) is zero, and b expresses the rate at which QD declines when the price rises. This equation holds true only for linear demand curves.

Change in quantity demanded
A change in the quantity buyers are willing and able to purchase that results from a change in the price of the good, other things being equal; a movement along the demand curve.

Change in demand
A change in the quantity buyers are willing and able to purchase, at any given price, that results from a change in some factor other than the price of the good; a shift in the demand curve.

Box 4.2 shows the effect of a rise in consumer income on the demand for wheat. Demand curve D_1 in this figure is the same as the demand curve in Box 4.1. According to this curve, the quantity demanded at a price of $2 is 2 billion bushels, and the quantity demanded at $1 is 2.5 billion bushels. Consumer income was one of the items covered by the "other things being equal" clause when this demand curve was drawn.

Suppose, however, that consumer income throughout the world rises. With higher income, people will want to buy more wheat-based foods than before at any given price. The greater demand for wheat-based foods will mean greater demand for wheat in the form of grain. Suppose that buyers of wheat are now willing to buy 3 billion bushels of wheat instead of 2 billion at a price of $2. This change is shown as a move from point A to point B in Box 4.2. Given the new, higher income, even more wheat would be bought if the price were $1. Instead of 2.5 billion bushels, as shown by D_1, buyers might now plan to purchase 3.5 billion bushels. This corresponds to a move from point C to point D.

Effect of an Increase in Consumer Income on the Demand for Wheat

BOX 4.2

Demand curve D_1 in this graph is the same as the demand curve shown in Box 4.1. It assumes some given level of consumer income. If their income changes, other things being equal, consumers will want to buy more wheat-based foods at any given price. This will shift the demand curve to the right, to, say, D_2. At $2 per bushel, the quantity demanded will be 3 billion bushels (B) rather than 2 billion (A); at $1 per bushel, the quantity demanded will be 3.5 billion bushels (D) instead of 2.5 billion (C); and so on.

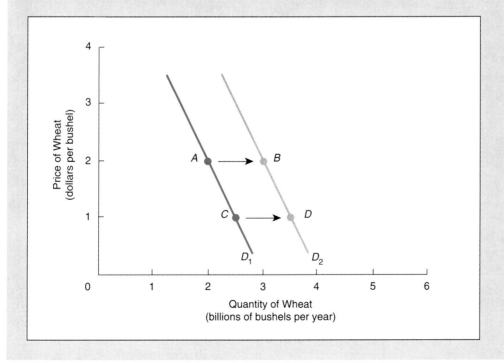

In both cases, the effects of a change in consumer income, at a given price, are shown by a movement off the original demand curve, D_1. Points B and D are on a new demand curve, D_2. We say that the increase in income has *shifted* the demand curve for wheat to the right. What if the price of wheat changes while income remains at the higher level? If this happens, the effects are shown as movements along the new demand curve.

In sum, there is a demand curve for each possible income level. Each of these demand curves represents a one-to-one relationship between price and quantity demanded, *given* the assumed level of income.

Normal and inferior goods

In the example just given, we assumed that an increase in income would cause an increase in the demand for wheat. Experience shows that this is what normally happens. Economists therefore call wheat a **normal good**, which means that when consumer incomes rise, other things being equal, people will buy more of it.

There are some goods, however, that people will buy less of if their incomes rise, other things being equal. When their incomes rise, people tend to buy fewer shoe-repair services; instead, they buy new shoes. And they tend to ride intercity buses less, since they would rather fly or drive. Goods such as shoe-repair services and intercity bus travel are called **inferior goods**. When consumer incomes rise, the demand curve for an inferior good shifts to the left instead of to the right.

Changes in the Prices of Other Goods

The demand for a good may be affected by changes in the prices of related goods as well as by changes in incomes. Look at Box 4.3, which shows demand curves for lettuce and cabbage. Either can be used to make salad. People's decisions about whether to eat tossed salad or cole slaw depend on many things, including the prices of lettuce and cabbage.

Suppose that the price of lettuce starts out at 69 cents a head and then rises to 99 cents a head. The effect of this change is shown in the left-hand figure as a movement along the lettuce demand curve from point A to point B. With the price of lettuce higher than before, consumers will tend to buy more cabbage than they otherwise would have. Suppose the price of cabbage is 49 cents a head. Before the price of lettuce went up, consumers would have bought 20 million heads of cabbage a week (point A' on the cabbage demand curve D_1). After the price of lettuce has gone up, they will buy 26 million heads of cabbage a week at the same price (point B' on the cabbage demand curve D_2).

In sum, an increase in the price of lettuce causes a *movement along* the lettuce demand curve and, at the same time, a *shift* in the cabbage demand curve.

Substitutes and complements

People tend to buy more cabbage when the price of lettuce goes up because they use it to replace lettuce in their salads. Economists say that such pairs of goods are **substitutes** because an increase in the price of one causes an increase in the demand for the other — a rightward shift in the demand curve. Consumers react differently to price changes when two goods tend to be used together. Tires and gasoline are an example. When the price of gasoline goes up, people drive less, so they buy fewer tires even if there is no change in the price of tires. An increase in

Normal good
A good for which an increase in consumer income results in an increase in demand.

Inferior good
A good for which an increase in consumer income results in a decrease in demand.

Substitute goods
A pair of goods for which an increase in the price of one causes an increase in the demand for the other.

Effects of an Increase in the Price of Lettuce on the Demand for Cabbage

BOX 4.3

An increase in the price of lettuce from 69 cents to 99 cents per head, other things being equal, results in an upward movement along the lettuce demand curve from point *A* to point *B*. This is called a decrease in the quantity of lettuce demanded. With the price of cabbage unchanged at 49 cents per head, consumers will substitute cabbage for lettuce. This will cause an increase in the demand for cabbage, which is shown as a shift in the cabbage demand curve from D_1 to D_2.

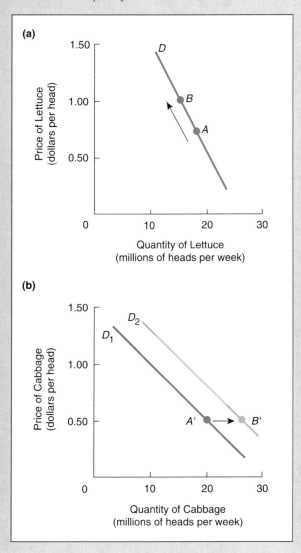

the price of gasoline thus causes a movement along the gasoline demand curve; at the same time, it causes a leftward shift in the demand curve for tires. Pairs of goods that are related in this way are known as **complements**.

Complementary goods
A pair of goods for which an increase in the price of one results in a decrease in the demand for the other.

Changes in Consumer Tastes

Changes in tastes are a third source of changes in demand. Sometimes these happen fast; this is the case, for example, in such areas as popular music, clothing styles, or nightclubs. The demand curves for these goods and services shift often. In other cases, changes in tastes take longer to occur but are more permanent. For example, for many years now, consumers have been more health conscious than they tended to be in the past; as a result, they have reduced their demand for high-cholesterol foods such as butter, eggs, and whole milk. This trend away from dairy products would be depicted as a leftward shift in the demand curve for dairy products, as depicted in Box 4.4.

As we will see later, one of the purposes of advertising and other marketing strategies is to increase consumers' desire or taste for a particular product, thus shifting the demand curve for that product to the right. This is essentially what the producers of in-line roller skates — the subject of this chapter's Preview — are attempting to do.

BOX 4.4 *Effects of a Change in Consumer Tastes on the Demand for Dairy Products*

A change in consumer tastes can cause a shift in the demand curve for a good. For example, during the 1970s, consumers became wary of high levels of cholesterol in their diets. As a result, they decreased their demand for dairy products. In this graph, the decrease in demand is shown as a shift in the demand curve from D_1 to D_2.

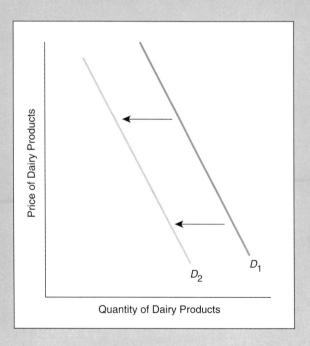

Changes in Population

A change in population will have two effects on the demand curve. First, it will likely change the demand curve for all products. More people with more income will tend to buy more of most products at current prices. Second, a change in population will likely produce a change in the mix of products that consumers want. An increase in the birth rate will increase the demand for baby carriages and nurseries more than it will increase the demand for some other products. A decrease in the death rate will increase the demand for products desired by older people.

We have discussed four major types of changes that cause the demand curve to shift: changes in consumer income, changes in the prices of other goods, changes in consumer tastes, and changes in population. There are other possible changes that can shift the demand curve as well, such as changes in the value of our currency, which will cause foreigners to increase or decrease their purchases of our goods, and changes in people's expectations. If, for example, prospective home buyers expect the prices of houses to rise in the near future, their demand for homes is likely to rise immediately, because they will want to beat the price increase.

Are There Exceptions to the Law of Demand?

Are there cases in which an increase in the price of a good causes people to use more of it? Theoretically, such exceptions are possible, although in practice they are quite rare. A famous example involves what the late American economist Thorsten Veblen called "conspicuous consumption," meaning that some people will buy more of some goods, such as jewellery and furs, at higher prices because a high price is a status symbol. The higher the price that you paid for your fur or diamond ring, the more some people will envy you when you meet them at cocktail parties.

While that kind of snobbery may increase the quantity demanded of such products as the price rises, most goods are bought in harmony with the law of demand.

Distinguishing between Shifts in and Movements along a Demand Curve

A failure to distinguish between shifts in demand curves and movements along a demand curve may sometimes cause us to believe that the law of demand is being broken.

Consider the following hypothetical example. At a certain Canadian university, tuition fees in 1980 were, on average, $700 a year. The number of student registrations that year was 4000. By 1990, average tuition fees at that university had risen to $1000. At the same time, student registrations increased to 5000. It appears at first glance that the demand for university education defies the law of demand: When tuition fees increased, the number of students "demanding" a university education also increased.

However, what we are likely dealing with here is not a single demand curve for university education that slopes upward to the right, but two different demand curves, one for 1980 and one for 1990, each of which behaves like a normal demand curve, sloping *downward* to the right. This is illustrated in the accompanying For Example. . . box.

FOR EXAMPLE...

Shifts in versus Movements along a Demand Curve

The demand curve D_1 represents a possible demand curve for university education in the year 1980. That year, 4000 students registered at our hypothetical university, with tuition fees set at $700. If tuition fees had been higher than $700 *that year*, fewer students would likely have registered. If they had been lower, more students might have enrolled. Changes in tuition fees that year would have created *movements along* the existing demand curve, D_1, in accordance with the law of demand. By the year 1990, a new demand curve, D_2, had emerged. In other words, in the ten-year interval between 1980 and 1990, the demand curve for university education had shifted to the right, possibly because of higher incomes, changing tastes (students preferred a university education to unemployment), and population growth. Despite a tuition fee of $1000, 5000 students registered. The dotted line connecting the two tuition prices, P_1 and P_2, with their respective enrolments, would suggest a demand curve sloping upward to the right, in defiance of the law of demand. However, what has happened is a shift in the demand curve, from one normal demand curve (D_1) in 1980 to another normal demand curve (D_2) in 1990.

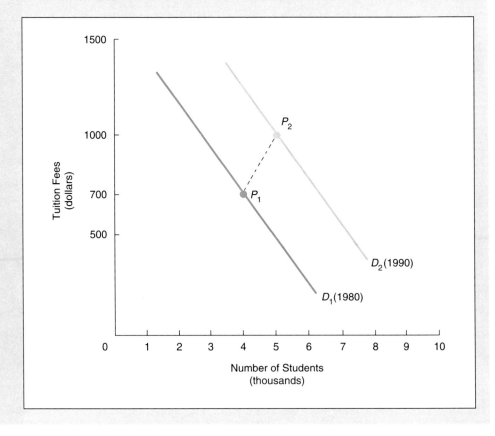

SUPPLY

We turn now from the demand side of the market to the supply side. As in the case of demand, we can construct a one-to-one relationship between the price of a good and the quantity of it that sellers intend to offer for sale, given the market conditions they expect.

Box 4.5 shows a supply curve for wheat. Like demand curves, supply curves are based on a *ceteris paribus* condition. The supply curve for wheat shows how sellers change their plans in response to a change in the price of wheat, assuming that there are no changes in the prices of other goods, in production techniques, in the prices of inputs, or in any other relevant factors.

Everyday experience suggests that, in order to induce sellers to increase the quantity of a good supplied, it is necessary, other things being equal, to offer them a higher price. When this is true, the supply curve for the good in question slopes upward. Box 4.5 shows a **supply schedule** and a corresponding upward-sloping **supply curve** for wheat. The supply curve can be expressed in equation form. The **supply equation** reads: $Qs = f(P)$, or $Qs = a + bP$. In Box 4.5, $Qs = 1 + \frac{1}{2}P$, or $P = -2 + 2\,Qs$. This type of equation holds true only for supply curves that are linear.

Supply schedule
A table showing the quantity of a good supplied at various prices.

Supply curve
A graphical representation of the relationship between the price of a good and the quantity of it supplied.

Supply equation
This equation expresses the idea that quantity supplied (Qs) is a function of price, or $Qs = a + bP$. This equation holds true only for linear supply curves.

The Slope of the Supply Curve

Why exactly is the supply curve for wheat expected to slope upward? There are a number of possible reasons, any or all of which may operate in a particular case. For one thing, a higher price gives farmers a greater incentive to devote more of their time and energy to wheat production. In addition, it may induce them to substitute wheat for other crops they had been producing. Furthermore, the higher price may make it possible to attract resources into wheat farming from other lines of production, perhaps even leading to the establishment of new farms. In short, just as we saw in Chapter 1, the higher price of wheat not only provides farmers with a key piece of information but also gives them an incentive to act on it.

Shifts in the Supply Curve

As in the case of demand, the effects of a change in the price of wheat, other things being equal, can be shown as a movement along the supply curve for wheat. This is called a **change in quantity supplied**. A change in some factor other than the price of wheat can result in a shift in the supply curve. This is referred to as a **change in supply**. Three sources of change in supply are worth noting.

Change in quantity supplied
A change in the quantity producers are willing and able to sell that results from a change in the price of the good, other things being equal; a movement along the supply curve.

Change in supply
A change in the quantity producers are willing and able to sell, at any given price, that results from a change in some factor other than the price of the good; a shift in the supply curve.

Technological change
A supply curve is drawn on the basis of a particular production technique. If a technological change reduces costs, producers will plan to sell more of the good than before at any given price. Box 4.6 shows how such an event would affect the wheat supply curve. Supply curve S_1 is the same as the one shown in Box 4.5. According to S_1, farmers will plan to supply 2 billion bushels per year at a price of $2 per bushel (point *A*).

Now suppose that new farming techniques reduce the cost of growing wheat. Using the new techniques, farmers will be willing to supply more wheat than before at any given price. They may, for example, be willing to supply 2.6 billion

BOX 4.5   *A Supply Schedule and a Supply Curve for Wheat*

Both the supply schedule and the supply curve for wheat show the quantity of wheat
supplied at various prices. An increase in the price of wheat induces farmers to supply a
greater quantity of it: It gives them an incentive to devote more time and energy to the
crop and to substitute it for other crops grown previously. A price increase might also
draw new resources (and even new farmers) into wheat production.

(a) Supply Schedule

	Price of Wheat (dollars per bushel)	Quantity of Wheat Supplied (billions of bushels per year)
	3.20	2.6
	3.00	2.5
	2.80	2.4
	2.60	2.3
	2.40	2.2
	2.20	2.1
A	2.00	2.0
	1.80	1.9
	1.60	1.8
	1.40	1.7
	1.20	1.6
B	1.00	1.5
	0.80	1.4

(b) Supply Curve

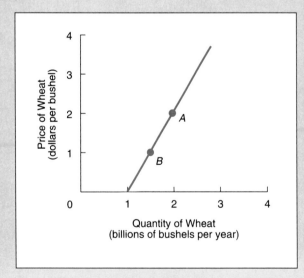

bushels of wheat at $2 per bushel (point *B*). The move from *A* to *B* is part of a shift in the whole supply curve from S_1 to S_2. Once the new techniques are established, an increase or decrease in the price of wheat, other things being equal, will result in a movement along the new supply curve.

Changes in input prices

Changes in input prices are a second factor that can cause supply curves to shift. An increase in input prices, other things being equal, tends to reduce the quantity of a good that producers plan to supply at a given price. Refer again to Box 4.6. Suppose that, starting from point *A* on supply curve S_1, the price of tractor fuel increases. No other changes occur to offset this increase in costs. Now, instead of supplying 2 billion bushels of wheat at $2 per bushel, farmers will supply, say, only 1.4 billion bushels at that price (point *C*). The move from *A* to *C* is part of a leftward shift in the supply curve, from S_1 to S_3.

If the price of fuel remains at the new level, changes in the price of wheat will cause movements along the new supply curve. For example, farmers could be induced to supply the original quantity of wheat — 2 billion bushels — if the price rose enough to cover the increased cost of fuel. As you can see in Box 4.6, that would require the price to rise to $3.20 per bushel (point *D*).

Shifts in the Supply Curve for Wheat   BOX 4.6

Several kinds of changes can cause the supply of wheat to increase or decrease. For example, a new production method that lowers costs will shift the curve to the right, from S_1 to S_2. An increase in the price of inputs, other things being equal, will shift the curve to the left, from S_1 to S_3. Changes in the prices of competing goods can also cause the supply curve to shift.

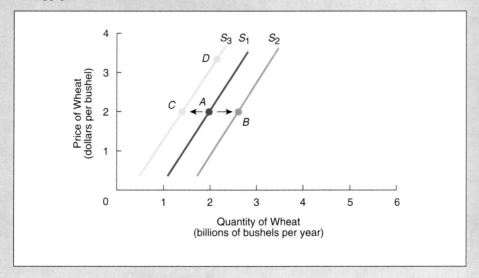

Changes in the prices of other goods

Changes in the prices of other crops can also produce a shift in the wheat supply curve. Suppose that the price of corn rises while the price of wheat stays at $2. The change in the price of corn gives farmers an incentive to shift some of their land from wheat to corn. The effect of the increase in the price of corn is to raise the opportunity cost of growing wheat; each bushel of wheat grown means a certain quantity of corn not grown, but the corn is now worth more. The effect of an increase in the price of corn can thus be shown as a leftward shift in the wheat supply curve.

THE INTERACTION OF SUPPLY AND DEMAND

As we have seen, markets transmit information, in the form of prices, to people who buy and sell goods. Taking these prices into account, along with other knowledge they might have, the buyers and sellers make their plans. As shown by the demand and supply curves, buyers and sellers plan to buy or sell certain quantities at any given price.

In each market, many buyers and sellers make different plans. When they meet to trade, some of them may be unable to carry out their plans. Perhaps the total quantity that buyers plan to purchase is greater than the total quantity that suppliers are willing to sell at the given price. In that case, some of the would-be buyers must change their plans. Or perhaps planned sales exceed planned purchases. In that case, some would-be sellers will be unable to carry out their plans.

Sometimes no one is disappointed: The total quantity that buyers plan to purchase exactly matches the total quantity that producers plan to sell. When the plans of buyers and sellers exactly match when they meet in the marketplace, no one needs to change plans. Under these conditions the market is said to be in **equilibrium**.

Market equilibrium
A condition in which the separately formulated plans of the buyers and sellers of some good exactly mesh when tested in the marketplace, so that the quantity supplied is exactly equal to the quantity demanded at the prevailing price.

Market Equilibrium

Supply and demand curves, which reflect the plans of sellers and buyers, can be used to give a graphic picture of market equilibrium. Box 4.7 uses the same supply and demand curves that we have seen before, but this time they are both drawn on the same diagram. If the quantity of planned sales at each price is compared with the quantity of planned purchases at that price — either the table or the graph can be used to make the comparison — it can be seen that there is only one price at which the two sets of plans match. This price — $2 per bushel — is the equilibrium price. If all buyers and sellers make their plans in the expectation of a price of $2, no one will be disappointed and no plans will have to be changed.

Shortages

What if, for some reason, buyers and sellers expect the market price to be something other than $2? Suppose, for example, that a price of $1 per bushel somehow becomes established in the market. Box 4.7 tells us that, at this price, producers will plan to supply wheat to the market at the rate of 1.5 billion bushels per year. At that price, buyers will plan to purchase at a rate of 2.5 billion bushels per year. When the quantity demanded exceeds the quantity supplied,

Equilibrium in the Wheat Market

BOX 4.7

When the quantity demanded of a product exceeds the quantity supplied, there is an excess quantity demanded, or a shortage, of the product. A shortage puts upward pressure on the price of the product. When the quantity supplied exceeds the quantity demanded, there is an excess quantity supplied, or a surplus, of the product. A surplus puts downward pressure on the price. In our example, it is only when the price of wheat is $2 per bushel that there is no shortage or surplus and no upward or downward pressure on price. At $2, the market is in equilibrium. In the graph, a surplus or shortage is indicated by the horizontal distance between the supply and demand curves. A surplus puts downward pressure on price and a shortage puts upward pressure on it, as indicated by the arrows following the supply and demand curves. The market is in equilibrium at the point where the supply and demand curves intersect.

(a)

Price (dollars per bushel) (1)	Quantity Supplied (billions of bushels) (2)	Quantity Demanded (billions of bushels) (3)	Shortage (billions of bushels) (4)	Surplus (billions of bushels) (5)	Direction of Pressure on Price (6)
3.20	2.6	1.4	—	1.2	Downward
3.00	2.5	1.5	—	1.0	Downward
2.80	2.4	1.6	—	0.8	Downward
2.60	2.3	1.7	—	0.6	Downward
2.40	2.2	1.8	—	0.4	Downward
2.20	2.1	1.9	—	0.2	Downward
2.00	2.0	2.0	0	0	Equilibrium
1.80	1.9	2.1	0.2	—	Upward
1.60	1.8	2.2	0.4	—	Upward
1.40	1.7	2.3	0.6	—	Upward
1.20	1.6	2.4	0.8	—	Upward
1.00	1.5	2.5	1.0	—	Upward
0.80	1.4	2.6	1.2	—	Upward

(b)

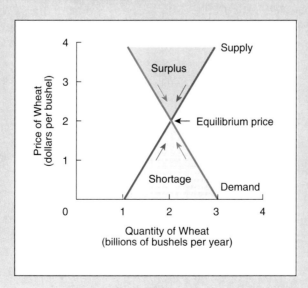

Excess quantity demanded, or shortage
The amount by which the quantity of a good demanded exceeds the quantity supplied when the price of the good is below the equilibrium level.

Inventories
Stocks of a finished good awaiting sale or use.

the difference between the two is called an **excess quantity demanded** or, more simply, a **shortage**. In the case of wheat, the shortage is 1 billion bushels per year when the price is $1 per bushel.

Shortages and inventories

In most markets, the first sign of a shortage is the depletion of **inventories** of the product available for sale. Under such circumstances, either sellers take the initiative to raise prices or buyers take the initiative to offer higher prices in the hope of getting part of the available quantity. In either event, the shortage puts upward pressure on price.

As the price of the product rises, producers begin to plan to sell more and buyers begin to plan to purchase less — in other words, the higher the price, the smaller the shortage. When the price of wheat in Box 4.7 reaches $2 per bushel, the shortage is entirely eliminated. With its elimination, there is no further upward pressure on prices. The market is in equilibrium.

Shortages and queues

In the markets for most goods, sellers have inventories of goods ready to be sold. There are exceptions, however. Inventories are not possible in markets for services — haircuts, tax preparation, lawn care, and the like. Also, some custom-made products, such as houses and specialized machine tools, are not held in inventories. Sellers in these markets do not begin production until they have a contract with a buyer.

In markets where there are no inventories, the sign of a shortage is a "queue" of buyers. The queue may take the form of a line of people waiting to be served or a list of names in an order book. The queue is a sign that buyers would like to purchase the good at a faster rate than producers have planned to supply it. Some plans cannot be carried out, at least not right away. Buyers are served on a first-come, first-served basis.

The formation of a queue of buyers has much the same effect on the market as a fall in inventories. Sellers react by increasing their rate of output or raising their prices or both. Buyers react to the rising price by reducing the quantity they plan to purchase. The result is a movement up and to the right along the supply curve and a simultaneous movement up and to the left along the demand curve, until equilibrium is reached.

Surpluses

Suppose instead that for some reason buyers and sellers expect the price of wheat to be higher than the equilibrium price — say, $3 per bushel. Box 4.7 shows that farmers will plan to supply 2.5 billion bushels of wheat per year at $3, but their customers will plan to buy only 1.5 billion bushels. When the quantity supplied exceeds the quantity demanded, there is an **excess quantity supplied**, or a **surplus**. As Box 4.7 shows, the surplus of wheat at a price of $3 per bushel is 1 billion bushels per year.

Surpluses and inventories

When there is a surplus of a product, sellers will be disappointed. They will not be able to sell all that they had hoped to sell at the planned price. As a result, their

Excess quantity supplied, or surplus
The amount by which the quantity of a good supplied exceeds the quantity demanded when the price of the good is above the equilibrium level.

inventories will begin to grow beyond the level they had planned to hold in preparation for normal changes in demand.

Sellers will react to the inventory buildup by changing their plans. Some of them will cut back their output. Others will cut their prices in order to reduce their extra stock. Many will do a little of both. The result of these changes in plans will be a movement down and to the left along the supply curve, following the arrow in Box 4.7.

As unplanned inventory buildup puts downward pressure on the price, buyers change their plans too. Finding that wheat costs less than they expected, they buy more of it. This is shown as a movement down and to the right along the demand curve. As this happens, the market is brought back into equilibrium.

Surpluses and queues

In markets where there are no inventories, surpluses lead to the formation of queues of sellers looking for customers. Taxi queues at airports are a case in point. At least at some times of the day, the fare for taxi service from the airport into the city is more than enough to attract a number of taxis equal to the demand. In some cities, drivers who are far back in the queue try to attract riders with offers of cut-rate fares. More often, though, there are rules against fare cutting. The queue then grows until a surge of business shortens it again.

Changes in Equilibrium Resulting from Changes in Demand and Supply

Assume that the market for wheat has achieved the equilibrium situation depicted in Box 4.7. The market price is $2 per bushel, and, at this price, quantity demanded exactly equals quantity supplied. Now assume that something happens to cause the demand for wheat to change. Perhaps there has been a population increase, or the price of a substitute grain, such as rye, has gone up. Consumers now desire to purchase more wheat, at every given price, than before, and the demand curve therefore shifts to the right. This change in demand is depicted in Box 4.8(a). In this diagram, the demand curve is shown as shifting to the right, from D_1 to D_2. The increased demand causes the price of wheat to rise, which in turn encourages farmers to increase the quantity of wheat they produce. The overall market result is a change from the initial equilibrium point, E_1, to a new equilibrium point, E_2. The equilibrium price has risen from $2 to $3 a bushel, and the equilibrium quantity has increased from 2 billion bushels to approximately 2.5 billion bushels. If, conversely, demand had decreased, causing the demand curve to shift to the left, the equilibrium price and quantity would both have fallen.

Now let us assume that there is a change in supply rather than demand. This alternative scenario is illustrated in Box 4.8(b), where an increase in supply causes the supply curve to shift to the right, from S_1 to S_2. Perhaps farmers have discovered a more efficient way of growing wheat, so that they are able to supply a greater quantity at every given price. The increase in supply shifts the equilibrium from E_1 to E_3 and results in lower prices and an increased quantity supplied. If, conversely, supply had decreased, shifting the supply curve to the left, prices would have risen and quantity would have fallen.

BOX 4.8   *Changes in Equilibrium Resulting from Changes in Demand and Supply*

In both graphs (a) and (b), the initial equilibrium point is E_1, at a price of $2 per bushel and a quantity of 2 billion bushels. In graph (a), the demand for wheat increases, shifting the demand curve to the right, from D_1 to D_2. This causes both price and quantity to rise, achieving a new equilibrium at E_2, at a price of $3 and a quantity of 2.5 billion bushels. If demand had *decreased*, shifting the demand curve to the left, the equilibrium price and quantity would have fallen. In graph (b), the supply of wheat increases, shifting the supply curve to the right, from S_1 to S_2. This reduces the equilibrium price from $2 to $1 and increases the equilibrium quantity from 2 billion to 2.5 billion bushels (at the new equilibrium point, E_3). If supply had *decreased*, the supply curve would have shifted to the left, increasing the equilibrium price and reducing the equilibrium quantity.

(a)

(b)

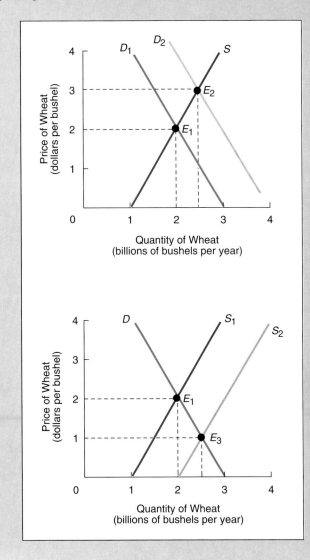

Interfering with Demand and Supply

Provincial rent controls

In the last decade, most provinces in Canada have chosen to interfere with the market price for apartments and other rental units by establishing some form of rent control. The purpose of such controls is to keep the price for an average apartment or other rental dwelling below what it would be in the absence of government intervention. Such a government-imposed maximum price, typically set below the market equilibrium price, is known as a **price ceiling**. The beneficiaries of price ceilings or rent controls are, of course, renters. However, some people who would like to rent an apartment or other dwelling may not benefit from such a program. At the control price, too few rental units may be supplied by builders. Vacancy rates may fall to zero, and some of those who would like to rent accommodation may not be able to. Some cities have experienced vacancy rates very close to zero under rent control programs.

As long as the control price is rigidly maintained below the market equilibrium price, shortages will persist. A new equilibrium will not be established. In order to avoid such persistent shortages, the control programs have generally permitted slight increases in rent, subject to review, and have permitted new rental dwellings to be exempt from the controls for a few years. In addition, builders of rental units have received special tax concessions, or "tax shelters," to encourage them to build more units than they otherwise would under rent controls. (See Review Question 9 at the end of this chapter.) Reduced taxes mean reduced costs, which cause the supply curve to shift down to the right, creating a new equilibrium at a lower price and a greater quantity. Box 4.9 shows hypothetical supply and demand curves for rental units and illustrates how rent controls prevent an equilibrium from being established.

Agricultural support programs

Governments in Canada, as well as in most other Western countries, have chosen to support the agricultural industry with many types of programs that interfere with the normal operation of demand and supply. **Price supports** are the most traditional and long-standing of all instruments of farm policy. Box 4.10 shows how they work, taking the market for wheat as an example. The market equilibrium price in Box 4.10 is $2 per bushel, and the equilibrium quantity of output is 2 billion bushels per year.

Suppose now that in order to raise farm incomes, the government declares a support price of $3 per bushel. A government-imposed minimum price of this kind, typically set above the market equilibrium price, is also known as a **price floor** (though it is commonly referred to as a *floor price*). At a floor price of $3 per bushel, farmers will produce 2.5 billion bushels of wheat, but consumers will buy only 1.5 billion bushels. The government will maintain the floor price by buying up the 1 billion bushels of surplus wheat and putting it in storage.[1]

Price ceiling
A maximum permissible price, usually imposed by the government and set below the market equilibrium price.

Price supports
Programs under which the government guarantees a certain minimum price to farmers by undertaking to buy any surplus that cannot be sold to private buyers at the support price.

Price floor
A minimum permissible price, usually imposed by the government and set above the market equilibrium price; commonly referred to as the *floor price*.

---

[1]Through the Canadian Wheat Board, the government allocates a wheat delivery quota to each farmer, and the wheat is sold by the board either at home or abroad. The farmer is paid an initial price (for example, $3 per bushel), which is, in effect, the support price. If demand on the world market enables the price to rise higher than $3, farmers receive additional payments.

BOX 4.9   Effects of Rent Controls

This graph shows hypothetical supply and demand curves for rental units. The equilibrium cost (or rent) of a unit in this example would normally be about $400, but rent controls keep the average monthly rent below equilibrium, at about $300. At this lower price, there will likely be a shortage of rental units. Vacancy rates will be at zero, and many people may not be able to obtain an apartment or other dwelling to rent.

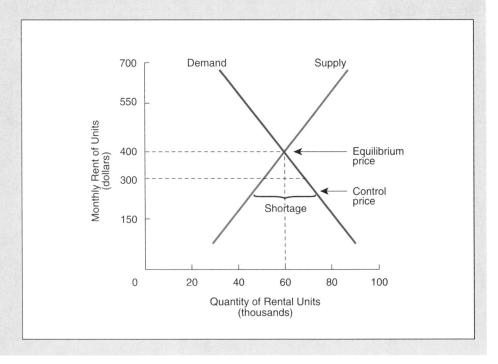

But what does the government do with the stored surplus wheat? During the 1960s, the quantities of wheat stored by the government became a national problem. Luckily, most of the vast accumulation (or at least the part of it that had not spoiled) was cleared out during the 1973 world food crisis. Because of the surplus problem, the government has experimented with other policies, which are designed to avoid the problem.

Land-use controls are one of the instruments intended to avoid the problem of surpluses. Box 4.11 shows how they work. The demand curve, D, and supply curve S_1 are the same as the demand and supply curves in Box 4.10. The objective of government policy is also the same: to raise the price of wheat from the market equilibrium level of $2 per bushel to the desired level of $3 per bushel.

The method of pushing the price up, however, is different this time. Instead of offering to buy any wheat that goes unsold at the price of $3 per bushel, the government attempts to restrict the quantity of wheat produced in order to drive the price up to the desired level. It does this by requiring each farmer to take some land out of wheat production.

The effect of the artificial restriction on the land used for wheat is to raise the cost of producing wheat. Ordinarily, farmers who want to grow more wheat will

Land-use controls
Policies designed to raise agricultural prices by limiting the amount of land on which certain crops can be grown.

The Effect of Price Supports

BOX 4.10

To carry out its price-support policy, the government agrees to pay $3 per bushel for all wheat that cannot be sold at that price in the open market. Because the support price is above the equilibrium price for a competitive market, this policy will reduce the quantity of wheat demanded and increase the quantity of wheat supplied. The resulting surplus will be purchased by the government and put into storage or otherwise disposed of.

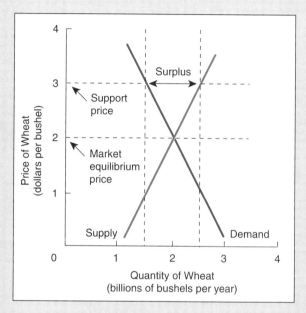

minimize their cost of production by adding a little more land, a little more labour, and a little more capital (machinery and fertilizer) in certain cost-mini-mizing proportions. Now those same farmers face a new constraint: they can use more labour and capital but *not* more land. It is still possible to grow more wheat if the price is high enough to justify the added cost, so the new supply curve, S_2, still has an upward slope. But the increased marginal cost resulting from the con-straint on farming practices causes a decrease in supply and shifts the supply curve to the left. If wheat production is restricted by just the right amount, as it is in Box 4.11, the same price ($3 per bushel) will be reached as the one achieved by means of price supports in the previous example.

SUMMARY

1. According to the *law of demand,* in any market, other things being equal, the quantity of a good demanded by buyers tends to rise as the price falls and to fall as the price rises. For any given market, the law of demand sets up a one-to-one relationship between price and quantity demanded, other things being equal. This relationship is graphically depicted as a downward-sloping *demand curve.*

BOX 4.11   *The Effects of Land-Use Controls*

This box shows how the government can raise the price of wheat to the desired level of $3 per bushel by means of land-use controls. Land-use controls raise the cost of producing wheat, shifting the supply curve to the left, from S_1 to S_2. The effect is to push the price of wheat up without creating a surplus. However, more resources must be used to produce each bushel of wheat than would have been the case without land-use controls.

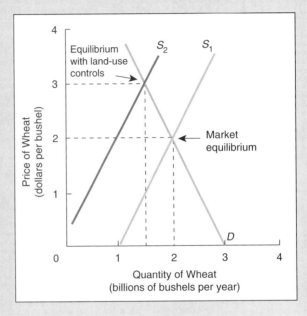

2. A movement along the demand curve, which is caused by a change in the price of the good, other things being equal, is known as a *change in quantity demanded*. A shift in the demand curve is known as a *change in demand*. Factors that can cause a shift in the demand curve include changes in income, changes in the prices of other goods, changes in consumer tastes, and changes in population.

3. If an increase in income causes the demand for a good to increase, it is a *normal good*. If an increase in income causes the demand for a good to decrease, it is an *inferior good*. If an increase in the price of one good causes the demand for another good to increase, the two goods are *substitutes*. If an increase in the price of one good causes the demand for another good to decrease, the two goods are *complements*.

4. In most markets, an increase in the price of a good will increase the quantity that producers are willing to supply. This relationship is graphically depicted as an upward-sloping *supply curve*.

5. A movement along the supply curve, which is caused by a change in the price of the good, other things being equal, is known as a *change in quantity supplied*. A shift in the supply curve is known as a *change in supply*. Factors

that can cause a shift in the supply curve include changes in production techniques, changes in the cost of inputs, and changes in the prices of other goods.

6. In a market with an upward-sloping supply curve and a downward-sloping demand curve, there is only one price at which the quantity that producers plan to supply will exactly match the quantity that buyers plan to purchase. This is known as the *equilibrium* price. If the price rises above the equilibrium level, an *excess quantity supplied*, or a *surplus*, will develop, causing an increase in *inventories* or the formation of a queue of sellers that will put downward pressure on the price until equilibrium is restored. If the price falls below the equilibrium level, an *excess quantity demanded*, or a *shortage*, will arise, causing a depletion of inventories or the formation of a queue of buyers that will put upward pressure on the price until equilibrium is restored.

7. When economic conditions change, supply curves and demand curves can shift. Normally, the price moves smoothly to a new equilibrium. However, *price floors* may lead to persistent surpluses, and *price ceilings* may lead to persistent shortages.

8. Governments sometimes choose to interfere with the normal operations of demand and supply, in order to provide support to groups such as farmers. Price supports and land-use controls are examples of government programs that alter the demand and supply conditions for certain farm products.

EFFECTIVE THINKING: PROBLEM 1

Rhino Poaching

Each of the effective-thinking problems in this book picks up on the material contained in the chapter it accompanies. In this chapter, you have learned about supply and demand. Rhino poaching is a problem that involves the supply of and the demand for rhinoceros horns. You are encouraged to find a solution to this problem using the ideas you have learned in Chapter 4.

In recent years, large numbers of rhinoceros in the wilds of Africa have been killed by poachers. The poachers kill the animals for their horns, which bring large sums of money on the black market, in part because they are believed to be an aphrodisiac. Poachers usually take only the animal's horn (or horns), leaving the rest of the body to rot. Game wardens have been unsuccessful in their efforts to protect the animals. As a result, the rhinoceroses' numbers have dwindled to the point that they have become an endangered species. As an economist, you are asked to help solve the problem of rhinoceros poaching.

Directions

Apply the twelve effective-thinking steps for successful problem solving (see the Appendix to Chapter 3 for a review and an example of the use of these steps). For Steps 10 through 12, assume that the plan you adopted in Step 9 is implemented.

An example of the thinking process an economist might go through using these twelve problem-solving steps appears in the section entitled Solutions to Effective-Thinking Problems, at the back of the book (see pages 783–94). Not all economists would produce identical answers for each step, but they would all draw on accepted principles of economics.

KEY TERMS

law of demand
ceteris paribus
demand schedule
demand curve
demand equation
change in quantity demanded
change in demand
normal good
inferior good
substitute goods

complementary goods
supply schedule
supply curve
supply equation
change in quantity supplied
change in supply
market equilibrium
excess quantity demanded, or
  shortage
inventories

excess quantity supplied, or
  surplus
price ceiling
price supports
price floors (floor price)
land-use controls

KEY BOX

Box 4.7 Equilibrium in the Wheat Market

REVIEW QUESTIONS

1. Consider the example of the in-line roller skates discussed in the Preview to this chapter. Use demand and supply curves in your answers to the following:

   a. Show what would happen to the price of in-line roller skates if the marketing strategies employed by the company shifted the demand curve to the right. (Assume that the supply curve slopes upward and to the right.)

   b. Sometimes, as in the case of VCRs and television sets, the price of a product declines as demand increases. Show under what conditions this might happen to the price of in-line roller skates.

   c. In some cities, police are cracking down on the use of roller skates on streets and sidewalks. What effect might this have on the price and quantity sold of in-line roller skates?

   d. Use recent financial journals to determine what actually happened to the market for in-line roller skates. Were the marketing strategies mentioned in the Preview article successful?

2. How does the concept of demand differ from the concepts of want and need?

3. What conditions are covered by the "other things being equal" clause in the law of demand? What effect does a change in any of these conditions have on the plans of buyers?

4. How do inventories put upward or downward pressure on prices when markets are not in equilibrium? How is equilibrium restored in markets in which there are no inventories of finished goods?

5. A vending machine company has studied the demand for soft drinks sold in cans from machines. In the firm's territory, consumers will buy about 2000 cans of pop at a price of 50¢ on a 20°C day. For each 5¢ by which the price is raised, the quantity sold falls by 200 cans per day. For each 3° rise in the temperature, the quantity sold rises by 150 cans per day. The corresponding relationships hold for decreases in price and temperature.

   Using this information, draw a set of curves showing the demand for soft drinks on days when the temperature is 17°C, 20°C, and 29°C.

6. Suppose there were a drought on the prairies, where the nation's wheat is grown. What would be the impact of the drought on the demand for and the supply of wheat? What would happen to the price of wheat? Why?

How would this be likely to affect the individual consumers of products containing wheat?

7. You are a member of the Metropolitan Taxi Commission, which sets taxi fares for your city. You have been told that long lines of taxis form at the airport during off-peak hours. At rush hours, on the other hand, few taxis are available and there are long lines of passengers waiting for cabs. It is proposed that taxi fares from the airport to downtown be cut by 10 percent during off-peak hours and raised by 10 percent during rush hours. How do you think these changes would affect the queuing patterns of taxis and passengers? Do you think the proposal is a good one from the point of view of passengers? From the point of view of cabbies? From the point of view of efficiency? Discuss.

8. If you were a wholesaler and you could see sooner than your competitors when the demand curve for the product you deal in was about to shift to the right, how could you use this advance knowledge to make money? Would you be benefiting anyone besides yourself in getting rid of the disequilibrium? Explain.

9. Suppose that rent controls have been placed on rental units such as apartments, and that tax authorities reduce the cost of building apartments by granting tax reductions to those who put their investment funds into new apartments. Illustrate, with reference to Box 4.9, how this would affect the supply curve for apartment units and possibly bring about a new equilibrium at the control price.

10. Assume that the highest price an emigrant to Antarctica will pay for a refrigerator is $500, while the lowest price at which a dealer will supply one is $1000. Draw demand and supply curves to depict this situation and indicate where the equilibrium price would be.

11. Draw a graph to illustrate each of the situations described below. Each situation involves one of the following: a shift in the demand curve, a movement along the demand curve, or no change at all in the demand curve for Pepsi-Cola. For each graph in which there is some movement, indicate whether there has been a change in demand or a change in the quantity demanded. Assume *ceteris paribus* in each of these situations, and assume also that Pepsi and Coke are normal goods.

    a. Pepsi-Cola announces a special summer sale on 2 L bottles.
    b. Coca-Cola raises the price of its product.
    c. A successful advertising campaign gets more people to drink Pepsi.
    d. A dedicated Pepsi drinker gets an increase in her income.
    e. A rumour is circulated that workers at the local Pepsi bottling plant are going on strike, and that Pepsi will not be available locally for a time.

12. Draw a graph to illustrate each of the situations described below. Each situation involves one of the following: a shift in the demand curve, a movement along the demand curve, or no change at all in the demand curve for the good or service under discussion. For each graph in which there is some movement, indicate whether there has been a change in demand or a change in the quantity demanded. Assume *ceteris paribus* in each of these situations.

    a. Members of the Roman Catholic church used to eat fish on Fridays because the church forbade eating meat on that day; then the church decided to allow its members to eat meat on Fridays.
    b. A jazz trombone ensemble, The Brass Connection, wins a Juno award, and people decide they want tapes and compact discs by the group.
    c. Technological advances lower the price of pocket calculators.
    d. A rumour spreads that Product X can cause cancer, even if it is used in moderation.

13. Draw a graph to illustrate each of the situations described below. Each situation involves one of the following: a shift in the supply curve, a movement along the supply curve, or no change at all in the supply curve for the good or service under discussion. For each graph in which there is some movement, indicate whether there has been a change in supply or a change in the quantity supplied. Assume *ceteris paribus* in each of these situations.

a. Bad weather causes a poor wheat crop on the Canadian prairies.

b. The price of beef increases, and farmers bring more cattle to market.

c. Oil prices raise the costs of production for a plastics manufacturing firm.

d. Technological advances reduce the cost of producing home computers.

14. A newspaper headline reports "Britons' love for tea declines, drink more coffee." Illustrate with two separate graphs what has happened to the demand for tea and the demand for coffee in Britain.

15. Plot supply and demand curves from the following market data:

Price (dollars)	Quantity Demanded	Quantity Supplied
2	8	2
4	6	4
6	4	6
8	2	8

a. What are the equilibrium price and quantity in this market?

b. What is the slope of the supply curve? Of the demand curve?

c. Over what range of prices would a surplus exist in this market? Over what range of prices would a shortage exist?

d. What would happen if the government imposed a price ceiling at a price of $3.50?

e. What would happen if the government imposed a price ceiling at a price of $7?

16. Plot supply and demand curves from the following market data:

Price (dollars)	Quantity Demanded	Quantity Supplied
1	9	2
5	5	4
9	1	6

a. What are the equilibrium price and quantity in this market?

b. What is the slope of the supply curve? Of the demand curve?

c. Over what range of prices would a surplus exist in this market? Over what range of prices would a shortage exist?

d. What would happen if the government imposed a price ceiling at a price of $4?

e. What would happen if the government imposed a price ceiling at a price of $8?

17. Consider each of the following developments and its effect on the market for hockey sticks.

a. Several years ago, Wayne Gretzky, a high-scoring NHL player, announced that he would use Titan brand hockey sticks exclusively. Before Gretzky announced his preference, Titan sticks ranked thirteenth in total hockey-stick sales; after his announcement, they became the number-one seller in wooden sticks. Use a demand curve (or curves) to illustrate the market for Titan sticks before and after Gretzky's announcement. Does your graph illustrate a change in demand or a change in the quantity demanded? Explain.

b. In early fall, 1990, Gretzky changed his mind, announcing that he now preferred Easton aluminum hockey sticks and that he would be using them exclusively. Illustrate graphically what you predict will happen to the demand for Easton sticks. Illustrate what you predict will happen to the demand for Titan sticks.

c. A group of wooden-hockey-stick manufacturers have indicated that they will ask the NHL to ban all metal sticks. How would such a ban affect the demand for wooden sticks? How would such a ban affect the demand for metal sticks? Illustrate your answers graphically.

A Closer Look at Demand

After studying this chapter, you will be able to

1. Explain what economists mean by the terms *utility* and *diminishing marginal utility*.

2. Explain the concept of consumer equilibrium.

3. Show how the effects of a price change on quantity demanded can be separated into an income effect and a substitution effect.

4. Apply the concepts of the substitution and income effects to the cases of normal and inferior goods.

5. Explain the concept of consumer surplus.

6. Define *elasticity* and distinguish among elastic, inelastic, and unit elastic demand curves.

7. Compute elasticity of demand, given data on changes in price and quantity demanded.

8. Show how revenue changes in response to a change in price under various conditions of elasticity.

9. Discuss the factors that determine the elasticity of demand.

10. Define and compute *income elasticity of demand, cross-elasticity of demand,* and *price elasticity of supply*.

A Preview   *The Demand for City Transit*

City planners in charge of bus services understand the law of demand: They know that if they increase bus fares, *ceteris paribus*, the number of bus riders will decline. But such knowledge is not enough. As the following article indicates, city planners need to be able to predict the impact of specific percentage increases in fares on the number of transit riders and on revenues. This requires them to look more closely at the nature of the demand for bus services.

Ridership Losses Bring Call for Probe

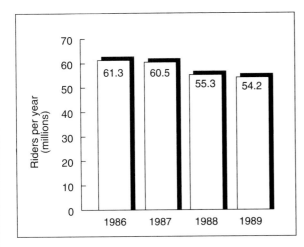

SOURCE: Paul Pihichyn/Winnipeg Free Press

Winnipeg Transit lost seven million riders between 1987 and 1989, prompting two city councillors to call for an investigation.

In separate interviews, Councillors Evelyne Reese and Harry Lazarenko, members of the works and operations committee that oversees transit, called for a full investigation of transit finances and operations.

Both Reese and Lazarenko said they didn't know of the ridership losses until Jeff Lowe, a consumer advocate and a transit critic, raised them at a recent committee meeting.

Lowe noted the biggest decline in ridership was in 1988, when it dropped by 5.2 million to 55.3 million after city council voted to increase the adult fare by ten cents to $1, breaking the so-called psychological barrier of cheap transit fares.

In 1987, transit had 60.5 million riders — 830 000 less than in 1986. Last year, ridership was 54.2 million — 1.1 million less than in 1988.

The three-year slide in ridership did not affect the annual revenue because of fare increases.

SOURCE: Radha Krishnan Thampi, "Ridership Losses Bring Call for Probe," *Winnipeg Free Press*, December 5, 1990, pp. 1, 4. Reproduced with permission.

LOOKING BEHIND THE DEMAND CURVE

When you have $10 to spend on hamburgers, pop, and french fries, why do you choose a particular combination of these things — say, two burgers, one large fries, and one large pop, rather than one burger, two large fries, and three pops? The answer may not seem important, but it is in fact essential to gaining an understanding of the factors at play behind *individual demand* curves.

People are used to the idea that when the price of a good goes down, the quantity of that good demanded by consumers tends to go up. The law of demand is easy to accept, because common sense and everyday experience show that it is the way things are. Still, knowing that a thing is so does not keep people from asking why it is so. In Newton's day, everyone knew that when apples fell from trees, they fell down and not up; but Newton asked why, and this led him to some valuable new insights about the laws of gravitation. In the same way, economists have often asked *why* people buy more of a good when its price falls. Trying to answer that question leads to some useful insights.

Many business firms take such insights about the factors that underlie individual consumers' behaviour very seriously. A soap manufacturer, for example, will survey consumers in stores to determine the price at which they would switch from its brand of soap to some other brand. The firm will take the results of such surveys into account when determining its pricing policies. Business firms are also able to determine the *market demand* for their products from studies of individual demand behaviour. This is usually done through surveys of selected market areas. Consumers in selected supermarkets in Regina, Saskatchewan, and London, Ontario, for example, may be polled to determine "typical" consumer response to a particular product in western and eastern Canada. A certain number of shoppers in each store will be asked how many bottles of a particular diet drink they would consume weekly at different prices. Individual A might buy four bottles at $3.00 each, while Individual B might buy none at that price. At $2.50, Individual A might buy six bottles, and Individual B would buy two. The *total* amounts demanded at various prices by all individuals surveyed — that is, all their individual demand curves added up horizontally — would result in a market demand curve for that product.

Consider the problems faced by bodies such as the Canadian Wheat Board, which is responsible for selling Canadian wheat abroad. It needs to know what will happen if it reduces the price of Canadian wheat — not just in general, but quite precisely. Presumably, a 10 percent cut in prices will increase sales, but by how much? By 5 percent, 10 percent, or more? In effect, the Canadian Wheat Board would like to know exactly how sensitive the demand curve for wheat is to price changes. If it knew this — if it could get *behind* the market demand curve for wheat — it would be much better equipped to make its pricing decisions.

This chapter takes us behind the demand curve, exploring the nature of both the individual's demand for particular goods and services, and the market's demand as a whole.

THE INDIVIDUAL'S CONSUMPTION AND UTILITY

The most basic question one can ask about the law of demand is why people demand goods and services at all. The answer seems to be that people want material goods and services because they get pleasure and satisfaction from them.

Utility
The economist's term for the pleasure, satisfaction, and need fulfilment that people get from the consumption of material goods and services.

A loaf of bread to eat, a warm bed to sleep in, or a book to read — each serves needs or desires in one way or another. Economists have their own term for this sort of thing. They say that the use or consumption of material goods gives people **utility**.

Utility and Psychological Needs

To a psychologist, just saying that people want things because they get utility from them would sound very shallow. Some psychologists, at least, would want to go into detail about the nature and sources of human wants. Followers of Abraham Maslow, for example, find it useful to think in terms of five basic levels of needs: (1) physiological needs; (2) safety and security needs; (3) affection and belonging needs; (4) the need for self-esteem and the esteem of others; and (5) the need for "self-actualization" or self-fulfilment.[1]

This simple list of needs raises some important questions for psychologists. Is each level of need equally important for all people? What factors in people's upbringing affect the needs they seek to satisfy in later life? Questions such as these, however, get very little attention from economists. Smith may buy a tennis racket to satisfy a physiological need for exercise; Jones may buy one in order to satisfy a need to belong by joining a tennis club; Baker may buy one in order to gain the esteem of others by playing in tournaments. What is true of tennis rackets is true of other goods and services too. People with different psychological needs all have one thing in common: They get utility of one sort or another from material goods. Most economists feel that they do not really need to know any more psychology than that.

Utility and Demand

Economists may not be interested in the origins of human wants, but they are interested in the intensity of those wants. The reason is that the intensity of people's wants for some goods relative to the intensity of their wants for others determines the quantities of those goods that they will demand in the marketplace. Whether a person wants a new car intensely enough to pass up the opportunity to spend the same funds on a three-week Caribbean cruise is clearly an economic as well as a psychological question. It is a question about the demand for automobiles.

Marginal utility
The amount of additional utility obtained from a one-unit increase in consumption of a good.

Principle of diminishing marginal utility
The principle that the greater the rate of consumption of some good, the smaller the increase in utility from a one-unit increase in the rate of consumption of that good.

Diminishing marginal utility
Economists made a major step forward in their understanding of the relationship between utility and economic behaviour when, in the late nineteenth century, they first clearly formulated the principle of diminishing marginal utility. The **marginal utility** of a good to a consumer means the amount of additional utility obtained from the consumption of one additional unit of the good in question. The **principle of diminishing marginal utility** says that the greater the quantity of any good consumed, the less the marginal utility from a one-unit increase in consumption.

---

[1]See Abraham Maslow, *Motivation and Personality*, 2d ed. (New York: Harper & Row, 1970).

William Stanley Jevons and Marginal Utility Theory

The English economist William Stanley Jevons is credited with the first systematic statement of the theory of marginal utility. Jevons was trained in mathematics and chemistry. With this background, it is not surprising that when his interest turned to economics he tried to restate economic theories in mathematical terms. It was this effort that led him to the theory of marginal utility.

In his *Theory of Political Economy*, published in 1871, Jevons set forth the principle of diminishing marginal utility in these words:

> Let us imagine the whole quantity of food which a person consumes on an average during twenty-four hours to be divided into ten equal parts. If his food be reduced by the last part, he will suffer but little; if a second tenth part be deficient, he will feel the want distinctly; the subtraction of the third part will be decidedly injurious; with every subsequent subtraction of a tenth part his sufferings will be more and more serious until at length he will be upon the verge of starvation. Now, if we call each of the tenth parts an *increment*, the meaning of these facts is that each increment of food is less necessary, or possesses less utility, than the previous one.

Jevons was the first economist to put the new theory into print, but he shares credit for the "marginal revolution" with at least three others who were working along the same lines at the same time. The Austrian economist Karl Menger published his version of marginal utility theory in 1871 as well. Three years later, the Swiss economist Leon Walras, who did not know of either Jevons' or Menger's work, came out with still another version. Finally, Alfred Marshall worked out the basics of marginal utility theory at about the same time in his lectures at Cambridge, although he did not publish them until 1890.

William Stanley Jevons (1835–1882)

For a simple but vivid example of the principle of diminishing marginal utility in action, imagine yourself in a blackberry patch eating berries by the handful. As you eat more and more berries, you get more and more satisfaction; but at the same time, the satisfaction from each additional handful diminishes. If you eat enough, you may even get to a point where more berries give you no additional utility at all. Then you stop eating berries, at least until the next day.

Utility, to be sure, is a very subjective concept. No one has yet invented a "utility meter" that can be hooked up to a person's skull to read utility like blood pressure. But suppose, to indulge in a bit of science fiction, that there were such a utility meter. If you allowed yourself to be hooked up to the meter during your spree in the blackberry patch, the results could be recorded in numerical or graphic form, as shown in Box 5.1. The table and the graphs in this box use the "util" as an imaginary unit for measuring utility. Both the table and the graphs show that, as the quantity of berries consumed per day increases, total utility increases — but at a decreasing rate. Marginal utility — that is, the additional utility obtained from each additional handful of berries — falls as the rate of consumption increases. For example, the third handful of berries increases utility by 2 units, from 5.5 to 7.5, whereas the fourth handful gives only 1.5 units more.

The consumer as economizer

For better or worse, the world is not one big blackberry patch where people can eat as much as they want without making choices. To put the principle of dimin-

BOX 5.1 *Diminishing Marginal Utility*

As the rate at which a person consumes some good increases, the utility derived from one additional unit decreases. The table and figures here show that as the rate of consumption of berries increases, total utility increases — but at a decreasing rate. In part (b), a smooth curve is drawn to join the points representing *total utility*, which are based on the data given in the table. Part (c) shows a *marginal utility* curve. The height of this curve at each point is equal to the slope of the total utility curve in part (b) at each corresponding point.

(a)

Quantity of Berries (handfuls per day)	Total Utility (utils)	Marginal Utility (utils per handful)
0	0	
		3.0
1	3.0	
		2.5
2	5.5	
		2.0
3	7.5	
		1.5
4	9.0	
		1.0
5	10.0	
		0.5
6	10.5	

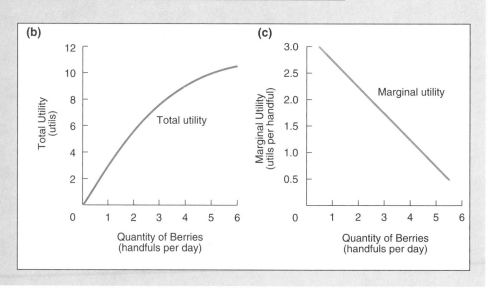

ishing marginal utility to work, one must look at a world more like the one that really exists. This is a world in which

1. There are many different desirable goods.
2. Consumers must pay for the goods they want.
3. Consumers have limited budgets.

In such a world, consumers who want to get the greatest satisfaction, given their limited budgets, have to economize: They have to make choices, each of which involves an opportunity cost. If people spend more on one good, they have less to spend on something else. What can be said about how consumers economize?

Solving the consumer problem

Begin with the consumer you know best — yourself. Suppose you are deciding how to divide your monthly spending between, say, food and clothing. If you spend an extra dollar a month on food, you get a certain added utility from doing so. At the same time, though, you must bear an opportunity cost equal to the utility you could instead have obtained by spending the dollar on clothing. Whether or not you actually think consciously in such terms, then, your choice will depend on which utility is greater — the extra dollar's worth of food or the extra dollar's worth of clothing.

Which is greater depends in turn on how much of each good you consume. If, relatively speaking, you have a lot of clothing and not much food, the marginal utility of clothing will tend to be low and that of food to be high. By shifting a dollar from clothing to food, you can give up a small utility and gain a large one, which will increase your *total* utility.

If, instead, you have relatively much food and relatively little clothing, the marginal utilities may be reversed. You will gain a lot of utility from spending an extra dollar on clothing and only a little from spending an extra dollar on food. Again, you can gain in total utility by shifting your pattern of expenditure, without spending more overall.

Consumer equilibrium

It is clear, then, that if the marginal utility of a dollar's worth of clothing is different from that of a dollar's worth of food, you have an incentive to change your pattern of consumption. There is only one condition under which you would *not* have an incentive to change your pattern of spending on food and clothing — that is, when the marginal utility per dollar's worth of the two goods is exactly the same.

Generalizing from this example, it can be said that consumers tend to shift their expenditures from one kind of good to another as long as they can increase their total utilities by doing so. When consumer expenditures are distributed among the various available goods in such a way that, for each consumer, the marginal utility of a dollar's worth of each good consumed is equal to the marginal utility of a dollar's worth of each *other* good consumed, no further increase in utility is possible within the given budget constraint. A state of **consumer equilibrium** is then said to prevail.

Consumer equilibrium
A state of affairs in which consumers cannot increase the total utility they obtain from a given budget by shifting expenditure from one good to another. (In consumer equilibrium, the marginal utility of a dollar's worth of one good must be equal to the marginal utility of a dollar's worth of any other good.)

An alternative statement

There is another, equivalent way to state the conditions for consumer equilibrium. Suppose that a person is consuming just the right quantities of, say, chicken and beef to make the marginal utility of a dollar's worth of chicken equal to the marginal utility of a dollar's worth of beef. It must be true, then, that the marginal utility of a kilogram of chicken divided by the price of chicken per kilogram is equal to the marginal utility per kilogram of beef divided by the price of beef per kilogram. In equation form, this comes out as follows:

$$\frac{\text{Marginal utility of chicken per kilogram}}{\text{Price of chicken per kilogram}} = \frac{\text{Marginal utility of beef per kilogram}}{\text{Price of beef per kilogram}}.$$

Suppose, for example, that chicken costs $1 per kilogram and beef costs $3. If the equation just given holds, then an extra kilogram of beef will give the consumer three times as much utility as an added kilogram of chicken. This means, as in the earlier statement of the conditions for consumer equilibrium, that the marginal utility of a dollar's worth (one kilogram) of chicken is equal to the marginal utility of a dollar's worth (one-third of a kilogram) of beef.

The equation can be extended to a world with any number of goods and services. MU_A, MU_B, and so on, stand for the marginal utilities of goods A, B, and so on. Likewise, P_A, P_B, and so on, stand for the prices of the various goods. The general expression for consumer equilibrium then becomes

$$\frac{MU_A}{P_A} = \frac{MU_B}{P_B} = \frac{MU_C}{P_C} = \frac{MU_D}{P_D} = \dots$$

From consumer equilibrium to the law of demand

The concepts of consumer equilibrium and diminishing marginal utility can be combined to give an explanation of the law of demand that is intuitively appealing, if not altogether precise. The explanation goes like this: suppose you have adjusted your pattern of consumption until you have reached an equilibrium in which, among other things,

$$\frac{\text{MU of chicken}}{\$1} = \frac{\text{MU of beef}}{\$3}.$$

As long as this equality holds, it will not be to your benefit to increase your consumption of beef; to do so would, according to the principle of diminishing marginal utility, quickly push down the marginal utility of beef. The marginal utility per dollar's worth of beef would drop below the marginal utility per dollar's worth of chicken, and you would be better off to switch back toward more chicken.

But what if the price of beef were to drop, say, to $2.50 per kilogram, upsetting the equality given above? To make the two ratios equal again, given the new price of beef, either the marginal utility of chicken would have to rise or the marginal utility of beef would have to fall. According to the principle of diminishing marginal utility, one way to get the marginal utility of beef to fall is to consume more beef, and one way to get the marginal utility of chicken to rise is to consume less chicken. Because chicken and beef are substitutes to most people, you would probably do a little of both — that is, cut back a little on chicken and consume a little more beef. In doing so, you would be acting exactly as the law of demand predicts: A fall in the price of beef would have induced you to buy more beef.

SUBSTITUTION AND INCOME EFFECTS AND THE LAW OF DEMAND

As we have noted, the argument just given links the principle of diminishing marginal utility to the law of demand in an intuitively appealing way, but it leaves a few too many loose ends dangling to suit all economists. Is there a way to rationalize the law of demand without relying directly on the slippery, unmeasurable concept of utility? There is. The alternative approach relies on a breakdown of the effects of a change in price into two separate components, known as the substitution effect and the income effect.

The Substitution Effect

Go back in the earlier example to the point where you had adjusted your purchases to an equilibrium, given a price of beef of $3 per kilogram and a price of chicken of $1 per kilogram. As before, suppose that the price of beef dropped to $2.50 per kilogram. With beef relatively cheaper than it was before (and chicken relatively more expensive than it was before), you would tend to substitute beef for chicken in your diet. You might substitute beef for other things, too; with the reduced price of a steak dinner, you might occasionally substitute an evening in a restaurant for an evening at the movies. This effect of the change in the price of beef is known as the substitution effect. In general terms, the **substitution effect** of the change in the price of a good is that part of the change in the quantity demanded attributable to the tendency of consumers to substitute relatively cheap goods for relatively expensive ones.

Substitution effect
The part of the increase in quantity demanded of a good whose price has fallen that is attributable to the tendency of consumers to substitute relatively cheap goods for relatively expensive ones.

The Income Effect

The substitution effect is not, however, the only reason that a drop in the price of beef would be likely to increase your consumption of beef. Suppose that with the price of beef at $3 per kilogram, you bought ten kilograms per month. The decline in the price to $2.50 per kilogram would be welcome to you not only because it would allow you to substitute beef for chicken in your diet, but for another reason as well: It would increase the purchasing power of your monthly budget. With beef at $2.50 per kilogram, you could buy the same quantities of all goods, including beef, and now have $5 left over at the end of the month to spend as you pleased. In short, a fall in the price of any good, other things being equal, produces an increase in real income.[2]

With your increased real income, you would tend to buy more of all normal goods and less of any inferior goods. For most people, beef is a normal good. Some of your new-found $5 in real income, then, would presumably go to the purchase of more beef. This effect of the change in the price of beef on the quantity of beef demanded is known as the income effect. In general terms, the **income effect** of a change in the price of a good is that part of the change in the quantity of the good demanded attributable to the change in real income resulting from the change in price.

Income effect
The part of the change in quantity demanded of a good whose price has fallen that is attributable to the change in real income resulting from the price change.

---

[2]Readers who have completed a course in macroeconomics will already be familiar with the concept of real income. For the benefit of those who have not taken such a course, *real income* means income adjusted for changes in prices to reflect actual purchasing power (recall the definition of the term *real* in Chapter 2). The same number of dollars represents more real income when prices fall and less real income when prices rise.

The Law of Demand for Normal and Inferior Goods

The concepts of the substitution and income effects of a price change are very helpful in understanding the law of demand itself and in understanding why the law of demand might, under rare circumstances, permit exceptions. Consider separately the cases of normal and inferior goods.

For a normal good, the law of demand holds absolutely, because the substitution and income effects work together to produce an increase in quantity demanded when the price of a good falls. The example given above is a case in point. When the price of beef dropped, you bought more beef partly because you substituted beef for chicken and for other goods and services that were now relatively more expensive than before. In addition, you bought more beef still because you spent part of your increased real income on beef — a normal good. Taking the two effects in combination, there is no doubt that a decline in the price of beef would increase the quantity of beef you demanded.

In the case of an inferior good, things are not quite so simple. Suppose that instead of considering a drop in the price of beef in general, you considered the effect of a drop in the price of hamburger only — with the price of all other cuts of beef held constant. Suppose further that you considered hamburger an inferior good — one that you would tend to phase out of your diet as your real income rose. A drop in the price of hamburger, as before, would tend to make you substitute hamburger for other foods that had become relatively more expensive. By itself, this would increase the quantity demanded. However, a drop in the price of hamburger would also produce a slight increase in your real income; and that, considered by itself, would tend to make you buy less hamburger. For an inferior good, then, the substitution and income effects operate in opposite directions. The law of demand holds for an inferior good only if the size of the substitution effect is larger than that of the income effect.

The theories of marginal utility and consumer equilibrium help us understand the universal economic problem of choosing among alternative uses for scarce resources. As we have already noted, they can also shed light on practical economic problems, though they don't necessarily lead to precise answers. The concept of *consumer surplus*, for example, is derived from utility theory and is useful in analyzing the effects on the welfare of consumers of changes in price.

Consumer Surplus

Consider the example depicted in Box 5.2. The demand curve there — John's demand curve for berries — is related in a general way to the marginal utility curve depicted in Box 5.1(c): John's demand curve slopes downward and to the right because he derives less marginal utility from each additional kilogram of berries he eats. The demand curve in Box 5.2 shows that John is willing to pay $3.50 for the first kilogram of berries, but only $3.00 for the second, and so on.[3]

---

[3]You will notice that the demand curve in Box 5.2 is not a straight line, though we often draw demand curves as straight lines for the sake of simplicity. In John's case, his willingness to purchase berries *usually* increases by one kilogram for every 50¢ drop in price, but when the price drops by only 25¢ from $2.50 to $2.25, he is willing to purchase another kilogram, and when it drops another 25¢ to $2.00, he increases his purchases again by one kilogram, for a total of five kilograms. Consumers often respond differently to price changes along different parts of the demand curve.

Consumer Surplus

BOX 5.2

John's demand curve for berries shows that he is willing to pay $3.50 for the first kilogram, $3.00 for the second, and so on. At the market price of $2.00, he purchases five kilograms, spending a total of $10.00. His demand curve shows, however, that he would actually be willing to pay $13.25 for five kilograms: $3.50 for the first, $3.00 for the second, $2.50 for the third, $2.25 for the fourth, and $2.00 for the fifth. The entire shaded area represents John's total satisfaction from consuming five kilograms of berries, while the rectangle under the price line represents the amount he actually pays for them. The shaded bars above the price line thus represent the satisfaction for which he does *not* pay, and which is known as his *consumer surplus*. In this case, the consumer surplus is $13.25 − $10.00 = $3.25.

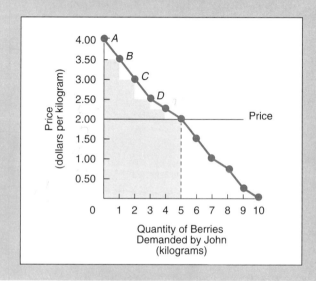

The amount he is willing to spend on each kilogram of berries gives some indication of the additional utility he derives from each.

Suppose that the price of berries is initially set by growers at $2.00 per kilogram. At this price, John will purchase five kilograms, and he will enjoy what economists call **consumer surplus**. This is the difference between what a consumer such as John is willing to pay for a certain quantity of a product and what he is actually required to pay. Look at John's demand curve once again. At $2.00 per kilogram, he will spend $10.00 on berries, purchasing five kilograms. But the demand curve also tells us that he would be willing to pay $3.50 for the first kilogram, $3.00 for the second, $2.50 for the third, $2.25 for the fourth, and $2.00 for the fifth kilogram — a total of $13.25. The difference between what he would be willing to pay ($13.25) and what he actually pays ($10.00) is his consumer surplus (in this case, $3.25). This surplus accrues to consumers because most goods are offered at a single price, which means that dealers cannot exploit the higher prices individual consumers might be willing to pay for smaller quantities.

We might say that John's total utility — his satisfaction from the berries — is depicted graphically in Box 5.2 by the entire shaded area under the demand

Consumer surplus
The difference between the amount a consumer is willing to pay for a good and the amount that is actually required.

curve, while the amount that he actually pays is represented by the rectangular portion of that shaded area, under the price line. The consumer surplus is the sum of the shaded bars above the price line.

Applying consumer surplus

To illustrate how the concept of consumer surplus can be applied to practical problems, assume that the berry growers in our example form a marketing board through which they can control the supply of berries and charge a higher price. Let's say they raise the price to $3.00 per kilogram. How does this affect John

BOX 5.3   *Elastic, Inelastic, and Unit Elastic Demand*

This diagram illustrates the relationship between changes in price and changes in revenue for three different demand curves. As the price of good A decreases from $5 to $3, revenue increases from $15 to $18; the demand for good A is elastic. As the price of good B decreases over the same range, revenue falls from $15 to $12; the demand for good B is inelastic. As the price of good C decreases, revenue remains unchanged; the demand for good C is unit elastic.

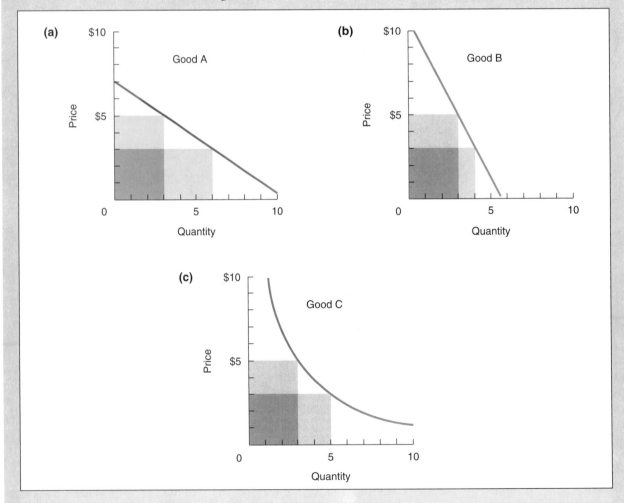

(and other consumers)? According to his demand curve, John will now buy only two kilograms of berries, cutting his expenditures on berries from $10.00 to $6.00. It is not clear that John is worse off than before: On the one hand, he now eats fewer berries than before; on the other, he has $4.00 more to spend on other goods. In terms of consumer surplus, however, John has clearly lost. As we have seen, he spends $6.00 on two kilograms of berries, but he would have been *willing* to spend $6.50 — $3.50 for the first kilogram and $3.00 for the second. His consumer surplus is now only 50¢, having fallen from the previous surplus of $3.25. Thus, our analysis has told us that our consumer's satisfaction has declined; in practice, however, there would likely be no way of telling by exactly how much.

ELASTICITY OF DEMAND

Economists in both private firms and government are particularly interested in the responsiveness of consumers to different prices. Will the quantity demanded increase quite sharply, as, say, the price of a soft drink falls from $2.00 to $1.80, or will it increase very little? The degree to which quantity demanded changes in response to a change in price is known as **elasticity**. This is one of the most important concepts associated with the theory of demand (as well as the theory of supply, as we will see at the end of this chapter and again in Chapter 6). It can be used to examine many practical problems, both in private business and in government policy making.

Elasticity can be measured in several ways. One way is to determine the impact of a change in price on the **total revenue** generated by the sale of a good. Total revenue is calculated as the quantity of the good sold multiplied by the price at which it is sold.

As Box 5.3 shows, a change in the price of a good can have one of three effects on total revenue, depending on the shape and position of the demand curve. In the case of good A, a decline in price from $5 per unit to $3 per unit increases the quantity demanded from three units to six units. Total revenue thus increases from $15 to $18 as the price falls. In the case of good B, the same decline in price from $5 to $3 is shown as increasing the quantity demanded by only one unit, from three units to four units. Total revenue thus decreases from $15 to $12. Finally, in the case of good C, a drop in price from $5 to $3 increases the quantity demanded from three units to five units, leaving total revenue unchanged at $15.

Such effects of changes in price on total revenue can be expressed in terms of the relationship between the percentage by which the quantity demanded changes and the percentage by which the price changes. The ratio of the percentage change in the quantity demanded of a good to the percentage change in the price of the good is known as the **price elasticity of demand**, or, simply, the **elasticity of demand**, for that good. If quantity demanded changes by a larger percentage than price, so that total revenue increases as the price decreases, as in Box 5.3(a), demand for the good is said to be **elastic**. If quantity demanded changes by a smaller percentage than price, so that total revenue decreases as the price decreases, as in Box 5.3(b), demand is said to be **inelastic**. And if price and quantity demanded change by the same percentage, so that total revenue remains unchanged, as in Box 5.3(c), demand is said to be **unit elastic**.

In addition to the cases of elastic, inelastic, and unit elastic demand illustrated in Box 5.3, there are two limiting cases illustrated in Box 5.4. Box 5.4(a) shows a demand curve that is perfectly vertical. No matter what the price, the quantity

Elasticity
The responsiveness of quantity demanded or supplied to changes in the price of a good or changes in other economic conditions.

Total revenue
The quantity of a good sold multiplied by the price at which it is sold.

Price elasticity of demand (elasticity of demand)
The ratio of the percentage change in the quantity of a good demanded to the percentage change in the price of that good.

Elastic demand
The situation in which quantity changes by a larger percentage than price along the demand curve, so that total revenue increases as price decreases.

Inelastic demand
The situation in which quantity changes by a smaller percentage than price along the demand curve, so that total revenue decreases as price decreases.

Unit elastic demand
The situation in which price and quantity change by the same percentage along the demand curve, so that total revenue remains unchanged as price changes.

Perfectly inelastic demand
The situation in which the demand curve is a vertical line.

Perfectly elastic demand
The situation in which the demand curve is a horizontal line.

demanded is a constant five units — no more, no less. Such a demand curve is referred to as **perfectly inelastic**. Box 5.4(b) shows a demand curve that is perfectly horizontal. Above the price of $5, none of the good can be sold. But as soon as the price drops to $5, producers can sell as much of the good as they care to produce without having to cut the price any more. A horizontal demand curve such as this one is described as **perfectly elastic**.

Measuring Elasticity of Demand

For many purposes, it is useful to put a numerical value on elasticity of demand, rather than simply to classify demand as elastic or inelastic. The basis for such numerical measurements is the definition of the *elasticity of demand* as the ratio of the percentage change in quantity demanded to the percentage change in price.

Percentage changes

In order to apply this definition to the measurement of elasticity, we need to be somewhat more precise than before about how to calculate percentage changes. Suppose, for example, that there is a $0.25 increase in the price of apple juice, from $0.75 per litre to $1.00 per litre. In everyday usage, we would call this a 33 percent increase in price ($0.25/$0.75 = 0.33). However, if we observed a $0.25 decrease in the price of apple juice, from $1.00 per litre to $0.75, we would call it a 25 percent decrease ($0.25/$1 = 0.25).

In measuring elasticity, it would be awkward to have to specify whether we were dealing with a price increase or a price decrease before calculating the per-

---

BOX 5.4 *Perfectly Elastic and Perfectly Inelastic Demand*

Part (a) of this diagram shows a demand curve that is a vertical line. No matter what the price, the quantity demanded is a constant five units. Such a demand curve is referred to as perfectly inelastic. Part (b) shows a perfectly elastic demand curve, which is a horizontal line. Above the price of $5, none of the good can be sold; at the price of $5, suppliers can sell as much of the good as they want without further reductions in price.

centage change. To get around this difficulty, we will adopt the convention of using the midpoint of the price range as a basis for calculating the percentage. The midpoint in this case is ($0.75 + $1)/2 = $0.875, so the percentage change, as we define it, becomes $0.25/$0.875 = 0.285 (approximately). Calculated this way, the percentage is the same for an increase as for a decrease over the specified range of price.

Using P_1 to represent the price before the change, and P_2, the price after the change, this convention for calculating the percentage change in price can be written in terms of a general formula as

$$\text{Percentage change in price} = \frac{P_1 - P_2}{(P_1 + P_2)/2}.$$

The same problem arises in defining the percentage change in the quantity demanded that results from a given change in price. Suppose that when the price of apple juice falls from $1.00 to $0.75 per litre, the quantity demanded increases from 100 L per day to 150 L. We can use the average of the higher quantity and the lower quantity to calculate the percentage change in quantity. If Q_1 and Q_2 are the quantities before and after a change in price, the formula for the percentage change can be written as

$$\text{Percentage change in quantity} = \frac{Q_1 - Q_2}{(Q_1 + Q_2)/2}.$$

Applying this formula to the example just given, we would say that either an increase in quantity from 100 L to 150 L or a decrease in quantity from 150 L to 100 L represents a 40 percent change in quantity:

$$\text{Percentage change in quantity} = \frac{150 - 100}{(150 + 100)/2} = 0.40.$$

An elasticity formula

Defining percentage changes in this way allows us to write a practical formula for calculating elasticities. The formula can be applied to the elasticity of either supply or demand. Using P_1 and Q_1 to represent price and quantity before a change, and P_2 and Q_2 to represent price and quantity after the change, the formula is as follows:[4]

$$\begin{array}{c}\text{Price}\\\text{elasticity}\\\text{of demand}\end{array} = \frac{(Q_1 - Q_2)/(Q_1 + Q_2)}{(P_1 - P_2)/(P_1 + P_2)} = \frac{\begin{array}{c}\text{Percentage change}\\\text{in quantity}\end{array}}{\begin{array}{c}\text{Percentage change}\\\text{in price}\end{array}}.$$

The following problem illustrates the use of this formula.

---

[4]Given the definition of percentage changes, we could write the elasticity formula as follows:

$$\frac{\dfrac{Q_1 - Q_2}{(Q_1 + Q_2)/2}}{\dfrac{P_1 - P_2}{(P_1 + P_2)/2}}$$

This is unnecessarily complicated, however, because the 2s cancel out. The formula given in the text is the simplified equivalent of this one.

Problem

A change in the price of apple juice from $1.10 per litre to $0.90 causes the quantity demanded to increase from 100 L per day to 150 L per day.

What is the price elasticity of demand for apple juice over the range of price and quantity indicated?

Solution

$$P_1 = \text{Price before change} \quad = \$1.10$$
$$P_2 = \text{Price after change} \quad = \$0.90$$
$$Q_1 = \text{Quantity before change} = 100$$
$$Q_2 = \text{Quantity after change} \quad = 150$$

$$
\begin{aligned}
\text{Elasticity} &= \frac{(100 - 150)/(100 + 150)}{(\$1.10 - \$0.90)/(\$1.10 + \$0.90)} \\
&= \frac{-50/250}{\$0.20/\$2.00} \\
&= -\frac{0.2}{0.1} \\
&= -2
\end{aligned}
$$

Note that the answer is a negative number. This is because demand curves have negative slopes: a decrease in price results in an increase in quantity demanded, and vice versa. The percentage changes in price and quantity will therefore have opposite signs, producing a negative number for demand elasticity. While this should be kept in mind, we will ignore the negative sign in our analysis for the sake of simplicity.

Elasticity Values and Changes in Revenue

The terms *elastic, inelastic, unit elastic, perfectly elastic,* and *perfectly inelastic demand* were introduced earlier in the chapter. They were defined in terms of the relationship between change in price and change in total revenue. Each of these elasticity terms corresponds to a certain numerical value or range of numerical values of elasticity as calculated according to the elasticity formula. A perfectly inelastic demand curve has a measured elasticity of zero, because any change in price produces no change in quantity demanded. The term *inelastic* (but not perfectly inelastic) *demand* applies to measured elasticities in the range from zero up to, but not including, one. *Unit elasticity*, as the name implies, means a numerical elasticity of exactly one. *Elastic demand* means any value for elasticity greater than one. *Perfectly elastic demand*, corresponding to a horizontal demand curve, is not defined numerically; as the demand curve approaches horizontal, the denominator of the elasticity formula approaches zero, so that the measured value of elasticity approaches infinity.

Demand Curves with Varying and Constant Elasticity

The formula just given for calculating the elasticity of demand shows the elasticity of demand over a certain range of price and quantity. Measured over some other range of price and quantity, the elasticity of demand for the same good may or may not be different. Whether the elasticity of demand for a good changes along the demand curve turns out to depend on the exact shape of the curve. This is illustrated in Boxes 5.5 and 5.6.

A linear demand curve

First consider Box 5.5(a), which shows a straight-line demand curve like most of those drawn in this book. The elasticity of demand is not constant for all ranges of price and quantity along this curve. Measured over the price range $8 to $9, for example, the elasticity of demand is 5.66. Measured over the range $2 to $3, it is 0.33. (The full calculations are shown in the box.)

This illustrates the general principle that elasticity declines as one moves down along a straight-line demand curve. It is easy to see why: With a straight-line demand curve, a $1 reduction in price always produces the same absolute increase in quantity demanded. At the upper end of the demand curve, though, a $1 change in price is a small percentage change, while the absolute change in quantity, as a percentage of the small quantity already demanded, is large. At the lower end of the curve, the situation is reversed. A $1 change is now a large percentage of the price, while the constant absolute increase in quantity has now become smaller in percentage terms. Because it is percentages, not absolute amounts, that count in elasticity calculations, the demand curve is less elastic near the bottom than near the top. Because elasticity changes along a straight-line demand curve, it makes sense to apply the formula only to small changes.

Note the relationship between the elasticity of demand and total revenue, as shown by Box 5.5(b). In the elastic range of the demand curve, total revenue increases as price decreases. Total revenue reaches a peak at the point of unit elasticity and declines again in the range of inelastic demand.

A constant-elasticity demand curve

If the demand curve is not a straight line, the results described above need not always apply. There is an important special case in which the demand curve has just the curvature needed to keep elasticity constant throughout its length. Such a curve is shown in Box 5.6. As the calculations in this box indicate, elasticity is exactly 1.0 everywhere on this curve. It is possible to construct demand curves with constant elasticities of any desired value. Such curves are often used in statistical studies of demand elasticity.

Determinants of Elasticity of Demand

Why is the price elasticity of demand high for some goods and low for others? One thing helping to determine the elasticity of demand for a good is the availability of substitutes or complements. If a good has close substitutes, demand for that good tends to be elastic, because when its price rises, people can switch to something similar. For example, the demand for olive oil is more elastic than it would be if other salad oils were not available as substitutes. Similarly, the demand for cars is less elastic than it would be if good public transportation were available everywhere, because cars and public transportation are reasonably close substitutes for each other. On the other hand, if something is a minor complement to an important good, its demand tends to be inelastic. For example, the demand for motor oil tends to be inelastic, because it is a complement to a more important good — gasoline. The price of gasoline is much more likely to influence the amount of driving a person does than is the price of motor oil.

BOX 5.5 *Variation in Elasticity along a Straight-Line Demand Curve*

This box shows how elasticity varies along a straight-line demand curve. At low quantities, demand is elastic; for example, in the range from 10 to 20 units, the elasticity of the demand curve shown in part (a) is 5.66. At 50 units of output (halfway down the curve), the point of unit elasticity is reached. From there to 100 units of output, demand is inelastic; in the range from 70 to 80 units, for example, elasticity is 0.33. Part (b) shows that total revenue increases as quantity increases over the elastic portion of the demand curve and decreases as quantity increases over the inelastic portion. Total revenue reaches a maximum at the point of unit elasticity.

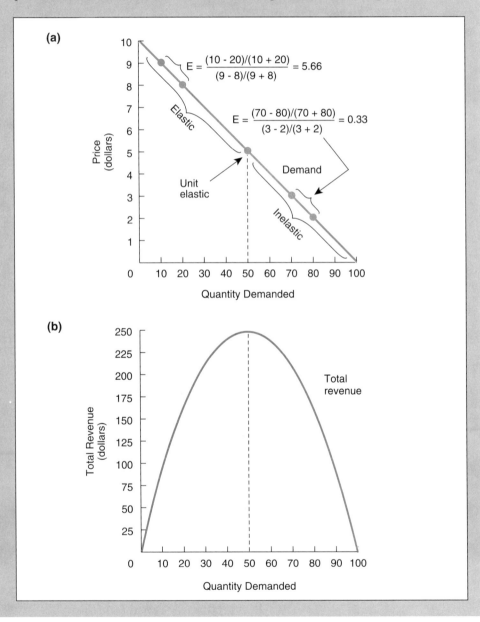

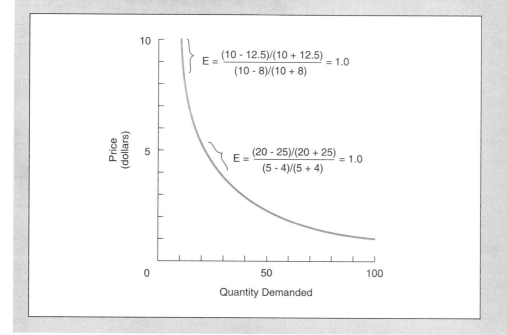

A Demand Curve with Constant Elasticity   BOX 5.6

It is possible for a demand curve to have constant elasticity throughout its length. The calculations below show that this curve has an elasticity of 1.0 wherever it is measured. This particular demand curve is a rectangular hyperbola with the formula $P \times Q = 100$.

Elasticity is also influenced by the portion of a person's budget spent on a good. Matches, for example, are no longer really a necessity, and good substitutes exist. Nonetheless, the demand for matches is thought to be very inelastic, just because people spend so little on them that they hardly notice a price change. In contrast, the demand for things like housing and transportation is not perfectly inelastic, even though they are necessities. Since they occupy a large part of people's budgets, changes in the prices of such things just cannot be ignored.

Finally, elasticity of demand is influenced by the time perspective being considered. Demand is often less elastic in the short run than in the long run. Consider the demand for home heating fuel, for example. In the short run, people find it hard to cut back the quantity they use when the price goes up. They are accustomed to living at a certain temperature, dressing a certain way, and so on. Given time, though, they may find ways to economize. They can put better insulation in their homes, get in the habit of dressing more warmly, or even move to a warmer climate.

Other Elasticities

The concept of elasticity has, up to this point, been applied only to the price elasticity of demand for a good, but there are many other common applications of the concept. All of them are based on the idea of the ratio of the percentage change in

FOR EXAMPLE...

Elasticity of Demand

The following article illustrates the case of a product for which demand is inelastic. University libraries find themselves having to pay very high prices for prestigious journals. The publishers know that they have a captive market for these journals, and they charge accordingly. If the demand were more elastic, they would be reluctant to charge such high prices.

Research Libraries — Over 40 000 Subscriptions Cancelled, More to Go

Canadian research libraries have cancelled thousands of subscriptions to journals over the past ten years, as currency-exchange rates and inflation have reduced buying power. Publishers' desire to generate larger profits is also a major reason for increased costs, librarians say.

Librarians are also convinced that publishers target specific journals for the largest price increases. The targeted journals are those that are of the highest quality, in the most demand, and that no academic library can afford to cancel if it is to retain its reputation as a research centre.

In short, publishers recognize that as far as these titles are concerned, academic and research libraries are captive audiences with little choice except to pay for the journal regardless of price.

For example, the journal *Current Genetics*, published by Springer, has had a 184 percent increase since 1985. *Synthetic Metals*, published by Elsevier, has jumped in price over three years by more than 200 percent.

SOURCE: *University Affairs*, Association of Universities and Colleges of Canada, February 1989, pp. 1, 2.

---

one variable to the percentage change in another. Three of the most commonly used types of elasticity, in addition to the price elasticity of demand, are income elasticity of demand, cross-elasticity of demand, and elasticity of supply.

Income elasticity of demand

As shown in Chapter 4 and again earlier in this chapter, changes in consumer income can cause changes in the demand for a good. Such changes are represented by shifts in the demand curve. The concept of elasticity, in the form of the income elasticity of demand, can be applied to measure the size and direction of such changes. The **income elasticity of demand** for a good is defined as the ratio of the percentage change in demand for the good to the percentage change in income. In measuring the income elasticity of demand for a good, the price of the good is assumed not to change. Income is usually measured in per-capita terms. Using Q_1 and Q_2 to represent quantities before and after the income change, and y_1 and y_2 to represent per-capita income before and after the change, the formula for income elasticity of demand can be written as follows:

Income elasticity of demand
The ratio of the percentage change in the demand for a good to the percentage change in the per-capita income of buyers.

$$\text{Income elasticity of demand} = \frac{(Q_1 - Q_2)/(Q_1 + Q_2)}{(y_1 - y_2)/(y_1 + y_2)} = \frac{\text{Percentage change in quantity}}{\text{Percentage change in income}}.$$

Income elasticity of demand is positive for a normal good and negative for an inferior good. Suppose, for example, that a study of meat-buying habits showed that for each 10 percent increase in income, the typical Canadian household tended to consume 12 percent more steak, 5 percent more chicken, and 2 percent less hamburger. One would conclude from these numbers that the income elasticity of demand was 1.2 for steak, 0.5 for chicken, and −0.2 for hamburger. Steak and chicken would thus be classified as normal goods and hamburger as an inferior good.

Cross-elasticity of demand

Another factor that can cause a change in the demand for a good is a change in the price of some other good. The demand for lettuce is affected by changes in the price of cabbage; the demand for motor oil is affected by changes in the price of gasoline; and so on. The concept of elasticity can be applied here also: The **cross-elasticity of demand** for a good is defined as the percentage change in demand for the good divided by the percentage change in the price of another good. The formula for cross-elasticity of demand is the same as the one for price elasticity of demand, except that the numerator shows the percentage change in the quantity of one good while the denominator shows the percentage change in the price of some other good.

Cross-elasticity of demand is related to the concepts of *substitutes* and *complements*. Because lettuce and cabbage are substitutes, an increase in the price of cabbage causes an increase in the demand for lettuce. The cross-elasticity of demand is positive. Because motor oil and gasoline are complements, an increase in the price of gasoline causes a decrease in the demand for motor oil. The cross-elasticity of demand is negative.

Cross-elasticity of demand
The ratio of the percentage change in the demand for a good to a given percentage change in the price of some other good, other things being equal.

Price elasticity of supply

The definition of the **price elasticity of supply** for a good closely resembles that of the price elasticity of demand: It is the percentage change in the quantity of the good supplied divided by the percentage change in the price of the good. The formula for price elasticity of supply is exactly the same as that for price elasticity of demand. Because price and quantity change in the same direction along a positively sloped supply curve, the formula gives a positive value for the elasticity of supply. Box 5.7 applies the elasticity formula to two supply curves, one with constant elasticity and the other with variable elasticity.

Price elasticity of supply (elasticity of supply)
The ratio of the percentage change in the quantity of a good supplied to the percentage change in its price.

SUMMARY

1. *Utility* refers to the pleasure and satisfaction that people get from goods and services. The added utility obtained from a one-unit increase in consumption of a good or service is its *marginal utility*. According to the *principle of diminishing marginal utility*, the greater the rate of consumption of a good, the smaller the increase in utility from an additional unit consumed.

2. Typically, a consumer must choose among many goods, given a fixed budget. *Consumer equilibrium* is said to occur when the total utility obtained from a given budget cannot be increased by shifting spending from one good to another. In equilibrium, the marginal utility of a dollar's worth of one good must be equal to the marginal utility of a dollar's worth of any other good.

BOX 5.7   Calculating Price Elasticities of Supply

This diagram gives four examples of how supply elasticities are calculated — two for each of the two supply curves shown. The supply curve S_1, which is a straight line passing through the origin, has a constant elasticity of 1.0. The supply curve S_2, which is curved, is elastic for low quantities of output and inelastic for larger quantities. For example, in the range from 20 to 30 units of output, the elasticity of S_2 is 3.4, and in the range from 80 to 90 units of output, the elasticity is 0.41.

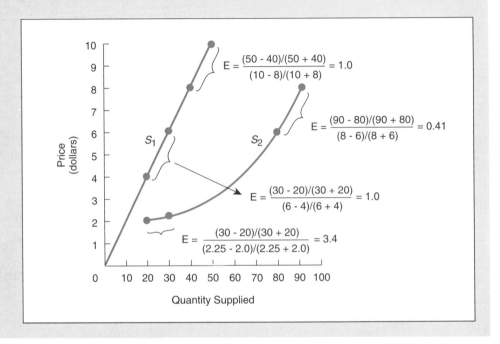

3. The change in quantity demanded that results from a change in the price of a good, other things being equal, can be separated into two parts. The part that comes from the tendency to substitute cheaper goods for more costly ones is the *substitution effect*. The part that comes from the increase in real income that results when the price of a good falls, other things being equal, is the *income effect*.

4. For a normal good, the substitution and income effects work in the same direction. The demand curves for normal goods therefore slope downward. For inferior goods, the income effect of a price change works in the opposite direction from the substitution effect. For inferior goods, therefore, the demand curve will slope downward only if the substitution effect outweighs the income effect.

5. *Consumer surplus* is a concept that recognizes that many consumers do not pay as much for a good as they would be willing to pay — in other words, that

their satisfaction, or total utility, from the good exceeds what they actually paid for it.

6. *Elasticity* is the responsiveness of quantity demanded or supplied to changes in the price of the good or to changes in other factors. If quantity demanded changes by a larger percentage than price, demand is said to be *elastic*. If quantity changes by a smaller percentage than price, demand is said to be *inelastic*. And if quantity and price change by the same percentage, demand is said to be *unit elastic*.

7. The *price elasticity of demand* between two points on a demand curve is computed as the percentage change in quantity divided by the percentage change in price. The formula for price elasticity of demand is

$$\frac{(Q_1 - Q_2)/(Q_1 + Q_2)}{(P_1 - P_2)/(P_1 + P_2)}.$$

8. If the demand for a good is elastic, a decrease in price will increase *total revenue*. If it is inelastic, an increase in price will increase total revenue. A straight-line demand curve is elastic at the upper end, reaches a point of unit elasticity in the middle, and becomes inelastic at the lower end.

9. A number of factors can affect the elasticity of demand for a good. Demand for goods that have ready substitutes tends to be elastic. Demand for goods that are minor complements to more important goods tends to be inelastic. Goods that account for a small portion of a person's budget tend to have inelastic demand. And demand tends to become more elastic the more time people are given to adjust to a change in price.

10. The concept of elasticity can be applied to many situations besides movements along demand curves. The *income elasticity of demand* for a good is the percentage change in the demand for a good divided by the percentage change in income. The *cross-elasticity of demand* between goods A and B is the percentage change in the demand for good A divided by the percentage change in the price of good B. And the *price elasticity of supply* is the percentage change in the quantity of a good supplied divided by the percentage change in its price.

KEY TERMS

utility	consumer surplus	unit elastic demand
marginal utility	elasticity	perfectly inelastic demand
principle of diminishing marginal utility	total revenue	perfectly elastic demand
consumer equilibrium	price elasticity of demand	income elasticity of demand
substitution effect	elastic demand	cross-elasticity of demand
income effect	inelastic demand	price elasticity of supply

KEY BOXES

Box 5.2 Consumer Surplus
Box 5.3 Elastic, Inelastic, and Unit Elastic Demand

Box 5.5 Variation in Elasticity along a Straight-Line
Demand Curve

REVIEW QUESTIONS

1. Assume that soft drinks cost 50¢ a cup and popcorn costs 75¢ a box. Under what conditions would a consumer be in equilibrium in the consumption of soft drinks and popcorn, assuming that at least some of each good is bought?

2. Packaged chocolate chip cookies are a normal good. Flour for baking cookies is an inferior good. Explain how the quantity demanded of each of these goods is affected by an increase in its price, taking into account both the substitution and income effects.

3. What role do the income and substitution effects play in determining the slope of the demand curve for a normal good? For an inferior good?

4. Is it true for all goods that more is always better than less, or are there some for which marginal utility could start out positive but then become negative?

5. Suppose that it would take eight rolls of wallpaper to decorate your kitchen. If someone gave you seven rolls of wallpaper, you would get only limited utility from them. An eighth roll, however, would bring great utility. Do you think this is a valid exception to the principle of diminishing marginal utility?

6. Martha Smith consumes two kilograms of pork and five kilograms of beef per month. She pays $1.50 per kilogram for the pork and $2 per kilogram for the beef. What can you say about the ratio of the marginal utility of pork to the marginal utility of beef, assuming that this pattern represents a state of consumer equilibrium for Smith? Is the ratio 3:4, 4:3, 5:2, 2:5, or none of these?

7. If you were the president of a union bargaining for a new contract and asking for higher wages, would you prefer that the demand for your firm's product were relatively elastic or relatively inelastic? Explain.

8. Suppose that Middle Eastern governments cut off exports of petroleum products to Canada and that the Canadian government imposed a price ceiling. Do you think the lines that might form at gas stations would be longer if the demand for gasoline were relatively elastic or if it were relatively inelastic?

9. Suppose that the supply of tobacco were relatively elastic and the demand relatively inelastic. Under these conditions, who do you think would protest an increase in the cigarette tax more strongly — consumers or producers? What if the elasticities were reversed?

10. The town manager of River City calls you in as a consultant to explain something puzzling. Last year, the city doubled its fares on its downtown buses. For a few months, the bus line reported a strong increase in revenues, but then the revenues began falling off and ended up lower than they had been to begin with. Does what you have learned about elasticity of demand and the determinants of that demand help you explain what happened?

11. Do you think it makes sense as a general principle to say that the demand for a broadly defined good, such as cars, clothing, or meat, will be less elastic than the demand for a corresponding narrowly defined good, such as Fords, Levi's, or pork chops? Explain.

12. Why would the slope of a demand curve not be just as good a measure as elasticity for the responsiveness of demand to price changes? Can you formulate a simple generalization relating the slope of a demand curve to the way in which total revenue changes when price changes?

13. Economists define the cross-elasticity of demand between good A and good B as the ratio of the percentage change in the quantity of good A to the percentage change in the price of good B. Suppose that the price of olive oil

was $5 per litre. Suppose also that a grocer found that customers bought 100 L of olive oil a month when the price of safflower oil was $3 per litre and 150 L of olive oil per month when the price of safflower oil was $4 per litre. What is the cross-elasticity of demand between olive oil and safflower oil? Are the two kinds of salad oil complements or substitutes for each other?

14. In the Preview to this chapter, it is stated that total revenue for the Winnipeg Transit did not change as fares went up. What appears to be the elasticity of demand for bus service in Winnipeg? As a city planner, would you recommend that fares be raised substantially?

15. Look back at Box 4.10, on page 111, which depicts a government support program for wheat. The market equilibrium price is $2 per bushel, but the government has guaranteed farmers a price of $3 per bushel (the support price). At this higher price, quantity supplied exceeds quantity demanded. How would the surplus change if demand for wheat were very elastic? In view of the determinants of demand discussed in the text, how elastic do you think the demand for wheat is in reality?

16. Calculate the price elasticity of demand for each of the following situations and identify each as representing elastic, unit, or inelastic demand.

  a. The price of a good increases by 20 percent, and the quantity demanded declines by 20 percent.

  b. Price increases from $6 per unit to $8, and the quantity demanded falls from six units to four units.

  c. Price falls from $5 per unit to $2, and the quantity demanded increases from four units to nine units.

17. Draw supply curves to illustrate the following situations. In each case, state whether the supply is perfectly elastic or perfectly inelastic.

  a. free clean air to breathe in Red Deer, Alberta

  b. original paintings by Picasso

  c. a $10 "all-you-can-eat" buffet at a restaurant

  d. hectares of land on an island in Ontario's cottage country

  e. federal/provincial income tax forms in April of each year

18. Draw demand curves to illustrate the following situations. In each case, state whether the demand is perfectly elastic or perfectly inelastic.

  a. demand for seats for the final game of the Stanley Cup series at a price of $20 per ticket

  b. demand for a pack of cigarettes by a confirmed smoker

  c. demand by a sick person for a drug prescribed by his or her doctor

  d. demand for clean air to breathe at a zero price

  e. demand for heroin by an addict starting to suffer from withdrawal symptoms

19. Suggest and give reasons for the probable price elasticity of demand faced by the firms or individuals in each of the following situations.

  a. a high-volume, relatively low price, automobile dealership that advertises more than most car dealers

  b. a drug company that has a patent on a drug that helps balding men grow hair

  c. a large warehouse store that sells canned and bottled food by the case at discount prices

  d. a firm that is the sole producer and distributor for tapes, records, and compact discs for a band that has recently become very popular with college and university students

20. A study of spending patterns in a developing country reveals that as per-capita income rises from $1100 to $1300, per-capita consumption of meat, *ceteris paribus*, rises from 75 kg to 125 kg per year. What is the income elasticity for meat in this country? Is meat a normal or inferior good?

21. Mr. Hacque is currently buying 12 units of good A. The price of good A is $2 per unit, and the last unit he buys brings him 10 utils of satisfaction. He is also buying good B, which costs $3 per unit. At the moment, he is buying 16 units of good B, and the last unit purchased brings him 18 utils of satisfaction. Assuming that Mr. Hacque buys only goods A and B, is he in an equilibrium position? If so, explain why.

If not, explain what he must do to reach an equilibrium. Assume he wants to maximize the satisfaction he receives from the goods he buys with his income.

22. An economics professor was once asked in an anonymous note passed to the front of the room, "Is it true that if the price falls low enough, some people will buy anything? If so, where did you get *that tie*?" Under what circumstances would it have made sense for the professor to buy the tie?

23. One day in mid-October of 1990, the price of gold fell sharply on international markets because of rumours that the Soviet Union planned to sell some of its large gold holdings. The Soviets were rumoured to be selling gold to buy Western grain and other commodities. Assume that the supply of gold on world markets on any one day is highly, if not perfectly, inelastic. Illustrate the gold-market situation before and after the rumours spread. Illustrate what would have occurred in the gold market if the Soviets had indeed gone through with a large sell-off of their gold supplies.

An Introduction to Indifference Curves

Chapter 5 gave two versions of the theory of consumer choice underlying the law of demand — one based on marginal utility, the other on income and substitution effects. This appendix gives a third version, using what are known as indifference curves. Indifference curves are not featured in this book, but they are used very frequently in intermediate- and advanced-level economic writing. Many students and instructors find it worthwhile to cover them at least briefly as part of an introductory course. This appendix will serve the needs of those who are interested.

Constructing an Indifference Curve

Begin by supposing that I am an experimenter and you are my experimental subject. I want to find out how you feel about consuming various quantities of meat and cheese. It would be convenient if I had a utility meter, but I do not. In order to find out your attitudes toward the consumption of meat and cheese, I instead present you with a number of food baskets (two at a time) containing various quantities of the two goods.

As I present each pair of baskets, I ask, Would you prefer the one on the left to the one on the right? The one on the right to the one on the left? Or are you indifferent between the two? If you play your role of experimental subject in good faith, I have a reasonable hope of getting a meaningful answer from you. In any event, I certainly have a better chance of getting a meaningful answer than I would if I asked you how many utils you would get from each basket.

At some point in the experiment, I offer you one basket (*A*) containing, say, eight kilograms of meat and three kilograms of cheese and another basket (*B*) containing, say, six kilograms of meat and four kilograms of cheese. I ask you the usual question, and you answer that you are indifferent between the two baskets. The extra kilogram of cheese in Basket *B*, you feel, just makes up for the fact that it has two kilograms less of meat than does Basket *A*. This gives me a very useful bit of information: It tells me that, for you, Basket *A* and Basket *B* belong to an **indifference set** — a set of consumption alternatives each yielding the same amount of satisfaction, so that no member of the set is preferred to any other. Exploring the matter further, I discover that two other baskets (*C* and *D*) also belong to the same indifference set, which now has the following four members.

Indifference set
A set of consumption alternatives, each of which yields the same utility, so that no member of the set is preferred to any other.

Basket	Meat (kilograms)	Cheese (kilograms)
A	8	3
B	6	4
C	5	5
D	4	7

With this information in hand, I thank you for participating in my experiment and get out a piece of graph paper. First, I draw a set of co-ordinate axes, as in Box 5A.1. Kilograms of meat are measured on the horizontal axis and kilograms of cheese on the vertical. Each basket of goods can be shown as a point in the area between the two axes. The points representing Baskets *A* through *D* are shown in their proper spots in the diagram. These points and all the points in between them lying on the smooth curve that has been sketched in joining them are members of the same indifference set. The curve itself is an **indifference curve** — a curve composed entirely of points that are all members of a single indifference set.

Indifference curve
A graphic representation of an indifference set.

Some Properties of Indifference Curves

Indifference curves have properties that reflect certain basic regularities in patterns of consumer preferences. Five of these properties are of particular interest.

1. *Indifference curves normally have negative slopes,* as illustrated in Box 5A.1. If both meat and cheese are desirable goods, it is impossible to have a positively

---

BOX 5A.1   *An Indifference Curve*

Each point in this diagram stands for a basket of meat and cheese. *A, B, C,* and *D* are all baskets among which a certain consumer is indifferent. All give equal utility. Those points and all the others on the smooth curve connecting them constitute an indifference set. An indifference curve, such as the one shown here, is a graphic representation of an indifference set.

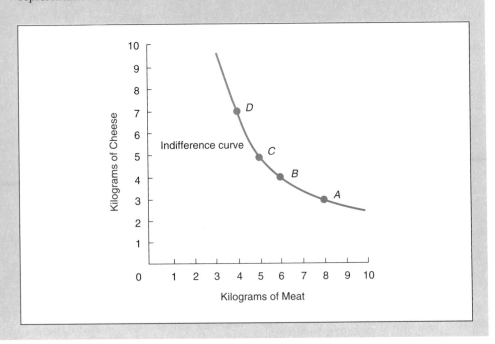

sloped indifference curve. This is demonstrated in Box 5A.2. The consumption basket shown by point *A* contains more of both goods than the one shown by point *B*. This implies that if greater quantities of meat and cheese give greater satisfaction, *A* must be *preferred* to *B*. It cannot then be a member of the same indifference set as *B*.

2. *The absolute value of the slope of an indifference curve at any point represents the ratio of the marginal utility of the good on the horizontal axis to the marginal utility of the good on the vertical axis.* For an example, refer back to Box 5A.1. Between *D* and *C*, the slope of the curve is approximately −2 (or simply 2 when the minus sign is removed to give the absolute value). This shows that the marginal utility of meat is approximately twice the marginal utility of cheese for the consumer — when the quantities consumed are in the area of Baskets *C* and *D*. Because the marginal utility of meat is twice that of cheese in this region, the consumer will feel neither gain nor loss in total utility in trading Basket *D* for Basket *C* — that is, in giving up two kilograms of cheese for one extra kilogram of meat. Because it shows the rate at which meat can be substituted for cheese without gain or loss in satisfaction, the slope of the indifference curve is called the **marginal rate of substitution** of meat for cheese.

> **Marginal rate of substitution**
> The rate at which one good can be substituted for another without gain or loss in satisfaction (equal to the slope of an indifference curve at any point).

Indifference Curves Cannot Slope Upward

BOX 5A.2

Indifference curves normally have negative slopes, as shown in Box 5A.1. The upward-sloping portion of the indifference curve shown here is impossible if both goods give increased satisfaction with increased quantity. *A* has more of both goods than *B*. Point *A* should thus be preferred to point *B*, and therefore it could not lie on the same indifference curve.

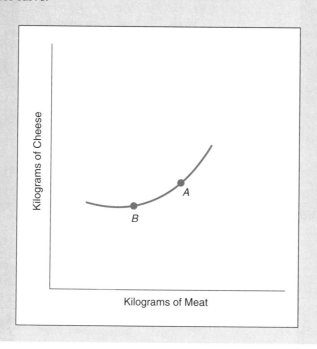

3. *Indifference curves are convex; that is, their slope decreases as one moves down and to the right along them.* This implies that the ratio of the marginal utility of meat to the marginal utility of cheese (also known as the marginal rate of substitution of meat for cheese) diminishes as one moves down and to the right along the curve. Look once more at Box 5A.1. In the region between *D* and *C*, the slope of the curve is approximately -2, indicating that the ratio of the marginal utility of meat to that of cheese is approximately 2:1. By comparison, in the neighbourhood between *B* and *A*, the slope is only about $-1/2$. The ratio of the marginal utility of meat to the marginal utility of cheese is now approximately 1:2.

4. *An indifference curve can be drawn through the point that represents any basket of goods whatsoever.* Consider Box 5A.3. Here is the same indifference curve as in Box 5A.1, but labelled I_1. Point *E*, representing a basket with seven kilograms of meat and five kilograms of cheese, is not a member of the indifference set represented by this curve. Because it lies above and to the right of point *B* and has more of both products than *B*, it must be preferred to *B*. There are other points, such as *F* and *G*, that have more cheese and less meat than *E* and, on balance, give the same satisfaction as *E*. The consumer is indifferent among *E*, *F*, *G*, and all other points on the curve I_2 and prefers all of these points to any of the points on I_1.

Any point taken at random, together with the other points that happen to be equally satisfactory, can form an indifference curve. Several other such

BOX 5A.3 *Multiple Indifference Curves*

An indifference curve can be drawn through any point. Here, the indifference curve I_1 represents an indifference set containing points *A*, *B*, *C*, and *D*, while I_2 represents a set containing points *E*, *F*, and *G*. All points on I_2 are preferred to all points on I_1. A representation selection of indifference curves such as the one shown here can be called an indifference map.

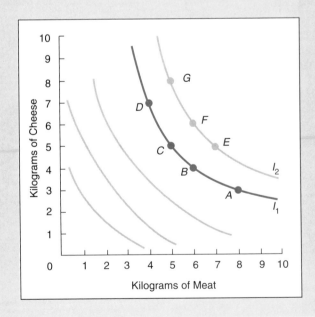

curves, unlabelled, are sketched in Box 5A.3. If all possible curves were drawn in, they would be so close together that the ink of the lines would run into a solid sheet entirely filling the space between the axes. A representative selection of indifference curves, showing their general pattern but leaving enough space to make the diagram easy to read, is called an **indifference map**.

Indifference map
A representative selection of indifference curves for a single consumer and pair of goods.

5. *Indifference curves do not cross, because consumer preferences are* **transitive** — which means that if you prefer *A* to *B* and *B* to *C*, you will prefer *A* to *C*. Looking at Box 5A.4, you can see that crossed indifference curves contradict this assumption of transitivity. Consider points *A*, *B*, and *C*. *A* and *B* both lie on the same indifference curve, I_1; hence, the consumer is indifferent between them. *A* and *C* both lie on I_2; hence the consumer is indifferent between them also. From the property of transitivity, if *B* is as good as *A* and *A* is as good as *C*, *C* is as good as *B*. But *C* lies above and to the right of *B*. It represents a combination of goods with more of both meat and cheese. If more is better, the consumer must prefer *C* to *B*. Since crossed indifference curves imply a contradictory set of preferences, the conclusion is that they cannot cross.

Transitivity
The situation where if *A* is preferred to *B* and *B* is preferred to *C*, then *A* must be preferred to *C*.

Crossing Indifference Curves Contradict the Assumption of Transitive Preferences

BOX 5A.4

Because consumer preferences are transitive, indifference curves do not cross. The impossible indifference curves shown here represent contradictory preferences. *A* and *B* are both on I_1, so the consumer must be indifferent between them. *A* and *C* are both on I_2, so the consumer must be indifferent between them, too. Transitivity implies that the consumer is indifferent between *B* and *C*, but this is impossible, because *C* contains more of both goods than does *B*.

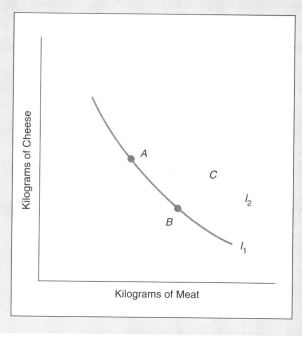

The Budget Line

The range of consumption opportunities open to a consumer with a given budget and with given prices can be shown on the same kind of graph that has been used for indifference curves. Box 5A.5 shows how this can be done. Suppose that you have a food budget of $10 per week, that the price of meat is $2 per kilogram, and that the price of cheese is $1 per kilogram. If you spend all your money on meat, you can have up to five kilograms of meat; if you spend all your money on cheese, you can have up to ten kilograms of cheese. Combinations such as two kilograms of meat and six of cheese or four kilograms of meat and two of cheese are also possible. Taking possible purchases of fractional kilograms of meat and cheese into account as well, these consumption opportunities can be shown on the diagram as a diagonal line running from 10 on the cheese axis to 5 on the meat axis. This diagonal line is called the **budget line** under the assumed conditions.

Budget line
A line showing the various combinations of goods that can be purchased at given prices within a given budget.

Using m to stand for meat and c to stand for cheese, the equation for the budget line can be written as $2m + 1c = 10$. This equation simply says that the number of kilograms of meat bought times the price of meat plus the number of kilograms of cheese bought times the price of cheese must add up to the total budget if no money is left unspent. Expressed in more general terms, the equation for a budget line for goods x and y — with P_x standing for the price of x, P_y for the price of y, and B for the consumer's total budget — is $P_x X + P_y y = B$. The

---

BOX 5A.5   *The Budget Line*

Suppose you have a budget of $10 per week. You can spend your money on meat at $2 per kilogram, on cheese at $1 per kilogram, or on some combination of the two goods. The consumption opportunity line — the budget line — shows all the possible combinations available to you, given these prices and your limited budget.

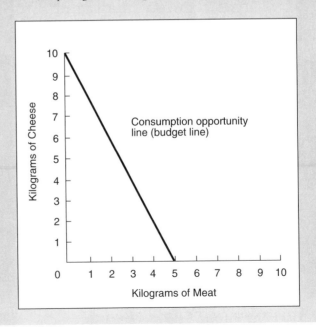

slope of such a budget line is $-P_x/P_y$. In the case illustrated in Box 5A.5, where the price of meat is $2 per kilogram and the price of cheese is $1 per kilogram, the slope of the budget line is -2.

A Graphic Representation of Consumer Equilibrium

Indifference curves and the budget line can be used to give a graphic representation of consumer equilibrium. Box 5A.6 shows the budget line from Box 5A.5 superimposed on an indifference map similar to that shown earlier in Box 5A.3. Preferences and consumption opportunities can thus be compared easily. For example, point *B* is preferred to point *A* because it lies on a "higher" indifference curve (one that at some point, such as *C*, passes above and to the right of *A*). By similar reasoning, point *D* is inferior to point *B*. Of all the points on or below the budget line, it is clear that point *E*, representing 2.5 kg of meat and 5 kg of cheese, is the most preferred, because all the other points on the budget line lie on lower indifference curves. Every point that is better still, such as *F*, lies outside the range of consumption opportunities.

Because *E* is the point giving the highest possible satisfaction under the conditions set, it is the point of consumer equilibrium. At *E*, the relevant indifference

Graphic Demonstration of **Consumer Equilibrium**   *BOX 5A.6*

Given the indifference curves and the budget line shown, *E* is the point of consumer equilibrium in this example. All points that are better than *E* (such as *F*) lie outside the boundary of the budget line. All other points for goods that the consumer can afford to buy (such as *A* and *D*) lie on lower indifference curves than does *E* and are thus less preferred.

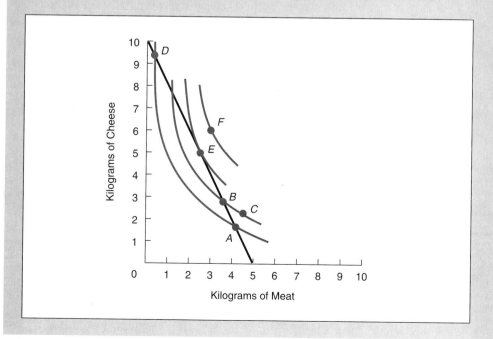

curve is just tangent to the budget line; this means that the slopes of the indifference curve and the budget line are the same at this point. The slope of the indifference curve, as shown earlier, is equal to the ratio of the marginal utility of meat to the marginal utility of cheese. The slope of the budget line is equal to the ratio of the price of meat to the price of cheese. It follows that, in consumer equilibrium,

$$\frac{\text{Marginal utility of meat}}{\text{Marginal utility of cheese}} = \frac{\text{Price of meat}}{\text{Price of cheese}}.$$

This is the condition for consumer equilibrium given in Chapter 5 (see page 123).

Graphic Derivation of the Demand Curve

We conclude this appendix with a discussion of how a demand curve for meat can be derived graphically from a set of indifference curves. Together with the indifference curves, Box 5A.7(a) shows a whole family of budget lines. Each budget line is based on the assumption that the price of cheese is $1 per kilogram and that the consumer's budget is $10, as before. Now, though, each budget line assumes a different price, P, of meat. The budget line running from 10 on the vertical axis to 2.5 on the horizontal axis assumes $P = $4. The budget line running from 10 on the vertical axis to 5 on the horizontal axis assumes $P = $2 (this is the same budget line as those drawn in Boxes 5A.5 and 5A.6). The other two budget lines are based on $P = $1.50 and $P = $1, respectively.

The equilibrium consumption pattern for the consumer will be different for each price of meat, other things being equal. When $P = $4, point A, representing six kilograms of cheese and one kilogram of meat, is the best the consumer can do; when $P = $2, point B is the most preferred point; and so on.

Given this information on consumer equilibrium under different price assumptions, it is a simple matter to draw the consumer's demand curve for meat. Box 5A.7(b) shows a new set of axes, with the quantity of meat on the horizontal axis as before, but with the price of meat now on the vertical axis. From Box 5A.7(a), when $P = $4, the consumer chooses the consumption combination A, which includes one kilogram of meat. In Box 5A.7(b), point a is thus marked as the quantity of meat demanded at a price of $4. Then point b (corresponding to point B in part [a]) is added, and so on. Drawing a smooth line through points a, b, c, and d in Box 5A.7(b) thus gives the consumer's demand curve for meat. As expected, it has the downward slope that is consistent with the law of demand.

Box 5A.7 can be adapted to illustrate the substitution and income effects noted earlier in this chapter. These effects are illustrated in Box 5A.8. Recall that, when the price of a good falls, two things happen: The good becomes cheaper in relation to other goods, and the real income of consumers increases. The first is known as the substitution effect, the second as the income effect. In Box 5A.8, the consumer is initially at A, when the price of cheese is $1 per kilogram and the price of meat is $4 per kilogram. We noted that, as the price of meat falls to $2 per kilogram and the price of cheese remains constant, the consumer will move from A to B. The consumption of cheese falls from 6 kg to 5 kg and the consumption of meat increases from 1 kg to 2.5 kg. In each case, the consumer spends an income of $10. Note again that at point A, the consumer's first budget line was tangent to indifference curve I_1, while at B, the consumer's second budget line is tangent to a

Graphic Derivation of a Demand Curve

Part (a) of this diagram shows a consumer's indifference map for meat and cheese and a set of budget lines. Each budget line corresponds to a different price, *P*, of meat, as shown. All four budget lines assume the price of cheese to be $1 per kilogram and the total budget to be $10. Points *A*, *B*, *C*, and *D* in part (a) show the choices the consumer makes at meat prices of $4, $2, $1.50, and $1, respectively. In part (b) of the diagram, the information on consumption of meat at the various prices is plotted on a new set of axes. The smooth line connecting points *a*, *b*, *c*, and *d* is the consumer's demand curve for meat.

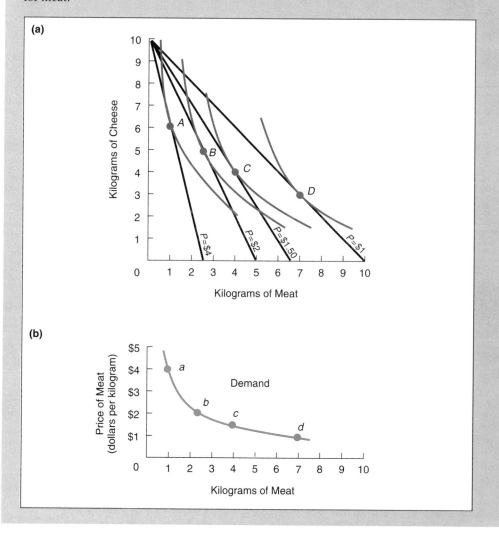

higher indifference curve. *The movement from* A *to* B *is actually made up of two effects that must now be isolated and identified.* Suppose that, after the drop in the price of meat, the consumer's income was reduced just enough to force him or her to remain on indifference curve I_1. In other words, the consumer is not able to enjoy an increase in welfare, or in real income, even though the price of meat has fallen. This is tantamount to giving the consumer a budget line parallel to his or

BOX 5A.8 *Income and Substitution Effects*

When the price of meat falls relative to the price of cheese, the consumer moves from point *A* to point *B*. If he were not allowed to enjoy any increase in real income (represented by a move to a higher indifference curve), he would move from *A* to *A'*, where the budget line based on the new price ratios of meat and cheese is tangent to the original indifference curve, I_1. This is the substitution effect. If, now, the individual were given his increase in real income, he would move from *A'* to *B*, illustrating the income effect resulting from the decrease in the price of meat.

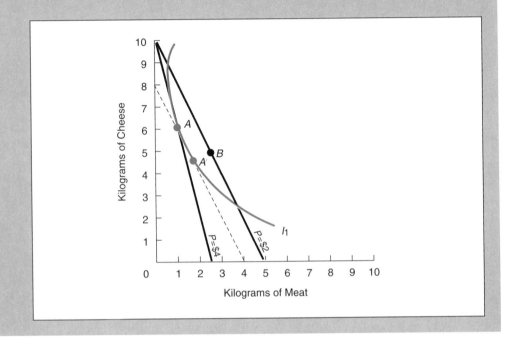

her second budget line (since it would have the same price ratios, and hence the same slope, as the second budget line) but tangent to indifference curve I_1. This budget line is represented by the dotted line in Box 5A.8. It is tangent to I_1 at *A'*. At *A'*, the consumer has reacted to the relatively lower price of meat by buying more meat and less cheese, simply because of the relative change in prices and not because of any increase in real income. This movement, then, represents the substitution effect. If, after moving from *A* to *A'*, the consumer were now given his or her real-income increase, the consumer would move from *A'* to *B*. This is the income effect. Therefore, the movement from *A* to *B* illustrated in Box 5A.7 is actually made up of two effects: a substitution effect, which in Box 5A.8 is portrayed as a movement from *A* to *A'*, and an income effect, represented in Box 5A.8 by the movement from *A'* to *B*.

KEY TERMS

indifference set
indifference curve

marginal rate of substitution
indifference map

transitivity
budget line

KEY BOXES

Box 5A.6 Graphic Demonstration of
         Consumer Equilibrium

Box 5A.8 Income and Substitution Effects

REVIEW QUESTIONS

1. A consumer takes $6 to the supermarket to
    buy bread and milk. The price of bread is $1
    per unit and the price of milk $1.50 per unit.
    Construct a budget line for this consumer. Put
    quantity of bread on the vertical axis and
    quantity of milk on the horizontal axis. Draw
    several hypothetical indifference curves for this
    consumer, and indicate the quantity of milk
    and bread that should be purchased to
    maximize satisfaction within the $6 budget, at
    the prices given.

    a. Illustrate what would happen to the budget
        line and to consumer equilibrium if the
        price of both milk and bread doubled.

    b. Illustrate what would happen to the budget
        line and to consumer equilibrium if the
        price of milk doubled and the price of bread
        remained the same.

    c. Illustrate what would happen to the budget
        line and to consumer equilibrium if the
        price of milk was cut in half and the price of
        bread remained the same.

A Closer Look at Supply:
The Theory of Cost

WHAT YOU WILL LEARN IN THIS CHAPTER

After studying this chapter, you will be able to

1. Distinguish between implicit and explicit costs, and between pure economic profit and accounting profit.

2. Explain the concepts of short run and long run in terms of fixed and variable inputs.

3. Show how output increases as the amount of a variable input is increased for a typical production process.

4. State and illustrate the law of diminishing returns.

5. Construct a family of short-run cost curves for a typical firm, given data on the firm's fixed and variable costs.

6. Explain how average costs vary in the long run as output varies for a typical firm.

7. Discuss the concept of economies of scale in terms of long-run cost curves.

A Preview   *Starting a New Business*

Each year, thousands of Canadians start new businesses and thousands go from one business to another or abandon their attempts to succeed in business altogether. The dream of owning one's own business is strong. Putting the dream into practice can be exciting, but it also involves careful calculation of costs and a good knowledge of the market — as the Martin family discovered.

The Martin Family: Hopeful Entrepreneurs

Andrea and Ralph Martin shared a dream with millions of Canadians: to operate a business of their own. For some, that dream means a hamburger franchise, a dry-cleaning shop, or a couple of hundred hectares of soybeans. The Martins were more ambitious: They dreamed of having their own computer company.

The Martins had no illusions about the life of the entrepreneur. They knew that starting their own firm would take hard work and sacrifice. Both were engineers with high-paying jobs at large corporations. On their combined income of $150 000 a year, they could have lived the good life — a house in the suburbs, a BMW in the driveway, a condominium in Florida. Instead, they lived in a small apartment and saved every dollar they could to build a nest egg with which to start their firm.

The Martins knew they couldn't take on IBM in hand-to-hand combat. They needed to find a corner of the computer market where they could start small and offer customers something new. Ralph's job with an oil company gave him an idea. On his visits to refineries and drilling sites, he often carried a notebook-sized computer to record data and make on-the-spot computations. But all the small computers available on the market were designed for use in offices. Out in the heat and dust of the field, they often broke down. Ralph was sure there would be a market for a more ruggedly built computer for use under field conditions. Andrea was sure she could design one.

The design for the new machine took shape on paper. The company, Fieldcom Inc., took shape on paper too. Then one day it was time to take the plunge. The Martins quit their jobs, hired two technicians and an office manager, and went into production. Their factory was an abandoned service station available at a rock-bottom price. Within a month, the first of their new products, the Fieldcom I, rolled off the assembly line.

THE NATURE OF COSTS

In this chapter and the next one, we will use the firm described in the Preview — Fieldcom Inc. — as a case study around which to build a theory of supply in competitive markets. Along with the theory of consumer choice that underlies the demand curve, this theory will give us a better understanding of the factors that affect equilibrium prices and quantities in a market economy. The first step, which we will take in this chapter, will be to develop a theory of cost. In the next chapter, we will show how costs interact with demand conditions to determine the amount of output that firms supply.

One of the most basic ideas in economics is that all costs arise from the need to choose among possible uses of scarce resources. All costs, in other words, are opportunity costs. The true measure of the cost of doing something is the value of the best alternative use of the same resources.

Implicit and Explicit Costs

The opportunity costs that a firm such as Fieldcom faces include the payments it must make to suppliers of parts, materials, and services, plus the incomes it must provide to workers, investors, and owners of resources in order to attract factors of production away from alternative uses. These costs are of two kinds — explicit and implicit.

Explicit costs are opportunity costs that take the form of payments to outside suppliers, workers, and others who do not share in the ownership of the firm. These include payments for the labour and raw materials used in production, the services of hired managers and salespeople, insurance, legal advice, transportation, and a great many other things.

Explicit costs
Opportunity costs that take the form of payments to outside suppliers, workers, and others who do not share in the ownership of the firm.

Implicit costs are the opportunity costs of using resources owned by the firm or contributed by its owners. Like explicit costs, they represent real sacrifices by the firm. Unlike explicit costs, however, they do not take the form of explicit payments to outsiders. When a firm uses a building that it owns, it doesn't have to make a payment to anyone, but it gives up the opportunity to receive payments from someone else to whom it could rent the building. To take another example, if the proprietor of a small firm works along with the firm's hired employees, he or she gives up the opportunity to earn a salary by working for someone else. Firms do not normally record implicit costs in their accounts, but that does not make them any less real.

Implicit costs
Opportunity costs of using resources owned by the firm or contributed by its owners.

Costs and Profits

The distinction between explicit and implicit costs is important for understanding the concept of profit. As economists use the term, profit means the difference between a firm's total revenues and its total costs, including both explicit and implicit costs. This concept is often called **pure economic profit**. In this book, the term *profit* always means pure economic profit.

Special care must be taken to keep the economic concept of profit in mind, because the language of business and accounting uses the term in a quite different sense. There, profit means revenue minus explicit costs only. Economists call this concept **accounting profit** to distinguish it from the pure economic profit

Pure economic profit
The sum that is left when both explicit and implicit costs are subtracted from total revenue.

Accounting profit
Total revenue minus explicit costs.

just defined. Putting the two definitions together gives us the following relationship:

$$\text{Pure economic profit} = \text{accounting profit} - \text{implicit costs.}$$

An example

Box 6.1 uses the example of Fieldcom Inc. to illustrate the difference between pure economic profit and accounting profit. The box shows Fieldcom earning total revenues of $600 000 in 1989. Explicit costs — materials purchased and salaries paid to employees — come to $380 000. This leaves an accounting profit of $220 000.

These explicit costs do not include all of the firm's opportunity costs, however. Both Andrea and Ralph Martin gave up high-paying jobs to start the firm. Their combined former income of $150 000 is listed in Box 6.1 as an implicit cost of production. Also listed as an implicit cost is $20 000 of interest income forgone. This is the amount of interest the Martins could have earned on their savings if they had left them in a high-yield bank account rather than investing them in Fieldcom's plant and equipment.

When both implicit and explicit costs are subtracted from revenue, the firm is left with a pure economic profit of $50 000. This sum is profit, not cost, because it is what the Martins earned from their new company over and above the $170 000 needed to attract their labour and capital away from the best alternative uses. It is their reward for acting as entrepreneurs — that is, for recognizing and entering a profitable niche in the computer market that no other entrepreneur had yet entered.

PRODUCTION AND COSTS IN THE SHORT RUN

Having pinned down the economic meaning of cost, our next step is to build a theory of cost. The job of this theory is to explain how costs vary as the amount of output produced by a firm varies and, in doing so, to provide a basis for the firm's supply curve. Our discussion of the theory of cost will be divided into two parts, corresponding to two time ranges — the short run and the long run. We will explain this distinction before presenting the theory of cost itself.

BOX 6.1   *Accounts of Fieldcom Inc.*

Total revenue	$600 000
Less explicit costs	
Wages and salaries	320 000
Materials and other	60 000
Equals accounting profit	220 000
Less implicit costs	
Forgone salary, Andrea Martin	75 000
Forgone salary, Ralph Martin	75 000
Interest forgone on invested savings	20 000
Equals pure economic profit	$ 50 000

The Long Run and the Short Run

A firm uses many kinds of inputs to produce its output. The amounts of inputs it uses vary with the amount of output it generates. The amount of some inputs used can be adjusted quickly, but others are not as easy to adjust.

The inputs that cannot be adjusted quickly as output changes are those that were built to achieve a certain output capacity, such as the plant building and the machinery. These are known as **fixed inputs**. In some cases, the services of employees — but only of those who cannot be replaced easily — can also be viewed as fixed inputs.

In addition to fixed inputs, the firm uses **variable inputs** — those that can be adjusted quickly and easily within a plant of a given size as output changes. Raw materials, energy, and hourly labour are variable inputs for most firms. It should be kept in mind that the status of inputs as fixed or variable depends on the situation. As the accompanying For Example. . . box shows, inputs that are variable for some firms may be fixed for others.

The distinction between fixed and variable inputs is the basis for the distinction between the short run and the long run in cost theory. The **short run** is a time range that is too short to change the size of a firm's plant, so changes in output can come about only as a result of changes in the amounts of variable inputs used. The **long run**, by contrast, is a time range that is long enough to permit changes in the amounts of fixed inputs and the size of the firm's plant.

Fixed inputs
Inputs that cannot easily be increased or decreased in a short time.

Variable inputs
Inputs that can easily be varied within a short time in order to increase or decrease output.

Short run
A time range within which output can be adjusted only by changing the amounts of variable inputs used while fixed inputs remain unchanged.

Long run
A time range that is long enough to permit changes in all inputs, both fixed and variable.

FOR EXAMPLE...

Labour Costs — Fixed or Variable?

The following excerpt from a *Wall Street Journal* article illustrates a situation in which labour, generally viewed as a variable input, is considered fixed.

High Cost of Liquidation Keeping Some Money-Losing Plants Open

Hourly labour is considered to be a variable cost of production. When demand for a firm's product declines, layoffs of hourly workers are often one of the first steps taken to adjust to a lower rate of output. However, some firms' contracts with their unions make hourly labour a fixed rate rather than a variable cost, at least in part.

The big steel firms' contract with the United Steel Workers is a case in point. This contract calls for pensions, health and life insurance, unemployment benefits, and severance pay when a plant is closed. The benefits can cost up to $70 000 for each employee.

If labour costs remain fixed even when a plant is closed, it may make sense to keep a plant running even though it is losing money. For example, in 1980, Kaiser Steel's directors voted to keep 11 000 workers on the job because shutting down would have cost the company more than $350 million in benefits.

In another case, the need to treat labour costs as fixed prompted a firm to adopt an unusual strategy to get rid of a money-losing operation. In 1981, National Steel decided that it could no longer afford to invest in its Weirton, West Virginia, steel division. Closing the plant would have cost the firm about $320 million in benefits for former employees. To escape this burden, National sold the Weirton operation to its 10 000 employees. They have kept the plant open and are hoping that wage cuts and increases in productivity will make it profitable again.

Production with One Variable Input

Most firms have many inputs that can be varied. A change in any one of them will have some effect on output, other things being equal. Let's turn once again to Fieldcom for an example.

One of the main variable inputs that Fieldcom uses in making small computers is labour. Box 6.2 shows what happens to the rate of production as the number of labour units is varied over the range of zero to ten workers per day.

If no worker is hired, no production can take place. Our example assumes that it will take a minimum of two workers in the plant to get it into production. Hiring just one worker won't help. When two workers are hired they can get a few of the necessary machines into operation, though only one computer will be built. Increasing the number of workers to three and then four per day has a dramatic impact on output. Finally, the machines in the plant are being used effectively. The fifth and sixth workers help still more. Work is now better coordinated, and morale rises. Hiring a worker each day increases output to a level that the technicians find just right. At that point, their output reaches thirteen computers a day.

What happens if still more labour is hired? Nothing much. When the eighth worker is hired, output remains the same. The extra worker is wasted, but causes no harm either. Output remains at thirteen computers a day. Of course, it could be raised further by varying *other* inputs — by giving the workers better equipment, stocking more parts, and so on. But for the moment we are looking at the effects on output of varying just one input, other things being equal.

Marginal physical product

Marginal physical product
The additional amount of output, expressed in physical units, produced by each added unit of one variable input, other things being equal.

The graph in Box 6.2 and columns 1 and 2 of the table show the relationship between rate of labour use and rate of output. In the range of one to seven units of labour, output increases as labour input increases, but not at a constant rate. Column 3 of the table shows how much output is added by each additional unit of labour. This is called the **marginal physical product** of the variable input. As labour use is increased from one unit per day to two, the marginal physical product is one unit of output. As labour use is stepped up from two units per day to three, marginal physical product rises to two units of output, and so on. The step from three units of labour to four gives the greatest boost to output. After that, output increases at a diminishing rate with each added unit of labour.

Finally, after the number of workers reaches seven per day, the marginal physical product drops to zero.

The law of diminishing returns

Law of diminishing returns
The principle that, as one variable input is increased, with all others remaining fixed, a point will be reached beyond which the marginal physical product of the variable input begins to decrease.

The example of labour use at Fieldcom illustrates one of the most useful principles in all of economics, the **law of diminishing returns**. According to this principle, as the amount of one variable input is increased, with the amounts of all other inputs remaining fixed, a point will be reached beyond which the marginal physical product of the input will decrease.

The law of diminishing returns applies to all known production processes and to all variable inputs. It applies in manufacturing, as can be seen in the Fieldcom case. But the law could be illustrated just as well by an example from farming with, say, fertilizer as the variable input: As more fertilizer is added to a field, output increases, but beyond a certain point, the gain in output brought about by an additional tonne of fertilizer tapers off. (Too much fertilizer might even poison

Response of Output to Changes in One Variable Input   BOX 6.2

The table and graph below show how the output of computers at Fieldcom Inc. responds to changes in one variable input, labour. All other inputs remain constant while the number of workers in the plant varies. If too few workers are hired, little or no production will be possible. Output improves as the number of workers increases. But when more than seven workers per day are hired, the existing space and equipment have already been fully utilized, and there is no further gain in output. Column 3 of the table shows the amount of additional output that results from each added unit of labour used. This is known as the marginal physical product of the variable input.

(a)

Input (workers per day)	Output (units per day)	Marginal Physical Product (units of output per added unit of input)
0	0	
		0
1	0	
		1
2	1	
		2
3	3	
		4
4	7	
		3
5	10	
		2
6	12	
		1
7	13	
		0
8	13	
		0
9	13	
		0
10	13	

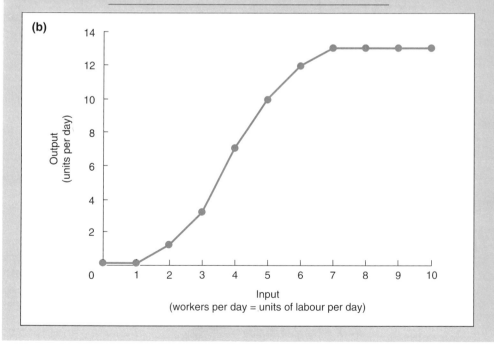

(b)

the plants, in which case marginal physical product would become negative.) Oil refineries, power plants, barbershops, government bureaus — in fact, any production process whatsoever — could be used to illustrate the law of diminishing returns.

From Marginal Physical Product to Marginal Costs

Marginal cost
The increase in cost required to increase the output of some good or service by one unit.

Out next step is to move from the marginal physical product of an input to the **marginal cost** of output. Marginal cost means the increase in cost required to increase the output of a good or service by one unit. As before, we will use Fieldcom as an example.

Some conclusions about marginal cost can be drawn from the example of labour. Box 6.2 showed how output increased as labour increased. Box 6.3 shows how the same data can be read in reverse to show the cost, in terms of labour, of making one more computer over various output ranges. Two units of labour have to be used before the first unit of output can be produced. The next unit of labour adds two units to output — a marginal cost of half a unit of labour per unit of output. Over the next range, adding a unit of output costs only a quarter of a unit of labour.

Beyond four units of labour and seven units of output, the marginal physical product of labour begins to fall. At this same point, the marginal cost of added computers, measured in terms of labour, begins to rise. Over the output range of seven to ten computers a day, each added computer costs a third of a unit of labour. From ten to twelve computers, the marginal cost rises to a half unit of labour per unit of output. The thirteenth unit of output costs another whole unit of labour. The result is a marginal-cost curve that is roughly U-shaped.

More than One Variable Input

It is time to drop the assumption that only one input can be varied at a time. In practice, short-run increases or decreases in Fieldcom's output would require changes in many inputs, although not in all of them. For example, if the firm wanted to raise its output from 13 to 26 units a day, it might have to burn more fuel to keep the shop heated longer each day, and double the rate at which it ordered parts. At the same time, its costs for an office manager and the opportunity costs of plant and equipment would remain fixed.

Taking more variable inputs into account, and allowing them to be varied in smaller steps, creates a smoother cost curve than the single-variable-input curve shown in Box 6.3. Box 6.4 shows how total and marginal costs respond to changes in output when all variable inputs are taken into account. The result is a total-variable-cost curve with a smooth reverse-S shape and a smooth U-shaped marginal-cost curve.

A Set of Short-Run Cost Curves

The marginal-cost and total-variable-cost curves shown in Box 6.4 are only two of a set of short-run cost curves that can be constructed for Fieldcom. The complete set is shown in Box 6.5. This box also contains some often-used formulas and abbreviations that pertain to cost curves.

Marginal Cost and Output with One Variable Input BOX 6.3

This box shows how the cost of production at Fieldcom Inc. changes as output changes. The table and graph are based on the same data that were used for Box 6.2, but here they are recast to stress marginal cost — the added cost of making each added unit of output. The cost is stated in terms of units of labour per unit of added output. For example, increasing the units of labour from three to four raises output from three computers per day to seven. Over this range, then, the cost of each added computer is one-quarter of a unit of labour. The graph shows a marginal-cost curve for the firm that is roughly U-shaped.

(a)

Output (units per day)	Input–Labour (workers per day)	Marginal Cost (units of input per added unit of output)
0	0	
		2.0
1	2	
		0.5
3	3	
		0.25
7	4	
		0.33
10	5	
		0.5
12	6	
		1.0
13	7	

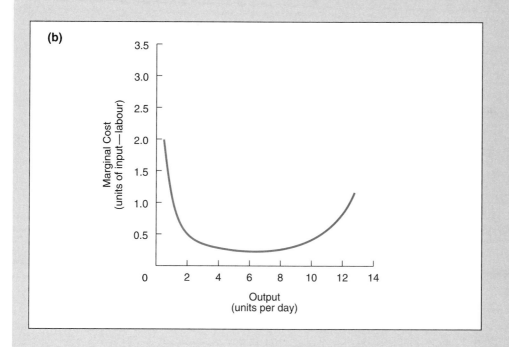

(b)

BOX 6.4 Marginal-Cost and Total-Variable-Cost Curves

This box shows the relationship between cost and output for Fieldcom Inc. under less restrictive assumptions than those used in Box 6.3. Now several inputs (labour, materials, fuel, etc.) are allowed to vary, although some others (office staff, test equipment, rent) remain fixed. This added flexibility creates a smoother U-shaped marginal-cost curve. The corresponding total-variable-cost curve has a reverse-S shape. The slope of the total-variable-cost curve is equal to the height of the marginal-cost curve at every given point. The minimum point on the marginal-cost curve corresponds to the inflection point of the total-variable-cost curve — that is, the point at which it stops becoming flatter and begins to become steeper. Note: The slope of the TVC curve at 9 units of output $= \dfrac{\Delta TVC}{\Delta Q} = $ approx. $\dfrac{\$2500 - \$700}{9 - 0} = \dfrac{\$1800}{9} = \$200$. This is equal to the marginal cost of $200 at 9 units in the bottom diagram.

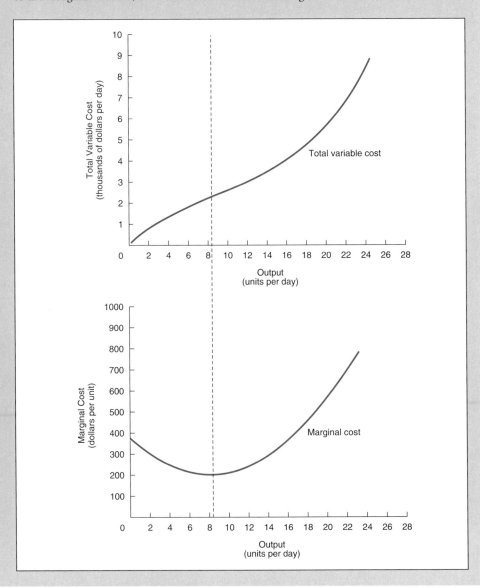

Total variable cost, from Box 6.4, appears in column 2 of part (c) of Box 6.5(c). Not all costs are variable in the short run. Fixed costs (office manager, test equipment, and so on) are assumed to be $2000 per day, as shown in column 3. Adding fixed cost to variable cost gives short-run total cost, which is shown in column 4.

The three total-cost curves — total variable cost, total fixed cost, and total cost — are shown graphically in part (a) of Box 6.5. Because fixed cost, by definition, does not vary as output varies, the total-fixed-cost curve is a horizontal line $2000 above the horizontal axis. Adding fixed cost to variable cost gives total cost. The total-cost curve parallels the total-variable-cost curve at a higher level. The distance between the total-cost and total-variable-cost curves is equal to total fixed cost.

The next column in part (c) of Box 6.5 is marginal cost, again taken from Box 6.4. These data appear on lines between the total-cost entries in order to stress the fact that marginal cost shows how total cost changes as the level of output changes. The marginal-cost curve drawn in part (b) of Box 6.5 is the same as the one in Box 6.4.

The last three columns in part (c) of Box 6.5 are all average-cost concepts: average variable cost, average fixed cost, and average total cost. *Average variable cost* is equal to total variable cost divided by quantity of output; *average fixed cost* is equal to total fixed cost divided by output; and *average total cost* is equal to total cost divided by output. The three average-cost curves also appear in part (b) of Box 6.5.

Some Geometric Relationships

If we examine parts (a) and (b) of Box 6.5, we will find some important geometric relationships among the cost curves. First, compare the marginal-cost curve with the total-variable-cost curve drawn above it (these are the same two curves that appear by themselves in Box 6.4). The bottom of the U-shaped marginal-cost curve lies at exactly the level of output at which the slope of the reverse-S-shaped total-variable-cost curve stops getting flatter and starts getting steeper. This occurs because the slope of the total-variable-cost curve is the *rate* at which that curve is rising, just as marginal cost measures the *rate* at which total variable cost is rising. In graphic terms, then, the *height* of the marginal-cost curve is always equal to the *slope* of the total-cost curve.

A second feature of the cost curve in Box 6.5 deserves comment. The marginal-cost curve intersects both the average-variable-cost and average-total-cost curves at their lowest points. This is not a coincidence. It is the result of a relationship that can be called the **marginal-average rule**. This rule can be explained as follows: Beginning at any given point, ask what the cost of making one more unit will be. The answer is given by marginal cost. Then ask whether this cost is more or less than the average cost of all units produced up to that point. If the added cost of the next unit made is less than the average cost of previous units, then making that unit will have the effect of pulling down the average. If the next unit costs more, its production will pull the average up. It follows that whenever marginal cost is below average-variable-cost, the average-variable-cost curve must be falling (that is, negatively sloped); and whenever marginal cost is above average variable cost, the average variable cost curve must be rising (that is, positively sloped). This in turn implies that the marginal-cost curve cuts the average-variable-cost curve at its lowest point. All this is equally true of the relationship between marginal cost and average total cost.

Marginal-average rule
The rule that marginal cost must be equal to average cost when average cost is at its minimum.

BOX 6.5   *A Set of Short-Run Cost Curves*

A whole set of short-run cost curves can be derived from data on fixed and variable costs, as this box shows. The data are presented in the form of a table and a pair of graphs. The box also contains a list of several useful abbreviations and formulas.

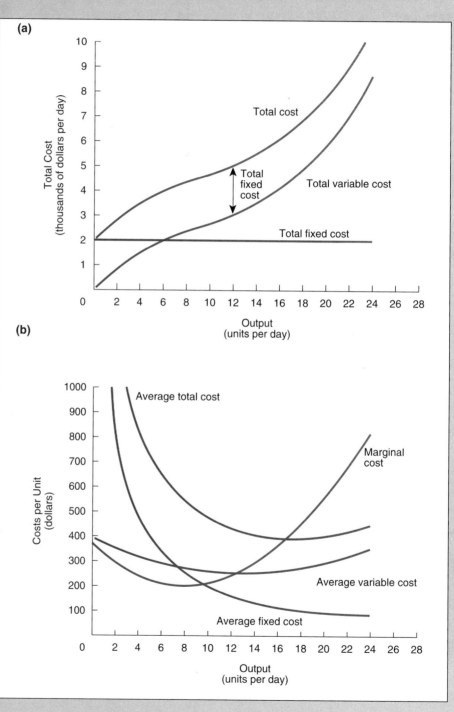

(c) *Common abbreviations:*

Q	Quantity of output
TC	Total cost
TFC	Total fixed cost
TVC	Total variable cost
MC	Marginal cost
AVC	Average variable cost
AFC	Average fixed cost
ATC	Average total cost

Useful formulas:

$$TC = TFC + TVC$$

$$MC = \frac{\text{Change in TC}}{\text{Change in Q}} = \frac{\text{Change in TVC}}{\text{Change in Q}}$$

$$AVC = \frac{TVC}{Q}$$

$$AFC = \frac{TFC}{Q}$$

$$ATC = \frac{TC}{Q}$$

Quantity of Output (units) (1)	Total Variable Cost (2)	Total Fixed Cost (3)	Total Cost (4)	Marginal Cost (dollars per unit) (5)	Average Variable Cost (dollars per unit) (6)	Average Fixed Cost (dollars per unit) (7)	Average Total Cost (dollars per unit) (8)
0	$ 0	$2000	$ 2000	—	—	—	—
				$380			
1	380	2000	2 380		$380	$2000	$2380
				340			
2	720	2000	2 720		360	1000	1360
				305			
3	1025	2000	3 025		342	667	1009
				275			
4	1300	2000	3 300		325	500	825
				250			
5	1550	2000	3 550		310	400	710
				230			
6	1780	2000	3 780		296	333	629
				215			
7	1995	2000	3 995		285	286	571
				205			
8	2200	2000	4 200		275	250	525
				200			
9	2400	2000	4 400		266	222	488
				205			
10	2605	2000	4 605		260	200	460
				215			
11	2820	2000	4 820		256	181	437
				230			
12	3050	2000	5 050		254	169	421
				250			
13	3300	2000	5 300		254	154	408
				275			
14	3575	2000	5 575		255	143	398
				305			
15	3880	2000	5 880		259	133	392
				340			
16	4220	2000	6 220		264	125	389
				380			
17	4600	2000	6 600		271	118	389
				425			
18	5025	2000	7 025		279	111	390
				475			
19	5500	2000	7 500		289	105	394
				530			
20	6030	2000	8 030		302	100	402
				590			
21	6620	2000	8 620		315	95	410
				655			
22	7275	2000	9 275		331	91	422
				725			
23	8000	2000	10 000		348	87	435
				800			
24	8800	2000	10 800		367	83	450

The marginal-average rule is not unique to economics; it can be seen in many everyday situations. Consider, for example, the effect of your grade in this course on your grade-point average. You could call your grade in this course your "marginal grade," because it represents the grade points earned by taking one more course. If your grade in this course (that is, your marginal grade) is higher than your average grade in other courses, the effect of taking this course will be to pull your average up. Your grade-point average must be rising if your marginal grade exceeds your average grade. If you do worse than average in this course, your grade-point average will fall. When your marginal grade falls short of your average grade, your grade-point average must be falling. This is the same as the relationship between marginal cost and average cost. If the cost of making one more unit is less than the average cost of making previous units, the average is pulled down; if it is more, the average is pulled up.

Some people find it easier to remember the relationships among the various cost concepts when they are presented as formulas. If you are such a person, you may find the formulas in Box 6.5 useful. The box also gives some common abbreviations. Although these are used only sparingly in this textbook, you may want to use them in your note taking, and your instructor will probably use them in lectures.

LONG-RUN COSTS AND ECONOMIES OF SCALE

It is sometimes said that firms operate in the short run and plan in the long run. This maxim reflects the distinction between variable and fixed costs; in the short run, a firm varies its output within a plant of fixed size: in the long run, it plans (and carries out) expansions or contractions of the plant itself.

The previous section, then, can be thought of as an analysis of the cost factors that affect operating decisions. Many key aspects of economics turn on the operating decisions that firms make within plants of given sizes. How will farmers change the quantities of the crops they grow? During a recession, by how much will a firm reduce its output, and how many workers will it lay off? Should a moving-and-storage company charge higher rates during its peak moving season? Any change in prices or quantities supplied that does not involve a change in plant size will be affected by the shape and position of the short-run cost curves of the firms involved.

In many other cases, however, we need to know something about the factors that affect firms' plans for expansion or contraction of their plant. We might want to know, for example, how the price of milk would be affected by a reduction in federal dairy subsidies, once farmers had eliminated their surplus production capacity. We might want to know how coal output would respond to increases in oil prices once time had been allowed for new mines to be opened and new equipment installed. Such questions require an analysis of long-run costs, to which we now turn.

Planning for Expansion

Put yourself in the position of an entrepreneur just setting out to establish a small firm such as Fieldcom. You think it will be wise to start with just a small plant, but you want to do some long-range planning too. After consulting with production engineers and other specialists, you sketch some average-total-cost curves for various possible sizes of plant. Five such curves are drawn in Box 6.6. The first

Alternative Short-Run Average-Total-Cost Curves BOX 6.6

The position of the short-run average-total-cost curve for a firm depends on the size of the plant it constructs. In the long run, the firm has a choice of operating with any size plant it chooses. Each plant size can be represented by a different U-shaped short-run average-total-cost curve. Five such curves are shown in this box. A new firm might begin with a plant corresponding to a curve such as the first one shown here. Then, as demand for its product expanded, it might move to those farther to the right.

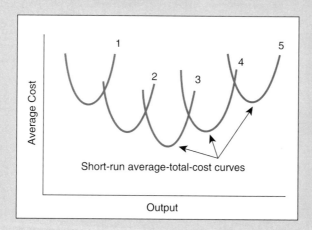

one shows short-run average costs for the range of output that is feasible with a very small plant, the second one corresponds to a slightly larger plant, and so on. As you build up the market for your product, you hope to able to expand your plant and move from one of these curves to the next.

Of course, the five short-run cost curves in the box represent only a sample of plant sizes. Intermediate positions are also possible. The size of plant you actually choose to build will depend, in the long run, on the quantity of output you expect to produce. For any given level of output, you will choose the size of plant that will permit that output to be produced at the lowest possible average total cost.

The Long-Run Average-Cost Curve

As your firm gradually expands, then, you can envision moving along a *long-run average-cost curve* of the kind shown in Box 6.7. This curve is the "envelope" of all possible short-run average-cost curves. The size of plant chosen in the long run for each output will be the one that produces a short-run average-total-cost curve just tangent to the long-run average-total-cost curve at that point.

Boxes 6.6 and 6.7 make clear that there is one best plant size for any given level of output that the firm plans to produce in the long run. Typically, a plant designed for one level of output can be run at a higher or lower level of output only at a penalty in terms of cost. As a young firm expands, it must build more or larger plants as it moves along the downward-sloping portion of the long-run average-total-cost curve. Likewise, a firm that is planning to reduce its output will eliminate some plant rather than keep production facilities operating at lower levels of output than they were designed for.

BOX 6.7   *Derivation of a Long-Run Average-Cost Curve*

A firm can build a plant of any size, and each possible plant size implies a different short-run average-total-cost curve. Here we have a large number of possible short-run average-cost curves, but even these curves are only a sample of all the possible curves. As the firm expands, in the long run, it moves from one curve to another, always choosing the size of plant that minimizes the average total cost for the output the firm plans to produce at any particular time. The path along which a firm will expand — the firm's long-run average-cost curve — is thus the "envelope" of all the possible short-run average-total-cost curves.

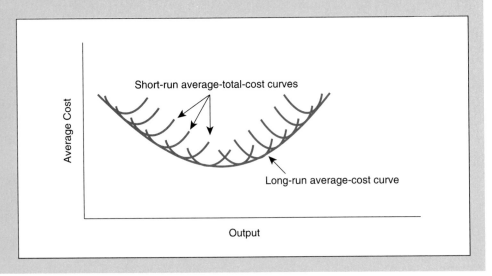

Economies of Scale

Economies of scale
A phenomenon said to occur whenever long-run average cost decreases as output increases.

Economists have developed some special terminology to describe what happens to long-run average costs as output increases. In any range of output where long-run average cost *decreases* as output increases, the firm for which the cost curves are drawn is said to experience **economies of scale**. In any range of output where long-run average cost *increases*, the firm is said to experience **diseconomies of scale**. Finally, if there is any range of output for which long-run average cost does not change as output changes, the firm is said to experience **constant returns to scale** in that range.

Diseconomies of scale
A phenomenon said to occur whenever long-run average cost increases as output increases.

The long-run average-cost curve in Box 6.7 is smoothly U-shaped, but that is not the only possible shape for such a curve. In fact, statistical studies suggest that L-shaped long-run average-cost curves are the rule, at least in many manufacturing industries. Such a curve appears in Box 6.8, which shows an initial range of economies of scale followed by a range of approximately constant returns to scale. The curve could turn out to be a flat-bottomed U if it were followed far enough (as the broken extension of the curve in Box 6.8 indicates). In any single industry, however, there may be no firms large enough to show diseconomies of scale. If there are none, that range of the curve remains invisible to statistical observation.

Constant returns to scale
A phenomenon said to occur when long-run average cost remains constant as output increases.

An L-shaped Average-Cost Curve Showing Minimum Efficient Scale

BOX 6.8

Statistical studies of long-run average cost suggest that long-run average-cost curves are often L-shaped, as shown here. The point at which economies of scale are exhausted and the curve begins to flatten out is called the minimum efficient scale for the firm. Probably, if a firm continued to expand without limit, long-run average costs would eventually begin to rise. However, in many industries, there are no firms operating at a sufficiently large scale to make the range of decreasing returns to scale visible to statistical observation. The upward-sloping portion of the curve is thus shown here as a broken line.

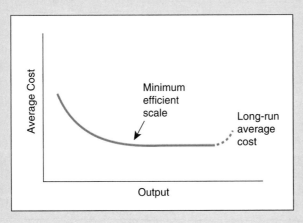

Statistical studies of long-run average cost often concentrate on measuring the level of output at which economies of scale are exhausted and constant returns to scale begin. This level is called the **minimum efficient scale** for the firm. As shown in Box 6.8, it corresponds to the point where the L-shaped long-run average-cost curve stops falling and begins to level out. If the cost curve does not have a sharp kink at this point — and there is no reason to think it must have — the minimum efficient scale can be identified only approximately. This is not a major problem, however, since statistical studies of cost must deal in approximations in any event.

Minimum efficient scale
The level of output at which economies of scale are exhausted.

Where do economies of scale come from? Why is it ever true that a large firm can produce at a lower unit cost than a smaller firm? Economists who have investigated these questions have found that there is no single source of economies of scale for all industries. Rather, there are a number of different sources, some of which are important in certain industries and others in other industries.

Sources of economies of scale

When most people think of economies of scale, what probably comes to mind first is an automobile assembly plant or a large steel mill. Costs per unit tend to decrease with the rate of output per plant per day in such industries as automobiles and steel for a number of reasons. One is that a metal-forming machine or a steel furnace capable of producing twice as much as a smaller or less powerful version usually costs less than twice as much to build. Another is that larger plants can take advantage of a more specialized division of labour. The automobile assembly line, on which each worker performs a single operation on each car as it moves by, is the classical example of this effect. Economies of scale associated with the rate of output per plant per day can be referred to as *plant-level* economies of scale.

Not all economies of scale are associated with increases in the rate of output of a single plant. Sometimes, for example, they have their origin in the total quantity of a product or model produced rather than in the rate at which it is produced. With a long production run, costs associated with product design, equipment set-up, and specialized training can be spread over a large number of units. A comparison of General Motors with Volkswagen can serve to illustrate the difference between economies of scale associated with the rate of production and those associated with the volume of production. General Motors achieves important economies of scale through a high rate of production but changes models frequently. Volkswagen, by comparison, produces fewer cars per year but keeps each model in production longer. Its famous Beetle, for example, was produced with minor variations for more than four decades.

In addition to the rate and volume of production at a single plant, attention must be given to economies of multiplant operation. The McDonald's hamburger chain provides a good example. The minimum efficient scale for a single plant (a single restaurant) is obviously very small in the fast-food industry. Nonetheless, McDonald's apparently realizes important economies by operating many restaurants as an integrated system. Some of the economies are production economies: individual food items and ingredients can be produced in efficient centralized kitchens, personnel can be trained at the famous "Hamburger University," and so on. A multiplant firm such as McDonald's also realizes significant economies of scale with such functions as finance, advertising, and marketing.

LOOKING AHEAD

This chapter has only scratched the surface of the theory of cost. Advanced books on the subject go into a wealth of extensions, additional details, mathematical formulations, and special cases. Nonetheless, the limited treatment given here will serve quite well as a basis for the analysis of individual firms and industries in the following chapters.

Chapter 7 will show how short-run and long-run cost curves can be used to derive supply curves for an industry in which there are a large number of competing firms. Chapter 8 will then use cost curves to analyze business behaviour in markets where a single firm has a monopoly. Chapter 9 will turn to the case of markets dominated not by a single firm but by a relatively small number of firms. At that point, the discussion will return to the theme of economies of scale, which are an important factor in determining the number of firms that exist in the market for a given product. Later chapters deal with public policies that may be necessary to counteract some negative results of certain types of market structures.

SUMMARY

1. *Explicit costs* of production take the form of payments to workers, suppliers, and other non-owners of the firm. *Implicit costs* are opportunity costs of using resources owned by the firm or contributed by its owners. Profit is often calculated by subtracting only explicit costs from revenue. This concept is called *accounting profit.* Economists use the term *profit* to mean revenue minus all costs, both implicit and explicit. This concept is called *pure economic profit.*

2. *Fixed inputs* are those that cannot be easily increased or decreased in a short time. They are linked with the size of the firm's plant. *Variable inputs* can be quickly and easily varied in order to increase or decrease output. Hourly labour, energy, and raw materials are variable inputs. The *short run* is a period within which only variable outputs can be adjusted. In the *long run,* changes can be made in fixed inputs, including plant size.

3. As the amount of one input to a production process is increased while the amounts of all other inputs remain fixed, output will increase, at least over some range. The amount of output added by each one-unit increase in the variable input is known as the *marginal physical product* of that input.

4. According to the *law of diminishing returns,* as the amount of one variable input used in a production process is increased (with the amounts of all other inputs remaining fixed), a point will be reached beyond which the amount of output added per unit of added variable input (that is, the marginal physical product of the variable input) will begin to decrease. This principle applies to all production processes.

5. A whole set of cost curves can be constructed for a firm, given data on its fixed and variable costs. The most commonly used cost curves are total cost, total fixed cost, total variable cost, average fixed cost, average variable cost, average total cost, average total cost, and *marginal cost.* Following the *marginal-average rule,* the marginal-cost curve cuts the average-variable-cost and average-total-cost curves at their lowest points.

6. In the long run, a firm can adjust the amounts of fixed inputs that it uses by expanding or reducing its plant. Each possible plant size has a U-shaped short-run average-total-cost curve. The firm's long-run average-cost curve is a shallower U-shaped curve based on a set of short-run curves.

7. When long-run average cost decreases as output increases, the firm is said to experience *economies of scale.* When long-run average cost increases as output increases, the firm is said to experience *diseconomies of scale.* If there are neither economies nor diseconomies of scale, the firm is said to experience *constant returns to scale.* The level of output at which economies of scale are exhausted and constant returns to scale begin is called the *minimum efficient scale.*

KEY TERMS

explicit costs
implicit costs
pure economic profit
accounting profit
fixed inputs
variable inputs

short run
long run
marginal physical product
law of diminishing returns
marginal cost

marginal-average rule
economies of scale
diseconomies of scale
constant returns to scale
minimum efficient scale

KEY BOXES

Box 6.2 Response of Output to Changes in One
         Variable Input
Box 6.3 Marginal Cost and Output with One
         Variable Input
Box 6.5 A Set of Short-Run Cost Curves

Box 6.6 Alternative Short-Run
         Average-Total-Cost Curves
Box 6.7 Derivation of a Long-Run
         Average-Cost Curve

REVIEW QUESTIONS

1. List the basic costs of owning and operating an automobile. Which are explicit costs? Which are implicit costs? Does driving an automobile create any opportunity costs for the economy as a whole that do not show up on your list as either implicit or explicit costs? If so, what are they?

2. Divide the costs of owning and operating an automobile into fixed and variable costs. Suppose you were deciding whether to drive to a football game at a nearby university or to take the bus instead. Would you take both fixed and variable costs into account? Suppose you were deciding which of two houses to buy — one in a neighbourhood where you could walk to work or one where you would have to buy a second car to drive to work every day. Would you then take both fixed and variable costs into account? Explain the difference between the two situations.

3. Do you think the business of running a university is subject to economies or diseconomies of scale? Which aspects of the university's operation (e.g., library, dormitories, faculty salaries, moving students between classes, and so on) are subject to economies of scale, diseconomies of scale, or constant returns to scale?

4. Take a piece of graph paper and draw a set of co-ordinate axes. Label the *x* axis "quantity of output" (0 to 20 units) and the *y* axis "cost" (0 to 20 units). Plot the following (*x*, *y*) points on your graph: (0, 4); (2, 6); (4, 7); (7, 8); (9, 9); (11, 11); (13, 14). Connect these points with a smooth curve and label it "total cost." Working from this curve, construct a total-fixed-cost curve and a total-variable-cost curve for the same firm.

5. On another piece of graph paper, draw a second set of co-ordinate axes. Label the horizontal axis "quantity" (0 to 20 units) and the vertical axis "cost per unit" (0 to 2 units, in tenths of a unit). Using the total-cost, total-variable-cost, and total-fixed-cost curves you drew for Question 4 as a basis, construct the following curves on your new graph: marginal cost, average total cost, average variable cost, and average fixed cost.

6. Turn to Box 6.7. Copy the diagram onto a sheet of graph paper, drawing the long-run average-total-cost curve and one of the short-run average-total-cost curves. Use the curves you have drawn to construct the matching long-run and short-run total-cost curves. The total-cost curves should both be reverse-S-shaped, and they should be tangent to each other at the same level of output for which the average-total-cost curves are tangent.

7. Suppose you look into the relationship between the amount of coal burned per week

in a certain power plant and the amount of electricity generated per week. You find the following: With tiny amounts of coal, not even enough to bring the boiler up to the temperature needed to make steam, no electricity can be produced. After a certain minimum amount of coal is burned, the plant begins to operate. From that point on, the added amount of electricity generated with each additional tonne of coal burned is constant over a wide range. Then a ceiling is reached beyond which burning more coal produces no more electricity at all. Sketch the total-physical-product curve for this plant, and draw a graph showing how marginal physical product varies as output varies. Does this production process obey the law of diminishing returns?

8. It has been said that if it were not for the law of diminishing returns, all the food that the world needs could be grown in a flowerpot. Discuss this statement. (*Suggestion*: Think of land as the only fixed factor and fertilizer as the only variable factor. How much food could be grown in the flowerpot if the marginal physical product of fertilizer were constant regardless of the amount of fertilizer used per unit of land?)

9. **Case for Discussion**
The early 1980s were hard times for the tractor industry. Farm incomes were low and farmers were burdened with debt, marking it hard for them to buy new equipment. By 1984, output had fallen to a third of the peak level reached in 1979.

The tractor market was expected to improve somewhat in the later 1980s, but most observers thought the 1979 sales peak would not be reached again any time soon. This forecast caused the leading tractor manufacturers to scramble to cut their losses. Plant closings were a major factor in the strategies of most firms. Massey-Ferguson had built $700 million worth of new plant. After 1980, half of the firm's total plant was scrapped or sold. Ford closed its European headquarters and began to assemble tractors at fewer locations. Even John Deere, the strongest firm in the market, was forced to close a combine plant. J.I. Case, the fifth-largest tractor maker, was reported to be thinking of leaving the industry altogether.

Questions:
a. Faced with the prospect of a permanent drop in sales, why would a tractor firm shut down some plants rather than keep all of its plants running at reduced levels of output? Would the firm react in the same way to a temporary drop in sales? Why or why not?
b. The tractor slump is forcing all firms to cut back their level of operations. Why might this situation force Case, the smallest of the major tractor makers, out of the business entirely? Suggest an explanation that makes use of cost theory.

10. a. Fill in the missing cost figures for the firm represented in the table below.
b. Using the cost data in the completed table, graph the firm's cost curves. At what dollar value does the marginal-cost curve cut the average-variable-cost curve? At what dollar value does it cut the average-total-cost curve?

Quantity of Output	Fixed Cost	Variable Cost	Total Cost	Marginal Cost	Average Fixed Cost	Average Variable Cost	Average Total Cost
0	_____	0	100	_____	_____	_____	_____
1	_____	_____	_____	_____	_____	90	_____
2	_____	170	_____	_____	_____	_____	_____
3	_____	_____	_____	70	_____	_____	_____
4	_____	_____	_____	_____	_____	_____	100
5	_____	_____	470	_____	_____	_____	_____
6	_____	450	_____	_____	_____	_____	_____
7	_____	_____	_____	90	_____	_____	_____
8	_____	_____	750	_____	_____	_____	_____
9	_____	_____	_____	_____	_____	86.67	_____
10	_____	_____	_____	_____	_____	_____	103

11. Explain why it is always the case that the marginal-cost curve cuts the average-variable-cost and the average-total-cost curves at their minimum point.

12. Firms make adjustments in their production decisions for either the long run or the short run. Which of the following are long-run adjustments and which are short-run?

    a. Eaton's hires 25 part-time employees for the December holiday season.

    b. Air Canada decides to buy six more passenger planes.

    c. A market gardener increases the amount of organic fertilizer on her tomato crop.

    d. A bank pays tuition and expenses for two employees who are enrolling in a two-year training program.

    e. A firm signs a contract with a builder to add an additional 3000 m² to its factory.

13. A jeweller who has been earning $30 000 a year working for a large firm decides to open his own business. He uses some retail space that he already owns but that he had been renting out for $1000 a month. To start the business, he uses $5000 of his own money and borrows another $5000 from the bank at an interest rate of 10 percent per year. Two employees are hired for the store, and each is paid an annual salary of $20 000. Utilities cost $2000 for the year, and advertising in the local paper costs $1800. The cost of supplies and merchandise to sell in the store is $35 000. During his first year in business, the jeweller takes in total revenues of $98 000.

    a. What are the implicit and explicit costs for this business in its first year of operation?

    b. Is this business making an accounting profit? Is it making a pure economic profit? Show your calculations.

14. In February 1991, "General Motors announced a program involving a capital-spending cut of $500 million (U.S.) a year during 1991–94 and a 47 percent reduction in its annual dividend. The program involved a 15 percent cut in [the number of white-collar workers employed in the United States and Canada] by the end of 1993. The company had one of its worst years in 1990 because of slumping car and truck sales" (*Globe and Mail*, February 21, 1991, p. B6). Draw two graphs, one with hypothetical average- and marginal-cost curves for GM and one with hypothetical total-cost curves. Sketch probable changes in the cost curves resulting from GM's announced cost cuts. Classify each of the proposed cuts by type of cost — fixed or variable — before you start to sketch your graphs.

Cost and Output with Two Variable Inputs

In this chapter, we looked at the relationship between cost and output when just one input is varied, with all other inputs remaining constant. In this appendix, we will extend the theory of cost to the case in which more than one input is varied.

Substitution of Inputs

The main new feature of situations in which more than one input is varied is the possibility of substituting one input for another. Consider the case of Leo Lewchuk, a farmer who makes his living growing corn. Lewchuk spends all his time working on his farm and does not hire anyone to help him. The amount of labour used in growing corn is, for him, a fixed input. In addition to fixed amounts of labour and machinery, he uses two variable inputs: land, which he rents, and fertilizer, which he buys.

Lewchuk can grow any given quantity of corn — say, 200 bushels — in many different ways. Some of the possibilities are shown in Box 6A.1. One way to grow 200 bushels of corn is to use 2.5 tonnes of fertilizer and 10 hectares of land. This is represented by point P on the graph. If Lewchuk wants to grow the same amount of corn on less land, he can substitute fertilizer for land. For example, at point Q, he can grow 200 bushels of corn on 5 hectares by using 5 tonnes of fertilizer. By substituting still more fertilizer for land, he can move to point R, where the 200 bushels are grown on just 2.5 hectares, using 10 tonnes of fertilizer.

Diminishing Returns in Substitution

In the chapter, we defined the law of diminishing returns as it applies to a situation in which one input is varied while all others remain constant. In that situation, after a certain point, the amount of the variable input needed to make an extra unit of output increases. (This is another way of saying that the marginal physical product of the variable input decreases.) A similar principle applies when one input is substituted for another in such a way that output is kept at a constant level: As the amount of input x is increased, the amount of x needed to replace one unit of y increases.

The example in Box 6A.1 illustrates this principle. In moving from point P to point Q, 2.5 tonnes of fertilizer replace 5 hectares of land, while output stays constant at 200 bushels. But in moving from point Q to point R, 5 more tonnes of fertilizer are needed to replace just 2.5 hectares of land.

As a result of the law of diminishing returns in substituting one input for another, the line connecting points P, Q, and R becomes flatter as one moves downward and to the right along it. This reflects the decreasing ratio of the marginal physical product of fertilizer to the marginal physical product of land as more fertilizer is substituted for land.

177

BOX 6A.1   An Isoquant

This graph shows an isoquant for the production of 200 bushels of corn. The variable inputs are land and fertilizer. The other inputs, labour and machinery, are assumed to be fixed. Points *P*, *Q*, and *R* represent various ways of growing the given quantity of corn. A movement downward along the isoquant represents the substitution of fertilizer for land while output is maintained at 200 bushels per year. As more and more fertilizer is substituted for land, the isoquant becomes flatter because of diminishing returns.

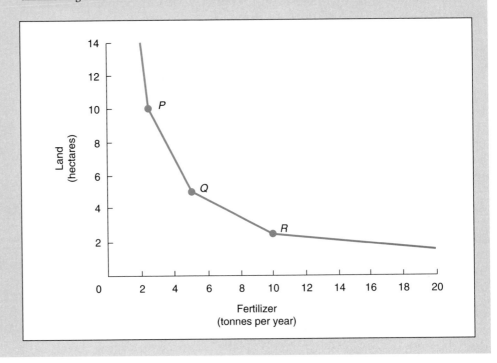

Choosing the Least-Cost Method of Production

An isoquant
A line showing the various combinations of variable inputs that can be used to produce a given amount of output.

The line connecting points *P*, *Q*, and *R* in Box 6A.1 is called an **isoquant**. The prefix *iso* comes from a Greek word meaning "equal," and an isoquant shows the various combinations of inputs that can be used to produce a given — or "equal" — amount of output. But while all the points on the isoquant are equal in terms of output, they are not equal in terms of cost. To see how a producer can choose the least-cost method of producing a given level of output, we need to know the prices of the inputs.

In the appendix to Chapter 5, we used budget lines to give a graphic picture of the prices of consumer goods. As Box 6A.2 shows, the same technique can be used to represent the prices of inputs. The graph assumes a cost of $50 a tonne for fertilizer and a rental price of $50 per hectare per year for land. The sum of $400 can buy 8 tonnes of fertilizer and no land, 8 hectares of land and no fertilizer, or

Finding the Least-Cost Method of Production

This graph shows how the least-cost method of production can be found from among the points on an isoquant, given the prices of the variable inputs. Here, the price of fertilizer is assumed to be $50 a tonne and the rental price of land $50 per year. A set of budget lines is drawn to represent various levels of spending on inputs. Line *A*, which corresponds to a total variable cost of $400, does not provide enough inputs to produce 200 bushels of corn. Line *C*, which corresponds to a total variable cost of $625, provides enough inputs to grow 200 bushels of corn using methods *P* or *R*. Line *B*, which corresponds to a total variable cost of $500, permits the 200 bushels to be grown using method *Q*, which is the least-cost method given these input prices.

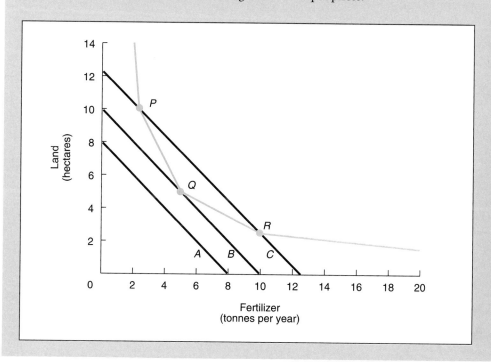

any of the other points on line *A*. The sum of $500 will buy 10 tonnes of fertilizer, 10 hectares of land, or any of the other points on line *B*, and so on.

When the isoquant for 200 bushels of corn is drawn on top of a set of budget lines for the inputs, it is easy to see the least-cost method of producing that level of output. It is the method that uses 5 tonnes of fertilizer and 5 hectares of land. This corresponds to point *Q* on the graph, where the isoquant just touches budget line *B*. Points *P* and *R* are possible ways of growing 200 bushels of corn, but they lie on budget line *C*, which corresponds to a cost of $625. And a budget of less than $500 (say, $400, as shown by budget line *A*) is not enough to reach the 200-bushel isoquant no matter how it is split between fertilizer and land.

The Response to Changes in Input Prices

If input prices change, the least-cost combination of inputs is also likely to change. Suppose that the suburbs begin to expand in the direction of Farmer Lewchuk's farm, driving up the price of land. Now land that used to rent for $50 per hectare per year rents for $200 per hectare. The price of fertilizer remains unchanged at $50 a tonne.

The results of the increase in the price of land are shown in Box 6A.3. Now $500 will not be enough to buy the combinations of inputs that fall along budget line B. Even if all of the money were spent on land, only 2.5 hectares could be rented. The new $500 budget line is D, which does not reach the 200-bushel isoquant at any point.

To grow 200 bushels, Lewchuk must now spend more than $500. As he increases his budget for land and fertilizer, the budget line shifts upward but stays

BOX 6A.3 Effects of a Change in Input Prices

If the rental price of land increases from $50 to $200 per hectare per year while the price of fertilizer remains fixed at $50 a tonne, 200 bushels of corn can no longer be produced for $500. The $500 budget line shifts from position B to position D, and it now falls short of the 200-bushel isoquant. Increasing the amount spent on variable inputs to $1000 shifts the budget line up to position F, where it just touches the isoquant at point R. The increase in the price of land thus not only raises the total variable cost of growing 200 bushels of corn but also causes fertilizer to be substituted for land, which is now relatively more costly.

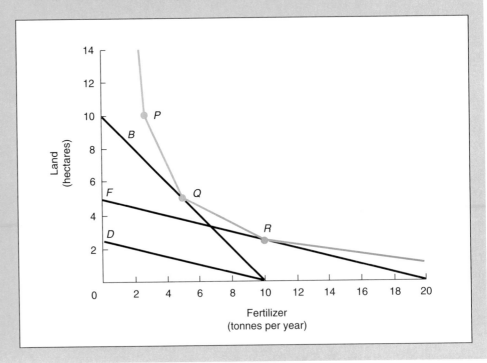

parallel to line *D*. When the budget line reaches *F*, which corresponds to spending $1000 on inputs, it just touches the isoquant at *R*. We see, then, that $1000 is the lowest cost at which 200 bushels of corn can be grown, given a price of $50 a tonne for fertilizer and $200 per hectare for land. At those prices, *R* is the least-cost combination of inputs.

The effect of an increase in the price of an input in this case is typical. Less of the input whose price has gone up is used, and the other input, which has become relatively less costly, is substituted for it.

Varying Output

The isoquant technique can also be used to analyze variations in output with two variable inputs. Turn to Box 6A.4. Part (a) of that box shows an isoquant "map" on which three sets of points have been drawn that correspond to three levels of output. As before, *P*, *Q*, and *R* represent three ways of growing 200 bushels of corn. Points *S*, *T*, and *U* represent three ways of growing 100 bushels, and points *V*, *W*, and *X* are three ways of growing 300 bushels. An isoquant has been drawn through each of these sets of points.

In this box, we return to the assumption that land costs $50 per hectare and fertilizer $50 a tonne. Using these prices, a set of three budget lines has been drawn, each of which corresponds to a different total variable cost — $300, $500, and $1000.

As the graph clearly shows, there is a least-cost method for producing each level of output, given these prices. Point *T* is the best way of producing 100 bushels; *Q* is best for 200 bushels; and *W* is best for 300 bushels. Other levels of output would also be possible. These would lie along the line drawn from the origin through points *T*, *Q*, and *W*. This is called the firm's *expansion path*. As the firm moves along its expansion path, more of both the variable inputs, land and fertilizer, is used. Meanwhile, the fixed inputs — labour and machinery, in Lewchuk's case — remain constant.

Deriving a Cost Curve from the Isoquant Map

Once the expansion path has been identified, it is easy to construct a total-variable-cost curve. All we need to do is construct a graph that links each of the points on the expansion path with the variable-cost level of the corresponding budget line. This is done in part (b) of Box 6A.4. At the origin, output is zero and total variable cost is zero. At point *T*, output is 100 bushels and total variable cost is $300. At *Q*, we have 200 bushels and $500; and at *W*, 300 bushels and $1000. Plotting these points and connecting them gives the firm's total-variable-cost curve.

Note that this curve has the same reverse-S shape as do the total-cost curves for Fieldcom Inc. shown in the chapter (see Boxes 6.4 and 6.5). This shape is a result of the law of diminishing returns, applied to the case in which two inputs vary while all others remain fixed. Beyond point *Q*, the amounts of inputs needed to produce each additional unit of output begin to rise, just as they did when only one input was allowed to vary. Only if all inputs are allowed to vary and none remains fixed can a firm escape the effects of the law of diminishing returns.

BOX 6A.4 Expansion of Output and Total Variable Costs

Part (a) of this box shows three isoquants for the production of corn, corresponding to outputs of 100, 200, and 300 bushels. Assuming input prices of $50 per hectare for land and $50 a tonne for fertilizer, budget lines can be drawn to show the minimum total variable cost for each level of output. As output expands, the firm will move from T to Q and then to W along the expansion path. Part (b) of the box plots the amount of output and the total variable cost for each of these points. The result is a reverse-S-shaped total-variable-cost curve that shows the effects of diminishing returns for levels of output above 200 bushels per year.

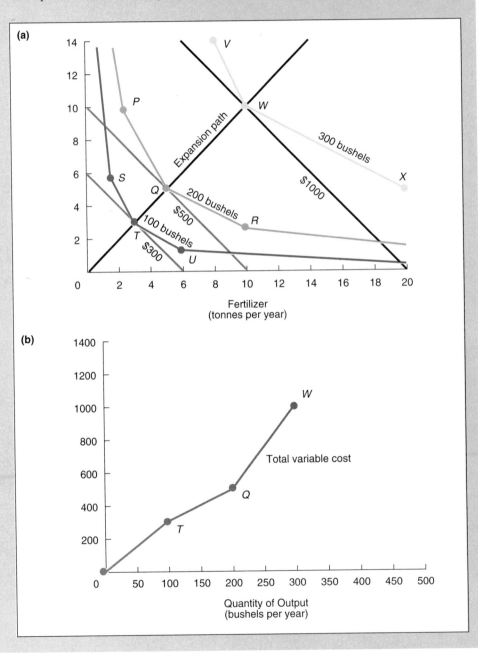

KEY TERM

an isoquant

KEY BOXES

Box 6A.1 An Isoquant

Box 6A.2 Finding the Least-Cost Method
of Production

Setting Price and Output under Perfect Competition

WHAT YOU WILL LEARN IN THIS CHAPTER

After studying this chapter, you will be able to

1. Describe the market structure of perfect competition.

2. Show how the profit-maximizing output for a perfectly competitive firm is determined in the short run.

3. Explain the conditions under which a perfectly competitive firm will stay open or shut down in order to cut its losses.

4. Draw a supply curve for a perfectly competitive firm, given its cost curves.

5. List the conditions for long-run equilibrium for a perfectly competitive firm.

6. Show how a perfectly competitive industry adjusts to long-run changes in demand.

7. Explain what is "perfect" about perfect competition.

185

A Preview   *The Perils of Competition*

Our economy is based on competition. One often hears businesspeople boast that they thrive on competition — they love to "fight it out" with their business rivals. But competition may eliminate the chance to make above-average profits, as the Martins discovered, and is therefore an unpleasant experience for businesses.

The Martins Face Reality

When Ralph and Andrea Martin started Fieldcom Inc., they thought they had the world by the tail. They believed that their rugged portable computer, the first one that was designed for use under hot and dusty field conditions, would be a sure source of profits. With only a small investment, they quickly got their firm off the ground and their computer into production.

Then came the competition. What the Martins hadn't taken into account was that the very factors that made the portable-computer market easy for them to enter would make it easy for everyone else to enter too. As soon as their machine proved that there was a market for rugged portable computers, copies sprang up on all sides. Makers of office-type portable computers beefed up their carrying cases and shock-mounted their components. Other start-up firms brought out machines that, from the user's point of view, were just as good as Fieldcom's. Equipment-supply dealers contracted little-known electronics firms in the Far East to produce rugged portable computers to be sold under the dealers' own brand names.

Within a year, there were many similar products available, none of which was able to capture a dominant share of the growing market. The pressure to trim prices was relentless. At the end of two years in business, the Martins were working hard and earning almost no profit, if the full opportunity costs of their firm were taken into account.

THE STRUCTURE OF PERFECT COMPETITION

In Chapter 6, we looked at Fieldcom by itself, but firms such as the Martins' do not operate alone in the real world. They face competition. Competition may take the form of a struggle between giants such as General Motors and Honda for domination of a market. Or it may take the form of advertising campaigns by rivals trying to woo fickle consumers. Sometimes it takes the form of rapid expansion in the number of available brands and styles, as often happens in the markets for breakfast cereal or clothing.

In the next few chapters, we will look at all of these kinds of competition, but here we will deal with a simpler case. This is the type of competition faced by Fieldcom, in which many small firms with similar products share a market that is easy to enter and easy to leave. This is the case that economists call *perfect competition.*

Let's begin with a more formal definition of perfect competition. Economists classify types of competition by the structure of the markets in which firms operate. **Market structure** in this sense means such factors as the number of firms in each industry, the extent to which the products of those firms differ, and the ease or difficulty of getting into and out of the market.

As a market structure, **perfect competition**, the subject of this chapter, has four defining features.

1. There are many buyers and sellers, each of whom buys or sells only a small fraction of all that is bought and sold in the market.

2. The product traded in the market is *homogeneous*; that is, the product sold by one firm is just like the product sold by any other.

3. All participants in the market, buyers and sellers alike, are well informed about prices, sources of supply, and so on.

4. Entry into and exit from the market are very easy.

Market structure
The key traits of a market, including the number of firms in each industry, the extent to which the products of different firms are different or similar, and the ease of entry into and exit from the market.

Perfect competition
A market structure characterized by a large number of relatively small firms, a homogeneous product, good distribution of information among all market participants, and freedom of entry and exit.

The Demand Curve of the Perfectly Competitive Firm

These four characteristics of perfect competition, taken together, ensure that all firms in the market will be **price takers** — firms that sell their outputs at fixed prices determined entirely by forces beyond their control. If a firm makes, say, steel nails, and steel nails sell for $1.50 per kilogram, that is that. The firm makes all its decisions and all its plans as if nothing it can do will change the $1.50 price tag.

It is easy to understand why firms operating in a perfectly competitive market are price takers. Because each producer contributes only a small fraction of the total output, its individual supply decisions will have no significant effect on the total quantity supplied in the market — and thus no significant effect on the market price as determined by supply and demand. Because the product is homogeneous, buyers are just as happy to buy from one firm as from another. Thus, a firm that raised its price even a fraction above what its competitors were charging would quickly lose all its customers. And because all buyers and sellers are well informed, no one would, out of ignorance, be willing to pay or attempt to get a price higher than the prevailing one.

Price taker
A firm that sells its outputs at fixed prices that are determined entirely by forces beyond its control.

Horizontal demand curve
The demand curve of a perfectly competitive firm, which can sell no output above the given market price and cannot increase sales by lowering its price.

This situation creates a unique demand curve for a perfectly competitive firm — a **horizontal demand curve** (a demand curve that is perfectly elastic). Each firm can sell whatever it produces at the going market price. At a higher price, it will be unable to sell any output at all, and lowering the price will not allow it to sell greater quantities of output. Each firm's demand curve is therefore a horizontal line at the level of the market price.

Under perfect competition, then, the decisions facing individual firms are very simple. The firm does not have to decide at what price to sell because price is completely beyond its control. It does not have to worry about product design or marketing decisions because, by definition, the product is the same for all firms and never changes. The only decision the firm needs to make is about quantity — how much to produce.

Perfect Competition: The Ideal and the Reality

Perfect competition, as defined here, is an abstraction, or an ideal. Economists study it because it is a theoretically interesting benchmark, useful in evaluating the performance of real-world industries. No industry meets all the conditions of perfect competition in every detail. Agriculture is often considered to come close, because it involves thousands of independent producers of almost completely undifferentiated products. However, farmers have reduced the competitiveness of their industry through the creation of marketing boards.

Before continuing further, we must take note of a paradox associated with perfect competition — that is, that perfect competition, as defined, is in many respects the exact opposite of competition as many people think of it in everyday business life. When we think of business competition, we ordinarily think of rivalry and struggle. We think of Pepsi and Coke battling for shares of the market. We think of advertising people talking up one product and putting down another. We think of Kodak working in secrecy to build an instant camera as good as Polaroid's.

Perfect competition, though, is none of these things. In a perfectly competitive market, there is no reason to battle for market share because there is plenty of room for each small firm to sell as much as it wants at the going price. There is no advertising in such a market, because buyers are already well informed, and goods are perfectly homogeneous — not only in fact but in the eyes of their consumers as well. There is no need for secrecy about techniques or innovations, because all technical knowledge is widespread and there are no innovations. The market environment is still competitive in the sense that any firm that fails to make its cost and supply decisions as accurately as its rivals may be forced out of the market. Firms are not sheltered from that kind of competition by any special privileges. Nonetheless, many of the more colourful or more personalized aspects of competition are absent. Much more will be said about the relationship of "perfect" competition to real-world competition in the next few chapters.

SHORT-RUN SUPPLY UNDER PERFECT COMPETITION
Short-Run Profit Maximization for a Typical Firm

Now that the concept of perfect competition has been introduced, it is time to turn to the main subject of the chapter — what lies behind the supply curve in a perfectly competitive market. The investigation will begin at the level of the individual firm, using Fieldcom as a typical example. The discussion will assume throughout that this firm and all others in the market make their production decisions with the object of earning maximum economic profits for the firms' owners, given prevailing prices of inputs and outputs and the production technology available. If prevailing market conditions make it impossible to earn positive economic profits, the firms will try to minimize losses.

A simple numerical example will show how a perfectly competitive firm adjusts the quantity of output it supplies in order to maximize profits. Box 7.1(a) shows short-run cost data for Fieldcom (as first given in Chapter 6). It also shows the revenue earned by Fieldcom from the sale of each quantity of output, assuming a constant price of $500 per unit. The price per unit does not vary as output per day varies because it is assumed, for the sake of discussion, that the computer produced by Fieldcom is essentially the same as that produced by a large number of other companies in this perfectly competitive market. The company is thus a price taker.

Subtracting total cost in column 3 from total revenue in column 2 gives the total profit the firm earns at each level of output. At a production level between eight and nine units a day, the firm reaches a break-even point, where there are neither losses nor profits. The maximum profit (since the costs of the firm include a "normal" return on invested capital, "normal" profits would be realized at the break-even point) is reached at nineteen units per day, where $2000 profit per day is earned. Nineteen units per day is thus the quantity the firm will choose to supply at the price of $500 per unit, assuming that it wants to earn the maximum profit.

This profit-maximizing quantity of output is also identified graphically in Box 7.1(b). In that diagram, the firm's total profit is indicated by the vertical distance between the total-revenue and total-cost curves. As shown, that distance is greatest at nineteen units of output.

A marginal approach

As an alternative to comparing total cost and total revenue, a marginal approach can be used to determine the profit-maximizing level of output for the competitive firm. Turn first to columns 5 and 6 of Box 7.1(a). Column 5 gives data on marginal cost. As in Chapter 6, these data are printed between the rows of entries in the first four columns to indicate that marginal cost is the *change in cost* as output moves from one level to another. Column 6 presents a new concept — marginal revenue. **Marginal revenue** is the amount by which total revenue increases when output increases by one unit. For a firm that is a price taker, as this one is, marginal revenue is equal to the price of the product. Each extra unit of output sold by Fieldcom thus adds $500 to total revenue. In Box 7.1(b), the marginal-revenue line, or the price line, is also the demand curve for the firm. It is a horizontal line at the level of the market price — $500.

As we can see from the table in Box 7.1, every unit increase in output at Fieldcom adds to both total cost and total revenue. If the increase in revenue exceeds the increase in cost (that is, if marginal revenue is greater than marginal cost), increasing output by one unit increases total profit. If the increase in cost exceeds the increase in revenue (that is, if marginal cost is greater than marginal revenue), increasing output by one unit reduces profit. It follows that, in order to maximize profit, a competitive firm should expand output as long as marginal revenue exceeds marginal cost. It should stop as soon as marginal cost begins to exceed marginal revenue. A comparison of columns 5 and 6 of Box 7.1 shows

Marginal revenue
The amount by which total revenue increases as the result of a one-unit increase in quantity.

BOX 7.1   Short-Run Profit Maximization under Perfect Competition

This box shows the profit-maximizing quantity of output chosen by a perfectly competitive firm, Fieldcom. This level of output can be found by comparing total cost and total revenue in columns 2 and 3 of part (a). This approach is shown graphically in part (b), where total profit appears as the gap between the total-revenue and total-cost curves. Alternatively, the profit-maximizing output can be found by comparing marginal cost and marginal revenue in columns 5 and 6 of part (a). Profit increases up to the point where marginal cost begins to exceed marginal revenue, and it declines thereafter. Part (c) of the box gives a graphic representation of the marginal approach. Whatever approach is used, the break-even point, where there are no profits and no losses, occurs between eight and nine units per day, the profit-maximizing output is nineteen units per day, and the maximum profit per day is $2000.

(a)

Quantity of Output (1)	Total Revenue (2)	Total Cost (3)	Total Profit (2) − (3) (4)	Marginal Cost (5)	Marginal Revenue (6)
0	$ 0	$ 2 000	$ −2000	—	—
1	500	2 380	−1880	$340	$500
2	1 000	2 720	−1720	305	500
3	1 500	3 025	−1525	275	500
4	2 000	3 300	−1300	250	500
5	2 500	3 550	−1050	230	500
6	3 000	3 780	−780	215	500
7	3 500	3 995	−495	205	500
8	4 000	4 200	−200	200	500
9	4 500	4 400	100	205	500
10	5 000	4 605	395	215	500
11	5 500	4 820	680	230	500
12	6 000	5 050	950	250	500
13	6 500	5 300	1200	275	500
14	7 000	5 575	1425	305	500
15	7 500	5 880	1620	340	500
16	8 000	6 220	1780	380	500
17	8 500	6 600	1900	425	500
18	9 000	7 025	1975	475	500
19	9 500	7 500	2000	530	500
20	10 000	8 030	1970	590	500
21	10 500	8 620	1880	655	500
22	11 000	9 275	1725	725	500
23	11 500	10 000	1500	800	500
24	12 000	10 800	1200		

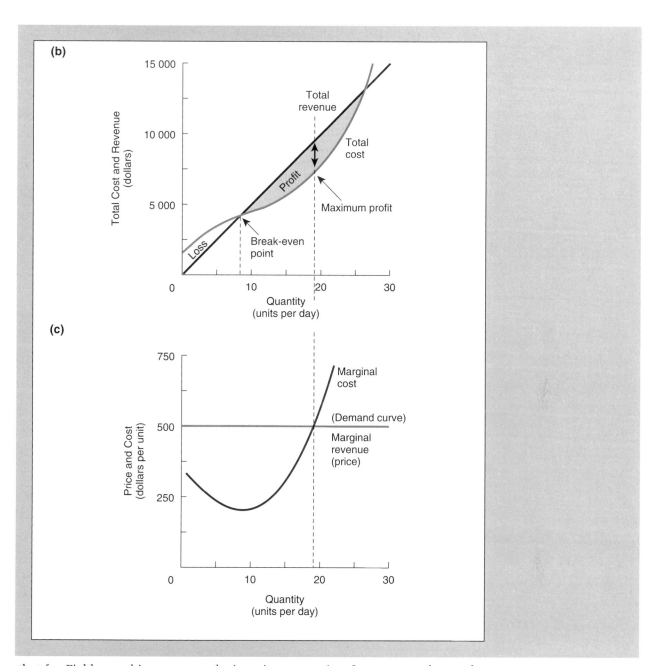

that for Fieldcom, this means producing nineteen units of output per day — the same number that are arrived at through a comparison of total cost and total revenue.

The marginal approach to short-run profit maximization is represented graphically in Box 7.1(c). Up to nineteen units of output, the marginal-cost curve lies below the marginal-revenue curve, so that each added unit of output increases profit. Beyond nineteen units, the marginal-cost curve is above the marginal-revenue curve, so that each added unit of output reduces profit. Note that the point of profit maximization, where the marginal-cost and marginal-revenue curves intersect, corresponds exactly to the point in part (b) where the spread between total revenue and total cost is greatest.

Minimizing short-run losses

In the example just given, Fieldcom was able to make a comfortable profit at the prevailing market price of $500 per unit. But market conditions need not always be so favourable. Suppose, for example, that the market price dropped to $300. The firm, being a price taker, could do nothing about the price and would simply have to adjust its quantity of output as best it could to meet the new situation. The necessary adjustments can be determined from the table and graphs of Box 7.2. The table shows that there is no level of output at which the firm can earn a profit. *Unable to earn a profit, the firm must turn its attention to minimizing losses.* With a price of $300 per unit, the minimum loss occurs at fourteen units of output. As in the previous case, this is the level of output beyond which marginal cost begins to exceed the price of the product.

BOX 7.2   *Short-Run Loss Minimization under Perfect Competition*

If the product price is too low for the firm to earn a profit, the firm must turn its attention to minimizing losses. The same techniques illustrated in Box 7.1 can be used to find the loss-minimizing level of output, which is fourteen units of output for a price of $300 per unit, as shown here. Part (c) of the box shows that the marginal-revenue curve intersects the marginal-cost curve at a point higher than average variable cost but lower than average total cost. Thus, each of the fourteen units sold at $300 earns more than its share of average variable cost but not enough to pay its share of average fixed cost.

(a)

Quantity of Output (1)	Total Revenue (2)	Total Cost (3)	Total Profit or Loss (4)	Average Total Cost (5)	Average Variable Cost (6)	Marginal Cost (7)	Marginal Revenue (8)
0	$ 0	$2000	$ −2000	—	—		
						$380	$300
1	300	2380	−2080	$2380	$380		
						340	300
2	600	2720	−2120	1360	360		
						305	300
3	900	3025	−2125	1009	342		
						275	300
4	1200	3300	−2100	825	325		
						250	300
5	1500	3550	−2050	710	310		
						230	300
6	1800	3780	−1980	629	296		
						215	300
7	2100	3995	−1895	571	285		
						205	300
8	2400	4200	−1800	525	275		
						200	300
9	2700	4400	−1700	488	266		
						205	500
10	3000	4605	−1605	460	260		
						215	300
11	3300	4820	−1520	437	256		
						230	300
12	3600	5050	−1450	421	254		
						250	300
13	3900	5300	−1400	408	254		
						275	300
14	4200	5575	−1375	398	255		
						305	300
15	4500	5880	−1380	392	259		
						340	300
16	4800	6220	−1420	389	264		
						380	300
17	5100	6600	−1500	389	271		

The two graphs in Box 7.2 give additional insight into the loss-minimizing supply decision under the given market conditions. Box 7.2(b) shows clearly why the firm cannot earn a profit: the total-cost curve is higher than the total-revenue curve at every unit of output. Nonetheless, total revenues come closest to meeting total costs at fourteen units of output.

Box 7.2(c) is perhaps the most helpful of all for understanding why it is worthwhile for the firm to produce fourteen units of output even though it loses money by doing so. In addition to the marginal-cost and marginal-revenue curves, it shows average-variable-cost and average-total-cost curves. Notice that

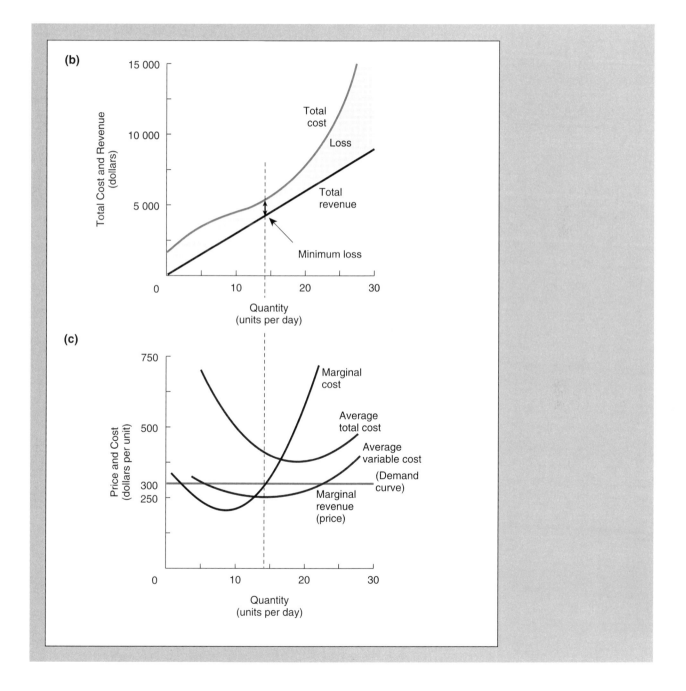

the point where marginal cost is equal to price lies between the two average-cost curves. The vertical distance between the average-variable-cost and average-total-cost curves is equal to average fixed costs. Thus, at fourteen units of output, the price of $300 is more than enough to cover each unit's share of variable costs but not quite enough to cover each unit's share of fixed costs.

The firm's loss-minimizing decision corresponds to simple common sense. Assume that the only variable input for Fieldcom is labour, and substitute the term *payroll* for the term *variable cost*. Similarly, assume that the firm's only fixed input is its factory building, and substitute *mortgage payment* for *fixed costs*. Clearly, with a price of $300, the firm is better off producing fourteen units of output than no units of output, because each unit more than pays for its share of the payroll and makes at least some contribution toward paying the mortgage.

BOX 7.3 Shutting Down to Minimize Short-Run Losses

Sometimes the price of a firm's output may drop so low that the firm must shut down altogether to minimize short-run losses. That possibility is illustrated here, at the price of $225 per unit. Notice that eleven units of output yield a smaller loss ($2345 per day) than any slightly greater or smaller output. However, the loss can be reduced to just $2000 per day if the firm shuts down. Notice also that in part (c) of the box, the marginal-cost curve intersects the marginal-revenue curve at a point below minimum average variable cost. That is the signal to shut down.

(a)

Quantity of Output (1)	Total Revenue (2)	Total Cost (3)	Total Profit or Loss (4)	Average Total Cost (5)	Average Variable Cost (6)	Marginal Cost (7)	Marginal Revenue (8)
0	$ 0	$2000	$ −2000	—	—		
						$380	$225
1	225	2380	−2155	$2380	$380		
						340	225
2	450	2720	−2270	1360	360		
						305	225
3	675	3025	−2350	1009	342		
						275	225
4	900	3300	−2400	825	325		
						250	225
5	1125	3550	−2425	710	310		
						230	225
6	1350	3780	−2430	629	296		
						215	225
7	1575	3995	−2420	571	285		
						205	225
8	1800	4200	−2400	525	275		
						200	225
9	2025	4400	−2375	488	266		
						205	225
10	2250	4605	−2355	460	260		
						215	225
11	2475	4820	−2345	437	256		
						230	225
12	2700	5050	−2350	421	254		
						250	225
13	2925	5300	−2375	408	254		
						275	225
14	3150	5575	−2425	398	255		
						305	225
15	3375	5880	−2505	392	259		
						340	225
16	3600	6220	−2620	389	264		
						380	225
17	3825	6600	−2775	389	271		

Shutting down to minimize short-run losses

What would happen if the price dropped even lower? Would it always be worth while for the firm to keep grinding out computers even though it was losing money? The answer, as shown in Box 7.3, is no.

Box 7.3 is based on an assumed price of $225 per unit. The table in part (a) shows that there is no way for the firm to make a profit with the price so low. Any supply decision will produce a loss. But this time, the loss can be minimized at a zero level of output. The best thing for the firm to do in the short run is to

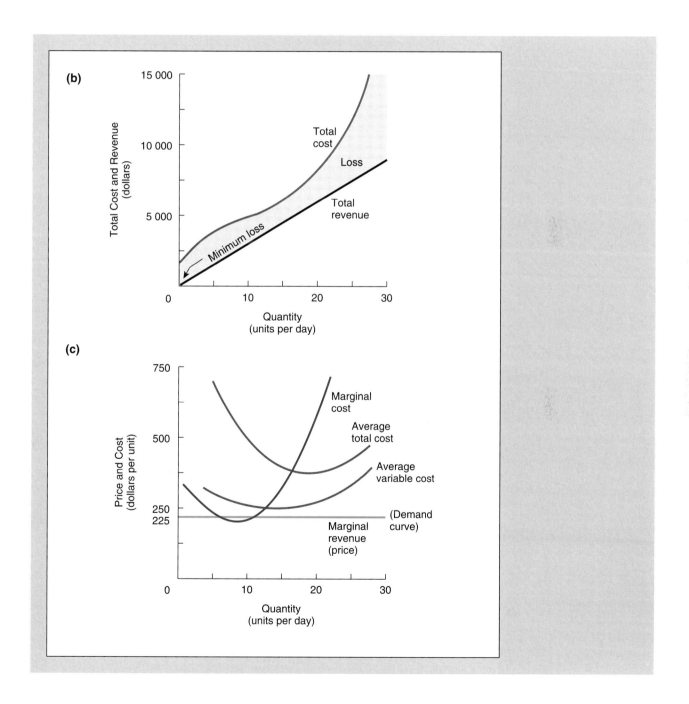

shut down. If things get better and the price rises again, the firm can restart production. If things never do get better, then, in the long run, the firm will have to wind up its affairs and go out of business altogether.

Notice that in this case it can be misleading to look only at the marginal-revenue and marginal-cost columns of the table. After seven units of output, marginal cost drops below the price of $225 and stays below until an output of eleven units is reached. *If* the firm were to stay in production, eleven units of output would give it a slightly smaller loss than would any slightly greater or smaller level of output. But in this case, the firm takes a still smaller loss by not producing at all.

As in the previous examples, the graphs tell the same story as the table. Box 7.3(b) shows once again that the total-revenue curve never reaches the total-cost curve. It comes fairly close at eleven units of output but not as close as it comes at zero output.

Box 7.3(c) shows that marginal cost and price are equal at eleven units of output. However, even at eleven units, the price does not cover average variable cost. Losses are minimized by shutting down. Once again, it may help to put the problem in terms of payroll and mortgage. If the firm produced eleven computers a day and could sell them only at $225 apiece, it would not earn enough even to meet its payroll. Better to send the workers home, suffer a loss equal to the mortgage payment, and hope for things to get better.

The Firm's Short-Run Supply Curve

The preceding examples supply everything needed to construct a short-run supply curve for the profit-maximizing firm in a perfectly competitive market. Box 7.4 shows how this curve is constructed.

Let us work through this graph, beginning with a price of $500 (at the marginal-revenue curve MR_1, or the demand curve D_1). As before, Fieldcom would choose to produce nineteen units of output at this price. Point E_1 of the firm's short-run marginal-cost curve must therefore be a point on the firm's supply curve.

Suppose now that the market price of the firm's product begins to fall as a result of forces beyond its control. As it does, the point where price equals marginal cost moves down along the firm's marginal-cost curve. Soon Point E_2 is reached — the point where marginal cost and average total cost are equal. This occurs at an output of approximately seventeen units and a price of approximately $385. At this price, the best the firm can do is break even, at seventeen units. A greater or a smaller output would result in a loss.

If the price falls still lower, the firm's problem becomes one of minimizing loss rather than maximizing profit. At a price of $300, for example, the firm minimizes losses by producing fourteen units, at point E_3. In the range of prices lying between minimum average total cost and minimum average variable cost, the supply curve continues to follow the marginal-cost curve.

Below a price of about $254, a change occurs. As before, when price is lower than the lowest point on the average-variable-cost curve, the firm minimizes losses by shutting down, rather than continuing to produce up to the point where marginal cost begins to exceed price. For a price of $254, then, Point E_4 on the vertical axis is the preferred point of operation. This point must then be a point on the firm's short-run supply curve. As the diagram shows, for this and all lower prices, the supply curve coincides with the vertical axis.

Derivation of the Short-Run Supply Curve BOX 7.4

This diagram traces Fieldcom's short-run supply curve. When the price is $500, the firm will produce at point E_1. As the price falls, the firm moves down along its short-run marginal-cost curve, as shown by points E_2 and E_3. The firm will continue to produce where price equals marginal cost until marginal cost falls below average variable cost. At that price, the firm will do just as well to shut down — that is, to produce at point E_4.

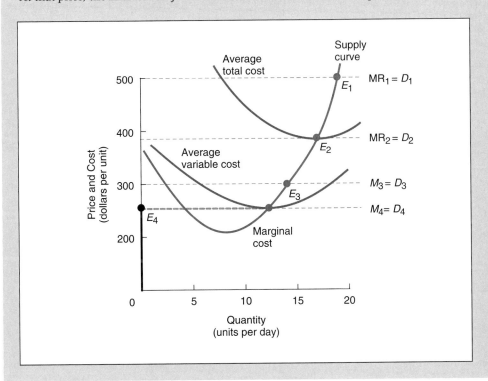

All that has been learned so far about the firm's short-run supply decision can now be stated in the form of an important generalization: *The short-run supply curve for a profit-maximizing firm operating in a perfectly competitive market coincides with the upward-sloping part of the marginal-cost curve lying above its intersection with the average-variable-cost curve.*

The Short-Run Industry Supply Curve

The supply curve for a whole industry can now be constructed on the basis of the supply curves of the individual firms. As a first approximation, an industry supply curve can be obtained by the horizontal addition of individual firms' supply curves, as shown in Box 7.5. It is necessary to make one qualification, though. The assumption has been that any individual firm can expand output without any change in input prices; but if all firms in an industry expand simultaneously, input prices will rise unless the supply curve of the input is perfectly elastic. If input prices rise as industry output expands, the short-run industry supply curve will be somewhat steeper than the sum of the individual supply curves.

BOX 7.5   *Approximate Derivation of the Short-Run Industry Supply Curve*

An approximation of the short-run industry supply curve can be obtained by means of a horizontal summation of the individual firms' supply curves. Here, the method of summation is shown for an industry with just three firms. If the prices of inputs vary as industry output varies, it will be necessary to make an adjustment in the industry supply curve.

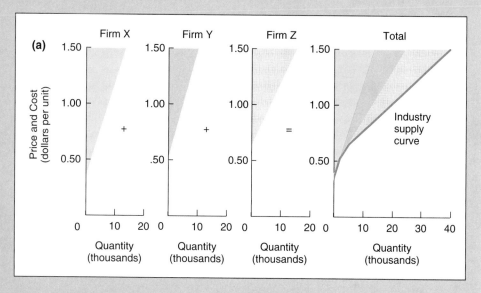

(b)

Price	Quantity Supplied			
	Firm X	Firm Y	Firm Z	Total
$0.40	1 500	0	0	1 500
$0.80	5 500	3 000	3 333	11 833
$1.20	9 500	7 000	10 000	26 500
$1.50	12 500	10 000	15 000	37 500

LONG-RUN EQUILIBRIUM UNDER PERFECT COMPETITION

Entry and Exit

For the individual firm, the long run is distinguished from the short run by the fact that *all* inputs can be varied, not just some of them. In the long run, firms can go out of business entirely. (Sometimes, firms go peaceably, with the owners selling off the assets and banking what is left. Other times, they go with a crash, leaving their creditors to collect perhaps only pennies on the dollar for the mortgages, bonds, and other debts they hold.) Also in the long run, new firms can come into a market, building new plants and buying new equipment, which then become their short-run fixed inputs. As firms enter and exit, whole industries expand and contract.

One of the defining characteristics of perfect competition is that there must be no barriers to this free flow of firms into and out of the industry. This characteristic played no direct role in the discussion of a firm's short-run supply decision, but free entry and exit are crucial to explaining how a competitive market works in the long run.

Equilibrium

Equilibrium, as explained in this book in many different contexts, is a state of affairs in which economic decision makers have no incentive to change their current patterns of behaviour. In a perfectly competitive industry, short-run equilibrium means that each firm must have no incentive either to increase or to decrease its quantity of output. That requires the firm to adjust its output to the point where marginal cost is equal to the price of the product. (Keep in mind that a perfectly competitive firm is a price taker, so price and marginal revenue are always equal.) In the long run, equilibrium in a perfectly competitive industry requires two other things as well. One is that each firm have no incentive to change the size of plant it uses to produce its current output, and the other is that firms have no incentive either to enter or to leave the industry.

Box 7.6 shows graphically how all these requirements are satisfied simultaneously in long-run equilibrium for a perfectly competitive firm. First, marginal cost is equal to price at the equilibrium quantity of output. This equality ensures that there is no incentive in the short run either to increase or to decrease output.

Second, the firm is operating with a plant of just the size necessary to make short-run average total cost equal to minimum possible long-run average cost at the equilibrium quantity of output. No change in the quantity of fixed inputs employed can reduce average cost, so the firm has no long-run incentive to change its plant size.[1]

Third, average total cost (both long-run and short-run) is equal to price at the equilibrium quantity of output. As always, average total cost includes an allowance for a normal rate of return on capital — no more, no less. Thus, when average total cost is equal to price, there is no incentive for firms either to enter the industry (to seek pure economic profit in excess of the normal rate of return on capital) or to leave the industry (in order to avoid pure economic loss — that is, a rate of return on capital less than the normal rate).

The long-run equilibrium conditions shown graphically in Box 7.6 can also be expressed in the form of the following equation:

$$\text{Price} = \frac{\text{Marginal}}{\text{cost}} = \frac{\text{Short-run}}{\text{average}}_{\text{total cost}} = \frac{\text{Long-run}}{\text{average}}_{\text{cost}}$$

If any part of this equation does not hold, there will be an incentive for firms to change the quantity of output they are producing within their current plants, to

---

[1]The reader may wish to review Boxes 6.6 and 6.7, which show the relationship between short-run and long-run average-cost curves for various plant sizes.

BOX 7.6   *The Typical Perfectly Competitive Firm in Long-Run Equilibrium*

Long-run equilibrium in a perfectly competitive industry requires that the typical firm (1) have no short-run incentive to change the quantity of output currently produced, (2) have no long-run incentive to change the size of plant used to produce its current output, and (3) have no long-run incentive to enter or leave the industry. This requires that price, short-run marginal cost, short-run average total cost, and long-run average cost all have the same value in equilibrium, as shown.

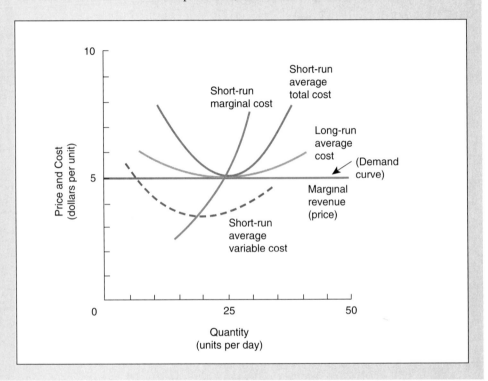

change the size of the plants they are using to produce their current output, or to enter or leave the industry. In other words, unless all parts of the equation hold, the market cannot be in long-run equilibrium.

Industry Adjustment to Falling Demand

A particular position of long-run equilibrium, such as the one shown in Box 7.6, can continue undisturbed only as long as outside conditions remain unchanged. Box 7.7, for example, shows how a perfectly competitive industry reacts to a long-run decrease in the demand for its product.

The box consists of two parts. Part (a) shows a set of cost curves, much like those shown in Box 7.6, for a typical individual firm in the industry. Part (b) is a supply-and-demand diagram representing the market in which the typical firm sells its output. The curves drawn there are short-run industry supply curves built up from the short-run supply curves of all the individual firms in the market (see

Long-Run Adjustment to a Decline in Demand

BOX 7.7

In this box, part (a) represents a single typical firm, and part (b), the entire industry. Initially, both the firm and the industry are in long-run equilibrium at a price of $5. Then something happens to shift the demand curve leftward from D_1 to D_2. In the short run, the price falls to $4, at the intersection of D_2 and S_1. The firm's short-run reaction is to retreat down along its marginal-cost curve. Eventually, some firms (not the one shown) get tired of taking losses and exit from the industry. Their exit causes the supply curve to shift toward S_2 and the market price to recover. The typical firm returns to break-even operation. The market has traced out part of its long-run supply curve, as shown by the long arrow.

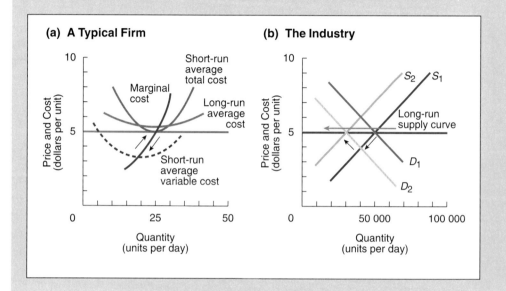

Box 7.5). The demand curves are short-run market demand curves of the usual kind.

Suppose that, initially, short-run supply curve S_1 and short-run demand curve D_1 applied. That would produce a market equilibrium price of $5. The individual firm would take this price as given and adjust its output accordingly, producing 25 units of output, as shown. At this price and output, the firm would be just breaking even. Remember, though, that breaking even in the economic sense means earning enough to cover all costs, including the implicit cost of a normal rate of return on the owner's invested capital.

Suppose now that something happens — say, a change in consumer tastes or incomes — that shifts the demand curve to the new position, D_2. The short-run result of this demand shift will be a drop in the market price to $4 per unit. The individual firm, being a price taker, will consider this decline in price as something beyond its control and will adjust to it as best it can. As shown in part (a) of the box, this means cutting back output a little to minimize loss but not shutting down completely. The movement of each individual firm back down along its marginal-cost curve is what produces the movement of the market as a whole down and to the left along short-run supply curve S_1.

But the situation in which the market now finds itself cannot prevail in the long run. The reason is that the typical firm and its fellows are operating at a loss. They are not giving their owners the normal rate of return they need to make an investment in this industry worth while. If the demand curve does not show any hope of shifting back to the right, some owners will become discouraged and will pull their capital out of the industry. Perhaps their firms will actually go bankrupt, or perhaps they will sell off their plant and equipment and get out while the going is good. Perhaps they will keep their firms intact but set to work to produce other goods for other, more profitable, markets. The particular form of exit does not much matter.

There is no real way to tell which firms will be the first to go; but, for convenience, assume that the typical firm shown in the box is not one of the first. Look what happens to it now as some of the others leave. As some firms withdraw, the market loses the contribution to total supply that those firms made. The market supply curve, now representing the sum of fewer individual supply curves, shifts to the left toward S_2. As it does so, the market price begins to rise up along the demand curve D_2. When the price gets all the way back up to $5, the firms still left in the industry will no longer be losing money. The exodus from the industry will stop, and the market will have reached a new long-run equilibrium. In the new equilibrium, price, marginal cost, short-run average total cost, and long-run average cost will once again be equal.

Long-run industry supply curve
A curve that traces the output response of all firms in an industry to persistent changes in demand over a period of time long enough for firms to adjust their plant size, if necessary, and for entry to and exit from the market to occur.

The entire sequence of events has traced out a portion of this industry's **long-run industry supply curve**, as shown by the arrow. A long-run supply curve for an industry shows the path along which equilibrium price and quantity move in response to persistent changes in demand, given time for individual firms to adjust the sizes of their plants, if necessary, and given time for entry and exit to occur. The long-run supply curve shown in Box 7.7 is perfectly elastic, at least in the region below the long arrow. In the long run, the leftward shift of the demand curve causes no change in price, only a decrease in the quantity supplied.

Industry Adjustment to Rising Demand

Freedom of entry plays the same role in the long-run adjustment of a perfectly competitive market to rising demand as freedom of exit plays in the adjustment to falling demand. This is illustrated in Box 7.8.

The starting position in this example is exactly the same as the one in Box 7.7. Short-run supply curve S_1 and demand curve D_1 give an equilibrium price of $5. The individual firm just breaks even producing 25 units of output at this price. Now follow what happens as the demand curve shifts to the *right* of D_1, to position D_3.

The short-run result of the shift in the demand curve is an increase in the market price to $6. The typical firm adjusts to this new price by moving up along its marginal-cost curve to a somewhat higher level of output. As all firms do this, the market moves up and to the right along short-run supply curve S_1.

But again, this short-run adjustment does not result in a state of affairs that can last in the long run. For now, all the firms are making profits in excess of the minimum needed to attract capital to the industry. Entrepreneurs elsewhere in the economy will soon spot this healthy, expanding market as a prime investment opportunity. Some of them may start brand-new firms to produce for this market. Others may shift plants and equipment previously used to produce some-

Long-Run Adjustment to an Increase in Demand   BOX 7.8

In this box, both the firm and the industry are again initially in equilibrium at a price of $5. Then something happens to shift the demand curve to the right, to D_3. In the short run, the price rises to $6, at the intersection of D_3 and S_1. The firm's short-run reaction is to move up along its marginal-cost curve, earning higher-than-normal profits. These high profits eventually attract new firms into the industry. As new firms enter, the supply curve shifts toward S_3. Profits for the typical firm return to normal, and entry activity ceases. Again, the market has traced out part of its long-run supply curve, as shown by the long arrow.

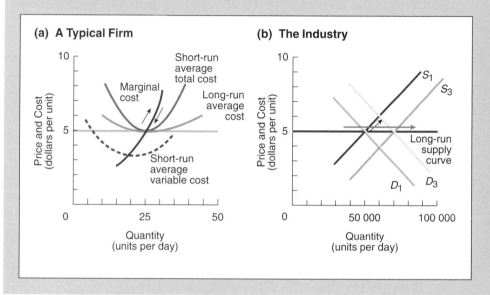

thing else to making goods for this industry. It does not matter whether the entry is by brand-new firms or by firms already existing in other industries that devote part of their capital to this particular market for the first time. In either case, new entry will cause the supply curve to shift to the right, toward S_3.

As the supply curve shifts, the price falls. It does not fall far enough to drive the new entrants back out again, but it does fall enough to drive everyone's profits back to the normal level. Entry will stop, and the market will be in a new long-run equilibrium at the intersection of S_3 and D_3.

Once again, a portion of the long-run supply curve for the industry has been traced out, as shown by the long arrow. And once again, this long-run supply curve is horizontal in the region investigated. A rightward shift in the demand curve has, in the long run, produced an increase in quantity supplied but no increase in price.

Long-Run Supply Curves with Changing Costs

In the examples just given, the industry long-run supply curve was a horizontal straight line, at least in the region examined. That is not the only possible shape such a supply curve can take, however. Box 7.9 shows some other possibilities — upward-sloping, downward-sloping, and U-shaped curves.

BOX 7.9   *Possible Long-Run Supply Curves for a Competitive Industry*

The shape of an industry's long-run supply curve depends largely on what happens to the prices of the industry's inputs as demand and output expand in the long run. If input prices do not change significantly, the long-run supply curve will be horizontal, as in part (a). If input prices rise, the long-run supply curve will slope upward, as in part (b). Falling input prices will produce a downward-sloping long-run industry supply curve, as in part (c). Finally, mixed cases, where the long-run supply curve first falls and then rises, are also possible, as shown in part (d).

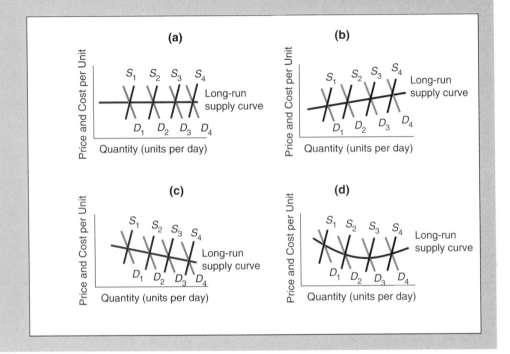

The shape that the long-run industry supply curve takes depends primarily on what happens to the industry's input prices in the long run as output expands. If the long-run supply curve for all inputs is perfectly elastic, the price of those inputs will not change as the quantity of them demanded by the industry increases. Or perhaps the industry will use such a small part of the total supply of each unspecialized input that whatever change in input price does occur will be negligibly small. Industry output can thus expand without affecting the underlying costs of the individual firms, and the long-run supply curve of the industry using the outputs will be perfectly horizontal (that is, perfectly elastic). This is the case in Boxes 7.7 and 7.8. Box 7.9(a) shows a succession of short-run supply and demand curves lying along such a horizontal long-run supply curve. Each pair of short-run curves represents one stage in the industry's long-run expansion.

Suppose, though, that the industry uses some specialized input, the supply of which cannot easily be increased. Perhaps some special skilled labour is needed, and more workers can be induced to acquire the skill only by bidding up the wage rate. The rising price of this important input will cause an upward shift in the cost curves of all the firms in the industry as new firms enter the industry and output expands. In this case, the long-run industry supply curve will slope upward, as in Box 7.9(b).

It is also possible that the price of some important input can decrease as industry output expands. For example, as sales of electronic equipment grow, the firms making the components that go into that equipment may be able to adopt cheaper methods of production. If this occurs, the cost curves for all firms will drift downward as new firms enter the industry. The long-run supply curve will then slope downward, as in Box 7.9(c).

Finally, it is possible that a combination of forces can be at work. In the industry shown in Box 7.9(d), long-run supply is at first influenced by the falling price of one specialized input, but beyond a certain point, some other specialized input creates a bottleneck that causes the long-run supply curve to bend upward. Many variants are possible. Only actual observation of particular industries can determine which situation exists.

WHAT IS PERFECT ABOUT PERFECT COMPETITION?

Our discussion of perfect competition is now very nearly complete. We have a fairly good picture of how perfectly competitive markets work. But there is one remaining question that deserves more attention than it has yet been given: What is so perfect about perfect competition?

As suggested early in the chapter, the answer is not that such a market is the perfect place to observe all forms of business rivalry. Far from it. Many familiar forms of rivalry are completely absent from perfectly competitive markets. Under perfect competition, business managers go blandly about their pure economizing without caring a whit what any particular other firm in the industry does. After all, those other firms cannot, by definition, be big enough to have any individual impact on market prices. They cannot, by definition, be getting ready to introduce a new, distinctive version of the industry's product. And they cannot, by definition, have any secrets. So it is not in any of these senses that perfectly competitive markets are perfect.

Instead, they are perfect in another sense. Think, for a moment, about just what a market really is. Very simply, it is a mechanism for getting buyers and sellers together to carry out mutually beneficial transactions. It would seem to make sense, then, to say that *a perfect market is one in which all potential mutually beneficial transactions are in fact carried out — a market in which no opportunity for such a transaction is missed*. That is exactly the sense in which perfectly competitive markets are perfect.

To see why, look at Box 7.10. This is a quite ordinary supply-and-demand diagram (long-run variety), just like many of the ones shown before. But now look at it in a slightly different way.

Start with the demand curve. Usually, one thinks of a demand curve as showing the quantity that consumers are willing and able to buy at any given market price. But, as you will recall from our discussion of consumer surplus in Chapter 5, the demand curve can also be thought of as showing the maximum amount consumers are willing to pay for a marginal unit of the good, given the quantity

BOX 7.10   *Why Perfectly Competitive Markets Are Perfect*

As noted earlier, in Chapter 5, one can think of the demand curve as showing how much consumers would be willing to pay for *additional* units of output. Similarly, one can think of the supply curve as showing how much producers would have to be offered to supply these additional units. If production were limited to a rate of 100 units per period, many opportunities for mutually beneficial exchange would be passed up. Consumers would be willing to pay nearly $12 for the 101st unit, while producers would have to be given barely more than $6 to produce it. Only once output had reached 150 units would all such worthwhile trades have taken place. The shaded area provides a rough measure of the opportunities for mutual benefit that would be wasted if production were limited to 100 units. But a competitive market would carry output all the way to 150 units.

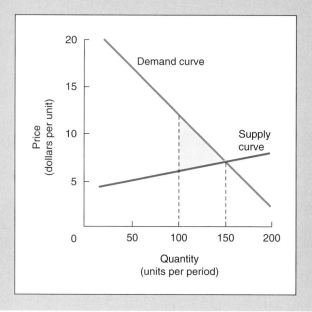

already available. This particular demand curve, for example, has a height of $12 at 100 units of output. That means someone is willing to pay barely $12 for the marginal 100th unit and someone is willing to pay almost, but not quite, that much for the 101st.

The supply curve can be interpreted in much the same way. Usually, one thinks of it as showing how much producers are willing to supply at a given price. But it also shows the minimum amount necessary to induce producers to supply the marginal unit. The supply curve in this box, for example, has a height of $6 at an output of 100 units. That means someone is barely willing to supply the 100th unit for $6 and that no one will supply a 101st unit unless offered just a little bit more.

Now, suppose that, for some reason, producers in fact are supplying goods to this market at a rate of only 100 units per period. At that level of output, the demand curve is above the supply curve. Some consumer out there is willing to pay nearly $12 for the 101st unit. And some producer is willing to supply it for anything just over $6. If production stops at 100 units, then, buyers and sellers will be passing up an opportunity for a mutually beneficial transaction. The market will not be perfect.

The same will be true, to a slightly lesser degree, if output stops at 101, 110, or 149 units. Even the production and sale of the 150th unit represents a mutually beneficial exchange, although only barely so. It can be said, then, that the whole shaded area in the graph gives a measure of the accumulated potential for mutual benefit that will be wasted if production stops short at 100 units.

Now we can see the sense in which perfectly competitive markets, when they are in equilibrium, are perfect. In such markets, production is carried out up to, but not beyond, the point where the long-run supply and demand curves intersect. All possible mutually beneficial transactions between consumers and producers are thus carried out. And, as we saw earlier in the chapter, each firm in long-run perfectly competitive equilibrium produces at the minimum possible average total cost. That means no further gains are possible on the production side, at least within the limits of current technology. With no improvements possible through changes in either the quantity of output traded or the way in which that output is produced, the market does as well as it can in satisfying the needs of consumers. In that sense, it is a perfect market.

Some Qualifications

It would be tempting to draw some broad conclusions from the preceding section. Would an economy in which all markets were perfectly competitive be the best of all possible worlds? Although perfectly competitive markets work well in some cases, a few qualifications should be noted.

One qualification is that technology does not co-operate. In many industries, economies of scale make it impractical to spread production among a large number of small firms. In such markets, a perfectly competitive structure is not efficient.

A second qualification is that consumers are not always indifferent between the products of different firms. For many goods — cars, clothing, restaurants — consumers want to have a choice. Forcing all firms to make an identical product in the name of perfect competition would cost more in lost consumer satisfaction than it would gain in lower production costs.

A third qualification is that perfect competition leaves little or no room for entrepreneurship. It does not allow for innovation or changing tastes. It assumes that all buyers and sellers are informed, even though in the real world, information is one of the scarcest and most valuable goods. Do markets with large numbers of small firms guarantee efficient decision making in a world of change and uncertainty? Are such markets most likely to produce new and better ways to satisfy human wants? The theory of perfect competition says nothing one way or the other in answer to these questions. Later chapters will return to them.

When all is said and done, perfect competition must be understood for what it is — a powerful economic model, but nothing more. It yields many useful insights. It allows us to think more clearly about what lies behind the law of supply and demand. It provides some insights into how well an industry would perform if it *were* perfectly competitive. And for some markets, it is not so far from reality in a descriptive sense. Even so, perfect competition is not the whole story by any means.

SUMMARY

1. A *perfectly competitive* market has the following traits: (a) There are many buyers and sellers, each of whom is small compared with the market as a whole; (b) the product is homogeneous; (c) all buyers and sellers have access to complete information; and (d) entry into and exit from the market are easy. These traits combine to create a situation that results in a *horizontal demand curve* for the perfectly competitive firm.

2. In the short run, the relationship between marginal cost and *marginal revenue* (price) determines the profit-maximizing level of output for a perfectly competitive firm. The firm should expand output to the point where marginal cost equals marginal revenue, provided that marginal revenue is at least equal to average variable cost at that point.

3. If marginal revenue is less than average total cost at the point where marginal cost and marginal revenue are equal, the firm cannot earn a profit. It will keep its loss to a minimum in the short run by staying open if marginal revenue is greater than average variable cost at that point. If marginal revenue is less than average variable cost at the point where marginal cost and marginal revenue are equal, the firm will minimize loss by shutting down.

4. The short-run supply curve for a perfectly competitive firm is the upward-sloping part of the marginal-cost curve above its intersection with the average-variable-cost curve.

5. Long-run equilibrium for a perfectly competitive firm requires that price, marginal cost, short-run average total cost, and long-run average cost all be equal.

6. A perfectly competitive industry adjusts to long-run decreases in demand through exit of firms, and to long-run increases in demand through entry of new firms. If input prices do not change as the industry's output changes, the industry's *long-run supply curve* will be flat. If input prices rise, the long-run supply curve will have a positive slope; if they fall, it will have a negative slope.

7. A perfectly competitive market is "perfect" in the sense that it allows all mutually beneficial transactions to be carried out. Nonetheless, perfect competition is not the best structure for all markets.

KEY TERMS

market structure
perfect competition

price taker
horizontal demand curve

marginal revenue
long-run industry supply curve

KEY BOXES

Box 7.1   Short-Run Profit Maximization under
          Perfect Competition
Box 7.4   Derivation of the Short-Run
          Supply Curve
Box 7.6   The Typical Perfectly Competitive Firm in
          Long-Run Equilibrium

Box 7.7   Long-Run Adjustment to a Decline
          in Demand
Box 7.9   Possible Long-Run Supply Curves for a
          Competitive Industry
Box 7.10 Why Perfectly Competitive Markets
          Are Perfect

REVIEW QUESTIONS

1. What is the relationship between the total-cost and total-revenue curves at the point of short-run profit maximization for a perfectly competitive firm? What is the relationship between the marginal-cost and marginal-revenue curves at the same point?

2. Under what conditions will a perfectly competitive firm find it worth while to operate even though, in the short run, it operates at a loss?

3. What part of the perfectly competitive firm's supply curve coincides with its marginal-cost curve in the short run? What part of the supply curve does not coincide with the marginal-cost curve?

4. List four quantities that must be equal for a perfectly competitive firm to be in long-run equilibrium.

5. Under what conditions will the long-run supply curve for a perfectly competitive industry be perfectly elastic? Under what conditions will it slope upward or downward?

6. Explain what is "perfect" about perfect competition.

7. Fieldcom buys some automated equipment in order to speed up production of its computers. The equipment adds $500 per day to the firm's fixed costs, but it saves $50 per unit in variable costs. Rework the graph in Box 7.4 to show how the new equipment affects Fieldcom's supply curve. (You may want to rework the table in Box 7.1 as a basis for the new supply curve.) What is the minimum price the firm now needs to charge in order to continue to operate in the short run? What is the lowest price at which it can break even?

8. Box 7.8 shows the long-run adjustment of a competitive industry to an increase in demand in the case in which input prices do not change as output changes. Assume instead that input prices rise as output rises. Draw a new set of diagrams to show how a typical firm and the industry as a whole respond to an increase in demand. When demand first increases, the industry will move upward along its short-run supply curve as before. When that happens, what will happen to the typical firm's cost curves? How will the typical firm's new equilibrium point compare with its starting point?

9. The restaurant industry has many firms, each of which is small. Entry into and exit from the industry are easy. However, the industry is not perfectly competitive because the product is not homogeneous — there are Italian restaurants, French restaurants, hamburger huts, and so on. Suppose a national restaurant commission decides to enforce perfect competition in the industry by requiring all restaurants to have the same menu. Do you think this action will increase consumer satisfaction? Why or why not?

10. If the government imposes a price ceiling on some product, does that make the firms that sell the product price takers, regardless of whether their industry fits the market structure of perfect competition? Explain.

11. Refer back to the cost table you completed for Review Question 10 at the end of Chapter 6, and assume that the firm represented in that table is a perfect competitor in the market for its product. Three different market prices for the product sold by this firm are given below. Determine, for each price, whether the firm is making a profit or suffering a loss. If the firm is operating at a loss, should it stay in business in the short run or shut down? Explain how you arrived at each of your answers. (You may want to graph the cost and price values, but it is possible to arrive at the correct answers from the table itself, with the addition of a price column.)
    a. $70   c. $130
    b. $80

12. It is stated in the text that the point of profit maximization (or loss minimization) for a firm occurs at the level of output beyond which marginal cost begins to exceed marginal revenue. Students often ask why it is not equally desirable to produce one unit less than the quantity at which marginal cost equals marginal revenue, since costs are equal to revenues for the last item. If you were the economics professor, how would you explain why a firm benefits from producing up to and including the level of output at which marginal cost equals marginal revenue? (*Hint*: When costs are calculated they include a fair return to factors of production.)

The Theory of Monopoly

WHAT YOU WILL LEARN IN THIS CHAPTER

After studying this chapter, you will be able to

1. Define the terms *monopoly* and *cartel*.

2. Show how marginal revenue is related to price for a monopoly, and construct a monopolist's marginal-revenue curve given a straight-line demand curve.

3. Demonstrate the process of profit maximization for a monopolist.

4. Explain why monopoly is viewed as an imperfect market structure.

5. List the conditions required for a monopoly to practise price discrimination and discuss the effects of price discrimination on consumers.

6. Explain why cartels encounter problems of cheating and instability.

A Preview   *Why Do Diamonds Cost So Much?*

In Chapter 7, we saw that competition can be both inconvenient and painful: It is inconvenient because it prevents business firms from setting as high a price as they would like, and it is painful because it can threaten firms with extinction. Small wonder, then, that business firms would relish the opportunity to protect themselves against competition by creating monopolies, as Cecil Rhodes did.

The Diamond Monopoly of Cecil Rhodes

Cecil Rhodes was one of the leading imperialists of the nineteenth century. He brought most of southern Africa under British control. Although he did all he could to expand the British Empire, he saw himself as a man of peace and took pride in his ability to bring warring factions together. He once settled a dispute between the British government and a tribal army by riding alone and unarmed into hostile territory to listen to the grievances of local chiefs.

The British Empire is gone, and the country once called Rhodesia no longer bears Rhodes's name; it is now Zimbabwe. But De Beers Consolidated Mines, Ltd., a diamond-mining concern that Rhodes founded in 1888, lives on. Today, De Beers controls the marketing of more than 80 percent of the world's uncut diamonds. Over the years, diamond producers have been an assorted lot, culturally and politically; they have included black-ruled Zaire and white-ruled South Africa, as well as the former, communist Soviet Union and Australia with its democratic-socialist government. Yet under De Beer's leadership, these diverse producers have worked together toward the shared goal of keeping diamond prices high. And for more than a hundred years, through good times and bad, De Beers has never had to cut its listed price for diamonds.

THE STRUCTURE OF PURE MONOPOLY

Any market that is dominated by a single seller is known as a **monopoly**. A single firm that makes and sells 100 percent of the output of a product is a **pure monopoly**. There is no distinction between the firm and the industry in this case; the firm is the industry. An organization such as De Beers, through which producers co-operate to control the sale of all or most of the output of a product, is known as a *cartel*. We discuss pure monopolies and cartels together in this chapter because the rules for profit maximization are the same for both. Toward the end of the chapter, however, we will see that cartels face problems of organization that do not affect pure monopolies.

As a market structure, pure monopoly is the opposite of perfect competition. In a perfectly competitive market, each firm has so many small rivals that no single firm, acting alone, can affect the market price. A pure monopolist, by contrast, has no competitors at all.

What is more, the pure monopolist is shielded against the entry of competitors. Sometimes the barriers to entry take the form of control of a unique natural resource. In other cases, the monopolist may be protected by law, as in the case of monopolies based on patents, licences, and permits. As later chapters will show, the government sometimes fights monopoly and sometimes promotes it.

Whatever their origin, monopolies differ from perfectly competitive firms in an important way: They are not price takers. The fact that a monopolist's choice of a level of output directly affects the product's price is the starting point of the theory of monopoly.

Monopoly
A market that is dominated by a single seller.

Pure monopoly
A market structure in which a single firm makes and sells 100 percent of the output of a product.

PROFIT MAXIMIZATION FOR THE PURE MONOPOLIST

Output, Price, and Marginal Revenue under Monopoly

For an example of the relationships among output, price, and revenue under monopoly, look at Box 8.1. Columns 1 and 2 of the table give data on the demand for the product of a pure monopolist. The data are also presented as a demand curve. As both the table and the graph make clear, the greater the output, the lower the price at which buyers will be willing to purchase the entire amount produced.

As the monopolist raises or lowers output, changes in both price and quantity affect the firm's total revenue. For any output, total revenue is equal to price times quantity. Starting from zero, the box shows that as output increases, total revenue first rises, then reaches a maximum at about seventeen units of output, and then falls. With a straight-line demand curve like the one in Box 8.1, the upper half is elastic, and the lower half, inelastic. That accounts for the shape of the "revenue hill" drawn as a separate graph below the demand curve.

The relationship between output and revenue for a pure monopolist can also be viewed in marginal terms. Chapter 7 defined *marginal revenue* as the change in total revenue that results from a one-unit increase in a firm's output. Column 4 of the table in Box 8.1 gives data on marginal revenue for the firm in this example. The figures in the column are the differences between the entries in column 3. Part (b) of the box shows the firm's marginal-revenue curve. The

BOX 8.1 Demand, Total Revenue, and Marginal Revenue for a Pure Monopolist

This box shows the relationships among demand, total revenue, and marginal revenue for a typical monopolist. Total revenue is found by multiplying price times quantity at each point on the demand curve. Marginal revenue is the increase in total revenue resulting from a one-unit increase in output. Part (b) of this box shows the demand curve and the marginal-revenue curve in graphic form. Note that for a straight-line demand curve, the marginal-revenue curve lies halfway between the demand curve and the vertical axis and that it cuts the horizontal axis at the point where price elasticity of demand is equal to one. This point corresponds to the point of maximum total revenue, as shown in part (c).

(a)

Quantity (1)	Price (2)	Total Revenue (3)	Marginal Revenue (4)
1	$10.00	$10.00	
			$9.40
2	9.70	19.40	
			8.80
3	9.40	28.20	
			8.20
4	9.10	36.40	
			7.60
5	8.80	44.00	
			7.00
6	8.50	51.00	
			6.40
7	8.20	57.40	
			5.80
8	7.90	63.20	
			5.20
9	7.60	68.40	
			4.60
10	7.30	73.00	
			4.00
11	7.00	77.00	
			3.40
12	6.70	80.40	
			2.80
13	6.40	83.20	
			2.20
14	6.10	85.40	
			1.60
15	5.80	87.00	
			1.00
16	5.50	88.00	
			0.40
17	5.20	88.40	
			−0.20
18	4.90	88.20	
			−0.80
19	4.60	87.40	
			−1.40
20	4.30	86.00	
			−2.00
21	4.00	84.00	
			−2.60
22	3.70	81.40	
			−3.20
23	3.40	78.20	
			−3.80
24	3.10	74.40	
			−4.40
25	2.80	70.00	
			−5.00
26	2.50	65.00	
			−5.60
27	2.20	59.40	
			−6.20
28	1.90	53.20	
			−6.80
29	1.60	46.40	
			−7.40
30	1.30	39.00	
			−8.00
31	1.00	31.00	
			−8.60
32	0.70	22.40	
			−9.20
33	0.40	13.20	
			−9.80
34	0.10	3.40	

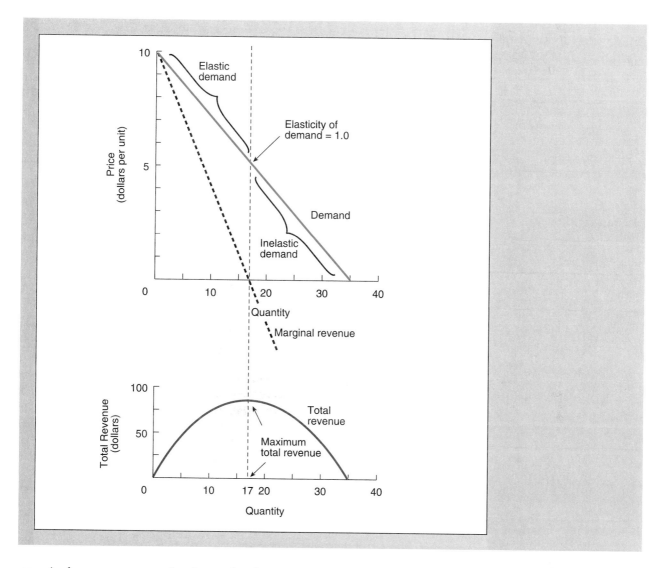

marginal-revenue curve is above the horizontal axis when total revenue is increasing (elastic demand) and below it when total revenue is decreasing (inelastic demand). It intersects the horizontal axis at the point of maximum total revenue.[1]

Notice that the marginal-revenue curve is always below the demand curve. This means that the increase in total revenue that the monopolist gets from the sale of one additional unit is less than the price at which that unit is sold. The reason is that the monopolist must cut the price on all units sold, not just on the last unit sold, in order to increase total sales volume. The price cut on earlier units thus partly or wholly offsets the revenue gain from increasing the amount sold.

[1]Here is an easy rule that will help in sketching the marginal-revenue curve that corresponds to any straight-line demand curve: *The marginal-revenue curve for a straight-line demand curve always cuts the horizontal distance from the demand curve to the vertical axis exactly in half.* This rule does not work for curved demand curves, but the examples in this book will be confined to simple, straight-line curves.

Profit Maximization

The relationship between output and revenue for a pure monopolist forms the basis for an analysis of short-run profit maximization. The best way to present such an analysis is through the use of a numerical example like the one we used in discussing perfect competition.

Box 8.2 takes the demand and revenue data from Box 8.1 and adds data on the firm's total and marginal costs. One way to determine the profit-maximizing level of output for the firm is to compare total cost and total revenue. Subtracting total cost (column 6) from total revenue (column 2) gives total profit (column 7). A glance at column 7 shows the profit-maximizing level of output to be thirteen units. The total-revenue–total-cost approach to profit maximization is

---

BOX 8.2 *Profit Maximization for a Pure Monopolist*

This box demonstrates that a pure monopolist maximizes profits by producing that quantity of output for which marginal cost is equal to marginal revenue. Notice that maximizing profit is not the same as maximizing revenue. In this example, the profit-maximizing output is thirteen units. In the range from thirteen to seventeen units of output, total revenue continues to increase. But because total cost increases even faster in this range, profits decline. Notice also that the profit-maximizing price for the monopolist is determined by the height of the demand curve (not the marginal-cost or the marginal-revenue curve) at the profit-maximizing quantity of output.

(a)

Output (1)	Price (2)	Total Revenue (3)	Marginal Revenue (4)	Marginal Cost (5)	Total Cost (6)	Total Profit (7)
1	$10.00	$10.00			$23.80	− $13.80
			$9.40	$3.40		
2	9.70	19.40			27.20	− 7.80
			8.80	3.05		
3	9.40	28.20			30.25	− 2.05
			8.20	2.75		
4	9.10	36.40			33.00	3.40
			7.60	2.50		
5	8.80	44.00			35.50	8.50
			7.00	2.30		
6	8.50	51.00			37.80	13.20
			6.40	2.15		
7	8.20	57.40			39.95	17.45
			5.80	2.05		
8	7.90	63.20			42.00	21.20
			5.20	2.00		
9	7.60	68.40			44.00	24.40
			4.60	2.05		
10	7.30	73.00			46.05	26.95
			4.00	2.15		
11	7.00	77.00			48.20	28.80
			3.40	2.30		
12	6.70	80.40			50.50	29.90
			2.80	2.50		
13	6.40	83.20			53.00	30.20
			2.20	2.75		
14	6.10	85.40			55.75	29.65
			1.60	3.05		
15	5.80	87.00			58.80	28.20
			1.00	3.40		
16	5.50	88.00			62.20	25.80
			0.40	3.80		
17	5.20	88.40			66.00	22.40

shown in the graph in part (b) of Box 8.2. Total profit is shown as the vertical gap between the total-cost and total-revenue curves. It reaches a maximum at thirteen units of output, where the two curves are farthest apart.

Note that maximizing profit is not the same thing as maximizing revenue. Between thirteen and seventeen units of output, total revenue continues to rise. But total cost rises even faster, so profit falls.

The profit-maximizing level of output for the pure monopolist can also be found by comparing marginal cost and marginal revenue, as shown in columns 4 and 5 of the table in Box 8.2. Marginal revenue is the amount by which total revenue increases when output is increased by one unit, and marginal cost is the amount by which total cost increases. It follows that as long as marginal revenue exceeds marginal cost, adding one more unit of output will add more to total revenue than to total cost and hence will add to total profit. Beyond thirteen units of output, marginal revenue falls below marginal cost, so any further expansion of output reduces total profit.

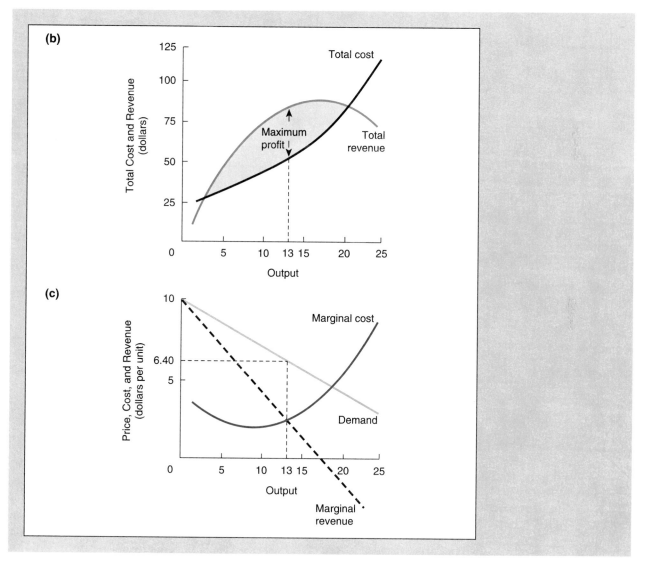

Part (c) of Box 8.2 compares marginal revenue and marginal cost in graphic terms. The profit-maximizing quantity is found where the marginal-cost and marginal-revenue curves intersect. It matches the point of maximum profit, which is shown in part (b) of Box 8.2 as the point where the gap between the total-revenue and total-cost curves is greatest.

The intersection of the marginal-cost and marginal-revenue curves in Box 8.2 gives the profit-maximizing level of output for the firm; the profit-maximizing price is given by the height of the demand curve for that level. For a pure monopolist, this price is always above marginal cost. For the firm in the example, marginal cost at thirteen units of output is $2.60 per unit, but according to the demand curve, consumers are willing to buy thirteen units for as much as $6.40. Therefore, $6.40 is what the monopolist will charge for the thirteen units of output in order to earn the maximum profit.

Profit Maximization or Loss Minimization?

Just as in the case of the perfectly competitive firm, the monopoly firm must sometimes settle for loss minimization in place of profit maximization, at least in the short run. Whether there are actual profits to be made or only losses to be minimized depends on the position of the demand curve relative to the monopolist's average-cost curves.

One possibility is illustrated in Box 8.3. Here, demand is high enough relative to average cost for the monopolist to make a pure economic profit, above and beyond the normal rate of return on capital that is built into the definition of average total cost. As in Box 8.2, the profit-maximizing quantity, at the intersection of the marginal-cost and marginal-revenue curves, is roughly thirteen units of output. The demand curve indicates that the profit-maximizing price for that quantity of output is approximately $6.40 per unit.

At thirteen units of output, average total cost is only $4 per unit. That means the monopolist earns a pure economic profit of $2.40 per unit above and beyond all costs, including the implicit cost of a normal rate of return on invested capital. At thirteen units of output, total profit is $31.20. This is shown graphically in Box 8.3 as the shaded rectangle. The base of the rectangle is equal to the quantity of output (thirteen units). Its height is equal to the difference between the price of $6.40 per unit and the average total cost of $4 per unit — that is, to the $2.40 average profit per unit that the firm earns.

Under less favourable demand conditions, however, the same firm may be able to do no better than to minimize losses. This possibility is illustrated in Box 8.4. The demand curve in the diagram lies below the average total cost curve at all points. This can happen, for example, during a severe recession, when consumer incomes are abnormally low. Following the usual rule, the loss-minimizing quantity of output is found to be about ten units, as Box 8.4 is drawn. According to the demand curve, that much output can be sold for $4 per unit, but average total cost at ten units of output is $4.75. At a price of $4 per unit, the monopolist will lose $0.75 on each unit sold. The total loss is shown in the graph by the shaded rectangle.

Although the monopolist suffers a loss at ten units of output, no other choice of output will yield a smaller loss. As Box 8.4 is drawn, $4 per unit is more than enough to cover average variable costs. The monopoly firm, like the perfectly competitive firm, is better off staying in production in the short run, even at a loss, so long as the price at which the output can be sold is greater than the

A Pure Monopolist Earning Positive Profits

BOX 8.3

The profit actually earned by a pure monopolist depends on the relationship of price to average total cost. In this example, the monopolist's demand curve is high enough to enable a pure economic profit to be earned. Total profit is shown in the diagram as the shaded rectangle with a width equal to the profit-maximizing quantity of output and a height equal to the difference between price and average total cost at that quantity of output.

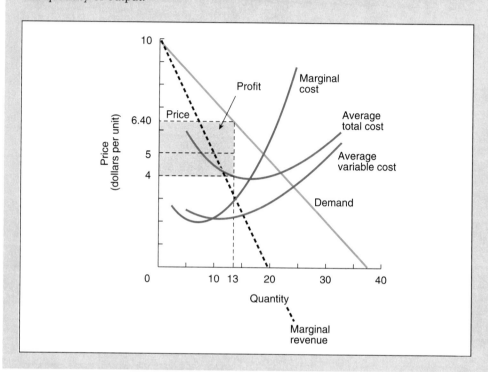

average variable cost. If the demand curve shifts so far to the left that it falls below the average-variable-cost curve at all points, the pure monopoly firm, like the perfectly competitive firm, will minimize short-run losses by shutting down. In the long run, if demand conditions do not improve, the firm will go out of business.

Long-Run Profit Maximization under Pure Monopoly

One of the most important conclusions reached in Chapter 7 was that, in the long run, pure economic profits are impossible under perfect competition. The reason is that if an increase in demand for the product raises the market price above average total cost, new firms will be attracted into the industry. As the new firms enter, the total quantity supplied to the market increases, driving the market price back to the level of average total cost.

BOX 8.4   Short-Run Loss Minimization for a Pure Monopolist

Sometimes demand may not be sufficient to permit a pure monopolist to earn a pure economic profit. In this example, the demand curve lies below the average-total-cost curve at all points. The best the monopolist can do, in the short run, is to minimize losses by producing at the point where marginal cost equals marginal revenue. If the demand curve were to shift downward even farther, so that the firm could not obtain a price covering average variable cost, the short-run loss-minimizing strategy would be to shut down.

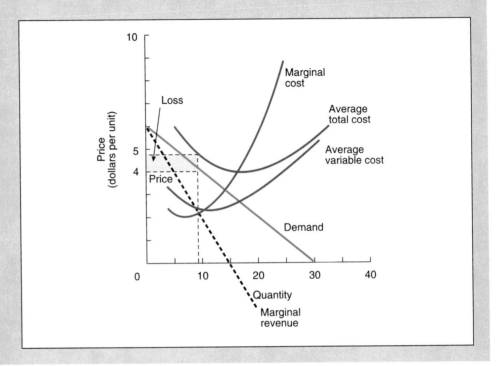

Under pure monopoly, in contrast, pure economic profits can continue indefinitely if demand conditions are favourable. The reason is that a monopolist is assumed to be protected against competition by barriers to entry. Even if short-run demand conditions permit a higher-than-normal rate of return on capital, as in Box 8.3, no other firm can enter the market. If nothing happens to disturb the favourable position of its cost and demand curves, a pure monopolist can earn pure economic profits above and beyond the normal rate of return even in the long run.

Indirect Competition and Long-Run Profits

Although protection from direct competition makes it possible in some cases for pure monopolists to earn pure economic profits in the long run, there are other cases in which long-run profits are eroded by indirect competition. In one limiting case, a monopoly firm faced with indirect competition might find itself in the position pictured in Box 8.5. In the graph there, the demand curve just touches the average-total-cost curve at the quantity of output for which marginal revenue equals marginal cost, so the best the firm can do is break even. It earns sufficient revenue to cover all its costs, including a normal rate of return on capital, but nothing more.

Two kinds of indirect competition in particular might push a monopolist toward this long-run break-even position. One is competition in the process of establishing a monopoly in the first place. A firm may have to bid competitively for a key patent or for access to key natural resources in order to establish its monopoly. Perhaps it will have to hire expensive lawyers and consultants to convince a government agency that it, and not some other firm, should get a key licence or permit. If entrepreneurs compete vigorously to establish a monopoly, it may very well turn out that the winner never does better than break even. Its initial efforts, although successful, may cost so much that it ends up in the position shown in Box 8.5.

The Break-Even Position for a Pure Monopolist   BOX 8.5

Although pure economic profit is possible under pure monopoly in the long run, it is not guaranteed. This graph shows a monopoly that is only breaking even (that is, earning no more than a normal rate of return on invested capital). Among other possibilities, this could be the result of high costs incurred in obtaining or defending the firm's monopoly position or of an erosion of demand caused by indirect competition from substitute products.

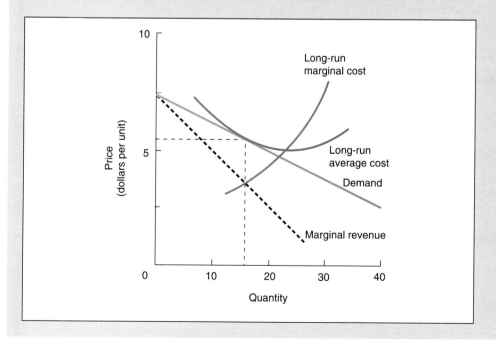

Competition from substitute products can also force a monopolist to the break-even position. A firm with a monopoly over steel production, for example, may find that, over time, clever entrepreneurs in the aluminum or plastics industry are stealing away more and more of its customers. The competition of substitutes may gradually erode demand for the monopolist's own product until, in the limiting case, the demand curve falls all the way to tangency with the average-cost curve.

The likelihood of actually reaching the limiting position of zero profits depends on the closeness of the substitutes offered by the other firms. For example, a firm whose monopoly consists in owning the only Italian restaurant in town will clearly feel more competitive pressure than will a firm owning the only restaurant of any kind. In fact, when a firm's "monopoly" is so narrowly based that many competing firms offer products that are very close substitutes, economists no longer classify the market structure as a pure monopoly. Instead, they call a market structure in which a large number of firms offer products that are relatively close substitutes for one another monopolistic competition. This type of monopoly is discussed in Chapter 9.

Monopoly as an Imperfect Market Structure

Chapter 7 showed that production is carried out in a perfectly competitive market up to the point where price is equal to marginal cost. This, it was argued, makes perfect competition a "perfect" market form, in the sense that all potential mutually beneficial transactions are carried out. Beyond the point of competitive equilibrium, consumer welfare cannot be further improved without imposing an actual loss on producers.

Under pure monopoly, by contrast, production stops short of the quantity necessary to bring market price down to the level of marginal cost. Consider Box 8.6, for example. There, the monopolist maximizes profit by producing 2000 units of output per month and selling each unit for $3. At a rate of output of 2000 units per month, marginal cost is only $1 per unit. There is a $2 gap between marginal cost and the market price. This gap represents a market imperfection; it indicates that some potential mutually beneficial transactions are not being carried out.

One way to understand the nature of this market imperfection is to think of the monopolist as an intermediary standing between the consumer and resource owners. The height of the demand curve at 2000 units of output in Box 8.6 represents what consumers are willing to pay for the 2000th unit of output. The height of the marginal-cost curve at this point represents what the firm has to pay resource owners for the various inputs necessary to produce the 2000th unit. Clearly, production of the 2000th unit is worth while; consumers value it at $3, and resource owners value the resources used up in producing it at only $1.

Reasoning in the same way, it would also be worth while to produce a 2001st unit of output. Consumers would value the 2001st unit at only slightly less than $3, and resource owners would be willing to release the necessary inputs for only a little more than $1. If it were feasible for consumers to negotiate directly with resource owners for production of the 2001st unit, that unit would presumably be produced at a mutually agreeable price, such as $2. In this case, however, consumers do not deal with resource owners directly. They deal instead through the monopolist as an intermediary, and it is not worth while for the monopolist

Why Monopoly Markets Are Imperfect

BOX 8.6

A perfect market is one in which all potential mutually beneficial exchanges are carried out and none is missed. Monopoly markets are not perfect in this sense. In the case illustrated here, a pure monopolist will maximize profits at a quantity of 2000 units per month and a price of $3 per unit. But at that price and quantity, there is a gap between the demand curve and the marginal-cost curve, which indicates that, in principle, further production could be carried out to the mutual benefit of consumers and resource owners. The shaded triangular area indicates the value of the potential benefits that are under monopoly in this example.

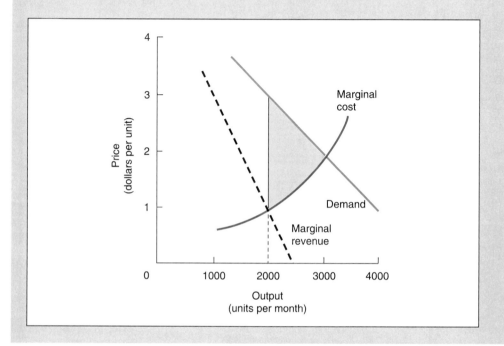

to produce a 2001st unit of output. Even though the 2001st unit could be sold at a price higher than its marginal cost, the marginal revenue earned by the monopolist from the transaction would be less than marginal cost. And it is not profitable for the monopolist to increase output beyond the point at which marginal revenue falls below marginal cost.

What is true of the 2001st unit is also true of the 2002nd, the 2003rd, and all units up to and including the 3000th. Each of these units could be produced and sold at a price higher than marginal cost — that is, at a price high enough to fully compensate resource owners and low enough still to be agreeable to consumers. But as long as consumers deal with resource owners only at arm's length, through the agency of the monopolist, this potential mutual benefit, represented in Box 8.6 by the shaded triangle, will not be realized. It is in this sense that pure monopoly is an imperfect market structure. Problems associated with monopoly are given additional treatment in the appendix to this chapter.

Price Discrimination

This is a good place to emphasize an assumption that has been only implicit in the discussion to this point — the assumption that the pure monopolist sells all units of output at a uniform price. Such a pricing policy is forced on the monopolist whenever the nature of the product makes resale among buyers possible. For example, it is highly unlikely that your campus bookstore (a monopoly on many campuses) could get away with selling economics textbooks at list price to third-year students and at a 25 percent discount to everyone else. If it tried to do so, it would not be long before some enterprising first-year student went into buying books for resale to third-year students at some split-the-difference price. The bookstore's list-price sales would soon fall to zero.

Price discrimination
The practice of charging different prices for the same product, when the price differences are not justified by differences in the cost of serving different customers.

Some firms, however, do not sell their product to all customers at the same price. Such sellers are said to practise **price discrimination**. Two things are required for price discrimination to be possible. First, resale of the product among consumers must be impossible, or at least inconvenient. And second, the seller must be able to classify potential customers into two groups, one with highly inelastic demand, who can be charged high prices, and one with more elastic demand, who will be driven away unless offered low prices. The accompanying For Example. . . box presents a case study on price discrimination in action.

Pros and Cons of Price Discrimination

Price discrimination is widely perceived as unfair, especially by those who pay a high price while others pay less. Attempts have been made to outlaw price dis-

FOR EXAMPLE...

Price Discrimination in Private Schools

Private schools in Canada very commonly practise price discrimination in selling their main product — education. It usually works as follows: First, the school's business office sets tuition at some ambitiously high level, while the admissions office gives its stamp of approval to a certain number of qualified applicants. Then, the financial-aid office gets busy working out a price-discrimination strategy. The strategy consists of offering selective price rebates, called scholarships, to those students who it thinks will not be willing or able to attend if charged full tuition.

A private school is in an ideal position to practise price discrimination. For one thing, the product is completely nontransferable. If you are admitted to both Upper Canada College in Toronto and Lower Canada College in Montreal, you can't sell your Upper Canada College admission to someone who didn't get into either place! Furthermore, the school collects a great deal of information that allows it to classify students according to willingness and ability to pay.

If the price-discrimination strategy is successful, everyone involved may benefit. Students who would not have been able to attend a private school at all without financial aid probably benefit most. Students who pay full tuition find their school experience enriched by the diversity of the student population, which represents a wider variety of backgrounds and abilities than could have been attracted without a scholarship program. Meanwhile, the school itself benefits by keeping its classrooms full with the help of scholarship students and its budget balanced with tuition and fees collected from those without scholarships.

crimination in some markets. However, as the For Example. . . box suggests, price discrimination should not be condemned before the alternatives are considered.

The key question to ask in evaluating any price-discrimination scheme is whether it moves the market closer to or farther from the ideal state in which all potential mutually beneficial trades are carried out. When price discrimination allows buying by those who are willing to pay a price at least equal to marginal cost but not as high as what a nondiscriminatory monopolist would charge, it may very well be beneficial. For example, price discrimination makes it possible for some students to attend schools they otherwise could not afford. It allows parents to take their young children to the movies. And it makes it possible for standby passengers, who could not afford the full fares that business travellers pay, to fill airplane seats that would otherwise go empty. These forms of price discrimination almost certainly represent improvements in market performance compared with what would realistically be possible under uniform pricing.

On the other hand, price discrimination can sometimes be carried too far. In particular, it is important that the lowest price charged not fall below marginal cost. If that were to happen, another kind of market imperfection would be introduced: Output would be too large, rather than too small, in comparison with a perfectly competitive market. Too many, rather than too few, resources would be attracted to the industry in question. For example, public utility commissions in some areas encourage electric utilities to discriminate against industrial users, and in favour of residential users, even to the point that some power for residential use is sold below long-run marginal cost. Many economists believe that this has encouraged wasteful use of electricity by homeowners and has thus made it necessary for utilities to overexpand their generating capacity.

CARTELS

Monopolies and Cartels

To the extent that it is motivated by profit maximization, every firm would like to be a monopolist. But most firms have no realistic chance of becoming pure monopolists. In most markets, firms face competitors that are far too numerous and far too vigorous ever to be bought up or driven away. Furthermore, in most markets, decreasing returns to scale would make it highly inefficient to concentrate all production in a single firm.

For would-be monopolists in such markets, there is a tempting alternative to the pure, single-firm monopoly. That alternative is a **cartel** — a group of independent suppliers of a product who agree to stop competing and, instead, to coordinate their supply decisions so all of them will earn a monopoly profit; together, they control the sale of most or all of the product available on the market.

Cartel
A group of independent suppliers of a product who agree to co-ordinate their supply decisions in an attempt to ensure that they will all earn monopoly profits; together, they control the sale of all or most of the output of a product.

How Cartels Work

A simple example will show just how cartels work. Imagine an industry composed of one hundred identical small firms. For simplicity, assume that the marginal cost of production for all firms in the industry is a constant $1 per unit, regardless of the quantity produced. Because marginal cost is the same for all units of output, the marginal-cost curve also serves as the long-run average-cost curve and the long-run supply curve for the industry. This perfectly elastic long-run supply curve is shown, together with a hypothetical demand curve for the industry, in Box 8.7.

The equilibrium price and quantity of output of the industry depend on how the market is organized. Suppose initially that all firms behave as perfect competitors. Under the theory set forth in Chapter 7, this situation will result in an equilibrium in which the market price is $1 per unit (equal to long-run average cost and long-run marginal cost) and in which 400 000 units of output are produced each month. In this equilibrium, each firm earns a normal rate of return on its capital and earns no pure economic profit.

Suppose now that the heads of the hundred firms get together one day to form a cartel. It is their hope that by replacing competition with co-operation, they can advance their mutual interests. They elect one of their number as cartel manager. The manager is instructed to work out a production and marketing plan that will maximize total profits for the industry and distribute these profits fairly among the members.

BOX 8.7   The Effects of a Cartel

This graph represents an industry composed of one hundred identical firms, each producing at constant long-run average and marginal cost. If the firms behave as perfect competitors, the industry will be in equilibrium where the demand curve and the marginal-cost curve intersect. If the firms form a cartel, however, they can jointly earn economic profits by restricting output to the point where marginal cost is equal to marginal revenue, and raising the product price from $1 to $2.

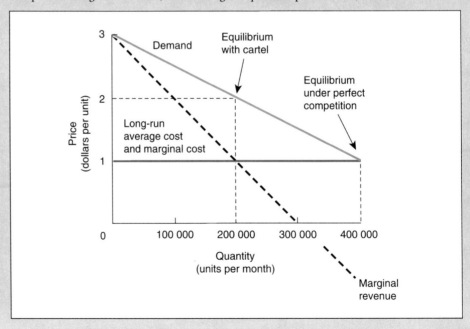

The profit-maximizing problem faced by the cartel manager is exactly the same as that faced by a pure monopolist. Industry profits are maximized at the level of output at which marginal revenue for the industry equals marginal cost. That output is 200 000 units per month in this example. By restricting output to that quantity, the cartel can raise the price of the product to $2 per unit, and $200 000 per month of pure economic profit will be generated. To share this profit fairly among all cartel members, the manager will assign each firm an output quota of 2000 units a month — half as much as it had been producing as a competitor. By this arrangement, the member firms will reap the benefits of pure monopoly despite their small size and large numbers.

The Stability Problem for Cartels

For its members, a successful cartel is a wonderful thing. Each firm is able to share in the profits of a monopoly while maintaining its organizational independence. But for buyers of the product, a cartel is clearly no blessing. In this example, buyers end up spending the same amount of money on the product, overall, as they do under competition, but getting only half the quantity.

Fortunately for consumers, relatively few markets are organized as cartels. In part, this is so because cartels that affect prices or production unduly are illegal under Canadian law. Even more importantly, though, cartels suffer from two big built-in problems that often prevent them from being formed at all or from surviving for long if they are formed.

Control over entry

The first problem affecting cartels is that of control over entry. As long as competition in an industry keeps price down to the level of long-run average cost, membership in the industry tends to be stable. As soon as a cartel raises price above this level, however, the industry becomes a magnet for new entrants. The entry of new firms does not increase the total quantity that the cartel can sell at the profit-maximizing price; it increases only the number of members among whom profits have to be shared. Unless there is some way for a cartel to control entry into its market, it cannot effectively serve the interests of its members.

Enforcement of output quotas

The second, even more serious, built-in problem of cartels is that of enforcing output quotas. In every cartel, each individual member always has an incentive to cheat on its quota by producing extra, unauthorized output. Take the cartel in Box 8.7. The quota for each of the one hundred members is 2000 units per month, just half of what each firm would produce under competitive conditions. What would happen if any single firm cheated on its quota by stepping up output to the pre-cartel level while the others continued to play by the rules?

The answer is simple. An extra 2000 units per month by one firm would have a negligible effect on the market price, because it would represent only a 1 percent increase in industry output. By producing 4000 units a month, the cheater would double its monthly profit — as long as others did not cheat too.

What if the others did cheat? What if all the other 99 firms stepped up output to 4000 units while only one firm stuck to its quota? With industry output at 398 000 units, the price would be forced down virtually all the way to the competitive level of $1. The firm that played fair would gain nothing for its honesty.

The conclusion to which this leads is that each member of a cartel will have an incentive to cheat if it expects other members to play fair — and to cheat if it expects others to cheat, too.

No cartel is free from the problems of entry by new firms and of cheating on quotas. The accompanying For Example. . . box describes the problems faced by OPEC, one of the world's best-known cartels. Even De Beers, a much older cartel, has not been free of these problems. In 1979, De Beers faced the threat of a major new entrant, the gigantic Argyle mine that had just been discovered in Australia. Two years later, it faced another crisis when Zaire tried to make a quick killing by selling more diamonds than its quota allowed. De Beers managed to bring both Zaire and Australia into line, but only at great cost. To keep the cartel intact, it had to accept a lower quota for its own South African mines, and it agreed to give Australia more freedom of action within the cartel than had ever been allowed before. In the end, the De Beers cartel was able to hang together only because the Soviet Union strongly backed the South Africans.

Domestic Cartels: The Farm Sector

As we noted in Chapter 7, agriculture offers a good example of a perfectly competitive industry. Farmers have suffered serious problems as a result of it: Prices can fluctuate dramatically, resulting in periods of low income for producers. However, the demand curve for many farm products is inelastic, so, if farmers could co-ordinate their output decisions, keeping supply down in order to raise prices, they would be in a strong position to increase their total revenue and their profits. They could, in other words, benefit from a cartel.

FOR EXAMPLE...

OPEC and Cartel Theory

At the end of 1982, the Organization of Petroleum Exporting Countries (OPEC) faced a crisis of overproduction and falling prices. The following passages are taken from an article that appeared in the *Wall Street Journal* at that time.

The Decline of the OPEC Cartel

When they meet in December, the members of OPEC will decide whether they can hold their cartel together for another year, or whether their attempt to keep both prices high and all production going has failed. The OPEC countries currently produce only about 60 percent of the oil they pumped before the quadrupling of prices in 1973, and now even prices are under pressure. Indeed, a strong case can be made that OPEC is declining just the way cartels have always declined.

To understand what is happening to OPEC, it is helpful to review the rules of cartel theory, first formulated in 1905 by a young German economist, Robert Liefmann, in his book *Die Kartelle* — and validated by all subsequent experience.

The first of these rules is that a cartel is always the product of weakness. Growing industries don't form cartels; only declining ones do.

At first, it was assumed that the rule did not apply to OPEC. It was assumed that OPEC could raise prices so astronomically because oil consumption had been growing exponentially and was slated to grow even faster.

But study after study since the price explosion of 1973 shows that the developed countries had previously been growing *less* dependent on petroleum. From 1950 to 1973, the energy required to produce an additional unit of manufactured output in developed countries declined by 1.5 percent per year; since then the decline has been much more rapid.

According to the second rule of cartel theory, if a cartel succeeds in raising the price of a commodity, it will depress the prices for all other commodities of the same general class. When OPEC raised oil prices in 1973, it was generally believed that the prices of all other primary commodities — agricultural products, metals, and minerals — would rise in parallel with the petroleum price. But a year later, the prices of all other primary products began to go down. They have been going down ever since.

A cartel, according to the third rule, will begin to unravel as soon as its strongest member — the largest and the lowest-cost producer — must cut production by 40 percent to support the smaller and weaker members. Even a very strong producer will not and usually cannot cut further. The weaker members will then be forced to maintain their production by undercutting the cartel price. In the end, the cartel will collapse into a free-for-all. Or the strongest member will use its cost advantage to drive the weaker and smaller members out of the market.

OPEC has been singularly lucky. Its second-strongest member, Iran, has been forced to cut output by more than 50 percent as a result of revolution and war. Even so, the largest producer, Saudi Arabia, has had to cut its output by more than 40 percent to prevent the collapse of the cartel price.

The other, weaker members, as predicted by the theory, have begun to sell petroleum at substantial discounts of as much as 15 percent below the posted price.

In the meantime, as the fourth of the cartel rules predicts, OPEC has lost its dominance of the oil market. "Any cartel undermines the market shares of its members within 10 years or so," Liefmann concluded in 1905. In 1973, the OPEC countries accounted for almost 60 percent of the oil supply of the industrialized countries. Their share nine years later has fallen to about 45 percent. As predicted by cartel theory, OPEC is losing market position to newcomers outside it such as Mexico, Britain, and Gabon.

The final rule is that the end of a cartel permanently impairs the position of the product, unless it cuts prices steadily and systematically — as did the only long-lived monopolists on record, the explosives cartel before World War I and the Bell Telephone System from 1910 through 1970. However, the experience of most past cartels, for example, the European steel cartel between wars, suggests that for a long time to come, petroleum will lose markets fast when it becomes more expensive and will not regain markets by becoming cheaper.

One cannot yet rule out what all the energy specialists predict: that the oil market is different, and OPEC will behave differently than other cartels. The test will come with the first sustained economic upturn in the developed countries. We will then know whether petroleum consumption will go up as fast as the economy, or whether, as cartel theory predicts, it will rise much more slowly or perhaps not at all.

SOURCE: Peter F. Drucker, "The Decline of the OPEC Cartel," *Wall Street Journal*, November 26, 1982, p. 12. Reprinted with permission of *The Wall Street Journal*. © Dow Jones & Company, Inc., 1982. All rights reserved.

Three years later, by 1985, the economic upturn had occurred. OPEC was still in crisis. Oil prices had fallen. Saudi Arabia's production fell to as low as 25 percent of capacity in some months, and many small OPEC members were selling below the agreed-upon price.

But organizing a system of agricultural cartels on a private, voluntary basis would be a completely hopeless undertaking. As we have seen, cartels have built-in stability problems. To be successful, a cartel must be able to restrict the entry of nonmembers into the industry, and it must be able to enforce rules among its members. Because the number of farms is so large and the barriers to entry so low, these problems would quickly prove fatal for any privately organized agricultural cartel.

Since farmers were unable to overcome problems of low income and erratic prices through voluntary co-ordination, it is not surprising that they turned to governments for help. The federal government created the Canadian Wheat Board in 1935 to set prices for wheat (as well as for a few other grains) and to organize its overseas marketing. The Agricultural Prices Support Act of 1944 permitted price supports for a broader range of farm products.

Both federal and provincial governments have assisted farmers by imposing price controls (that is, setting prices above the market-equilibrium level) or by establishing marketing boards. The latter resemble cartels in that they control the output, and sometimes the price, of the products involved. There are now more than a hundred farm marketing boards in Canada, covering more than half of gross farm sales.

Some Qualifications

It would be tempting to wrap up this chapter with a sweeping comparison of monopoly and competition: Competition is perfect; monopoly is flawed. But not so fast. The conclusions that can safely be drawn from a comparison of the two market structures are more limited than this initial treatment might suggest. Indeed, much more groundwork must be laid before any reliable conclusions can be drawn.

For one thing, our analysis of perfect competition and pure monopoly has hardly taken such factors as technology, product quality, and consumer tastes into account. Before we reach any conclusions on the merits of various market structures, we need a more complete picture of these other aspects of competition.

Second, up to this point, we have compared two different markets—one competitive and the other monopolistic. That is not the same as considering how the performance of any one market would be affected under each of the two market structures. Going from one market structure to another involves increasing or decreasing the number of firms in the industry, and that is likely to affect costs and product quality as well. If, for example, competition reduces costs and improves the quality of the product, its advantage over monopoly may be much greater than the little triangle in Box 8.6 would suggest. By contrast, if dividing production among many firms raises costs or detracts from quality, those effects may more than outweigh the benefits of competition.

Having said all of this, however, we must nonetheless stress that the *theoretical* case against monopoly and other forms of imperfect competition (which we shall examine in the next chapter) is a strong one. Further support for this assertion can be found in the appendix to this chapter.

SUMMARY

1. Any market that is dominated by a single seller is a *monopoly*. A single firm that makes and sells 100 percent of the output of a product is a *pure monopoly*. An organization of producers who act together to control the sale of all or most of the output of a product is a *cartel*.

2. A monopolist is not a price taker. As output is increased or decreased, both price and quantity change, causing changes in total revenue. For a firm with a straight-line downward-sloping demand curve, marginal revenue is always below price. In such a case, the marginal-revenue curve cuts the horizontal distance from the demand curve to the vertical axis in half.

3. A monopolist makes the maximum profit by producing at the level of output at which marginal cost equals marginal revenue. The price is determined by the height of the demand curve at the profit-maximizing level. If a monopoly cannot earn a profit in the short run, it will try to keep its loss to a minimum. If the loss-minimizing price is above average variable cost, the firm will continue to operate in the short run. If the loss-minimizing price is below average variable cost, the firm will shut down.

4. Monopoly is said to be an imperfect market structure because the amount of output produced by a monopoly firm is less than the amount necessary to bring market price down to the level of marginal cost. This means that, under monopoly, consumers who would be willing to pay a price greater than marginal cost for the additional output are not able to do so. In other words, the gap between marginal cost and the market price indicates that some potential mutual benefit is forgone.

5. A monopoly firm can practise *price discrimination* if its product cannot be resold by buyers and if it has some way of classifying buyers according to the elasticity of their demand. Although price discrimination is resented by those buyers who have to pay higher prices, it may increase efficiency by allowing some of the customers who would otherwise have been shut out of the market to buy the product.

6. In theory, a cartel can restrict the output of its members and raise prices to levels that benefit all of them. In practice, cartels face two disruptive forces: (1) the threat of new firms coming into the cartel, and (2) the threat of cheating by existing members. Because of these problems, few cartels are successful in the long run.

KEY TERMS

monopoly
pure monopoly

price discrimination
cartel

KEY BOXES

Box 8.3 A Pure Monopolist Earning
            Positive Profits

Box 8.6 Why Monopoly Markets Are Imperfect
Box 8.7 The Effects of a Cartel

REVIEW QUESTIONS

1. What is the difference between a pure monopoly firm and a cartel?

2. Is there any difference in the profit-maximizing price and quantity for the two market structures, under given cost conditions?

3. Why is marginal revenue always less than price for a monopolist? Under what elasticity conditions will marginal revenue be positive, negative, or zero?

4. Given data on cost and demand, how is the profit-maximizing level of output for a monopolist determined? Given the profit-maximizing output, how is the price determined?

5. Why is monopoly thought to be an imperfect, or inefficient, market structure?

6. Under what conditions can a monopolist practise price discrimination? Who gains and who loses from price discrimination? Is price discrimination always inefficient?

7. "A monopoly firm can always make a profit because, with no competition, it can charge any price it wants to." Do you agree? Why or why not?

8. The form of price discrimination discussed in the text involves charging different customers different prices when the price difference is not justified by differences in costs. Can you think of any examples in which different prices *are* justified by differences in costs? Discuss.

9. In what ways do labour unions resemble cartels? In what ways do they differ? Do you think labour unions ever suffer from the instability that plagues product-market cartels? (We will return to the subject of labour unions in Chapter 13.)

Cases for discussion

10. Some postal services have traditionally maintained a special low rate for the shipment of books. Can you think of any likely economic reasons for this particular instance of price discrimination? Do you think the policy is a desirable one? Explain.

11. Most airlines regularly charge business travellers more than other travellers, and they frequently use special discount prices that are considerably lower than regular economy rates. Why do you think they do this? Is the policy desirable? Discuss.

12. In October 1990, an official in the federal government's Bureau of Competitions Policy stated that "Canadian business can no longer tolerate the cost of doing business in a global market having to face costs imposed on them by price-fixing cartels." The statement came after the *Globe and Mail* alleged widespread price fixing in the cement, compressed gas, and road-paving industries in Ontario. What costs to Canadian business are likely to result from some firms' engaging in price fixing of factor inputs? Specifically, how would domestic price fixing affect Canadian attempts to do business in global markets?

13. In 1987, nutmeg producers in Grenada and Indonesia formalized an agreement to set world nutmeg prices. Producers in these two countries account for 98 percent of the world's nutmeg production. On hearing of this agreement, an official of an association of spice producers said that any price changes would have little impact on the demand for nutmeg, because bakers cannot easily substitute other spices for it.

    a. What formal name is given to the market structure agreed upon by these nutmeg producers?

    b. What do you think happened to nutmeg prices as a result of the agreement?

    c. What problems are likely to develop within this voluntarily organized market structure? Explain why.

Another Look at the Costs of Monopoly

In Box 8.6, we examined the cost of monopoly in terms of benefits lost to society. If production stops short of the point where the cost of the last unit of output equals the price consumers are willing to pay for that unit, the potential mutual benefits to be derived from that product have not been realized.

What this analysis did *not* show is the loss suffered by a particular group, consumers. This loss can be measured in terms of *consumer surplus*, a concept that was introduced in Chapter 5. This way of describing the cost of monopoly is illustrated in the article reproduced in Box 8A.1. The article also explains how part of this loss in consumer benefits becomes a gain for the monopoly firm in the form of **monopoly rent** — that is, the economic profit that is made under monopoly but that is not available to perfectly competitive firms. However, not all of the consumer benefits are transferred to the monopolist; some are lost to society altogether, and represent what is known as **deadweight loss**.

The article goes on to explain an economic theory that holds that this deadweight loss underestimates the actual loss of resources that occurs with the creation of monopolies. According to economist Jagdish Bhagwati and other scholars, monopolies spend significant resources on creating and defending their profit-earning, monopoly position rather than on creating useful output. Bhagwati used the term **directly unproductive profit seeking (DUP)** to describe, as the article puts it, "all ways of seeking a profit that do not contribute to the output of goods and services." The article then cites several examples of such wasteful, rent-seeking activities. In many cases, the role of government in such activities is significant, a fact that has in turn led economists to develop a theory of government decision making known as **public-choice theory**. Box 8A.1 explains this theory briefly.

Monopoly rent
The earnings of a monopoly firm in excess of what it would make as a competitive firm.

Deadweight loss
The part of consumer surplus that is lost under monopoly and is not transferred to the monopolist in the form of monopoly rents; it represents an overall loss of benefits to society.

Directly unproductive profit seeking (DUP)
The profit-seeking activities of a firm that do not contribute to the output of goods and services.

Public-choice theory
A branch of economics that applies economic theory to political decision making, casting voters in the role of customers and government in the role of entrepreneur.

Monopoly and Theories of Rent Seeking

BOX 8A.1

This brief in our series on the modern classics of economics looks at theories of "rent seeking" — the use of resources to make profits without creating any useful output. These theories have changed the way economists think about monopolies and government.

You do not need to be a professional economist to know that monopolies are inefficient: the idea is widely understood. Only quite recently, however, have most economists begun to see that they had long underestimated the economic harm that monopolies do. More recently still, they have started to see that this particular sort of harm is exceptionally widespread — and by no means confined to straightforward cases of monopoly.

"The Welfare Cost of Tariffs, Monopolies and Theft," published in 1967 by Gordon Tullock, then at the University of Virginia, was the first contribution to this reappraisal. Mr. Tullock was already attracting attention as a leader of the public-choice school of economic theorists (see the last section of this box). While glancing at the traditional theory of monopoly, he spotted the gap that the theory of rent seeking would be needed to fill.

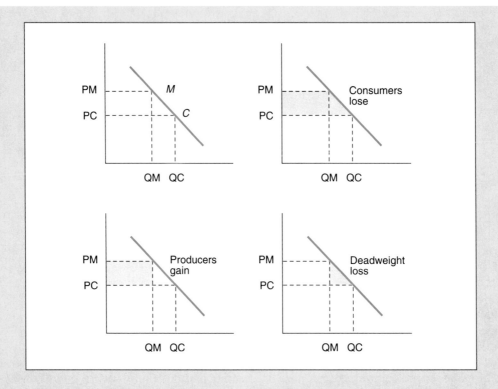

The graphs show, in simple terms, how the traditional theory analyzes the losses caused by monopoly. Part (a), with price on the vertical axis and quantity on the horizontal axis, shows a familiar downward-sloping demand curve: As the price of a good falls, the quantity demanded rises. Suppose that point *C* represents the outcome for an industry with competitive suppliers: a price of PC and a quantity demanded of QC. Also suppose that *M*, with a price of PM and a quantity of QM, represents the outcome under monopoly. *M* is higher up the curve than *C* because, as is well known, monopolists reduce output to drive up their price.

This obviously hurts consumers. Their loss can be represented geometrically by the shaded area in part (b). The monopolist, on the other hand, gains — to the tune of the shaded area in part (c). This is called the *monopoly rent*. Parts (b) and (c) show that consumers lose more than producers gain. As a result, the economy as a whole suffers a net penalty that economists call the *deadweight loss*; this is shown in part (d).

Note that, according to this traditional view, the monopolist's gain is not in itself a loss to the economy: It is simply a redistribution of income from consumers to producers. Only the smaller shaded area in part (d) counts as an overall loss.

Mr. Tullock pointed out that this cannot be right. Monopolies rarely, if ever, arise spontaneously. They have to be created, and then they have to be defended against the competitive pressures that immediately try to break them down. Both tasks involve the use of scarce resources.

Governments can and do bestow monopoly power (either in the strict form of allowing only one producer, or in the weaker form of granting the power to drive prices higher than they would be under free competition). In effect, governments have monopoly rents in their gift.

Willing to Pay

Any sensible would-be monopolist will be happy to pay to get hold of them. But how much will he be willing to pay? Even if he spent all his potential rent to grab and hang on to the monopoly, he would be no worse off than a competitive supplier. The only upper limit on what he is willing to "invest" is the shaded rectangle in part (c). From the economy's point of view, this investment is likely to be pure waste — as useless as the traditional theory's deadweight loss, and a lot bigger.

Where governments are corrupt, the waste may take the form of transfers to *bureaucrats* whose only function is to receive them, and who would otherwise have to find economically useful employment. Where governments are honest, the waste may take the form of employing teams of lawyers (and economists) to *lobby* the government. In either case, large amounts of real resources will be spent in the mere distribution of rents. The traditional theory's harmless transfer from consumers to producers may, in practice, be almost entirely economic loss.

Wherever You Look

These and other strands of thinking united into a thriving branch of modern economics after 1982, when Jagdish Bhagwati of Columbia University revealed the full scope of rent seeking.* He called it *directly unproductive profit seeking (DUP)* — a precise, if unattractive, term that covers a much wider range of activities than the rent seeking discussed above.

Mr. Bhagwati's DUP encompasses all ways of seeking a profit that do not contribute to the output of goods and services.

- Lobbying to obtain a bigger share of *government spending* is one form of DUP. Most governments spend enormous sums on education, health, roads, defence, and so on. They also spend smaller amounts on a far longer list of assorted good causes — everything from roof insulation to opera. Lobbies will compete to win bigger shares of all these budgets.

- If governments use their *tax systems* to favour certain groups and activities over others — and all of them do — there is also income to be had in tilting these preferences in the appropriate direction. Resources will again be used to that end.

- The lobbyists are interested not just in spending and taxes, but also in government *regulation*. A manufacturer of seatbelts finds it worth while to support laws making their use compulsory; makers of patented drugs campaign for stricter rules to stop competing treatments from coming quickly to the market.

- Another economically important category of policy-related DUP aims to *evade government policy*, rather than to profit from it. Tax avoidance (which is legal) and tax evasion (which is not) are both examples of this. Each requires that effort and ingenuity be turned to an economically unproductive purpose.

Thanks to the efforts of Mr. Bhagwati and others, the idea of DUP is now firmly embedded in the economic literature.

Public-Choice Theory: Rational Economic Bureaucrats

The theory of DUP challenges the surprisingly popular fallacy that governments are disinterested champions of the public interest; it sees them instead as dispensers of favours and takers of bribes. Theories of DUP are therefore part of a broader literature on public choice, led since the 1960s by James Buchanan and Gordon Tullock, who both worked for many years at the University of Virginia.

According to public-choice theory, in Mr. Tullock's words, "the voter is thought of as a customer and the politician as an entrepreneur." Civil servants vary according to the setting; but in the middle reaches of a Western bureaucracy (where political masters have no control of appointments and dismissal is out of the question), they are a law unto themselves. Some will work hard for pleasure (they are known as "hobbyists"); others will do no work at all, or expand their departments, or gather perks. This is rational, self-interested behaviour. In short, public-choice theory applies economics to government.

Most public-choice theorists want to give voters more power, but not because they regard voters as especially thoughtful or well informed — quite the opposite. According to the theory, individual voters cannot affect decisions, so they have no incentive to take much interest. If they do, they will focus on the narrow issues that affect them directly (farmers care mainly about farm support; teachers, teachers' pay).

Despite this, public-choice theorists argue in favour of more voter-power. The reason is simple: democracy exists to serve the citizens' interests, and voters are the only people in political life who are not systematically biassed against that aim. "They may be badly informed," says Mr. Tullock, "but what they want is their own well-being." Elsewhere in the system, there is a clash between the interests of men in grey suits and those of the citizenry. Most public-choice theorists therefore want to dilute political power. They favour more proportional representation; bigger-than-simple majorities for the passage of new legislation extending government powers; more government by referendum; more competition within and among government departments; and more "contracting-out" of government-provided services.

---

*Jagdish Bhagwati, "Directly Unproductive Profit-Seeking Activities," *Journal of Political Economy* 90 (October 1982).

SOURCE: "School Brief," *The Economist,* February 9, 1991, pp. 75–76.

KEY TERMS

monopoly rent
deadweight loss

directly unproductive profit
    seeking (DUP)

public-choice theory

KEY BOX

Box 8A.1 Monopoly and Theories of Rent Seeking

Oligopoly and Monopolistic Competition

After studying this chapter you will be able to

1. Distinguish oligopoly from other market structures.

2. Define the term *monopolistic competition.*

3. Explain how market concentration is measured and discuss the factors that cause it.

4. Discuss the many aspects of competition involved in marketing.

5. Discuss the effects of advertising on market structure and performance.

6. Illustrate the concept of oligopolistic interdependence.

7. List some of the factors that affect the performance of oligopolistic markets.

8. Describe the nature of long-run equilibrium under monopolistic competition.

9. Compare perfect competition and monopolistic competition in terms of efficiency and consumer satisfaction.

A Preview   Ganging Up on the Competition

In their efforts to protect themselves from competition, firms are seldom able to create pure monopolies. More often, a few of the largest firms in an industry get together and "co-operate" in setting prices and keeping rival firms out. This article describes such a situation, which economists term *oligopoly*.

A Crack in the Cement Club

Gordon Bailey's mind is a sort of built-in cement calculator — unerring knowledge of prices, strengths, markets, factories, and the quirks of the players. All of this experience led him to the conclusion that Ontario provides a business opportunity big enough to drive a seven-metre ready-mix truck through.

Cement in Ontario is about the most expensive in the world. In Toronto, at the beginning of this year, a tonne of Portland cement powder listed for about $130 (U.S.$110). Just across the border, in New York State, the same stuff goes for U.S.$70. Offshore, it is cheaper still. Given that the main ingredients in cement are limestone and energy, both of which are in bountiful supply in Ontario, the huge price difference points to another powerful market force at work.

Call it an oligopoly. Cement in Ontario, and to a lesser extent in other parts of the nation, is controlled by four players with more than 90 percent of the local business. They are St. Lawrence Cement Inc., 59.7 percent owned by Holderbank Financière Glaris Ltd. in Switzerland; Lafarge Canada Inc., controlled by Paris-based Lafarge Coppée, the world's second-largest cement maker; Essroc Canada Inc. (formerly Lake Ontario Cement Ltd.), controlled by Société des ciments français; and the sole Canadian of the lot, Toronto-based St. Marys Cement Corp., privately controlled by the Lind and Rogers families in Toronto.

Concentration is the nature of the cement business itself. Throughout the world, a handful of major players have emerged dominant in the industry, with the French often at the forefront. This is a mature industry, where gradual and expensive improvements in efficiency supplant technological leaps as the major determinant of success. Hence, the

barriers to entry are imposing. Building a modern green-field cement powder plant in Canada could cost upwards of $150 million these days.

In Ontario, two different parties have shown intense interest in the local cement price phenomenon. One is industry veteran Bailey and his partner Lorne Leibel, president of Canada Homes Inc. — one of the country's largest home builders. Rather than fight the system, the two decided it made much better commercial sense to find an external source of cement and sell it within the existing price structure. To do this they set up their own cement company, Chieftain Cement Inc.

The second party is perhaps even less welcome to the oligopoly: the federal Bureau of Competition Policy. In the spring of 1990, it obtained a search warrant that states that a conspiracy to fix prices and rig bids in the cement and ready-mix concrete industry in the Toronto area existed from May 1976 to July 1988. Federal officials obtained this warrant to search the offices of the four major players in the Ontario cement industry, which together dominate the local cement market. The parent companies named in the warrant were: St. Lawrence Cement, Lafarge Canada, Lake Ontario Cement, and St. Marys. The federal investigation continues.

From the beginning, Chieftain's strategy has been *not* to wage heroic battle against the mammoth cement manufacturers. It calls for peaceful co-existence with the major players to reap advantage from the very pricing umbrella provided by the oligopoly. "I don't want to do enough business to make the Big Four want to push me out," says Bailey. "I do 100 000 tonnes a year. They do 4.5 million tonnes. What's the point of them cutting the price for all their sales just to get my 100 000 tonnes out

of the market?"

Bailey can likely land cement in Oshawa for U.S.$50 to U.S.$55 a tonne (pretax), or about half the list price in Toronto.

A question mark is the reaction of the Big Four. For now, they seem to regard Chieftain as something of a curiosity. "We know [it's] there," says Mike Doran, general manager of Essroc's Great Lakes cement division. "It's a highly integrated market, so there's only so much business it can go after. I can't say it is regarded as a threat, though it could have a minor impact on prices."

Though it remains unspoken, the major players might secretly be relieved by the arrival of new participants, particularly ones obviously not inclined to upset the juicy pricing structure. After all, the federal Bureau of Competition Policy may be more sympathetic to an industry open to all comers than what previously amounted to a closed shop.

Chieftain declares itself satisfied with a small slice of the pie. "If we don't take a lot," says Bailey, "they shouldn't get too upset."

SOURCE: Excerpted from Dunnery Bast, "A Crack in the Cement Club," *Canadian Business*, March 1991, pp. 64–69. Reproduced with permission.

BETWEEN PURE MONOPOLY AND PERFECT COMPETITION

In the Ontario cement industry, as we learned in the Preview, four firms dominate the market. They are neither pure monopolists nor perfect competitors. They compete with one another to supply the construction industry with cement, and are bothered by pesky newcomers such as Chieftain. They have evidently been unable to form a monopoly cartel. However, while they are not free to behave the way monopolists do, neither does their behaviour resemble that of the perfectly competitive firms we described in Chapter 7. For one thing, they are able to strike fear into potential competitors, making entry into the industry quite difficult. Also, they have considerable influence over the price of their product. Even firms whose costs are lower than those of the four industry giants are reluctant to disturb the prices they have established.

Thus, the Ontario cement industry operates somewhere between our two extreme models of monopoly and perfect competition—as do many other industries in Canada. The article in the Preview refers to the Ontario cement industry as an **oligopoly** — an industry in which a few firms (two or more, but fewer than, say, a dozen) account for a major part of the industry's output. The dominant position of these few firms causes them to behave in unique ways that have long been of interest to economists and economic policy makers.

Oligopoly represents an imperfect form of competition. So, too, does another type of industry structure, which economists call **monopolistic competition**. This paradoxical term refers to industries that have many small firms, as do industries under perfect competition, and virtually no barriers to entry. However, under monopolistic competition, unlike perfect competition, the goods produced or sold by the firms are not homogeneous. Each firm is able to create a small market for itself (and so, in effect, has a small demand curve of its own) by making its product distinct in some way from others. Restaurants and clothing stores are good examples of such firms.

This chapter will explore the major characteristics of these two forms of imperfect competition in greater detail. First, however, consider Box 9.1, which provides a brief summary of these characteristics and compares them with those of perfect competition and monopoly.

> **Oligopoly**
> A market structure in which there are two or more firms, at least one of which has a large share of total sales.
>
> **Monopolistic competition**
> A market structure in which many small firms offer differentiated products.

OLIGOPOLY: COMPETITION AS RIVALRY

The term *competition* has two meanings in economics. In the phrase "perfect competition," it refers to market structure. A market is perfectly competitive if it has large numbers of small firms, a homogeneous product, well-informed buyers and sellers, and easy entry and exit of firms. In its second meaning, competition refers to business rivalry — that is, to a type of behaviour rather than a market structure. Two firms are said to compete if they treat each other as rivals in their efforts to do the best they can in the marketplace.

As we pointed out in Chapter 7, there is no rivalry in perfectly competitive markets because each firm sees every other firm as too small to have much of an impact on market conditions. Rivalry is absent from pure monopoly because there is only one firm in the market. And as long as members obey the rules they have agreed upon, rivalry is absent in a cartel.

In an oligopoly — the cement industry is a case in point — it matters very much to each firm what its rivals do, and not just in relation to price. In many

BOX 9.1   Four Types of Market Structures

Characteristics	Perfect Competition	Monopoly	Oligopoly	Monopolistic Competition
Number of firms in industry	Many	One	Few	Many
Product	Homogeneous	Unique	Differentiated or identical	Somewhat differentiated
Barriers to entry	None	Large	Fairly large	Fairly small
Firm's control over prices	None	Considerable	Some	A little
Marketing/ advertising	None	Some, to enlarge market	Considerable	Some
Concentration	Close to 0 percent	100 percent	High	Low
Examples	Wheat (individual farmers) Beans	Hydro Post office	Cement Automobiles	Restaurants Retail clothing stores

markets, an oligopoly firm must also be prepared to respond to moves that its competitors make in terms of product changes, technical innovations, customer service, and advertising.

The need to focus on the interaction of many firms rather than on the behaviour of each firm in isolation makes it difficult to formulate a completely satisfactory theory of oligopoly. Rather than presenting a single, unified theory, then, the first part of this chapter will look at a number of fragmentary theories all tied together by one central question: *Is perfect competition necessary for satisfactory market performance, or is competition among a few large rival firms good enough?* Some economists have argued that, even without explicitly agreeing to do so, oligopolists can co-ordinate their actions to restrict output and raise prices almost as effectively as do members of formal cartels. Others reject this idea and argue instead that competition among the few works very efficiently to serve consumer needs. Still others hedge their bets by saying that some oligopolies seem to perform better than others for reasons that are not completely understood. Although the controversy cannot be settled here, at least a map of the territory can be provided. We shall start with the central concept of market concentration.

MARKET CONCENTRATION: MEASUREMENT AND DETERMINANTS

The main purpose of this section is to develop some insight into the performance of oligopolistic markets, but two preliminary questions need to be asked. First, how many markets are really dominated by just a few firms (and how many is "a few")? And second, what determines the number of firms in a market and the size of their market share? Knowing the answers to these questions will make it easier to understand both the operation of different markets and the rationale behind government policy toward monopoly and oligopoly.

Measuring Market Concentration

Concentration ratios provide a rough-and-ready measure of the extent to which markets are dominated by a few firms. The most common of these ratios are the four-firm concentration ratio (which measures the percentage of sales attributed to the top four firms in a given market) and the eight-firm concentration ratio (which measures the market shares of the top eight firms). Box 9.2 gives four-firm concentration ratios for several Canadian industries. The first three industries are classic oligopolies; they consist of a handful of firms that control virtually the entire market. In the case of such industries as agriculture and construction, there are many firms, each of which is small relative to the size of the market. All in all, more than one-half of Canadian manufacturing output comes from markets in which the top four firms control half the market or more. The Macdonald Royal Commission found that Canadian industries tend to be more highly concentrated than their counterparts in the United States. It observed that "in total, nearly four-fifths of U.S. economic activity is essentially competitive. The estimate for Canada is substantially lower, amounting to only two-fifths of economic activity as measured by GNP."[1]

Concentration ratio
The percentage of an industry's total sales contributed by the four or eight largest firms in the industry.

Four-Firm Concentration Ratios for Selected Industries   BOX 9.2

Concentration ratios measure the percentage of industry sales made by the largest firms in the industry. This selection of several major industries in Canada shows the percentage of overall industry sales made by the four largest firms in each industry.

Industry	Concentration Ratio		
	1965	1982	1985
Breweries	94.5	—	97.7
Motor vehicles	93.3	—	95.1
Tobacco products	—	91.8	—
Petroleum refining	84.8	—	64.0
Rubber products	—	58.4	—
Construction	—	5.4	—
Agriculture, forestry, and fishing	—	5.0	—

Note: Imports are not included.

SOURCE: Adapted from Statistics Canada, *Annual Report of the Minister of Industry, Trade and Commerce under the Corporations and Labour Unions Returns Act*, Part 1: Corporations, 1982, p. 49, Catalogue no. 61–210, and Christopher Green, *Canadian Industrial Organization and Policy* (Toronto: McGraw-Hill Ryerson, 1990), p. 80.

---

[1]*The Report of the Royal Commission on the Economic Union and Development Prospects for Canada 2* (Ottawa: Minister of Supply and Services, 1985), p. 217.

An interesting question, but one that is difficult to answer, is whether industry has become more or less concentrated in Canada over time. In 1985, the Macdonald Royal Commission noted in its report that concentration, as measured by the percentage of total shipments account for by the four largest enterprises in the industry, had increased in most major sectors between 1957 and 1980. The increases were most notable in retail trade (5.1 percent), transportation and communications and utilities (7.8 percent), and services (7.6 percent). By the early 1980s, 82 percent of all manufactured goods were being produced by industries with four or fewer firms.

In aggregate terms, the top 1 percent of Canadian enterprises accounted for 69.5 percent of all sales in 1987.[2] This figure had held relatively constant throughout the decade of the eighties. It is likely, however, that the sharp increase in corporate mergers in Canada during the late 1980s has resulted in an increase in concentration levels.

The Determinants of Market Concentration

The next important question is, Why are some industries more concentrated than others? The phenomenon of economies of scale provides a logical starting point for answering this question.

Economies of scale

Chapter 6 introduced the concept of economies of scale. A firm is said to experience economies of scale if its long-run average costs decline as its scale of output increases. Shapes of long-run average-cost curves vary from one industry to another, but statistical studies have indicated that many industries fit the pattern of an L-shaped long-run average-cost curve. Such a cost curve shows economies of scale initially, followed by a range of constant returns to scale.

The point at which the average-total-cost curve stops falling and begins to flatten out is known as the minimum efficient scale for the firm, and it is an important determinant of market concentration. The study of economies of scale in Canada in the late 1950s by Eastman and Stykolt, from which the data in Box 9.3 are taken, indicates that many industries appeared to have *too many* plants, each of which was too small to produce at the output level of minimum efficient scale. In contrast to U.S. firms, which often build plants that appear to be larger than required by economies of scale, Canadian firms often build plants that are smaller than what would be necessary to realize such economies. The concentration ratio in industries in which this is the case might be said to be too low rather than too high. In view of the relatively small Canadian market and the reality of economies of scale, much of Canadian industry may indeed lend itself to an oligopolistic market structure.

A more recent study of economies of scale notes that Canadian labour productivity in manufacturing (as measured by value-added-per-employee) was 21 percent lower than U.S. productivity in the 1961–65 period, and 16 percent lower in the 1976–80 period. About one-third of the inefficiency was attributable to

[2]Statistics Canada, *Annual Report of the Minister of Industry, Science and Technology under the Corporations and Labour Unions Returns Act*, Part 1: Corporations, 1987, p. 73, Catalogue no. 61–210. Used with permission of the Minister of Supply and Services Canada, 1992.

Minimum Efficient Scale for Sixteen Industries BOX 9.3

This table presents the results of a study of Canadian industries in the late 1950s and early 1960s. Column 1 shows the number of plants that the existing Canadian market could contain if each plant were the smallest efficient size (that is, if each plant were operating at the point where the average-cost curve stops falling and begins to level out). Column 2 shows the actual number of plants in each industry. Column 3 shows the percentage of industry output produced by the plants that were actually operating at the most efficient level.

Industry	Year of Study	Number of Plants of Smallest Efficient Size That Could Be Contained (1)	Actual Number of Plants (2)	Percentage of Output Produced by Plants Operating at Most Efficient Level (3)
Fruit canning	(1958)	4	13	0
Vegetable canning	(1958)	24	43	50
Cement	(1957)	17.8	18	80
Containerboard	(1960)	4.7	10	57
Shipping containers	(1958)	28	37	72
Synthetic solid detergents	(1959)	7	3	100
Synthetic liquid detergents	(1959)	49	?	75
Refrigerators	(1960)	0.6	10	0
Electric ranges	(1960)	0.9	23	0
Wringer washing machines	(1960)	8	14	58
Newsprint	(1958)	36	39	80
Beef packing	(1959)	42	47	68
Pork packing	(1959)	16	45	9
Petroleum refining	(1956)	7	40	0
Primary steel	(1955)	4	4	0
Rubber tire	(1959)	7	9	20

Note: These results are generally confirmed by more recent studies. See, for example, P. Gorecki, *Economies of Scale and Efficient Plant Size in Canadian Manufacturing Industries* (Ottawa: Department of Consumer and Corporate Affairs, 1976), and John R. Baldwin and Paul K. Gorecki, *The Role of Scale in Canada–U.S. Productivity Differences in the Manufacturing Sector, 1970–1979*, Royal Commission on the Economic Union and Development Prospects for Canada, Collected Research Studies 6 (Toronto: University of Toronto Press, 1985).

SOURCE: H.C. Eastman and S. Stykolt, *The Tariff and Competition in Canada* (Toronto: Macmillan, 1967).

less-than-optimal plant size. Short production runs, diversity of output, and other factors accounted for the remaining two-thirds of the difference.[3]

One of the reasons Canadian firms build plants that are too small to achieve economies of scale may be that they are reluctant to expand capacity because,

---

[3]John R. Baldwin and Paul K. Gorecki, *The Role of Scale in Canada–U.S. Productivity Differences in the Manufacturing Sector, 1970–1979*, Royal Commission on the Economic Union and Development Prospects for Canada, Collected Research Studies 6 (Toronto: University of Toronto Press, 1985), p. 12.

given a relatively small market, substantial increases in capacity might require considerable reductions in price. Price reductions would threaten the profit margins of the firms in the industry.

It should also be noted that the production costs of individual plants are not the only criteria used by firms in deciding the most efficient scale of operation. A study of the Canadian food-processing industry observes that "plants that are too small to minimize production costs are often optimal in the sense of minimizing overall costs of production, assembly, and distribution."[4] Small tomato-canning plants in Ontario, for instance, survive because they are able to locate close to the raw materials they use and because they can specialize. Factors such as these lead the multiplant firms that we have in meat-packing, fish-processing, and dairy-processing industries to assume the higher production costs associated with small operations while retaining the advantages of size in bargaining, raising capital, advertising, and spreading out the burden of overhead. Given such multiplant economies, more industries may be operating at or close to their minimum efficient scale than might initially appear to be the case.

Nonetheless, it is unlikely that the market concentration ratios presented in Box 9.2 are determined by economies of scale alone. Many Canadian economists are convinced that, while a large number of industries have more plants in operation than are warranted by considerations of efficiency, there are simultaneously fewer firms in those industries than desirable. In other words, a relatively small number of firms, often operating numerous production or distribution units of less-than-efficient size, have come to dominate many Canadian industries. Determinants other than efficiency must account for the survival of such market structures and for the absence of new rivals to challenge existing firms. It is thus necessary to consider some of the other possible determinants.

Other Barriers to entry

One reason that an industry may be more concentrated than economies of scale alone would account for is that there may be barriers to the entry of new firms. Even if profits in the industry are unusually high, prospective entrepreneurs may for some reason be unable to duplicate the performance of existing firms. As demand for the product expands, then, growth can come only through the expansion of existing firms, even after all economies of scale have been exhausted, or even if existing firms merely duplicate undersized production units.

Legal barriers. As in the case of pure monopoly, barriers to entry into oligopolistic industries are sometimes created on purpose by federal, provincial, or municipal government policy. In such industries, policy stops short of creating a pure franchised monopoly but still limits the number of competitors to fewer than would exist under free entry. For example, entry into the various segments of the broadcasting industry was for years tightly controlled by the Canadian Radio-television and Telecommunications Commission (CRTC). Despite some recent reforms, these legal barriers to entry have still not been entirely disman-

---

[4]John Morris, "The Competitive Characteristics of the Canadian Food-Processing Industry," in *Competition and Public Policy on Competition in the Canadian Food Industry,* Proceedings of the Agricultural and Food Marketing Forum, ed. R.M.A. Lyons and R.L. Louks, Department of Agricultural Economics and Farm Management, University of Manitoba, Occasional Series no. 7, May 1977.

tled. At the provincial level, entry into many professions and trades—law, medicine, plumbing, hairdressing, and dozens of others — is limited by licensing boards. Entry into rental housing or retailing in many communities is limited by local zoning regulations. The list of such legal barriers also includes patents and copyrights, which limit the access of prospective entrepreneurs to new technology and ideas.

Ownership of resources. A second kind of barrier to entry is ownership of some nonreproducible resource. For example, entry into the ski-resort industry is limited by the availability of suitable mountains. Entry into extractive industries is, in at least some cases, limited by ownership of the best available natural resources by existing firms. In other markets, the nonreproducible resources in question are human. Entry into the movie industry might be difficult, for example, if the top-quality stars were all under contract to existing firms. Whatever the reason, ownership of a nonreproducible resource gives existing firms an advantage over new entrants and thus constitutes a barrier to entry not directly related to economies of scale.

Market power. A third barrier to entry is market power. Market power is not the same as market performance, though in cases where economies of scale exist, it may depend at least partly on efficient performance. By **market power**, economists mean the strength that a firm may possess for reasons primarily other than technical efficiency — for example, exclusive control of resources, prior buildup of profits, networks of influence and command, or massive advertising — that gives it an advantage over potential rivals.

The following hypothetical example illustrates one aspect of market power. A young engineer in Montreal develops a new method of manufacturing paper, which, he claims, can reduce the cost of producing a certain type of paper by one-third. He arranges the financing, builds the plant, installs his new equipment, and hires the necessary employees. On the day he opens his plant, he announces a price for his paper that is one-third lower than the price charged by the large, single, long-established paper mill in the area. This larger mill cannot produce paper at that price, but, relying on its accumulation of past profits and its network of paper mills across the country, it cuts its price in the Montreal area by half. The new firm will now be driven out of business, not because it is unable to achieve efficient operation — it is *more* efficient than its rival — but because it doesn't have the market power of its older rival. The established firm does not lose much money, because it can retain higher prices in its other markets, and it does not lose money for long, because it can raise the price again as soon as the challenger declares bankruptcy. Incidentally, the practice of the hypothetical established firm in this case would be a violation of Canadian law. It is an example of "predatory pricing," meaning the temporary, localized use of below-cost prices to drive a rival out of business. However, such practices are difficult to prosecute, and the fines levied may be a small price to pay for the elimination of a competitor.

Firms may increase their market power by appointing bank presidents or other persons with specialized knowledge and influence to their boards of directors. Such appointments may give them advantages when it comes to examining new markets or arranging their financing. Several Canadian sociologists have documented the existence of a "corporate elite" in Canada: a social and economic

Market power
The strength that a firm possesses for reasons other than technical efficiency — for example, exclusive control of resources, prior buildup of profits, networks of influence and command, or massive advertising — that gives it an advantage over its rivals.

network of about a thousand business leaders who occupy most of the important directorships in the country.[5] It is safe to assume that the social and economic connections thus established provide benefits to the participants that place them at an economic advantage over those who operate outside the network.

Firms may also attempt to expand their power and control through formal mergers. Mergers can take many forms. A firm can merge *vertically* with a supplier or purchaser of its products, or *horizontally* with a competitor. It can engage in a *conglomerate* merger with firms producing completely different types of products and services. Horizontal mergers may result in economies of scale, and conglomerate mergers may give the firms involved more stability by reducing the dangers inherent in having all their eggs in one basket. Almost always, however, one objective of mergers is to increase market power, and, from the point of view of potential competitors, the result may be increased barriers to entry.

The largest conglomerate in Canada is BCE Inc. (the Bronfman group), which controls 360 firms, each with at least $10 million in assets. Next in size is Canadian Pacific Ltd., which employs more than 100 000 people directly or through its 167 subsidiaries. Businesses such as these are able to "pyramid" their investments from one company to another in order to establish effective control over a large business empire without formal mergers.

In recent years, there have been more mergers in Canada than in much larger economies, such as Germany or Japan. In 1989 alone, almost 1200 mergers and acquisitions, involving $30 billion in assets, took place in Canada, and nearly half of them involved foreign firms. Some of these mergers might be considered necessary to enable smaller Canadian companies to benefit from economies of scale and thereby to compete with larger foreign firms. However, the results of a recent Economic Council of Canada research project suggest that, in many instances, there are no such clear-cut benefits from mergers. Economist Abe Tarasofsky observes that roughly a dozen large conglomerates represent about 20 percent of the entire Canadian corporate sector, compared with only about 10 percent in 1980. Asked whether these recent mergers had improved the productivity of the firms involved (measured in terms of profitability), he replied, "On the whole, the profitability of the acquired assets remains about the same as it was before. . . . I have found that about four acquired firms out of ten improved their performance. An equal four out of ten recorded deteriorated performances, and the other two remained where they were before."[6] Thus, while there is no evidence to suggest that mergers generally result in improved economic performance, it is unfortunately clear enough that they do limit the entry of potential competitors and consequently, in the long run, prevent the emergence of cheaper and better methods of production.

Another way in which companies seek to secure market power in order to enhance their strength in a given industry is through the use of extensive advertising and other marketing techniques. Indeed, marketing is so important to modern business that it warrants a more detailed examination.

---

[5]The classic study of this phenomenon remains John Porter, *The Vertical Mosaic* (Toronto: University of Toronto Press, 1965). See also Wallace Clement, *The Canadian Corporate Elite: An Analysis of Economic Power* (Toronto: McClelland and Stewart, 1975), and Peter Newman, *The Canadian Establishment* (Toronto: McClelland and Stewart, 1977), vol. 1.

[6]Economic Council of Canada, "Mergers and Acquisitions," *Au Courant* 10, no. 4 (1990): 14–15. Reproduced with permission of the Chairman of the Economic Council of Canada, 1992.

The Economics of Marketing

Marketing is the process of finding out what customers want and channelling a flow of goods and services to satisfy those wants. Marketing consists of four activities: creating a *product* that will meet consumer needs; getting it to a *place* where consumers can conveniently buy it; *promoting* the product through advertising, personal selling, and other means; and putting the right *price* on the product. These four activities are often called the "four P's" of marketing. As Box 9.4 shows, the costs of the four P's account for about half of all consumer spending. Let's look at the role that each of these activities plays in a competitive economy.

Marketing
Finding out what customers want and channelling a flow of goods and services to satisfy those wants.

Competition and the product

In a perfectly competitive market, the product — wheat, trucking services, or whatever — is thought of as a constant. Some oligopolies also have products that change little from year to year — the aluminum and cement industries are examples. But there are many oligopolistic markets in which shaping the product to fit consumer needs is a key part of competition.

Innovation is one major aspect of product competition. Consider the example of stereo equipment. It is clear what customers want: They want music in their living rooms that sounds like a live performance. That is an ideal that is never

Marketing Costs and Consumer Spending   BOX 9.4

As this chart shows, marketing costs account for about half of all consumer spending. The costs and profits of wholesale and retail trade are the largest single item, followed by freight transportation. Advertising, although it is the most visible of marketing activities, accounts for only about 3 percent of the cost of consumer goods and services. All aspects of marketing are important to the process of competition.

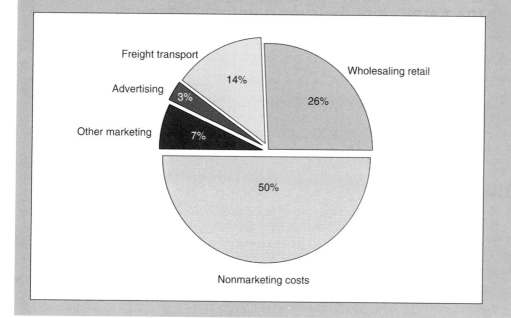

quite reached, but long-playing records, metal-oxide cassette tapes, Dolby noise-suppression systems, and compact discs each represent a step closer to the ideal. The first competitor to take each step has at least a temporary advantage.

Diversity is another aspect of product competition. Consumers have different needs and tastes. Economists talk about "the market" for cars, but this market is really composed of many segments: the markets for economy cars, vans, sports cars, and so on. Competition ensures that products will be made that will meet the needs of consumers in each segment; a neglected segment would soon attract a firm in search of profits.

Quality is still another aspect of product competition — one that has been getting more attention in recent years. The quality of many goods made in North America has been improving for years: Tires last longer; fabrics wash more easily; contact lenses give better vision. However, the demand for quality seems to have risen even faster than the supply. Foreign firms — especially Japanese firms — have gained a competitive advantage in many markets by being the first to respond to this demand for quality. As North American firms scramble to catch up, consumers are the winners.

Competition in distribution

The second of the four P's of marketing — place — refers to all the activities needed to get a product to consumers. It includes transportation and other aspects of physical distribution and, even more important, the services of wholesale and retail firms.

Innovation and diversity affect distribution systems as much as they affect products themselves. Such tried-and-true methods of retailing as supermarkets and department stores (which were innovations earlier in the century) have come under pressure in recent years. On the one hand, specialized boutique-type retailers and direct-mail companies have won a bigger share of the wealthiest consumers. On the other hand, discount stores, off-price retailers, and warehouse-type food stores have made inroads among budget-conscious consumers. Often the prize in competition among manufacturing firms goes to those that have the best distribution networks.

Competition in promotion

Promotion — which includes advertising, personal selling, store displays, and public relations — is the most visible aspect of competition in many markets. Promotion is the communication link between producers and their customers.

A major part of promotion is spreading information. The theory of consumer choice and perfect competition assumes that consumers are well informed about the choices available to them, but, in the real world, information is a scarce resource. Advertising, personal selling, and other promotional activities lower the cost to consumers of learning about prices, product features, and where to buy desired goods and services.

It is well known, however, that advertising does more than just inform consumers. It also shapes their tastes and even their perceptions. The power of advertising to shape tastes and perceptions has made this aspect of marketing a subject of controversy. Economists such as John Kenneth Galbraith argue that a distinction should be made between true wants and those that are created by advertising. In the view of such critics, advertising that goes beyond a simple statement of the facts about a product is at best a waste and at worst harmful to consumer welfare. Other observers doubt that there are such things as true or natural wants other than the very basic needs for food, clothing, and shelter. All other wants are "created" in one way or another by myriads of cultural and historical factors. Advertising may affect which goods people choose to satisfy various needs and wants. It may cause them to choose round-toed boots rather than square-toed boots to keep their feet dry, but that does no harm. Economists who take this point of view believe that efforts to limit consumer choice in the name of giving people what they "truly" want are a greater threat to consumer welfare than advertising is.

Advertising as a barrier to entry

In the case of oligopoly, advertising is seen as a barrier to entry by new firms. As such, it is said to lead to high levels of market concentration. And concentration, in the view of some economists, is linked with poor market performance.

The way in which advertising acts as a barrier to entry is by creating brand loyalties. Consumers who might otherwise treat all cola drinks as close substitutes are divided into opposing camps, some fiercely loyal to Pepsi, others to Coke. Each firm can raise its price with little fear that doing so will cause its customers to go elsewhere. And neither firm needs to worry about the resulting high profits' attracting new firms to the market, since new firms would have to spend money not only to build plants and hire workers but also to mount tremendously expensive advertising campaigns.

Another kind of reasoning comes from studies of the ways in which advertising is used by firms. For example, it has been shown that, on the whole, new products are advertised more heavily than established products. This may indicate that makers of established products tend to depend on consumer loyalty and that advertising is a way of breaking down that loyalty. Perhaps even more interesting are the results of real-life experiments in which advertising has been introduced into markets where it was not permitted before. One study compared the price of eyeglasses in areas where advertising was restricted with their price in areas where they could be advertised freely. It found the price in areas that restricted advertising to be more than twice as high.[7] And so the debate goes on.

Economists are often more suspicious than business people of the alleged benefits of advertising, because their perspective is different. A business firm that manages to take a share of the market away from a competitor through advertising and to raise its revenues and profits in the process will naturally praise the benefits of advertising. However, the economist is more concerned about advertising's benefits for society, and from that perspective, the results are much more ambiguous. Business firms are driven very strongly to triumph over their rivals, and advertising can certainly be an effective weapon in such warfare, but since winning the war brings no clear savings in costs — in fact, quite the contrary — and no improvements in products or services, the consumer seldom benefits in the long run.

Price as a marketing tool

This brings us to price, the last of the four P's of marketing. Marketing specialists agree with economists that good pricing decisions are vital to a firm's success. But in the real world, they say, the right price can't be found by picking a point on a

---

[7]Lee Benham, "The Effect of Advertising on the Price of Eyeglasses," *Journal of Law and Economics* 15 (October 1972): 337–52.

graph. Instead, pricing decisions have to be co-ordinated with other marketing decisions if a product is to succeed in the marketplace.

Take quality and variety, for example. Some consumers are willing to pay top price for top quality, while others would prefer less than the top quality at a lower price. Some are willing to pay high prices to satisfy unusual tastes, while others will accept cheaper, mass-produced goods. Pricing is a key factor in distribution, too. Often the same goods are available at different prices in swanky boutiques and barnlike off-price outlets. Some consumers prefer one, some the other. Finally, price and promotion interact. While some consumers will pay extra for advertised brands, others prefer low-priced generic goods that bear no brand name.

In sum, when all aspects of marketing are taken into account, competition begins to look like a much more complex process than it appears to be on a graph, where price and quantity are the only two variables under consideration.

OLIGOPOLY: INTERDEPENDENCE AND CO-ORDINATION

It is much more difficult to state a theory of oligopoly than it is to state a theory of pure competition or monopoly. The theories of competition and monopoly presented in Chapters 7 and 8, respectively, focus on decision making by a single firm under given conditions. Those conditions, which include technology, input prices, and the demand curve for the product, are assumed not to be affected by the decisions the firm itself makes. Under pure competition, it is possible to isolate the firm's actions, because the firm is so small; under monopoly, the firm being studied is assumed to be isolated from rivals. The ability to isolate the decisions of a pure competitor or a monopolist greatly simplifies the task of theory building.

Industries that are dominated by a few large firms, in contrast, raise the problem of **oligopolistic interdependence**. This refers to the need for each firm to take the likely reactions of its rivals into account when planning its market strategy. Even with given cost and demand conditions, there is no "best" price and quantity decision for the oligopolist. Instead, there are a number of possible strategies, each of which is more or less suitable, depending on what the firm's rivals do.

The case of gasoline pricing is a good example of oligopolistic interdependence (see the accompanying For Example. . . box). In that market, the prices each firm sets depend on the prices its rivals set, and vice versa. In such a market, any changes made by one firm are likely to touch off a long series of moves and countermoves. No simple theory can say when a given price move should be made or predict the outcome of a series of moves by a firm and its rivals.

Oligopolistic interdependence
The need, in an oligopolistic market, to pay close attention to the actions of one's rivals when making price or production decisions.

FOR EXAMPLE...

Oligopolistic Interdependence

This article provides an illustration of the effects of oligopolistic interdependence in gasoline pricing. Similar patterns are evident in the setting of air fares and in other oligopolistic markets.

"Who's Pumping Whom?" Motorists Ask of Gas Hike

Like other motorists digesting the sudden jump in Winnipeg gas prices yesterday, Tim Taylor wants to know who's pumping whom.

"How can it (the price) go up six or seven cents in one day?" Taylor asked after pulling into a Portage Avenue Petro-Canada station. "It's unbelievable."

Prices for regular gas jumped six to eight cents, hitting 53.9 cents a litre at some stations.

The increase was met with surprise and cynicism.

"What makes it (the price) fluctuate so dramatically in one week? It makes you wonder who is playing with the prices," Marcia Cels said while filling up at an Esso station that had joined the pricing frenzy.

The jump at the pump brought calls from the provincial New Democrats for price regulation.

"I didn't really believe it when I first heard it — nine cents?" Jim Maloway (Elmwood) said, noting the price of oil has risen only sixteen cents a barrel.

"They (the province) regulate the price of utilities, pre-arranged funerals, Autopac — why can't they do it for gasoline?"

Consumer and Corporate Affairs Minister Linda McIntosh rejected the idea.

"For starters, the opposition doesn't like to talk about the fact that where there is regulation, the prices haven't dropped below sixty cents," she said.

Shell Canada outlets led the way in the price surge, but managers and employees of other stations warned they may soon follow the leader.

"I stay competitive," said Al Wiebe, manager of a Petro-Canada station on Cottonwood Road. "If Shell increased to 53.9, that's what I'll be."

The new Shell price of 53.9 cents was set by the multinational's Calgary office, said an employee of a Shell station on Archibald Street.

SOURCE: " 'Who's Pumping Whom?' Motorists Ask of Gas Hike," *Winnipeg Free Press*, June 26, 1991, p. 1. Reproduced with permission.

Oligopoly and Shared Monopoly

Although the simple theories of monopoly and perfect competition do not fit the complex world of oligopolistic interdependence, they do provide a framework within which we can discuss the theory of oligopoly. Such a framework is given in Box 9.5. A similar diagram was used in Chapter 8 to show the effects of a cartel, but now we shall assume that a formal cartel does not exist.

We shall also assume that the industry in our example is dominated by a few large firms, with perhaps some small ones on the fringe. Profits are maximized for these firms at a price of $2 and an output of 150 000 units per month, which corresponds to a point directly above the intersection of the marginal-cost and marginal-revenue curves. At this point, the firms can be said to enjoy a **shared monopoly**. Such a monopoly is, in effect, a cartel without formal agreement or enforcement mechanisms.

The opposite extreme is *cut-throat competition* — price competition so complete that pure economic profit is impossible. This extreme is shown in Box 9.5 by the

Shared monopoly
The situation that exists when firms in an oligopoly co-ordinate their activities in order to earn maximum profits for the industry as a whole.

BOX 9.5 *Range of Possible Prices and Output Levels for an Oligopoly*

The cost and demand curves given here are those of an oligopolistic industry. If the firms co-operate, they can, at one extreme, achieve a *shared monopoly*. At the other extreme, they can compete so fiercely that pure economic profit is impossible and the price is driven down to the level of cost. This extreme is labelled "cut-throat competition." In practice, co-operation becomes increasingly risky as the industry moves upward along the demand curve toward the shared-monopoly position. The likely outcome is a price somewhere between the $1 and $2 limits on the graph.

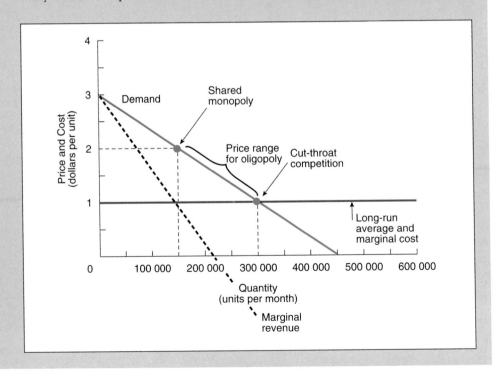

intersection of the demand curve and the marginal-cost curve. Cut-throat competition among oligopolists would duplicate the price–output performance of perfect competition. In the long run, no lower price could be sustained without driving firms and resources out of the industry.

The range of price–output combinations that an oligopoly can achieve, then, includes the extremes of shared monopoly and cut-throat competition and the segment of the demand curve between the two extremes. Where along this range will any given oligopoly end up? The answer depends on the balance struck between the risks and benefits of the co-operation needed to achieve shared monopoly.

The risks are of three kinds. First, there is a risk that the rivals with whom one seeks to co-operate will not respond in kind. Second, there is a risk that even if a firm does achieve a degree of co-operation with its present rivals, the fruits of the effort will have to be shared with new firms attracted by the resulting higher profits. And third, there is a risk that if co-operation is pursued too openly, the firms will be found in violation of Canada's competition laws. (These laws will be discussed in detail in Chapter 10.) The benefits of shared monopoly are sufficiently desirable to keep cut-throat competition at bay at least some of the time, but the risks increase as the rival firms edge their way upward and to the left along the demand curve. As a result, it seems likely that most oligopolies operate somewhere between the two extremes shown in Box 9.5.

Informal Theories of Oligopoly

In the light of the discussion so far, the goal of a theory of oligopoly might be viewed as that of finding the point on the demand curve at which any given industry is likely to operate. There have been many attempts to construct formal theories that would solve this problem. But before examining a few of the formal theories, let us consider some of the so-called informal theories, which amount to a description of some general conditions that influence the ability of oligopolists to act independently of their rivals or to co-operate with them. We shall look at several of the conditions in turn.

Number and size of firms

There is little doubt that the number and size of the firms in a market make a lot of difference. Co-operation is easier in a market with only two or three big firms of roughly equal size than in a market where a dozen firms of equal size have half the market and the other half is divided up among smaller firms. A major reason is that the larger the number of firms, the more likely it is that any one firm can cut prices under the table.

The relative size of the various firms in the market is also important. Many observers have suggested that tacit co-ordination of prices is easier in an industry in which there is one dominant firm. That firm may be able to act as a price leader. Under the strongest form of **price leadership**, firms are no longer uncertain about how their rivals will react to price changes. The leader knows that the others will follow it either up or down. The others know that they are safe if they follow the leader, because others will too; but if they raise or lower prices on their own, others will *not* follow. When it works, this arrangement results in a shared monopoly.

However, tacit co-ordination cannot always be inferred from a coincidence in the timing of price changes. In any industry, someone has to be the first to change

Price leadership
In an oligopoly, the situation that exists when increases or decreases in price initiated by one dominant firm, known as the price leader, are matched by all or most other firms in the market.

prices if market conditions change. Even if one firm is usually the first to make a move, its role may be no more than that of a barometer, telling the others that the pressure of demand or cost has made a price change necessary.

Nature of the product
The nature of the product also affects the ease or difficulty of co-ordination. A homogeneous product with a smooth flow of orders tends to make co-ordination easier, while a variable product with an irregular flow of orders tends to make it more difficult. With a variable product, there are simply too many factors to co-ordinate. It is not enough that all firms tacitly agree to sell at the same price: They also have to agree on a set of price adjustments for variations in quality, fast or slow delivery, size of order, and so on. Under these conditions, an agreement to raise the price above the competitive level, even if it can be sustained, is unlikely to lead to higher profits. It is more likely to lead to an outbreak of competition in terms of quality, scheduling, volume discounts, and so on, which will gradually add to the cost of doing business until excess profits disappear.

Information
Co-ordination under oligopoly, if possible at all, is likely only in a market where firms have fairly good information about what their rivals are doing. Clearly, there can be no tacit understanding that all firms will charge the same price or follow a price leader if prices are kept secret. So there is little doubt that secrecy is an enemy of co-ordination under oligopoly.

Growth and innovation
The rates of growth and innovation in a market are a final factor that is likely to affect the ease or difficulty of co-ordination among rival oligopolists. In a market where product features, production techniques, and the personalities of buyers and sellers do not change from year to year, an agreement among firms, whether tacit or overt, will never have to be revised. In a market where things change quickly, any agreement will soon be made obsolete by changing conditions or disrupted when new buyers or sellers enter the market. Given the uncertainties of tacit agreements and the fact that overt ones are illegal, one would expect that the faster the pace of growth and change, the less success rival firms will have in co-ordinating their activities.

Formal Theories of Oligopoly

Over the years, many economists have tried to state a formal theory of oligopoly. The goal of such a theory would be to determine the equilibrium price and level of output for an oligopolistic firm and its industry, given such aspects of market structure as the number of firms involved, the concentration ratio, costs and technology, and the nature of the demand curve. No general theory has been developed, but some useful partial theories and clever analyses of special cases exist. These provide some insight into the broader problem of oligopoly. The three theories discussed in this section are a sample from the literature on formal theories of oligopoly.

The Cournot theory and its variations
The oldest attempt at a theory of oligopoly began with a work published by Augustin Cournot in 1838. Cournot recognized the problem of oligopolistic inter-

dependence — the need for each firm to take its rivals' behaviour into account when deciding on its own market strategy. The way to understand the behaviour of rival firms, Cournot thought, was to make a simple assumption about the way each firm would react to the moves of its rivals.

In his initial statement of the problem, Cournot assumed that each firm would act as if it did not expect its rivals to change their levels of output even if it changed its own output level. Later theorists who expanded Cournot's theory, however, usually made price rather than quantity the crucial variable. In the price-based version of the Cournot theory, each firm is assumed to set its price as if it expected other firms in the industry to leave their prices unchanged.

Box 9.6 shows how the price-based Cournot theory might work for an industry with just two firms. Each firm has a definite price that will yield maximum profits for each possible price that its rival may charge. These prices are shown in the form of the firms' *reaction curves*. For example, Firm 1's reaction curve indicates that it will charge $60 if its rival charges $50 (point *S*). If Firm 2 charges $150, Firm 1 will charge $130 (point *T*). In the limiting case, Firm 2 may charge so much that it will price itself out of the market, leaving Firm 1 with a pure monopoly. In that case, Firm 1 will maximize its profits by charging $150, as shown by the broken line labelled "Firm 1's monopoly price." Firm 2's monopoly price is shown in the same way. The two reaction curves can be derived from the

The Cournot Theory of Oligopoly *BOX 9.6*

The Cournot theory assumes that each firm will set its price as if it expects its rival's price to remain fixed. The reaction curves show the best price for each firm, given the other's price. For example, point *S* on Firm 1's reaction curve indicates that Firm 1 should charge $60 if Firm 2 charges $50. If Firm 1 has a monopoly, it will set a price at $150. If Firm 2 then enters the market, it will touch off a price war, moving the industry step by step to points *A*, *B*, *C*, *D*, and finally *E*. Point *E* is a stable equilibrium.

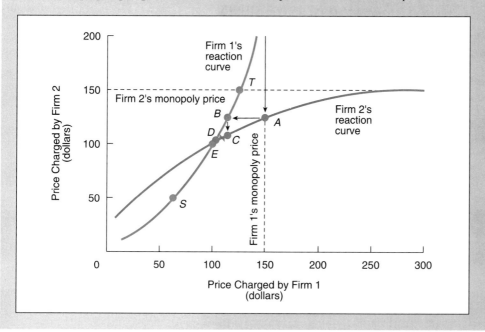

cost and demand curves of the two firms. The derivation is not given here, but it can be found in many advanced texts.

Given these reaction curves, the oligopoly story, according to Cournot, can be told somewhat as follows: Imagine that, at first, Firm 1 is the only producer of the good in question. Since it has a pure monopoly, it maximizes profits by setting a price of $150. Then Firm 2 enters the market. According to the Cournot theory, Firm 2 will set its price as if it expected Firm 1 to go on charging $150 forever. Given this assumption, Firm 2 sets its price at $125, as shown by point *A* on Firm 2's reaction curve.

At this point, Firm 1 begins to notice its rival. Seeing that Firm 2 has taken away many of its customers with its much lower price, it moves to point *B* on its reaction curve, cutting its own price to $115.

Firm 2, which entered the market on the assumption that Firm 1 would maintain its price at $150, must react next. Given Firm 1's $115 price, Firm 2 cuts its price to $108 (point *C*). That sparks a price cut by Firm 1, which goes to $107 (point *D*). After a series of ever-smaller moves and countermoves, the prices of the two firms converge at an equilibrium of $100 at point *E*.

Two things are appealing about the Cournot theory. First, it gives a stable equilibrium. At prices above the intersection of the two reaction curves, each firm has an incentive to undercut its rival's price. At prices below the intersection, each firm has an incentive to charge more than its rival does. Thus, given the assumptions, there is only one price that the market can reach.

A second appealing feature of the Cournot theory is that, as it is expanded to allow three-, four-, and multifirm oligopolies, it shows that the equilibrium price moves steadily away from the monopoly price and toward a price equal to marginal cost. Thus, the Cournot equilibrium for an industry with one firm is equal to the monopoly price; the Cournot equilibrium for an industry with an infinite number of firms is equal to the competitive price; and the Cournot equilibriums for oligopolies of various sizes are ranged along a continuum between these two extremes.

Still, there is one feature of the Cournot theory that has always bothered economists. The structure of the theory depends on each firm's assuming that its rival will not react to its price changes. Yet daily life in the Cournot world proves this assumption to be wrong. In our example, Firm 2 enters on the assumption that Firm 1 will pay no attention to the fact that it comes in and takes away a large chunk of its sales. But Firm 1 does react, as does Firm 2. Instead of this mindless price war, wouldn't each firm have second thoughts about its price cutting, fearing its rival's reaction? The Cournot theory refuses to face up to this possibility.

The kinked-demand-curve theory

A century after Cournot, in 1939, another major theory of oligopoly came along. This was the so-called *kinked-demand-curve theory*, which was proposed at about the same time by the British economists R.L. Hall and C.J. Hitch and the American economist Paul M. Sweezy. Like the Cournot theory, the kinked-demand-curve theory begins from a simple assumption about how oligopolists will react to price changes made by their rivals. Each firm is supposed to assume that if it cuts its price, its rivals will match the cuts, but if it raises its price, no other firms will follow. Box 9.7 shows how the market looks to an oligopolist who makes these two assumptions. Let *P* be the price ($1.70 in this case) that happens to prevail in the market. If the firm cuts its price below *P*, other firms will also lower their

The Kinked-Demand-Curve Theory of Oligopoly   BOX 9.7

An oligopoly firm will have a kinked demand curve if its rivals will follow any price decrease it makes but not any increase. There is a sharp step in the marginal-revenue curve that corresponds to the kink in the demand curve. Here the marginal-cost curve crosses the marginal-revenue curve just at the step. This makes the equilibrium very stable.

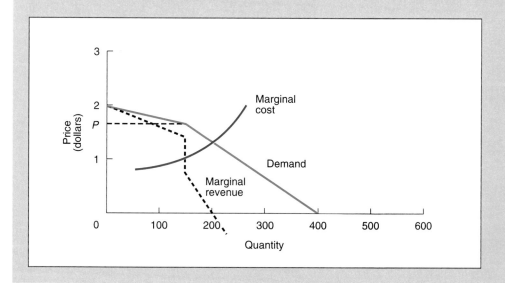

prices. Sales in the industry as a whole will expand. The firm in question will keep about the same share of the market and will move down the lower slope of the demand curve. In contrast, if the firm raises its price, the others will not follow suit. Instead of keeping its share of the market, our firm will lose customers to its rivals. As a result, the part of the firm's demand curve above price *P* is much more elastic than the part below *P*.

Now bring marginal cost and marginal revenue into the picture. Give the firm a short-run marginal-cost curve with the usual upward slope. The marginal-revenue curve has a step in it that corresponds to the kink in the demand curve. To the left of the step, marginal revenue is very high, showing that revenue will be lost quickly if the firm moves up the very elastic part of the demand curve. To the right of the step, marginal revenue is much lower, showing that little extra revenue can be obtained by moving down the less elastic part of the demand curve. As it is drawn, the marginal-cost curve cuts the marginal-revenue curve right at the step. The prevailing price is an equilibrium price for the firm, since it will be unprofitable to move in either direction.

The kinked-demand-curve equilibrium for an oligopoly firm is a very stable kind of equilibrium. Unlike a pure monopoly firm, the oligopoly firm with a kinked demand curve will not change its price or output in response to small- or medium-sized changes in costs. The level of marginal cost shown in Box 9.7 can move by as much as 30 cents in either direction, and the firm will not change its price or output. The marginal-cost curve will still cross the marginal-revenue curve at the step. Only if marginal cost changes by more than 30 cents per unit will the firm break with the prevailing price.

Like the Cournot theory, the kinked-demand-curve theory is simple and elegant. Its assumptions about the way each oligopolist views its rivals' actions are clearly more plausible than Cournot's. But the kinked-demand-curve theory has a major flaw of its own. Although it explains why an oligopolist might be reluctant to change its price once the price was set, it fails to explain how the price comes to be set at any particular level in the first place. The theory thus provides an answer to a question that is not central to the analysis of oligopoly.

Game theory

Oligopoly, it has often been remarked, is really a game of sorts — one in which, as in chess or poker, each player must try to guess the opponent's moves, bluffs, countermoves, and counterbluffs as many moves ahead as possible. Hence, economists who specialize in oligopoly theory were very excited by the appearance in 1944 of a thick, highly mathematical book entitled *The Theory of Games and Economic Behavior*.[8] Could it be that the authors, John von Neumann and Oskar Morgenstern, had at last solved the oligopoly puzzle?

Clearly, von Neumann and Morgenstern had taken a major step. Instead of using as their starting point an assumption about how one firm would react to the other's moves, they decided to ask, in effect, what *optimal assumption* each firm should make about its rivals' behaviour.

A simple example of an oligopoly game will convey the spirit of the von Neumann–Morgenstern approach. Imagine a market in which there are only two firms — Alpha Company and Zed Enterprises. Their product costs $1 a unit to make. If both firms set their price at $5 a unit, each will sell 100 units per month at a profit of $4 a unit, for a total monthly profit of $400. If both firms set their price at $4 a unit, each will sell 120 units at a profit of $3 a unit, for a total profit of $360. Which price will the firms actually set? Clearly, $5 is the price that will maximize their joint profits, but under oligopoly, this price may not be a stable equilibrium.

Box 9.8 shows why. It presents the pricing strategies available to Alpha Company. Besides the two already mentioned, Alpha must consider two more. One is to cut its price to $4 while Zed holds at $5. That will allow Alpha to take away a lot of Zed's customers and to sell 150 units, for a profit of $450. The other new possibility is for Alpha to hold its price at $5 while Zed cuts its price to $4. Then Zed will take away a lot of Alpha's customers and leave Alpha selling only 60 units, for a total profit of $240.

So what will happen? One way to seek an answer is to look at the effects of different assumptions that each firm might make about the other's behaviour. If Alpha assumes that Zed will charge $5, then Alpha will be best off charging $4. If Alpha assumes that Zed will charge $4, then Alpha will again be best off charging $4. It looks as if Alpha will be best off charging $4 regardless of what Zed does. Alpha will also be aware that Zed's view of the game is the mirror image of its own. After thinking about the likely effects of the different assumptions, each firm will see that it is rational to assume the worst. Unless the two firms can agree

---

[8]John von Neumann and Oskar Morgenstern, *The Theory of Games and Economic Behavior* (Princeton, N.J.: Princeton University Press, 1944).

*Profits for Alpha Company under Various
Pricing Strategies*

BOX 9.8

This table shows the profits that Alpha Company would earn under various pricing strategies for Alpha and its rival, Zed Enterprises. If both firms set their price at $5, each earns $400. If both cut their price to $4, they continue to split the market, and each earns $360. If Alpha cuts its price while Zed does not, Alpha steals many of Zed's customers and earns $450. If Zed cuts its price while Alpha's remains at $5, Zed steals many of Alpha's customers, leaving Alpha with only $240 in profits.

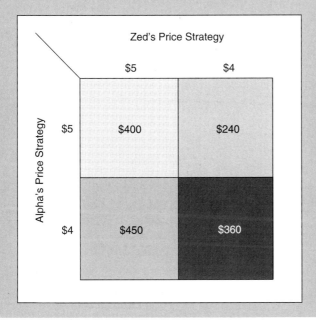

to keep the price at $5 (and such agreements are assumed to be against the rules of the game as it is played here), it seems that $4 is the equilibrium price.

Despite the high hopes of oligopoly theorists, however, it turned out that game theory could not be used to solve the general problem of oligopoly. Some games had a structure that made it impossible to come up with the kind of determinate solution that our example gives. And efforts to expand the game to three or more players quickly bogged down in a swamp of mathematical complications. Alas, game theory has remained little more than a brilliant solution to an extremely small set of special cases.

Measuring Market Performance under Oligopoly

Neither the formal nor the informal theories of oligopoly give conclusive answers to the question asked at the beginning of the chapter — whether rivalry among a few firms in a concentrated market is enough to secure good market performance. In this context, good market performance means performance like that of a perfectly competitive market, with prices equal or close to marginal cost. Poor performance means performance like that of a monopoly or cartel, in which prices remain higher than marginal cost.

Not being able to answer questions about market performance by means of pure theory, economists turn to statistical methods. Because it is hard to measure directly whether a gap exists between a firm's output prices and its marginal costs, the most common approach is an indirect one. If firms in concentrated industries can be shown, on the average, to earn higher-than-normal rates of return on capital, one can infer that they are behaving more like monopolists than like perfect competitors. If, on the other hand, firms in concentrated industries earn rates of return no higher, on the average, than firms in less concentrated industries, it can be inferred that oligopolies perform about as well as more competitive industries.

Unfortunately, different statistical studies have produced conflicting results. Early studies revealed a weak but discernible link between high profits and concentration, but later studies seemed to refute this result. The general conclusion now is that larger firms in more concentrated industries indeed earn higher-than-normal rates of return on capital. However, the source of these profits may be lower costs rather than higher prices.[9]

MONOPOLISTIC COMPETITION

The theory of monopolistic competition blends monopolistic and competitive aspects. The theory can be understood with the help of Box 9.9, which shows short- and long-run equilibrium positions for a typical firm under monopolistic competition.

The demand curve for a firm under monopolistic competition, like that for a firm under pure monopoly, slopes downward. Each firm's product is a little different from those of its competitors. Each firm can therefore raise its price at least a little without losing all its customers, because some customers attach more importance than others to the special style or location or other marketing advantage the firm offers. Given this downward-sloping demand curve, the short-run profit-maximizing position shown in the box is found in the same way as that for a pure monopolist: The level of output is determined by the intersection of the marginal-cost and marginal-revenue curves, and the price charged is determined by the height of the demand curve at the point.

But this short-run equilibrium cannot also be a long-run equilibrium under monopolistic competition. The reason is freedom of entry. In the short-run position shown in part (a) of Box 9.9, the firm is earning a pure economic profit. This is shown by the fact that price exceeds average total cost. But high profits attract new firms. As new firms enter the market, the demand curves of firms that are already there will shift downward. The reason is that although the new firms' products are not the same, they are to some extent substitutes for those of the original firms. If the original firms improve their products or market them more aggressively, those efforts will raise their average total costs. The downward shift in the demand curve of the original firms or the upward shift in their cost curves, or both, will continue until there are no more profits to attract new firms. The

[9]See Bradley T. Gale and Ben Branch, "Concentration and Market Share: Which Determines Performance and Why Does It Matter?" *Antitrust Bulletin* 27 (Spring 1982).

Short-Run and Long-Run Equilibrium under Monopolistic Competition

BOX 9.9

Under monopolistic competition, each firm has a downward-sloping demand curve, but there are no barriers to entry by new firms. In the short run, a firm that produces at the point where marginal cost is equal to marginal revenue can earn pure economic profits, as shown in part (a). In the long run, however, new firms are attracted to the market. This diverts part of the demand from the firms that are already in the market, thus lowering the demand curve of each. Also, those firms may fight to keep their share of the market, using means that increase their costs. Entry by new firms will continue until a long-run equilibrium is reached in which profits are eliminated, as shown in part (b).

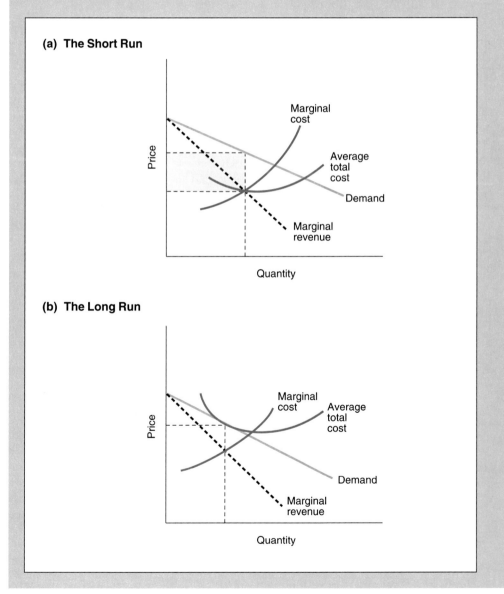

result will be the long-run equilibrium position that is shown in part (b) of Box 9.9.

This long-run equilibrium position is sometimes said to be a sign of poor performance. For one thing, as under pure monopoly, each firm turns out too little of its product. The gap between price and marginal cost indicates potential added production that would increase economic efficiency. In addition, under monopolistic competition, a firm does not operate at the lowest point on its long-run average-cost curve. If there were fewer firms, each producing a greater amount of output, the same quantity of goods could be provided at a lower total cost. The hallmark of monopolistic competition, then, is too many clothing stores, supermarkets, and restaurants, each operating at a fraction of capacity and each charging inefficiently high prices. Yet, despite the high prices, each earns the minimum return needed to stay in business.

Are Perfect Competition and Monopolistic Competition Different?

Not all economists accept the criticisms of monopolistic competition that we have just noted. Many articles have been written on the subject, and many variations on the theory have been suggested. Setting aside differences in detail, most of what is said in favour of monopolistic competition comes down to the idea that monopolistic competition and perfect competition are not really very different.

One argument is that the belief that there is a difference comes from a mistaken idea about the nature of the product being sold. Take restaurants, for example. The restaurants in any town sell meals that are highly varied according to location, cuisine, atmosphere, service, and many other features. But perhaps meals are not really the product. Instead, think of all restaurants as selling a homogeneous good called dining pleasure. The differences among restaurants should be thought of not as differences in product but as differences in the methods used to produce dining pleasure, as well as differences in the packages of dining pleasure being sold. Likewise, different farmers grow potatoes in assorted sizes and use a variety of farming methods, but the potato market is still thought to be close to perfectly competitive. The dining-pleasure market, by this line of reasoning, is just like the potato market.

A variation on this argument admits that there are differences among products but points out that such differences are valuable in themselves. Suppose it were true, as the theory of monopolistic competition suggests, that prices would be a little lower if there were fewer barbershops, each one not quite as conveniently located; or fewer supermarkets, each one a little more crowded; or fewer flavours of ice cream. Would a move in that direction benefit consumers? Not if consumers are willing to pay something for variety. Imagine that there were some way to split the market for, say, ice cream into two markets — one for the good called ice cream and the other for the good called variety. If that were possible, then each good could have its own price, and each market could be perfectly competitive. But this isn't possible. In the real world, a single market for both goods, with the structure known as monopolistic competition, is as close as one can come to the ideal.

LOOKING AHEAD

The last three chapters have looked at the connection between market structure and performance. Before we go on to the next two chapters, which look at public policies that deal with competition and market structure, it will be useful to summarize two key controversies that economic theory has not resolved.

The first has to do with the extent to which perfect competition, or something close to it, can be viewed as the natural state of the economy. If a great deal of concentration is needed in most markets for firms to take advantage of economies of scale, perfect competition will be very rare. If, in industries that are not highly concentrated, a large amount of product variety is needed to meet consumer demand, there will be even less room for perfect competition. However, if both market concentration and product variety are in fact consequences of market imperfections, caused by such factors as advertising and barriers to entry, there may indeed be room to expand the area of perfect competition.

The second controversy concerns the question of whether perfect competition, or something close to it, is a necessary or even a sufficient condition for good market performance. If, in concentrated markets, shared monopoly is rare and active competition is the rule, perfect competition may not be necessary. And if, at least in some markets, concentration is needed to achieve economies of scale, perfect competition may not even be a sufficient condition for good market performance.

As we will see in the following chapters, these controversies underlie many debates on matters of public policy.

SUMMARY

1. An *oligopoly* is a market in which there are two or more firms, at least one of which has a large share of total sales. In an oligopoly, deciding how to react to the actions of rival firms with regard to price, output, and product features is a major aspect of decision making.

2. A market structure in which each of many small firms makes a product that is a little different from those of its competitors is known as *monopolistic competition*. Both oligopoly and monopolistic competition are examples of imperfect competition.

3. *Concentration ratios* are a common measure of the degree to which a market is dominated by a few firms. The most commonly used ratios measure the share of total sales in the market accounted for by the top four or eight firms in the market. More than one-half of all manufacturing output in Canada comes from markets in which four firms control more than half of the total output.

4. Economies of scale can represent a barrier to entry to an oligopolistic industry, in that there may be room for only a small number of large firms if the lowest possible costs are to be achieved. But there are also various other barriers to entry, including legal barriers; restricted ownership rights to nonreproducible resources; and *market power*, which is the result of superior financial strength, well-developed connections in the business world, and massive advertising.

5. *Marketing* means finding out what customers want and channelling a flow of goods and services to meet those wants. It consists of four activities: creating a product that will meet consumer needs; getting it to a place where consumers can conveniently buy it; promoting it through advertising, personal sell-

ing, and other means; and putting the right price on it. All aspects of marketing are important to competition.

6. Some economists view advertising as a barrier to entry into a market by new firms and as a source of monopoly profits. Others dispute these claims, contending that advertising is in fact more extensively used by new firms entering a market than by firms that are already established in that market.

7. *Oligopolistic interdependence* refers to the need for each firm in an oligopoly to pay close attention to the actions of its rivals.

8. A major question in oligopoly theory is how well oligopolies perform — that is, how closely they approach the outcome of perfect competition, in which equilibrium prices equal marginal cost, as opposed to that of *shared monopoly*. Among the factors that are thought to affect market performance are the number and size of firms, the presence or absence of *price leadership*, the nature of the product (homogeneous or varied), access to information, and the pace of growth and innovation.

   Early studies suggested that firms in industries with high concentration ratios earned higher profits than those in less concentrated industries. This was taken as a sign that firms in concentrated industries engaged in tacit coordination and earned joint monopoly profits. More recent research suggests that the connection is not so simple, and that at least part of the higher profits in more concentrated industries is accounted for by the fact that firms with dominant market shares tend to have lower production costs than smaller firms.

9. In long-run equilibrium, each firm within a market structure of monopolistic competition produces at a point where its demand curve is tangent to its long-run average-total-cost curve.

10. Monopolistic competition is said to be inefficient, in that price exceeds marginal cost in long-run equilibrium. This means that fewer firms, each producing more output, could supply the market at a lower average total cost. If this were the case, however, consumers would have to give up some variety, so they would not necessarily be better off.

EFFECTIVE THINKING: PROBLEM 2

Small Business

This effective-thinking problem is based on material from Chapter 6, which relates to supply costs, and Chapter 9, which deals with imperfectly competitive market structures. A small business has to make decisions about its costs and levels of output based on the market structure within which it operates.

   Assume that a friend of yours has just completed a furniture-design course, and has a new design for an avant-garde living-room chair. She is considering starting a small company to produce the chair, which she hopes she can sell at a profit. Since you have an economics background, she wants advice from you on the economic aspects of the business. All of your friend's money will go into the company, but she offers to pay you a percentage of the profits for your advice. However, since she will be risking a great deal of time and money on the basis of that advice, she also wants you to pay a percentage of the losses, should there be any.

Output of Chairs	Total Variable Cost	Total Fixed Cost	Price
0	$ 0	$2000	$ 0
1	180	2000	1200
2	520	2000	1160
3	825	2000	1120
4	1100	2000	1080
5	1350	2000	1040
6	1580	2000	1000
7	1795	2000	960
8	2000	2000	920
9	2200	2000	880
10	2405	2000	840
11	2620	2000	800
12	2850	2000	760
13	3100	2000	720
14	3375	2000	680
15	3680	2000	640
16	4020	2000	600
17	4400	2000	560
18	4825	2000	520
19	5300	2000	480
20	5830	2000	440
21	6420	2000	400
22	7075	2000	360
23	7800	2000	320
24	8600	2000	280

You have arrived at the figures in the accompanying table based on estimated information that your friend has supplied in response to your questions about production costs and probable demand for this sort of a chair.

Directions

Decide what economics-related problems your friend's new company faces. Use the twelve effective-thinking steps for successful problem solving to address those problems (see the Appendix to Chapter 3 if you need to review the steps). For Steps 10 through 12, assume that the plan you adopt in Step 9 is implemented. Illustrate your solution(s) with a graph. (*Hint*: Base your solution(s) on the economic theory you have studied in Chapters 6–9.)

An example of the thinking process an economist might go through using these twelve problem-solving steps appears at the back of the book (see pages 783–94). Not all economists would produce identical answers for each step, but they would all draw on accepted principles of economics.

KEY TERMS

oligopoly	market power	shared monopoly
monopolistic competition	marketing	price leadership
concentration ratio	oligopolistic interdependence	

KEY BOXES

REVIEW QUESTIONS

1. What is the difference between rivalry and competition? What does it mean to say that rivalry is a matter of conduct, while competition is a matter of structure?

2. What key traits distinguish an oligopoly from a perfectly competitive market? From a monopoly? From a cartel?

3. Evaluate the following statement: Barriers to entry are lower in the restaurant industry than in the airline industry, because a restaurant requires only a few workers and a few thousand dollars in capital, while even a small airline requires hundreds of workers and millions of dollars in capital.

4. Would you consider the market for university education to be an oligopoly? What factors do you think determine the structure of the university "industry"? How important are economies of scale? Barriers to entry?

5. How is the performance of an oligopoly affected by the number and size of the firms in the industry? By the nature of the product? By access to information? By the pace of growth and innovation?

6. Total motor-fuel consumption in Canada rose slightly between 1974 and 1984, but the number of service stations fell sharply. One explanation runs as follows: Before the 1973–74 oil-price shock, buyers of gasoline tended to be strongly brand loyal. The shortages of the 1970s forced consumers to shop around and buy gasoline wherever they could find it. In doing so, they found that their cars ran just about the same on any gas. They therefore ceased to be loyal to any brand.

   Assume that reduced brand loyalty means a flatter demand curve for any given gas station. Based on what you know about monopolistic competition, explain why this would lead to a new equilibrium with a reduced number of service stations, even if conditions did not change in other ways?

7. **a.** Critics of advertising blame it for creating brand loyalty. This in turn is said to create barriers to entry into oligopolistic industries, and to make the demand curves of firms in monopolistic competition less elastic than they would otherwise be. In both cases, advertising is thought to contribute to poor market performance. What does this case suggest about the connection between advertising and brand loyalty? Does it support a policy of setting limits on advertising as a means of improving market performance in the beer industry?

   b. Economies of scale have led to a high degree of concentration in the brewing industry. That industry is now an oligopoly dominated by a few major brewers. Yet those brewers still produce a great many brands of beer. If one looked only at the number of brand names displayed in a typical store, one would think brewing was an example of monopolistic competition. What does brand loyalty have to do with this market structure? Do you think market performance would be improved by limiting each large firm to just one brand? By returning to a situation in which each brand was made by a different firm? Discuss.

8. Why is monopolistic competition said to be inefficient? What would consumers give up if average costs were lowered by reducing the number of firms in such a market?

9. The Calgary Co-operative Association Ltd. owns thirteen supermarkets and is the second-largest food chain in Calgary. Safeway is the largest chain and Superstore is the third-largest. The *Financial Times* reports that while "many food chains . . . are cutting prices by cutting costs and customer service, the Calgary Co-op is heading in the opposite direction. Calgary Co-op doesn't have the lowest prices in town. Instead, it offers free classes in microwave cooking, barbecuing, lawn care, and car repair" (January 28, 1991, pp. 8–9). The Co-op also bags customers' groceries. Co-op profits are about 4.4 percent of sales, which is far above the industry average of 1 to 2 percent. Since it is a co-op, the store distributes a certain percentage of the profits among its owner-customer members. The Co-op and its competitors would likely be operating in what type of market structure? Explain how the Co-op can experience such a high rate of profit without having to cut costs the way its competitors are doing. Does the Co-op's record go against the cost theory presented in the text? Explain your answer.

10. Before Terminal 3 opened at Toronto's Pearson International Airport, restaurants were asked to bid for the planned food-service outlets. The outlets were grouped as follows: (a) fourteen café/bars; (b) two sit-down restaurants along with two nearby café/bars; and (c) outlets in the fast-food court. Many firms bid for the outlets, but in the end, the Toronto-based firm Bitove was awarded the contract for all the outlets in all three groupings. What market structure is suggested by the Bitove win in the bidding process? Do you think giving all the outlets to one firm was a good idea? Explain your answers.

11. During February 1991, gasoline prices in Toronto and major Western cities dropped by between four and seven cents per litre. Price drops resulted in a price war among major energy companies. Independent gas dealers — those not associated with a major Canadian energy company — were said to be importing gasoline from the United States to undercut major Canadian retailers. Does game theory, the kinked-demand-curve model, or the Cournot theory explain this type of behaviour among gasoline companies? Explain your answer.

12. What market structure best describes individual gas stations? What market structure best explains major Canadian energy companies? Explain why you picked the structures you did.

13. During the February gasoline price war described in Question 11, gasoline price decreases varied by province. Prices in Toronto and major Western cities were tumbling, but prices in Atlantic Canada declined by lesser amounts. Even when adjustments were made for provincial taxes and regulations, some provinces had higher gasoline prices than others. Using theory from the text, develop a plausible explanation for this difference in prices.

14. What is the difference between a shared monopoly, as discussed in Chapter 9, and a cartel, as discussed in Chapter 8? Would total industry output and price be the same in both situations? Why or why not?

15. The large automobile companies tend to produce cars year after year that are similar in design, features, and price. Is this evidence that the firms are colluding or have some sort of shared-monopoly arrangement? If not, how can you explain the similarities that occur year after year?

PART THREE

Market Failure

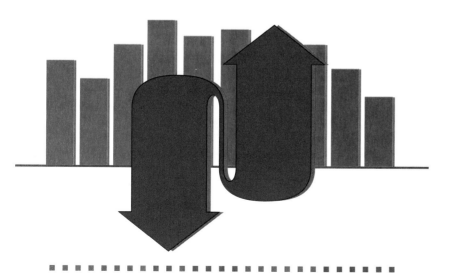

Breakdowns in Competition and Government Regulation

WHAT YOU WILL LEARN IN THIS CHAPTER

After studying this chapter, you will be able to

1. Describe the various types of market failure.

2. Distinguish between direct and indirect government regulation of business.

3. Define *natural monopoly* and explain why such monopolies are either regulated or taken over by governments.

4. Discuss some of the major problems associated with the direct regulation of natural monopolies.

5. Discuss the development of Canada's competition laws.

6. Describe the social, political, and economic goals of competition policy.

A Preview *When Competition Breaks Down*

Business firms often resent government interference in the economy. They fear that governments will destroy a competitive market economy. However, as the following article indicates, it is sometimes the firms themselves that destroy the competitiveness of the market, and it is government, paradoxically, that tries to protect it.

A Watchdog with Bite:

The Competition Bureau's Delicate Balance

His favourite sport is tennis — and by all accounts, Howard Wetston is a fiercely competitive player. But to the dismay of some business leaders, Wetston displays the same tenaciousness off the court, as director of the federal government's Bureau of Competition Policy. In March, he challenged two of the country's major corporate players, Canada Packers Inc. of Toronto and John Labatt Ltd. of London, Ont., by refusing to sanction the merger of their flour-milling operations. Each of the food giants has since strongly criticized the bureau's decision, arguing that it will undermine their ability to compete with larger, American firms. But Wetston told *Maclean's* that he stands by his decision. "The flour industry in Canada," he added bluntly, "has been operating like a cartel for years."

The flour-milling decision was easily the most controversial case to come before the 44-year-old German-born lawyer since he became Canada's competition watchdog in October 1989. It also dramatized the opposing pressures on the competition bureau at a time when trade barriers around the world are gradually coming down. Wetston's primary responsibility, as set out by the 1986 Competition Act, is to ensure that consumers' interests are protected and that businesses do not gain an overwhelming share of the domestic market for their products. But at the same time, many companies say that they need to grow, sometimes at the expense of competition, in order to take on large,

foreign-owned firms, particularly those based in the United States.

The proposed merger of Canada Packers' and Labatt's milling and baking interests, announced in September 1990, would have created the largest bakery in Canada and the fifth-largest in North America, with annual sales of more than $850 million. But Wetston argued that the deal would have hurt consumers, who rely on competition in the flour industry to maintain stable prices for bread, other baked goods, and pasta.

The battle with Canada Packers and Labatt is not the only fight that Wetston has on his hands these days. Several companies are challenging the constitutional authority of the competition bureau. Among other things, they maintain that Wetston and his officials have exceeded their authority.

Despite those pressures, Wetston vows to continue enforcing the competition law. Although he likes to play acoustic guitar and reads Russian novels in his spare time, he says that the bureau is his home for as many as 75 hours a week, including most weekends. Says Wetston, who is unmarried: "The job requires that kind of commitment." That fierce dedication suggests that his most recent run-in with corporate Canada will not be his last.

SOURCE: Nancy Wood, "A Watchdog with Bite: The Competition Bureau's Delicate Balance," *Maclean's*, June 17, 1991, p. 40. Reproduced with permission.

A MORE CRITICAL LOOK AT THE MARKET

Why does Canada need a competition watchdog such as Howard Wetston? Should companies in a market economy not be allowed to compete in the way they wish, without government interference? The flour-milling companies mentioned in the Preview certainly resent such interference. They would like to grow bigger in order to compete more effectively with large American firms. The Canadian government, however, through its Bureau of Competition Policy, argues that they are large enough, and that their expansion would not be in the interests of the Canadian consumer, presumably because their behaviour would come to resemble that of monopolists.

Howard Wetston believes, along with most economists, that the market is indeed a wondrous thing. Business firms that are allowed to compete according to its unwritten laws are likely to produce, at the lowest possible prices, the goods and services that consumers most want. But a free market has a critical failing: It is always in danger of destroying itself. The firms that succeed in the daily competitive struggle may eventually decide to thwart the attempts of others to compete against them. Successful firms may praise the virtues of competition, but, having achieved a position of strength, they are often inclined to reduce the threat of competition by erecting such barriers to entry into their industry as were described in Chapter 9. If they succeed in this, they can increase their profit margins by charging higher prices. The market performs well only as long as there is real competition among rival firms; it fails to protect the consumer when competition breaks down. The government is called on to perform a paradoxical role when that occurs: It must interfere with the workings of the market in order to save the market from itself. Hence, the purpose of the Bureau of Competition Policy is not to destroy the market but to protect it.

Some years ago, a young economist on his first assignment with the Bureau of Competition Policy took part in a "raid" on several private companies that were suspected of price fixing. He was issued a special permit to search the files of one of the firms. As he reviewed the files of the company's president, the latter scolded him: "Haven't you guys heard of Adam Smith? He objected to government snoopers' interfering with the market. Why don't you leave us alone?" The government "snooper" could appreciate the discomfort of the businessman, but couldn't resist replying, "If we prove that you have been fixing prices, then it is we and not you who will have been acting in the spirit of Adam Smith. Smith himself warned that business firms will often try to destroy competition in the market, and when they do, the government has a duty to restore it." Minutes later, the economist found an incriminating document: It indicated that the company was indeed involved in a price-fixing scheme with other firms in the industry. Instead of competing with one another — that is, engaging in behaviour that ultimately benefits the consumer — these firms were colluding to enhance their position at the *expense* of the consumer.

Market Failure

Chapter 1 devoted considerable attention to the recent economic and political failure of a number of socialist states, and reflected on the apparent superiority of the performance of certain market economies. In this chapter and the next one, we shall take a more critical look at our own market economy. This will involve examining several different kinds of **market failure**, a term that refers

Market failure
The inability of firms in a market economy to provide goods and services in a socially optimal way.

to the inability of the market to provide goods and services in a socially optimal way.

First it is necessary to review briefly what it is that markets are *intended* to do. We learned in previous chapters that, in a perfectly competitive market system, the price of a product will, in the long run, equal the lowest average cost of a firm. In addition, at this price, the producer's opportunity cost in making the last unit of output will equal the consumer's evaluation of the worth of that unit. All possible mutually beneficial transactions between consumers and producers will thus have been carried out, and the market will in this sense have operated in a socially optimal way.

This potentially good result, however, is thwarted by the existence of monopoly or *imperfect competition* in some markets, as discussed in Chapters 8 and 9. In many cases, such imperfect market conditions seem to develop in defiance of economic necessity and society's good. This, then, is the first type, and the first category, of market failure: the failure to achieve the social benefits of perfect competition.

All other types of market failure fall into a different category, in that they can occur even when the market is operating at, or close to, the level of perfect competition. The second type of market failure that we consider is a case in point: A perfectly competitive market may, in the course of production, create side effects that are detrimental to society. It is possible, for instance, that the firms in the pulp and paper industry are extremely competitive and cost-efficient, and yet there is nothing within the market system to prevent those firms from polluting the environment. Economists refer to such side effects as *negative externalities* or *negative spillovers* from economic activity. Brain tumours caused by toxins released in the course of production are an example of a negative spillover effect. We shall explore this second type of market failure in detail in Chapter 11, which addresses the question: Why does the market economy fail to produce a mix of goods that would provide society with what it needs while at the same time minimizing the negative side effects of production? (We shall also see in Chapter 11 that some types of production can produce *positive externalities*.) It will be shown that the market by itself may not be able to deal adequately with some of the externalities it creates; government regulations of some kind are often required.

A third type of market failure involves society's need for what economists call *public goods* (see Chapter 3). These are goods that cannot be provided to one consumer without being provided to other consumers at the same time, a condition that may make their profitable production by private firms difficult, perhaps impossible. Yet such goods may be important for society. Radio broadcasting is an example of a public good. If one person can receive a broadcast, anyone can. How does the producer of such a good obtain sufficient revenue from all potential consumers to justify the expense of building a broadcasting facility? In some countries, no direct attempt is made to charge radio users as such. The government either provides the service and pays for it out of general tax revenues (which is largely true of the CBC) or permits private firms to obtain sufficient revenue from advertisers to pay for the broadcasts. In Canada, both methods are used. In still other countries, the government imposes a special tax on radios and uses the revenues from that tax to subsidize radio broadcasters. In the case of certain public goods, such as national defence, the government may be required to take over most of the responsibility for their provision; in the case of others, such as broadcasting, a mixture of government and private initiatives

CHAPTER 10 / Breakdowns in Competition and Government Regulation • **275**

may work well. The fact remains that there are a number of important goods and services that, because of their peculiar characteristics, might not be produced in sufficient quantity in a market system that relies entirely on the competitive efforts of private firms.

A fourth type of market failure is related to the *instabilities* that markets sometimes create. Healthy competitive markets will be characterized by the frequent introduction of new products and techniques and by the replacement of old firms by new ones that have more innovative ideas. As we noted in Chapter 3, Joseph Schumpeter called this phenomenon "creative destruction." The instability it creates for the least-imaginative enterprises might be described as a necessary and healthy type of instability, which is ultimately beneficial to most people in society. However, market economies are also characterized by instabilities that are not so beneficial. They do not result from inefficient enterprises' being replaced by more efficient ones, but from forces over which individual participants in the economy have little control. Under this heading, economists include the cyclical behaviour of market economies (recall the discussion of *business cycles* in Chapter 2), which requires government intervention in the form of stabilization policies (to be discussed in detail in the macroeconomics portion of this textbook). Industries such as agriculture may also experience persistent instability problems, associated with variations in supply caused by forces over which individual producers have little control (for example, the weather). The market may not be able to correct such failures by itself.

The four types of failures noted here — *imperfect competition, externalities, public goods,* and *instabilities* — have caused governments to intervene more and more in the operation of market economies.[1] This chapter and the next one describe the scope and character of some of the many types of regulations that governments have instituted to cope with such failures.

THE SCOPE OF GOVERNMENT REGULATIONS

The scope of government regulation in Canada affecting economic activity is illustrated in Box 10.1. It would be impossible to provide details here on the nature and impact of such regulations on each of the sectors listed. A distinction can be made, however, between **direct regulation**, which involves government control over price, rate of return, supply, or entry and exit conditions in a specific industry, and **indirect** or **social regulation**, which is aimed at controlling the attributes of a product or service, providing better information, improving working conditions, and protecting workers and consumers. Social regulation usually cuts across many industries, providing such things as health and safety standards, quality standards, and laws against air and water pollution. It has been estimated by the Economic Council of Canada that in excess of 25 percent of Canada's GDP is subject to some form of direct regulation of prices and production.[2] An even larger proportion comes under some form of indirect legislation. Very similar

Direct regulation
Government regulation of one or more of price, rate of return, and entry and exit conditions, usually in a specific industry.

Indirect or social regulation
Government regulation of the attributes of a product or service, information, methods of production, sale, and employment.

---

[1]As Chapter 3 indicated, there are other reasons for government intervention in the economy as well, such as the requirements of nation building, which are not directly related to the market failures discussed here. Another type of failure, to be discussed separately in Chapter 14, is that of markets to distribute income as equally as the majority of citizens might wish.

[2]Economic Council of Canada, *Responsible Regulation: An Interim Report*, 1979, p. 11.

BOX 10.1 *The Scope of Regulation in Canada*

A wide range of federal, provincial, and municipal regulations has been developed in Canada to determine rates, entry and exit conditions, quality of output, health and safety, accuracy of information, and environmental effects in dozens of industries in Canada. Almost 30 percent of the nation's GDP is affected by direct regulations.

- **Communications**
  Broadcasting
    Radio (AM, FM)
    Television
  Telecommunications
    Telephone
    Telegraph
    Satellite
    Cable TV

- **Consumer Protection/Information**
  Disclosure (product content label-
    ling, terms of sale, etc.)
  False and misleading advertising
  Sales techniques (merchandising)
  Packaging and labelling
  Prohibited transactions, e.g.,
    pyramid sales, referral sales
  Weights and measures

- **Cultural/Recreational**
  Residency requirements
  Language (bilingualism)
  Canadian content in broadcasting
  Horse racing
  Gambling (lotteries)
  Sports
  Film, theatre, literature, music
    (e.g., Canadian content)

- **Energy**
  Nuclear
  Natural Gas
  Petroleum
  Hydro-electric
  Coal

- **Environmental Management**
  a. *Pollution control*
    air
    water
    solid-waste disposal
  b. *Resource development*
    minerals
    forestry
    water
  c. *Wildlife protection*
    hunting
    fishing
    parks/reserves
    endangered species
  d. *Land use*
    planning/zoning
    development approval
    subdivision
    strata-title
  e. *Weather modification*

- **Financial Markets and Institutions**
  Banks
  Nonbanks
    Trust companies
    Management companies
    Finance companies
    Credit unions/
      Caisses populaires
  Pension plans
  Securities/commodities
    transactions
  Insurance

- **Food Production and Distribution**
  a. *Agricultural products*
      marketing
    pricing
    grading
    storage
    distribution
    entry
    supply
  b. *Fisheries (marine, freshwater)*
    price
    entry
    quotas
    gear

- **Framework**
  Competition policy
  Antidumping laws
  Foreign Investment Review
  Bankruptcy laws
  Corporation laws
  Intellectual and industrial
      property
    copyright
    industrial design
    patents
    trademarks
  Election laws
    contributors
    spending
    reporting

- **Health and Safety**
  a. *Occupational health and safety*
  b. *Products — use*
    explosives
    firearms
    chemicals

  c. *Product characteristics*
    purity
    wholesomeness
    efficacy
    accident risk
  d. *Building codes*
  e. *Health services*
    nursing homes
    private hospitals
    emergency services
  f. *Animal health*
  g. *Plant health*

- **Human rights**
  Antidiscrimination legislation
    with respect to hiring, sale of
    goods or services, etc.
  Protection of privacy, personal
    information reporting

- **Labour**
  Collective bargaining
  Minimum-wage laws
  Hours of work, terms of employment

- **Liquor**
  Characteristics (e.g., alcoholic
    content)
  Distribution and sale

- **Professions/Occupational Licensure**
  Certification/licensure
  Registration
  Apprenticeship

- **Transportation**
  Airlines (domestic, international)
  Marine (domestic, international)
  Railways
  Intercity buses
  Taxis
  Pipelines
  Trucking (inter- and intraprovincial)
  Urban public transit
  Postal express

- **Other**
  Rent control
  Metrification
  General wage and price controls

SOURCE: Adapted from Economic Council of Canada, *Responsible Regulation: An Interim Report*, 1979, p. 11. Reproduced with permission of the Chairman of the Economic Council of Canada, 1992.

results were found for the United States, where, however, public ownership is much less extensive than it is in Canada.

In the past decade, the federal government has attempted to streamline the regulatory process and to reduce the extent of government regulation in specific industries. Such regulatory reforms have been implemented particularly in transportation, telecommunications, and finance. In the transportation industry, railways, trucks, and airlines are much freer than before to set their own rates, and it is now much easier for new firms to enter the industry. Similar changes have occurred in the telephone industry and are currently underway in the whole telecommunications sector, including within the broadcast media. Major regulatory changes in the financial sector are discussed in Chapter 22.

In this chapter, we examine both direct and indirect ways of promoting competition in Canada. Direct regulations involve the control of what are considered "natural monopolies," such as hydro-electric and natural-gas firms. Indirect regulations refer to attempts by the federal government's Bureau of Competition Policy to foster a more competitive climate in Canadian industry.

DIRECT GOVERNMENT REGULATION OF NATURAL MONOPOLIES

A **natural monopoly** is an industry in which the minimum efficient scale of operation is so large relative to the size of the market that the industry has room for only one firm operating at this minimum efficient level of output. With only one producer serving the whole market, total costs are kept to a minimum. Gas, electric, and water services are typical examples of a natural monopoly. It is easy for a single company in any such utility to hook up more customers once it has run its lines into their neighbourhood, whereas it would be wasteful and costly for different companies to run lines down the same street.

> **Natural monopoly**
> An industry in which the minimum efficient scale of operation is so large relative to the size of the market that the industry has room for only one firm operating at this minimum efficient level of output.

Although the term *natural monopoly* is well established in economics, it should be interpreted with care. New technology, for example, may alter the conditions under which an industry operates, making it possible for more firms to function effectively within it. This appears to be happening to long-distance telephone service, where the introduction of fibre-optical systems, satellite communications, and microwave relays has eliminated reliance on cable services, which were best handled by a single firm. In the United States, these technological developments have already resulted in the breakup of the giant AT&T's monopoly on long-distance services, and in Canada, they are producing pressure for a similar segmentation of the market.

The Regulatory Problem

The policy problem raised by natural monopolies is how to keep the firm from taking advantage of its monopoly to raise prices and restrict output. Competition policies of the type that we discuss in the next section won't work. Those policies aim to prevent the growth of a monopolistic market structure, but in the case of a natural monopoly, no other structure would permit an efficient scale of production.

Consider the example in Box 10.2. The firm shown there, an electric utility, has constant marginal costs and an L-shaped long-run average-cost curve. The demand curve intersects the long-run average-cost curve at quantity Q_1, not far from the minimum efficient scale of production. If this output were divided between even two firms, each of which produced half of quantity Q_1, the cost per unit would be a lot higher — and it would be higher still if there were more than two firms.

BOX 10.2   *Regulation of a Natural Monopoly*

This graph shows the cost and demand curves for a natural monopoly such as an electric utility. As an unregulated monopolist, the firm would make the maximum profit by charging price P_2 and selling quantity Q_2. If regulators impose a maximum price of P_1, the firm will find it worth while to produce quantity Q_1.

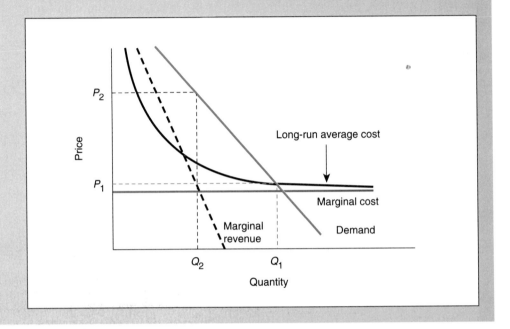

If one unregulated firm operates in a market, it can be expected to act like a pure monopolist. Instead of producing Q_1, it will produce Q_2, which corresponds to the intersection of the firm's marginal-revenue curve with its marginal-cost curve. The price that corresponds to this output is P_2, which is far above marginal cost. This is too small an output and too high a price for efficient production.

The Regulatory Solution

The analysis up to this point indicates that in a natural monopoly, competition by two or more firms is inefficient, and so is monopoly pricing by a single firm. The traditional solution is to allow just one firm to operate and to regulate the price at which it can sell its output.[3] For example, the firm may be limited to a price no higher than P_1, the price at which the demand curve intersects the long-run average-cost curve in Box 10.2. With this price ceiling in force, the firm becomes a price taker for levels of output up to Q_1, because keeping output below that level no longer enables it to raise the price. The maximum profit is earned

[3]Such regulation may be accomplished either by regulating the prices of a private firm or by having the government own the monopoly. In the latter case, the government-appointed managers have access to more information on cost and demand than is usually available to the government regulators of private monopolies, but the task of finding and setting the most efficient price levels remains essentially the same.

under the regulated price by producing Q_1 units of output. This is a lower price and a greater quantity than would result either from an unregulated pure monopoly or from dividing production among two or more competing firms.

To make the market perfectly efficient, the price would have to be reduced to the level of marginal cost, which is slightly lower than P_1. At any price less than P_1, however, the firm would suffer a loss. It could survive, in the long run, only if it were subsidized. By allowing the firm to charge price P_1, which is high enough to cover all costs, the regulators avoid the need for a subsidy while giving up only a small degree of efficiency.

Rate of return as a focus of regulation

It is easy to see the correct regulated price in Box 10.2, since the shapes and positions of the demand and cost curves are right there on the page. In the real world, however, regulators do not have complete information about demand and cost. Lacking this information, they must set the price by considering the information that they can observe.

In practice, this means focussing on the **rate of return** earned by the firm. The rate of return is the firm's accounting profit expressed as a percentage of its net worth. Regulators aim to set a price that will make the regulated firm's rate of return equal to the average earned by comparable firms in unregulated markets. This average is assumed to represent the opportunity cost of capital.

Because accounting profit includes the opportunity cost of capital contributed by the firm's owners, setting the rate of return at a "normal" level is equivalent to setting pure economic profit equal to zero — the level of pure economic profit that would prevail under the ideal of perfect competition. If the regulators set the price too high, the firm will earn a pure economic profit. That implies a rate of return higher than the opportunity cost of capital — more than the minimum needed to attract capital from other uses. On the other hand, if the price is set too low, the firm will suffer a pure economic loss. This means that the accounting profit will not be high enough to cover the opportunity cost of capital, so that people will not be willing to invest in the firm. A price just equal to average total cost, then, will permit a rate of return just equal to the opportunity cost of capital. Any lower price will not allow the firm to raise capital, whereas any higher price will permit the firm's owners to earn a pure economic profit by taking advantage of the firm's monopoly position. (Government-owned firms may deliberately set higher prices to earn higher revenues for the government — a practice that amounts to another form of taxation.)

Armed with this reasoning, the regulators proceed in five steps:

1. They measure the value of the firm's capital, which for the firm in the box is, say, $1.2 million. This is called the rate base.

2. They measure the average rate of return for the economy, which turns out to be, say, 15 percent per year. (In practice, neither of these two steps is as easy as it sounds, but for our purposes, the regulators can be given the benefit of the doubt.)

3. They multiply the rate base by the permitted rate of return to figure out a total cost of capital for the firm — $180 000 per year in this case. This sum should be enough both to make interest payments on the portion of the firm's capital that was acquired by borrowing and to give an accounting profit that is high enough to compensate the owners for their investment in the firm.

Rate of return
A firm's accounting profit expressed as a percentage of its net worth.

4. The regulators then ask the firm to propose a price (or a set of prices) that it thinks will allow it to meet its capital costs.

5. As time goes by, they keep track of the firm's actual rate of return, cutting the price if it rises too high and allowing it to rise if returns fall below the target.

Limits on rate-of-return regulation

For a number of reasons, rate-of-return regulation may not always achieve its goals of lower prices and greater output. One possible reason is that regulators may be guided by goals other than economic efficiency. This may occur, for example, if regulated firms "capture" the regulatory agency by gaining control over the appointment of regulators, or if regulators follow lax policies in the hope of finding well-paid jobs in the industry after their terms as regulators end (or, as has been observed, if the firm is government-owned and becomes, in effect, a revenue producer for the government). On the other hand, regulatory agencies in some areas have been "captured" by political groups that purport to represent the interests of consumers. They seek the short-run political gains that come from keeping rates low without regard for the regulated firm's long-run capital needs.

Another possible problem is that regulators may not know enough about the industry to control its rate of return. It is by no means easy to measure such factors as the regulated firm's stock of capital, its rate of return, and the opportunity cost of capital. The more the regulators have to rely on guesswork, the less likely they are to be effective.

Finally, there is the fact that regulation, by having the firm operate on a cost-plus basis, distorts incentives. If a firm is allowed to earn revenues that exceed costs by a certain amount and no more, why should the firm try to minimize its costs at all? Minimizing costs is hard work for managers. Why not relax and take things easy? Why not take Wednesday mornings off for golf? Install new carpets on the boardroom floor? There is a reduced incentive to put effort into keeping costs down.

Distortions caused by average-cost pricing

Even if regulators are able to adjust the rate of return of regulated firms to just the right level, regulation can still lead to inefficiency. One source of inefficiency arises from the use of average-cost rather than marginal-cost pricing. Box 10.2 glosses over this problem by assuming that the marginal cost of producing electric power is constant and that it is not very different from average total cost at the level of output where the utility operates.

In practice, many utilities have plants of different ages that operate at different levels of marginal cost. Regulatory agencies tend to look at the historical costs of these plants when they set prices. Plants built many years ago are listed at the cost that was paid for them at the time they were built, even though this may be far below the cost of replacing them or adding to their capacity. Average cost as measured in historical terms falls far short of marginal cost, since the cost of generating an added kilowatt hour means the cost of generating it in new facilities. Setting prices below marginal cost can lead to wasteful use: For example, it does not provide enough incentive for firms to implement conservation measures, such as installing insulation and thermostat timers, or to shift electricity use from peak periods, when the least-efficient generators must be brought on line, to periods when generating costs are lower.

Cross-subsidization is another problem that is created by average-cost pricing. Cross-subsidization is the practice of covering total costs, on the average, by charging some customers more than the cost of their services while charging others less. Telephone service is a case in point: Long-distance customers are usually charged prices that exceed the cost of their long-distance service, while local customers pay less than the cost of their local service. On the average, telephone rates cover total costs. Such cross-subsidization is, of course, much loved by those who make mostly local calls and disliked by those (often business firms) who are required to make many long-distance calls. Partly on grounds of fairness, the practice is being reconsidered by regulatory bodies in Canada.

Cross-subsidization raises other economic and social issues as well. Economic theory suggests that in cross-subsidization cases of the type just described, it is generally best to set higher prices on services that have an inelastic demand and relatively lower prices on services that have an elastic demand. A higher price set on a service with inelastic demand will, for example, affect the quantity demanded relatively little. However, consider the pricing of telephone services from this perspective: It is generally believed that the demand for local service is more inelastic than the demand for long-distance service. However, the price of local calls is kept down through cross-subsidization from long-distance calls, which have their prices set at artificially high levels. This practice, therefore, runs counter to what economic theory suggests would be most efficient for society.[4]

However, other considerations also come into play in evaluating such a cross-subsidization policy. A Canadian study has shown, for example, that local service has a larger budget weight for lower-income groups than for higher-income groups, and lower prices for local services may therefore have a positive effect on social welfare. In setting rates, government regulatory bodies must balance such conflicting objectives. What seems fair and perhaps even efficient from one perspective may not appear to be socially desirable from another perspective.

Canadian governments regulate many industries in the manner described in Box 10.2. Railways, electricity, gas, and telephone utilities (both private and government-owned), banks, pipelines, trucking companies, airlines, taxicabs, broadcasting companies, securities, and insurance firms are all subject to government regulation. In some cases, for example, railways and telephone companies, there is close scrutiny of prices, profits, and levels of service. In others, such as insurance, banking, and securities, the regulatory authorities are interested mainly in financial integrity and do not control prices and profits. In broadcasting, the chief concern seems to be with service.

As indicated earlier, considerable deregulation has taken place in several Canadian industries in the past decade. In the transportation industry, a new federal National Transportation Act was passed in 1988. On the one hand, this act provided for more *indirect* regulation of the industry, by imposing stricter safety codes on the industry. On the other hand, it gave limited power to the newly created regulatory body, the National Transportation Agency, to intervene *directly* in the industry. In particular, there is now less regulation of rates and of entry into the industry.

Cross-subsidization
The practice of covering total costs, on the average, by charging some customers more than the cost of their services while charging others less than the cost of their services.

---

[4]This analysis is based on Keith Acheson's very useful survey article, "Economic Regulation in Canada," in *Canadian Industrial Policy in Action*, ed. Donald McFetridge, Royal Commission on the Economic Union and Development Prospects for Canada, Collected Research Studies 4 (Toronto: University of Toronto Press, 1985), pp. 155–93. The article also contains numerous references to further research, including the reference in the following paragraph.

Significant changes have also taken place in the telecommunications industry. Until recently, the telephone industry in Ontario and Quebec was dominated by a private company, Bell Telephone, while in most of the other provinces government monopolies provided telephone service. Before the recent changes, Bell Telephone had its rates regulated by the federal government while the rates of the provincial monopolies were regulated by public utility bodies. Telephone rates continue now to be regulated by public bodies, but new companies have been permitted to provide competition in the provision of telephone services.

INDIRECT REGULATION TO PROMOTE COMPETITION

The Development of Competition Laws

Competition laws
A set of laws, including the acts of 1889 and 1923 and subsequent amendments, that seek to protect a competitive market structure and to control the competitive behaviour of firms.

Legislative attempts to curb monopoly in Canada — **competition laws** — go back to the Act for the Prevention and Suppression of Combinations in Restraint of Trade, of 1889, which made it a misdemeanour "to conspire, combine, agree or arrange unlawfully to unduly limit the transportation, production, or storage facilities for any trade commodity, to restrain the trade of such a commodity, or to unduly prevent or lessen competition in the production, sale, or price of any commodity."

In 1892, this act became a part of the Criminal Code, and an offence under the act became indictable. Subsequently, in 1910 and 1923, 1951, and 1960, further competition laws were enacted and amended, providing investigative and administrative support for prosecutions carried out under the Criminal Code. The act was eventually renamed the Combines Investigation Act.

When one compares the Canadian legislation with the Sherman Act and other competition laws in the United States (where they are known as "antitrust laws"), it becomes clear that the Canadian approach to controlling monopoly is much less aggressive than the American.

L.A. Skeoch, a Canadian expert on competition law, has noted that "perhaps the most striking aspect of the history of the legislation dealing with restraints on competition in Canada is the mixed character of the economic beliefs and policies it discloses. For example, the early debates in the House of Commons on the Combines Investigation Act — and the more recent debates for that matter — display no broad support for a general policy of competition."[5]

Canadian economic development, as we noted in Chapter 3, was promoted by the creation of virtual monopolies, such as the Hudson's Bay Company and Canadian Pacific Railways. Although there was considerable resentment over the abusive practices of these companies, there was also a widespread belief that large companies were necessary to develop the chief resources of the country. Hence, there was no strong commitment to what Skeoch calls "a general rule of competition."

This helps to explain several important features of the development of our competition policy. First, no attempt was ever made in Canada to break up existing monopolies, as was done with Standard Oil of New Jersey in the United States in 1911. Here, the law was primarily concerned with the prevention of

---

[5]L.A. Skeoch, *Restrictive Trade Practices in Canada* (Toronto: McClelland and Stewart, 1966), p. 3. Much of this section is based on this book.

such individual abuses as price fixing and price discrimination. Second, large sectors of the economy — banking and real estate, for instance — were until recently exempt from prosecution. Third, the limited financial resources allotted by the government to combines investigation never permitted more than a token approach to the problem.

Until 1967, combines investigation and prosecutions were carried out through a special branch of the Department of Justice. Then, in 1967, the Department of Consumer and Corporate Affairs assumed responsibility for investigating and prosecuting combines, mergers, monopolies, and other forms of restraint of trade. A new Competition Bill, before Parliament since 1977, was finally passed in 1986. It contains some radically new provisions, which will be discussed later in this section.

Types of Offences under the Law

Over the years, the federal government has relied on its competition legislation to deal with two types of offences: those considered illegal *per se* and those that could be declared illegal only if it was shown that they had been detrimental to the public.

The pursuit of ***per se* offences** has led to numerous successful prosecutions. Such offences include *price fixing* (where firms agree to sell their similar products at a set price), *price discrimination* (charging different customers different prices for no justifiable economic reason), and *exclusive dealing and tied selling* (product supplied on condition that the purchaser buy only from the one supplier and buy other products from that supplier as well). It is interesting to note that *resale price maintenance*, a form of vertical restraint wherein manufacturers or wholesalers try to force a certain price on the retailer, is illegal in Canada (there can be only a "suggested price"), while in many American states, the practice is protected by law. Canadian law seems to favour the consumer, while the law in the United States is more concerned about protecting small businesses.

> *Per se* **offence**
> An act that is declared illegal in itself, without having to be proved harmful to someone.

Prosecutions of offences involving mergers and monopolies — that is, offences that had to be proved harmful to the public before they could be deemed illegal — were less common and less successful. Before World War II, there was only one prosecution of a merger offence — the Western Fruits and Vegetables case — and it resulted in an acquittal. In 1959, charges were brought against Canadian Breweries and the Western Sugar Company, but both of these cases ended in acquittal as well. The Electric Reduction Company of Canada Ltd. pleaded guilty to a merger charge in 1970. K.C. Irving Ltd., a Maritimes conglomerate, was convicted of merger charges in 1974, but the decision was reversed by the Supreme Court of Canada on grounds that detriment had not been proved. In Canada, therefore, there has never been a conviction after a full trial that was not reversed on appeal. Very often, new and tougher legislation was stymied by strong business groups, calling into question the ability of a modern industrial democracy to curb the power of important economic interests.[6]

That there was a significant problem was recognized by the federal government as early as 1966, when it asked the Economic Council of Canada to examine existing competition legislation and to recommend new competition policies.

---

[6]For a fuller discussion of this problem, see Roy Vogt, "Corporate Power and the Development of New Competition Policies in Canada," *Journal of Economic Issues* (June 1985): 551–58.

In 1969, the council recommended several changes to the existing law, which became the subject of vigorous debate inside and outside Parliament for more than a decade.

The council had two major concerns: to create more effective legislation for dealing with *mergers* and to apply competition laws to firms selling *services* (such as insurance companies) as well as to those that produced commodities.

With regard to mergers, three basic changes were recommended:

1. Merger cases should be transferred to civil jurisdiction from criminal jurisdiction. Criminal law was considered inappropriate for dealing with the complex economic issues that merger cases often involve.

2. Under civil jurisdiction, a semilegal tribunal, *not* a court, should handle merger cases. A semilegal tribunal adjudicating cases with economic implications could be made up of such experts as economists and business people, as well as judges.

3. Such a tribunal should be informed in advance of planned mergers, and be empowered to prevent undesirable mergers from occurring.

These recommendations were endorsed by the government, and legislation to enact them was introduced into Parliament in 1971. However, business reaction was hostile and vigorous, and the legislation was delayed for years. In 1976, the portion of the new bill that extended the application of competition laws to some services was passed, but the provisions for dealing with mergers did not become law until 1986.[7]

The New Competition Act

In 1986, most of the recommendations originally proposed by the Economic Council of Canada were enacted into law with the passage of the Competition Act and the Competition Tribunal Act. The Competition Tribunal, consisting of both federal judges and business experts and operating under civil law, now handles merger cases.

Companies planning a merger of a certain size (more than $400 million of combined sales) are required to notify the tribunal 21 days in advance. Banks now come under the law, joining other service industries that were included in 1976. Crown corporations are also now subject to the law.

Between 1986 and 1990, the new Bureau of Competition Policy investigated about 800 of the more than 4000 mergers that took place in Canada. In about 100 of those 800 cases, the companies involved were required to make changes suggested by the bureau before the mergers could be completed. In two of the most prominent cases, Canada Safeway was required to sell about half of the Woodward food stores that it planned to purchase, and Imperial Oil Ltd. was prevented from purchasing Texaco until it agreed to sell the Texaco stations in the Atlantic region.

---

[7]Action toward passage of the bill was given new impetus in 1981, however, when the cabinet minister responsible for competition policy observed that "the Canadian economy is now in the position of having one of the highest levels of concentration of all the Western industrial countries and, at the same time, the weakest laws on mergers" (Roy Vogt, "Corporate Power and the Development of New Competition Policies in Canada," 551–58).

In all merger cases, the bureau and the Competition Tribunal, to which the bureau refers its cases, must first determine whether the proposed merger is likely to lessen competition. Then, they must examine whether the merger is likely to produce increased efficiencies and whether the benefits from them are likely to outweigh the harm that could come from decreased competition. If the answer to both of the latter questions is yes, the merger cannot be held up. This "improved efficiency" test is a way of ensuring that firms will not be prevented from growing through merger if there is a good chance that they will thereby be able to compete more effectively with other large firms.

Under the 1986 legislation, the Bureau of Competition Policy has also tried to curb many other forms of anticompetitive behaviour. Some of the actions it has taken are described in the accompanying For Example. . . box. The Canadian branches of three large transnational companies, Xerox, NutraSweet, and Chrysler, were forced by the bureau to give up practices that were designed to harm competitors. Xerox was refusing to supply parts to smaller companies that repaired Xerox copiers and that thereby created competition for new Xerox products. NutraSweet, whose Canadian patent on its artificial sweetener, aspartame, expired in 1987, had compelled large users of aspartame, such as Coca-Cola Ltd. and Pepsico, Inc., to sign exclusive worldwide deals to ensure supply. Companies producing rival sweeteners were consequently unable to sell their products to these formerly potential buyers. This sort of action is now prohibited in Canada. Chrysler refused to supply parts to a dealer who had been buying them for many years and selling them to overseas buyers. Chrysler now wanted to handle all overseas sales itself, without competition from other sellers of its parts. The Competition Tribunal ruled that this was anticompetitive behaviour, and Chrysler was ordered to resume selling parts to the dealer it had cut off.

In one of the most spectacular cases to come before the bureau, three large flour mills were forced to pay $1 million in fines each — the largest fines ever imposed in Canada — because they had rigged bids to buyers of flour for the Third World. They had secretly agreed on the price each would charge and the quantity of flour each would supply to the Canadian International Development Agency for distribution in hunger relief.

In 1990, several companies in Canada launched successful court cases against the Bureau of Competition Policy and the Competition Tribunal. The courts ruled that the Competition Tribunal, which adjudicates merger cases, was unconstitutional, that it did not have the authority to punish firms for contempt, and that the provisions of the Competition Act for outlawing business conspiracies were biassed against business. These rulings, however, were appealed, and in 1992 the Supreme Court of Canada upheld the constitutionality of the new competition legislation, thereby strengthening the Bureau of Competition Policy.

Can Competition Be Enforced?

The market is a wonderful instrument for satisfying most consumer needs in the most efficient way. To function properly, it depends vitally on strong competition among rival firms, yet it is always vulnerable to the restrictive actions of the most powerful.

There are economists who argue that firms in oligopolistic industries in particular are virtually forced to find some means of co-operation with other firms in order to survive. They are doubtful that effective measures for counteracting such pressures can ever be found. In their view, to prevent an oligopolist from

FOR EXAMPLE...

The Competition Act in Practice

The following excerpts from newspaper articles give some idea of the ways in which Canadian companies try to prevent competition, and the actions that the Bureau of Competition Policy has taken against them.

'Refusal-to-Deal' Case Goes Against Chrysler

A precedent-setting Competition Tribunal ruling appears to give new ammunition to small independent marketers in their dealings with major suppliers.

The tribunal, in a decision released Friday, has ordered Chrysler Canada Ltd. to resume supplying parts to a small Montreal-based exporter, Richard Brunet, who had been cut off by the international auto giant since 1986.

SOURCE: David Hatter, " 'Refusal-to-Deal' Case Goes Against Chrysler," *Financial Post*, October 16, 1989, p. 3. Reproduced with permission.

NutraSweet Wages Bitter Court Battle

Canadian consumers of diet soda, sugarless gum, and low-calorie candies, and the soft drink industry all have a stake in the outcome of a court battle being waged over the business practices of NutraSweet Co., the world's largest manufacturer of aspartame.

NutraSweet uses its commanding position in the marketplace to keep competitors at bay, Canada's competition watchdog says.

SOURCE: Alan Toulin, "NutraSweet Wages Bitter Court Battle," *Financial Post*, January 15, 1990, p. 3. Reproduced with permission.

Xerox Must Sell Parts to Competitor

For the second time in four weeks, the federal Competition Tribunal has ordered a powerful multinational company to allow competition from a much smaller firm.

Toronto-based Xerox Canada Inc. was ordered on Friday to supply parts to an independent photocopier company. The ruling follows an early October tribunal decision forcing NutraSweet Co. to loosen its grip on the market for the sweetener aspartame.

SOURCE: John Geddes, "Xerox Must Sell Parts to Competitor," *Financial Post*, November 5, 1990, p. 3. Reproduced with permission.

Flour Firms Fined $1 Million Each for Bid-Rigging

An Ontario judge Friday slapped Canada's biggest flour makers with the heftiest fines for bid-rigging in Canadian history — $1 million each — in connection with the sale of flour earmarked for hunger relief.

Justice John O'Driscoll of the Ontario Court, general division, levied the fines against Maple Leaf Mills Ltd., Ogilvie Mills Ltd., and Robin Hood Multifoods Ltd.

SOURCE: Colin Languedoc and John Geddes, "Flour Firms Fined $1 M Each for Bid-Rigging," *Financial Post*, December 10, 1990, p. 3. Reproduced with permission.

colluding in some way with other oligopolists is as futile as prohibition. What is necessary instead, they argue, is vigorous competition from outside — that is, from the world market. As we will see in Chapter 16, this has been a factor motivating the movement toward free trade in Canada. What the Bureau of Competition Policy cannot do, increased competition with foreign firms might just be able to accomplish.

However, as the examples that we have considered in this chapter illustrate, many of the anticompetitive actions that have been prosecuted in Canada were perpetrated by multinational firms using their international leverage to curb competition within Canada. It is therefore not at all clear that international competition will solve the problem of breakdowns in competition. The problem will undoubtedly remain with us, as many observers insist, but that is no reason to avoid doing whatever can be done to fight it — in Canada's case, using the Bureau of Competition Policy to maintain, to the extent that it is able, a competitive climate within Canadian history.

SUMMARY

1. Although competitive markets are remarkably efficient in satisfying consumer wants, their competitiveness can be restricted in various ways. Breakdown of competition is one of several forms of *market failure* — that is, the failure of the market to operate in a socially optimal way. Other types of market failure, such as the existence of externalities, the need for public goods, and market instabilities, can occur even in an environment of nearly perfect competition.

2. A *natural monopoly* is an industry in which total costs are kept to a minimum because a single producer serves the entire market. This happens when the minimum efficient scale of operation in the industry is as large as, or larger than, demand when output is sold at a price equal to average total cost.

3. The policy problem raised by natural monopoly is how to keep the single producer from exploiting its monopoly power to raise prices and restrict output. Government regulation of natural monopolies focusses on a firm's *rate of return*, because its cost and demand curves cannot be directly observed. If the rate of return is set too high, the firm has an incentive to attract more resources than it needs; if it is set too low, the firm may fail to acquire or maintain as much plant and equipment as it needs in order to do its job. Government-owned firms face some but not all of these problems.

4. Many industries are regulated even though they are not natural monopolies. As noted in Chapter 4, for example, the agricultural industry is heavily regulated.

5. *Competition laws* represent an indirect form of government regulation designed to protect a competitive market structure in Canada and to control the competitive behaviour of firms.

6. The foundations of competition policy in Canada go back to the first anti-combines act of 1889. This act, eventually renamed the Combines Investigation Act, was variously amended and interpreted over the years. It placed constraints on business behaviour, the most important of which was the prohibition of price fixing. In addition, laws prohibiting certain kinds of vertical restraints — such as tied-selling contracts and resale price maintenance — and many forms of price discrimination were also enforced with some success. However, attempts to limit the growth of companies through merger largely failed, because, until 1986, merger cases were tried under the Criminal Code and the mergers had to be proved, beyond a reasonable doubt, to be harmful to the public.

7. Attempts by the federal government to establish a tribunal consisting of both judges and lay experts to adjudicate mergers and other forms of enterprise

co-ordination under civil (as opposed to criminal) jurisdiction finally met with success only in 1986, with passage of the new Competition Act and the Competition Tribunal Act. These laws are currently being tested and interpreted through the courts. Economists are far from united on the course that competition policy should take in the future.

KEY TERMS

market failure
direct regulation
indirect or social regulation

natural monopoly
rate of return
cross-subsidization

competition laws
per se offence

KEY BOX

Box 10.2 Regulation of a Natural Monopoly

REVIEW QUESTIONS

1. Compare competition policy and direct regulation as ways of dealing with monopoly. When is each type of policy appropriate?

2. In some Canadian provinces, utilities such as electric companies, telephone systems, and gas pipelines are government-owned. What do you think are the advantages and disadvantages of government ownership compared with direct regulation of private monopolies?

3. Draw cost and demand curves for a natural monopoly. What is the connection between demand and minimum efficient scale?

4. List the steps in rate-of-return regulation for a natural monopoly.

5. "Economic analysis provides no firm conclusions on which the government can base policies relating to competition." Discuss.

6. It is sometimes said that collective restrictive agreements (such as price fixing) give rise to the disadvantages associated with monopoly without any of the latter's advantages. Discuss.

7. Discuss the advantages and disadvantages of a resale-price-maintenance law that prevents manufacturers from enforcing the prices at which their products are sold by distributors.

8. In 1987, nutmeg producers in Indonesia and Grenada, who together control 98 percent of world nutmeg production, finalized an agreement to set world nutmeg prices. In 1984, the price of nutmeg averaged $0.68 (U.S.) per pound; by 1986, the average was $1.72 (U.S.). The price now averages $3.14 (U.S.) per pound. On the basis of this information, answer the following questions:

   a. What type of market organization is operating in the market for nutmeg?

   b. Would you suspect that the demand for nutmeg is elastic or inelastic?

   c. What problems often arise for producers in this type of market organization?
   Explain all parts of your answer.

9. In an article on price fixing in the cement industry, the *Globe and Mail* commented on the structure of the industry in Canada: "The giant cement makers (four firms) own about 90 percent of all the users of cement powder in the Toronto area — ready-mix concrete makers, concrete-block makers, and concrete-pipe makers. . . . [This] makes it easy to maintain artificially high prices" (October 12, 1990, p. A1). Is the ownership of a large percentage of the users of a product by the

firm that supplies the product the sort of thing that a concentration ratio measures? If not, how is it different?

10. An expert on government regulation and competition has stated that the Bureau of Competition Policy "has done a good job prosecuting business crime within the confines of grotesquely weak competition law," and that, because of the latter problem, "business crime pays in Canada. Executives who conspire to fix prices and rig markets have more to fear from their lawyer's bills than [from] a judge's fine. . . . [The] fines companies pay have been ridiculous [that is, very low]" (*Globe and Mail*, October 13, 1990, p. A6). Discuss the possible consequences and benefits of increasing fines for Canadian firms found guilty of price fixing.

11. In January 1991, Don Knoerr, president of the Canadian Federation of Agriculture, said the removal of agricultural supply-management systems "would eliminate the bargaining power of farmers and give (food) processors virtually all the control of the price of their inputs. Farmers, like processors, have to be able to get returns for their work if they're going to stay in business. Pricing has to be a balance between the interest of the farmers and [that of] the processors." What assumptions does Mr. Knoerr make in saying that the removal of supply management would give processors virtually all the control over the price of their inputs? Explain your answer. *Note:* You may want to refer back to Chapter 8 and the section entitled "Cartels and the Farm Sector" before you answer this question.

Sustainable Development

WHAT YOU WILL LEARN IN THIS CHAPTER

After studying this chapter, you will be able to

1. Understand some of the problems associated with environmental damage.

2. Define externalities and describe how they create differences between private and social costs.

3. Discuss various methods for dealing with both negative and positive externalities.

4. Discuss the impact of transaction costs on market solutions to externalities.

5. Explain why trading pollution credits is viewed by many as the most efficient approach to pollution reduction.

6. Define and illustrate the special problems of common property.

7. Define and discuss the concept of sustainable development and the problems associated with it.

A Preview   *The Real Cost of Doing Business*

The costs of doing business cannot be measured only by adding up a firm's internal costs; its costs to society must also be considered. Business activity can, for example, harm the environment or use up resources too quickly and thereby harm future generations. The costs to society in such cases exceed the private costs of the firms. Some way must be found to hold firms accountable for both private and social costs, but, as the following article indicates, this is not always easy to do.

The Politics of Pollution

The dark, lethal liquid spills from the depths of the pulp and paper mill and stains the banks of Blackbird Creek. The dirty flow crosses the Trans-Canada Highway three times as it meanders fourteen kilometres to the slate-grey waters of Moberly Bay, carved in the northern shore of Lake Superior.

Nothing lives in Blackbird Creek. A visitor is said to have mistaken the bubbling waters for a hot spring and jumped in. He survived. Fish are less fortunate. None exist, even in the five square kilometres of the bay.

The mill is run by Kimberly-Clark of Canada Ltd., a subsidiary of the U.S. multinational. For 40 years, it has operated in Terrace Bay, a tidy community of 2600 in northwestern Ontario. The mill makes bleached kraft pulp used in facial tissues and disposable diapers. It is the town's main industry, employing 1600 mill workers and woodsmen.

The pollution of Terrace Bay has become the new focus of an old debate on jobs and the environment. The story is familiar: The government orders a company to clean up. The company says it cannot afford to comply, and threatens to close down. Faced with the loss of jobs, the government relents.

This time, environmentalists in Ontario expected to hear a different refrain. They saw Kimberly-Clark as a test of will of the fledgling Liberal government and its commitment to fight industrial pollution.

Directed by Environment Minister Jim Bradley, Ontario has imposed heavy fines on polluters, forced them to clean up spills, and set limits on acid rain

emissions. Its record on the environment has been called the strongest in Canada.

But its response to Kimberly-Clark has soiled that image. In late January, after weeks of tense, fitful negotiations, the government agreed to give the company until 1989 to reach pollution standards it was to have met last year. Critics, dismayed by the extension, called it a failure of resolve. They fear the ruling — which will be the subject of a public meeting in Terrace Bay this week — suggests that industry can pollute and get away with it.

SOURCE: Andrew Cohen, "The Politics of Pollution," *Financial Post*, February 16, 1987, p. 17. Reproduced with permission.

MARKET ECONOMIES AND THE DESTRUCTION OF THE ENVIRONMENT

Why is it so difficult to prevent the kind of pollution described in the Preview? Why has the threat of a global environmental catastrophe become one of the most important economic and social problems of our time?

People are beginning to care about the impact of economic growth on the earth's ecology, but they have reason to wonder why the problem has been allowed to develop for so long and what can really be done to solve it. From space shuttles 300 km above the earth, astronauts can observe the destruction of the Brazilian rain forests, the slow movement of slimy rivers toward the ocean in virtually every part of the globe, and the ugly gashes that mark the destruction of large parts of the British Columbia forest. Closer to the earth, trained observers discern even more destruction: the pollution of many of our lakes and streams, the declining fish populations, the impact of acid rain on plant and animal life, the growing number of persons with respiratory disorders caused by foul air, and the increasing incidence of cancer and other diseases.

Canada is now in the forefront of countries raising concerns about the environment, but its own record is being criticized both at home and abroad. A German television documentary entitled "A Paradise Despoiled" focusses on pollution in Canada, in general, and on the destruction of British Columbia's forests, in particular, calling British Columbia the "Brazil of the North." The British journal *The Economist* notes that Canada emits more greenhouse gases per capita than any other Western industrialized country. These are the carbon dioxide gases that are thought to contribute to global warming.

Why are these things happening? Largely, it seems, because of our unrelenting commitment to economic growth and our failure to measure some of the costs of such growth. Most people, focussing on the benefits it brings, want growth. Take, for example, the Canadian forest industries — logging, wood, paper, and allied industries. Together, they represent Canada's largest single industry. Forestry produces $43 billion worth of products annually, accounts for 17 percent of Canada's exports, and generates jobs for about 900 000 people. The prospect of having the development of this industry curbed because of damage done to the environment poses a major threat to a large part of Canada's work force. For this reason, the pollution caused by forestry is also a major political problem, just as is the pollution caused by other industries. Secure jobs and incomes are usually of greater concern to governments than are changes in the environment and other negative effects of economic activity.

The question posed by economists is this: Are the growing problems of environmental destruction the result of basic flaws in the market economy? In other words, does the market economy fail, in some fundamental way, to produce the right mix of goods and services — that is, a mix that would provide us with what we want without creating a lot of undesirable side effects? In this chapter, we shall examine this question from two perspectives. The first has to do with the right mix of goods for the present generation: To what extent, and why, are we failing to use resources in such a way that their negative consequences are minimized during our own lifetime? (As we shall see, this question has a flip side: To what extent are we failing to take advantage of the positive side effects produced by certain resources?) The second perspective has to do with the effect of our current use of resources on future generations. This inquiry leads to the concept of *sustainable development*, examined in the last section of the chapter.

EXTERNALITIES: QUESTIONING THE MEANING OF EFFICIENCY

Welfare economics
The branch of economics that tries to define the optimal outcome of economic activity.

Earlier in this textbook, in Chapter 2, we referred briefly to the basic elements of what economists call **welfare economics** — a branch of economics that seeks to define the optimal outcome of economic activity. A core proposition of welfare economics is that, under certain basic assumptions, a perfectly competitive market, operating efficiently, uses resources in such a way that no change is possible that could make one person better off without making another person worse off. This, as noted in Chapter 2, is called *Pareto optimality* and signifies that the economy is operating without waste — in other words, that it is operating on its production possibilities frontier.

As we have pointed out throughout the last three chapters, however, economies in the real world do not operate under conditions of perfect competition. This in itself would arguably make the propositions of welfare economics irrelevant. Our concern in this chapter, however, is to show that problems such as environmental destruction are attributable not to breakdowns in competition, but to an inherent flaw in the market system itself. In other words, such problems would exist even within a perfectly competitive market structure. Another way of stating our task is this: We shall show that Pareto's definition of well-being is in fact insufficient, and that the efficiency achieved by an economy operating on its production possibilities frontier, producing goods and services as cheaply as possible, is perhaps not good enough.

Private costs and benefits
The costs incurred and benefits reaped by those who actually produce a good.

Social costs and benefits
The total cost or benefit to society of producing a good, including both private and external costs or benefits.

Externality (external cost or benefit)
An unintended side effect of the use of resources that is either a cost to society (a negative externality) or a benefit (a positive externality); the market neither extracts compensation from those who generate negative externalities nor compensates those who produce positive externalities.

Pareto optimality assumes that private costs and benefits are the same as social costs and benefits — but, in practice, this is often not the case. The market failure examined in this chapter results from the differences between **private costs and benefits** and **social costs and benefits**; specifically, we examine the failure of the market to take adequate account of this difference. The difference to which we refer is known in economics as an **externality**. Externalities are the social side effects of private business activity. Problems arise in market economies when the market does not compensate those who produce positive side effects, or positive externalities, and when it does not assess costs to those who produce negative externalities. When the market fails in this way, it is in effect failing to produce the right mix of goods: It produces more than the socially optimal quantity of goods with negative externalities, and less than the socially optimal quantity of goods with positive externalities.

As an example of a negative externality, consider the pollution that accompanies the production of a good such as paper. The chemicals that are released into the environment, if they go unchecked, will likely reduce the income of fishermen and of people who depend on the tourist industry. The market does not force the producer of such pollution to compensate the victims.

From the point of view of the economist, such a situation is not only unfair but inefficient as well. A simple, hypothetical example will help to illustrate economic reasoning in such a case.

Negative Externalities: The Private and Social Costs of a Paper Mill

Assume that the costs and the demand curve for a private, competitive pulp and paper operation are as shown in Box 11.1. In the table, several different types of costs are shown. There are, first of all, the direct costs of operation paid for

Privately and Socially Optimal Output Levels of a Pulp and Paper Mill

BOX 11.1

The table below indicates the private and external costs associated with a hypothetical pulp and paper mill. It is assumed that for every 1000 t of paper produced, enough pollution is generated to cause $25 000 in damages to others. Therefore, the external cost *per tonne* is always $25. This external marginal cost is added to the marginal private operating costs, and the result is called the *marginal social cost.* The diagram shows that the firm will choose to produce between 3000 t and 4000 t of paper, where the price per tonne is equal to the additional private cost of producing each tonne. However, from society's point of view, output ought to be cut back to the point where the price is equal to the marginal social cost of production — that is, between 2000 t and 3000 t.

			Quantity (tonnes)			
Costs	0	1000	2000	3000	4000	5000
Total private costs	$0	$100 000	$175 000	$275 000	$400 000	$550 000
Total external costs	0	25 000	50 000	75 000	100 000	125 000
Total social costs	0	125 000	225 000	350 000	500 000	675 000
Marginal private costs per tonne	$100	$ 75	$100	$125	$150	
Marginal external costs per tonne	25	25	25	25	25	
Marginal social costs per tonne	125	100	125	150	175	

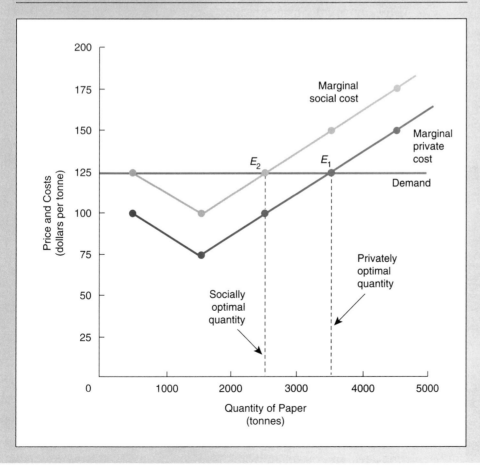

by the paper mill. These are referred to as *private costs*. Second, there are *external costs*, which represent the damage done to persons and institutions affected negatively by the operation of the paper mill, such as fishermen and tourist operators. Such costs will, of course, be difficult to calculate, but they are nevertheless very real. Private and external costs are added to obtain the *social costs* of operating the paper mill, which represent the total cost to society of producing paper at that mill.

The table in Box 11.1 indicates that it costs this mill $100 000 to produce 1000 t of paper (total private costs = $100 000). Each 1000 t of paper creates damages of $25 000 to others through pollution, so the total social cost of producing 1000 t of paper is $125 000. As output increases, private and external costs increase as shown in the table. These total costs are translated into marginal costs in the bottom part of the table — that is, the additional private, external, and social costs of producing each additional tonne of paper. Because it costs $100 000 to produce the first 1000 t of paper, the *marginal private cost* per tonne of the first 1000 t equals $100 (the additional cost of *each* tonne). The marginal external cost of the first 1000 t is $25 (it is assumed that this remains the same for each level of output), so that the *marginal social cost* of producing paper in the range of the first 1000 t is $125. The other marginal costs are calculated in the same way.

Now, according to economic theory, a business firm will maximize its profit by producing that level of output at which marginal (private) cost equals marginal revenue. Assume that this paper firm faces a horizontal demand curve (because it is one of many competitive firms producing a homogeneous product), meaning that it can sell any quantity at the existing market price. We will assume that this price is $125, which therefore also represents the firm's demand curve and its marginal-revenue curve. The firm will maximize its profit (or minimize its losses) by producing between 3000 t and 4000 t, where marginal private costs equal marginal revenue.

However, this privately optimal point of production is *not* the optimal point of production for society. Between 3000 units and 4000 units, according to the diagram in Box 11.1, the *marginal social cost* of the last unit is $150, or $25 higher than marginal revenue. If the price of the product reflects the marginal benefit derived by each consumer from using the product and if the marginal social cost is an accurate reflection of the marginal cost to society of producing the product, then an output level of between 3000 t and 4000 t is *not* socially optimal. The additional costs of the last units at that quantity are greater than the additional benefits.

It would be in society's interest to find some way of forcing this private paper mill to incorporate *both* private and external costs into its cost calculations. In other words, the producer should be required to consider the *marginal social cost* of production in determining the optimal production level. The diagram in Box 11.1 indicates that if this were done, output would be reduced from between 3000 t and 4000 t to between 2000 t and 3000 t, because marginal social cost equals marginal revenue at the latter output point.

Positive Externalities

As we noted earlier, the external effects of production can be positive as well as negative. Take, as a first example, the construction of a railway system. The building of a railway obviously involves huge capital outlays. A private entrepreneur contemplating such an enterprise might easily be discouraged from proceeding because of the enormous amount of revenue that a railway would have to generate in order to match its costs. If, however, such a project produced substantial, positive externalities, an economic case could be made for subsidizing it with government revenues. For example, rail passenger service offers an alternative to travelling by car, and might therefore lessen the need to build more highways and also reduce automobile pollution and congestion. The benefits to society in this case may be greater than the benefits that accrue only to rail passengers, and yet, as long as only the latter are required to pay for the service, the revenue generated may not be high enough to warrant building the railway line. In other words, the market price that railways can charge their passengers will be too low in relation to the marginal social benefits. Society may be justified in eliminating this gap between marginal cost and marginal social benefit either by lowering the cost through subsidies to the railways or by subsidizing consumers to enable them to pay a higher price. As we have seen previously, the Canadian government has often used the first policy to stimulate railway building in this country.

To clarify the chain of reasoning that we have just used, take another product, education, as an example of a good that likely produces positive externalities. Imagine a situation in which governments assume no responsibility for the schooling of children, and the marketplace is supposed to take care of this need by itself. The only "consumers," or purchasers, of this product we call "schooling" are going to be the parents of children. It is their responsibility to hire contractors who will build and staff the schools.

Box 11.2 illustrates what might happen in such a case. In the graph, the marginal-private-cost (MPC) curve indicates the additional costs that a private contractor would incur for each additional "pupil-place" or "unit of schooling" provided. The demand curve indicates the price that parents are willing to pay for each such unit. Assuming that the contractors operate in a perfectly competitive situation, the price of $700 offered by parents is also the marginal revenue that contractors obtain for each pupil-place provided. According to Box 11.2, contractors will provide 2000 pupil-places, because that is where their marginal private costs will be equal to their marginal revenue (at E_1).

However, what if schooling provides an external benefit of $100 per pupil to society at large. Presumably property owners experience less vandalism when young people are in school, and employers benefit from the skills that students have learned. Perhaps also — though this is debatable — better-educated persons are generally more productive than others, so that society as a whole benefits.

In any case, assume that society is justified in attributing an external benefit of $100 per student. The marginal social cost of producing "schooling" will then be lower than the marginal private cost. Remember, marginal social cost equals marginal private cost plus marginal external cost. In the case of a negative externality, there is an additional external cost, which will show up as a positive number — that is, as a real cost addition. In the case of a positive externality, however, the additional external cost is really a *benefit* and should be recorded as a negative number — that is, as a real cost reduction. In our example, the marginal external benefit of each pupil is exactly $100, so that the marginal-social-cost curve will be precisely $100 below the marginal-private-cost curve.

From society's point of view, the optimal production of schooling occurs where marginal *social* cost is equal to marginal revenue. In our example, this occurs at E_2, where each contractor will provide 3000 school places instead of only 2000. The trick now is for somebody to get the contractor to adopt society's point of view.

BOX 11.2   *Private and Social Costs of Providing a Good or Service with Positive Externalities*

In the case of positive externalities, where there is an external benefit rather than an external cost, marginal social cost is lower than marginal private cost by the value of the external benefit. The social costs of providing an education for children may therefore be less than the private costs, once external benefits have been subtracted from private costs. In such a case, a market system might produce too little of the good, since it does not take external benefits into account.

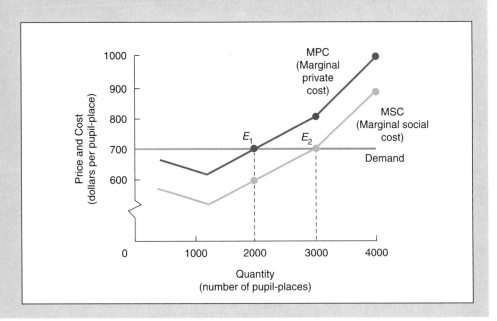

MAKING PRODUCERS RESPONSIVE TO SOCIAL COSTS AND BENEFITS

How can business firms be made to consider social costs and benefits in determining optimal levels of output? More than three decades ago, Ronald Coase of the University of Virginia wrote a classic article[1] in which he argued that the potential exists within the market itself to force producers to take account of externalities. To illustrate his point, he used the example of the negative environmental effects of wood-burning locomotives: The sparks from such locomotives would often set farmers' fields on fire. The solution, Coase maintained, lay neither in the banning

---

[1]Ronald Coase, "The Problem of Social Cost," *Journal of Law and Economics* 3:1–44.

of wood-burning locomotives by government, nor even in government enforcement of more stringent pollution regulations, but simply in granting *farmers* the right to force railway companies to operate their locomotives without spewing sparks. In the economic literature, the granting of such rights to individuals or groups is said to bestow special **property rights** on them. As long as property rights exist and are appropriately assigned, so the theory goes, externality problems should correct themselves. In Coase's example, farmers would have the legal right to force railway owners to put spark suppressants on their locomotives. By pitting private farmers against private railway owners, the market could solve this type of problem on its own, without the need for government intervention. The government would merely create the appropriate rules — in this case, by assigning property rights — and enforce them.

In 1973, Steven Cheung, then of the University of Washington, applied Coase's line of reasoning to a positive externality: the pollination services provided for growers of flowers and fruit by bees in the course of their honey production.[2] The prevailing view on this issue was that beekeepers would not be able to charge for these services, and that they would therefore keep less than an optimal number of bees in production. However, when he examined the beekeeping industry in Washington, Cheung found that beekeepers had indeed found ways of charging flower and fruit growers for nectar and pollination. This meant that bee production was probably operating at or near its socially optimal level.

These seemingly minor examples, and others like them, have led many economists to conclude that the market is capable of handling a wide range of negative and positive externalities with a minimum of government intervention. In other words, the market may not fail nearly as often, or as inevitably, as some had feared.

Then why, it might be asked, are there serious environmental problems in most market economies, and why is the government frequently called on to intervene? One answer lies in the existence of **transaction costs**. It is simply too difficult and too expensive for thousands of victims of pollution to bring (that is, to "transact") formal complaints against particular polluters. It would also be difficult and expensive to verify the extent of the damage being claimed in each case, and it would certainly involve great expense to try each of the claims through the courts. It seems clear that, in the majority of cases, it would be easier and cheaper to have governments act on behalf of all victims, either forcing polluters to install equipment to reduce or eliminate the pollution they generate or raising taxes on polluters to pay for cleaning it up. In terms of Box 11.1, either of these government actions would raise the paper mill's private costs to the level at which they would equal social costs. (In other words, the social costs of pollution would be paid for by the polluter.) In this way, the socially optimal level of output would be reached, and much less pollution would be generated than before.

A similar argument can be made for some government intervention in cases of positive externalities. Look back at the example of schooling depicted in Box 11.2. To ensure the provision of the socially optimal number of "pupil-places," at least two different types of strategies could be used. First, the government could give parents a grant of $100 per pupil, enabling them to pay $800 instead of $700

Property rights
Rights that pertain to the permissible use of resources.

Transaction costs
The costs, other than price, that are incurred in trading goods or services.

---

[2]Steven N.S. Cheung, "The Fable of the Bees: An Economic Investigation," *Journal of Law and Economics* 16 (April 1973): 11–33.

for each child enrolled in school. This would effectively push the demand curve up to $800, causing it to cross the marginal-private-cost curve at the socially optimal output level of 3000 pupil-places. Alternatively, the government could leave the demand curve where it was and lower the marginal-private-cost curve by $100, to the level of the marginal-social-cost curve, by granting a subsidy of $100 per pupil-place to the contractors commissioned to build the schools. The new marginal-private-cost curve would then cross the old demand curve at the socially optimal output level of 3000 pupil-places.

It should be noted that, in the case of both negative and positive externalities, these solutions require only a minimal amount of participation by governments as tax collectors and dispensers of grants or subsidies; in neither case are governments required to "manage" the producers (that is, the polluting firms or the school contractors) directly. In the case of grants to parents in the schooling example, for instance, the parents could increase their influence by pooling their grants; for the combined funds, they could require the contractors to build the kinds of schools they wanted, develop curriculums that met their standards, pay teachers, and so on, without direct government involvement. Our actual school systems in Canada have much more government involvement than is required in order to deal with the problem of externalities alone.

The Costs of Dealing with Externalities

In Canada, governments participate heavily in the financing and operation of a wide range of services that are considered to generate positive externalities, such as medical care, education, and social work. The assumption behind this involvement is that the market, left to its own devices, would not produce socially optimal quantities of such services. At the same time, governments are participating more and more in programs to reduce negative externalities, hoping thereby to reduce the output of goods whose production generates such externalities to a socially optimal level.

The cost of such programs runs into the billions of dollars. In 1990, all governments in Canada combined spent about $140 billion, or about 50 percent of their entire budgets, on health, education, and social welfare. In addition, governments are spending several billions of dollars each year cleaning up air and water pollution and enforcing a growing number of pollution regulations. This is not surprising when one considers, for example, that the cost of cleaning up only a small part of the chemical pollution in the Niagara area is estimated at about $300 million or that it could cost more than $20 billion to effect an appreciable reduction in the acid-rain problem. Most Western countries now spend about 1 percent of their annual GDP dealing with pollution problems (for Canada, this amounts to more than $6 billion). Such activity is having some effect: Many lakes and streams, including Lake Erie, are once again open for swimming; fish populations are slowly being restored; and reforestation programs are reclaiming some of the lands that suffered the worst deforestations of the past.

Governments are also experimenting with new forms of pollution controls. One of the most important — and most controversial — of these new ideas, recommended in the federal government's recent Green Plan (see the accompanying For Example. . . box) involves the use of tradeable pollution credits.

Trading Pollution Credits

As the article in the For Example. . . box explains, the federal government has introduced a plan whereby business firms will be able to trade pollution credits. To many members of the public, the prospect of firms' actually being given the *right* to pollute is quite disturbing. But the government now sees this as the most efficient way to reduce pollution, and the notion is sufficiently important and complex to warrant our careful attention and analysis.

To understand the reasoning behind this approach, it is necessary to consider several facts about pollution in the world today:

1. In many industries, it is impossible to eliminate pollution entirely — at least, it would be prohibitively expensive to do so.

FOR EXAMPLE...
Tradeable Pollution Credits

In its attempts to find the most efficient way to reduce pollution, Canada is considering a new method that allows companies to buy and sell one another's pollution credits.

A Green Plan for Smog Credits

Ottawa took its first tentative steps toward creating a market in tradeable pollution credits in the Green Plan, its $3 billion, five-year environmental strategy.

The 174-page document, released this week, calls for tradeable credits to be incorporated into federal–provincial urban smog control agreements as early as 1993 — if the concept proves feasible.

But some of the plan's critics say Environment Minister Robert de Cotret has shown little faith in one of the most powerful tools to control pollution — the market.

Under an "emissions-trading" system, permits or credits are distributed to polluters in an area, allowing them to discharge certain amounts of a compound based on an overall pollution target for that region.

Demand in the market is supposed to come from companies for which controlling pollution is expensive. They will have the cheaper option of buying credits to maintain or even increase their emissions.

Those credits will come from their cleaner competitors, who can cut their emissions more cost-effectively. As they reduce their pollution, they will be able to sell their leftover credits for cash.

The overall number of credits available can be cranked down over time to achieve stricter emission standards and encourage the development of new pollution-control technologies.

"The idea . . . is to reduce the number of regulations and allow industries to make the decisions themselves, the most cost-effective way they can," said Tom Brydges, an Environment Canada scientist working on the plan.

"The same environmental benefit as a regulation is gained, but often at a fraction of the cost."

Variations on this system have been tried many times over the past fifteen years in the United States, not always successfully. But the concept has shown enough promise there to form the principal means of cutting acid-rain-causing sulphur dioxide emissions by 50 percent over the next ten years in the recently approved U.S. Clean Air Act.

Emissions trading has never been attempted in Canada, although federal and provincial officials have studied the idea for more than a year. Researchers think it could work to control some industrial sources of smog, such as the production of solvents used in everything from paint to hairspray.

SOURCE: John Fox, "A Green Plan for Smog Credits," *Financial Post*, December 17, 1990, p. 3. Reproduced with permission.

2. The cost of reducing pollution differs from one industry to another, and even from one firm to another within an industry, depending on the nature and age of the technology being used or on the prevailing external conditions (for example, the type of fuel that is available to a firm or the difficulties it must overcome in extracting a particular resource).

3. For most industries or firms, the cost of reducing pollution rises the closer its complete elimination is approached.

These conditions are reflected in the graph in Box 11.3. The cost of reducing pollution is measured on the vertical axis and the amount of pollution created by different firms in a given industry is measured on the horizontal axis. The curve labelled MCRP (marginal cost of reducing pollution) illustrates the cost of eliminating successive "units" of pollution. It rises to the left, indicating that the cost of reducing a unit of pollution rises as more and more reductions occur — that is, as one approaches the complete elimination of pollution. Assume now that Firm X is producing Q_1 units of pollution and that Firm Y is producing Q_2 units of pollution. Next, suppose that the government issues an order that all firms must cut their pollution in half. The order seems fair enough at face value, but, in fact, the cost of the reductions will be very different for the two firms. Firm X, the heavier polluter, will have to cut pollution to Q_3, at a cost equal to the area under the MCRP curve between points Q_1 and Q_3. Firm Y, the lesser polluter, will have to cut pollution from Q_2 to Q_4, at a cost equal to the area under the MCRP curve between Q_2 and Q_4. Although Firm Y must reduce pollution by a smaller amount than Firm X, its costs may actually be greater than those of Firm X because the costs of reducing pollution are higher closer to the point at which it is eliminated. (Note that Firm Y's costs will be greater than Firm X's as long as the shaded area between Q_3 and Q_4 is greater than the shaded area between Q_1 and Q_2.)

The government could get around this perverse result by imposing a pollution tax, T, on each firm (as shown in Box 11.3) rather than ordering the 50 percent cut in pollution. Both firms would then find it expedient to reduce pollution to Q_5 units, since the tax on pollution would be greater than the cost of reducing pollution to that point. Neither firm, however, would reduce pollution to less than Q_5 units, because the costs of reduction in that range exceed the cost of the tax. Under this policy, Firm X, the heavier polluter, would have to reduce pollution by a greater amount than Firm Y, and would, justly, have to pay more than Firm Y for doing so.

A similar result can be achieved without involving the government in the expense of raising taxes, by issuing pollution permits or credits. Suppose each firm is given the "right," in the form of a permit, to pollute just half as much as it did before. However, firms are free to reduce pollution by more than this, and sell their excess pollution rights to others. To understand why it might pay them to do this, assume once again that we have the two firms, X and Y, depicted in Box 11.3. Firm X is permitted Q_3 units of pollution, equal to half of its current pollution of Q_1, while Firm Y is permitted only Q_4 units of pollution, equal to half of its current level of Q_2. Assume next that both firms reduce pollution to the required levels. Firm X might then reason as follows: "It would pay me to reduce pollution even further from Q_4 to, say, Q_5, if I could sell the surplus pollution rights gained by such a move to someone else for a price equal to T." Observe that in moving from Q_3 to Q_5, Firm X has excess pollution permits equal to the distance Q_3 to Q_5. The cost of reducing pollution from Q_3 to Q_5 is less than price T per unit of pollution. Therefore, if Firm X can sell its excess permits for a price of T per unit of pol-

The Cost of Reducing Pollution

BOX 11.3

In this graph Firm X produces Q_1 units of pollution, and Firm Y produces Q_2 units. Both firms have the same MCRP curve. If both firms are required to cut pollution in half, Firm X will go down to Q_3 units, and Firm Y to Q_4. Although Firm Y does not pollute as much as Firm X, it may have to pay more than Firm Y to reduce its pollution by 50 percent. If, instead, a pollution tax, T, is imposed, both firms will reduce pollution to Q_5, and Firm Y will do so at a lower cost than Firm X. A similar result would be obtained by requiring firms to buy permits to produce half of their current level of pollution. The buying and selling of these permits would result in a decrease in pollution to Q_5 units for all firms.

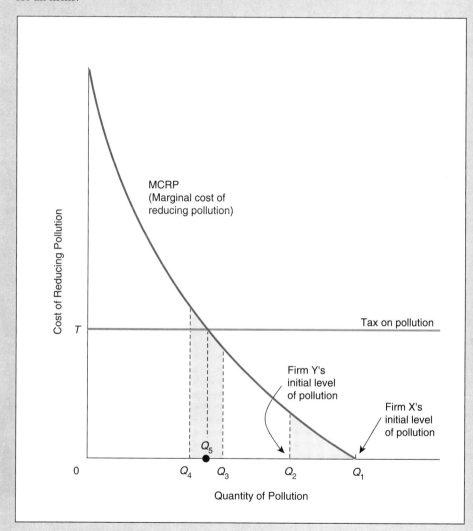

lution, it will be making money. The question is, would another firm be willing to buy these permits at a price of T? Yes, Firm Y would. Firm Y was required to reduce pollution from Q_2 to Q_4. Box 11.3 shows that the cost of eliminating the last few units of pollution, from Q_5 to Q_4 exceeded price T. Therefore, it would pay

Firm Y to buy pollution permits from Firm X at a price of T, and increase pollution to Q_5. The overall reduction in pollution by both firms would be the same as it was under the pollution tax policy.

While this method has been used in the United States with some apparent success, its application in Canada has yet to be tested. There is a possibility that the idea of "pollution rights" could be interpreted, not only by the general public, but even by some businesses, as a right to pollute *more* — a possibility that could produce some unexpected deviations from the goals of the plan.

PROBLEMS ASSOCIATED WITH COMMON-PROPERTY RESOURCES

Environmental damage is a matter not only of pollution but also of depletion. Some resources, such as coal, became depleted over time because they are not renewable. Even some renewable resources, however, such as fish and forest products, are in danger of depletion because of a peculiar problem — the problem of **common-property resources**. These are resources that are owned by no one in particular and that can therefore be used by anyone.

Common-property resources
Resources that are not privately owned and that can therefore be used by anyone.

Several decades ago, the Manitoba government was alerted to the fact that the fish populations of several Manitoba lakes were diminishing at an alarming rate. The income of fishermen on these lakes was also declining. It was observed that fishing is an industry that exploits a common-property resource: The fish belong to everyone and, therefore, to no one in particular. In calculating their costs of fishing, individual fishermen took into account only their outlays on boats, nets, and other supplies, and ignored the impact of their own catches on the potential catches of others. They also ignored the impact of their combined fishing efforts on the long-run stock of fish. In other words, they failed to take into account the negative externalities of their individual efforts. Because social costs were ignored, the actual annual catch far exceeded the socially optimal catch.

The solution to the overuse of common-property resources such as fish is similar to the solutions suggested earlier in this chapter for curbing pollution: charge a substantial fee — say, in the form of a licence — so that marginal private costs begin to approximate marginal social costs. This should have the effect of reducing the number of fishermen and, therefore, the overall number of fish caught.

SUSTAINABLE DEVELOPMENT: PRODUCTION WITH A VIEW TO THE FUTURE

Our discussion of the problems associated with depletable and common-property resources leads us naturally to the second major question of this chapter: How can society ensure production of the right mix of goods and services now, so that future generations will benefit from a hospitable environment? In other words, how can society ensure **sustainable development** — development that meets present needs without reducing the ability of future generations to meet their needs?

Sustainable development
Development that meets present needs without reducing the ability of future generations to meet their needs.

The concept of sustainable development embodies questions that have concerned people for a long time — for example, whether we can go on enjoying economic prosperity, and whether we can help the billions of poor people in the world improve their standard of living, without using up or destroying the earth's resources.

In the year 1798, the British economist Thomas R. Malthus published a book entitled *An Essay on the Principle of Population*, in which he argued against the common view of his time that rapid population growth promoted prosperity. His research indicated, he said, that the opposite was true: Unrestrained population growth would eventually produce mass starvation, because population would grow more quickly than the food supply that would be required to feed it. Malthus maintained that food supplies increased in an arithmetic progression, while population grew in a geometric progression.

The Malthusian spectre of population's outstripping food resources has haunted economists and social-policy makers ever since. Nonetheless, the experience of more than a century (at least, that of most parts of the Western world) seemed to have proved his predictions wrong. The Industrial Revolution of the nineteenth century led to major improvements in resource use, which raised rather than lowered people's standard of living. Growing prosperity did not induce a more rapid population growth, as Malthus had predicted it would, but a fairly steady, manageable rate of growth. However, in many parts of the world, famine often did occur, reminding the rest of the world that it was really not sustaining itself on a worldwide basis. Then, in 1972, another book drew the Western world's attention to a growing crisis in its own midst. Published by a private economic think tank called The Club of Rome, this book, entitled *The Limits to Growth*, argued that rapid industrial growth and a rapidly growing world population could exhaust the supply of many natural resources, such as oil, copper, and coal, by the end of another century.[3] This, together with inadequate food supplies, would lead to a major economic crisis. The study, together with others that followed it, generated a far-ranging debate that stimulated renewed interest in the question of sustainable development.

In the last decade, most governments of industrialized countries have established commissions to study, and policies to implement, ways of reducing the use of basic resources and improving the environment. In Canada, federal and provincial governments have established so-called round tables, made up of environmental experts in various fields, to advise them on environmental policy. "Green plans" have been formulated, and the federal government is establishing a major centre for the study of sustainable development in Winnipeg.

In 1987, the United Nations' World Commission on Environment and Development (known as the Brundtland Commission after its chairman) issued a 400-page document, *Our Common Future*, which committed member countries to more vigorous action in the interest of sustainable development. The report established four basic goals:

1. To reduce population growth.

2. To increase the stock of renewable resources.

3. To improve energy efficiency.

4. To bridge the gap between rich and poor nations.[4]

---

[3]Donald H. Meadows et al., *The Limits to Growth* (New York: Universe Books, 1972), pp. 125–26.

[4]From a three-part series of articles by John Fox: "A Sustainable Cure for a Suffering Planet," *Financial Post*, July 16, 1990, p. 5; "Economics Can't Ignore the Environment," *Financial Post*, July 17, 1990, p. 14; "New Technology Could Help Save Energy," *Financial Post*, July 18, 1990, p. 12. Used with permission.

The data in Box 11.4 provide some idea of how expensive efforts to meet these goals will be. The Worldwatch Institute of Washington estimates that it will cost at least $1.371 trillion (U.S.) (above and beyond amounts already being spent on existing environmental programs) to put the world on a sustainable-development course by the year 2000. The World Bank is even less optimistic: It predicts that Western countries will need to contribute at least $800 billion by the end of this century just to help Third World countries develop energy resources sufficient to give them a strong industrial base.[5]

The prospects for substantial improvement do seem rather bleak. Past trends and attitudes are always difficult to change. World economic activity has grown twentyfold since 1900, and most of that growth has occurred during the last forty years. The population of the world was about two billion in 1960 and will increase to six billion by the year 2000; it is estimated that if it doubles in the next fifty years, the use of resources will have to increase at least fivefold to provide an adequate standard of living. In the meantime, as will be shown in Chapter 29,

---

BOX 11.4 *The Costs of Achieving Sustainable Development by the Year 2000*

The Worldwatch Institute, an environmental think tank based in Washington, D.C., has put together the following rough estimates of the costs of efforts that will be required, in addition to existing environmental-protection projects, to put the world on a course of sustainable development by the year 2000. As indicated in the table, such efforts include protecting topsoil and reforesting, as well as implementing measures to slow population growth, improve energy efficiency, and reduce the debt of the Third World.

Year	Protecting Cropland Topsoil	Reforesting the Earth	Slowing Population Growth	Raising Energy Efficiency	Developing Renewable Energy	Retiring Third World Debt	Total
	(billions of dollars)						
1990	4	2	13	5	2	20	46
1991	9	3	18	10	5	30	75
1992	14	4	22	15	8	40	103
1993	18	5	26	20	10	50	129
1994	24	6	28	25	12	50	145
1995	24	6	30	30	15	40	145
1996	24	6	31	35	18	30	144
1997	24	6	32	40	21	20	143
1998	24	7	32	45	24	10	142
1999	24	7	32	50	27	10	150
2000	24	7	33	55	30	0	149

SOURCE: Worldwatch Institute, *State of the World Report* (Washington, D.C.: Worldwatch Institute, 1988). Reproduced with permission.

---

[5]Much of the information in this section is based on John Fox's three-part series of articles (see footnote 4).

many parts of the world, particularly sub-Saharan Africa, are experiencing serious reductions in what is already a precarious economic existence.

Nevertheless, many Western governments, individuals, and business firms seem strongly committed to the goals of sustainable development, and the next few decades will be a crucial test of their ingenuity and resolve. The For Example. . . box illustrates just how powerfully such ideas can affect activity at the local level — and thereby provide at least some basis for hope for the future.

FOR EXAMPLE...
Local Initiatives for Sustainable Development

The following article illustrates the impact at the local level of environmental-protection ideals and world efforts toward sustainable development.

Co-operating with Nature

"Do what is right and the dollars will follow," says Ohio farmer Valentine Yutzy.

Some might question both the economics and theology of that motto, but Yutzy thinks he can prove it.

For him, doing what is right includes practising environmental agriculture on his 272-acre [110-hectare] farm near Plain City in central Ohio. This means extensive conservation tactics ranging from water and topsoil protection to a complex program of crop rotation and plant nutrition.

One of the first things a visitor might notice is that Yutzy's farm doesn't smell, despite the presence of 75 cows. He'll gladly demonstrate an ingenious method of cross ventilating his dairy barns, which he devised to gently diffuse odours so they don't offend neighbours. Less obvious are the numerous subsurface techniques he uses to safeguard the local water supply and the nutritional value of the soil.

One of Yutzy's goals is to have no nonfiltered surface water run off into a public stream. To accomplish this, he's built a catch basin under his fertilizer storage and mixing plant to make sure no accidental spill can get into public streams. He's also constructed a settling basin with an overflow for the area used to wash equipment, load fertilizer, and fill the sprayer. Waterways are grassed so that water running through his farm won't take soil with it.

Yutzy also pays a lot of attention to soil life and tilth management. He incorporates all plant and animal residues into the aerobic soil layer. This is done so the soil microflora and earthworms can convert the organic matter into humus for plant nutrients for the next crop. Not only does he believe this approach encourages micro-organisms to help feed the crops, but "soils that are biologically alive have . . . [fewer] erosion problems."

The Yutzy farm uses no harsh chemicals, except in emergencies. No caustic chemical fertilizers are used. He uses a few herbicides, insecticides, and fungicides as possible. His ultimate goal is to use none at all.

A ten- or eleven-year crop rotation is used, alternating corn, small grains, alfalfa, and soybeans. Yutzy has found this to be a natural way to break up the life cycle of many harmful pests and weeds. "When you have continuous crops of the same kind, you generally have a buildup of pests of one kind or another," he says.

Manure is Yutzy's primary supplemental fertilizer. He sees it as a natural resource. "We don't call manure a waste product around here," he says. He'll often tinker with it, however, adding small amounts of molasses, calcium nitrate, and liquid fish to enhance the bacterial life in the soil.

The crop and animal sections of the farm are completely balanced in a closed-loop system. "We feed all that we raise and raise all that we feed," says Yutzy.

Yutzy concedes that his farming methods are not understood by all. "Some people think I'm crazy," he says.

That should not surprise him, for when Yutzy first heard of biological farming several years ago, he thought he was listening to "voodoo doctors." But he gave them enough benefit of the doubt to study what they were saying and soon became not only a convert himself but also an expert who is frequently called upon to address university groups.

SOURCE: "Cooperating with Nature," *The Marketplace*, October 16, 1990, pp. 14–16.

SUMMARY

1. The production of some goods and services results in external benefits or costs called *externalities*. The market does not compensate those who generate positive externalities (external benefits) and does not charge those who generate negative externalities (external costs).

2. Even a perfectly competitive market will not produce the optimal quantities of such goods and services from the viewpoint of society. Without some mechanism for charging the producers of negative externalities and for rewarding producers of positive externalities, the market will produce more than the socially optimal quantity of goods and services with negative externalities and less than the socially optimal quantity of those with positive externalities.

3. The proper adjustments for such externalities may on occasion be made through private negotiations between the parties involved, but in many cases, it is more efficient to have the government intervene to encourage production up to the point where marginal social costs equal marginal social benefits.

4. *Common-property resources* entail special problems, such as overuse and depletion, which may best be solved by charging fees to users of such resources.

5. Many countries have embraced the goals of *sustainable development* in order to create conditions that will avoid jeopardizing the ability of future generations to meet their needs.

EFFECTIVE THINKING: PROBLEM 3
Pickled-Cocktail-Onion Firm

You have learned that negative externalities such as pollution can be part of the process of production. This effective-thinking problem describes the negative externalities caused by a small firm's production process and deals with the ways that the firm and society might choose to handle the situation. You may want to refer back to Chapter 7 before working through this problem.

A firm that produces pickled cocktail onions estimates its output and costs to be as shown in the accompanying table. The firm finds that it is able to sell all the output it produces at a price of $22 per case. The firm is currently producing 90 cases per week, but the owners wonder if this is in fact their profit-maximizing (or loss-minimizing) output level. The firm's owners hire you as an economic consultant to advise them on this question.

In addition to its concerns about its profit-maximizing level of output, the firm has other problems: People living near the onion-picking plant are complaining that chemicals from the pickling process get into the air and make their eyes water. (See the table for an estimate of the total costs to the neighbours resulting from the plant's production.) Some people have suggested that the government should make the onion plant economically responsible for the discomforts it is causing its neighbours; others believe that the plant should be forced to shut down completely because its production process bothers some people. In addition

Output (cases per week)	Firm's Fixed Costs	Firm's Variable Costs	Estimated Total External Costs to the Neighbours
30	$1000	$ 240	$100
40	1000	360	150
50	1000	500	200
60	1000	720	250
70	1000	1050	300
80	1000	1440	350
90	1000	1980	400
100	1000	2700	450

to advising the firm about its output levels, make some suggestions to the government, from an economic perspective, about the situation with the neighbours. For instance, advise the government on the socially optimal level of output for this firm.

Directions

Use the twelve effective-thinking steps for successful problem solving to advise (1) the onion firm, on its profit-maximizing (or loss-minimizing) level of output, and (2) the government, on economic solutions to the plant's problems with its neighbours. (See the Appendix to Chapter 3 if you need to review the twelve steps.) For Steps 10 through 12, assume that the plan you adopt in Step 9 is implemented. Make any calculations and draw any graphs you think might help you to reach an answer or to formulate appropriate policy for this situation.

An example of the thinking process an economist might go through using these twelve problem-solving steps appears at the back of the book (see pages 783–94). Not all economists would produce identical answers for each step, but they would all draw on accepted principles of economics.

KEY TERMS

welfare economics
private costs and benefits
social costs and benefits

externalities
property rights
transaction costs

common-property resources
sustainable development

KEY BOXES

Box 11.1 Privately and Socially Optimal Output
　　　　　Levels of a Pulp and Paper Mill
Box 11.2 Private and Social Costs of Providing a
　　　　　Good or Service with Positive Externalities

Box 11.3 The Cost of Reducing Pollution

REVIEW QUESTIONS

1. The Great Lakes are severely polluted. Among the people hurt by this pollution are the owners of lakefront property. Do you think these owners should be permitted to bring legal suit against any company polluting the lake on which their property is located? If such suits were permitted, do you think many would be brought? Should property owners who won such cases against polluters be able to obtain cease-and-desist orders stopping all further pollution, or should they simply be awarded monetary damages? Explain.

2. If a case were to be made for government intervention in the field of education, would it be sufficient to have the government impose taxes and redistribute the revenue to either parents or contractors, or would it be necessary to have the government become involved in the provision of educational services?

3. **Case for Discussion**
   On Monday, Main Street property owners in Steinbach overwhelmingly rejected a proposal to rebuild utilities, sidewalks, and boulevards along the thoroughfare at an estimated cost of well over $1 million.

   The merchants told town council at a special meeting called to assess property owners' opinions on the proposal that the price of reconstruction is too steep during a period of economic recession.

   Realtor George Penner added that some property owners also believed the town's taxpayers at large should pay for a portion of Main Street improvements, since he felt all residents benefited from an attractive downtown appearance.

   Questions:
   Based on the information in this excerpt from the Steinbach, Manitoba, newspaper, *The Camillon* (vol. 38, no. 2, p. 1), would it be necessary for the municipal government to undertake the described improvements on its own in order to get them done? What is the actual minimum function that governments must assume in such situations?

4. A chemical plant releases chemical pollutants into the air as part of its production process. The atmosphere can safely dissipate only a certain amount of these chemicals. As production at the plant increases, the polluted air begins to damage plant, animal, and human life in a twenty-kilometre radius around the plant. Government regulators are attempting to determine the socially optimal level of output for this plant, which provides hundreds of jobs for local residents.

   a. Complete the table below by calculating total social costs, marginal private costs, marginal external costs, and marginal social costs per tonne of chemicals produced. Plot the values for marginal private costs and marginal social costs on a graph.

   b. What is the external cost per tonne of chemicals produced for this firm?

   c. Assuming the firm has a perfectly elastic demand curve for its products at a price of $350 per tonne, what is the privately optimal level of output?

   d. Based on the same assumption as in Question 4(c), what is the socially optimal level of output?

Costs		Quantity (tonnes)			
	0	200	400	600	800
Total private costs	$0	$100 000	$140 000	$200 000	$280 000
Total external costs	0	20 000	40 000	60 000	80 000
Total social costs	0	____	____	____	____
Marginal private costs per tonne	____	____	____	____	
Marginal external costs per tonne	____	____	____	____	
Marginal social costs per tonne	____	____	____	____	

5. In some large urban areas, commercial airliners are prohibited from landing and taking off between certain hours, when most people are sleeping. What is the problem with unrestricted landing times? How, other than prohibiting landing, could this situation be dealt with?

PART FOUR

Factor Markets and Income Distribution

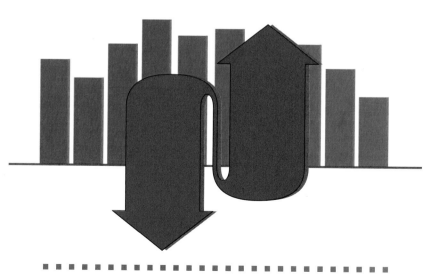

Factor Markets and Marginal Productivity Theory

WHAT YOU WILL LEARN IN THIS CHAPTER

After studying this chapter, you will be able to

1. Explain how factor markets help determine how and for whom goods and services are produced.

2. Explain how marginal revenue product is related to the amount of a factor used in the case of perfectly competitive and monopolistic firms.

3. Discuss the concept of derived demand and list causes of shifts in factor demand curves.

4. Discuss the labour supply curve for the economy as a whole and for an individual labour market.

5. Discuss competitive equilibrium in labour markets and the marginal productivity theory of distribution.

6. Demonstrate factor market equilibrium under conditions of monopsony.

7. Explain how relative wages may be affected by discrimination and other noneconomic factors, and how affirmative action programs and the concept of "equal pay for work of equal value" are responses to this.

8. Apply supply-and-demand analysis to pure economic rent.

9. Discuss the determination of interest rates in terms of the supply and demand for loanable funds.

10. Discuss three theories of the origins of pure economic profit.

A Preview *Some Are More Equal Than Others*

The slogan of the ruling pigs in George Orwell's famous satire, *Animal Farm*, is "All animals are equal, but some animals are more equal than others." In economic life, something similar appears to hold true for people: Even when men and women perform the same kinds of jobs, they are often paid at different wage rates. The following article, from the British journal *The Economist*, reviews a current Canadian approach to dealing with this age-old problem.

Pay Equity: Papering Over the Sex Gap

The Canadian province of Ontario is discovering that paying women the same wages as men is less simple than it sounds. This month, Ontario extended the world's toughest pay-equity law to include all of the 8000 firms and government agencies in the province which employ more than 100 workers. The year-old law had previously applied only to employers of 500 or more, but even among big employers it has sown confusion. The law will be extended over the next two years to factories, offices, and shops with as few as ten workers. Employers covered by the law must draw up plans for paying the same wages to men and women for work of comparable value.

Employers must also set aside at least 1 percent of their total payroll each year to close the sex gap. Advertisements on Toronto buses and subway trains encourage workers to complain to the pay-equity commission if their employers fail to meet the deadlines. A pay-equity tribunal, whose chairwoman is a former trade-union lawyer, has favoured workers rather than employers in most of the 125 cases it has heard so far.

The law has already brought handsome benefits to thousands of women. Hospitals and schools have made the biggest adjustments. The province's 224 public hospitals set aside $50 million in 1990 for pay-equity wage hikes. They expect to budget similar amounts for the next three or four years. Individual pay increases of 30–50 percent are common.

In a less tangible sense, the law has created a greater awareness of the value of many jobs done by women. Brigid O'Reilly, the province's pay-equity commissioner, notes that "it has brought home to people that the decisions which clerical, administrative, and secretarial staff make are often quite complex." She points to a school which raised its secretary's salary by about $300 a month after determining that her job had the same value as that of the audio-visual technician. The pay-equity exercise has led many companies to revise their entire job-evaluation and compensation systems.

But pay equity has also soured relations between some employers and their workers, and even opened rifts among workers themselves.

A feature of the Ontario system is that it requires a job-by-job comparison between men and women, rather than the "wage-line" system favoured elsewhere, which can be just as arbitrary, but allows proportional wage adjustments where there are no exact job comparisons— for example, a cleaner might be deemed to be worth 30 percent of an accountant. Under the Ontario system, companies must grade all jobs according to four criteria: skill, effort, responsibility, and working conditions. Those where women predominate are then compared with jobs of equal value held by men, and wages for the two groups must be brought into line.

Job-by-job comparison has bred much discontent. The women who stick labels on bottles at a Seagram's distillery have complained that they deserve better than being compared with male labourers who move packing cases around the factory floor. One hospital's nursing assistants received no extra pay because their salaries already matched that of the apprentice electrician whose job was deemed to be of equal value. But the assistants at another hospital just ten miles away received increases of more than $200 a month to bring them into line with a male laboratory technician.

The heart of the problem is the difficulty of identifying suitable "male comparators." Many of the biggest employers of women — such as hospitals, day-care centres, libraries, and the clothing industry — do not have a big enough range of male-dominated occupations against which to measure their female staff. About a fifth of Ontario's female workers are thus excluded from the pay-equity process.

Trade unions are finding a way around this problem — and at the same time ensuring maximum benefit from the system — by pushing for the definition of an employer to be cast as widely as possible. In its most celebrated case so far, the pay-equity tribunal decided that fifty nurses in southwest Ontario could compare their pay to that of policemen, because the two groups' employers are financed by the same local authority. More such arbitrary comparisons, and the dissension that goes with them, can be expected soon. Ontario's left-wing government, which took office last September, has promised to find a way of quickly bringing all of the province's 1.7 million women workers within pay-equity's ambit.

SOURCE: "Pay Equity: Papering Over the Sex Gap," *The Economist*, January 12, 1991, pp. 62–63. Reproduced with permission.

AN INTRODUCTION TO FACTOR MARKETS

The average salary for a woman working full-time in Ontario in 1987 was $20,710, while the average for a man working full-time was $32,120 — a 36 percent difference.

Why is there such a discrepancy between male and female wages? And why does the gap appear to be particularly large in Canada? A survey of nineteen countries in 1977 found that only Japan and Ireland had a bigger gap between the earning power of men and that of women than Canada.[1]

Concerns about this phenomenon have produced a movement for *pay equity* in Canada. But what does "pay equity" mean? Are women receiving lower wages than men because they get paid less than men for the same job? Such outright discrimination may be relatively rare, and will become even rarer under recent human rights legislation. Pay equity, in the form of equal pay for the same job, will do little to close the pay gap between men and women. The problem is more complex. What has happened, basically, is that the system of wage payment in Canada has produced higher pay for jobs in which men predominate, and lower pay for jobs in which women predominate. Is there anything unfair about this? Won't there always be some jobs that pay more than others—for good economic reasons—and can anyone be accused of discrimination because women tend to gravitate to the jobs that pay less?

Recent advocates of pay equity maintain that there *is* something unfair about this system. They define *pay equity* in terms of *equal pay for work of equal value* (or, for work of *comparable worth*), and they argue that our factor markets do not necessarily perform well in equalizing pay on the basis of job value. From their point of view, a clerk typist, who will most often be a woman, may be performing work that is of equal value to that of a steam-shovel operator, who will normally be a male, and yet our factor market system will reward them very differently.

Why do our factor markets produce the kind of wage disparities that they do, and how would advocates of pay equity correct the disparities that they see?

The pay-equity issue draws attention to an important set of markets to which we have referred only indirectly up to this point. That set of markets is **factor markets** — the markets in which labour, capital, and natural resources are bought and sold. Factor markets perform two major functions in a market economy: They help determine how goods and services are produced and they determine income distribution.

Factor markets are important in determining how goods and services are produced because most goods and services can be produced in more than one way. Wheat, for example, can be grown by extensive cultivation of large areas of land with a lot of machinery and little labour or by intensive cultivation of small areas with little machinery and much labour. The choice of production methods depends on the relative prices of the various factors. As those prices change, production methods can change too. Factors that are relatively cheap are used intensively, while those that are relatively expensive are used sparingly.

At the same time, factor markets help determine income distribution, because most people earn their incomes by selling whatever factors of production they own. The greatest number sell their labour services. Many also sell or rent land or capital that they own. Because markets determine factor prices, they also deter-

Factor markets
The markets in which the factors of production — labour, natural resources, and capital — are bought and sold.

---

[1]Frances Russell, "Apples vs. Oranges," *Winnipeg Free Press*, July 14, 1986, p. 7.

mine how much of the total product will go to the owners of labour services, capital, and natural resources.

This chapter and the next two will explore both of these functions of factor markets. The first part of this chapter outlines marginal productivity theory — the foundation of the economic theory of factor markets. Later parts of the chapter apply this theory to the determination of relative wages of various occupations, and to the determination of such other incomes as rent, interest, and profits. Chapter 13 discusses the role of unions in determining wage income. Finally, Chapter 14 will take up the problem of poverty. It will show how the operation of factor markets helps determine the incidence of poverty and will discuss government policies aimed at reducing or eliminating poverty.

FACTORS OF PRODUCTION: DEMAND AND SUPPLY

In many ways, factor markets are much like the product markets already studied. The theories of supply and demand and the tools of marginal analysis apply to factor markets just as they do to product markets. But factor markets do differ from product markets in one major respect: In factor markets, it is firms that are the buyers and households that are the sellers, rather than the other way around. A theory of the demand for factors of production must be based on the same considerations of price, revenue, and profit that determine the supply of products. A theory of factor supply must be an extension of the theory of consumer choice.

In taking the first steps toward a theory of factor demand, we shall once again assume that firms aim to maximize profits. Each profit-maximizing firm must take three things into account when it makes its hiring decisions: (1) the quantity of output produced by a unit of the factor in question; (2) the revenue derived from the sale of the output that will be produced; and (3) the cost of obtaining the factor.

Marginal Physical Product

Chapter 6 defined the *marginal physical product* of a factor as the increase in output resulting from a one-unit increase in the input of that factor when the quantity of all other factors used remains unchanged. For example, if employing one additional worker hour of labour in a light-bulb factory yields an additional output of five light bulbs, when no other inputs to the production process are increased, the marginal physical productivity of labour in that factory is five bulbs per hour. To take another example, if giving a farmer one more hectare of land makes it possible for the farmer to produce twenty more bushels of wheat per year — without any increase in the amount of work performed, the amount of machinery used, or anything else — the marginal physical product of land on that farm is twenty bushels per hectare. Finally, if having one extra dollar of capital allows a taxi company to carry one extra passenger one extra kilometre each year, that puts the marginal physical product of capital for the company at one passenger kilometre per dollar's worth of capital.

Law of diminishing returns

As Chapter 6 showed, the marginal physical product of a factor varies as the quantity of the factor used varies, other things being equal. In particular, as the quantity of a single variable factor increases, with the quantities of all other factor inputs remaining fixed, a point will be reached beyond which the marginal physical product of the variable factor will decline. This principle is known as the *law of diminishing returns.*

Box 12.1 shows total and marginal physical product curves for a firm subject to the law of diminishing returns throughout the range of zero to twenty units of factor input. (At this point, it does not matter whether the factor in question is labour, capital, or natural resources; the principle is the same for all.) As the quantity of this one factor is increased, with the quantities of all other factors used held constant, output increases — but at a diminishing rate. The first unit of

---

Total and Marginal Physical Product of a Factor of Production

BOX 12.1

As the quantity of one factor increases while that of other factors remains unchanged, total physical product increases, but at a decreasing rate. Marginal physical product, as part (c) of this box and column 3 of the table in part (a) show, decreases as the quantity of the factor employed increases. This decrease in marginal physical product is a direct consequence of the law of diminishing returns.

(a)

Quantity of Factor (1)	Total Physical Product (2)	Marginal Physical Product (3)
0	0	
		20
1	20	
		19
2	39	
		18
3	57	
		17
4	74	
		16
5	90	
		15
6	105	
		14
7	119	
		13
8	132	
		12
9	144	
		11
10	155	
		10
11	165	
		9
12	174	
		8
13	182	
		7
14	189	
		6
15	195	
		5
16	200	
		4
17	204	
		3
18	207	
		2
19	209	
		1
20	210	

(b)

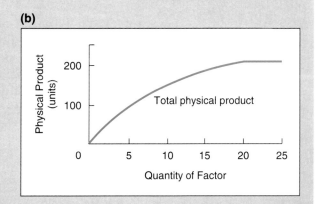

(c)

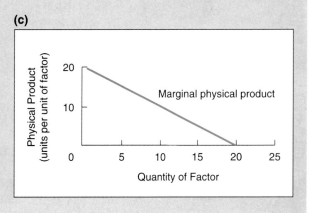

the factor yields a marginal physical product of twenty units of output, the second a marginal physical product of nineteen units, and so on. After the twentieth unit of factor input, as the example is constructed, marginal physical product drops to zero. This implies that some absolute capacity ceiling has been reached, so that adding more of the variable factor cannot produce more output unless the quantities of some of the fixed factors are also increased. For example, if the variable factor in question is labour, it may be that adding more than twenty workers will do nothing to increase output unless, say, the quantity of machinery available for use by the workers is also increased. Note that beyond twenty units of input where the marginal physical product of the variable factor drops to zero, the total-physical-product curve becomes horizontal.

Marginal Revenue Product

Marginal revenue product (of a factor) The change in revenue resulting from the sale of the product produced by one additional unit of factor input.

To determine what quantity of each factor of production it should hire to maximize profit, a firm must take into account the revenue that will be earned from the sale of the product of an added unit of factor input, as well as the size of the marginal physical product. Here, a new term will be useful. The change in revenue resulting from the sale of the product produced by one additional unit of factor input is called the **marginal revenue product** of that factor.

Marginal revenue product for a competitive firm

What happens to the marginal revenue product of a factor as the quantity of that factor is varied depends on what happens to both the marginal physical product of the factor and the marginal revenue earned by selling each additional unit of the product. The simplest case to consider is that of a perfectly competitive firm. Because such a firm is a price taker, as shown in Chapter 7, the quantity of output it produces has no effect on the price at which its output is sold. Marginal revenue for the competitive firm is thus equal to the price of the firm's output, which is constant for all quantities of output. To calculate the marginal revenue product of a factor for such a firm, then, the marginal physical product of the factor is multiplied by the price of the output.

Box 12.2 gives an example of how marginal revenue product is calculated for a perfectly competitive firm. The marginal physical product schedule is the same as that given in Box 12.1, and a constant price of $1 per unit of output is assumed.

Marginal revenue product for a monopolist

If the firm in question is not perfectly competitive, the price at which it sells its output will tend to vary as the quantity of output varies. Suppose, for example, that the firm is a pure monopolist. As Chapter 8 demonstrated, a pure monopoly firm must decrease the price at which its product is sold each time it wants to increase the quantity sold, in accordance with the downward-sloping demand curve for its product. Because the price per unit decreases as output increases, marginal revenue per unit of output is always less than price per unit for a monopolist.

Hence, to calculate the increase in revenue resulting from a one-unit increase in factor input for a monopolist, we must take into account changes in both marginal physical product and marginal revenue. Box 12.3 illustrates how this is done, using the same total-physical-product schedule as the one in Boxes 12.1 and 12.2, but assuming, this time, that the firm is a monopolist. Column 3 gives the firm's demand curve, showing that the price at which output can be sold

Marginal Revenue Product for a Typical Price-Taking Firm

BOX 12.2

For a price-taking firm, the marginal revenue product of a factor is equal to the factor's marginal physical product times the marginal revenue (price) of the product. This table is constructed on the assumption that the product price is $1 per unit and the marginal physical product is the same as in Box 12.1. *Note*: Although it is not explicitly shown in this table, marginal revenue product can also be calculated as the difference in *total revenue* between two successive units of output.

Quantity of Factor (1)	Total Physical Product (2)	Marginal Physical Product (3)	Marginal Revenue (Price) (4)	Marginal Revenue Product (5)
0	0			
		20	$1	$20
1	20			
		19	1	19
2	39			
		18	1	18
3	57			
		17	1	17
4	74			
		16	1	16
5	90			
		15	1	15
6	105			
		14	1	14
7	119			
		13	1	13
8	132			
		12	1	12
9	144			
		11	1	11
10	155			
		10	1	10
11	165			
		9	1	9
12	174			
		8	1	8
13	182			
		7	1	7
14	189			
		6	1	6
15	195			
		5	1	5
16	200			
		4	1	4
17	204			
		3	1	3
18	207			
		2	1	2
19	209			
		1	1	1
20	210			

drops from $1.40 per unit at 20 units of output to $0.45 at 210 units of output. Multiplying price times total physical product gives the total revenue corresponding to each quantity of factor input, shown in column 4.

The differences between successive entries in the total-revenue column give the marginal-revenue-product data, shown in column 5. For example, as the quantity of factor input increases from 4 units to 5 units, the total output increases from 74 units to 90 units, while the price falls from $1.13 per unit to $1.05. As column 4 shows, total revenue increases from $83.62 when 4 units of

BOX 12.3   Marginal Revenue Product for a Monopolistic Firm

This box shows how marginal revenue product varies as the quantity of factor input varies for a pure monopoly firm. As column 3 shows, price falls as output increases, in accordance with the demand for the firm's product. Total revenue begins to decline after ten units of factor input, because although marginal physical product is still positive after that point, marginal revenue (that is, revenue per additional unit of output) becomes negative. Marginal revenue product can be calculated either as the difference between successive entries in the total-revenue column or as the product of marginal physical product and marginal revenue.

Quantity of Factor (1)	Total Physical Product (2)	Price of Output (3)	Total Revenue (4)	Marginal Revenue Product (5)	Marginal Physical Product (6)	Marginal Revenue (5) ÷ (6) (7)
0	0	—	0			
				$28.00	20	$1.40
1	20	$1.40	$28.00			
				23.09	19	1.22
2	39	1.31	51.09			
				18.45	18	1.03
3	57	1.22	69.54			
				14.08	17	0.83
4	74	1.13	83.62			
				10.88	16	0.68
5	90	1.05	94.50			
				7.88	15	0.53
6	105	0.98	102.38			
				5.32	14	0.38
7	119	0.91	107.70			
				3.18	13	0.25
8	132	0.84	110.88			
				1.44	12	0.12
9	144	0.78	112.32			
				0.06	11	0.01
10	155	0.73	112.38			
				−1.00	10	−0.10
11	165	0.68	111.38			
				−1.76	9	−0.20
12	174	0.63	109.62			
				−2.24	8	−0.28
13	182	0.59	107.38			
				−2.48	7	−0.35
14	189	0.56	104.90			
				−2.52	6	−0.42
15	195	0.53	102.38			
				−2.38	5	−0.48
16	200	0.50	100.00			
				−2.08	4	−0.52
17	204	0.48	97.92			
				−1.66	3	−0.55
18	207	0.47	96.26			
				−1.16	2	−0.58
19	209	0.46	95.10			
				−0.60	1	−0.60
20	210	0.45	94.50			

Note: Figures in columns 3, 4, 5, and 7 are rounded to the nearest cent.

factor input are used to $94.50 when 5 units of factor input are used. This gives a marginal revenue product of $10.88 in the range from 4 to 5 units of factor input.

As the price continues to fall, marginal revenue eventually becomes negative. Beyond that point, additional units of factor input, even though they increase total physical product, reduce total revenue. The turning point comes at 10 units of factor input in our example. Beyond that point, marginal revenue product is negative, even though marginal physical product remains positive.

At every level of factor input, the marginal revenue product of the factor is equal to the marginal physical product times the marginal revenue (that is, revenue per additional unit of output). This relationship is shown in columns 5 through 7 of Box 12.3. Note that the marginal-revenue figures in column 7 are expressed in terms of dollars per additional unit of output, whereas the marginal-revenue-product figures in column 5 are expressed in terms of dollars per unit of factor input.

Marginal Factor Cost

The third consideration a firm must take into account to determine the profit-maximizing quantity of a factor is the cost of obtaining each additional unit of that factor — that is, the factor's **marginal factor cost**.

To keep things simple for the moment, consider only the case wherein a firm is a price taker in the market in which it buys its factors of production. This will happen if the firm is only one among a large number of firms competing to hire that particular factor and if the quantity of the factor it uses is only a small fraction of the total used by all firms. For a firm that buys as a price taker, marginal factor cost is simply equal to the market price of the factor. If, for example, the market wage rate for data-entry clerks is $7 per hour, then the marginal factor cost for this particular type of labour is $7 per hour for any firm that is a price taker in the market for data-entry clerks.

Marginal factor cost
The amount by which a firm's total factor cost must increase in order for it to obtain an additional unit of that factor.

Profit Maximization

Profit maximization requires that a firm hire just enough of each factor of production to equalize marginal revenue product and marginal factor cost. If marginal revenue product exceeds marginal factor cost, hiring one more unit of the factor will add more to the revenue than to the cost and hence will increase profit. If marginal factor cost exceeds marginal revenue product, reducing input of the factor by one unit will reduce cost by more than revenue and hence will also increase profit. Only when marginal revenue product and marginal factor cost are equal will it be impossible for any change in factor input to raise profit. This rule applies to both perfectly competitive and monopolistic firms.

Box 12.4 illustrates this profit-maximization rule. The table and corresponding graph in the box are based on the assumption that the firm is a perfect competitor in the output market and that it sells its product at $1 per unit, as in Box 12.2. The firm is also assumed to be a price taker in the factor market, buying inputs of the factor at $5 per unit. Notice that profit rises as more of the factor is hired — up to the fifteenth unit of input. The firm just breaks even on the hiring of the sixteenth unit of input, and profit declines thereafter. It is between the fifteenth and sixteenth units of factor input that marginal revenue product becomes exactly equal to marginal factor cost.

Factor Demand Curves

It follows from this analysis of profit maximization that a firm's marginal-revenue-product curve for a factor is also the firm's demand curve for that factor. A demand curve must indicate the quantity demanded at each price, and it has just been shown that the quantity of the factor demanded will be whatever quantity makes the factor's price (more precisely, its marginal factor cost) equal to marginal revenue product.

BOX 12.4 Profit Maximization for a Price-Taking Firm

Profit maximization requires that a firm hire just enough of each factor of production to equalize marginal revenue product and marginal factor cost. Here it is assumed that the firm is a price taker, as in Box 12.2. The point of profit maximization falls between fifteen and sixteen units of the factor.

(a)

Quantity of Factor (1)	Marginal Revenue Product (2)	Marginal Factor Cost (3)	Total Factor Cost (4)	Fixed Costs (5)	Total Revenue (6)	Total Profit (7)
0			$ 0	$100	$ 0	−$100
	$20	$5				
1			5	100	20	−85
	19	5				
2			10	100	39	−71
	18	5				
3			15	100	57	−58
	17	5				
4			20	100	74	−46
	16	5				
5			25	100	90	−35
	15	5				
6			30	100	105	−25
	14	5				
7			35	100	119	−16
	13	5				
8			40	100	132	−8
	12	5				
9			45	100	144	−1
	11	5				
10			50	100	155	5
	10	5				
11			55	100	165	10
	9	5				
12			60	100	174	14
	8	5				
13			65	100	182	17
	7	5				
14			70	100	189	19
	6	5				
15			75	100	195	20
	5	5				
16			80	100	200	20
	4	5				
17			85	100	204	19
	3	5				
18			90	100	207	17
	2	5				
19			95	100	209	14
	1	5				
20			100	100	210	10

(b)

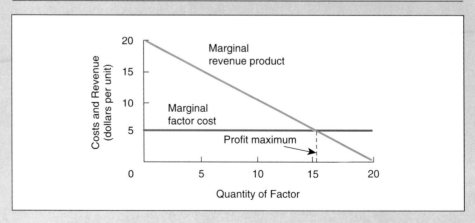

Individual firms' demand curves for a factor of production can be added together to get a market demand curve for that factor. Such a market demand curve is said to be a *derived demand* curve, because the demand for a factor of production does not arise from the usefulness of the factor services themselves. Instead, it is derived indirectly from the usefulness of the products the factor can produce. The market demand for farmland is derived from the market demand for food, the market demand for printers from the market demand for books, and so on.

Changes in Factor Demand

The demand for factors, like the demand for products, changes in response to changes in economic conditions. Consider Box 12.5. Suppose that the demand curve D_0 is the market demand curve for some factor of production. A change in the market price of that factor will cause a *change in the quantity demanded* of the factor. This is represented by a movement along the demand curve (indicated by the arrow drawn parallel to D_0). Changes in economic conditions other than a change in the factor's price can cause a *change in demand* for a factor — for example, a shift in the demand curve from D_0 to D_1 or D_2.

Three kinds of changes in particular are capable of causing shifts in the demand curve for a factor of production. First, an increase in demand for the product that the factor produces will shift the factor demand curve to the right. Similarly, a decrease in demand for the product will cause the factor demand

---

Movements along and Shifts in a Factor Demand Curve   **BOX 12.5**

Changes in the price of a factor, other things being equal, will produce movements along a given factor demand curve, as shown by the arrow. Other kinds of changes can cause a shift in the factor demand curve. An increase in demand for the product produced by the factor might shift the curve from D_0 to D_1. An increase in the price of another factor that is a complement to the given factor might shift the curve from D_0 to D_2.

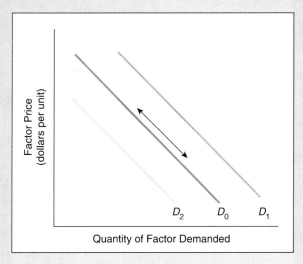

curve to shift to the left. Second, a change in the price of another factor of production used in combination with the given factor can also cause the demand curve for the given factor to shift. An increase in the price of a factor that is a substitute for the given factor will cause the demand curve for the given factor to shift to the right, while an increase in the price of a factor that is a complement to the given factor will cause the demand curve of that factor to shift to the left. Third, any change in technology that increases the marginal physical productivity of a factor will cause its demand curve to shift to the right, other things being equal, while a decrease in the marginal physical product of the factor will shift the curve to the left.

SUPPLY AND DEMAND IN THE LABOUR MARKET

Up to this point, marginal productivity and factor demand have been discussed in general terms. It is time now to turn to the specifics of markets for particular factors — labour, land, and capital. With this section, we begin our analysis of such markets by looking at the supply and demand for labour. The discussion will be limited at first to the case of individual workers' competing with one another for jobs. The next chapter will take up the case of organized labour markets, where workers join together into unions to bargain with employers rather than competing with one another for jobs on an individual basis.

The Labour Supply Curve

The general analysis of factor demand in the preceding section can be applied to the labour market without special modification. A labour supply curve is now needed to go with the labour demand curve. A look at the labour supply decision for an individual worker will begin the analysis.

Individual labour supply

The decisions people as individuals make regarding how much labour to supply to the market are part of the general problem of consumer choice and can be analyzed in terms of the theory developed in Chapter 5. The best way to approach the problem is to think in terms of a trade-off between two alternative sorts of utility — the utility derived from not working (leisure) and the utility derived from working, which might include job satisfaction as well as the goods and services that earnings from work can purchase. Leisure is valued for relaxation, recreation, and the accomplishment of assorted household tasks. But time spent at leisure is time taken away from work and, consequently, from earning income that can be used to buy goods and services as well as from gaining job satisfaction. Within the limits of a 24-hour day, people balance the relative advantages of work and leisure to achieve a consumer equilibrium in which, ideally, the marginal utility per hour of leisure exactly equals the marginal utility of the goods that can be bought with an hour's earnings or the satisfaction that can be gained from an hour's work.

The hourly wage rate can be thought of as the price — or, more, precisely, the opportunity cost — of leisure to the worker, in that it represents the dollar equivalent of the goods and services and the job satisfaction that must be sacrificed in order to enjoy an added hour of leisure. As the wage rate increases, it affects work-versus-leisure decisions in two ways. First, there is a substitution effect; the increased wage rate provides an incentive to work more, because each hour of work now produces more income to be spent on goods and services. In effect, purchased goods and services are substituted for leisure. Second, however, the increase in the wage rate has an income effect that tends to *reduce* hours worked. The higher wage rate, assuming that the prices of goods and services in general remain unchanged, increases workers' real incomes. With higher real incomes, they tend to consume more of all goods that are normal goods and less of those that are inferior goods. Leisure is a normal good. Other things being equal, people generally seek more leisure, in the form of shorter working hours and longer vacations, as their incomes rise. Taken by itself, then, the income effect of a wage increase is the reduction of the quantity of labour supplied by workers.

It can be seen, therefore, that the net effect of an increase in the wage rate on the quantity of labour supplied by an individual worker depends on the relative strength of the substitution and income effects. It is generally believed that for very low wage rates, the substitution effect predominates, so that the quantity of labour supplied increases as the wage increases. As the wage rises even higher, however, the income effect may become relatively stronger. People tend to treat leisure as a luxury good; after they have assured themselves of a reasonable material standard of living, they begin to consider "spending" any further wage increases on increased time away from work. The labour supply curve for an individual to whom this generalization applies has a backward-bending shape, like the one shown in Box 12.6. Over the positively sloped low-wage section, the substitution effect of wage changes predominates, and over the negatively sloped high-wage section, the income effect predominates.

An Individual's Labour Supply Curve   BOX 12.6

At relatively low wage rates, increases in wages tend to increase the amount of work an individual is willing to do, because the extra money compensates for time taken away from leisure activities. At relatively high wage rates, however, increases in wages tend to allow a person to take more time off work and still enjoy a high standard of living. Together, the two effects give the individual labour supply curve the backward-bending shape shown here.

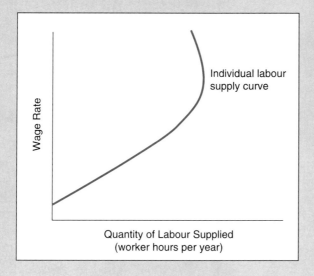

Market labour supply

Even though the labour supply curves for all individual workers may bend backward (at least over a large range of wages), the supply curve for any particular type of labour as a whole is likely to be positively sloped throughout. Consider, for example, the supply of electrical engineers in Vancouver, the supply of data-entry clerks in Montreal, or the supply of farm labourers in Saskatchewan. Each individual engineer or clerk or labourer might, beyond some point, respond to an increased wage by cutting back on hours worked; but for the market as a whole, this tendency would be more than offset by new workers' being drawn by the wage hike into that particular labour market from other occupations or areas. Thus, other things being equal, if the wage rate for electrical engineers in Vancouver rose, more engineering students would take up that specialty; if the wage rate for data-entry clerks in Montreal rose, more people would become data-entry clerks than, say, office receptionists; and if the wage for farm labourers in Saskatchewan rose, workers would be drawn in from Alberta, Manitoba, and Ontario. As a result, for any discussion of the market for a particular category of labour at a particular time and place, it is reasonable to draw the labour supply curve with the usual positive slope, as in Box 12.7, regardless of the shape of the individual labour supply curves underlying it.

Competitive Equilibrium

Determining the wage rate in a labour market that is fully competitive on both sides is a straightforward exercise in supply-and-demand analysis. Box 12.8, for example, shows supply and demand curves representing the labour market for

---

BOX 12.7 *Hypothetical Supply Curve for Data-Entry Clerks*

Although each individual data-entry clerk may have a backward-bending supply curve, the supply curve for data-entry clerks in any particular local market will have the usual upward-sloping shape. As the wage rises, people will be drawn into this occupation from other kinds of work or from other localities.

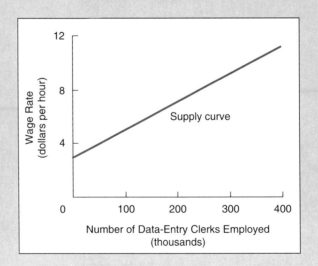

Determination of the Equilibrium Wage in a Competitive Labour Market

BOX 12.8

When both employers and workers are price takers in the labour market, the point of equilibrium is found where the supply and demand curves intersect. Here the equilibrium wage rate is $7 per hour, and the equilibrium quantity of labour is 200 000 data-entry clerks employed.

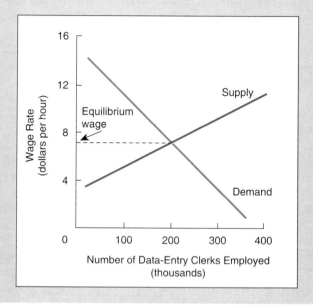

data-entry clerks in Montreal. It assumes that a large number of data-entry clerks compete with one another for jobs and that a large number of employers compete with one another for data-entry clerks, so that both are price takers. The demand curve for data-entry clerks is the employers' combined marginal revenue curve. The supply curve is the same as that in Box 12.7.

Equilibrium in this market requires a wage rate of $7 per hour, with 200 000 data-entry clerks employed. If the wage rate were lower, there would be a shortage of data-entry clerks. Some firms, unable to fill all their job openings, would offer premium wages to workers from other jobs or other regions. The wage rate would be driven up to the equilibrium level. If, on the other hand, the wage rate were above $7 per hour, there would be a surplus of data-entry clerks. Many people would be looking for data-entry jobs and not finding them. After sufficient fruitless search, some would become willing to accept work at lower-than-expected wages, thus pushing the wage rate down toward equilibrium. Others would drift into other occupations or regions.

In a labour market such as this one, where both employers and employees are price takers, the equilibrium wage rate is equal to the marginal revenue product of labour. In the special case where all employers are price takers (perfect competitors) in the market in which they sell their output as well as in the market in which they purchase inputs, the equilibrium wage rate is equal to the marginal physical product of labour times the price per unit of output.

Monopsony

Not every factor market has a large number of buyers competing with one another. The extreme situation where there is only one buyer in a market is called **monopsony**.

There is an important difference between the case of competition and the case of monopsony. For a monopsonist, marginal factor cost is not equal to the price of the factor. Box 12.9 shows why. The table and graph in this box represent the supply side of the market for data-entry clerks in a small town that has only one big employer — an insurance company — which employs all or almost all the town's data-entry clerks.

The supply schedule of data-entry clerks shows that no one will work in data entry if the wage rate is $3 per hour or less. Above that wage, each extra two cents per hour will attract one more worker. Suppose that the monopsonistic employer has hired 150 clerks, paying them $6 per hour. The total labour cost for a labour force of this size is $900 per hour. What will happen to the firm's total labour cost if it expands its labour force by one additional worker?

According to the supply curve, to hire 151 clerks requires a wage of $6.02 per hour. That wage must be paid not just to the 151st worker but to all workers. The total cost of a labour force of 151 clerks, then, is $6.02 times 151, or $909.02. The addition of one more worker has raised the total labour cost from $900 to $909.02, a marginal factor cost of $9.02. Similar results can be obtained by choosing other starting points from the table. *In every case, the marginal factor cost for the monopsonist is greater than the factor price (the wage rate).*

Box 12.9(b) shows a marginal-factor-cost curve based on the marginal-factor-cost column of the table in part (a). This curve lies above the supply curve at every point. The relationship between the supply curve and the marginal-factor-cost curve for a monopsonist, as shown in this figure, is analogous to the relationship between the demand and marginal-revenue curves for a monopolist.

Monopsony Equilibrium

Given the monopsonist's marginal-factor-cost curve — derived from the factor's market supply curve — determining the equilibrium level of employment for the firm is a matter of routine. Box 12.10 shows the monopsonistic employer's marginal-revenue-product curve along with the labour supply and marginal-factor-cost curves from Box 12.9. Following the general rule that profit is maximized where marginal factor cost is equal to marginal revenue product, it can be seen that the monopsonist will hire 150 data-entry clerks at a wage rate of $6 per hour.

Note that when a labour market is in monopsony equilibrium, the wage rate is lower than the marginal revenue product of labour. In the example shown, the equilibrium wage rate is $6 per hour, although the marginal revenue product is $9 per hour. Despite the gap between the wage rate and the marginal revenue product, this increase in the quantity of labour hired will not increase revenue by enough to offset higher labour costs. The reason is that the cost of hiring another worker is not just the $6.02 per hour that must be paid to the 151st worker but that sum plus the extra two cents per hour by which the wages of all 150 previously hired workers must be raised. The complete marginal factor cost for the 151st worker is thus $6.02 + $3.00, or $9.02 per hour. We see, then, that the

Marginal Factor Cost under Monopsony *BOX 12.9*

Under monopsony, marginal factor cost exceeds factor price. Consider the increase in quantity from 150 to 151 units of labour in the example given below. The wage rate must be raised from $6 to $6.02 not just for the 151st employee but for all the previous 150 as well. Marginal labour cost in this range is thus $9.02 per hour, not $6.02 per hour.

(a)

Quantity of Labour Supplied (1)	Wage Rate (2)	Total Factor Cost (3)	Marginal Factor Cost (4)
1	$3.02	$ 3.02	
			$ 3.06
2	3.04	6.08	
			3.10
3	3.06	9.18	
150	6.00	900.00	
			9.02
151	6.02	909.02	
			9.06
152	6.04	918.08	
200	7.00	1400.00	
			11.02
201	7.02	1411.02	
			11.06
202	7.04	1422.08	

(b)

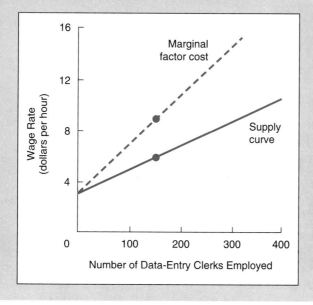

marginal productivity theory of distribution does not apply in a monopsonistic labour market. In such a market, workers are paid a wage that is less than their contribution, at the margin, to the employer's revenue.

BOX 12.10   *Wage Determination under Monopsony*

Here are a monopsonist's marginal-revenue-product curve for labour, labour supply curve, and marginal-factor-cost curve. The quantity of labour required to maximize profits is found where the marginal-revenue-product curve and the marginal-factor-cost curve intersect. Note that the equilibrium wage rate is *not* shown by the intersection of the marginal-factor-cost and marginal-revenue-product curves. Instead, the rate is equal to the height of the supply curve directly below that intersection.

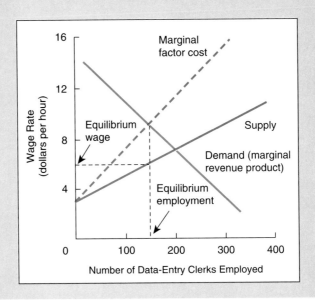

A Summary of Results: Determining Wages and Employment under Different Market Structures

We have now examined the determination of wages and employment under two different product market structures — perfect competition and monopoly — and two different labour market structures — perfect competition and monopsony. This gives us four logical possibilities for the market-structure combinations within which firms determine the wages they will pay and the number of workers they will hire. These are summarized in Box 12.11. For firms operating in perfectly competitive labour markets, wages are determined by the interaction of the market demand and market supply curves (situations 1 and 3). Under monopsony (situations 2 and 4), firms set the wage rate equal to the height of the labour supply curve at the point at which marginal factor cost equals marginal revenue product. In all situations, the number of workers to be hired is determined by the point at which marginal factor cost equals marginal revenue product — but because marginal factor cost is equal to the wage rate in perfectly competitive labour markets, we say that the amount of labour hired in such markets is determined by the point at which the wage rate equals the marginal revenue product.

Wage and Employment Determination in Different Product and Labour Markets

BOX 12.11

If firms operate in product markets of two different structures (perfect competition and monopoly) and in labour markets of two different structures (perfect competition and monopsony), there are logically four different market-structure combinations in which different firms determine wage rates and the number of workers to be hired. These alternatives are illustrated in the following table.

Situation	Structure of the Firm's Product Market	Structure of the Firm's Labour Market	Determination of Wage Rate	Determination of Number of Workers
1	Perfect competition	Perfect competition	Determined for the firm by the market	Set at the point where the wage rate equals the marginal revenue product
2	Perfect competition	Monopsony	Set by the firm, equal to the height of the labour supply curve at the point where marginal factor cost equals marginal revenue product	Set at the point where marginal factor cost equals marginal revenue product
3	Monopoly	Perfect competition	Determined for the firm by the market	Set at the point where the wage rate equals the marginal revenue product
4	Monopoly	Monopsony	Set by the firm, equal to the height of the labour supply curve at the point where marginal factor cost equals marginal revenue product	Set at the point where marginal factor cost equals marginal revenue product

ARE ALL WAGE DIFFERENCES JUSTIFIED?

The marginal productivity theory of income determination helps to explain the economic factors that result in different wage rates for different types of work. The various demand curves for labour, based on differences in "revenue productivity," interact with various supply curves, based on the differing desires and abilities of people to respond to wage offers, to produce labour markets with different equilibrium wages. This presumably explains why, in general, engineers are paid more than data-entry clerks and doctors are paid more than engineers.

However, there are wage differences that are not so easily explained by marginal productivity theory, and they are therefore not easily justified in economic terms.

The monopsony example has already alerted us to a situation in which workers are not paid in accordance with their economic contribution. The lesson is important: *Wage rates, and wage differences, may be influenced by market forces that are not directly related to marginal productivity.* This takes us back to the issue discussed in the Preview to this chapter: Why do many jobs that are typically held by men pay more than apparently comparable jobs held mainly by women?

Affirmative Action and Pay Equity

Marginal productivity theory would suggest that if there are wage differences between jobs, then the jobs must not really be comparable. For example, according to the theory, a steam-shovel operator earns more than a data-entry clerk because, on the demand side, the operator has greater revenue-productivity than the clerk and, on the supply side, fewer people are willing to become steam-shovel operators than data-entry clerks. Furthermore, if, under these circumstances, women choose to be data-entry clerks and men choose to be steam-shovel operators, their differences in pay will be fully justified. In other words, a nondiscriminatory market produces a nondiscriminatory result.

At least two different lines of argument have developed in opposition to this conclusion. The first basically accepts the tenets of marginal productivity theory but maintains that results are often not in line with the theory because factor markets do not provide equal opportunities to all. Maybe steam-shovel operators deserve higher wages on the basis of productivity, but certain groups, such as women, are discriminated against because they don't have the same opportunity as men to become operators. Their failure to enter such occupations may have many sources: subtle hiring discrimination by male supervisors who can't imagine a woman handling such a job; intimidation by male superiors; and the belief, in some cases still held by women themselves and certainly fostered by the whole culture, that women are not suited for such occupations. Advocates of this view recommend both short- and long-run solutions to such discrimination. In the long run, the attitudes of both male and female participants in the work force must be changed. In the short run, a program of *affirmative action* — that is, of deliberately opening more jobs to women through some form of quota system in order to overcome existing imbalances as quickly as possible — is advocated.

Good jobs
Specialized, stable, and well-paid jobs in the dynamic sectors of industry.

Bad jobs
Part-time, temporary, and low-paid jobs in less-dynamic sectors of industry.

In 1990, the Economic Council of Canada classified jobs in the Canadian economy as "good jobs" and "bad jobs."[2] **Good jobs** are highly specialized, stable, and well-paid jobs in "dynamic services" such as transportation, communication, utilities, business services, and finance. **Bad jobs** are those to which the council referred as "nonstandard" — usually part-time, temporary, and low-paid. Women, because of family responsibilities and fewer opportunities for training, have taken bad jobs, with their negative consequences, in disproportionate numbers. The Economic Council made it clear that a wide range of new programs, including family-support, training, and affirmative-action programs, would be needed to correct the situation.

---

[2]Economic Council of Canada, *Good Jobs and Bad Jobs: Employment in the Service Economy* (Ottawa: Economic Council of Canada, 1990).

A second line of argument against the position that the principles of marginal productivity theory yield nondiscriminatory results calls into question one of the apparent assumptions of the theory, namely, that wages are paid strictly according to productivity. Critics who espouse this line of argument point out that the wage scales of many occupations reflect an observance of criteria that have little to do with the actual productivity of workers — for example, the objectively unwarranted value with which people arbitrarily invest certain types of work and the power that certain groups undeservedly gain within their occupation. The market, because it is often imperfect, doe not necessarily correct such anomalies by itself. Arthur Earle, the first head of the London School of Business Studies, has documented that corporations often reward their top executives on the basis of criteria that have little to do with performance. In many cases, the executives determine their own salaries, which have been known to rise appreciably even in years when the company performs very badly.[3]

It is also a fact that in many occupations, particularly in the service sector (which now accounts for 70 percent of all jobs), it is difficult, if not impossible, to measure productivity. How, for example, would one measure a teacher's productivity? By the number of students taught? What if all the students perform poorly on exams? Should that be factored in? It is the awareness of such grey areas that has prompted critics of our wage system to propose another way of establishing appropriate financial rewards. Advocates of this position identify certain objective *qualities* that different jobs have — qualities that may be linked only indirectly to productivity — and they maintain that wage rates, and wage differences, should be determined on the basis of an evaluation of such qualities. This group calls for "equal pay for work of equal value," but defines *value* as something other than the purely economic value that appears to be assumed in marginal productivity theory.

The first group of critics — those who call for affirmative action — might agree with the view that the jobs of steam-shovel operators and data-entry clerks are not strictly comparable and that wage differences between them are therefore justifiable. What they want is more women steam-shovel operators. The second group of critics is more likely to argue that the two jobs *are* comparable and that the wages they bring should therefore be equal. In the opinion of this second group, just as apples and oranges *appear* different because of surface qualities such as shape and colour, but are in fact quite similar in terms of more basic qualities such as calories and vitamins, so different jobs — such as those of data-entry clerks and steam-shovel operators — may appear different in terms of operating environment and current wage scales, but are in fact quite similar in terms of other qualities. These other qualities include such factors as education and skill levels required, degree of responsibility involved, accountability, and working conditions. Advocates of equal pay for work of equal value — or, perhaps more accurately, for work of "comparable worth" — maintain that such qualities *can* be identified, measured, and compared in different jobs, but that the market, left to itself, does not do a good job of allocating different wage rates on the basis of such comparisons. They therefore call for legislation to implement this method of determining wages.

---

[3]Quoted in Frances Russell, "Tycoons Set Own Salaries and Keep Them Secret," *Winnipeg Free Press*, November 21, 1990, p. 7.

The ideas of this second group are far from new. Several U.S. states have had pay-equity programs in the public sector for a number of years. The state of Minnesota allocates nearly 1 percent of its payroll annually to adjust wages in line with criteria such as those mentioned above, and it has apparently narrowed the gap between male and female wages considerably. In Canada, the Royal Commission on the Status of Women first proposed such a program twenty years ago. Ontario, as the Preview article states, now has "the world's toughest pay-equity law," recently extended to include all firms and government agencies with more than a hundred employees. Manitoba has legislated the application of equal pay for work of equal value to its public servants, and Quebec and the federal government have adopted the principle as policy, without legislation.

The accompanying For Example. . . box illustrates how pay-equity principles were applied to two different jobs in an Ontario auto company. After rating the jobs according to working conditions, education requirements, degree of responsibility involved, and other criteria, the company found they were virtually equal in value. This result required the equalization of wages for the two types of workers.

FOR EXAMPLE...
Pay Equity in Practice

The table below shows how one Toronto auto company, in accordance with Ontario's pay-equity legislation, evaluated two different jobs — those of receptionist and warehouseman — using a pay-equity point system. Points were assigned in categories such as working conditions, education, and responsibility, and jobs rated within three points of each other were considered of equal value. The receptionist's job was rated only three points lower than the warehouseman's. Consequently, according to the legislation, the company would have to equalize the wages paid for the two jobs within five years.

Job	Receptionist	Warehouseman
Hourly wage	$8.01	$11.01
Education	106	80
Experience	79	86
Complexity	81	76
Supervision of others	0	0
Independence of action	55	55
Consequence of errors	46	51
Confidentiality	14	0
Contacts	48	33
Physical skill and effort	44	76
Working conditions	19	38
Total	492 points	495 points

SOURCE: Coopers & Lybrand Consulting Group.

SOURCE: *Financial Post*, August 21, 1989, p. 4. Reproduced with permission.

One question, however, remains: Are the advocates of this new way of determining wages calling the basic theory of wage determination, as developed in this chapter, into question, or is their criticism directed primarily at the existing *operation* of labour markets? We have suggested that the affirmative-action advocates might be said to oppose the current operation of the system while the pay-equity advocates question, in a more radical way, the basic underlying assumptions of the system. However, a closer examination of the ideas of the latter group indicates that their concern may be less radical than it at first appears, and that they too are more at odds with the actual operation of many of our labour markets than with the underlying theory of wage determination. According to this traditional theory, such job characteristics as working conditions, ability (including training), and degree of responsibility *do* have an impact on relative wages. Poor working conditions, for example, induce a smaller number of workers to apply for a job, and thereby drive up the wage. Theoretically, then, there is no need for a special agency to set wages that take account of poor working conditions. However, in practice, wage rates in many labour markets may have developed over time in ways that do not reflect existing conditions, but that perhaps do reflect the kinds of discrimination mentioned earlier. It could therefore be argued that agencies are needed to adjust wages in order to make them conform more closely to results that are indeed justified by economic theory.

Few markets, if any, operate perfectly. When they are perceived to perform poorly, any citizen is justified in calling for change. Sometimes the best kind of change may be to unshackle market forces so that they can do their job properly. Entry into many jobs in Canada is currently restricted by the self-licensing privileges (and tenure rules) of groups such as doctors, lawyers, and professors, and quite probably also by subtle forms of discrimination. A lessening of these restrictions would be helpful to many. At the same time, especially in the absence of such reforms, a second type of change may also be required — namely, to propel the disadvantaged into better positions through some form of affirmative action, and to reclassify jobs and wages on the basis of criteria to which the market *should* be responding, but, for whatever reason, is not.

RENT, INTEREST, AND PROFITS

Wages and salaries are a big part of the income-distribution picture in the Canadian economy. Recently, they have accounted for some three-quarters of all net national income. They are not, however, the whole picture.

The remaining quarter of personal income (excluding transfer payments) is composed of rent, interest, and profits. These sources of income, although relatively small, deserve the same careful analysis that we gave wages and salaries. Rent, interest, and profits play a key role in the resource-allocation process. They also play an important role in determining the overall distribution of personal income, since they are distributed somewhat less equally than labour income.

Economic Rent

Pure economic rent is the income earned by a factor of production that is in completely inelastic supply. The classic example of such a factor is land, which in this context refers to the natural productive powers of the earth and the locational advantages of particular sites. Things such as artificial improvements, creation of new land through reclamation, and destruction of the soil through erosion

Pure economic rent
The income earned by any factor of production that is in perfectly inelastic supply.

are not taken into consideration in the definition of land as a factor of production in perfectly inelastic supply.

Box 12.12 shows how rent is determined by supply and demand in a competitive market. It considers a particular category of land — Saskatchewan wheat land. The supply curve for Saskatchewan wheat land is a vertical line, because the quantity of land supplied is assumed not to vary as the rent that it earns varies. The demand curve is the marginal-revenue-product curve for that land as seen by Saskatchewan wheat farmers. Because of diminishing returns, the marginal revenue product of land declines as more land is used in combination with fixed quantities of labour and capital. The demand curve thus slopes downward to the right.

The rent that the land earns is determined by the intersection of the supply curve, representing the scarcity of land, and the demand curve, representing its productivity. If the rent is higher than the equilibrium shown, not all land will be put to use. The rent will then fall as landowners compete with one another to find tenants. If the rent is lower than the equilibrium rate, farmers will be unable to find all the land they want. They will bid against one another for the limited available supply, and thereby drive rents up.

BOX 12.12   *Determination of Rent by Supply and Demand*

Pure economic rent is earned only by a factor that has a perfectly inelastic supply curve. This figure shows hypothetical supply and demand curves for Saskatchewan wheat land. No account is taken of any possibilities for creating or destroying such land, so the supply curve is vertical. The demand curve, as for other factors, is based on the land's marginal revenue product.

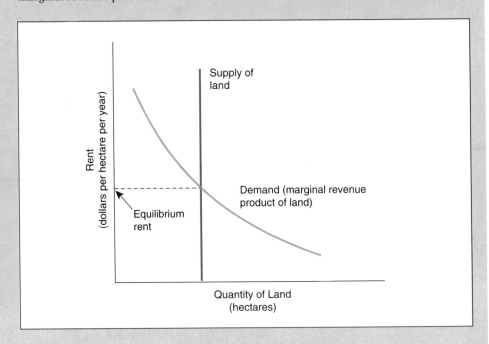

Capitalization of rents

The price of land is called rent; often, of course, land is not rented by a tenant from a landlord, but is used by the person who owns it. That use does not change the way supply and demand determine the value of land. It does mean, though, that it is sometimes convenient to speak of the price of land in terms of a lump-sum sales price rather than as a rent per month or year.

There is a simple relationship between the value of a parcel of land expressed as a rent and the price at which that parcel can be sold in the market. The market price of a parcel of land is said to be the **capitalized value of its rent** — that is, the sum that would earn an annual return equal to the annual rent if it were invested at the market rate of interest.

Capitalized value of a rent
The sum of money that, if invested at the current market rate of interest, would earn a periodic interest return equal to the rent for the same period.

Consider, for example, a piece of land with an expected real rental value of $1000 per year in perpetuity. If the expected real rate of interest were 5 percent per year, a buyer would be willing to pay $20 000 for title to the land ($20 000 × 0.05 = $1000, or $1000 ÷ 0.05 = $20 000). If the expected real rate of interest were 2 percent per year, the price of the land would rise to $50 000 ($1000 ÷ 0.02 = $50 000), and so on. In general, the price of a parcel of land having a perpetual expected real annual rental value of R dollars per year, capitalized at the real rate of interest, r, is given by the formula R/r.

Other rents

The term *rent* can refer to the market return earned by any factor of production that is unique or that is in perfectly inelastic supply. Consider the very high incomes of people with unique talents, such as athletes, singers, actors, and some executives. These incomes are more plausibly thought of as rents earned on talents rather than as wages earned for work done. Artificially created legal privileges can also be said to earn rents. For instance, part of the earnings of a taxicab can be counted as rent earned from the licence that gives it the legal privilege to operate, so long as the supply of licences is strictly limited by city authorities.

The hallmark of pure economic rent is inelasticity of supply. Pure economic rent should not be confused with what is loosely called the rental income earned by manufactured assets that are not in perfectly inelastic supply. Consider the rental income that accrues to an apartment-house owner, for example. It may in part be pure economic rent earned by some uniquely convenient site on which the building is located. In addition, though, the owner's income includes implicit wages for any custodial work done in the building, implicit interest on the money invested to build it, and so on.

What is pure economic rent and what is not depends in part on the time frame within which the income is considered. In the short run — say, a period too short for new buildings to be constructed — a case could be made for considering part of the income earned from buildings as a pure economic rent. In the long run, however, when additional buildings can be supplied at a price, such "rental" income is clearly not a pure economic rent.

INTEREST AND CAPITAL

Two Aspects of Interest

The theory of capital and interest is in many ways the most complicated part of factor market theory, and care must be taken to understand the relationship between two different aspects of interest. The term *interest* is used to express both the price paid by borrowers to lenders for the use of loanable funds and the market return earned by capital as a factor of production. A person who loans $1000 to another in return for a payment of $100 per year (plus eventual repayment of the principal) is said to earn 10 percent interest per year on the money. At the same time, a person who buys a machine for $1000 and earns $100 a year by employing the productive services of that machine is said to earn 10 percent interest on capital.

Consumption Loans

Our discussion of interest and capital will begin by looking at how credit markets work in a simplified economy where households are the only suppliers of credit — that is, of loanable funds. Savers are households that earn incomes now but consume less than they earn in order to put something aside for expected future needs. The money they save becomes loanable funds, and savers are in this sense suppliers of credit. Not all households in the economy are savers, however; some want to consume more than their current incomes permit. The latter may be households that want to tide themselves over a temporary decrease in income, or they may be households with steady incomes that simply do not want to wait to buy a car or take a vacation. These and other households that borrow for any number of reasons are one source of demand for loanable funds. The loans they take out are called consumption loans.

The Productivity of Capital

Nothing has yet been said about capital as a factor of production. Opportunities to use capital as a factor of production are a second source of demand for loanable funds, in addition to the demand for pure consumption loans. To understand the demand for loans of this kind, it is necessary to understand why capital is productive.

Using capital means using a roundabout method of production rather than a direct method. Consider, as an example, a person who owns a brick-making business. There are two ways to make bricks. The direct way is to form them by hand out of raw clay scooped up from the ground and to bake them over an open fire. Suppose that by using this method, a worker can make 100 bricks per month. The alternative way of making bricks is more roundabout. The brickmaker first spends a month forming bricks by hand and putting them together to make a kiln. When the kiln is completed, its hotter fire and lower fuel consumption make it possible to produce 110 bricks per month from then on. The roundabout method that involves investing in capital equipment (the kiln) lengthens the period between the time work starts and the time finished bricks begin to appear. In return, it increases the eventual rate of output. That is the sense in which capital is productive.

The brick maker's experience is repeated in a more elaborate way whenever a firm makes a capital investment. Producing automobiles on an assembly line is a roundabout method of production compared to producing them one by one with hand tools. Constructing a building in which to hold economics classes is a roundabout method of education compared with holding classes in the woods under a tree. In every case, time is taken to construct aids to production in order to produce more effectively later on.

Investment Loans

The brick maker in the example invested directly by actually building the needed capital equipment. In a market economy, firms need not build their own capital equipment. Anyone who sees an opportunity for increasing output by using a more capital-intensive (that is, a more roundabout) production process can borrow money and buy capital. The productivity of capital thus creates a source of demand for loanable funds in addition to the demand for consumption loans. Loans for increasing productivity can be called *investment loans*.

Box 12.13 shows how the rate of interest is determined when the demand for investment loans is added to the demand for consumption loans. The demand curve for loans is downward sloping because consumers experience diminishing satisfaction from extra consumption and will borrow more, in order to finance increased consumption, only if they can do so at lower rates of interest. Because of the diminishing marginal productivity of capital, businesses will be inclined to borrow more money for building more capital equipment only if they can do so

---

The Interest Rate with Consumption and Investment Loans

BOX 12.13

This box shows how the interest rate is determined in a market in which there are both consumption and investment loans. In this case, the demand for investment loans is added to the demand for consumption loans to get the combined demand for loan funds. The equilibrium interest rate is higher than it would be if only consumption loans were taken into account.

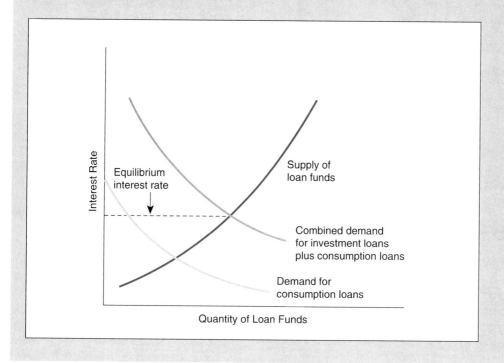

at lower interest rates. The supply of loanable funds slopes upward to the right because those who provide the funds sacrifice current consumption. The more they sacrifice, the more painful it becomes, and the greater will be the interest they demand in compensation. The equilibrium interest rate is simply the price that those who supply the funds exact for their sacrifice, and a reflection of the increased benefits anticipated by those who borrow the funds. In other words, at the equilibrium interest rate, supply equals demand.

PROFIT AND ENTREPRENEURSHIP

The term *pure economic profit* was introduced in Chapter 6 to refer to the income, if any, remaining to owners of a firm after they have deducted all implicit and explicit costs of production. Explicit costs include factor payments to workers, resource owners, and suppliers of capital, together with the cost of semi-finished inputs, if any, purchased from other firms. Implicit costs include a normal rate of return on capital supplied by owners of the firm plus the opportunity costs of using natural resources or labour supplied by owners of the firm or owned by the firm itself. What is left over is pure economic profit.

This definition of profit leaves unanswered two very important questions that have not yet been raised. Why does a firm ever earn any pure economic profit at all? Why is the entire value of the product of all firms not divided up among the owners of the labour, natural resources, and capital used in the production process? These are subtle questions that have occupied the minds of many great economists, but no answer has yet been offered with which everyone can agree. Still, it will be worth while to look at some of the kinds of answers that have been suggested.

Theories of Profit

Risk and profit

According to one theory, profits are a reward that the owners of business receive for bearing risk. Every business venture is subject to the risk of failure. That is the nature of economic life in a world where the future is not known with certainty. People who merely hire out their factor services largely escape risk. A new business is usually expected to offer workers contractual guarantees that the payroll will be met even if the firm loses money. It is also expected to offer security against default to banks or bondholders who provide capital. The owner or owners of the firm (the shareholders, if the firm is organized in the corporate form) bear most of the risk of loss if the firm fails. In return, they get the privilege of keeping the profits if revenues turn out to be more than enough to pay off the firm's obligations to hired factors. Why is it, though, that the profits earned by successful risk takers are not exactly offset by the losses of the unsuccessful? The answer has to do with people's attitudes toward risk.

It is possible that some people are indifferent to risk. A person who is indifferent to risk will be indifferent to the opportunity to earn $10 000 a year with absolute certainty and the opportunity to try for $20 000, subject to a fifty–fifty chance of failing and earning nothing. People who are indifferent to risk may launch new businesses even when the expected profit if the business succeeds is exactly offset by the expected loss if the business fails.

In practice, though, most people dislike risk. If they know they can earn a secure $10 000 a year, they will not launch a business with a fifty–fifty chance of failure unless that business, if successful, will pay more than $20 000. Because most people dislike risk, somewhat fewer business ventures are launched than would be otherwise. That makes opportunities a little more favourable, on the average, for those who are willing to bear some risk. When successes and failures are averaged out over the whole economy, profits can therefore more than offset losses. The excess of profits over losses is the reward earned by the people who bear business risks. And factor owners, to the extent that they are shielded from these risks, are willing to accept less than the whole value of the product of the firm.

Profits as arbitrage

A second theory equates profits with the activity of **arbitrage** — buying a good at a low price in one market and selling it at a higher price in another. Examples of pure arbitrage can be found in markets for agricultural commodities, precious metals, foreign currencies, and other markets where completely standardized goods are traded at different points in the world.

Arbitrage
The activity of earning a profit by buying a good for a low price in one market and reselling it for a higher price in another market.

Consider, for example, the gold markets in London and Hong Kong. Economic policies, daily news developments, and other events may initially affect supply and demand in these two gold markets differently. A political crisis in the British government, for example, might prompt an increase in demand in the London market, sending the price of gold there up relative to the price in Hong Kong. Before the prices got far apart, however, alert arbitrageurs in Hong Kong would start buying gold at the low Hong Kong price for resale at the higher London price. This activity would raise demand in Hong Kong and increase supply in London until the price in the two markets was equalized. (In practice, because of various transaction costs, the prices would be only approximately equalized on any given day.) In the process of acting as a crucial link in the international transmission of information through the price system, the arbitrageurs would turn a handy profit.

Arbitrage cannot often be seen in as pure a form as that represented by the international gold market. However, as economists Israel Kirzner pointed out in his influential book, *Competition and Entrepreneurship*, there is an element of arbitrage in every profit-making transaction.[4] Consider the entrepreneur-owner-manager of, say, a small shoe factory. This person buys inputs in one set of markets at the lowest prices possible and, after combining the inputs to form finished shoes, sells the product in other markets at the highest price possible. In a hypothetical world where all markets were in perfectly competitive long-run equilibrium, it would be no more possible to make a profit by buying labour and leather in one market and selling shoes in another than it would be by buying gold in Hong Kong and selling it in London. In such a world, the price of the leather and labour would be bid up to just equal the price of the finished shoes. In the real world, though, the alert entrepreneur can find arbitrage opportunities in a great variety of markets and can earn profits accordingly.

Profits and innovation

A third theory associates profit with the activity of innovation. This theory has achieved considerable popularity through the writings of Joseph Schumpeter.[5] In

---

[4]Israel Kirzner, *Competition and Entrepreneurship* (Chicago: University of Chicago Press, 1974).

[5]See, for example, Joseph Schumpeter, *Capitalism, Socialism, and Democracy* (New York: Harper & Bros., 1942).

subtle contrast to the entrepreneur as arbitrageur, taking advantage of spontaneously occurring opportunities to buy low and sell high, the entrepreneur as innovator creates new profit opportunities by devising a new product, a new production process, or a new marketing strategy. If successful, the entrepreneur achieves a position of temporary monopoly that permits pure economic profits to be earned until rival firms catch on or leap ahead with innovations of their own.

Further Comments on the Nature of Profit

Entrepreneurship as a factor of production

It is probably pointless to try to determine which of the three theories of profit just discussed is the correct one. The economic activity called entrepreneurship is best thought of as an inseparable blend of risk taking, alertness to opportunities for arbitrage, and innovation.

Because entrepreneurs, like workers, resource owners, and suppliers of capital, earn a reward for their contribution to production, entrepreneurship is sometimes spoken of as a fourth factor of production. In some ways, it is indeed a little like the three factors of production — labour, natural resources, and capital. First, entrepreneurship, like the others, is scarce. Not everyone possesses the ability to organize business undertakings and recognize new economic opportunities. Second, entrepreneurs do earn an income in the form of the profit that remains after all the costs of their firms have been covered. Third, as is true for labour, natural resources, and capital, production cannot take place without entrepreneurship.

There is a limit, however, to how far the parallel between entrepreneurship and other factors can be pushed. The main problem is that entrepreneurship is an intangible, and therefore not subject to measurement. There is no quantitative unit of entrepreneurship and hence no way to determine a price per unit. Applying supply-and-demand analysis to this fourth factor of production just does not work.

Monopoly profits

Up to this point, no distinction has been made between the profits earned in the short run by a competitive firm (before those profits are eroded by the competition of new entrants) and the profits earned by a monopolist (which under proper conditions of demand can persist indefinitely). Some writers have suggested that monopoly profits are a separate category of income that cannot be explained either as a reward to labour, capital, or natural resources or in terms of the entrepreneurial activities of risk bearing, arbitrage, and innovation. On closer inspection, however, it turns out that most, if not all, of monopoly profit can be explained without introducing a special new category of income.

Consider, for example, the case of a monopoly based on a patented invention. When such a firm's explicit costs are subtracted from its revenues, more than enough is left over to provide a normal rate of return on capital. The firm can be said to earn a pure economic profit, but it would be more accurate to say that it earns an implicit rent as owner of the patent. It could, after all, sell or lease the patent rights to some other firm, in which case the patent owner would earn an explicit rent and the firm using the patent would earn only a nominal return on capital after paying to acquire the patent. The opportunity cost to a monopolist of not renting the patent to another firm should thus be counted as an implicit cost, not as part of pure economic profit. The same applies to firms that have a monopoly based on any other unique advantage that is in perfectly inelastic supply, such as a government franchise, a uniquely suitable location, or a unique natural resource.

If a monopolistic firm does not possess any unique advantage, its monopoly cannot be more than temporary. Sooner or later, other entrepreneurs will enter into competition with the firm and begin the process of reducing its pure economic profits to zero. Temporary monopoly profits of this type are not a separate category of income; they are simply the return earned by the monopolistic entrepreneur who was alert enough to get into the market before any competitors did so.

LOOKING AHEAD

In this chapter, we have examined some of the basic theories developed by economists to explain the remuneration of factors of production. The abstract theory of how factor markets work was supplemented by a brief analysis of criticisms voiced by advocates of change. The next chapter attempts to add to the realism of our discussion by looking more closely at the actual structure of the labour market in Canada, with a special focus on the role of unions.

SUMMARY

1. *Factor markets* play an important role in determining how goods and services are produced. When factor prices change, firms tend to modify their production methods, using less of factors that have become more expensive and more of those that have become cheaper. At the same time, factor markets help determine for whom goods and services are produced, since payments for the services of labour, capital, and natural resources are the main source of income for most households.

2. For a perfectly competitive firm, the *marginal revenue product* of a factor is equal to the factor's marginal physical product times the price of the product. For a monopolistic firm, it is equal to marginal physical product times marginal revenue. In both cases, the firm makes the maximum profit by buying each factor up to the point at which marginal revenue product equals *marginal factor cost*. Thus, the marginal-revenue-product curve is the factor demand curve for a firm that is perfectly competitive in the factor market.

3. The demand for a factor of production is said to be a derived demand because it depends on the demand for the goods or services that the factor produces. An increase in demand for the product shifts the factor demand curve to the right; a decrease in demand for the product shifts the factor demand curve to the left. Changes in the prices of factors that are substitutes or complements for a given factor, as well as changes in technology, can also cause shifts in factor demand curves.

4. Labour supply curves depend on the trade-off that people make between leisure and the goods and services they can buy with income earned at work, as well as the satisfaction they can derive from work. The labour supply curve for an individual worker, and perhaps for the economy as a whole, may bend backward above a certain wage rate. However, the supply curve for a single

labour market (say, the supply of data-entry clerks in Montreal) is positively sloped throughout its length.

5. In a labour market in which employers compete for workers and workers compete for jobs, the equilibrium wage rate will be equal to the marginal productivity of labour. This is known as the marginal productivity theory of distribution. If employers are also perfect competitors in the market in which they sell their output, then the equilibrium wage rate will be equal to the value of the marginal product.

6. *Monopsony* refers to a situation in which there is only one buyer of factor services in a given market. The marginal-factor-cost curve for such a firm lies above the supply curve of labour. Equilibrium is established at the intersection of the marginal-factor-cost curve and the marginal-revenue-product curve. In such a market, the equilibrium wage is not equal to marginal revenue product.

7. Other "failures" of factor markets can be attributed to discrimination and to other practices that prevent some individuals and groups from earning income that is comparable to others in a similar job or with similar ability, training, and responsibility. Such strategies as affirmative action and "equal pay for work of equal value" are being advocated and legislated to correct these imbalances.

8. *Pure economic rent* is the income earned by any factor of production whose supply is completely inelastic. Land is the classic example of a factor that earns a pure economic rent. The *capitalized value of rent* determines the market price of land. Rent can also be said to be earned by other factors whose supply is perfectly inelastic, such as the special talents of athletes or performing artists.

9. The term *interest* expresses both the price paid by borrowers to lenders in credit markets and the income earned by capital as a factor of production. The interest rate is determined in credit markets. The supply of credit depends on the willingness of savers to lend. The demand for credit is composed of the demand for consumption loan plus the demand for investment loans.

10. There are several theories about the nature of profits. One theory holds that profit is the reward that entrepreneurs earn for bearing risks. Another sees profit as earned mainly through *arbitrage*. Still another stresses innovation. In practical terms, profit can be thought of as income derived from a mixture of these three sources.

KEY TERMS

factor markets	monopsony	pure economic rent
marginal revenue product	good jobs	capitalized value of a rent
marginal factor cost	bad jobs	arbitrage

KEY BOXES

Box 12.8 Determination of the Equilibrium Wage
 in a Competitive Labour Market

Box 12.10 Wage Determination under Monopsony

Box 12.11 Wage and Equipment Determination in
 Different Product and Labour
 Markets

REVIEW QUESTIONS

1. What is the relationship between the marginal revenue product of a factor of production and the price of the product when the firm is a perfect competitor in the market where it sells its output? When it is a monopolist in the market where it sells its output?

2. What is the factor market equilibrium condition for a profit-maximizing firm?

3. Why is it possible for one person's labour supply curve to have a negatively sloped section above a certain wage rate? Why do the labour supply curves for individual labour markets not have such negatively sloped sections?

4. According to the marginal productivity theory of distribution, what is the relationship between the wage rate and the value of the product in equilibrium?

5. In what way is the factor market equilibrium condition for a monopsonistic firm like that for a competitive firm? In what way is it different?

6. How do the proposals of advocates of affirmative action differ from those of advocates of equal pay for work of equal value?

7. Use supply and demand curves to show the difference between the pure economic rent earned by a factor of production whose supply is completely inelastic and the income earned by, say, the owner of an apartment building.

8. What do we mean when we say that using capital means using a roundabout method of production? Under what conditions will it be worth while for a firm to invest in new capital equipment?

9. Do you think there is any close connection between the value of what somebody produces and the amount that person earns? Consider these specific examples: an auto worker; a real estate salesperson; a rock star; your economics professor. Why does the connection between earnings and product seem closer in some cases than in others?

10. Suppose a friend said to you that it was just fine to let factor markets determine how things were produced, but the matter of for whom they are produced ought to be handled according to the principle of "to each according to need." Sketch a reply to this remark that begins: "But that won't work. If you don't let markets determine *for whom*, they won't be able to determine *how*. . . ."

11. In his historical novel *Chesapeake*, James Michener describes the unsuccessful efforts of early European colonists to run their plantations with hired Native American labour. Among the many factors that led to the breakdown of relationships between the planters and local tribes were some economic problems. For example, Michener reports the frustration of a planter who finds that an offer of higher wages does not prevent his Native workers from quitting their jobs in the fields after a few weeks of work. In fact, the workers seem to quit sooner when their pay is raised. Does what you have learned in this chapter shed any light on this problem? Discuss.

12. "Equal pay for equal work is not enough. Employers must also be required to follow affirmative-action guidelines or hiring quotas for members of disfavoured groups." Comment on this statement in the light of what you have learned in this chapter.

13. This chapter has suggested that part of the income of people with unique talents might be considered a form of pure economic rent. Suppose you observe that a certain baseball player is paid $2 million a year. How would

you distinguish the part of the player's income that is rent from the part that is a return on investment in human capital in the form of training for the sport?

14. Suppose you decide to start a Christmas tree farm. You already own a suitable piece of land. You get seeds from pine cones that you gather in the woods. You plant the seeds with your own hands. Five years later you sell the trees for $30 each. How should your revenue be divided up among wages, rent, interest, and profit?

15. A contractor places an ad for labourers in the newspaper, offering to pay them $10 per cubic metre for removing rocks and dirt from a cellar hole. Four workers show up and start the job. Celine is a person of average build. She uses a simple shovel and bucket and manages to earn $20 a day. Bill, a giant of a man, also uses a shovel and bucket but is able to earn $50 a day. Marcel uses a wheelbarrow and earns $60 a day even though he is no stronger than Celine. Donna uses a bucket and shovel too, and at first she earns only $20 a day. Not satisfied with this income, she takes a month off to complete a muscle-building course. When she comes back, she earns $50 a day. How should the income of each worker be classified in terms of wages, rent, interest, and profit?

16. a. Using the data supplied in the table below, calculate the marginal physical product and the marginal revenue product of labour for Firms A and B. (Assume that two firms have the same marginal physical product.)

b. Plot the total-physical-product curve and the marginal-physical-product curve using the data in the completed table.

Units of Labour	Total Physical Product for Firms A and B	Marginal Physical Product for Firms A and B	Marginal Revenue for Firm A	Marginal Revenue for Firm B	Marginal Revenue Product for Firm A	Marginal Revenue Product for Firm B
0	0					
		_____	$10	$30	$_____	$_____
1	20					
		_____	10	25	_____	_____
2	30					
		_____	10	20	_____	_____
3	35					
		_____	10	15	_____	_____
4	38					
		_____	10	10	_____	_____
5	39					

17. a. Based on the data in Question 16, is Firm A a perfect or imperfect competitor in the product market? Is Firm B a perfect or imperfect competitor in the product market? What information did you use to arrive at your answers?

b. What purpose does the marginal-revenue-product curve serve for a firm that has to decide how many workers to hire?

c. If Firm A has to pay a wage of $30 for each additional worker, how many workers should it hire, assuming it wants to maximize profits and minimize costs? How many workers should Firm B hire under the same circumstances? Explain your answers.

18. a. Complete the table below by calculating the total cost of labour for the firm represented, the marginal factor cost of labour, and the marginal revenue product of labour.

b. Plot the marginal-factor-cost curve and the supply curve for labour, as well as the firm's demand curve for labour.

19. a. Based on the data in Question 18, how many workers will this firm hire? How did you determine your answer?

b. What wage will the firm pay the last worker it hires? How did you determine this amount?

c. What is the value to the firm of the last worker it hires? How did you determine this?

20. a. Based on the data in Question 18, is this firm a perfect or imperfect competitor in the product market? How can you tell?

b. Is the firm a perfect or imperfect competitor in the factor market for labour. How can you tell?

Number of Workers	Price of Each Worker Hired	Total Cost of Labour	Marginal Factor Cost of Labour	Marginal Physical Product of Labour	Marginal Revenue from the Sale of Output	Marginal Revenue Product
0	$ 1	$ 0				
			$_____	7	$2	$_____
1	2	_____				
			_____	6	2	_____
2	3	_____				
			_____	5	2	_____
3	4	_____				
			_____	4	2	_____
4	5	_____				
			_____	3	2	_____
5	6	_____				
			_____	2	2	_____
6	7	_____				
			_____	1	2	_____
7	8	_____				
			_____	0	2	_____
8	9	_____				
			_____	−1	2	_____
9	10	_____				

Labour Unions and Collective Bargaining

WHAT YOU WILL LEARN IN THIS CHAPTER

After studying this chapter, you will be able to

1. Provide information on union membership and union structure and organization in Canada.

2. Review the history of labour unions in Canada.

3. Summarize the main elements of Canadian labour law.

4. Use supply-and-demand analysis to show the effects of labour unions in competitive and monopsonistic markets.

5. Compare the results of collective bargaining in the public and private sectors.

6. Evaluate the extent of labour–management conflict in Canada and assess problems associated with such conflict.

A Preview   *Are Labour Unions Still Important for Workers?*

Many Canadians think of labour unions as extremely strong organizations that seriously challenge the rights of management in most businesses. The fact is, however, as the following article indicates, that the percentage of unionized workers among all Canadian workers has been on the decline and that the union movement is indeed vulnerable to economic conditions that occasion high unemployment and loss of job security.

Old Wounds Still Fester

Lynn Williams, president of the United Steelworkers of America, maintains he was joking last September when he said he was glad to be talking about the 1990s; they couldn't be any worse than the 1980s. But Williams' Ontario counterpart, Leo Gerard, has the same message — and he is grimly serious. "The 1980s were clearly the most consistently difficult period for the trade union movement since its birth," he says.

Aggressive demands for wage concessions, crumbling job security, judicial challenges under Canada's Charter of Rights and Freedoms — labour was under siege at the bargaining table and in the courts. It looked like the once-powerful Canadian institution was in decline.

But Gerard and other labour stalwarts have kept the faith. On the eve of the 1990s, they present evidence of a revitalized labour movement. As of January, the year-over-year increase in the number of unionized employees in Canada was 2.7 percent, even though Canada's 3.9 million unionized workers, as a percentage of all nonagricultural paid workers, declined to 36.2 percent in 1989 from 40 percent in 1982. As small as those gains may be, they beat the U.S. record of the last ten years. There, the level of unionism slipped to a fifty-year low of 16.8 percent of the work force in 1988.

"The [Canadian] union movement has continued to make itself relevant, not just at the bargaining table, but as an instrument of social and political justice. I think we have come out of the 'eighties

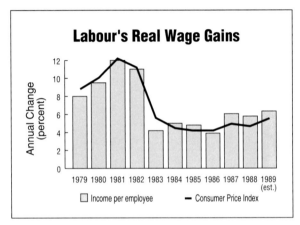

Labour's Real Wage Gains

Annual Change (percent)

☐ Income per employee   — Consumer Price Index

SOURCE: Statistics Canada; *The Financial Post.*

stronger, and with a higher level of acceptance," Gerard says.

Yet, as one of the most challenging decades in labour's history draws to an end, many of the fundamental problems of the 1980s remain unresolved. . . . Coming to terms with the changing nature of the work force was one of the struggles of the 1980s that awaits resolution in the 1990s.

SOURCE: David Estok, "Old Wounds Still Fester," *Financial Post Report on the Nation*, 1989, p. 42. Reproduced with permission.

LABOUR UNIONS IN CANADA

As the Preview article indicates, large numbers of Canadian workers belong to labour unions. Drawn by the prospect of higher wages, better fringe benefits, and possibly better job security, about 36 percent of all nonagricultural paid workers in this country were members of unions in 1989 — about 3.9 million workers in total.

However, as the Preview article also explains, these figures represent a drop in the unionized portion of the country's total nonagricultural labour force, from about 40 percent in 1982 to 36 percent in 1989. During approximately the same period, the unionized sector of the United States' nonagricultural labour force shrank even more, dropping to a very low 16.8 percent. The growth of public-sector unionism in both countries in recent decades has not altered overall declines in the private sector.

In the past, a majority of Canadian union members belonged to unions with headquarters outside Canada — most commonly in the United States. As we shall see later in the chapter, American labour organizations and ideologies have had a profound impact on the Canadian labour movement. In recent years, however, the importance of "international" unions in Canada — those with headquarters in the United States — has declined significantly. In 1988, their share of Canada's total union membership was only about 32 percent, a sharp decline from the 46 percent share they could claim in 1980.

Although unionized workers in Canada belong to hundreds of different unions — a fact that has led observers to characterize the Canadian union movement as highly fragmented — a substantial proportion belong to roughly a dozen very large unions. This is illustrated in Box 13.1, which lists the ten largest unions (in 1988), along with their affiliations. Almost 40 percent of all unionized workers belong to these unions. Unions such as the Canadian Union of Public Employees (CUPE) and the Public Service Alliance of Canada (PSAC) have successfully unionized public-sector employees throughout the country (nearly all civil servants in Canada are unionized). CUPE and PSAC are affiliated with the Canadian Labour Congress (CLC), an umbrella organization. Public-sector unions operating at the provincial level, such as the Fédération des affaires sociales of Quebec and the Ontario Public Service Employees Union, are either independent or belong to a provincial body such as the Confederation of National Trade Unions (CNTU), or Confédération des syndicats nationaux (CSN), of Quebec. Workers in the private sector are organized in unions such as the United Steel Workers — blue-collar unions affiliated with both a U.S. federation (the AFL/CIO) and a Canadian federation (the CLC).

Some industries have proved to be much easier to unionize than others, as the following review of Canadian labour history will show. Virtually no one in agriculture belongs to a union, while the public sector and the construction and transportation industries have become heavily organized. Box 13.2 illustrates the relative strength of the union movement in various industries in Canada.

So much for generalities. These statistics and observations are enough to show that Canadian unions, although not as strong as the labour organizations of some other countries, are sufficiently large to play a significant role in the economy. Let us now turn to a more detailed look at their origins and functions.

BOX 13.1 Membership and Affiliation of Canada's Ten Largest Unions

Almost 40 percent of unionized workers in Canada belong to the country's ten largest unions. Among the very largest are public-sector unions, affiliated with Canadian labour federations. Some private-sector employees, such as steelworkers and food and commercial workers, belong to unions affiliated with federations operating in both the United States and Canada.

Union	Affiliation	1988 Membership
1. Canadian Union of Public Employees	CLC	362 453
2. United Food and Commercial Workers International Union	AFL-CIO/CLC	178 066
3. United Steelworkers of America	AFL-CIO/CLC	166 001
4. Public Service Alliance of Canada	CLC	152 674
5. Canadian Auto Workers Union	CLC	103 999
6. Quebec Teaching Congress	Independent	101 056
7. Fédération des affaires sociales (Social Affairs Federation)	CNTU (CSN)	96 983
8. International Brotherhood of Teamsters	AFL-CIO	88 206
9. Service Employees International Union	AFL-CIO/CLC	81 336
10. Ontario Public Service Employees	CLC	75 045

Note: CLC — Canadian Labour Congress; AFL-CIO — American Federation of Labor–Congress of Industrial Organizations; CNTU — Confederation of National Trade Unions (CSN — Confédération des syndicats nationaux).

SOURCE: Statistics Canada, *Annual Report of the Minister of Industry, Trade and Commerce under the Corporations and Labour Unions Returns Act*, Part 2, *Labour Unions*, 1988, p. 48. Reproduced with permission of the Minister of Supply and Services Canada, 1992.

The History of Canadian Unionism

The history, structure, and philosophy of Canadian unions have been shaped by various forces that we have noted earlier in this book: the extreme regional disparities of the country; the large-scale development of resources requiring considerable capital investment and resulting in concentration levels higher than those in the United States; the extreme seasonal and cyclical fluctuations; and the country's economic dependence on the United States. These factors have, in the words of one scholar, "all worked to produce a Canadian labour movement that could be described as decentralized, fragmented, relatively weak, and strongly influenced by American international unions."[1]

---

[1] M. Saunderson, "Labour Relations in Canada," in *The Canadian Economy: Problems and Policies*, ed. G.C. Ruggeri (Toronto: Gage, 1977), pp. 274–75. For a more recent study of Canadian labour relations, see W. Craig Riddell, *Canadian Labour Relations*, Royal Commission on the Economic Union and Development Prospects for Canada, Collected Research Studies 16 (Toronto: University of Toronto Press, 1985).

Percentage of Workers Unionized, by Industry BOX 13.2

The table below ranks various sectors of the Canadian economy by degree of unionization. The public sector has become the most thoroughly unionized.

Industry	Percentage of Workers Unionized
1. Public administration	76.4
2. Transportation	56.6
3. Construction	52.8
4. Forestry	47.3
5. Manufacturing	36.8
6. Service industries	33.4
7. Mines and oil wells	28.6
8. Trade	10.4
9. Finance	3.4

SOURCE: Statistics Canada, *Annual Report of the Minister of Industry, Trade and Commerce under the Corporations and Labour Unions Returns Act*, Part 2, *Labour Unions*, 1988, p. 40. Reproduced with permission of the Minister of Supply and Services Canada, 1992.

The development of local unions in Great Britain and the United States at the beginning of the nineteenth century found an echo in scattered industrial centres in Canada by the 1820s and 1830s. Small **craft unions**, which were unions of skilled workers all practising the same craft, were formed in the shops of tailors, printers, and foundry operators in several places in Quebec, the Maritimes, and Ontario. These early attempts at unionization usually failed, because of sharp opposition from owners, generally hostile courts, and poor organization. In 1873, in Toronto, the first attempt was made to form a co-ordinating body, the Canadian Labor Union. It lasted only until 1877. A somewhat more successful effort was made by an American union, the Knights of Labor, which began to organize Canadian unions shortly after Confederation. It was founded as a secret society (the Noble Order of the Knights of Labor), but its growth began only after it abandoned secrecy in 1878. It reached a peak membership of about 12 000 in Canada in 1887.

Many local unions of skilled craftsmen were affiliated with the Knights of Labor, but the Knights' principles went far beyond the narrow bounds of craft unionism. They welcomed anyone who worked for a living, including farmers and unskilled labourers. In this they resembled an **industrial union**, which is a union of all workers in an industry, including both skilled and unskilled workers and workers practising various trades. Only such "undesirables" as bankers, liquor dealers, Pinkerton detectives, and lawyers were excluded by the Knights. Their program was not limited to narrow economic concerns. It stressed workers' education and producer co-operatives that would help counteract the "evil of wealth."

The Knights ran into conflict with other craft unions and declined rapidly after they were associated (without proof) with the killing of a policeman during Chicago's Haymarket Riot of 1886.

Despite the ultimate failure of the U.S.-based Knights of Labor, many Canadian workers found it advantageous to turn to American unions for financial and

Craft unions
Unions of skilled workers practising a single craft.

Industrial union
A union representing all workers in an enterprise, regardless of trade.

organizational support in establishing unions in their craft. Naturally, most of these unions became affiliates of the American unions. For example, the United Brotherhood of Carpenters and Joiners in the United States had dozens of affiliates in Canada, from Nova Scotia to British Columbia, by 1890.

One of the first successful confederations of labour in Canada, the Trades and Labor Council of Canada (TLC), was founded in 1886, and affiliated itself with the rapidly growing American Federation of Labor (AFL). Thereafter, the philosophy of the AFL, as expressed by its founder, Samuel Gompers, came to dominate much of the Canadian labour scene (see the accompanying Profile box). Indeed, no Canadian labour leader ever influenced the philosophy of unionism in Canada as profoundly as this powerful American unionist did. Gompers sought to avoid the mistakes that had led to the downfall of the Knights of Labor. The AFL owes its success largely to three features of its organization and philosophy that were prominent from its earliest years:

1. The AFL was based solidly on the principle of craft unionism. Its leaders thought that the dangers of economic depressions and employer opposition could be overcome only by relying on skilled workers who could not easily be replaced during strikes. The AFL itself was, in effect, an umbrella organization of national craft unions.

PROFILE   Samuel Gompers, Founder of the AFL

Samuel Gompers
(1859–1924)

Samuel Gompers was born in a London tenement, the son of a skilled cigar maker. When he was thirteen, his family moved to the United States and settled in New York. Gompers followed his father into the cigar trade.

Although his formal education ended at the age of ten, Gompers was very active in the workers' self-education movement of the time. In the cigar-making shops, jobs were organized on a piecework basis. Groups of workers would have one of their members read to them while they worked, "paying" the reader by making his cigars for him. Gompers became acquainted with the works of Marx, Engels, and other European socialists in this way. Often he was chosen as the reader.

The cigar makers' union to which Gompers belonged fell apart during the depression of 1873. Gompers rebuilt it as a model of the craft unions he was later to unite under the American Federation of Labor. Key features of this union were high membership dues, central control of funds, national officers with control over local unions, and union-organized accident and unemployment benefits for members.

Gompers became disillusioned with radical socialism. The main role of unions, in his view, was to watch after the economic interests of their members. He wrote as follows:

> Unions, pure and simple, are the natural organizations of wage workers to secure their present material and practical improvement and to achieve their final emancipation. . . . The working people are in too great need of immediate improvements in their condition to allow them to forgo them in the endeavour to devote their entire energies to an end however beautiful to contemplate. . . . The way out of the wage system is through higher wages.

During the 1890s, a socialist faction emerged within the AFL. It adopted a program calling for the collective ownership of all means of production and other radical measures. Gompers opposed the group, and in the 1895 election for the AFL presidency, he was defeated. He fought back, however, and succeeded in regaining the presidency the next year. He remained president until his death in 1924.

2. The AFL emphasized business unionism; that is, it devoted most of its energies to bread-and-butter issues of pay and working conditions. Unlike many European labour unions, it was content to work within the capitalist system. It did not seek to eliminate private property or to establish socialism.

3. The AFL limited its political role to that of a lobbyist on labour's behalf. Again in contrast to European labour movements, it did not found a labour party. Gompers thought that excessive political involvement would lead to internal conflict within the labour movement and would weaken its ability to achieve concrete economic objectives.

The TLC, through its affiliation with the businesslike and highly successful AFL, was the guiding force for unionism in Canada for half a century after its founding.

Partly in reaction to the overwhelming strength of the international unions affiliated with the TLC and the AFL, several rival, autonomous confederations were established on a provincial basis, notably the B.C. Federation of Labor, in 1911, and the Federation of Catholic Workers of Canada (Quebec), in 1921. Until the rise of strong, independent public workers' unions after World War II, these provincial federations formed the main bulwark against the complete dominance of the TLC.

The period 1914 to 1919 saw the development of a more radical form of unionism. Union membership increased sharply in this period, partly as a result of the increased union activity permitted by the federal government in all industries devoted to the war effort. The war itself brought Canadian union members in touch with more militant forms of industrial conflict in Europe, particularly the aims and methods of the 1917 Bolshevik Revolution. There is also evidence that rising prices immediately after the war, and a poor job market, led to a decline in real wages for many workers. The results of the combination of such new opportunities, ideas, and economic pressures included growing political action by labour in British Columbia, the formation of the One Big Union (OBU) by Western radicals in 1918, and the most dramatic event in Canadian labour history — the Winnipeg General Strike of 1919. The police put down the strikers in Winnipeg, and imprisoned several of them, including J.S. Woodsworth, who would later become founder of the CCF (the Co-operative Commonwealth Federation), which was the precursor of the NDP. In 1920, eleven labour members were elected to the Manitoba legislature, and J.S. Woodsworth became a member of Parliament for Central Winnipeg.

Despite — or, perhaps, because of — the new radicalism and the political successes, the union movement made few new advances in the interwar period. The Great Depression of the 1930s caused massive unemployment, accompanied by new labour–management conflict. In the Estevan coal miners' strike of 1931, for example, three workers were killed. There were approximately 400 000 union members in Canada in 1920, and about the same number in 1940. As we shall see, social, legal, and legislative changes were required to give the union movement new momentum.

New union structures were also needed. The TLC and the AFL had turned their backs on the type of industrial unionization that had been favoured by the Knights of Labor. In the 1920s and 1930s, several unions in Canada and the United States promoted industrial unionism and laid the foundation for a major change in union strategy. In the United States, the fight was carried on by the

Congress of Industrial Organizations (CIO), led by the mine workers' leader, John L. Lewis. In Canada, the Canadian Brotherhood of Railway Employees (CBRE) led the way, first creating the All-Canadian Congress of Labour (ACCL) and then assisting, in 1940, in the formation of the Canadian Congress of Labour (CCL). The CCL, in turn, affiliated with the CIO, but never came to be dominated by it (unlike the TLC, which was clearly subservient to the AFL).

After World War II, the AFL in the United States modified its stand on craft unionism and began to espouse industrial unionism. This led to the merger of the AFL and the CIO in 1955. A similar merger occurred in Canada in 1956, when most of the members of the TLC and the CCL joined together to create one confederation of labour, the Canadian Labour Congress (CLC). Most unions outside Quebec are now affiliated with the CLC. In Quebec, the Confederation of National Trade Unions (CNTU), or the Confédération des syndicats nationaux (CSN), continues to represent most of the provincial trade unions.

As this brief historical survey has made clear, the Canadian labour union movement has been deeply influenced by ideas and organizations originating outside Canada, particularly in the United States. Today, the unions to which about 32 percent of all unionized Canadian workers belong are affiliated with unions based in the United States. Although many of them are also affiliated with the Canadian Labour Congress, their main direction comes from their U.S. affiliates. While it has already been noted that the proportion of unions based in the United States has declined considerably, those unions remain a strong force in the Canadian labour movement and constitute a major economic link between Canada and the United States.

Public Policy toward Unions

What should be the government's policy toward unions? This question has been a topic of impassioned political debate ever since unions were first created. Some have argued that all unions should be suppressed as illegal restraints on trade. Others have advocated government support for unions, in order to promote industrial stability and high living standards for all. Still others have favoured a laissez-faire policy, letting workers and management bargain without government interference. The debate has been clouded by disagreement about the true effects of unions on relative and absolute wages and on industrial efficiency. Without taking a position, the next section will survey the changing course of government policy over time, showing how first one and then another opinion has become dominant.

Unions had trouble with the courts from their earliest days. Under precedents from English common law, they were often treated as illegal conspiracies in restraint of trade. In most cases, businesses were able to get the support of the courts to have the unions declared illegal. Often they didn't bother resorting to the courts: Workers who were caught participating in the formation of a union or even listening sympathetically to a union organizer were summarily fired. Such workers were often blacklisted, so that they had trouble getting a job anywhere else. Confrontations were often violent, both in Canada and the United States. Some employers used "yellow-dog" contracts, whereby workers signed an agreement not to engage in union activity. This often became a condition of employment.

In the United States, the Sherman Antitrust Act was used vigorously against unions as a form of restraint of trade, but in Canada, competition legislation was not used in a similar fashion. Canadian governments, both provincial and federal, created few laws either for or against unions, so that unions neither suffered the disadvantages of legislation such as the Sherman Act nor benefited from the advantages of pro-union laws such as those passed in the United States in the 1930s. Parliament passed an act in 1900 that set out a framework of conciliation to handle disputes between labour and management. This was followed by the Industrial Disputes Investigation Act of 1907, which included the acceptance of the right of workers to organize and bargain collectively, but did not require management to recognize a union.

It was only in 1939 that changes in the Criminal Code made it an offence for an employer to harass employees who were unionizing. During World War II, a special Order-in-Council laid the basic foundation for collective bargaining by forcing management to bargain with an elected union "in good faith."

A unique Canadian decision made in 1946 by Mr. Justice Ivan Rand of the Supreme Court of Canada, who had been appointed to arbitrate and settle a bitter strike at the Ford Motor Company, gave unions a new type of power and security. The ruling, which has come to be known as the Rand Formula, required both union and nonunion members at Ford to pay union dues. This set a precedent in support of the practice of compulsory union dues.

Since World War II, unions have enjoyed the right to organize, to bargain collectively with the employer, and to strike if a settlement cannot be reached. The right to strike was extended to public-sector unions in the 1960s (unlike the case in the United States, where public-sector unions have largely been denied the right to strike).

Since 1925, when the Privy Council ruled that labour relations fall under property and civil rights and should therefore be under provincial jurisdiction, most unions are subject to provincial laws and operate under provincial labour boards. About 15 percent of unionized workers currently fall within the jurisdiction of federal law.

COLLECTIVE BARGAINING AND WAGE RATES

Union Goals

Labour unions have won many benefits for their members and have pursued many different goals. They have bargained for shorter working hours and better health and safety conditions. They have established pension funds for their members, promoted worker education, and engaged in party politics. For Canadian unions, however, the number-one goal has long been to achieve higher wages for their members. This section will look at the means unions have at their disposal to achieve higher wages; later sections will examine how successful they have been in doing so.

The Union in a Competitive Market

Our discussion will begin with the case of a union formed in a previously competitive market, which now seeks higher wages through the threat of a strike. Consider Box 13.3. This figure shows a labour market in which the competitive equilibrium wage rate is $8 per hour and the equilibrium level of employment is 300 000 worker hours per year (see point E_1 in the graph).

BOX 13.3   *Effect of Unionization in a Competitive Labour Market*

A union formed in a previously competitive labour market can use a strike threat to bargain for higher wages. Here, the union threatens to strike unless the wage is raised from its competitive level of $8 per hour ($E_1$) to $10 per hour. With the strike threat in force, the supply curve of labour to employers becomes horizontal at $10 per hour up to 400 000 labour hours per year. A new equilibrium is reached at E_2, where the new supply curve intersects the demand curve. The wage is higher than it was initially, but the quantity of labour employed is smaller.

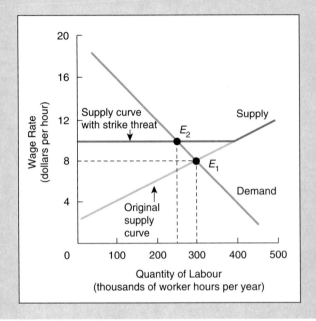

Suppose that the newly organized workers in this industry tell employers that they want $10 per hour, or else they will go on strike. The strike threat is represented in the graph by a change in the shape of the supply curve. Originally, the supply curve had the usual upward-sloping shape. After the strike threat, employers face a supply curve with a kink in it. The horizontal left-hand branch of the new kinked supply curve indicates that if the employer does not pay at least $10 per hour, no workers at all will be available. Up to 400 000 worker hours will be supplied at $10 per hour. To hire more labour than that, the wage will have to be raised higher than the amount the union is demanding.

Suppose the employers decide they have no choice but to accept the union demand. They will react by shifting to a new equilibrium at point E_2 in Box 13.3, where the demand curve and the horizontal part of the new supply curve intersect. There, they will hire 250 000 worker hours per year at $10 per hour. The union will have succeeded in raising the wage of its members, but only at the expense of reducing the amount of work available from 300 000 worker hours per year to 250 000 worker hours per year.

The trade-off in this example between increased wages and reduced employment is a rather general one when workers bargain collectively with competitive employers. Given the inevitable trade-off, just how far back along the employers' demand curve for labour should the union try to push?

There is no easy answer — no easy way to calculate an optimal wage demand. If the union wants to keep as many of its workers employed as possible, it may simply accept the competitive wage and confine its bargaining to nonwage issues. Perhaps, though, the union wants to raise the total income of its members. If the demand curve is inelastic in the region of the competitive wage, this can be done by pushing the wage up a bit. Although employment will fall, total labour income will increase.

In Box 13.4, the labour demand curve is inelastic up to a wage of $10 per hour, unit elastic at that point, and elastic beyond it. The $10 wage thus gives the largest possible total labour income — $2.5 million per year. Unfortunately, keeping the wage at this level creates a surplus of labour. Workers will be willing to supply 400 000 hours per year, but only 250 000 hours will be demanded. The union can either allow workers to compete for jobs on a first-come, first-served basis and not worry about those who cannot get a job, or it can try to parcel out the available work among all those who want a job in the industry. In the latter case, the union would have to restrict the number of hours that each worker put in. Whichever route is taken, a union that keeps the wage above the equilibrium level must be sufficiently well organized to prevent nonunion workers from undercutting its negotiated wage.

The Wage–Job Trade-off

BOX 13.4

Unions facing employers who are price takers may choose various ways of dealing with the wage–job trade-off. If the union's objective is to maximize employment, it will not bargain for a wage higher than the market-equilibrium wage. If the labour demand curve is inelastic at the competitive-equilibrium point, total income of union members can be increased by raising the wage to the point where the demand curve becomes unit elastic. If the union restricts membership to a limited elite group, it may push wages even higher.

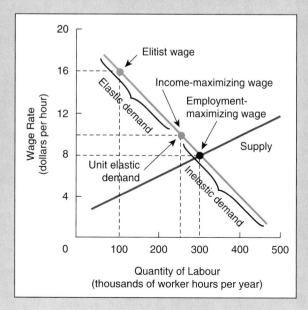

Sometimes, a strong union will ask for a wage even higher than the one that gives the maximum labour income. Suppose, for example, that the union takes an elitist attitude, restricting membership to certain racial or ethnic groups or to friends and relatives of current members. Look at Box 13.4 again. An elite group of workers may push the wage up to, say, $16 per hour, if 100 000 hours per year is all the work members of the group want. To hold a card in such a union, need-less to say, will be a jealously guarded privilege.

Featherbedding

The practice of negotiating purposefully inefficient work rules so that more workers will be needed to do a job.

Sometimes powerful unions try to get around the trade-off between wages and jobs through the practice of **featherbedding** — insisting on purposefully ineffi-cient work rules so that more workers will be needed to do a job. There have been some notorious examples of featherbedding in Canadian industry. For instance, there was a time when railway unions required firemen (workers who tended the fires that drove steam engines) on diesel locomotives.

If featherbedding simply means that some workers stood idly by while others worked normally, it would be just another form of work sharing. To the extent that it involves technical restrictions that lower productivity, though, it creates problems that simple work sharing does not. Lowering productivity means shift-ing the labour demand curve to the left. In the end, total earnings for a group of featherbedding workers must be lower than earnings for an equal number of workers who practise a form of work sharing that does not restrict productivity.

The Union in a Monopsonistic Labour Market

There is one exception to the trade-off between jobs and wages — the case where a union faces a monopsonistic employer. Consider Box 13.5. This figure shows a labour market in which a monopsonistic employer faces a group of workers who are initially unorganized. The wage rate in equilibrium is $6.50 per hour, and only 220 000 hours of labour per year are hired. This point is labelled E_1.

Now consider what happens if a union confronts the monopsonist with a demand for a wage of $10 per hour and backs the demand with a strike threat. As in Box 13.3, this demand puts a kink in the labour supply curve. What is more important, along the horizontal part of the new labour supply curve, the monop-sonist's marginal labour cost is equal to the wage rate. The union says, in effect, that the firm can hire as many workers as it wishes at no more and no less than $10 per hour — which means that changes in the quantity of labour hired no longer require changes in the wage rate. One more worker hour raises total labour costs by no more and no less than $10.

Suppose that the union is strong enough to make the monopsonist accept its wage demand on a take-it-or-leave-it basis. The new equilibrium will then be found where the new marginal-labour-cost curve intersects the demand curve, at point E_2. The wage rate there is $10 per hour, and 240 000 worker hours per year are employed. Both the wage rate and employment are higher than they were in the previous monopsonistic equilibrium.

Notice, however, that there is a limit on the power of a union facing a monop-sonist to raise wages without losing jobs. This limit is set by the extent to which the original monopsony wage fell short of the competitive wage. Once the wage rate begins to exceed the level where the supply and demand curves intersect, further raises reduce employment. In fact, as Box 13.5 is drawn, the wage of $10 per hour is already in the trade-off region. Maximum employment is achieved with a wage rate of $8 per hour, equal to the competitive wage.

The Effects of Unionization in a Monopsonistic Labour Market

BOX 13.5

When a union faces a monopsonistic employer, it can sometimes raise both wages and employment. Here, the original monopsony equilibrium wage is $6.50 per hour with 220 000 worker hours per year (E_1). A strike threat puts a kink in the monopsonist's marginal labour-cost curve, because the union's take-it-or-leave-it $10 per hour bargaining position makes the employer a price taker in the labour market at that wage rate. The new marginal-labour-cost curve intersects the demand curve at 240 000 worker hours per year, which becomes the new equilibrium point, E_2. Both the wage rate and the quantity of labour employed are higher than they were at E_1.

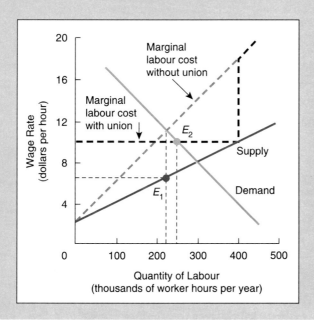

Bilateral Monopoly

The example just given assumes that the monopsonistic employer will accept the union demand on a take-it-or-leave-it basis. Not all employers react this way. A strong employer may counter the union demand with the threat of a lockout or of some take-it-or-leave-it offer of its own. The kind of bargaining situation that develops when neither party to the labour contract acts competitively and neither passively accepts the demands of the other is called **bilateral monopoly**. The outcome of bargaining under bilateral monopoly is impossible to predict with the type of analysis used here. Economic theory can only specify a range of outcomes within which a settlement can take place. The actual outcome depends simply on the relative bargaining strength and skill of the two sides. The headline-making disputes in which "big labour" clashes with "big business" often fall into the category of bilateral monopoly. Bilateral monopoly is also characteristic of the increasingly important negotiations between large public-sector unions and the governments they confront.

Bilateral monopoly
A market in which both buyer and seller exercise monopoly power and neither passively accepts the demands of the other.

Relative Wages

How successful a union will be in raising the relative wages of its members depends primarily on three things: (1) whether the union is strong enough to make a credible strike threat; (2) how willing it is to sacrifice jobs in order to gain higher wages; and (3) what the demand conditions are in its sector of the labour market. No purely theoretical analysis can tell which unions will be able to win higher relative wages and which will not. This is an empirical question that has drawn the attention of many economists.

In the United States, a 1963 study by H.G. Lewis indicated that unions were able to raise the wages of their members above those of nonunion workers in the same industry, especially in the first few years of the union's existence. However, only rarely were unions able to raise union wages more than 25 percent above the nonunion level. The increases generally achieved ranged from about 5 to 20 percent above the nonunion wage.[2] A Canadian study by G. Starr indicated that for production workers in Ontario, the increase in relative wages for union members ranged from 10 to 17 percent.[3]

One circumstance that must be taken into account, of course, is that firms may set the wages of nonunion workers in accordance with those negotiated by union members in the same or a related firm or industry, usually in an effort to prevent unionization. In such cases, it may be only in times of economic slack, when employees are being laid off and management can afford to alienate some of its staff, that the value of the union's protection of its members becomes apparent.

DO PUBLIC-SECTOR UNIONS POSE SPECIAL PROBLEMS?

We noted earlier that public-sector unions are extremely important in Canada. Many Canadians seem to feel that they pose special problems. In its surveys of attitudes about the state of the economy from 1982 to 1985, the Royal Commission on the Economic Union and Development Prospects for Canada (the Macdonald Commission) found that Canadian business people in particular felt that public-sector unions were able to negotiate considerably higher wages than those negotiated in the private sector. Public-sector negotiations were also believed to be less subject to such market pressures as unemployment and inflation. Furthermore, higher wage settlements in the public sector were thought to have an adverse effect on negotiations in the private sector, because private-sector unions viewed them as precedent setting.

The special studies of the Macdonald Commission indicated that (1) government employees earned about 5 to 10 percent more than their counterparts in the private sector; (2) wage negotiations in the public sector were about as sensitive to market forces as those in the private sector; (3) there was a very limited spillover effect from the public to the private sector; and (4) in the preceding decade and a half, wage increases in the government (noncommercial) sector had been remarkably similar to those in the private (commercial) sector.[4] This last

---

[2]H.G. Lewis, *Unionism and Relative Wages in the U.S.* (Chicago: University of Chicago Press, 1963).

[3]G. Starr, *Union–Non Union Wage Differentials* (Toronto: Ontario Ministry of Labour, 1973).

[4]Royal Commission on the Economic Union and Development Prospects for Canada, *Report*, 3 vols. (Toronto: University of Toronto Press, 1985), 2: 681–82 (hereafter cited as Macdonald Commission, *Report*).

Annual Average Wage Changes in the Public and Private Sectors

BOX 13.6

This graph shows the annual average wage changes in the public (noncommercial) and private (commercial) sectors, not including cost-of-living adjustment clauses. It is evident that, between 1968 and 1983, wage increases in the public and private sectors in Canada followed very similar patterns.

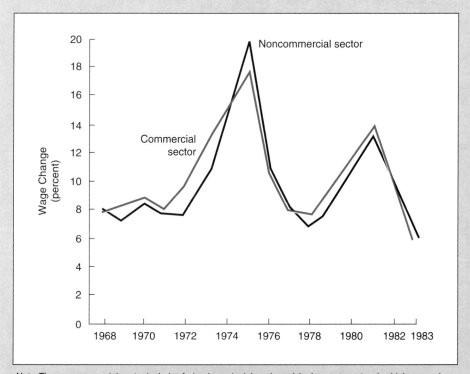

Note: The noncommercial sector includes federal, provincial, and municipal governments, plus highway and bridge maintenance, water systems and utilities, welfare organizations, education and related services, and hospitals. The commercial sector includes *all* other enterprises, some of which (for example, Crown corporations such as the CBC and Canada Post) might elsewhere be considered as part of the public sector. To include these in the noncommercial sector would not significantly alter the averages.

SOURCE: Canada, Labour Canada, *Wage Developments Resulting from Major Collective Bargaining Settlement*; Macdonald Commission, *Report* 2: 684. Reproduced with permission.

finding is illustrated in Box 13.6. Thus, according to the commission's studies, labour unions in the public sector behave very much like those in the private sector, and achieve quite comparable results.

WHAT ELSE DO UNIONS DO?

To focus entirely on the effects unions have on wages would be misleading; unions do many other things besides bargain over wages. This has been true from the earliest days of unionism, when the Knights of Labor campaigned for worker education and self-improvement, to the present, when unions bargain for such essential "fringe benefits" as pensions and accident insurance, organize social activities, help members with personal and family problems, and serve as a channel for participating in politics.

Some of the things that unions do extend beyond the scope of economics. But even on the economic level, unions affect more than wages. For one thing, unions give workers a voice in how the workplace is run. In an economy based on free labour markets, a worker can always seek another job if he or she does not like the way the workplace is run. But unions offer an alternative. They can bargain with the employer over health and safety conditions in the workplace. They can help settle the workers' grievances in matters ranging from job assignments to company policy, to conflicts with supervisors. They can bargain over issues of fairness, such as the role of seniority in layoffs and recalls.

Such bargaining, of course, often produces serious conflicts between the union and management. The ultimate power of the employer is the power to fire the worker. The ultimate power of the union is to withhold services — to strike. The vast majority of union–management conflicts are resolved through peaceful negotiation. However, on many occasions, perhaps because of the intransigence of both union leaders and management, or simply because their perception of what is possible in terms of increases in wages and fringe benefits differs radically, negotiations break down and a strike ensues. In general, there is nothing particularly alarming about this. The right to strike was given to unions precisely so that, when exercised, it could bring about a fairer solution than would otherwise have been possible. However, what is of concern to many observers in Canada is the relatively large number of strikes that occur in this country, and the large number of working days lost due to labour–management conflict.

BREAKDOWNS IN THE COLLECTIVE-BARGAINING PROCESS

Despite the peaceful resolution of most potential conflicts between management and labour, the Canadian experience in management–labour relations has, in recent decades, been one of the most disappointing among Western industralized nations.

Union leaders in Canada have generally frowned on the cozy relationships that some American union leaders seem to have maintained with their employers — relationships that may have made the American unions less militant and that may also have led to the many glaring abuses of power by American union leaders that have come to light over the years. At the same time, both union and management are sceptical of experiments in "industrial democracy" in such countries as Sweden and Germany, where a greater spirit of co-operation has been developed between employers and employees by granting workers considerable rights in the management of companies.

Canadian labour and management seem to prefer the adversary system of bargaining, based on the assumption of class conflict. The result is continued industrial strife, millions of hours of work lost through strikes and lockouts, and the use of tactics that sometimes seem to fall just short of war. Time lost through labour–management disputes is small in absolute terms; it amounts to about one day per worker per year — roughly the time lost through the celebration of Victoria Day each May. Moreover, it is considerably less than the time lost to occupational accidents, illness, and absenteeism.

Nonetheless, in relative terms, Canada's record is not enviable. As the Macdonald Commission noted, "We Canadians are now among the most dispute-prone of the industrialized nations."[5] A study prepared for the Macdonald Commission concluded that Canada's relatively high number of strikes and lockouts and the increased incidence of work stoppages over the last few decades can be explained in terms of several factors. One relates to the information required of, and available to, the negotiating parties. Within many Canadian companies, there appear to be very poor mechanisms for exchange of information among employers, employees, and the union management. Other factors include the cyclically unstable resource industries that are characteristic of Canada and the decentralized nature of our collective-bargaining system.

None of these factors, unfortunately, can be changed easily or quickly. In the meantime, increasing pressure is being placed on government to interfere with the collective-bargaining process by legislating workers back to work. In the period 1965–74, federal and provincial governments together passed 23 back-to-work acts. In the period 1975–84, they passed 41 such acts. Contrary to some popular opinion, the public sector's propensity to strike is lower than the private sector's. Legislative actions may provide a short-run solution to work stoppages that seem particularly injurious to the public, but in the long run, it is clear that Canada needs to *improve* its bargaining procedures — not kill them with legislation — in order to reduce its serious labour–management problems.

PROBLEMS AHEAD

The greatest problem facing unions today is the need for a major labour-organization breakthrough in the fast-growing service sector, particularly in such dynamic branches as finance, business services, and trade. Only 3.4 percent of workers in the area of financial services are currently unionized. Almost all of the country's new jobs are appearing in small business firms in these growing sectors — sectors that are among the most expensive and difficult to organize.

SUMMARY

1. In 1989, about 36 percent of Canada's nonagricultural workers belonged to labour unions, compared with 40 percent in 1982. Although union density is not unusually high in Canada, the growth of union membership has been unusually high in the last few decades.

2. Some of the largest unions in Canada are public-sector unions; indeed, the public sector has become more thoroughly unionized than the private sector. A majority of Canadian unions are affiliated with the Canadian Labour Congress (CLC). A significant but declining minority are affiliates of unions based in the United States.

3. The first local *craft unions* in Canada were established in the early decades of the nineteenth century. In the 1870s and 1880s, the U.S.-based Knights of Labor tried to establish a confederation of labour here. They were soon suc-

---

[5]Macdonald Commission, *Report* 2: 695.

ceeded by the Trades and Labor Council of Canada (TLC), in affiliation with the AFL in the United States. The philosophy and practice of the latter were shaped by the strong leadership of Samuel Gompers. The TLC emphasized craft unionism and concentrated on the bread-and-butter issue of higher wages. *Industrial unionism* had some early successes in a few provinces and in some independent unions, but it became widespread only with the formation of the Canadian Congress of Labour (CCL) in 1940, in affiliation with the CIO in the United States. At first, the TLC and the CCL feuded bitterly, but in 1956, following the merger of the AFL and the CIO, the two organizations united and formed the Canadian Labour Congress (CLC).

4. The strike threat is a union's ultimate weapon in bargaining with employers for higher wages. A union wage demand backed by a strike threat has the effect of bending the labour supply curve so that it becomes horizontal at the level of the wage demand. In a market where employers are price takers, a higher wage can usually be won only at the expense of jobs lost.

5. Sometimes *featherbedding* or other kinds of work sharing are used to spread available work among all union members.

6. Within certain limits, a union can win both higher wages and higher employment from a monopsonistic employer.

7. *Bilateral monopoly* refers to a market in which both buyer and seller exercise monopoly power.

8. Empirical studies show that many unions succeed in raising the wages of their members above nonunion wage levels. Often, though, the relative wage advantage of union members amounts to only a few percentage points. Unions provide for their members in many other ways, negotiating improved fringe benefits and better working conditions.

9. Public policy toward unions has gone through several phases. Until the 1930s, courts were generally hostile toward unions. Unions gained the legal rights they now enjoy over the course of half a century: the earliest price of legislation addressing labour–management disputes was passed in 1900, but real gains were made only in the late 1930s and during World War II. The Rand Formula of 1946 provided the foundation for the compulsory payment of union dues, a source of new security for unions. Despite legislative progress, labour and management operate in a sometimes fierce adversary system, resulting in a comparatively high rate of days lost through industrial disputes.

KEY TERMS

craft unions
industrial union

featherbedding

bilateral monopoly

KEY BOXES

Box 13.3 Effect of Unionization in a Competitive
           Labour Market
Box 13.4 The Wage–Job Trade-off

Box 13.5 The Effects of Unionization in a
           Monopsonistic Labour Market

REVIEW QUESTIONS

1. Use supply and demand curves to show how a union affects wages and employment in a competitive labour market.

2. Under what conditions do labour unions have the greatest influence on the incomes of their members?

3. "A labour union can increase the incomes of its members only at the cost of reducing the number of jobs." Discuss.

4. Why do you think unions are stronger in the public sector and in construction than in private service industries and in such sectors as agriculture?

5. In what ways do unions resemble cartels? In what ways do they differ from cartels? Do you think public policy should treat unions and producer cartels differently? Discuss.

6. Refer to Box 13.5, which illustrates the effects of unionization in a monopsonistic labour market. Using the demand and supply curves depicted in that box, identify the maximum wage that a union might get while keeping employment at 220 000. Alternatively, what would be the maximum employment level if wages were held to $6.50 per hour by the union?

7. How many different unions are represented on your campus? Assuming that your initial investigation reveals that there are several, examine why — or whether — more than one union was necessary.

8. Under what labour market conditions would an increase or a decrease in demand for workers with a certain skill leave the equilibrium wage rate unaffected? Illustrate your answer with a graph.

9. a. A medium-sized pharmacy/gift store in a large city decides to hire a few extra part-time clerks for the December holiday season. Would the labour market for these clerks be competitive? How would the wages that the store would have pay to attract clerks be determined? Explain your answers.

   b. If individuals who worked part-time during the December holiday season were unionized, would the number of workers hired and the wage rate be different than they would be without a union? (Assume the union's goal is to maximize the number of workers hired.)

10. a. Draw a graph showing the situation that exists when a strong union faces a relatively weaker monopsonistic employer, and the union sets its wage demand above the competitive wage. What does the supply curve look like, assuming that nobody is willing to work for less than the union wage?

    b. What happens to the firm's marginal-labour-cost curve in this situation?

    c. Assuming the union's wage demands are met, how will the quantity of workers hired be determined?

    d. What wage rate will be paid?

    e. Has the union maximized the total wages paid or the number of workers employed, or neither?

Income Distribution and the Problem of Poverty

WHAT YOU WILL LEARN IN THIS CHAPTER

After studying this chapter, you will be able to

1. Provide a summary profile of income distribution in Canada.

2. Explain how a Lorenz curve and the Gini coefficient can be used to illustrate income inequality.

3. Explain how poverty is defined in Canada.

4. Summarize some of the main statistics on poverty and discuss various explanations for them.

5. Describe some of the most important government programs designed to help the poor and to redistribute income.

6. Assess the apparent effects of such programs.

7. Describe the Macdonald Commission's proposal for providing a better income-security system.

A Preview   *Rich and Poor: A Considerable Difference*

When people discuss how well-off they are, they usually think only of their annual income, and perhaps the money they have in the bank. However, as this article indicates, many people have a great deal more wealth than they think, tied up in such things as real estate, stocks, and bonds. Many Canadians, in fact, are very wealthy. Unfortunately, there are also great differences in wealth among different groups of people throughout the country, as well as from region to region. Consider, as you read the article, that more than three million Canadians live in poverty, including 60 percent of all single mothers.

More Millionaires Than Ever

Canadians have entered this recession with far more wealth to cushion the pain than in any other, a new study shows.

Thanks to soaring real estate values and the steady growth of money socked away in registered retirement savings plans, average Canadian household wealth more than doubled between 1983, just after the last recession, and 1989. The growth has left almost one in every twenty households a millionaire, the study by management consultants Ernst & Young says.

The average Canadian household's net worth — total assets such as houses and stock portfolios minus liabilities such as mortgage debt — was $261 400 at the end of 1989, compare to $115 000 at the end of 1983.

Three-quarters of household wealth is locked up in nonliquid assets such as real estate, farms, private businesses, pension plans, and jewellery. Liquid assets, including bank deposits, stocks, and bonds, make up the remainder. Real estate alone, principally homes, made up 43 percent of the total.

Reasons behind the rapid accumulation of wealth include soaring real estate values in such markets as Vancouver and southern Ontario, the strong performance of stocks in the 1983–89 period, and the huge popularity of RRSPs.

Ontario stands far above all other provinces, with average household wealth of $329 500. The Western provinces come next, with average wealth ranging from $229 600 to $263 000, then Quebec, at $204 000, and the Atlantic provinces, ranging from $161 600 in Newfoundland to $189 900 in Nova Scotia.

Average Household Wealth across Canada, December 1989
(thousands of dollars)

Newfoundland	161.6
New Brunswick	180.7
P.E.I.	188.6
Nova Scotia	189.9
Quebec	204.0
Manitoba	229.6
Alberta	244.8
Saskatchewan	257.3
CANADA	**261.4**
British Columbia	263.0
Ontario	329.5

SOURCE: Ernst & Young Management Consultants. Reproduced with permission.

SOURCE: Excerpted from Greg Ip, "More Millionaires Than Ever," *Financial Post*, December 17, 1990, p. 3. Reproduced with permission.

CANADA: A WEALTHY NATION, BUT . . .

In all international comparisons of standards of living, Canada consistently ranks as one of the half-dozen wealthiest countries in the world. At present, one in twenty Canadian families owns assets exceeding $1 million. One may record this with a sense of accomplishment.

However, even a relatively wealthy country such as Canada faces substantial income-related problems. The first problem to be noted is that income is very unevenly distributed, across both families and regions. This is the main problem that concerns us in this chapter. However, the problem of income *distribution* has been compounded, since about 1978, by a slowdown in the rate of growth of income. Wealth may be increasing as assets appreciate in value, but annual income is not growing as rapidly. As long as the total income "pie" is growing, everyone can get a larger slice, and the relative size of each person's slice can remain unchanged. But when the pie stops growing, and even shrinks, some people can get a larger slice only at the expense of others. It then becomes extremely difficult to solve the problem of income distribution.

Box 14.1 provides data on the historical growth of family income (part [a]) and personal income (part [b]) in Canada in the last few decades. Part (a) indicates that family income grew very rapidly in the three decades from 1951 to 1981, averaging about 35 percent per decade. By contrast, in the nine-year period from 1981 to 1989, it grew by only 7.1 percent.

Family income includes all sources of income, such as wages, salaries, interest, and rent. When only income from wages and salaries is considered, the results are even less encouraging. Box 14.1(b) contrasts the growth of three types of employee income since 1961: personal income, including all sources of income; wages and salaries only; and personal disposable income (income from all sources after taxes and transfer payments). All three grew dramatically between 1961 and about 1977, but tailed off abruptly after that. The red and green lines show that personal income and personal disposable income grew slightly through the 1980s. Real wages and salaries per employee, however, actually declined. In other words, workers who depend largely on wages and salaries for their income actually had a lower standard of living in 1989 than they did in 1977. It is against this rather bleak development that the problem of income distribution must be examined.

POVERTY AND INCOME DISTRIBUTION

Inequality of Income

As we emphasized at the beginning of Chapter 13, factor markets not only determine how goods and services are produced but also help determine income distribution. Workers and owners of capital and natural resources are rewarded according to the productivity of the factors they contribute (at least, when the market is operating as close to perfectly as possible). Entrepreneurs earn profits or losses according to their degree of success in finding and taking advantage of new opportunities. Since people differ in skills and talents, in the amount of capital and natural resources they control, and in luck and entrepreneurial ability, their incomes differ. Some earn nothing; others earn millions of dollars a year.

The factor markets that we have been studying distribute income very unequally among Canadian families. A distressingly large number of families live in

BOX 14.1 The Growth of Income in Canada

Statistics Canada offers the following historical summary of the trends indicated in the table in part (a) below:

> Between 1951 and 1989, family incomes increased more than one-and-a-half times in real terms (161.8 percent). However, close to three-fifths of the total increase occurred between 1951 and 1971 (93.9 percent). Per-capita family income increased by two times from 1951 to 1989 (211.2 percent). This was greater than the family-income growth due to a decrease in [average] family size (−15.9 percent).
>
> The 1960s was clearly the decade of greatest growth, followed by the 1950s. During the 1970s, the real increase was still significant, though down sharply from the growth of the previous decade. The 1980s have seen much less growth compared to the previous three decades.

The graph in part (b) documents trends in personal income (income from all sources), wages and salaries only, and personal disposable income (income from all sources *after* taxes and transfer payments) from 1961 to 1989. High interest rates in the 1980s contributed to the growth of personal income, but wages and salaries have actually declined since 1978.

(a)

| | Percentage Change in: | | |
	Family Income	Family Size	Family Income per Capita*
1951–61	32.8	+4.2	27.4
1961–71	46.0	−4.6	53.0
1971–81	26.1	−11.2	41.9
1981–89	7.1	−4.8	12.5
1951–89	161.8	−15.9	211.2

*Per-capita family income is average family income divided by average family size.

SOURCE: Statistics Canada, *Income After Tax, Distribution by Size in Canada*, 1989, p. 19, Catalogue no. 13-207. Reproduced with permission of the Minister of Supply and Services Canada, 1992.

(b)

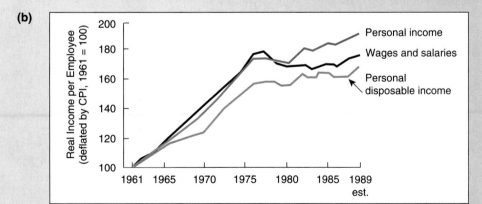

SOURCE: Catherine Harris, "A Peek inside Our Pocketbooks," *Financial Post Investor's Guide*, Fall 1989, p. 60; data for graph from Statistics Canada, *National Income and Expenditures Accounts*, Catalogue no. 13-001; *National Income and Expenditures Accounts, Annual Estimates*, Catalogue no. 13-531; and *Historical Labour Force Statistics, Actual Data, Seasonal Factors, Seasonally Adjusted Data*, Catalogue no. 71-201. Reproduced with permission of the Minister of Supply and Services Canada, 1992.

poverty. (*Poverty* will be defined and examined more closely later in this chapter.) The *general inequality* of income in Canada can be understood by comparing the lowest and highest-income groups with the *average family income*. The average family income in Canada in 1990 was $51 633. This figure, like most averages, masks substantial differences. Regionally, average family income ranged from a high of $57 027 in Ontario to a low of $39 701 in Prince Edward Island. In terms of family structure, average family income was almost three times as high for two-income families as it was for one-income families headed by single mothers ($58 202 for the former versus $21 961 for the latter).

Measuring Inequality by Quintile Shares

One common way of measuring the inequality of income distribution is to divide the population into equal groups ranked from poorest to richest. If, for example, the population is divided into five equal groups, each group is called a *quintile*. Box 14.2 gives the income share for each quintile of Canadian families for the years 1971, 1980, and 1989. If income were distributed equally in our society, each quintile would receive 20 percent of total family income. This is clearly not the case.

The share of total family income received by the richest fifth of families in Canada is consistently about six or seven times greater than the share received by the lowest fifth. What is perhaps most remarkable is the stability of the distribution pattern over time: In fact, there has been very little change in it since World War II. The lowest fifth has consistently received about 6 percent of family income, the second fifth about 13 percent, and the highest fifth between 38 and 40 percent. It is nonetheless worth noting that, since 1971, the lowest quintile has slowly but steadily increased its share from 5.6 percent to 6.5 percent.

Income Shares of Canadian Families by Quintiles, 1971–1989   BOX 14.2

This table divides Canadian families into five equal groups, or *quintiles*. There are the same number of families in each group, and the groups are ordered from poorest to richest. The table indicates, for each year, the percentage of total before-tax income that went to each group. For example, in 1989, the poorest fifth of families in Canada received only 6.5 percent of family income, while the richest fifth received 39.3 percent, or about 6 times as much. This unequal distribution of income remained relatively constant between 1971 and 1989.

Year	Lowest 20 Percent	Second Quintile	Third Quintile	Fourth Quintile	Top 20 Percent	Total
1971	5.6	12.6	18.0	23.7	40.0	100.0
1980	6.2	13.0	18.4	24.1	38.4	100.0
1989	6.5	12.6	17.8	23.8	39.3	100.0

SOURCE: Statistics Canada, *Income After Tax, Distribution by Size in Canada*, 1989, p. 147, Catalogue no. 13-207. Reproduced with permission of the Minister of Supply and Services Canada, 1992.

The Lorenz Curve and the Gini Index of Inequality

Lorenz curve
A curve that graphs the cumulative percentage of income household units along the horizontal axis and the cumulative percentage of income received by those units along the vertical axis.

In 1905, M.O. Lorenz demonstrated a method of illustrating income inequality that has been used extensively by economists ever since. In Box 14.3, a **Lorenz curve** is developed by plotting the cumulative percentage of family units along the horizontal axis and the cumulative percentage of income received by those families along the vertical axis. The data from Box 14.2 (for 1989) can be used for this purpose. *A* is the point at which the poorest 20 percent of family units received 6.5 percent of family income; *B* is the point at which the poorest 40 percent received 19.1 percent of family income (6.5 + 12.6); and *C* is the point at which the poorest 60 percent of families received 36.9 percent of family income (6.5 + 12.6 + 17.8); and so on. Connecting these points enables us to approximate a Lorenz curve for Canadian families. If income were broken down into many more income intervals, a more accurate curve would be possible.

If every quintile had the same share of income (that is, 20 percent), the Lorenz curve would be the straight line, *OE*. The distance from the line *OE* to the actual Lorenz curve connecting points *A*, *B*, *C*, and *D* provides us with a measurement

BOX 14.3 *The Lorenz Curve and the Gini Coefficient of Inequality*

This Lorenz curve for Canada for Canada for 1989 is derived from the data in Box 14.2. The percentage of income units (households), measured cumulatively, is plotted along the horizontal axis, and the percentage of income received by those units, again measured cumulatively, is plotted along the vertical axis. Points *A*, *B*, *C*, *D*, and *E* are derived in this way. If each family quintile received 20 percent of total income, the Lorenz curve would be the line *OE*. The deviation of the actual Lorenz curve, *OABCDE*, from that line represents the degree of income inequality in the society. This is measured numerically by the Gini coefficient, which is the ratio of the actual inequality (given by the shaded area) to the greatest possible inequality (which would be given by the area of the entire triangle *OPE*).

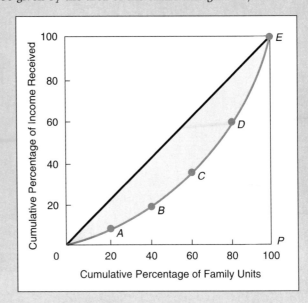

of the income inequality in the country. In 1912, Corrado Gini proposed that the extent of inequality in a society could be measured by determining the ratio of the area between the actual Lorenz curve for a society and the *OE* line (the shaded area in Box 14.3) to the area of the entire triangle *OPE*. The greater the inequality, the larger the shaded area would be and the more it would approximate the entire area of the *OPE* triangle. Therefore, the ratio, known as the **Gini coefficient**, would also be greater.

In summary, the lower the Gini ratio, or coefficient, the greater the *equality* of income within a society; the higher the ratio, the greater the *inequality*. In the early 1970s, the Gini coefficient for families in Canada was calculated to be 0.348, while for the United States, it was 0.369. Canada's coefficient of inequality was about halfway between that of the most unequal country among Western industrial nations, France (0.417), and that of the most equal, the Netherlands (0.264).[1]

Gini coefficient
The ratio of the area between the Lorenz curve and the line *OE* to the area of the entire triangle *OPE*.

GOVERNMENT INCOME-REDISTRIBUTION PROGRAMS

The previous box, we should note, records only the distribution of before-tax money income, including government transfer payments. It does not indicate how the distribution has been affected by those transfer payments, or how it will be affected by Canada's tax system.

Ever since the Great Depression, but particularly since World War II, governments have employed a wide range of so-called welfare expenditures, insurance programs, and taxation measures to construct an income-security system for Canadians.

With respect to tax measures, federal and provincial governments have sought to redistribute income, in order to provide a "safety net" for low-income earners, in two ways: by implementing a progressive schedule for tax rates (one that applies higher tax rates to higher-income earners) and by introducing a series of tax exemptions and credits, such as the child tax credit, the marital exemption, and registered retirement savings plans (RRSPs).

In addition to tax policy, governments have used tax revenues, as well as insurance premiums, to support a large number of expenditures (transfer payments) in aid of the poor, the physically or mentally challenged, and the unemployed.

At least a dozen transfer programs are currently in existence, and they provide some form of assistance to almost two million Canadians. In 1989, government transfers to families accounted for 9.9 percent of average family income. This represented a drop in the rate of transfers from a high of 10.7 percent in 1984. (Prior to that, the rate had been on an upward trend, rising from 7.3 percent in 1980.) In 1989, transfers represented 50.4 percent of the income of the lowest fifth of Canadian families, and the percentage rose to 77.9 for families with an income of less than $10 000. Individuals without families received 17.9 percent of their income, on average, from government transfers.

Here, we shall concentrate briefly on a few of the major transfer programs. These include family allowance (FA); the guaranteed income supplement (GIS), which provides income-tested benefits for the elderly, financed by the federal

---

[1] This information and some of the preceding analysis are derived from Lars Osberg, *Economic Inequality in Canada* (Toronto: Butterworths, 1981).

government under the Canada Assistance Plan (CAP); provincially delivered welfare payments (PWP), financed jointly, and roughly equally, by the federal and provincial governments (the federal portion comes out of the CAP), but administered by the provinces and their municipalities; unemployment insurance benefits (UI), financed through premiums paid to the federal government; the Old Age Security pension (OAS), which provides benefits to all citizens 65 years of age or older, and the Canada and Quebec Pension Plans (CPP and QPP), which provide pension benefits to those who have contributed premiums at work.

The distributional impact of these government tax and expenditure programs, by income class, is illustrated in Box 14.4. The data in this box were derived in a special study, conducted by Michael Wolfson in 1985, of the family incomes of 1800 families.[2] These families are broken down into ten percentile groups

---

BOX 14.4 The Effect of Income Taxes and Transfer Payments on Family Income, 1985

Columns 1 and 2 of the table below indicate that in 1985, the poorest 10 percent of families had an average annual income of $2590. This is the money income they received before taxes and before receiving government transfer income. (Note, however, that most of these families would not have owed any taxes.) Column 3 shows that after taxes and transfer income, the average income of this group increased to $6570. Similar calculations are made in columns 1–3 for successively higher income groups. Columns 4–5 show the effect of an income-security plan proposed by the Macdonald Commission, which is discussed later in the chapter.

| | Average Family Incomes (dollars) | | | |
(1) Disposable Income Percentile	(2) Current Pre-Tax, Pre-Transfer Disposable Income	(3) Current After-Tax After-Transfer Disposable Income	(4) After-Tax Income as Changed by UISP	(5) Percentage Change in After-Tax Income by UISP
0–10	2 590	6 570	8 100	23.3
10–20	4 410	10 210	10 840	6.1
20–30	8 860	13 740	14 500	5.5
30–40	14 230	17 790	18 380	3.3
40–50	19 580	21 420	21 860	2.0
50–60	25 820	25 430	25 180	−1.0
60–70	32 810	30 050	29 390	−2.2
70–80	40 190	35 120	33 950	−3.3
80–90	49 480	41 270	40 240	−2.5
90–95	61 580	49 860	48 990	−1.7
95–100	89 110	67 580	66 690	−1.3
ALL	27 330	26 030	26 030	0.0

Note: "Current" means 1985 tax and transfer structure.

SOURCE: Small-scale microsimulation model applied to a sample of 1800 composite households; Michael Wolfson, "A Guaranteed Income," *Policy Options*, January 1986, p. 36.

---

[2]Michael Wolfson, "A Guaranteed Income," *Policy Options*, January 1986, p. 36.

(instead of the five 20 percent groups we have encountered thus far), with even finer breakdowns at the upper levels. Wolfson's main concern was to examine the potential impact of several new proposals on the distribution of family income. These included proposals put forward by the Macdonald Commission (labelled UISP, for Universal Income Security Program, in Box 14.4) and Wolfson's own proposal. Consideration of the latter is not possible in a book of this scope, but the Macdonald Commission's suggestions are reviewed later in the chapter.

For the moment, we will focus attention on columns 1–3 of Box 14.4. We can see from the first row that, in 1985, the poorest 10 percent of all families had an average money income, before taxes and transfer income from government, of $2590. The second-lowest group (the 10–20 percentile group) had an average income of $4410. The third column indicates that after taxes and after receipt of transfer income from the government (note that most of these families would not have paid taxes), the average income of these lowest groups rose appreciably. Because of government programs, the average income of the lowest-percentile group, for example, increased from $2590 to $6570, or by 154 percent. In contrast, because of those same programs, the average family income of the top 5 percent of families decreased from $89 110 to $67 580. In general, the income of the bottom 50 percent of families was increased by government programs, while that of the top 50 percent was reduced. Other studies have shown that this redistribution of income occurs not because of the tax system — which, when all tax shelters and exemptions are taken into account, is really only slightly progressive — but because of government expenditures that favour lower-income groups.

Despite such significant redistribution of income, the poverty problem remains an important one in Canada. Its dimensions will now be examined more closely.

A PROFILE OF POVERTY IN CANADA

If we are to discuss poverty as a policy problem, we must know how income distribution and poverty are related. We might say that, in one sense, income distribution is a matter of numbers, while poverty is a matter of people and values. Measuring income distribution is just a routine task of positive economics. Measuring poverty, however, requires a normative judgement. It requires us to decide how far down the income scale a family can fall before they no longer have enough or have less than they ought to have.

Definitions of Poverty

There is no single definition of poverty that everyone accepts. Some call for an absolute income figure that indicates the minimum income a household would need to satisfy its basic wants. Others see poverty in relative terms: When income in general is rising, the income of the poor may also rise, but if their *relative* position remains unchanged, their sense of being poor will also remain. By such a definition, it is possible to have "poor" people in Canada who are better off than the "rich" in some other countries. They are poor in relation to the rest of their own society, with which they will inevitably compare their situation.

Statistics Canada and the Economic Council of Canada have tried to establish absolute "poverty lines" for different-sized families in different locations. These lines were originally calculated on the basis of studies in the 1960s that indicated

Canadian families spent, on average, about half their income on the basic essentials of food, clothing, and shelter. It was arbitrarily decided that a family that spent a considerably greater proportion of its income on these essentials — say, 70 percent — could be considered poor. The poverty line (to which Statistics Canada officially refers as the "low-income cutoff" level) was drawn at that point, and any household spending 70 percent or more on essentials was considered to be below it. Since then, with rising real incomes, the line has been lowered to those income levels at which 58.5 percent of income or more is spent on food, shelter, and clothing. Box 14.5 indicates the level of income that households of various sizes, in rural and urban areas, needed in order to operate above the low-income cutoff level in 1989.

There is, of course, much room for debate about the validity of such figures. Some critics contend that the low-income cutoff levels are too high, because, for example, some households that fall below them still seem to be able to afford cars and television sets. Others argue that the figures are too low, because people do not live "by bread alone" and many families close to the poverty line are unable to share in the cultural and social amenities that their society offers. The debate will never be settled, but the figures at least give social planners something definite to work with. We shall use them in other parts of this chapter.

Who Are the Poor?

In 1990, about 3.8 million Canadians, or about 14.6 percent of the population, were living below the poverty line. This represents a slight increase over the 1987 figure of 14.1 percent.

The incidence of poverty across the country is uneven in both geographic and social terms. Box 14.6 provides information on the regional incidence of poverty in 1989. In Ontario, only 5.2 percent of families lived below the poverty line, while in Quebec the proportion was 8.9 percent.

BOX 14.5 *Incomes at the Poverty Line, by Household Size and Location, 1989*

Persons per Household	Poverty Line Large Cities (500 000 +)	Rural Areas
1	$13 511	$ 9 198
2	18 314	12 469
3	23 279	15 849
4	26 803	18 247
5	29 284	19 936
6	31 787	21 640
7 or more	34 188	23 275

SOURCE: Statistics Canada, *Income Distribution by Size in Canada*, 1989, p. 178, Catalogue no. 13-207. Based on 1986 Family Expenditure Survey. Reproduced with permission of the Minister of Supply and Services Canada, 1992.

The Geographical Distribution of Poverty in Canada, 1989

BOX 14.6

Region	Percentage of Families below Poverty Line
Atlantic Provinces	8.7
Quebec	8.9
Ontario	5.2
Prairie Provinces	8.7
British Columbia	7.6

SOURCE: Statistics Canada, *Income Distribution by Size in Canada*, 1989, p. 168, Catalogue no. 13-207. Reproduced with permission of the Minister of Supply and Services Canada, 1992.

Box 14.7 provides data that associate various social factors with the incidence of poverty. For example, 31.1 percent of households headed by a woman, usually widowed or divorced, lived in poverty, as compared with only 5.2 percent of households headed by a man. Age is also shown to be an important factor: Very young families (family head under 25 years of age) had a very high poverty rate. (The rate is also very high among single elderly people, but the relevant data are not included in this table.) The level of education of the head of the family is also important: Only 3.7 percent of families in which the head had a university degree lived in poverty, compared with 14.3 percent of those in which the head had 0–8 years of schooling.

Incidence of Poverty by Selected Characteristics, 1989

BOX 14.7

Characteristics	Percentage of Families below Poverty Line
Sex of Family Head	
Male (under 65)	5.2
Female (under 65)	31.1
Age of Family Head	
24 and under	21.7
25–34	10.0
35–44	7.1
45–54	4.8
55–64	6.3
65 and over	3.7
Education of Family Head	
0–8 years	14.3
Some high school, no postsecondary	8.3
University degree	3.7

SOURCE: Statistics Canada, *Income Distribution by Size in Canada*, 1989, pp. 164, 168, Catalogue no. 13-207. Reproduced with permission of the Minister of Supply and Services Canada, 1992.

In 1971, the Special Senate Committee on Poverty determined in the course of extensive hearings that the poor can be classified in three general categories:

1. About one-quarter of the poor are unable to work because of severe disability.

2. About one-half of the poor are working, but are not able to earn an adequate income.

3. The remaining quarter of the poor are seemingly able to work but can't or won't find employment.[3]

The first group can be helped through special assistance programs and personal charity. The second group, that of the working poor, poses many special problems. Its members are the victims of erratic employment patterns related to swings in the business cycle; low-productivity jobs and low pay, often associated with low levels of education; and low mobility (see the accompanying For Example. . . box).

The third group, made up of those who are not working but are potentially able to work, also poses acute problems. To what extent are they simply not motivated to work, either because of generous social-assistance programs that reduce the penalty for not working or because of an absence of inner drive or a sense of responsibility? To what extent are they unable to sell their limited skills in the prevailing job market? We simply don't have reliable answers to these

FOR EXAMPLE...
The Dilemma of the Working Poor

Melvin Bender (a fictitious name, used to protect the identity of a real person) is a 49-year-old man living in a small Saskatchewan town. Throughout his adult life, he has been unable to find steady work. For a few years, he worked as a stock clerk in a grocery store, but the owner, having calculated that Melvin's marginal productivity was not equal to the minimum wage he was drawing, fired him.

Melvin has completed only four years of school. He is subject to epileptic seizures, for which he requires regular medication and which prohibit him from driving a car or operating many types of electrical machines and equipment. He would like very much to work. After having been released from several jobs, he has finally landed a part-time position with an apartment owner, for whom he mows the lawn and does other odd jobs. He manages to earn about $400 a month and qualifies for about $200 a month in social assistance, which leaves him with a monthly shortfall of about $300. His family helps him make up the difference. If he quit working, his monthly social allowance would be increased to about $600, meaning that his monthly shortfall would not increase. But Melvin Bender *wants* to work, and he resents the strong pressures put on him — not least by government social agencies — to quit.

_____

[3]Canada, Special Senate Committee on Poverty, *Poverty in Canada* (Ottawa: Minister of Supply and Services, 1971). See also T. Courchene, "Some Reflections on the Senate Hearings on Poverty," in *Economics Canada: Selected Readings*, ed. B.S. Keirstead et al. (Toronto: Macmillan of Canada, 1974), pp. 205–206.

questions. Some feel that generous welfare programs, along with unemployment insurance provisions, have contributed to some of the unemployment in the country. However, a study of welfare policy in Manitoba observed that, "contrary to a popular view, the typical individual on welfare is not an able-bodied person with a large family who prefers living in idleness drawing his welfare cheque to taking a job and supporting himself. Indeed, insofar as the provincial welfare rolls are concerned, the employable category makes up only a small proportion of the total, usually five percent or less."[4]

WHAT IS TO BE DONE ABOUT POVERTY?

This profile of poverty in Canada gives us an idea of the dimensions and complexity of the problem. However, while poverty may be difficult to define or measure, it is a painful reality to those who are poor. The question remains, what can be done about it?

Earlier in the chapter, we looked at some of the measures and programs that governments in Canada have developed to cope with the problem. A great deal of money is being spent in this aim, and, as Box 14.4, showed some redistribution of income from the richest to the poorest is indeed being effected by it.

There are many Canadians who feel that we are already doing enough — that we may even have gone too far in the direction of becoming what they call a "welfare state." We may, in fact, be spending enough — or at least as much as Canadian taxpayers will tolerate — but we may not be spending it in the right ways. The facts show that there is still a high incidence of poverty in the country and that, in recent years, it has been growing rather than diminishing.

What should be changed? In its examination of what it calls our "income-security system," the Macdonald Commission identified a number of serious weaknesses in the current system. It faulted the system as follows:[5]

1. It is ineffective. In spite of an expenditure of billions of dollars, there are still many Canadians living in poverty, while many income-security payments are made to people who are not poor.

2. It is too complex. There are too many programs and too many people administering them. It is often difficult for Canadians to discover what benefits they qualify for, and the interaction of programs results in many unforeseen pitfalls for beneficiaries.

3. It creates work disincentives. This situation may derive from three problems. Benefits are unrealistically high for some recipients or are paid for too long a period. The marginal tax or reduction rate of the system is extremely high, sometimes more than 100 percent. The benefits paid may encourage people to remain tied to unproductive or noncompetitive industries and may actively discourage them from taking advantage of better employment opportunities.

---

[4]Clarence L. Barber, *Welfare Policy in Manitoba*, A Report to the Planning and Priorities of Cabinet Secretariat, Province of Manitoba, December 1972, p. 8.

[5]Royal Commission on the Economic Union and Development Prospects for Canada, *Report*, 3 vols. (Toronto: University of Toronto Press, 1985), 2: 783.

4. It is inequitable. Because significant parts are based on tax exemptions rather than on direct transfers or tax credits, more benefits go to some high-income than to some low-income families. This anomaly appears, particularly, when the entire tax and transfer system is taken into account, including all of the tax breaks generally used by middle- and upper-class Canadians.

5. The sustainability of the system is sometimes claimed to be uncertain because of the age structure of our population, projections of continuing high levels of unemployment, and assumed perverse effects of demographic change.

In keeping with these criticisms, the commission recommended sweeping changes, involving a closer matching of benefits to needs, more incentives for the recipients of aid to continue working, and a simplification of the system.

A comprehensive approach to poverty through changes to the Income Tax Act, using "negative taxes" and a guaranteed base income, was proposed by the Macdonald Commission. This approach was related to what is known as a Guaranteed Annual Income policy (GAI) for Canada, which had come about as follows: In November 1970, the federal government published a White Paper, "Income Security for Canadians," calling for study of "an overall guaranteed-income program for the whole population." The government agreed to co-operate with provincial governments in researching the feasibility of such a program. The only provincial government to take up the offer was Manitoba, which launched a three-year research project in 1975. In 1973, the federal government issued its "Working Paper on Social Security in Canada," which gave broad support to new initiatives in the area of social security, including a negative-income-tax approach. Before examining the specific proposal of the Macdonald Commission, we shall outline the basic principles of a guaranteed-income program.

A Guaranteed-Income Program

Negative income tax
A general name for transfer systems that emphasize cash benefits: A basic benefit is available to households with zero earned income and is then reduced at a rate of substantially less than 100 percent as income is earned.

Economists concerned about the disincentive effects of the present welter of poorly co-ordinated transfer programs have long advocated "cashing out" all in-kind transfers and rolling all transfer programs into a single negative-income-tax program. The basic idea behind a negative income tax is very simple. Under a positive income tax — the kind currently used — individuals pay the government an amount that varies according to how much they earn. A **negative income tax** puts the same principle to work in reverse. It makes the government pay individuals an amount that varies in proportion to their earnings.

Box 14.8 shows how a negative income tax could be set up. The horizontal axis of the figure measures the income a household earns. The vertical axis measures what it actually receives after payments from or to the government. The 45° line represents the amount of disposable income households would have if there were no tax of any kind. The negative- and positive-income-tax schedules show the disposable income of families with the negative-income-tax program in force.

As the graph is drawn, the benefit received by a family with no earned income is $6000, which presumably is the amount required for survival. The family receives this income as a transfer payment from the government. Starting from zero earned income, transfer payments are reduced by $0.50 for each $1 earned. The earnings themselves are not taxed until they have reached $12 000. This means, for example, that when a family earns $3000, its total received income will be its earned income of $3000, plus $6000 in transfer payments, minus a

A Possible Negative-Income-Tax Schedule   BOX 14.8

In the graph below, families are not taxed on earned income that is less than $12 000. Instead, when earned income is zero, they receive a transfer payment (a so-called *negative tax*) of $6000. This transfer payment is reduced by half the earned income as earned income exceeds zero. When earned income reaches a level of $12 000, the earned income is still not taxed, but transfer payments will have been reduced to zero (by half of the earned income). A *positive* income tax of 50 percent is first applied to earnings above $12 000.

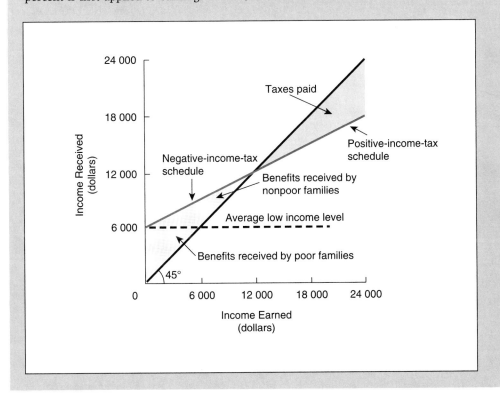

reduction in transfer payments of $1500 (the reduction being equal to half of the earned income). This gives the family a total received income of $7500.

When earned income equals $12 000, or twice the amount considered necessary for survival, a break-even point is reached. Earned income is still not taxed, but transfer payments will have been reduced to zero (by half of the earned income). Therefore, received income will be $12 000. Beyond an earned-income level of $12 000, a positive income tax kicks in. All additional earnings are taxed at 50 percent.

The negative income tax has the great advantage of maintaining work incentives for all beneficiaries. In our example, the marginal tax rate for poor families is only 50 percent. This rate is presumably low enough to prevent widespread withdrawal of effort. Note, however, that the cost of the program is still much greater than the initial size of the aggregate income deficit. All but the very poorest families receive more than the minimum they need to reach the low-income cutoff. What is more, many nonpoor families — those with earned incomes in the $6000 to $12 000 range — also receive benefits.

Many practical questions about the cost and workability of a negative income tax cannot be answered by economic theory. They can be answered only on the basis of actual experience with running such a program.

The UISP (Universal Income Security Program) of the Macdonald Commission

In its search for a better income-security program, the Macdonald Commission ultimately recommended a comprehensive reform, which it called a Universal Income Security Program (UISP). Though the proposal is quite a simple one, and closely resembles the negative-tax, or guaranteed-income, programs that we have just been discussing, it was designed to accomplish a number of things:

1. An adequate level of benefits for those who are unable to work.

2. Income supplements for the working poor.

3. A marginal tax-back rate that will not discourage those who may be able to work their way out of the need for benefit payments.

4. Basic equity among Canadians in different family and life situations.

Concretely, the UISP recommendations were as follows:

1. The elimination of certain programs that existed at the time, such as the Guaranteed Income Supplement (GIS), Family Allowances, Child Tax Credits, Married Tax Exemptions, and Child Exemptions.

2. The creation of a universally available income transfer. Several amounts were suggested. In Option B, which the commission itself recommended and which will be used here for analysis, the personal tax exemption would be retained and each adult in a family would be guaranteed a basic income of $2750, with an additional $750 per child under eighteen. Single parents would receive an extra $2000 (the first child being treated, in effect, as an adult), and single elderly individuals would receive an extra $1075. Therefore, there would be guarantees of $5500 and $3825 for a single parent with child and a single elderly person, respectively.

3. The guarantees would then be reduced or taxed back at the rate of 20 percent of total family income.

4. The provincial governments should "top-up" the income of the most needy from their current assistance budgets.

The Macdonald Commission itself noted that these proposals differed from many Guaranteed Annual Income proposals in that the guarantees the commission proposed were relatively low, while simultaneously the effective tax rate (or tax-back) was also low.

Possible Effects of the UISP

Michael Wolfson, in a study to which we referred earlier (see the discussion of Box 14.4), tried to assess the possible effects of the UISP on the current distribution of income in Canada. Using Option B, but modifying it slightly for purposes of analysis, he determined that it would add significantly to the income of the poorest families in Canada. These results are given in columns 4 and 5 of Box 14.4. Column 4, for example, indicates that the lowest 10 percent of income families would have their average income increase from $6570 to $8100 under the UISP, which represents an increase of 23.3 percent in their income (the percentage figure is given in column 5).

Other low-income families would also receive increases in income, but not by nearly as much. The families in the top 50 percent of the income scale would see slight decreases in their incomes (in percentage terms).

What are some of the potential problems with such a program, and what are the chances that it might be implemented?

One potential problem is posed by the diversity of living standards in different parts of the country. The business of setting benefits would be greatly complicated by the need to reconcile regional interests. A further problem is how the UISP would actually relate to other programs. Many economists believe that it would make great sense to use a comprehensive guaranteed income to replace all existing social-insurance and public charity programs. Existing programs are not easy to eliminate, however. Each has its own army of lobbyists among beneficiaries, politicians, and public officials. But simply to tack a guaranteed income onto the existing welter of programs would increase rather than reduce the total cost of all transfer programs. It would also increase rather than reduce the complexity, overlaps, and conflicting incentives that characterize the current system. For the moment, it appears that political realities may keep the UISP in the textbooks, but interest in the scheme has become so widespread that it may not stay there forever.

CONCLUSIONS

The economics of poverty is, in many ways, the most discouraging branch of economics to study. Economists, of course, have plenty of simple and elegant solutions. If we really want to eliminate poverty, what we need to do is abolish all existing programs and replace them with a single, streamlined negative income tax, or something like it. But our political system is not built to pursue a goal such as eliminating poverty in a straightforward, single-minded way. It is a system of give and take that responds to many opposing interests, and the current array of poverty programs is the natural income.

SUMMARY

1. Income is distributed unequally in Canada. The *Lorenz curve* and the *Gini coefficient* provide useful measurements of the extent of inequality.

2. Governments at all levels use taxation and expenditure programs to alleviate poverty and reduce income inequality. A considerable amount of redistribution occurs through government programs, but the poverty problem has not been solved. Indeed, it seems to be getting worse.

3. In 1989, more than three million Canadians were classified as poor, according to the most commonly used measure of poverty. This measure, officially called the "low-income cutoff" but popularly referred to as the "poverty line," is the amount of income that allows a family to spend no more than

58.5 percent of income on the basic necessities of food, shelter, and clothing. The amount of income that constitutes the poverty line differs with family size and location.

4. There are different types of poor people. About one-quarter of the poor are unable to work, one-half work but are unable to earn a sufficient income, and the remaining quarter are seemingly able to work but cannot or will not find employment. Different strategies are required to meet the needs of each group.

5. Many proposals for reform of our income-security programs have been advanced, including a radical negative-income-tax, or guaranteed-income, program. The strongest support for such a proposal in recent years came in 1985 from the Macdonald Commission, which recommended a Universal Income Security Program (UISP). The very lowest income groups would receive a sizable boost to their income under this program. It remains to be seen, however, whether the UISP has a greater chance of being implemented than similar suggestions have had in the past.

KEY TERMS

Lorenz curve   Gini coefficient   negative income tax

KEY BOXES

Box 14.3 The Lorenz Curve and the Gini Coefficient of Inequality

Box 14.8 A Possible Negative-Income-Tax Schedule

REVIEW QUESTIONS

1. What is the shape of the Lorenz curve for an economy in which income is distributed equally? How does the Lorenz curve for the Canadian economy compare with this standard?

2. How is poverty defined in Canada? By this definition, can we ever solve the poverty problem?

3. What has been the trend of poverty in Canada during the 1980s and early 1990s? (Consult sources in your library for current data.) How do you account for this?

4. What are the major income-security programs in Canada?

5. Describe briefly the main features of the UISP.

6. It is sometimes said that poverty is not the fault of individuals, but of society. Do you agree? What do you think the statement means? Because "society" is itself composed of individuals, does it mean that certain individuals who are not poor are responsible for the poverty of those who are? If so, which individuals are responsible? Do you think that any of your own actions may contribute to causing someone else to be poor?

7. According to the logic of the federal government's low-income standard, an officially poor family is likely not to be able to afford an adequate diet. Do you think it

odd that so many poverty-level families, who cannot afford adequate nutrition, do seem able to afford cars, television sets, clothes dryers, and air conditioners? Is it natural and reasonable that a poor family should own such things? Would you favour legislation that attempted to force poor families to spend more on food and less on seemingly unessential items such as the appliances listed above? Could the data on appliances indicate a defect in the official method of measuring poverty?

8. Suppose that there were a universally effective guaranteed-income program in force, so that measured poverty was entirely eliminated. Would you then be willing to see other social-insurance programs, including social security (retirement), unemployment insurance, and medicare, abolished? Why or why not?

9. Discussions of "waste" in poverty programs often focus on the fact that some benefits go to families whose incomes are above the poverty line. After reading this chapter, do you agree that it is wasteful to pay benefits to some nonpoor families? Would you favour a program that cut off all benefits as soon as the poverty line was reached? In what ways might such a program itself be wasteful? Discuss.

10. The Russian Revolution, with its overthrow of the czar and the government as well as its takeover of land and other factors of production, was partly designed to reallocate income and wealth. Assuming that the revolution accomplished this, at least in part, draw probable Lorenz curves to illustrate the situation in Russia before and after the revolution. What would have happened to the Gini coefficient as a result of the revolution?

11. Using the current minimum-wage rate in your province, calculate the annual earnings of a person who works a 40-hour week, 52 weeks a year. From this amount, subtract estimates of (1) reasonable costs for transportation to and from work (for example, the cost of a monthly bus pass times twelve); (2) the cost of an adequate one-bedroom apartment; (3) the cost of a sufficient amount of groceries each month; (4) the monthly cost of a telephone; (5) an amount for newspapers and perhaps a couple of magazines, as well as an occasional movie; and (6) a reasonable amount for clothing, taking into consideration that winter clothing can be expensive. How well do you think this hard-working, reliable individual who holds down a full-time job could live on these wages? Do you think that he or she could do a reasonable job of supporting a dependent child?

12. Under a proposed negative-income-tax scheme to eliminate poverty, the lowest income level a family would receive is set at $8000 per year.

a. If the marginal benefit reduction is set at 50 percent, after what level of income would taxes become positive?

b. If a family had an *earned income* of $8000, what total income would they receive under this scheme?

Canada in the International Market

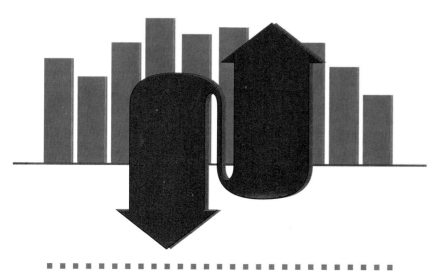

Canada's International Trade and Balance of Payments

WHAT YOU WILL LEARN IN THIS CHAPTER

After studying this chapter, you will be able to

1. Apply the principle of comparative advantage to international trade.

2. Discuss the issues involved in the protectionism versus free trade debate.

3. Discuss recent trends in Canada's trade policy.

4. Describe the basic features of the balance of payments.

5. Show how foreign-exchange rates are determined.

6. Describe the purchasing-power parity theory of exchange rates.

7. Define *balance of payments equilibrium.*

8. Examine the connection between interest-rate policy and foreign-exchange rates.

A Preview   *Canada's Role in the World Economy*

If Canada depended less on other countries, Canadians might breathe more easily. However, as this article indicates (and as the chapter will explain), Canada purchases many of the things it needs from other countries and it depends on others to buy many of the things it produces. The question is not *whether* we should trade with other countries, but how best to organize this trade.

Canada's Trade Outlook Cloudy

Canada's trade performance in the past couple of years has been uninspiring.

And that's no wonder, given the high value of the Canadian dollar vis-à-vis the U.S. dollar, which is eroding our competitiveness. Our surplus on goods trade slipped to $6.9 billion in 1989 from $10.1 billion the year before.

This year, however, we're doing better, but not because of any fundamental improvement in our competitiveness. Rather, we're benefiting from a surge in grain exports combined with weak import demand as the economy slips into recession.

Three major factors overhang the world trading system at the moment: the December 31 due date for a new pact under the General Agreement on Tariffs & Trade; U.S. protectionist forces, currently slumbering but not dead; and the emergence of giant trading blocs.

A new GATT agreement is key to keeping U.S. protectionist forces at bay and ensuring that the emerging trading blocs are outward, not inward, looking. Similarly, containment of U.S. protectionist forces is critical in making sure that the new, integrated European Community market won't earn the nickname "Fortress Europe" when it emerges at the end of 1992.

Canada is — and always has been — a strong advocate of an open world trading system. Exports are our lifeblood, amounting to about a quarter of gross domestic product. But we have to protect ourselves as well. That's why we pursued and signed the Free Trade Agreement with the United States and why we've joined in the U.S.–Mexico free-trade talks.

Should we end up with a North American trading bloc, it would rival the EC in population — 360 million versus the EC's 350 million — though it would not come close in terms of trade volume. The EC accounts for almost 40 percent of world trade (excluding the Soviet Union), while Canada, the United States, and Mexico combined account for less than 20 percent. One reason for the smaller trade flows in North America is Mexico's low income; another is the United States' self-sufficiency. Exports of goods are equivalent to just 7 percent of U.S. gross national product versus 22 percent in Canada, 8 percent in Mexico, and an average 23 percent in the EC.

However, neither the current Canada–U.S. Free Trade Agreement, nor a possible future Canada–U.S.–Mexico pact, is sufficient to guarantee Canada a bright future as an exporter.

Indeed, the expected benefits of the Canada–U.S. free-trade deal may not materialize because of the high Canadian dollar. There's not a lot of hard evidence of damage from the high Canadian dollar yet. Indeed, Canada's surplus on goods trade with the United States is likely to be a little higher this year than last.

But there are lots of indications that the high Canadian dollar is doing damage — mounting numbers of plant closures, stories of companies moving or considering moving to the United States. Even more worrisome is the concern that more and more companies on both sides of the border will choose the United States for most of their new plants.

Obviously, if the Canadian dollar comes down — as many economists expect — the damage can be stemmed

or even reversed. A value of 80¢ (U.S.) would probably leave most companies in a competitive position, and many will probably be able to manage with the Canadian dollar between 81¢ (U.S.) and 82¢ (U.S.).

But even if the Canadian dollar moves to the low 80¢ (U.S.) range, the 1990s don't promise to be great years for Canadian trade. Resource prospects are middling, with excess supply likely to keep grain prices down and environmental concerns adding to the costs of forestry and mining efforts.

But when we move into the twenty-first century, the picture could brighten considerably as the developing world becomes more industrialized, bringing with it greater demand for the resources we have in such abundance.

SOURCE: Catherine Harris, "Canada's Trade Outlook Cloudy," *Financial Post*, October 13, 1990, p. 18. Reproduced with permission.

CANADA IN THE INTERNATIONAL MARKET

Much has been said in this book about markets — about the market economy in general and the Canadian market system in particular. We have considered several types of markets within Canada, particularly the service sector and the labour market. It is time now to examine Canada's position within the international market. The Canadian economy, much more than that of most countries, is tied into a vast network of other economies. In 1990, Canada sold 27 percent of the goods and services it produced to other countries, and bought from others 30 percent of the goods and services it consumed. The Canadian economy depends in particular on the economy of the United States, and it is this unique interdependence with our neighbour to the south that forms part of the subject matter of this chapter, and the core of the next.

As we will see in Chapter 16, global changes are taking place in international economic relations. Three major trading blocs appear to be developing: a European bloc, dominated by a large, united Germany; an Asian bloc, dominated by Japan; and a North American bloc, consisting of Canada, the United States, and Mexico and dominated by the United States. These developments are of profound significance for Canada, and therefore receive special treatment in Chapter 16.

First, however, it is important that we know something about the need for, and the mechanics of, international trade: Why should a country engage in international trade at all? On what basis should it participate? How is international trade conducted? We must be able to answer all these questions, as well as those raised in the Preview: Why, for example, it is not good enough for Canada to have a $6.9 billion trade surplus with the United States? And how is the value of the Canadian dollar actually determined? Furthermore, how does that value affect our economy? This chapter will explore these and many other questions arising from Canada's involvement in international trade.

The basic rationale for both domestic and international trade was in fact examined in Chapter 2, with its discussion of opportunity cost and comparative advantage. (You might find it helpful to review those concepts before proceeding with the discussion in this chapter.) In Chapter 2, however, the notion of comparative advantage was not applied specifically to international trade, and arguments for and against its application have not yet been examined. This will now be done. In addition, a closer look at Canada's trade with other countries will help us to appreciate the important role that international trade plays in determining the level of economic activity in Canada. Not only the exchange of goods and services but also the purchase and sale of international bonds and stocks are important to our economy. It is this complex of international transactions that we describe in this chapter.

AN INTERNATIONAL APPLICATION OF COMPARATIVE ADVANTAGE

We saw in Chapter 2 that trade between regions or countries is economically beneficial whenever such regions or countries have a comparative advantage in the production of some goods. They have such an advantage when they can, in comparison with other regions, produce a good at lower *opportunity cost*, measured in terms of other forgone goods. The concept was illustrated numerically in Chapter 2 with the example of two farmers picking strawberries and peas (see page 40). On the basis of their opportunity costs, we determined that Farmer A should pick peas, and Farmer B, strawberries. If, subsequent to such specialization, they wished to consume both goods, they would have to engage in trade with each other.

The concept of comparative advantage can be illustrated graphically, using a set of production possibilities frontiers for two countries, rather than two people. This is done, using the example of Spain and Norway, in Box 15.1, which shows three production possibilities frontiers. Part (a) is the production possibilities frontier for Spain. It is assumed that Spain can produce up to 500 t of grain per year if it produces no fish (point *B*). If it produces no grain, it can catch up to 250 t of fish per year (point *D*). The combinations of grain and fish that Spain can possibly produce are thus represented by the line running from *D* to *B*.

Box 15.1(b) shows the corresponding production possibilities frontier for Norway. If Norwegians devote all their time to fishing, they can catch up to 200 t of fish per year (point *B'*). If they devote all their time to farming, they can grow up to 200 t of grain (point *D'*). The line joining points *B'* and *D'* thus represents the Norwegian production possibilities frontier.

Pretrade production and consumption

Let us assume that before trade begins, Spain produces and consumes 350 t of grain and 75 t of fish. This is shown as point *A* on Spain's production possibilities frontier. Correspondingly, Norway is assumed to produce and consume 100 t each of fish and grain. This is shown by point *A'* on Norway's frontier.

The world production possibilities frontier

A production possibilities frontier for the world as a whole (consisting of just these two countries in our example) can be constructed as in Box 15.1(c). The world frontier is constructed as follows. First, assume that both countries devote all their labour to grain. That gives 500 t of grain from Spain plus 200 t from Norway, or 700 t of grain in all (point *R* in Box 15.1[c]). Starting from there, assume that world fish output is to be increased. For maximum efficiency, Norwegian farmers should be the first to switch to fishing, because the opportunity cost of fish is lower in Norway (1 t of grain per tonne of fish) than it is in Spain (2 t of grain per tonne of fish). As Norwegians switch to fishing, then, world production moves up and to the left along line segment *RQ*.

When all Norwegians have abandoned farming for fishing, the world will have arrived at point *Q* — 500 t of grain (all Spanish) and 200 t of fish (all Norwegian). From that point on, the only way to get more fish is to have Spanish farmers switch to fishing. At the opportunity cost of 2 t of grain per tonne of fish, this moves the economy along line segment *QS*. When all Spanish farmers are fishing, the world arrives at point *S*, where 450 t of fish and no grain are produced. The production possibilities frontier for the world as a whole is thus the kinked line *RQS*.

The effects of trade

The pretrade production point for the world as a whole lies inside the world production possibilities frontier. Adding the quantities of fish and grain from *A* and *A'* together, we arrive at point *P* in Box 15.1(c) — 450 t of grain and 175 t of fish. This is inefficient; the world economy as a whole could produce more of both goods. To improve efficiency, both countries must specialize.

Suppose that Spain shifts its production from 350 t of grain and 75 t of fish (point *A*) to 500 t of grain and no fish (point *B*). It then trades the extra 150 t of

A Graphic Illustration of Comparative Advantage

BOX 15.1

This box shows production possibilities frontiers for Spain, Norway, and the two countries combined (World). Before trade, Spain produces and consumes at point *A*, and Norway at point *A'*. Together, these correspond to "world consumption" point *P*, which is inside the world production possibilities frontier. After trade begins, Spain specializes in producing grain (point *B*) and trades part of the grain for fish, moving to point *C*. Norway specializes in producing fish (point *B'*) and reaches point *C'* through trade. As a result, world efficiency is improved, and point *Q* is attained on the world production possibilities frontier.

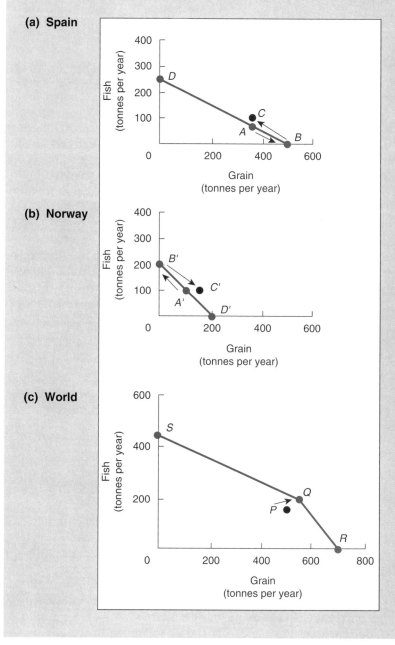

grain for 100 t of Norwegian fish. Spain's consumption thus ends up at point *C*, while its production remains at *B*.

At the same time, Norway shifts its production from *A'* to *B'*, specializing entirely in fish. The extra 100 t of fish are traded for the 150 t of Spanish grain, thus moving Norwegian consumption to point *C'*.

As the result of specialization plus trade, then, both Spain and Norway have moved to points that lie outside their own national production possibilities frontiers. As they do so, the world as a whole moves from point *P*, inside its production possibilities frontier, to point *Q*, on the world frontier. As in the numerical example, specialization improves world efficiency, increases world production of both goods, and leaves both countries better off than they would have been in the absence of trade.

PROTECTIONISM VERSUS FREE TRADE

Our illustration of the theory of comparative advantage has been for a very simple, two-country trading world. However, the theory has been extended many times to cover more complex and realistic situations. The extensions have covered situations in which there are more than two countries, in which there is more than one factor of production and more than two commodities, and in which production possibilities frontiers are not straight lines, to name just a few. The result of all this additional theoretical work has been to show that the theory of comparative advantage is very general. Regardless of the initial assumptions or the complexity of the situations, international trade, following the principles of comparative advantage, offers all countries involved an opportunity for mutual gain compared with the no-trade alternative.

But if international trade is so unequivocally beneficial, why do free-trade policies always and everywhere face opposition? Why does every government feel pressure to create **protectionist** policies, such as **tariffs** and **import quotas**, that will restrict the free importation of goods from abroad? The sources and logic of protectionism form the subject of this section.

The Terms-of-Trade Argument

One argument in favour of trade restrictions concerns the possibility of manipulating the international terms of trade. In our example of Spain and Norway, we supposed that the terms of trade of grain for fish would be set by competitive bargaining and haggling by private traders from each country. Such a process might not always result in the exact 1.5:1 trading ratio of grain to fish assumed in the example, but it would not be surprising to see the gains from trade divided fairly evenly when the terms of trade are competitively set.

In the real world, however, a country may sometimes find reason to interfere with the competitive determination of the terms of trade. Note, for example, that Canada is one of the world's leading producers and exporters of nickel (producing about 35 percent of world output) and a leading importer of textiles. To take advantage of its partial monopoly power in the nickel market, Canada might restrict nickel exports, hoping to drive up the world price. Similarly, to take advantage of its buying power in the textile market, it might restrict textile imports, hoping to drive the world price down. The export and import restrictions would, of course, have the effect of reducing the total volume of trade. Worldwide gains from trade would thus be less than they would be in the absence of

Protectionism
Policies of shielding domestic industry from foreign competition.

Tariff
A tax levied on imported goods.

Import quota
A limitation on the quantity of a good that can be imported in a given time period.

protectionist measures. Nonetheless, manipulating the terms of trade might leave Canada with a bigger share of the smaller world total gains from trade, making Canadians better off, on balance, than under a free-trade policy.

However, the terms-of-trade argument for protectionism, which has been known for more than a hundred years, has its limitations. One major limitation concerns the possibility of retaliation by trading partners. If other countries react to Canadian trade restrictions by imposing trade restrictions of their own, the attempt to manipulate the terms of trade may well fail. The volume of world trade will then shrink even more, and all countries will be left worse off than under free trade.

The Income-Distribution Argument

A more complete understanding of the origins of trade restrictions requires consideration of their effects on the distribution of income within each trading country. Take, as an example, the effects on the Canadian economy of increased imports of Chinese textiles after a period in which such imports were somewhat restricted. The impact of increased textile imports can be divided into three parts. First, all consumers of textiles in Canada will benefit because textiles will be cheaper than before. Second, the Chinese may increase their purchases of Canadian goods, which will benefit workers in Canadian export-oriented industries. Finally, Canadian textile workers and manufacturers will suffer a decreased demand for their products.

Textile workers and manufacturers with relatively mobile skills or assets can escape most of the impact by moving to other industries. Some workers, however, are less mobile because of personal circumstances or the specialization of their skills. They are likely to suffer a loss of income that will more than offset the benefits they receive as consumers of cheaper textiles. In the aggregate, the loss to the group adversely affected may be more than offset by the gains to others in the economy. But this fact is not likely to make much impression on unemployed textile workers. They will see free trade as a threat and will campaign for protection. The government will then have a difficult political decision to make. Suppose that the government decides that the textile workers deserve consideration. Does this mean protectionism should be supported? Not necessarily. The policy of protection might be compared with alternative policies that could have the same distributive effects. One such alternative may be to subsidize the retraining and relocation of textile workers who lose their jobs. Another may be simply to offer these workers cash compensation.

How do these alternatives rate? In terms of efficiency, they are not perfect, but probably they are better than tariffs or quotas. They seem to offer two advantages. One is that benefits are more precisely concentrated on the people who need them. The other is that the tax burden required to fund the alternative programs is likely to be distributed more equitably than the burden of higher textile prices would be.

The National-Security Argument

Another argument advanced for the restriction of trade involves considerations of nation building and defence. It was pointed out in Chapter 3 that Canada and the United States experimented with free trade on certain products for twelve years, between 1854 and 1866. Following the American Civil War, a wave of nationalism led the United States to build tariff barriers against other countries, including

Canada. Canada retaliated with barriers of its own, also in the name of nationalism. It was felt that tariffs would help industry in central Canada to grow more quickly, and a strong industrial base was considered essential for the building of a Canadian nation. Exponents of such views are not deterred by counterarguments that their policies may lead to inefficiency. In their view, it is more important to have a relatively inefficient *Canadian* industry than a more efficient non-Canadian industry. In time of emergency, it is argued, it would be important to have adequate Canadian supplies of strategic goods such as energy and basic metals. One problem is that tariffs may actually result in *more* foreign ownership of Canadian industries, as foreigners try to get behind the Canadian tariff wall.

The Infant-Industry Argument

Canada appears to have a strong comparative advantage in the production of natural resources, which it has in abundance and to which it has attracted considerable capital, and a comparative disadvantage in the production of many manufactured goods, particularly those that are labour intensive. Does this mean that Canada is destined forever to have a weak manufacturing sector? There are those who argue that this need not be the case. Some industries, it is argued, might fare well after a while if they received support during their development or infant phase, until they were mature enough to compete with the industries of other countries. The Canadian steel industry, for example, is as efficient in some of its branches as comparable branches of that industry are in other countries. It has been permitted, so the argument runs, to develop expertise and capital over the long run to make itself competitive. This argument may well be sound for some industries, but many industries in Canada, for resource or climatic reasons, may never be able to compete. How can one distinguish one request for protection from another, or know which infants will eventually thrive? Once the protection is given, how easily can it be taken away? These are difficult practical problems that must be faced in evaluating this argument for trade restrictions.

CANADA IN INTERNATIONAL TRADE: SOME FACTS

Exports and Imports

Canada's relative strength in international trade is indicated in Box 15.2. In 1990, Canada had a large trade surplus (that is, it exported more than it imported) in such products as energy, forestry, and agricultural and fish products, while it had a substantial deficit (that is, it imported more than it exported) in machinery and equipment and consumer goods.

Canada's Trading Partners

It is not surprising that a large proportion of Canada's trade is with the United States, its closest neighbour and the world's largest economy. This trade generates a healthy surplus for Canada in most years — tempting business people and politicians in the United States to press for protection against Canadian trade, and conversely tempting Canadians to bargain for even more access to the U.S. market. (Note particularly the huge Canadian surplus in forestry products in Box

15.2. It is no coincidence that recent U.S. calls for protection have occurred precisely in this sector.)

Box 15.3 indicates that, in recent years, Canada has relied on the U.S. market for 75 percent of its exports. At the same time, about 70 percent of its imports come from the United States. This dependency on the U.S. market increased considerably over the course of the 1980s. In the mid-1970s, Canada's exports to the United States represented only about 65 percent of its total exports, and imports from the United States accounted for about the same percentage of its total imports. Canada has made overtures to such trading blocs as the European Community to increase its trade, and it is paying more attention to what are known as the Pacific Rim countries, but the actual development of its trade in recent times indicates that, so far, such efforts at a wider geographical dispersion of trade have been largely fruitless.

CANADA'S BALANCE OF PAYMENTS

Balance of payments
A measure of all economic transactions between Canada and other countries in a given year. The balance of payments is in surplus when receipts in the current and capital accounts exceed total payments to foreigners. It is in deficit when such receipts are less than total payments.

Canada records its exports and imports of goods and services, along with other international transactions, in a series of accounts that together document the country's **balance of payments** — a measure of all the annual business transactions between Canada and the rest of the world. In the balance-of-payments accounts, Canada's international receipts and payments are broken down into three categories: (1) transactions in goods and services produced in the current year, summarized in what is called the *current account*; (2) transactions in short- and long-term securities and bonds, summarized in the *capital account*; and (3) changes in official holdings of reserves, recorded in the *official-reserve account*.

Canada's Trade Balance by Commodity Groups, 1990 — BOX 15.2

This box shows that in 1990, as in most years, Canada exported more commodities than it imported. Its overall trade balance in commodities was $10.7 billion. The largest positive balances were achieved in natural resources. While some industrial sectors had a small positive balance, the machines and equipment and consumer goods sectors produced significant negative balances.

Commodity	Exports	Imports	Balance
	(billions of dollars)		
Agricultural and fish products	12.8	8.7	+4.1
Energy products	14.4	8.1	+6.3
Forest products	20.8	1.3	+19.5
Industrial goods	30.0	26.1	+3.9
Machines and equipment	28.8	42.5	−13.7
Automobile products	33.9	30.5	+3.4
Consumer goods	2.8	15.8	−13.0
Other	2.5	2.3	+0.2
Total	146.0	135.3	+10.7

SOURCE: Adapted from Statistics Canada, *Canadian Economic Observer*, May 1991, pp. 5.1.1, and 5.1.2, Catalogue no. 11-010. Reproduced with permission of the Minister of Supply and Services Canada, 1992.

BOX 15.3   *Where Canada Exports*

As the map below indicates, Canada depends on one market, the United States, to purchase about 75 percent of its exports. This dependency has been increasing: In the mid-1970s, countries outside North America bought 35 percent of Canada's exports; by 1990, that figure had dropped to 25 percent. Similarly, Canada imported 33 percent of its goods from outside North America in the mid-1970s, compared with 30 percent in 1990.

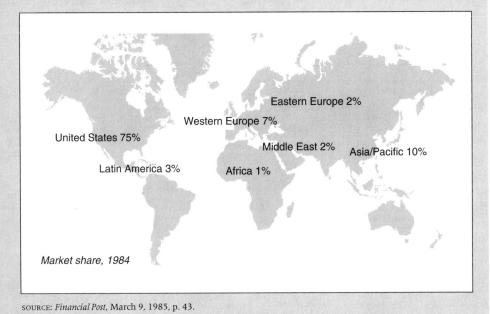

Eastern Europe 2%

Western Europe 7%

United States 75%

Middle East 2%   Asia/Pacific 10%

Latin America 3%   Africa 1%

Market share, 1984

SOURCE: *Financial Post*, March 9, 1985, p. 43.

The Current Account

Current account
The account that records all transactions involving imports and exports of goods and services, plus international unilateral transfer payments.

Box 15.4 illustrates the relationship among these accounts for the year 1990, showing the entries in the **current account** at the top. In that year, Canada ran a current-account deficit of $15 989 million. In merchandise trade, it exported considerably more than it imported (as it usually does), so that it had a sizable surplus in this part of the account (see line 2). However, as is also quite customary, it had deficits in its service transactions (line 3) and in the area of investment income and transfers (line 4) that were large enough to more than offset the surplus in merchandise trade. Services include travel, in which Canada normally has a deficit, and investment income and transfers include receipts and payments for interest and dividend transactions. Canada normally pays much more to foreigners in the form of interest and dividends than it receives from them, indicating that foreigners have invested much more in the Canadian economy than Canadians have invested abroad. The deficit on the current account of $15 989 million means that Canadians were required in 1990 to obtain at least that much foreign currency from sources other than trade to pay for their purchases of foreign goods and services. Fortunately, the capital account provides such an alternative source.

Canada's Balance of Payments, 1990 — BOX 15.4

This box shows, in simplified form, the actual Canadian balance of payments in 1990. In the current account, a surplus of $10 798 million in merchandise trade was more than offset by large deficits in service transactions, investment income, and transfers, creating an overall deficit in the current account of $15 989 million. In the capital account, capital inflows exceeded capital outflows by $20 959 million (as a result of Canada's high interest rates in 1990, among other things). This surplus of foreign funds offset the current-account deficit, creating an addition of $4970 million (including errors of estimate) in the official-reserve account, referred to as Official Holdings of International Currencies in this table.

Account	Item	Receipt	Payments	Balance
		(millions of dollars)		
1. Current Account	Merchandise exports	146 057	—	
	Merchandise imports	—	135 259	+10 798
	Services	22 378	30 205	−7 827
	Investment income and transfers	19 313	38 274	−18 961
	Balance on Current Account	187 748	203 738	−15 989
2. Capital Account	Capital inflows	30 255	—	
	Capital outflows	—	9 296	
	Balance on Capital Account			+20 959
3. Official Holdings of International Currencies (including errors of estimate)				+4 970

SOURCE: Statistics Canada, *Canadian Economic Observer*, May 1991, p. 5.20, Catalogue no. 11-010. Reproduced with permission of the Minister of Supply and Services Canada, 1992.

The Capital Account

Current-account transactions are not the only transactions that take place between residents of different countries. We must also consider international lending and borrowing and international sales and purchases of assets, which are recorded in the **capital account**. A Canadian company might, for example, obtain a short-term loan from a Milwaukee bank to finance the purchase of a shipload of beer for import to Canada. The Ontario government might get a long-term loan from Citibank of New York to help finance construction of a hydro-electric project. A Canadian millionaire might open an account in a Swiss bank. Or an oil-rich Middle Easterner might purchase Saskatchewan farmland or shares in a Canadian corporation.

All these transactions and others like them are called "transactions on capital account." Purchases of Canadian assets by foreigners and borrowing by Canadians from foreigners (through the selling of bonds to foreigners, for example) create a flow of currency into Canada and are therefore called **capital inflows**. Purchase of foreign assets by Canadians and loans by Canadians to foreigners

Capital account
The account that records all transactions involving international borrowing and lending and all international purchases and sales of assets for investment purposes.

Capital inflows
Purchases of domestic assets by foreigners and borrowing by domestic residents from foreigners.

Capital outflows
Purchases of foreign assets by domestic residents and borrowing by foreigners from domestic sources.

(through the purchase of foreign bonds, for example) create a flow of currency out of Canada and are therefore called **capital outflows**.

As Box 15.4 shows, in 1990, there was a *net* capital inflow (inflows minus outflows) of $20 959 million into the Canadian economy. Much of this inflow can be attributed to the fact that interest rates were much higher in Canada than in the United States, encouraging Americans and others to buy Canadian bonds, and thereby increasing the flow of currency into Canada.

The Official-Reserve Account

Official-reserve account
The account that records transactions involving purchases and sales of reserves of foreign currency by central banks.

The net capital-account inflows exceeded the current-account deficit in 1990 by $4970 million, which means that in the third account, the **official-reserve account**, our foreign-currency holdings went up by that amount (net of statistical errors, which always creep into these accounts).

The balance of Canada's international payments can be summed up as follows: Canada traditionally buys more goods and services from others than it sells. This shows up as a deficit on the current account. This deficit is usually financed by a net inflow of foreign currency on the capital account. Deficits in one or more of the accounts within the balance of payments are matched by surpluses in other accounts (and if, for example, there were deficits in both current and capital accounts, they would be matched by a corresponding change in the reserve account); thus, the overall account is always in balance.

The Current Account Reviewed

While the overall balance is always in balance, the perennial deficit in Canada's current account deserves special consideration. Within the current account, Canada generally has a favourable balance on trade in goods, known as the merchandise balance. This balance has been negative in only two years since 1960. However, in the service sector, particularly in the receipts and payments associated with travel and interest and dividend transactions, Canada almost always has a deficit more than large enough to counteract the favourable merchandise balance.

This situation poses unique and severe problems for the Canadian economy. It means that Canada is constantly under pressure to borrow enough foreign currency through its capital account to pay for the deficit experienced in the current account. For this purpose, interest rates must be kept at a level high enough to entice foreign lenders, but perhaps too high to generate enough domestic investment to create full employment. Problems of this kind will be discussed in greater detail in the macroeconomics portion of the text.

THE THEORY OF EXCHANGE-RATE DETERMINATION

How Supply and Demand Determine the Short-Run Value of the Canadian Dollar

One of the most popular topics of conversation among Canadians (next to the weather) is the fluctuating value of the Canadian dollar. Why was our dollar worth more than the U.S. dollar for many years prior to 1976, and why has it become much less valuable since then? The supply-and-demand analysis described in Chapter 4 helps to explain this.

At any given time, there is a demand for our dollars by foreigners who wish to make purchases from us: The Canadians from whom foreigners make their purchases want to be paid in Canadian dollars. Foreign purchasers must go to the foreign-exchange market to obtain Canadian dollars for their transactions. This results in a demand for Canadian dollars in the foreign-exchange market. On the other hand, each time a Canadian purchases goods or services from abroad, he must exchange Canadian dollars in the foreign-exchange market for the currency of the country from which the purchase is being made. This results in a supply of Canadian dollars in the foreign-exchange market, and a corresponding demand for other currencies. The value of our dollar is determined through such demand and supply forces.

The term **foreign-exchange market** refers to the whole complex of institutions, including banks, specialized foreign-exchange dealers, and official government agencies, through which the currency of one country may be exchanged for that of another.

Foreign-exchange market
The complex of institutions through which the currency of one country may be exchanged for that of another.

The Supply of and Demand for Foreign Exchange

All kinds of goods and services are exchanged by countries, as we have noted. Payments on *current account* consist of payments for imports of goods and services, including payments of interest and dividends to foreigners for past loans and investments. For the moment, assume that no other transactions occur among the citizens of the various countries of the world.

Suppose, now, that a U.S. clothing importer wants to buy a shipment of parkas from Canada. The importer plans to finance the purchase with U.S. dollars held in a New York bank account. However, the parka manufacturer wants to be paid in Canadian dollars, which can be used to meet payrolls and buy materials in Canada. The U.S. bank sells the necessary quantity of U.S. dollars on the foreign-exchange market, receiving Canadian dollars in return. These are then forwarded to the Canadian manufacturer to pay for the parkas.

Meanwhile, thousands of other Canadians and Americans are also buying and selling dollars for their own purposes. The overall activity in the foreign-exchange market, like that in any other market, can be characterized in terms of supply and demand curves, as shown in Box 15.5. This market has been drawn to show the supply of and demand for Canadian dollars, with the price (that is, the exchange rate) given in terms of U.S. dollars per Canadian dollar. But it could equally well have been drawn to show the supply of and demand for U.S. dollars, with the price given in Canadian dollars per U.S. dollar.

Look first at the demand curve for Canadian dollars that appears in this market. The shape and position of the demand curve for Canadian dollars depends on how U.S. demand for Canadian goods varies as the exchange rate varies, other things being equal. It is easy to see that the demand curve will normally be downward sloping. Suppose, for example, that parkas sell in Canada for $50. At an exchange rate of one U.S. dollar per Canadian dollar, American consumers would have to pay $50 U.S. They might buy a total of, say, 200 000 parkas per year, thus generating a demand for 10 million Canadian dollars in the foreign-exchange market. If the exchange rate were to fall to 0.8 U.S. dollars per Canadian dollar while the parka price remained unchanged, American consumers

BOX 15.5 *Equilibrium of Demand and Supply in the Foreign-Exchange Market*

The demand curve for Canadian dollars (*D*) indicates that Americans will desire a greater quantity of Canadian dollars as the cost per U.S. dollar declines. The quantity supplied (S_1) increases at higher exchange rates. When only current-account transactions are considered, the process by which equilibrium is maintained in the foreign-exchange market is very simple. Suppose that a sudden increased preference among Canadians for travel in the United States shifts the supply curve of Canadian dollars to the right, from S_1 to S_2. This creates an excessive supply of dollars and puts downward pressure on the exchange rate. As the exchange rate falls, Americans are induced to spend more on Canadian goods, and Canadians to spend less on American goods. The exchange rate reaches a new equilibrium at 0.8 U.S. dollars per Canadian dollar.

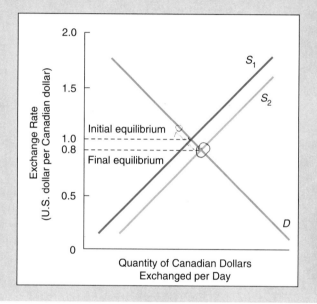

would be able to buy parkas more cheaply for U.S. dollars. At that lower price, they would presumably buy a greater quantity — say, 510 000 parkas. The demand for Canadian dollars on the foreign-exchange market would thus increase to $25.5 million.

The supply curve for dollars S_1 in Box 15.5 is drawn with an upward slope, indicating that more Canadian dollars will be supplied to the foreign-exchange market as the price of Canadian dollars, in terms of U.S. dollars, rises. When the value of the Canadian dollar rises, Canadian demand for American goods increases and more Canadian dollars are actually spent and supplied to Americans. Suppose, for example, that a certain U.S.-built motor home has a price of $20 000 U.S. At an exchange rate of one U.S. dollar per Canadian dollar, the motor home would sell for $20 000 in Canada (forgetting about shipping costs and other charges). If, say, 5000 of the motor homes per year were sold at that price, Canada would have to supply 100 million Canadian dollars to the foreign-exchange market in order to get the 100 million U.S. dollars needed to pay the U.S. manufacturer. Suppose next that the exchange rate rose to 1.25 U.S. dollars per Canadian dollar, so that Canadian buyers could get the motor home for just

16 000 Canadian dollars. If the quantity imported rose to 7500 per year as a result of the increase in the value of the Canadian dollar, Canadians would supply 120 million Canadian dollars to the exchange markets.

Box 15.5 also helps to illustrate how exchange rates can change as a result of shifts in demand and supply. As that graph is drawn, the foreign-exchange market is initially in equilibrium at an exchange rate of one U.S. dollar per Canadian dollar. Suppose, then, that some change in Canadian spending habits occurs. Canadians might decide to travel more in the United States and pay more to Americans in the form of interest and dividends. This could increase the supply of Canadian dollars in the foreign-exchange market, at the existing exchange rate. This is shown in Box 15.5 as a shift in the Canadian dollar supply curve from S_1 to S_2. The shift in the supply curve initially creates an excess quantity supplied of Canadian dollars, which tends to depress the exchange rate. As the exchange rate falls, Canadian goods become cheaper for Americans to buy, encouraging an increase in the quantity demanded of Canadian dollars. This is presented by a movement down along the demand curve in Box 15.5. At the same time, American goods become more expensive for Canadian buyers, somewhat decreasing the quantity of Canadian dollars supplied. This appears as a downward movement along the new Canadian dollar supply curve. As the figure is drawn, the supply and demand for Canadian dollars comes into equilibrium again at an exchange rate of 0.8 U.S. dollars per Canadian dollar.

In the terminology of foreign-exchange markets, the Canadian dollar is said to **depreciate** when its price falls in terms of foreign currency, as in the example above. Seen from the U.S. point of view, a fall in the price of the Canadian dollar in terms of U.S. dollars is equivalent to a rise in the price of the U.S. dollar in terms of Canadian dollars. The U.S. dollar, then, can be said to have **appreciated** against the Canadian dollar.

Depreciation and appreciation of the exchange rate
The Canadian dollar is said to depreciate when its price falls in terms of foreign currency, and to appreciate when its price rises in terms of foreign currency.

Foreign-Exchange Markets with Current and Capital Accounts

When only current-account transactions were considered, equilibrium in foreign-exchange markets required that every dollar's worth of goods or services imported be paid for by a dollar's worth of goods or services exported. Once capital-account transactions are introduced, however, this need no longer be the case. Imports of goods or services can now be paid for either by exports, or by capital inflows; that is, by borrowing from foreigners or selling assets to foreigners. Similarly, a country can export more goods and services than it imports, as long as it provides its trading partners with the means to do so, by making loans to them or buying assets from them.

Consider once again the accounts in Box 15.4. In 1990, the year for which these accounts are drawn, Canada is shown as importing more in goods and services than it exports, and running a current-account deficit of nearly $16 billion. At the same time, however, borrowing from foreigners plus sales of Canadian assets to foreigners (capital inflows) exceed loans to foreigners plus purchases of foreign assets (capital outflows) by nearly $21 billion. Canada thus has a $21 billion capital-account surplus that more than balances the current-account deficit.

It is not necessary to draw a new set of foreign-exchange supply and demand curves to take both current and capital transactions into account. There is still just one supply curve of Canadian dollars, one demand curve for Canadian dollars, and one exchange rate for the Canadian dollar in terms of any other currency, such as the U.S. dollar. However, there are now additional sources of shifts in the supply and demand curves, such as a rise in Canadian interest rates. One immediate effect of this would be to make Canadian securities more attractive to foreign buyers, since they would now yield a higher return. The increased demand by foreigners for Canadian dollars with which to buy these securities would show up as a rightward shift in the demand curve for Canadian dollars in the foreign-exchange market. That would tend to cause the Canadian dollar to appreciate against the U.S. dollar. As will be discussed later in this chapter, the Bank of Canada might deliberately cause interest rates in Canada to be higher than those in the United States, in order to get the demand curve for the Canadian dollar to shift to the right. The exchange rate would then rise above 0.8 U.S. dollars per Canadian dollar. (See the accompanying For Example. . . box, which describes a consequence of high interest rates.) It is shifts in the type of international transactions just described that explain, through demand-and-supply analysis, how the value of our dollar changes in the short run.

So far, only the mechanics of exchange-rate determination have been discussed; exchange rates, like other prices, are determined by supply and demand. The next step is to look beyond the supply and demand curves for a theory explaining why, at any particular time, the curves intersect at one exchange rate rather than another. Once that step has been taken, the next section will discuss the conditions for equilibrium in both the domestic and foreign sectors of the economy. This will then be followed by an examination of how and why governments use interest-rate policies to intervene in foreign-exchange markets.

FOR EXAMPLE...
Why Exporters Fear High Interest Rates

The following article indicates how, in early 1990, Canada's high interest rates were keeping the value of the Canadian dollar well above the level desired by many Canadian manufacturers and exporters. The high value of the dollar was discouraging exports and encouraging imports.

Canadian Dollar Key to Economy's Future

The Canadian economy has proved more resilient than expected. Despite high interest rates, it grew almost 3 percent in 1989 and was still exhibiting signs of strength in the first quarter. This is both good and bad.

On the plus side, there is clearly a lot of business and consumer confidence which augurs well for longer-term growth. The problem is that much of the increased demand in the past year has been supplied by imports.

Wide differential

The problem is the high Canadian dollar. Pushed up by the wide Canada–U.S. interest-rate differential —

three to four percentage points for most of 1989 and five points at the tail end — the Canadian dollar average 84.5¢ (U.S.) last year. That is well above the 80¢ (U.S.) at which economists say most Canadian firms are competitive.

The question is whether this is a temporary or a long-term problem. The answer will determine how well the economy will do in the first half of the 1990s.

SOURCE: Catherine Harris, "C$ Key to Economy's Future," *Financial Post*, March 26, 1990, p. 6. Reproduced with permission.

THE LONG RUN: PURCHASING-POWER PARITY

The leading theory of exchange-rate determination in the long run is the so-called **purchasing-power parity theory**. According to this theory, the price of a unit of Currency A in terms of Currency B (that is, the exchange rate) will, in the long run, tend to equal the ratio of the price level in Country B to the price level in Country A.

In a world where all goods and services were traded internationally, with no transportation costs or other barriers to trade, the purchasing-power parity theory would presumably hold exactly. Suppose, for example, that the Canadian and German domestic price levels are such that $100 will buy exactly twice as large a market basket of goods in Canada as can be bought for 100 marks in Germany. The purchasing-power parity theory will then imply that the exchange rate must be 2 marks per dollar. If a dollar could be exchanged for more than 2 marks, Canadian consumers would all try to turn in their dollars and do their shopping in Germany. Their attempt to do so would immediately drive the price of the dollar back down to 2 marks. Similarly, if a dollar could be purchased for less than 2 marks, Germans would try to turn in all their marks for dollars and shop in Canada. This would quickly push the price of the dollar up to 2 marks. In such a world, in fact, the expressions "100 dollars" and "200 marks" would simply be different names given in Germany and Canada to equal-sized lumps of abstract purchasing power.

In practice, exchange rates do not always reflect purchasing-power parities exactly (see the accompanying For Example. . . box). The difference can be explained in part by the fact that purchasing-power parities reflect the prices of all goods and services, while exchange rates tend to reflect the value of goods and services traded internationally.

Also, deviations of exchange values from present purchasing-power parities may reflect future expectations as much as current realities. For example, if participants in foreign-exchange markets come to expect future inflation in Canada to consistently average higher in relation to German inflation than they had expected in the past, they may "speculate" against the dollar by shifting out of dollar-denominated assets into mark-denominated assets. These capital-account transactions can depress the value of the dollar even before enough actual inflation takes place to justify the new exchange rate in terms of purchasing-power

Purchasing-power parity theory (of exchange rates) The theory holding that the price of a unit of Currency A in terms of Currency B will, in the long run, tend to be equal to the ratio of the price level in Country B to the price level in Country A.

FOR EXAMPLE...
Currency-Value Deviations from Purchasing-Power Parities

The Economist's survey of Big Mac prices around the world indicates in a simple way how currency values may deviate from their purchasing-power parity. Compare, for example, the price of a Big Mac in the United States — $2.25 (U.S.) — and in Canada — $2.35 (Cdn). Based on this price comparison alone, the U.S. dollar is worth more than the Canadian dollar, because it takes fewer U.S. dollars to buy a Big Mac. In fact, the U.S. dollar should equal 1.04 Canadian dollars ($2.35/$2.25). However, at the time the survey was taken, the U.S. dollar was actually worth 1.15 Canadian dollars. Therefore, as the article notes, the U.S. dollar was too high in relation to the Canadian dollar — or, to put it another way, the Canadian dollar was too low in relation to the U.S. dollar — insofar as Big Macs were concerned.

Big Mac Currencies

It is time for our annual update of *The Economist's* Big Mac index, a rough-and-ready guide to whether a currency is under- or overvalued. It was launched five years ago in the hope of making economic theory more digestible.

The index is based on the theory of purchasing-power parity (PPP), which argues that, in the long run, the exchange rate between two currencies should equate the prices of an identical basket of goods and services in the respective countries. Our "basket" is McDonald's Big Mac hamburger, made locally to a rigorous standard in more than fifty countries. Its local prices are less likely to be distorted by international transport and distribution costs than if we used, say, the price of *The Economist* in different countries.

So once again our correspondents have been gorging themselves on Big Macs. In four American cities, they paid, on average, $2.25. In Tokyo, the Big Mac costs ¥380, equivalent to $2.81. This implies that the dollar is 20 percent undervalued against the yen: It should, on our Big Mac PPP basis, buy ¥169 (the yen price divided by the dollar price) not the ¥135 prevailing when we made our survey. Similarly, it is 13 percent undervalued against the D-mark; it should be worth DM 1.91.

Indeed, on Big Mac PPP grounds, the dollar looks undervalued against most currencies, so its recent rally could have further to run. The exceptions are the Australian, Canadian, Hong Kong, and Singapore dollars, the Hungarian forint and the Yugoslav dinar, which all look too low in dollar terms.

The Real Test

Hamburger Prices				
Country	Price* in Local Currency	Implied PPP† of the Dollar	Actual Exchange Rate 9.4.91	% Over (+) or Under (−) Valuation of the Dollar
Australia	A$2.45	1.09	1.27	+17
Belgium	BFr100	44.44	34.50	−22
Britain	£1.67	0.74	0.56	−24
Canada	C$2.35	1.04	1.15	+11
Denmark	DKr26.75	11.89	6.42	−46
France	FFt18.00	8.00	5.65	−29
Germany	DM4.30	1.91	1.67	−13
Holland	F15.25	2.33	1.88	−19
Hong Kong	HK$8.90	3.96	7.79	+97
Hungary	Forint115	51.11	75.12	+47
Ireland	I£1.40	0.62	0.62	—
Italy	Lire3600	1600	1239	−23
Japan	¥380	169	135	−20
Singapore	S$2.80	1.24	1.77	+43
S. Korea	Won2100	933	721	−23
Soviet Union	Rouble10	4.44	1.74**	−61
Spain	Ptas350	155	103	−34
Sweden	SKr26	11.56	6.04	−48
United States††	$2.25	—	—	—
Yugoslavia	Dinar32	14.22	15.12	+6

*Prices may vary locally **Commercial rate †Purchasing-power parity in local currency: local price divided by dollar price ††New York, Chicago, San Francisco and Atlanta.   SOURCE: McDonald's; *Economist* correspondents.

SOURCE: "Big MacCurrencies," *The Economist*, April 13, 1991, p. 78. Reproduced with permission.

parities. Similarly, if participants in foreign-exchange markets speculate that the character of future real economic growth will cause the demand for a country's exports to increase more rapidly than its demand for imports, the present exchange rate for its currency may be bid up in anticipation of the expected future improvement in its current-account balance.

With the necessary reservations, as noted, the purchasing-power parity theory can be thought of as determining exchange rates in the long run.

CANADA'S DILEMMA IN THE FOREIGN MARKET

Most of our international transactions are conducted with the United States, and Canada's basic problems in the foreign market can best be illustrated by referring to our dealings with that country.

Canada's balance-of-payments position vis-à-vis the United States can be summarized briefly. We almost always have a deficit in our current account with the United States. This is largely due to the interest and dividends on investments in Canada that we pay to U.S. investors. These investors want to be paid in U.S. dollars, so companies in Canada paying interest and dividends to them must purchase U.S. dollars on the foreign-exchange market. Doing so pushes up the value of the U.S. dollar. Therefore, our heavy dependence on U.S. investment has created a perennial problem for us, by saddling us with heavy debt payments that push down the value of our dollar. In order to stabilize the value of the dollar around **par**, we have tried to lure more investment into Canada by keeping our interest rates above those prevailing in the United States. Because of our higher interest rates, Americans are induced to buy our securities in preference to their own. It is operations of this kind that have counterbalanced the negative impact that the normal deficits in our current account have on the value of our dollar.

The reasons for the high-interest-rate policy and the concern to keep the value of the Canadian dollar near par with the U.S. dollar are explored more fully in the macroeconomics portion of this textbook. The problems mentioned here, however, are part of a larger set of problems in our foreign trade that have prompted Canadian policy makers to explore new ways for Canada to participate in the international market. In the next chapter, we examine a few of the dramatic changes that have been implemented as well as others that are being contemplated for the future.

Par
The point at which one unit of a currency is traded for exactly one unit of another currency.

SUMMARY

1. A country is said to have a comparative advantage in the production of any good that it can produce at a lower opportunity cost than that of its trading partners. Trading nations can realize mutual benefits if each specializes in products for which it has a comparative advantage. Such specialization can give consumers in each country more of all goods than they would have without international trade.

2. Although the theory of comparative advantage shows that all countries benefit from free international trade, a country with selling or buying power in international markets can sometimes manipulate the terms of trade by using *tariffs* or *quotas*. The resulting improvement in terms of trade can theoretically more than offset the loss in efficiency. However, if other countries retaliate

with *protectionist* measures of their own, all can end up losers. Similar dangers are present with most other protectionist measures.

3. Some of the arguments for protection — the infant-industry argument, for example — are not without merit, but most economists favour the freest possible trade on the basis of the theory of comparative advantage.

4. The many kinds of international transactions that take place in the world economy can conveniently be classified into three accounts, which, taken together, provide a measure of a country's *balance of payments*. The first is the *current account*, which comprises imports and exports of goods and services and unilateral transfers. The second is the *capital account*, which includes all international borrowing and lending and all international purchases and sales of assets for investment purposes. The third is the *official-reserve account*, which is made up of central bank purchases and sales of foreign-currency reserves. Because all international transactions are included in one account or another, the sum of the surpluses or deficits on these three accounts must always be zero.

5. Canada depends on foreign trade for almost one-third of its total purchases and sales. It normally has a positive balance on merchandise trade, but its current account is usually in deficit because of service payments. This deficit requires either a surplus in the capital account or a drawing down of its official reserves.

6. The mechanics of exchange-rate determination in the short run can be explained by means of supply-and-demand analysis of the various shifts in the sorts of international transactions that are recorded in the current and capital accounts — that is, of activity in the foreign-exchange market. In the long run, international exchange rates tend to reflect, at least approximately, changes in the *purchasing-power parity* of various national currencies.

7. Canada has historically faced a persistent problem in its transactions with the United States — that is, a large deficit in our current account due largely to the interest and dividends on investment that we owe U.S. investors. This has forced Canada to attract inflows of U.S. capital through relatively high interest rates.

KEY TERMS

protectionism
tariff
import quota
balance of payments
current account

capital account
capital inflows
capital outflows
official-reserve account
foreign-exchange market

depreciation and appreciation of
   the exchange rate
purchasing-power parity theory
par

KEY BOXES

Box 15.1 A Graphic Illustration of Comparative
            Advantage
Box 15.4 Canada's Balance of Payments, 1990

Box 15.5 Equilibrium of Demand and Supply in
            the Foreign-Exchange Market

REVIEW QUESTIONS

1. Consider the following statement: "The European Community (EC), Japan, Russia, all areas of the world are beating us. . . . It's no longer economical for us to produce anything." On the basis of what you have learned about the principle of comparative advantage, do you think it is really possible to reach a point at which it is no longer economical to produce anything — that is, at which it is economical to import everything? Explain.

2. Simple trade theory suggests that countries will export goods in the production of which they have a comparative advantage and import goods in the production of which they have a comparative disadvantage. In fact, countries often import the same kinds of goods they export. For example, most countries that are big exporters of automobiles are also importers of automobiles. Why do you think that happens?

3. Is the current-account balance the same as the merchandise balance? Explain.

4. On the basis of Box 15.5, explain what kinds of transactions result in demand by Canadians for foreign currency and what kind result in a supply of foreign currency to Canadians.

5. Why might it be better to subsidize workers who are harmed by freer trade than to protect them by imposing tariffs on foreign imports?

6. If the Canadian dollar depreciates against the U.S. dollar, it is assumed that Americans will buy more Canadian goods and services and Canadians will buy fewer American goods and services. This increase in exports and decrease in imports should help to restore the imbalance that may have prompted the depreciation in the first place. However, what would happen if Americans actually spent less on Canadian goods than before? (*Note*: Americans can now buy Canadian dollars more cheaply than before. Therefore, though they will likely buy more Canadian goods, their outlay on these goods might actually decline.) Conversely, what would happen if Canadian outlays (expenditures) on American goods increased?

7. Use a supply–demand diagram for the Canadian dollar to illustrate the following situations. In each case, indicate if the Canadian dollar has appreciated or depreciated relative to the other currency mentioned in the question. To avoid confusion, be sure that all parts of your graph represent Canadian dollars.
   a. The introduction of the GST drives scores of Canadian shoppers to the United States for shopping.
   b. Canadian tourists flock to Mexico during an especially long, cold winter.
   c. Large numbers of American tourists come to see and to shop at the West Edmonton Mall.
   d. American corporations increase their direct investment in Canada.

8. Using the scenarios described in Question 7, graph the changes that occur in the foreign-exchange markets for the non-Canadian currency in each case. In other words, graph the foreign-exchange market for the U.S. dollar in parts (a), (c), and (d) and for the Mexican peso in part (b).

9. To which of Canada's balance-of-payments accounts does each of the following belong? Indicate, for each transaction, whether it represents an inflow or an outflow of funds for Canada.
   a. Japanese business people buy three Vancouver hotels.
   b. Canadian investors purchase a shopping mall in Tucson, Arizona.
   c. Canadian tourists head to Mexico in record numbers during an especially long, cold winter.
   d. American tourists don't come to Canada as much because of the depreciation of the U.S. dollar relative to the Canadian dollar.

10. Assuming Canada has a deficit in its current account, which of the following would reduce the deficit? If any of the following would not reduce the current-account deficit, explain why.
   a. France buys more lumber from Canada.
   b. Canada buys more oil from OPEC nations.
   c. Saudi Arabians buy five Canadian thoroughbred racehorses from Ontario breeders at an average price of $700 000 each.
   d. An American corporation invests $5 million in a new factory in New Brunswick.

CHAPTER 16

Free Trade

After studying this chapter, you will be able to

1. Outline Canada's new economic position in the midst of the ongoing fundamental restructuring of the world economy.

2. Define concepts such as *globalization, regionalization,* and *decentralization.*

3. Describe Canada's wavering commitment to economic independence.

4. Understand the role of the GATT.

5. Distinguish between direct and portfolio investment, and understand the importance of the former in Canada's dependence on the U.S. economy.

6. Understand the objectives of the Free Trade Agreement with the United States and describe some of its initial problems.

A Preview   *Closer Links with an Old Partner*

Are nation-states such as Canada obsolescent? Are we bound to disintegrate into a number of smaller states or regions, as the Soviet Union and Yugoslavia have done, or are we bound to be swallowed up by the United States? The following article, by Marshall Cohen, president and chief executive officer of Molson Cos. Ltd., raises some of these important questions, and the chapter focusses in particular on our new and troubling economic relationship with the United States.

Regional Economies Could Open Pathway to Global Liberalization

There are a number of unique elements in Canada's history that have helped to shape it, stemming from the co-existence of two founding peoples. But the things that make Canada unique compared to most other industrialized nations are outweighed by the things that make us similar.

Many Canadians fear that Canada is following the Soviet or Yugoslavian model of ethnic disintegration. But this idea is too simplistic. It misses the basic reality that decentralization and regionalization are taking place not just in the Soviet Union and Eastern Europe, but also in the United States and Western Europe.

All major countries — not just Canada — are experiencing pressures of external integration. And all major countries — not just Canada — are at the very same time experiencing severe pressures of downward disintegration. We see this in strong and persistent demands for local autonomy — even sovereignty — in regions throughout the industrialized world.

What seems to be happening is that as the primacy of nation-states erodes, old identities and loyalties are beginning to reassert themselves. The Scottish nationalist movement is one example of that; we see other examples in Germany, Italy, France, Spain — ironically at the very same time that people in Europe are taking on a sense of European identity, and European Community institutions are beginning to assert a substantial impact on their lives.

Indeed, one of the greatest sources of pressure for regionalism within nations is globalization. Globalizing financial markets are making cities like London, New York, and Tokyo more and more like each other, and less and less like the countries of which they are a part.

The reduced economic role of the nation-state, and the increased prominence of regional groupings of nations, leads many to see a grave danger — the potential fragmentation, rather than integration, of global trade. The concern is that in the creation of Europe 1992 and the North American free-trade area, we are creating a Fortress Europe and a Fortress North America.

My view is that while regional protectionism is a danger, it is not inevitable. Rather than spawn a new wave of protectionism, the new regional trade relationships we are seeing could become a new source of progress in trade liberalization.

In the U.S.–Canada agreement, the dispute-settlement mechanism constitutes a major innovation — one that was only possible in the context of that accord's objectives.

In both Europe and North America, we are heading down similar paths; our goal must be to make sure that our paths meet.

Throughout the world, we are coming to terms with a new reality: The borders of the economy are no longer the borders of the state. Europe has a head start over North Americans in recognizing that fact and dealing with it. We will have an opportunity to learn from Europe, and I hope Europe will have an opportunity to learn from us as well.

SOURCE: Marshall Cohen, "Insight: Regional Economies Could Open Pathway to Global Liberalization," *Financial Post*, June 17, 1991, p. 10. Marshall Cohen is president and chief executive officer of Molson Cos. Ltd. This is from his address to the Canada–U.K. Chamber of Commerce Joint Committee annual conference in London.

CANADA'S FRAGILE ECONOMIC AUTONOMY

Chapter 15 showed that the Canadian economy has vital links to many other economies, particularly the United States. At the present time, these links are expanding dramatically, raising serious doubts about the long-run autonomy of the Canadian economy.

Our Preview, written by the head of one of Canada's largest transnational corporations — and therefore a prime actor in the changes taking place — explores some of the implications of these changes for Canada. Three different types of changes can be identified, as follows:

1. **Globalization**, which refers to the greater openness of most national economies to the entire world economy. In particular, it refers to the growing tendency of companies within a particular country to plan their location and output strategies on a global basis. Some Canadian companies, for example, no longer ask, "How shall we expand or consolidate our operations in Canada in order to increase our profits?" but "In what locations throughout the world should we expand or consolidate our operations in order to maximize our profits?" Although it is not new, the practice of global corporate planning seems to be rapidly accelerating.

2. **Regionalization**, which refers to the integration of national economies, such as Canada, with other national economies, such as the United States. The result is regional trading blocs, such as the European Community (EC) — an alliance of twelve West European economies — and the trade area recently created by the Canada–U.S. Free Trade Agreement.

3. **Decentralization**, which refers to the fragmentation of national economies and the reduced power of central national governments. This, too, is happening in many parts of the world, particularly in Eastern and Central Europe, but also in countries such as Belgium and Canada. The potential separation of Quebec from the rest of Canada is a dramatic symbol of the decentralizing forces that have long threatened Canada's national economy.

Globalization
The growing tendency of corporations to conduct their business on a global basis, without regard to the special interests of the country in which their headquarters are located.

Regionalization
The tendency of countries to form regional trading blocs such as the European Community and the trade area created by the Canada–U.S. Free Trade Agreement.

Decentralization
The fragmentation of national economies into smaller units or the general reduction of the power of central national governments.

All of these changes — globalization, regionalization, and decentralization — are bound to have a profound impact on the Canadian economy. The first two threaten Canada's economic autonomy, and the third, its viability as a nation. All three are presenting the country with new political and economic challenges. The focus of this chapter, however, is on regionalization, because this is the process that has been given new impetus with the Canada–U.S. Free Trade Agreement (which may soon be extended to include Mexico) and because, as such, it is also helping to accelerate the other two forces of change.

In order to appreciate these forces more fully and to anticipate more accurately where they might lead Canada, we must first consider a brief historical overview of past trends. The chapter will then proceed to a description and analysis of Canada's regional alliance with the United States, and the possible extension of that alliance to Mexico.

A LONG-STANDING CONFLICT: INDEPENDENCE VERSUS DEPENDENCE

As we noted in Chapter 3, before Confederation in 1867, the regions that we now call Canada were heavily dependent on other countries for their economic development. A large proportion of their staple products were sold in European markets, particularly in France and Great Britain. Until the 1840s, they were granted special access to the British market. Then, in the years leading up to Confederation, the British North American colonies turned increasingly to the U.S. market, to the point that a limited free-trade agreement — the Reciprocity Treaty of 1854 — was signed. Only after successive rebukes from Great Britain and the termination of the treaty with the United States in 1865 did the colonies decide to integrate their local economies into a new national economy called Canada.

After 1867, great efforts were made to ensure Canada's independence. But the two major parties, the Liberals and the Conservatives, adopted conflicting policies. In 1879, just into their second term in office, the Conservatives, under the leadership of John A. Macdonald, implemented the first phase of their National Policy, which was based on tariff protection for Canadian industry and financial support for nation-building efforts, primarily the transcontinental railway. The Liberals tended to follow a north–south continental policy, favouring free trade and closer economic ties with the United States. However, whenever the Liberals formally proposed economic reciprocity with the United States, as they did in 1891 and again in 1911, they either lost an election or were voted out of office.

Although the idea of economic reciprocity with the United States was dropped after 1911, closer economic ties were nonetheless forged through U.S. investment in Canada. Such investment was encouraged, particularly during the Great Depression of the 1930s, when tariffs on many Canadian goods were raised. This prompted more foreign firms interested in the Canadian market to build branch plants in Canada.

Toward Freer Trade under the GATT

After World War II, Canada began to dismantle its tariff structure and modify many of its other protectionist policies in accordance with the aims of the worldwide trade-liberalization movement it had joined. The major Western trading nations (now numbering more than ninety) joined together in the **General Agreement on Tariffs and Trade (GATT)**, to promote freer trade throughout the Western world. After almost eight rounds of negotiations, including the current Uruguay negotiations (so named because they began in Punta del Este, Uruguay, in 1986), Canada's average tariff has been reduced to 9.2 percent. By 1987, 85 percent of all goods traded between Canada and the United States were tariff-free.

General Agreement on Tariffs and Trade (GATT) An international trading agreement that involves more than ninety countries and limits trade restrictions among them.

This move toward freer trade in the Western world has contributed over the years to a tremendous growth in international trade. The figures for Canada are impressive: Since 1947, its population has doubled, its real gross domestic product has increased fivefold, and the volume of its foreign trade has increased sevenfold. In 1990, Canada was the world's eighth-largest exporter of merchandise (Germany was first, followed by the United States and Japan), and accounted for 3.8 percent of world merchandise exports.

Growing Involvement with the United States

Coinciding with Canada's growing involvement in international markets through trade was a dramatic increase in the United States' involvement in the Canadian economy — an involvement that was developing primarily on two fronts. First, as we saw in Chapter 15, Canada's trade began to depend more and more on exports to (and imports from) the United States. In 1947, the United States bought 38 percent of Canada's exports; by 1990, that figure had risen to 75 percent. Second, U.S. investment in Canada, particularly *direct investment,* was growing rapidly.

Direct investment refers to the outright purchase of a firm (which then becomes a wholly owned subsidiary) or the purchase of at least one-third of a firm's voting shares — the minimum percentage required to gain controlling interest in the firm. **Portfolio investment**, by contrast, refers primarily to bond holdings, which do not carry voting rights. Most British investment in Canada in the pre–World War I period was of the portfolio variety, with Canadian bonds being sold in the London market. Portfolio investment might be viewed as more in the nature of a loan. For example, Canadian utilities such as Hydro-Québec and Ontario Hydro finance much of their expansion by selling bonds in the New York market. Such sales do not give Americans control over these utilities because the bonds carry no voting rights.

As we noted above, then, U.S. investors tended to make a large part of their foreign investments direct investments. They either bought Canadian companies outright or purchased enough voting shares to gain effective control over them. By 1970, foreign countries (but primarily the United States) controlled the assets of 37 percent of all nonfinancial industries in Canada. Over the course of the next fifteen years, that figure declined to about 23 percent, as a result, in part, of Canadian government buy-back programs. However, since 1985, foreign control of Canadian business has once again been on the rise, climbing to an average level of 25 percent by 1987. In some industries, the figure was much higher than the average: 45.6 percent of the assets in Canadian manufacturing, for example, and 30.6 percent in mining, were under foreign control.[1] Comparisons show that a greater proportion of Canada's economy is foreign-owned than that of any other Western industrialized economy.

Box 16.1 lists the fifteen largest foreign-owned corporations in Canada in 1990. Although some of these corporations are managed by Canadians, their ultimate investment strategy and long-term planning are controlled by their foreign headquarters. And while it can be argued that Canada has benefited from foreign investment in various ways — reaping the benefits, for example, of new American and Japanese technology and management skills — there is also no doubt that foreign investment has had the effect, over time, of slowly eroding Canada's economic and, perhaps, political autonomy.

It is important to note, however, that the interdependence of the U.S. and Canadian economies has also been furthered by large Canadian investments in the United States. In the last few decades, Canada has invested about one-third as much in the United States as the United States has invested in Canada. And given that the Canadian economy is only one-tenth the size of that of the United States, this means that a greater *proportion* of Canadian resources are flowing into the United States than vice versa. However, this picture overstates Canada's relative strength, because it does not take into account the reinvestment in the Canadian economy of funds earned within Canada by American corporations.

A somewhat clearer picture of Canada's position in the field of foreign investment is given in Box 16.2. It is stated there that, in 1989, the United States earned more from its investments abroad than it paid out to foreign countries for

Direct investment
Business investment that gives the investor controlling interest in a firm.

Portfolio investment
Business investment that does not give the investor controlling interest in a firm; refers primarily to bond holdings.

---

[1]Statistics Canada, *Annual Report of the Minister of Industry, Science and Technology under the Corporations and Labour Unions Returns Act,* Part I, *Corporations,* 1987, Catalogue no. 61-210. Reproduced with permission of the Minister of Supply and Services Canada, 1992.

BOX 16.1 *Largest Foreign-Owned Companies in Canada, 1990*

This table lists the fifteen largest foreign-owned companies in Canada — which also rank among Canada's fifty largest corporations, as indicated in the column headed "Financial Post 500 Rank."

Rank	Company	1990 Sales (thousands of dollars)	Financial Post 500 Rank	Foreign Ownership (percent)	Parent	Country
1	General Motors of Canada	18 458 171	1	100	General Motors	U.S.
2	Ford Motor of Canada	13 706 200	3	94	Ford Motor	U.S.
3	Imperial Oil	10 223 000	6	70	Exxon	U.S.
4	Chrysler Canada	7 067 000	10	100	Chrysler	U.S.
5	Shell Canada	5 508 000	16	78	Shell Petroleum	Netherlands
6	IBM Canada	4 578 000	22	100	IBM	U.S.
7	Sears Canada	4 571 100	23	61	Sears Roebuck	U.S.
8	Amoco Canada Petroleum	4 444 000	24	100	Amoco	U.S.
9	Canada Safeway	4 317 951	25	100	Safeway	U.S.
10	Total Petroleum (N.A.)	3 179 929	37	52	Total Compagnie Française des Pétroles	France
11	Canada Packers	3 092 238	38	56	Hillsdown Holdings	Britain
12	Mitsui & Co. (Canada)	2 728 680	43	100	Mitsui	Japan
13	United Westburne	2 563 522	44	69	Dumez	France
14	Honda Canada	2 454 476	46	100	Honda 50.2%; American Honda 49.8%	Japan/U.S.
15	F.W. Woolworth	2 321 791	50	100	Woolworth	U.S.

SOURCE: *Financial Post 500*, June 1991, p. 176. Reproduced with permission.

their investments in the United States. The situation is very different for Canada: Its deficit on investment income reached a record-high level of $20 billion in 1989 — a substantially greater amount than that owed by any other Western nation.

The developments described above have for some time caused economists and other observers to question Canada's economic autonomy. It is clear that long before passage of the Free Trade Agreement (FTA) with the United States in January 1988, the Canadian economy had become strongly linked to that of the United States through trade, investment, and corporate strategies. Nevertheless, the agreement represented a considerable departure from past government policy — especially from the early policies of the Conservative party, which now promoted it — and remains sufficiently controversial, and sufficiently central to the country's economic future, to deserve special consideration.

THE CANADA–U.S. FREE TRADE AGREEMENT

After a period of unprecedented public debate, the Canadian government signed the Free Trade Agreement with the United States in January 1988, and it went into effect on January 1, 1989. An agreement of this nature had been endorsed earlier by the Senate Standing Committee on Foreign Affairs, and had been recommended by the Macdonald Commission in 1985.

Canada's Investment-Income Deficit BOX 16.2

Although Canadians invest relatively heavily in the United States, they have, for
several decades, welcomed much more foreign investment into Canada. For this
reason, Canada has a high and growing deficit on foreign investment income — a
measure of its dependence on foreign economies.

Foreign Investment Income

America is by far the world's biggest debtor, with a net
foreign debt at the end of 1989 of more than $600
billion. Yet last year it was still in rough balance on its
foreign investment income, down from a surplus of $25
billion in 1985. This paradox is partly explained by the
fact that America's direct investment abroad is older
than foreigners' investment in the United States. This
means that America's investment earns a higher rate

of return. It also means that, if investment abroad was
valued at current market prices rather than historic
prices, America might not be a net debtor after all.
Japan now has the world's biggest surplus on
investment income ($29 billion), followed by
Switzerland ($14 billion). At the other extreme,
Canada's deficit on investment income has risen from
$11 billion in 1985 to $20 billion last year.

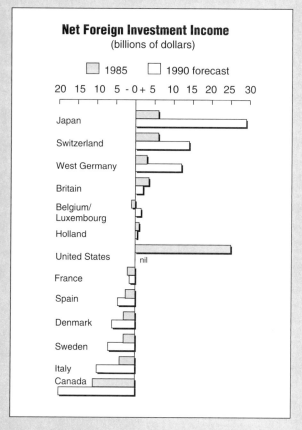

SOURCE: OECD

SOURCE: *The Economist*, August 11, 1990, p. 98. Reproduced with permission.

Reasons for Entering into the Agreement

Several factors seem to have led to the ultimate adoption of free trade with the United States as government policy. There was, first, a growing awareness that other trading blocs were developing in the world, possibly replacing the global system of rules under the GATT. In the early 1970s, Canada had tried, without much success, to establish more favourable links to the European Community. In the view of parts of the government and much of the business community, it appeared increasingly clear that Canada must strengthen its position vis-à-vis other alliances through a special alliance with the United States. One concrete sign of the potential breakdown of the world trading system was the growing use by many countries of "hidden" protectionist measures, such as subsidies. GATT had managed to reduce tariffs among member countries and to counteract other obvious protectionist weapons such as quotas, but it seemed almost helpless in face of these more subtle forms of protection. The accompanying For Example. . . box provides information on current subsidy programs among leading trading nations, including Canada. It points out that when subsidies are measured in terms not only of actual cash outlays, but also of soft loans, tax concessions, and government equity participation, the subsidies of some countries amount to more than 10 percent of the value of their industrial output. It takes wealth to counteract this kind of protectionism (to pay large subsidies), as well as a strong bargaining position. Canada on its own has some of the first but little of the second.

A second reason often given for entering into the FTA was a fear that the United States would itself become more protectionist and more antagonistic in its trade dealings with Canada. Indeed, serious disputes involving lumber, fish, and many other Canadian trade products had erupted in the period leading up to the agreement. "Better to join the enemy than fight him" was the lesson drawn by some from this experience.

A third reason, given by a number of academic economists and certain business groups, was that a new world trading order was emerging, led by strong multinational corporations with tremendous competitive advantages. Unless Canada learned to be more competitive itself, through a freer trade agreement with the United States, it would not fare well with either the United States or other large trading nations or blocs. Partial evidence for such a view is provided in Box 16.3, which shows that despite increased trade in the last few decades, Canada's *share* of world exports actually shrank from 5.3 percent in 1971 to 3.9 percent in 1987. The same diagram shows that the United States' share also declined, while the shares of Japan and other Asian countries grew. This suggests that a closer alliance with the United States would not necessarily correct the situation for Canada; nonetheless, in many quarters, the United States was still seen as a model of competitiveness from which Canada could learn.

The Nature of the Agreement: Basic Objectives and Main Features

The Free Trade Agreement is much more than an agreement about trade. Indeed, if its main objective had been the reduction of tariffs between Canada and the United States, continuing negotiations within the GATT might have done the job just as well. The basic Canadian objectives were as follows:

1. To achieve more open access to U.S. markets for Canadian goods and services.

FOR EXAMPLE...
Hidden Barriers to Trade

The following article from *The Economist* explains the threat of hidden barriers to trade and documents the true extent of such barriers in several European countries. Unfortunately, data on subsidies in the form of soft loans, tax concessions, and government equity participation were not available for Canada.

From the Sublime to the Subsidy

Fingers crossed, the 1990s will see a lowering of trade barriers. But free-traders will need to stay alert: As barriers crumble, governments may be tempted to rely more on subsidies to protect favoured firms.

During the 1970s, OECD governments pumped more and more subsidies into industries, to prop up those in decline and to encourage so-called sunrise ones. In the 1980s, this came to a halt: The average rate of industrial subsidy stabilized and even fell in some countries. Three cheers, shout free-market economists, who worry that subsidies divert labour and capital into less productive uses. But it is too early to start popping champagne corks. Subsidies could start to rise again in the 1990s.

For one thing, the rich countries enjoyed sustained expansion in the 1980s, so governments were under less pressure to save lame ducks. If the world were to plunge into recession, many governments would again be tempted to intervene.

More worrying, the greater the success of multilateral negotiations to reduce tariff barriers, the greater will be the incentive to use subsidies instead. Governments may try to convince themselves that subsidies are more respectable than tariffs as a way to protect industries. In fact, they are more dangerous, being less transparent. There is no internationally agreed standard for measuring subsidies. If trade wars are not simply to turn into subsidy wars, there needs to be multilateral surveillance of subsidies.

The OECD Industry Committee hopes to start work soon on collecting internationally comparable data. Meanwhile, a recent OECD working paper . . . reviews existing data.

Start first with national accounts. In most countries, government subsidies to industry (that is, excluding agriculture and public services) amounted to 2–3 1/2 percent of the value of industrial output in 1986 (the latest year for which full figures are available). The average rate of subsidy in Europe dwarfed that in America (0.5 percent) and Japan (1.0 percent), ranging from just below 2 percent in West Germany and Britain to as much as 6–7 percent in Sweden and Ireland. (Note, though, that subsidies

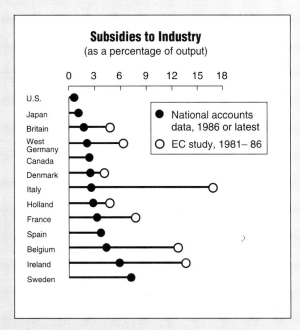

Subsidies to Industry
(as a percentage of output)

● National accounts data, 1986 or latest
○ EC study, 1981– 86

have since fallen sharply in Sweden, with the closure of all state-owned shipyards.)

Official figures on subsidies should carry a health warning. The national-accounts figures cover only cash grants; they exclude soft loans, tax concessions (for example, to encourage investment), and government equity participation, which in many countries are more important than grants. France and Denmark, for example, channel most of their subsidies through soft loans and equity participation; West Germany and Ireland rely heavily on tax concessions.

A more comprehensive survey by the European Commission estimated the value of these other types of subsidy. The average rate of industrial subsidy in the EC in 1981–86 was 8.6 percent of output — two to three times as large as the national-accounts figures. Britain, Denmark, and Holland all had subsidy rates below 5 percent, while the big culprits were Italy and Luxembourg, with rates of 16–17 percent. There are no comparable figures for America.

SOURCE: "Economics Focus: From the Sublime to the Subsidy," *The Economist*, February 24, 1990, p. 71. Reproduced with permission.

BOX 16.3 Canada's Share of World Exports

This diagram shows that Canada's share of world exports declined significantly between 1971 and 1987, dropping from 5.3 percent to 3.9 percent during that period. This relatively poor performance is one sign of Canada's apparent loss of competitiveness on the world market and one of the reasons given by some observers for exposing Canada to freer trade through the Canada–U.S. Free Trade Agreement.

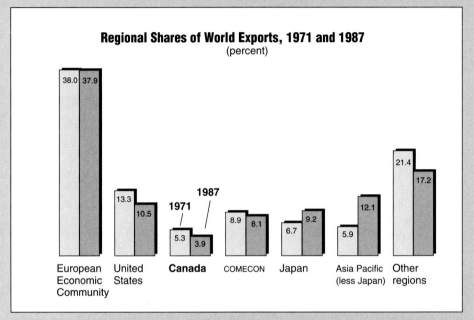

Regional Shares of World Exports, 1971 and 1987
(percent)

SOURCE: Economic Council of Canada, *Au Courant* 11, no. 2 (1990): 5. Reproduced with permission of the Chairman of the Economic Council of Canada, 1992.

2. To achieve more secure access to U.S. markets.

3. To secure special provisions for sensitive sectors of the Canadian economy.

More open access to U.S. markets meant, first of all, reduced tariffs on Canadian goods entering the United States and, second, fewer restrictions on Canadian firms bidding on contracts to supply goods or services to the U.S. military and other U.S. government agencies. *More secure access* to U.S. markets meant, primarily, access without excessive harassment and threat of penalties. This objective would be achieved by means of more clearly defined rules pertaining to access and more reliable and impartial arbitration procedures for settling disputes. *Special provisions for sensitive sectors* of the Canadian economy meant the exemption of certain sectors, such as culture and health, from the provisions of the FTA.

The negotiations that led up to the signing of the agreement arrived at the following terms for meeting these Canadian objectives: With regard to more open access, negotiators agreed to a major reduction of tariffs. Since Canadian tariffs were about twice as high as those imposed by the United States, greater reductions by Canada were called for. A gradual reduction was planned, resulting in the virtual elimination of all tariffs by 1998. (Sixty-three percent of Canadian tariffs are to be eliminated by 1993.) An equally comprehensive solution was *not* achieved with regard to the removal of nontariff barriers. Similarly, barriers to Canadian firms' tendering on U.S. government purchases were reduced but not eliminated.

With regard to more secure access, the major innovation was a new dispute-settlement mechanism. It is not clear that the dispute-settlement mechanism is working well, although some observers feel that it is a substantial improvement over previous dispute-settlement arrangements. Nonetheless, the U.S. government, under pressure from U.S. interest groups, has objected to many Canadian trade initiatives, and the dispute-settlement panels appear to be much less immune to political pressure than was originally hoped. Furthermore, the Free Trade Agreement did not settle issues relating to unfair pricing, subsidies, and dumping (selling at a lower price in a foreign market than at home), which are to be resolved by 1997. This means that, for the present, Canada remains subject to the kinds of uncertainties in these areas that existed in the past, and that the agreement was intended to resolve.

Under the terms of the agreement, "sensitive" sectors, such as agriculture, culture, health, and the automotive trade, seem to have been assured the protection that Canada sought for them. However, some fear that these sectors could again become vulnerable when the issue of subsidies is raised in subsequent discussions or when extension of the agreement (for example, to include Mexico) is negotiated.

Results, Anticipated and Actual

Before the Free Trade Agreement was signed, the Economic Council of Canada tried in a substantial study to forecast the results of such an agreement.[2] Unfortunately, the agreement that was finally signed differed in some important respects from the version that the Economic Council used in its projections. However, the projections themselves were not seriously affected by the changes, and it is worth while considering them here.

The council produced several different sets of projections, based on several different assumptions about the ability of companies to respond to new competitive pressures and about the general growth of the Canadian economy. A middle-range projection on the cautious side was as follows: The FTA would

1. create about 76 000 new jobs (net of jobs lost) between 1988 and 1998 (in other words, thousands of jobs would be lost, but even more thousands would be gained);

2. increase real gross domestic product by 0.7 percent in the same time period;

3. reduce the Consumer Price Index by 3.3 percent;

4. increase exports by 0.9 percent;

5. increase imports by 2.3 percent.

---

[2]Economic Council of Canada, *Venturing Forth* (Ottawa: Economic Council of Canada, 1988).

More specifically, in this series of projections, the Economic Council predicted that employment and output in the primary and service sectors would grow modestly during this period (by less than 1 percent in the primary sector and by approximately 1 percent in services), while both output and employment would decline slightly in the manufacturing sector.

The initial effects of the FTA are extremely difficult to measure, in large part because the Canadian economy has suffered a major recession since 1990 and the value of the Canadian dollar has been maintained at a relatively high level — at approximately $0.86 (U.S.). Both factors work against the positive results predicted by supporters of the FTA.

So far, what we have is a lot of "impressionistic" evidence of the kind offered in the accompanying For Example. . . box, with its description of the difficulties experienced by Canada's furniture industry. While losses in this industry seem attributable to the Free Trade Agreement, the question remains, Will such losses ultimately be offset by gains in other industries? In other words, What kind of general picture is emerging? In the first few years after the introduction of the FTA, the general picture has not been encouraging. The Canadian economy experienced a serious recession, marked by the loss of hundreds of thousands of jobs, particularly in the manufacturing sector. Unfortunately, it is impossible to determine how much of this was a direct result of the FTA and how much was attributable to a similar recession in the United States, which seriously reduced our net exports, as well as to other factors, such as the high value of the Canadian dollar.

In summary, it is probably accurate to say that most economists are in favour of free trade because of their commitment to the theory of comparative advantage. That theory by its very nature supports a global view of resource allocation and trade. Nonetheless, nation-states have emerged in the course of history for many important social, political, and economic reasons, and it is precisely because it conflicts with those reasons that the Free Trade Agreement with the United States is controversial and warrants critical analysis. In addition, it reduces Canada's control over some of its resources, such as energy, and it renders helpless those industries that were not prepared for the complete elimination of trade barriers. It is noteworthy, for example, that the federal government virtually ignored the recommendation of the Macdonald Commission that an adjustment fund be established to assist those industries and workers who would be hardest hit by the effects of the agreement. Since such adjustment costs were not factored into the government's assessments of the agreement's costs and benefits, it cannot be said that Canadians were given an accurate appraisal of its potential impact.

PROSPECTS FOR A NORTH AMERICAN FREE-TRADE ZONE

Although the jury is still out on the success of the FTA, the United States and Mexico have begun free-trade discussions of their own, and have invited Canada to participate. The Canadian government has responded positively, and a preliminary free-trade agreement involving Canada, the United States, and Mexico was reached in the summer of 1992. This is yet another sign of the immense changes taking place in world trading relationships — and challenging even further the economic autonomy of Canada.

FOR EXAMPLE...
Identifying the Effects of the FTA

The difficulties of the Canadian furniture industry since the signing of the FTA may be attributed at least in part to that agreement. They may also indicate that the ability of Canadian companies in many industries to compete successfully on "a level playing field" with U.S. companies — a prospect rarely doubted by those who supported the FTA — was an illusion.

Furniture Makers Feel Squeeze

Outgunned by U.S. competitors and threatened by menacing economic forces, Canada's furniture industry is retrenching in a battle for survival.

On its southern flank lie U.S. manufacturers, who are launching an aggressive assault on the Canadian market through openings provided by the Free Trade Agreement. This comes at a time when the Canadian industry's defences are weakened by a high Canadian dollar and soaring interest rates.

Adding to these woes are forecasts of a worsening economic downturn and the dampening effect of the federal government's goods and services tax.

"Shipments this year are down significantly in every sector," George Sinclair, executive director of the Ontario Furniture Manufacturers' Association, says. "When interest rates on credit cards get up past 20 percent, people just stop buying."

Privately owned

Plant closings and decreased production have already claimed at least 2000 jobs in an industry that directly employs 62 000 people and ships more than $5 billion worth of goods annually, says Robert Diguer, executive vice-president of the Canadian Council of Furniture Manufacturers. The vast majority of the industry is controlled by privately owned companies in Ontario and Quebec.

One study predicts that the eradication of Canada's high tariff wall by 1994 will result in a loss of 3500 jobs. "At the pace we're at now, we're going to exceed that 3500," Diguer says.

The council contends that jobs are migrating to the United States as free-trade provisions kick in. Canadian exports to the United States are dwindling at a time when imports are soaring, a trend that pushed Canada's furniture balance of trade into the negative last year for the first time since 1981. Canada enjoyed a $268 million furniture trade surplus in 1986.

Some Canadian furniture makers are looking south to relocate or build new plants — particularly to the U.S. southeast, where labour and material costs are comparatively low. At least ten Canadian firms have set up facilities in the United States in recent years.

SOURCE: Don Hogarth, "Furniture Makers Feel Squeeze," *Financial Post*, April 16, 1990, p. 7. Reproduced with permission.

SUMMARY

1. Canada is currently experiencing major changes in its economic relations with other countries and in its internal economic and political relationships. Three types of changes can be identified, as follows: (a) *globalization*, which refers to the growing tendency among corporations to conduct their business on a global basis, without regard to the special interests of the country in which they are based; (b) *regionalization*, which refers to the emergence of regional trading blocs, such as the European Community and the trading area created by the Canada–U.S. Free Trade Agreement; and (c) *decentralization*, which refers to the fragmentation of national economies, a process represented in Canada by the possible separation of Quebec from the rest of the country.

2. The main focus of the chapter is on regionalization, and especially on Canada's long-standing "regional" relationship with the United States. Until recently, all attempts since Confederation to establish a free-trade area with the United States failed. Instead, Canada reduced its trade barriers on a multilateral basis through the *General Agreement on Tariffs and Trade (GATT)*.

3. The increased interdependence of the U.S. and Canadian economies after World War II was characterized by a growing proportion of Canadian exports going to the United States and by increased U.S. investment in Canada, particularly *direct investment*, which gave U.S. firms control over the companies in which they invested. Canadian investment in the U.S. economy also grew significantly.

4. The Free Trade Agreement (FTA) between Canada and the United States came into effect on January 1, 1989. Its purpose, from the Canadian perspective, was to give Canada more open and more secure access to the U.S. market by reducing tariffs and other barriers to the entry of Canadian goods into the United States and by establishing an improved dispute-settlement mechanism to handle trade disputes between the two countries. The severe recession that followed the signing of this agreement has been linked by some to the agreement itself. While such allegations are difficult to prove, promised improvements have clearly failed to materialize in the first few years since the agreement came into effect.

KEY TERMS

globalization	General Agreement on Tariffs and Trade (GATT)	direct investment
regionalization		portfolio investment
decentralization		

Understanding a National Economy: Macroeconomics

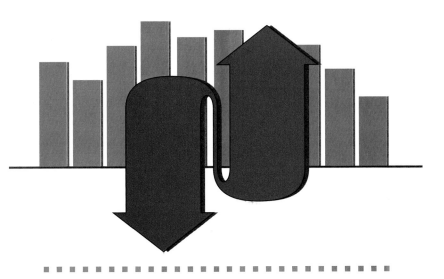

CHAPTER 17

The Anatomy of a Modern Economy: The Circular Flow of Income and Product

WHAT YOU WILL LEARN IN THIS CHAPTER

After studying this chapter, you will be able to

1. Describe the basic anatomy of a modern economy.

2. Outline the circular flow of income and product in an economy made up of households and firms.

3. Distinguish between stocks and flows in the economy.

4. Define domestic income and domestic product and explain how they are related.

5. Show how saving and investment fit into the circular flow of income and product.

6. Explain what is meant by *aggregate expenditure* and *aggregate output*.

7. Apply the concept of *equilibrium* to the circular flow of income and product.

8. Show how the government sector fits into the circular flow.

9. Show how imports and exports fit into the circular flow.

10. Explain the concepts of *leakages* and *injections* and the relationship between them.

A Preview   *Linking Cause and Effect in a National Economy*

Most Canadians would probably agree that the issues that really matter in an economy are jobs, output, and prices. These issues form the main subject matter of macroeconomics. Economists specializing in this field have tried to discover what causes employment, output, and prices to change from month to month and from year to year. They search for linkages between causes and effects.

The Interaction of Spending, Output, and Employment

Graph (a) gives an example of the type of "effect" that macroeconomists investigate — the behaviour of the annual rate of employment growth in the Canadian economy between 1986 and 1990. What caused this effect? Graphs (b)–(d) may provide some clues. They show that in the years 1986 to 1988, when employment grew quite rapidly (by about 3 percent annually), output, business investment, and consumer spending also grew rapidly. After 1988, when the rate of employment growth declined,

the rates of output growth and of business and consumer spending dropped off as well. What is the connection among these phenomena? In macroeconomics, we try to discover the answers to such questions.

SOURCE: Based on data from Statistics Canada, *Canadian Economic Observer, Historical Statistical Supplement 1989/90*, pp. 7, 23, 34, Catalogue no. 11-210. Used with permission of the Minister of Supply and Services Canada, 1992.

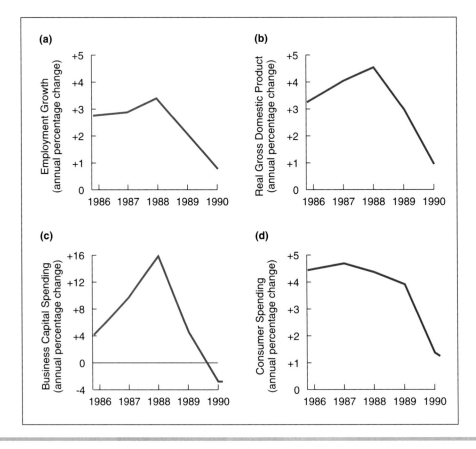

AN INTRODUCTION TO MACROECONOMICS

The Preview provides us with a thumbnail sketch of the aims and interests of the field of **macroeconomics**. The data in the four graphs refer to nationwide phenomena: the output of the entire Canadian economy (gross domestic product, or GDP), the combined expenditures of all consumers and of all business firms in Canada, and changes in employment across the economy. These data are derived from the activities of the millions of consumers and business firms whose *individual* behaviour is the subject of study of microeconomics. The purpose of macroeconomics is to examine how the output and spending decisions of all those individual entities combine to produce spending and output flows on a national level.

Economists — and, of course, many other observers — want to know not only how an individual firm such as General Motors decides how many cars to produce, what prices to charge, and how many workers to hire, but how output, prices, and employment are determined across the entire Canadian economy, and how those combined decisions relate to the problems of inflation and unemployment.

But in order to diagnose problems such as inflation and unemployment, economists first had to examine and describe the anatomy of a modern economy. Modern economies are extremely complex organisms, and it has taken several centuries of scholarly work to produce a fairly satisfactory outline of their anatomy. In some ways, as will become clear in this chapter, an economy closely resembles the circulatory system of the human body. Until William Harvey described the circular flow of blood through the human body in the seventeenth century, the medical profession had no reliable way of diagnosing human ills or of prescribing cures for them. Similarly, until economists identified the basic "flows" in a modern economy, it was difficult to make sense of the periodic fluctuations of prices, employment, and output. Even with its better understanding of the human body, modern medicine has not found a cure for all human ills; even with our better understanding of an economy's anatomy, there remain economic problems for which there are no satisfactory solutions. Nevertheless, there has been considerable progress in understanding. This chapter details the anatomy of a modern economy.

Macroeconomics
The study of large-scale, nationwide economic phenomena, such as inflation, unemployment, and economic growth.

THE STRUCTURE OF THE CIRCULAR FLOW

A modern economy is made up of a **circular flow of income and product**. The lifeblood of this system is *spending*. The job that I have depends on the spending of others. The income I earn in this job enables me in turn to purchase goods and services, and my spending provides jobs for others. The economy is a vast circular flow of production, income, and spending.

A Simple Economy

To see the circular flow in its simplest form, imagine an economy made up of only households and business firms — a two-sector economy with no government, no financial markets, and no imports or exports. To make things simpler still, assume that households live entirely from hand to mouth, spending all of their income on consumer goods as soon as that income is received. Similarly, assume that firms sell their entire output to consumers as soon as it is produced.

Circular flow of income and product
The flow of goods from firms to households and of factor services from households to firms, counterbalanced by the flow of expenditures from households to firms and of factor payments from firms to households.

The circular flow of income and product for this ultra-simple economy is shown in Box 17.1. The diagram is drawn with real goods and services flowing clockwise and the corresponding money payments flowing counterclockwise.

Two sets of markets link households to firms. Product markets, which appear at the top of the diagram, are those in which households buy goods and services produced by firms. Factor markets, which appear at the bottom, are those in which firms obtain the labour services, capital, and natural resources they need from households.

The clockwise flows of goods and services through these markets are balanced by counterclockwise flows of money payments. Households make payments for the things they buy in product markets. Firms make factor payments — wages, interest payments, rents, royalties, and so on — in exchange for the factor services they buy.

BOX 17.1   *The Circular Flow in a Simple Economy*

In this simple two-sector economy, households spend all their income on consumer goods as soon as they receive it, and firms sell all their output to households as soon as they produce it. Physical goods and factor services flow clockwise, while corresponding money payments flow counterclockwise.

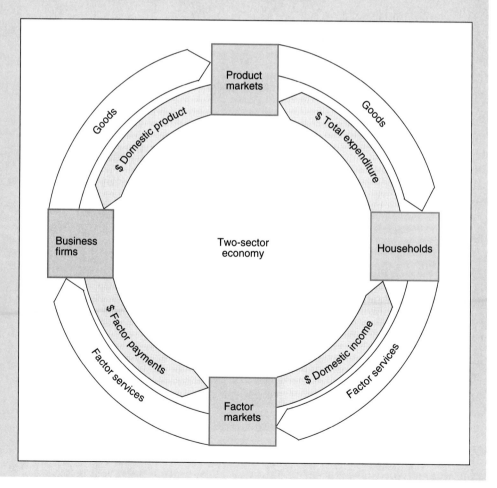

By convention, when firms use labour, capital, or natural resources that they themselves own, they are counted as "buying" those factors from the households that are the ultimate owners of the firms. All costs of production can therefore be viewed as factor payments. If a firm has something left over after it meets all its costs, it earns a profit. Profits too are counted as flowing directly to the households that own the firms, even though some profits may be retained by a firm to increase the owner's equity rather than being paid out as dividends. For purposes of the circular flow, then, profit is lumped together with other factor payments to make up total factor payments.

Stocks and Flows

Having said this much, let's pause for a moment to concentrate on a word used several times already. Economists call all of the things shown in Box 17.1 **flows** because they are processes that occur continuously through time. Flows are measured in units per time period — for example, in dollars per year, litres per minute, or tonnes per month. Measurements of flows are measurements of the rate at which things are happening.

Flows
Processes occurring continuously through time, measured in units per time period.

The technical language of economics distinguishes carefully between flows and stocks. A **stock** is an accumulated quantity of something existing at a particular time. (The word *stock* in this general sense has nothing to do with the kind of stocks that are bought and sold on Bay Street.)

Stocks
Accumulated quantities existing at a particular time, measured in terms of units alone.

For an illustration of the difference between stocks and flows, we can think of a bathtub filling up with water. When we talk about how fast the water is running, we are talking about a *flow*, measured in litres per minute. When we talk about how much water is in the tub at a given moment, we are talking about a *stock*, measured only in litres. Similarly, in the world of economics, we might talk about the rate of housing construction in Toronto in terms of new units per month (the flow) as distinct from the actual number of houses in Toronto as of January 1, 1991 (the stock).

Domestic Income and Product

Two of the flows in Box 17.1 deserve special attention and have special names. The first is **domestic income** — the total of all wages, rents, interest payments, and profits received by households. Domestic income is shown in the diagram as an arrow aimed at the box representing households. The second important flow is **domestic product** — a measure of the total value of the final goods and services produced. In the diagram, domestic product is shown as an arrow passing from the box representing product markets to the box representing firms.

Domestic income
The total of all incomes, including wages, rents, interest payments, and profits, received by households.

Domestic product
The total value of all goods and services supplied in the economy.

In this economy, domestic income and domestic product are equal, simply because of the way they are defined.[1] This equality can be verified in either of two ways. First, consider household expenditures as a link between domestic income and domestic product. Households are assumed to spend all of their income on consumer goods as soon as they receive it, and firms are assumed to

---

[1]Chapter 18 will show that, given the way domestic income and domestic product are actually measured by the official statisticians of the Canadian government, the equality between them does not hold precisely. However, these differences are not important for the current discussion.

sell all of their output to consumers as soon as it is produced. The payments made by buyers must equal the payments received by sellers, so domestic product must equal domestic income.

Alternatively, consider factor payments as a link between domestic income and domestic product. When firms receive money for goods they sell, they use part of it to pay the workers, natural-resource owners, and others who contributed factors of production to make the goods. Anything left over is profit. Factor payments, including profits, account for all the money received by firms, so total factor payments must be equal to domestic product. Factor payments also account for all of the income received by households, so total factor payments must be equal to domestic income. It again follows that domestic income and domestic product must be equal.

Saving and Investment

The circular flow shown in Box 17.1 is so simple that not very much of interest can be said about it. To build a theory that will be useful for understanding the real-world economy, a few complications must be introduced.

The first change will be to drop the requirement that households immediately spend all of their income to purchase consumer goods and, instead, to permit them to save part of what they earn. The rate of **saving** by households, under this assumption, is simply the difference between domestic income and household consumption expenditures.

The second change will be to drop the requirement that firms immediately sell all of their output to consumers. Instead, they will be permitted to sell some products to other firms and to let some accumulate in inventory before selling them to anyone. When firms buy newly produced capital goods (for example, production machinery, newly built structures, or office equipment) from other firms, they are said to engage in **fixed investment**. When firms increase the stock of finished products or raw materials that they keep on hand, they are said to engage in **inventory investment**. The rate of inventory investment can be less than zero in periods when firms are decreasing their stocks of goods or raw materials on hand. The sum of fixed investment and inventory investment will be called, simply, **investment**.

Note that investment is defined more narrowly in economics than in everyday usage. In everyday usage, people talk about "investing" in bonds or stocks. In actual fact, they are only "saving" their money in a different way. In the economist's terms, money becomes investment only when a firm uses it to purchase newly produced capital goods or new additions to inventory.

Circular flow with saving and investment

Box 17.2 shows how the circular flow of income and expenditure looks when saving and investment are added. (The clockwise arrows showing the flows of goods and services have been omitted to simplify the diagram.) Hypothetical numbers are used to illustrate how payments to factors of production become the income of households, and how this income, in turn, becomes expenditure on goods and services. Of the $100 000 income received by households, it is assumed that $80 000 is spent directly on consumption, while the other $20 000 is saved. This saving supplies a source of funds for firms to use in making investment expenditures.

Saving
The part of household income not used to purchase goods and services or to pay taxes.

Fixed investment
Purchases by firms of newly produced capital goods, such as production machinery, newly built structures, and office equipment.

Inventory investment
Changes in the stocks of finished products and raw materials that firms keep on hand. If stocks are increasing, inventory investment is positive; if they are decreasing, it is negative.

Investment
The sum of fixed investment and inventory investment.

The Circular Flow with Saving and Investment   BOX 17.2

When saving and investment are added to the circular flow, there are two pathways by which expenditures can travel on their way from households to product markets. Some income is spent directly on consumer goods. The rest is saved and passes to firms via financial markets. The firms then may or may not choose to use the investment expenditures in the product markets. The clockwise flows of goods and services have been left out of this diagram. Only flows of funds are shown.

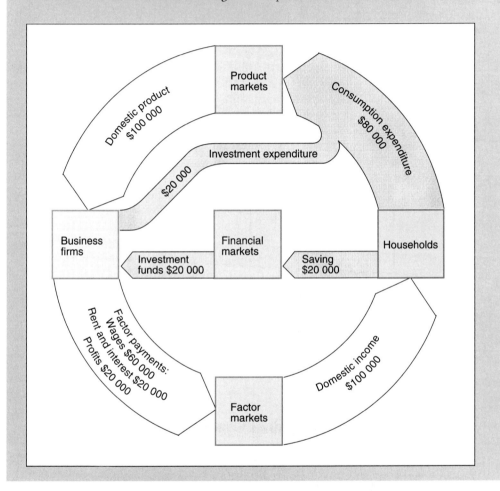

On the way from households to firms, the flow of saving passes through a set of financial markets. These markets include a great variety of financial institutions — chartered banks, trust and loan companies, credit unions and caisses populaires, the stock and bond markets, insurance companies, and other institutions that act as intermediaries between households that save and firms that make investment expenditures. Households supply funds to these financial markets. Firms can then borrow from financial markets to obtain the funds they need to make investment expenditures. (Chapter 22 will discuss the operation of financial markets in detail.)

Equilibrium and disequilibrium in the circular flow

Adding saving and investment to the circular flow raises an entirely new issue: can total expenditure still be counted on to provide an equalizing link between domestic income and domestic product? There are now two entirely different sets of people making expenditure decisions. Households decide how much to spend on consumption, and firms decide how much to spend on investment. How can we be sure that when these two kinds of expenditures are added together, the total will just equal the total value of all goods produced?

Aggregate Output and Expenditure

Aggregate output/
Aggregate supply
The value of all final goods and services produced by all firms.

Aggregate expenditure/
Aggregate demand
The value of all final goods and services purchased in a whole economy.

The term **aggregate output**, or **aggregate supply**, refers to the value of all final goods and services supplied by all firms in the economy.[2] There is already another term for the same thing: domestic product. Following the same terminology, **aggregate expenditure**, or **aggregate demand**, can be used to mean all final goods and services purchased in the whole economy. In defining *aggregate expenditure* this way, though, care must be taken in the way the term *expenditure* is used. Aggregate expenditure refers here to the total desired, or planned, expenditures of all buyers on all final goods and services produced in the economy. We refer to the amount that consumers, business firms, and other buyers *intend* to spend in the economy as their *desired*, or *planned, expenditures* (the two words are used interchangeably to express the intentions of buyers).

The desired expenditures of buyers may differ in the end from their *actual* expenditures. This happens, as we shall see, when desired expenditures (aggregate expenditure) do not equal the total value of all goods and services produced by an economy (aggregate output).

A numerical example

A numerical example will show how aggregate output can be compared with aggregate expenditure. Assume that the various firms in our hypothetical economy, represented in Box 17.3, have plans to produce consumer goods, such as apples and radios, at a rate of $80 000 per year. They also produce capital goods, such as machinery, at a rate of $20 000 per year. As all firms carry out their plans, output flows at a rate of $100 000 per year. This flow, which can be called either domestic product or aggregate output, is detailed in lines 1 to 3 of parts (a) and (b) of the table.

While producers are busy carrying out their plans, buyers make plans too. Consumers desire to buy consumer goods at a rate of $80 000 per year, and at the same time, the various firms plan to buy machinery at a rate of $20 000 per year. No firm plans either to increase or to decrease the stocks of finished products held in inventory, so planned inventory investment is zero. All these buying plans are expressed in lines 4 to 8 of Box 17.3(a). The total dollar value of all desired

---

[2]It is assumed here that values are expressed in current prices, unadjusted for inflation. These are defined as "nominal" values in Chapter 1. "Final goods and services" refers to goods and services that are not used up during the course of production. They include consumer and capital goods, but not raw materials. As will be explained in Chapter 18, it is necessary to restrict the measurement of domestic product to final goods in order to avoid double counting.

A Numerical Example of a Simple Economy in Equilibrium and Disequilibrium   *BOX 17.3*

This box shows a simple economy under conditions where (a) aggregate output is exactly equal to aggregate expenditure and (b) where output is not equal to expenditure. In the first case, the plans or desires of buyers and sellers exactly mesh and no unplanned inventory changes take place. In the second case, the plans don't mesh and unplanned inventory changes do occur.

(a) The Case of Equilibrium

Output Resulting from Producers' Plans

1.	Total domestic product (aggregate output)		$100 000
2.	Consumer goods (apples, radios)	$ 80 000	
3.	Capital goods (machinery)	20 000	

Expenditures Resulting from Buyers' Plans

4.	Total desired consumption expenditure		$ 80 000	
5.	Planned investment expenditure on machinery	$ 20 000		
6.	Planned inventory investment	0		
7.	Total planned investment expenditure		20 000	
8.	Total planned (or derived) expenditure (aggregate expenditure)			$100 000

(b) The Case of Disequilibrium

Output Resulting from Producers' Plans

1.	Total domestic product (aggregate output)		$100 000
2.	Consumer goods	$ 80 000	
3.	Capital goods	20 000	

Expenditures Resulting from Buyers' Plans

4.	Total desired consumption expenditure		$ 75 000	
5.	Planned investment expenditure on machinery	$ 15 000		
6.	Planned inventory investment	0		
7.	Unplanned inventory investment (unsold consumer goods of $5000 + unsold capital goods of $5000)	10 000		
8.	Total planned and unplanned investment		25 000	
9.	Total planned and unplanned expenditure (aggregate expenditure)			$100 000

Summary of Disequilibrium Case

10.	Total domestic product		$100 000
11.	Total domestic expenditure		100 000
12.	Planned	$ 90 000	
13.	Unplanned	10 000	

expenditures (consumption plus capital investment on machinery plus planned inventory investment) is listed on line 8 as total planned (or desired) expenditure.

Comparing line 1 with line 8 in Box 17.3(a), we see that the desires of buyers and sellers exactly mesh. Aggregate output and aggregate expenditure are equal. When the desires of buyers and sellers mesh this way, we say that the circular flow as a whole is in equilibrium, just as we say that an individual market is in equilibrium when the plans of its buyers and sellers mesh.

However, in practice, the plans, or desires, of buyers and sellers need not always fit together as neatly as they do in Box 17.3(a). It would be surprising if they did. After all, buyers and sellers do not often consult one another before production takes place. Often, production plans are set before buyers' desires are even formed.

As an example of what happens when buyers' and sellers' desires do not mesh, consider Box 17.3(b). The situation there is the same as in Box 17.3(a), except that now consumers plan to buy only $75 000 worth of consumer goods, and firms plan to buy only $15 000 worth of capital goods (machinery). Thus total planned, or desired, expenditure (the total of lines 4 and 5 in Box 17.3[b]) is only $90 000, even though aggregate output (line 1) is $100 000.

There are, therefore, some disappointments in store for producers: $5000 worth of consumer goods and $5000 worth of capital goods will be left over. What will happen to these unsold goods? Once produced, they cannot vanish into thin air. Instead, they will accumulate as inventories in the warehouses of the business firms. Those firms did not *plan* to make any inventory investments, but they find themselves making such investments despite their plans. The $5000 of unsold consumer goods and the $5000 of unsold capital goods are thus listed in line 7 of Box 17.3(b) as *unplanned* inventory investments.

The Equality of Domestic Product and Total Desired Expenditure

When aggregate buying plans do not mesh with aggregate production plans, the circular flow is said to be in *disequilibrium*. Aggregate output and aggregate expenditure are not equal: domestic product and total desired expenditure are not equal. One crucial equality does hold, though. Domestic product is still equal to total expenditure *when both planned and unplanned expenditures are taken into account*. The reason is that goods that are produced and not sold *must* be added to inventories, whether firms planned to put them there or not. As long as unplanned inventory investment is counted as part of total expenditure — and it is — total expenditure is by definition equal to domestic product. Thus, in Box 17.3(b), consumption expenditures of $75 000 (line 4) plus planned investment expenditure of $15 000 (line 5) *plus unplanned* inventory investment of $10 000 (line 7) equal $100 000, making total expenditure equal to domestic product. In equation form, this is written as follows:

$$\text{Domestic product} = \text{Total desired expenditure} + \text{Unplanned inventory investment} = \text{Total expenditure}$$

Another way to write exactly the same thing is:

$$\begin{matrix} \text{Aggregate} \\ \text{output} \end{matrix} = \begin{matrix} \text{Aggregate} \\ \text{expenditure} \end{matrix} + \begin{matrix} \text{Unplanned} \\ \text{inventory} \\ \text{investment} \end{matrix}$$

Reactions to disequilibrium

In the numerical example outlined in Box 17.3(b), aggregate expenditure fell short of aggregate output. Because buyers' and sellers' plans or desires failed to mesh, there was an unplanned accumulation of inventories. Firms would not want this unplanned rise in inventories to go on and on. In order to stop it, they would reduce their rate of output, or lower prices in order to stimulate sales, or both. These reactions would amount to a reduction in aggregate expenditure. The size of the circular flow would begin to shrink as the number of dollars received by firms for their products and the number of dollars paid out to workers fell.

At another time, aggregate expenditure might exceed aggregate output. With total desired expenditures greater than domestic product, unplanned inventory depletion would take place. Firms would react in a way opposite to their reaction to an excess of aggregate output over aggregate expenditure. They would either increase output to rebuild inventories or take advantage of the high level of aggregate expenditure to raise prices, or both. Whichever they did, the size of the circular flow would grow as incomes and expenditures rose.

Finally, it is entirely possible that when the desires of buyers and sellers were tested in the market, they would turn out to mesh. In that case, with production and desired expenditure equal, no unplanned inventory investment would occur, and no corrections would be necessary. The circular flow would be in equilibrium.

The Equality of Domestic Product and Domestic Income

Having shown that domestic product is equal to total expenditure in this economy, we also need to remind ourselves that domestic product is equal to domestic income. Go back for a moment to the situation in Box 17.2. Firms are shown to be producing $100 000 worth of goods a year. To produce those goods, they make factor payments (including profits) of $100 000 to households, which means that domestic income is also $100 000. The value placed on goods and services by producers (which equals domestic product) is, in fact, determined by the payments made to all factors of production. Thus, the domestic product is equal to domestic income.

Adding Government to the Circular Flow

When government enters the circular flow of income, expenditure, and product, things become slightly more complicated. Box 17.4 shows how the circular flow looks when government is added. Two new pathways along which expenditures can flow from households to the product market are opened up.

BOX 17.4 The Circular Flow with Government Included (Three-Sector Economy)

With government added to the circular flow of income and product, there are two new channels along which funds can flow from households to product markets. Some income is diverted to government in the form of net taxes and then used to finance government purchases. Alternatively, if the government runs a budget deficit, it may borrow from the public via financial markets and use the borrowed funds to finance its expenditures. If the government runs a budget surplus, the flow of funds along this pathway may be reversed, in which case the arrow from government to financial markets will point in the opposite direction from that shown.

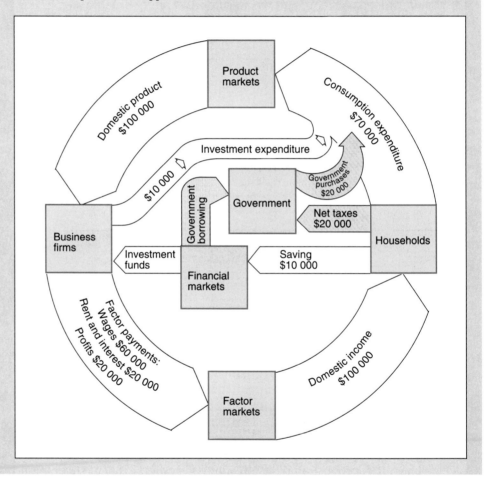

First, governments take in revenue from taxes they levy on households. Some of that revenue is immediately returned to households in the form of pension payments, family allowances, and other forms of government assistance called, as a group, *transfer payments*. The difference between what governments take in as tax revenue and what they pay out as transfer payments is called **net taxes**. Funds thus flow from households to government as net taxes and then from government to product markets as government purchases.

Second, if government purchases of goods and services exceed net taxes, the government may need to borrow from the public through financial markets. In

Net taxes
Total tax revenues collected by government at all levels minus total transfer payments disbursed.

this case, the government budget is said to be in **deficit**. When the government runs a deficit, funds flow from households to financial markets as saving, then from financial markets to the government as government borrowing, and finally from government to the product markets as government purchases. Sometimes, the government budget is in **surplus** rather than deficit. In that case, government's borrowing from the public is less than its repayment of past debts. The net flow of funds between government and financial markets is then the reverse of what is shown in Box 17.4

Box 17.4 shows the government with a balanced budget. It receives $20 000 in net taxes and spends $20 000 on goods and services. The box also shows the economy in equilibrium: Domestic product of $100 000 is exactly matched by expenditure of $100 000. Consumers spend $70 000 (after reducing their savings from $20 000 to $10 000 in order to pay net taxes of $20 000 out of their household income of $100 000), governments spend $20 000, and businesses have planned investment expenditures of $10 000.

Adding the Foreign Sector to the Circular Flow

The final step in constructing the circular flow of income and product is to add the foreign sector, as we have done in Box 17.5. This box shows that some of the expenditures made by consumers, firms, and governments do not flow to domestic product markets, but rather to foreign economies to pay for imports of goods and services. It is assumed that $5000 of government expenditures (G) and $5000 of business investment expenditures (I) are in the form of imports. In addition, $10 000 worth of goods bought by consumers (C) are imports, contributing to total imports of $20 000. These expenditures are shown by the arrow labelled *imports* in the diagram. At the same time, some expenditures on domestically produced goods and services are made by foreigners. These are shown in the box by the arrow labelled *exports*, which passes from the foreign-economy sector to domestic product markets.

Remember that the arrows in Box 17.5 all represent flows of funds, not flows of physical goods and services. The imports arrow thus shows the flow of funds out of the Canadian economy to pay for imported goods and services, and the exports arrow shows the flow of funds into the Canadian economy in payment for exports of goods and services. As we learned in Chapter 15, if imports exceed exports, the Canadian economy is said to run a trade deficit. This deficit must be paid for by borrowing from foreigners — hence the arrow labelled *loans from foreigners to finance trade deficit*, which points from foreign economies to the domestic financial markets. If, instead, Canadian exports exceed imports, Canada is said to run a trade surplus. In this case (not shown), foreign buyers of Canadian goods have to pay for them by borrowing funds in Canadian financial markets, and the direction of the arrow is reversed. In Box 17.5, exports are assumed to equal imports, and the whole economy is pictured as being in equilibrium.

Leakages and injections

The first section of this chapter described a highly simplified economy in which households spent all their income on consumption goods, so that all expenditures flowed directly from households to domestic product markets. As financial markets, government, and foreign economies were added, however, it was shown that in the real world, three kinds of purchases of goods and services do not originate directly in domestic households: investment (purchases of capital goods and

Deficit
In referring to government budgets, an excess of government purchases over net taxes.

Surplus
In referring to government budgets, an excess of net taxes over government purchases.

BOX 17.5   *The Circular Flow with Government and Foreign Sector (Four-Sector Economy)*

This box adds a foreign sector to the circular flow with government that was shown in Box 17.4. Some consumption, investment, and government purchases are for goods produced abroad; this is shown as the triple arrow labelled *imports* pointing toward the foreign-economies sector. At the same time, some expenditures on domestically produced goods are made by foreigners; these are shown as the arrow labelled *exports* running from the foreign sector to domestic product markets. If imports exceed exports, the excess imports must be paid for by borrowing from abroad; this is shown by the arrow labelled *loans from foreigners to finance trade deficit*. If exports instead exceed imports, there is a trade surplus, and the direction of that arrow is reversed. Note that all the arrows in this box represent flows of funds, not of physical goods and services. That is why the exports arrow points into the domestic economy and the imports arrow points away from it.

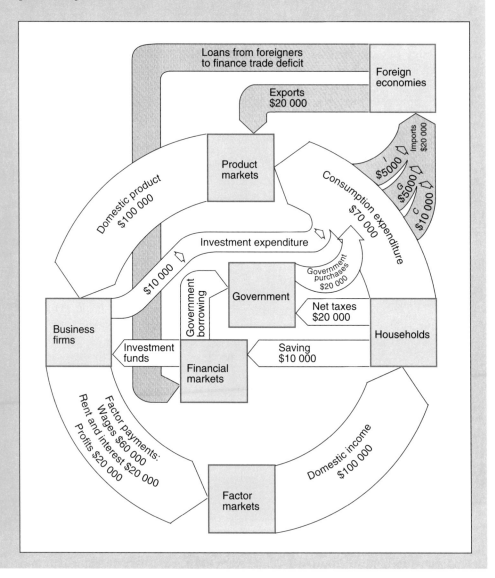

goods for inventory by domestic business firms), government purchases, and exports (purchases of domestic goods and services by foreigners). From now on, these three kinds of purchases will be referred to collectively as **injections** into the circular flow of goods and services.

Offsetting these injections are imports (expenditures by households, business firms, and units of government on goods produced abroad), plus saving and net taxes (the use of household income for purposes other than the direct purchase of goods and services). From now on, saving, net taxes, and imports will be referred to collectively as **leakages** from the circular flow.

Injections
The part of total expenditures that does not originate in domestic households — that is, investment, government purchases, and exports.

The equality of domestic income and domestic product

Another numerical example will show that adding the government and foreign sectors, with their associated injections and leakages, to the economy does not disturb the fundamental equality between domestic income and domestic product on which the circular flow is based. Box 17.6 shows an economy in which consumption is $70 000, investment is $12 000, government purchases are $20 000, and exports are $8000. Of the consumption, investment, and government purchases shown, $10 000 is spent on imported goods, which cannot be counted as part of the domestic product of the country represented in the box. Domestic product is thus shown as the total of consumption, investment, and government purchases, plus expenditures on domestic goods by foreigners (exports), minus that part of consumption, investment, and government purchases not spent on domestic goods and services (imports). As the economy represented in Box 17.6 is constructed, the total comes to $100 000.

Leakages
The part of domestic income not devoted to consumption (saving plus net taxes), plus domestic expenditures on foreign-made goods (imports).

The Equality of Domestic Income and Domestic Product BOX 17.6

This numerical example shows that the equality of domestic income and domestic product is maintained when the government and foreign sectors, with their associated injections and leakages, are added to the economy. Domestic product is a measure of the goods and services produced in the domestic economy. To arrive at its total, we add consumption, investment, and government purchases of all kinds, plus foreign purchases of domestically produced goods (exports), and we subtract the portion of consumption, investment, and government purchases devoted to foreign-made goods (imports). Using the term *net exports* to stand for exports minus imports, we could say that domestic product equals consumption, plus investment plus government purchases plus net exports. This is equal to domestic income, which is divided among consumption, saving, and net taxes — as shown in the second part of the table.

Consumption	$ 70 000
Plus investment	12 000
Plus government purchases	20 000
Plus exports	8 000
Less imports	− 10 000
Equals domestic product	$100 000
Consumption	$ 70 000
Plus saving	15 000
Plus net taxes	15 000
Equals domestic income	$100 000

Net exports
Total exports minus total imports.

The production of $100 000 of domestic product (represented by the symbol Y) generates $100 000 in factor payments for domestic households. As the bottom part of the table in Box 17.6 shows, this amount is divided among consumption ($70 000); saving ($S$) ($15 000), and net taxes (T_n) ($15 000). Introducing the term **net exports** (X_n) to represent exports minus imports, the relationships shown in Box 17.6 can be written in equation form as follows:

$$\text{Domestic product} = \text{Consumption} + \text{Investment} + \text{Government purchases} + \text{Net exports}$$

$$(\text{or, } Y = C + I + G + X_n)$$

$$= \text{Consumption} + \text{Saving} + \text{Net taxes}$$

$$(\text{or, } Y = C + S + T_n)$$

$$= \text{Domestic income}$$

Note that consumption, saving, and net taxes, taken together, constitute the way that total income is used by the recipients. On the other hand, consumption, investment, government purchases, and net exports are the expenditures that provide the source of income for the recipients.

The equality of leakages and injections

It follows from the relationship between domestic income and domestic product that total injections must equal total leakages. Beginning with the equation shown above, consumption can be subtracted from both sides, and imports (M) can be added to both sides. The result is as follows:

$$\text{Investment} + \text{Government purchases} + \text{Exports} = \text{Saving} + \text{Net taxes} + \text{Imports}$$

$$(\text{or, } I + G + X = S + T_n + M)$$

$$\text{Total injections} = \text{Total leakages}$$

In terms of the circular-flow diagrams, which were built up sector by sector, the leakages and injections appear as follows:

Economy	Injections	Leakages
Two-sector	I	S
Three-sector	$I + G$	$S + T_n$
Four-sector	$I + G + X$	$S + T_n + M$

Note that this relationship holds even though, in the numerical example of Box 17.6, no individual pair of items on the leakages and injections list exactly matches up. In that example, saving exceeds investment by $3000, imports exceed exports by $2000, and net taxes fall short of government purchases by $5000. The reason total injections must always equal total leakages is that injections include unplanned inventory investment as a balancing item. Suppose, for example, that beginning from the position shown in Box 17.6, government purchases suddenly rose by $5000, while planned expenditures by households, firms, and foreigners remained constant. The additional purchases made by government could not come out of thin air; unless or until production of goods and services increased, they would have to come out of inventory. Total investment, including unplanned inventory disinvestment, would thus fall by $5000 to compensate for the rise in government purchases.

Or suppose, again starting with the situation shown in Box 17.6, that foreigners suddenly decided to buy $2000 less of Canadian goods. Exports would fall, and the $2000 worth of goods that would otherwise have been exported would then accumulate as unplanned inventories of Canadian firms, once again maintaining the required equality.

LOOKING AHEAD

The circular-flow model presented in this chapter gives a good overview of the macroeconomy, but it leaves many questions unanswered. One question that must be dealt with is how domestic product, domestic income, and so on, can actually be measured. This matter will be dealt with in Chapter 18. Other unanswered questions have to do with the government's control over the volume of the circular flow through policy tools such as spending, taxes, and monetary policy. Just how are these policy tools used? How significant are their effects, individually and in combination? And how do the various tools interact? Such questions will be answered in Chapters 19–26.

Still another set of questions has to do with the connections among changes in nominal domestic product, real domestic product, and the average level of prices. We have said many times that when aggregate expenditure rises, firms respond by increasing real output or raising prices, or doing some of both. What conditions will determine their choice of option? The answer is crucial for the achievement of the macroeconomic goals of full employment, price stability, and real economic growth. This set of questions will be given a preview in the next chapter and will be dealt with more fully in Chapters 19 and 27.

SUMMARY

1. The *circular flow of income and product* is the flow of goods and services between households and firms, balanced by the flow of money payments made in exchange for those goods and services. In the simplest case, households spend all their money on consumer goods produced by firms, and firms use all the proceeds of the sales to pay wages, rent, interest, and profits to households.

2. In economics, the term *flow* refers to any process that occurs continuously through time. For example, the rate at which the automobile industry produces cars, measured in units per year, is a flow. A *stock* is the total amount of something that exists at a point in time. For example, the total number of cars registered in Canada as of a certain date is a stock.

3. *Domestic product* is the total value of all goods and services produced in the economy. *Domestic income* is the total income received by households, including wages, rents, interest payments, and profits. The two are always equal because for every dollar that firms receive from the sale of their products, they pay out a dollar in factor payments and profits.

4. *Saving* is the part of income that households do not spend on consumer goods or use to pay taxes. *Investment* refers to purchases of newly produced capital goods or the building up of inventories by firms. Saving passes from households to financial markets; firms borrow funds through financial markets to finance investment.

5. *Aggregate output* is the total value of goods and services produced in the economy, measured in terms of the prices at which they are sold. It means the same thing as domestic product. *Aggregate expenditure* is the current dollar value of all planned, or desired, expenditures in the economy.

6. The circular flow is said to be in equilibrium when aggregate output and aggregate expenditure are equal. In this case, there are no unplanned changes in inventories. If aggregate expenditure exceeds aggregate output, there will be unplanned decreases in inventory (negative inventory investment). Firms will tend to react by raising output, raising prices, or doing some of both. The circular flow will then expand. If aggregate output exceeds aggregate expenditure, there will be unplanned increases in inventories. The reactions of firms will cause the circular flow to shrink.

7. The government sector is connected to the circular flow in three ways. First, households pay *net taxes* (taxes minus transfer payments) to the government. Second, the government buys goods and services in product markets. And third, the government borrows from financial markets to finance a *deficit*, or supplies funds to financial markets when it runs a *surplus*.

8. The foreign sector is also connected to the circular flow in three ways. First, households pay foreign sellers for imported goods. Second, foreign buyers make payments to domestic firms for exported goods. And third, foreign lenders supply funds to domestic financial markets if the country has a trade deficit, or borrow from domestic financial markets if the country has a balance-of-payments surplus.

9. Saving, net taxes, and imports are known as *leakages* from the circular flow. Investment, government purchases, and exports are known as *injections*. When both planned and unplanned investments are included, leakages must equal injections. In a three-sector economy (households, firms, and government), this means that saving + net taxes = investment + government purchases. In an economy that is connected to the rest of the world, it means that saving + net taxes + imports = investment + government purchases + exports. The various pairs of leakages and injections need not balance; only the totals have to be equal.

KEY TERMS

macroeconomics	saving	net taxes
circular flow of income and product	fixed investment	deficit
flows	inventory investment	surplus
stocks	investment	injections
domestic income	aggregate output	leakages
domestic product	aggregate expenditure	net exports

KEY BOXES

Box 17.5 The Circular Flow with Government and Foreign Sector (Four-Sector Economy)

Box 17.6 The Equality of Domestic Income and Domestic Product

REVIEW QUESTIONS

1. Explain why domestic income and domestic product are equal. Why, when profits are included, do the payments made by firms to households exactly equal the value of the products that firms produce?

2. Sketch a circular flow for an economy in which there are households, firms, and financial markets. Include the pathways along which saving and investment travel.

3. What is the link between aggregate output and domestic product? Between aggregate expenditure and domestic product?

4. What does it mean to say that the circular flow of income and product is in equilibrium? What does inventory investment have to do with equilibrium and disequilibrium in the circular flow?

5. Sketch a circular flow for an economy in which there are households, firms, financial markets, and government. Show the three connections between the government sector and the rest of the economy.

6. Contrast the flow of money you put into your bank account each payday with the stock of money indicated by the balance in your bankbook. How are the flow and stock related? Why is one referred to as a *flow* and the other as a *stock*?

7. Not all inventory investment is unplanned. Why would a firm plan to increase or decrease its inventories? How would you plan your inventories over the year if you were a seller of children's toys? Of air conditioners? How would you plan your inventories of auto parts if you were a dealer in a town with a steadily growing, or steadily shrinking, population?

8. Rework Box 17.3(b) for the case of excess aggregate expenditure. What role do inventory adjustments play in establishing the equality of domestic income and domestic product? How would producers tend to adjust to these inventory changes?

9. Beginning from a state of equilibrium, as in Box 17.6, trace the effects of each of the following through the circular flow. What happens to inventories? What reactions do firms tend to have? What happens to the size of the circular flow, measured in nominal terms?

   a. Business managers, suddenly becoming more optimistic about the future, decide to increase investment in order to expand productive capacity.

   b. The federal government cuts income taxes.

   c. Good crops throughout the world reduce foreign demand for Canadian farm products.

10. Rework Box 17.6 for the following cases:

    a. Planned investment exceeds saving by $5000, and the government runs a $10 000 budget deficit.

    b. Imports exceed exports by $6000, and the government budget is exactly balanced.

    c. Saving exceeds investment, and net taxes exceed government purchases.

11. *Bonus question*: Can you work out an example where saving exceeds investment, the government runs a budget surplus, and imports exceed exports? If not, why not?

12. In a particular year, producers and buyers have the following plans:

Production of capital goods	$120 000
Total planned investment expenditure	50 000
Output of consumer goods	70 000
Total planned consumption expenditure	90 000

    a. Calculate aggregate expenditure and aggregate output. Is this economy in equilibrium or disequilibrium?

    b. Calculate unplanned inventory investment.

    c. What is the total domestic product?

Measuring Macroeconomic Performance

WHAT YOU WILL LEARN IN THIS CHAPTER

After studying this chapter, you will be able to

1. Define gross domestic product (GDP) and explain how it is measured.

2. Distinguish between gross domestic product and gross national product (GNP).

3. Distinguish between gross domestic product and net domestic income.

4. Define *personal income* and *personal disposable income.*

5. Use the GDP deflator as a measure of the changing level of average prices.

6. Compare the GDP deflator and the Consumer Price Index.

7. Discuss the usefulness and completeness of the Canadian national-income accounts.

8. Define *labour force, unemployment,* and the *unemployment rate,* and identify and explain three types of unemployment.

A Preview   *Measuring Inflation*

Rapidly rising prices — a phenomenon to which we refer as inflation — pose a threat to those whose incomes do not keep pace. But how is this threat measured? The following article provides some clues, leading into a more detailed treatment of the various kinds of macroeconomic measurements discussed in this chapter.

Inflation: Is the Cure Worsening the Disease?

Scarcely a day passes without a politician or business person warning of the threat that inflation poses to the Canadian economy. The Bank of Canada, besieged with pleas for lower interest rates, steadfastly reiterates the importance of "price stability."

But inflation comes in many forms — it's barely rising in some sectors of the economy — and it is measured in many ways. And, ironically, some of the cures prescribed for it may actually be worsening the disease.

Most Canadians associate inflation with rises in the Consumer Price Index. But Statistics Canada also tracks an industrial products price index — a tally of wholesale prices on goods ranging from soft drinks to machine tools — and a raw materials price index.

And, to track inflation for the economy as a whole, economists calculate an implicit price index, or "GDP deflator," which includes prices paid by governments and business and on exports and imports as well as by consumers.

Examining these indices since 1981 shows that consumer prices have consistently risen more than all other prices, by 5.3 percent on a compound annual average. By contrast, the GDP deflator has risen an average of 4.4 percent a year, industrial product prices have risen 3.4 percent, while raw material prices didn't grow at all. Even without oil and gas, whose prices plunged in 1986, raw material prices only advanced an average of 0.9 percent a year.

SOURCE: Greg Ip, "Inflation: Is the Cure Worsening the Disease?" *Financial Post*, April 2, 1991, p. 1. Reproduced with permission.

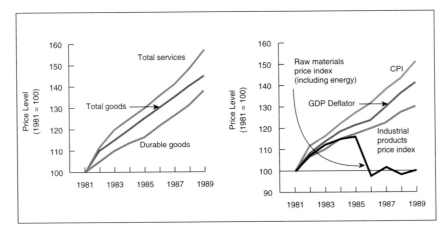

SOURCE: Based on data from Statistics Canada, *Canadian Economic Observer, Historical Statistical Supplement 1989/90*, p. 47, Catalogue no. 11-210. Used with permission of the Minister of Supply and Services Canada, 1992.

MEASURING INCOME AND PRODUCT

A famous American writer once revealed that his early ambition in life had been to become an astronomer — he had been fascinated with stars as a young man. Once at university, however, he lasted only a few months in his introductory course. Why? Because, he said, he hadn't expected the study of stars to involve so many mathematical measurements.

Indeed, the same problem adheres to many exciting and important ideas: They may be fascinating in a general sort of way, but in order to examine them seriously, one has to dig down into the dirt of detail and work with figures and measurements.

The behaviour of output and income, the price level, and the level of employment is of interest to most Canadians. We want to know *why* we suffer from periodic bouts of unemployment and inflation, as well as from declining output. But before we can embark on an analysis of the causes of such phenomena, we must know how to define and measure them. That is the purpose of this chapter. We begin by examining how income and output are measured, then we move on to prices, and, finally, we consider the definition and measurement of unemployment.

Gross Domestic Product

National-income accounting begins with the measure of total production known as **gross domestic product (GDP)**. GDP is the dollar value at current market prices (that is, the nominal value) of all final goods and services produced annually within the boundaries of a nation.

Until 1986, a slightly different measure, known as **gross national product (GNP)**, was used to measure our economy's output. The difference can be explained briefly as follows: Gross domestic product measures output produced *within Canada* (and the income flowing from that output) in a given year regardless of who owns the production units — Canadians or foreigners. Gross national product measures production *by Canadian nationals* both inside and outside Canada. For example, investment income received by Canadians from abroad is included in GNP but not in GDP, while investment income paid to foreigners arising from income produced in Canada is included in GDP but not in GNP. Since people typically think of economic activity as the output produced within their own country, most Western nations have come to use GDP as the measure of their output. Until recently, Canada and the United States, by using GNP measurements, were two major exceptions to this practice. As of 1986, Canada has joined the majority of Western nations in using the GDP as the prime measure of output, though measurements of GNP will continue to be made as well. (The United States continues to use GNP as its main measure of output and income.)

Since investment income (in the form of interest and dividend payments) received by Canadians from their foreign investments is less than the investment income paid to non-Canadians for their investments in Canada, GNP is less in Canada than GDP. The difference in 1990 was as follows:

Gross domestic product (GDP)
The dollar value at current market prices of all final goods and services produced within a country in a given year.

Gross national product (GNP)
The dollar value at current market prices of all final goods and services produced by citizens of a country both at home and abroad.

Gross domestic product (GDP) (including investment income earned by foreigners in Canada)	$677.9 billion
Minus investment income paid to foreigners	− 32.9 billion
Plus investment income earned by Canadian nationals abroad	+ 8.7 billion
Equals gross national product (GNP)	653.7 billion

In most countries, the difference between GDP and GNP is much smaller than it is in Canada — usually less than 1 percent. However, both in Canada and elsewhere, the annual growth rates of the two measures seldom differ much. Therefore, for purposes of macroeconomic analysis, it does not matter very much which measure of output and income is used. Since GDP has now been adopted as the primary measure for Canada, it will be used most often in the remainder of this text, though at times reference may be made to GNP for specific purposes.

Why We Measure *Final* Goods

Final goods and services
Goods and services that are sold to (or are ready to be sold to) parties that will use them for consumption, investment, export, or as government purchases.

It is now time to look more closely at the actual construction of the GDP figures. Our definition states that GDP measures all *final* goods and services produced in a given year in Canada. The term **final goods and services** is actually a key part of the definition of gross domestic product. The purpose of GDP is to measure the sum of the economic contributions of each firm and industry in the country, without missing anything and without counting anything twice. To do this, care must be taken to count only goods and services sold to *final users* — parties that will use them for domestic consumption, investment, export, or as government purchases. *Intermediate goods* — those that are purchased to be used as inputs in producing other goods or services — are excluded.

Box 18.1 shows why counting both final and intermediate goods would overstate total production. The example traces the process of producing a loaf of bread

---

⇅ **BOX 18.1** *Value Added and the Use of Final Products in Measuring GDP*

This table shows why GDP must include only the value of final goods and services if it is to measure total production without double counting. The value of sales at each stage of production can be divided into the value added at that stage and the value of purchased inputs. The selling price of the final product ($1 for a loaf of bread, in this case) is equal to the sum of the values added at all stages of production.

Final stage: baking		
Value of one loaf of bread	$1.00	
Minus value of flour	−0.60	
Equals value added in baking	$0.40	→ $0.40
Next to final stage: milling		
Value of flour	$0.60	
Minus value of wheat	−0.35	
Equals value added in milling	$0.25	→ $0.25
Second from final stage: farming		
Value of wheat	$0.35	
Minus value of fuel, fertilizer, and so on	−0.20	
Equals value added in farming	$0.15	→ $0.15
All previous stages		
Value added in fuel and fertilizer industries, plus value added by suppliers to those industries, and so on	$0.20	→ $0.20
Total value added		$1.00

that sells for $1 at retail. The final stage of bread production is baking, but the baker does not do a dollar's worth of work. Instead, the baker takes 60 cents' worth of flour, turns it into a loaf of bread, and gets 40 cents in exchange for the labour, capital, and other factors of production used in the process of baking. The 60 cents' worth of flour is an intermediate good; the 40-cent contribution made by the baker is the **value added** to the product at its final stage. (Of course, in practice, other intermediate goods, such as yeast, fuel for the oven, and so on, are used in baking. It is only to simplify the example that we assume that bread is made solely from flour plus the effort of the baker.)

The next section of Box 18.1 shows the next-to-last stage of production, milling the flour. The miller buys 35 cents' worth of wheat, produces flour that sells for 60 cents, and gets 25 cents in exchange for the work of milling. The value added at the milling stage is 25 cents.

Going still farther back, we come to the stage at which the wheat was grown. To grow 35 cents' worth of wheat, some farmer bought 20 cents' worth of fuel, fertilizer, and so on, and kept 15 cents in exchange for the effort of growing the wheat. That makes 15 cents more of value added.

Clearly, the process of making bread could be traced back to ever-more-removed stages. The last section of the box sums up the value added at all stages of production prior to farming—by the fuel and fertilizer suppliers, the suppliers of those suppliers, and so on. If production were traced back far enough, every penny could be attributed to the value added somewhere in the chain of production.

Now compare the first and last lines of the box. Lo and behold, the value of the final good, bread, turns out to be an exact measure of the sum of the values added at each stage of production. That is why only final goods are counted in GDP. Adding together the dollar's worth of bread plus the 60 cents' worth of flour plus the 35 cents' worth of wheat and so on would far overstate the true rate of productive activity (the true total value added) in the economy.

Value added
The dollar value of an industry's sales less the value of intermediate goods purchased for use in production.

The Expenditure Approach to Measuring GDP

In principle, GDP could be measured by adding together the value of each final good or service sold or by adding up the value added at each stage of production, as shown in Box 18.1. To simplify the process, however, national-income accountants[1] take advantage of the equality of domestic product and total expenditure. It is easier to gather data on the total expenditures of households, investors, governments, and buyers of exports on final goods produced in the domestic economy than it is to stand at factory gates and count goods as they roll off assembly lines. This way of measuring GDP is known as the **expenditure approach**. Box 18.2 shows how it works, using 1990 data for the Canadian economy.

Expenditure approach (to measuring GDP)
A method of estimating nominal aggregate economic activity by adding together the various expenditures on final goods and services produced domestically.

Consumption expenditure
The first line of Box 18.2 gives total household consumption of both domestically produced and imported goods and services — totalling $402.1 billion in 1990.

[1]Reference is still made in Canada to the *national*-income accounts (which contain the data on both GDP and GNP) and to *national*-income accountants, even though gross *domestic* output has become the main measure of economic activity.

BOX 18.2 Gross Domestic Product by Type of Expenditure, 1990

Gross domestic product is estimated using the expenditure approach. This involves adding together the values of expenditures on newly produced final goods and services made by all economic units in Canada to obtain a measure of aggregate economic activity.

Item	Amount (billions of dollars, at current prices)
1. Personal expenditure on consumer goods and services	402.1
2. Government current expenditure on goods and services	132.5
3. Gross fixed capital investment	141.1
4. Change in inventories	−2.7
5. Exports of goods and services	168.4
6. Imports of goods and services	−165.5
7. Statistical discrepancy	2.0
8. *Gross domestic product at current prices*	677.9

SOURCE: Adapted from Statistics Canada, *Canadian Economic Observer*, June 1991, p. 5.3, Catalogue no. 11-010. Reproduced with permission of the Minister of Supply and Services Canada, 1992.

Both the goods and the services components of consumption contain some items that do not pass through the marketplace on their way to consumers. One such item is an estimate of food produced and consumed on farms. Another is an estimate of the rental value of owner-occupied homes. As we shall see later in this chapter, however, by no means are all nonmarket goods and services captured in the national-income accounts.

Government expenditure

Line 2, government current expenditure, measures the contribution that all levels of government — federal, provincial, and municipal — make to gross domestic product. This figure poses some special problems. Ideally, the government contribution should be measured in terms of the value of the services that governments produce, such as education, national defence, police protection, and all the rest. However, since very few government services are actually sold to consumers and businesses, there are no market prices in terms of which to value them. Instead, national-income accountants use government purchases of goods and services to approximate the contribution of government to gross domestic product.

Government expenditure on goods and services includes the wages and salaries of all civilian and military personnel hired by government plus the value of all the buildings, computers, paper clips, assault rifles, and so on, used by those employees. Presumably, all the government workers using all that equipment produce an output at least as valuable as the same inputs could have produced in the private sector. In any event, that is the assumption that justifies inclusion of government purchases in GDP. Note that government transfer payments are not included, since they do not represent expenditures made to purchase newly produced goods or current services.

Investment expenditure

The item in Box 18.2 called *gross fixed capital investment* is the sum of all firms' purchases of newly produced capital goods, by both government and private firms. This includes machinery and office equipment and new construction of business structures and residential housing. Separate account is kept of inventory investment, called *change in inventories*. As noted in Chapter 17, this refers to changes in the stock of finished products and raw materials that firms keep on hand. If such stocks are increasing, inventory investment is positive; if they are decreasing, it is negative.

Net-export expenditure (exports minus imports)

Line 5 of Box 18.2 shows exports of goods and services for 1990. These must be added in because they are goods and services produced in Canada, even though they are bought and consumed elsewhere. On the other hand, imports must be subtracted (line 6) because some of the expenditures on consumer goods, investment goods, and government purchases that have already been added in were for imported goods. However, because these goods were not produced in Canada, they must now be subtracted.

The statistical discrepancy

The final item in the calculation of GDP is a minor irritant called the *statistical discrepancy*. It arises because, each year, the GDP is measured in two different ways: on the basis of *expenditures* (as illustrated in Box 18.2) and on the basis of *income* (as illustrated in Box 18.3). Conceptually, these two approaches should give the same results, but in practice, the thousands of more-or-less reliable information sources that must be used in calculating GDP yield results that never quite agree. The problem is solved by subtracting half of the difference from the larger number and adding half of the difference to the smaller number. In this way, a uniform GDP figure is produced each year for the two measurements. The balancing figure is called the *statistical discrepancy*.

The Income Approach to Measuring GDP

Domestic Income

We turn now to the income approach to GDP measurement. As the name implies, the **income approach** measures the overall rate of the circular flow by adding up all the different kinds of incomes earned by households. This is done in Box 18.3. The various incomes add up to what is known as **net domestic income**, or, simply, *domestic income*. The categories of income used in the derivation of domestic income require further clarification.

The category *wages, salaries, and supplementary labour income* includes not only wages and salaries but also employer contributions to such social benefits as pensions and unemployment insurance as well as such supplementary income as various fringe benefits and rental income.

The category *corporation profits* includes all income earned by the owners (that is, the shareholders) of corporations, whether the owners actually receive that income or not. Dividends are the part of that income that the owners actually receive. Another part goes to pay the taxes on corporate profits, while yet another is retained by corporations to use for investment purposes. Dividends

Income approach
(to measuring GDP)
A method of estimating nominal aggregate economic activity by adding together the various incomes earned by all households.

Net domestic income
The total income received by a nation's productive factors resulting from production within the nation's boundaries. It is equal to GDP minus capital-consumption allowances, indirect business taxes, and the statistical discrepancy.

BOX 18.3 *Net Domestic Income and Gross Domestic Product, 1990*

Nominal gross domestic product is measured using the income approach. First, net domestic income is derived by adding together the values of all forms of income earned by households from production in Canada. This includes dividends paid to nonresidents out of profits generated in Canada, as well as some portions of corporate profits, such as retained earnings and corporate profit taxes, that are not actually received by households. Indirect taxes (less subsidies) plus capital-consumption (depreciation) allowances and the statistical discrepancy are added to net domestic income to obtain gross domestic product. The total obtained using the income approach is the same as the GDP calculated by the expenditure approach (after the statistical discrepancy has smoothed out the initial difference).

Item	Amount (billions of dollars, at current prices)
1. Wages, salaries, and supplementary labour income	383.2
2. Corporation profits before taxes	47.9
3. Interest and miscellaneous investment income	58.0
4. Net income of farm operators from farm production	2.7
5. Net income of nonfarm unincorporated business, and rent	37.2
6. Inventory valuation adjustment	−2.5
7. *Net domestic income*	526.5
8. Indirect taxes (less subsidies)	76.5
9. Capital-consumption allowances	76.9
10. Statistical discrepancy	−2.0
11. *Gross domestic product at current prices*	677.9

SOURCE: Adapted from Statistics Canada, *Canadian Economic Observer*, June 1991, p. 5.2, Catalogue no. 11-010. Reproduced with permission of the Minister of Supply and Services Canada, 1992.

paid to nonresidents are included because they represent income derived from production within Canada, while dividends received by Canadians from abroad are excluded because that income was not generated in Canada.

Line 3 of Box 18.3, *interest income*, excludes interest paid by governments on the public debt, which is considered a transfer payment. Miscellaneous investment income includes profits or losses on government business enterprises.

Items 4 and 5 represent all income earned by farmers, small unincorporated businesses, and self-employed professionals. No attempt is made to sort this income into wages, interest, or profits. Rental income is the income of persons acting as landlords.

The sixth item, *inventory-valuation adjustment*, refers to the artificial increase in the value of inventories that results from price increases (inflation). An appropriate deduction is made for this.

Adding together all these items gives us net domestic income (line 7).

From domestic income to GDP: reconciling the income and expenditure approaches

The results we have obtained thus far do not seem to agree with those that we observed in the circular-flow diagrams of Chapter 17. In those simplified diagrams, the income produced by an economy (defined here as net domestic income) was always equal to the value of output (GDP). This is not the case, however, for the 1990 income figures for the Canadian economy that we just itemized. As we saw in Box 18.2, the GDP for that year, based on the expenditure approach, was $677.9 billion. In Box 18.3, line 7, we discovered that the incomes generated by that domestic output totalled only $526.5 billion, which is more than $150 billion short of the value of output. Why is net domestic income considerably less than gross domestic product? This can be explained as follows: The GDP as derived via the expenditure approach is based on the purchase of all newly produced final goods *valued at current prices*. These prices, in turn, are based on all the costs incurred in producing the good or service, including profit. To give a simple example, if a firm produces only one unit of a good, and if the costs for that unit are $100 for wages, $50 for interest and rent, and $50 for profit, that good will be priced at $200. If the output of the economy consisted of that good alone, the GDP would be $200. Note now that all the costs of this particular product are transformed into an equivalent amount of income. The total of wages, interest, rent, and profit is $200, and all of this will be income to someone. This is the kind of situation that we described in Chapter 17. However, in the real world, not all the costs of doing business (and, hence, not all the costs that make up the price of a product) generate an equivalent amount of income. For example, the indirect taxes that business firms pay are added to other costs in determining price, but they do not accrue as income to producers in the economy. They are treated differently from the corporate profits tax, which is viewed as being earned by owners and then taken from them by the tax collector. Therefore, the amount of such indirect taxes will not be included in income, but it *will* be included in the value of goods produced that year (because, as a cost, it will add to the price of those goods). Therefore, net domestic income will fall short of gross domestic product by at least this amount, and, in order to "reconcile" the former with the latter, an amount equivalent to indirect taxes will have to be added to net domestic income (line 8).

Something similar takes place with capital-consumption (depreciation) allowances. Such allowances "capture" that part of the year's investment that was made solely to replace worn-out or obsolete equipment (capital "consumed" or used up). Such expenditures are counted as costs by the firms that make them, and add to the price of the product (and hence to the value of GDP), but they do not show up as proprietors' or shareholders' income. Therefore, net domestic income will fall short of gross domestic output (measured on the basis of expenditures) not only by the value of indirect taxes but also by an amount equal to total capital-consumption allowances. This amount must therefore be added to net domestic income as well, in order to reconcile it with GDP. This is done in line 9 of Box 18.3. By adding both these items to net domestic income, plus the statistical discrepancy, we arrive via the income approach at a value for GDP that is exactly equal to the value of GDP as measured by the expenditure approach.

From Net Domestic Income to Personal Disposable Income

Net domestic income, as mentioned several times, is a measure of income earned by households, whether or not those households ever actually get their hands on it. For some purposes, it is more important to measure what households

Personal income
The total of all income, including transfer payments, actually received by households before payment of personal income taxes and other transfer payments to government.

Personal disposable income
Personal income minus personal taxes.

actually receive than what they earn. The total income actually received by households is called **personal income**.

Box 18.4 shows the steps required to transform domestic income into personal income. First, two items that are earned by households but not received by them are subtracted. These items are corporate profits taxes and undistributed corporate profits. Next, transfer payments — payments received by households although not earned by them — are added. The result is personal income.

One further income measure is shown at the bottom of Box 18.4: **personal disposable income** (or *disposable income*, for short). This is what households have left of their personal income after they pay personal taxes of various kinds to federal, provincial, and municipal governments, including transfer payments to government, such as pension and unemployment-insurance contributions.

This completes our discussion of the major items in the national-income account, measured in current prices. In the next section, we turn our attention to the problem of making adjustments for changing prices.

MEASURING REAL INCOME AND THE PRICE LEVEL

Real Gross Domestic Product and the Deflator

In the ten-year period 1981–90, Canadian gross domestic product, measured in nominal terms (that is, at current prices), rose from $356 billion to $677.9 billion.

BOX 18.4   *Net Domestic Income and Personal Income, 1990*

Domestic income is a measure of all income earned by households, while personal income is a measure of the income households actually receive. To go from domestic income to personal income, subtract corporate profits taxes and undistributed corporate profits, then add transfer payments. If personal taxes and transfer payments to government are subtracted from this figure, the result is personal disposable income.

Item	Amount (billions of dollars, at current prices)
Net domestic income	526.5
Minus corporate profits taxes	− 14.2
Minus undistributed corporate profits	− 2.7
Plus transfer payments*	83.5
Equals personal income	593.1
Minus personal taxes and transfer payments to government	− 135.1
Equals personal disposable income	$458.0

*Includes government and consumer interest payments and business transfer payments

SOURCE: Adapted from Statistics Canada, *Canadian Economic Observer*, June 1991, pp. 5.7, 5.8, and estimates, Catalogue no. 11-010. Reproduced with permission of the Minister of Supply and Services Canada, 1992.

To anyone who lived in Canada during those years, however, it is clear that even though nominal GDP almost doubled, the real output of goods and services increased much less. Some of the increase in the dollar value of GDP reflected an increase in the prices at which goods and services were sold. To know what really happened to output in those years, then, we need to adjust the growth of nominal GDP to take inflation into account.

What we need is a measure of the price level in order to make this adjustment — a measure of the change in the average prices of all goods and services. The most broad-based measure of the price level for the Canadian economy is the one known as the **GDP deflator**. The appendix to this chapter explains how the GDP deflator is calculated, but for now, it is enough to say that it is a *price index* that covers all final goods and services that go to make up the GDP. A **price index** is a weighted average of the prices of goods and services expressed in relation to a base-year value of 100.

GDP deflator
A price index that covers all final goods and services produced in the economy.

Price index
A weighted average of the prices of goods and services expressed in relation to a base-year value of 100.

In discussions of economic theory, the price level is expressed in relation to a base-year value of 1.0. Official government statistics, however, commonly use a base-year value of 100. In the late 1980s and early 1990s, the base year used in calculating the GDP deflator was 1986; in other words, the value of the GDP deflator for 1986 was 100. By 1990, its value had reached 118.8. This means that the 1990 "market basket" of goods — so many litres of gasoline, so many loaves of bread, so many trips to the hairdresser, and so on — cost 18.8 percent more than it would have if sold at the prices of 1986.

To calculate real GDP — GDP adjusted for inflation — for 1990, we divide 1990 nominal GDP by the ratio of the 1990 GDP deflator to the 1986 GDP deflator, and arrive at a value of $570.7 billion. This figure can also be referred to as the value of 1990 GDP measured in constant 1986 dollars. By comparing the 1990 real GDP of $570.7 billion with the 1981 real GDP of $440.1 billion (Box 18.5), we can see that the real output of goods and services rose by only about 29.7 percent over the ten-year period. The remaining part of the near doubling of nominal GDP represented pure inflation.

Using the GDP deflator

Box 18.5 shows nominal GDP, real GDP, and the GDP deflator for Canada in each year from 1981 to 1990. To convert nominal GDP for any year to real GDP stated in constant 1986 dollars, we simply divide nominal GDP by the ratio of the deflator for that year to the base-year deflator. For convenience, we can refer to the year for which we are making the adjustment as the *current year*. In equation form, then, the rule for adjustment can be stated as follows:

$$\text{Current-year real GDP} = \frac{\text{Current-year nominal GDP}}{\text{Current-year deflator/Base-year deflator}}.$$

As Box 18.5 shows, applying this formula to current years after 1986 gives values for real GDP that are less than current-year nominal GDP. Applying the formula to current years before 1986, when the GDP deflator had values that were less than 100, gives values for real GDP in 1986 dollars that exceed nominal GDP for those years.

The shrinking dollar

As long as we speak in nominal terms, a dollar is a dollar. When we begin to speak in real terms, as we have just been doing, a 1990 dollar is no longer the same as a 1981 dollar or a 1986 dollar. The reason is that inflation shrinks the

BOX 18.5   *Nominal GDP, Real GDP, and the GDP Deflator for Canada, 1981–1990*

At the time of writing (1992), the base year for the GDP deflator is 1986. To calculate real GDP in constant 1986 dollars for any current year, divide current-year nominal GDP by the ratio of the current-year GDP deflator to the base-year GDP deflator.

Year	Nominal GDP (billions of dollars, at current prices)	GDP Deflator	Real GDP (billions of constant 1986 dollars)
1981	356.0	80.9	440.1
1982	374.4	87.9	426.0
1983	405.7	92.3	439.4
1984	444.7	95.2	467.2
1985	478.0	97.7	489.4
1986	505.7	100.0	505.7
1987	551.3	104.8	526.1
1988	603.4	109.8	549.2
1989	651.6	115.2	565.7
1990	677.9	118.8	570.7

SOURCE: Adapted from Statistics Canada, *Canadian Economic Observer*, June 1991, pp. 5.2, 5.3, 5.4, Catalogue no. 11-010. Reproduced with permission of the Minister of Supply and Services Canada, 1992. Also, *Financial Post Report on the Nation*, Winter 1990, p. 50. Reproduced with permission.

purchasing power of the dollar each year. The GDP deflator (or any of the other price indexes to be discussed) can be used to measure the shrinking value of the dollar, beginning from any year we choose. The purchasing power of the dollar in a given current year relative to some other year is calculated by dividing $1 by the ratio of the current-year GDP deflator to the GDP deflator in the year for which the comparison is being made. For example, to calculate the purchasing power of the 1990 dollar relative to that of the 1981 dollar, we first calculate the ratio of the 1990 GDP deflator to the 1981 GDP deflator. That ratio is 118.8 ÷ 80.9 = 1.47. Dividing $1 by 1.47 gives 68 cents. In 1990, the dollar was worth only 68 cents compared with its value in 1981. (The choice of 1981 as a year from which to measure the shrinking value of the dollar is arbitrary; any other year could be used instead.)

The Consumer Price Index

Consumer Price Index (CPI)
A price index based on the market basket of goods and services purchased by a typical urban household.

Although the GDP deflator is the broadest-based price index for the Canadian economy, it is not the best-known one. That honour belongs to the **Consumer Price Index (CPI)**. Rather than taking into account the prices of all final goods and services, as the GDP deflator does, the Consumer Price Index considers only the goods and services that make up the "market basket" purchased by a typical urban household.

The Consumer Price Index measures the prices of about 400 goods and services purchased by private households in Canadian urban centres with a population of 30 000 or more. The current index is based on a "basket" of goods selected in 1986. This basket was linked to a previous basket that provided a basis for the index in 1981. Since a fairly constant basket of goods and services is maintained, a continuous price index is possible.

The basket of goods and services typically purchased by consumers is determined through regular family-expenditure surveys. Once the basket has been selected, the price of each item in the basket is monitored monthly. Each item is given a "weight," depending on its importance in consumer purchases. The price change of each item multiplied by its weight determines the change in the CPI for a given month. The weights are now changed every four years, reflecting changing consumer tastes and buying patterns. Box 18.6 provides a breakdown of the major items contained in the CPI and the weights derived for those items in the years 1967 and 1990. Note that basic items such as food accounted for a much smaller proportion of the average family's expenditure in 1990 than they did in 1967, while housing and other items represented a larger proportion.

The importance of the Consumer Price Index

The CPI is the most widely used price series produced by Statistics Canada. Its importance derives from its usefulness in measuring the purchasing power of the consumer dollar. All income earners would like to increase their dollar income each year, but what they are most interested in knowing is whether such dollar increases are sufficient to maintain or increase their purchasing power. The latter

"Weights" of Major Items in the Consumer Price Index   BOX 18.6

The Consumer Price Index is calculated by measuring the price changes of a wide range of goods and services. The items in a typical consumer basket are given "weights" based on the relative amount spent on each item. Since consumer spending patterns change over time, these weights must be changed periodically. Below are the weights for 1967 and 1990, reflecting the percentage of total consumer expenditures spent on major goods and services.

Item	Weight (percent) 1967	1990
Food	24.8	18.1
Housing	31.4	36.3
Clothing	11.3	8.7
Transportation	15.2	18.3
Health and personal care	4.5	4.2
Recreation, reading, and education	6.9	8.8
Tobacco and alcohol	6.0	5.6

SOURCE: Statistics Canada, *Canadian Economic Observer*, June 1991, p. 5.41, Catalogue no. 11-010. Reproduced with permission of the Minister of Supply and Services Canada, 1992.

could not be determined without a measuring stick such as the CPI. The purchasing power of the dollar is related inversely to movements in the CPI. According to the CPI, the price of a typical basket of goods in Canada rose from $75.50 in 1981 to $119.50 in 1990. This means that prices rose by 58 percent during that period, and anyone whose income did not rise by at least 58 percent during the same period actually lost purchasing power. Another way of expressing this is to say that the purchasing power of a dollar in 1990 relative to that of a 1981 dollar was 63 cents:

$$100 \text{ cents} \times \frac{75.5}{119.5} = 63 \text{ cents.}$$

Because of its usefulness in measuring the real purchasing power of the dollar, the CPI serves as the bottom line in many salary and wage negotiations; workers insist on getting increases at least equal to the price increases indicated by the CPI. Many collective agreements contain clauses that guarantee that wages will increase in line with increases in the CPI. Similar cost-of-living-adjustments (COLAS) are often incorporated into pension schemes. Federal social insurance payments, such as Old Age Security, the Canada Pension Plan, and Family Allowances, are indexed to the CPI. The federal government also adjusts income tax exemption levels on the basis of the CPI.

It should be noted that the CPI measures price increases experienced by a sample population in selected areas of the country, so it may not precisely reflect the experience of other groups in other places. It also assumes, by maintaining a "fixed" basket of goods, that there is no quality change in goods and that consumers do not switch to cheaper substitutes for goods and services in the basket. Because substitutes *are* made, the CPI may overstate the price inflation experienced by many consumers. Studies indicate, however, that this factor is not very significant.

HOW GOOD ARE THE GDP FIGURES?

We have now looked in some detail at the ways in which nominal and real GDP are measured. We have also learned how the Consumer Price Index and the GDP deflator are used to change nominal to real values. In conclusion, it is necessary to make several points about the limitations of GDP measurements.

First, much economic activity is not included in GDP at all. There are whole industries — gambling, bootlegging, narcotics, prostitution — whose multi-billion-dollar sales go unreported because they are illegal. Some legal economic activity also goes unreported for purposes of tax evasion. Other market activity — such as babysitting and casual yard work — goes unreported because it is too scattered to keep track of, even though the total sums involved may be quite large. The size of the underground market economy is surely large, constituting perhaps as much as 10 percent of reported GDP. Even this does not count the enormous amount of nonmarket economic activity that takes place, including such highly valuable services as unpaid housekeeping and child care.

Second, even if real GDP did accurately measure the level of market and non-market economic activity, it would still not be a very good measure of overall welfare or satisfaction. For example, the way income is distributed may affect the level of satisfaction. The level of real GDP per capita does not directly reflect the number of families in poverty or the relative income status of high- and low-income groups.

Third, fewer and fewer labour hours per worker are devoted to producing real GDP as the years go by. It is plausible to think that more leisure will cause satisfaction to rise. Leisure is evidently a scarce economic good valued by workers. However, the substantial increase in the leisure of the Canadian worker in this century is not explicitly reflected in GDP calculations.

Fourth, real GDP is a measure only of currently produced goods and services. Satisfaction can also be derived from durable consumer goods that were produced in the past but that are still in use. Surely, the larger the present stock of consumer durables, the higher consumer satisfaction must be.

Fifth, the market prices at which goods are sold do not accurately reflect external costs or benefits — those that affect third parties not directly involved in the exchange. For example, as we discussed in Chapter 11, negative externalities, such as the environmental pollution caused by certain productive activities, detract from welfare. Pollution adversely affects people who are neither buyers nor sellers of the goods whose production created it. Like several of the non-market goods discussed above that affect satisfaction, pollution is not entered into GDP calculations. Unlike those goods, however, pollution would have to be counted as a negative value. Annual additions to the amount of pollution should, in principle, be subtracted from GDP; but practical problems make such an adjustment impossible.[2]

Sixth, an increase in output does not necessarily imply an increase in welfare, even if none of the problems mentioned thus far is present. An unseasonably cold winter, for example, or an epidemic of infectious disease could cause purchases of heating fuel or medical services to rise dramatically. Yet the resulting increases in real GDP would hardly represent an increase in satisfaction! Wartime defence expenditures provide another example of the lack of direct correspondence between output and welfare. We could argue that, in principle, these kinds of expenditures are for the maintenance of the stock of human beings and should be treated just like investment expenditures that offset depreciation of the capital stock; that is, they should be subtracted from real GDP to get real new output. Putting this idea into practice, however, would be difficult.

Finally, many aspects of human welfare are not related at all to the flow of economic goods and services or to the economic satisfaction obtained from them. While everyone would agree that people do not live by bread alone, obtaining agreement about exactly what else is important would not be easy. How important are unspoiled natural areas, unalienating work, loving human contact, social justice, income equality, economic growth, and freedom? These are normative questions that each person must answer individually. The economist could never hope to incorporate these social and economic conditions into an objective measure of social welfare.

For all these reasons, then, real GDP should not be interpreted as a complete measure of social welfare. Still, it is far from worthless. It provides a roughly accurate picture of the economy's annual production of final goods and services, which, of course, is all that it was ever intended to do. As will be seen, it is valuable for several purposes, even given its limitations.

---

[2]The best that could probably be done would be to subtract from GDP the total expenditures made solely to abate or prevent pollution. Even after such clean-up expenditures, however, enough pollution remains to affect welfare adversely.

MEASURING UNEMPLOYMENT

One of the main purposes of economic activity is to create jobs — and, hence, to generate income — for people. An economy that is functioning well is able to provide jobs with adequate pay for all those who want to work. In other words, in a healthy economy, employment should be at or close to its maximum potential level, with unemployment at or close to zero.

Before we examine how employment and unemployment are measured in Canada, we must specify the approach that we are taking — namely, that in much of the macroeconomic analysis in this text, we try to limit the number of variables under examination at any given time. We therefore make the simplifying assumption in the present discussion that growth in employment is closely related to growth in output; indeed, we use the behaviour of output as a proxy for the behaviour of employment. In reality, the causes of employment and unemployment are much more complex, and relate to issues that we shall explore toward the end of this book (Chapter 27).

The current focus of employment policy in Canada is the unemployment rate, as measured by Statistics Canada and published in a monthly bulletin entitled *The Labour Force*. To calculate this rate, Statistics Canada first surveys about 55 000 Canadian households each month to determine how many Canadians are members of the **labour force**. The labour force is made up of people fifteen years of age and older who, at the time of the survey, were either *employed* (which means, among other things, that they were working at least one hour per week as paid employees) or *unemployed* (which means that they were actively but unsuccessfully looking for work). The **unemployment rate** is the percentage of people in the labour force who are not currently employed but are actively looking for employment. Persons under fifteen years of age, adults not actively seeking employment, military personnel, and certain institutionalized persons are counted as outside the labour force, and thus as neither employed nor unemployed.

The monthly measurement of unemployment in Canada indicates the degree to which potential labour resources in the country are not being utilized. For example, if one million people are recorded as unemployed, it would seem to follow that the country is not making use of the potential labour of exactly one million people, no more and no less. But the unemployment figures are actually too optimistic about the amount of potential labour lost to the economy. This is so for two reasons. First, the unemployment figures do not include the labour lost through the part-time employment of people who would prefer to be employed full time. As long as such people work only a few hours a week, they are counted as "employed." The "underemployment" of such people should somehow be added to the unemployment figures in order to estimate more accurately the current underutilization of the country's potential labour resources. Second, the unemployment figures do not record the number of people who have been discouraged from applying for a job because they are aware of the large number of people already looking for work. Such "discouraged" workers don't enter the labour force, and therefore are not added to the list of the unemployed. Their labour, however, is lost to the economy, and should be added to any estimate of how much potential labour is not being utilized.

Box 18.7 shows changes in the labour force, employment, and unemployment over the course of one year, from March 1990 to March 1991. During that year, two forces combined to increase the unemployment rate substantially: The labour

Labour force
All members of the noninstitutionalized civilian population fifteen years of age and older who are either officially employed or looking for employment.

Unemployment rate
Percentage of the labour force who are not employed but are actively looking for employment.

The Labour Force, Employment, and Unemployment in Selected Months

BOX 18.7

The labour force includes everyone in Canada who is fifteen years of age or older and who is able and willing to work. The "employed" are all those who actually have jobs, whether full-time or part-time. The "unemployed" are all those in the labour force who, at the time of the monthly survey, do not have a job but are looking for one (column 3 minus column 4). The unemployment rate measures the unemployed (column 5) as a percentage of the labour force (column 3).

The selected data show that between March 1990 and March 1991, the number of people who wanted to work increased from 13.574 million to 13.733 million. However, during that period, the number of persons actually holding jobs dropped from 12.596 million to 12.291 million, meaning that unemployment grew substantially, and the unemployment rate increased from 7.2 percent to 10.5 percent.

(1) Year	(2) Month	(3) Labour Force	(4) Employed (thousands)	(5) Unemployed	(6) Unemployment Rate (percent)
1990	March	13 574	12 596	978	7.2
1991	March	13 733	12 291	1442	10.5

SOURCE: Adapted from Statistics Canada, *Canadian Economic Observer*, June 1991, p. 5.24, Catalogue no. 11-010. Reproduced with permission of the Minister of Supply and Services Canada, 1992.

force grew, while the number of persons with jobs declined. This indicates that both the rate of growth of the labour force *and* the rate of growth of jobs contribute to changes in unemployment.

Clearly, the goal of providing a job for everyone who is willing and able to work implies that the officially measured unemployment rate should be kept low. But how low is low? Because of the way the unemployment rate is defined, a zero unemployment rate is impossible: Even when the economy is performing smoothly and efficiently, there will be a certain number of people who have voluntarily quit their jobs to look for better ones, or who have entered the labour force for the first time and have not yet found a job. The process of job search, through which workers are matched to the jobs to which they are best suited takes time.

Types of Unemployment

Frictional unemployment

The term **frictional unemployment** refers to the short periods of unemployment that occur when job seekers are being matched up with available jobs within the mainstream of the economy. Much of this short-term unemployment is voluntary. It involves people who have quit old jobs to look for new ones, people taking a week or so to move or go on vacation before starting a newly found job, and people who have entered occupations such as construction work, in which temporary layoffs are a part of life but earnings are good on a year-round basis. Economists view a certain level of frictional unemployment as necessary to match workers with jobs in a labour market where information is incomplete and transaction costs are often high.

Frictional unemployment Short periods of unemployment, that occur when job seekers are being matched up with available jobs within the mainstream of the economy.

Structural unemployment

Structural unemployment
Long periods of unemployment that occur when workers' skills do not match those required by available jobs; a result, in part, of shifts in the structure of the economy that make certain skills obsolete.

The term **structural unemployment**, by contrast, refers to people who are spending long periods of time out of work, often with little prospect of ever finding an adequate job. These workers faced prolonged joblessness in part because the shifting structure of the economy has made their skills obsolete. The structurally unemployed also include people with few skills and little work experience. Teenagers and some minority groups are especially affected by this type of unemployment. For these people, structural unemployment is not merely a problem of lack of jobs. Certain types of jobs — hospital-orderly jobs, fast-food work, and car washing, for example — are almost always available and require few specific skills. But structurally unemployed workers either avoid these kinds of jobs or work at them only for short periods before quitting. Working for short periods at dead-end jobs tends to build up a pattern of poor work habits and absenteeism that makes many structurally unemployed people unattractive to most employers.

Cyclical unemployment

Cyclical unemployment
The part of unemployment that can be attributed to cyclical fluctuations in the economy, such as downturns or expansions of demand.

Frictional plus structural unemployment make up what might be termed, at any one time, the economy's virtually unavoidable rate of unemployment (although, as we shall point out in Chapters 27 and 28, structural unemployment might be reduced substantially with better government policies). However, the actual unemployment rate may be above or below the rate normally attributed to frictional and structural factors, depending on cyclical factors such as downturns or expansions of demand in the economy. The unemployment caused by cyclical fluctuations is called **cyclical unemployment**.

In practice, it is extremely difficult to distinguish between these different types of unemployment. Frictional and cyclical unemployment should, normally, be short-run phenomena, while structural unemployment is a long-run problem. A 1982 study by the Economic Council of Canada found that "unemployment spells exceeding three months accounted for 45 percent of total unemployment."[3] This might indicate that almost half of the unemployment in Canada is due to structural factors, which require particular types of social and economic policies to correct, while slightly more than half is frictional or cyclical. The minimization of cyclical unemployment is one of the primary concerns of macroeconomic policy.

SUMMARY

1. *Gross domestic product* is the main measurement of aggregate economic activity now used in Canada. It is defined as the dollar value at current market prices of all *final goods and services* produced within a nation in a given year.

2. Gross domestic product can be measured by an *expenditure approach*, adding together the total of consumption, investment, government purchases, and net exports (exports minus imports). It can also be derived by the *income*

---

[3]Economic Council of Canada, *In Short Supply: Jobs and Skills in the 1980s* (Ottawa: Economic Council of Canada, 1982), p. 50.

approach. *Net domestic income* is measured by adding together the total of wages, profits, and other forms of income, including payments to nonresidents for productive activity within Canada (and excluding payments to Canadian residents for activity outside Canada). GDP and net domestic income differ by the total value of capital-consumption allowances, indirect taxes, and the statistical discrepancy.

3. *Personal income* is the total income that households receive, as opposed to domestic income, which is the total that they earn. Personal income includes transfer payments, which households receive but do not earn, and excludes corporate profits taxes and undistributed corporate profits, which they earn but do not receive. Personal income less personal taxes equals *personal disposable income*.

4. The *GDP deflator* is the broadest-based measure of the price level. It can be thought of as an average of the prices of all final goods and services that go into GDP. The GDP deflator can be used to calculate real GDP for any year, expressed in terms of constant dollars of the base year. To find current-year real GDP in terms of a chosen base year, divide current-year nominal GDP by the ratio of the current-year deflator to the base-year deflator.

5. The GDP deflator takes the prices of all final goods and services into account. The *Consumer Price Index (CPI)* includes only the market basket of goods purchased by a typical household.

6. Real GDP does not attempt to measure welfare or satisfaction; it measures only the output of goods and services. It does not even do that job perfectly because of sampling errors, omitted items, and biases in price indexes (which are discussed in the appendix to this chapter). It is important to remember that a great many things contribute to overall human welfare that are not in any way measured by GDP.

7. The *labour force* measures the number of people fifteen years of age and older who are willing and able to be employed. The *unemployment rate* measures the percentage of those in the labour force who are without jobs, but seeking work. There are three major types of unemployment: *frictional, structural,* and *cyclical.*

EFFECTIVE THINKING: PROBLEM 4
Cost-of-Living Adjustments

This effective-thinking problem deals with a debate between a firm and some of its workers concerning cost-of-living adjustments. Before you tackle the problem, you might want to read the appendix to this chapter: It will help you understand price indexes and may suggest a solution to the cost-of-living debate.

A group of employees working in northern Manitoba for a Winnipeg-based firm believe that they were not given the proper cost-of-living adjustments to their salaries over a four-year period. The firm had promised the northern workers an adjustment to their salaries that would reflect the changes in the cost of living that they experienced while working in the north.

Year	CPI for Canada	GDP Deflator for Canada	CPI for Winnipeg, Manitoba	Canadian Wholesale Price Index	CPI for Yellowknife, NWT
1	104	105	103.5	103.8	105
2	108	108	107	107.5	109.5
3	111	111	110.5	110.8	113
4	116	117	115	116.5	117.8

Over the four-year period in question, price indexes listed in the accompanying table were calculated by Statistics Canada. (Assume that year 0, or the base year, for these indexes was set at a value of 100.) No separate price index exists for the area of northern Manitoba where the workers were employed. The cost-of-living increases that the workers received during this period were as follows: 3.5 percent in years, 1, 2, and 3, and 4.5 percent in year 4.

You have been hired as an economist by this group of northern workers to help them present a case for a cost-of-living salary adjustment that reflects the true cost-of-living increases in northern Manitoba over the four years in question. The workers hope to win a lump-sum payment from the firm if it is proved that they have been undercompensated.

Directions

Use the twelve effective-thinking steps for successful problem solving to determine whether the northern workers are justified in their complaint and, if they are, to assist them in presenting their case. (See the Appendix to Chapter 3 if you need to review the effective-thinking steps.) For Steps 10 through 12, assume that the plan you adopt in Step 9 is implemented. Show any calculations you make to reach a solution to this problem.

An example of the thinking process an economist might go through using these twelve problem-solving steps appears at the back of the book (see pages 783–94). Not all economists would produce identical answers for each step, but they would all draw on accepted principles of economics.

KEY TERMS

gross domestic product (GDP)
gross national product (GNP)
final goods and services
value added
expenditure approach
income approach

net domestic income
personal income
personal disposable income
GDP deflator
price index
Consumer Price Index

labour force
unemployment rate
frictional unemployment
structural unemployment
cyclical unemployment

KEY BOXES

Box 18.1 Value Added and the Use of Final
Products in Measuring GDP

Box 18.2 Gross Domestic Product by Type of
Expenditure, 1990

Box 18.3 Net Domestic Income and Gross
Domestic Product, 1990

Box 18.7 The Labour Force, Employment, and
Unemployment in Selected Months

REVIEW QUESTIONS

1. In 1981, wages and salaries per employee averaged $17 980. By 1990, they had increased to $30 550. However, between 1981 and 1990, the Consumer Price Index rose from 75.5 to 119.5. What were real wages and salaries in 1981 and 1990, adjusted by the CPI? By 1990, by what percentage had they increased over wages in 1981?

2. If all parents in Canada exchanged child-care services with their neighbours, received a wage for doing their neighbours' work, and hence did none of their own child care, what would happen to GDP as measured by national-income accountants? Who, if anyone, would be better off with a situation in which everyone got paid? Explain.

3. Do you think transfer payments should be included in the measure of GDP? Explain.

4. In 1933, net fixed business investment was equal to about −$300 million. How could this have been possible?

5. A firm gets rid of its inventory of $10 000 worth of shoes by having a sale to the public. What happens to GDP in this case? What happens to each of its components?

6. If the government increased the unemployment-insurance deduction, what would happen to GDP, net national income, and personal disposable income?

7. Classify each of the following expenditures of an individual's own earnings as consumption, saving, investment, or something else:

   a. the purchase of a new home

   b. the purchase of a new automobile for cash

   c. payment of a monthly instalment on a loan

   d. the purchase of an item of clothing for $4 plus $0.60 sales tax

   e. the purchase of common shares in a corporation

   f. paying the children a weekly allowance

   g. the payment of tuition for additional education

   h. a tip at a restaurant.

8. In Box 18.7, what would the unemployment rate in March 1991 be if

   a. the labour force had not grown between March 1990 and March 1991, but the number of employed had changed as shown?

   b. the labour force had grown as shown, but the number of employed had remained at the March 1990 level?

9. In a particular year, producers and buyers have the following plans:

Production of capital goods	$110 000
Total planned investment expenditure	80 000
Output of consumer goods	60 000
Total planned consumption expenditure	90 000

   a. Calculate aggregate expenditure and aggregate output. Is this economy in equilibrium or disequilibrium?

   b. What is the value of unplanned inventory investment in this economy?

10. Calculate GDP for an economy characterized by the following:

Investment income paid to foreigners	$13.3 million
Investment income earned abroad by nationals	8.5 million
GNP	432.6 million

11. Calculate GNP for an economy characterized by the following:

Investment income paid to foreigners	$13.3 million
Investment income earned abroad by nationals	8.5 million
GDP	432.6 million

12. Using the following data, calculate nominal GDP using (1) the expenditure approach and (2) the income approach. Also calculate nominal net domestic income as part of your totals. *Note*: There is no statistical discrepancy in this example. (Amounts are given in millions of dollars.)

Government expenditures on goods and services	$148
Wages and salaries	392
Exports of goods and services	150
Personal expenditure on consumer goods and services	425
Inventory evaluation adjustment	−5
Interest and miscellaneous investment income	63
Indirect taxes less subsidies	64
Corporation profits before taxes	46
Gross fixed capital investment	131
Imports of goods and services	158
Change in inventories	−6
Net income of farm operators from farm production	5
Net income of nonfarm unincorporated businesses and rent	34
Capital-consumption allowances	91

Computation of Price Indexes

This appendix provides further details about the GDP deflator and the Consumer Price Index. Knowing these details will make it easier to see the differences between the two and to understand the source of the substitution bias, which affects the two indexes differently.

The GDP Deflator for a Simple Economy

A much simpler economy than that of Canada will serve to illustrate the computation of price indexes. Box 18A.1 shows price and quantity data for two years for an economy in which only three goods are produced: movies, apples, and shirts. The box shows that nominal GDP grew from $400 in 1975 to $1000 in 1990. But what do these figures mean? Do they mean that people really had more of the things they wanted in 1990 than in 1975? More precisely, do they mean that people had 2.5 times as much? These questions cannot be answered easily by looking at the box as it stands.

A line-by-line comparison of the data for the two years shows that the figures on nominal product do not tell the whole story. Clearly, prices went up sharply between 1975 and 1990. Movies cost twice what they used to, apples three times as much, and shirts half again as much. We notice also that the amounts of goods produced have changed. Twice as many movies and shirts were produced in 1990 as in 1975, but only half as many apples.

Nominal GDP for a Simple Economy   BOX 18A.1

In this simple economy, in which only three goods are produced, nominal domestic product grew from $400 in 1975 to $1000 in 1990. Prices also went up in that time, though, so people did not really have 2.5 times as many goods in 1990 as they did in 1975.

1975	Quantity	Price	Value
Movies	50	$ 2.00	$ 100
Apples	1000	0.20	200
Shirts	10	10.00	100
1975 Nominal GDP			$ 400

1990	Quantity	Price	Value
Movies	100	$ 4.00	$ 400
Apples	500	0.60	300
Shirts	20	15.00	300
1990 Nominal GDP			$1000

If we want to know how much better off people were in 1990 than in 1975, we need a way to separate the quantity changes that have taken place from the price changes. One way to do this is to ask how much the total value of output would have changed from 1975 to 1990 if prices had not changed. This approach gives the results shown in Box 18A.2. There we see that the 1990 output of 100 movies, 500 apples, and 20 shirts, which had a value of $1000 in terms of the prices at which the goods were actually sold, would have had a value of only $500 in terms of the prices that prevailed in 1975. The $500 is thus a measure of real GDP for 1990. It is this measure that should be compared to the 1975 GDP of $400 if we want to know what really happened to output between the two years. Rather than having 150 percent more output in 1990 than in 1975, as indicated by the change in nominal GDP from $400 to $1000, the people in this simple economy really had only about 25 percent more, as indicated by the change in real GDP from $400 to $500.

We have now seen how to compute real GDP for 1990 directly from price and quantity data, without using a price index to convert nominal values into real values. But although we have not explicitly used a price index, we have created one implicitly. This implicit index, or implicit GDP deflator, is the ratio of current-year nominal GDP to current-year real GDP times 100, as expressed by the following formula:

$$\text{GDP deflator} = \frac{\text{Current-year output valued at current-year prices}}{\text{Current-year output valued at base-year prices}} \times 100.$$

Applying the formula to the data in Boxes 18A.1 and 18A.2 gives a value of 200 for the deflator.

BOX 18A.2 Nominal and Real GDP for a Simple Economy

This table shows how the figures from Box 18A.1 can be adjusted to take changing prices into account. The 1990 quantities are multiplied by 1975 prices to get the value of 1990 GDP as it would have been had prices not changed. The total of 1990 quantities valued at 1975 prices is a measure of real GDP for 1990 stated in constant 1975 dollars. The implicit GDP deflator for 1990, calculated as the ratio of 1990 nominal GDP to 1990 real GDP, multiplied by 100, has a value of 200.

	1990 Quantity	1990 Price	Value at 1990 Price	1975 Price	Value of 1990 Output at 1975 Price
Movies	100	$ 4.00	$ 400	$ 2.00	$200
Apples	500	0.60	300	0.20	100
Shirts	20	15.00	300	10.00	200
		1990 Nominal GDP =	$1000		1990 Real GDP = $500

The Consumer Price Index for a Simple Economy

The Consumer Price Index differs from the GDP deflator in two ways. First, as mentioned in the body of the chapter, it takes into account only the prices of goods and services consumed by a typical urban household. Second, it is calculated according to a formula that uses base-year quantities rather than current-year quantities. The first difference does not matter for this simple economy, in which all goods are consumer goods, but the second difference does matter, as Box 18A.3 shows.

To calculate the CPI for this economy, instead of asking how much current-year output would have cost at base-year prices, we begin by asking how much base-year output would have cost at current-year prices. The index is then calculated as the ratio of the two different valuations of base-year quantities:

$$\text{Consumer Price Index} = \frac{\text{Base-year market basket valued at current-year prices}}{\text{Base-year market basket valued at base-year prices}} \times 100.$$

The CPI is calculated using base-year quantities partly because current-price data are easier to collect than current-output data. That is why this index can be announced every month with little delay.

Comparing the CPI and the GDP Deflator

As Box 18A.3 shows, the CPI for 1990 in our simple economy had a value of 237.5, whereas the GDP deflator for 1990 was only 200. Both indexes were calculated using the same data, and both used 1975 as a base year. Which, if either, is the true measure of the change in prices between the two years?

A Consumer Price Index for a Simple Economy   *BOX 18A.3*

The Consumer Price Index can be calculated as the base-year market basket of goods valued at current-year prices divided by the base-year market basket valued at base-year prices, multiplied by 100. This table shows how such an index can be calculated for a simple economy. The 1975 output cost $400 at the prices at which it was actually sold. If it had been sold at 1990 prices, it would have cost $950. The CPI for 1990 is thus 237.5.

	1975 Quantity	1975 Price	Value of 1975 Quantity at 1975 Price	1990 Price	Value of 1975 Quantity at 1990 Price
Movies	50	$ 2.00	$100	$ 4.00	$200
Apples	1000	0.20	200	0.60	600
Shirts	10	10.00	100	15.00	150
			$400		$950

The answer is that neither the CPI nor the GDP deflator is the only correct measure of change in the price level. Instead, each is the answer to a different question. The GDP deflator is the answer to the question How much more did the 1990 output cost at the prices at which it was actually sold than it would have cost if it had been sold at 1975 prices? The CPI, by contrast, is the answer to the question How much more would the 1975 output have cost if it had been sold at 1990 prices instead of 1975 prices?

A close look at the data shows why the answers to the two questions are not the same. In 1975, lots of apples and not very many shirts were produced compared with 1990. Yet between the two years, the price of apples increased 200 percent while the price of shirts increased only 50 percent. Because the CPI uses base-year quantities, it gives a heavy weight to apples, which showed the greatest relative price increase, and not much weight to shirts, which showed only a modest price increase. In contrast, the GDP deflator uses current-year quantities, thereby decreasing the importance of apples and increasing that of shirts.

We see now why it is that the CPI tends to have an upward substitution bias relative to the GDP deflator. But that does not make the GDP deflator a true measure of change in the cost of living. It could just as well be said that the GDP deflator has a downward substitution bias relative to the CPI or that each has an opposite bias from some "true" price index. No foolproof way has yet been found to calculate the true cost-of-living index, although some interesting attempts have been made.

A discussion of these more complex types of price indexes would take us far beyond the scope of this book. However, the basic types of price indexes covered here are the ones most commonly used for policy purposes.

REVIEW QUESTION

1. The following table shows output and prices for a simple economy in 1986 and 1990. Use the data to calculate both the CPI and GDP deflator for 1990, using 1986 as the base year.

	1986 Quantity	1986 Price	1990 Quantity	1990 Price
Cars	1000	$ 2 500	2000	$ 4 000
Houses	100	20 000	150	40 000
Hospital services (total days of care)	500	100	550	250

The Equilibrium Level of Domestic Income

WHAT YOU WILL LEARN IN THIS CHAPTER

After studying this chapter, you will be able to

1. Understand the impact of the Great Depression on the development of macroeconomic theory.

2. Discuss Say's law and the background to the emergence of Keynesian economics.

3. Explain the connection between income and desired consumer spending.

4. Define *autonomous desired consumption* and the *marginal propensity to consume*, and explain how a consumption schedule is constructed.

5. Show how the saving schedule is linked to the consumption schedule.

6. Construct an aggregate expenditure schedule, given a consumption schedule plus information on taxes, desired investment expenditure, desired government expenditure, and desired net-export expenditure.

7. Construct an income–expenditure equilibrium line and explain its use.

8. Use a 45° line diagram to find the equilibrium level of real domestic income.

9. Compare the leakages–injections approach and the income–expenditure approach to determining domestic income.

A Preview   *The Canadian Economy in Recession*

The Canadian economy experienced a serious recession in 1990 and 1991. The following article describes the decline of gross domestic product in the first few months of 1991. Output in manufacturing was particularly hard hit; the report attributes this to "declining demand in all the major sectors of the economy — household spending, business investment, and exports." It is this connection between spending and output that we shall explore in detail in this chapter.

Output (GDP) Tumbles Again in March

The monthly measure of real gross domestic product contracted by 0.2 percent in March. Following no change in February and a 1.1 percent drop in January, this left output for the first quarter down 1.5 percent, the steepest quarterly decline of the current recession.

The slack in goods production was widespread, with sharp declines in all major industry groups except forestry. Most other primary industries and construction posted drops of about 2 percent, while the rate of decline in manufacturing accelerated to 1.6 percent.

Manufacturers continued to be affected by slack demand and too much inventory and, as a result, they posted their eighth straight drop. Manufacturing output has declined by almost 14 percent since its peak in May 1989.

The breadth of the cutback in manufacturing output reflected declining demand in all the major sectors of the economy — household spending, business investment, and exports.

SOURCE: Excerpted from Statistics Canada, "Output (GDP) Tumbles Again in March," *Canadian Economic Observer*, June 1991, pp. 1.5–1.6, Catalogue no. 11-010. Reproduced with permission of the Minister of Supply and Services Canada, 1992.

AN OVERVIEW OF GDP GROWTH IN CANADA

The decline of real output in Canada in the first few months of 1991, which the Preview briefly outlines, confirmed the worst fears of Canadians: It meant that Canada was indeed in a recession, the length of which no one could predict.

Although the growth rate of real output (GDP) in Canada fluctuates considerably from month to month and from year to year, it is very seldom negative. In fact, measured on an annual basis, Canada's real GDP has declined only four times since World War II: in 1946, 1954, 1982, and 1991. As shown in Box 19.1, real GDP increased more than twelvefold between 1926 and 1991, from $35.6 billion to roughly $460 billion. Despite this impressive growth record over a 66-year period, the Canadian economy has been badly shaken several times, most notably in the early 1930s and again in the last decade and a half.

Box 19.1(a) illustrates the growth of real GDP during the 25 years from 1926 to 1951. These years witnessed the most dramatic changes ever known in the Canadian economy. Real output grew rapidly from 1926 to 1929, then plunged sharply as the Canadian economy entered what has come to be known as the Great Depression. The depression bottomed out in 1933, but recovery was slow: It was only in 1938 that the economy restored itself to the 1929 level of output. Ten years of growth had been lost, along with hundreds of thousands of jobs. The Dirty Thirties produced the worst economic hardships suffered by Canadians since Confederation. Most other countries were equally hard-hit.

Box 19.1(a) illustrates not only the dramatic decline of the Depression years but the equally dramatic recovery that occurred during World War II. If, in the ten-year period from 1929 to 1938, the economy registered no overall growth whatsoever, in the seven-year period from the beginning of 1939 to the end of 1945, it skyrocketed: Real GDP increased by 70 percent, from $42.3 billion to $72.1 billion. At the end of the war, the economy faltered for a few years, and people feared that the war had merely interrupted the Depression and that the economy would quickly sink back into it. In 1945 and again in 1946, real GDP declined slightly; indeed, in the four-year period 1944–48, output grew by less than 2 percent. Beginning in 1949, however, the economy began to grow more rapidly again, initiating a period of about thirty years of unprecedented growth.

Box 19.1(b) illustrates the growth of real GDP between 1951 and 1991. Following a period of somewhat uneven growth during the 1950s, real GDP grew steadily until 1982. Its growth rates by decade were as follows: 1951–60: 50 percent; 1961–70: 60 percent; 1971–80: 50 percent; and 1981–90: 30 percent. The lower growth rates of the 1980s and the recessions of the early 1980s and early 1990s are a sad contrast to the steady, often high rates of growth experienced between the mid-1950s and the end of the 1970s. The relatively poor performance of the Canadian economy in the last decade is given special attention in Chapter 27. Its causes are related to new kinds of economic problems that economists are still trying to understand.

THE BIRTH OF MODERN MACROECONOMIC THEORY

Modern macroeconomic theory was born as a response to the shock of the Great Depression. The 1930s were traumatic not only for the economy but for the economics profession as well. Economic theory seemed powerless to explain

BOX 19.1   *The Growth of Real GDP, 1926–1991*

The graph in part (a) illustrates the dramatic changes in real gross domestic product that occurred in Canada during the Great Depression of the 1930s and, later, during World War II. The Depression was a tremendous shock to all Canadian citizens — and to the economics profession. The dramatic decline in GDP in the years 1930–33 called for a new understanding of macroeconomics. Part (b) illustrates the impressive growth of real income and output in the Canadian economy between 1951 and 1991. During that forty-year period, real GDP increased more than fivefold, rising from $88.6 billion in 1951 to $460.3 billion in 1991. But there were several years of recession as well, marked by absolute downturns in 1954, 1982, and 1991.

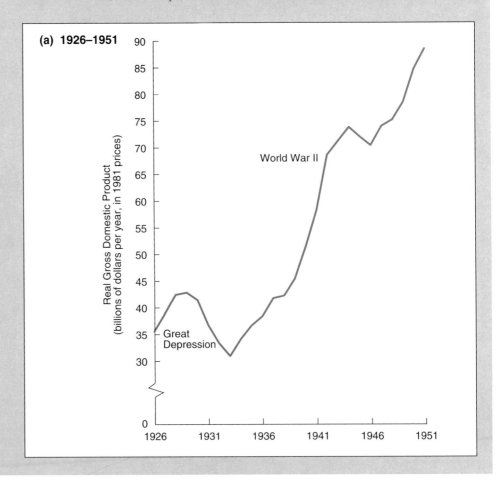

what was happening, let alone to find a cure. The profession needed to find a new approach to macroeconomic phenomena — indeed, it had to rediscover macroeconomics. The eighteenth- and nineteenth-century classics of economics, by such thinkers as Adam Smith, David Ricardo, Thomas Malthus, and Karl Marx, concerned themselves with the performance of national economies. Smith's pioneering work, for example, explored the wealth of nations. But in the late nineteenth and early twentieth centuries, most leading economists turned

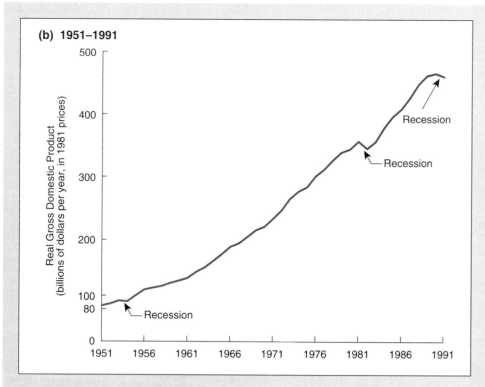

(b) 1951–1991

SOURCE: Based on data from Statistics Canada, *Canadian Economic Observer, Historical Statistical Supplement 1988/ 89*, p. 3, Catalogue no. 11-210, and *Canadian Economic Observer*, June 1991, p. 1.1, Catalogue no. 11-010. Reproduced with permission of the Minister of Supply and Services Canada, 1992.

their attention to microeconomic problems — that is, to the behaviour of consumers and individual firms. As a well-known modern economist noted,[1] macroeconomics seemed to retreat into the underworld. The Great Depression of the 1930s forced economists to redirect their attention to macroeconomic problems, in order to explain how national economies could experience falling output and rising unemployment for years at a time.

The Macroeconomic Equilibrium Problem: Does Supply Equal Demand?

The Depression presented an apparent paradox: While the economy was clearly able to produce far more than it was actually producing, firms could not find buyers for their output. The problems was not, strictly speaking, that people

---

[1]Robert Heilbroner, *The Worldly Philosophers*, 6th ed. (New York: Simon & Schuster, 1987). This is still, after forty years, one of the finest introductions to the world of economic ideas.

Say's law
The proposition that producing a given level of domestic product will automatically generate an equal level of aggregate demand.

could not afford all that the firms could produce. It had long been known that the process of production automatically yields a domestic income equal to the value of domestic product. And with **Say's law**, a proposition put forward by the French economist Jean Baptiste Say in the early nineteenth century, the notion of the equality of domestic income and domestic product within the circular flow had been extended into the idea that supply creates its own demand. Specifically, Say's law suggests that households, which receive wages, rents, interest, and profits from firms, will desire to use all of that income to buy the goods produced by the firms. Although later followers of this doctrine recognized that the savings of households represented an apparent leakage from spending flows (meaning that not *all* income was available to be spent on the economy's output), they did not consider this to be a serious problem. They reasoned that virtually all households placed their savings in financial institutions, which channelled those funds, as loans, to other consumers (to finance spending beyond their current income) or to business firms (to finance investment). If the amount saved still exceeded the demands of such borrowers, the interest rate charged for borrowing could be lowered to a point where the demand for savings exactly matched the supply of savings. It was in this way, proponents of the theory argued, that the circular flow was kept in equilibrium: The total value of goods and services produced in an economy in a given year created an equal amount of income, which then generated an equal amount of desired spending.

It was argued that, for similar reasons, unemployment could not become a major problem. If the demand for jobs temporarily exceeded the supply of jobs, producing unemployment, wages would be reduced, and business firms would thereby be encouraged to hire more workers. It was this generally accepted way of looking at macroeconomic problems that had led most economists to conclude that major, sustained declines in output, as well as major, sustained increases in unemployment, were virtually impossible in market economies.

The stock-market collapse of 1929 and the severe downturn that most Western economies experienced in its wake naturally caused economists in a number of countries to question the conventional macroeconomic wisdom. They began to look for alternative theories and solutions. This search for a new kind of economics was led by the British economist John Maynard Keynes (see the accompanying Profile box).

The Keynesian Challenge

Keynes challenged Say's law — and traditional macroeconomics (to which he referred as the "classical" tradition) — by arguing that the income of households would not necessarily be equalled by the desired spending of households and firms. Keynes's doubt found its source in the fact that aggregate demand is the result of spending decisions by individual firms and households that do not coordinate their plans in advance. As we saw in Chapter 17, part of domestic income goes into various leakages from the circular flow, including saving, net taxes, and imports. If firms, governments, and buyers of the nation's exports do not plan to inject enough spending back into the economy to balance those leakages, aggregate demand will fall short of aggregate supply. And while it is true that governments can normally be counted on to spend their total tax revenues, there is no mechanism in a market economy to ensure that the value of exports will match the value of imports. Keynes also maintained that there is no mechanism that can be relied upon to make consumers' and firms' borrowings

John Maynard Keynes and the General Theory

John Maynard Keynes was born into economics. His father, John Neville Keynes, was a lecturer in economics and logic at Cambridge University. John Maynard began his own studies at Cambridge in mathematics and philosophy, but his talent for economics so impressed Alfred Marshall that the distinguished teacher urged him to concentrate on that subject. In 1908, after Keynes had completed his studies and done a brief stint in the civil service, Marshall offered him a lectureship in economics at Cambridge, which he accepted.

John Maynard Keynes
(1883–1946)

Keynes is remembered above all for his *General Theory of Employment, Interest and Money*, published in 1936. Although this was by no means his first major work, Keynes's reputation as the outstanding economist of his generation rests on it, since it represented a fundamental departure from current mainstream theory. Its major features are a bold theory based on broad macroeconomic aggregates and a strong argument for activist and interventionist policies.

Keynes was no "narrow" economist. He was an honoured member not only of the British academic elite but also of Britain's highest financial, political, diplomatic, administrative, and even artistic circles. He had close ties to the renowned "Bloomsbury group" of London's literary world, counting among his friends Virginia Woolf, E.M. Forster, and Lytton Strachey. In 1925, Keynes married the ballerina Lydia Lopokova. He seemed to be a dazzling success at whatever he attempted, from mountain climbing to financial speculation. As a speculator, he made a huge fortune for himself, and as bursar of King's College, he turned an endowment of £30 000 into one of £380 000.

Keynes wrote in his *General Theory* that

> the ideas of economists and political philosophers, both when they are right and when they are wrong, are more powerful than is commonly understood. Indeed, the world is ruled by little else. Practical men, who believe themselves to be quite exempt from any intellectual influences, are usually the slaves of some defunct economist. Madmen in authority, who hear voices in the air, are distilling their frenzy from some academic scribbler of a few years back. . . . There are not many who are influenced by new theories after they are twenty-five or thirty years of age, so that the ideas which civil servants and politicians and even agitators apply to current events are not likely to be the newest.*

Keynes's words are ironic, in that he himself has become one of the economists of the past whose ideas remain influential, even though they are no longer the most up-to-date.

*John Maynard Keynes, *The General Theory of Employment, Interest and Money* (London: Macmillan, Papermac 12, 1964), pp. 383–84.

---

equal households' savings. If, for example, consumers and business firms were pessimistic about the future of the economy, even a very low rate of interest might fail to induce them to borrow — and then to spend — the available savings.

Keynes argued that when desired, or planned, spending does fall short of output, a downward economic spiral may develop. Firms will cut output, reducing income and spending even further. Jobs will be cut, and wages will fall — but possibly not far enough to encourage firms to hire more workers. Keynes considered wages to be generally "stickier" than the classical economists had assumed, meaning that wages would not fall enough to maintain previous employment levels. In any case, substantial reductions in wages might exacerbate rather than alleviate the problems of the economy: If the total amount paid out in wages declined, spending might be cut even more, thereby intensifying the downward spiral of the economy.

Today this reasoning seems straightforward enough. To readers of Keynes's *General Theory of Employment, Interest and Money*, however, it provided the new theoretical framework they needed to understand the Great Depression. As we study the determinants of the equilibrium level of output in this and later chapters, we will, in a sense, retrace the steps taken by Keynes and his followers in developing modern macroeconomic theory.

THE BASIC MACROECONOMIC MODEL

To keep things simple, in this chapter and throughout the macroeconomics portion of the book, we will make several assumptions that eliminate certain differences between the circular-flow models of Chapter 17 and the official national-income accounts of Chapter 18. First, we will drop the distinction between gross domestic product and net domestic income by assuming that capital-consumption allowances, indirect business taxes, and the statistical discrepancy are zero. Second, we will assume undistributed corporate profits to be zero so that personal disposable income will be equal to domestic income minus net taxes. These assumptions can be expressed in equation form as follows:

Disposable income + Net Taxes = Personal Income = Domestic product.

Another assumption we make for the sake of simplicity, one that will hold for this chapter only, is that the prices are constant. This means that the analysis involves *real* income and *real* expenditures, unaffected by price changes. We drop this assumption in Chapter 20, which examines specifically the impact of varying prices.

THE DETERMINANTS OF AGGREGATE DESIRED EXPENDITURE

Keynesian macroeconomic analysis focusses on aggregate expenditure. It is based on the premise that if a full-employment level of output is to be sustained over any length of time, it must be matched by an equivalent amount of spending. This premise has prompted economists to devote significant attention to the causes, or the determinants, of aggregate spending. Chapters 17 and 18 identified four major components of aggregate desired expenditure (ADE): consumer spending on goods and services, business investment, government spending, and net exports. It is now time to examine each of these components in greater detail, in order to develop a more complete analysis of the nature of the whole — that is, of aggregate desired expenditure.

Before we embark on our examination of the first component — desired consumption expenditure — it is necessary to point out that what interests economists and policy makers most with regard to aggregate expenditure is how much the different decision makers in the economy *plan*, or *desire*, to spend in a given period of time. Determining, at the end of each year, how much was *actually* spent is a relatively straightforward matter; it is more difficult — and, with respect to theory and policy, more important — to predict annual spending *intentions*. As our analysis will show, it is spending intentions that ultimately determine what the income and output level of the economy will be.

In the following analysis, the term **desired expenditures** will be used to describe the spending intentions of the various groups in the economy that make expenditure decisions. The term **realized expenditures** will be used in reference to actual expenditures, as recorded in the national-income accounts. Desired expenditures are also known as **ex ante expenditures** (expenditure plans, made in advance of actual expenditures), while the realized expenditures recorded in Canada's national-income accounts represent **ex post facto expenditures** (expenditures recorded after the fact). It should be noted that ex ante decisions are often based on past experience; hence, our exploration of the ways in which decision makers arrive at their *desired* expenditures will naturally involve consideration of past experience as it is recorded in the national-income accounts.

DESIRED CONSUMPTION EXPENDITURE

The single most important component of aggregate desired expenditure is consumer spending on goods and services. In an average year, Canadian consumers spend the equivalent of about 55 percent of GDP. Since some of this spending "leaks" out of the economy as payment for imports, not all of it actually supports the output of goods and services within the country. Still, about 40 percent of the goods and services produced in Canada are bought by Canadian consumers.

What determines the amount that consumers desire to spend each year? And how can we account for the changes in their expenditure plans from year to year? Keynes made the reasonable assumption that the major determinant of consumption expenditure is likely to be the income that consumers have at their disposal. The close connection between real disposable income and consumption expenditure in Canada over the course of a recent ten-year period is shown, ex post facto, in Box 19.2. In that period, disposable income increased by 33.1 percent, while consumer expenditure rose by 32.6 percent.

The Consumption Schedule

Taking the close connection between disposable income and desired consumption as his starting point, Keynes proposed a relationship between the two that resembled the one shown in Box 19.3. This box shows how desired consumption changes in response to short-run changes in disposable income — not for the actual Canadian economy but for a simple economy in which households spend exactly 75 cents of each dollar of added disposable income. The relationship shown in Box 19.3 is known as the **consumption schedule** or **consumption function**.

Autonomous desired consumption

Notice that the consumption schedule in Box 19.3 does not pass through the origin, but intersects the vertical axis at a level slightly higher than zero. This indicates that even when disposable income is zero, desired consumption does not drop to zero. The amount of desired consumption associated with a zero level of disposable income (equal to the height at which the consumption schedule intersects the vertical axis) is called **autonomous desired consumption**.

Desired expenditures
The spending intentions of the various decision makers in an economy; desired expenditures are *ex ante expenditures.*

Realized expenditures
The actual expenditures made in a given year, as recorded in the national-income accounts; realized expenditures are *ex post facto expenditures.*

Ex ante expenditures
Expenditure plans, made in advance of actual expenditures.

Ex post facto expenditures
Expenditures recorded after the fact.

Consumption schedule (consumption function)
A graphic or numerical schedule that shows how desired consumption expenditure varies as disposable income varies, other things being equal.

Autonomous desired consumption
The part of total desired consumption expenditure that is independent of the level of disposable income; for any given consumption schedule, autonomous desired consumption is equal to the level of desired consumption associated with zero disposable income.

Taken at face value, the $100-billion level of autonomous desired consumption shows that aggregate desired consumption expenditure is $100 billion even if aggregate disposable income is zero. In practice, of course, disposable income never falls to zero for the economy as a whole. Individual households, however,

---

BOX 19.2 *Personal Disposable Income and Personal Consumption Expenditure, 1981 to 1990*

As we can see in the graph below, personal consumption expenditure represents a fairly constant percentage of personal disposable income (87 to 88 percent), and changes from year to year in fairly close step with changes in disposable income. Between 1981 and 1990, real personal disposable income increased by 33.1 percent, and real consumption expenditure, by 32.6 percent. This close relationship led economists to develop the so-called *consumption function*, which links changes in desired consumption to changes in income.

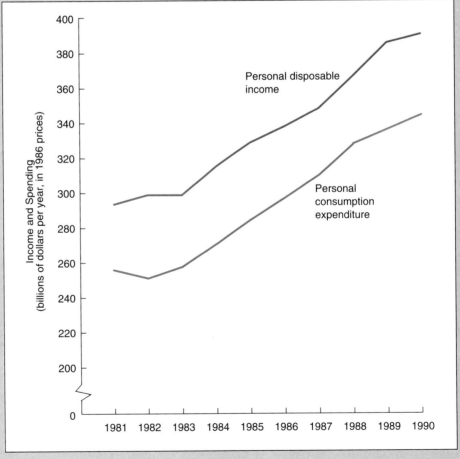

SOURCE: Based on data from Statistics Canada, *Canadian Economic Observer, Historical Statistical Supplement 1988/89*, pp. 1.3, 1.5, Catalogue no. 11-210, and *Canadian Economic Observer*, June 1991, pp. 1.2, 1.5, Catalogue no. 11-010. Reproduced with permission of the Minister of Supply and Services Canada, 1992.

The Consumption Schedule

BOX 19.3

The table and graph both offer a simple example of the connection between real disposable income (Y_d) and desired consumption (C). The level of autonomous desired consumption is shown on the graph by the height of the intersection of the consumption schedule with the vertical axis. The slope of the consumption schedule is equal to the marginal propensity to consume.

(a)

(1) Real Disposable Income (Y_d)	(2) Desired Consumption Expenditure (C)	(3) Change in Real Income	(4) Change in Desired Consumption	(5) Marginal Propensity to Consume	(6) Average Propensity to Consume
		(billions of dollars per year)			
$ 0	$ 100				—
		$100	$75	0.75	
100	175				1.75
		100	75	0.75	
200	250				1.25
		100	75	0.75	
300	325				1.08
		100	75	0.75	
400	400				1.00
		100	75	0.75	
500	475				0.95
		100	75	0.75	
600	550				0.92
		100	75	0.75	
700	625				0.89
		100	75	0.75	
800	700				0.88
		100	75	0.75	
900	775				0.86
		100	75	0.75	
1000	850				0.85
		100	75	0.75	
1100	925				0.84
		100	75	0.75	
1200	1000				0.83

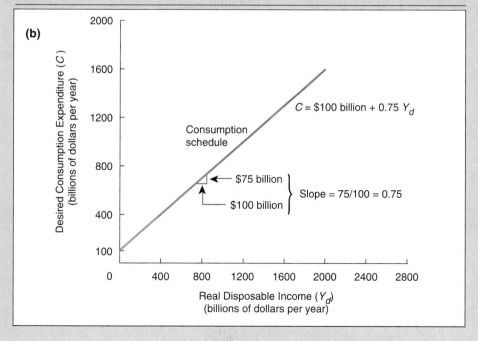

(b)

$C = \$100\text{ billion} + 0.75\, Y_d$

Consumption schedule

$75 billion

$100 billion

Slope = 75/100 = 0.75

may experience zero income, and when they do, they do not cut desired consumption to zero. They may even draw on past savings or borrow against future income to try to make the minimal level of desired consumption attainable.

The marginal propensity to consume

Turn now to columns 1–4 of Box 19.3. They show that whenever disposable income rises, some of the additional income is spent on consumption above and beyond autonomous desired consumption. The fraction of each additional dollar of disposable income that goes to additional consumption is called the **marginal propensity to consume (MPC)**. (The term *marginal* refers here, as elsewhere, to the effects of a small increase or decrease in some economic variable — in this case, disposable income. A *propensity* is simply a tendency.)

The box shows, for example, that a $100-billion increase in disposable income, from $500 billion to $600 billion, raises desired consumption by $75 billion, from $475 billion to $550 billion. Likewise, a $100-billion decrease in disposable income, from $500 billion to $400 billion, causes desired consumption to fall by $75 billion, from $475 billion to $400 billion. The value of the marginal propensity to consume for this example thus is 0.75 ($75 billion divided by $100 billion).

In geometric terms, the marginal propensity to consume is equal to the slope of the consumption schedule. In part (b) of Box 19.3, a horizontal movement of $100 billion in disposable income corresponds to a vertical movement of $75 billion in desired consumption. The slope of the consumption schedule is thus $75/100 = 0.75$, the same as the marginal propensity to consume.

We can now express the consumption function in algebraic terms. Let C represent desired consumption; Y_d, disposable income; a, autonomous desired consumption; and b, the marginal propensity to consume. In a general form, then, the consumption function is written as follows: $C = a + bY_d$. The particular consumption function used in our model is expressed algebraically as follows: $C = \$100$ billion $+ 0.75\ Y_d$.

Marginal versus average propensity to consume

It is important to distinguish the marginal propensity to consume from the average propensity to consume. The **average propensity to consume (APC)** for any level of income is equal to total desired consumption divided by income. APC is shown in column 6 of Box 19.3. For levels of income below $400 billion APC consumption exceeds disposable income, so that the average propensity to consume is greater than one. As disposable income rises, the average propensity to consume falls. But because total desired consumption always includes a constant level of autonomous desired consumption, at least in the short run, the average propensity to consume is always greater than marginal propensity to consume.[2]

Short run versus long run

The actual values of both the average and the marginal propensity to consume depend in practice on the time horizon. In Canada, consumption spending

---

Marginal propensity to consume (MPC)
The fraction of each additional dollar of disposable income that people desire to spend on consumption.

Average propensity to consume (APC)
Total desired consumption for any level of income divided by total disposable income.

---

[2]The relationship between average and marginal propensity to consume can be shown through a comparison of algebraic expressions, as follows: As we have seen, the consumption schedule can be written as $C = a + bY_d$, where b is the marginal propensity to consume. The average propensity to consume can be expressed as $C/Y_d = (a + bY_d)/Y_d = a/Y_d + b$. The last expression shows clearly that the average propensity to consume exceeds the marginal propensity to consume as long as autonomous desired consumption is greater than zero.

(measured ex post facto) has tended to rise over long periods by about 90 cents for each dollar increase in disposable income, which implies a long-run marginal propensity to consume of about 0.9. Also, the long-run level of autonomous consumption, as implied by historical data, approaches zero. As a result, the average and marginal propensities to consume are equal in the long run.

In the short run (a year or less), consumption tends to increase by less than 90 cents for each dollar increase in income. Also, autonomous consumption is positive in the short run, so the marginal propensity to consume is less than the average propensity to consume.

One reason for this is that year-to-year changes in disposable income are not always permanent. People tend to make smaller changes in their spending plans in response to temporary changes in income than they do in response to permanent ones. For example, a household that is accustomed to a $20 000 annual income would no doubt cut back its spending plans somewhat in a year when its income temporarily dropped to $18 000; as long as it expected times to return, however, it would probably reduce its spending plans by less than if it expected the lower income level to be permanent. As long as the drop in income was seen as temporary, the household could plan to offset it to some degree by dipping into past savings or by borrowing.

Even permanent changes in income are not always perceived as permanent in the short run. Thus, a household that experiences a permanent increase in income of $2000 per year might at first tend to treat part of the added income as temporary and might consequently plan to spend less of it than it would otherwise. Over a longer period, as the household came to accept that the increase in income was permanent, it might plan to consume more of it.

Because this book focusses mainly on short-run economic stabilization policy, the examples in this and later chapters will use a marginal propensity to consume of 0.75, somewhat lower than the observed long-run marginal propensity to consume for Canada. There is nothing sacred about the value of 0.75, however. Under different short-run conditions, a higher or lower value might be appropriate. Box 19.4, for example, shows consumption schedules for marginal propensities to consume of 0.9, 0.66, and 0.5. A $100-billion level of autonomous desired consumption is assumed for each of these schedules, so they differ only in their slope: The higher the marginal propensity to consume, the steeper the consumption schedule.

The Saving Schedule

In the basic macroeconomic model that we are constructing, leakages from the spending flow are also important. Household savings are one form of leakage. Fortunately, once we know the level of desired consumption that corresponds to each level of real disposable income, we can easily calculate the level of desired saving. The relationship between desired saving and disposable income, called the **saving schedule**, is given in numerical form in part (a) of Box 19.5, and in graphic form in part (b). Desired saving at each level of real disposable income is calculated by simply subtracting desired consumption from disposable income.

Dissaving, or negative desired saving, occurs when desired consumption exceeds disposable income. In this example, a $100-billion dissaving occurs when real disposable income is zero. Desired saving at zero disposable income is the negative of autonomous desired consumption.

The break-even point, at which there is neither desired saving nor dissaving, occurs at $400 billion of real disposable income. At levels of disposable income

Saving schedule
A graphic or numerical schedule that shows how desired saving varies as disposable income varies, other things being equal.

Dissaving
Negative desired saving, which occurs when desired consumption exceeds disposable income.

BOX 19.4 *Consumption Schedules for Various Marginal Propensities to Consume*

The slope of the consumption schedule is equal to the marginal propensity to consume. Here, consumption schedules are shown for marginal propensities to consume of 0.9, 0.66, and 0.5. Autonomous desired consumption of $100 billion is assumed for all the curves.

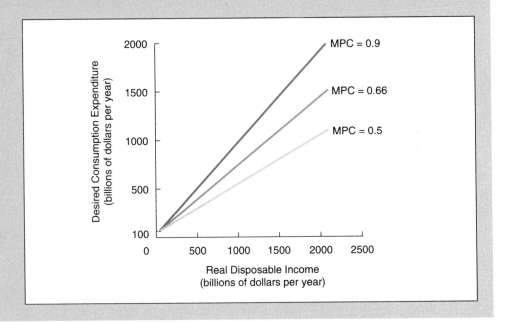

below $400 billion, desired saving is negative; at levels above $400 billion, it is positive.

The fraction of each additional dollar of disposable income that people plan to save is called the **marginal propensity to save (MPS)**. Because all disposable income is intended to be either saved or consumed, it follows that the marginal propensity to save is equal to one minus the marginal propensity to consume, or, in equation form,

$$MPS = 1 - MPC.$$

In geometric terms, the marginal propensity to save is equal to the slope of the saving schedule, which is 0.25 in part (b) of Box 19.5.

Marginal propensity to save (MPS)
The fraction of each dollar of additional income that people desire to save.

Shifts in the Consumption Schedule

The consumption schedules that we have drawn so far show the link between disposable income and desired consumption spending in real terms (that is, in constant dollars). A movement along the consumption schedule shows how real desired consumption spending changes as real disposable income changes, other things being equal. In this section, we will consider the factors covered by the other-things-being-equal clause — that is, the factors that can cause a shift in the consumption schedule.

The Saving Schedule

BOX 19.5

The saving schedule shows the connection between desired saving and income. In part (a), desired saving is found by subtracting desired consumption from real disposable income. In part (b), the saving schedule is depicted in graphic form. When real disposable income is less than $400 billion, desired saving is negative (that is, dissaving occurs), and when real disposable income exceeds $400 billion, desired saving is positive.

(a)

(1) Real Disposable Income	(2) Desired Consumption	(3) Desired Saving
(billions of dollars per year)		
$ 0	100	−100
100	175	−75
200	250	−50
300	325	−25
400	400	0
500	475	25
600	550	50
700	625	75
800	700	100
900	775	125
1000	850	150
1100	925	175
1200	1000	200
1300	1075	225
1400	1150	250
1500	1225	275
1600	1300	300
1700	1375	325
1800	1450	350
1900	1525	375
2000	1600	400

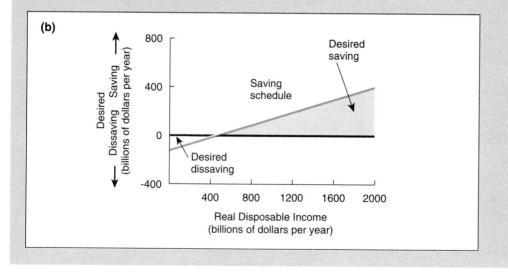

Wealth Effects

One factor that is assumed to remain constant as we move along the consumption schedule is *wealth*. Wealth is another term for a household's net worth — its assets (such as houses and cars, shares of stock and bonds) minus its liabilities. Of two households that have equal income, we expect the one with greater wealth to spend more freely (that is, to have a higher average propensity to consume) than the one with less wealth.

Because greater wealth leads to the consumption of a greater percentage of income, anything that happens to increase the total real wealth of all households will cause an upward shift in the consumption schedule. For example, many people hold some of their wealth in the form of shares of corporate stock. If the prices of stocks rise faster than other prices, the real value of the shares owned by households will increase, potentially producing an upward shift in the consumption schedule. If, however, stock prices remain steady while the Consumer Price Index rises, the real value of the shares held by households will decline, and the consumption schedule could shift downward.

Expectations

People's spending decisions depend not only on their current income and wealth but also on their expected future income and wealth. Any change in their expectations can cause a shift in the consumption schedule. When all consumers become pessimistic, as they tend to do during a recession, the consumption schedule can shift downward. When they become more optimistic, it can shift upward again.

Tax effects

Up to this point, we have drawn the consumption schedule with disposable income on the horizontal axis of the graph. For many purposes, however, it is more useful to plot domestic income on the horizontal axis. In a world with no taxes, this change would not affect the consumption schedule at all, because without taxes, domestic income and disposable income would be equal. Once we introduce taxes, however, the level of disposable income, on which consumption decisions depend, will differ from the level of domestic income. As a result, changes in taxes become another source of shifts in the consumption schedule. Let's see why this is true, first considering the case of so-called lump-sum taxes, then that of income taxes.[3]

Lump-sum taxes Taxes that do not vary as the taxpayer's income varies are called **lump-sum taxes**. Personal property taxes are a major example on the revenue side of the net tax picture. On the transfer side of net taxes, many items, from interest on the national debt to government pensions, are not directly linked to income changes.

Box 19.6 shows how the consumption schedule is affected by the introduction of a lump-sum tax of $100 billion into an economy that had no taxes before. The first two columns of the table, which are the same as those in Box 19.3, show real domestic income and the corresponding level of desired consumption when there are no taxes. The consumption schedule assumes autonomous

Lump-sum taxes
Taxes that do not vary with the level of real domestic income (for example, property taxes).

---

[3]We continue to assume that there are no indirect business taxes or corporate profits taxes. Only personal taxes, such as personal income taxes and personal property taxes, are taken into account. It therefore remains true that domestic income minus net taxes equals disposable income.

Domestic Income and Desired Consumption with Lump-Sum Taxes

BOX 19.6

Lump-sum taxes are taxes that do not vary with changes in the level of domestic income. This box shows how the introduction of a lump-sum tax of $100 billion shifts the consumption schedule downward, when the schedule is drawn with domestic income (as opposed to disposable income) on the horizontal axis. The amount of the shift is equal to the level of lump-sum taxes times the marginal propensity to consume.

(a)

(1) Real Domestic Income	(2) Desired Consumption without Tax	(3) Lump-Sum Tax	(4) Real Disposable Income	(5) Desired Consumption with Tax
		(billions of dollars per year)		
0	100	100	−100	25
100	175	100	0	100
200	250	100	100	175
300	325	100	200	250
400	400	100	300	325
500	475	100	400	400
600	550	100	500	475
700	625	100	600	550
800	700	100	700	625
900	775	100	800	700
1000	850	100	900	775
1100	925	100	1000	850
1200	1000	100	1100	925

(b)

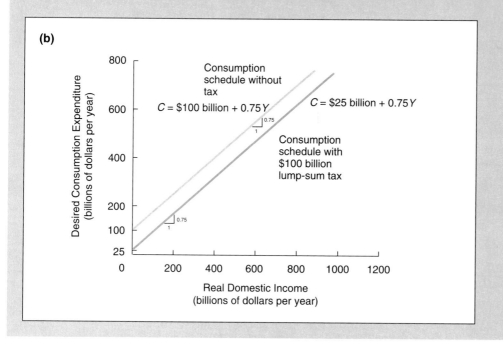

desired consumption of $100 million and a marginal propensity to consume of 0.75. Columns 3 and 4 of the table show that the $100-billion lump-sum tax reduces disposable income to a level $100 billion below that of domestic income. As column 5 shows, this $100-billion reduction of personal income cuts $75 billion from desired consumption at each income level, in accordance with the 0.75 marginal propensity to consume. The remaining $25 billion of the reduction in disposable income is reflected in a reduction in saving. As before, autonomous desired consumption is at the level of $100 billion when disposable income is zero. However, zero disposable income now corresponds to $100 billion of domestic income, as line 2 of the table shows. At a domestic income of zero, desired consumption with the lump-sum tax is $25 billion.[4]

Part (b) of Box 19.6 shows the effect of the new lump-sum tax in graphic terms. The introduction of the tax produces a downward shift in the consumption schedule, when the schedule is drawn, as it is here, with real domestic income (as opposed to disposable income) on the horizontal axis. The new schedule is parallel to the old one, but it has shifted downward by an amount equal to the marginal propensity to consume times the amount of the lump-sum taxes. In this case, the shift is $75 billion. The vertical intercept of the new schedule is equal to the initial level of autonomous desired consumption minus the product of the marginal propensity to consume times the level of lump-sum net taxes, which gives $25 billion in this case. The new consumption function can be written as $C = \$25$ billion $+ 0.75\ Y$.

Percentage income tax Lump-sum taxes are an important source of revenue for provincial and municipal governments, and lump-sum transfers are an important item on the expenditure side of the federal budget. The largest source of federal revenue, however, is the personal income tax, or **percentage income tax**, which is calculated as a percentage of income. This income-linked tax has a somewhat different effect on the consumption schedule, as Box 19.7 shows.

The table in part (a) of Box 19.7 assumes a 20 percent income tax on income from all sources, but lump-sum net taxes of zero. As columns 3 and 4 of the table show, this tax takes 20 cents of each dollar of domestic income, leaving 80 cents of disposable income. As columns 4 and 5 show, the marginal propensity to consume of 0.75 applies to this 80 cents of personal income. All told, then, of each dollar of domestic income, 20 cents goes to taxes, and of the remaining 80 cents, 60 cents goes to consumption and the other 20 cents to saving.[5]

Percentage income tax
A percentage tax placed on personal income, whereby the absolute amount taxed varies with income.

---

[4]In algebraic terms, we now have the following:
Let C represent desired consumption; Y_d, disposable income; T_n, net taxes; and Y, net domestic income. We know that $Y_d = Y - T_n$, and $T_n = \$100$ billion, so $Y_d = Y - \$100$ billion. Therefore:

$$C = \$100 \text{ billion} + 07.5\ Y_d$$
$$= \$100 \text{ billion} + 0.75\ (Y - \$100 \text{ billion})$$
$$= \$100 \text{ billion} + 0.75\ Y - \$75 \text{ billion}$$
$$= \$25 \text{ billion} + 0.75\ Y$$

[5]The relationship between desired consumption and domestic income with a percentage income tax can be explained simply as follows: If changes in desired consumption are always 75 percent of any changes in disposable income (as measured by the MPC), and disposable income is 80 percent of domestic income (as it is with a 20 percent tax), then changes in desired consumption will be 60 percent of any changes in domestic income (80 percent of 75 percent). Thus, the MPC is 0.75 in relation to disposable income and 0.6 in relation to domestic income.

The Consumption Schedule with an Income Tax   *BOX 19.7*

When the consumption schedule is drawn with real domestic income on the horizontal axis, the introduction of a percentage income tax reduces the slope of the schedule. This example assumes a marginal propensity to consume of 0.75 and a percentage tax of 0.2. The slope of the consumption schedule with the percentage income tax in effect is equal to MPC $(1 - t)$, where t is the marginal tax rate, or, in this case, $0.75 (1 - 0.2) = 0.75 (0.8) = 0.6$.

(a)

(1) Real Domestic Income	(2) Desired Consumption without Tax	(3) 20% Income Tax	(4) Real Disposable Income	(5) Desired Consumption with Tax
		(billions of dollars per year)		
0	100	0	0	100
100	175	20	80	160
200	250	40	160	220
300	325	60	240	280
400	400	80	320	340
500	475	100	400	400
600	550	120	480	460
700	625	140	560	520
800	700	160	640	580
900	775	180	720	640
1000	850	200	800	700
1100	925	220	880	760
1200	1000	240	960	820

(b)

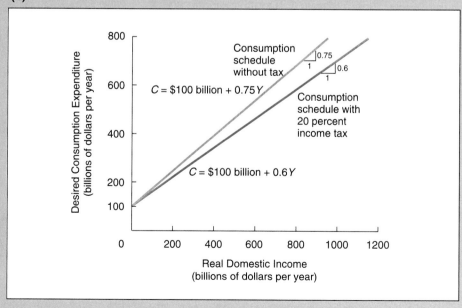

Part (b) of Box 19.7 shows the effect of the percentage income tax in graphic terms. Instead of a downward shift that leaves the new schedule parallel to the old one, the income tax reduces the slope of the consumption schedule. With no income tax in effect, the slope of the schedule is equal to the marginal propensity to consume (0.75 in this case). With a 20 percent income tax in effect, the slope is reduced to 0.6. The formula for the consumption schedule with a percentage income tax in effect is $C = \$100$ billion $+ 0.75 (Y - tY)$, where t represents the percentage income tax expressed as a fraction of domestic income. Thus, in our example,

$$
\begin{aligned}
C &= \$100 \text{ billion} + 0.75\,(Y - tY) \\
&= \$100 \text{ billion} + 0.75\,(Y - 0.2\,Y) \\
&= \$100 \text{ billion} + 0.75\,Y - 0.15\,Y \\
&= \$100 \text{ billion} + 0.6\,Y
\end{aligned}
$$

FROM DESIRED CONSUMPTION EXPENDITURE TO AGGREGATE DESIRED EXPENDITURE

The purpose of our discussion in this chapter is to examine the various expenditure decisions that make up aggregate desired expenditure. So far, we have examined desired consumption expenditure, relating it, through hypothetical examples, to both disposable income and domestic income. While consumers finance their expenditures out of disposable income, it will be more helpful, for the purposes of our further analysis, to continue to relate consumption expenditure decisions, as well as investment, government, and net-export expenditure plans, to domestic income, as we have just done.

The consumption schedule is the foundation of the aggregate desired expenditure function. The vertical intercept of the consumption schedule is equal to the level of autonomous desired consumption, adjusted, if need be, for lump-sum taxes. The slope of the consumption schedule is equal to the marginal propensity to consume, adjusted, if need be, for the marginal income-tax rate. In the sections that follow, we will gradually construct an aggregate expenditure schedule, based on total desired expenditures. Our analysis will involve the following two assumptions (in addition to those specified earlier in the chapter): (1) that there is no income tax and (2) that lump-sum taxes are fixed at $100 billion.

Desired Investment Expenditure

Business investment is the second major component of aggregate desired expenditure. As we explained in Chapter 17, it includes desired investment in fixed capital (buildings and machinery), as well as desired changes in inventories. Undesired or unplanned changes in inventories are not included in aggregate desired expenditure. In recent years, ex post facto investment, as measured in the national-income accounts, has represented, on average, roughly 20 percent of real GDP. However, our focus in this analysis is on ex ante investment — that is, on *desired* investment expenditure.

The level of desired investment depends on interest rates and business expectations. Interest rates represent the costs of obtaining funds for investment. These costs are weighed against the expected returns from the investments. Other things being equal, the lower the interest rate, the more people will desire to invest; similarly, the more optimistic business expectations are, the more planned investment there will be.

In Chapter 25, we will explore in greater detail the links among interest rates, expectations, domestic income, and investment, but for the time being, we will treat desired investment as *constant*. We assume constant interest rates and unvarying expectations, and allow investment to be independent of changes in domestic income. Thus, in this analysis, once we know the level of desired investment for a given year, we can simply add it to desired consumption spending as the second component of aggregate desired expenditure. Indeed, this is what we have done in Box 19.8.

In this box, we assume that desired investment is $110 billion at all levels of domestic income. The investment function (I) is therefore a horizontal line at $110 billion. The line labelled $C + I$ combines the desired consumption and

---

Desired Investment Expenditure and Aggregate Desired Expenditure

BOX 19.8

In this example, investment is assumed to remain constant, at $110 billion, regardless of the level of real domestic income. The investment schedule is therefore a horizontal line. When added to the consumption schedule, it creates the $C + I$ line, which illustrates how aggregate desired expenditure (ADE) changes as domestic income changes. The $C + I$, or ADE, curve shows, for example, that when real domestic income is $200 billion, $C + I$ will equal $285 billion ($C + I = \$135$ billion + [$0.75 \times$ real domestic income]).

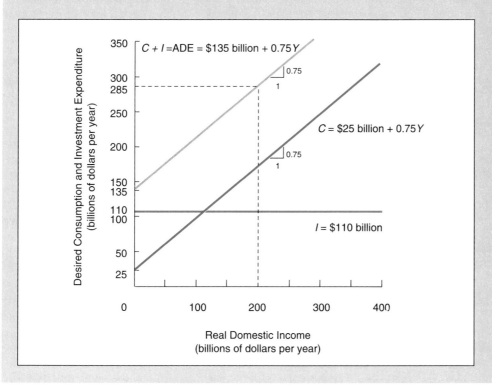

Real Domestic Income
(billions of dollars per year)

investment expenditure schedules, and thus represents aggregate desired expenditure for this two-component example. It intercepts the vertical axis at $135 billion, because when domestic income is zero, autonomous desired consumption is $25 billion and desired investment is $110 billion. Desired investment, in this example, does not rise with increases in domestic income, but desired consumption does — by 75 percent of any increase in domestic income. Therefore, as Box 19.8 shows, the $C + I$ line starts at a level of $135 billion and rises with a slope of 0.75.

Desired Government Expenditure

The third major component of aggregate desired expenditure, after consumption and investment, is government expenditure on goods and services. Expenditures by the various levels of government in Canada have often grown more rapidly than domestic output, although their growth rate has slowed in recent years. They account for more than 20 percent of gross domestic product.

Despite the importance of government purchases, macroeconomic analysis traditionally considers their desired level to be determined by political decision processes that are "outside" the economic system. This does not mean that the legislators and executives who make spending decisions at various levels of government are uninfluenced by such economic considerations as the level of domestic income or the rate of unemployment. On the contrary, our later analysis of fiscal policy will show that they are very much guided by such considerations. Nonetheless, the relationships among desired government spending and domestic income and unemployment are too indirect and too complex to be put into a simple theory. Therefore, in our initial hypothetical treatment of aggregate desired expenditure, we assume that desired government spending is constant. In Box 19.9, we arbitrarily assume that it is $150 billion at all levels of domestic income; hence, it is represented as a horizontal line at that expenditure level. The new aggregate desired expenditure line $(C + I + G)$ now intercepts the vertical axis at $285 billion (recall that, when domestic income is zero, autonomous desired consumption is $25 billion and desired investment is $110 billion, so $C + I + G$ = $25 billion + $110 billion + $150 billion), and it continues to have a slope of 0.75.

Desired Net-Export Expenditure

Net exports are the fourth and final component of aggregate desired expenditure. Net exports, as measured ex post facto in the national-income accounts, represent the difference between the value of goods and services exported to foreigners and the value of goods and services imported from foreign countries. As we showed in Chapter 15, foreign trade is extremely important to the Canadian economy, accounting for about 30 percent of Canada's GDP annually. It is important, therefore, to understand some of the factors that determine the levels of our imports and exports.

Before we examine these factors, however, it should be noted that it is the *difference* between exports and imports (*net* exports) that determines the impact that the foreign market will have on the Canadian economy. Net exports are normally only 1 or 2 percent of Canadian GDP, but that small size may understate their importance as a source of disturbances in aggregate desired expenditure, because net exports can be very volatile. For example, from 1987 to 1989, net

Desired Government Expenditure and Aggregate Desired Expenditure

BOX 19.9

In this graph, desired government expenditure on goods and services is built into the aggregate desired expenditure schedule. Desired government expenditure (G) is depicted as a horizontal line at $150 billion, because it is assumed to be constant and autonomous. (We assume that governments would plan to spend $150 billion even if domestic income were zero.) Total autonomous desired consumption, investment, and government expenditures now total $285 billion. The aggregate desired expenditure schedule therefore intercepts the vertical axis at that level and rises with income at a rate of 75 percent of income, giving the ADE curve its slope of 0.75. The ADE curve shows that when real domestic income is $600 billion, $C + I + G$ will equal $735 billion.

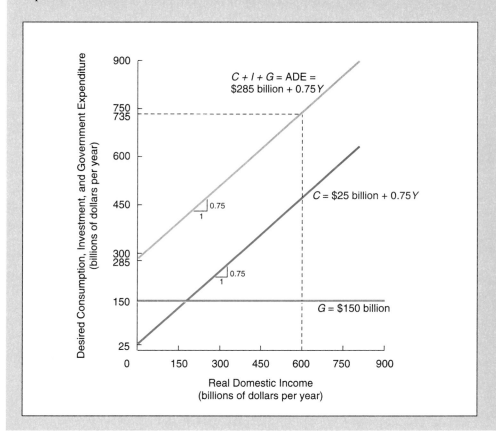

exports fell from zero to almost −$13 billion, a total swing equivalent to about 2.3 percent of GDP.

Desired imports are a part of total desired consumption, investment, and government expenditures. As such, they are the result of the same forces that underlie those expenditures: income, prices, interest rates, and a multitude of other factors.

Most imports into Canada result from consumer expenditures. Thus, in our analysis we will assume that desired imports are related to personal disposable

Import schedule
A graphic or numerical representation of how desired import purchases vary as real disposable income varies, other things being equal. It is assumed here that
$M = M_a + mY_d$,
where M is desired imports, M_a is autonomous desired imports, m is the marginal propensity to import, and Y_d is disposable income.

Marginal propensity to import (MPM)
The proportion of each additional dollar of disposable income (Y_d) that people desire to spend on imports.

$$\text{MPM} = m = \frac{\Delta M}{\Delta Y_d}$$

Autonomous desired imports
The value of imports planned even when disposable income is zero.

income, just as desired consumer expenditures are. The more disposable income we have, the more Japanese cameras and American computers we will plan to import.

In constructing an **import schedule**, we will also assume that desired imports like desired consumer expenditures, consist of both an autonomous element and an element that is related to disposable income. The value of the latter is determined by what we call the **marginal propensity to import (MPM)** — that is, the proportion of each additional dollar of disposable income that goes to additional imports. In the short run, the MPM has been found to be as high as 49 percent.[6] The term **autonomous desired imports** refers to the value of import purchases that are planned even when disposable income is at zero.

As with desired investment and government expenditures, we find it useful for purposes of analysis to relate changes in desired imports to changes in domestic income rather than disposable income. In our model, however, where the only difference between disposable income and domestic income is a lump-sum tax, the marginal propensity to import out of disposable income will be the same as the marginal propensity to import out of domestic income. The imposition of a lump-sum tax affects autonomous desired imports but not the marginal propensity to import.[7]

While *desired imports* are connected positively to income generated within our economy, *exports* are related primarily to the income of persons outside our economy (they are the *desired imports* of nonresidents, and therefore are related to *their* income). For this reason, exports are treated similarly to government purchases: as a very important expenditure component that is not connected directly to income flows within our country. A constant value is therefore assigned to exports.

The behaviour of imports and exports in our model is shown in Box 19.10. Exports equal $125 billion at each level of domestic income, while desired imports start at $50 billion when domestic income is zero and rise by $15 billion for every $100 billion increase in domestic income. This means that the marginal propensity to import is 0.15. Given these conditions, exports will equal desired imports at a level of domestic income of $500 billion (both will equal $125 billion). Note that at levels of income of less than $500 billion, exports will exceed desired imports; that is, net exports will be positive. At levels of income of more

---

[6] T.R. Robinson, "Canadian Imports and Economic Stability," *Canadian Journal of Economics* 1 (May 1968): 421. In another study, Robinson indicates that a longer-run MPM tends to be about half as large ("Foreign Trade and Economic Stability," *Studies of the Royal Commission on Taxation*, no. 5, Ottawa, 1967, p. 175).

[7] Assume, for example, that $M = M_a + m(Y_d)$, where M stands for desired imports; M_a, for autonomous desired imports; m, for the marginal propensity to import; and Y_d, for disposable income. (Assume also that values are given in billions of dollars.) If $M_a = \$65$ and $m = 0.15$, then

(1) $M = \$65 + 0.15 Y_d$.

Now, in our model, disposable income = domestic income (Y) minus net taxes (T_n), or $Y_d = Y - T_n$. Equation (1) can then be rewritten as follows:

$$M = \$65 + 0.15 (Y - T_n).$$

If we add a net tax of $100 to the other money values, $M = \$65 + 0.15 (Y - \$100)$, or $M = \$65 + 0.15 Y - \$15$. This simplifies to

(2) $M = \$50 + 0.15 Y$.

The two equations show that the marginal propensity to import (m) is the same for both Y_d and Y. What changes is the value of M_a.

Hypothetical Export, Import, and Net-Export Schedules   BOX 19.10

In the model below, exports equal $125 billion at all levels of domestic income. Desired imports are $50 billion when domestic income is zero, and rise by 0.15 of domestic income. When domestic income is $500 billion, exports and imports will be equal (net exports will be zero).

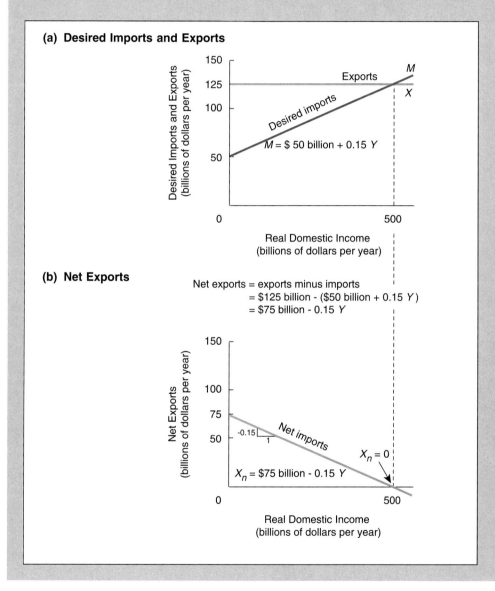

(a) Desired Imports and Exports

$M = $ \$ 50$ billion $+ 0.15 \, Y$

(b) Net Exports

Net exports = exports minus imports
= $125 billion - ($50 billion + 0.15 Y)
= $75 billion - 0.15 Y

$X_n = $75 billion - 0.15 Y

$X_n = 0$

than $500 billion, desired imports will be greater than exports, and net exports will be negative. Recall that *net exports* equal exports minus desired imports, or $X - M$.

This hypothetical example reflects the type of export and import behaviour that a country such as Canada can expect. As the level of income in Canada rises, imports may be stimulated more than exports, resulting in a growing deficit in the export-import balance, although, as became apparent in our more detailed discussion of the foreign sector in Chapter 15, many other factors, such as prices and foreign-exchange rates, seriously affect the actual balance between exports and imports in any given year.

We now need only to add net exports to desired consumption, investment, and government purchases in order to construct a schedule of aggregate desired expenditure. A note of caution about terminology before we proceed: You will find that, for the sake of convenience and simplicity, the word *desired* is often omitted in reference to an aggregate desired expenditure schedule, line, or curve. It is therefore important for you to remember that the *aggregate expenditure schedule* represents the total of all *desired* expenditures, unless otherwise stated.

THE AGGREGATE EXPENDITURE SCHEDULE AND INCOME DETERMINATION

Aggregate expenditure schedule
A table or graph showing the relationship between aggregate desired expenditure (the real value of total desired expenditure) and real domestic income.

The first step in constructing a theory of income determination is to prepare an aggregate desired expenditure schedule — or, simply, an **aggregate expenditure schedule** — which shows what the real level of total desired expenditure will be for each possible level of real domestic income. Box 19.11 indicates how such a schedule can be built up from the separate desired consumption, investment, government-purchase, and net-export components discussed above — indeed, it serves as a summary of the material we have just covered.

Look first at the tabular form of the aggregate expenditure schedule in Box 19.11(a). The consumption schedule in column 2 is based on an assumed marginal propensity to consume of 0.75, an autonomous desired consumption of $25 billion, and lump-sum net taxes of $100 billion. Interest rates and business conditions are assumed to remain constant and yield the $110 billion of desired investment expenditure shown in column 3. As before, this component of desired expenditure is assumed not to vary as domestic income varies. Desired government purchases (column 4) are also assumed not to vary.

Desired exports, imports, and net exports (columns 5–7) are assumed to vary as described in Box 19.11. Aggregate desired expenditure (column 8) is equal to the sum of desired consumption, investment, government purchases, and net exports.

BOX 19.11   *Construction of the Aggregate Expenditure Schedule*

Aggregate desired expenditure is the total value of all desired expenditures. This box shows how an aggregate expenditure schedule can be built up from its four separate components: desired consumption, investment, government purchases, and net exports. In the simplified economy represented in this box, desired consumption and imports are the only elements of desired expenditure that vary as real domestic income varies (net exports vary only because imports do). The slope of the aggregate expenditure schedule, represented by the curve $C + I + G + X_n$ in part (b), is thus equal to the marginal propensity to consume (0.75) minus the marginal propensity to import (0.15) — that is, 0.6.

(a)

(1) Real Domestic income (Y)	(2) Desired Consumption Expenditure (C)	(3) Desired Investment (I)	(4) Desired Government Expenditures (G)	(5) Desired Exports (X)	(6) Desired Imports (M)	(7) Desired Net Exports (X_n)	(8) Aggregate Desired Expenditure (ADE)
			(billions of dollars per year, with constant prices)				
0	25	110	150	125	50	+75	360
100	100	110	150	125	65	+60	420
200	175	110	150	125	80	+45	480
300	250	110	150	125	95	+30	540
400	325	110	150	125	110	+15	600
500	400	110	150	125	125	0	660
600	475	110	150	125	140	−15	720
700	550	110	150	125	155	−30	780
800	625	110	150	125	170	−45	840
900	700	110	150	125	185	−60	900
1000	775	110	150	125	200	−75	960
1100	850	110	150	125	215	−90	1020
1200	925	110	150	125	230	−105	1080
1300	1000	110	150	125	245	−120	1140
1400	1075	110	150	125	260	−135	1200
1500	1150	110	150	125	275	−150	1260
1600	1225	110	150	125	290	−165	1320

(b)

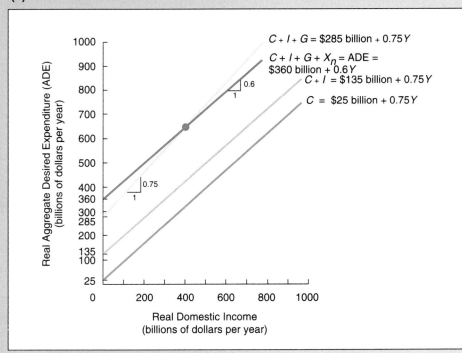

$C + I + G = \$285 \text{ billion} + 0.75\,Y$

$C + I + G + X_n = \text{ADE} = \$360 \text{ billion} + 0.6\,Y$

$C + I = \$135 \text{ billion} + 0.75\,Y$

$C = \$25 \text{ billion} + 0.75\,Y$

The procedure for constructing the graphic form of the aggregate desired expenditure schedule, shown in Box 19.11(b), is as follows: First, real domestic income is plotted on the horizontal axis and real desired expenditure on the vertical axis. Next, the consumption schedule is drawn, as given in column 2 of the table. This schedule is labelled C in Box 19.11(b).

Then, desired investment expenditure is added. Given the shape and position of the investment schedule and the rate of interest (which is assumed to be constant), desired investment is fixed at $110 billion and does not change as domestic income changes. A line, labelled $C + I$, is thus drawn parallel to the consumption schedule, separated from it by a distance equal to the level of desired investment.

The next component of aggregate desired expenditure to be added is government purchases, which are assumed to be constant at $150 billion. Adding this component gives a new line, labelled $C + I + G$.

Desired net exports are assumed in this example to have a value of $75 billion − 0.15 of domestic income, because net exports equal $X − M$, and $X = \$125$ billion and $M = \$50$ billion + 0.15 × domestic income. When domestic income is zero, X_n (net exports) adds $75 billion to aggregate desired expenditure. Thereafter, the gap between $C + I + G + X_n$ and $C + I + G$ declines as X_n declines. When domestic income is $500, X_n is zero and $C + I + G + X_n = C + I + G$. At higher levels of income, where X_n is negative, $C + I + G + X_n$ actually lies below $C + I + G$.

The aggregate expenditure schedule equals $C + I + G + X_n$, which in our example equals $25 + 0.75 (y) + \$110$ billion + $150 billion + $75 billion − 0.15 (y)$, where y = domestic income. Adding C, I, G, and X_n results in an aggregate expenditure schedule that equals $360 billion + 0.6 y.

The Equilibrium Level of Domestic Income

Having examined some of the determinants of aggregate desired expenditure, and having developed an aggregate expenditure schedule, we can now combine such a schedule with different levels of domestic income and output to determine what economists call the **equilibrium level of income**. This is the level of income that generates a level of aggregate desired expenditure exactly equal to the current level of domestic output.

To help understand this concept, recall from Chapter 17 that the circular flow is in equilibrium only when aggregate desired expenditure is equal to domestic product. From our analysis of the circular flow, we know that every dollar of domestic output generates a dollar of domestic income. The problem is this: Will that level of income in turn create an amount of aggregate desired expenditure that matches the level of output? If it does, the circular flow is in equilibrium; if it does not, the circular flow is in disequilibrium.

The income–expenditure diagram in Box 19.12 depicts a very unique aggregate expenditure schedule. It is a 45° line, which has the unique property that, at every point on the line, the level of income and output (measured on the horizontal axis) is exactly equal to aggregate expenditure (measured on the vertical axis). This is true, of course, of realized or ex post facto expenditures, so the 45° line is really a *realized expenditure schedule*. For example, assume that the current income and output level is $1200 billion. Locate this point on the horizontal axis, then move vertically upward to the 45° line (the aggregate realized

Equilibrium level of income
The level of income that generates a level of aggregate desired expenditure equal to the current level of domestic output.

The Income–Expenditure Equilibrium Line   *BOX 19.12*

In this graph, the 45° line (Z) represents a unique reference or line that equates domestic income and output (on the horizontal axis) with aggregate realized expenditure (on the vertical axis). If the aggregate desired expenditure were identical to this line, the circular flow would always be in equilibrium, regardless of the income and output level of the economy.

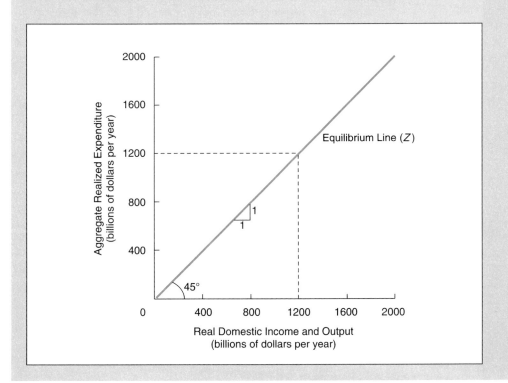

expenditure line). Aggregate realized expenditure at this point is also $1200 billion. The same equality between income and aggregate realized expenditure exists everywhere along the 45° line. Now, if aggregate *desired* expenditure (ADE) corresponded to this 45° line, it would be the same as aggregate realized expenditure no matter what level of income and output the economy produced, and both would equal income and output. In this case, the economy would always be in equilibrium, regardless of the level of income and output.

Aggregate desired expenditure, however, does not correspond to the 45° line. We have already seen that the typical aggregate expenditure curve has a slope of less than one, whereas the slope of the 45° line is exactly one.

This is illustrated in Box 19.13. In this diagram, to which we refer as a **45° line diagram**, we first plot a hypothetical aggregate desired expenditure curve, which intercepts the vertical axis at a height of $360 billion, then rises with a slope of 0.6. We then superimpose a 45° line (Z), which indicates what aggregate desired expenditure *would* be if the circular flow were in equilibrium. Observe that the actual aggregate desired expenditure curve crosses the 45° line at only one point, which in this case occurs at an income/output level of $900 billion. The point of intersection of the ADE curve and the 45° equilibrium line

45° line diagram
A diagram that uses a 45° line to depict equilibrium between aggregate desired expenditure and real income; also called an *income–expenditure diagram.*

BOX 19.13 Using the 45° Line to Determine Equilibrium Domestic Income

The aggregate desired expenditure curve (ADE) and the 45° line (Z) intersect at the equilibrium income point. This figure provides a simple way to determine the equilibrium level of real domestic income, given the assumptions concerning desired expenditure on which the aggregate desired expenditure curve is based. At any level of domestic income greater than the equilibrium level, there will be excess aggregate output, unplanned inventory accumulation, and downward pressure on domestic income. At any level of domestic income less than the equilibrium level, there will be excess aggregate desired expenditure, unplanned inventory depletion, and upward pressure on income and output.

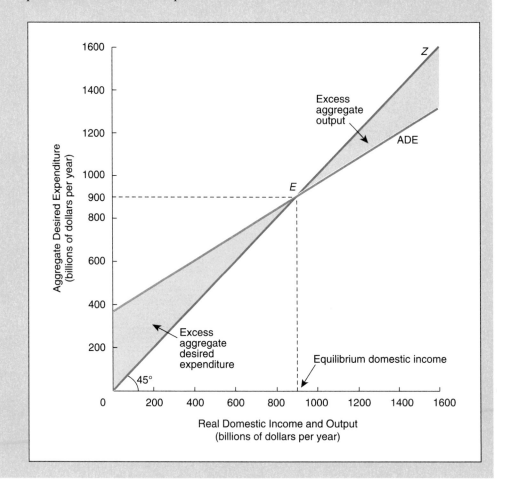

(Z) shows the exact level of domestic income and output that will permit aggregate desired expenditure to equal output. That point is marked *E* in Box 19.13 to indicate that it is the equilibrium point.

It is easy to see that no other level of real domestic income can represent equilibrium in the circular flow. If domestic income were lower than the equilibrium level — say, $600 billion — aggregate desired expenditure would exceed domestic product and domestic income. There would be unplanned depletion of business inventories equal to the vertical distance between the aggregate desired expenditure schedule and the Z line, as shown in Box 19.13. Firms would try to build inventories back up to their previous levels by increasing output, which would in turn cause real domestic income to rise until equilibrium was restored at point E.

If, on the other hand, real domestic income were higher than the equilibrium level — say, $1200 billion — then aggregate desired expenditure would fall short of domestic product. The unsold goods would go to unplanned inventory investment equal to the gap between the aggregate desired expenditure schedule and the Z line. Business firms would react to the buildup in inventories by cutting back on production. The cutback would cause output and income to fall until equilibrium was restored at point E.

As we noted earlier, our analysis in this chapter ignores price changes, and focusses on the *real* values of income, output, and desired expenditure. We have therefore assumed, in the preceding discussion, that when the economy experiences unplanned inventory depletion as a result of an excess of aggregate desired expenditure over domestic output, firms will respond by increasing real output. In the real world, of course, they are also likely to increase prices. Similarly, when unplanned inventory buildup occurs, firms may decrease real output, but they are likely to reduce prices as well. The "price" response to disequilibrium is examined in Chapter 20, where new tools of analysis are developed to take price changes into account.

A numerical approach The determination of equilibrium in the circular flow, depicted graphically in Box 19.13, is represented numerically in Box 19.14, which gives values for real domestic income, aggregate desired expenditure, and unplanned inventory change. The table confirms that $900 billion is the only level of domestic income that allows for equilibrium in the circular flow. Column 5 shows that domestic income tends to move toward equilibrium whenever it is at any level other than $900 billion.

Expenditure Changes

A great many economic factors can affect the level of aggregate desired expenditure. The aggregate expenditure schedule depicts the effects of changes in domestic income on desired expenditure. The effects of these changes are represented by movements along a given aggregate expenditure schedule.

Other factors also influence desired expenditure. Changes in consumer expectations and wealth may cause the level of autonomous desired consumption to vary. Changes in the expected real rate of interest or the expected real return on investment projects cause the level of desired investment to vary. Changes in policy cause the government-purchases component of aggregate desired expenditure to vary, and changes in desired consumption and in the world economy affect the volume of desired net exports. All the changes in desired expenditure that result from causes other than changes in domestic income must be represented by shifts in the aggregate desired expenditure schedule. The nature of such shifts and the adjustments that they require in terms of output, prices, and employment are the subject of Chapters 20 and 21.

BOX 19.14   *Finding Equilibrium Real Domestic Income:*
A Numerical Approach

This box represents numerically the determination of equilibrium real domestic income, based on the same assumptions that underlie the graphic representation in Box 19.13. At every level of real domestic income *except* the equilibrium level, real output either falls short of aggregate desired expenditure, causing unplanned inventory depletion, or exceeds aggregate desired expenditure, causing unplanned inventory accumulation. Unplanned inventory depletion stimulates firms to raise output, causing domestic income to increase; unplanned inventory accumulation causes firms to reduce output, causing domestic income to decrease.

(1) Real Domestic Income	(2) Aggregate Desired Expenditure	(3) Real Domestic Product	(4) Unplanned Inventory Change	(5) Tendency of Change in Real Domestic Income
		(billions of dollars per year, with constant prices)		
100	420	100	−320	Increase
200	480	200	−280	Increase
300	540	300	−240	Increase
400	600	400	−200	Increase
500	660	500	−160	Increase
600	720	600	−120	Increase
700	780	700	−80	Increase
800	840	800	−40	Increase
900	900	900	0	No change
1000	960	1000	+40	Decrease
1100	1020	1100	+80	Decrease
1200	1080	1200	+120	Decrease
1300	1140	1300	+160	Decrease
1400	1200	1400	+200	Decrease
1500	1260	1500	+240	Decrease
1600	1320	1600	+280	Decrease

SUMMARY

1. *Say's law* posits that the production of a given level of domestic product will automatically generate an equal level of aggregate desired expenditure. The truth of this proposition was challenged by the Great Depression of the 1930s, during which the economy was clearly able to produce more, but firms were unable to sell enough of their output. This situation set the stage for the work of John Maynard Keynes, who observed that although the process of production does generate enough income to buy all of the economy's output, there is no guarantee that people's plans will call for spending all of that income.

2. Keynes observed that as consumers' incomes increase, their desired spending also increases, but by less than a dollar for each dollar added to disposable income. Economists refer to this fraction as the *marginal propensity to consume*. The relationship between desired consumption and disposable income can

be shown in the form of a *consumption schedule*, which intersects the vertical axis at a level equal to *autonomous desired consumption* and which has a slope equal to the marginal propensity to consume.

3. Desired saving is the portion of disposable income that households do not wish to spend. When disposable income is zero, there is negative desired saving, or *dissaving*, equal to autonomous desired consumption. For each additional dollar of disposable income, desired saving increases by a fraction of a dollar, to which we refer as the *marginal propensity to save*. The marginal propensity to save is equal to one minus the marginal propensity to consume (MPS = 1 − MPC).

4. Aggregate desired expenditure consists of four major components: desired consumption, investment, government, and net-export expenditure. An *aggregate expenditure schedule* shows the relationship between aggregate desired expenditure and real domestic income. To construct such a schedule, we begin with the consumption schedule, drawn with real domestic income on the horizontal axis. If there are *lump-sum taxes*, the consumption schedule must be shifted downward to take them into account. The schedules for the next three components of aggregate desired expenditure are then added. We assume in this model that the value of the second and third components (desired investment and desired government expenditure), as well as of part of the fourth (exports), does not vary as the level of domestic income varies; desired imports, however, are related positively to income, as defined by the *marginal propensity to import*. Under these assumptions, the slope of the completed aggregate desired expenditure curve is equal to the marginal propensity to consume minus the marginal propensity to import.

5. The *45° line*, or the income–expenditure equilibrium line, shows the level of aggregate realized expenditure that corresponds to each level of real domestic income.

6. The *equilibrium level of real domestic income* is found at the point where the aggregate desired expenditure curve intersects the 45° equilibrium line. At any higher level of real domestic income, aggregate output exceeds aggregate desired expenditure, resulting in unplanned inventory buildup. The level of real domestic income will consequently tend to fall back toward the equilibrium level. At any lower level of real domestic income, aggregate desired expenditure exceeds output, resulting in unplanned inventory depletion. In this case, real domestic income will tend to rise until equilibrium is restored.

KEY TERMS

Say's law
desired expenditures
realized expenditures
ex ante expenditures
ex post facto expenditures
consumption schedule
   (consumption function)
autonomous desired
   consumption

marginal propensity to
   consume (MPC)
average propensity to consume
   (APC)
saving schedule
dissaving
marginal propensity to save
   (MPS)
lump-sum taxes

percentage income tax
import schedule
marginal propensity to import
   (MPM)
autonomous desired imports
aggregate expenditure schedule
equilibrium level of income
45° line diagram

KEY BOXES

Box 19.3 The Consumption Schedule
Box 19.8 Desired Investment Expenditure and
          Aggregate Desired Expenditure
Box 19.9 Desired Government Expenditure and
          Aggregate Desired Expenditure

Box 19.11 Construction of the Aggregate
           Expenditure Schedule
Box 19.13 Using the 45° Line to Determine
           Equilibrium Domestic Income

REVIEW QUESTIONS

1. What happens to desired consumption spending as the level of disposable income rises? What is the meaning of the slope of the consumption schedule? What is the meaning of the height at which the consumption schedule intersects the vertical axis?

2. Explain how a saving schedule can be constructed from the information given by the consumption schedule.

3. List the steps in constructing the aggregate expenditure schedule, given the consumption schedule, net taxes, desired government purchases, desired investment, and desired net exports. What is the slope of the aggregate expenditure curve?

4. What does the income–expenditure equilibrium line show? Why is it always a 45° line that passes through the origin?

5. Use a 45° line diagram to show the direction of unplanned inventory change at levels of real domestic income above and below the equilibrium level.

6. Suppose you won $1000 in a lottery. How much of the money would you spend and how much would you save? (Remember that debt repayment counts as saving.) Would you save more or less of this $1000 windfall than of the first $1000 of an annual pay increase that you expected to be permanent? Would it surprise you to learn that some surveys have found that the marginal propensity to consume from windfall income is smaller than the marginal propensity to consume from permanent income changes? Explain.

7. On a piece of graph paper, draw consumption schedules for the following values of autonomous desired consumption (*a*) and of the marginal propensity to consume (MPC): *a* = 1000, MPC = 0.5; *a* = 1200, MPC = 0.6; *a* = 500, MPC = 0.9. Next, draw saving curves for each of these sets of values.

8. On a sheet of graph paper, draw a consumption schedule assuming autonomous desired consumption of $100 billion and a marginal propensity to consume of 0.8. Label the horizontal axis "real domestic income." Now modify this schedule for the following tax assumptions:
   a. Lump-sum net taxes of $50 billion.
   b. A percentage income tax with a tax rate of 25 percent.
   c. Both of the above taxes at the same time.

9. On another sheet of paper, draw the consumption schedule using the same assumption as in Question 8. Now sketch the effect on the consumption schedule of a progressive income tax (wherein the tax rate rises as income rises), a regressive income tax (wherein the tax rate falls as income rises), and a proportional tax (wherein the tax rate does not vary with income level). For this question, you are concerned only with the general shape of the curve, not with exact values.

10. We have assumed that desired net exports vary as income varies. Assume that exports are constant but that households desire to spend ten cents of every dollar of disposable income on imported goods and services, and that imports and exports are equal at a real domestic income of $1000 billion. Sketch an aggregate expenditure curve that includes these assumptions. What would the slope of this aggregate expenditure curve be?

11. Kanadu is a small island in the middle of Hudson Bay, with its own economy. Total annual output of goods and services is $600 (= GDP = Y). There is initially no government, and the citizens are happy. Desired consumer expenditure in this economy is expressed by the equation $C = \$100 + 0.8\, Y_d$, where Y_d is personal disposable income. Since there are no taxes, and it is assumed that there is no depreciation, $Y_d = Y$. Assume further that business firms spend $100 annually on investment, exports bring in $100, and desired imports are expressed by the equation $M = \$20 + 0.2\, Y_d$. Determine the equilibrium level of output (Y) for this economy.

12. **a.** If autonomous desired consumption is $200 and the marginal propensity to consume is a constant 0.6, what is the value of desired consumption when real disposable income is $500? When real disposable income is $700? When real disposable income is $1000?

   b. Based on the assumptions above, beyond what level of real disposable income does desired saving become positive?

   c. Is this consumption schedule a straight line with a constant slope or does it rise and then flatten out? How can you tell?

13. **a.** If autonomous desired consumption is $500 and the marginal propensity to consume is 0.65, what is the value of desired consumption when real disposable income is zero? When real disposable income is $500? When real disposable income is $1000?

   b. If desired consumption is $600, what is the approximate level of real disposable income for this economy? If desired consumption is $2200, what is the approximate Y_d?

14. Based on the information in Question 13, what is the level of desired saving when desired consumption is $500? When desired consumption is $2200?

15. **a.** What is the value of desired consumption when autonomous desired consumption is $400, the marginal propensity to consume is 0.6, real domestic income is $1200, and the percentage income-tax rate is 0.25?

   b. If the percentage income-tax rate changes to 0.3, what happens to the level of desired consumption if real domestic income remains at $1200?

   c. What is the slope of the consumption function without a percentage income tax? What is its slope with an MPC of 0.6 and an income-tax rate of 25 percent? With an income-tax rate of 30 percent?

16. **a.** Assume that $C = \$40 + 0.8Y$; $I = \$165$; $G = \$210$; MPM $= 0.1$; and $X_n = \$40$. What is the value of aggregate expenditure when real domestic income is zero?

   b. What is the slope of the aggregate expenditure schedule?

   c. What is the value of aggregate expenditure when $Y = \$1200$?

APPENDIX TO CHAPTER 19

The Leakage–Injection Approach to Domestic Income Determination

The concepts of leakages and injections, introduced in Chapter 17, provide another means of determining the equilibrium level of real domestic income. As Box 19A.1 shows, the leakage–injection approach uses the savings schedule rather than the consumption schedule as its starting point. Columns 2–5 of the table show how real domestic income is divided into desired consumption, saving, net taxes, and imports. Desired saving, net taxes, and imports are all leakages from the circular flow. Their total appears in column 6. In part (b) of Box 19A.1, a sloping line is drawn to show how total leakages vary as real domestic income varies. This line, which is labelled $S + T_n + M$ on the graph, can be called a *leakage curve* and has a slope of 0.4, equal to the marginal propensity to save (0.25) plus the marginal propensity to import (0.15).

Columns 7–9 of the table show the components of desired injections: desired investment, government purchases, and exports. The total of desired injections is shown in column 10. Under the assumptions made in this chapter, none of these components varies as real domestic income varies. The desired injection curve (labelled $I + G + X$ in Box 19A.1) is therefore horizontal.

Desired leakages are the part of real domestic income that households do not desire to spend on domestically produced consumer goods. Desired injections are sources of income for domestically produced goods and services that do not arise directly from the household sector. At the point where the desired injection and desired leakage curves intersect, then, the portion of output that consumers do not desire to take from the market is absorbed by other users of final goods and services. At that point, and only at that point, the separate spending plans of households, businesses, units of government, and foreign buyers of exports exactly mesh with the production activities of domestic firms. There is neither unplanned inventory buildup nor unplanned inventory depletion. The circular flow is in equilibrium.

A comparison of Boxes 19.13 and 19A.1 shows that the equilibrium level of real domestic income is the same using both approaches. For nonequilibrium levels of real domestic income, the vertical gap between the aggregate expenditure curve and the equilibrium line is always the same as the vertical gap between the leakage curve and the desired injection curve. For both approaches, this gap is equal to the rate of unplanned inventory change (plus or minus) when the desires of buyers and sellers do not mesh.

The Leakage–Injection Approach to Domestic Income Determination

BOX 19A.1

This box shows how the equilibrium level of real domestic income can be determined by finding the point at which desired injections to the circular flow (desired investment plus government purchases plus exports) are equal to total desired leakages from the circular flow (desired saving plus net taxes plus imports).

(a)

(1) Real Domestic Income	(2) Desired Domestic Consumption	(3) Desired Saving	(4) Desired Net Taxes	(5) Desired Imports	(6) Total Desired Leakages	(7) Desired Investment	(8) Desired Government Purchases	(9) Exports	(10) Total Desired Injections
			(billions of dollars per year, with constant prices)						
100	100	−100	100	65	65	110	150	125	385
200	175	−75	100	80	105	110	150	125	385
300	250	−50	100	95	145	110	150	125	385
400	325	−25	100	110	185	110	150	125	385
500	400	0	100	125	225	110	150	125	385
600	475	25	100	140	265	110	150	125	385
700	550	50	100	155	305	110	150	125	385
800	625	75	100	170	345	110	150	125	385
900	700	100	100	185	385	110	150	125	385
1000	775	125	100	200	425	110	150	125	385
1100	850	150	100	215	465	110	150	125	385
1200	925	175	100	230	505	110	150	125	385
1300	1000	200	100	245	545	110	150	125	385
1400	1075	225	100	260	585	110	150	125	385
1500	1150	250	100	275	625	110	150	125	385

(b)

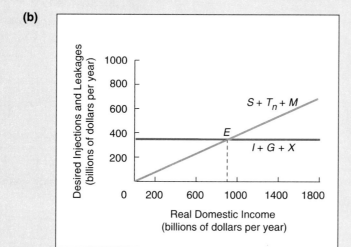

CHAPTER 20

Changes in Equilibrium and the Multiplier

WHAT YOU WILL LEARN IN THIS CHAPTER

After studying this chapter, you will be able to

1. Use the income–expenditure model to explain changes in income resulting from changes in aggregate desired expenditure.

2. Define *the multiplier* and explain its function.

3. Explain why and how changes in prices affect the impact of the multiplier.

4. Relate changes in income to the price level, as well as to changes in aggregate desired expenditure, by using aggregate demand and aggregate supply functions.

5. Define and discuss *macroeconomic equilibrium*.

6. Explain why the macroeconomic equilibrium level of income is not necessarily the most desirable level of income for the economy.

A Preview   *How Business Firms Adjust to Fluctuations in the Economy*

Total desired spending in the Canadian economy seldom equals total output, and desired spending on a particular product almost never matches the output of that product. Therefore, business firms — such as Canadian Heritage Designs, described in the following article — constantly have to adjust output, employment, and prices to the actual amount being spent on their products. This chapter examines such adjustments and the process by which the economy as a whole moves from one equilibrium to another.

What Kind of Recovery?

Now that the Canadian economy seems to be pulling out of the recession, economists and business people are debating another issue — whether the recovery will be weak or strong. Among the optimists is Paul Beaupré, the 45-year-old owner of Canadian Heritage Designs Ltd., a small Vancouver firm that makes reproductions of early Canadian pine furniture. Last fall, Beaupré's sales virtually dried up, forcing him to cut some prices and lay off five of his sixteen full-time employees. "I got the stuffing kicked out of me," he recalls, adding that the dearth of customers last February and March "was really scary." By contrast, Beaupré says that June was one of his best months in years, "and July is shaping up quite nicely." As a result, he plans to reintroduce a night shift this week and hire two more workers.

"The turnaround has been dramatic," he adds. "As soon as consumers feel confident about their savings or their credit-card overdrafts, they feel they can go out and spend."

For months now, similar signs of economic expansion have been cropping up across the country. Helped by lower interest rates, sales of new and existing houses rose sharply this spring in many cities — a clear signal that consumers were beginning to shrug off the worst effects of the slowdown. Meanwhile, Statistics Canada says that the country's gross domestic product jumped by 0.9 percent in April, the first significant increase since the recession began in the second quarter of 1990.

SOURCE: "What Kind of Recovery?" *Maclean's,* July 22, 1991, p. 30. Reproduced with permission.

THE EFFECTS OF MACROECONOMIC INSTABILITY

Most people are seriously affected by changes in an economy's income and output. When consumer spending in Canada declined in the fall of 1990, retail firms such as Paul Beaupré's Canadian Heritage Designs Ltd. found their sales declining drastically. Beaupré, for one, was forced to lay off staff and cut prices. Many other firms had to do the same, and Canada's unemployment rate began to rise, signalling the onset of a serious recession. By the summer of 1991, it appeared that recovery was on its way: spending had started to increase, and many firms had begun to rehire staff and increase production. Unfortunately, Beaupré and many others were mistaken in their forecasts. By the fall of 1991, signs of recovery had vanished and even the increased spending of the Christmas season was too slight to raise the economy out of the lingering recession that plagued it.

This chapter continues our analysis of some of the major problems faced by market economies such as Canada's. There is no mechanism in such economies to bring aggregate desired expenditure into line with real income and output. Aggregate expenditure, as we saw in Chapter 19, is the result of decisions made by millions of consumers, investors, government employees, and foreign buyers that are based, in most cases, on expectations regarding future incomes — expectations that no one is in a position to regulate.

Hence, the economy continues to fluctuate from year to year in terms of income, output, prices, and employment. The effects of such macroeconomic instability (to which we generally refer as *disequilibrium*) are, as we shall see again and again in the coming chapters, quite enormous. In 1991, close to 1.5 million Canadians could not find jobs, and the country's average real income fell. It is true that the plight of Western market economies, including our own, was dwarfed by that of the recently decentralized Eastern European economies, but that provided cold comfort for the unemployed and the financially ruined in the West.

Why Is Unemployment a Problem?

There are several reasons why unemployment poses severe problems for individuals and for the economy as a whole. For individuals, unemployment means loss of income and, perhaps equally significantly, loss of confidence and dignity. People work not only for the money: In many cases, it is through their work that they find much of the meaning in their lives. The loss of a job, or the failure to find one, can therefore be devastating both financially and psychologically.

For the economy as a whole, unemployment means loss of output, as well as increased social problems, including more crime. It is estimated that whenever the unemployment rate increases by 1 percent, real output in the economy declines by about 2.5 percent. Economists estimate that when the unemployment rate in Canada is 10.5 percent (as it was throughout most of 1991), it is about 4 percentage points higher than it needs to be under current economic policies and our current system of wage and price setting (such estimates are discussed in greater detail in Chapter 27). This means that, in 1991, *avoidable* unemployment cost the country about 10 percent in lost output — or about $80 billion, in current prices. Eliminating this unemployment would have provided an extra $3000 worth of goods and services for every man, woman, and child in Canada.

Why Is Inflation a Problem?

Inflation, by which we mean persistent increases in prices of, say, more than 3 or 4 percent a year, also poses significant problems, though they may be less obvious than those created by unemployment. Rising prices reduce the purchasing power of money. For those whose money income rises at the same rate as the price level, this is not a serious problem; for everyone else, it is. Inflation, in effect, redistributes real income from those who cannot adjust to it to those who can. For society as a whole, the losses of those who are unable to adjust to inflation are balanced by the gains of those who are, but this is no consolation to the losers, whose losses do not seem to be within their power to control.

Who loses during inflation, and who gains? The losers are those whose money incomes are relatively fixed. This may include workers who are in a weak wage-bargaining position, people on fixed incomes (for example, pensions that are not indexed to inflation), and creditors who have lent money at fixed rates of interest. Those who gain include, for one, workers who are in a strong wage-bargaining position: While they may lose initially, when prices start to rise, because they are locked into wage agreements based on earlier, lesser price increases, they have the power to catch up eventually by means of new agreements. Those who gain also include business firms that benefit from higher prices, pensioners whose pensions are indexed, and debtors whose fixed interest payments now cost less in terms of forgone purchasing power.

The real problem of inflation is the inequity of its effects. Those who benefit from it often do so not because of increased effort, but because of luck or power, or both. The losses of those who are harmed by it, conversely, are typically the result of a lack of bargaining power and sheer bad luck.

Some economists argue that, for the economy as a whole, a little bit of inflation may be a good thing. If prices rise at, say, 2 or 3 percent a year, business firms may be encouraged to expand operations in anticipation of the benefits of higher prices. Price increases that escalate from year to year, however, have the opposite effect: They create uncertainty and dampen business investment.

Because the effects of macroeconomic instability are so significant, it is important for us to understand the forces that create it, as well as the processes by which changes in income and output result in changes in prices and employment.

In this chapter, we examine the dynamic process by which an economy's output and income level adjusts to shifts in aggregate desired expenditure. At the outset, our analysis is based on the assumption that prices are constant; this assumption is dropped as the analysis progresses. Chapter 21 examines the problems of *unsatisfactory* equilibrium levels of output and the ways in which governments try to correct them.

THE MULTIPLIER EFFECT

To understand what happens to real income, output, and employment when aggregate desired expenditure changes, we begin with the situation depicted in Box 20.1. (Notice that our hypothetical economy in this example operates, for the sake of simplicity, not in billions but in hundreds of dollars.) Starting at an equilibrium level of income of $900, based on the aggregate expenditure curve ADE_1. Box 20.1 shows the effects of a $100 increase in desired expenditure at all levels of income. For the moment, it does not matter whether this increase originates in the desired consumption, investment, government, or net-export expenditure component of aggregate desired expenditure. The effect in any case is to shift the aggregate expenditure schedule upward by $100, from position ADE_1 to position ADE_2. While ADE_1 intercepts the vertical axis at a height of $360, ADE_2 starts at a height of $460, then rises parallel to ADE_1, remaining $100 higher throughout.

What happens to the equilibrium level of domestic income when the aggregate expenditure schedule shifts upward by $100? The immediate effect is that aggregate desired expenditure exceeds domestic product, so that inventories start to be depleted. Firms react to this unplanned inventory depletion by increasing output, and possibly employment as well. Real domestic income rises to its new equilibrium level of $1150, at the point where ADE_2 crosses the 45° equilibrium line (Z).

Notice what has happened: A $100 upward shift in the aggregate expenditure schedule has induced a $250 increase in equilibrium domestic income. This ability of a given shift in aggregate desired expenditure to create a larger increase in equilibrium domestic income is the famous **multiplier effect**, a conceptual pillar of Keynesian macroeconomics.

Multiplier effect
The ability of a $1 shift in the aggregate expenditure schedule to induce a change of more than $1 in the equilibrium level of real domestic income.

The Multiplier Effect of a Shift in the Aggregate Expenditure Schedule

BOX 20.1

A shift in the aggregate expenditure schedule produces a greater-than-equal change in equilibrium real domestic income. This is known as the multiplier effect. Here, a $100 upward shift in the aggregate expenditure schedule produces a $250 increase in equilibrium real domestic income, from $900 to $1150. The multiplier—that is, the ratio of the change in equilibrium income to the original change in aggregate desired expenditure—thus has a value of 2.5 in this example.

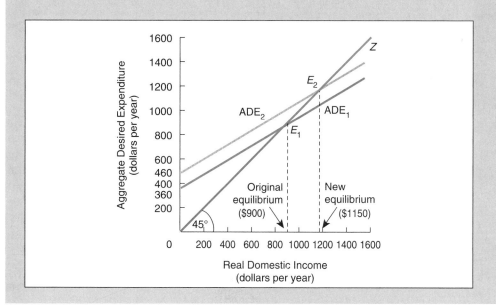

Round by Round

A good way to view the multiplier effect is to imagine the effects of the initial upward shift in aggregate desired expenditure percolating down through the economy "round by round." Suppose that the original shift is caused by a $100-per-year increase in government purchases and that these purchases are all made within Canada. The aggregate expenditure function shifts upward by $100. In response to the $100 increase in desired expenditure, business firms increase output enough to cause a $100 increase in real domestic product. The increase in domestic product results in $100 of additional real income for some people in the form of higher profits, wages, rents, or interest payments. It might also increase employment and reduce unemployment. All of what has happened so far can be called the first-round effect of the shift in aggregate desired expenditure on domestic goods and services.

The second round consists of the *effects* produced by the entry into the economy of the $100 in new income that was generated by the first round. Given an assumed marginal propensity to consume of 0.75 and a marginal propensity to import of 0.15, the people who receive this income will spend $75 of it on consumer goods and services, of which $15 will be spent on imports. The net effect is to increase the aggregate desired expenditure on domestic goods and services by $60 more and, consequently, to generate $60 in new factor payments and income, and possibly more employment.

In the third round, three-quarters of the newly generated income of $60 — that is, $45 — is spent, $9 of it going to imports. This means that the aggregate desired expenditure on domestic goods and services increases by $36. Domestic income will go up by the same amount. In the fourth round, aggregate desired expenditure will increase by $27 (0.75 × $36), $5.40 of which (0.15 × $36) will go to imports. Aggregate desired expenditure on domestic goods and services will therefore rise by $21.60 in the fourth round, as will domestic income. This will continue until the increments become too small to worry about. When all the increments to income induced by the original $100 upward shift in the aggregate expenditure schedule are added together, we arrive at

$$\$100 + \$60 + \$36 + \$21.60 + \$12.96 + \$7.78 \ldots = \$250,$$

just as expected. This round-by-round version of the multiplier effect is summarized in Box 20.2.

The Multiplier Defined

Box 20.2 shows quite clearly that as income increases in response to the original upward shift in the aggregate expenditure schedule, domestic income "catches up" with desired expenditure. For each $1 increase in real domestic output, there is an equivalent increase in income, but desired expenditure on domestic output increases by only a fraction of a dollar. The fraction is equal to the marginal propensity to consume minus the marginal propensity to import. At the new equilibrium, the difference between desired expenditure on domestic goods and services and domestic income is eliminated.

The ratio of the induced increase in domestic income to the original increase in desired expenditure on domestic output is called the **multiplier**.[1] The value

Multiplier
The ratio of an induced change in the equilibrium level of domestic income to the initial change in desired domestic expenditure that caused it. For an economy in which imports play an important role, the value of the multiplier is given by the following formula:

Multiplier =
$$\frac{1}{1 - (MPC - MPM)}$$

or $\dfrac{1}{1 - MPC_D}$

where MPC_D is the marginal propensity to consume domestic output.

$$MPC_D = \frac{\Delta C}{\Delta Y_d} - \frac{\Delta M}{\Delta Y_d}$$

---

[1]An algebraic derivation of the multiplier formula is given in the appendix to this chapter.

The Multiplier Effect, Round by Round

BOX 20.2

This box shows the round-by-round multiplier effects of an initial $100 upward shift in the aggregate expenditure schedule for domestic goods and services. Each increase in aggregate desired expenditure on domestic output produces an equal increase in real domestic income. Each $1 increase in real domestic income in turn produces $0.75 of new consumer spending, which includes a $0.15 increase in expenditures on imports. This means that each $1 increase in domestic income produces $0.60 of new spending on domestic goods and services. In total the infinite series of rounds produces a $250 increase in aggregate expenditure on domestic output, and the same increase in domestic income. In comparing this box with Box 20.1, note that the original $100 increase in aggregate expenditure corresponds to the upward shift in the aggregate expenditure schedule, whereas the subsequent increases in aggregate expenditure for domestic goods and services correspond to movements along the new schedule.

(1) Round	(2) Increase in Aggregate Desired Expenditures	(3) Increase in Imports	(4) Increase in Aggregate Desired Expenditure on Domestic Goods and Services	(5) Increase in Real Domestic Income
1	$100.00	$ 0	$100.00	$100.00
2	75.00	15.00	60.00	60.00
3	45.00	9.00	36.00	36.00
4	27.00	5.40	21.60	21.60
5	16.20	3.24	12.96	12.96
6	9.72	1.94	7.78	7.78
7	5.84	1.17	4.67	4.67
8	3.50	0.70	2.80	2.80
All later rounds	5.24	1.05	4.19	4.19
Totals	$287.50	$37.50	$250.00	$250.00

of the multiplier depends on the fraction of each added dollar of income that goes to added expenditure on domestically produced goods and services. More precisely, the multiplier is given by the formula:

$$\text{Multiplier} = \frac{1}{1 - (\text{MPC}_D)}, \text{ where MPC}_D = \text{MPC} - \text{MPM}.[2]$$

---

[2]If the foreign market were not so important to Canada, one could ignore the effect of income on desired imports and derive a simpler multiplier using only the MPC. This simpler multiplier, used in many U.S. texts, is $1/1 - \text{MPC}$. In our original example, when MPC = 0.75 and MPM = 0.15, the multiplier was 2.5; using the simpler formula, it is 4. In other words, introducing import leakages reduces the multiplier. The "Buy Canadian" campaigns that are occasionally promoted on billboards are prompted by the desire to lessen the leakage of spending from the Canadian economy.

MPC stands for the marginal propensity to consume; MPM, for the marginal propensity to import; and MPC_D, for the marginal propensity to consume domestic output. Applying the figures used previously, we obtain the following:

$$\text{Multiplier} = \frac{1}{1 - (0.75 - 0.15)} = \frac{1}{0.4} = 2.5$$

As the formula for the multiplier indicates, the value of the multiplier is related to that portion of any change in income that is spent on domestic goods and services (MPC minus MPM).

Alternatively, the multiplier can be related to that portion of any change in income that is *not* spent on domestic output, a portion equal to the marginal propensity to save (MPS) *plus* the marginal propensity to import (MPM). This suggests the following alternative formula for the multiplier:

$$\text{Multiplier} = \frac{1}{\text{MPS} + \text{MPM,}}$$

which, using the figures from our original example, gives

$$\text{Multiplier} = \frac{1}{0.25 + 0.15} = 2.5$$

Income Taxes and the Multiplier

The multiplier formulas given above are valid only for an economy that has no income tax. It is not difficult to modify the formula to take the income tax into account, however. First, we recognize that for an economy with no income tax, the element $1 - MPC_D$ in the denominator of the multiplier formula is equal to one minus the slope of the aggregate expenditure schedule. Thus, the formula can also be written as follows:

$$\text{Multiplier} = \frac{1}{1 - \text{slope of aggregate expenditure schedule}}$$

Next, we recall that an income tax changes the slope of the aggregate expenditure schedule from MPC_D to $MPC_D(1 - t)$, where t is the percentage tax rate. The formula for the multiplier in an economy with a percentage income tax imposed at a percentage tax rate of t is thus

$$\text{Multiplier with an income tax} = \frac{1}{1 - \text{MPC}_D(1 - t)}$$

If, for example, $MPC_D = 0.6$ and $t = 0.25$ (that is, 25 percent of domestic income, Y), we obtain

$$\text{Multiplier with an income tax} = \frac{1}{1 - 0.6(1 - 0.25)} = \frac{1}{1 - 0.6 + 0.15}$$
$$= \frac{1}{0.55} = 1.8$$

The Multiplier Effect in Reverse

Box 20.2 illustrated how an increase in aggregate desired spending of a certain amount can ultimately cause real income and output to increase by an even greater amount. The opposite, of course, is also true. A decrease in aggregate desired expenditure can lead to a dramatic decline in income and output.

The downward shift of the aggregate expenditure schedule, resulting, for example, from a decrease in desired investment, will create an even greater decrease in income and output. To confirm this, return to Box 20.1 and imagine a new ADE line — call it ADE_3 — below and parallel to ADE_1. If, for example, ADE_3 is $100 below ADE_1, intercepting the vertical axis at $260, it will cross the Z line (the equilibrium line) at a domestic-income level of $650. This means that the original $100 decrease in aggregate desired spending on domestic goods causes equilibrium income to fall by $250, from the initial level of $900 to the new level of $650, as a result of the effect of a multiplier of 2.5.

The multiplier effect plays a central role in Keynesian economic theory and policy analysis. It implies that even small changes in desired spending will have magnified effects on the domestic economy. Early Keynesian economists saw the instability of private desired spending, magnified by the multiplier effect, as the main reason for the boom-and-bust cycles that had plagued market economies since at least the nineteenth century.

EXTENDING THE MODEL: CHANGES IN PRICES AND EMPLOYMENT LEVELS

The income–expenditure model that we have been developing up to this point helps explain the general causes of fluctuations in domestic income and domestic output. It is, however, a very simplified model, which sheds little light on two problems that are of prime concern to economists. First, it cannot tell us anything about the changes that, in reality, can normally be expected to accompany the income and output changes occurring in response to changes in desired expenditures.

Our analysis thus far has assumed constant prices, suggesting, for example, that a real change in aggregate desired expenditure of $100 will, because of the multiplier of 2.5 in our example, generate a real increase in output of $250. Hence, our model has needed to plot the relationship between only two variables, real aggregate desired expenditure and real domestic income. We must now make additions to the model that will allow both real changes in income and price changes to be identified explicitly and clearly.

The second limitation of our existing model is that it cannot tell us what happens to employment and the unemployment rate as domestic income and output change. This dynamic also requires further examination, which we shall initiate in this chapter and pursue in greater detail in Chapter 27.

THE DETERMINATION OF REAL OUTPUT, EMPLOYMENT, AND PRICES

Two basic propositions underlie the analysis of this section:

1. When aggregate desired expenditure changes, it produces a multiple change in income and output, such that both prices and real output may change.

2. Changes in employment are related positively to changes in real output — that is, employment rises as real output rises, and vice versa. Conversely, the unemployment rate is related negatively to changes in real output, meaning that when real output in the economy increases, the unemployment rate falls, and vice versa.

Box 20.3 uses a very simple hypothetical example to illustrate these propositions. The numbers in Box 20.3(a) show that, in Year 1, our hypothetical economy's aggregate expenditure schedule is expressed by the equation ADE = $360 + 0.6Y, where Y represents real domestic income and 0.6 is the slope of the ADE curve. This schedule is identical to ADE$_1$ in Box 20.1. The nominal equilibrium value of Y in Year 1 is $900, meaning that real income and output is $900 (column 6) when the average price for each of 900 goods and services sold in the economy is $1 (column 5). Column 7 records an unemployment rate of 12 percent for Year 1. In Year 2, the aggregate expenditure schedule jumps by $100, from $360 + 0.6Y to $460 + 0.6Y, which, with a multiplier of 2.5, results in a new nominal income of $1150. Column 5 for Year 2 shows that the price

BOX 20.3 *Changes in Real Output and Employment with Constant and Rising Prices*

The first two rows of the table in part (a) show how real output and unemployment change as aggregate desired expenditure increases by $100 and prices remain constant. The bottom row of the table describes an alternative scenario, in which prices increase, on average, from $1.00 to $1.15. The figure in part (b) illustrates the results graphically. Notice that ADE$_3$ reflects a downward shift induced by the effects of rising prices on real wealth and net exports, as explained in Box 20.4.

(a)

(1) Curve in Graph	(2) Year	(3) Aggregate Desired Expenditure	(4) Nominal Income (Y)	(5) Price Level	(6) Real Income (Y)	(7) Unemployment Rate (UR)
ADE$_1$	1	$360 + 0.6Y	$900	$1.00 (P$_1$)	$900	12%
ADE$_2$	2	$460 + 0.6Y	$1150	$1.00 (P$_1$)	$1150	8%
ADE$_3$	Alternative Year 2	$460 + 0.6Y (with subsequent downward shift)	$1150	$1.15 (P$_2$)	$1000	10.5%

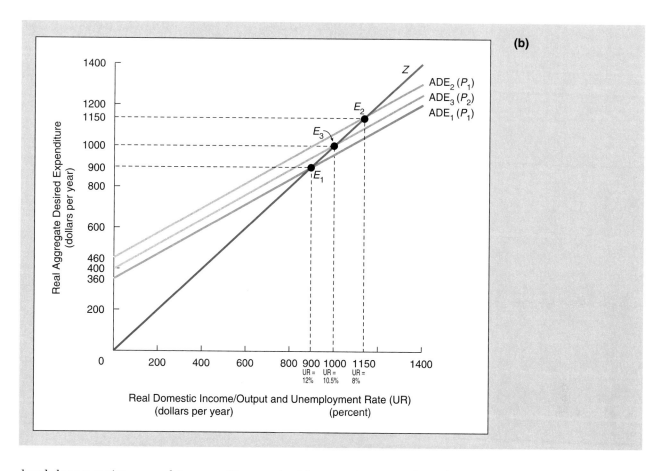

level does not rise, so real income, like nominal income, increases from $900 to $1150 (column 6). This is the same result as the one we obtained in Box 20.1. Because real output has risen substantially — by more than 25 percent of its initial level — the unemployment rate falls substantially, from 12 percent in Year 1 to 8 percent in Year 2 (column 7). This change in the unemployment rate reflects the second of the two propositions underlying this analysis — namely, that the unemployment rate varies inversely (or negatively) with changes in real income and output. To put it another way, the more real goods and services an economy produces, the more jobs it will create.

These numerical results are depicted graphically in Box 20.3(b). Curves ADE_1 and ADE_2 are identical to those in Box 20.1, except that, in this case, we indicate (in parentheses) that the price level remains constant at P_1 ($1) and we record (on the horizontal axis) the unemployment rate (UR) associated with each equilibrium level of real income.

Let us now return to the table in Box 20.3(a), and consider the last row (Alternative Year 2). It shows what would happen if, after the aggregate expenditure curve shifted upward by $100, prices as well as real output began to rise. If nominal income once again increased to $1150, but prices also rose, on average, to $1.15 (column 5), real income would rise to only $1000, because real income is equal to nominal income divided by the price level, or $1150 ÷ $1.15. The result — $1000 — is recorded in column 6. This means that real output has risen by only about 11 percent — less than half the percentage increase experienced when prices remained constant. The price increase also diminishes the change in the unemployment rate, which falls from 12 percent to 10.5 percent, rather than to the 8 percent level to which it had dropped when prices remained constant. These results are depicted graphically by the curve labelled ADE_3 in Box 20.3(b). Notice that, when prices rise from P_1 to P_2, the real aggregate expenditure curve ADE_3 rises by less than $100 above ADE_1. To understand this, assume that, initially, ADE_3 does rise by the full $100 to intercept the vertical axis at $460 rather than at $360. However, the price increase has other effects, which are explained in Box 20.4 and which ultimately cause the aggregate expenditure curve to shift downward. (Read Box 20.4, on the impact of rising prices on real wealth and net exports, then review Box 20.3 once again.) The ADE_3 curve finally settles somewhere between $360 and $460 on the vertical axis and, in our example, intersects the equilibrium line at point E_3 — that is, at a real-income level of $1000 and an unemployment rate of 10.5 percent.

With these added features, the income–expenditure model becomes versatile enough to suggest not only how income and output change with changes in real

BOX 20.4 *The Effect of Changing Prices on Aggregate Desired Expenditure*

The aggregate expenditure schedule relates aggregate desired expenditure to changes in real income. When the price level in an economy changes (for example, when average prices rise), real income changes as well, since real income is the current money income divided by the price level. Such a change in real income is represented by a *movement along* the aggregate desired expenditure curve, rather than by a *shift in* the curve, since the ADE schedule is designed precisely to show how desired expenditures change as real income changes. In the case of an increase in prices, real income declines and the economy moves downward to the left along the ADE curve.

Nonetheless, changing prices *can* shift the aggregate expenditure curve through their effect on *wealth* and on *net exports*. As we noted in Chapter 19, a household's assets (such as houses and stock or bonds) constitute a stock of wealth that has an effect on the level of desired consumption expenditure, but is not part of the income flow against which changes in desired consumer expenditure are plotted. Changes in wealth will, however, affect the position of the consumption expenditure curve and, therefore, of the aggregate expenditure curve. For example, rising prices will cause a decline in real wealth, and this will cause the aggregate expenditure curve to shift downward. The decline in real wealth occurs because assets such as bonds have a fixed return, and will ultimately be sold at a fixed price. When the general price level is rising, the real value of the bond declines, because the purchasing power that it will yield to its owner once it is sold is declining. A decline in wealth will prompt the holders of wealth to save more, thereby reducing their desired consumption.

Price changes affect the position of the aggregate expenditure curve through their impact on desired net exports as well. For example, an increase in the domestic price level will make exports more expensive and imports relatively cheaper. If foreign-currency rates do not adjust for such price changes, there will be a downward shift in desired net exports, and a corresponding downward shift in the aggregate expenditure schedule.

The reverse of the dynamics just described also holds true: Decreases in domestic prices have the effect of increasing the real value of wealth, as well as increasing exports and reducing imports, thus causing the aggregate expenditure curve to shift upward.

aggregate desired expenditure, but how prices and employment may change as well. The model might be used, for example, to show what happens when aggregate desired expenditure declines because of a sudden drop in exports to the United States caused by a recession in the U.S. economy, or to show how both real income and employment are likely to fall in the Canadian economy, assuming both fixed and flexible prices.

While the income–expenditure model has the great merit of demonstrating the link between income and desired expenditures and while it can, with appropriate adaptations of the kind we have just made, *suggest* how prices and employment will be affected by changes in expenditures and income, it can do little more than hint at such effects.

The basic cause-and-effect relationship illustrated by the income–expenditure model is, as the name suggests, the relationship between income and desired expenditures. The horizontal axis shows changes in income, and the vertical axis, changes in desired expenditures. The model does not recognize the price level explicitly, and is therefore unable to demonstrate the relationship among changes in desired expenditures, income, and prices explicitly. As it has been developed to this point, the income–expenditure model has thrown little light on *why*, and under what conditions, prices will change as income and desired expenditures change. For example, to the extent that the model does not help us predict by how much prices may rise as the aggregate expenditure curve shifts upward, it is unable to tell us by how much real income can be expected to rise. And since changes in employment are related to changes in real income, a model that cannot tell us much about changes in real income (versus changes in prices) is also severely limited in explaining changes in the unemployment rate.

For these reasons, it is necessary to combine the income–expenditure model with another model in which the connection among changes in income, expenditure, *and* prices can be shown explicitly. The model that serves this purpose is the *real aggregate demand and aggregate supply* model, which essentially relates demand (aggregate desired expenditure) to prices rather than to income, just as the demand curves that we studied in the microeconomics portion of this textbook do. Furthermore, the model introduces a supply curve (aggregate domestic output and income), which is also related to prices. In the next section, the demand and supply components of this model are developed and explained separately, and then combined into an integrated model with the income–expenditure model.

REAL AGGREGATE DEMAND AND SUPPLY

The Aggregate Demand Curve

The purpose of this section is to create a model of macroeconomic behaviour that links real domestic income and output to price. The first step in building such a model is shown in Box 20.5, which describes how an **aggregate demand curve**, which relates domestic income to price, can be derived from our previous income–expenditure model. It is possible to match the two models by placing one on top of the other, because, in both cases, real domestic income is measured on the horizontal axis.

To understand how the aggregate demand curve is derived and what it means, let us first examine what is happening in the income–expenditure diagram in

Aggregate demand curve
A curve that relates real domestic income and the price level.

Box 20.5(a). We assume that the initial aggregate expenditure schedule for our hypothetical economy is ADE$_1$, which intersects the equilibrium line at point E_1 — that is, at an equilibrium income level of $1150. Although it is not shown explicitly in this diagram, the equilibrium price level is assumed to be $1.00. Now let us move down from point E_1 in part (a) to the corresponding point E_1 in part (b). Point E_1 in the bottom diagram indicates that the $1150 level of real income, shown on the horizontal axis, relates explicitly to a price level of $1.00 on the vertical axis. Next, we return to the top diagram, and assume that prices begin to rise. For reasons explained earlier (see Box 20.4), this general price increase will shift the aggregate desired expenditure curve in part (a) of Box 20.5 downward, to ADE$_2$, resulting in a new equilibrium at point E_2 and a new equilibrium income level of $1000. Moving down from E_2 to the diagram in part (b) of Box 20.5, we see that the new real income of $1000 is linked, by point E_2, to a price level of $1.15. Once again, we return to the top diagram and assume that the price level continues to rise, shifting the aggregate expenditure curve down even farther, to ADE$_3$. This downward shift causes the equilibrium level of income to fall to $600, at point E_3. Moving down from this point to the lower diagram, we see that the new real income level of $600 is linked to a price level of $1.50.

Joining together the three points in Box 20.5(b) gives us our aggregate demand (AD) curve. As we can see from this example, the aggregate demand curve slopes upward to the left (or downward to the right), because as prices rise, real domestic income declines (or as prices fall, real domestic income rises).

Shifts in the aggregate demand curve are caused by changes other than changes in price. For example, if equilibrium income rises or falls at a given price level, the aggregate demand curve will shift to the right or to the left, respectively. Consider the hypothetical situation depicted in Box 20.6. In the top diagram, we being with E_1 and an equilibrium real income level of Y_1. The initial aggregate demand curve (AD$_1$) in Box 20.6(b) shows that the price level at this equilibrium income point is P_1. Now let us assume that in part (a), the aggregate expenditure curve shifts upward to ADE$_2$ because of an increase in autonomous desired expenditure. In our diagram real income rises by an even greater amount (as a result of the multiplier effect), to Y_2. If prices do not rise, the aggregate demand curve in part (b) will shift to the right, to AD$_2$, where point E_2 reflects the new income, Y_2, and the original price level, P_1. Should the price level subsequently rise, the aggregate desired expenditure curve in Box 20.6(a) will fall to ADE$_3$, lowering the real equilibrium income level to Y_3. In terms of the aggregate demand curve in the bottom diagram, this change is reflected by a *movement along* the AD$_2$ curve, upward and to the left, to the new income level of Y_3 and the new price level of P_2.

BOX 20.5   *The Aggregate Demand Curve*

We start with the aggregate expenditure curve labelled ADE$_1$ in the top diagram, which intersects the Z line at point E_1 — giving an equilibrium income level of $1150. Successive price increases cause the aggregate expenditure curve to shift downward, first to ADE$_2$, then to ADE$_3$, causing equilibrium real income to fall first to $1000 and then to $600 (point E_3). The changes in price that cause these shifts are shown explicitly in the bottom diagram, where the aggregate demand (AD) curve relates the successively lower levels of real income to successively higher prices.

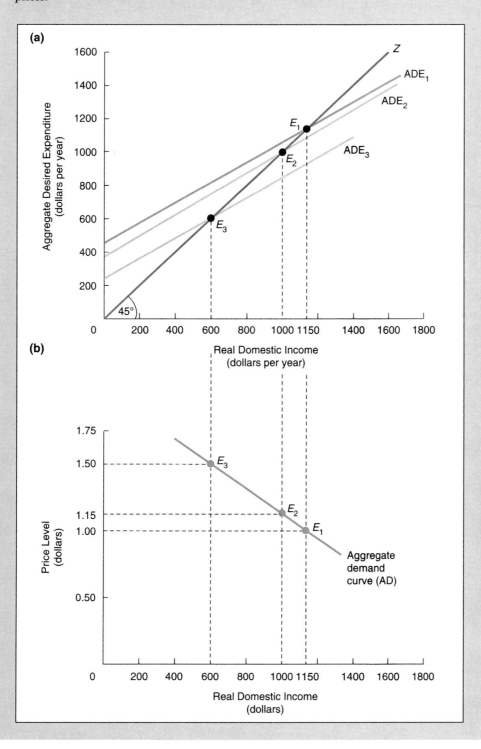

BOX 20.6   *Shifts in the Aggregate Demand Curve*

The diagrams below show how changes in aggregate desired expenditure cause shifts in aggregate demand. As the aggregate expenditure curve shifts upward from ADE_1 to ADE_2 in part (a), the aggregate demand curve in part (b) shifts to the right, from AD_1 to AD_2. It is assumed initially that the price level remains constant, as reflected by point E_2 on aggregate demand curve AD_2. But if prices should rise as a result of increased spending, the aggregate expenditure curve will shift downward, to ADE_3, resulting in a lower income level. In terms of aggregate demand, as shown in the bottom diagram, this involves a movement upward to the left along AD_2 to the new equilibrium point, E_3, at the new income level of Y_3 and the new price level of P_2.

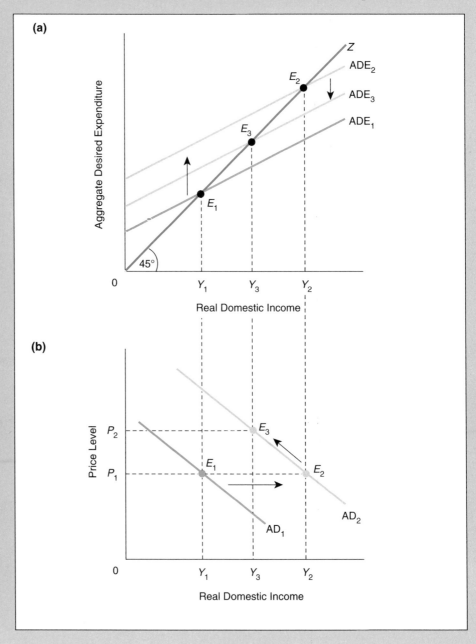

The Aggregate Supply Curve

We now come to a critical question: When the aggregate expenditure curve shifts upward as in Box 20.6(a) and the aggregate demand curve shifts to the right, as it does in Box 20.6(b), what determines whether prices will rise or remain constant? To answer this question, we must introduce the aggregate supply curve. The **aggregate supply curve** traces the relationship between the price level and the real quantity of goods and services supplied for the economy as a whole, much as the supply curve for, say, wheat traces the relationship between price and the quantity of wheat supplied for that particular single market. If the supply curve is horizontal, output can increase without any increase in prices, but if the supply curve slopes upward to the right, prices will rise as output increases.

What, then, determines the slope of the supply curve? At this stage of our analysis, we will assume a short-run situation, in which the prices of inputs are fixed, so that the supply curve does not rise upward as a result of rising input prices (long-run changes are considered in Chapter 27). Under this condition, two factors determine the slope of the aggregate supply curve: (1) the productivity of factors of production as the level of output changes and (2) the state of the economy. Let us consider productivity first: Most firms encounter diminishing marginal returns as they increase output in response to an increase in demand, causing the cost of each unit of output to rise. This in turn causes the firms to charge higher prices for their products. If diminishing returns were not encountered, cost and output prices could remain unchanged.

Whether or not diminishing returns are encountered depends partly on the second reason for the upward slope of the aggregate supply curve — namely, the state of the economy. When the economy is in a recession, with many firms using only part of their plant, as well as only part of their full labour capacity, output can be expanded without incurring higher unit costs. Moreover, even if costs do rise slightly, firms might be so desperate to sell their output that they will do so at existing prices. However, in most industries, as the economy recovers and output increases and plant capacity and employees come to be fully utilized, further expansion will lead to diminishing returns from factors of production. This raises the costs of production and forces business firms to raise their prices.

It is therefore reasonable to expect that the aggregate supply curve will have a different slope at different levels of income and output. When income is relatively low, as it is during periods of recession, and there is considerable unused capacity of capital and labour, the aggregate supply curve might be horizontal, indicating that output and income can be increased without raising prices. However, as expansion takes place and as diminishing returns set in once factors of production come to be more fully utilized, an increase in quantity supplied will mean higher prices, and the aggregate supply curve will begin to slope upward to the right. This scenario is depicted in Box 20.7. It shows how the shape of the aggregate supply curve determines the price, output, and employment effects of a change in aggregate demand.

> **Aggregate supply curve**
> A curve that relates the total supply of goods and services in an economy to the price level.

Combining Demand and Supply: Price, Output, and Employment Effects of a Shift in Aggregate Demand

In Box 20.7(a), the aggregate expenditure curve labelled ADE_1 produces an equilibrium income level of Y_1. At this level of real income, the unemployment rate is assumed to be very high — 13 percent. The bottom diagram shows that income level Y_1 is linked to a price level of P_1 on aggregate demand curve AD_1. Let us assume now that, in Box 20.7(a), the aggregate expenditure curve shifts upward to ADE_2, producing a new equilibrium income of Y_2 and reducing the unemployment rate to 10 percent. This prompts the aggregate demand curve in part (b) of the diagram to shift to the right, to AD_2, along the aggregate supply curve (AS). The aggregate supply curve is horizontal in this range because of continuing high unemployment and unused capacity in the economy. Therefore, at the new aggregate supply–demand equilibrium — point E_2 in Box 20.7(b) — the price level remains constant.

Now let us assume that the aggregate expenditure curve in part (a) shifts upward once more, to ADE_3, creating a higher equilibrium income of Y_3 and reducing the unemployment rate to 7 percent. At this point, a more complex situation may develop. As shown in Box 20.7(b), the aggregate supply curve may begin to slope upward slightly, because the unemployment rate is declining and, with declining excess capacity and diminishing marginal productivity, costs increase, prompting firms to raise output prices. *Before* prices rise above P_1, though, the economy may move briefly to Y_3 and E_3 in the bottom diagram. Then, as the price level does rise to P_2, the aggregate expenditure curve in Box 20.7(a) will fall to ADE_4, lowering equilibrium income to Y_4. It is likely that the unemployment rate will consequently rise slightly above 7 percent. In Box 20.7(b), the economy moves upward to the left along the AD_3 curve, to the point where that curve crosses the aggregate supply curve (at point E_4). Aggregate demand and supply will thus reach a final equilibrium at an income level of Y_4 and a price level of P_2.

Combining the income–expenditure model with the aggregate demand and aggregate supply model makes it easier to understand not only how changes in desired expenditures produce changes in real income and employment, but also how — and why — prices may change. It is the shape of the aggregate supply curve that ultimately determines the extent to which a change in desired aggregate expenditure will affect real income *and* prices.

This model also helps us see how rising prices reduce the effect of the expenditure multiplier. For example, in Box 20.7, if prices had remained constant, income would have risen with the full effect of the multiplier, from Y_2 to Y_3, as aggregate desired expenditure rose from ADE_2 to ADE_3. However, price increases reduced real income, so the *net* increase in income was limited to the amount represented by the distance from Y_2 to Y_4. There is still a multiplier effect with

---

BOX 20.7   *Aggregate Demand and Supply Combined*

Box 20.7(b) introduces the aggregate supply (AS) curve, which is horizontal in the range E_1 to E_2, but rises thereafter. Initially, the aggregate expenditure curve in part (a) shifts from ADE_1 to ADE_2, raising the equilibrium level of real income from Y_1 to Y_2. It is assumed that this increase in real income causes the unemployment rate to fall from 13 percent to 10 percent. Simultaneously, the increase in income causes the aggregate demand curve in part (b) to shift to the right, from AD_1 to AD_2. Real output and income expand along the AS curve, from E_1 to E_2, *without* an increase in prices (because unused capital and labour capacity keep costs from rising). As aggregate desired expenditure rises again, shifting the curve in part (a) from ADE_2 to

ADE_3 and raising the income level to Y_3, the picture changes somewhat. First, it is assumed that the unemployment rate falls to 7 percent, which will eventually cause prices to rise. Before they do, however, the aggregate demand curve in part (b) shifts to the right again, from AD_2 to AD_3, to reach a new equilibrium at point E_3. Next, once prices do start to rise, they will cause a downward shift in the aggregate expenditure curve in part (a), from ADE_3 to ADE_4, reducing equilibrium income to Y_4 and forcing the unemployment rate above 7 percent. This causes the economy to move, in part (b), from E_3 to E_4, upward and to the left along the AD_3 curve. At E_4, aggregate demand and supply are in equilibrium, at price level P_2 and income level Y_4.

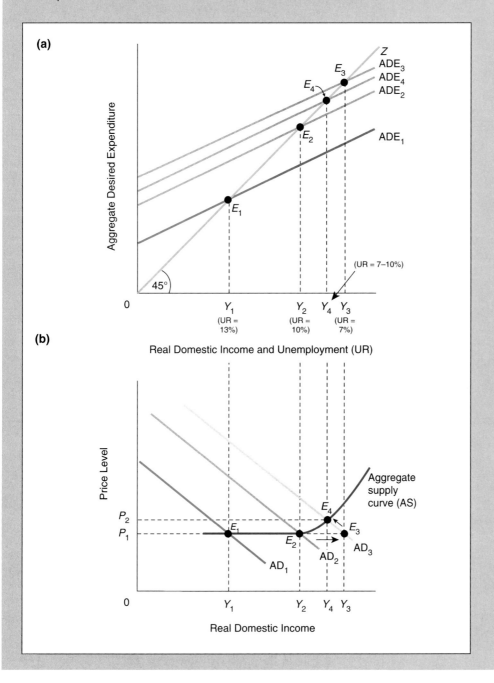

rising prices (the horizontal distance from Y_2 to Y_4 is greater than the vertical distance from ADE_2 to ADE_4), but the full potential effect of increased aggregate desired expenditure on real income is not realized.

TWO DEFINITIONS OF EQUILIBRIUM

The tools of analysis developed in this chapter allow us to understand equilibrium in two ways: (1) as the point at which aggregate desired expenditure equals real income and output (depicted in Box 20.7[a]), and (2) as the level of real income at which aggregate real demand equals aggregate real supply (Box 20.7[b]).

The example in Box 20.7 showed us that unless aggregate real demand and aggregate real supply are in equilibrium, no equilibrium achieved between aggregate desired expenditure and real income can be sustained. To clinch this important point, note once again that E_3 in Box 20.7(a) *seemed* to represent a new equilibrium point, at an income level of Y_3 and an unemployment rate of 7 percent. However, at the corresponding point E_3 in Box 20.7(b), aggregate demand did not equal aggregate supply. The diagram shows that when the aggregate demand curve moved to the right of E_2, the supply curve sloped upward, eventually forcing prices to rise. Therefore, it was only after prices had risen to P_2, and after income had fallen, that aggregate demand and aggregate supply achieved equilibrium (at point E_4). Furthermore, it was only at E_4 in Box 20.7(a), at an income of Y_4, that the equilibrium between real income and aggregate desired expenditure became stable. We call this *stable* equilibrium **macroeconomic equilibrium**, and define it as the income level at which aggregate desired expenditure equals real domestic income *and* aggregate demand equals aggregate supply.

Macroeconomic equilibrium
The income level at which aggregate desired expenditure equals income *and* aggregate demand equals aggregate supply.

Problems Associated with Macroeconomic Equilibrium

Although macroeconomic equilibrium may be considered highly desirable because of its stability, it is not necessarily the best situation for an economy to be in. Note, for example, that in Box 20.7, the economy finally achieves macroeconomic equilibrium at point E_4, after numerous spending shifts and a price adjustment. Note also that, at income level Y_4, the unemployment rate is higher than 7 percent. In this sense, the economy is not achieving its real potential. (In terms of microeconomic analysis, as discussed in Chapter 2, it is operating *within*, rather than *on*, its production possibilities frontier.) When the economy is operating at a stable macroeconomic equilibrium, people may still clamour for government action to improve the performance of the economy and to reduce the unemployment rate, and policy makers may try to meet those demands by searching for ways to increase real income levels in order to reduce unemployment.

It must also be noted that macroeconomic equilibrium can occur when prices are rising, as they are at point E_4 in Box 20.7(b). An equilibrium achieved during inflation may also be deemed undesirable. In the next chapter, we shall apply the tools of analysis developed in this chapter to examine some of the policies that governments can use to combat both undesirably low levels of income (associated with high unemployment) and rising prices.

SUMMARY

1. Things are seldom at rest in a market economy. Aggregate desired expenditure will often be either less than or greater than current levels of income and output, resulting in constant fluctuations in output, income, employment, and prices.

2. Changes in aggregate desired expenditure can create major changes in the level of real domestic income. For example, when aggregate desired expenditure increases by $100 billion, the equilibrium level of real income and output increases by more than $100 billion. This is known as the *multiplier effect*.

3. The ratio of an induced increase in real domestic income to the original increase in aggregate desired expenditure that caused the increase in income is called the *multiplier*. Its value is given by the formula $1/(1 - MPC_D)$, where MPC_D is the marginal propensity to consume minus the marginal propensity to import. In an economy that has a percentage income tax, the formula is $1/[1 - MPC_D (1 - t)]$, where t is the percentage tax rate.

4. If prices rise as aggregate desired expenditure increases, the new aggregate expenditure curve will shift downward, because higher prices reduce real wealth and net exports. This diminishes (but does not altogether eliminate) the multiplier effect of increased desired spending on real income.

5. Relating employment to real income and output allows us to examine the impact of changes in income on the unemployment rate. The latter is assumed to vary inversely with changes in real income and output.

6. While any changes in price that may accompany changes in aggregate desired expenditure can be assumed, or regarded as implicit, in the income–expenditure model, they can be shown explicitly in an aggregate demand–aggregate supply model. In this model, the *aggregate demand (AD) curve* relates real domestic income to the price level, and the *aggregate supply (AS) curve* relates the total amount supplied in an economy to the price level.

7. The aggregate demand curve slopes upward to the left because rising prices cause real income to decline. The aggregate supply curve may be horizontal over a certain range, but even in the short run, when input prices are assumed to be constant, it is likely to rise as it moves to the right because of diminishing marginal returns and fewer unused productive resources as the economy expands.

8. In Chapter 19, equilibrium was defined as the income level at which the aggregate expenditure curve crossed the 45° equilibrium line — that is, where aggregate desired expenditure exactly matched income and output. The aggregate demand–aggregate supply model shows us that for equilibrium to be stable, another condition must be met: Aggregate demand must equal aggregate supply. The price level will fluctuate, causing the aggregate expenditure curve to shift, until this condition is met. This more comprehensive version of equilibrium is defined as *macroeconomic equilibrium*.

9. Macroeconomic equilibrium can occur at undesirable levels of unemployment. Economic policy makers may therefore have to develop strategies that help move the economy to higher income levels. Macroeconomic equilib-

rium may also be undesirable if it is accompanied by rapidly rising prices (inflation). Special policy initiatives may also be required to correct this situation.

KEY TERMS

multiplier effect
multiplier

aggregate demand curve
aggregate supply curve

macroeconomic equilibrium

KEY BOXES

Box 20.1 The Multiplier Effect of a Shift in the Aggregate Expenditure Schedule
Box 20.3 Changes in Real Output and Employment with Constant and Rising Prices

Box 20.4 The Effect of Changing Prices on Aggregate Desired Expenditure
Box 20.5 The Aggregate Demand Curve
Box 20.6 Shifts in the Aggregate Demand Curve

REVIEW QUESTIONS

1. Assume that the marginal propensity to import is 0.25. What is the value of the multiplier when the marginal propensity to consume is
   a. 0.8
   b. 0.75
   c. 0.5

2. Assume that autonomous desired expenditure is $100 billion and the MPC_D is 0.75. Draw the aggregate expenditure curve on graph paper and determine the equilibrium level of income. (Alternatively, solve the problem using algebra, as shown in the appendix to this chapter.)

3. Based on the data in Question 2, what will the multiplier and the new equilibrium level of income be if the government imposes an income tax at a rate of 25 percent?

4. a. On the model of Box 20.2, illustrate the first three rounds of the multiplier effect when the aggregate desired expenditure schedule is shifted upward as the result of a $500 million increase in desired government spending. Assume that the marginal propensity to save is 0.15 and the marginal propensity to import is 0.1.

   b. What is the value of the multiplier?
   c. What is the total increase in aggregate desired expenditure on domestic goods and services after all rounds of the multiplier effect have been added together?

5. a. If the slope of the aggregate expenditure schedule for an economy is 0.8, what is the value of the multiplier?

   b. How large a change in the level of real domestic income would result from a downward shift of $250 in the aggregate expenditure schedule?

6. a. If an income tax of 20 percent were imposed on the economy in Question 5, what would the multiplier be?

   b. What would be the approximate effect of a $200 increase in aggregate desired expenditure?

7. a. If an economy's marginal propensity to consume domestic output (MPC_D) is 0.85 and its marginal propensity to save is 0.05, what is the slope of its aggregate expenditure schedule?

   b. What is the multiplier?

c. If aggregate desired expenditure declined by $100, what would be the effect on real domestic income?

8. a. If a percentage income tax of 10 percent were imposed on the economy of Question 7, what would the multiplier be?

b. What would be the effect of a $100 decrease in aggregate desired expenditure?

An Algebraic Approach to Income Determination and the Multiplier

All the theoretical propositions illustrated with graphs and numerical examples in Chapters 19 and 20 can also be expressed in terms of elementary algebra. Let us begin with the consumption schedule. Using a for the constant term in the schedule (autonomous desired consumption), b for the marginal propensity to consume, C for desired consumption expenditure, T_n for net taxes, Y for real domestic income, M for desired imports, M_a for autonomous desired imports, and m for the marginal propensity to import, the consumption schedule and the import schedule can be written as follows:

$$C = a + b(Y - T_n) \tag{20A.1}$$
$$M = M_a + m(Y - T_n).$$

Note that the expression $(Y - T_n)$ represents real disposable income.

With the consumption schedule as a basis, the aggregate desired expenditure (ADE) schedule is put together by adding desired investment (I), government purchases (G), and exports (X) and subtracting imports (M). This gives

$$ADE = C + I + G + X - M. \tag{20A.2}$$

Substituting in Equations 20A.1, we obtain

$$ADE = a + b(Y - T_n) + I + G + X - M_a - m(Y - T_n). \tag{20A.3}$$

It is convenient to rewrite this equation by grouping the constant terms, so that it becomes

$$ADE = (a - bT_n + mT_n + I + G + X - M_a) + bY - mY. \tag{20A.4}$$

The element in parentheses in Equation 20A.4 represents the constant term, or vertical intercept, of the aggregate expenditure schedule; and b, the marginal propensity to consume, minus m, the marginal propensity to import, represents its slope.

This equation can now be used to determine the equilibrium level of real domestic income. The theory set forth in Chapter 19 showed that for the economy to be in equilibrium, domestic income must be equal to desired expenditure, so that there is no unplanned inventory accumulation or depletion. This equilibrium condition can be written as follows:

$$Y = ADE. \tag{20A.5}$$

Substituting Equation 20A.4 into Equation 20A.5, the equilibrium condition becomes

$$Y = [a - bT_n + I + G + X - (M_a - mT_n)] + bY - mY. \tag{20A.6}$$

Solving Equation 20A.6 for Y then gives the following formula for the equilibrium value of real domestic income:

$$Y^* = \left(\frac{1}{1 - b_d}\right)[a - bT_n + I + G + X - (M_a - mT_n)], \qquad (20A.7)$$

where b_d is the marginal propensity to consume domestic output which equals $b - m$.

The asterisk after the Y in this formula is a reminder that the equation holds only for the equilibrium value of real domestic income.

Equation 20A.7 can now be applied to solve a number of problems.

Problem 1
Use Equation 20A.7 to derive the formula for the multiplier.

Solution
The multiplier was defined in Chapter 20 as the ratio of an induced change in the equilibrium level of real domestic income to an initial shift in the aggregate expenditure schedule for domestic output. In algebraic terms, a shift in the aggregate expenditure schedule means an increase or decrease in the intercept term $[a - bT_n + I + G + X - (M_a - mT_n)]$. For ease in notation, let A represent this intercept term:

$$A = [a - bT_n + I + G + X - (M_a - mT_n)]. \qquad (20A.8)$$

Equation 20A.7 then becomes

$$Y^* = \left(\frac{1}{1 - b_d}\right) A. \qquad (20A.9)$$

Suppose now that this constant term changes from an initial value of A_0 to a new value, A_1, thereby producing a shift in the aggregate expenditure schedule of $A_1 - A_0$. This increases the equilibrium value of real domestic income from

$$Y_0^* = \left(\frac{1}{1 - b_d}\right) A_0$$

to a new value of

$$Y_1^* = \left(\frac{1}{1 - b_d}\right) A_1.$$

The multiplier, as the ratio of the change in equilibrium income to the shift in the aggregate expenditure schedule, can now be calculated as follows:

$$\text{Multiplier} = \frac{Y_1^* - Y_0^*}{A_1 - A_0}$$

$$= \frac{(A_1 - A_0)/(1 - b_d)}{A_1 - A_0} = \frac{1}{1 - b_d}.$$

Fiscal Policy and the Public Debt

WHAT YOU WILL LEARN IN THIS CHAPTER

After studying this chapter, you will be able to

1. Discuss the use of income/output targets in making fiscal policy.

2. Explain how a change in government purchases can be used to control the equilibrium level of domestic income.

3. Discuss the effectiveness of tax changes and changes in government purchases as means of controlling aggregate desired expenditures.

4. Explain how the federal budget deficit is affected by changes in fiscal policy as well as by changes in unemployment, inflation, and interest rates.

5. Discuss the debate over the dangers of a large budget deficit and a growing national debt.

A Preview   *Concern about the Public Debt*

The excerpt that follows indicates that concern about the public debt is starting to interfere with the government's ability to conduct fiscal policy in Canada. Is such concern justified? This chapter examines that question, after discussing the nature of both fiscal policy and public debt.

One Opinion: "Debt Is a Time Bomb Set for the 1990s"

High debt levels have put a straitjacket on the conduct of fiscal policy in Canada.

The debt squeeze is being felt most acutely at the federal level. But since the provinces and municipalities depend on Ottawa for a large chunk of their revenues, those governments are going to find themselves looking for new ways to secure funds for higher spending on health, education, and infrastructure in the 1990s.

Finance Minister Michael Wilson, like his Group of Seven colleagues, is fond of chastising the United States about its large public deficits. But among the G7 nations, only Italy is accumulating public debt.

There is some disagreement among economists over how serious a problem large public debts will prove to be, but many remain sceptical that Ottawa can balance its budget within the next decade. All agree, however, that the conduct of fiscal policy is being hampered by high levels of public indebtedness. Expensive national objectives, such as day care and the protection of Arctic sovereignty, are getting sideswiped by uncontrollable public interest charges.

SOURCE: Excerpted from Ted Jackson, "Debt Is a Time Bomb Set for the 1990s," *Financial Post Report on the Nation*, Winter 1989, p. 19. Reproduced with permission.

GOVERNMENT INTERVENTION TO IMPROVE THE ECONOMY

As we noted in Chapter 20, some equilibrium levels of income are more desirable than others. An income level may be considered undesirable if it is accompanied by high rates of unemployment or rising prices — or both. (The first and second of these situations are called, as we know, recession and inflation, respectively. The third is known as *stagflation*.) An equilibrium income level accompanied by substantial imbalances in net exports or by substantial increases in government debt may also be considered undesirable. The problem of stagflation is considered in Chapter 27, and imbalances in net exports receive our attention in Chapter 26. In this chapter, our analysis focusses on three problems: recession, inflation, and government debt.

Since World War II, most central governments, including Canada's, have assumed a large part of the responsibility for improving macroeconomic performance. They have tried especially to achieve a low level of unemployment and to keep prices stable. Two broad sets of policies have been adopted to attain these goals: fiscal policy and monetary policy. The latter is the subject of the next few chapters; fiscal policy forms the main focus of this chapter.

FISCAL POLICY IN ACTION

As our Preview indicates, the growth of government deficits in recent years has brought **fiscal policy** — that is, the management of aggregate desired expenditure through changes in net taxes and government purchases — to centre stage as a topic of national debate. This chapter uses the Keynesian multiplier model, with some of the modifications noted in Chapter 20, to explore the economics of fiscal policy.

When government policy makers set out to improve the performance of the economy, they have in mind some sort of a target or standard that they aspire to achieve. We will assume in this discussion that the goal of fiscal policy is to achieve a **target level of domestic income** (or an *income target*, for short) that will create full employment without inflation.

If, at any time, the equilibrium level of real domestic income is equal to the target level, no active fiscal policy is called for. To see fiscal policy in action, we need to look at the more interesting cases in which equilibrium domestic income either falls short of or exceeds the income target.

Fiscal policy
Management of aggregate desired expenditure through changes in net taxes and government purchases.

Target level of domestic income
The level of domestic income judged by policy makers to be most compatible with such goals as full employment and price stability; also called an *income target*.

A Deflationary Gap: Recession

Consider the case illustrated in Box 21.1. The way the aggregate expenditure curve, ADE, is drawn in this figure, it crosses the equilibrium line, Z, at an income level of $900. Suppose that this is, in fact, the current level of income and, hence, that the economy is in equilibrium. Suppose also, however, that the unemployment rate is at an unacceptably high level of 13 percent. (You may notice that this analysis follows closely the example developed in Box 20.7[a].) In other words, the economy is in a recession. Policy makers decide to increase the level of income and output in order to reduce the unemployment rate. Assume that an income target of $1200 is chosen — one at which, it is hoped, unemployment will be reduced to a satisfactory level.

BOX 21.1   A Deflationary Gap

A deflationary gap is said to occur whenever aggregate desired expenditure is less than domestic product at the target level of domestic income. Under this condition, the equilibrium level of real domestic income is below the target level. If domestic income were at the target level, unplanned inventory accumulation would put downward pressure on the level of income and cause it to contract.

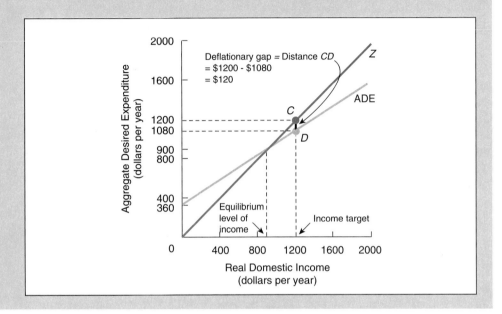

Suppose for a moment that the government is able to persuade business firms to increase their output (and income) to this higher level of $1200, without any increase in government expenditure (or in any other component of aggregate desired expenditure). If the aggregate expenditure curve remained where it was, business firms would find at the end of the year that they were unable to sell all of their $1200 worth of output. Box 21.1 indicates that, at an output/income level of $1200, desired domestic expenditures would amount to only $1080. (To verify this, move up to point *D* on the ADE curve from the $1200 point on the horizontal axis.) Aggregate desired expenditure would therefore fall $120 short of domestic output.

Whenever desired expenditure is less than domestic output at the target level of income, there is a **deflationary gap**. The size of the gap represents the rate of unplanned inventory accumulation that will take place at the target level of income with the given aggregate expenditure schedule. Geometrically, the gap is measured by the vertical distance between the aggregate expenditure curve and the equilibrium line at the target level of domestic income. The word *deflationary* refers to the fact that unplanned inventory accumulation tends to cause the level of real domestic income to fall. The gap may also be called a "recessionary gap," since aggregate desired expenditure (and, hence, the sustainable level of income and output) is too low to reduce unemployment.

Deflationary gap
The difference between desired expenditures and the target level of domestic income when domestic income exceeds aggregate desired expenditure at that level.

An Inflationary Gap

Alternatively, the equilibrium level of real domestic income may be higher than the target level. Such a case is shown in Box 21.2, where the aggregate expenditure schedule is $160 higher than necessary to achieve the income target of $1200. Instead of unplanned inventory accumulation and a deflationary gap at the target income, there is unplanned inventory depletion and an **inflationary gap** of $160.

To understand the problems posed by an inflationary gap, examine the situation depicted in Box 21.2(a). Assume that a real income level of $1200 is considered desirable because, at the level, prices are stable and the unemployment rate is low — say, 4 or 5 percent. There is neither inflation nor recession. Assume that the economy actually achieves such an equilibrium for a time, based on desired expenditure as represented by curve ADE_1, which crosses the equilibrium line at $1200. Note that this curve is matched in Box 21.2(b) by aggregate demand curve AD_1, which crosses the aggregate supply curve at E_1 — that is, at a real income of $1200 and a price level of $1.00. Assume next that, for some reason, the aggregate expenditure curve in Box 21.2(a) is pushed upward, to ADE_2. Perhaps desired investment has risen sharply and unexpectedly, or there has been a sharp increase in foreign demand for Canadian products. The vertical intercept of ADE_2 is $160 higher than that of ADE_1. This means that if business firms continue to produce $1200 worth of final goods and services, aggregate desired spending will exceed this amount by $160. Note in Box 21.2(a) that at an income level of $1200, aggregate desired spending in equilibrium should also equal $1200, which is represented by point D. However, if ADE_2 is the current aggregate expenditure curve, desired spending will actually be $1360, at point C. The distance CD, or $160, is the extent to which aggregate desired spending currently exceeds the income target, and it is this gap to which we refer as the inflationary gap.

Why is an inflationary gap a problem? In fact, it would not be a problem if the economy could actually increase real income significantly without incurring a great deal of inflation. In this case, as we can see in Box 21.2(a), real income would increase to $1600, reaching a new equilibrium at point E_2. This theoretical possibility is reflected in Box 21.2(b), where the aggregate demand curve has shifted to the right, to AD_2, because of the increase in aggregate desired expenditure depicted in Box 21.2(a). If the aggregate supply curve in part (b) were a horizontal line, the economy could achieve equilibrium at point E_2, where AD_2 crosses the aggregate supply curve at a real income of $1600 and at the same price level as before ($1.00). But this, in fact, cannot happen: To the right of point E_1, the aggregate supply curve slopes sharply upward, so that, as aggregate demand shifts to the right, from AD_1 to AD_2, prices begin to rise. A new equilibrium is reached at point E_3, at a real-income level of only slightly more than $1200 and a price level of $1.25. The reason the aggregate supply curve is likely to slope upward, as depicted in this example, is that, at E_1, the economy is very near full employment, so that firms experience diminishing returns and higher costs as they try to expand their output.

Let us return now to Box 21.2(a). The higher prices accompanying the upward shift of the aggregate expenditure curve from ADE_1 to ADE_2 ultimately push the curve back down to the position represented by ADE_3. As you will recall from Chapter 20 (Box 20.4), this occurs because higher prices reduce real wealth and

Inflationary gap
The difference between desired expenditures and the target level of domestic income when aggregate desired expenditure exceeds domestic income at that level.

BOX 21.2   *An Inflationary Gap*

The curve labelled ADE₁ in part (a) creates an equilibrium at *D*, or *E*₁, with a real-income level of $1200. We assume that something causes aggregate expenditure to increase, resulting in an upward shift from ADE₁ to ADE₂. Now, at an income level of $1200, aggregate desired expenditure is $1360, exceeding income by $160. This difference, represented by distance *CD*, is known as the *inflationary gap*. In the absence of any price effects, the economy might seek a new equilibrium at point *E*₂, with an income level o $1600. However, as part (b) illustrates, prices rise sharply as a result of the increase in aggregate desired expenditure. The result is a shift to the right of the aggregate demand curve, from AD₁ to AD₂, and a movement upward along the aggregate supply curve to *E*₃, where prices are substantially higher (at $1.25) than they were originally. This development is parallelled in part (a) by a downward shift of the aggregate expenditure curve, from ADE₂ to ADE₃, caused by the impact of higher prices on wealth and net exports. Little has actually been achieved: Real income has risen slightly, but at the expense of a great deal of inflation.

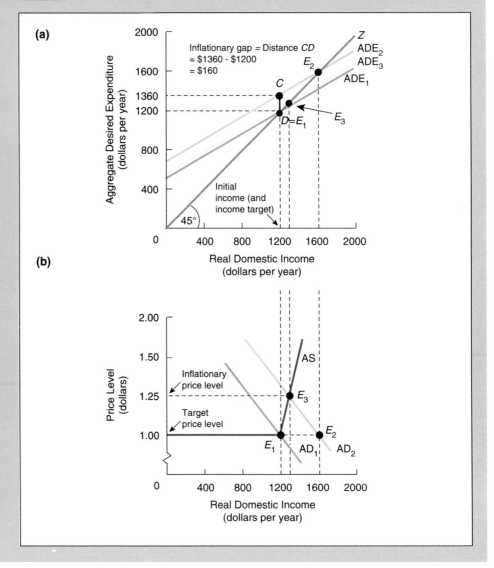

net exports. Thus, final equilibrium is achieved at point E_3, at an income level of slightly more than $1200.

What, then, has been achieved by the initial increase in aggregate desired expenditure from ADE_1 to ADE_2? Very little, in fact: Real output has increased only slightly, meaning that the unemployment rate cannot have dropped by a very significant amount. What has happened instead is a sharp increase in prices. For this reason, the excess aggregate desired expenditure of $160 that was created at the initial equilibrium income level of $1200 is aptly called the inflationary gap. Its consequences are not desirable, and economic policy makers will do well to return the economy, if they can, to an income level of $1200 and a stable price level.

Eliminating a Deflationary or an Inflationary Gap

When there is an inflationary or a deflationary gap in the economy, fiscal policy can be used to eliminate it. In the case of a deflationary gap, desired consumption, investment, government purchases, and net exports combined are less than domestic income at the target level. Policy makers can try to eliminate the gap directly, by increasing government purchases, or indirectly, by stimulating consumption through reduced taxes. In the case of an inflationary gap, desired consumption, investment, government purchases, and net exports combined are greater than domestic income at the target level. Policy makers then try to eliminate the gap by cutting government purchases or discouraging consumption with a tax increase.

Eliminating a deflationary gap by increasing government expenditure

We begin with a simple case in which the government eliminates a deflationary gap by increasing government purchases. In Box 21.3, initial conditions are represented by the aggregate expenditure curve ADE_1. The consumption schedule on which this curve is based assumes a marginal propensity to consume of 0.75, autonomous desired consumption of $100, and lump-sum taxes of $100. Interest rates and business conditions generate $110 of desired investment expenditure, and desired government purchases are $150. Desired net exports are $75 − 0.15 of domestic income. The result is an initial equilibrium real domestic income of $900. There is a deflationary gap of $120, measured vertically at the target level of domestic income of $120.

Policy makers want to eliminate the deflationary gap, and one way to do so is by increasing government purchases. Suppose policy makers authorize spending an extra $120 to accelerate the completion of a stretch of interprovincial highway. If the policy is to work, this added spending must be paid for not by increasing taxes, but by borrowing from the public. The consequences of the increased spending can be assessed with the aid of the round-by-round approach. Assume that spending $120 on the highway project creates $120 in new income for the construction workers, which raises total domestic income in the first round from $900 to $1020. Given a marginal propensity to consume of 0.75, the workers save one-quarter of their new income and spend the rest ($90) on, say, clothing. Because 15 percent of the increased income ($18) is spent on clothing produced outside the country, the increased expenditure generates $72 of new

BOX 21.3   *Using Fiscal Policy to Eliminate a Deflationary Gap*

This box illustrates the use of fiscal policy to eliminate a deflationary gap and to move equilibrium real domestic income to the target level of $1200. In the 45° diagram, it is shown that a $120 increase in government purchases results in a $300 increase in equilibrium real domestic income, taking the economy to its target level.

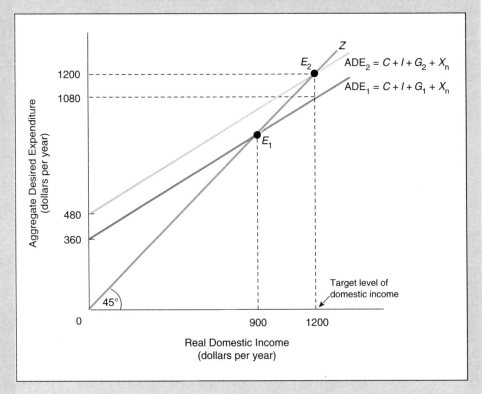

income for domestic clothing workers and retailers, which raises total income to $1092 in the second round. In the third round, clothing workers spend three-quarters of their new income on something else, including 15 percent on imports, which adds $43.20 more to the stream of income and expenditure. As further rounds progress, the target level of $1200 domestic income is approached more and more closely.

The final result of this process is depicted in Box 21.3, which shows the effects of the increased government purchases in terms of the 45° diagram. The decision to spend $120 on the highway project shifts the aggregate expenditure schedule upward by $120, from ADE_1 to ADE_2. Now, desired expenditures exceed the $900 of domestic income —, and hence, of domestic product — by $120. This added desired expenditure initially causes inventories to decline unexpectedly. In response, firms step up output, which causes real domestic income and domestic product to increase. The unplanned depletion of inventories is not eliminated entirely until the new equilibrium level of real domestic income is reached — at the point where the new aggregate expenditure schedule intersects the equilibrium line (Z). This new equilibrium occurs at the target income of $1200.

The multiplier   The preceding analysis shows that when government purchases are increased while taxes, desired investment, the net-export schedule, and the consumption schedule remain unchanged, equilibrium real domestic income changes by an amount equal to the change in government purchases times the multiplier. In this case, the multiplier is as follows:

$$\text{Multiplier} = \frac{1}{1 - \text{MPC}_D} = \frac{1}{1 - (0.75 - 0.15)} = \frac{1}{0.4} = 2.5$$

Hence, with a $120 change in government purchases and a multiplier of 2.5, the change in equilibrium income is $2.5 \times \$120 = \$300$. This can also be written as follows:

$$\frac{\text{Change in}}{\text{domestic income}} = \frac{1}{1 - \text{MPC}_D} \times \frac{\text{Change in}}{\text{government purchases}}$$

$$\$300 = 2.5 \times \$120$$

Eliminating a deflationary gap by means of tax policy

Fiscal-policy authorities can stimulate aggregate desired expenditure by lowering net taxes rather than by increasing government purchases. Net-tax policy is potentially as capable as government-purchase policy of eliminating a deflationary gap, but the chain of effects through which it operates is sufficiently different to warrant a separate discussion.

Net taxes and desired consumption expenditure   The major difference between the two types of fiscal policy is that changes in government purchases are themselves changes in aggregate desired expenditure, whereas changes in net taxes operate on aggregate desired expenditure only indirectly — through changes in desired consumption expenditures. The immediate effect of a $1 tax cut is a $1 increase in the part of domestic income left to households as disposable income. The effect of this change on aggregate desired expenditure (on domestic goods and services) depends on the marginal propensity to consume and the marginal propensity to import. If the marginal propensity to consume is 0.75 and the marginal propensity to import is 0.15, as assumed in recent examples, a $1 tax cut produces a $0.75 increase in desired consumption expenditure, other things being equal, and a $0.15 increase in desired imports, or a $0.60 increase in desired expenditure on domestic goods and services.

Geometrically, this initial effect of a tax cut appears as an upward shift in the aggregate expenditure schedule. With a marginal propensity to consume of 0.75 and a marginal propensity to import of 0.15, each $1 cut in taxes shifts the aggregate expenditure schedule up by $0.60. Once the aggregate expenditure schedule has shifted, the multiplier process takes over. The $0.60 in new first-round expenditure on domestic goods and services stimulated by each $1 cut in net taxes becomes someone's second-round income. Sixty percent of this second-round income is spent on further domestic output, which generates third-round income, and so on. Equilibrium is reestablished only when the economy has moved along the new, higher aggregate expenditure curve to the point where it intersects the 45° equilibrium line.

The net-tax multiplier The change in equilibrium real domestic income produced by a change in taxes is equal to the multiplier times the amount of the shift in the aggregate expenditure curve produced by the tax change. This shift is opposite in direction to the tax change (up for a tax cut, down for a tax increase) and equal in magnitude to the amount of the tax change times the marginal propensity to consume domestic output (MPC_D). With a marginal propensity to consume of 0.75 and a marginal propensity to import of 0.15, the multiplier has a value of 2.5. A $1 tax cut shifts the aggregate expenditure curve up by $0.60. Multiplying this by 2.5 gives an increase in equilibrium real domestic income of $1.50. (Similarly, a $1 tax increase shifts the aggregate expenditure curve *down* by $0.60, which produces a $1.50 drop in equilibrium domestic income.)

This analysis of the effects of a change in taxes can be used to define the **net-tax multiplier** — the change in equilibrium domestic income resulting from a $1 change in net taxes. The net tax multiplier is negative because a change in net taxes causes an opposite shift in the aggregate expenditure curve. It is also smaller than the previous multiplier, because the size of the shift in the aggregate expenditure curve produced by each $1 change in disposable income is equal to only $1 times the marginal propensity to consume minus the marginal propensity to import. Using MPC to represent the marginal propensity to consume, MPM to represent the marginal propensity to import, and MPC_D to represent the marginal propensity to consume domestic output (MPC − MPM), the formula is as follows:

$$\text{Net-tax multiplier} = -\frac{(MPC - MPM)}{1 - (MPC - MPM)}, \text{ or } -\frac{MPC_D}{1 - MPC_D}.$$

If MPC = 0.75, MPM = 0.15, and MPC_D = 0.6, then the net-tax multiplier is

$$-\frac{0.6}{1 - 0.6} = -\frac{0.6}{0.4} = -1.5.$$

Taxes and transfers A final comment on net-tax policy: The term *net taxes*, as explained earlier, means taxes collected by government minus transfer payments. The net-tax multiplier thus applies to changes in transfer payments as well as to changes in taxes paid. A $1 increase in transfer payments is a $1 decrease in net taxes, and a $1 decrease in transfer payments is a $1 increase in net taxes. With a marginal propensity to consume of 0.75 and a marginal propensity to import of 0.15, a $1 increase in transfer payments can be expected to produce a $1.50 increase in equilibrium real domestic income. This is the result of applying the net tax multiplier of −1.5 to the change in net taxes of −$1.

In our earlier example of the use of fiscal policy to eliminate a deflationary gap (Box 21.3), we saw that, in order for the equilibrium level of domestic income to increase by $300 (from $900 to $1200), government expenditures had to increase by $120. By what amount would net taxes have to *decrease* in order to achieve the same result? The answer to this question is found by dividing the desired change in income by the net-tax multiplier. Thus, if the desired change in income is $300 and the net-tax multiplier is −1.5, the required change in net taxes is $300 ÷ −1.5 = −$200. In other words, for the equilibrium level of income to rise by $300, net taxes would have to decrease by $200. The government could achieve this goal either by cutting taxes by $200 or by increasing

Net-tax multiplier
A multiplier showing the change in equilibrium domestic income resulting from a change in net taxes. The formula for the net-tax multiplier is as follows:

$$-\frac{(MPC - MPM)}{1 - (MPC - MPM)} \text{ or }$$

$$-\frac{MPC_D}{1 - MPC_D}$$

transfer payments by $200, or by implementing some combination of these two options. The important point here is that the result of either a tax cut or a transfer increase is to raise the level of disposable income by $200. With a marginal propensity to consume of 0.75, consumers would then wish to spend an additional $150 (0.75 × $200), of which (at an MPM of 0.15) $30 would go to imports. Thus, the first-round effect of the $200 decrease in net taxes on aggregate desired *domestic* spending is $120 — the same effect achieved by means of a $120 increase in government expenditure on domestic output. It is this initial increase in aggregate desired domestic expenditure (shown in Box 21.3 as the shift from $360 to $480 in the vertical-axis intercepts of ADE_1 and ADE_2) that, when multiplied by the expenditure multiplier of 2.5, eventually increases equilibrium income by $300.

Changes in price when the deflationary gap is eliminated

Until now, we have assumed in our numerical example that prices remain constant as the level of income rises from $900 to its target level of $1200. We have therefore been discussing a *real* change in income and, consequently, a substantial reduction in the unemployment rate. However, as we have observed before, it is possible that prices will begin to rise as income increases and as the unemployment rate falls. When this does occur, the aggregate expenditure curve may fall slightly, because net exports and the real value of wealth decline as prices rise. This possibility is examined in Box 21.4. As before, it is assumed that the shift in aggregate desired expenditure from ADE_1 to ADE_2 shifts equilibrium income from E_1 to E_2, or from $900 to $1200. Now, however, we recognize that price increases may cause the aggregate expenditure curve to shift downward, to ADE_3, causing income to fall to E_3, or $1100.

This example shows that price increases can undermine the full impact of fiscal policy on real equilibrium income. If real income rises by only $200 because of price increases, unemployment will not fall by as much as policy makers had anticipated. The government might respond by increasing its purchases or by further reducing net taxes, but such changes might be accompanied by growing inflation. Hence, a good use of fiscal policy is often accompanied by unpleasant side effects.

Using fiscal policy to eliminate an inflationary gap

We shall now consider, with the aid of Box 21.5, how the *reverse* of the policies that we discussed in the context of eliminating a deflationary gap can be employed to eliminate an *inflationary* gap. You may find it helpful at this point to review the discussion of an inflationary gap provided in Box 21.2.

In Box 21.5, we start with the aggregate expenditure curve ADE_1 and an undesirable equilibrium income of $1600 (at point E_1). At this level of income, the economy would be experiencing serious inflation, so policy makers have selected a target level of income of $1200. The policy makers decide that by reducing aggregate desired expenditure by $160 — and thereby causing the aggregate expenditure curve to shift down to the position represented by ADE_2 — they can restore price stability. A reduction in government spending of $160 should eventually take the economy to the target income level of $1200, at point E_2. (The drop in spending of $160, combined with the multiplier of 2.5, reduces income by $400.)

The same result could be obtained by increasing net taxes by $266.67, which would decrease disposable income by the same amount. Assuming, as we have

BOX 21.4   *Price Changes and the Elimination of a Deflationary Gap*

If the government is able to shift the aggregate expenditure curve upward by $120, from ADE_1 to ADE_2, by means of increased government expenditure or net-tax cuts, or both, equilibrium income will rise by $300, from $900 to $1200 (from E_1 to E_2). However, if prices rise as a result of rising expenditures and falling unemployment, the aggregate expenditure curve will shift downward, to ADE_3, forcing the equilibrium income level down as well, to $1100 (at point E_3). The effects of fiscal policy on real income can thus be dampened by price changes.

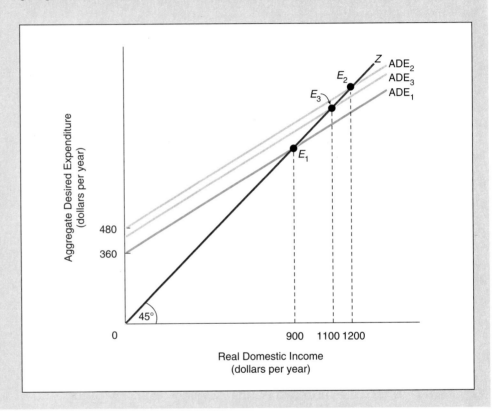

in previous examples in this chapter, that the marginal propensity to consume domestic output is 0.6 in this economy, a reduction of $266.67 in disposable income would result in a decline in consumer expenditures of $160 (that is, 0.6 × $266.67). The aggregate expenditure curve would fall by that amount.

If the government uses the correct combination of net-tax increases and expenditure cuts, it may indeed reduce income to $1200. However, the effects of price changes must also be taken into account: As prices fall, the real value of wealth increases and net exports increase, causing the aggregate expenditure curve to move upward, to ADE_3. Thus, income may not fall precisely to the target level, but the government may nevertheless succeed in reducing inflation considerably. Another problem that emerges from this analysis is the likely negative impact on the unemployment rate that would result from such an anti-infla-

Using Fiscal Policy to Eliminate an Inflationary Gap   BOX 21.5

The equilibrium income level in this diagram is $1600 (at point E_1, where ADE$_1$ crosses the Z line). The government, however, wishes to lower the income level in order to reduce inflation, and decides to decrease its spending on domestic output by $160, causing the aggregate expenditure curve to shift down to position ADE$_2$. Policy makers could achieve the same outcome by increasing net taxes by $226.67. Either approach would cause equilibrium income to fall to $1200, at point E_2. But if prices do indeed fall, the aggregate expenditure curve may shift upward again, to ADE$_3$, thereby offsetting some of the desired decline in income and prices.

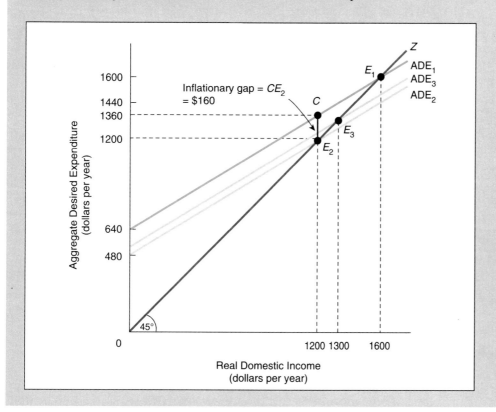

tionary policy. Once again, we see that fiscal policy produces side effects that complicate the pursuit of desired outcomes. Such problems receive closer attention in Chapter 27.

The Multipliers Compared

Two multipliers have been introduced in our analysis. Throughout our examples, we have assumed a marginal propensity to consume of 0.75 and a marginal propensity to import of 0.15, and hence a marginal propensity to consume domestic output of 0.6, which has given us a multiplier related to changes in desired expenditures of 2.5 and a net-tax multiplier of −1.5. If the marginal propensity to consume were 0.9 and the marginal propensity to import remained at 0.15, the expenditure multiplier would be 4 and the net-tax multiplier would be −3.[1]

However, these multipliers should be interpreted with caution. A change in government spending is the most powerful tool of fiscal policy, in the sense that it takes advantage of the full value of the multiplier. That power does not mean, though, that a change in government spending is necessarily the best way to eliminate an inflationary or a deflationary gap. Government-spending and net-tax policies can be equally effective, so long as the latter involves a sufficiently large change in taxes or transfer payments.

The Balanced-Budget Multiplier

The fact that the multiplier for an increase in government expenditures is greater than the net-tax multiplier opens up the interesting possibility that a balanced increase in both government spending and net taxes will have a *net* stimulative effect on the economy. A government need not go into debt in order to move the economy toward a full-employment equilibrium when a deflationary gap exists.

To understand this possibility, imagine an initial situation in which domestic income is at its equilibrium level and the federal budget is exactly in balance. Beginning from this position, suppose that government purchases are raised by $100 and that, at the same time, net taxes are increased by a lump sum of $100. This combination of policy moves will leave the budget exactly in balance at the initial level of domestic income.

However, using the same multipliers as before, the $100 increase in government spending will increase the real income level by $250, while the tax increase of $100 will reduce income by only $150 (the net-tax multiplier of −1.5 multiplied by the change in tax). The net result should be a $100 increase in the equilibrium level of real domestic income.

Balanced-budget multiplier effect
The ability of an increase in government purchases, matched dollar for dollar by an increase in taxes, to raise the equilibrium level of real domestic income. Using the expenditure and net-tax multiplier, the formula for the balanced-budget multiplier is as follows:

$$\Delta Y = \frac{\Delta G - MPC_D(\Delta T_n)}{1 - MPC_D}$$

If $\Delta G = \Delta T_n$, then,

$$\Delta Y = \frac{\Delta G - MPC_D(\Delta G)}{1 - MPC_D}$$

or $\Delta Y = \dfrac{\Delta G\,(1 - MPC_D)}{1 - MPC_D}$

∴ the multiplier = $1 \times \Delta G$.

The ability of an increase in government purchases, matched dollar for dollar by an increase in taxes, to raise the equilibrium level of real domestic income is known as the **balanced-budget multiplier effect**. If a tax increase (or cut) initially reduces (or increases) desired consumption by the full amount of the marginal propensity to consume, a dollar change in government purchases matched by a dollar change in net taxes will produce a dollar change in equilibrium real domestic income. In this case, the value of the balanced-budget multiplier is 1.

At a time when balanced federal budgets are just a fading memory, the balanced-budget multiplier effect might seem to be little more than a theoretical curiosity. Not so: The balanced-budget multiplier operates whenever net taxes and government purchases are changed by equal amounts, whether or not the budget is initially in equilibrium.

Box 21.6 summarizes the various multipliers introduced in our analysis.

---

[1]In Chapter 20, we also introduced the multiplier for an economy in which there is a percentage income tax, *t*. The formula for this multiplier is $1/1 - MPC_D(1 - t)$. The higher the value of *t*, the smaller is the multiplier. Using this formula, one can calculate a change in equilibrium real domestic income resulting from any change in the percentage tax rate.

Summary of Multipliers   *BOX 21.6*

The first three multipliers given below are consistent with lump-sum taxes but require further adaptation for use with a proportional tax (that is, a percentage tax). The fourth multiplier is specifically designed for use with a proportional tax.

1. The Expenditure Multiplier

$$\frac{1}{1 - MPC_D}$$

2. The Net-Tax Multiplier

$$\frac{-MPC}{1 - MPC_D}$$

3. The Balanced-Budget Multiplier

$$1 \times \Delta G, \text{ or } 1$$

4. The Proportional-Tax Multiplier

$$\frac{1}{1 - MPC_D(1 - t)}$$

Note: MPC_D stands for the marginal propensity to consume domestic output, or $MPC - MPM$; and t, for the proportional tax rate.

DISCRETIONARY FISCAL POLICY AND AUTOMATIC STABILIZERS

Up to this point, we have assumed that policy makers are free to adjust taxes and government purchases as they please, for no other purpose than to manipulate aggregate desired expenditure. Policy actions of this type are characteristic of **discretionary fiscal policy**. As we shall see, the ability or willingness of policy makers to use such policies may depend on the extent to which the government is currently in debt.

Much fiscal policy is *not* of a discretionary nature. Some policy changes occur automatically, in the absence of any positive action by Parliament or the federal cabinet. Although ignored in the simplified examples we have used up to this point (which assumed the presence of only lump-sum taxes), these automatic changes are quite important in practice. For example, many kinds of taxes — including corporate and personal income taxes, payroll taxes, and sales taxes — automatically increase as the level of domestic income increases. Also, many kinds of transfer payments tend to decrease as domestic income increases. Unemployment benefits are a case in point.

Because these nondiscretionary changes in taxes and transfer payments tend to have a contractionary influence when the economy is expanding and an expansionary influence when it is contracting, they are called **automatic stabilizers**. In effect, these stabilizers reduce the value of the multiplier for the economy. Because of them, the economy is less sensitive than it would be oth-

Discretionary fiscal policy
Changes in the levels of taxes, transfers, or government purchases made for the specific purpose of economic stabilization.

Automatic stabilizers
Changes in taxes, transfers, and government purchases that occur automatically as GDP rises or falls.

erwise to unexpected changes in desired investment, government purchases, autonomous consumption expenditure, and net exports.

Many economists attribute the severity of the Great Depression of the 1930s to the weakness of automatic stabilizers at that time. In 1929, the total expenditure of all levels of government represented only 16 percent of GDP; today, it accounts for more than 40 percent. The most powerful of the automatic stabilizers — the federal income tax and unemployment compensation — were insignificant in the 1930s. The strength of these automatic stabilizers in the post–World War II period is believed to have prevented the recurrence of a depression as severe as the Great Depression.

FISCAL POLICY AND THE FEDERAL BUDGET

So far, we have said very little about the impact of fiscal policy on government budgets. Both provincial and federal governments engage in fiscal policy, deliberately varying taxes and expenditures to change income and output levels. The budgets of these governments are never in balance. When a government spends more than it takes in, thereby running a budget deficit, it must borrow in financial markets. When it takes in more than it spends, it runs a budget surplus; then, by paying off old debt, it becomes a net supplier of funds to financial markets.

Our concern in this chapter is primarily with the fiscal policy and budget experience of the federal government. Such policy is largely the responsibility of the federal minister of finance.

According to Keynesian fiscal theory, governments should plan to spend more than they take in during periods of recession, to eliminate the deflationary gap. By contrast, in years when the economy is doing well, they should plan to run up surpluses. If this were done, and if good times were matched by bad times, governments should be able to balance their budgets in the long run.

Unfortunately, with the exception of a few provincial governments in Western Canada that succeeded for a number of years in channelling budgetary surpluses into special funds to be used during recessions, most governments in Canada have run deficits much more often than they have run surpluses. Indeed, since 1969, the federal government has had *only* deficits. The accumulation of such deficits has produced a steadily rising national debt.

Budget Deficits versus the National Debt

Budget deficit or surplus
A budget *deficit* or *surplus* refers to an *annual* negative or positive difference between government revenues and expenditures.

National debt
The *total indebtedness* of the federal government (or of all levels of government) as a result of all past borrowings.

It should be noted that **budget deficits or surpluses** are the *annual* amounts by which government revenues fall short of or exceed government outlays. The **national debt** is the cumulative total of all annual federal budget deficits (minus surpluses).

Box 21.7 indicates how annual federal government expenditures, revenues, and budgetary balances changed, as a percentage of GDP, between 1966 and 1990. In 1966, expenditures and revenues each represented roughly 16 percent of GDP, so that the budget was practically in balance. The two figures rose to about 20 percent by 1974, showing only small deficits in most years along the way. However, after that, things changed considerably. In the late latter half of the 1970s, revenues fell as a percentage of GDP because of reductions in federal taxes, while the ratio of expenditures to GDP remained more or less constant.

Total Federal Government Revenues, Expenditures, and Budget Balances as a Percentage of GDP, 1966 to 1990

BOX 21.7

When government expenditures and revenues grow at a more rapid rate than GDP, their ratio to GDP increases; conversely, when they grow at a slower rate than GDP, their ratio to GDP declines. This graph shows that, in the ten-year period 1965–75, the ratios of both revenues and expenditures to GDP increased, but because they generally kept pace with each other, annual deficits were small. In the latter half of the 1970s, annual deficits grew because the ratio of revenues to GDP dropped while that of expenditures to GDP remained relatively stable. Then, in the early 1980s, flat revenues combined with rapidly growing expenditures resulted in even larger annual deficits. By the latter half of the 1980s, although the rate of growth of expenditures slowed and that of revenues picked up slightly, decreasing annual deficits, the accumulated national debt nonetheless exceeded $400 billion.

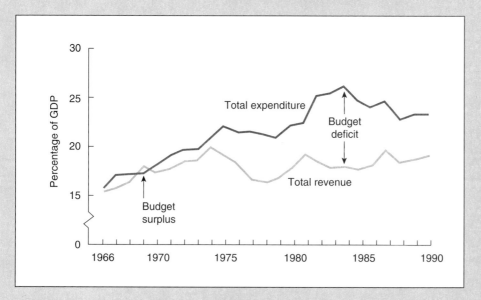

SOURCE: Statistics Canada, *Canadian Economic Observer*, June 1991, p. 3.7, Catalogue no. 11-010. Reproduced with permission of the Minister of Supply and Services Canada, 1992.

This caused annual budget deficits to grow. In the first half of the 1980s, the ratio of revenues to GDP changed little, while that of expenditures to GDP increased considerably (to about 25 percent), because of the recession of that period and the government's use of discretionary fiscal policy. Thus, as a result of flat revenues and rising expenditures, the deficit ratio rose sharply. In the latter half of the 1980s, government expenditures, as a percentage of GDP, declined, while tax revenues rose at a more rapid rate than GDP; consequently, the deficit ratio decreased slightly. By 1991, however, the cumulative total of successive years of high deficits had resulted in a *national debt* of more than $400 billion, which alarmed many citizens and exerted pressure on the government to adopt deficit-reducing measures.

This situation has given rise to a widespread debate over fiscal policy. Since the debate promises to be a long-running one, it will be worth our while to look at some economic principles that shed light on changes in the deficit.

The Structural Deficit versus the Cyclical Deficit

The first distinction that needs to be made concerns the origins of the federal deficit. In part, the deficit is a result of policy decisions made by the government. But policy makers do not determine the exact levels of government receipts and expenditures. Instead, they pass general laws setting tax rates, benefit formulas for transfer payments, and programs for purchases of goods and services. These laws determine general directions, but the actual levels of receipts and expenditures are strongly affected by the stage of the business cycle in which the economy finds itself. In a recession, for example, tax collections tend to fall and payments for unemployment compensation tend to rise, causing the deficit to grow. During a recovery, tax collections rise and transfer payments fall, reducing the deficit. Changes in interest rates and the rate of inflation also affect the levels of receipts and expenditures.

The structural deficit

It is possible to distinguish, at least approximately, the effects of policy changes from the effects of the business cycle by calculating what the federal surplus or deficit would be if a standard level of unemployment prevailed. An unemployment rate of 7–8 percent is commonly used as benchmark. This is lower than the rate characteristic of the trough of a recession but higher than the rate that has been reached at the peak of many past recoveries.

Structural deficit
The federal budget deficit that would prevail if the economy were operating at a constant benchmark rate of unemployment.

The budget deficit (or surplus) that the federal government would run given a 7–8 percent benchmark rate of unemployment is called the **structural deficit**. Changes in the structural deficit are interpreted as representing changes in policies pertaining to taxes, transfer payments, and government purchases. These policy changes represent the use of discretionary fiscal policy. During recession, the actual deficit is greater than the structural deficit.

The cyclical deficit

Cyclical deficit
The difference between the actual federal deficit in a given year and the structural deficit for that year.

The difference between the actual deficit and the structural deficit is called the **cyclical deficit**. When unemployment rises above the 7–8 percent benchmark level, the cyclical deficit becomes positive, since the actual deficit exceeds the structural deficit. When unemployment falls below the 7–8 percent benchmark, the actual deficit is less than the structural deficit. At such times, the cyclical deficit is negative. Changes in the cyclical deficit reflect changes in receipts and expenditures that occur automatically as real output and unemployment change. These changes in the deficit are the result of the operation of the automatic stabilizers discussed earlier.

According to one Canadian study, only about $9 billion of the $30.5 billion federal deficit of 1984 should be considered a structural deficit — due to what might be called "excessive" government spending. The rest of the deficit was due to cyclical factors — namely, a continuing recession that reduced government revenues and prompted larger outlays from built-in government programs.[2]

---

[2]Pierre Fortin and John McCallum, "Structural Deficit May Go on Its Own," *Financial Post*, June 6, 1984, p. 7.

Problems of the Deficit and the National Debt

As far back as the 1930s, when the Keynesian idea of using discretionary fiscal policy for economic stabilization was first gaining popularity, fiscal conservatives became worried about the asymmetry of fiscal policy. They issued a warning: If the government allows larger and more frequent deficits than surpluses, it will run up an endlessly growing national debt that could lead to financial ruin. They also raised some important questions: Can the government go on spending beyond its means forever? Should the government be required to balance its budget each year, financing all programs on a pay-as-you-go basis, in order to avoid bankruptcy? Even if debts are paid on time, does financing today's spending programs with borrowed money create distortions in the economy of today and place an unfair burden on future generations?

Almost half a century after Keynes, these questions are still being asked — perhaps with an even greater urgency, imparted by the growing size of the debt. Many economists (and noneconomists, as well) regard the ballooning deficits and the growing debt with foreboding. Before turning to the reasons for their concern, however, we shall look briefly at the thinking of a group of economists who believe that the federal deficit is not a serious problem.

Reasons not to worry about the deficit

In the opinion of fiscal activists, the important thing is to provide the right amount of stimulus or exercise the right amount of restraint each year to help move the economy toward the goals of full employment, price stability, economic growth, and balance-of-payments stability. If this requires running budget deficits more often than surpluses, then so be it. There is no reason to make controlling the size of the national debt a separate goal of policy. No one is hurt if the national debt grows, so nothing should be sacrificed in order to keep it small. The following four arguments underlie this position:

Trend of the national debt   The first argument holds that the national debt, as a percentage of gross domestic product, has generally been declining, *not* rising. If ever the national debt was a burden, it was at the end of World War II. In 1946, the national debt stood at an all-time high of 135 percent of GDP. By the mid-1970s, it had been reduced to less than 25 percent of GDP.[3] Although the ratio had increased to 60 percent by 1991, it was still well below the rates that prevailed in the 1940s.

The power of taxation   A second argument against being concerned about the size of the national debt is that the federal government need never worry about bankruptcy, no matter how large its debt becomes. The federal debt is backed by the federal power of taxation, which is enormous. As long as the power of taxation exists, people will continue to lend the government money to refinance the debt as it becomes due, confident that they will be repaid on time, in full, and with interest.

---

[3]In 1816, during the Industrial Revolution, England's national debt was more than twice the size of its gross national product (Arthur Redford, *The Economic History of England, 1760–1860* [London: Longmans, 1960], p. 103).

We owe it to ourselves   The third argument is that the size of the national debt is not a matter of serious concern because it is a debt that the Canadian people owe largely to themselves. It is a mere bookkeeping entry that can be cleared by shuffling funds from one account to another with no net drain on the real resources of the country. From the point of view of the circular flow, interest payments on the national debt are only transfer payments.

Can't build today's houses with tomorrow's bricks   Finally, it is said that there is no reason to be concerned that the national debt will put an unfair burden on future generations. Even if those in authority want to do so, the argument goes, today's houses cannot be built with tomorrow's bricks. Real goods and services, that is to say, cannot be transferred from the future to the present. No matter how government spending is financed today, annual real income consists in the real goods and services we produce — no more and no less. The same has been true at every time in the past and will be true at every time in the future.

Beware false comparisons   Taken together, these arguments add up to a warning not to make false comparisons between the national debt and the debts of individual families or private firms. Individuals and private firms can go bankrupt if their debts get larger than their ability to repay. Repayments of private debts (unless they are debts to people within the same family or firm) are not mere bookkeeping entries, but real flows of purchasing power from those within to outsiders. Thus, private debts do represent a real burden on the future consumption or investment capacity of the unit that incurs them. But none of these things, it is said, holds true for the national debt.

Reservations about deficit spending

While acknowledging that the four arguments for deficit spending are valid as far as they go, modern fiscal conservatives nonetheless have grave reservations about the wisdom of unlimited deficit spending and limitless growth of the national debt. They raise four points of their own.

Reversal of the trend   First, although they admit that there was a downward trend in the national debt relative to GDP after World War II, fiscal conservatives are alarmed by the apparent break in the trend that became evident in the late 1970s, 1980s, and early 1990s. The debt has grown steadily during those years in relation to GDP, and the size of the annual deficits — which measure the *rate* at which new debt is accumulated — reached a postwar high. Furthermore, the growing debt ratio was accompanied by interest rates that had risen to historic highs, so that the proportion of GDP needed to service the debt was much higher than it had been at the end of World War II. These disturbing trends are illustrated in Box 21.8. The second column of the table shows the trend of the federal debt as a percentage of GDP. This ratio declined steadily in the postwar period, but between 1982 and 1991, it jumped from 40.5 percent to 60 percent.

Limits on fiscal policy   Second, growing government debt increases the interest charges on the debt, forcing governments to use an increasing part of their annual budgets for the payment of interest on the debt (see column 3 of the table in Box 21.8). This in turn reduces the government's ability to use government revenues for more creative fiscal-policy measures.

Ratios of National Debt and Interest on the Debt to GDP, Selected Years BOX 21.8

The second column of this table indicates that Canada's federal government had a higher debt-to-GDP ratio in the 1950s and early 1960s than it did in the mid-1980s. Nonetheless, the ratio has risen appreciably since 1977. Column 3 shows that interest payments on the debt (that is, the carrying charges of the debt) have also increased sharply as a percentage of GDP.

Year	Ratio of National Debt to GDP (percent)	Ratio of Interest Payments on Debt to GDP (percent)
1952	80.1	1.3
1962	56.3	1.1
1972	43.5	1.0
1982	40.5	2.0
1984	50.4	3.0
1991	60.0 (est.)	6.0 (est.)

SOURCE: Department of Finance, *Economic Review*, Ottawa, April 1985, p. 128; 1991 figures adapted from Statistics Canada, *Canadian Economic Observer*, June 1991, p. 3.1, Catalogue no. 11-010. Reproduced with permission of the Minister of Supply and Services Canada, 1992.

The ratio of debt charges to government revenue more than doubled for the federal government between the mid-1970s and the early 1990s, from about 12 percent to 30 percent. Some economists think that interest payments are poised for "explosive" growth. If they are right, the government's freedom to conduct fiscal policy could be seriously curtailed.

Limits to taxation   Third, those people who are concerned about the size of the national debt are sceptical of assurances that taxes can be raised without limit to repay debts. There are examples of cities, such as New York and Cleveland, that have already found their taxing power insufficient to repay past debts on schedule. Cities in Canada have not yet reached this crisis stage, but they too are severely pinched by a narrow tax base and growing demands for services. The federal government does have one power that makes it more able than provincial and municipal governments to meet debt payments, but it is not the power of unlimited taxation. Rather, it is the power to create money. This power, discussed in coming chapters, does indeed guarantee that the federal government need never default on its debts; in the long run, however, its use can impart an inflationary bias to stabilization policy.

Possible burdens on future generations   Fourth, critics of excessive deficit spending are not convinced that borrowing to finance government spending imposes no burden on future generations. True, it is impossible to build today's houses with tomorrow's bricks. But future generations may indeed be burdened with the necessity of exporting some of those future bricks to pay off today's borrowing from abroad. (Gross federal debt owed to foreigners had risen to $100 billion by 1990.) In addition, heavy government borrowing today may indirectly cause real domestic product to be lower in the future than it otherwise would have been. The reason is that the government and private firms must compete in financial markets for the same pool of funds created by savers. At some point, government borrowing may begin to crowd out the private investment on which future economic growth depends. (More on this subject will appear in later chapters.)

To summarize, modern fiscal conservatives accept the arguments used in defence of deficit spending by fiscal activists only up to a point. The national debt — at least that part of it held by people within Canada — is indeed not strictly comparable to private debts. The federal government is admittedly not in danger of literal bankruptcy. Nonetheless, there is a danger that excessive short-run reliance on deficit spending as a means of promoting full employment may in the long run threaten the ability of the economy to achieve price stability and real economic growth.

CONCLUSIONS

Our discussion of stabilization policy has now been taken about as far as it can be on the basis of multiplier theory alone. Already, the discussion of the controversy over the national debt has had occasion to mention money and the federal government's power to control the supply of money. Monetary policy is, in fact, the second side of stabilization policy, and it is as important as fiscal policy. The next three chapters will discuss the banking system and monetary policy. Then, Chapter 25 will take a fresh look at what this chapter has explained and will discuss the interactions between monetary policy and fiscal policy.

FOR EXAMPLE...
Increasing Tax Revenues to Lower the Deficit

Many Canadians feel that their taxes are much too high, not only in absolute terms but in comparison with taxes in other countries. The following chart indicates that, in 1990, Canada ranked fifteenth among 24 countries reporting to the OECD in terms of its ratio of total tax revenues to GDP (in other words, 14 of the 24 countries had a higher tax-to-GDP ratio than Canada). One of the most dynamic economies in the world, Germany, has a higher ratio than Canada, while another, Japan, has a lower one. Those who fear that our tax burden is stifling economic growth may point to countries such as Japan and the United States to support their case, but the example of such countries as Germany and Austria, to name just two, weakens their argument considerably.

Recent tax initiatives in Canada, particularly the introduction of the *Goods and services tax (GST)* in 1991, were designed partly to satisfy those Canadians who wanted the government to do something about the public debt and partly to improve Canada's competitiveness in export markets. The GST is a comprehensive sales tax on both goods and services and replaces a sales tax on manufactured goods that had placed exporters of such goods at a disadvantage relative to foreign producers of similar goods. The GST has evoked strong negative reactions from Canadian consumers, not only because it adds to their impression that they are being taxed excessively, but because it affects more of their necessary purchases and because it has not been accompanied by significant decreases in the prices of the manufactured goods from which the earlier federal sales tax was dropped.

Tax Revenues

The ratio of total tax revenues to GDP is a measure of a country's tax burden. On that basis, Scandinavian countries top the tax league. Sweden has the highest taxes, equivalent to 57.7 percent of GDP in 1990, up from 49.1 percent in 1980. A long way behind, in second and third places, are Denmark (48.1 percent last year) and Norway, which was the only country to reduce its tax burden significantly, from 47.1 percent in 1980 to 46.2 percent in 1990. Despite the much trumpeted "tax cuts" in the 1980s in America and Britain, the tax burdens of both countries actually increased. Britain's taxes rose from 35.3 percent of its GDP in 1980 to 36.8 percent in 1990; America's edged up from 29.5 percent to 30.1 percent. America and Australia have the lowest tax burdens among the OECD economies.

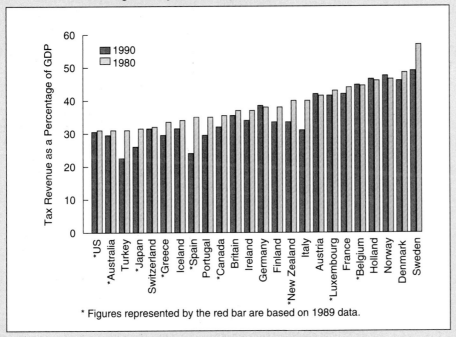

* Figures represented by the red bar are based on 1989 data.

SOURCE: *The Economist*, September 21, 1991, p. 123. Reproduced with permission.

SUMMARY

1. The planning of *fiscal policy* is a forward-looking process. The first step is to project what the equilibrium level of domestic income is likely to be under the current budget — that is, if no changes are made in tax or spending laws. Next, a *target level of real domestic income* is chosen, taking effects on employment and prices into account. Finally, a set of tax and spending policies is chosen that will bring the projected level of domestic income in line with the income target.

2. To eliminate a *deflationary gap*, the government may increase its purchases, causing an upward shift in the aggregate expenditure schedule. This leads to

excess aggregate desired expenditure, which causes the circular flow, measured in real terms, to expand. The new equilibrium level of real domestic income is higher by an amount equal to the increase in government purchases times the expenditure multiplier. In case of a decrease in government purchases (used to eliminate an *inflationary gap*), the whole process is reversed.

3. A cut in lump-sum net taxes or a reduction in the income-tax rate also has an expansionary effect on the economy. Each dollar of tax reduction increases disposable income by a dollar. This, in turn, adds a fraction of a dollar to consumption expenditure, shifting the aggregate expenditure curve upward.

4. Changes in taxes, transfers, or the level of government purchases made for the specific purpose of achieving the goal of economic stabilization constitute *discretionary fiscal policy*. In addition to discretionary fiscal policy, other changes in taxes, transfers, and even government purchases occur automatically as the level of domestic product varies. Examples are changes in income taxes and unemployment benefits. These are called *automatic stabilizers*.

5. At least since the 1930s, there has been a running controversy between fiscal conservatives, who would like to see the federal government balance its budget — that is, avoid or at least minimize the annual *budget deficit* — at least most of the time, and fiscal activists, who think that persistent deficit spending is no real cause for worry. The issue centres largely on whether the *national debt* (and the repayment of it) imposes a real burden, present or future, on the economy. The fiscal activists have succeeded in establishing that naive fears of national bankruptcy are based on misleading analogies between private debt and the national debt. But fiscal conservatives counter that, in the long run, excessive government borrowing and indebtedness can pose a threat to economic growth and price stability.

EFFECTIVE THINKING: PROBLEM 5

Target Income

In order to meet fiscal-policy goals, policy makers sometimes try to increase or decrease the level of domestic income and output — that is, they try to achieve an income target. This problem deals with attempts to change the level of total economic output.

Assume that an economy is faced with the levels of output, income, desired expenditures, saving, and lump-sum taxes given in the accompanying table.

At the present equilibrium level of real domestic income, unemployment is at an unacceptable level of 15 percent. Some economists think that if gross domestic product (GDP) were increased to $560 billion, unemployment would be reduced to an acceptable level without causing an increase in inflation.

As an economic adviser to the federal finance minister, what fiscal-policy measures would you suggest to ensure a healthy economy with acceptable levels of unemployment?

GDP = Y	Taxes	C	S	I	G	X	M
		(billions of dollars per year)					
380	45	350	−15	25	40	40	15
400	45	365	−10	25	40	40	20
420	45	380	−5	25	40	40	25
440	45	395	0	25	40	40	30
460	45	410	5	25	40	40	35
480	45	425	10	25	40	40	40
500	45	440	15	25	40	40	45
520	45	455	20	25	40	40	50
540	45	470	25	25	40	40	55
560	45	485	30	25	40	40	60
580	45	500	35	25	40	40	65

Directions

Use the twelve effective-thinking steps for successful problem solving to help the economy reduce unemployment to acceptable levels (see the Appendix to Chapter 3 if you need to review the steps). For Steps 10 through 12, assume that the plan you adopt in Step 9 is implemented. Make any calculations and draw any graphs you think might help you to reach an answer or to formulate appropriate policy for this situation.

An example of the thinking process an economist might go through using these twelve problem-solving steps appears at the back of the book (see pages 783–94). Not all economists would produce identical answers for each step, but they would all draw on accepted principles of economics.

KEY TERMS

fiscal policy
target level of domestic income,
   or income target
deflationary gap
inflationary gap

net-tax multiplier
balanced-budget multiplier
   effect
discretionary fiscal policy
automatic stabilizers

budget deficit or surplus
national debt
structural deficit
cyclical deficit

KEY BOXES

Box 21.1 A Deflationary Gap
Box 21.2 An Inflationary Gap
Box 21.3 Using Fiscal Policy to Eliminate a
      Deflationary Gap
Box 21.4 Price Changes and the Elimination of a
      Deflationary Gap

Box 21.5 Using Fiscal Policy to Eliminate an
      Inflationary Gap
Box 21.6 Summary of Multipliers

REVIEW QUESTIONS

1. As a policy maker, what factors would you take into account in deciding whether the projected level of real domestic income for the coming year was too high, too low, or just right?

2. If the projected level of real domestic income is below the target level for the coming year, what sort of change in government purchases would be called for?

3. Why is a $1 change in government purchases thought to have a greater impact on aggregate desired expenditure than a $1 change in net taxes?

4. How are federal revenues and expenditures affected by changes in output, unemployment, inflation, and interest rates? How is the federal budget deficit affected by an increase in domestic income?

5. What has been the trend over the last ten years in the size of the federal budget deficit, expressed as a percentage of gross domestic product? What has been the trend in the size of the national debt relative to GDP?

6. Is the target level of domestic income always the level of domestic income at which there will be equilibrium?

7. Should the major tool of fiscal policy be changes in government spending or changes in taxation? Justify your position.

8. Rework the graph in Box 21.3 to show the effects of a cut in government purchases or an increase in lump-sum taxes.

9. What importance does the size of the marginal propensity to consume and of the marginal propensity to import have for the effectiveness of fiscal policy in closing both inflationary and deflationary gaps?

10. It has been proposed from time to time that a law or constitutional amendment should be passed that would force the federal government to balance its budget every year. Do you think it would be possible to keep the actual budget deficit at zero every year? Or should an amendment aim only to keep the structural deficit at zero? Discuss.

11. If there were a deflationary gap, would there be some advantage in simply paying workers to dig ditches and then fill them in? Under what circumstances would this policy be beneficial?

12. Do you think that there is an inflationary gap in the economy right now (as you are taking this course)? A deflationary gap? How can you tell? What is the government doing about the gap if there is one?

13. The current equilibrium level of real domestic income is $1200, but the target income is $1500. The marginal propensity to save in the economy is 0.15 and the marginal propensity to import is 0.1.
    a. Does an inflationary gap or a deflationary gap exist in the economy?
    b. What change in government spending would be required to remove the gap and bring the economy to equilibrium at a real domestic income of $1500?

14. The present equilibrium level of real domestic income is $1200, but the target income is $1000. The marginal propensity to save in the economy is 0.15 and the marginal propensity to import is 0.1.
    a. Does an inflationary gap or a deflationary gap exist in the economy?
    b. What change in government spending would be required to remove the gap and bring the economy to an equilibrium at a real domestic income of $1000?

15. a. Using the information given in Question 13, what change in net taxes would be required to reach the target income of $1500?
    b. Using the information given in Question 14, what change in net taxes would be required to reach the target income of $1000?

16. Government policy makers decide to build roads costing $150 million and to raise taxes by the same amount to finance the road construction. If the marginal propensity to save is 0.2 and the marginal propensity to import is 0.2, what change in real domestic income will result from these policy decisions?

Money and Canada's Financial System

WHAT YOU WILL LEARN IN THIS CHAPTER

After studying this chapter, you will be able to

1. Define *money* in terms of the function it serves.
2. Explain how the quantity of money is measured.
3. List the main assets and liabilities of a chartered bank.
4. Discuss sources of stability and instability in the banking system.
5. Describe the basic purpose and functions of the Bank of Canada.
6. Discuss the role and importance of other major financial institutions in Canada.

A Preview   *What Is Money?*

The topic of this chapter is money. But what is money? Even in Canada's relatively brief history, many different objects — from beaver pelts to playing cards — have served as "money."

In the early 1680s, the colony of New France faced a shortage of money in the form of gold coins, or specie. As historians William Marr and Donald Paterson recount, the colony came up with a unique solution.

When New France Used Playing-Card Money

In 1685, the intendant of New France undertook bold action to surmount this problem. He declared a money which only indirectly had gold backing. This money, in the form of simple playing cards appropriately denominated, was essentially a substitute for specie which the French government owed as military pay and civil servants' salaries.

The playing-card experiment of New France was remarkably successful between 1685 and 1717. It fulfilled the vital function of money as a medium of exchange because it could be redeemed in Quebec, once specie arrived from France and it became generally accepted. In fact, when France financed the war of the early 1700s by over-issue of playing-card money in New France and debasement of the coinage at home, the playing-card money depreciated less in value than its nominal backing. This is strong testimony for the argument that money is what people accept as money.

SOURCE: William L. Marr and Donald G. Paterson, *Canada: An Economic History* (Toronto: Gage, 1980), p. 246.

MONEY: WHAT IT IS AND WHAT IT DOES

As the case of playing-card money in New France shows, money can take many different forms. We have mentioned money many times in this book. In this chapter and the following two, money will take centre stage. We will begin with a formal definition of money and a brief discussion of the not-so-simple matter of measuring how much of it there is in the economy. Next, we will describe the banking system and, then, the broader financial system in Canada. In Chapter 23, we will look at the ways in which the Bank of Canada, a government agency, can control the stock of money. In Chapter 24, we will turn to a discussion of the demand for money and the ways in which that demand interacts with supply in financial markets. This will take us to the central question of why money matters. We will see that changes in the stock of money can have a strong impact on the decisions of households, firms, and units of government. This fact makes monetary policy a very powerful weapon in the fight for price stability, full employment, and economic growth. Without further introduction, then, let's begin our study of monetary economics.

Money is best defined in terms of what it does: It serves as a means of payment, a store of purchasing power, and a unit of account. Money serves these functions regardless of its name or form — Canadian dollars, Japanese yen, or playing cards.

Money
An asset that serves as a means of payment, a store of purchasing power, and a unit of account.

The Functions of Money

As a *means of payment*, money reduces the costs of making transactions. Using money avoids the drawbacks of barter. In a money economy, we don't have to find out what the dentist wants for dinner before we go to get our teeth fixed. Instead of taking a steak or a basket of potatoes with us, we take money; the dentist then visits the supermarket on the way home and picks out whatever looks good, similarly paying for it with money (not dental services).

As a *store of purchasing power*, money makes it possible to arrange economic activities in a convenient manner over time. Income-producing activities and spending decisions do not have to occur at the same time. Instead, we can accept payment in money for our productive efforts and keep the money handy until we decide how to spend it. The Canadian dollar is a fairly good store of purchasing power, although its purchasing power has been hurt by inflation in recent decades. The Mexican peso, by contrast, is a very poor store of purchasing power. At the high annual inflation rates of the mid-1980s, people were forced to spend pesos almost as fast as they earned them, or else they wouldn't be able to buy much with them at all.

Finally, as a *unit of account*, money makes it possible to measure and record economic stocks and flows. A household's needs for food, shelter, and clothing can be expressed in dollar terms in planning a household budget. The nation's output of movies, apples, and weapons can be added together in dollar terms to provide a basis for planning economic policy. Without money as a unit of account, private and public economic planning would be impossible.

Money, the Liquid Asset

Any asset that a household, firm, or unit of government owns is a store of purchasing power in that it can be sold and the proceeds from it used to buy something else. Money, however, has two important traits that no other asset has, or at least not to the same extent. One is that money itself can be used as a means of payment, without first having to be exchanged for something else. A house, a bond, or a blast furnace may have great value, but can rarely be traded without first being exchanged for an equivalent amount of money. The other trait is that, because money serves as a unit of account, it can, by definition, neither gain nor lose in nominal value. A house, a bond, or a blast furnace may be worth more or fewer dollars next year than this year, but the nominal value of a dollar is always a dollar, no more and no less.

Liquidity
An asset is said to possess liquidity if it can be used directly as a means of payment and if it does not vary in nominal value.

An asset that can be used directly as a means of payment and that is protected against gain or loss in nominal value is said to have **liquidity**. No other asset is as liquid as money. In fact, a comparison of the definition of money (an asset that can be used as a means of payment and that serves as a unit of account) and the definition of liquidity (usefulness as a means of payment plus unchanging value relative to the nominal unit of account) suggests that any perfectly liquid asset is, by definition, a form of money.

Measuring the Stock of Money

For purposes of economic policy, it is important not only to know what money is but also to be able to measure how much of it there is. In all modern economies, the amount of money is controlled by government. As we will see, when governments fail to supply enough money, real output and employment decline. Indeed, some economists believe that the Great Depression was caused, or at least exacerbated, by such a failure. On the other hand, flooding the economy with too much money can be highly inflationary. Many economists blame the wild inflation in countries such as Mexico and Argentina on excessive growth of the money stock.

Although Canada's economy since World War II has been free from major depressions and extreme rates of inflation, its performance in recent years has not been as good as we might wish. If it is to improve in the future, better monetary policy will be needed. And because the money supply cannot be controlled if it cannot be measured, the problem of measurement is more important now than ever before.

Currency
Coins and paper money.

Types of Money

Demand deposits
Deposits at chartered banks that permit the depositor to make payments to others by writing a cheque against the deposit.

In modern economies, currency and demand deposits perform all three of the basic functions of money. By **currency** we mean coins and paper money. **Demand deposits** are the accounts in chartered banks that we commonly call chequing accounts. By conventional definition, money is held only by households and firms other than banks. No currency or demand deposits that belong to the Bank of Canada or to chartered banks are included in the definition of money. When we speak of the economy's stock of money in this book, this is what we mean: the total currency outside banks plus the public's holdings of demand deposits in chartered banks. This total is generally called **M_1**.

M_1
The money supply defined as total currency outside banks plus demand deposits held by the public in chartered banks.

Currency

Bank of Canada
Canada's government-owned central bank, responsible for monetary policy and the policies of the chartered banks.

Since 1945, the **Bank of Canada** has been solely responsible for issuing the nation's currency. Prior to 1945, this privilege was shared with the chartered banks. Before the establishment of the Bank of Canada in 1934, the federal government and the chartered banks were in charge of currency issues.

Paper money and coins are no longer backed by any intrinsically valuable commodity. The Bank of Canada will not give anything in exchange for a $10 bill other than $10 in paper money and/or coins — which represent, simply, another promise to pay. Until the beginning of World War II, the Bank of Canada supported the currency with gold. It was required to hold the equivalent of 25 percent of its note and deposit liabilities in gold. This provision was suspended during the war, because the money supply had to be increased substantially to support the war effort. The requirement was abolished in 1967. We now have a currency whose value is based entirely on the public's faith that it can be exchanged for all kinds of goods and services.

Demand deposits

Demand deposits are non-interest-bearing deposits in **chartered banks**. They represent the obligations of these banks to their depositors. As shown in Box 22.1, demand deposits account for some 52 percent of the money supply (M_1), but this figure actually understates their importance. Demand deposits turn out to be used to conduct some 90 percent of the dollar volume of all transactions in the economy. Although demand deposits are issued by chartered banks, there are, as we shall see, limits on the volume of such deposits that banks can create.

In addition to demand, or chequing, deposits, both private individuals and business firms have substantial savings, or notice, deposits that are also quite liquid. They can be used almost as easily as chequing deposits for making payments and are therefore added to M_1 to make up a second measure of money, called **M_2**.

Chartered banks
Financial intermediaries given a government charter to provide a broad range of banking services, including accepting demand deposits and making consumer and business loans.

M_2
A second definition of money, including currency, demand deposits, daily-interest chequable and non-personal (business) notice deposits, and personal savings deposits.

Components of the Canadian Money Stock, July 1991 — BOX 22.1

This table breaks the Canadian money supply down into its component parts as of July 1991. The most liquid assets — currency and demand deposits — make up the most commonly used money supply measure, M_1. To this are added daily-interest chequable and nonpersonal notice deposits, as well as personal savings deposits, to give M_2. Foreign-currency deposits hold by chartered banks for Canadian residents, plus fixed-term deposits of business firms, are added to M_2 to give M_3.

	Amount (billions of dollars)
Currency	20.2
Plus demand deposits	21.5
Equals M_1	41.7
Plus personal savings deposits and nonpersonal notice deposits	232.8
Equals M_2	274.5
Plus foreign-currency deposits in Canadian banks and nonpersonal fixed-term deposits	48.9
Equals M_3	323.4

SOURCE: Bank of Canada, *Bank of Canada Review*, August 1991, Table E1. Reproduced with permission.

M₃
Equals M₂ plus foreign-currency deposits in chartered banks.

There are other deposits in chartered banks that are quite liquid and, depending on their degree of liquidity, they are added to M_2 to produce additional measures of "money." Thus, **M_3** equals M_2 plus the fixed-term deposits of business firms and foreign-currency deposits held in chartered banks by Canadian residents.

Near-Moneys

Near-moneys
Assets that are less-than-perfectly liquid but still liquid enough to be reasonably close substitutes for money.

People hold many other forms of assets that can be used to perform the three functions of money. This is especially true of deposits held in institutions other than chartered banks — for example, chequing and savings deposits held in credit unions and trust companies. Funds in such accounts are sometimes referred to as **near-moneys**. Near-moneys might also include such assets as government bonds and securities, which are often quite liquid.

Credit and Credit Cards

In their efforts to make transactions ever more convenient for their customers, bankers have succeeded in blurring not only the distinction between money and near-moneys but also the distinction between money and credit. A case in point is the "plastic money" that almost everyone carries these days — Mastercard and Visa and all the rest. But money and credit cards are different things, and it is important to understand why.

What distinguishes a credit card from both money and near-moneys is that it is not a store of purchasing power, but simply a document that makes it easy for its holder to obtain a loan. When you go into a store, present your credit card, and walk out with a can of tennis balls, you have not yet paid for your purchase. What you have done, instead, is borrow money from the bank that issued the credit card. Simultaneously, you have instructed the bank to turn over the proceeds of the loan to the merchant. Later, the bank will send money to the merchant, thus paying for the tennis balls; later still, you will send money to the bank to pay off the balance on your credit-card account.

Schedule 1 banks
Banks in which no individual can own more than 10 percent of the shares; to date, all are Canadian-owned.

THE CANADIAN BANKING SYSTEM

Every year, Canadian citizens (along with some foreigners) pour billions of dollars of savings into a variety of Canadian financial institutions — banks, credit unions, trust companies, life insurance companies, and other such institutions. The financial institutions then lend these large sums to private individuals and business firms, or invest them directly in projects that promise a safe return. In this vast system of buying and selling money, the chartered banks play the most important role, although the role of other financial institutions, as we will note shortly, is also very significant.

Schedule 2 banks
Banks that can be narrowly held and that are currently almost exclusively subsidiaries of foreign-owned banks.

Bank Act
The federal act, passed in 1935 (and amended several times since), under which banks in Canada are chartered and reviewed.

Schedule 1 and Schedule 2 Banks

The Canadian banking system consists (at the time of writing, in late 1991) of two types of banks, known as **Schedule 1 banks** and **Schedule 2 banks**. Both types of banks are chartered under the **Bank Act**, which subjects them to review and ultimate control by Parliament. The differences between them, however, are substantial. Schedule 1 banks must be widely held; no individual investor can own more than 10 percent of the shares of a Schedule 1 bank and no group of foreign investors, except U.S. citizens (since passage of the Free Trade Agreement with the United States), can own more than 25 percent of any class of shares. This means that, at least until the Free Trade Agreement, Schedule 1 banks were, by definition, Canadian-owned banks. (Consequently, they were — and still are — often referred to as domestic banks.) Since passage of the Free Trade Agreement, a group of U.S. citizens could theoretically obtain majority interest in a so-called domestic bank, but none has in fact done so to date.

Schedule 2 banks are allowed to be more narrowly held, and, with one exception (the Laurentian Bank of Canada), they are all subsidiaries of foreign banks.

There are currently 8 domestic banks in Canada, 7 of which are Schedule 1 banks. In addition, there are 59 Schedule 2 banks, of which 58 are subsidiaries of foreign banks. Our main, though not exclusive, concern here is with the 8 domestic banks, and particularly with the 6 largest, which account for almost 90 percent of total Canadian bank assets of $584 billion. By comparison, the 59 Schedule 2 banks had combined assets of only $65 billion.

Canada's Major Chartered Banks

Box 22.2 lists the six largest Schedule 1 banks, ranked by size in terms of assets. Although these banks represent a great concentration of assets in Canada, it is worth noting that they are relatively small on an international scale. In 1990, the largest Canadian bank, the Royal Bank of Canada, ranked only 54th among all the banks in the world. The five largest banks were all in Japan, and the assets of the smallest of these were more than three times the size of the assets of the Royal Bank.

Assets of the Six Largest Schedule 1 Banks in Canada, 1990 BOX 22.2

In 1984, there were fourteen domestic banks in Canada. Because of bank failures and mergers, the number was reduced to eight by 1988. The six banks listed below clearly dominate the industry, accounting for almost 90 percent of total bank assets.

Bank	Assets (billions of dollars)
Royal Bank of Canada	125.9
Canadian Imperial Bank of Commerce	114.2
Bank of Montreal	87.4
Bank of Nova Scotia	87.2
Toronto Dominion Bank	66.9
National Bank of Canada	35.9

SOURCE: *Financial Post 500*, Summer 1991, p. 154.
Reproduced with permission.

It is also worth noting that, because of the way the United States' banking system is organized, only two U.S. banks are larger than Canada's Royal Bank. Indeed, the Canadian banking system resembles the British system and is very different from the banking system of the United States, which has 15 000 separate banks. The amalgamation of banks, and the creation of a branch system such as ours, has been discouraged in the United States. The power of large, multi-branch banks is feared, and the objective instead has been to make banks serve the needs of industry in local communities. By contrast, in Canada, a very few large banks operate about 7400 branches. The emphasis here has been on consolidation and safety. Mangers are moved around frequently to prevent local branches from losing their objectivity in advancing loans to local business. Credit unions and other financial institutions have often taken advantage of this situation by providing the kind of local service that small banks in the United States provide.

Chartered banks are financial intermediaries that accept a wide variety of deposits from firms and households and in turn make loans to the public in a wide variety of forms. They are, in many respects, the most important and least specialized of financial intermediaries. Their prime function is to store the savings of households in the form of deposits, then to channel those savings into the various loans and securities from which they make their income. In 1990, Canadian chartered banks held about 62 percent of all money deposits in Canada, while trust companies held 25 percent, and credit unions, 13 percent. This 62 percent share of deposits held by the banks was a decline from the average 68 percent that they had had in the 1960s and 1970s. During the 1980s, the trust companies increased their share from 18 percent to 25 percent, while the credit unions' share declined slightly, from 14 percent to 13 percent.

Chartered banks supply most of the consumer and commercial credit in Canada. The main types of loans they provide, in order of importance, are business loans, mortgage loans (to finance real-estate purchases), and consumer loans. Small businesses in particular rely on the banks; larger corporations are more likely to finance their operations through the issue of shares and bonds, and such transactions are negotiated through different financial institutions. Nonetheless, when bond and stock markets are weak, as they were in the late 1980s, larger corporations may also rely heavily on bank financing.

The best way to get an idea of how chartered banks operate is to look at their total balance sheet. This will make clear just where the funds handled by banks come from and where they go.

A Balance Sheet for Chartered Banks

Box 22.3 shows the consolidated balance sheet of Canada's chartered banks as of June 1991. Like all balance sheets, this one is divided into two columns. The left-hand column lists all the banks' *assets* — all the things to which the banks hold legal claim. The right-hand column shows the banks' *liabilities* — all the claims held against the banks by outsiders — and their *net worth* — the difference between assets and liabilities. Net worth represents claims against the banks' assets by the owners of the banks. It includes shareholders' equity and reserves for losses.

Because of the way the terms are defined, the right-hand and left-hand columns exactly balance — hence the term *balance sheet*. For all balance sheets,

Consolidated Balance Sheet of All Canadian Chartered Banks, June 1991

BOX 22.3

Listed as assets are all the things that the banks own. Liabilities are all the claims against the banks, held by individual firms or institutions. The banks' net worth is obtained by subtracting liabilities from assets.

Assets (billions of dollars)		Liabilities and Net Worth (billions of dollars)	
Bank of Canada reserve deposits and notes	5.0	Canadian demand deposits	23.0
Treasury bills	22.6	Canadian savings/notice deposits	208.3
Mortgages	116.2	Deposits held by foreigners	
General loans	180.7	(foreign-currency liabilities)	202.1
Canadian securities	19.8	Other liabilities	141.3
Foreign securities and deposits with foreign banks	187.5	Total liabilities	574.7
Other assets	76.3	Net worth	33.4
Total assets	608.1	Total liabilities plus net worth	608.1

SOURCE: Based on data originally published in Bank of Canada, *Bank of Canada Review*, August 1991, pp. S32–S35. Reproduced with permission.

whether of banks or of any other financial unit or aggregate, it must always be true that

$$\text{Assets} = \text{Liabilities} + \text{Net worth.}$$

The balance sheet shows that most of the assets held by banks are financial claims against others. These claims are mostly loans granted to individuals and businesses, and securities issued by business and federal, provincial, and municipal governments. On the liability side of the balance sheet, the biggest items are demand and notice deposits, which are claims against the bank owned by depositors. The net-worth figure represents what would be left to the owners of the bank if they were to sell all their assets and pay off all their liabilities at "book" values.

The rate of growth of bank assets is determined largely by the ability of banks to meet the credit demands of the public. Loans are the primary assets of the banks. In order to increase their loans, banks must attract more savings. As we have seen, the share of deposits held by banks declined during the 1980s. However, the banks have managed to attract savings in other forms. They have, for example, increased their share of the $10 billion to $12 billion that Canadians save each year in the form of Registered Retirement Savings Plans (RRSPs). The banks now account for 37 percent of that market, compared with 34 percent for trust companies.

As a result of both increased competition from other sectors of the financial industry and losses sustained by some banks in recent years (as we shall discuss shortly), the banks' rate of profit was not very high during the 1980s. Their average return on equity was 10.3 percent, compared with 12 percent for other sectors of the financial-services industry. This rate of return placed the banks in eighteenth place among 34 corporate sectors. However, their profit position seems to be improving, and in 1990, the six largest chartered banks reported an average return of close to 14 percent on their equity.

Reserves

Reserves
Money held by chartered banks as cash or as non-interest-bearing deposits with the Bank of Canada.

The **reserves** item on the asset side of the balance sheet deserves some further explanation. Historically, the reason that banks hold some of their assets in the form of reserves is that depositors may want to withdraw their money from the bank at any moment, either by writing a cheque to someone who will deposit it in another bank or by walking up to the teller's window and asking for currency. In Canada's so-called *fractional-reserve* banking system today, the quantity of reserves that banks hold is not left up to the judgement of individual bankers. Instead, the Bank Act sets certain reserve requirements for chartered banks. These take the form of fixed percentages of deposits that banks must hold as reserves. These percentages are called **required-reserve ratios**. They vary according to the type and size of deposits, and are set down in the Bank Act, which is reviewed every ten years. The rates at the time of the 1980 review were 12 percent for demand deposits and 4 percent for notice deposits. By 1991, they had declined to 10 percent and 3 percent, respectively. Required-reserve ratios play an important role in the expansion and contraction of Canada's money supply, which we shall discuss in Chapter 23.

Required-reserve ratios
Legally required minimum quantities of reserves, expressed as ratios of reserves to total funds held in various types of deposits.

Some Risks of Banking

Banks are able to earn a profit only because they lend out or invest most of the deposits they accept at an interest rate higher than the rate they pay to depositors. They keep only a fraction of their total deposits, as required by the Bank of Canada, in the form of non-interest-bearing reserves. Banks have been doing business in much the same way for hundreds of years, but it entails some well-known risks.

One is the risk of loan losses. What happens if a bank makes a loan to a customer who is unable to repay the loan? When a loan goes bad, the loss is at first absorbed by the net worth of the bank's owners. (In balance-sheet terms, the bad loan is a reduction in assets. Liabilities — that is, deposits and borrowings — do not change. Thus, net worth, which is equal to assets minus liabilities, must fall.) If loan losses are too great, however, the bank's net worth may be used up. At that point, the bank no longer has enough assets to pay off its depositors and other creditors, and it is in real trouble. Technically, a bank whose liabilities exceed its assets is said to be *insolvent*.

A second risk that banks face is the loss of deposits. When a depositor withdraws funds, the bank must dip into its reserves or other cash assets. This is not a problem under normal conditions, when new deposits more or less offset withdrawals. If there is a wave of withdrawals, however, the bank may have to convert some of its earning assets into cash to pay off depositors. Some assets, such as short-term government securities, are easy to convert into cash, but others, such as long-term business or mortgage loans, may be more of a problem. At that point, the bank is in a different kind of trouble — it is *illiquid*.

Whether the bank's troubles begin with loan losses or deposit losses, there is a danger that they may trigger a *run on the bank*. This refers to a situation in which depositors begin to withdraw their funds from a bank because they fear it may not be able to honour all of its liabilities. Fearing that the bank may be able to pay only the first depositors in line, they all compete to be first in line. Their fears become self-fulfilling, and the bank fails.

In the worst possible case, not just one bank but the whole banking system can get into trouble. When many banks face loan losses or runs at the same time, they cannot help each other out through temporary loans of reserves. If large banks fail, smaller banks, which keep deposits in the large ones or make other loans to them, may be brought down as well. If many banks try to meet deposit outflows by selling their holdings of securities at the same time, the market price of the securities may fall, adding to their losses. A general bank *panic* can ensue in which the stability of the whole system is threatened.

How safe is the banking system?

During the nineteenth century, recessions touched off a number of bank panics in Canada. After World War I, the economy went through another period of instability, producing a notable bank failure in 1923. However, for more than half a century thereafter, not a single chartered bank failed in Canada — not even during the Great Depression of the 1930s — a record that was the envy of many countries in the world. This result was attributable in part to the system of a few large banks with many branches scattered across the country. A branch experiencing difficulties in one region could easily be bailed out by its headquarters, which could draw on the resources of its other branches. In more recent decades, the monitoring function of the Bank of Canada, as well as of other federal agencies, may also have contributed to the stability of the Canadian banking system.

However, the severe recession of the early 1980s, which was characterized by a particularly serious downturn in the Alberta economy, brought about by falling oil prices, put new strains on the banking system. Several Western-oriented banks were suddenly faced with heavily depreciated assets and unredeemable loans.

In the fall of 1985, Canadians were shocked by the failure of two banks in western Canada — the Canadian Commercial Bank and the Northland Bank. In the following year, several other banks, including the Mercantile Bank of Canada (which was merged into the National Bank of Canada) and the Bank of British Columbia (which was bought by Hong Kong investors) were saved only by being bailed out by others. Hundreds of millions of dollars of government money was used to reimburse depositors in the first two banks, in order to ensure the public that bank deposits continued to be a safe form of saving.

Foreign liabilities of Canadian banks

Canadian banks have developed a substantial amount of business in other countries, setting up more than two hundred foreign branches. Considerable loan losses have been experienced by Canadian banks in several Eastern European and Third World countries, a development that has raised concerns about the viability of overseas loans in general.

Box 22.4 indicates that, at the end of 1990, Canadian bank liabilities in foreign countries totalled $207.5 billion, or more than one-third of the total assets of the banks ($609.9 billion). Foreign assets, at $200.2 billion, did not quite match foreign liabilities. Although Canadian banks have successfully written off past losses

BOX 22.4 *Foreign Assets and Liabilities of Canadian Banks, End of 1990*

Canadian banks have weathered more than a decade of substantial losses in Eastern Europe and the Third World, and have built up sizable reserves against future losses. Nevertheless, their foreign liabilities, at $207.5 billion, remain at high levels, representing more than one-third of total bank assets. These liabilities are not quite covered by foreign assets of $200.2 billion.

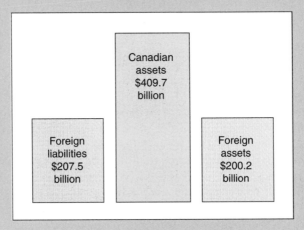

SOURCE: Canada, Ministry of Industry, Science, and Technology, *Banking: Industry Profile*, Ottawa, 1991, p. 2, figure 1.

and have created larger reserves against future losses, the foreign position of many banks leaves them unduly exposed to future risks.

THE BANK OF CANADA

Reference has already been made several times to one of the most important institutions in the Canadian banking system — the Bank of Canada. The major responsibilities of this bank are considered in the next chapter, where its role in managing Canada's money supply is examined, but a brief description of its purpose and functions is in order here.

The Bank of Canada is Canada's central bank. It was created in 1934, in the middle of the Great Depression, in order to lend stability and leadership to Canada's banking system. It has become the main institution through which the federal government controls Canadian banks and the Canadian money supply.

Initially, all shares of the Bank of Canada were sold to the public, making it a private bank. The first governor, Graham Towers, and the directors of the Bank were appointed by the government, but provision was made for future election of the directors by the private shareholders. However, political pressure developed to make the Bank more subject to government control. Therefore, in 1936, the federal government acquired 51 percent of the Bank's shares, and in 1938, it bought the rest. The Bank of Canada thereby became a true government bank.

Structure of the Bank of Canada

The structure of the Bank of Canada is simple. The Bank is managed at the top by a board of directors, consisting of the governor, the senior deputy governor, and twelve directors. The deputy minister of finance is also on the board as a nonvoting member. The directors are appointed for three-year terms by the minister of finance, with the approval of the federal cabinet. Unlike the Federal Reserve System in the United States, the Bank of Canada does not have formal regional divisions, but the directors on the board are usually chosen on a regional basis, and periodical meetings are held across the country. In addition, the Bank has branch offices in all major Canadian cities.

The governor and senior deputy governor are appointed by the board of directors, with cabinet approval, to seven-year terms. (See the Profile box on the Bank's governors on page 580.) An executive committee, consisting of the governor, senior deputy minister, and two directors selected by the board, plus the nonvoting deputy minister of finance, is the real power within the Bank and meets weekly to implement board policy. The full board is called together at least eight times a year to review and ratify policy.

Functions of the Bank of Canada

The Bank of Canada is expected to formulate and execute monetary policy for Canada, and it is designed to be reasonably free from political interference. When it attempts, for example, to control inflation by cutting down on the amount of money that people have to spend, it may run into considerable opposition from members of the public. The government may then be pressured into changing the Bank's policy. It obviously wouldn't do for the Bank to give in to such pressure whenever it develops. The governors of the Bank of Canada have tried to maintain a certain tradition of independence, especially the second governor, James Coyne, who (as described in the accompanying Profile) refused to follow government policy and was eventually forced to resign in 1961.

The government, of course, as the sole shareholder of the Bank and as the body responsible for overall economic policy, has ultimate control over the Bank. There is regular, close consultation between the minister of finance and the governor, and in case of serious disagreement, it is clearly the minister who holds the upper hand. Some argue that the Bank should be a mere arm of the government, a division of the Department of Finance, since the elected representatives of the government are answerable to the people and should formulate all economic policy for the country. Others point to evidence that, the more independent its central bank, the more successful a country will be in fighting inflation. In a study of seventeen major industrial countries, Prof. Alberto Alesina of Harvard University documented what appears to be a fairly strong link between central-bank independence and low inflation. The Bank of Canada, for example, was ranked seventh in terms of independence, and the Canadian inflation rate was also the seventh-lowest among the seventeen countries between 1973 and 1986.[1] However, the inflation rate is only one criterion by which to assess economic performance, and overall Bank performance should be judged by other measures as well,

---

[1] Alberto Alesina, "Politics and Business Cycles," *Economic Policy* 8 (Cambridge: Harvard University Press).

PROFILE Governors of the Bank of Canada

Graham F. Towers
(1897–1975)

James E. Coyne
(1910–   )

Louis Rasminsky
(1908–   )

Gerald K. Bouey
(1920–   )

John W. Crow
(1937–   )

From its establishment in 1934 to the present day, the Bank of Canada has had only five governors. The first governor was Graham F. Towers, a native of Montreal and an economist and accountant by training. He served longer than any other governor, from 1934 to 1954, and developed for the Bank of Canada a worldwide reputation for monetary responsibility and imaginative direction. International recognition of his work led to his appointment as alternate governor of the International Monetary Fund from 1946 to 1954. In the post–World War II period, Towers followed an expansionary policy and maintained low interest rates in order to stimulate investment. He was criticized in the early 1950s for not fighting growing signs of inflation with a more restrictive policy, but he remained primarily concerned with the possibility of recession.

His successor, James Coyne, a lawyer and a native of Winnipeg, was criticized in the late 1950s for following a much more restrictive course at a time when the government and many economists felt that the economy needed some stimulation. The minister of finance, Donald Fleming, asked Coyne to change course, and when Coyne refused, the minister asked for his resignation. Coyne refused to resign, whereupon the government initiated action in Parliament to declare his office vacant. After an appearance before the Senate and before being evicted by the government, Coyne did resign, on July 13, 1961.

James Coyne was succeeded by the third governor, Louis Rasminsky, an economist from Montreal. Upon taking the office, he publicly declared that, while the Bank of Canada has the responsibility for monetary policy, if the government disapproves of this policy and asks the Bank to change it, the governor of the Bank is faced with only one choice: He must either change his mind and follow the government's advice, or resign.

When the Bank Act was revised in 1967, it provided for closer and more continuous consultation between the minister of finance and the governor of the Bank of Canada and clarified the steps to be taken in case of a disagreement.

The fourth governor, Gerald K. Bouey, an economist from Saskatchewan, took over from Louis Rasminsky in 1973. About the time that Governor Bouey assumed his duties, Canada came to be plagued by unusually high rates of inflation *and* unemployment. The years since 1973 have been marked by a vigorous debate among economists and government advisers about which of these problems poses the greater danger to the Canadian economy.

The fifth and current governor, John Crow, an economist born in London, England, assumed the duties of governor in 1987. He has thus far pursued an approach similar to that of his predecessor, Gerald Bouey, in stressing that the main objective of the Bank of Canada is to foster price stability, even at the cost of high interest rates.

such as unemployment and growth rates (to which we shall turn our attention in Chapters 27 and 28).

The regional diversity of Canada makes a broadly acceptable monetary policy extremely difficult to achieve. Growing inflation, for example, may be the main problem of the central provinces, while unemployment is the prime concern of eastern Canada and the Prairies. For this reason, the constitutional debates of 1991 proposed measures that would give the various regions more control over central-bank policies.

The work of the Bank is carried out through several departments, including Securities (to handle open-market operations, which will be explained in Chapter 23), Research, and International Transactions. Through its nationwide network of offices and its role as the ultimate clearing agency, the Bank not only manages to regulate monetary operations in the country, but it is one of the few government agencies that regularly produces a profit on its operations. Probably the most visible function of the Bank is its currency processing. While the Royal Canadian Mint is responsible for coins, the Bank of Canada is the sole issuer of paper currency. Each year, it produces more than 600 million new bills, of which more than 90 percent are used to replace worn-out bills.

The chartered banks are required to submit regular reports on their operations to the minister of finance and the Bank of Canada. Their most closely watched duty is to keep reserve deposits with the Bank of Canada.

OTHER MAJOR FINANCIAL INSTITUTIONS

Banks are by no means the only financial institutions active in the economy. Many other institutions — including trust and mortgage-loan companies, credit unions and caisses populaires, and consumer-loan companies — perform some, although not all, of the same functions that banks do. In particular, these institutions function as go-betweens for savers with funds to lend and investors with the need to borrow. For this reason, they are considered financial intermediaries, as are banks.

The various financial intermediaries can be classified into several groups: near-banks, contractual savings institutions, and securities markets.

Near-Banks

The most familiar financial intermediaries, after the chartered banks, are the so-called **near-banks**. They include trust and mortgage-loan companies, credit unions, caisses populaires, and the Quebec savings banks. These institutions accept deposits on which cheques can be written, but they are currently not subject to reserve requirements with the Bank of Canada. With some exceptions, they are subject to provincial regulations. In recent years, credit unions alone have accounted for personal or consumer loans to Canadians equal to more than 25 percent of the loans issued by chartered banks.

Contractual Savings Institutions

Contractual savings institutions are financial intermediaries such as insurance companies and pension funds, to which individuals and groups commit savings on a long-term, contractual basis. More savings are committed to such

Near-banks
Institutions that accept deposits on which cheques can be written but that are not chartered banks and are not subject to direct control by the Bank of Canada.

Contractual savings institutions
Financial intermediaries, such as insurance companies and pension funds, to which individuals and groups commit savings on a long-term, contractual basis.

institutions annually than to the near-banks. Since the important role played by these institutions is not always clearly understood, a further description of some of their functions is in order.

The insurance industry

The insurance industry is really two industries. One part of the business of an insurance company is selling protection against risk. The other is operating as a financial intermediary.

Risk protection   Insurance companies sell protection against risk on the principle that although exposure to risk is inherently unpredictable for any single individual, it is highly predictable for large numbers of individuals. No family, for example, can be certain that its house will not burn down during the coming year. An insurance company, however, can predict quite accurately, on the basis of past experience, that, say, one in every thousand houses in a given type of neighbourhood will burn down each year. Knowing this, it can sell insurance. Each family pays a premium each year equal to a thousandth of the value of its house, and the pool of funds thus collected is used to compensate the unlucky one family in a thousand whose house burns down.

Today, one can buy insurance against risks of almost any kind. Fire insurance, automobile accident insurance, and health insurance are the most common types. All of them protect the buyer against losses that might never occur but that would be very costly if they did.

Life insurance is a very important kind of insurance. Superficially, it differs somewhat from the other kinds of insurance mentioned thus far in that the risk it appears to insure against — death — is something certain to befall everyone. On closer examination, however, it turns out that what life insurance really does is protect the buyer against the risk of *premature* death. Although everyone can be certain of dying sometime, death during any given year is a risk, not a certainty — much like the risk of having a house burn down.

Pensions and annuities are closely related to life insurance. They are arrangements under which a person pays in a premium each year up to a given age, say, 65 years of age, and then receives a fixed sum each year until death. In a sense, pensions and annuities insure people against the risk that they will live too long. Pension premiums and benefits are based on participants' average life expectancy at retirement. Those who die sooner than expected will, in a sense, not get their money's worth out of the program. But those who live longer than expected will receive payments totalling more than the value of the premiums they paid in.

Insurance companies as financial intermediaries   This picture of what insurance companies do is, of course, an extremely simplified one. If the companies actually paid out benefits as rapidly as they took in premiums, they would not be able to cover administrative expenses, let alone make a profit. In part, insurance companies allow for administrative expenses and profit by charging premiums that are somewhat higher than the level dictated by the exact probability of risk. (In the earlier example, this would mean collecting from each purchaser of a fire-insurance policy somewhat more than a thousandth of the value of the insured home.) But insurance companies and pension funds have another important source of income as well — namely, their operations as financial intermediaries.

Insurance companies are able to operate as financial intermediaries because all insurance involves an element of saving. This is so because premiums are collected before benefits are paid out, which generates in the meantime a pool of funds controlled by the insurance company. In the case of life insurance and pension funds, the lag between receipt of premiums and payment of benefits is often particularly long, which gives these companies billions of dollars to put to work in financial markets. The assets of life-insurance companies alone are nearly as large as the assets of savings institutions.

These vast quantities of funds are put to work principally through the purchase of securities such as corporate stocks and bonds. Insurance companies and pension funds also often buy commercial mortgages and sometimes invest directly in real estate. Certain types of life-insurance policies also permit policyholders to take out personal loans from these companies at advantageous interest rates.

Securities Markets as Financial Intermediaries

Throughout this book, we have mentioned government and corporate securities — bills, bonds, stocks, mortgage notes, and the like — without mentioning the important class of financial intermediaries with which they are associated — the markets in which such securities are bought and sold. These institutions also play an important role in channelling savings from households to business and government borrowers. Conceptually, the securities markets can be divided into two classes, primary and secondary.

Primary securities markets are those in which new borrowing takes place. Suppose, for example, that General Motors wants to build a new assembly plant or a new testing facility. It might finance the project with a bank loan, but it has an alternative that is often more attractive: It can sell newly issued bonds or shares of stock to the public. Bonds are a promise to repay a fixed nominal amount at a later date, with periodic interest payments to be made in the meantime. Stocks represent a share in the ownership of the firm, including the right to receive part of future profits in the form of dividends.

Primary securities markets
Markets in which companies sell new shares of stock and bonds for borrowing purposes.

A corporation seeking to raise money through the sale of shares or bonds does not normally approach individual households directly. Instead, it uses the services of brokers and underwriters — specialists in putting individuals and firms with funds to lend in touch with companies wishing to sell newly issued bonds and stocks. Brokers and underwriters thus act as financial intermediaries. Since the purchaser of the new securities may itself be a bank, savings institution, or insurance company, the funds involved may pass through a chain of two or more financial intermediaries on their way from the original saver to the ultimate borrower.

When most people think of securities markets, however, it is not these primary markets that they have in mind. Instead, they think of highly publicized institutions such as the New York Stock Exchange or the Toronto Stock Exchange. These exchanges are called **secondary securities markets**; they stand in relation to the primary markets discussed above exactly as used-car dealers stand in relation to new-car dealers. The sellers in secondary securities markets are typically not the issuers of bonds or shares of stock but savers or financial institutions who own and now wish to sell shares or bonds issued by firms or government units at some time in the past.

Secondary securities markets
Markets, such as stock markets, that deal in previously issued securities.

Strictly speaking, then, secondary securities markets are not financial intermediaries. Rather than channelling money from savers to investors, they permit savers to exchange "used" securities for money or money for securities. Indirectly, however, these markets are very important to the operation of the economy's system of financial intermediaries. They give households, banks, savings institutions, insurance companies, pension funds, and all the rest a much-needed flexibility in their financial operations.

A corporation makes a long-term financial commitment with the sale of a new bond or share of stock, but the buyer need not make an equally long-term commitment. Because the secondary market with its network of brokers is always there, the buyer can resell the security tomorrow, obtaining cash to spend on goods, services, or some different kind of asset.

An Overview of Canada's Financial System

The relative strengths of the various sectors of Canada's financial-services industry are illustrated in Box 22.5. The assets of the forty largest financial companies represented in this box totalled $899.4 billion in 1990, an amount considerably greater than Canada's gross domestic product. The ten largest banks accounted for 60 percent of this amount, and for 67.6 percent of forty firms' total profits, but the other financial institutions also pooled sizable amounts of public savings.

CONCLUSIONS

This chapter has wandered rather far from macroeconomic policy — but for a reason. Chartered banks and other financial intermediaries play a crucial role in regulating the circular flow of income and product, which is what macroeconomic policy seeks to stabilize. The focus here has been on their function of channelling funds from savers to investors. The next chapter will look at the function

---

BOX 22.5   *Assets and Net Income (Profits) of the Ten Largest Banks, Life Insurance Companies, Trust Companies, and Credit Unions in Canada, 1990*

The assets of the ten largest banks, insurance companies, trust companies, and credit unions totalled $899.4 billion in 1990, an amount greater than Canada's GDP. The ten largest chartered banks account for 60.3 percent of these assets, and for 67.6 percent of the total profits of these forty largest financial institutions. However, the assets of the other institutions are also substantial and represent a major pool of saving and credit in the economy.

The Ten Largest	Assets		Net Income	
	(billions of dollars)	(% of total)	(millions of dollars)	(% of total)
Banks	542.2	60.3	3715.9	67.6
Life-insurance companies	169.3	18.8	1118.8	20.4
Trust companies	134.0	14.9	280.2	5.1
Credit unions and caisses populaires	53.9	6.0	382.1	7.0
	899.4	100.0	5497.0	100.0

SOURCE: *Financial Post 500*, Summer 1991, pp. 158, 160. Reproduced with permission.

of banks as creators of money and at the Bank of Canada as the regulator of the money supply.

SUMMARY

1. *Money* is an asset that serves as a means of payment, a store of purchasing power, and a unit of account. Because it can be used directly as a means of payment, and because it has a fixed nominal value, it is said to have *liquidity*.

2. In practice, many kinds of assets have some or all of the features of money. The two assets that fit the definition of money most closely are *currency* (coins and paper money) and *demand deposits* (chequing accounts). Together, these make up the measure of the money supply known as M_1. Other definitions of money are also used. For example, when daily-interest chequable and notice deposits are added to M_1, the result is the measure of the money supply known as M_2.

3. Financial intermediaries are institutions that channel funds from savers to investors. They are a necessary part of the circular flow of income and product because the needs of individual lenders and borrowers do not necessarily match in terms of quantity of funds, length of commitment, and degree of risk.

4. *Chartered banks* are the least specialized and most important class of financial intermediary. They accept demand deposits, savings deposits, and time deposits from households and firms and earn income by making loans and purchasing securities. Banking practices are regulated by the *Bank Act* and by federal and provincial regulatory bodies. One of the most important Bank Act regulations is that chartered banks must maintain *reserves* with the *Bank of Canada*.

5. A fractional-reserve banking system faces a potential problem in that it uses short-term liabilities, such as deposits, as a basis for longer-term, less liquid assets, such as commercial and mortgage loans. If depositors suddenly decide to withdraw their funds from a bank, it may fail. A bank can also fail because of loan losses or operating losses.

6. A number of nonbank financial intermediaries also operate in the Canadian economy. They include savings institutions, insurance companies, and organized securities markets. Each plays an important role in channelling funds from savers to investors.

KEY TERMS

money	M_2	reserves
liquidity	M_3	required-reserve ratio
currency	near-moneys	near-banks
demand deposits	Schedule 1 banks	contractual savings institutions
M_1	Schedule 2 banks	primary securities markets
Bank of Canada	Bank Act	secondary securities markets
chartered banks		

KEY BOX

Box 22.1 Components of the Canadian Money
          Stock, July 1991

REVIEW QUESTIONS

1. Money serves three functions: It is a means of payment, a store of purchasing power, and a unit of account. How does inflation undermine each of these functions?

2. Look in your library for news articles or other accounts of a country that has experienced very rapid inflation — what is sometimes called *hyperinflation*. Argentina, Brazil, Bolivia, and Israel are recent examples; Germany in the 1920s is a historical example. How did this experience affect the functions performed by money in the country you have researched?

3. For most purposes, compared with barter (the direct exchange of one good or service for another), money lowers the cost of making transactions. However, barter has not disappeared, even in an advanced economy such as Canada's. Can you give an example of the use of barter in the Canadian economy today? Why is barter used instead of money in this case?

4. Do you use any credit cards? Does the use of credit cards reduce the amount of money you need? What forms of money do you need less of because you have a credit card?

5. A recent report on Canada's banking system notes that banks are deriving more and more of their profit from fees rather than from the difference between what they pay in interest on deposits and what they receive in interest from loans. About one-third of bank revenue is now obtained from fees, compared with 22 percent ten years ago. Using your understanding of elasticity of demand, try to explain this recent bank behaviour in terms of the apparent elasticity of demand for bank loans for bank services. (Consider the interest rate to be the price of loans and fees to be the price of bank services.)

6. Calculate M_1, M_2, and M_3 for an economy with the following money components:

Component	Amount (millions of dollars)
Foreign currency deposits in domestic banks	19.8
Demand deposits	27.4
Nonpersonal fixed-term deposits in domestic banks	22.6
Currency	32.6
Personal savings deposits and nonpersonal notice deposits	184.6

7. Calculate total assets and total liabilities plus net worth for a banking system with the following items on its balance sheet:

Item	Amount (millions of dollars)
Central bank reserve deposits and notes	6.2
Deposits held by foreigners (foreign-currency liabilities)	84.8
Foreign securities and deposits with foreign banks	200.2
Canadian securities held	18.4
Canadian demand deposits	26.4
General loans	186.2
Treasury bills held	14.0
Domestic savings/notice deposits	211.5
Mortgage loans	120.6
Net worth	_____

The Bank of Canada and the Supply of Money

WHAT YOU WILL LEARN IN THIS CHAPTER

After studying this chapter, you will be able to

1. Understand what can (and what cannot) change a nation's stock of money.
2. Describe how the Bank of Canada can change the supply of money through open-market operations.
3. Discuss how the Bank of Canada uses other means to change the money supply.
4. Explain the limits of money expansion and contraction.

A Preview   *How Money Affects the Economy*

We saw in Chapter 22 that most of Canada's money stock consists of deposits with the chartered banks. In the narrowest measure of the money stock, M_1, demand deposits account for slightly more than half of the total money supply. In the broader measure M_2, savings deposits represent the major part of the money stock.

Economists are particularly interested in *changes* in M_1 and M_2, because such changes may have a major impact on economic growth. The following article explains that growth in M_1 usually *precedes* changes in spending, while growth in M_2 *coincides with* changes in spending. The net growth rate of these two ($M_1 - M_2$) seems to act as a money meter, accurately predicting increases in GDP. Whether this will always be the case, and why precisely it has been the case to date, is not entirely clear, but the phenomenon highlights a major concern of this chapter — to understand the causes and effects of changes in Canada's money supply.

Money-Supply Figures Point to Economic Upturn in Spring

"Never forecast, especially about the future." Good advice perhaps, but not easy to follow.

For better or for worse, efforts to peer ahead in time occupy the minds of millions. A key concern of many Canadians at present is the future course of the economy. With the country now evidently in recession, it is natural to wonder when we will see a recovery.

The usual way to approach this type of question is to turn to a complex model of income and expenditure in the economy, and try to get a sense of what consumers are doing, how strong investment is, how exports are faring, and what is happening to inventories. But this approach has problems. An enormous amount of information is needed, while many of the numbers are difficult to measure and subject to large revisions. Moreover, although these models often give a good sense of the strength of continuing trends, they do poorly when it comes to signalling turning points.

Interestingly, however, there is a model that forecasts turning points quite well. Better yet, it uses only two numbers — measures of the money supply — which are published weekly by the Bank of Canada and are almost never significantly revised: M_1 (currency in circulation and in chequing accounts) and M_2 (a broader

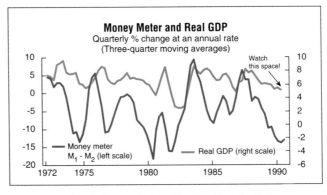

Money Meter and Real GDP
Quarterly % change at an annual rate
(Three-quarter moving averages)

SOURCE: Reproduced with permission of the C.D. Howe Institute.

measure, which also includes savings accounts).

M_1 is money used primarily for transactions. It tends to signal changes in the spending intentions of individuals and businesses, reacts very quickly to changes in the Bank of Canada's monetary policy, and usually moves in advance of total spending in the economy. M_2 also includes less liquid forms of money. It tends to vary contemporaneously with total spending. Comparing growth of M_1, the leading indicator, with growth of M_2, the coincident indicator, produces a "money meter" that signals changes in the economy quite reliably, as the accompanying chart illustrates.

The green line in the chart is the money meter; growth in M_1 minus growth in M_2 (quarterly changes at

annual rates). The blue line represents growth of real gross domestic product. (Both lines are three-quarter moving averages.) As the chart shows, the money meter generally changes direction ahead of the economy, with a lead averaging two quarters. Since the early 1970s, it has given only one serious wrong signal. (Financial innovations in an environment of persistently high interest rates after the 1981–82 recession caused growth of M_1 — most of which pays no interest — to be very weak in 1983, and it failed to signal the economy's continued strength in 1984.)

SOURCE: William Robson, "Money Supply Figures Point to Economic Upturn in Spring," *Financial Post*, October 1, 1990, p. 6. Reproduced with permission.

WHY MONEY MATTERS

Money obviously matters to everyone. The best things in life may be free, but most of the thousands of little things that we need in our daily lives have a price, and we must have money to acquire them. During the Depression, many Canadian communities found themselves short of money, in the form of both currency and bank deposits. In desperation, many business firms created their own money in the form of light metal disks imprinted with the firm's name. These disks soon circulated through the local economy as a means of payment. As we saw in Chapter 22, almost anything can serve as money as long as other people accept it as such.

When economists ask whether and why money matters, they have something a little different in mind from this universal need to carry out daily purchases. They ask, for example, how changes in the stock of money affect the performance of an entire economy. The Preview has already suggested that economic performance may indeed be linked to changes in the money supply. But before we embark on a more complete explanation of this relationship (in Chapters 25 and 26), we must first gain some understanding of what causes a nation's money supply to change. This is the main purpose of this chapter.

A second question that economists ask is Why do people choose to save, or "hold," money rather than to spend it on a good that brings them pleasure or an asset that increases their earnings? To understand the nature of this question, it is necessary to recall that money, by definition, does not directly produce either pleasure or profits (except to those who take delight in hearing the jingle of currency or watching their bank balance grow). Money (M_1) is defined either as currency, which lies uselessly in a purse or wallet until it is spent, or as a bank deposit that earns little or no interest. It is only when we *give up* money, in exchange for goods or profit-earning assets, such as bonds and shares of stock, that we increase our pleasure and our earnings. So why hold money if it can be put to much better use when it is *not* held? People's desire to hold money — which economists call the *demand for money* — is therefore not as obvious a phenomenon as one might suppose. This demand, which is explored in the following chapter, interacts with the forces of supply, which we examine in this chapter, and together they have a significant impact on the performance of a modern economy.

CHANGES IN THE SUPPLY OF MONEY

In Chapter 22 (Box 22.1), we saw that the stock of money in Canada (M_1) was exactly $41.7 billion in July 1991. Of this amount, 48 percent was held outside banks in the form of currency, and 52 percent consisted of chequing deposits in chartered banks. In most years, this stock of money grows. Between September 1990 and September 1991, for example, M_1 grew by 7.8 percent. What are the causes of such growth?

It might seem to people that the stock of money grows every time they get a paycheque, because the cheque increases their bank balance or their supply of currency, or both. But this, of course, is not the case. When a worker deposits her employer's cheque in her bank account, the bank account of the employer is reduced almost immediately by the same amount. The transaction has not changed the nation's stock of money; it has merely redistributed the stock between the worker and her employer. Virtually all our money transactions are of this kind: Money changes hands, but there is no net change in its total amount. What is required to increase the stock is an infusion of "new" money: a receipt of money by persons within the economy that is not counterbalanced by an equal deduction elsewhere in the economy.

There are two main ways in which "new" money can enter an economy. First, it can come from outside the economy — for example, through the sale of export goods. Second, it can result from the creation of money by an institution within the economy, which, because of its unique character, does not produce a counterbalancing reduction of money. The first type of infusion of new money, from outside the economy, is not very significant. (We discuss it in Chapter 26.) The second type is very important, and we explore it here.

The unique institution that is able to infuse new money into the economy is the government's central bank, the Bank of Canada. It has the power to increase the money supply very directly by printing more currency, but this is not actually what it does when it wants to change the stock of money. It acts instead on the other major component of M_1 — the demand deposits held in chartered banks. The Bank of Canada is able to control the volume of such deposits by means of five policy tools: open-market operations, moral suasion, draw-downs and redeposits, changes in the interest rate that it charges when lending reserves to banks, and changes in required-reserve ratios. Each of these will be described briefly, later in the chapter but our attention will be devoted primarily to open-market operations, through which the Bank of Canada most frequently alters the money supply.

Open-Market Operations

Open-market operations
A purchase of securities from the public or a sale of securities to the public by the Bank of Canada for the purpose of altering the quantity of reserves available to chartered banks.

Open-market operations involve the purchase or sale of securities (bonds) by the Bank of Canada. If the Bank wants to expand the money supply, it instructs its open-market trading desk, operating in the money markets, to buy government securities. This is known as an open-market purchase. The Bank pays for the securities with a cheque that it writes on its own account. When the person or firm selling the securities deposits the cheque in a bank, those funds are added to the reserves of the banking system. And, as we shall see, each dollar of reserves added to the banking system permits the volume of transactions deposits to expand by several dollars.

If the Bank of Canada wants to decrease the money supply, it reverses this process. It instructs the trading desk to carry out an open-market sale of securities. If a member of the public buys securities from the Bank of Canada and pays for them with a cheque written on a chartered bank, reserves are drained from the banking system.

Box 23.1 provides a summary of the actual balance sheet of the Bank of Canada for June 1991. It shows on the asset side that the Bank deals extensively in the purchase and sale of government bonds. In that month, its holdings of such bonds exceeded $20 billion. On the liabilities side, the item that interests us most in this context is the $1.5 billion in chartered bank deposits that the Bank of Canada held that month. As we shall see, this is the amount that the chartered banks keep with the Bank of Canada as required reserves. These funds are owed by the Bank to the chartered banks and are therefore recorded as a liability.

Balance Sheet of the Bank of Canada, June 1991 — BOX 23.1

The Bank of Canada has liabilities to both the general public (in the form of currency in circulation) and the chartered banks (in the form of reserve deposits). The Bank's main assets are government bonds.

Assets (millions of dollars)		Liabilities and Net Worth (millions of dollars)	
Treasury bills	13 090	Bank notes in circulation	22 135
Other government bonds	9 375	Chartered bank reserve deposits	1 512
Other assets	2 381	Other liabilities and net worth	1 199
Total	24 846	Total	24 846

SOURCE: Data derived from Bank of Canada, *Bank of Canada Review*, August 1991, pp. S24–S25. Reproduced with permission.

A simplified example will now help us to see how, on the basis of its bond transactions and the reserve deposits of chartered banks, the Bank of Canada is able to increase or diminish the nation's money supply.

CREATION OF MONEY BY BANKS

As we have seen, the major part of the Canadian money supply consists of the liabilities of banks. We turn now to a discussion of the way these institutions create money on the basis of reserves controlled by the Bank of Canada.

A Simplified Banking System

We could not possibly cover all the details of money creation in the actual Canadian economy, given its various types of financial institutions and different forms of money. To keep things manageable, we will therefore limit our discussion to a simplified banking system, as defined by the following:

1. The system consists of ten banks, all of which are identical.

2. The banks' only assets are reserve deposits, securities, and loans.

3. The banks' only liabilities are demand deposits; net worth is zero.

4. Demand deposits are the only form of money in the banking system.

5. The system is regulated by a simplified Bank of Canada that has the power to set uniform reserve requirements on all deposits.

6. The Bank of Canada's only assets are government securities, and its only liabilities are the reserve deposits of chartered banks. Banks do not borrow reserves from the Bank of Canada in this system.

Simplified though it is, this ten-bank system can tell us a great deal about the mechanics of money creation in the Canadian banking system.

Reserves: Required and Excess

As we have seen, the Bank of Canada regulates bank reserves. It does so by setting a minimum percentage of certain deposits that each bank must hold in the form of reserve deposits either with the Bank of Canada or as vault cash. As we noted in Chapter 22, these are called *required reserves*, and the ratio of required reserves to deposits is called the *required-reserve ratio*. If the bank holds more than the minimum required reserves, the balance is called **excess reserves**. For our simplified banking system, we will assume a required-reserve ratio of 10 percent on all deposits. This is somewhat above the average required-reserve ratio for transactions deposits in the Canadian banking system.

Excess reserves
Total reserves minus required reserves.

Balance-sheet equilibrium

If a bank's reserves fall below its required-reserve level, it must make up the difference. It can do this either by selling assets or by borrowing. Legally, a bank can hold more than the required level of reserves, but there is a strong incentive not to do so: Reserves earn no interest. As profit-seeking firms, banks want to earn all the interest they can, so they normally use up almost all excess reserves by making loans or buying securities. In recent years, the excess reserves of Canadian banks have tended to be less than 2 percent of total reserves.

The situation in which total reserves equal required reserves can be thought of as a state of equilibrium. In our simplified banking system, excess reserves may exist for a while, but we will assume that banks reduce them to zero as promptly as possible.

Creation of Money in the Simplified Banking System

We come now to the central topic of this short course in money mechanics: creation of money by the banking system. As the following example will show, money creation is governed by the required-reserve ratio, the amount of reserves supplied, and the efforts of banks to maximize their profits.

Initial balance sheets

To begin with, we will assume that each of the banks in the system starts out with a balance sheet that looks like Box 23.2(a). The simplified Bank of Canada will begin with a balance sheet that looks like Box 23.2(b).

The process of deposit creation

The stage is now set in such a way that the Bank of Canada has control over the total quantity of reserves at chartered banks. This in turn makes it possible for the Bank of Canada to control the quantity of money supplied by the banking system in the form of demand deposits. Suppose, for example, that the Bank of Canada decides to increase the quantity of money available to the economy. Here is how it might typically proceed.

An open-market purchase injecting reserves The easiest way for the Bank of Canada to set in motion an expansion of demand deposits is through an *open-market operation* — an open-market purchase in this case. Suppose, for example, that the Bank of Canada's securities department decides to buy $10 000 in securities from a member of the public (see Box 23.3[a]). The Bank of Canada pays for

---

Initial Balance Sheets in the Simplified Banking System BOX 23.2

The following are the initial balance sheets of (a) one of the ten identical chartered banks in our simplified banking system, and (b) the simplified Bank of Canada.

(a)

Assets			Liabilities	
Reserves		$10 000	Demand deposits	$100 000
Required	$10 000			
Excess	0			
Loans		90 000		
Total assets		$100 000	Total liabilities	$100 000

(b)

Assets		Liabilities	
Canadian government		Chartered bank	
securities	$100 000	reserve deposits	$100 000

---

these securities with a cheque — a special cheque drawn on itself, not on one of the chartered banks. The seller of the securities deposits this special Bank of Canada cheque in his or her local chartered bank account. To help keep track of things, we shall call this bank the Alberta Bank. That bank in turn deposits the cheque in its account with the Bank of Canada, at which point the objective of injecting $10 000 of reserves into the system has been accomplished (see Box 23.3[b]). After all this has taken place, the balance sheets of the Bank of Canada and the Alberta Bank look like the ones in Box 23.3.

Balance-Sheet Changes in the Deposit-Creation Process BOX 23.3

(a)

Assets		Liabilities	
Canadian government		Chartered bank	
bonds	$110 000	reserve deposits	$110 000
	(+10 000)*		(+10 000)*

*Here and in subsequent balance sheets, *changes* are shown in parentheses.

(b)

Assets			Liabilities	
Reserves at Bank			Demand deposits	$110 000
of Canada		$20 000		
		(+10 000)		(+10 000)
Required	$11 000			
	(+1 000)			
Excess	9 000			
	(+9 000)			
Loans		90 000		
Total assets		$110 000	Total liabilities	$110 000
		(+10 000)		(+10 000)

Notice how the $10 000 in new reserves in the Alberta Bank is distributed between required reserves and excess reserves. Since deposits have gone up by $10 000, the bank must hold $1000 more in required reserves. The other $9000 is not required to be held as reserves, so it is listed as excess reserves. The bank is no longer in equilibrium; it can increase its income by putting its excess reserves to work. What happens when it does is the subject of the next section.

Making a new loan   Suppose that the Alberta Bank decides to put its $9000 to work by making a new loan of $9000. It does this simply by crediting $9000 to the chequing account of the borrower, Amar Singh. Box 23.4 shows the Alberta Bank's balance sheet at the moment the loan is completed.

The bank now has $9000 in new assets (loans) matched by $9000 in new liabilities (the increase in the borrower's demand deposits). Required reserves have increased sufficiently to maintain a level of 10 percent of deposits. The bank still has excess reserves of $8100, but it does not make further new loans, because it knows that the situation is only temporary. Singh did not borrow $9000 just to leave it sitting idle in this chequing account; he borrowed it to buy a car.

Chequing away the proceeds of the loan   Singh pays for the car by writing a cheque on his account in the Alberta Bank. The dealer from whom he buys the car — Françoise Bernard — has her account at the Brandon Bank.

When Bernard deposits Singh's Alberta Bank cheque in her Brandon account, the Brandon Bank sends it to the Bank of Canada for collection. The Bank of Canada credits $9000 to Brandon's reserve account and debits (subtracts) $9000 from Alberta's reserve account. Then it puts the cheque itself (the actual piece of paper) in the mail so that the Alberta Bank can eventually forward it to Singh for his personal records. Box 23.5 shows the balance sheets of the two banks when all these transactions have taken place. No further changes take place in the Bank of Canada's balance-sheet totals.

Now we can see why the Alberta Bank could not lend out more than its initial $9000 of excess reserves. It knew that the new $9000 deposit it created by the loan was not likely to stay there for long. As soon as the cheque cleared, Alberta lost $9000 in total reserves. Its required reserves went down by only $900 (10 percent of the amount of the loss in deposits), so the $8100 of the excess

BOX 23.4   *Balance-Sheet Changes in the Deposit-Creation Process*

Assets			Liabilities	
Reserves		$20 000	Demand deposits	$119 000
Required	$11 900			(+9 000)
	(+900)			
Excess	8 100			
	(−900)			
Loans		99 000		
		(+9 000)		
Total assets		$119 000	*Total liabilities*	$119 000
		(+9 000)		(+9 000)

Balance-Sheet Changes in the Deposit-Creation Process   BOX 23.5

(a) Alberta Bank

Assets			Liabilities	
Reserves		$11 000	Demand deposits	$110 000
		(−9 000)		(−9 000)
Required	$11 000			
	(−900)			
Excess	0			
	(−8 100)			
Loans		99 000		
Total assets		$110 000	Total liabilities	$110 000
		(−9 000)		(−9 000)

(b) Brandon Bank

Assets			Liabilities	
Reserves		$19 000	Demand deposits	$109 000
		(+9 000)		(+9 000)
Required	$10 900			
	(+900)			
Excess	8 100			
	(+8 100)			
Loans		90 000		
Total assets		$109 000	Total liabilities	$109 000
		(+9 000)		(+9 000)

reserves that Alberta had immediately after making the loan was needed to make up the difference.

Keeping the expansion going with another loan   When all transactions were completed, the Alberta Bank ended up with $10 000 more in deposits as well as $10 000 more in assets. But that is not the end of the story. The $8100 in excess reserves that the bank lost did not disappear from the banking system. The Brandon Bank's excess reserves rose by exactly the same amount that Alberta's fell. Brandon gained $9000 in deposits and $9000 in reserves, of which only $900 were required reserves. The remaining $8100 became excess reserves for Brandon.

To increase its earning assets to the maximum, Brandon must put its excess reserves to work. Assume that, like the Alberta Bank, it makes a new loan of $8100. We now know that the proceeds of this loan will be chequed away quickly, so we will skip the intermediate balance sheet. After Brandon's borrower has written a cheque for $8100, which is deposited in, say, the Cornwall Bank and cleared through the Bank of Canada, Brandon's and Cornwall's balance sheets will appear as shown in Box 23.6.

The multiple expansion of deposits

We really do not have to trace much farther the effect of the Bank of Canada's initial injection of $10 000 of new reserves into the chartered banking system. A clear pattern is beginning to emerge. Bank A received a deposit of $10 000, of

BOX 23.6 *Balance-Sheet Changes in the Deposit-Creation Process*

(a) Brandon Bank

Assets		Liabilities	
Reserves	$10 900	Demand deposits	$109 000
	(−8 100)		
Required	$10 900		
	(no change)		
Excess	0		
	(−8 100)		
Loans	98 100		
	(+8 100)		
Total assets	$109 000	Total liabilities	$109 000

(b) Cornwall Bank

Assets		Liabilities	
Reserves	$18 100	Demand deposits	$108 000
	(+8 100)		(+8 100)
Required	$10 810		
	(+810)		
Excess	7 290		
	(+7 290)		
	(+7 290)		
Loans	90 000		
Total assets	$108 100	Total liabilities	$108 100
	(+8 100)		(+8 100)

which it set aside 10 percent as required reserves and used the remainder to finance a loan of $9000. Bank B received a deposit of $9000, of which it set aside 10 percent as required reserves and used the remainder to finance a loan of $8100. Bank C received a deposit of $8100, of which it put aside $810 as required reserves. It used the remaining $7290 to finance another loan. Each bank makes new loans equal to 90 percent of the deposits it receives, thereby generating new deposits for the next bank in line. Total new deposits generated by the initial injection of $10 000 of new reserves is thus equal to the sum of the infinite series $10 000 + $9000 + $8100 + $7290 + $6561 + $5905 + ... = $100 000. The whole process is referred to as the multiple expansion of deposits by the chartered banking system.

A summary

Just to check what we have learned, we can go back to the beginning and look at the effects of the injection of new reserves, using a shortcut method based on the consolidated balance sheet for all ten member banks. The initial purchase by the Bank of Canada of $10 000 in securities from a member of the public puts $10 000 in new reserves into the banking system. The first bank to get those reserves holds on to only the required portion (10 percent) and passes the remainder on to some other bank. Ten percent of these reserves come to rest as required reserves in the second bank, another 10 percent of the remainder in the third, and so on.

The multiple expansion of deposits continues in this way until all reserves have eventually come to rest as required reserves in one bank or another. But no matter how often the reserves are passed from hand to hand, the total increase in the quantity of reserves in the banking system remains $10 000. Total deposits have to rise by enough to convert all of the initial $10 000 of excess reserves into required reserves. With a 10 percent required-reserve ratio, this takes $100 000 in new deposits. In the eventual equilibrium position, the consolidated balance sheet for the ten identical member banks in our simplified banking system will be as shown in Box 23.7.

Contraction of the Money Supply

If the Bank of Canada withdraws reserves from the simplified banking system, the whole process works in reverse. Suppose, for example, that the Bank of Canada begins by selling $1000 in securities to a member of the public. The seller pays for the securities with a cheque drawn on the Dalhousie Bank. Dalhousie loses $1000 in deposits and $1000 in reserves. That leaves it $900 short of required reserves, as the balance sheet in Box 23.8 shows (assuming the same initial balance sheet for the Dalhousie Bank as for all the banks in the previous example).

In order to meet its legal reserve requirements, the Dalhousie Bank must somehow obtain $900 in new reserves. One obvious way to do this is to reduce its loans, perhaps demanding immediate payment on a "demand" loan (a loan that must be paid on demand). The person who makes such a loan repayment may write a cheque on another bank, say the Edmonton Bank. This bank then loses $900 in deposits and $900 in reserves, leaving it with an $810 shortfall from required reserves. Edmonton in turn calls in loans to meet its requirements, and the operation of the multiple contraction process continues until it causes a total loss of $10 000 in deposits.

The Money Multiplier

We will conclude our analysis of the simplified banking system by drawing an important generalization from both the expansionary and contractionary exam-

---

Consolidated Balance Sheet of All Chartered Banks (Final Position)

BOX 23.7

Assets		Liabilities	
Reserves	$110 000 (+10 000)	Demand deposits	$1 100 000 (+100 000)
Required	$110 000 (+10 000)		
Excess	0		
Loans and securities	990 000 (+90 000)		
Total assets	$1 100 000 (+100 000)	Total liabilities	$1 100 000 (+100 000)

BOX 23.8 *Balance-Sheet Changes in the Deposit-Contraction Process*

Dalhousie Bank

Assets			Liabilities	
Reserves		$9 000	Demand deposits	$99 000
		(−1 000)		(−1 000)
Required	$9 900			
	(−100)			
Excess	−900			
Loans		90 000		
Total assets		$99 000	*Total liabilities*	$99 000
		(−1 000)		(−1 000)

ples just given: In every case, the ultimate change in total demand deposits (and hence in the total money supply) in the simplified chartered banking system must be equal to the initial change in reserves divided by the required-reserve ratio. The ratio of the change in the money supply to the initial change in reserves can be called the **money multiplier** for the banking system. (More precisely, it can be called the *demand-deposits-to-total-reserves multiplier*.)

In the simplified banking system, the formula for the money multiplier is

$$\text{Money multiplier} = \frac{1}{\text{Required-reserve ratio}}.$$

Money multiplier
The ratio of the quantity of money to the total reserves in a banking system. Various money multipliers can be defined, depending on the definition of money used. In the simplified banking system, the formula for the money multiplier is

$$\text{Money multiplier} = \frac{1}{\text{Required-reserve ratio}}.$$

With the required-reserve ratio of 0.1 that we have used in our examples, the money multiplier is 10. Hence, the injection of $10 000 in new reserves results in a $100 000 expansion of the money supply, and a $1000 withdrawal of reserves results in a $10 000 contraction. In equation form, then,

$$\text{Change in the money supply} = \text{money multiplier} \times \text{change in reserves}$$
$$\$100\,000 \qquad = \qquad 10 \qquad \times \qquad \$10\,000$$

OTHER INSTRUMENTS OF MONETARY POLICY, AND SOME PRACTICAL PROBLEMS

We turn now from the simplified banking system to the real world. On the surface, everything looks similar. Demand deposits still make up the most important part of the money supply, although not all of it. The Bank of Canada still has the power to control bank reserves and to impose reserve requirements. And changes in the total reserves of the banking system still result in multiple expansions or contractions of the money supply.

On closer examination, however, the actual banking system of Canada differs from that of the simplified economy in a number of details, which, taken together, crucially affect both the methods used by the Bank of Canada to control the nation's money supply and the success of those methods.

Other Instruments of Monetary Policy

As we noted earlier in the chapter, the Bank of Canada uses five major instruments to orchestrate its monetary policy: (1) *open-market operations* (sales and purchases of government securities in the open market): (2) *moral suasion* (attempts by the Bank of Canada to persuade the chartered banks to follow a certain policy); (3) *draw-downs and redeposits* (transfers of government deposits between the Bank of Canada and the chartered banks); (4) changes in the *bank rate* (the interest rate paid by chartered banks to borrow reserve funds from the Bank of Canada); and (5) changes in the *required-reserve ratios* for chartered banks.

The preceding section illustrated open-market operations in a simplified banking system in some detail. By the purchase and sale of securities, the Bank of Canada can inject new reserves directly into the banking system or withdraw reserves from it. Something more must now be said about the other monetary-policy tools employed by the Bank of Canada.

Moral suasion

Because the number of chartered banks in Canada is so small, the Bank of Canada can easily contact their presidents to obtain their support in implementing a certain policy. This may be done through general discussion or special directives. The Bank of Canada might request, for example, that the chartered banks tighten up on their loans or raise their interest rates. Because of its legal supervisory powers, the Bank of Canada has considerable clout when it engages in such **moral suasion**.

Moral suasion
Direct attempts by the Bank of Canada to influence the practices of the chartered banks.

Draw-downs and redeposits

The federal government has substantial deposits with the Bank of Canada and the chartered banks. With the permission of the minister of finance, the Bank of Canada can transfer government deposits from itself to the chartered banks, thereby increasing the reserves of the banks, or it can reduce those reserves in support of a tight monetary policy by transferring government deposits from the chartered banks to the Bank of Canada. These **draw-downs and redeposits** have become one of the most important short-term techniques used by the Bank of Canada in implementing monetary policy.

Draw-downs and redeposits
Transfers of government deposits between the Bank of Canada and the chartered banks.

The bank rate

Another policy instrument that the Bank of Canada can use is to change the **bank rate** (or discount rate, as it is called in the United States). A rise in the bank rate, other things being equal, has the effect of discouraging chartered banks from borrowing to augment their reserves. A decline in the bank rate has the opposite effect.

Actually, the chartered banks in Canada rarely borrow from the Bank of Canada to augment their reserves. They can call in loans or sell assets in the market to satisfy the reserve requirements. Changes in the bank rate act more as a signal to the chartered banks, telling them whether the Bank of Canada would like them to raise or lower their own interest rates. Most market interest rates, including the "prime rate" that chartered banks charge their best customers, tend to follow the bank rate. In the late 1950s and again in the 1980s and early 1990s, the Bank of Canada allowed this rate to "float" in relation to the interest rate that applied

Bank rate
The interest rate paid by chartered banks to borrow reserve funds from the Bank of Canada; also acts as a signal to the chartered banks as to the interest rates *they* should charge.

on short-term government bonds. Since the rate on such bonds is itself affected by the Bank's open-market operations, market interest rates were still effectively subject to the Bank of Canada's influence.

Changes in required-reserve ratios

The fifth instrument of monetary policy — changing required-reserve ratios — is more powerful in the United States than it is in Canada. In Canada, the rates for so-called cash or primary reserves are set when the Bank Act is reviewed. The Bank of Canada actually lost its right to vary primary reserve ratios when the Bank Act was amended in 1967. Instead, it was given the right to establish secondary reserve requirements for the chartered banks, and to vary these requirements. Chartered banks can now be required to hold up to 12 percent of their total Canadian deposits in the form of such liquid, interest-bearing assets as short-term treasury bills and day-to-day loans. These are the secondary reserves. The Bank of Canada has, since 1967, varied the secondary reserve ratio from 5 percent to 9 percent.

Practical Problems of Monetary Policy

The Bank of Canada has relied on the major tools of monetary policy described in the preceding section to control the growth of the money supply for many years, but only relatively recently has it begun to publicize its monetary-growth targets in advance.

During the rapid inflation of 1975, the Governor of the Bank of Canada, Gerald Bouey, followed the example of other central bankers and announced annual growth targets for M_1, the most immediately spendable money. High growth rates in the money supply were linked in the minds of many economists with the rapidly increasing inflation of the period. The target growth rate in the money supply for the first few years was set at 10 percent to 15 percent annually. By the end of 1979, this target had been reduced to a 5 percent to 9 percent annual growth rate. Since 1982, no specific money targets have been set.

Despite the variety of policy instruments available, and despite the announced targets, monetary policy in practice is a far more imprecise affair than in the simplified economy described earlier in this chapter. The real world is full of many problems and pitfalls that we have not yet mentioned. As a result, the Bank of Canada, even with the best of intentions, has had only mixed success in meeting the monetary-policy objectives it has set for itself.

Variations in money multipliers

The key to control over the money supply in the simplified banking system was a fixed money multiplier, equal to the reciprocal of the required-reserve ratio on demand deposits. In the real world, the closest equivalent to this multiplier is the so-called M_1-to-total-reserves multiplier (the M_1 multiplier, for short). As the name implies, this multiplier is the ratio of M_1 to total reserves of the chartered banking system. It is more complicated and subject to more variation than the money multiplier that we desired for our simple banking system.

Structure of reserve requirements One major reason for the greater complexity of this real-world money multiplier is that required-reserve ratios vary from one kind of deposit to another. Some reserves must be used to support savings deposits that are not counted as part of M_1. Other things being equal, the greater the ratio of savings and time deposits to demand deposits at banks, the lower the M_1 multiplier.

Near-banks A second major reason for variations in the M_1 multiplier is the existence of near-banks, such as trust companies and credit unions. They offer savings and term deposits that compete with those offered by chartered banks, but their deposits are not considered part of the money supply. Hence, shifts in deposits among banks and near-banks are also a source of variability in the money multiplier.

Excess reserves Yet a third reason for variability in the M_1 multiplier is the fact that real-world banks, unlike those in the simplified banking system, cannot always keep their excess reserves exactly at zero. Banks sometimes find it hard to keep up with unexpected deposit flows, resulting in excess reserves. Such excess reserves, while only a small amount on average, do show some variation over time.

Currency The Bank of Canada allows chartered banks to count currency on hand (so-called vault cash) as reserves, which means that when individuals or firms withdraw money from their banks in the form of currency, they drain total reserves from the banking system. When this happens, a multiple contraction of the money supply takes place, unless the Bank of Canada offsets the shift with an injection of new reserves.

In addition, currency is a form of money that is not a liability of the banking system and thus is not itself subject to reserve requirements. Even if the Bank of Canada maintains the level of reserves, the larger the fraction of their money balances people choose to hold as currency, the larger the M_1 multiplier.

CONCLUSIONS

This chapter has examined in some detail a few questions concerning the supply of money: how money is created by the banking system, and how the Bank of Canada attempts to exercise control over the money supply. Now it is time to return to a theme sounded briefly at the beginning of the chapter — the relationship between monetary policy and the goals of full employment, price stability, economic growth, and balance-of-payments stability. It is the importance of money to these goals of stabilization policy, after all, that justifies the attention to technicalities in this chapter.

The next chapter will turn from the supply side of the money market to the demand side and will examine the effect of variations in money demand and supply on real domestic income and product. Chapters 25 to 28 will show how monetary and fiscal policy together affect the success or failure of stabilization policy as a whole.

SUMMARY

1. The stock of money in an economy does not change as a result of most money transactions, wherein one party's receipt of money is matched by another's loss of it. Additions to the money supply must come either from

outside the economy or through the operations of a financial institution within the economy whose infusions of money are not counterbalanced by reductions.

2. The Bank of Canada is just such an institution. By interacting with the chartered banks through *open-market operations* — that is, by altering the reserves of the banks — it is able to expand or contract the money supply.

3. In a simplified banking system, an injection of new reserves sets off a multiple expansion of deposits and, hence, of the money supply. Each bank receiving new reserves makes loans or buys securities equal to its *excess reserves*. In that way, it passes along part of the reserves to the next bank in line. The process continues until deposits have risen enough to convert all the new reserves into required reserves. The ratio of money to reserves is known as the *money multiplier.*

4. In the actual Canadian banking system, the Bank of Canada has available five main instruments of monetary policy: *open-market operations* (buying and selling securities on the open market); *moral suasion* (efforts by the Bank of Canada to get the chartered banks to follow a proposed policy; *draw-downs and redeposits* (transfers of government deposits between the Bank of Canada and the chartered banks); changes in the *bank rate* (the rate charged to chartered banks for loans of reserves from the Bank of Canada); and changes in *required-reserve ratios.*

5. The Bank of Canada's instruments of monetary policy do not give it precise control of the money supply. A major reason is that the money multiplier can change as a result of factors that are not under the direct control of the Bank of Canada. Shifts of funds from one type of bank to another, from banks to near-banks, from one type of deposit to another within banks, and from deposits to currency can all affect the money multiplier. So can changes in banks' excess reserves. In addition, shifts of funds from chartered bank deposits to currency can alter the total reserves available to the banking system.

KEY TERMS

open-market operations
excess reserves

money multiplier
moral suasion

draw-downs and redeposits
bank rate

KEY BOXES

Box 23.1 Balance Sheet of the Bank of Canada,
　　　　　June 1991

Box 23.7 Consolidated Balance Sheet of All
　　　　　Chartered Banks (Final Position)

REVIEW QUESTIONS

1. Using the same starting position given in the text for the simplified banking system, work through the multiple expansion (or contraction) process for the following policy actions:

   a. An injection of $5000 in new reserves via an open-market purchase.

   b. A withdrawal of $500 in new reserves via an open-market sale.

   c. A selective reduction in the required-reserve ratio for the Alberta Bank only — from 10 percent to 8 percent. (Assume that once the expansion process gets under way, no one ever deposits new reserves in the Alberta Bank but uses only the other nine banks.)

   d. A general reduction in the required-reserve ratio for all banks from 10 percent to 8 percent.

2. Go to your library and obtain copies of the *Globe and Mail* business section or the *Financial Post*. Usually, these papers contain short news items or columns reporting weekly changes in the money supply announced by the Bank of Canada. Locate such an item and describe what is happening to the money supply. What comment does the paper make regarding Bank of Canada policy?

3. In a simplified banking system with a 6 percent required-reserve ratio, open-market operations by the central bank add $200 million to reserves.

   a. What is the resulting change in the money supply?

   b. Would the central bank have to buy or sell securities on the open market to add $200 million to reserves?

4. In a simplified banking system with an 8 percent required-reserve ratio, the central bank redeposits $150 million of government funds into the chartered bank reserve accounts that it is holding. What is the resulting change, if any, in the money supply?

5. In a simplified banking system with a 10 percent required-reserve ratio, open-market operations by the central bank reduce chartered bank reserves by $400 million.

   a. What is the resulting change in the money supply?

   b. Would the central bank have to buy or sell securities on the open market to reduce reserves by $400 million?

6. A simplified banking system has a required-reserve ratio of 5 percent. As part of monetary policy, central-bank authorities draw down by $15 million government deposits currently held in the central bank as reserves of the chartered banks (that is, the government funds are transferred from the chartered bank reserves to the central bank). At the same time, the central bank sells $10 million of securities on the open market. What is the net change in the money supply as a result of these two monetary-policy actions?

The Demand for Money and Money-Market Equilibrium

WHAT YOU WILL LEARN IN THIS CHAPTER

After studying this chapter, you will be able to

1. Explain the equation of exchange and the concept of velocity.

2. Show how interest rates and real domestic income affect the demand for money, using the portfolio-balance theory.

3. Draw a money demand curve and explain the causes of shifts in the curve.

4. Use money supply and money demand curves to explain the reaction of the money market to a change in the money supply.

5. Use money supply and demand curves to explain the reaction of the money market to a change in real domestic income.

6. Show how changes in the Bank of Canada's monetary-control strategy affect the shape of the money supply curve.

7. Trace the response of the money stock and interest rates to changes in money demand under different monetary-control strategies.

A Preview   *Inflation and the Demand for Money*

The following excerpt from a Bank of Canada research paper explains how inflation reduces the purchasing power of money, and how this in turn causes people's demand for money — that is, their desire to hold money — to decline. Such ideas are at the core of this chapter.

Why Inflation Causes People to Hold Less Cash

An anticipated decrease in the purchasing power of money imposes a direct cost on the economy because it causes economic agents to hold less money, and therefore individuals "spend more time in ATM [automatic-teller machine] line-ups" replenishing cash balances. Individuals also spend more time rearranging their portfolios to seek out the highest rate of return on their assets.

The reason that inflation causes economic agents to hold less cash is that it increases the opportunity cost of holding money through higher money interest rates. Interest rates rise with inflation because lenders demand compensation for reductions in the purchasing power of money, and borrowers provide this compensation without curbing their appetite for debt because they expect to repay with money that has lost its value. In effect, interest rates rise to reflect an inflation premium. When interest rates rise, people increase their holdings of assets bearing interest payments and reduce their holdings of non-interest-bearing money.

SOURCE: Excerpted from Jack Selody, *The Goal of Price Stability: A Review of the Issues,* Bank of Canada Technical Report no. 54, pp. 4–5. Reproduced with permission.

THE DEMAND FOR MONEY

Chapter 22 defined money and discussed the various things that serve as money and near-moneys in the Canadian economy, and Chapter 23 explained how the supply of money is determined. This chapter turns first to the determination of the demand for money and then to the interaction of the supply and demand for money in the money market. It will lay the groundwork for the discussion of the interaction of monetary and fiscal policy in Chapter 25.

In examining the demand for money, as in dealing with other subjects in economics, it is important to distinguish between stocks and flows. The demand for money is the demand for a stock. It is not a question of how much money people would like to spend per day or per month; that would be a matter of a flow of money. Instead, the demand for money is a matter of how large a share of their total wealth people would at any point in time like to hold in the form of money — that is, as currency or demand deposits — rather than in the form of assets such as securities, real estate, or consumer durables.

Early Views of the Demand for Money

One early view of the demand for money arose from the so-called **equation of exchange**. This equation can be written in the form

$$MV = PY,$$

where M stands for the quantity of money, V for the **velocity** of money (that is, the average number of times each dollar of the money stock is spent each year for income-producing purposes), P for the price level, and Y for real domestic income (assuming constant prices). This equation must always hold, given the way the term *velocity* is defined. Suppose, for example, that real domestic income is $1000 billion and that the price level is 1. Real domestic income thus will be $1 \times \$1000$ billion, or $1000 billion per year. If each dollar is spent an average of five times a year, a money stock of $200 billion will be required to sustain the $1000-billion-per-year domestic income. Sustaining that income with a smaller money stock would require each dollar to be used more than five times a year. If the money stock were larger, the same level of real domestic income could be sustained with a velocity of less than five. In short, the stock of money times the velocity of money must always, because of the way *velocity* is defined, equal domestic income.

The equation of exchange itself is not a theory; it simply shows the relationships among money, velocity, real income, and the price level. An early step toward a theory of the demand for money, however, was to assume that velocity is a constant. This constant number of times that each dollar could be spent each year was thought to be determined by custom and certain other factors, such as how often workers were paid and how fast banks could clear cheques. With constant velocity, the amount of money required to sustain any given level of real domestic income could be found by dividing real domestic income by velocity. In equation form, using MD to stand for **money demand**, PY to stand for domestic income, and V to stand for velocity, this theory of money demand could be written as follows:

$$MD = \frac{PY}{V}$$

Equation of exchange
An equation that shows the relationships among the money stock (M), the velocity of money (V), the price level (P), and the level of real income (Y), written $MV = PY$.

Velocity
The ratio of real domestic income to the money stock; a measure of the average number of times each dollar of the money stock is used each year for income-producing purposes.

Money demand (MD)
The amount of money people wish to hold (in the form of currency and liquid bank deposits), usually measured in relation to different rates of interest.

Keynes on the Demand for Money

When John Maynard Keynes began work on his *General Theory of Employment, Interest and Money*, he was not content with the simple view that the demand for money would be proportional to domestic income because equilibrium velocity was constant. Instead, he developed a more complex theory based on three motives for holding money.

Keynes called the need to hold money as a means of payment the **transactions motive**. Besides holding money for day-to-day purchases, people may also hold some extra money to deal with unexpected events. Keynes called this the **precautionary motive** for holding money. He believed that both the transactions and the precautionary motives were roughly proportional to income, as suggested by the equation of exchange.

Keynes also believed that people had a third motive for holding money, one that was somewhat different from the other two. People may want to hold part of their wealth in the form of money, Keynes said, if they think other forms of wealth are temporarily too risky. Suppose, for example, that interest rates are unusually low. An unusually low level of interest rates implies unusually high prices for bonds. Under these conditions, people may hesitate to hold bonds for fear that their prices will fall. Thus, when bond prices are unusually high, Keynes suggested, people may prefer to hold much of their wealth in the form of money, hoping to exchange the money for bonds after interest rates rise and the price of bonds falls. Keynes called this the **speculative motive** for holding money.

The price of bonds and the rate of interest

A short digression on the subject of bonds is necessary at this point. **Bonds** are simply IOUs of firms and government units. They have been mentioned several times without explanation of one of their important features — the inverse relationship between their price and the rate of interest.

In Canada, long-term corporate bonds are often issued in denominations of $1000. The issuing firm promises to pay the bondholder a certain sum per year for a certain number of years (usually twenty to thirty years) until maturity and, upon maturity, to repay the initial $1000. The annual sum the bondholder receives until maturity is set according to the rate of interest prevailing at the time the bond is issued. If the interest rate is 8 percent, the annual payment on a $1000 bond will be $80; if the interest rate is 10 percent, the payment will be $100; and so on.

In Canada, there are active secondary markets in which bonds of this type can be bought and sold. The original purchaser need not hold the bond until maturity. There is no guarantee, however, that the bond can be sold in the secondary market "at par" — that is, at its original purchase price of $1000. Instead, the price at which the bond can be resold depends on what has happened to the interest rate between the date of issue and the date of resale.

Suppose a certain firm issues a 25-year bond at a time when the interest rate on such bonds is 10 percent, agreeing to pay $100 per year for 25 years plus $1000 on maturity. The original purchase price is $1000. A year later, the original buyer wants to sell the bond; but in the meantime, the interest rate has gone up to 12.5 percent. That means that brand new $1000 bonds are scaled to pay their purchasers $125 per year, so no one is willing to buy last year's bond with the $100 payment unless its price is cut to approximately $800 — since $100 is 12.5 percent of $800. The original buyer of the bond with the $100 annual payment suffers a capital loss of $200 in selling the bond.

Transactions motive
A motive for holding money arising from the convenience of using it as a means of payment for day-to-day transactions.

Precautionary motive
A motive for holding money arising from its usefulness as a reserve of liquid funds for use in emergencies or in taking advantage of unexpected opportunities.

Speculative motive
A motive for holding money arising from its fixed value, when the value of alternative assets is expected to decline.

Bond
A promise, given in recognition of a loan, to make a fixed annual or semiannual payment over a period of years plus a larger final payment equal to the sum initially borrowed.

If, instead, the interest rate had fallen, say, to 5 percent, new bonds would be paying only $50 per year. In that case, the old bond carrying a $100 annual payment could be sold at a premium in the secondary market — for roughly $2000, in fact.

Many short-term government bonds, known as treasury bills (or T-bills), are sold by auction in Canada. The price at which a bond is sold, when calculated in relation to the price at which the government will buy the bond back at maturity, establishes the interest rate for that bond. For example, if a $100 T-bill, redeemable in three months ($100 being the price the government will pay for it after three months) is currently sold for $97.70, the interest rate is 2.35 percent for three months and about 9.4 percent on an annual basis. If that same bond had fetched a higher auction price, say, $98, the annual interest rate would have been lower, at about 8.2 percent.

The important point illustrated by these two examples is this: When interest rates are rising, the price paid for existing bonds in the secondary markets and for newly auctioned bonds will fall. On the other hand, when interest rates are falling, the prices of such bonds will rise. (Canada Saving Bonds are an exception to this practice: They are paid at fixed interest rates.)

That is why, to return to the Keynesian speculative demand for money, when bond prices are unusually high, people may prefer to hold more money and fewer bonds, hoping to exchange money for bonds when bond prices fall (and interest rates rise).

In sum, Keynes thought that the demand for money depends both on the level of domestic income and on interest rates. As domestic income rises, other things being equal, the demand for money will increase because of the transactions and precautionary motives. But given the level of real domestic income, the speculative motive will tend to make the quantity of money demanded increase as interest rates fall and decrease as interest rates rise.

The Portfolio-Balance Theory of Money Demand

Today, most economists accept the notion that the demand for money responds to changes in both real domestic income and interest rates. Keynes's three-way classification of motives for holding money is widely viewed as too rigid, however, and his concept of the link between interest and money demand is seen as too narrow.

Economists today find it useful to talk about the demand for money in terms of the concept of **portfolio balance**. A *portfolio* is simply the collection of assets of all kinds that a person owns. Balancing the portfolio means adjusting the proportions of currency, chequing-account funds, savings deposits, securities, real estate, and so on, to best suit the interests of the portfolio holder. Money is held because of its liquidity.

An asset is said to be liquid, we recall, if it can be used directly as a means of exchange. There is thus a potential advantage to holding a liquid asset such as money instead of less liquid assets such as stocks, bonds, or real estate. The real advantage is that liquidity reduces transaction costs. One doesn't want to have to make a trip to a bank or a broker each week in order to exchange stocks or bonds for money to buy groceries.

Portfolio balance
The balance among the various kinds of assets that a person owns — including money, consumer durables, stocks, and bonds — shifting from one kind of asset to another as economic conditions change.

The opportunity cost of liquidity

Offsetting the advantage of liquidity is a major disadvantage: the more liquid an asset, the less interest it generally tends to pay. Currency and demand deposits in chartered banks generally pay little or no interest. Some of the assets included in M_2 will pay higher interest rates, but even these assets tend to pay a smaller return than such alternatives as shares of stock or long-term bonds when yields are averaged over an extended period. The loss of the higher interest rates available on alternative assets is an opportunity cost of holding money, to be weighed against the advantages of money's liquidity.

A Money Demand Schedule

In the portfolio-balance theory of money demand, the amount of money that people want to hold depends on both their domestic income and the various interest rates on nonmonetary assets. Other things being equal, an increase in real domestic income increases the demand for money. This is because, with higher incomes, people will make more transactions, and they will need more money if they are to do so conveniently. At the same time, other things being equal, an increase in the interest rate will decrease the amount of money demanded. The reason is that an increase in the interest rate increases the opportunity cost of holding money.

The relationship of the amount of money demanded to the interest rate and the level of real domestic income is known as the **money demand schedule**. An example of a money demand schedule for a simple economy is shown in Box 24.1. The entries in the second and third columns of the table give the amount of money demanded when the interest rate is as shown in the first column and the level of real domestic income is as shown at the top of the table. For example, when the interest rate is 10 percent per year and the level of real domestic income is $600 billion, the amount of money demanded is $72 billion. If income remains at $600 billion, but the interest rate falls to 4 percent, the amount of money demanded rises to $180 billion.

Box 24.1 also presents the money demand schedule in graphic form. At any given level of income, the relationship between the amount of money demanded and the interest rate takes the form of a downward-sloping curve that looks much like any other demand curve. For example, the curve labelled MD_1 shows how money demand varies as the interest rate varies when real domestic income is $600 billion. This curve is based on the data in the $600 billion column of the table.

The table and graph also show that when income changes, there is a shift in the money demand curve. The table shows an increase in income to $1200 billion in column 3. When such an increase in income occurs, money demand is higher at every given rate of interest. In fact, when income doubles, money demand doubles. This increase in money demand is illustrated in the graph as a shift of the money demand curve from MD_1 to MD_2. Note, for example, that at an interest rate of 4 percent, MD_2 is at $360 billion while MD_1 is at $180 billion.

The Stability of Money Demand

In Box 24.1, the money demand curve shifts as a result of a change in the level of real domestic income, but there are other factors that can cause the curve to shift as well. Economists are interested in these factors because, as we shall see,

Money demand schedule
A schedule showing the quantity of money that people desire to hold in their portfolios given various values for the interest rate and the level of real domestic income.

A Money Demand Schedule for a Simple Economy   BOX 24.1

The table and graph below show how the amount of money demanded varies in a simple economy as the interest rate (on a representative nonmonetary asset) and the level of real domestic income vary. The entries in columns 2 and 3 of the table show the amount of money demanded at each of the interest rates given in column 1 and at the real domestic income levels shown at the top of the table. Columns 2 and 3 can be graphed to show the money demand curves for levels of real domestic income of $600 billion ($MD_1$) and $1200 billion ($MD_2$).

(a)

(1) Interest Rate (percent)	(2) Money Demand at Real Domestic Income Level of	(3)
	$600 billion	$1200 billion
	(billions of dollars)	
2	360	720
4	180	360
6	120	240
8	90	180
10	72	144
12	60	120
14	51	102

(b)

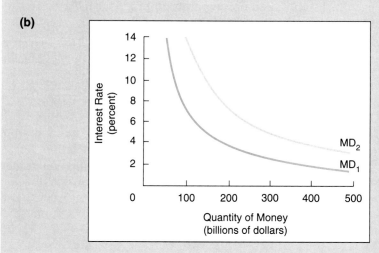

the *stability* of money demand is an important determinant of the effectiveness of monetary policy.

Changes in the velocity of money

In addition to changes in income, changes in the velocity of money can cause the money demand curve to shift. Velocity has already been defined as the number of times each dollar of the money stock is used each year. It is measured as the ratio of domestic income to the money stock. As we saw earlier (page 607), this relationship can be derived from the equation of exchange, $MV = PY$, and the equation for the theory of money demand (assuming constant velocity),

MD = *PY/V*. Inverting the latter equation, we obtain *V* = *PY*/MD (velocity = domestic income/money demand).

Now, let us consider Box 24.1 once more, applying these relationships to money demand when the rate of interest is 6 percent, income is $600 billion, and money demand is $120 billion. Applying our equation for velocity, we see that, at this particular rate of interest, the velocity of money is 5 (*V* = *PY*/MD = $600 billion/$120 billion). The velocity of 5 tells us that people in this economy are able to "turn over" their money stock five times in the course of a given period of time. In other words, they require a stock of money of only $120 billion to carry out transactions totalling $600 billion.

At any given level of income, the velocity of money varies with interest rates. Thus, at an income level of $600 billion, velocity is 5 when the interest rate is 6 percent, but rises to 10 when the interest rate is 12 percent (*V* = *PY*/MD = $600 billion/$60 billion). This tells us that, at such a high interest rate, people choose to hold less money — indeed, they turn it over at twice the rate they did before.

The velocity of money is determined not only by interest rates but also by institutional factors, such as the relative ease with which people can shift back and forth between money and nonmoney assets. Many innovations in the handling of money have been introduced in recent years by both individuals and business firms. The number of available nonmoney options for holding assets even on a very short-term basis — say, a few days or weeks — has increased immensely. For example, rather than putting most of their paycheques into chequing deposits that pay no interest (and form a major part of M_1), people can now deposit those cheques into daily-interest chequing accounts, or savings accounts that allow for withdrawals. The level of income does not change, and the number of transactions being carried out in a given period remains the same, but the amount of money stock required to finance those transactions is reduced. The result is an increase in velocity.

An increase in velocity will shift the money demand curve to the left. This means that at a given level of domestic income, and at any given rate of interest, less money needs to be held for purposes of transactions and speculation. This is illustrated in Box 24.2. In part (a), column 2 reproduces the income and money demand conditions associated with MD_1 in Box 24.1. The income level is $600 billion and, at an interest rate of 6 percent, for example, money demand is $120 billion and velocity, as we discovered, is 5. Column 3, which assumes that domestic income is still $600 billion, shows how money demand changes with an increase in velocity. At an interest rate of 6 percent, for example, money demand is now only $75 billion. At a higher rate of interest, say, 12 percent, money demand has fallen from $60 billion at the initial velocity to $30 billion. This change in money demand resulting from an increase in money velocity is illustrated in the graph in Box 24.2(b) as a shift to the left in the money demand curve, from MD_1 to MD_2.

Thus, as we have seen, the money demand curve will shift to the right as domestic income rises, but it will shift to the left as financial innovations increase the velocity of money. These shifts will, to some extent, counteract each other. In the Canadian economy over the last two decades, however, real domestic income has not increased very rapidly, while financial innovations have. The net effect has been a slight shift to the left of the money demand curve. In other words, at roughly similar interest rates of, say, 8–10 percent, less money is needed per dollar of real domestic income today than was needed in the past.

A Shift in Money Demand Resulting from an Increase in Velocity BOX 24.2

Column 2 of the table below represents the same income and money demand conditions as those that define MD_1 in Box 24.1. Income is $600 billion and, at an interest rate of, say, 6 percent, money demand is $120 billion and velocity is 5. In column 3, the same income level is associated with a lower money demand (for example, at the same interest rate, money demand is only $75 billion), because *velocity* has increased. People now "turn over" their money a greater number of times in any given period. Part (b) illustrates this change as a leftward shift in the money demand curve, from MD_1 to MD_2.

(a)

(1) Interest Rate (percent)	(2) Money Demand at $600 billion Real Domestic Income, with	(3)
	Initial Money Velocity	Increased Money Velocity
	(billions of dollars)	
2	360	250
4	180	125
6	120	75
8	90	60
10	72	45
12	60	30
14	51	20

(b)

EQUILIBRIUM IN THE MONEY MARKET

Thus far, we have discussed the demand and supply of money separately. In this section and the next one, we will put supply and demand together. The result is a graph such as the one shown in Box 24.3. The horizontal axis shows the stock of money; the vertical axis shows the interest rate. The interest rate is the "price" of holding money — or, as explained earlier, the opportunity cost of holding part of a portfolio of assets in the form of non-interest-bearing money rather than in the form of a representative nonmonetary interest-bearing asset.

BOX 24.3 *Equilibrium in the Money Market*

The money demand curve shown here is based on the data given in Box 24.1, assuming a real domestic income level of $1200 billion. The money supply curve assumes that the Bank of Canada sets a money supply target of $180 billion and adjusts total reserves to maintain this quantity of money regardless of what happens to interest rates. Under these conditions, the equilibrium interest rate is 8 percent.

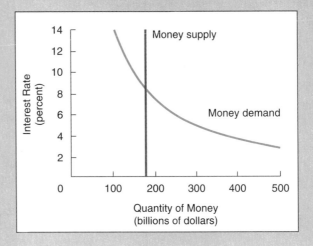

The money demand curve in Box 24.3 shows the amount of money that people want to hold at each given interest rate. An increase in real domestic income will shift the money demand curve to the right; a decrease in real domestic income will shift it to the left. Other factors, such as changes in velocity, can also cause the demand curve to shift, as we have seen.

The shape of the money supply curve depends on the policy of the Bank of Canada. The supply curve in Box 24.3 assumes that the Bank of Canada sets a target for the money stock ($180 billion, in this case) and adjusts reserves to hold the money stock on target regardless of what happens to the interest rate. This assumption results in a vertical money supply curve. (In the final section of this chapter, we will discuss other kinds of money supply curves.)

We will refer to a supply–demand situation such as the one shown in Box 24.3 as the "money market," but it should be understood that this is not a market in quite the usual sense. We usually think of a market as a place where people buy and sell things — that is, where they exchange things for money. People do not "buy" and "sell" money in this sense. Despite these unusual features, supply and demand do interact in the so-called money market to produce an equilibrium much as they do in markets of the more familiar kind.

The supply and demand curves in Box 24.3 intersect at an interest rate of 8 percent. At that interest rate, the amount of money supplied by the banking system (which is determined, in turn, by the amount of reserves supplied by the Bank of Canada to the banking system) is just equal to the amount that people want to hold in their portfolios. There is neither upward nor downward pressure on interest rates.

No other interest rate would permit such an equilibrium. Suppose, for example, that the interest rate were only 4 percent. With such a low opportunity cost of holding money, people would want to hold more of it. An individual or a firm can add money to a portfolio by selling some other asset—shares of stock, bonds, treasury bills, or real goods. Let us consider bonds as an example. If a large number of people try to sell bonds for money at the same time, the price of bonds will tend to fall. As has been explained, a fall in the price of bonds means an increase in the yield on bonds. If people were trying to sell other kinds of assets to get money, yields on those assets would rise too. In time, the whole family of interest rates would rise back up to 8 percent, bringing the money market back to the equilibrium depicted in Box 24.3.

Note that, the way the graph in Box 24.3 is drawn, a rising interest rate brings the market back into equilibrium by reducing the amount of money demanded, not by increasing the amount of money supplied. As long as the Bank of Canada does not provide more reserves to the banking system, banks cannot supply any more money. People's or firms' adding money to their portfolios by selling other assets does not affect the amount of money in the banking system as a whole. It just moves reserves from the buyers' banks to the sellers' banks.

Exactly the same story can be told in reverse for the case in which the interest rate is higher than its equilibrium value. In that case, people will want to hold less money. They will try to get rid of money by buying other assets. This will drive the price of those assets up, consequently driving interest rates down. But as long as the Bank of Canada keeps the total reserves of the banking system constant, all this buying and selling will only move money from one bank to another; it will not change the money stock as a whole.

Effects of a Change in the Money Supply

The description we have given of the money market is useful for a number of purposes. Let's begin by using it to analyze the effects of changes in the money supply.

Box 24.4 shows the money market in equilibrium at point E_1, with a money supply of $180 billion and an interest rate of 8 percent. Starting from this point, the Bank of Canada decides to increase the money supply to $360 billion. Assuming a money multiplier of 10, it can do this by injecting $18 billion of new reserves into the banking system by means of open-market purchases.

The immediate impact of the open-market operation is to boost banks' excess reserves. In order to restore their balance sheets to equilibrium, banks set out to convert the excess reserves into earning assets. In part, this means buying securities. The increased demand for securities pushes up their price and pushes down their yield. The banks also convert their excess reserves into earning assets by making new loans. Competition among banks in making loans tends to push down interest rates on loans.

As banks work off their excess reserves, the money supply expands, as explained in Chapter 23. In Box 24.4, this is shown as a shift in the money supply curve from MS_1 to MS_2. At point E_1, people were content to hold the original quantity of money, $180 billion, in their portfolios. Now, falling interest rates reduce the opportunity cost of holding money, making people willing to absorb the increased quantity that banks supply. Thus, as the injection of reserves shifts the money supply curve to the right, falling interest rates cause people to move downward and to the right along their money demand curve. In time, a

BOX 24.4   *Effects of an Increase in the Money Supply*

The money supply starts out at $180 billion, putting the money supply curve in the position MS₁. An open-market purchase by the Bank of Canada injects new reserves into the banking system. Efforts by banks to put the new reserves to work by buying securities and making loans drive the interest rate down as the money supply expands. At the new equilibrium, E_2, the interest rate has fallen by enough to make people willing to hold the larger quantity of money.

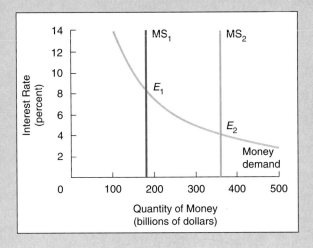

new equilibrium is reached at point E_2, where the stock of money is greater and the interest rate is lower than it was before.

If the Bank of Canada withdraws reserves from the banking system through an open-market sale, the same process happens in reverse. Banks find themselves with less than the required quantity of reserves. They respond by selling securities or reducing their volume of loans — actions that tend to raise the interest rate. As the money supply curve shifts to the left, rising interest rates make people content to hold only the reduced quantity of money in their portfolios. A new equilibrium is reached at a point where the money supply is smaller and the interest rate higher than it was before.

Effects of an Increase in Income

In discussing the effects of a change in the money supply, we assumed that the level of real domestic income stayed constant. Let's reverse that assumption and see what happens to the money market when real domestic income changes while the money supply remains constant.

Box 24.5 sets the stage. It shows the market in equilibrium at point E_1, with an interest rate of 4 percent and a money supply of $180 billion. Real domestic income is assumed to be $600 billion, which puts the money demand curve in the position MD₁.

Effects of an increase in Real Domestic Income   BOX 24.5

A real domestic income of $600 billion puts the money demand curve at MD_1. The equilibrium interest rate is 4 percent, given this income and the money supply of $180 billion. If an increase in real income to $1200 billion shifts the money demand curve to MD_2, there will be an excess demand for money at the initial interest rate. People will try to increase the quantity of money in their portfolios by selling other assets. In the process, the prices of those assets are bid down and interest rates rise.

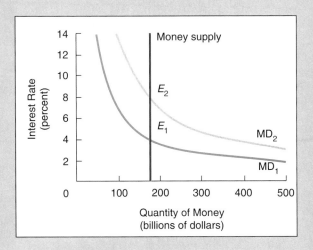

Assume now that real domestic income rises to a level of $1200 billion. As we saw earlier in the chapter, an increase in real domestic income, other things being equal, shifts the money demand curve to the right. The new position of the money demand curve is MD_2.

At the new, higher income level, people will be making a greater volume of transactions than before. Other things being equal, they would want more money to carry out the extra transactions — but the supply of money is limited to $180 billion by Bank of Canada policy. Because banks are not supplying more money to support the higher income, people try to get the extra money by selling other assets. This does not increase the money supply as a whole, but it does drive up interest rates. The higher interest rates make people willing to get along with the limited money supply that is available, despite the fact that their incomes are now higher. Thus, the economy moves to a new equilibrium at point E_2. There, real domestic income and the interest rate are higher than they were before, and the money supply has not changed.

If real domestic income falls, the same process occurs in reverse. With lower incomes, people do not need as much money for transactions. They buy other assets to replace money in their portfolios. Doing this tends to push interest rates down. When interest rates fall enough to make people content to hold the existing stock of money even at a lower level of real domestic income, the money market will be back in equilibrium. The interest rate and real domestic income will be lower than they were before, and the money supply will be unchanged.

MONETARY-CONTROL STRATEGIES AND INTEREST RATES

Our analysis of the money market suggests that traders in the bond and stock market — and anyone who is interested in interest rates — need to pay attention to what the Bank of Canada is doing. In this section, we shift our point of view from that of private individuals and firms to that of the Bank of Canada.

Exactly what role interest rates should play in planning and carrying out monetary policy is a matter of considerable debate. Some economists believe that the Bank of Canada's job is to keep the money supply under control; having done that, it should let interest rates go wherever the market sends them. Other economists, along with many business people, think that part of the Bank of Canada's job should be to prevent sharp upswings and downswings in interest rates. Large swings in interest rates, they say, can disrupt business planning, thereby hurting employment and productivity. In this section, we will explore three different strategies of monetary control and their relationship to interest rates.

Three Monetary-Control Strategies

Box 24.6 shows three possible monetary control strategies, each represented by a different money supply curve.

1. *Monetary-supply targetting* The first strategy is one of strict money-supply targetting. This is the strategy that was assumed in the last section and that was followed by the Bank of Canada from 1975 to 1982: The Bank of Canada selects a target for the money supply and adjusts the level of bank reserves to maintain the money supply at the target level regardless of what happens to interest rates. This strategy is represented by the vertical money supply curve, MS_1. With the money demand curve in the position MD, a money supply of $200 billion would, as shown, result in an equilibrium interest rate of 8 percent.

2. *Interest-rate targetting* The second strategy is one of interest-rate targetting. In this strategy, the Bank of Canada begins by deciding what it would like the interest rate to be. It then uses open-market operations to adjust the money supply so that the equilibrium interest rate will be at the target level. This strategy is represented by a horizontal money supply curve. If the interest-rate target is 8 percent, the money supply curve will be in the position MS_2. Given the money demand curve MD, the Bank of Canada would have to allow the money stock to settle at $200 billion to hit the 8 percent target. If the money demand curve were to shift to the right or left, the Bank of Canada would use open-market purchases or sales to adjust the money stock along the path MS_2.

3. *No specific target* The third strategy is the one represented by MS_3. In this case, the Bank of Canada targets neither the money supply nor the interest rate. Instead, it allows the money supply to expand whenever the interest rate rises, but not enough to offset the rise in the interest rate entirely.

LOOKING AHEAD

This completes our initial discussion of the supply and demand for money. The important next step — to apply this theory to the problem of domestic-income

Three Monetary-Control Strategies

BOX 24.6

The slope of the money supply curve depends on the Bank of Canada's monetary-control strategy. The Bank of Canada can set a target for the money supply and stick to it regardless of what happens to interest rates. In this case, the money supply curve will be vertical (MS₁). Alternatively, the Bank can set a target for the interest rate and use open-market operations to stabilize the rate (at least in the short run), regardless of what happens to the money stock. In this case, the money supply curve is horizontal (MS₂). Finally, the Bank of Canada can allow the money supply to expand as the interest rate rises. This results in an upward-sloping money supply curve (MS₃).

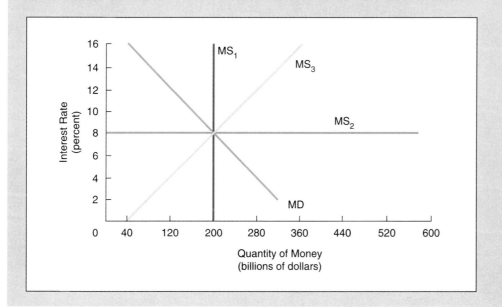

determination — is the aim of the next chapter. That chapter will show how the inclusion of the money market in the analysis of domestic-income determination leads to some important modifications of the multiplier theory and sets the stage for the discussion of inflation and unemployment.

SUMMARY

1. Using M for the quantity of money, V for the velocity of money, P for the price level, and PY for real domestic income, the *equation of exchange* can be written $MV = PY$. The term *velocity* means the average number of times each year that each dollar of the money stock is used for income-producing purposes.

2. According to the modern theory of *money demand*, people hold part of their *portfolios* — that is, their assortment of assets — in the form of money in order to gain the benefits of liquidity. Since most forms of money pay either no interest or a lower rate of interest than less liquid assets pay, the interest rate can be thought of as the opportunity cost of holding money. Other things

being equal, a decrease in the interest rate tends to increase the amount of money demanded. Also, other things being equal, an increase in real domestic income tends to increase the demand for money.

3. The demand for money can be represented by a downward-sloping curve on a graph in which the horizontal axis measures the quantity of money and the vertical axis measures the interest rate. An increase in real domestic income shifts the money demand curve to the right; a decrease in real domestic income shifts it to the left. Other factors, particularly changes in velocity, can also cause shifts in the money demand curve.

4. The money market can be represented by a vertical money supply curve and a downward-sloping money demand curve. If the quantity of money is increased while domestic income remains constant, the market will move to a new equilibrium at a lower rate of interest. The lower interest rate is needed to induce people to hold the greater quantity of money.

5. If real domestic income rises while the quantity of money remains constant, there will be an excess demand for money. This will cause people to try to adjust their portfolios, selling other assets in order to obtain money. In the process, interest rates will be pushed up and the money market will move to a new equilibrium. A decrease in real domestic income will cause an excess supply of money, leading to a fall in interest rates.

6. The slope of the money supply curve is determined by the Bank of Canada's money-control strategy. If the Bank of Canada chooses a target for the money supply and sticks to it regardless of what happens to interest rates, the money supply curve will be vertical. If it sets an interest-rate target, the money supply curve will be horizontal. In cases in which the interest rate is allowed to vary but an increase in the interest rate is partly offset by an increase in the money stock, the money supply curve will slope upward to the right.

KEY TERMS

equation of exchange
velocity
money demand (MD)
transactions motive for holding
   money

precautionary motive for
   holding money
speculative motive for holding
   money

bond
portfolio balance
money demand schedule

KEY BOXES

Box 24.1 A Money Demand Schedule for a Simple Economy
Box 24.2 A Shift in Money Demand Resulting from an Increase in Velocity
Box 24.3 Equilibrium in the Money Market

Box 24.4 Effects of an Increase in the Money Supply
Box 24.5 Effects of an Increase in Real Domestic Income
Box 24.6 Three Monetary-Control Strategies

REVIEW QUESTIONS

1. If the quantity of money is $100 billion and real domestic income is $500 billion, what is the velocity of money? If real domestic income remains constant while velocity increases to 10, what will happen to the money demand schedule?

2. According to the portfolio-balance theory, how does a change in the interest rate affect the demand for money? How does a change in real domestic income affect the demand for money?

3. Are the effects of an increase in real domestic income best shown by a movement along the money demand curve or by a shift in the curve? In which way are the effects of a change in the interest rate best shown?

4. Are the effects of an open-market purchase by the Bank of Canada best shown by a rightward shift in the money supply curve, a leftward shift in the curve, or a movement along the curve? How does the interest rate change in response to an open-market purchase, other things being equal?

5. Are the effects of an increase in real domestic income, with no change in the money supply, best shown by a rightward shift in the money demand curve, a leftward shift in the curve, or a movement along the curve? What happens to interest rates as a result of an increase in real domestic income?

6. What is the shape of the money supply curve when the Bank of Canada pursues a strategy of setting a strict target for the money supply? A strategy of setting an interest-rate target? An intermediate strategy, setting neither the money supply nor the interest rate?

7. Using the *Bank of Canada Review* or some other source, find the most recent values for the money supply (both M_1 and M_2), the price level (use the GDP deflator), and real domestic income. Use the equation of exchange to determine the velocities of M_1 and M_2. Which velocity is greater?

8. Rework the example given in Box 24.4 for the case of a decrease in the money supply from $180 billion to $120 billion.

9. Rework the example given in Box 24.5 for the case of a decrease in real domestic income from $600 billion to $400 billion. (Create a hypothetical money demand schedule to determine the demand curve at a real domestic income of $400 billion.)

10. Discussions of monetary policy often refer to "tight" or "easy" policy. If the Bank of Canada pursues a strategy of strict money-supply targetting, the meaning of these terms is simple: Tightening policy means shifting the money supply curve to the left, while easing policy means shifting it to the right. If the Bank of Canada is using a strategy of interest-rate targetting, tightening policy means raising the interest-rate target and easing policy means lowering it. Sketch a graph that shows the effects of tightening and easing policy, using a horizontal money supply curve and assuming no shift in the money demand curve. If the Bank of Canada is pursuing an intermediate policy, tightening means a shift upward and to the left in the sloping money supply schedule and easing means a shift downward and to the right in the sloping money supply schedule. Sketch these cases as well.

11. In mid-summer of 1991, financial newspapers ran articles over the course of several days suggesting that a possible fall in the value of the Canadian dollar relative to the U.S. dollar might cause a rise in Canadian interest rates. The concern was that the Bank of Canada might increase the bank rate.

    a. Why would the Bank of Canada consider raising the bank rate when the value of the Canadian dollar was falling?

    b. What difference would higher interest rates make to the economy?

    Explain your answers.

12. Assume that the level of domestic income is $1000, and use the equation of exchange and the money demand equation to answer the following:

    a. If the velocity of money is 8, what is the demand for money?

    b. If velocity increases to 10, how will the demand for money change?

    c. Assuming that the level of domestic income remains at $1000, what could cause the velocity of money to increase?

13. a. What effect, if any, is the increased velocity described in Question 12 likely to have on the money demand curve?

b. Assuming a vertical and fixed money supply curve, what will happen to the interest rate as a result of the increase in velocity?

The Interaction of Monetary and Fiscal Policy

WHAT YOU WILL LEARN IN THIS CHAPTER

After studying this chapter, you will be able to

1. Explain how a firm balances the opportunity costs of investments against the benefits of those investments.

2. Draw an investment schedule for the economy and explain movements along the schedule and shifts in it.

3. Describe the main linkages between the money market and the circular flow of income and product.

4. Use Keynesian theory to find equilibrium values for real domestic income and interest rates under given conditions.

5. Use Keynesian theory to explain the effects of fiscal policy on real domestic income and interest rates.

6. Use Keynesian theory to show how monetary policy affects real domestic income and interest rates.

7. Discuss problems of co-ordinating monetary and fiscal policy.

8. Outline the Keynesian–monetarist debate over the transmission mechanism.

Economic policy is a team effort. Numerous players are involved, led by the federal government's Department of Finance and the Bank of Canada. Unfortunately, the efforts of these players are often not sufficiently well co-ordinated. Sometimes, as the following article suggests, one player is asked to take on more than its fair share of responsibility.

"Too Much Is Expected from Monetary Policy Alone"

In the past half century, the Bank of Canada has been a major player in all Canadian economic developments. Using open-market operations, moral suasion, and an iron hand in velvet glove, the central bank's monetary policies have played a key role in determining the environment for economic activity, the pace of business, and our standard of living.

Of course, as the Bank itself has attested on many occasions, its actions have not always produced economic results satisfactory to all. Though the Bank is at times blamed for being "too late" with a just-right policy, it is only one agent influencing the economic climate. In addition, it has only one effective control — adjusting the cash reserves of the banking system and, ultimately, the growth in the money supply.

The limitation, of course, is the other policies, most particularly the government's fiscal policies, with which the central bankers must work. "In my mind," former governor Louis Rasminsky says, "too much is expected from monetary policy alone. What you have to be concerned with is the whole mix of policies.

Over the years, people have learned that monetary policy is not a panacea; you can't make up for the deficiencies of other policies through monetary policy. It is the whole complex of policies that determines what our situation is and you can't look to the central bank to have continuous prosperity."

SOURCE: Barry Critchley, *Financial Post*, July 7, 1984, p. 13.

EXPLORING THE INTERACTION OF TWO SETS OF POLICIES

As our Preview suggests, the federal government can use a broad mix of policies to try to control prices, the level of output, and other major economic forces in the economy. Fiscal policy (Chapter 21) comprises the taxation and spending measures used by the government to control economic activity. In Chapter 23 we devoted our attention to another set of policies—monetary policies—which are largely under the control of the Bank of Canada. Neither of these two sets of policies can be used very effectively on its own.

In this chapter, we will examine the interaction of monetary and fiscal policy. We will then be prepared to consider in greater detail how changes in the level of real domestic income and employment can be effected through a mix of fiscal and monetary policies.

In exploring the interaction of fiscal and monetary policy, we will begin with a theoretical framework based on the work of Keynes and his followers. Recent experience has cast doubt on the usefulness of many of the Keynesians' specific policy suggestions. Still, the theoretical framework set forth by Keynes in his *General Theory of Employment, Interest and Money* remains alive and well. It is the language in which Keynesians, neo-Keynesians, anti-Keynesians, and post-Keynesians conduct their debates.

THE KEYNESIAN THEORY OF INCOME DETERMINATION

In discussing fiscal and monetary policy, we have looked at different sectors of the economy without explaining how they interact. One is that of the circular flow of domestic income and product. Here, we deal with markets for goods and services. Another is the monetary sector, which is concerned with the supply and demand for such assets as money, bonds, and other securities.

We know in a general way that financial markets and the circular flow are linked, because we know that investment funds flow through financial markets on their way from households to firms.

Now it is time to look more closely at how events in the monetary sector affect the circular flow of income and product and how these sectors interact to produce an equilibrium level of real domestic income. The interaction occurs particularly through investment and the rate of interest; hence, our starting point in linking these sectors will be a simple theory of investment. At first, we will limit our discussion to an economy in which there is no inflation. All changes in income will take the form of changes in *real* income. This assumption is justified not because it is always realistic, but simply because it is easier to take things one at a time.

A Simple Theory of Investment

Business firms must constantly invest. They must acquire new plant and equipment to replace what wears out each year. They must invest in more plant and equipment in order to grow and to adapt to changing conditions, such as foreign competition and higher energy costs. They must invest in inventory to smooth out variations in the timing of input purchases, rates of production, and sales of final products. To do all this, they must somehow acquire the needed funds. Many firms are fortunate enough to have a steady flow of profits, some of which can be used for investment before the balance is paid out to owners. Other firms obtain funds by borrowing, either directly from the public or through financial intermediaries. Still others bring in new partners or shareholders as a means of raising funds for investment.

The opportunity cost of capital

Whatever the source of a firm's investment funds, acquiring new fixed capital or inventories always involves an opportunity cost. The opportunity cost of capital is the interest rate that must be paid for funds that are obtained from outside the firm or that could be earned by investing the firm's own funds elsewhere. There is no free capital. A firm that spends its own profits on new office equipment could have earned interest on those funds by depositing them in a bank, buying government securities, or lending them to another firm. A firm that borrows to buy its capital goods must pay the interest rate charged by the lenders. And a firm that obtains investment funds by drawing in new partners or shareholders must offer those new owners a rate of return on the capital they bring with them that is at least equal to what they could have obtained by putting their funds to work elsewhere.

How much to invest?

At any given time, dozens or hundreds of investment opportunities may present themselves to a firm. A regional sales office may be built in a distant city. Production equipment may be modernized. Larger supplies of raw materials may be kept on hand to guard against supply disruptions. Somehow, the firm's managers must decide which projects to undertake and how far to carry each one. In doing so, they must weigh the potential benefits, in terms of increased profits, against the opportunity cost of capital — that is, of obtaining the needed investment funds.

The investment schedule

Marginal efficiency of investment
The expected rate of return on an additional dollar of planned investment.

Investment schedule
A downward-sloping schedule that shows the connection between desired investment and the interest rate, other things being equal.

Two basic principles underlie all theories of investment: First, as a firm's investment outlays increase, the expected rate of return on the last dollar invested tends to fall. In the language of economics, the **marginal efficiency of investment** is said to decrease as the annual flow of investment increases. Second, it is profitable for a firm to expand its investment outlays up to, but not beyond, the point at which the marginal efficiency of investment drops below the opportunity cost of capital, as measured by a representative rate of interest.

Putting these two principles together makes it possible to draw an **investment schedule** for an entire economy. Such a schedule shows the amount of desired investment for all business firms associated with each rate of interest. The way the investment schedule in Box 25.1 is drawn, a 20 percent interest rate is associated with $200 billion of desired investment spending for the economy as a whole. The marginal efficiency of investment in this economy is such that the first $200 billion of investment will yield a return greater than 20 percent. Business firms can therefore afford to invest this amount when the interest rate is 20 percent. The return on investments beyond $200 billion is expected to be less than 20 percent, so investment spending reaches its limit at $200 billion when the rate of interest — which represents the opportunity cost of investment — is 20 percent.

An Investment Schedule for an Entire Economy BOX 25.1

This graph shows that desired investment is related negatively to the rate of interest. Because the rate of return — the marginal efficiency of investment — is assumed to decline as investment increases, spending on investment will rise only as the opportunity cost of investing, as represented by the rate of interest, declines.

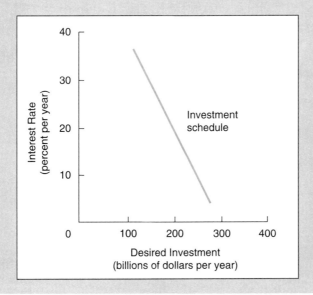

Any change in the interest rate, other things being equal, will produce a movement along the investment schedule. In Box 25.1, a decrease in the interest rate to 10 percent will cause desired investment to increase to $250 billion. It now pays business firms to invest in projects whose rate of return (marginal efficiency of investment) is no less than 10 percent. By contrast, an increase in the interest rate to 25 percent will cause total desired investment to shrink to $175 billion.

Shifts in the investment schedule

Any change in the conditions covered by the "other things being equal" clause will shift the investment schedule.

As a general rule, anything that increases the expected rate of return on investment will shift the investment curve upward and to the right, and anything that decreases the expected return will shift it downward and to the left. Sometimes, technological advances can spur investment in a major sector of the economy, as was the case with railways in the nineteenth century and automobiles early in this century. Today, investment in "high-tech" equipment, ranging from word processors to welding robots, is booming. More broadly, expectations about long-term growth trends and population trends affect the level of desired investment. In the short run, forecasts of business conditions can strongly affect the timing of fixed investments and can even more strongly influence the level of planned inventory investment. Whatever the source, an increase in confidence regarding the long- or short-run economic future will tend to shift the investment schedule upward and to the right. A decrease in confidence will tend to shift the investment schedule downward and to the left.

Linkages between the Money Market and the Circular Flow

Transmission mechanism
The mechanism through which monetary policy affects the equilibrium level of real domestic income.

In the Keynesian theory of income determination, the investment schedule serves as the linkage, or **transmission mechanism**, through which monetary policy acts on the circular flow of income and product. In turn, changes in the level of income within the circular flow have a feedback effect on the money market. In Box 25.2, these effects are represented by arrows.

The interest rate–investment transmission mechanism

First look at the arrow running from the money market to the investment schedule to the aggregate expenditure curve. The intersection of the money supply and the money demand curves determines the equilibrium interest rate — 8 percent in this example. Given the position of the investment schedule, the interest rate determines the volume of desired investment spending — $100 billion a year in this case. This $100 billion of desired investment then becomes the I of $C + I + G + X - M$ — that is, of aggregate desired expenditure. Finally, the intersection of the aggregate expenditure curve and the 45° line (Z) determines the equilibrium level of real domestic income within the circular flow.

Any change in the interest rate will be transmitted through this channel. For example, an increase in the interest rate, other things being equal, will cause a movement upward and to the left along the investment schedule. This will reduce the level of desired investment. As the I component of aggregate desired expenditure falls, the entire aggregate expenditure curve will shift downward. The equilibrium level of real domestic income will thus be reduced.

A decrease in the interest rate, other things being equal, will produce a movement downward and to the right along the investment schedule. This will increase the investment component of aggregate desired expenditure and shift the aggregate expenditure curve upward. The point at which the aggregate expenditure curve and the equilibrium line (Z) intersect will move to the right, indicating an increase in the equilibrium level of real nominal domestic income.

Feedback from domestic income to the money market

The second arrow in Box 25.2 shows the feedback from real domestic income to the money demand curve. As we learned in Chapter 24, the position of the money demand curve depends on the level of domestic income. An increase in income shifts the money demand curve to the right, and a decrease shifts it to the left.

The position of the money demand curve, as determined by the level of real domestic income, determines the point at which it intersects the money supply curve. A rightward shift in the money demand curve (caused by an increase in real domestic income) will raise the equilibrium interest rate; a leftward shift (caused by a decrease in real income) will lower the equilibrium interest rate.

Finding the Equilibrium Values of Real Domestic Income and the Interest Rate

Because the money market and the circular flow are so closely linked, they can be in equilibrium together only when certain values of real domestic income and the interest rate prevail. Let the required level of real domestic income be Y, and

The Interaction of Money and Real Domestic Income   BOX 25.2

The money market and the circular flow can be in equilibrium at the same time only if a certain pair of values for real domestic income and the interest rate prevail. The large arrows in this diagram show how the interest rate and real domestic income interact. The equilibrium interest rate determines the equilibrium level of desired investment, thereby determining the position of the aggregate desired expenditure curve. The intersection of the aggregate expenditure curve and the equilibrium line (Z) determines the equilibrium level of real domestic income, which in turn determines the position of the money demand curve.

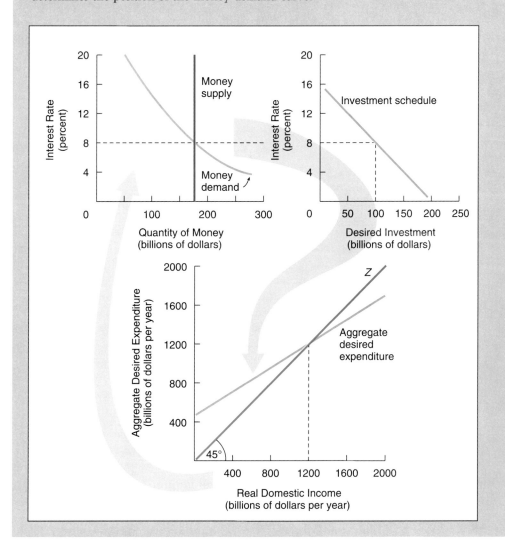

the required interest rate, *r*. The value of *r* must be just right to induce the level of desired investment needed to put the equilibrium level of real domestic income exactly at the level *Y*, and the value of *Y* must be just right to put the money demand curve in the position needed to keep the equilibrium interest rate at *r*.

The way the graphs in Box 25.2 are drawn, an interest rate of 8 percent and a real domestic income of $1200 billion are called for. The aggregate expenditure schedule is drawn on the assumptions that autonomous desired consumption is $100 billion, the marginal propensity to consume is 0.75(based on disposable income), government purchases are $280 billion, net exports are $75 billion −0.15 of domestic income, and net taxes[1] are $100 billion. Desired investment must therefore be $100 billion in order for equilibrium real domestic income to be $1200 billion. A check of the investment schedule reveals that an interest rate of 8 percent is needed to encourage just that amount of investment.

In the money market, where a money supply of $180 billion is assumed, the money demand curve must be in exactly the position shown in Box 25.2 for the equilibrium rate of interest to be 8 percent. This position corresponds to a real domestic income of $1200 billion. Thus, $r = 8$ percent and $Y = \$1200$ billion are an equilibrium pair of values for the interest rate and real domestic income. Any higher level of real domestic income would put the money demand curve too far to the right, giving too high an interest rate, and any lower level would put it too far to the left, giving too low an interest rate. In the next section, we examine what happens when this complex equilibrium between the money market and the income–expenditure market (the circular flow) is upset.

MONETARY AND FISCAL POLICY IN THE KEYNESIAN MODEL

In previous chapters, we have discussed fiscal and monetary policy under assumptions that left out interactions between the money market and the circular flow. In Chapter 21, for example, when we looked at the effects of changes in taxes and government purchases, we assumed that these policy changes would leave private desired investment unchanged. In Chapter 24, we looked at the effects of changes in the money supply while assuming that the money demand curve did not move. Now we will relax these assumptions to take into account the economic interactions shown in Box 25.2. The result will be a modification of our earlier conclusions regarding both fiscal and monetary policy.

A Revised Look at the Effects of Fiscal Policy

Effects of a change in government purchases

In Chapter 21, we concluded that when government purchases increase while net taxes, investment, net exports, and the consumption schedule stay the same, equilibrium domestic income will change by an amount equal to the change in government purchases times the multiplier (assuming no change in prices). If interactions between the level of real domestic income and the level of desired investment are taken into account, however, this conclusion must be revised.

Suppose that the economy starts out in equilibrium with interest rate r and real domestic income Y. Fiscal-policy makers then decide to increase government purchases by $100 billion, with no change in net taxes. What are the effects of this policy as they work their way through the economy?

---

[1]Throughout this discussion, all taxes are assumed to be lump-sum taxes.

The first effect of the increase in government purchases is to shift the aggregate expenditure schedule upward by $100 billion. Desired expenditure now exceeds domestic product at the initial income level. This causes unplanned depletion of inventories, to which firms respond by increasing output. Therefore, the level of real domestic income begins to rise.

Money-market effects

As real domestic income rises, the change in fiscal policy begins to affect the money market. The increase in domestic income causes the money demand curve to shift rightward. In Box 25.3, this is shown as a shift of the money demand curve from its initial position, MD_1, to a new position, MD_2. The money demand curve shifts to the right because when incomes rise, people tend to want more money in their portfolios. Because the money supply does not increase, people's attempts to get more money by selling securities simply drive down the prices of these securities, thereby driving up interest rates. In sum, then, the effect on the money market of the increase in government purchases is to push up the interest rate.

The crowding-Out effect

Let us turn now to the investment schedule shown in Box 25.3. Increased demand for money has driven up the interest rate. As a result, firms find it more costly to undertake fixed investment projects and to increase their inventories of raw materials or finished goods. They therefore reduce their desired investment

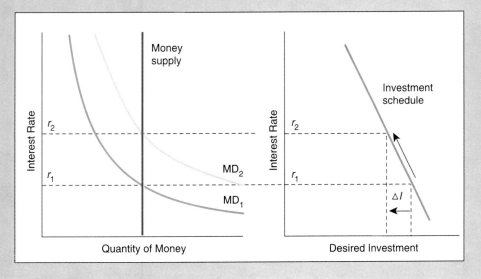

The Crowding-Out Effect   BOX 25.3

An increase in government purchases causes real domestic income to rise via the multiplier effect. The increase in income shifts the money demand curve from its initial position, MD_1, to a new position, MD_2. The equilibrium interest rate rises from r_1 to r_2. An amount of private investment equal to ΔI is crowded out.

Crowding-out effect
The tendency of an increase in desired government purchases to increase the interest rate and thereby decrease the level of desired investment.

spending. This is shown by a movement upward and to the left along the investment schedule. This decrease in desired investment as a result of an increase in government purchases is called the **crowding-out effect**. The amount of investment crowded out is labelled ΔI (that is, "change in desired investment") in the graph.

The change in desired investment that results from crowding out has an effect, in turn, on aggregate desired expenditure. This is shown in Box 25.4, where the original position of the aggregate expenditure curve is shown as ADE_1. Taken by itself, the increase in government purchases would have pushed the schedule all the way up to position ADE_2 (again, ignoring possible price increases). That position is never reached, however. When the crowding-out effect is taken into account, it is clear that the upward shift in aggregate desired expenditures is less than the amount of the increase in government purchases. If ΔG stands for the increase in government purchases, and ΔI, for the amount of investment that is crowded out, the upward shift is reduced to $\Delta G - \Delta I$. This puts the highest and final position reached by the aggregate expenditure curve at ADE_3 rather than ADE_2.

If we look at Boxes 25.3 and 25.4 together, we can see that both income and the interest rate have changed as a result of the increase in government purchases. The new equilibrium interest rate, r_2, and the new equilibrium domestic income, Y_2, are higher than they were to begin with, but private desired investment is lower.

BOX 25.4   *The Crowding-Out Effect*

Here, the crowding-out effect is shown from the standpoint of aggregate desired expenditure and real domestic income. Taken by itself, the increase in government purchases (ΔG) would push the aggregate expenditure curve from ADE_1 to ADE_2. The crowding-out effect chops ΔI off desired investment, however, so the actual shift is from ADE_1 to only ADE_3, a distance equal to $\Delta G - \Delta I$.

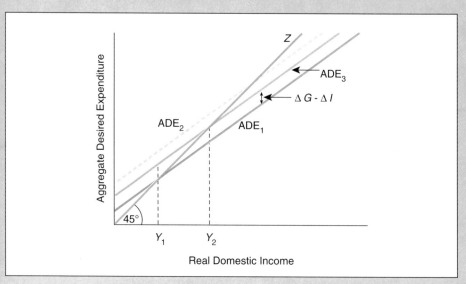

Crowding out and the multiplier

Because an increase in government purchases crowds out some private investment, real domestic income does not increase by the full amount of the multiplier times the increase in government purchases (even when the effect of possible price changes is ignored). This fact does not directly contradict the conclusion reached in Chapter 21, however. That conclusion was based on the assumption that desired investment would not change when the level of real domestic income changed. However, as we have now seen, that assumption must be revised when the interactions between the money market and the level of real domestic income are taken into account. This means that we have to modify the way the multiplier theory is applied to the analysis of fiscal policy. The multiplier must now be applied not just to the change in government purchases but to the changes in government purchases minus the induced change in private desired investment.

The new way of applying the multiplier theory can be put in the form of a simple equation. Using ΔY to represent the change in real domestic income resulting from a change in government purchases (ΔG) and using $1/(1 - \text{MPC}_D)$ to stand for the multiplier, we find that

$$\Delta Y = \frac{1}{1 - \text{MPC}_D} \times (\Delta G - \Delta I)$$

Crowding out and tax policy

There can also be a crowding-out effect when taxes are changed. As we saw in Chapter 21, a tax cut, with government purchases unchanged, tends to shift the consumption component of the aggregate expenditure schedule upward. As aggregate desired expenditure expands, the money demand curve is shifted to the right, just as it was when the expansion began with increased government purchases. The resulting rise in the interest rate and decline in desired investment partly offset the expansionary impact of the tax cut. In the Keynesian theory, then, a tax cut, like an increase in government purchases, will cause both the equilibrium level of real domestic income and the interest rate to rise.

Is there a crowding-out effect in Canada?

Studies in the United States indicate that a growing government debt has had an impact on interest rates and on investment. In Canada, studies by the Economic Council of Canada[2] reveal a somewhat weaker connection between government debt, interest rates, and investment. Interest rates in Canada seem to move more in response to changes in interest rates in the United States (for reasons that will be explained in Chapter 26) than to changes in government borrowing. However, the studies, while inconclusive, do not rule out the danger of growing government deficits for private investment.

A Revised Look at the Effects of Monetary Policy

Chapter 24 described the effects of a change in the money supply, given the assumption that the money demand curve would remain fixed when the money

---

[2]Economic Council of Canada, *Steering the Course: Twenty-First Annual Review*, 1984, pp. 46–48.

supply curve shifted. In this section, we will look at the effect of a money supply change within the framework of the Keynesian theory, taking interactions between the money market and the level of domestic income into account.

Effects of an open-market purchase

To be precise, suppose that the Bank of Canada begins an expansion of the money supply by means of an open-market purchase of securities. (Expanding the money supply by cutting the bank rate or reserve requirements would have the same effect.)

The initial effect of the open-market purchase is to create an increase in bank reserves. Banks set to work to convert their excess reserves into earning assets by buying securities and making loans. In the process, as explained in Chapter 24, the money supply expands and interest rates fall. This is shown in Box 25.5 by the shift in the money supply curve from the position MS_1 to the position MS_2. The decrease in interest rates causes people to move downward along money demand curve MD_1 toward its intersection with the new money supply curve, MS_2.

Effects on income and investment As the interest rate begins to fall, firms increase their desired investment. This is shown by a movement downward and to the right along the investment schedule. The increase in desired investment

BOX 25.5   *Money Market and Investment Effects of an Increase in the Money Supply*

An increase in the money supply shifts the money supply curve from MS_1 to MS_2. The immediate effect of this shift is a movement downward along money demand curve MD_1 toward its intersection with the new money supply curve. The interest rate falls and desired investment increases. This pushes up real domestic income via the multiplier effect. The rise in income in turn shifts the money demand curve to a new position, MD_2, cutting short the drop in the interest rate. A new equilibrium is reached with interest rate r_2.

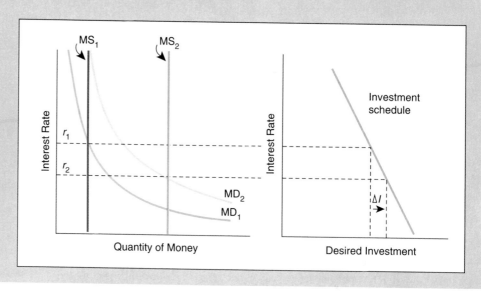

shifts the aggregate expenditure schedule upward, as shown in Box 25.6. Desired expenditure now exceeds real domestic income and, by the multiplier process, domestic income begins to increase.

As real income increases, the money market is affected again. Now the money demand curve begins to shift to the right, moving toward the position marked MD_2 in Box 25.5. This shift cuts short the fall in the interest rate, and a new equilibrium interest rate is reached where MD_2 and MS_2 intersect. The new money demand curve is higher than the old one, but it is not high enough to prevent the interest rate from falling at least somewhat.

Once interest rate r_2 is reached, desired investment stops expanding. The aggregate expenditure schedule comes to rest at a new equilibrium position, ADE_2, as shown in Box 25.6. This means that the new equilibrium interest rate will be lower than before and the new equilibrium real domestic income will be higher.

Co-ordination of Monetary and Fiscal Policy

Although we have looked at monetary and fiscal policy separately to this point, in practice, both kinds of policy are carried on at once. During certain periods of Canada's economic history, they have been closely co-ordinated. During others, the Bank of Canada has defied the Department of Finance and conducted monetary policies that were counter to the trend of fiscal policy.

The Effects of an Increase in the Money Supply on Real Domestic Income

BOX 25.6

An increase in desired investment caused by an increase in the money supply shifts the aggregate expenditure curve upward. The amount of the shift is equal to the change in desired investment, ΔI. A new equilibrium is reached with real domestic income rising from Y_1 to Y_2.

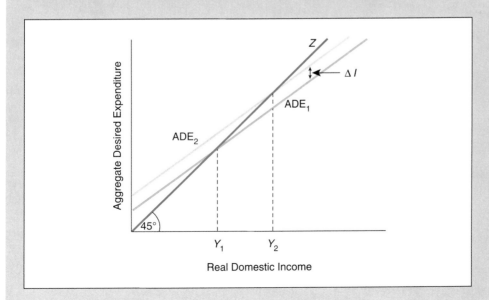

Monetary policy and deficits in the 1980s and early 1990s

In the 1980s and early 1990s, federal budget deficits of record size put a new focus on the interaction between monetary and fiscal policy. The results of the large deficits were much as Keynesian theory would lead us to expect: They helped to stimulate the economy, so that the economy recovered from the 1981–82 recession. By the end of the 1980s, the inflation rate increased, and the Bank of Canada seemed to be using a tight monetary policy to combat it. However, to understand what was happening, and to shed more light on the complex relationship between monetary policy and inflation, it is necessary to distinguish between real and nominal interest rates.

Real versus nominal interest rates

The key to understanding the relationship between monetary policy and interest rates during the 1980s is the distinction between **real and nominal interest rates**. This distinction was ignored earlier in the chapter, where we assumed zero inflation. It is time now to drop that assumption and to look at the effects of monetary policy on interest rates in a world where the price level is variable. In such a world, the long-run effect of increasing the rate of money-supply growth, at least beyond a certain point, will be higher, rather than lower, nominal interest rates. The reasoning behind this statement is as follows.

First, although there is no practical limit to the rate at which monetary policy can cause nominal domestic income to expand, there is a limit to how fast real domestic income can expand. This limit is established by trends in technology, capital accumulation, and the labour force. The trend rate of growth of real GDP in Canada has been in the neighbourhood of 3 percent per year. In the long run, then, if expansionary monetary policy forces the rate of growth of nominal GDP above 3 percent, the excess growth must take the form of inflation.

The next step in the reasoning has to do with the reaction of asset holders to inflation (as noted in the Preview to Chapter 24). In deciding how to balance their portfolios, potential buyers of fixed-interest securities, especially long-term bonds, will look closely at the real rate of interest they expect to earn — that is, at the nominal rate of interest minus the expected rate of inflation. For any given nominal rate of interest, an increase in the expected rate of inflation will drive the expected real rate of interest down, making bonds less attractive. Investors will try to reduce their holdings of bonds by selling them off, thereby driving down their prices and driving up their nominal yields. The effect is an increase in nominal interest rates.

The appearance of high nominal interest rates at the end of the 1980s seemed to signify an overly tight monetary policy, but, as has been shown, this wasn't necessarily the case. Critics of the Bank of Canada urged it to ease its monetary policy, but the Bank was reluctant to ease monetary policy as much as some of its critics wanted. If monetary policy were eased while fiscal policy remained expansionary, it warned, growth of aggregate desired expenditure would further outrun growth of real productive capacity. The result would be higher inflation. This would push nominal interest rates higher without necessarily reducing real interest rates. As we shall see in Chapter 26, the Bank of Canada was also reluctant to expand the money supply and lower the nominal rate of interest because of the impact that this might have on the value of the Canadian dollar.

This analysis calls attention to a broader conclusion that can be drawn from the Keynesian model: For any given real domestic income target, there is a trade-

---

Real and nominal interest rates
Nominal rates of interest are actual current rates; real rates of interest are the nominal (current) rate minus the current rate of inflation.

off between monetary and fiscal policy. The desired growth of real domestic income can be achieved by an expansionary fiscal policy together with a tight monetary policy; by an expansionary monetary policy combined with a tight fiscal policy; or by a balanced program somewhere between these two extremes. According to the Keynesian model, the main difference between the two strategies would be in the level of interest rates and investment. With an easy money/tight fiscal policy approach, both real and nominal interest rates would be relatively low and investment would be relatively high as a share of GDP. With a tight money/easy fiscal policy approach, both nominal and real interest rates would be higher, while consumption and government purchases would be larger in relation to GDP.

BEYOND KEYNES'S GENERAL THEORY: MONETARISM VERSUS KEYNESIANISM

Keynes's general theory of employment, interest, and money was intended to be "general" in the sense that it would take into account both monetary and fiscal factors. However, in the first years after Keynes's work appeared, it was not the general theory as a whole that dominated the thinking of economists. Instead, some economists stressed desired expenditure and de-emphasized the role of money. Early followers of Keynes saw the events of the Great Depression as justifying the view that "money doesn't matter." The fact that monetary policy failed to prevent both the large decline in real domestic income and the increase in unemployment to 24 percent of the labour force between 1929 and 1933 was due, in their opinion, not to poor conduct of monetary policy but to the ineffectiveness of such policies. Their view seemed to be supported by the fact that the Depression did not end until World War II brought on a massive increase in government spending.

After the war, many of the early Keynesians forecast a new depression and economic stagnation. They thought that private investment would dry up with the end of wartime spending. They were wrong. The postwar recovery of Canada, the United States, and Western Europe was rapid. Central banks in most of the major economies pursued easy monetary policies during those years, and inflation was more widespread than depression. The countries that were able to control inflation did so only by using standard monetary policies. Economists started to wonder whether money didn't matter after all and began to look again at the general Keynesian theory as a whole.

The Monetarists

The reaction against the one-sided theories of the early Keynesians received major support during the 1950s and 1960s from a group of economists led by Milton Friedman of the University of Chicago. Research led him to believe that movements in the money supply had a much greater effect on economic events than the early Keynesians had been willing to admit. It seemed to be possible to explain even the Great Depression in terms of faulty monetary policy — especially the 25 percent decrease in the narrowly defined money supply that the

Federal Reserve Board (the U.S. central bank) allowed between 1929 and 1933. Because of the emphasis they gave to monetary policy, Friedman and his followers came to be known as monetarists.

Monetarism
A school of economic thought that emphasizes changes in the money supply as a determinant of prices, income, and employment.

The economics profession did not immediately convert to **monetarism**. In fact, in some ways, the 1960s were the heyday of Keynesian policy. In the United States, many leading Keynesians left their university posts to join the Council of Economic Advisers under Presidents Kennedy and Johnson. Even so, the ideas of the monetarists proved influential in persuading the Keynesians to return to the original concept of general theory, in which monetary and fiscal policy played equal roles. And the work of the monetarists in the 1950s and the 1960s paved the way for extensions of economic theory in the 1970s and 1980s. These have blurred the distinction between the two schools of thought.

In Canada, economists such as David Laidler, Thomas Courchene, and Michael Parkin, all originally of the University of Western Ontario, and Jack Carr of the University of Toronto, among others, began to provide a monetarist critique of Canadian economic policy in the 1970s. A number of them are graduates of the University of Chicago.[3] A famous Canadian economist, the late Harry G. Johnson (see the Profile box opposite), took an eclectic, Keynesian–monetarist approach to the analysis of economic change. Many economists similarly elude classification into a single school of thought.

Monetarist ideas began to make an impact on government and Bank of Canada policy. Courchene, who had earlier criticized the Bank of Canada for contributing to the inflation of the early 1970s, noted with delight in 1976 that "the Bank of Canada has embraced the tenets of the monetarist approach to stabilization policy."[4]

Monetarism versus Keynesianism: unresolved issues

Today, the theoretical gap between monetarism and Keynesian economics has been narrowed but not altogether eliminated. The analysis presented in the first part of this chapter can be used as a framework for discussing some of the important unresolved issues, including the following:

1. What is the relative importance of monetary and fiscal policy in determining real domestic income?

2. How are the effects of monetary-policy actions transmitted through the economy?

3. To what extent is monetary policy a determinant of the rate of inflation, in both the long run and the short run?

4. What kind of monetary and fiscal policies are best suited to the goals of economic stabilization?

---

[3]Students are sometimes surprised to discover how the ideas of their professors can apparently be traced back to the schools in which they studied. The influence of Friedman and the so-called Chicago School can now be traced through two generations in Canada. As mentioned, a number of monetarists at the University of Western Ontario received their training at Chicago. In turn, one of the more vocal young monetarists, Michael Walker, chief economist of the Fraser Institute in Vancouver, studied economics at Western.

[4]Thomas J. Courchene, *Monetarism and Controls: The Inflation Fighters* (Montreal: C.D. Howe Research Institute, 1976), p. 1. However, Courchene subsequently criticized the Bank for its very narrow monetary strategy.

Harry G. Johnson: Between Monetarism and Keynesianism

Harry G. Johnson
(1923–1977)

One of the world's most famous interpreters of macroeconomics, until his death in May 1977 at the age of 53, was Harry G. Johnson. Johnson was born in Toronto and, after studying economics at the University of Toronto and Cambridge University, taught economics for several years in Canada. After completing his Ph.D. at Harvard University in 1958, he became Professor of Economics at the University of Chicago. For a number of years, from 1966 to 1973, he was also Professor of Economics at the London School of Economics, jetting back and forth across the Atlantic to teach and advise students at both universities. At the time of his death, he was professor at the University of Geneva as well as at Chicago.

Johnson was a prodigious worker and a prolific writer. One colleague observed that "he seemed to be intellectually 'all Muscle.' Physically, too, he gave an impression of tremendous power under easy self-control. He was broad, thick-chested, inclined toward a solid plumpness."* During his brief career, he published hundreds of articles on economics and more than a dozen books, dealing largely with the interpretation and application of Keynesian theory.

Though most of Johnson's career was spent outside Canada, he retained a lively interest in the Canadian economy, as evidenced by several of his major books (for example, *The Canadian Quandary* and *Canada in a Changing World Economy*) and the numerous lectures that he gave in this country. Just a year before his death, he gave the Harold Innis Lecture at the meetings of the Canadian Economics Association, on the topic "Keynes's General Theory: Revolution or War of Independence?" In keeping with his previous work, he argued in this lecture that Keynes had produced some new and interesting ideas for economists to follow, but that they did not amount to a revolution in economic thought. Johnson felt that pre-Keynesian ideas still had considerable validity, as shown by, among others, one of his colleagues at the University of Chicago, Milton Friedman. Johnson felt that Keynes's view was oriented primarily to the short run. For example, not enough attention was given in Keynes's work on the multiplier process to the shocks and adjustments that affect the process over time. However, Johnson thought that Keynes had revitalized the study of economics and had provided it with helpful new tools and new directions.

As a result of his cosmopolitan experience and outlook, Johnson was very critical of Canadian nationalism. He firmly believed in the benefits of free trade and competition and decried the defeatist, defensive attitude that he detected among many Canadians. He was frequently invited to lecture in less-developed countries, and there, too, he was outspoken in his criticism of centralized direction of the economy and the extreme nationalism of some of those countries. He will be remembered by most of his students and readers as one of the clearest interpreters of macroeconomics since Keynes.

*Edward Shils, "Harry Johnson, Memoir," *Encounter*, November 1977, p. 87.

The first two of these issues will be discussed in the remainder of this chapter. The third and fourth will be left for Chapters 26 to 28.

How large a crowding-out effect?

The debate over the relative importance of monetary and fiscal policy as determinants of real domestic income is, to a considerable extent, a debate over the importance of the crowding-out effect. Box 25.7 shows why. Suppose that the money demand curve has the steep shape shown by MD$_1$, indicating that the demand for money is not very sensitive to changes in the interest rate. If this is the case, large changes in the rate of interest will be occasioned by the portfolio adjustments that occur when the money demand curve shifts relative to the money supply curve (as when real income changes) or when the money supply curve shifts relative to the money demand curve (as a result of monetary policy). Suppose that, at the same time, the investment schedule is relatively flat, like I_1, so that a change in the rate of interest will induce a large change in desired investment expenditure.

Taken together, the curves MD$_1$ and I_1 tend to give the sort of results expected by monetarists. An expansion of government purchases leads to a large increase in the rate of interest, a large drop in private desired investment spending, and hence a large crowding-out effect. Also, an increase in the money supply leads to a large decline in the rate of interest and a large increase in desired investment spending. Therefore, given curves of these shapes, fiscal policy tends to be relatively ineffective and monetary policy relatively effective.

By contrast, if the money demand curve has the shape of MD$_2$, and the investment schedule the shape of I_2, the situation is reversed. Fiscal policy will have relatively little impact on interest rates; and interest rates, in turn, will have relatively little impact on private desired investment. Changes in taxes or government purchases will then operate on aggregate desired expenditure without

BOX 25.7 *Alternative Views of Monetary- and Fiscal-Policy Effectiveness*

If the money demand curve has a shape like that of MD$_1$, while the investment schedule is shaped like I_1, monetary policy will tend to be more effective than fiscal policy. A change in the money supply will have a big impact on desired expenditure, while fiscal policy will be severely hampered by the crowding-out effect. By contrast, a money demand schedule shaped like MD$_2$, with an investment schedule shaped like I_2, will give the advantage to fiscal policy. Changes in the money supply will have little impact on desired investment spending, and the crowding-out effect will be small.

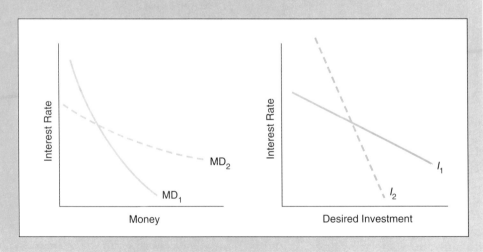

much hindrance from the crowding-out effect. At the same time, the economy will become much less sensitive to changes in the money supply. The world will behave more in the way that a Keynesian would expect it to.

The transmission mechanism

In addition to disagreeing about the size of the crowding-out effect, monetarists and Keynesians continue to disagree about the nature of the mechanism by which the effects of monetary policy are transmitted through the economy.

Keynesians tend to emphasize the chain of causation running from changes in monetary policy to changes in interest rates to changes in desired investment spending. This is the transmission mechanism emphasized so far in the chapter. Keynesians also suggest that there may be a secondary chain of causation running from a decrease in interest rates to an increase in share prices and, hence, via an increase in wealth, to an increase in desired consumer spending.

Monetarists, without disagreeing that interest rates and desired investment play an important role in transmitting the effects of monetary policy, tend to emphasize that changes in the money supply affect the economy in many other ways as well. In particular, they point out that it can be very misleading to think in terms of a world in which money and bonds and perhaps shares are the only assets that people hold in their portfolios — however convenient such a two- or three-asset economy may be as an expositional device for writers of textbooks.

Instead, when the Bank of Canada injects new money into the economy — more money than people initially want to hold — those who first receive the new money are likely to try to rebalance their portfolios by purchasing a broad variety of assets. These assets might include not only bonds of various types and maturities as well as shares, but also productive capital equipment, housing, and even consumer durables. Increased demand for all these assets tends to drive their prices up, which in turn stimulates construction firms to build more houses, corporations to issue new shares and purchase new capital equipment, and durable-goods makers to increase production to replace depleted inventories. The effects of expansionary monetary policy are thus transmitted through a great variety of channels, including some that are not adequately reflected in market interest rates, to many parts of the economy. The implication is that monetary policy may thus be more effective than the traditional Keynesian transmission mechanism would imply.

Evidence

Not surprisingly, a number of attempts have been made to bring empirical evidence to bear on the Keynesian–monetarist controversy. These efforts have succeeded in narrowing, although not entirely closing, the gap between the two schools of thought. As we have already seen, the crowding-out effect does not appear to be as significant in Canada as monetarists have supposed. As to the impact of monetarism on the Canadian economy, a number of Canadian economists are disillusioned about the effects of so-called monetarist policies in the last decade. There is considerable disagreement about the extent to which monetarism was really practised, and whether it was subject to disturbing forces — such as changes in money-holding patterns — which were largely beyond its control. Despite the problems that have been encountered, most economists probably agree that money "matters" more than it was assumed to matter a few decades earlier.

LOOKING AHEAD

This completes our discussion of monetary and fiscal policy. We now have a fairly clear picture of the ways in which these policy tools can be used together to control the level of aggregate desired expenditure and, thus, the equilibrium level of real domestic income. However, as we have pointed out many times, control over real income is not the only goal of macroeconomic policy. It is time now to focus directly on the linkages between changes in aggregate desired expenditure and real income, on the one hand, and inflation and unemployment, on the other. That will be the job of the next four chapters.

SUMMARY

1. The opportunity cost of capital for a firm is the interest rate that must be paid for funds obtained from outside the firm or the rate that could be earned by investing the firm's own funds elsewhere. A firm should invest up to the point at which the expected rate of return obtained from the last dollar of investment (the *marginal efficiency of investment*) falls below the opportunity cost of capital.

2. The economy's *investment schedule* is a downward-sloping curve that shows total desired investment for each interest rate. A change in the interest rate, other things being equal, causes a movement along the schedule. An increase in the expected rate of return on investment shifts the schedule upward and to the right. A decrease in the expected rate of return shifts it downward and to the left.

3. The money market is linked to the circular flow of income and product in two ways. First, a change in interest rates brought about by a shift in money supply or demand will affect desired investment and, hence, the position of the aggregate expenditure curve. Second, a change in the level of real domestic income will affect the position of the money demand curve and, hence, the equilibrium interest rate.

4. Keynesian theory takes the linkages between the circular flow and the money market into account. According to this theory, any given set of conditions results in a unique equilibrium pair of values for real domestic income and the interest rate.

5. In the Keynesian theory, an expansionary fiscal policy shifts the aggregate expenditure curve upward and raises the equilibrium value of real domestic income. Rising domestic income shifts the money demand curve to the right, raising the interest rate. The rise in the interest rate causes a drop in desired investment. This partly offsets the upward shift in the aggregate expenditure curve — a phenomenon known as the *crowding-out effect*. The final result of an expansionary fiscal policy is a higher level of real domestic income and a higher interest rate.

6. In the Keynesian theory, an increase in the money supply shifts the money supply curve to the right and drives down the interest rate. This stimulates desired investment. The rise in desired investment pushes up the aggregate expenditure curve, thus raising the equilibrium value of real domestic income. The increase in real domestic income shifts the money demand

curve to the right, thus partly offsetting the drop in the interest rate. The result is a higher level of real domestic income and a lower interest rate. However, when inflation is taken into account, this result must be modified. In the long run, a rate of money growth so high that it causes inflation will cause the *nominal interest rate* to rise, not fall.

7. Monetary and fiscal policy both affect real domestic income and interest rates. This means that a variety of policy mixes can be used to achieve any given domestic income target: a tight fiscal policy combined with an easy monetary policy; a tight monetary policy combined with an easy fiscal policy; or moderate use of both types of policies. According to the Keynesian theory, a mix that combines tight fiscal policy and easy monetary policy will, other things being equal, result in lower nominal and real interest rates than will the opposite mix.

8. The term *monetarism* refers to a school of thought that places more emphasis on monetary policy than Keynesian economists do. The two schools differ in their views of the *transmission mechanism* of monetary policy. Keynesians stress the linkage from interest rates to desired investment to aggregate desired expenditure.

   Monetarists also call attention to other portfolio effects, wealth effects, and credit-rationing effects.

KEY TERMS

marginal efficiency of
   investment
investment schedule

transmission mechanism
crowding-out effect

real and nominal interest rates
monetarism

KEY BOXES

Box 25.2 The Interaction of Money and Real
   Domestic Income
Box 25.3 The Crowding-out Effect
Box 25.4 The Crowding-out Effect
Box 25.5 Money Market and Investment Effects
   of an Increase in the Money Supply

Box 25.6 The Effects of an Increase in the Money
   Supply on Real Domestic Income
Box 25.7 Alternative Views of Monetary- and
   Fiscal-Policy Effectiveness

REVIEW QUESTIONS

1. Why does the interest rate represent the opportunity cost of capital for a firm that finances a project with funds retained from its own earnings?

2. In the Keynesian theory, why does a shift in the position of the aggregate expenditure

curve cause a shift in the position of the money demand curve? Why does a change in the interest rate cause a shift in the aggregate expenditure curve?

3. In the Keynesian model, how does an expansionary fiscal policy affect real domestic

income and the interest rate? How does a contractionary fiscal policy affect them?

4. In the Keynesian model, how does an expansionary monetary policy affect real domestic income and the interest rate? How does a contractionary monetary policy affect them? How is the relationship between monetary policy and interest rates affected when inflation is taken into account?

5. If the Bank of Canada wants to maintain low interest rates, is its job made easier or harder by an expansionary fiscal policy?

6. What lessons about monetary policy did Keynesians tend to draw from the events of the Great Depression? What lessons did monetarists tend to draw from the same events?

7. Your college football stadium is sold out for ten games each year. Tickets cost $20 each. The school is thinking of adding a new section to the stands that would hold 1000 more people. Building the section would cost $1 million. The school can borrow the money at an interest rate of 14 percent. Should it do so? If it keeps adding seats, at some point it will not be possible to fill them all for every game. What does this imply about the marginal efficiency of investment in stadium seats?

8. Rework the graphs in Boxes 25.3 and 25.4 for the case of a tax increase. Trace the sequence of events step by step. Will the interest rate be higher or lower in the new equilibrium? Will real domestic income be higher or lower? Assume that the full marginal propensity to consume applies to changes in disposable income that result from changes in taxes.

9. Make two more sets of graphs like the ones in Boxes 25.3 and 25.4. In one of them, make the money demand schedule steeper than MD_1 and the investment schedule flatter. In the other, make the money demand schedule flatter and the investment schedule steeper. Now trace the effects of an increase in government spending through both sets of graphs. In which case is the crowding-out effect greater? Why?

10. Make yet another set of graphs like the ones in Boxes 25.3 and 25.4. This time, assume

that the Bank of Canada follows a policy of holding interest rates constant by allowing the money supply to expand each time money demand increases. (You can represent this policy with a horizontal money supply curve drawn at the interest rate r_1.) Now trace the effects of an increase in government spending. Is there a crowding-out effect? Why or why not?

11. Rework the graphs in Boxes 25.5 and 25.6 for the case of a decrease in the money supply. What will this do to interest rates? To real domestic income? To the position of the money demand curve?

12. As in Question 9, prepare two sets of graphs with different slopes for the money demand curve and the investment schedule. Using the graphs, trace the effects of an increase in the money supply. In which case do the results match monetarist predictions more closely? In which case are they closer to Keynesian predictions? Why is there a difference?

13. As part of an expansionary fiscal-policy initiative, the government increases its spending by $200 million. At the same time, the Bank of Canada lowers the bank rate, causing the interest rate to decline and desired investment to increase by $75 million. If the marginal propensity to consume domestic output (MPC_D) is 0.8 in this economy, what is the net affect on real domestic income of the monetary and fiscal policies?

14. As part of a contractionary fiscal-policy initiative, the government decreases its spending by $200 million. At the same time, the Bank of Canada lowers the bank rate, causing the interest rate to decline and desired investment to increase by $75 million. If the marginal propensity to consume domestic output (MPC_D is 0.75 in this economy, what is the net effect on real domestic income of the monetary and fiscal policies?

15. The government cuts taxes by $100 million as part of fiscal-policy action, but the Bank of Canada keeps the money supply fixed.

a. Using the linkages between the money market, desired investment, and aggregate desired expenditure, describe possible changes in money demand, interest rates, desired investment, desired consumption, aggregate desired expenditure, and real domestic income.

b. How might monetary policy be co-ordinated with the tax cut to eliminate any possible ill effects of the fiscal policy?

16. a. If the tax cut described in Question 15 occurred when the Bank of Canada was following a monetary policy that kept interest rates constant, what would the money supply curve look like?

b. What effect would the tax cut have on desired investment?

c. What effect would the tax cut have on money demand?

The Elementary Algebra of Money and Income Determination

This appendix is a continuation of the Appendix to Chapter 20, which developed a simple algebraic version of the multiplier theory. It adds no new theory to what has been presented in the body of Chapter 25. Nonetheless, students who feel comfortable with elementary algebra may find the approach presented here useful in consolidating their understanding of the general theory of real-income determination. Throughout this appendix, the rate of inflation is assumed to be zero (as was assumed in most of this chapter).

Aggregate Desired Expenditure

The basic equation for aggregate desired expenditure is as follows:

$$\text{ADE} = C + I + G + X - M. \tag{25A.1}$$

In the Appendix to Chapter 20, the C in this equation was replaced with a consumption schedule, which was written as

$$C = a + b(Y - T_n), \tag{25A.2a}$$

and the M was replaced with an imports schedule, written as

$$M = M_a + m(Y - T_n), \tag{25A.2b}$$

where a and b were constants representing autonomous desired consumption and the marginal propensity to consume, respectively; $Y - T_n$ stood for disposable income; M_a was autonomous desired imports; and m was the marginal propensity to import. Now, I in Equation 25A.1 will also be replaced with a simple investment schedule:

$$I = c + dr, \tag{25A.3}$$

where I stands for desired investment and r for the interest rate, and where c and d are constants. The constant d, which is the reciprocal of the slope of the investment schedule, will have a negative value, because desired investment increases as the rate of interest falls.

Putting together Equations 25A.1, 25A.2a and b, and 25A.3, we obtain the following general expression of the aggregate expenditure schedule:

$$\text{ADE} = a + c + b(Y - T_n) + dr + G + X - M_a - m(Y - T_n). \tag{25A.4}$$

Money Demand

For a general equilibrium analysis of real-income determination, a money demand schedule is also needed. The one used in Chapter 24 gave a money demand curve in the shape of a rectangular hyperbola. To retain this kind of money demand schedule would involve the use of quadratic equations and would unnecessarily complicate the arithmetic, so we replace it here with a linearized money demand schedule written as

$$MD = e + fY + gr, \qquad (25A.5)$$

where MD stands for the quantity of money demanded; r, for the interest rate; and Y, for income; and where e, f, and g are constants. The constant g is the reciprocal of the slope of the money demand schedule. It is negative because money demand decreases when the interest rate rises.

The reader is cautioned that this linear formulation of the money demand function has certain drawbacks. One is that, except for a certain central range of the variables, algebraic solution of the equilibrium equations (to be presented below) may produce negative values for income or the interest rate. Such negative values have no reasonable economic meaning. Care will be taken to keep within the safe range of values in the examples.

Numerical Values

The constants in these equations can be replaced with representative numerical values to show how the algebraic formulations of desired expenditures and money demand can be put to work. Using $a = 100$, $b = 0.75$, $c = 210$, $d = -500$, $e = 80$, $f = 0.2$, $m = 0.15$, and $g = -400$, Equations 25A.4 and 25A.5 can be rewritten as

$$ADE = 310 + 0.75(Y - T_n) - 0.15(Y - T_n) - 500r + G + X - M_a \quad (25A.6)$$

and

$$MD = 80 + 0.2Y - 400r. \qquad (25A.7)$$

Equilibrium Conditions

As shown in the text of Chapter 25, the economy as a whole can be in equilibrium only when both the money market and the circular flow are in equilibrium. Money-market equilibrium requires that money supply equal money demand, and equilibrium in the circular flow requires that domestic product be equal to aggregate desired expenditure. These equilibrium conditions can be written as follows:

$$MS = MD \qquad (25A.8)$$

for the money market, where MS stands for the money supply, and

$$Y = ADE \qquad (25A.9)$$

for the circular flow.

Substituting Equation 25A.7 into Equation 25A.8, and Equation 25A.6 into Equation 25A.9, we obtain

$$MS = 80 + 0.2Y - 400r \qquad (25A.10)$$

and

$$Y = 310 + 0.75 (Y - T_n) - 0.15(Y - T_n) - 500r + G + X - M_a, \qquad (25A.11)$$

which simplifies to

$$Y = 775 - 1.5T_n + 2.5(G + X - M_a) - 1250r. \qquad (25A.12)$$

Equilibrium in the economy is possible only for pairs of values for r and Y that simultaneously satisfy Equations 25A.10 and 25A.12.

Policy Variables

Besides r and Y, there are five variables in Equations 25A.10 and 25A.12 for which numerical values have not yet been specified. Two of these values are X (exports) and M (imports). The problems that follow assume that exports (X) are autonomous, while desired imports (M) are partly autonomous (M_a) and partly related to disposable income $(m[Y - T_n])$. The remaining three variables are G (government purchases), T_n (net taxes), and MS (the money supply). These are collectively referred to as policy variables, because they stand for the elements of the economy that are under the direct control of the government. The following problems will show how the manipulation of these variables can be used by policy makers in their attempts to hit their economic targets.

Problem 1   Government policy makers set their policy variables at the values $G = 125$, $T_n = 100$, MS $= 300$, $M_a = 50$, and $X = 245$. Apply Equations 25A.10 and 25A.12 to determine the equilibrium values of r and Y.

Solution   Equation 25A.10 becomes

$$300 = 80 + 0.2Y - 400r$$

and Equation 25A.12 becomes

$$Y = 775 - 150 + 800 - 1250r.$$

Simplifying and setting the equations equal to zero, we obtain

$$220 - 0.2Y + 400r = 0$$
$$1425 - Y - 1250r = 0.$$

The usual methods for solution of simultaneous equations give the pair of values $r = 0.1$ and $Y = 1300$ as the equilibrium levels for interest rate and domestic income.

Problem 2   Using the solution to Problem 1 as a starting point, assume that the authorities want to raise the equilibrium level of domestic income to a target level of $1400, using monetary policy alone. How much will the money supply have to be increased to accomplish this objective?

Solution   Substitute $Y = 1400$, $G = 125$, $T_n = 100$, $X = 245$, and $M_a = 50$ into Equation 25A.12 in order to find the required equilibrium value for r. The substitution gives

$$1400 = 775 - 150 + 800 - 1250r,$$

which simplifies to

$$25 - 1250r = 0.$$

The solution to this last equation is $r = 0.02$.

   Next, substitute the equilibrium values $Y = 1400$ and $r = 0.02$ into Equation 25A.10 in order to determine the money supply necessary to give a 0.02 rate of interest when domestic income is $1400. This gives

$$MS = 80 + 0.2(1400) - 400(0.02) = 352.$$

The solution to the problem, then, is that the money supply must be increased by $52 — from $300 to $352 — in order to raise domestic income to $1400.

Problem 3   Using the solution to Problem 1 as a starting point, show that an increase of $26 in government purchases will be more effective in raising the equilibrium level of domestic income if the Bank of Canada pursues an accommodating monetary policy than if it leaves the money supply unchanged.

Solution   An accommodating monetary policy is one that expands the money supply enough to keep the interest rate unchanged — in this case, equal to 0.1. Substitute the values $T_n = 100$, $G = 151$, $M_a = 50$, $X = 245$, and $r = 0.1$ into Equation 25A.12 to get the new value that equilibrium domestic income will reach if accommodating monetary policy is pursued. Without going into details, the new equilibrium Y with accommodating monetary policy is $1365. (Further substitution of $Y = 1365$ and $r = 0.1$ into Equation 25A.10 shows that the money supply would have to be increased to $313 to achieve this result.)

   Without accommodating monetary policy, the new values of Y and r are found by going through the same steps outlined in the solution to Problem 1, using $G = 151$. Again without going into details, the solution turns out to be $Y = \$1340$ and $r = 0.12$. Substitution of the new, higher value of the interest rate into the investment schedule ($I = 210 - 500r$) shows that $10 of the original $160 in private desired investment is crowded out by the $26 increase in government purchases. This accounts for the lower equilibrium value of Y when accommodating monetary policy is not used.

CHAPTER 26

Fiscal and Monetary Policy in an Open Economy

WHAT YOU WILL LEARN IN THIS CHAPTER

After studying this chapter, you will be able to

1. Define and discuss *balance-of-payments equilibrium*.

2. Discuss the conditions of general equilibrium in an open economy.

3. Discuss the relative merits of flexible and fixed exchange rates.

4. Describe the so-called J-curve effect.

5. Discuss Canada's involvement in international monetary arrangements.

6. Examine the connection between interest-rate policy and foreign-exchange rates.

A Preview *Balancing Several Objectives Simultaneously*

This excerpt from the 1990 annual review of the Economic Council of Canada summarizes part of the controversy surrounding Canada's monetary policy in recent years. It also gives us a sense of the difficulties policy makers face in the trying to meet different kinds of policy objectives, from domestic objectives such as price stability and low unemployment to objectives that involve the international market, such as a balance-of-payments equilibrium and an appropriate value for the Canadian dollar. In the terminology of economic theory, they face the daunting task of achieving equilibrium in several markets at once.

Conflict over the Value of the Dollar

The current controversy over monetary policy reflects a struggle between conflicting short-term policy priorities, and much of the debate centres around the value of the Canadian dollar. The dollar appreciated to the 87-cent (U.S.) range during the summer of 1990 — well above the range that would be anticipated on the basis of relative rates of inflation and productivity growth. This has had positive consequences for the trend in inflation in Canada, as the high dollar has made imported goods cheaper. But in a sense, the high dollar has borrowed price stability from the future. Because there are an additional 2 to 3 percentage points of inflation waiting to emerge when the dollar returns to more normal levels, the central bank will be reluctant to see an early depreciation. In effect, interest rates will tend to err on the high side over the next few years in order to prevent a falling exchange rate from unleashing this hidden inflation.

At the same time, industry is anxious to see an early decline in the value of the dollar. A strong currency raises the price of exported goods, putting producers at a competitive disadvantage on foreign and domestic markets and discouraging the investment in plant and equipment that is needed now to modernize Canadian firms preparing for global competition in the future. There is a serious risk that, if they are sustained too long, a strong dollar and high interest rates will neutralize the positive effects of the Canada–U.S. trade agreement and other measures taken to improve this country's competitive position.

SOURCE: Economic Council of Canada, *Transitions for the 90s: Twenty-Seventh Annual Review*, Ottawa, 1990, pp. 22, 24. Reproduced with permission of the Chairman of the Economic Council of Canada, 1992.

THE INTERACTION OF MONEY, DOMESTIC INCOME, AND THE BALANCE OF PAYMENTS

The Conditions for General Equilibrium

Our earlier discussion of Canada's role in the international economy (Chapters 15 and 16), and the survey of macroeconomics featured in the last nine chapters, indicate that the Canadian economy operates simultaneously in three separate (though overlapping) markets. One of these is the international market, involving imports and exports of goods and services, and capital inflows and outflows. The international market is extremely important for Canada. As we saw, Canadians import about 30 percent of all the goods and services they consume, and they rely on foreign countries to purchase almost 30 percent of Canadian output. In addition, foreign investment has been significant in funding Canadian industry, and many Canadian companies invest heavily abroad. For this reason, Canada is considered to have an unusually "open" economy. The other two markets are the domestic circular flow of real goods and services, and the money market. The latter market tries to bring into balance the demand and supply of money.

In each market, we have identified counter-balancing forces of demand and supply. When these forces are brought into balance in each market, a condition of *equilibrium* is said to exist.

It was shown in Chapter 25 that the money market and the circular flow can be in equilibrium only if there is a perfect matching of interest rates and domestic income. Box 25.2 illustrated a general equilibrium situation for the money market and the circular flow. No consideration, however, was given to equilibrium in the international market, where equilibrium is identified as a balance within Canada's balance of payments.

It was observed in Chapter 15 that, in a purely accounting sense, the balance of payments will always be shown to be in equilibrium, because in principle the sum of the current, capital, and reserve accounts will always be exactly zero. However, economists define a **balance-of-payments equilibrium** as a situation in which there are no changes in reserves. That is, the balance of payments is considered to be in equilibrium when the capital account exactly balances the current account. This means that any loss of foreign currency required to pay for a deficit on the current account is matched by a net capital inflow of the same amount, while a surplus in the current account will be utilized to finance net capital outflows. If such balancing occurs, there will be no loss or build-up of foreign-currency reserves.

As we have seen (Chapter 15), Canada usually runs a deficit on its current account. An equilibrium in Canada's balance of payments can be said to exist only when capital inflows exceed capital outflows by the amount of the current-account deficit. (When capital inflows do exceed capital outflows, it is defined as a positive *net* capital inflow.) This kind of equilibrium might be considered a minimal objective. Even more desirable would be a balance or near-balance in the current account itself, with exports equalling imports, easing the pressure to increase inflows of foreign capital to help pay for a current-account deficit. However, we will consider only the minimal objective here.

To achieve a balance-of-payments equilibrium, either negative net exports (deficit on current account) must be matched by positive net capital inflows (surplus on capital account) or positive net exports must be matched by negative net capital inflows.

Balance-of-payments equilibrium
A situation in which transactions in the capital account exactly match transactions in the current account, so that there is no loss or build-up of foreign-currency reserves.

The requirements for equilibrium in the balance of payments are illustrated in Box 26.1. A net-export schedule is depicted in part (a). Because we assume that autonomous exports exceed autonomous desired imports, net exports in our example have a positive autonomous element. However, because imports increase with domestic income, while exports are assumed not to increase, *net* exports decline as domestic income rises. Thus, the current account becomes negative at high levels of domestic income.

In our example, exports are assumed to be $125 regardless of income, autonomous desired imports are $50, and the marginal propensity to import is 0.15. Net exports (exports minus imports) therefore equal $125 − $50 + 0.15Y, or $75 − 0.15Y. (Note that, for the sake of convenience, we are once again dealing in dollars, rather than billions of dollars, in the examples throughout this chapter.) As the graph in Box 26.1(a) indicates, at a domestic income level of $500, net exports are zero, and at income levels above $500, they become negative. We assume that real domestic income in this economy is at the $1200 level, which, as we can see in the graph, means that net exports are −$105. (We can confirm this result by substituting $1200 for Y in the net-export schedule given above: $75 − 0.15 [$1200] = −$105.) In other words, the current account has a deficit of $105.

To achieve a balance-of-payments equilibrium under these conditions, there must be a positive net capital inflow of $105 to match the negative net exports.

BOX 26.1   *A Balance-of-Payments Equilibrium*

To achieve a balance-of-payments equilibrium, net exports (recorded in the current account) must be balanced by net capital flows (recorded in the capital account). Part (a) below illustrates a hypothetical net-export schedule, $75 − 0.15 Y. At an income level of $1200, net exports will be −$105. Payment of this deficit on the current account will deplete the country's holdings of foreign currency by $105. To counteract this loss, there must be a capital inflow of $105 on the capital account, which will be contingent on an interest rate that is high enough to attract capital into the country. Part (b) shows that the necessary interest rate in this case is 8 percent; at lower rates, net capital inflows will fall short of the needed $105 inflow.

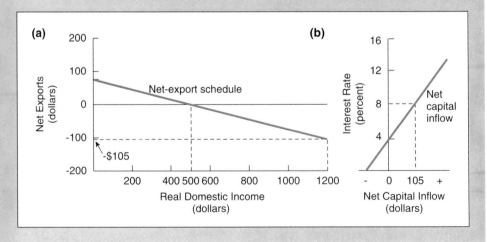

Box 26.1(b) illustrates a hypothetical **net capital inflow function**, which relates capital flows to domestic rates of interest. In our example, we assume that at low rates of interest — below 4 percent — capital outflows exceed capital inflows, leading to a negative *net* capital inflow; at an interest rate of 4 percent, capital inflows equal capital outflows, so net capital inflows are zero; and at interest rates above 4 percent, capital inflows exceed capital outflows, creating a positive net capital inflow. We assume also that the money market, which is not depicted here, has created an interest rate of 8 percent, which happens to be the rate that results in a net capital inflow of $105.[1] This exactly matches the negative net exports in part (a) and, hence, the loss of foreign reserves in the current account, meaning that the balance of payments in this example is in equilibrium. Note that, at any other rate of interest, net capital inflows would not equal the deficit in the current account, so that a balance-of-payments equilibrium would not be achieved.

To summarize, a minimal equilibrium in the balance of payments can be achieved only when net exports are balanced by net capital inflow. Capital inflows are related primarily to interest rates. The higher our interest rates are compared with those of other countries (for example, the United States), the more inclined Canadians will be to borrow in those countries (thus raising capital inflows) and the less inclined foreigners will be to borrow in Canada. What is important is not the absolute level of our interest rates but the differential between our rates and those of other countries. However, it will be assumed here that, as our rates go up, the differential increases. Net capital inflows will then be related positively to the rate of interest.

It follows from these assumptions that, at a specific level of real domestic income, which produces a particular level of net exports, one particular rate of interest is required to create capital flows that exactly match the net exports. Therefore, equilibrium in the foreign market requires a matching of interest rates and real domestic income, just as a matching of interest rates and domestic income was required to create equilibrium simultaneously in the money market and in the circular flow. In fact, as we shall see, *general equilibrium in an economy requires that the money market, the circular flow, and the balance of payments all be brought into equilibrium simultaneously by a unique combination of interest rates and real domestic income.*

General Equilibrium Including the Foreign Market

The nature and necessity of such a general equilibrium in the money market and in the circular flow of income and product were illustrated in Box 25.2. An interest rate of 8 percent caused the demand for money to be equal to the supply of money. Simultaneously, that interest rate resulted in investment spending of $100 billion, which, together with the other spending flows in the economy, was consistent with a domestic income of $1200 billion. Therefore, that interest rate,

Net capital inflow function
A function relating desired net capital inflows (inflows minus outflows) to domestic interest rates.

---

[1]The net capital inflow function used here is expressed by the equation $F = \$105 + 2625r$, where F is net capital inflow, $105 is the autonomous net capital inflow, and the number 2625 expresses the rate at which F will change in relation to interest rates (r). For example, if $r = 0.08$, $F = -\$105 + 2625 (0.08) = -\$105 + \$210 = \$105$.

in combination with that particular level of domestic income, created equilibrium in both the money market and the circular flow.

However, nothing was said in that example about equilibrium in the foreign market — that is, in the balance of payments. For that reason, it was not really correct to refer to that example as a situation of *general* equilibrium.

The requirements for simultaneous **general equilibrium** in the money market, the circular flow, and in the balance of payments are illustrated in Box 26.2. It is assumed first (part [a]) that a rate of interest of 8 percent is established in the money market through the interaction of money demand and money supply, equating money demand with money supply. Next (part [b]), this rate of interest creates a net capital inflow of $105 in the balance-of-payments capital account. The 8 percent rate of interest also produces $100 of desired investment via the investment function (part [c]). This level of desired investment, together with other desired expenditures (as noted earlier, in Box 25.2), produces a level of real domestic income of $1200 (part [d]), which in turns results in negative net exports of $105. Fortunately, going back to the capital account depicted in part (b), this deficit in the current account is balanced by the positive net capital inflow of $105.

We thus have the following simultaneous-equilibrium conditions:

1. In the money market, supply and demand forces have been brought into equilibrium at a rate of interest of 8 percent. Given those forces, only that rate of interest will produce equilibrium.

2. In the circular flow, the 8 percent rate of interest helps to create expenditures (through the investment function) that produce an equilibrium level of real domestic income of $1200. Given a rate of interest of 8 percent, no income level other than $1200 will produce an equivalent level of desired expenditures. Therefore, the circular flow is uniquely in equilibrium at a rate of interest of 8 percent and a real domestic income of $1200.

3. In the foreign market, the 8 percent rate of interest creates a net capital inflow of $105. Simultaneously, the real domestic income of $1200 results in a current-account deficit of $105. Equilibrium in the foreign market, therefore, results from a perfect matching of interest rates and real domestic income.

The important result is this: A unique combination of a particular rate of interest and a particular level of income is required to produce a general equilibrium

---

BOX 26.2 *A General Equilibrium View of the Money Market, the Foreign Market, and the Circular Flow*

Demand and supply forces in the money market interact to create an interest rate of 8 percent. This interest rate generates a positive net capital inflow of $105 (part [b]). The 8 percent rate of interest simultaneously generates $100 of desired investment (part [c]). This level of desired investment, together with the other spending flows in the economy, generates a real domestic income of $1200 (part [d]). It so happens that a domestic income of $1200 produces a $105 deficit on the current account (part [d]) which is exactly matched by the net capital inflow of $105 (part [b]). Note that a different rate of interest would have led to a different net capital inflow *and* to a

---

General equilibrium
A situation in which money supply equals money demand in the money market, aggregate desired expenditure equals domestic output in the circular flow, and there is a balance-of-payments equilibrium in the foreign market.

different level of domestic income (via desired investment) and a different current-account deficit.

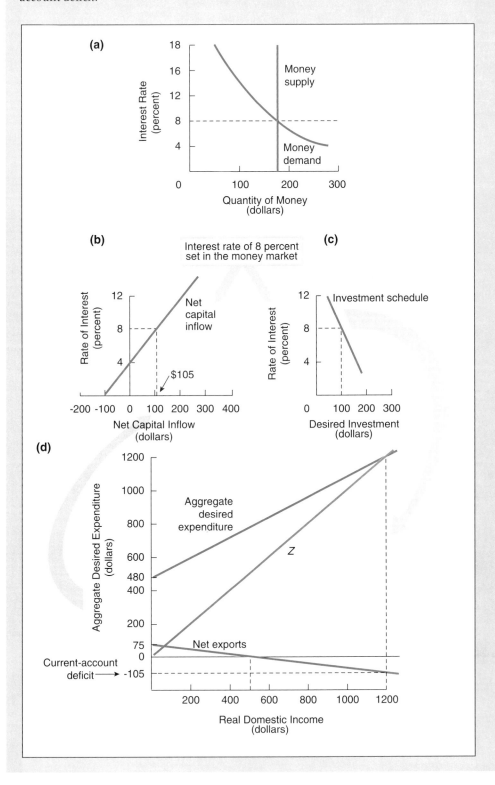

Fixed exchange rates
Exchange rates that are set by government and not permitted to move freely in response to imbalances in the foreign sector.

Floating, or flexible, exchange rates
Exchange rates that are determined by the forces of supply and demand in the foreign-exchange market.

for the economy. Government policy may be able to establish interest rates and income levels that achieve equilibrium in two markets but not in all three. Failure to achieve equilibrium in one may frustrate policies designed to maintain equilibrium in the others. As we shall see, this is strictly true only when **exchange rates** are **fixed** rather than **floating, or flexible** — that is, when they are not permitted to move freely in response to imbalances in the foreign sector. (It should also be noted that the general equilibrium sought here is assumed to be the most desirable one — namely, one with full employment, low inflation, and a balance of payments achievable on the basis of policies that promote the overall objectives.)

The Difficulty of Achieving General Equilibrium Using Monetary Policy (under Fixed Exchange Rates)

To understand the difficulty of achieving equilibrium, let us consider a situation in which the government has decided to increase real domestic income, because there is too much unemployment when domestic income is $1200. Suppose that, to help achieve this end, the Bank of Canada increases the money supply, and thereby reduces interest rates to 4 percent. This is depicted in Box 26.3(a) as a shift in the money supply curve to the right, from MS_1 to MS_2. The lower rate of interest causes desired investment to rise to $150, as shown in part (c), and that $50 increase in turn causes the level of domestic income to rise, via the multiplier, by $125, from its previous level of $1200 to $1325. This is shown by the shift in the aggregate expenditure schedule in part (d), from ADE_1 to ADE_2, creating a new equilibrium at an income level of $1325.

If we were considering only the circular flow and the money market, we would assume that the economy was in equilibrium at this point. But since we are now also taking the foreign market into account, we must look at what happens to equilibrium in it. At a rate of interest of 4 percent, net capital inflow falls

BOX 26.3   *Attempting to Create a New General Equilibrium via Monetary Policy (under Fixed Exchange Rates)*

It is assumed here that the Bank of Canada increases the money supply, from MS_1 to MS_2 in part (a), thereby reducing the interest rate to 4 percent. This causes desired investment to rise to $150 (part [c]), which brings the level of domestic income up to $1325 (part [d]). A new equilibrium is thus achieved in the money market and the circular flow, but the foreign market is no longer in equilibrium: At an income level of $1325, net exports will be −$123.75 (part [d]), while at an interest rate of 4 percent, net capital inflow will be reduced to zero (part [b]). Under fixed exchange rates, there are no "natural" forces creating a balance-of-payments equilibrium at an income level of $1325. Instead, the economy will likely be forced back to its original income level of $1200.

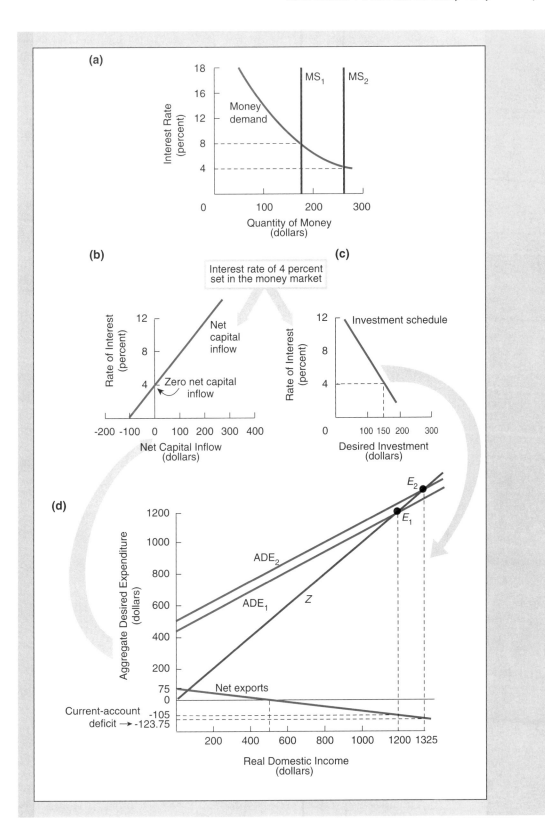

to zero, while simultaneously, at the income level of $1325, net exports fall to $-\$123.75$ ($X_n = \$75 - 0.15[\$1325]$). The current-account deficit has grown larger as a result of the monetary policy, but at the same time, the net capital inflow required to pay for the deficit has diminished. The balance of payments is in serious disequilibrium.

What is likely to happen in an economy in which the foreign market is in serious disequilibrium, perhaps because of a monetary policy designed to lower interest rates and increase income? *If the exchange rate is fixed*, and the interest rate remains at 4 percent, the deficit in the balance of payments will not be self-correcting. (As will be shown below, flexible exchange rates might correct the imbalance "automatically"; the imbalance would reduce the value of the dollar, which would stimulate exports and reduce the current account deficit.) Instead, the Bank of Canada will have to use up its reserves of foreign currency to pay for the imbalance. In the process of selling foreign currency to the private dealers who need it to pay for the excess imports that constitute the current-account deficit, the Bank will receive cheques in Canadian currency from those dealers, which will reduce the deposits of the chartered banks. This will reduce the money supply, thereby increasing interest rates once again and lowering the level of income. Unless the Bank of Canada counterbalances such reductions in the money supply with new infusions of money, the economy will revert to its old equilibrium level, and the monetary policy designed to increase the level of income and reduce the level of unemployment will have been completely undermined. *Monetary policy, therefore, may be made ineffectual by fixed exchange rates.*

Achieving General Equilibrium Using Fiscal Policy (under Fixed Exchange Rates)

If, on the other hand, *fiscal policy*, without accommodating monetary policy, were used to increase domestic income, the effects would be more positive with regard to achieving general equilibrium. The rise in income would increase the current-account deficit, but in the absence of any increase in the money supply, it would also raise interest rates. Higher interest rates, in turn, would increase net capital inflow, and major balance-of-payments problems would thereby be avoided. Fiscal policy can thus be effective in achieving general equilibrium under fixed exchange rates.

Fiscal and Monetary Policy under Flexible Exchange Rates

Very different results are possible under flexible exchange rates. If, through monetary policy, the money supply is increased, causing the current-account deficit to grow while net capital inflow declines, the value of the Canadian dollar will decline. This will happen because the *supply* of Canadian currency in the foreign-exchange market will *increase* (as Canadians react to lower interest rates and higher incomes by exchanging more Canadian dollars for foreign currency, in order to purchase more bonds and goods and services from foreigners), and the *demand* for Canadian dollars will *decrease* (as foreigners react to our lower interest rates by buying fewer bonds from us). The decline in the value of our dollar should reduce the current-account deficit. Foreigners will find our goods and services cheaper than before, while Canadians will find that foreign goods and services have become more expensive.

In terms of Box 26.3, the net-export schedule in part (d) will shift upward to the right, because, at any given level of income, more will now be exported and less imported. In fact, it can be assumed that the value of the Canadian dollar will keep dropping until net exports and net capital inflow are equal (meaning that the net-export schedule in Box 26.3 shifts so far to the right that net exports equal zero at an income level of $1325). The foreign market will then have achieved a new equilibrium, at an interest rate of 4 percent and the target income level of $1325. With flexible exchange rates, policy makers have some hope of moving the economy in the desired direction. Even monetary policy is effective with flexible exchange rates.

Flexible exchange rates may appear to make fiscal policy more potent than our earlier examples of the multiplier effect (in Chapter 20) suggested. Partly because of import leakages, the multiplier in our example was only 2.5 for an increase in desired government expenditures. However, if the government uses an expansionary fiscal policy to increase income, the increased deficit on the current account resulting from higher desired imports may result in a depreciation of our currency. This will decrease imports and increase exports, thereby increasing the demand forces and the level of income. Yet, higher interest rates will accompany this increased demand, in the absence of increases in the money supply, and the higher rates will attract more foreign capital, driving the exchange rate back up. At the same time, the higher interest rates will discourage domestic investment. The result is therefore indeterminate. However, fiscal policy remains an effective stabilization tool under flexible exchange rates.

Exchange-Rate Policy in Canada

In general, flexible exchange rates are favoured by most economists because they eliminate imbalances in the foreign sector that might result from monetary and fiscal policy, so that domestic stabilization policies can be pursued without too much worry about repercussions in the balance of payments.

However, the real world is one in which other considerations also play an important role, so that fixed or semi-fixed exchange rates are more often the rule than the exception. In the 1950s (until 1961), Canada allowed its exchange rate to fluctuate freely; in the 1960s, it operated with fixed exchange rates; and in the 1970s, 1980s, and early 1990s, rates were semi-flexible, being controlled partly by special purchases and sales of foreign currency by the Bank of Canada.

The Case for and against Fixed Rates

Real effects of currency disturbances

The first point made by proponents of fixed rates is that variations in exchange rates have significant real effects on the economy. When a country's currency appreciates, its export industries find it harder to compete in world markets. At the same time, industries that face import competition find it difficult to compete in domestic markets. When a country's currency depreciates, in contrast, export and import-competing industries boom, but industries that rely on imported energy or imported raw materials suffer. If the appreciation or depreciation in question reflects fundamental long-term changes in patterns of world trade, these adjustments in import and export industries may be necessary and desirable. But it is argued that short-term random, cyclical, or speculative changes in exchange rates should not be allowed to disturb the domestic economy. After all, labour and other factors of production cannot make costless moves from sector to sector at a moment's notice.

The J-curve effect

J-curve effect
The short-term increase in the current-account deficit following a currency devaluation.

A second reason frequently advanced for fixing exchange rates is that, in the short run, the depreciation of a country's currency may worsen rather than improve its balance of payments on current account. This is known as the **J-curve effect**, and is illustrated in Box 26.4. When a country's currency first depreciates, few additional export sales are made immediately, and importers do not or cannot immediately reduce the quantity of goods they purchase. At the lower exchange rates, however, importers do have to offer greater quantities of the domestic currency in order to obtain the foreign currency they need to buy the unchanged physical quantity of imports. The current-account balance thus moves toward deficit, putting further downward pressure on the exchange rate. Eventually, the lower exchange rate attracts new export buyers and encourages importers to find domestic substitutes. Supporters of fixed rates emphasize the possible negative short-term effects of flexible rates. Supporters of flexible rates can argue that, in the long run, such rates do produce favourable results. Something like this appears to have happened after Canada's dollar fell sharply in value toward the end of 1976. It took some time before the foreign market benefited from the exchange-rate depreciation.

BOX 26.4   *The J-Curve Effect*

The so-called J-curve effect occurs because a devaluation may initially worsen a country's balance of payments on its current account before eventually improving it. Here, the country has been experiencing a moderate current-account deficit for some time. At the point shown, it devalues its currency. At first, the current account drops farther into deficit, but eventually it rises into surplus, following the J-shaped path shown.

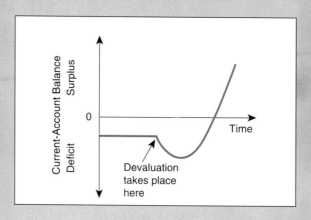

Inflationary effects

A third argument in favour of fixed exchange rates is based on the relationship between exchange-rate variations and inflation. Countries experiencing relatively rapid inflation can expect their currencies to depreciate — in accordance with the purchasing-power parity theory. However, the causation may also run the other way; a currency depreciation may cause inflation. This occurs in part directly, because the prices of imported goods and raw materials rise, and in part indirectly, because domestic import-competing industries feel free to raise their prices when the prices of imports rise.

Under the proper conditions, a vicious cycle that runs something like this can be touched off: Inflation in, say, Canada causes the dollar to depreciate. Depreciation brings a round of inflation. International asset holders see the worsening inflation and react by pulling their funds out of Canadian banks and securities, thereby creating a capital-account deficit. Especially if the J-curve effect of the depreciation is creating a current-account deficit at the same time, the value of the dollar can plunge out of control in the absence of official intervention.

Meanwhile, a less inflationary country — say, Switzerland — enters a "virtuous" cycle that is the mirror image of the vicious cycle described for Canada. Currency appreciation lowers import prices, further dampening inflation. International investors rush to put their funds in the ultra-safe Swiss franc, thereby creating a capital-account surplus that causes further appreciation. But while the banks of Zurich grow fat, Swiss watchmakers find themselves increasingly priced out of the world market on which their livelihood depends.

The way to prevent such runaway vicious–virtuous cycles, it is said, is to prevent exchange-rate fluctuations in the first place. Rather than letting differential rates of inflation disturb exchange markets, countries should use the time gained by exchange-rate intervention to undertake domestic policies to control inflation.

Arguments for floating, or flexible, rates

Floating-rate advocates begin by pointing out that fixed rates do not truly protect the domestic economy from the real effects of international disturbances. For example, if inflation occurs under a fixed-rate system, foreign competition may prevent prices from rising in industries facing strong international competition. As costs and prices rise in other sectors of the domestic economy, the industries facing foreign competition will be squeezed and resource allocation will consequently be disturbed. As was indicated previously, the J-curve effect is likely a short-term one. In the long run, it is not really an argument for fixed rates.

Floating-rate advocates are similarly unconvinced by the argument that currency depreciation creates a vicious cycle through inflation. The impact of exchange-rate fluctuations on domestic inflation depends on whether the domestic money stock is held constant or increased. If the money stock is held constant instead of being increased to accommodate the inflationary impact of currency depreciation, price increases in some markets will tend to be offset by price decreases elsewhere. Floating-rate advocates concede that in a floating-rate world, central banks would not always have the necessary discipline to avoid inflationary monetary policy, but they suggest that the blame should be placed on the banks, not on the monetary system.

It is time now to turn from theory to a brief review of the postwar history of the international monetary system.

THE INTERNATIONAL MONETARY SYSTEM

Toward the end of World War II, in 1944, the major trading nations of the world met, under the auspices of the United Nations, at Bretton Woods, New Hampshire, to forge a new world monetary system based on forced exchange rates. The Bretton Woods conference also set up the International Monetary Fund (IMF), with headquarters in Washington, D.C., to administer the system. The rules of the international monetary game as it was played under the **Bretton Woods system** are presented here.

It was not quite an ideal fixed-rate system. Instead, it featured what might best be called an "adjustable peg." Par values for each currency were established in terms of the U.S. dollar. Exchange rates were pegged at the par values; thus, they were allowed to fluctuate under the influence of supply and demand within a narrow range of 2.25 percent above par to 2.25 percent below par. (These limits were extended from a mere 1 percent only after December 1971.) When the value of a currency rose to the upper limit or fell to the lower one, the government of the country in question was obligated under IMF rules to intervene and prevent further movement. A government faced with an excess demand for its currency at the limit rate had to sell enough of its own currency in exchange for dollars to soak up the excess demand. A government faced with an excess supply of its currency had to buy it in exchange for dollars if necessary to keep its price from slipping below the limit.

Although governments were supposed to intervene in exchange markets to counteract temporary disturbances, they had another option if they felt the disturbances reflected fundamental long-term changes. In the face of such changes, they could adjust the peg — change the par values of their currencies. This could be done in either of two slightly different ways. One way was to declare immediately a new par value above or below the initial value. The other was to float the currency temporarily, letting it find a new equilibrium value under the influence of supply and demand without government intervention. Once things appeared to have settled down, a new par value would be fixed at the market-determined rate. (A few countries, notably Canada, let their currencies float for years at a time in the postwar period. This, however, was considered to be in violation of at least the spirit, if not the letter, of IMF rules.)

Problems of the Bretton Woods System

Resisting adjustment

Under the Bretton Woods system, a country whose currency fell to the lower limit of the permissible range was supposed to either buy its own currency in an amount sufficient to correct the imbalance or adjust the peg, make a new start at a new par value, and try to keep serious imbalances from arising again in the future. Unfortunately, governments often did neither when faced with downward pressure on their currencies. Fearing unemployment and high interest rates, they refused to make purchases of their own currency. And, concerned about possible sectoral effects, they resisted downward adjustment of their par value. In desperate attempts to prop up their currencies, they engaged in all sorts of trade restrictions. They imposed tariffs and quotas to try to improve current-account balances, and they slapped on foreign-exchange controls to prevent free international movements of capital, all in the hope of improving the capital account. But these mechanisms usually did little more than postpone the day of reckoning.

Bretton Woods system The monetary system created at Bretton Woods toward the end of World War II; it involved "pegging" currencies in relation to the U.S. dollar.

Crises

Because adjustments were seldom fully automatic, the system was crisis-prone. Too often, governments resisted making the small adjustments that would have been only slightly painful. Instead, they waited for pressures to build up, and those pressures eventually tore the system apart.

Here is the scenario for the kind of international monetary crisis that repeatedly occurred under the Bretton Woods rules: Some country, say, the United Kingdom, runs a persistent balance-of-payments deficit. A chronic excess supply of British pounds sterling appears on the world's exchange markets. The British government is forced to support the pound. It resists monetary restraint. Gradually, dollar reserves are run dangerously low, and the British government is forced to borrow from the IMF or the U.S. Treasury. It may try to impose exchange controls or other trade restrictions, but its efforts are met with threats of retaliation and domestic political resistance. It becomes harder and harder to keep the pound from breaking through the floor. The final scene in the sterling crisis is set when speculators, observing the decline in the value of the pound, start to pour hundreds of millions of pounds into the foreign-exchange markets. The excess supply of sterling becomes overwhelming. An actual devaluation is triggered by the speculative pressure that occurs in anticipation of the devaluation.

The End of the Bretton Woods System

In early 1973, an especially severe crisis occurred, involving the U.S. dollar, the German mark, and the Japanese yen. In response to this crisis, the major trading nations took the bold step of abandoning the adjustable peg and allowing their currencies to float relative to one another. The relative values of the yen, the dollar, and the mark were allowed to find their own levels under the influence of supply and demand.

The international monetary system that emerged from the crisis of 1973 is still a mixed system. It contains a number of features that do not conform exactly to a pure floating-rate system. Although it is much more flexible than the adjustable peg, two important restrictions must be kept in mind.

First, not every currency floats against every other currency. Rather, the system is one in which major blocks of currencies float against one another. A number of Western European countries have attempted to peg their currencies against one another in an arrangement known as the European Monetary Union. Countries with strong trading ties to the United States have pegged their currencies to the dollar. Those with strong ties to Britain have pegged theirs to the pound, and recently, several European countries have tied their currency to the German mark. Movements between blocks have been substantial, though. Because increased flexibility has been introduced, several currencies have swung by as much as 20 to 30 percent. Occasionally, there have been swings of 2 to 3 percent in a single day.

Second, governments have not taken a strictly hands-off attitude toward exchange rates. Instead, they have frequently intervened in foreign-exchange markets to dampen what they perceive to be temporary or unjustified fluctuations in exchange rates. Such intervention, however, is not guided by any specific rules, as was the case under the Bretton Woods agreements. The present mixture of floating rates and sporadic intervention is often referred to as a "dirty float."

During much of the postwar period, the Canadian dollar has been allowed to float within limits, so that its value has been set largely by the forces of demand and supply.

CANADA AND THE FOREIGN MARKET: POLICY OPTIONS

As we pointed out in Chapter 15, a large part of Canada's international trade involves the United States. We can therefore use the example of our dealings with that country to illustrate the nature of Canada's basic problems in the foreign market. Let us begin by reviewing what we discussed in Chapter 15 about Canada's balance-of-payments position in relation to the United States: First, Canada typically has a current-account deficit with the United States, attributable in large part to the interest and dividends on U.S. investments in Canada that we must pay in U.S. dollars purchased on the foreign-exchange market. Such purchases push up the value of the U.S. dollar. Thus, because of our dependence on U.S. investment, we are saddled with heavy debt payments that push down the value of our own dollar. In order to stabilize the value of our dollar around 80 cents (U.S.), we have tried to lure more investment into Canada by keeping our interest rates above those that prevail in the United States. Such policies have helped to counterbalance the negative effect on the value of our dollar of the normal deficits in our current account.

In 1976, several factors converged to bring about a substantial decline in the value of our dollar. First, our interest rates fell, approaching those that prevailed in the United States. Consequently, fewer Canadian bond issues were sold in the United States, and there was therefore little to counter the normal downward pressure on the dollar. Second, our inflation rate rose above that of the United States, creating additional problems in our current account. Third, the victory of the Parti Québécois in Quebec, which threatened the unity of the country, probably led to some speculative action against the dollar by people anticipating the diminution of Canadian resources that would occur if Quebec seceded.

As we can see from the graph in Box 26.5, the value of the dollar continued to fall throughout the late 1970s and early 1980s, taking a sharp downward turn in the mid-1980s and even dropping below 70 cents (U.S.) for a brief period in 1986. Since then, as a result of a combination of actions by the Bank of Canada and a weakening of the U.S. dollar in international markets, the Canadian dollar has climbed back up to the 80–90-cent (U.S.) range.

The Bank of Canada has kept Canadian interest rates several percentage points higher than U.S. rates throughout this most recent period to prevent the value of the Canadian dollar from falling too far below that of the U.S. dollar. This high-interest-rate policy has created considerable controversy among economists and business people (see the For Example. . . box on page 668). High interest rates, say the critics, discourage investment and add to unemployment; furthermore, by increasing the cost of doing business, they contribute to inflation. By attracting foreign capital, high interest rates also add to the large interest payments that already create problems in the current account. Our borrowings in the capital account add to the interest payments in the current account.

The Bank argues that high interest rates are necessary to prevent a massive outflow of capital from Canada to the United States and other countries into which Canadians channel their money. Unless we resorted to foreign-currency

The Behaviour of Canada's Exchange Rate (Relative to the U.S. Dollar), 1973–1991

BOX 26.5

This graph shows how the value of the Canadian dollar has changed relative to the U.S. dollar from 1973 to 1991. Our dollar was at par with the U.S. dollar in 1973, but then, especially after 1976, its value began to decline, plummeting to a low of less than 70 cents (U.S.) in 1986. Since then, it has climbed back up to the 80-cent (U.S.) range as a result of Bank of Canada interest-rate policy and a weakening of the U.S. dollar in international markets.

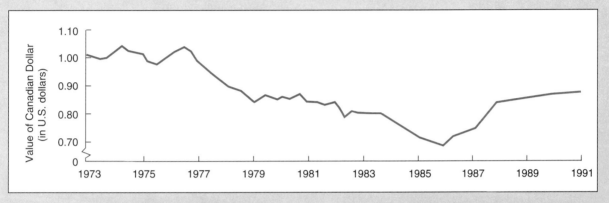

SOURCE: Department of Finance, *Economic Review*, Ottawa, April 1985.

controls, which are judged to be very difficult to manage, such an outflow would seriously drain this country of funds for investment. Furthermore, the Bank argues, if Canada's exchange rate were allowed to drop freely in response to market pressures, our cost of imports would rise, thus adding to Canada's inflation rate. In recent years, the Bank of Canada has relied in particular on the anti-inflation argument to justify its high-interest-rate policy.

What, then, is the solution? It is not clear that a devaluation of the Canadian dollar would be disastrous, in terms of either increased inflation or massive capital outflows. As our discussion of purchasing-power parity theory in Chapter 15 showed, the long-run value of the Canadian dollar relative to the U.S. dollar should settle at a ratio equal to the ratio of the Canadian dollar's purchasing power to that of the U.S. dollar. Therefore, although our dollar might fall to below 75 cents (U.S.) in the short run (in the absence of higher interest rates), in the long run, it should move in a range between 75 and 80 cents (U.S.), reflecting the fact that costs in the United States — and, hence, prices — are considered to be about 20 to 25 percent lower than in Canada. It will not be easy to solve our problems in the international sector, but we might be better advised to put up with the pain of short-run currency devaluations than to endure the greater debilitation of increasing deficits and high interest rates in the long run.

CONCLUSIONS

As the international economy moves through the 1990s, the world of Bretton Woods fades more and more into history. The academic debates over fixed versus

FOR EXAMPLE...
Controversy over Bank of Canada Policy

The following article documents the ongoing arguments about the value of the Canadian dollar. Note that Thomas Courchene is advocating not only a lower value for the dollar but a fixed exchange rate as well.

Eighty-Cent Dollar Urged as Expert Calls for Ending Inflation War

Canada should give up its war on inflation and peg the dollar at 80 cents (U.S.) before the country as we know it is destroyed, says leading economist Thomas Courchene.

"The real tragedy is that we did not peg the rate at 80 cents in 1988," Courchene told the Canadian Exporters' Association annual meeting yesterday.

Courchene said allowing the dollar to float to current levels of more than 88 cents (U.S.) has turned opportunities in the Canada–U.S. free-trade deal into "an economic nightmare."

The exporters' association has been a vocal critic of Bank of Canada inflation-fighting policies that have boosted the dollar and made [domestic] goods more expensive for foreign customers.

Those policies have been blamed for the 1990–91 recession and unemployment of more than 10 percent.

"If the bank holds to its course and if there is something special economically, socioculturally and politically about the upper half of North America, then this Canada will be history before it is competitive."

Courchene, director of the School of Policy Studies at Queen's University, in Kingston, Ontario, is a former chairman of the Ontario Economic Council.

He was also critical of the federal government's constitutional proposal released last month to make zero inflation the prime goal of the Bank of Canada.

"Constitutions ought to enshrine structures and principles, not economic policy," he added.

John Crow, governor of the central bank, has been keeping Canadian interest rates three-to-five percentage points higher than those in the United States to dampen consumer and business spending.

The side-effect of high interest rates has been a strong dollar as foreigners snap up high-yielding Canadian bonds.

Courchene said the Bank of Canada simply hasn't the clout to pursue a policy of zero-inflation independent of the United States.

A set of inflation targets were set in the federal budget in February with a goal of bringing down inflation to two percent by the end of 1995.

The annual inflation rate in August was 5.8 percent.

Finance Minister Don Mazankowski has stated repeatedly that zero-inflation is the foundation of his economic policies.

Although a high dollar hurts exporters, it brings down prices in Canada for imported goods.

But Courchene said Canada should follow the example of Europe where countries have been fixing exchange rates and now are pursuing a single European currency.

"The best way to think about all of this is that Canada will be tied, inflation-wise, to the U.S., just as is California."

Lloyd Atkinson, chief economist at the Bank of Montreal, told the meeting the high value of the dollar has been overestimated as a factor in Canada's declining competitiveness.

He said Canada's sluggish manufacturing productivity is a greater problem, one that's making for an anemic recovery from the year-long recession.

SOURCE: Clyde Graham, "80-Cent Dollar Urged as Expert Calls for Ending Inflation War," *Winnipeg Free Press*, October 8, 1991, p. 21.

floating exchange rates that characterized the 1950s and 1960s have been over-taken by events. At present, it is clear that the float is here to stay for quite a while. Critics of free-floating exchange rates argue that such rates have been tried and found wanting; supporters counter that floating rates have not been given enough of a chance, especially recently, to allow us to judge whether or not they could do the job.

Canada's current approach — the so-called dirty float, which allows our dollar to move up and down as long as it stays above 80 cents (U.S.) — involves the Bank of Canada's intervening in the foreign-exchange markets whenever the dollar threatens to fall too drastically. Hence, we may not know for some time whether truly flexible rates would solve some of our serious economic problems.

SUMMARY

1. Despite the inevitable zero balance for all the accounts in our balance of payments, an imbalance, or disequilibrium, can be said to exist whenever deficits or surpluses in the current account are not balanced by surpluses or deficits in the capital account. Such an imbalance will require the use of foreign-currency reserves and, under a system of *floating exchange rates*, will be reflected in exchange-rate fluctuations.

2. A unique combination of interest rates and real domestic income is required to produce a *balance-of-payments equilibrium. General equilibrium* can be said to exist only when the money market, the circular flow, and the foreign market are all in equilibrium. Under *fixed exchange rates*, monetary policy will create disequilibrium in the foreign sector, which will negate the effectiveness of such policies. Both fiscal and monetary policy can be more effective with flexible exchange rates.

3. From 1944 to 1973, the international monetary system operated under a system of fixed exchange rates. Many observers of the international economy continue to favour such a system. They argue that (1) it shields the domestic economy from international financial disturbances; (2) under flexible rates, depreciation of a currency does not necessarily improve the current-account balance in the short run; and (3) a depreciating exchange rate can cause, as well as be caused by, inflation, thereby creating the danger of a vicious–virtuous cycle.

4. Advocates of floating rates dispute each of these arguments and contend that fixed-rate proponents exaggerate the inherent instability of the international economy. They see the unwillingness of governments to play by the rules of the game as a fatal flaw in all fixed-rate systems.

5. Canada usually has a current-account deficit with the United States, which is attributable in large part to the interest and dividend payments that we owe on U.S. investments in Canada and which compels the Bank of Canada to follow a high-interest-rate policy in order to attract inflows of U.S. capital.

EFFECTIVE THINKING: PROBLEM 6

Monetary Policy

When formulating monetary policy, policy makers must consider existing Canadian fiscal policy as well as the economic policy and conditions of other nations with which Canada trades. The economic theory discussed in Chapters 25 and 26 is relevant to the following problem, which addresses the considerations involved in co-ordinating domestic fiscal and monetary policy with foreign-market factors.

You've been asked for your advice as an economic staff member in the policy-planning section of the Bank of Canada. The situation is as follows: The federal government and most provincial governments have been conducting expansionary fiscal policy during the past year. These governments have been borrowing money by issuing bonds to finance their increased spending. Inflation and nominal interest rates have been rising gradually, but the unemployment rate has declined throughout the nation.

Over the past year, the Bank of Canada has kept the money supply relatively constant and the bank rate stable at about 9 percent. The Bank is starting to be concerned about possible increasing rates of inflation. (The governor of the Bank has stated that his primary goal for monetary policy is to lower inflation rates.) The Federal Reserve's discount rate in the United States has been rising gradually over the past year and now stands at 8 percent. The U.S discount rate is predicted to continue to rise slowly.

Surveys show that Canadians expect an inflation rate of about 5 percent per year. The current level of inflation is 4 percent per year. The current exchange rate between the Canadian dollar and the U.S. dollar is $1 Cdn. = $0.84 U.S. The reserve ratio required of chartered banks by the Bank of Canada is 6.25 percent (0.0625); the marginal propensity to consume domestic output (MPC_D) is 0.7; and the marginal propensity to save (MPS) is 0.1. The money demand curve (MD) and the investment schedule (*I*) are estimated by the Bank to have the slopes shown in the accompanying graphs, and the money supply (MS) is $40 billion while desired investment is $120 billion, also as shown there. (Note that the bank rate and the nominal interest rate are different, and that the nominal interest rate is not the same as the expected real interest rate. Remember that the nominal interest rate equals the expected real interest rate plus the expected rate of inflation.)

Directions

As a Bank of Canada policy adviser, formulate monetary policy to meet the primary goal of monetary policy as stated by the governor of the Bank — that is, to lower the rate of inflation. Other monetary-policy goals such as low rates of

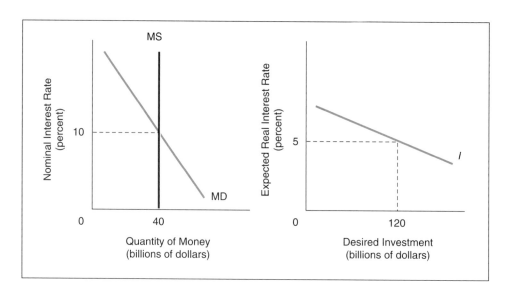

unemployment, steady growth of real GDP, and balance-of-payments stability can also be considered, but fighting inflation should be viewed as the central goal. Use the numbers given in the problem for any calculations you might make or graphs you might draw, but bear in mind that it is impossible to obtain exact results on the basis of the limited information supplied and with the large number of unpredictable variables involved. The concepts you have learned in several of the macroeconomics chapters in this book will be useful to you in working with this situation. Use the twelve effective-thinking steps for successful problem solving in formulating the appropriate monetary policy in this situation (see the Appendix to Chapter 3 if you need to review the steps). For Steps 10 through 12, assume that the plan you adopt in Step 9 is implemented. Although monetary-policy *concepts* will be the main tool you need in working through this situation, you may create data based on reasonable assumptions if you would also like to make calculations as a part of your solution.

An example of the thinking process an economist might go through using these twelve problem-solving steps appears at the back of the book (see pages 783–94). Not all economists would produce identical answers for each step, but they would all draw on accepted principles of economics.

KEY TERMS

balance-of-payments
    equilibrium
net capital inflow function
general equilibrium

fixed exchange rates
floating, or flexible, exchange
    rates

J-curve effect
Bretton Woods system

KEY BOXES

Box 26.1 A Balance-of-Payments Equilibrium

Box 26.2 A General Equilibrium View of the
            Money Market, the Foreign Market,
            and the Circular Flow

REVIEW QUESTIONS

1. Using Box 26.2 as your model for analysis, assume that the government increases its desired expenditures on goods and services by $100 and that the multiplier is 2.5. Also assume that the Bank of Canada "accommodates" the new fiscal policy by increasing the money supply to prevent interest rates from rising, so that interest rates remain at 8 percent.

    a. By how much would real domestic income increase?

    b. Would the foreign sector be in equilibrium at the new level of income? Explain precisely what would happen to the current and capital accounts.

    c. If the Bank of Canada refuses to allow the exchange rate to fall, what would it have to do to interest rates to correct any imbalances that might exist? How does this compare with recent Bank of Canada policy in Canada?

    d. How would any imbalances be solved through flexible exchange rates?

2. If the Canadian dollar depreciates against the U.S. dollar, it is assumed that Americans will want to buy more Canadian goods and services and Canadians will want to buy fewer American goods and services. This increase in exports and decrease in desired imports should help to restore the imbalance that may have prompted the depreciation in the first place. However, what would happen if Americans actually spent less on Canadian goods than they did before? (*Note*: Americans can now buy Canadian dollars more cheaply than before. Therefore, although they will likely buy more Canadian goods, their outlay on these goods might actually decline.) Conversely, what would happen if Canadian outlays (expenditures) on American goods increased?

3. Assume that, at the current interest rate, net capital inflow is $250. If the net-export function is $80 = 0.1Y$, what level of real domestic income is required in order to achieve a balance-of-payments equilibrium?

4. If real domestic income is currently $1250 and the net-export function is $85 - 0.15Y$, what must the net capital inflow be for the balance of payments to be in equilibrium?

5. The government cuts taxes by $200 million as part of fiscal-policy action, and there is no change in the money supply. Using the linkages among the money market, desired investment, and aggregate desired expenditure, describe possible changes in desired consumption, money demand, interest rates, desired investment, aggregate desired expenditure, real domestic income, net exports, net capital inflow, and the exchange rate (assuming it is flexible).

Stabilization
Problems
and Strategies

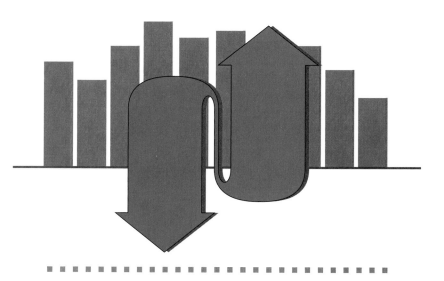

The Inflation–Unemployment Problem

WHAT YOU WILL LEARN IN THIS CHAPTER

After studying this chapter, you will be able to

1. Explain what is meant by the economy's *noninflationary level of real output.*

2. Use aggregate supply and demand curves to show how a drop in aggregate demand causes a recession and to illustrate two ways in which the economy can recover from a recession.

3. Define *demand-pull inflation* and explain how it affects real output.

4. Define *cost-push inflation* and show how it can lead to an inflationary recession.

5. Discuss the basic characteristics and relevance of the Phillips curve.

A Preview   *The Spectre of Stagflation*

The following "snapshots of the economy" were taken by the *Financial Post* in mid-1991. At that time, both inflation and unemployment were considered significant problems in the Canadian economy. It was forecast that, by 1992, the inflation rate would decline to more acceptable levels, but the unemployment rate would remain at approximately 10 percent of the work force. In this chapter and the next one, we will focus on the twin problems of inflation and unemployment.

Snapshots of the Economy

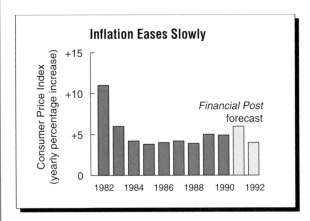

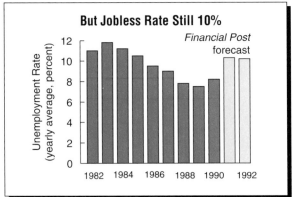

Inflation will moderate next year but, with the Consumer Price Index still running 4 percent above year-earlier levels, the battle won't be won.

Sluggish economic growth will mean only a slow reduction in unemployment, with the jobless rate likely to average 10 percent in 1992.

SOURCE: *Financial Post*, August 19, 1991, p. 5. Reproduced with permission.

THE INFLATION–UNEMPLOYMENT DILEMMA: A LONG-TERM PROBLEM

As we have noted in previous chapters, Canada's economic policy makers must attempt to achieve several goals simultaneously: price stability, full employment, economic growth, a smaller public debt, and — as we stressed in Chapter 26 — a balance-of-payments equilibrium and an appropriate value for the Canadian dollar. There are several reasons for treating the first three of these goals in greater depth. First, the general public is affected most directly, and most dramatically by price inflation, unemployment, and economic growth. Second, it appears that the government's economic policies have largely failed to produce satisfactory results in these areas, particularly in the last few decades. Third, performance in any one of these three areas has a significant effect on performance in the other two.

In this chapter, we show how unemployment and inflation are linked, and why it is so difficult to achieve adequate levels of performance in these two areas simultaneously. Chapter 28 describes a set of policies that could be used in conjunction with fiscal and monetary policies to achieve better results. Chapter 29 then examines economic growth, comparing Canada's performance with that of other countries.

Canada's failure to achieve satisfactory levels of inflation and employment has tended to be more pronounced than that of most other leading industrial nations. Box 27.1 shows that among the Group of Seven — the world's seven leading market economies — Canada had the highest unemployment rate (10.6 percent) in mid-1991, and the second-highest inflation rate (at 5.8 percent). Canada's position in mid-1991 was indicative of its relative performance over the course of the past decade, except that, for much of that decade, the United Kingdom's rate of inflation was slightly higher than Canada's, and its unemployment rate was almost as high.

Inflation and Unemployment Rates in the Group of Seven Countries, 1991 — BOX 27.1

Among the seven leading Western industrial nations, Canada had the highest unemployment rate in mid-1991 and, following Italy, the second-highest inflation rate.

Country	Unemployment Rate (percent)	Inflation Rate (one-year percentage increase in Consumer Price Index)
Canada	10.6	5.8
France	9.5	3.0
Germany	6.4	4.1
Italy	9.9	6.3
Japan	2.2	3.5
United Kingdom	8.5	4.7
United States	6.8	3.8

SOURCE: *The Economist*, September 28, 1991, p. 115. Reproduced with permission.

In mid-1991, Canada's inflation rate was coming down, but there seemed to be little prospect of a substantial reduction in the unemployment rate. It was apparent that the government's economic policies were not providing satisfactory solutions in 1991, and had not been doing so for some time before. In our discussion of this persistent dilemma, we will focus on the nature of the disease in this chapter and on the adequacy — or inadequacy — of attempted cures in the next.

EXPLAINING INFLATION AND UNEMPLOYMENT

In Chapters 20 and 21, we examined some of the reasons for inflation and unemployment with the aid of the Keynesian income–expenditure model and the modern tools of aggregate demand–aggregate supply analysis. Before proceeding any further, we shall review briefly the essential features of this body of theory.

Inflation and Unemployment in the Short Run

Box 27.2, which resembles Box 20.6, provides a concise introduction to our further analysis. We assume in part (a) that the economy is initially in equilibrium at a real-income level of Y_1 (where the aggregate expenditure curve ADE_1 crosses the equilibrium line, Z), and has an unemployment rate of 10 percent. Box 27.2(b) shows that income level Y_1 is related to price level P_1, as indicated by the intersection of aggregate demand curve AD_1 and the aggregate supply curve, AS. Now let us assume that something causes aggregate desired expenditure, as depicted in part (a), to increase. Such an increase could result from a number of factors: new fiscal policy measures that involve increases in desired government expenditures or decreases in taxes, or both; new monetary policies that increase the money supply or reduce interest rates, or both; growth in net exports; increases in desired business investment; or a decrease in the personal saving rate and a corresponding increase in desired consumer expenditures. Any of these or some combination of them, could cause the aggregate expenditure curve to shift upward, from ADE_1 to ADE_2. At the point where curve ADE_2 crosses the Z line, a new equilibrium income, Y_2, is attained. We shall assume that the increase in income is not accompanied by inflation *initially*. Thus, since the whole of the multiplier effect is "real," there is a substantial decline in the unemployment rate — to 7 percent.

Now, as shown in Box 27.2(b), the increase in aggregate desired expenditure has caused the aggregate demand curve to shift to the right, from AD_1 to AD_2. If prices remain at the level P_1, a new equilibrium will be established at point E_2 on AD_2 (at real-income level Y_2). However, as we saw in our analysis in Chapter 20, the upward-sloping aggregate supply curve does not allow for equilibrium at this point. Evidently, as output expands, costs rise, forcing producers to charge higher prices. We assume at this point that costs rise not because of increased input prices, but because of diminishing marginal productivity as output expands. (Costs may also rise because more use is made of overtime. Labour costs will therefore increase, but not because wage *rates* have risen.) As prices rise, aggregate desired expenditure declines, as shown by the downward shift from ADE_2 to ADE_3 in Box 27.2(a). This in turn forces a decline in aggregate quantity demanded, which is indicated by a movement upward and to the left along AD_2

Explaining Inflation and Unemployment Using the Income–Expenditure Model and Aggregate Demand–Aggregate Supply Analysis

BOX 27.2

Part (a) uses the basic Keynesian income–expenditure model to show how an initial equilibrium income is established at Y_1, with an unemployment rate of 10 percent. An expenditure increase shifts ADE_1 to ADE_2; as a result, income rises to Y_2 and unemployment falls to 7 percent. However, part (b) shows that the increase in desired expenditure causes the aggregate demand curve to shift to the right (from AD_1 to AD_2), so that it intersects the upward-sloping aggregate supply curve at point E_3, raising prices from P_1 to P_2. Macroeconomic equilibrium is thus finally established. The ultimate result of the increase in desired expenditure is a drop in unemployment but an increase in prices.

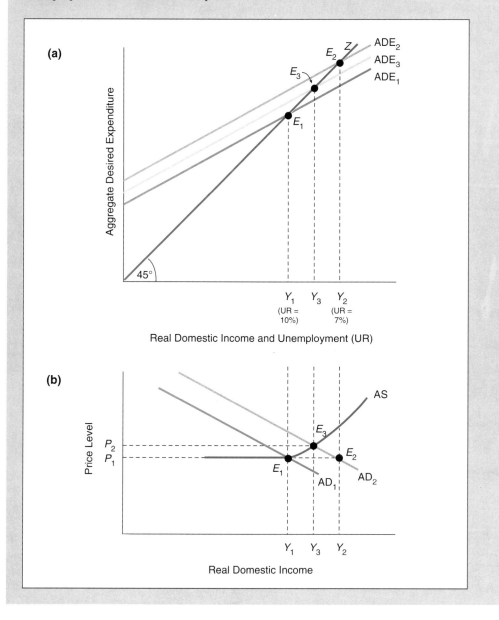

in part (b). A new macroeconomic equilibrium is achieved at point E_3, where aggregate demand equals aggregate supply.

The end result of the increase in aggregate desired expenditure is a decrease in unemployment (to a level somewhere between 10 percent and 7 percent) and an increase in prices (from P_1 to P_2). The reduction in unemployment may be attributed to two factors:

1. The increase in aggregate desired expenditure, which increases real output.

2. The fact that, as aggregate desired expenditure increases, costs rise, but not enough to absorb the whole increase in real output. This is an important new point to which we will return in a moment. However, it may be clear even without the aid of formal theory that, if the aggregate supply curve in Box 27.2(b) were vertical at E_1 rather than gradually upward sloping, the increase in aggregate demand would produce no increase in real output and, hence, no drop in the unemployment rate.

The increase in prices may also be attributed to two factors:

1. The increases in aggregate desired expenditure, which causes the aggregate demand curve to shift upward and to the right, where it intersects the upward-sloping aggregate supply curve at a higher price level. This phenomenon will be described later as "demand-pull inflation."

2. The fact that the aggregate supply curve slopes upward. If the aggregate supply curve remained horizontal at point E_1 in Box 27.2(b), the aggregate demand curve could shift to the right and settle at point E_2, occasioning no increase in the price level.

Since several conditions must be satisfied simultaneously in order to increase output and reduce unemployment — and to do both without inflation — it should be seen already that neither fiscal nor monetary policy can guarantee lower rates of unemployment or price stability. Both operate essentially on the demand side of the economy, while changes in output, employment, and prices are the result of both demand and supply forces. We will return to this theme in the next chapter where policy solutions are examined more closely.

So far, our analysis of how aggregate demand and aggregate supply interact to increase output, reduce unemployment, and, in all likelihood, increase prices has been confined to the short run. We have defined the short run in this case as a situation in which input prices remain fixed. The aggregate supply curve that we have used thus far is based on the assumption that input prices are constant; we will continue to assume that this is the case for all short-run supply curves. However, it is important to observe what happens in the long run, when input prices *do* change and cause the economy to shift from one short-run aggregate supply curve to another.

Long-Run Shifts in the Aggregate Supply Curve

In explaining how firms react in the short run to an increase in aggregate demand, it is necessary to observe their expectations about input prices. The aggregate supply curve AS_1 in Box 27.3, which is similar to the aggregate supply curve in Box 27.2(b), is based on the assumption that firms expect input prices to remain at levels corresponding to an average price level of $1.00 for *all* goods.

Aggregate Supply in the Long Run, and Long-Run Equilibrium

BOX 27.3

The upward-sloping aggregate supply curve applies only in the short run because, sooner or later, each firm's increases in output prices become increases in other firms' input prices. As this happens, firms revise their plans in order to take the higher costs into account. The increase in the expected level of input prices shifts the aggregate supply curve upward. Assuming that the aggregate demand curve remains fixed, the economy will move upward along AD_2 as the aggregate supply curve shifts upward. In time, the economy will reach a new long-run equilibrium at E_3. At that point, the price level will have risen fully in proportion to the increase in demand. Real output will then have returned to its NILO of $1000. Expected input prices will have risen to a level consistent with the new average level of output prices, $1.10.

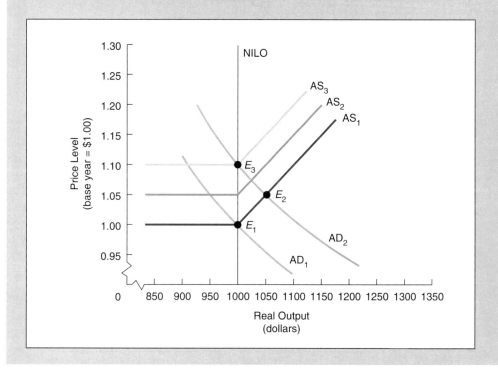

Given this expectation, when the aggregate demand curve shifts from AD_1 to AD_2, firms move from point E_1 to point E_2 along the aggregate supply curve.

It is important to note that curve AS_1 is horizontal up to a real-output level of $1000, and only then begins to rise. The output level of $1000, beyond which prices begin to rise as output increases, is known in economic theory as the **noninflationary level of (real) output (NILO)**. It is the point at which long-run equilibrium with stable prices is possible.

The NILO is not an absolute limit to what the economy can produce. Output can rise above it for a brief period if more people than usual go to work, if firms add overtime work, and if standby plant capacity is brought into use. Conversely, in a period of recession when resources lie idle, real output falls below the noninflationary level.

Noninflationary level of (real) output (NILO)
The level of output at which long-run equilibrium with stable prices is possible.

The concept of the NILO is closely related to that of the production possibilities frontier introduced in Chapter 2. Points on the frontier represent different possible mixes of output within the noninflationary level of overall output. If resources are not used fully, the economy will fall inside its production possibilities frontier, that is, below the NILO. Output above the NILO corresponds to points outside the production possibilities frontier. Such points may be reached temporarily through overtime work, the use of standby capacity, and so on. But a permanently higher level of real output requires an expansion of the frontier as the result of investment, technological advance, or the like.

In our previous analysis, the point E_2 was seen as a point of macroeconomic equilibrium (the same point was labelled E_3 in Box 27.2[b]). But E_2 is not a point of *long-run equilibrium*. The reason is that the rise in the general price level (from \$1.00 to \$1.05, as Box 27.3 is drawn) will inevitably cause firms to revise their initial expectations about input prices. This happens because the prices of each firm's output affect the prices of other firms' inputs.

In the case of firms that make intermediate goods, the relationship between input prices and output prices is simple and direct: If steel mills raise the prices of their sheet steel and beams, auto makers and construction firms will face an increase in their input prices. But there is also a pass-through from output prices to input prices in the case of firms that make consumer goods. In this case, the linkage runs from the price of consumer goods to the cost of living to the level of wages. If firms that make shirts and radios and potato chips raise their prices, workers will face an increase in the cost of living. To maintain their standard of living, they will seek higher wages. Sooner or later, this increase in wages will raise the costs of all firms.

At E_2, then, the price level has risen to \$1.05. Recall that aggregate supply curve AS_1 assumed a level of input prices corresponding to an average level of output prices of \$1.00. As the prices of each firm's outputs begin to be passed through to increases in the input prices of other firms, the expected level of input prices begins to rise. In Chapter 4, we saw how an increase in the prices of inputs used in the production of a good — say, the fuel, fertilizer, and machinery used in the production of wheat — would cause an upward shift in the supply curve for that good. In much the same way, an increase in the expected average price of all inputs causes the economy's aggregate supply curve to shift up.

In this case, the price level has risen to \$1.05. If firms now expect a level of input prices corresponding to this new average level of output prices, the aggregate supply curve will shift up to position AS_2. The curve shifts upward by exactly the same amount that the expected price level has risen.

For the moment, we assume that firms base their expectations regarding input prices on the average level of output prices that prevailed in the previous year. Applying this rule will make it easy to keep track of what is going on as aggregate supply and demand conditions change.

Long-Run Equilibrium

Still using Box 27.3, we can now trace the economy's path to a new long-run equilibrium. In doing so, we assume that the aggregate demand curve remains in the position AD_2. As the aggregate supply curve shifts to AS_2, reflecting a higher expected level of input prices, firms do not find it profitable to expand their output as much as they initially did. As the quantity supplied in each market is reduced, prices rise even higher. As a consequence, there is a movement up and to the left along aggregate demand curve AD_2.

As this happens, the price level moves higher than the level of $1.05 that had been reached at E_2. As ongoing increases in output prices continue to affect the input prices of other firms, the aggregate supply curve shifts still higher. In the long run, if there is no further change in demand, the economy will reach the point E_3, where the aggregate supply curve has shifted all the way to AS_3. At that point, the price level has risen to $1.10, and real output has fallen back to its original level of $1000 — that is, to the noninflationary level of output.

At E_3, the entire increase in demand has been converted into price increases. There is no reason for firms to expect input prices to rise more unless something new happens to demand. At this point, the expected level of input prices has finally been brought back into line with the average level of output prices. Only such a point, at which the intersection of the aggregate supply and aggregate demand curves occurs at the noninflationary level of output, can be a point of long-run equilibrium.

APPLICATIONS OF AGGREGATE SUPPLY AND DEMAND THEORY TO CONDITIONS OF RECESSION AND INFLATION

Aggregate supply and aggregate demand curves make it possible to deal with a number of policy issues. They allow us to go beyond the effects of monetary and fiscal policy on real variables. With the help of our new tools, we can see the effects these policies have on real output *and* the price level directly. In this section, we will begin by looking at the economy in a period of recession. After that, we will look at two kinds of inflation. Throughout the discussion, we will be careful to distinguish between the short-run and long-run effects of economic policy. Also, while we will assume that it is changes in aggregate desired expenditure that bring about changes in aggregate demand, we will focus on the latter in showing what happens to prices, output, and employment.

The Economy in Recession

A classic recession is brought about by a drop in aggregate demand. Box 27.4 illustrates the process. The story begins with the economy in equilibrium at E_1. This corresponds to the assumed NILO of $1000 and a price level of $1.00. Suppose now that something causes aggregate desired expenditure to fall to $900. Whatever the cause, falling aggregate desired expenditure shifts the aggregate demand curve from AD_1 to AD_2.

The first effect of the drop in demand will be unplanned inventory buildup as sales fall short of output rates. As in the case of an increase in aggregate demand, we will assume that firms at first expect no change in input prices. This being the case, they will react just as they would if their industry were the only one affected by the decline in demand. As firms in each industry move to the left along their own industry supply curves, the economy as a whole will move to the left along the aggregate supply curve.

As this happens, real output falls, though prices may remain constant at $1.00 (point E_2). Firms reduce their output or shut down. Workers are laid off and

BOX 27.4   The Economy in Recession

This graph shows a recession that is assumed to have been brought on by a decrease in aggregate desired expenditure (not shown here) from $1000 to $900. As the aggregate demand curve shifts from AD_1 to AD_2, the economy moves to the left along aggregate supply curve AS_1 to point E_2. As it does so, real output falls below its noninflationary level and unemployment rises. The economy can recover from the recession through a return of aggregate demand to its initial level. If that does not occur, the aggregate supply curve will shift downward progressively, to AS_2 and AS_3, and the economy will return to its NILO at a lower price level (at point E_4). This process can, however, be very slow.

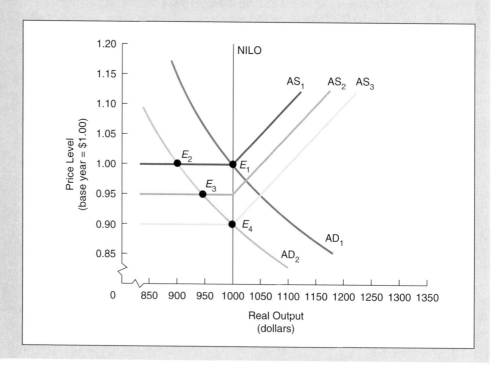

have trouble finding new jobs. The unemployment rate rises, and the economy approaches the low point of a recession.

Two paths to recovery

From E_2, there are two paths that the economy can take to return to the noninflationary level of real output. The first possibility is that aggregate desired expenditure remains at its new level of $900. If this happens, the economy will not remain at E_2. Price cuts will be made by some firms, and as the economy falls into recession, these will increasingly come to represent cuts in other firms' input prices. As this happens, the expected level of input prices will fall, and the aggregate supply curve will shift downward, to AS_2. As it does so, the economy will slowly work its way down along aggregate demand curve AD_2 toward a new short-run equilibrium at E_3. The last drop in prices may reduce input prices even further, causing the aggregate supply curve to shift again, to AS_3. The economy will again work its way down aggregate demand curve AD_2, to a long-run equilibrium at point E_4. There, real output will return to its NILO of $1000. The price level will have fallen from $1.00 to $0.90, in proportion to the drop in aggregate desired expenditure. And the expected level of input prices will be brought into line with this new, lower average level of all prices.

The other path by which the economy can return to the noninflationary level of real output is by way of a rebound of aggregate desired expenditure. If desired expenditures return to their initial level, the aggregate demand curve will shift back to position AD_1. If the original shift in aggregate desired expenditure was caused by a temporary drop in desired consumption, investment, or net exports, the rebound in demand may take place without government action. If it does not, an expansionary fiscal or monetary policy can be used to speed the recovery. In either case, a quick recovery by aggregate demand will allow the economy to move back up along the aggregate supply curve to E_1 before the supply curve has time to begin to shift downward.

Which path out of a recession is better? Many economists favour a policy of restoring aggregate desired expenditure, using active fiscal or monetary policy if necessary. They think that recovery through falling prices would take too long. For a number of reasons — some psychological, some having to do with long-term contracts — firms tend to raise prices more readily than they cut them. And workers seem to accept cuts in nominal wages much less willingly than they accept wage increases.

Recent recessions in Canada have not lasted long enough to bring about reductions in the general price level. (Wages and prices in hard-hit sectors such as lumber, steel, or copper often fall during recessions, but in recent recessions, these have been offset by price increases in other sectors, such as services.) During the Great Depression, however, both prices and real output fell dramatically. It took a whole decade for the economy to recover. Since that time, policy makers have tried to deal with recessions by restoring aggregate desired expenditure as quickly as possible.

Demand-Pull Inflation

The opposite of recession is **demand-pull inflation**, which refers to an increase in the price level caused by an expansion of aggregate demand relative to the economy's noninflationary level of real output. Box 27.3 gave us a first look at demand-pull inflation, although we did not use the term there. Now Box 27.5 continues the story.

> **Demand-pull inflation**
> An increase in the price level caused by an increase of aggregate demand relative to the noninflationary real output level.

The onset of demand-pull inflation

The economy starts out in equilibrium at E_1, where the price level is $1.00 and real output is equal to its NILO. Then, an increase in aggregate desired expenditure shifts the aggregate demand curve to AD_2. The surge in demand results in unplanned inventory depletion. Expecting to be able to restock their inventories at an unchanged level of input prices, firms in each industry move up along their industry supply curves. As this happens, the economy moves up along aggregate supply curve AS_1 toward a new short-term equilibrium at E_2.

This is the first stage of demand-pull inflation. The increase in demand has pulled prices up, although not fully in proportion to the increase in demand. As we stressed earlier, however, E_2 is not a point of long-run equilibrium. Soon, the output-price increases that have taken place on the way to E_2 will become increases in other firms' input prices. Then firms will revise their expectations of input prices, and the aggregate supply curve will begin to shift upward.

BOX 27.5   *Demand-Pull Inflation*

Demand-pull inflation occurs when aggregate demand increases relative to the NILO. In this graph, the economy starts out at E_1, where real output is at its NILO. An increase in demand shifts the aggregate demand curve to AD_2. Both prices and real output rise as the economy moves upward along AS_1. This is the first phase of demand-pull inflation. If aggregate demand did not increase further, the economy would return to the noninflationary level of real output at E_3 as the aggregate supply curve shifted upward. However, a continued expansionary policy may allow the aggregate demand curve to keep pace with the rising aggregate supply curve. In that case, the economy moves upward along the path shown by the arrow. Real output remains above its NILO, but the economy continues to experience demand-pull inflation.

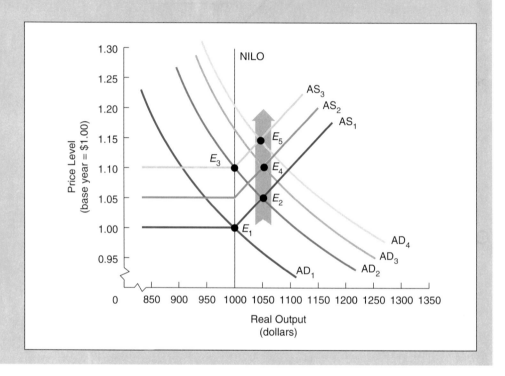

Continuing demand-pull inflation

There are two ways in which events can unfold from this point. One was shown in Box 27.3, where aggregate demand was assumed to remain fixed at its new level. In that case, the aggregate demand curve stays in the position AD_2, and the economy drifts up along it toward E_3. As it does so, the increase in real output that took place during the initial phase of demand-pull inflation is reversed.

Alternatively, expansionary fiscal or monetary policy might allow aggregate demand to continue to grow. In this case, as the aggregate supply curve is driven upward by firms' expectations of rising input prices, the aggregate demand curve keeps up with it. Real output does not fall back toward its NILO. Instead, the whole increase in aggregate demand is being reflected in higher prices.

This is the second phase of demand-pull inflation, in which rising aggregate demand and expectations of a rising price level keep pace with each other. The aggregate demand and supply curves both shift upward, and the economy follows a path from E_1 to E_2 to E_4 and so on, as shown by the arrow in Box 27.5.

Policy implications

Box 27.5 has major implications for economic policy. It suggests that, in the short run, starting from a state of equilibrium, an expansionary fiscal or monetary policy is an effective way to stimulate real economic growth and lower unemployment. In the short run, the cost of such a policy is a small amount of inflation. However, according to the theory, the benefits of demand-pull inflation are not permanent.

After the first benefits of the expansion have been enjoyed, policy makers face a dilemma. One choice is to stop the stimulus. If they do this, inflation will slow again, but output will fall and unemployment will rise. The other choice is to continue the expansionary fiscal or monetary policy. In this case, the theory holds, real output can be held above its NILO for some time. Choosing this path, however, means continuing inflation.[1]

Cost-Push Inflation

Demand-pull inflation occurs when the aggregate demand curve shifts upward while the aggregate supply curve either remains fixed or shifts upward at an equal rate. But inflation is also possible when the aggregate supply curve shifts upward while the aggregate demand curve either stays in place or shifts upward at a slower rate. This type of inflation is known as **cost-push inflation** because upward shifts in the aggregate supply curve are linked with increases in firms' costs of production.

Cost-push inflation
Inflation that is caused by an upward shift in the aggregate supply curve while the aggregate demand curve remains fixed or shifts upward more slowly.

Supply shocks

Box 27.6 shows the economy starting out in long-run equilibrium at point E_1. The price level is $1.00 and real output is at its noninflationary level of $1000. At this point, something happens that abruptly raises input prices for all or most firms, and also raises workers' cost of living. The sudden increases that occurred in 1974 and 1979–80 in the cost of natural resources, including oil, are examples of such an event. A major crop failure or natural disaster would be another example. Such an upward push to the price level from an outside source is known as a **supply shock**.

The effect of a supply shock — let's say, of an abrupt increase in imported-oil prices — is to raise the level of input prices above the level that firms had expected. As firms see what has happened and adjust their expectations accordingly, the aggregate supply curve shifts upward from AS_1 to AS_2, as shown in Box 27.6. With the higher expected level of input prices but with no matching increase in demand, firms must revise their plans. They find that it is no longer profitable to produce as much as they did before. As they cut back their output, each industry moves up and to the left along its industry demand curve. As this

Supply shock
An event, such as an increase in the price of imported oil, a crop failure, or a natural disaster, that raises input prices for all or most firms and pushes up workers' cost of living.

---

[1]The way Box 27.5 is drawn, the rate of inflation is steady from year to year as the economy moves up along the path from E_2 to E_4 to E_5. However, later, when we take a closer look at the process of inflation, we will show that the policy implications of demand-pull inflation are even more discouraging than is suggested here. We will show that a steady rate of inflation is not enough to keep real output above its NILO for a prolonged period. Instead, a steadily accelerating rate of inflation is required.

BOX 27.6 *Effects of a Supply Shock*

A supply shock is an event, such as an increase in the price of imported oil, that drives up input prices. In this graph, the economy starts out in equilibrium at point E_1. Then a supply shock pushes the aggregate supply curve upward, from AS_1 to AS_2. As a result, the economy moves from E_1 to E_2. The latter, however, is not a point of long-run equilibrium, since real output is below its NILO. If the aggregate demand curve stays in the position AD_1, the economy will eventually return to E_1 as the relative prices of nonenergy products fall. This will bring the average price level back to $1.00. The economy can recover from the supply shock faster if aggregate demand is increased, shifting the aggregate demand curve to AD_2. This will move the economy to point E_3. However, the result of responding to a supply shock with an increase in demand is a higher price level.

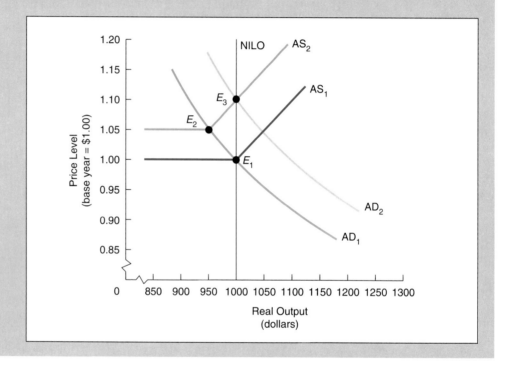

happens, the economy as a whole moves upward and to the left along aggregate demand curve AD_1 to point E_2. There, real output is below its NILO. The economy cannot remain in this position, but what happens next depends on what is done with aggregate demand.

If aggregate demand remains at $1000, the aggregate demand curve will stay at AD_1. In this case, the excess capacity of firms and excess unemployment will tend to put downward pressure on wages and prices. Some unemployed workers will accept jobs at lower wages than they had hoped for. Firms will find that, although energy prices remain high, the average level of input prices is not as high as they had initially expected it to be. This will give them a little room to cut their prices in order to boost sales. In time, the economy will move back down along AD_1, from E_2 to E_1. The price level will fall back to where it was before oil prices rose, and output will return to its noninflationary level.

This path to recovery from a supply shock is likely to be quite slow, however. To follow this path, average prices — output prices as well as the expected prices of inputs — must fall while energy prices, the assumed source of the supply shock, remain high. This means that there must be a major adjustment in relative prices. Real wages and the prices of goods and services other than energy must fall more than the average to bring the average down. This is likely to be a painful process for everyone.

There is, however, another way to recover from a supply shock. This is through expansion of aggregate desired expenditure. If aggregate desired expenditure is raised from $1000 to $1100, the aggregate demand curve in Box 27.6 will shift upward, from AD_1 to AD_2. The economy can then move to an equilibrium at E_3, where output will be back at its NILO.

In fact, if the expansion of aggregate desired expenditure follows the supply shock quickly enough, the economy may be able to avoid any major loss of real output. Instead of moving to E_2, it will move straight up along the noninflationary level of real output from E_1 to E_3.

Recovery from a supply shock through expansion of demand is likely to be faster than recovery through adjustment of relative prices. Also, the cost of recovery in terms of lost real output is likely to be less. But the cost in terms of inflation is greater. If policy makers respond to the supply shock by raising aggregate demand, the price level will end up being permanently higher. If they keep the lid on aggregate demand, the impact of the supply shock on the average price level will be only temporary. After the adjustment is complete, the reduction in the prices of goods and services other than energy will be large enough to offset the increase in energy prices, so that there will be no lasting increase in the price level.

There is no general agreement on the best way to react to supply shocks. The option selected depends in part on policy markers' relative degree of tolerance for inflation, on the one hand, and unemployment, on the other. Some economists have suggested that temporary supply shocks such as crop failures or natural disasters should not be met by raising aggregate demand. The reasoning is that the aggregate supply curve will soon shift back down as the damage is repaired. But, they suggest, a long-lasting supply shock such as the oil-price increases of the 1970s might best be at least partially accommodated by raising aggregate demand. It may be worth suffering the resulting permanent increase in the price level in order to avoid a prolonged transition period of low real output and high unemployment before relative prices are able to adjust.

Inflationary expectations

Supply shocks are not the only source of cost-push inflation. Cost-push inflation can also be caused by inflationary expectations, fuelled by the experience of demand-pull inflation in the past. To get this result, we need to modify our assumptions about the way firms form their expectations about the level of input prices. Up to this point, we have assumed that firms expect input prices in the current year to be at a level consistent with the level of output prices in the previous year. However, this assumption is probably unrealistic in an economy that has experienced inflation for several years in a row. Under conditions of continuing inflation, it is likely that firms will expect the level of input prices to increase this year by a percentage equal to last year's rate of inflation. To put it another way, it is likely that when firms have seen inflation in the past, they will expect more inflation in the future, and will make their plans accordingly.

Box 27.7 shows what happens when inflationary expectations become established in the economy. We begin from a situation of continuing demand-pull inflation. An expansionary fiscal or monetary policy has held output above its noninflationary level for some time. The economy is moving upward along the arrow through E_1 and E_2. After several years of inflation, firms and workers expect more inflation in the future. They have adjusted their plans to cope with it as best they can. Their plans are reflected in a series of upward-shifting aggregate supply curves that keep pace with the upward-shifting aggregate demand curve.

What happens now if the government decides to stop inflation by stopping the growth of aggregate desired expenditure? (Note that we are not talking about *reducing* the level of aggregate desired expenditure, but only about stopping its

BOX 27.7 *Inflationary Recession (Stagflation)*

In this graph, the economy has been experiencing demand-pull inflation, moving along the arrow from E_1 to E_2. At that point, a shift in fiscal and monetary policy stops the growth of aggregate desired expenditure. The aggregate demand curve becomes fixed in the position AD_2. Firms and workers expect inflation to continue, pushing up input prices and the cost of living. As a result, the aggregate supply curve continues to shift upward. As the aggregate supply curve shifts from AS_3 to AS_4, the economy experiences an inflationary recession, or stagflation, in which prices continue to rise while real output drops below its NILO.

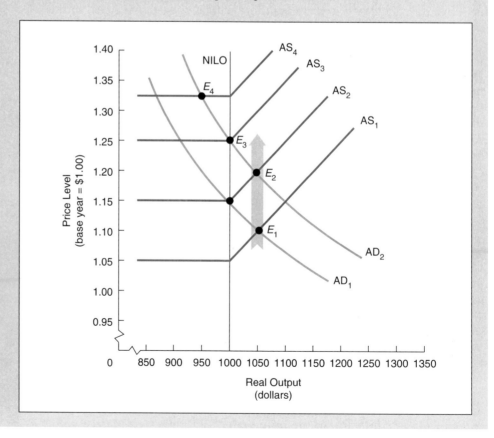

growth.) In terms of the graph, the effect would be to stop the upward shift of the aggregate demand curve, leaving it in the position AD$_2$.

Stopping the growth of aggregate desired expenditure would not stop inflation in its tracks. We have assumed that firms and workers have grown accustomed to inflation and expect it to continue. Workers expect their cost of living to rise and have negotiated contracts with their employers that give them offsetting wage increases each year. Firms expect their input prices to rise and have become accustomed to passing the increases along to their customers. As long as firms expect their input prices to rise and set their prices and output plans on that basis, the aggregate supply curve will continue to drift upward.

Inflationary recession

With the aggregate supply curve moving upward while the aggregate demand curve stays put, real output will start to fall and unemployment will start to rise. Meanwhile, the price level will keep going up. Soon, the economy will reach point E_3 in Box 27.7, where real output has returned to its NILO. This is not the end of the story, however. Inflation is still going on, and there is no reason for firms or workers to expect it to stop. Because firms and workers expect prices to continue to rise, they continue to make their plans on that basis, and the aggregate supply curve keeps on drifting upward, as shown by AS$_4$ in Box 27.7.

As the economy moves along the aggregate demand curve toward point E_4, it enters an **inflationary recession** (sometimes referred to as *stagflation*). This is a situation in which inflation, high unemployment, and depressed real output all occur at the same time.

Policy implications

What can be done to bring the economy out of an inflationary recession? A "cold turkey" approach is to keep the lid on aggregate desired expenditure, and wait. Rising unemployment, slowing sales, and an unplanned inventory buildup will, in time, cause firms and workers to revise their inflationary expectations. Prices of raw materials will begin to fall. Workers will eventually accept lower wages. Slowly, the economy will slip back down along the aggregate demand curve toward an equilibrium at E_3. But the experience will be a painful one.

A more moderate approach would be to slow the growth of aggregate demand gradually rather than stopping it cold. With luck, this could bring the economy to a "soft landing" at the noninflationary level of real output. It might take longer to slow inflation this way, but a severe inflationary recession might, with luck, be avoided.

In practice, though, there is a danger that policy makers will overreact to an inflationary recession. Instead of easing the growth of demand gradually and bringing the economy to a soft landing, they may step on the accelerator with a burst of expansionary fiscal and monetary policy. Such a policy of "reflation" may restore economic growth, but only at the expense of continuing price increases.

The truth of the matter is that one knows a quick, painless way to stop inflation once it has become part of public expectations. As we will see, many economists think the best hope is not to let inflation get started in the first place. This is a theme to which we will return in the next chapter.

Perhaps the best way to understand how inflation and unemployment are likely to develop is to examine their behaviour over time, and then to use our tools of analysis to explain that behaviour.

Inflationary recession
A situation in which real output falls below the NILO, while rapid inflation continues; sometimes referred to as *stagflation*.

THE BEHAVIOUR OF INFLATION AND UNEMPLOYMENT OVER TIME IN CANADA

The hypothetical behaviour of output, prices, and unemployment that we have examined with the aid of aggregate demand and supply analysis reveals a rather complex relationship between inflation and the rate of unemployment. There is often, but not always, an inverse relationship between the two, at least in the short run. For example, if aggregate demand increases, output will temporarily increase, prices will rise, and unemployment will fall (the latter as a result of the increase in output). Prices and unemployment therefore move in opposite directions. Conversely, if demand falls, prices and output will tend to fall, and unemployment will rise. Again, there is an inverse relationship between price inflation and the unemployment rate. However, in the absence of further increases (or decreases) in demand, shifts in supply, which are caused by the increase in input prices, will tend to force output, and unemployment, back to their original levels while prices continue to rise (or fall) for a period of time. During this time, unemployment and prices will tend to move in the same direction. However, if demand continues to increase (or decrease), prices and unemployment may go on moving in opposite directions for some time.

In the presence of inflationary expectations, which we examined briefly in the preceding section, a change in the relationship between inflation and unemployment will almost inevitably take place over time (refer back to Box 27.7). Initially, as output and prices both increase, unemployment will fall — creating an inverse relationship between inflation and unemployment. However, as inflationary expectations develop and cost-push inflation reinforces demand-pull inflation, output will fall even below its original level (pushing the unemployment rate above its initial level), while prices continue to rise. For an indefinite time, therefore, the unemployment rate and the inflation rate may move upward together, a phenomenon that has come to be called *stagflation*.

A Hypothetical Phillips Curve

Phillips curve
A curve showing the relationship between the rate of inflation and the level of unemployment. Inflation, usually represented on the vertical axis of such a figure, can be measured in terms of either the rate of change in wages or the rate of change in a price index.

Recent experience with stagflation, and earlier brief episodes of a positive inflation–unemployment relationship, have upset what economists previously thought was a fairly stable and persistent *inverse* relationship between inflation and unemployment. In fact, a special curve, known as **Phillips curve**, came into general use in economics to illustrate such a relationship. It was named after economist A.W.H. Phillips, who in 1958 published a study of the British economy that showed an inverse relationship between changes in prices and changes in unemployment in the period from 1861 to 1957. (Actually, Phillips plotted a relationship between changes in *wages* and changes in unemployment, but since higher wages tend to be correlated with higher prices, it was the relationship between *prices* and unemployment that came to characterize what was soon to become known as the *Phillips curve*.) Based on Phillips's findings, economists began to examine their own economies to discover evidence of a Phillips curve.

A typical Phillips curve is illustrated in Box 27.8. At point *R* on this curve, the economy is experiencing an unemployment rate of 5 percent and an inflation rate of 1 percent. By increasing aggregate desired expenditure, it might be possible to move the economy to a point such as *D*, where unemployment has fallen to less than 3 percent. However, if the Phillips curve is correct, this will happen only at the expense of higher inflation. At *D*, prices are rising by 4 percent. It is

A Hypothetical Phillips Curve

BOX 27.8

A Phillips curve postulates an inverse relationship between inflation and unemployment. At point *R* on the curve below, the unemployment rate is 5 percent and the inflation rate is 1 percent. An increase in aggregate desired expenditure might help to take the economy to point *D*, where unemployment has been reduced to less than 3 percent. However, the inflation rate has risen to 4 percent. There is a trade-off between inflation and unemployment: A drop in unemployment is obtained at the expense of higher prices.

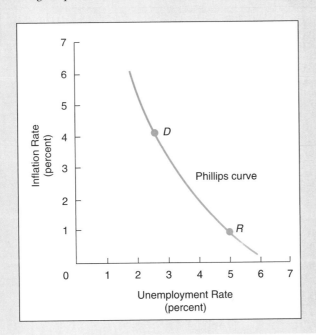

this trade-off between inflation and unemployment that the Phillips curve highlights.

The Phillips Curve in Recent Canadian History

Turning from the realm of theory to the real world, one can find some similarities between the hypothetical Phillips curve and recent experience with inflation and unemployment in Canada, but there are also significant differences.

Box 27.9 plots the relationship between the unemployment rate and the inflation rate in Canada between 1954 and 1991. What we see is a series of loops, rather than a clearly defined Phillips curve. However, in the twists and turns of those loops, it is possible to discern segments of typical Phillips curves, as, for example, in the movement of prices and unemployment from 1961 to 1966 (a movement up and to the left along a Phillips curve) and again from 1969 to 1971 (a movement down and to the right along such a curve).

However, as our analysis has suggested, the relationship between price movements and changes in output and unemployment depends on such dynamic fac-

BOX 27.9 *Canada's Experience with Inflation and Unemployment, 1954–1991*

This box presents actual data on inflation and unemployment in Canada from 1954 to 1991. Although it is possible to discern a series of Phillips curves in the twists and turns of the loops in the graph, it is obvious that no single Phillips curve exists to explain the relationship between movements in prices and unemployment in Canada.

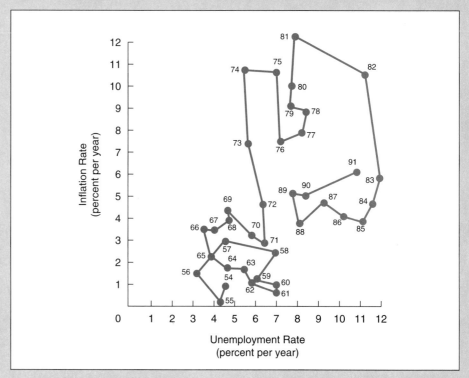

SOURCE: Department of Finance, *Economic Review,* Ottawa, April 1982, pp. 159, 171, and *Financial Post Report on the Nation,* October 1990, p. 51. Reproduced with permission.

tors as whether or not initial changes in demand and supply conditions are sustained or reversed, and whether demand and supply changes come to reinforce each other through changes in inflationary expectations. To examine such forces in detail is beyond the scope of this text. Nevertheless, the tools of aggregate demand and supply developed in this chapter can throw considerable light on the behaviour of inflation and unemployment recorded in Box 27.9.

As the graph in Box 27.9 indicates, between 1961 and 1966, the unemployment rate dropped from 7 percent to less than 4 percent, while at the same time, inflation increased from 1 percent to more than 3 percent. This was the result of increases in demand in the economy, prompted partly by expansionary government policies, and is consistent with the movement from point E_1 to point E_2 in Box 27.5 — a case of demand-pull inflation. From 1967 to 1969, there were increases in both prices and unemployment — a case of stagflation, which is illustrated by the move from point E_1 to point E_4 in Box 27.7. Between 1969 and 1971, restrictive government policies reduced the inflation rate but also increased unemployment — similar to the movement from point E_1 to point E_3 in Box 27.4. Then, in 1971, domestic demand began to increase, aided by an expansionary monetary policy. By the following year, prices were beginning to rise (as they do in the move from E_1 to E_2 in Box 27.5), accompanied by a small decrease in the unemployment rate. From 1972 to 1974, the inflation rate was accelerating, while unemployment continued to fall slightly. What happened was that domestic demand was now being reinforced by sharply increased foreign demand for our agricultural products and other primary resources. This also meant higher input prices for many of our manufacturers. Evidence indicates that profit margins and wages began to increase as well, pushing the aggregate supply curve to the left (as illustrated, for example, in Box 27.6). Prices, of course, shot up even more, and now the inflation was accompanied by virtually no change in the unemployment rate. The time was ripe for an inflationary recession (Box 27.7).

However, at this point, in October 1975, the federal government stepped in with wage and price controls. This seemed to dampen inflation for a few years, albeit at the expense of increases in unemployment. After 1977, another inflationary process began, fuelled largely, it seems, by increases in the costs of food and energy resources (there was a second wave of oil-price increases, promoted by OPEC policies). This cost-push inflation, or supply shock (see Box 27.6), generated higher and higher inflation rates between 1979 and 1981, with no appreciable drop in unemployment. The government began to use restrictive monetary policy to fight this new inflation, and the inflation finally began to recede in 1982, but, once again, at the expense of unemployment. In 1983, the unemployment rate reached a postwar high of 11.9 percent, while the inflation rate fell from 10.8 percent in 1982 to 5.8 percent in 1983.

Between 1983 and 1990, the inflation rate hovered in the 4–6 percent range, while unemployment fell, slowly but consistently, to less than 8 percent by 1989. Restrictive government policies appear to have helped bring inflationary pressures under control, while lower wage demands by labour and lower profit margins among business firms helped to reduce unemployment at the same time. In 1990, another bout of stagflation began, with both rising prices and rising unemployment.

THE POLICY DILEMMA

Macroeconomic theory demonstrates the powerful role that monetary policy and fiscal policy play in the modern economy. "Demand management" through such policies undoubtedly contributed a great deal to the rapid growth and stability of the Canadian economy in the first 25 years after World War II. However, since the early 1970s, growing instability — as measured by unusually large increases in both inflation and unemployment — has prompted economists to search for new tools of analysis and prescription.

The new prescriptions that are needed will have to take into account the way in which costs and prices are determined in our economy. Fiscal and monetary policies will continue to play a vital role in determining our level of economic activity, but their effectiveness will continue to depend on the institutional framework within which costs and prices are established. This framework, with suggested policy changes, is examined in Chapter 28.

SUMMARY

1. Canada's performance in terms of unemployment and inflation has been relatively poor in recent years compared with that of other leading industrial nations.

2. Inflation and unemployment result largely from the interaction of forces of aggregate demand and aggregate supply. Therefore, the tools of aggregate demand and supply analysis are particularly useful in studying these two basic macroeconomic problems.

3. As an economy moves closer and closer to full employment, increases in aggregate demand tend to increase both real output and prices. The demand curve moves up along the short-run supply curve as the economy experiences increased costs due to diminishing returns.

4. If demand pressures continue to grow, and prices continue to increase, inflationary expectations are created, and input prices begin to go up. A change in input prices causes the aggregate supply curve to shift upward to the left. This can also happen as the result of adverse supply shocks, such as oil price increases or crop failures. On the other hand, improvements in productivity and economic growth shift the aggregate supply curve downward to the right, permitting further reductions in unemployment without inflationary pressures.

5. In the short run, a decrease in aggregate demand moves the economy down and to the left along its aggregate supply curve. The result is a recession. Similarly, an increase in aggregate demand moves the economy up and to the right along the supply curve, causing *demand-pull inflation*. If no further changes take place in the level of aggregate demand following a recession or an episode of demand-pull inflation, expectations may eventually adjust to the new situation, producing a shift in the aggregate supply curve. The result will be a new equilibrium, in which real output returns to its previous level and the price level changes in proportion to the initial change in aggregate demand.

6. *Cost-pull inflation* occurs when the aggregate supply curve shifts up or to the left. An upward shift can be caused by the momentum of inflationary expectations following an episode of demand-pull inflation. A leftward shift can be caused by a supply shock. If aggregate demand remains fixed while the supply curve shifts up or to the left, the immediate result is an inflationary recession, in which real output falls, unemployment increases, and the price level rises, all at the same time.

7. The existence of cost-push inflation tends to undermine the proposition that there is an inverse relationship between unemployment and inflation, as originally described by A.W.H. Phillips.

KEY TERMS

noninflationary level of (real) output (NILO)
demand-pull inflation

cost-push inflation
supply shock

inflationary recession (stagflation)
Phillips curve

KEY BOXES

Box 27.2 Explaining Inflation and Unemployment Using the Income–Expenditure Model and Aggregate Demand–Aggregate Supply Analysis
Box 27.3 Aggregate Supply in the Long Run, and Long-Run Equilibrium

Box 27.4 The Economy in Recession
Box 27.5 Demand-Pull Inflation
Box 27.6 Effects of a Supply Shock
Box 27.7 Inflationary Recession (Stagflation)
Box 27.8 A Hypothetical Phillips Curve

REVIEW QUESTIONS

1. When the level of aggregate demand falls, what happens to real output, unemployment, and the price level in the short run? What is likely to happen to them in the long run?

2. Describe how cost-push inflation can lead to an inflationary recession.

3. Use an inflation–unemployment chart to trace an inflationary recession. Explain why is it possible for both the rate of inflation and the unemployment rate to rise in the same year?

4. Tax cuts are an established technique for stimulating aggregate desired expenditure. Some tax cuts may also stimulate aggregate supply by providing greater incentives to work and invest. Using aggregate supply and demand curves, compare the effects of the following:

   a. A one-time tax rebate with no significant incentive effects.

   b. A permanent cut in income-tax rates that provides an immediate incentive to work harder and produce more.

   Assume that the effects of the two on aggregate demand are identical.

5. Using the aggregate demand and supply curves developed in this chapter, indicate what would happen to real output, prices, and unemployment under the following circumstances:

   a. An increase in productivity due to a more skilled labour force.

   b. An increase in net exports.

   c. A decrease in the money supply.

   d. Increased government expenditures accompanied by sharp increases in the general wage level.

6. Assume that in a country where everything else is fine, there is suddenly an outbreak of hoof-and-mouth disease that sharply decreases the supply of beef cattle. Would the resulting rise in the price of beef be a case of true cost-push inflation? Trace this kind of inflation through the marketing chain for beef. At what points would it look different from demand-pull inflation? At what points would it be hard to tell the difference?

7. Assume that aggregate demand has been growing for several years while real output has remained steady at its NILO. The result has been steady inflation. If the government wants to stop inflation by suddenly stopping the growth of aggregate demand, should it

   a. go quietly about the necessary fiscal and monetary policy moves with as little fanfare as possible?

   b. explain and publicize its program as widely as possible?

How would the effects of the two alternatives differ? Why might one be better than the other in terms of the major goals of stabilization policy?

8. **a.** If the aggregate expenditure curve shifts upward as a result of an increase in government purchases, and the aggregate supply curve is horizontal, will the equilibrium level of real domestic income change by the full amount of the multiplier effect? Why or why not?

    b. If the aggregate supply curve is upward sloping when the aggregate expenditure curve shifts upward, will the full multiplier effect be felt? Why or why not?

9. In Questions 8a and 8b, what is likely to happen to the rate of unemployment when aggregate desired expenditure increases? Would you expect the change in unemployment to be different in the case described in Question 8a than in the one described in Question 8b? Explain your answer.

10. Fear of a recession causes a decline in the desired investment and desired consumption components of aggregate desired expenditure.

    a. What will happen to the aggregate demand curve in this situation?

    b. What would you expect to happen to the real output level in the economy?

    c. If the recession continues and aggregate demand remains constant, what is likely to happen to the aggregate supply curve? Why might this occur?

    d. Assuming that the equilibrium level of real output is below the NILO for the economy, what is likely to happen to the price level?

Expectations Hypotheses

Rational Expectations and Economic Policy

The theory outlined in this chapter is built on the idea of an upward-sloping aggregate supply curve along which the economy moves, in the short run, when aggregate demand rises or falls. We explained the aggregate supply curve by saying that, when demand rises, firms do not, at least at first, expect the prices of their inputs to rise. As a result, each firm behaves as if the increase in aggregate demand were affecting its industry alone. Firms move up along their industry supply cures, and real output rises along with the price level.

Is it reasonable for firms to behave this way? Is this the way they do behave? These questions are a matter of debate in economics today — a debate that hinges on how people form their expectations.

The Adaptive-Expectations Hypothesis

The simplest view about expectations is that people expect the future to be like the past, and adapt their plans accordingly. The theory presented in this chapter is based on this view, which has come to be known as the **adaptive-expectations hypothesis**. In the early part of the chapter, we assumed that firms expected the level of input prices each year to be consistent with the level of output prices the previous year. In our discussion of inflationary recession, we modified the hypothesis by assuming that firms expected not the level of prices, but rather the rate of inflation, to be the same in a given year as it was in the previous year. More complex economic models often assume that expectations are based on weighted average of rates of inflation over several years in the past. But these assumptions are all variations on the theme that people form their expectations of the future primarily on the basis of past experience.

Adaptive-expectations hypothesis
The hypothesis that people form their expectations about future economic events mainly on the basis of past economic events.

There is a good deal of common sense in this view. If it simply means that people learn from experience and adjust their plans on that basis, it would be hard to disagree with it. What is more, the experience of the Canadian economy in the 1970s seems to bear this hypothesis out, at least in general terms. When inflation first began to get serious in the early 1970s, people were caught off guard. They didn't know how to react. As inflation continued, however, people began to expect more inflation. They changed their plans and their ways of doing business. When inflation slowed in the mid-1980s, they did not go right back to the old ways of doing business. The memory of high rates of inflation influenced their plans for a time even after inflation slowed.

The adaptive-expectations hypothesis is also useful because it produces the kind of aggregate supply curve that is quite typical — one that slopes upward in the short run and shifts upward in the long run. Adaptive expectations thus provide a basis for a plausible theory of recession and inflation. Even so, many economists are not happy with the adaptive-expectations hypothesis.

699

The Rational-Expectations Hypothesis

The main challenge to the adaptive-expectations hypothesis has come from a group of economists who see past experience as only one of a number of factors that affect people's expectations. In forming their expectations about the future, they say, rational people should look to the future as well as the past. In particular, they should look at what government policy makers are saying and doing, and take into account the likely effects of current policy on future economic events. This view, promoted by economists such as Robert Lucas, Thomas Sargent, and Robert Barro, has come to be known as the **rational-expectations hypothesis**. Suppose, for example, that the economy has experienced an inflation rate of 10 percent for the last year or two, and that political pressure has built up for policy makers to do something about it. The prime minister responds with a hard-hitting television speech saying that the government is going to whip inflation now. What will people expect to happen?

Rational-expectations hypothesis
The hypothesis that people form their expectations about future economic events not only on the basis of past events but also on the basis of their expectations about economic policies and their likely effects.

The adaptive-expectations hypothesis assumes that people will expect inflation to continue in the future just as it has in the past, regardless of what the prime minister says. The rational-expectations hypothesis takes a different view. It assumes that people are not simple-minded. They will listen to the prime minister and then try to find out what policies are being undertaken to back up his statements.

Suppose they conclude that the prime minister has no influence on Parliament and will not be able to control government spending. They also see that the Bank of Canada is not concerned about inflation and is continuing to pump up the money supply at ever-faster rates. In this case, it is unlikely that they will expect inflation to slow; in fact, they will expect it to speed up. Firms will therefore base their plans on the expectation of a higher rate of inflation. Unions will negotiate contracts that protect their members against future inflation. Households will take inflation into account when buying houses or cars. It would be irrational for people not to act this way.

Conversely, say backers of the rational-expectations hypothesis, people might listen to the prime minister's speech and conclude that it will be followed up by strong action. Suppose Parliament cheers the prime minister's statements and promises to restrain government spending. Suppose the Bank of Canada joins the anti-inflation campaign by slowing the growth of the money supply. In this case, according to the rational-expectations theory, firms, workers, and households will modify their plans to prepare for a slowdown in inflation.

Policy Implications of Rational Expectations

The rational-expectations hypothesis has strong implications for economic policy. It suggests that the effects of policy moves that are expected by the public will be quite different from the effects of policy moves that are unexpected. Look at Box 27A.1, for example. This box, which is similar to Box 27.3, deals with the effects of an increase in aggregate demand. Under the adaptive-expectations hypothesis, firms would at first respond to the shift in the aggregate demand curve by moving upward from E_1 along AS_1 to E_2. As this happened, the price level would rise. As firms adapted their plans to the higher price level, the aggregate supply curve would shift upward, and in time, the economy would move to a long-run equilibrium at point E_3. Meanwhile, however, the economy would

Policy Implications of Rational Expectations   *BOX 27A.1*

According to the rational-expectations hypothesis, the economy will respond differently to increases in demand that are expected than to those that come as a surprise. Suppose that the aggregate demand curve shifts from AD_1 to AD_2. If the shift is unexpected, the economy will, in the short run, move upward along AS_1 to E_2. Real output will rise and unemployment will fall. Only later, as input-price expectations adapt to the inflation that has taken place, will the aggregate supply curve shift to AS_2. Then the economy will move to a long-run equilibrium at E_3. However, if the shift in aggregate demand is fully expected, the result will be different. Firms and workers will expect costs to go up and will change their plans right away. The aggregate real supply curve will shift directly to AS_2, and the economy will move straight up from E_1 to E_3. There will be no change in real output or unemployment, only a change in the price level.

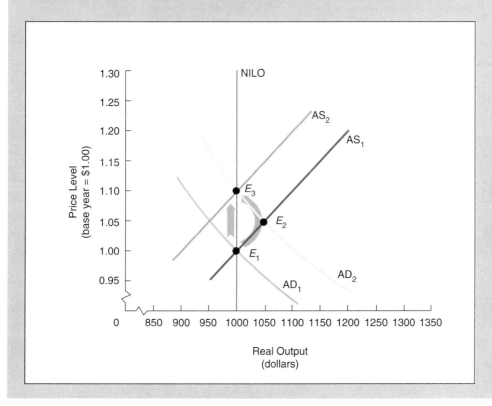

have gained something in return for the experience of inflation. From the time of the initial increase in demand until the economy finally reached E_3, real output would have been above its NILO.

Supporters of the rational-expectations hypothesis say that this sequence of events will take place only if the cause of the increase in aggregate demand is unexpected — say, an unexpected surge in consumer spending or investment. But if the increase in demand is caused by a shift in fiscal or monetary policy that has been publicized and is therefore expected by firms and households, the outcome will be different. This might be the case, for example, if the Bank of Canada announced an increase in its target for the money supply or in aggregate demand for the coming year.

An expected change in policy, according to the rational-expectations hypothesis, will affect the plans that firms make for dealing with the increase in demand. They will know that an expansionary policy will soon cause a rise in prices, including the prices of their inputs. Workers will expect the cost of living to increase and will demand higher wages. If firms learn about the policy in advance and expect it to raise input prices, they will no longer each react as if their industry is the only one affected by the increase in demand. They know the whole economy is going to be affected, and knowing this, they modify their plans accordingly. As a result, the aggregate supply curve will shift upward to AS_2 the moment the policy goes into effect. Instead of moving from E_1 to E_2, the economy will move directly from E_1 to E_3. The expansionary policy will have little or no effect on real output. Instead, it will only push prices up, and it will do so very soon.

In sum, say supporters of the rational-expectations hypothesis, the economy will follow an upward-sloping aggregate supply curve only when shifts in aggregate demand come as a surprise. If they are expected, the upward-sloping aggregate supply curve does not apply. Instead, the shift in demand will affect only prices, while real output will remain at its NILO. In effect, under the rational-expectations hypothesis, the economy's aggregate supply curve in the case of anticipated policy changes is a vertical line that coincides with the NILO. Thus, expected changes in macroeconomic policy have no effect on real output or employment.

Doubts about Rational Expectations

The rational-expectations hypothesis has had a big impact on macroeconomic thinking in a fairly short time. However, many economists have doubts about this hypothesis, or at least about its policy implications. Some think it expects too much of firms, workers, and consumers. Do people really pay much attention to what fiscal and monetary policy makers are doing? Do they understand what policy shifts imply for prices, interest rates, and so on? Can ordinary people form rational expectations about the future course of the economy when even professional forecasters so often disagree?

Supporters of the rational-expectations hypothesis say that they don't require every farmer and shopkeeper to have a Ph.D. in economics. They just say that people don't ignore what they read in the papers and see on the news. This information has an impact on their economic decisions — more of an impact than the adaptive-expectations hypothesis takes into account. And many key economic decision makers — major corporations, stock-market traders, banks, union leaders, and so on — do act on the basis of professional economic advice.

A more telling criticism focusses on the policy implications of rational-expectations theory rather than on the way in which expectations themselves are formed. In practice, the critics point out, shifts in economic policy seem to affect more than just the price level. On the average, according to one estimate, a one-percentage-point change in the growth rate of aggregate demand has a first-year effect on prices of only 0.44 percent. The remaining 0.56 percent takes the form of a movement in real output.[2] In part, this estimate may reflect the result of averaging episodes of expected demand shifts with episodes of unexpected demand shifts. But economists who are not hard-line rational-expectationists think there are reasons why even expected shifts in aggregate demand have major effects on real output and unemployment, at least in the short run.

First, they point out, prices do not respond immediately to every change in demand because it is often costly to adjust prices. True, there are some markets, such as the commodity exchanges where grain and metals are traded, in which prices respond to demand minute by minute. But in other markets, price responses are more sluggish. For example, it tends to be more costly to change prices in markets for goods that have many styles and sizes, such as clothing and auto parts. Catalogues and price tags for such goods are changed only periodically. In other markets, sellers are reluctant to change prices too often for fear of offending steady customers. In still other markets — unionized labour markets being a case in point — prices are subject to long-term contracts. They are rarely changed before the contracts expire.

A second reason for gradual price changes is that inventories slow the rate at which demand shifts are transmitted from one sector of the economy to another. Any increase in aggregate demand tends to be felt first by sellers of final goods. For example, a shoe store may quickly see the effect of a tax cut in the form of a surge of customers. But instead of raising its prices right away, the store will probably be glad to sell more shoes, thereby running down its inventory. When the shoe store puts in an order to restock, the manufacturer will feel the increase in demand. But it probably will not raise its prices right away either. Instead, it will make more shoes to fill the retailer's order. Sooner or later, its inventories of leather will be depleted, and it too will have to put in an order to restock. Only then will raw-materials markets feel the increase in demand.

At that point, prices may begin to move. When the shoe manufacturers' buyers go out to get more leather, they will find only a limited supply of hides on the market. The market for hides is one in which prices respond quickly to changes in demand. So the buyers will go back to the factory and say, "We'll have to raise our shoe prices because the price of leather has gone up." The next time the retailer puts in an order, the price increase will be passed along. Then the customer will be told, "We have to raise our shoe prices because the wholesale price has gone up." But the whole process takes time because of the cushioning effect of inventories at each stage.

Finally, there is the fact that firms get information about demand for their own products faster than they get information about changes in aggregate demand for the economy as a whole. When a shoe store sees its inventories drop, it does not know at first whether this is an isolated piece of luck or whether demand is booming throughout the economy. If the firm thinks the demand increase is something local, it is less likely to think the increase in demand will push its input prices up. It responds at first by increasing output. Only later, when the price increases of other firms are passed through to affect input prices, does the firm revise its plans.

---

[2]Robert J. Gordon, "Output Fluctuations and Gradual Price Adjustment," *Journal of Economic Literature* 19 (June 1981): 493–530.

This kind of reasoning leads to a middle ground between the rational-expectations and adaptive-expectations hypotheses. In this view, the rational-expectations hypothesis is seen as correct in stressing that people take available information into account when they make their economic plans. It is correct in saying that the response to expected changes in policy may not be the same as the response to unexpected changes. Even so, there are many frictions and adjustment lags in the economy. Because of these, people do not respond right away to every bit of news that comes their way. In practice, then, an economy with rational expectations but also with many frictions and lags does not work much differently than one in which expectations are formed adaptively. In both cases, the economy will follow an upward-sloping aggregate supply curve in the short run.

KEY TERMS

adaptive-expectations hypothesis

rational-expectations hypothesis

Strategies for Economic Stabilization

WHAT YOU WILL LEARN IN THIS CHAPTER

After studying this chapter, you will be able to

1. Describe how Canada has perceived the inflation–unemployment problem and how it has tried to treat it.

2. Contrast supply-side with demand-side solutions to the problem.

3. Discuss the elements of incomes policies and describe Canada's recent experience with wage and price controls.

4. Outline the basic thesis of the share economy.

5. Define *industrial democracy* and its possible relevance for Canada.

A Preview   *Macroeconomics Is Not Enough*

The following articles argue that much of the difficulty that we are experiencing in coping with the twin problems of inflation and unemployment arises from our failure to devise better ways of setting wages and prices on the microeconomic level — that is, within each individual firm. As the second piece below maintains, some countries outside North America are doing a much better job of this than Canada.

Behind Macroeconomic Problems Lie Basic Microeconomic Problems

Throughout the last two decades, unemployment and inflation have become more and more tightly intertwined. Periods of high joblessness and periods of high inflation now alternate, and both frequently occur together.

The principal economic problems of our day have at their core not *macro* but profoundly *micro* behaviours, institutions, and policies. The war against stagflation cannot be won at the lofty antiseptic plane of pure macroeconomic management. . . . What is most desperately needed is an improved framework of incentives to induce better output, employment, and pricing decisions at the level of the firms.

SOURCE: Martin L. Weitzman, *The Share Economy* (Cambridge, Mass.: Harvard University Press, 1985), pp. 1–3.

Some Countries Are Coping Better than Canada

One might be tempted to infer from the Canadian experience in the 1980s that only a severe recession and a long period of restrictive monetary policy will serve to reduce or control inflation, even though such a remedy has strong adverse effects on the labour market and on regional economies. Yet certain countries — Austria, Sweden, Norway, and Japan, in particular — have managed for more than twenty years to contain inflation without creating unemployment. These countries appear to have been able to make the necessary adjustment and adaptation, and to record overall good economic performance without causing major dislocations in labour markets. Thus, it may be possible to draw some lessons from a comparison of the approaches of these countries to the quest for full employment with the Canadian experience, in an effort to see whether or not the Canadian strategy toward the fight against inflation and unemployment could be improved.

SOURCE: Economic Council of Canada, *Transitions for the 90s: Twenty-Seventh Annual Review*, Ottawa 1990, p. 40. Reproduced with permission of the Chairman of the Economic Council of Canada, 1992.

FROM DIAGNOSIS TO PRESCRIPTION

Most of our time to this point has been spent on a *diagnosis* of the nature and problems of the Canadian economy. We have developed and applied tools of analysis to enable us to understand Canada's macroeconomic performance. In the course of our investigation, several problems have been detected, including the debt position of Canadian governments, persistent deficits in Canada's current account, and high levels of inflation and unemployment relative to the levels that characterized our earlier postwar experience and to those that prevail in other leading industrialized countries. Chapter 27 provided a detailed diagnosis of the twin problems of inflation and unemployment. The time has now come to move from diagnosis to prescription, from an analysis of the problems to potential solutions. We must note that this shift in focus takes us out of the realm of positive economics and into that of normative economics, where value judgements will inevitably come into play.

Before considering policies that Canada might adopt to improve its macroeconomic performance, however, we must engage in just a little more diagnosis: Specifically, we must critically examine the prescriptions of the past before we can suggest new ones. In the course of this final diagnosis, we will address several questions pertaining to Canada's past economic-stabilization policies. First, have the country's economic problems in fact been taken seriously enough? Second, has the diagnosis focussed on the right issues? The comments by Martin L. Weitzman that are presented in the Preview suggest that economists have, to some extent, been looking in the wrong places: They have focussed their attention too much on macroeconomic behaviour and not enough on microeconomic behaviour. Third, have past prescriptions been so misguided that entirely new ones are required, or have they been merely insufficient, calling now for a supplementary set of remedies? Finally, can Canada learn from the experience of other countries, as the second item in the Preview, from the Economic Council of Canada, suggests?

Our discussion in this chapter will move from diagnosis and analysis to prescription in the course of addressing these questions. In other words, our recommendations for achieving economic stability will emerge step by step from our analysis of past policies and from our consideration of policies being pursued elsewhere in the world. We begin with a brief exploration of the history behind our current set of stabilization policies and an evaluation of the degree of seriousness that has characterized the official approach to the problems of unemployment and inflation.

IN PURSUIT OF FULL EMPLOYMENT AND PRICE STABILITY

Canada's White Paper on Employment and Income

In Chapter 19, we described how the Great Depression affected macroeconomic policy making and economic thought in general. One of the consequences of these changes was to give governments increased responsibility for economic

White Paper on Employment and Income
The 1945 federal government document committing the government to the promotion of economic stability and high levels of employment.

stabilization. In 1945, Canada's federal government published its **White Paper on Employment and Income**, in which it made a commitment to pursue policies that would promote price stability and high levels of employment. Since governments in the past had never *officially* assumed such responsibilities, the White Paper represented a fairly radical step on the government's part.

However, in a recent review of government actions in support of this commitment, the Economic Council of Canada concluded that "Canada has never made more than a timid commitment to full employment. In recent years, inflation and the government deficit have taken turns at being the chief priority of policy in Canada, and those two problems rank higher than unemployment at the present time."[1]

Indeed, the Economic Council observes that, right from the beginning, the government's commitment to full employment was rather tentative. There was even a reluctance on the part of the government to speak of full employment; the preferred expression was "high levels of employment." The original draft of the White Paper called for "full employment" but the government minister in charge of implementing the proposals, C.D. Howe, insisted that the phrase be dropped.

The Meaning of Full Employment

The government's fear that full employment might be unattainable has since found an echo in some of the analytical work on unemployment conducted by economists. A debate has developed about the meaning of the term *full employment*, as described in the accompanying For Example. . . box. On one side of this debate are those who believe that it should be possible to eliminate all but frictional unemployment in a healthy economy. (Refer back to Chapter 18 if you need to review the different types of unemployment.) Following this assumption, as the article in the For Example. . . box notes, the Canada Employment and Immigration Advisory Council estimates that Canada should be able to achieve a standard of full employment in which not more than 4 percent of the labour force is unemployed.

Nonaccelerating-inflation rate of unemployment (NAIRU)
The unemployment rate associated with a noninflationary level of real output.

On the other side of this debate are economists who concede that it might indeed be possible to achieve a level of full employment with 4 percent or less of the labour force unemployed, but who argue that this is possible only at the expense of unacceptably large increases in prices. Their work has led to the concept of a **nonaccelerating-inflation rate of unemployment (NAIRU)**, which refers to the lowest level of unemployment that can be attained without unleashing inflationary forces in the economy. Recent studies have placed the NAIRU for the Canadian economy at between 7.6 percent and 8.0 percent. In other words, it appears that, when the unemployment rate drops to these levels, the economy has begun to "heat" up sufficiently to trigger a new round of inflation. The lowest nonaccelerating-inflation rate of unemployment is also referred to as the "natural rate of unemployment," a term that suggests that this rate is somehow inherent in the make-up of the economy.

The economists who believe that all but frictional unemployment can be eliminated dispute such a conclusion.[2] They admit that a NAIRU of 7.6 percent to

---

[1]Economic Council of Canada, *Transitions for the 90s*, p. 45.

[2]See, for example, Goran Therborn, *Why Some People Are More Unemployed than Others* (London: Verso, 1986).

FOR EXAMPLE...
Defining Full Employment

The following excerpt from the Economic Council of Canada's *Transitions for the 90s: Twenty-Seventh Annual Review* outlines two definitions of full employment — the "institutional" definition and the "technical" definition.

What Is Full Employment?

What exactly is meant by full employment? At the risk of oversimplifying, one can distinguish two basic approaches to the concept. The first, which might be called "institutional," describes the concept as it has been applied in the adoption of full-employment strategies by certain European countries. Diane Bellemare and Lise Poulin-Simon have proposed the following definition in *Le défi du plein emploi:*

> In a democratic society that seeks to improve standards of living, full employment refers to a situation in which every person who wants to work — at the prevailing wage rate, in a job for which he or she is trained, and in a job located close to his or her place of residence — has the opportunity to do so.[1]

Generally speaking, therefore, championing full employment amounts to calling for measures to eliminate involuntary unemployment.

As Bellemare and Poulin-Simon also point out, however, a precise statistical definition of full employment presents a number of difficulties. For example, the unemployment rate does not take into account the labour market participation rate. The government could theoretically reduce the rate of unemployment by introducing measures to induce large numbers of workers to withdraw from the labour market (e.g., high taxes on employment earnings). But could this truly be considered full employment? On the other hand, the full-employment objective might include the goal of removing the barriers that prevent certain people not in the labour force from actively looking for work (e.g., availability of adequate day-care services and deductibility of day-care costs, better fringe benefits for part-time employment, and so on).

In a situation of full employment, unemployment figures would normally reflect only the situation of those people who are frictionally unemployed, the rate then being about 2 or 3 percent. The Canada Employment and Immigration Advisory Council recently recommended that "four percent unemployment continue to be construed as a state of 'full employment' in Canada."[2]

The other definition corresponds to a "technical" conception of full employment and is the fruit of developments in economics over the past few decades; it serves as the basis for the current stance of economic policy in countries such as Canada, the United States, and Great Britain. Full employment is defined in terms of what governments can do, in the short term, to eliminate unemployment without sparking a new round of inflation. Thus, whatever unemployment cannot be attributed to insufficient aggregate demand is the level of unemployment under full employment.

In the 1980s, full employment was thus identified by many economists with the natural unemployment rate or the nonaccelerating-inflation rate of unemployment (NAIRU). The most recent estimates place the NAIRU between 7.6 percent[3] and 8.0 percent.[4] The present situation in Canada in 1990, therefore, can be viewed more or less as a situation of full employment, according to the "technical" definition of full employment.

SOURCE: Economic Council of Canada, *Transitions for the 90s*, p. 43. Reproduced with permission of the Chairman of the Economic Council of Canada, 1992.

[1] "Dans une société démocratique qui vise une amélioration des niveaux de vie, le plein emploi désigne une situation réalisée lorsque toute personne qui veut travailler au taux de salaire courant, dans un travail pour lequel elle a été formée et à proximité de son lieu de résidence, a la possibilité de le faire." Bellemare and Poulin-Simon, *Le défi du plein emploi*, p. 330.

[2] Canada Employment and Immigration Advisory Council, *Full Employment Is an Achievable Goal* (Ottawa: Employment and Immigration Canada, April 1990), p. 3.

[3] See Andrew Burns, "The Natural Rate of Unemployment: A Regionally Disaggregated Approach," Working paper no. 2, Economic Council of Canada, Ottawa, 1990.

[4] See David E. Rose, "The NAIRU in Canada: Concepts, Determinants and Estimates," Technical report no. 50, Bank of Canada, Ottawa, 1990.

8.0 percent may be the lowest attainable under current government policies, but argue that different policies would make a much lower rate possible. They point out, for example, that a number of countries — most notably Austria, Sweden, Norway, Japan, and Switzerland — have managed to maintain rates of unemployment of less than 5 percent for long periods of time *without* experiencing accelerating inflation. Hence, in their opinion, there is nothing inevitable or "natural" about the higher rates of unemployment experienced in Canada, or about a NAIRU of 7.6–8.0 percent.

Achieving Full Employment without Inflation

The fact remains that, according to our best evidence, at the present time, under current policies, accelerating inflation is likely to occur whenever the Canadian unemployment rate falls to the 7.6–8.0 percent level. What, then, would it take to achieve lower rates of unemployment without accelerating inflation? Some possible answers to this question are illustrated in Box 28.1.

The aggregate demand and supply curves in this box are similar to those developed in previous chapters. Let us assume that the economy is initially at a real-income–real-output level of $1000 — a level that we previously took to represent the noninflationary level of output (NILO). This time, however, rather than focussing on the output level, we will concentrate on the rate of unemployment associated with it. We assume that, at an income level of $1000, the unemployment rate is 8 percent, and that this represents the NAIRU for the economy. Let us assume further that, at a real-income level of $1150, the unemployment rate could be reduced to 4 percent. The problem, of course, is to find a way to move the economy to that output level *without incurring accelerating inflation*.

We saw in Chapter 27 that, if an increase in aggregate desired expenditure shifts the aggregate demand curve to the right from a point of equilibrium at a NILO, the economy will experience rising prices. We assume in Box 28.1 that the NILO ($1000) is coincident with the NAIRU (8 percent), and that any attempt to reduce the unemployment rate below 8 percent will trigger a new round of inflation. If, for example, starting from equilibrium point E_1, the aggregate demand curve shifts to the right, from AD_1 to AD_2, the economy will move up along aggregate supply curve AS_1 to a new equilibrium at point E_2. At E_2, real output has increased slightly and unemployment has fallen, but prices have risen, as predicted by those who emphasize the existence of a nonaccelerating-inflation-rate of unemployment. As we learned in Chapter 27, this initial increase in prices will create inflationary expectations and cause increases in input prices, eventually shifting the aggregate supply curve all the way up to AS_2, and creating a new equilibrium at point E_3. Real output will fall back to the noninflationary level of $1000, unemployment will return to the nonaccelerating-inflation rate of unemployment of 8 percent, and the inflation rate may once again be under control. It is important to note that these developments occur essentially as a result of the behaviour of aggregate supply.

To reduce unemployment without triggering inflation, the economy must meet the following two conditions:

1. It must have a short-run aggregate supply curve that does not shift upward and to the left when the aggregate demand curve moves to the right of an equilibrium point with a nonaccelerating-inflation rate of unemployment.

Growth with Stable Prices

BOX 28.1

If aggregate demand shifts to the right, from AD_1 to AD_2, the economy will first move from E_1 to E_2, and eventually to E_3, where prices are higher than they were before but output and unemployment have not changed. If something could be done to prevent the aggregate supply curve from shifting upward and to the left, or if that curve could be made to shift downward and to the right, to AS_3, through economic growth, it would be possible to reduce the unemployment rate below the NAIRU of 8 percent.

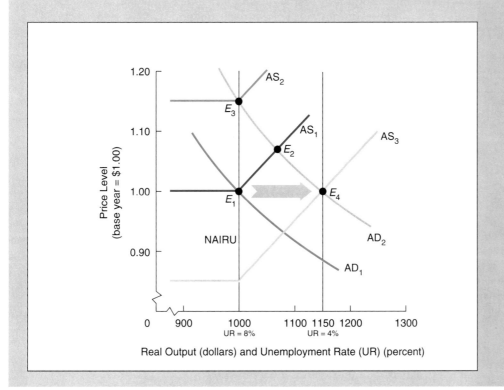

2. It must have a long-run aggregate supply curve that is horizontal to the right of such an equilibrium point.

Condition 1 recognizes that, in the short run, it may be impossible to avoid at least some increase in prices as the economy is induced to move to the right through increased aggregate demand. Specifically, it may be impossible to bring more variable resources, such as labour, into the production process without incurring higher costs (resulting from diminishing marginal productivity combined with, for example, a greater reliance on costly overtime labour as well as inadequately trained additional personnel). Hence, while Condition 1 recognizes that the short-run supply curve is likely to *slope* upward, it suggests the possibility of preventing the *shift* of the curve upward and to the left in the longer run. In other words, it suggests that policy makers take some sort of action to prevent the initial price increase from producing inflationary expectations and thus *accelerating* inflation. We shall see that there may indeed be strategies capable of accomplishing this goal.

Condition 2 involves the economy's moving to the right of its NAIRU point (or, in terms of our discussion in Chapter 2, to the right of its production possibilities frontier) through economic growth. If growth could be accomplished without increasing costs, the long-run aggregate supply curve could be horizontal, permitting a movement in Box 28.1 from E_1 from E_4 because of the shift of the short-run AS curve downward and to the right, from AS_1 to AS_3. The strategies that are able to accomplish such a development are noted later in this chapter, and receive fuller attention in Chapter 29.

As you can see, our treatment of this subject involves the implication that, if the nonaccelerating-inflation rate of unemployment is seen as a limitation placed on the Canadian economy not by "natural" or immutable conditions but by stabilization policies pursued in the past, it may be possible to implement strategies that could overcome it. The very fear that it would be impossible to achieve full employment at unemployment rates lower than 7–8 percent may itself have prevented the formulation of policies capable of giving better results.

Where Is the Source of the Problem?

We suggested earlier that the inflation–unemployment problems may not be responding well to recent treatment because policy makers are looking for the causes of the problem in the wrong places. As economist Martin Weitzman contends (as quoted in this chapter's Preview), "The principal economic problems of our day have at their core not *macro* but profoundly *micro* behaviours, institutions, and policies."

After World War II, the adoption of a Keynesian orientation to economic problems such as inflation and unemployment led to a focus on aggregate demand strategies. Keynesianism attributed unemployment to insufficient aggregate demand, and successive governments, under the influence of this orientation, sought to maintain high employment by ensuring sufficient aggregate desired expenditure in the economy.

The Economic Council of Canada observes that

> the approach that emerged was pragmatic, apolitical, and technocratic, and it had little impact on Canada's institutions and political practices. There was no need for planning boards or regulatory bodies. Since economic management was to be carried out by experts, there would be no need for popular participation in decision making or for the implementation of consensus-building machinery.[3]

What Martin Weitzman and the Economic Council of Canada, along with many other economists, are suggesting is that economic policy since World War II has focussed too much on the forces of demand in the economy and not enough on the forces of supply. This one-sided orientation has led to a neglect of the more subtle microeconomic forces that underlie the supply side of the economy: the behaviour of labour markets, the productivity, flexibility, and motivation of labour, and the price-setting practices of management—all those things that, to use the terms of the preceding analysis, cause the aggregate supply curve to behave in such a way that the unemployment rate cannot be brought below 7–8 percent without unleashing accelerating inflation.

---

[3]Economic Council of Canada, *Transitions for the 90s*, p. 45. Reproduced with permission of the Chairman of the Economic Council of Canada, 1992.

What has happened in the last few decades in Canada as a result of this focus on the demand side of the economy is that whenever an inflationary spiral has developed, or has threatened to develop, monetary policy in particular has been used to bring it under control, at the expense of rising unemployment. The problems of rising unemployment has been met largely through income-assistance programs, which may ease the pain of the unemployed but do nothing to eliminate the problem of unemployment itself. There is obviously a need for policies that will address the unemployment problem more aggressively, by focussing in much more intently on the supply side of the economy.

NEW ECONOMIC STRATEGIES

The foregoing critique of economic policies designed to address the inflation–unemployment problem does not mean to suggest that demand management in the Keynesian or monetarist tradition should be abandoned. At times of high unemployment, increasing aggregate demand remains the most important first step in bringing the unemployment rate down. However, as our analysis has shown, demand management must be accompanied by appropriate responses on the supply side if it is to achieve its goals.

Our analysis thus far suggests three types of policies that could improve the supply-side performance of the economy:

1. Policies that reduce the steepness of the short-run aggregate supply curve, so that when aggregate demand pushes the economy to the right, past the equilibrium point at the NILO and the NAIRU, the labour force can be increased and used more intensively without incurring substantial diminishing returns.

2. Policies that inhibit the development of inflationary expectations after the economy has begun to move up the short-run aggregate supply curve.

3. Policies that encourage rightward shifts of the short-run aggregate supply curves, so that the long-run supply curve can be virtually horizontal, thereby permitting economic growth without inflation.

We devote the remainder of this chapter to an exploration of the first two types of policies, which involve moving the economy closer to its production possibilities frontier. The third type — long-term economic-growth strategies — involves *shifting* the production possibilities frontier to the right, as Chapter 29 demonstrates.

1. Reducing the slope of the aggregate supply curve   Why is it that the aggregate supply curve in the Canadian economy slopes upward to the right when increases in aggregate demand temporarily push the unemployment rate below 7–8 percent? Why can additional labour resources not be hired without creating undesirable increases in prices? The reasons we had given thus far is that the economy begins to experience diminishing marginal returns at this point. In other words, the hiring of additional labour at this point goes hand in hand with diminishing marginal productivity and higher marginal costs. But why should this be so? In a series of studies summarized in its 1990 Annual Review, the Economic Council of Canada has suggested that a large part of the problem is attributable to Canada's lack of attention to the creation of a versatile, well-trained labour force. Too many people who would like to work are incapable of responding effectively to increased demands for workers.

Box 28.2 indicates that Canada, in comparison with countries that are meeting with greater success in solving the inflation–unemployment problem, spends a relatively small proportion of its GDP on **active labour-market measures** — that is, on measures designed to improve the performance of the labour force. Active measures involve, in particular, the training or retraining of workers, and their reintegration into the labour force. Canada spends, in total, more than 2 percent of its GDP on labour-market support — a comparatively high figure — but at least three-quarters of this amount supports passive programs, such as unemployment compensation. By contrast, countries such as Sweden, Norway, and West Germany spend at least half of such funds on active measures.

The Economic Council of Canada notes that, with the introduction of the Canadian Jobs Strategy in 1985, and the Labour Force Development Strategy, added in 1989, the federal government has indicated a greater interest in active labour-market measures, which may help in the future to reduce the slope of the aggregate supply curve in the Canadian economy.

Active labour-market measures
Measures designed to assist in the training or retraining of workers, and their re-integration into the labour force.

BOX 28.2   *Public Expenditures on Labour-Market Programs (as a Percentage of GDP), Selected Developed Countries, 1989*

Canada spends more than 2 percent of GDP in support of the labour market, but unlike countries such as Sweden, Norway, and Germany, much of this amount is spent on income support rather than on active measures such as retraining.

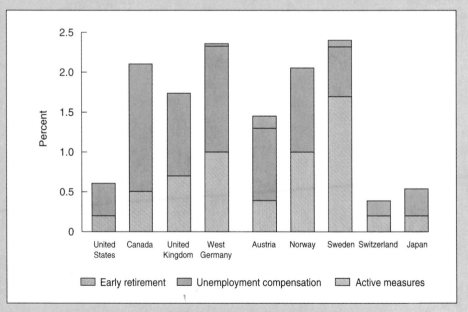

SOURCE: Organization for Economic Co-operation and Development, *A New Framework for Labour Market Policies* (Paris, May 1990); reprinted in Economic Council of Canada, *Transitions for the 90s*, p. 46. Reproduced with permission of the Chairman of the Economic Council of Canada, 1992.

2. Policies to restrain inflationary expectations Another set of policies that could help improve the supply-side performance of the economy aims to contain or inhibit the development of inflationary expectations: On several occasions over the past few decades, when initial increases in aggregate desired expenditure or supply shocks began to force prices up, labour and management reacted in ways that were perfectly reasonable for each, but ended up being destructive to both. Seeing that prices were rising, workers asked for wage increases. Management, in response to those demands, as well as to the higher prices of other inputs, increased prices again. A vicious price spiral thus began, frustrating any attempt to reduce unemployment without accelerating inflation. If a mechanism could be found to restrain the impulse on both sides to keep up with, or stay ahead of, current inflation, it might be possible to reduce unemployment without the threat of escalating inflation.

Two basically different methods have been developed by a number of market economies to counteract such inflationary pressures. One involves the compulsory (or near-compulsory) adoption of wage and price controls, which is sometimes referred to as incomes policy. The other is a long-term, voluntary system of negotiations, often involving labour, management, and government, that seeks to develop a common strategy for containing inflation.

Incomes Policies

An **incomes policy** is any policy that directly controls wages, salaries, and earnings for the purpose of fighting inflation. Ordinarily, such a policy also includes direct controls on wholesale and retail prices. Canada has experimented with incomes policies, and they have become a permanent feature of economic life in many Western European countries. It will be worth while to look at how these policies work and why they are highly controversial.

Incomes policy
A policy that attempts to control wages, salaries, earnings, and prices directly in order to fight inflation.

The case for controls

The case for wage and price controls is strongest when they are used as a temporary measure to fight an inflationary recession. When policy makers apply the brakes after a period of rapid inflation, firms and workers do not expect inflation to stop right away. Their inflationary expectations push the aggregate supply curve upwards, causing cost-push inflation. In effect, the expectation of more inflation becomes a self-fulfilling prophecy. The result is an inflationary recession.

Suppose now that just as the growth of aggregate demand is slowed, the government imposes a program of strict wage and price controls. This is done with great fanfare and a show of firm resolve to lick inflation once and for all. What is hoped is that workers and firms will believe that the controls are really going to stop inflation. If they do, they will revise their inflationary expectations much sooner than they would if they had to learn from experience.

This reduction in expected inflation, if it happens, will remove the cost-push element from the inflationary recession. Workers will know that they do not have to push for high wages to beat inflation, so they will accept controls. Firms will know that their input prices will not be rising, so they will keep the prices of their output in line. A larger part of the slowdown in the growth of GDP will take the form of a slowdown in price increases than would otherwise be the case. The drop in real output and the rise in unemployment will be less than they would otherwise have been. As a result, the transition to price stability will be faster and less painful than it would have been without controls.

Problems with controls

So much for theory. The problem is that wage and price controls are often used not as a supplement to demand-management policy but as a substitute for it. The government either tries to use wage and price controls to fight inflation without also slowing the growth of aggregate demand, or leaves controls in force after the transition is over and a new boom is under way. If this is done, wage and price controls will either be ineffective or lead to shortages, rationing, and black markets.

Canadian Experience with Wage and Price Controls

There have been several experiments with wage and price controls in the Canadian economy. One was during World War II, when huge wartime government spending made it impractical to control aggregate demand. The effects of controls under those conditions were what we might expect: After rationing was introduced, shortages and black markets became widespread. All this was tolerated because people felt that rationing was the fairest way to distribute essentials during the emergency. As soon as the war was over, controls were abandoned with a sigh of relief.

Another experiment, of an entirely voluntary nature, was attempted in the late 1960s, when prices started to rise after a period of price stability. The government suggested in 1966 that wage increases should not exceed 6 percent annually. However, these guidelines were soon broken by the government itself, when it granted a 15 percent increase to members of the Seafarers' Union after a long strike.

In 1969, the government tried to reestablish a voluntary program of restraint by creating a Prices and Incomes Commission. This commission made some thorough studies of the causes of inflation and sought voluntary support for a restraint program, but labour unions, which felt that wages would be more closely monitored than profits, refused to co-operate. These attempts came to an end with the abolition of the commission in 1972.

The third, and most ambitious, experiment with controls was initiated by the Trudeau government in October 1975, after prices in the previous year had risen by more than 10 percent. There is some evidence that inflationary pressures were beginning to ease just at the time the controls were set up. Nonetheless, the government established the Anti-Inflation Board, with a mandate — and considerable powers — to reduce annual price increases to 4 percent by 1978. The price and wage controls applied to about 50 percent of the economic activity of the country. (Foodstuffs, imports and exports, and public services were not subject to the controls.) By late 1976, the wages of roughly 2.4 million workers were controlled by the board. Controls were restricted to the profits and prices of firms employing more than 500 employees. However, direct price controls were eliminated altogether in June 1976, because of the complex problems that had arisen in enumerating the huge variety of goods and services. Corporations were still required to justify price increases, and large profit margins were viewed as evidence of excessive price changes and as grounds for ordering price rollbacks.

The Anti-Inflation Board and the control program were discontinued in the spring of 1978, meaning that the experiment had been in effect for about two-and-a-half years. In terms of its major objective — the substantial reduction of annual price increases—the program must be considered a failure. Although the inflation rate dropped considerably in 1976, to 7.5 percent, the annual rate of increase was up to 9 percent by 1978, instead of down to the target of 4 percent.

There were several reasons for this outcome. First, many goods, particularly imports and foodstuffs, on which the Canadian consumer is heavily dependent, were not controlled at all. In late 1976, the problem of import prices was compounded by a serious and prolonged decline in the exchange rate of the Canadian dollar. This helped to boost exports and ease some of the demand pressure on imports, but it also meant a substantial increase in the effective price that Canadians paid for their imports.

The failure of governments to control utility prices also contributed to the persistence of high inflation. In addition, because many income earners were not monitored at all or, at least, not as closely as those who were subject to union–management negotiations in large corporations, unions understandably did not support the program. Therefore, cost-push factors were not eased nearly as much as had been hoped.

Whether the program helped to diminish inflationary expectations is not clear. Inflation continued to run high until 1981, and both wages and rates of return on investment rose sharply as well. We cannot know how inflation would have behaved if the program had not existed or if it had been more systematically enforced. But the results of this radical incomes-policy experiment in Canada, like the results of similar programs in other countries, were not very satisfying.

In 1982, the federal government implemented a program limiting wage increases for public-sector employees to 6 percent and 5 percent over two successive years (hence, the "six-and-five program"). Inflationary pressures were reduced, but labour resented this one-sided approach (controlling wages and not prices) and no similar program has been developed since. In 1991, wage restraints were again imposed on public-sector employees, but the immediate objective in this case was to contain the growth of the public debt.

It should be noted that fixed prices and wages represent a fundamental distortion of the market system and must be viewed strictly as emergency stopgap measures. They have noting in common with the voluntary wage and price restraints that have been worked out through negotiations in other countries.

A New Incomes Proposal

Most income controls have been imposed *after* an inflationary cycle has started, and, as we have just indicated, their long-run effectiveness is questionable. In 1985, economist Martin L. Weitzman (whose words were quoted in the Preview to this chapter) proposed a more subtle form of income control, designed to *prevent* both high rates of inflation and unemployment.

As indicated in the Preview, Weitzman is disillusioned with the orthodox macroeconomic demand-management approach to these problems, and believes that the root problem is located within individual firms, where wage and price policies are made. He maintains that changing the way in which labour is remunerated for its services would solve the unemployment problem and eliminate the need for macroeconomic demand management. He calls his system of remuneration a "share system." In his words, a share system differs from a typical wage system in the following way:

> In a share system, a worker's compensation is directly and automatically adjusted by some index of the firm's well-being, such as profits per worker or product

price. In a wage system, the worker's compensation is not directly tied to any such firm-specific index.[4]

The essence of Weitzman's system, which has received considerable attention from other economists, is that when unemployment begins to threaten an economy and output and profits begin to decline, firms will be induced to hire *more* labour, not less. This is because the cost of hiring additional labour will automatically fall (since the rate paid to labour is tied to the firm's profitability).

The case that Weitzman makes seems quite convincing. One real problem, however, is that, under his system, the wages of those workers currently employed would decline in order to make room for additional workers. In the absence of some compensating inducement, it seems unlikely that labour would accept such a solution.

Experiments with Industrial Democracy

Incomes policies generally seek to *impose* a solution on workers and employers, trying to coerce them into more "rational" forms of behaviour. This type of policy appears at times to be necessary in countries where there is no natural form of co-operation between labour and management, or no mechanism through which they can work at certain problems co-operatively.

Several industrialized countries have tried in the last few decades to create mechanisms to permit labour and management to work at mutual solutions, without destroying their ability to bargain over matters such as wages and working conditions. Such efforts have come to be described as experiments in **industrial democracy**. This is a very broad term and refers to a wide range of practices that share the common objective of increasing the participation of workers in economic decision making within their plant and enterprise and, in the process, encouraging greater co-operation between workers and employers.

Industrial democracy
Arrangements whereby workers are able to participate more fully in economic decision making.

The countries that have advanced quite far in this direction are Sweden, Norway, Japan, Austria, the Netherlands, and Germany. Before we describe some of the features of their experiments and examine briefly the motivation behind them, let us consider how the economic performance of these countries has differed from our own.

Two Canadian economists found that, in the control of inflation and unemployment, there is a substantial difference between countries such as those listed above and countries that have *not* developed similar forms of consensus, such as Canada, Australia, the United States, and France: Specifically, the latter have suffered far higher rates of both inflation and unemployment.[5] The difference in performance is illustrated quite vividly in Box 28.3. As one of the authors of the study has noted, "the six successful countries have not only superior tools [of demand management] but also superior social consensus. These are the countries with the lowest average strike rates over the whole postwar period and with the most effective system of labour–management co-operation at the plant level (works councils)."[6]

---

[4]Weitzman, *The Share Economy*, pp. 82–83.

[5]Clarence Barber and John McCallum, *Controlling Inflation: Learning from Experience in Canada, Europe and Japan* (Toronto: James Lorimer & Company, 1982).

[6]John McCallum, "We Need a Way as Well as a Will," *Financial Post*, November 20, 1982, p. 10.

Inflation and Unemployment with and without Industrial Democracy

BOX 28.3

Countries represented in the bottom left-hand corner, with relatively low rates of unemployment and inflation in the late 1970s and early 1980s, are compared with the countries in the upper right-hand corner, which have higher inflation and unemployment. A basic difference between the two sets of countries is that the former have developed forms of social consensus between groups such as labour and management, while the latter have not.

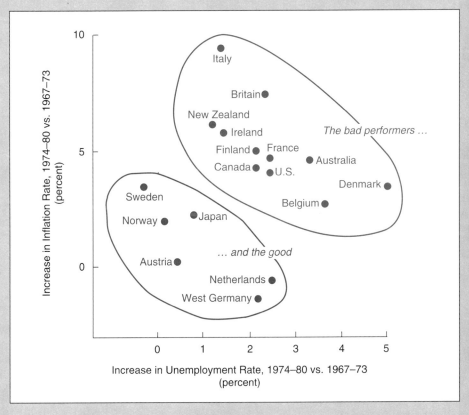

SOURCE: John McCallum, "We Need a Way as Well as a Will," *Financial Post*, November 20, 1982, p. 10.

No one would pretend that these countries have found a panacea for all their major economic problems. Indeed, in the case of West Germany and Japan, unemployment worsened considerably in the 1980s. They are clearly not impervious to some of the strong current affecting us. But the empirical evidence is too ample for us to ignore: Some of these countries have developed a system of setting wages and prices and settling other matters involving workers and employers that is quite different from ours, and this system appears to have an impact on their macroeconomic performance.

The systems now in place usually grant workers more rights on at least two different levels:

1. Within the plant where the worker is employed, decisions involving working conditions, including holiday time, pay schedules (though not usually pay rates, which are bargained for collectively), overtime, dismissals, and layoffs are regulated by agreements between management and labour worked out in plantwide labour bodies, often called workers' councils. Grievances are subject to binding arbitration.

2. At the level of the whole enterprise, which might have many plants or other subunits within it, workers are allowed to be members of the highest company board, which decides matters such as plant relocations, new investments, and the hiring of management. This practice has been carried farthest in Germany, where the highest board is called the supervisory board. The following description gives some indication of the ambitious scope of the German attempts at industrial democracy:

> The Co-Determination Act of 4 May 1976 establishes three different forms of worker participation on supervisory boards. In the first type, in stock companies with up to 2000 employees (outside coal and steel), one-third of the seats on the supervisory board are allocated to workers' representatives. In the second type, in stock companies with more than 2000 employees (outside coal and steel), the board consists of an equal number of workers' and shareholders' representatives. On a board with twenty members, six of the ten workers' representatives must be white- and blue-collar personnel elected by the workers, three are union representatives nominated by the union and elected by the workers, and one must be an executive legal "worker" nominated by all senior executives and voted for by all executives. The chairman is to be elected with a two-thirds majority vote of the board. Failing that, he is elected by the shareholders' representatives. He casts an additional vote in the event of a tie. These boards came into full effect on 1 July 1978. The third type exists in the coal mining and iron- and steel-producing industries (based on the Stock Act of 1965 and the Mining Co-Determination Act of 21 May 1951). The board consists of an equal number of shareholders' and workers' representatives, plus a "neutral" chairman agreed upon by both sides.[7]

Famous German companies such as Volkswagen are organized this way, and operate very successfully. Workers on the company board have access to all financial information about the company. In fact, they are provided with funds by the company to hire their own lawyers and accountants to make sure they understand what is happening. When the company is doing badly, no one has to tell them — they know it for themselves. Several times in Volkswagen's history, the workers have held back wage increases or even taken a cut when the company was in jeopardy. Conversely, they have benefited from good years, knowing precisely how good they were and what the company could afford. The wages of German workers have risen more than the average for workers in Europe. Furthermore, when Volkswagen wanted to build an assembly plant in the United States in the 1970s, it was required that a detailed "social" plan be worked out in advance with workers, providing satisfactory remuneration for those who would be laid off if such a move were made, and the chance to move to the new location for workers who so desired.

---

[7]Roy Vogt, "Property Rights and Employee Decision Making in West Germany," *Journal of Economic Issues* 15 (June 1981): 383.

Salary negotiations are carried out on the national level, keeping in mind the needs of each industry and overall problems in the economy. Government may get involved in this process, reminding the parties that for the sake of German exports and full employment, wage and price settlements should not go above a certain level.

Countries such as Germany have developed such models of mutual decision making for a number of reasons. First, they think it will improve efficiency, by helping the worker to identify more closely with the company. Second, it is hoped that decision made will be more "rational," that is, corresponding to both worker and management goals and also to the needs of the economy. Third, it is considered a worker's *right* to be involved in decision making. The worker commits time, energy, and talent to the company, and is clearly more involved in it than the average shareholder. Why should workers not be able to have a greater say in the institutions to which they are most committed?

Can Canada Learn from Others?

There is no reason to think that the changes described above could not be adopted in Canada, and that they would not prove beneficial. In 1982, the Manitoba government appointed two workers to the board of Manitoba Forestry Resources, one of its Crown corporations. Chrysler made headlines a few years ago when, in the midst of a financial crisis, it appointed the head of the United Automobile Workers to its board, in order to seek worker co-operation.

Parliament authorized a subcommittee in 1982 to study the possibility of encouraging more profit-sharing plans for workers and to examine "alternate forms of employee participation on boards of directors and in company decision making generally."[8]

Unfortunately, both business and labour leaders are often apprehensive about these developments. Management thinks that such changes are an encroachment on their rights, and that workers will use increased power irresponsibly. Union leaders fear that they will be "co-opted" into serving management goals. Co-operation may appear to be an act of surrender to those who are accustomed to thinking almost entirely in adversarial terms.

In a careful study of late-nineteenth-century workers' response to industrial capitalism, Gregory J. Kealey showed that workers initially sought to retain co-decision-making powers with management.[9] They had had considerable power over the setting of prices, determining the quality of their product, and setting their working hours and wages under the old handicraft system, and they wished to retain an equal footing with management. They did not want to be pushed into a separate class of people called "employees," because it seemed to them an essential human right to have some basic say about working conditions. Workers were, however, pushed into a lower, less powerful class, and eventually they joined unions to fight against a new adversary.

Perhaps the time has come to break down the barriers that were created then and to restore some of the rights that were taken away. With a new way of

---

[8]House of Commons standing Committee on Finance, Trade, and Economic Affairs, *Report of the Sub-Committee to Promote Profit Sharing by Employees in Business*, Ottawa, June 1982.

[9]Gregory S. Kealey, *Toronto Workers Respond to Industrial Capitalism, 1867–1892* (Toronto: University of Toronto Press, 1980).

setting our wages and prices, in a more trusting environment in which essential information is available to all participants, and in which both local and national objectives can be considered, we may discover at least one other method of solving some of our current problems. Our examination of macroeconomics ends where it should: in a concern not only for better economic performance but for the methods that should be used in achieving such performance. As the accompanying For Example. . . box indicates, our failure to develop better methods has proved very costly.

FOR EXAMPLE...
The Costs of Poor Labour–Management Relations

The distrust between labour and management in Canada and the failure to develop better labour–management relations undoubtedly contribute to the high number of working days lost through strikes in this country. This is one of the direct costs of poor microeconomic policies and contributes to poor price and output performance on the macroeconomic level.

Acrimonious Labour-Relations Climate

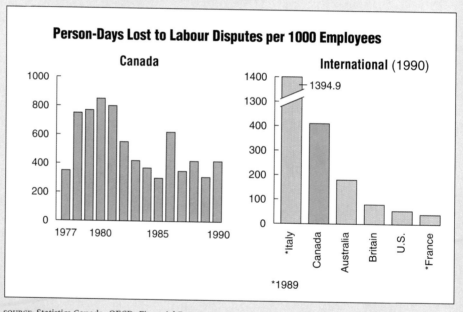

Person-Days Lost to Labour Disputes per 1000 Employees

SOURCE: Statistics Canada, OECD, Financial Post

Canada spends its Labour Day weekend in the midst of a national strike by postal workers and the threat of one by federal public servants. Last year, Canada lost 5.2 million person-days to strikes and lockouts, the highest since 1986, equivalent to 410 days per 1000 employees. That's a big improvement from the 9 million days lost in 1980, or 740 per 1000 employees. But it is still acrimonious by other countries' standards. Although international comparisons are difficult because of spotty data, Canada appears to have one of the industrial world's worst records on labour relations. The level of days lost due to labour disputes was the second-highest of six major industrial countries for which data are available.

SOURCE: Greg Ip, "EconoChart: Acrimonious Labor Relations Climate," *Financial Post*, September 2, 1991, p. 3. Reproduced with permission.

CONCLUSIONS

Macroeconomics as it is now known was born in the crisis of the Great Depression. Before that time, the distinction between the two areas now called macroeconomics and microeconomics was not as sharp as it later became. In particular, part of what made Keynes's ideas catch on was their macroeconomic nature. To the followers of Keynes, it seemed that the really important features of national economic life could be captured in a few key relationships between broad aggregate quantities. Macroeconomics meant building with big blocks labelled "consumption," "investment," "aggregate supply," "money," and so on. The demand-management policies of the 1960s grew out of this macroeconomic approach.

Today, the distinction between macroeconomics and microeconomics is once more becoming blurred. One thing more than any other unites the critics of the theory and policy of the past — a belief in the great importance of understanding the detailed microstructure of economic life. This is as true of economists who are liberals as of those who are conservatives. It is as true of neo-Keynesians as it is of monetarists. And it is true of those who simply look for the truth with no labels attached.

The exciting topics of macroeconomics today are such microeconomic questions as How can we understand unemployment in terms of the job training and skills of workers? How is cost-push inflation generated? How do workers and business people form their expectations and plans for the future? How can they learn to make decisions together that will benefit both groups in the long run?

We are back, it seems, to the theme with which the book began. Economics is about people. It is not about aggregate demand or inflationary gaps or Phillips curves — except when these things are understood as expressions of the way individual people think and act and plan.

SUMMARY

1. In examining Canada's record in combatting inflation and high unemployment, it is useful to ask four questions: Have these problems been taken seriously enough? Has the diagnosis been accurate? Do past prescriptions need to be replaced or merely supplemented? Can Canada learn from the experience of other countries?

2. Governments and many economists have doubted the ability of the Canadian economy to achieve unemployment rates of less than 7–8 percent without accelerating inflation (in other words, 7–8 percent has been estimated as Canada's *nonaccelerating-inflation rate of unemployment*, or *NAIRU*). This belief seems to be at least partly responsible for a relative neglect of the unemployment problem in Canadian policy making.

3. To some extent, the diagnosis of the inflation–unemployment problem in Western market economies since World War II has been faulty. Economists and policy makers assumed that the source of the problem was located in the demand side of the economy, and failed to pay sufficient attention to the supply side.

4. Demand management continues to be important, but must be supplemented by supply-side strategies. These include *active labour-market measures*, designed to reduce the slope of the aggregate supply curve, as well as policies aimed at inhibiting inflationary expectations, from *income policy* to voluntary arrangements among labour, management, and government that fall within the realm of *industrial democracy*.

5. Several Western European countries that have developed programs of industrial democracy have met with greater success than Canada in tackling the inflation–unemployment problem. Canada could learn a great deal from them.

KEY TERMS

White Paper on Employment and Income

nonaccelerating-inflation rate of unemployment (NAIRU)

active labour-market measures

incomes policy

industrial democracy

KEY BOX

Box 28.1 Growth with Stable Prices

REVIEW QUESTIONS

1. In 1982–83, the inflation rate began to show significant declines, but unemployment rates remained high. How would you explain this, in view of the theory developed in the last three chapters?

2. At the moment that you are reading this, what do you perceive to be the main problem in the country — inflation or unemployment?

How would you propose to cope with the problem if you were advising the minister of finance? Do you think that more co-operative relationships between labour and management would help? Why or why not?

3. "We have political democracy, but very little economic democracy." What do you think is meant by this assertion? Discuss its validity.

The Global Economy

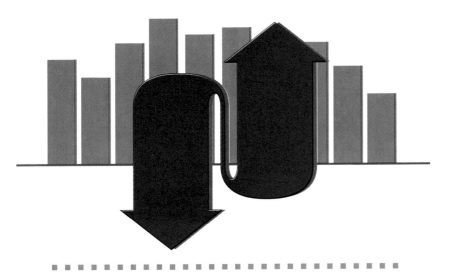

The Global Economy: Problems of Uneven Development

WHAT YOU WILL LEARN IN THIS CHAPTER

After studying this chapter, you will be able to

1. Define and explain *economic development*.

2. Compare the income levels of different countries, and describe the differences in growth patterns.

3. Discuss the gap between rich and poor countries.

4. Describe the problem of income distribution within low-income countries as compared with high-income countries.

5. Discuss possible reasons for the weak performance of poor economies.

6. Examine the performance of different countries in terms of factor productivity.

7. Discuss the impact of population growth on development.

8. Describe the problem of Third World debt.

9. Discuss strategies used by the World Bank and other agencies to solve the problem of uneven development.

A Preview   *Rich and Poor Countries:*
Why the Vast Difference between Them?

Many Canadians live below the poverty line and are therefore acquainted with economic hardship. However, as the following story indicates, the hardships of most Canadians pale beside the economic plight of many other of the world's peoples. The story challenges us to determine why the discrepancy is so great, and what might be done to change the situation.

Two Families, Two Worlds

Mary is a typical middle-class Canadian. She earns $49 000 a year as a teacher in Toronto, and her husband earns $35 000 as a clerk in the Ontario government. They have two healthy children, two cars, and a four-bedroom, two-bathroom house. They are happy to live in one of the richest countries in the world. It bothers them, however, that they are not as well off as they thought they would be. Some quick calculations tell them that their real income (after adjusting for inflation), and hence their real purchasing power, has scarcely increased in the last ten years. Half of their after-tax income is spent on their monthly mortgage payments of $1600. If one of them were laid off, they would probably have to sell their house. They seem to have less security than their parents had, and less freedom to enjoy the things they do have.

Alberto and his wife work on a tea plantation in Mozambique, a few hundred miles from the capital of Maputo. They are both in their thirties, but neither can read or write. Alberto's wife has given birth to six children; two died in infancy. The family has almost no cash income, but there is very little to purchase in the local markets in any event. A harsh drought a few years ago ruined many of the local farms, and an ongoing civil war has forced most able-bodied men, including Alberto, to spend much time away from the fields. Alberto and his family have less food to eat than they did ten years ago. Unless the war ends and the harvest improves, they are likely to starve to death within a year.

ONE PLANET, BUT DIFFERENT WORLDS

In 1990, approximately 5.3 billion people shared life on this planet. Modern technology in communications and transportation has contributed to the creation of what Marshall McLuhan termed a "global village," in which people have, in some ways, come to share more common goals and tastes. However, as the Preview indicates, within this shrinking globe, very different worlds continue to exist. And while the inhabitants of these different worlds may share certain aspirations and concerns, the conditions in which they live and their chances for actually achieving those goals differ in the extreme.

This book has focussed on the Canadian economy — on the ways in which it attempts to solve the problem of scarcity for its citizens and to determine what, how, and for whom to produce goods and services. This concluding chapter focusses on the global economy, stressing, in particular, the uneven development that characterizes it. Our analysis begins with a brief description of this uneven development pattern, proceeds to an investigation of its possible causes, and concludes with a few policy recommendations.

THE PATTERN OF UNEVEN DEVELOPMENT

The word *development* has many different meanings and must be used very cautiously. An observation, for example, that a nation is "highly developed" may be intended to mean only that it has an unusually creative culture, but may be understood to imply that it is therefore, in some broad sense, superior to other nations. To avoid such judgemental implications, which are generally unwarranted, the narrower term **economic development** is used here. This term refers to a country's standard of living, and is measured primarily, though not exclusively, in terms of per-capita income. A "developing" nation, in this narrower sense, is one in which per-capita income is low but growing, and is accompanied by improvements in other tangible conditions such as health care, life expectancy, and education.

Economic development
The growth of per-capita income, together with improvements in basic material conditions such as health care and education.

For many years, it was fashionable among students of economic development to divide the world into three development groups:

1. the so-called free-market economies of Western Europe and North America, as well as Japan, Australia, and New Zealand;[1]

2. the formerly centrally planned socialist economies of Eastern and Central Europe;

3. the rest of the world, consisting of "less developed" or "developing" countries and often referred to as the **Third World**, because of this ranking order.

A different set of categories has been developed by the International Bank for Reconstruction and Development (IBRD), commonly known as the World Bank, based in Washington, D.C. In its annual *World Development Report*, the latest of

Third World
The low-income countries of the world, which constitute a third "development group" after the high-income market economies and the middle-income, formerly centrally planned, socialist economies.

---

[1]These market economies belong to the Organization for Economic Co-operation and Development (OECD), with headquarters in Paris, which was set up in 1961 to develop economic and social policies.

Low-income economies
According to the World Bank, economies with a per-capita income of $580 or less in 1989.

Middle-income economies
According to the World Bank, economies with a per-capita income of more than $580 but less than $6000 in 1989.

High-income economies
According to the World Bank, economies with a per-capita income of $6000 or more in 1989.

which (1991) is used extensively in this chapter, the bank distinguishes between three types of countries, as follows:

1. **low-income economies**: economies with a per-capita GNP of $580 or less in 1989;

2. **middle-income economies**: economies with a per-capita GNP of more than $580 but less than $6000 in 1989 (a further division, at a per-capita GNP of $2335 in 1989, is made between lower-middle-income and upper-middle-income economies);

3. **high-income economies**: economies with a per-capita GNP of $6000 or more in 1989.

The low-income economies are found almost exclusively in Asia (which includes the world's two largest low-income countries, India and China) and sub-Saharan Africa (the portion of the continent south of the Sahara, excluding South Africa). The high-income countries, as already noted, are those in Western Europe and North America, along with Australia, New Zealand, Japan, and a few oil-rich countries in the Middle East. The middle-income economies consist of most of the market economies of South America, several countries in southern and northern Africa, and countries along the eastern Mediterranean as well as in Eastern Europe. While all of the high-income countries are market economies, the middle- and low-income countries are a mixture of various types of economies.

These broad groupings mask the great disparity between the incomes of the poorest and the richest countries. The poorest country in the world in 1989 was Mozambique, with a per-capita GNP of $80, followed by Ethiopia ($120) and Tanzania ($130). The richest country in the World Bank's ranking was Switzerland, with a per-capita income of $29 880, followed by Japan ($23 810) and Norway ($22 290). The United States was ranked sixth ($20 910), and Canada, ninth ($19 030). While such international comparisons are extremely difficult to make (because of fluctuating exchange rates and differing methods of national-income accounting), they nevertheless give a fair indication of the tremendous differences that currently exist among the income levels of different countries. The problem of unequal development may be summarized in one simple observation: In 1989, the average income of residents of the dozen or so poorest countries in the world was about $200, or about 1 percent of the average income of residents of the richest dozen countries.

Such differences in income are accompanied by other significant disparities. For example, in 1989, life expectancy in the poorest dozen countries was about 48 years, compared with 75 years in the richest dozen countries; the adult-literacy rate was about 60 percent in the former, compared with 100 percent in the latter; the infant-mortality rate was more than 100 per thousand in the former, compared with fewer than 10 per thousand in the latter; and, perhaps most important, the daily caloric intake was fewer than 2000 calories in the poorest countries, compared with more than 3000 in the richest. One economist described the situation this way:

> In 1989, the world had 157 billionaires, perhaps 2 million millionaires, and 100 million homeless. Americans spend $5 billion each year on special diets to lower their calorie consumption, while 400 million people around the world are so undernourished their bodies and minds are deteriorating. . . . The histories of

rich and poor diverged particularly sharply in the eighties. For industrial nations, the decade was a time of resurgence and recovery after the economic turmoil of the seventies. For the poor, particularly in Africa and Latin America, the eighties were an unmitigated disaster, a time of meagre diets and rising death rates.[2]

Are the Poorest Nations Starting to Catch Up?

Just how the position of the poorest countries relative to the richest has changed in the last few decades is, unfortunately, very difficult to determine. In general, the World Bank is fairly optimistic about long-term trends. Box 29.1, for example, shows that some countries, such as China and South Korea, have been able to double their output, and their income, in much less time in the latter half of this century than it took leading economies such as the United States and the United Kingdom to double theirs in the eighteenth and nineteenth centuries. Such changes have also been accompanied by substantial improvements in life expectancy and other indexes of development. In its 1991 developed report, the World Bank notes that no famines have occurred in Western Europe since the mid-1800s, in Eastern Europe since the 1930s, and in Asia since the 1970s. Only parts of Africa are still threatened by the prospect of mass starvation.

The Doubling of Output per Person, Selected Countries 　　*BOX 29.1*

This chart shows an accelerating rate of economic development for selected countries over the last two centuries. For example, it took the United Kingdom 58 years (1780–1838) to double its output, and the United States, 47 years (1839–86). In the latter half of this century, Brazil was able to double its output in 18 years. Even more recently, South Korea doubled its output in 11 years, and China, in only 10.

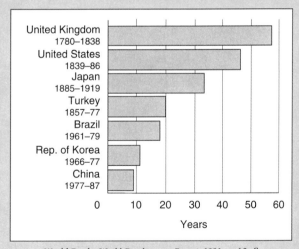

SOURCE: World Bank, *World Development Report, 1991*, p. 12, figure 1.1. Reproduced with permission.

[2]Alan B. Durning, "Ending Poverty," in Worldwatch Institute, *State of the World Report, 1990* (Washington, D.C.: Worldwatch Institute, 1991), p. 135. Reproduced with permission.

This sense of general progress, as well as of a lessening of the gap between rich and poor countries, is reinforced by the data in Box 29.2. Asian countries, led by China, South Korea, and Taiwan, achieved the highest growth rates in per-capita GDP between 1950 and 1989, averaging 3.6 percent per year. Other developing economies moved up within the middle-income category at an average annual rate of 2.7 percent. These rates of growth exceeded those of the high-income OECD economies, which averaged 2.3 percent per year. The OECD rates, in turn, were only slightly higher than the rates experienced by the socialist countries of Eastern Europe (2 percent) as well as by other countries in Europe (Portugal, Greece, and Turkey), the Middle East, and North Africa. Indeed, as our Preview suggested, and as we will see later in this chapter, citizens of many high-income countries, including Canada, are acutely conscious of what seem to be very disappointing improvements in their standards of living. The data in Box 29.2 confirm that a considerable narrowing of the gap between high- and low-income countries has been taking place. The major exceptions, also identified in Box 29.2, are the countries of sub-Saharan Africa and Latin America. In Latin America, growth rates averaged only 1.2 percent per year between 1950 and 1989 and, in sub-Saharan Africa, only 0.8 percent. In the latter economies, there was an absolute decline in per-capita income between 1973 and 1989.

BOX 29.2 *Trends in Per-Capita GDP, 1950–1989*

This table shows that most regions of the world have experienced considerable economic growth in the period 1950–89. Asia had the highest annual growth rates. Sub-Saharan Africa, which comprises all countries south of the Sahara except South Africa, had the lowest rates, and is the only region in which per-capita income actually declined in the period 1973–89, leaving it by far the poorest region in the world.

	Per-Capita GDP (1980 International dollars)			Average Annual Growth Rates 1950–1989
Region or Group	*1950*	*1973*	*1989*	*(percent)*
Asia*	487	1215	2 812	3.6
Latin America	1729	2969	3 164	1.2
Sub-Saharan Africa	348	558	513	0.8
Europe, Middle East, and North Africa**	940	2017	2 576	2.0
Eastern Europe	2128	4658	5 618	2.0
Developing economies	839	1599	2 796	2.7
OECD members**	3298	7396	10 104	2.3

Note: Data presented are simple averages of GDP per capita.
*Excluding Japan, which is included in the category "OECD members."
**In this table, the category "OECD members" includes only high-income market economies. Therefore, although Greece, Portugal, and Turkey belong to the OECD, they are included here in the "Europe, Middle East, and North Africa" category because they are middle-income economies.

SOURCE: World Bank, *World Development Report, 1991*, p. 14, table 1.1. Reproduced with permission.

A much less optimistic picture of growth trends is drawn by the Worldwatch Institute, a private research institute in the United States, which, in its 1990 *State of the World Report*, bases an alternative analysis of international income spreads on the work of two University of Pennsylvania researchers, Robert Summers and Alan Heston. Summers and Heston collected per-capita GDP figures (adjusted to reflect real purchasing power) for 130 countries; their findings are summarized in Box 29.3. Countries fall into four categories, based on per-capita income in 1985: rich (per-capita income greater than $6000); middle (per-capita income between $2500 and $6000); poor (per-capita income between $1000 and $2500); and poorest (per-capita income less than $1000). The data in this box indicate that, since 1950, the wealthy nations have nearly tripled their income, while the poorest have been able to increase theirs only very minimally. The gap between them has therefore widened considerably, according to this research. The results of this research differ substantially from the conclusions reached by the World Bank. This is due partly to the way in which per-capita income figures are arrived

An Alternative View of Trends in Per-Capita GDP, 1950–1988　　　　　　　*BOX 29.3*

This graph shows that the income gap between the richest and the poorest nations in the world widened considerably between 1950 and 1988. Real per-capita income nearly tripled in the wealthiest nations, but remained virtually unchanged in the poorest. The four categories shown in the graph are based on per-capita income in 1985.

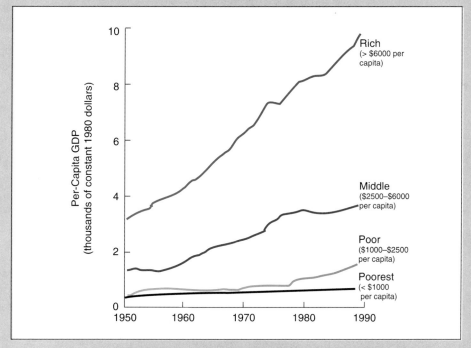

SOURCE: Worldwatch Institute, *State of the World Report, 1990*, p. 137, figure 8.1. Reproduced with permission.

at (the World Bank makes far less effort, apparently, to determine the actual purchasing power of different levels of per-capita income), and partly to the fact that the World Bank compares "regions," while the last study compares countries.

Income Disparities within Countries

Our picture of uneven development among countries should be supplemented by some consideration of income disparities *within* countries. In Canada and many other market economies, the richest fifth of the population earns between five and ten times as much as the poorest fifth. In the world's poorest countries, the disparity is often much greater, thereby accentuating the relative poverty of the poor.

Box 29.4 indicates that, in a number of middle- and low-income countries, such as Brazil, Ecuador, Panama, Peru, Turkey, Colombia, and Kenya, the richest fifth of the population receives more than twenty times as much income as the poorest fifth. Fortunately, in several of the world's fastest-growing countries, such as South Korea, Taiwan, and China, the ratio has fallen to less than ten to one, suggesting that income disparities within a country may decrease as the country develops. Nonetheless, for those countries with extreme disparities, average income figures understate the true position of the poor considerably. Consequently, their position relative to the rest of the world is also greatly understated by statistics based on group averages, such as the ones we have considered thus far.

EXPLAINING UNEVEN DEVELOPMENT

Various theories have been advanced to explain the differing rates of growth of different economies. Some scholars, following the lead of German economist and sociologist Max Weber, have emphasized the influence of culture and religion on economic development. They have argued, for example, that regions of Europe and America that were predominantly Protestant experienced more-rapid economic growth than other regions, possibly as a consequence of the so-called Protestant work ethic. Whether or not that particular theory is correct, common sense suggests that religious and cultural values are likely to have a significant effect on economic development. Some religions and cultures undoubtedly place more emphasis on material achievement than others, and it would be surprising if this did not have some impact on economic growth.

The role of geography and climate has also been emphasized. To what extent, for example, has Canada's relatively rapid economic development been attributable to the country's proximity to the United States? To its relatively harsh climate? How has production in Asian and African countries been affected by extreme heat? Such questions are not easily answered; nonetheless, the factors of geography and climate are clearly relevant.

The resource base of an economy is also significant. Japan is often cited as a country that has achieved remarkable economic growth in the absence of a rich natural-resource base. Even in Japan, however, growth might have been facilitated by better resources.

While they do not ignore such factors, economists have tended in recent decades to focus on the *process* of economic growth itself, as outlined in the following section.

Income Inequality and the Growth of GDP in Selected Economies, 1965–1989

BOX 29.4

This diagram shows that countries with above-average growth rates are also able to achieve an above-average level of income *equality*. For example, Singapore, South Korea, Taiwan, Hong Kong, and China had high rates of growth in the period 1965–89 (more than 5 percent annually), as well as a high degree of income equality: The richest fifth of the population in each had less than 10 times the income of the poorest fifth. The economies of countries such as Brazil, Ecuador, Panama, and Peru grew at a rate of less than 4 percent per year, and the income of the richest fifth of the population in each was more than 30 times greater than that of the poorest fifth.

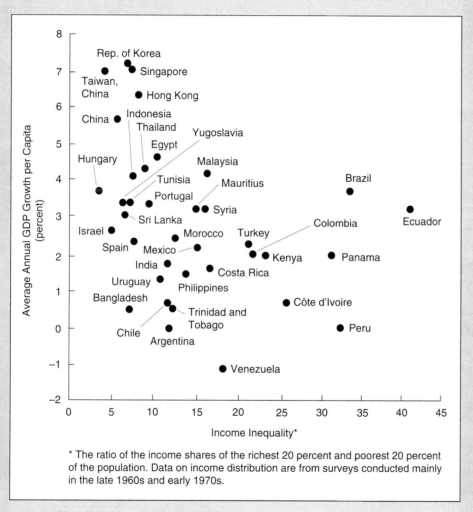

* The ratio of the income shares of the richest 20 percent and poorest 20 percent of the population. Data on income distribution are from surveys conducted mainly in the late 1960s and early 1970s.

SOURCE: World Bank, *World Development Report, 1991*, p. 137, figure 7.2. Reproduced with permission.

Total Factor Productivity

Put simply, the growth of output in an economy depends on the combined use of capital and labour in the production process. In other words, if these two factors are used effectively, and in effective combination, a society's production possibilities frontier will be pushed out to the right; otherwise, it will not. Growth, then, is seen to be the result of three forces:

1. increases in the labour force;

2. increases in the amount of capital used;

3. increased output per unit of labour and capital — that is, increased productivity.

If per-capita income is to be increased, these three forces must combine to increase output at a faster rate than the rate of population growth.

Economists identified the need to *measure* the combined input of labour and capital in order to determine the proportion of a country's economic growth that can be attributed to the use of increased amounts of both inputs (items 1 and 2 above) and the proportion that results from an improved use of the two inputs in combination — that is, from improved productivity (item 3 above). Box 29.5 describes the method economists use to do this, as well as its implications, in some detail. In Box 29.6, the method is applied to the Canadian economy in two different periods, 1954–74 and 1975–83. To see how the method is applied, let us focus on the first period, 1954–74. During that time, real output (GDP) grew by an average of 4.9 percent a year, the number of employed workers increased by 2.6 percent a year, and the capital stock grew by 5.6 percent a year. If we were to consider only the relationship between output growth and employment growth, we would derive a measure of labour productivity. In this case, the result would be very favourable: On average, each 2.6 percent increase in employed labour resulted in a 4.9 percent increase in output. But we can see from Box 29.7 that this result was attributable not only to the increase in labour but also to the increase in the capital that facilitated labour's efforts. Hence, a measure of labour productivity alone would give a misleading impression of the sources of growth in the economy — as would a measure of capital productivity alone. Indeed, it appears that, in the period 1954–74, increases in capital were used rather inefficiently: Annual increases in capital stock of 5.6 percent produced increases in output of only 4.9 percent. Was capital unproductive and labour very productive? Such conclusions were clearly absurd. To determine the contribution to growth of both capital and labour combined, economists saw that it was necessary to measure **total factor input**. As noted earlier, Box 29.5 outlines the method they found to do this. It might seem, on the surface, that the easy solution to measuring total factor input would be to add up the annual increases in both labour and capital and divide by two, thereby arriving at the average growth of both factors combined. This approach, however, ignores the relative importance of the two factors in the production process. In Canada, for example, labour accounts for roughly 60 percent of production, and capital for roughly 40 percent. The correct method of adding the two together, then, is to weight them according to these percentages: The actual increase in employment is multiplied by 0.6, and the increase in the capital stock is multiplied by 0.4. Applying this to the data for the period 1954–74 in Box 29.6 (2.6 percent employment growth and 5.6 percent capital-stock growth), we obtain a total factor input figure of 3.9 (that is, $2.6 \times 0.6 + 5.6 \times 0.4$).

In the absence of any increase in factor productivity, the 3.9 percent increase in total factor input would result in a 3.9 percent increase in output. Any increase

Total factor input
A measure of the weighted, combined input of capital and labour in the production process.

Total Factor Productivity in Economic Growth BOX 29.5

An important advance in economics of the past fifty years has been to identify and measure total factor productivity, which measures changes in output per unit of all inputs combined. Before, most analysis of productivity focussed on the growth of labour productivity, and, to a lesser degree, on the growth of the average productivity of capital.

Observe the following differences. The total output of the United States in the first part of the twentieth century grew at about 3.0 percent a year. Its capital stock also grew at about 3.0 percent, whereas the labour input (measured in worker-hours) grew at only about 1.0 percent a year. In the capital–labour mix, capital accounted for about one-third, and labour, two-thirds. So total factor inputs were rising about 1.7 percent a year: two-thirds times 1.0 percent plus one-third times 3.0 percent. Total factor productivity, or the residual, thus accounted for 1.3 percent in output growth: 3.0 percent (the rate of growth of output) minus 1.7 percent (the growth rate of inputs).

The early calculations of total factor productivity for different countries led to the conclusion — surprising at the time — that about half of growth in output was due to the residual, which was quickly baptized as technical change. What makes up the residual? Technological innovations have no doubt generated some improvements in total factor productivity. But the main additional element is in the quality of labour. If the additions to the labour force are more productive than the existing force, they will add more to output than they would under the formula based on labour's share. And the extra contribution from upgrading the quality of labour ends up in the residual.

Adjusting for labour quality makes it easy to identify the residual with technical change — defined very broadly. Technical change includes such obvious innovations as the mechanical cotton picker, the pneumatic tire, the hand-held calculator, the personal computer, the fork-lift truck, and the containerized shipping system.

But technical change also includes numerous ways of reducing real costs. These costs may fall as more discipline is instilled in the work force by a more demanding manager — or as the work force becomes more productive because a too-demanding manager has been fired. An assembly line might be made more productive simply by straightening it out — or a farm by introducing a different fertilizer. Productivity may also be increased by, for example, installing a facsimile machine, closing down unprofitable branches, or buying longer-lasting tires for trucks.

The way to understand more about what makes up the residual is to study the growth of total factor productivity in detail — product by product, industry by industry, sector by sector. Even with close study, not every source of cost reduction can be identified, but the most important ones surely can. This identification alone reveals the kaleidoscopic sources of growth encompassed in the residual.

SOURCE: World Bank, *World Development Report, 1991*, p. 42, box 2.3. Reproduced with permission.

in output beyond 3.9 percent, then, must be attributable to improvements in productivity. **Total factor productivity** is therefore defined as the difference between the growth in total factor input and the growth in output. Thus, subtracting the 3.9 percent increase in total factor input from the 4.9 percent increase in real GDP yields 1.0 percent of growth in total factor productivity (or, as the World Bank article in Box 29.5 refers to it, "the residual"). In other words, of the 4.9 percent annual increase in real output, 3.9 percent was attributable to increases in labour and capital, and 1.0 percent was the result of increases in factor productivity.

A look at the period 1975–83 shows that output grew less than did total factor input by an annual average of 0.8 percent, which means that total factor productivity actually declined by that percentage each year. This confirms the impression of those who — like Mary in our chapter Preview — perceive their

> **Total factor productivity**
> The difference between the growth of total factor input and the growth of total output.

BOX 29.6   *Aggregate Economic Growth in Canada, 1954–1974 and 1975–1983*

This table shows that average annual increases in real output dropped from 4.9 percent in the period 1954–74 to 2.1 percent in the period 1975–83. One of the main problems was the drop in total factor productivity, from 1.0 percent in the first period to −0.8 percent in the second.

	Compound Annual Growth Rate (percent)	
	1954–74	*1975–83*
Real GDP	4.9	2.1
Employment	2.6	1.8
Capital stock	5.6	4.4
Total factor input	3.9	2.9
Total factor productivity	1.0	−0.8

SOURCE: Gerald Stuber, *The Slowdown in Productivity Growth in the 1975–83 Period*, Bank of Canada Technical Report no. 43, Ottawa, October 1986, p. 5. Reproduced with permission.

common gains to be minimal: Although some growth is taking place in Canada, the *growth rate* is declining and we seem to be falling behind our earlier performance standards.

Factor-productivity analysis allows us to understand the basic conditions for economic growth. Such analysis has revealed that virtually every economy in the world has been experiencing growth problems for the past decade or longer. In the late 1980s, many Eastern European countries became so alarmed by their dismal growth records that they chose to make a radical change — to move away from central planning and to become market economies. This enormous transition is still in full swing, and the results are as yet inconclusive.

Box 29.7 applies factor-productivity analysis to various types of economies and shows that, while most countries performed poorly in the period 1960–87, Africa and Latin America fared especially badly. The total factor productivity (TFP) of these regions was exactly zero, meaning that the 3.3 percent average annual increase in GDP in Africa, for example, was entirely the result of increases in labour and capital inputs. Genuine improvements in the standard of living, as measured by increases in per-capita income, are virtually impossible under such circumstances.

Reasons for Low Productivity

Analyzing the mechanics of the growth process helps us understand *what* happened, but not *why* it happened. Economists in Western market economies have a difficult time explaining the reasons for the declining growth rates in their economies. Similarly, it remains difficult to explain why the growth rates of some developing nations have always been at or close to zero — and why some have even become *negative* in recent years.

Growth of GDP, Factor Inputs, and Total Factor Productivity in Developing and Industrial Economies, 1960–1987

BOX 29.7

Column 2 of the table shows the average annual rates of growth of GDP in the various groups of countries represented. Column 3 records the average annual increase in the capital stock, and column 4, the average annual increase in labour employment. These increases in factor inputs have then been combined, with proper weights (not shown here), allowing total factor productivity to be calculated (column 5). One of the main problems facing the low-income countries is highlighted in column 5: The African and Latin American countries show zero annual increases in factor productivity.

(1) Region, Group, or Economy	Average Annual Percentage Increase, 1960–87,* in			
	(2) GDP	(3) Capital	(4) Labour	(5) TFP
Developing economies				
Africa	3.3	6.3	2.2	0.0
East Asia	6.8	10.2	2.6	1.9
Europe, Middle East, and North Africa	5.0	7.6	1.7	1.4
Latin America	3.6	6.3	2.6	0.0
South Asia	4.4	7.7	2.1	0.6
68 economies	4.2	7.2	2.3	0.6
Industrial economies				
France	3.9	4.8	−0.2	1.7
Germany**	3.1	4.2	−0.6	1.4
United Kingdom	2.4	3.1	−0.2	1.2
United States	3.0	3.4	1.8	0.5

Note: Estimates for developing countries are based on a sample of 68 economies.
*Until 1985 for industrial economies.
**The Federal Republic of Germany before reunification with the former German Democratic Republic.

SOURCE: World Bank, *World Development Report, 1991*, p. 43, table 2.2. Reproduced with permission.

The Worldwatch Institute has isolated several possible reasons for low productivity.[3] It distinguishes among problems at the *local, national,* and *global* levels.

Problems at the local level Four problems are identified at the local level: (1) lack of ownership of resources by the poor; (2) physical weakness and illness; (3) population pressures; and (4) powerlessness.

Worldwatch notes that, in many poor countries, more than 80 percent of agricultural households are landless or near-landless. There is therefore little incentive to improve labour productivity. At the same time, most of these people suffer from malnutrition and assorted physical afflictions. In 1985, only 4.4 per-

---

[3]Worldwatch Institute, *State of the World Report, 1990*, pp. 140 ff.

cent of the deaths in advanced industrial countries were from infectious and parasitic diseases (which are debilitating long before death), while in poorer countries, such diseases accounted for 43.5 percent of all deaths.

Population pressure, resulting from unusually high birth rates, continues to pose serious problems. Partly because of above-average death rates, birth rates in these countries are high. One reason is that people want many children so that at least a few will survive into adulthood. The result is comparatively high birth rates, and rapid increases in population. In Mozambique, for example, the birth rate declined only slightly between 1965 and 1989, from 4.9 percent of the population to 4.6 percent (as compared with Canada's 1.4 percent), while the death rate declined from 2.7 percent to 1.7 percent (which is still considerably higher than Canada's 0.8 percent). The **rate of population growth** is measured as the difference between the birth rate and the death rate in any given year. Hence, in Mozambique, despite a slight decline in the birth rate, the rate of population growth increased from 2.2 percent in 1965 (4.9 percent − 2.7 percent) to 2.9 percent in 1989 (4.6 percent − 1.7 percent). While a rate of 2.9 percent is typical of many poor countries, it stands in sharp contrast to the average annual population increase of less than 1 percent that is typical of higher-income countries.

Social, political, and economic powerlessness is identified as the fourth factor retarding economic improvement on the local level. The problem is related in part to high rates of illiteracy. Unable to read, the poor may be easily intimidated or misled into signing away their rights to land, for example, and may be prey to various kinds of extortion.

Problems at the national level Local problems are often compounded by problems at the national level, where governments typically pass tax laws and regulations that favour the ruling class. (The best-paying jobs are also reserved, unofficially, for members of the inner circles of that class.)

Problems at the international level At the international level, poorer countries often find it difficult to obtain the capital and the technology that they need in order to improve productivity. Domestic saving rates are consequently low. There has been a hope that, through borrowing and international trade, domestic markets could be built up, and foreign currency could be obtained to purchase foreign technology. International agencies such as the World Bank and the International Monetary Fund have invested substantially in some of the developing countries, and such assistance has been supplemented by aid from many of the wealthier countries, including Canada. However, many of the hoped-for benefits of such international efforts have been nullified by other developments on the international scene. Escalating oil prices, for example, have added substantially to the cost of imports, and high interest rates on foreign debts have increased the indebtedness of many poor countries to levels that make the payment of debt out of export earnings impossible. In 1989, the low-income countries owed $1.12 trillion to industrial countries — nearly half of their collective GDP. While debts were escalating, the prices of the goods that these countries export were falling. (See Box 29.8, which compares the drastic drop since the early 1970s in the commodity price index of the low-income countries — that is, the price index for the commodities they export — with the sharp increase in Third World debt.) At the same time, a number of high-income countries were

Rate of population growth
The difference between the birth rate and the death rate in any given year.

Commodity Price Indexes and Total Third World Debt, 1970–1987

BOX 29.8

This graph shows that, between 1970 and 1987, the external debt of low-income countries increased from less than $200 billion to nearly $1200 billion. At the same time, the prices of commodities exported by these countries fell by about half, from an index value of close to 140 in 1974 to one of close to 70 in 1987. This has made it impossible for Third World countries to pay off their debt through trade.

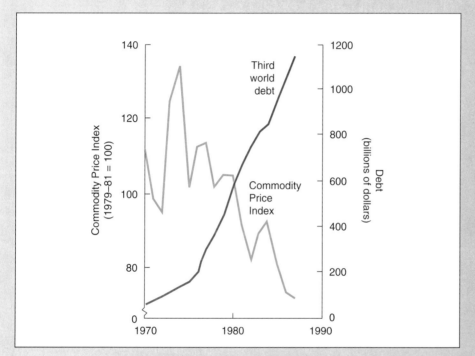

SOURCE: Worldwatch Institute, *State of the World Report, 1990*, p. 144, figure 8.2. Reproduced with permission.

raising trade barriers against the low-income countries. The European Community, for example, levies a tariff against cloth imported from poor, heavily indebted nations that is four times as high as the one on cloth imported from wealthy nations. World Bank figures suggest that industrial-country trade barriers cost developing countries $50 billion to $100 billion a year in the lost sales and in revenues lost because of depressed prices.[4] As a result of such developments in the international market, more foreign currency has been leaving the poor countries since the mid-1980s to finance debt payments and imports than has been entering them in the form of export earnings.

In its most recent diagnosis of development problems (*World Development Report, 1991*), the World Bank focusses on policy decisions. It argues, in effect, that the

---

[4]Worldwatch Institute, *State of the World Report, 1990*, p. 144.

policies pursued both by outside agencies, such as the World Bank, and by the governments of developing countries, are largely to blame for poor economic performance. It claims that the low-income economies suffer from too much government interference in the wrong places (hampering competition at the microeconomic level); flawed macroeconomic policies (that is, poor management of taxes and government expenditures); too little investment in education and health (which would directly improve the quality of the labour force); and too many barriers to international trade (on the part of both the developing countries and the higher-income countries).

The reasons for uneven development advanced by the World Bank are not necessarily at variance with those we considered earlier, although, in general, they place more emphasis on policy decisions within the developing countries and less on deep-rooted underlying conditions, which are not easy to correct. In the next section, which examines possible solutions, this diagnosis is analyzed further.

WHAT IS TO BE DONE?

Difficult problems seldom have easy solutions, and the problems of uneven development are no exception. As we have seen, many countries have, in fact, improved their economies dramatically since World War II. Recently, China, South Korea, and Taiwan have achieved rates of growth that have allowed them to double their income in little more than a decade.

Before we look at the lessons that might be learned from such success stories, a brief review of the attempts that have been made to stimulate economic growth in less successful areas may be useful. A number of international organizations, particularly the World Bank and the International Monetary Fund (IMF), as well as many local nongovernmental organizations (NGOs), have attempted since World War II to promote economic and social development in various parts of the world, especially in Asia, Africa, and Latin America. The focus here is on the strategies adopted by the World Bank and the IMF. These two organizations, with headquarters on opposite sides of 19th Street in Washington, D.C., were designed to be the twin pillars of the postwar economic order. The task of the World Bank was to promote development by making loans from its huge accumulation of member deposits, and that of the IMF was to set and maintain the basic rules of international economic relations. In the 1970s, when the Bretton Woods system of fixed exchange rates broke down and private capital markets expanded, the roles of the two organizations changed, and the lines between them became blurred. Both became involved in development programs and in helping to establish macroeconomic rules for developing countries, an arrangement that still persists today. Thus, while the operations of the two organizations remain distinct, it is valid to speak of a World Bank–IMF development strategy.

The World Bank–IMF strategy that exists today is the result of several significant modifications since World War II. Beginning in the late 1940s, massive industrialization projects were financed in a number of low-income countries, in the belief that rapid industrialization was the key to quick economic growth. Indeed, development was understood as, essentially, **industrialization**. Many of the funded projects, however, never got off the ground: Buildings and machines were soon lying idle. It appeared that neither the domestic economics

Industrialization
In the context of Third World development, the attempt on the part of Western development agencies in the postwar period to speed up the economic growth of low-income countries through industrial development.

nor foreign economies were ready for the implementation, and the consequences, of such projects. On the domestic level, there were often problems of labour that was insufficiently trained and of markets that were unprepared to use the products being generated. In addition, the projects were often extremely capital-intensive, in countries with an overabundant supply of labour. Compounding these problems was the fact that other countries were not prepared to open up their borders sufficiently to the industrial goods that these low-income countries were starting to produce.

In the early 1970s, new policies, which focussed on **depauperization**, were implemented. Depauperization involved attempts to reach the poorest of the poor through projects aimed at the grass-roots level. The emphasis now was on improving social programs, particularly in areas such as health care and education. While these efforts seemed to make a difference in some countries, results were slow to come in others. At the same time, the funds that the low-income countries had had to borrow to finance the earlier massive industrialization projects and then the new social programs began to accumulate into massive debts — debts that grew spectacularly as interest rates accelerated in the late 1970s and early 1980s. At that point, the World Bank and the IMF decided that a program of austerity and financial discipline was necessary. Countries that depended on these agencies' support were now required to initiate some or all of the following reforms:

Depauperization
Attempts to improve economic conditions in low-income countries through a broad range of social programs, particularly in the areas of health care and education.

1. devaluing the country's currency;

2. reducing the size and role of government in the economy;

3. encouraging the export sector by reducing tariffs and other foreign-trade restrictions and by discontinuing programs of import-substitution;

4. implementing microeconomic restructuring by allowing greater freedom in domestic markets for price changes;

5. implementing cutbacks in health, education, and welfare programs.

Some of these new policies seem to have been inspired by the success of the export strategies and strict macroeconomic policies that countries such as South Korea and Taiwan have been following. However, these countries have also relied quite heavily on government to subsidize domestic industries and to protect domestic markets against foreign competition, as well as for other types of interventions that diverge from the free-market policies espoused by the World Bank and the IMF in the 1980s.

More recently still, the World Bank and the IMF seem to have modified their position. In the Bank's *World Development Report, 1991*, emphasis is still being placed on more-competitive markets for developing countries, but a substantial and positive role is now being assigned to governments, less manipulation of exchange rates is envisaged, and more assistance to health care and education is again being advocated.

In view of the past failures of various development strategies, it is obvious that grand designs and general solutions to problems of uneven development are not viable. This chapter concludes, therefore, with a brief description of specific areas in which improvements are clearly necessary, and suggests a few ways in which solutions might be found.

Escaping the Population Problem

Concern about the population problem has led many governments and international agencies to stress population control as a key to development. Population-control programs have had some success in some countries, although they are by no means the only reason for falling birth rates. The potential for success of voluntary population-control measures is sometimes gauged by the "unmet need" for fertility control among couples of childbearing age. This term refers to the percentage of couples who do not want more children, or who want to space their children, but are not using contraception or other effective fertility-control methods such as prolonged breast-feeding. In many countries, as many as one-quarter or one-third of couples may have an unmet need for fertility control. As this need is met, birth rates can be expected to continue to fall.

Some countries have gone beyond voluntary methods of population control. In China, housing, jobs, and the availability of some goods and services are tied to keeping family size within the limits that the government defines. Such measures have helped reduce China's birth rate. However, compulsory population-control measures raise ethical questions and can provoke strong political resistance.

Creating the Conditions for Growth

Food and agriculture

Agriculture is a key to economic growth throughout the developing world. It accounts for one-third to one-half of all output and employment. Food production is also a key factor in the health of the population. Hence, it is a logical starting point for discussing the potential for economic growth.

There are some notable agricultural success stories in the developing world — in some countries of Southeast Asia, in India and Sri Lanka, and in several South American countries. However, agriculture has stagnated in other parts of the world, notably in sub-Saharan Africa. There, food production has hardly increased at all in the past decade; in fact, production of export crops has actually declined in many sub-Saharan countries, and food imports have soared.

Scale of agriculture   Domestic development plans and international aid efforts have stressed agriculture for some time. Between 1973 and 1980, the World Bank and other agencies channelled more than $5 billion into African agriculture. It is now thought that the limited success of that aid was due in part to too great a focus on large-scale, government-run projects. These projects, which involved heavy capital outlays for mechanization of irrigation, did not meet expectations. They were plagued by problems of management, overemployment of staff, underutilization of equipment, and maintenance problems.

In other parts of Africa, Tanzania being a prime example but not the only one, agricultural performance was hurt by programs of rural collectivization. In accordance with ambitious theories of social transformation, the rural population was moved from traditional farms and villages to new population centres. These policies were devastating to the output of small farmers and did not result in enough added output from new, large-scale projects to make up the difference.

Today, the World Bank recommends a focus on small-scale agriculture as the key to improved performance. Small farms are seen as capable of providing both food and jobs for the rural population, as well as a surplus for export and for feeding city dwellers. But the success of small-scale agriculture in Africa and elsewhere requires other policy changes as well.

Prices and incentives   In many countries, the biggest barrier to the growth of agriculture is the structure of prices and other incentives. Low food prices, designed to benefit the urban populations that represent the base of political support for the governments of many countries, are one part of the picture. Food prices are kept low both by official price controls and, in many countries, by massive import of wheat, rice, and other staples. With domestic food prices at one-half to one-third of world levels, farmers have little incentive to produce a surplus above the needs of their own families. A World Bank study of 27 rural development projects highlighted the importance of this factor: 7 of the 9 projects undertaken under favourable price conditions met or surpassed their output goals compared with only 5 of the 18 undertaken under unfavourable price conditions.

Low prices and a lack of incentives are a problem in the area of export crops such as coffee, cocoa, and cotton as well. Growers of these crops face a double burden in much of Africa. First, sales of these crops are heavily taxed, and second, high exchange rates reduce the proceeds of exports in terms of domestic currency. As a result, farmers typically receive only about 40 percent of what they would have received had they been able to sell their output freely on the world market. Under these conditions, exports of coffee, cocoa, cotton, and other crops have fallen steadily.

Marketing and procurement   A third major problem facing African farmers has been the lack of effective organizations for marketing agricultural outputs and for distributing agricultural inputs such as seeds and fertilizer. In many countries, these functions fall within the jurisdiction of state monopolies that are plagued by management problems, overstaffing, inadequate budgets (for everything except salaries), and other problems. Under these conditions, there are few countries in Africa in which farmers can count on the availability of essential farm inputs. As a result, Africa has largely been bypassed by the "green revolution" that brought new seed varieties, fertilizers, pesticides, and so on, to small farmers in many other parts of the world.

The key to reforming agricultural marketing and procurement, according to the World Bank, is to take advantage of domestic trading systems. These networks of traders already function effectively to supply rural market towns with a wide variety of goods that are not monopolized by state organizations. There is reason to believe that they could be equally helpful, if given a chance, in distributing farm goods and inputs.

Availability of capital

Capital is scarce in less-developed countries. This is true of all kinds of capital: structures and equipment for industry and agriculture: so-called social-overhead capital in the form of roads, communications networks, and health-care systems; and human capital in the form of well-educated and well-trained workers and managers.

Some low-income countries save as large a percentage of their national income as advanced countries do. In others, domestic saving is very low. In any case, because per-capita income is low to begin with, even a fairly high rate of domestic saving yields only a limited amount of new capital. As a result, most low-income countries, as we discussed earlier, have depended on capital inflows from abroad to help finance development. And, also as noted earlier, in the absence of good foreign trading markets and in the presence of reduced commodity prices and high interest rates, these capital inflows have, over time, resulted in the growth of a massive debt. The debt crisis has brought severe cutbacks in imports, public and private consumption, and standards of living. In many cases, countries have ended up poorer rather than richer, and certainly poorer than they would have been without the inflows of borrowed capital.

Foreign aid, in the form of grants and low-interest loans, has been another major source of capital for the less-developed countries. Millions of people throughout the world are alive or living better thanks to foreign aid. Even so, foreign aid, like capital flows, has its critics.

Two criticisms of past aid efforts stand out. First, donors often focussed their efforts on projects that were unsuited to the local economies in terms of size or technology. As a result, the poorest countries of the world are studded with factories that stand idle for lack of spare parts, imported materials, and labour and management skills. Second, in too many cases, foreign aid made it possible for governments to pursue domestic policies that clearly retarded development. These policies ranged from food subsidies for urban consumers to nationalization of industry and trade to waste of investment funds on "showcase" projects.

Canada provides foreign aid through the Canadian International Development Agency (CIDA). Such aid has recently averaged about $2 billion a year, or about 0.46 percent of Canada's GDP. This is far less than the 1 percent or more of GDP that Prime Minister Pearson set as a goal for Canada in the 1960s, but it is considerably higher, on a per-capita basis, than the amounts that some other countries, including the United States, are giving. Canada has concentrated much of its aid in the form of special development programs, assisted by more than 1500 Canadians serving abroad.

SUMMARY

1. *Economic development* is defined narrowly in terms of the growth of per-capita income, though improvements in other conditions of life such as health care, life expectancy, and education are also considered. The global economy is characterized by its uneven economic development.

2. The World Bank groups countries into three levels of development (based on 1989 per-capita incomes): *low-income economies* (per-capita GNP of $580 or less); *middle-income economies* (per-capita GNP of more than $580 but less than $6000); *high-income economies* (per-capita income of $6000 or more).

3. Broad groupings tend to hide wide variations in income levels. Furthermore, some researchers have shown that the gap between high- and low-income countries has been increasing since 1950, mostly because growth rates in the former have been far higher than in the latter.

4. Income inequality *within* the poorest countries is extremely high; as economies develop, income distribution appears to become more equitable.

5. Many factors may help to explain uneven development, from religious and cultural values to geography, climate, and a country's resource base — all of which affect the way in which productive resources are used.

6. The growth of an economy depends ultimately on the effective use of resources, particularly capital and labour. Economists have developed a way of combining capital and labour into a composite factor called *total factor input*. By subtracting increases in total factor input from increases in output, we obtain a measure of *total factor productivity*.

7. Low growth rates in many of the low-income countries are attributed to problems at the local, national, and international levels. At the local level, problems include the lack of ownership of resources by the poor, physical weakness and illness, high *rates of population growth*, and powerlessness. At the national level, these problems are often compounded by the wrong kinds of government intervention and by varying degrees of corruption. At the international level, foreign capital inflows have aided development, but international trade barriers and high interest rates have contributed to the creation of a serious debt problem.

8. Development strategies implemented by agencies such as the World Bank and the International Monetary Fund in the past have included rapid *industrialization* and *depauperization*. These programs were only partially successful. In an attempt to bring the crippling debt problem under control, the agencies tried, in the 1980s, to impose domestic and foreign "disciplines" on the poor economies, insisting on balanced government budgets, devaluations of currency, greater openness to foreign trade, and encouragement of competitive pressures at home. More recently, these approaches appear to have been softened somewhat, and greater emphasis is again being placed on government intervention and on the support of education and health care.

9. There is clearly no panacea for the ills of the low-income countries. The most pressing current requirements, however, are to reduce population pressures and to improve agricultural performance.

KEY TERMS

economic development
Third World
low-income economics
middle-income economies

high-income economies
total factor input
total factor productivity

rate of population growth
industrialization
depauperization

KEY BOXES

Box 29.2 Trends in Per-Capita GDP, 1950–1989

Box 29.7 Growth of GDP, Factor Inputs, and Total Factor Productivity in Developing and Industrial Economies, 1960–1987

REVIEW QUESTIONS

1. If labour accounts for 60 percent of output and capital for 40 percent, calculate
    a. total factor input if employment grows by 3 percent and the capital stock increases by 5 percent;
    b. total factor productivity if GDP grows by 4.8 percent;
    c. the increase in per-capita income if population increases by 2.0 percent.

2. In what ways are the problems of developing countries today similar to those faced by Canada in the nineteenth century? In what ways are they different?

3. People in Canada eat large amounts of meat, while people in many parts of the world go hungry. It takes about ten kilograms of grain to produce each kilogram of meat. Would poor people in the Third World be helped if Canadians simply stopped eating so much meat and ate more bread instead? How would the grain released from meat production in Canada get to the countries where it was needed, if at all? Would the world food market do the job? What policy changes might be needed?

4. Each year, thousands of immigrants come to Canada from the less-developed world, both legally and illegally. They benefit their home countries by sending money to their families. Even though the immigrants often take jobs that are low-paid by Canadian standards, they earn far more than they could have earned in their home countries. What is the effect of this immigration on worldwide income equality? What is the effect on the distribution of income among Canadian citizens? Would you favour or oppose a policy that allowed open immigration from developing countries, provided that the immigrants could prove that they could find jobs once they arrived in Canada? Discuss both positive and normative aspects of this question.

5. It is sometimes said that it is pointless to give money to developing countries, because this money will just end up lining the pockets of Saskatchewan farmers or Ontario industrialists without doing the low-income countries any good. Is this concern wholly or partly justified, or wholly unjustified? Why?

Credits and Permissions

Glossary

Absolute advantage The ability to produce a good or service at absolutely lower cost, measured in terms of factor inputs used per unit of output.   40

Accounting profit Total revenue minus explicit costs.   157

Active labour-market measures Measures designed to assist in the training or retraining of workers, and their re-integration into the labour force.   714

Adaptive-expectations hypothesis The hypothesis that people form their expectations about future economic events mainly on the basis of past economic events.   699

Aggregate demand curve A curve that relates real domestic income and the price level.   527

Aggregate expenditure/Aggregate demand The value of all final goods and services purchased in a whole economy.   438

Aggregate expenditure schedule A table or graph showing the relationship between aggregate desired expenditure (the real value of total desired expenditure) and real domestic income.   502

Aggregate output/Aggregate supply The value of all final goods and services produced by all firms.   438

Aggregate supply curve A curve that relates the total supply of goods and services in an economy to the price level.   531

Arbitrage The activity of earning a profit by buying a good for a low price in one market and reselling it for a higher price in another market.   343

Automatic stabilizers Changes in taxes, transfers, and government purchases that occur automatically as GDP rises or falls.   555

Autonomous desired consumption The part of total desired consumption expenditure that is independent of the level of disposable income; for any given consumption schedule, autonomous desired consumption is equal to the level of desired consumption associated with zero disposable income.   485

Autonomous desired imports The value of imports planned even when disposable income is zero.   500

Average propensity to consume (APC) Total desired consumption for any level of income divided by total disposable income.   488

Bad jobs Part-time, temporary, and low-paid jobs in less-dynamic sectors of industry.   334

Balanced-budget multiplier effect The ability of an increase in government purchases, matched dollar for dollar by an increase in taxes, to raise the equilibrium level of real domestic income. Using the expenditure and net-tax multiplier, the formula for the balanced-budget multiplier is as follows: 554

$$\Delta Y = \frac{\Delta G - \text{MPC}_D(\Delta T_n)}{1 - \text{MPC}_D}$$

If $\Delta G = \Delta T_n$, then,

$$\Delta Y = \frac{\Delta G - \text{MPC}_D(\Delta G)}{1 - \text{MPC}_D}$$

or

$$\Delta Y = \frac{\Delta G (1 - \text{MPC}_D)}{1 - \text{MPC}_D}$$

∴ the multiplier $= 1 \times \Delta G$.

Balance of payments A measure of all economic transactions between Canada and other countries in a given year. The balance of payments is in surplus when receipts in the current and capital accounts exceed total payments to foreigners. It is in deficit when such receipts are less than total payments.   401

Balance-of-payments equilibrium A situation in which transactions in the capital account exactly match transactions in the current account, so that there is no loss or build-up of foreign-currency reserves.   653

Bank Act The federal act, passed in 1935 (and amended several times since), under which banks in Canada are chartered and reviewed.   572

Bank of Canada Canada's government-owned central bank, responsible for monetary policy and the policies of the chartered banks.   570

751

Bank rate   The interest rate paid by chartered banks to borrow reserve funds from the Bank of Canada; also acts as a signal to the chartered banks as to the interest rates *they* should charge.   599

Bilateral monopoly   A market in which both buyer and seller exercise monopoly power and neither passively accepts the demands of the other.   363

Bond   A promise, given in recognition of a loan, to make a fixed annual or semiannual payment over a period of years plus a larger final payment equal to the sum initially borrowed.   608

Bretton Woods system   The monetary system created at Bretton Woods toward the end of World War II; it involved "pegging" currencies in relation to the U.S. dollar.   664

Budget deficit or surplus   A budget *deficit* or *surplus* refers to an *annual* negative or positive difference between government revenues and expenditures.   556

Budget line   A line showing the various combinations of goods that can be purchased at given prices within a given budget.   148

Business cycle   A cycle in which periods of growth of real output (which may be accompanied by inflation) alternate with periods of falling output (which tend to be accompanied by high unemployment).   48

Capital   All means of production created by people, including tools, industrial equipment, and structures.   10

Capital account   The account that records all transactions involving international borrowing and lending and all international purchases and sales of assets for investment purposes.   403

Capital inflows   Purchases of domestic assets by foreigners and borrowing by domestic residents from foreigners.   403

Capitalism   An economic system based on competition and individual achievement, market co-ordination of production and distribution, and private ownership of capital and land.   10

Capitalized value of a rent   The sum of money that, if invested at the current market rate of interest, would earn a periodic interest return equal to the rent for the same period.   339

Capital outflows   Purchases of foreign assets by domestic residents and borrowing by foreigners from domestic sources.   404

Cartel   A group of independent suppliers of a product who agree to co-ordinate their supply decisions in an attempt to ensure that they will all earn monopoly profits; together, they control the sale of all or most of the output of a product.   225

Ceteris paribus   A Latin expression often used in economics to express the condition "other things being equal."   92

Change in demand   A change in the quantity buyers are willing and able to purchase, at any given price, that results from a change in some factor other than the price of the good; a shift in the demand curve.   94

Change in quantity demanded   A change in the quantity buyers are willing and able to purchase that results from a change in the price of the good, other things being equal; a movement along the demand curve.   94

Change in quantity supplied   A change in the quantity producers are willing and able to sell that results from a change in the price of the good, other things being equal; a movement along the supply curve.   101

Change in supply   A change in the quantity producers are willing and able to sell, at any given price, that results from a change in some factor other than the price of the good; a shift in the supply curve.   101

Chartered banks   Financial intermediaries given a government charter to provide a broad range of banking services, including accepting demand deposits and making consumer and business loans.   571

Circular flow of income and product   The flow of goods from firms to households and of factor services from households to firms, counterbalanced by the flow of expenditures from households to firms and of factor payments from firms to households.   433

Common-property resources   Resources that are not privately owned and that can therefore be used by anyone.   304

Common share (or stock)   A share in the ownership of a corporation that gives the owner a vote in the selection of management and the right to share in any dividend payments.   71

Comparative advantage   The ability to produce a good or service at comparatively less cost than someone else.   40

Competition laws   A set of laws, including the acts of 1889 and 1923 and subsequent amendments, that seek to protect a competitive market structure and to control the competitive behaviour of firms.   282

Complementary goods   A pair of goods for which an increase in the price of one results in a decrease in the demand for the other.   97

Concentration ratio   The percentage of an industry's total sales contributed by the four or eight largest firms in the industry.   241

Conditional forecast A prediction of future economic events, stated in the form, "If A, then B, other things being equal." 16

Constant returns to scale A phenomenon said to occur when long-run average cost remains constant as output increases. 170

Consumer equilibrium A state of affairs in which consumers cannot increase the total utility they obtain from a given budget by shifting expenditure from one good to another. (In consumer equilibrium, the marginal utility of a dollar's worth of one good must be equal to the marginal utility of a dollar's worth of any other good.) 123

Consumer Price Index (CPI) A price index based on the market basket of goods and services purchased by a typical urban household. 462

Consumer surplus The difference between the amount a consumer is willing to pay for a good and the amount that is actually required. 127

Consumption schedule (consumption function) A graphic or numerical schedule that shows how desired consumption expenditure varies as disposable income varies, other things being equal. 485

Contractual savings institutions Financial intermediaries, such as insurance companies and pension funds, to which individuals and groups commit savings on a long-term, contractual basis. 581

Co-operative A firm that pools the resources of its members, as a corporation does, but grants only one vote to each member, regardless of the member's investment. 72

Co-ordinate axes The horizontal and vertical axes used to measure the *x* value and *y* value. 23

Corporation A firm organized as an independent legal entity, with ownership divided into equal parts called "shares." Each shareholder's liability is limited to the amount of his or her investment in the firm. 70

Cost-push inflation Inflation that is caused by an upward shift in the aggregate supply curve while the aggregate demand curve remains fixed or shifts upward more slowly. 687

Craft unions Unions of skilled workers practising a single craft. 355

Creative destruction The process within market economies whereby new firms or industries emerge to replace those that are in decline. 55

Cross-elasticity of demand The ratio of the percentage change in the demand for a good to a given percentage change in the price of some other good, other things being equal. 137

Cross-subsidization The practice of covering total costs, on the average, by charging some customers more than the cost of their services while charging others less than the cost of their services. 281

Crowding-out effect The tendency of an increase in desired government purchases to increase the interest rate and thereby decrease the level of desired investment. 632

Currency Coins and paper money. 570

Current account The account that records all transactions involving imports and exports of goods and services, plus international unilateral transfer payments. 402

Cyclical deficit The difference between the actual federal deficit in a given year and the structural deficit for that year. 558

Cyclical unemployment The part of unemployment that can be attributed to cyclical fluctuations in the economy, such as downturns or expansions of demand. 468

Deadweight loss The part of consumer surplus that is lost under monopoly and is not transferred to the monopolist in the form of monopoly rents; it represents an overall loss of benefits to society. 233

Decentralization The fragmentation of national economies into smaller units or the general reduction of the power of central national governments. 417

Deficit In referring to government budgets, an excess of government purchases over net taxes. 443

Deflationary gap The difference between desired expenditures and the target level of domestic income when domestic income exceeds aggregate desired expenditure at that level. 544

Demand curve A graphical representation of the relationship between the price of a good and the quantity of it demanded. 94

Demand deposits Deposits at chartered banks that permit the depositor to make payments to others by writing a cheque against the deposit. 570

Demand equation This equation can be written as $Qd = a - bP$, where Qd = quantity demanded, a = quantity demanded when the price (P) is zero, and b expresses the rate at which QD declines when the price rises. This equation holds true only for linear demand curves. 94

Demand-pull inflation An increase in the price level caused by an increase of aggregate demand relative to the noninflationary real output level. 685

Demand schedule A table showing the quantity of a good demanded at various prices. 94

Depauperization Attempts to improve economic conditions in low-income countries through a broad range of social programs, particularly in the areas of health care and education. 743

Depreciation and appreciation of the exchange rate The Canadian dollar is said to depreciate when its price falls in terms of foreign currency, and to appreciate when its price rises in terms of foreign currency. 407

Desired expenditures The spending intentions of the various decision makers in an economy; desired expenditures are *ex ante expenditures*. 485

Direct investment Business investment that gives the investor controlling interest in a firm. 419

Directly unproductive profit seeking (DUP) The profit-seeking activities of a firm that do not contribute to the output of goods and services. 233

Direct regulation Government regulation of one or more of price, rate of return, output, and entry and exit conditions, usually in a specific industry. 275

Discretionary fiscal policy Changes in the levels of taxes, transfers, or government purchases made for the specific purpose of economic stabilization. 555

Diseconomies of scale A phenomenon said to occur whenever long-run average cost increases as output increases. 170

Dissaving Negative desired saving, which occurs when desired consumption exceeds disposable income. 489

Division of labour, or specialization The division of the production process into numerous specialized functions for purposes of greater productivity. 40

Domestic income The total of all incomes, including wages, rents, interest payments, and profits, received by households. 435

Domestic product The total value of all goods and services supplied in the economy. 435

Draw-downs and redeposits Transfers of government deposits between the Bank of Canada and the chartered banks. 599

Economic development The growth of per-capita income, together with improvements in basic material conditions such as health care and education. 729

Economic planning Systematic intervention in the economy by government with the goal of improving co-ordination. 9

Economics The study of the choices people make and the actions they take in order to make the best use of scarce resources in meeting their wants and needs. 5

Economic system A type of economy characterized by a particular ideology and particular institutions and rules. 10

Economies of scale A phenomenon said to occur whenever long-run average cost decreases as output increases. 170

An economy The set of ideas, institutions, rules, and factors of production by means of which a society attempts to satisfy the needs of its members. 5

Efficiency A state of affairs in which, given the available knowledge and resources, no change can be made that would make one person better off without making another worse off. 36

Elastic demand The situation in which quantity changes by a larger percentage than price along the demand curve, so that total revenue increases as price decreases. 129

Elasticity The responsiveness of quantity demanded or supplied to changes in the price of a good or changes in other economic conditions. 129

Enterprise In one sense of the term, a group of corporations under common control. 72

Entrepreneurship The process of seeking out new possibilities: making use of new ways of doing things, being alert to new opportunities, and helping to expand existing limits. 43

Equation of exchange An equation that shows the relationships among the money stock (M), the velocity of money (V), the price level (P), and the level of real income (Y), written $MV = PY$. 607

Equilibrium level of income The level of income that generates a level of aggregate desired expenditure equal to the current level of domestic output. 504

Ex ante expenditures Expenditure plans, made in advance of actual expenditures. 485

Excess quantity demanded, or shortage The amount by which the quantity of a good demanded exceeds the quantity supplied when the price of the good is below the equilibrium level. 106

Excess quantity supplied, or surplus The amount by which the quantity of a good supplied exceeds the quantity demanded when the price of the good is above the equilibrium level. 106

Excess reserves Total reserves minus required reserves. 592

Expenditure approach (to measuring GDP) A method of estimating nominal aggregate economic activity by adding together the various expenditures on final goods and services produced domestically. 455

Explicit costs Opportunity costs that take the form of payments to outside suppliers, workers, and others who do not share in the ownership of the firm. 157

Ex post facto expenditures Expenditures recorded after the fact. 485

Externality (external cost or benefit) An unintended side effect of the use of resources that is either a cost to society (a negative externality) or a benefit (a positive externality); the market neither extracts compensation from those who generate negative externalities nor compensates those who produce positive externalities. 294

Factor markets The markets in which the factors of production — labour, natural resources, and capital — are bought and sold. 317

Factors of production The three basic inputs used in producing all goods and services — labour, capital, and natural resources. 9

Featherbedding The practice of negotiating purpose-fully inefficient work rules so that more workers will be needed to do a job. 362

Final goods and services Goods and services that are sold to (or are ready to be sold to) parties that will use them for consumption, investment, export, or as government purchases. 454

Fiscal policy Management of aggregate desired expenditure through changes in net taxes and government purchases. 543

Fixed exchange rates Exchange rates that are set by government and not permitted to move freely in response to imbalances in the foreign sector. 658

Fixed inputs Inputs that cannot easily be increased or decreased in a short time. 159

Fixed investment Purchases by firms of newly produced capital goods, such as production machinery, newly built structures, and office equipment. 436

Floating, or flexible, exchange rates Exchange rates that are determined by the forces of supply and demand in the foreign-exchange market. 658

Flows Processes occurring continuously through time, measured in units per time period. 435

Foreign-exchange market The complex of institutions through which the currency of one country may be exchanged for that of another. 405

45° line diagram A diagram that uses a 45° line to depict equilibrium between aggregate desired expenditure and real income; also called an *income–expenditure diagram*. 505

Frictional unemployment Short periods of unemployment, that occur when job seekers are being matched up with available jobs within the mainstream of the economy. 467

GDP deflator A price index that covers all final goods and services produced in the economy. 461

General Agreement on Tariffs and Trade (GATT) An international trading agreement that involves more than ninety countries and limits trade restrictions among them. 418

General equilibrium A situation in which money supply equals money demand in the money market, aggregate desired expenditure equals domestic output in the circular flow, and there is a balance-of-payments equilibrium in the foreign market. 656

Gini coefficient The ratio of the area between the Lorenz curve and the line *OE* to the area of the entire triangle *OPE*. 377

Globalization The growing tendency of corporations to conduct their business on a global basis, without regard to the special interests of the country in which their headquarters are located. 417

Good jobs Specialized, stable, and well-paid jobs in the dynamic sectors of industry. 334

Government purchases Expenditures made by federal, provincial, and municipal governments to purchase goods from private firms and to hire the services of government employees. 63

Gross domestic product (GDP) The dollar value at current market prices of all final goods and services produced within a country in a given year. 47, 453

Gross national product (GNP) The dollar value at current market prices of all final goods and services produced by citizens of a country both at home and abroad. 453

High-income economies According to the World Bank, economies with a per-capita income of $6000 or more in 1989. 730

Horizontal demand curve The demand curve of a perfectly competitive firm, which can sell no output above the given market price and cannot increase sales by lowering its price. 188

Ideology The shared ideas about acceptable forms of behaviour and goals around which a society is formed. 5

Implicit costs Opportunity costs of using resources owned by the firm or contributed by its owners. 157

Import quota A limitation on the quantity of a good that can be imported in a given time period. 398

Import schedule A graphic or numerical representation of how desired import purchases vary as real disposable income varies, other things being equal. It is assumed here that $M = M_a + mY_d$, where M is desired imports, M_a is autonomous desired imports, m is the marginal propensity to import, and Y_d is disposable income. 500

Income approach (to measuring GDP) A method of estimating nominal aggregate economic activity by adding together the various incomes earned by all households. 457

Income effect The part of the change in quantity demanded of a good whose price has fallen that is attributable to the change in real income resulting from the price change. 125

Income elasticity of demand The ratio of the percentage change in the demand for a good to the percentage change in the per-capita income of buyers. 136

Incomes policy A policy that attempts to control wages, salaries, earnings, and prices directly in order to fight inflation. 715

Indifference curve A graphic representation of an indifference set. 144

Indifference map A representative selection of indifference curves for a single consumer and pair of goods. 147

Indifference set A set of consumption alternatives, each of which yields the same utility, so that no member of the set is preferred to any other. 143

Indirect or social regulation Government regulation of the attributes of a product or service, information, methods of production, sale, and employment. 275

Industrial democracy Arrangements whereby workers are able to participate more fully in economic decision making. 718

Industrialization In the context of Third World development, the attempt on the part of Western development agencies in the postwar period to speed up the economic growth of low-income countries through industrial development. 742

Industrial union A union representing all workers in an enterprise, regardless of trade. 355

Inelastic demand The situation in which quantity changes by a smaller percentage than price along the demand curve, so that total revenue decreases as price decreases. 129

Inferior good A good for which an increase in consumer income results in a decrease in demand. 96

Inflation A sustained increase in the average price of all goods and services. 45

Inflationary gap The difference between desired expenditures and the target level of domestic income when aggregate desired expenditure exceeds domestic income at that level. 545

Inflationary recession A situation in which real output falls below the NILO, while rapid inflation continues; sometimes referred to as *stagflation*. 691

Injections The part of total expenditures that does not originate in domestic households — that is, investment, government purchases, and exports. 445

Institutionalists and Marxists Economists who work with models that use a wide range of data, including the effects of the prevailing social and political institutions, to explain economic behaviour. 16

Inventories Stocks of a finished good awaiting sale or use. 106

Inventory investment Changes in the stocks of finished products and raw materials that firms keep on hand. If stocks are increasing, inventory investment is positive; if they are decreasing, it is negative. 436

Investment The sum of fixed investment and inventory investment. 436

Investment schedule A downward-sloping schedule that shows the connection between desired investment and the interest rate, other things being equal. 626

An isoquant A line showing the various combinations of variable inputs that can be used to produce a given amount of output. 178

J-curve effect The short-term increase in the current-account deficit following a currency devaluation. 662

Labour The contributions to production made by people working with their minds and their bodies. 9

Labour force All members of the noninstitutionalized civilian population fifteen years of age and older who are either officially employed or looking for employment. 466

Land-use controls Policies designed to raise agricultural prices by limiting the amount of land on which certain crops can be grown. 110

Law of demand The principle that, other things being equal, the quantity of a good demanded by buyers tends to rise as the price of the good falls, and to fall as the price of the good rises. 91

Law of diminishing returns The principle that, as one variable input is increased, with all others remaining fixed, a point will be reached beyond which the marginal physical product of the variable input begins to decrease. 160

Leakages The part of domestic income not devoted to consumption (saving plus net taxes), plus domestic expenditures on foreign-made goods (imports). 445

Liquidity An asset is said to possess liquidity if it can be used directly as a means of payment and if it does not vary in nominal value. 570

Long run A time range that is long enough to permit changes in all inputs, both fixed and variable. 159

Long-run industry supply curve A curve that traces the output response of all firms in an industry to persistent changes in demand over a period of time long enough for firms to adjust their plant size, if necessary, and for entry to and exit from the market to occur. 202

Lorenz curve A curve that graphs the cumulative percentage of income household units along the horizontal axis and the cumulative percentage of income received by those units along the vertical axis. 376

Low-income economies According to the World Bank, economies with a per-capita income of $580 or less in 1989. 730

Lump-sum taxes Taxes that do not vary with the level of real domestic income (for example, property taxes). 492

M_1 The money supply defined as total currency outside banks plus demand deposits held by the public in chartered banks. 570

M₂ A second definition of money, including currency, demand deposits, daily-interest chequable and non-personal (business) notice deposits, and personal savings deposits.   571

M₃ Equals M₂ plus foreign-currency deposits in chartered banks.   572

Macroeconomic equilibrium The income level at which aggregate desired expenditure equals income *and* aggregate demand equals aggregate supply.   534

Macroeconomics The branch of economics that deals with large-scale economic phenomena, especially inflation, unemployment, and economic growth.   12, 433

Marginal-average rule The rule that marginal cost must be equal to average cost when average cost is at its minimum.   165

Marginal cost The increase in cost required to increase the output of some good or service by one unit.   162

Marginal efficiency of investment The expected rate of return on an additional dollar of planned investment.   626

Marginal factor cost The amount by which a firm's total factor cost must increase in order for it to obtain an additional unit of that factor.   323

Marginal physical product The additional amount of output, expressed in physical units, produced by each added unit of one variable input, other things being equal.   160

Marginal propensity to consume (MPC) The fraction of each additional dollar of disposable income that people desire to spend on consumption.   488

Marginal propensity to import (MPM) The proportion of each additional dollar of disposable income (Y_d) that people desire to spend on imports.   500

$$MPM = m = \frac{\Delta M}{\Delta Y_d}$$

Marginal propensity to save (MPS) The fraction of each dollar of additional income that people desire to save.   490

Marginal rate of substitution The rate at which one good can be substituted for another without gain or loss in satisfaction (equal to the slope of an indifference curve at any point).   145

Marginal revenue The amount by which total revenue increases as the result of a one-unit increase in quantity.   189

Marginal revenue product (of a factor) The change in revenue resulting from the sale of the product produced by one additional unit of factor input.   320

Marginal utility The amount of additional utility obtained from a one-unit increase in consumption of a good.   120

The market The network of business dealings through which a society's production and distribution decisions are co-ordinated.   8

Market equilibrium A condition in which the separately formulated plans of the buyers and sellers of some good exactly mesh when tested in the marketplace, so that the quantity supplied is exactly equal to the quantity demanded at the prevailing price.   104

Market failure The inability of firms in a market economy to provide goods and services in a socially optimal way.   273

Marketing Finding out what customers want and channelling a flow of goods and services to satisfy those wants.   247

Market power The strength that a firm possesses for reasons other than technical efficiency — for example, exclusive control of resources, prior buildup of profits, networks of influence and command, or massive advertising — that gives it an advantage over its rivals.   245

Market structure The key traits of a market, including the number of firms in each industry, the extent to which the products of different firms are different or similar, and the ease of entry into and exit from the market.   187

Microeconomics The branch of economics that deals with the choices and actions of small economic units — that is, households, business firms, and units of government.   11

Middle-income economies According to the World Bank, economies with a per-capita income of more than $580 but less than $6000 in 1989.   730

Minimum efficient scale The level of output at which economies of scale are exhausted.   171

Model A mathematical or graphic version of an economic theory.   15

Monetarism A school of economic thought that emphasizes changes in the money supply as a determinant of prices, income, and employment.   638

Money An asset that serves as a means of payment, a store of purchasing power, and a unit of account.   569

Money demand (MD) The amount of money people wish to hold (in the form of currency and liquid bank deposits), usually measured in relation to different rates of interest.   607

Money demand schedule A schedule showing the quantity of money that people desire to hold in their portfolios given various values for the interest rate and the level of real domestic income.   610

Money multiplier The ratio of the quantity of money to the total reserves in a banking system. Various money multipliers can be defined, depending on the definition of money used. In the simplified banking system, the formula for the money multiplier is: 598

$$\text{Money multiplier} = \frac{1}{\text{Required-reserve ratio}}.$$

Monopolistic competition A market structure in which many small firms offer differentiated products. 239

Monopoly A market that is dominated by a single seller. 213

Monopoly rent The earnings of a monopoly firm in excess of what it would make as a competitive firm. 233

Monopsony A market in which there is only one buyer; from the Greek words *mono* ("single") and *opsonia* ("buying"). 330

Moral suasion Direct attempts by the Bank of Canada to influence the practices of the chartered banks. 599

Multiplier The ratio of an induced change in the equilibrium level of domestic income to the initial change in desired domestic expenditure that caused it. For an economy in which imports play an important role, the value of the multiplier is given by the following formula:

$$\text{Multiplier} = \frac{1}{1 - (\text{MPC} - \text{MPM})}$$

or $\dfrac{1}{1 - \text{MPC}_D}$

where MPC_D is the marginal propensity to consume domestic output. 520

$$\text{MPC}_D = \frac{\Delta C}{\Delta Y_d} - \frac{\Delta M}{\Delta Y_d}$$

Multiplier effect The ability of a $1 shift in the aggregate expenditure schedule to induce a change of more than $1 in the equilibrium level of real domestic income. 519

National debt The *total indebtedness* of the federal government (or of all levels of government) as a result of all past borrowings. 556

Natural monopoly An industry in which the minimum efficient scale of operation is so large relative to the size of the market that the industry has room for only one firm operating at this minimum efficient level of output. 277

Natural resources Anything that can be used as a productive input in its natural state, such as farmland, building sites, forests, and mineral deposits. 10

Near-banks Institutions that accept deposits on which cheques can be written but that are not chartered banks and are not subject to direct control by the Bank of Canada. 581

Near-moneys Assets that are less-than-perfectly liquid but still liquid enough to be reasonably close substitutes for money. 572

Negative income tax A general name for transfer systems that emphasize cash benefits: A basic benefit is available to households with zero earned income and is then reduced at a rate of substantially less than 100 percent as income is earned. 384

Net capital inflow function A function relating desired net capital inflows (inflows minus outflows) to domestic interest rates. 655

Net domestic income The total income received by a nation's productive factors resulting from production within the nation's boundaries. It is equal to GDP minus capital-consumption allowances, indirect business taxes, and the statistical discrepancy. 457

Net exports Total exports minus total imports. 446

Net taxes Total tax revenues collected by government at all levels minus total transfer payments disbursed. 442

Net-tax multiplier A multiplier showing the change in equilibrium domestic income resulting from a change in net taxes. The formula for the net-tax multiplier is as follows: 550

$$-\frac{(\text{MPC} - \text{MPM})}{1 - (\text{MPC} - \text{MPM})} \text{ or}$$

$$-\frac{\text{MPC}_D}{1 - \text{MPC}_D}$$

Nominal In economics, a term used in reference to data that have not been adjusted for the effects of inflation. 47

Nonaccelerating-inflation rate of unemployment (NAIRU) The unemployment rate associated with a noninflationary level of real output. 708

Noninflationary level of (real) output (NILO) The level of output at which long-run equilibrium with stable prices is possible. 681

Normal good A good for which an increase in consumer income results in an increase in demand. 96

Normative economics The part of economics that makes judgements about economic policies or outcomes. 17

Official-reserve account The account that records transactions involving purchases and sales of reserves of foreign currency by central banks. 404

Oligopolistic interdependence The need, in an oligopolistic market, to pay close attention to the actions of one's rivals when making price or production decisions. 251

Oligopoly A market structure in which there are two or more firms, at least one of which has a large share of total sales. 239

Open-market operations A purchase of securities from the public or a sale of securities to the public by the Bank of Canada for the purpose of altering the quantity of reserves available to chartered banks. 590

Opportunity cost The cost of a good measured in terms of the lost opportunity to pursue the best alternative activity with the same time and resources. 38

Par The point at which one unit of a currency is traded for exactly one unit of another currency. 411

Partnership A firm jointly owned and operated by two or more persons. Each partner bears full legal liability for the debts of the firm. 69

Percentage income tax A percentage tax placed on personal income, whereby the absolute amount taxed varies with income. 494

Perfect competition A market structure characterized by a large number of relatively small firms, a homogeneous product, good distribution of information among all market participants, and freedom of entry and exit. 187

Perfectly elastic demand The situation in which the demand curve is a horizontal line. 130

Perfectly inelastic demand The situation in which the demand curve is a vertical line. 130

Per se **offence** An act that is declared illegal in itself, without having to be proved harmful to someone. 283

Personal disposable income Personal income minus personal taxes. 460

Personal income The total of all income, including transfer payments, actually received by households before payment of personal income taxes and other transfer payments to government. 460

Phillips curve A curve showing the relationship between the rate of inflation and the level of unemployment. Inflation, usually represented on the vertical axis of such a figure, can be measured in terms of either the rate of change in wages or the rate of change in a price index. 692

Portfolio balance The balance among the various kinds of assets that a person owns — including money, consumer durables, stocks, and bonds — shifting from one kind of asset to another as economic conditions change. 609

Portfolio investment Business investment that does not give the investor controlling interest in a firm; refers primarily to bond holdings. 419

Positive economics The part of economics that is limited to making statements about facts and the relationships among them. 17

Post-industrial society The third phase of a society's economic evolution, following the traditional, agrarian phase and the modern, industrial phase. The post-industrial society is based on services. 57

Precautionary motive A motive for holding money arising from its usefulness as a reserve of liquid funds for use in emergencies or in taking advantage of unexpected opportunities. 608

Preferred share (or stock) A share in the ownership of a corporation that gives the owner voting rights and a fixed return on investment, paid out from profits before any payment of dividends is made to owners of common shares. 71

Price ceiling A maximum permissible price, usually imposed by the government and set below the market equilibrium price. 109

Price discrimination The practice of charging different prices for the same product, when the price differences are not justified by differences in the cost of serving different customers. 224

Price elasticity of demand (elasticity of demand) The ratio of the percentage change in the quantity of a good demanded to the percentage change in the price of that good. 129

Price elasticity of supply (elasticity of supply) The ratio of the percentage change in the quantity of a good supplied to the percentage change in its price. 137

Price floor A minimum permissible price, usually imposed by the government and set above the market equilibrium price; commonly referred to as the *floor price*. 109

Price index A weighted average of the prices of goods and services expressed in relation to a base-year value of 100. 461

Price leadership In an oligopoly, the situation that exists when increases or decreases in price initiated by one dominant firm, known as the price leader, are matched by all or most other firms in the market. 253

Price supports Programs under which the government guarantees a certain minimum price to farmers by undertaking to buy any surplus that cannot be sold to private buyers at the support price. 109

Price taker A firm that sells its outputs at fixed prices that are determined entirely by forces beyond its control. 187

Primary securities markets Markets in which companies sell new shares of stock and bonds for borrowing purposes. 583

Principle of diminishing marginal utility The principle that the greater the rate of consumption of some good, the smaller the increase in utility from a one-unit increase in the rate of consumption of that good. 120

Private costs and benefits The costs incurred and benefits reaped by those who actually produce a good. 294

Production possibilities frontier (PPF) A graph showing the possible combinations of goods that can be produced by an economy, given the available resources and technology. 36

Property rights Rights that pertain to the permissible use of resources. 299

Protectionism Policies of shielding domestic industry from foreign competition. 398

Public-choice theory A branch of economics that applies economic theory to political decision making, casting voters in the role of customers and government in the role of entrepreneur. 233

Public goods Goods or services that (1) cannot be provided to one citizen without also being supplied to that person's neighbours, and (2) once provided for one citizen, cost no more to be provided to others. 64

Purchasing-power parity theory (of exchange rates) The theory holding that the price of a unit of Currency A in terms of Currency B will, in the long run, tend to be equal to the ratio of the price level in Country B to the price level in Country A. 409

Pure economic profit The sum that is left when both explicit and implicit costs are subtracted from total revenue. 157

Pure economic rent The income earned by any factor of production that is in perfectly inelastic supply. 337

Pure monopoly A market structure in which a single firm makes and sells 100 percent of the output of a product. 213

Rate of population growth The difference between the birth rate and the death rate in any given year. 740

Rate of return A firm's accounting profit expressed as a percentage of its net worth. 279

Rational-expectations hypothesis The hypothesis that people form their expectations about future economic events not only on the basis of past events but also on the basis of their expectations about economic policies and their likely effects. 700

Real In economics, a term used in reference to data that have been adjusted for the effects of inflation. 48

Realized expenditures The actual expenditures made in a given year, as recorded in the national-income accounts; realized expenditures are *ex post facto expenditures*. 485

Real and nominal interest rates Nominal rates of interest are actual current rates; real rates of interest are the nominal (current) rate minus the current rate of inflation. 636

Recession A period in which real output falls for six months or more. 48

Recovery A period of renewed growth of real output following a recession. 49

Regionalization The tendency of countries to form regional trading blocs such as the European Community and the trade area created by the Canada–U.S. Free Trade Agreement. 417

Required-reserve ratios Legally required minimum quantities of reserves, expressed as ratios of reserves to total funds held in various types of deposits. 576

Reserves Money held by chartered banks as cash or as non-interest-bearing deposits with the Bank of Canada. 576

Saving The part of household income not used to purchase goods and services or to pay taxes. 436

Saving schedule A graphic or numerical schedule that shows how desired saving varies as disposable income varies, other things being equal. 489

Say's law The proposition that producing a given level of domestic product will automatically generate an equal level of aggregate demand. 482

Scarcity A situation in which there is not enough of a resource to meet all of people's wants and needs. 5

Schedule 1 banks Banks in which no individual can own more than 10 percent of the shares; to date, all are Canadian-owned. 572

Schedule 2 banks Banks that can be narrowly held and that are currently almost exclusively subsidiaries of foreign-owned banks. 572

Secondary securities markets Markets, such as stock markets, that deal in previously issued securities. 583

Service sector The sector of an economy consisting of service industries, such as health and education services; communication and transportation services; and financial, legal, and trading services. 57

Shared monopoly The situation that exists when firms in an oligopoly co-ordinate their activities in order to earn maximum profits for the industry as a whole. 252

Short run A time range within which output can be adjusted only by changing the amounts of variable inputs used while fixed inputs remain unchanged. 159

Slope of a curved line At any given point, the slope of a straight line drawn tangent to the curve at that point. 26

Slope of a straight line The ratio of the change in the *y* value to the change in the *x* value between any two points in the line. 26

Social costs and benefits The total cost or benefit to society of producing a good, including both private and external costs or benefits. 294

Socialism An economic system based on co-operation and the advancement of the society as a whole, centrally planned co-ordination of production and distribution, and communal ownership of capital and land. 10

Sole proprietorship A firm owned and usually managed by one person, who receives all profits of the firm and who personally bears all the firm's liabilities. 69

Speculative motive A motive for holding money arising from its fixed value, when the value of alternative assets is expected to decline. 608

Stabilization policy Efforts by government to control the level of national income and the related conditions of inflation, unemployment, and the balance of payments, using taxation and expenditure as its tools. 67

Staple product A commodity on which the economy of a settlement or region concentrates much of its labour and capital. 60

Stocks Accumulated quantities existing at a particular time, measured in terms of units alone. 435

Structural deficit The federal budget deficit that would prevail if the economy were operating at a constant benchmark rate of unemployment. 558

Structural unemployment Long periods of unemployment that occur when workers' skills do not match those required by available jobs; a result, in part, of shifts in the structure of the economy that make certain skills obsolete. 468

Substitute goods A pair of goods for which an increase in the price of one causes an increase in the demand for the other. 96

Substitution effect The part of the increase in quantity demanded of a good whose price has fallen that is attributable to the tendency of consumers to substitute relatively cheap goods for relatively expensive ones. 125

Supply curve A graphical representation of the relationship between the price of a good and the quantity of it supplied. 101

Supply equation This equation expresses the idea that quantity supplied (Qs) is a function of price, or $Qs = a + bP$. This equation holds true only for linear supply curves. 101

Supply schedule A table showing the quantity of a good supplied at various prices. 101

Supply shock An event, such as an increase in the price of imported oil, a crop failure, or a natural disaster, that raises input prices for all or most firms and pushes up workers' cost of living. 687

Surplus In referring to government budgets, an excess of net taxes over government purchases. 443

Sustainable development Development that meets present needs without reducing the ability of future generations to meet their needs. 304

Target level of domestic income The level of domestic income judged by policy makers to be most compatible with such goals as full employment and price stability; also called an *income target*. 543

Tariff A tax levied on imported goods. 398

Theory An explanation of how facts are related. 15

Third World The low-income countries of the world, which constitute a third "development group" after the high-income market economies and the middle-income, formerly centrally planned, socialist economies. 729

Total factor input A measure of the weighted, combined input of capital and labour in the production process. 736

Total factor productivity The difference between the growth of total factor input and the growth of total output. 737

Total revenue The quantity of a good sold multiplied by the price at which it is sold. 129

Transaction costs The costs, other than price, that are incurred in trading goods or services. 299

Transactions motive A motive for holding money arising from the convenience of using it as a means of payment for day-to-day transactions. 608

Transfer payments All payments made by government to individuals that are not made in return for goods or services currently supplied. Social insurance benefits, welfare payments, and unemployment insurance benefits are major forms of transfer payments. 63

Transitivity The situation where if *A* is preferred to *B* and *B* is preferred to *C*, then *A* must be preferred to *C*. 147

Transmission mechanism The mechanism through which monetary policy affects the equilibrium level of real domestic income. 628

Transnational (or multinational) corporation A corporation that has branch operations in more than one country. 72

Unemployment rate Percentage of the labour force who are not employed but are actively looking for employment. 44, 466

Unit elastic demand The situation in which price and quantity change by the same percentage along the demand curve, so that total revenue remains unchanged as price changes. 129

Utility The economist's term for the pleasure, satisfaction, and need fulfilment that people get from the consumption of material goods and services. 120

Value added The dollar value of an industry's sales less the value of intermediate goods purchased for use in production. 455

Variable inputs Inputs that can easily be varied within a short time in order to increase or decrease output. 159

Velocity The ratio of real domestic income to the money stock; a measure of the average number of times each dollar of the money stock is used each year for income-producing purposes. 607

Welfare economics The branch of economics that tries to define the optimal outcome of economic activity. 294

White Paper on Employment and Income The 1945 federal government document committing the government to the promotion of economic stability and high levels of employment. 708

x **value** Corresponds to a point's horizontal distance from the vertical axis. 23

y **value** Corresponds to a point's vertical distance from the horizontal axis. 23

Name Index

Subject Index

Solutions to Selected Review Questions

APPENDIX TO CHAPTER 1

2. The slope of the line between points *A* and *B* is 2/2 = 1; between points *C* and *D* is −2/1 = −2; and between points *E* and *F* is 1/1 = 1.

3. The 45° line cuts the desired consumption function when both disposable income and consumption are approximately $575.

    a. $575; $575

    b. The 45° line marks out equal values on the horizontal and vertical axes.

CHAPTER 4

11. a. a downward movement along the demand curve resulting from a change in price; a change in the quantity demanded

    b. a rightward shift in the demand curve resulting from a change in the price of a substitute product; a change in demand

    c. a rightward shift in the demand curve resulting from a change in consumer tastes; a change in demand

    d. a rightward shift in the demand curve resulting from a change in income; a change in demand

    e. a rightward shift in the demand curve as people stock up on Pepsi; a change in demand

13. a. a leftward shift in the supply curve; a change in supply

    b. an upward movement along the supply curve; a change in the quantity supplied

    c. a leftward shift in the supply curve; a change in supply

    d. a rightward shift in the supply curve; a change in supply

15. a. $5, 5 units

    b. 1, −1

    c. at any price above $5; at any price below $5

    d. There would be a shortage of 3 units.

    e. The price ceiling would not affect the market, since it is above the equilibrium price of $5.

17. a. The demand curve for Titan sticks shifts to the right; this is a change in demand caused by a change in consumer preferences.

    b. The demand curve for Easton sticks should shift to the right; the demand curve for Titan sticks should shift to the left. Both are changes in demand resulting from a change in consumer preferences.

    c. A ban on metal sticks should cause the demand curve for wooden sticks to shift to the right, and the demand curve for metal sticks to shift to the left. Both would be changes in demand resulting from a change in consumer preferences.

CHAPTER 5

16. a. elasticity = 1; unit demand

    b. elasticity = 1.4; elastic demand

    c. elasticity = 0.9; inelastic demand

18. a. perfectly elastic at a price of $20

    b. perfectly inelastic at one pack

    c. perfectly inelastic at a quantity of one prescription

    d. perfectly elastic along the zero (e.g., horizontal) axis

    e. perfectly inelastic at one "fix" of heroin

20. The income elasticity for meat is 3 a positive coefficient value. Meat is a normal good, since meat consumption increases as income increases.

22. If the ratio of marginal utility to price for the tie was equal to the ratio of marginal utility to price for all the other goods and services the professor bought, "that tie" becomes a rational purchase.

APPENDIX TO CHAPTER 5

1. The budget line cuts the vertical axis (bread) at 6 and the horizontal axis (milk) at 4. Equilibrium occurs at the point of tangency between the budget line and the highest possible indifference curve.

  a. The budget line would cut the vertical axis (bread) at 3 and the horizontal axis (milk) at 2. Equilibrium occurs at the point of tangency between the budget line and the highest possible indifference curve.

  b. The budget line would cut the vertical axis (bread) at 6 and the horizontal axis (milk) at 2. Equilibrium occurs at the point of tangency between the budget line and the highest possible indifference curve.

  c. The budget line would cut the vertical axis (bread) at 6 and the horizontal axis (milk) at 8. Equilibrium occurs at the point of tangency between the budget line and the highest possible indifference curve.

CHAPTER 6

10. a. See the table below.

  b. The marginal-cost curve cuts the average-variable-cost curve at approximately $75 and the average-total-cost curve at about $91.

12. a. short-run
  b. long-run
  c. short-run
  d. long-run
  e. long-run

14. Graphs will vary depending on the classification of fixed and variable costs. The average-total-cost curve will fall for all levels of output, as will the average-variable-cost curve, as a result of the reduction in white-collar wages. If capital costs are considered fixed costs, then average fixed costs will fall for all levels of output, and so, likely, will marginal costs. The total-cost curve will fall for all levels of output because of the overall reduction in spending.

CHAPTER 7

11. a. At a marginal revenue (price) of $70, the firm should go out of business in the short run because it is not able to cover its average variable costs, which are $74 at the point where marginal cost equals marginal revenue — that is, at 5 units of output.

  b. At a marginal revenue (price) of $80, the firm is taking a loss but should stay in business in the short run because it is covering its average variable costs, which are $75 at the point where marginal cost equals marginal revenue — that is, at an output of 6 units.

  c. At a marginal revenue (price) of $130, the firm is making a profit. It is more than covering its average variable costs and its average total costs at the point where marginal cost equals marginal revenue — that is, at an output of 9 units.

Quantity of Output	Fixed Cost	Variable Cost	Total Cost	Marginal Cost	Average Fixed Cost	Average Variable Cost	Average Total Cost
0	100	*0*	*100*		—	—	—
				90			
1	100	90	190		100	*90*	190
				80			
2	100	*170*	270		50	85	135
				70			
3	100	240	340		33.33	80	113.33
				60			
4	100	300	400		25	75	*100*
				70			
5	100	370	*470*		20	74	94
				80			
6	100	*450*	550		16.67	75	91.67
				90			
7	100	540	640		14.29	77.14	91.43
				110			
8	100	650	*750*		12.50	81.25	93.75
				130			
9	100	780	880		11.11	*86.67*	97.78
				150			
10	100	930	1030		10	93	*103*

CHAPTER 8

12. Price fixing tends to benefit producers and raise costs for buyers. If Canadian firms buy inputs from price-fixing Canadian producers, their costs will be higher and so, consequently, will the prices they must charge. These higher prices make Canadian firms uncompetitive in global markets.

13. a. cartel

b. Nutmeg prices would increase dramatically as a result of the cartel agreement to restrict supply and set prices.

c. All cartels face the problem of having to police members to prevent them from selling more than their agreed-upon quota and from setting prices below the agreed-upon price.

CHAPTER 9

9. The Calgary Co-op and its competitors would be oligopolists. The Co-op has managed to differentiate its product through the provision of related services. Its high profit rate is possible because of both owner-customer loyalty and an apparent demand for its differentiated services. No, this does not go against the cost theory presented in the text.

11. Yes. Although the Cournot theory and game theory generally involve only two firms, the idea of a price war relates to both theories. The kinked-demand-curve theory is likely more applicable to this situation of multiple firms' competing in a price war by lowering prices. A price war involves lowering prices below the going market price and having others decide to follow the price cut or not.

13. While gasoline prices fell in general, the nation is divided into several different markets, and different prices are therefore possible. People in the Atlantic provinces do not have the option of buying in Toronto or major Western cities, so Atlantic gas suppliers need not lower their prices to meet Toronto prices.

14. A shared monopoly is an informal arrangement that exists through tacit agreement. It is possible that the two situations could produce similar price and output restrictions for "members." The end goal of each is to earn monopoly profits for all the firms involved.

CHAPTER 10

8. a. A cartel has been organized in the nutmeg market.

b. The demand for nutmeg is likely quite inelastic; otherwise, buyers would substitute other spices for it as its price rose.

c. The cartel will have problems making sure that none of its members sells nutmeg for less than the agreed-upon price. Also, nutmeg producers in other nations may want to join the cartel, which could reduce prices for all members, or, at least, limit the volume that each one was permitted to supply.

10. Higher fines would be more effective as an economic deterrent from violating competition laws. If the Canadian government is serious about increasing competition, then raising fines to deter firms from abusing the law may be a good idea.

12. a. If margarine remains an unappealing colour, consumers may continue to prefer butter. The colour restrictions are likely an attempt to reduce the substitution of margarine for the butter produced by dairies.

b. If margarine had a more appealing, butterlike colour, the demand for margarine as a substitute for butter might increase.

c. The demand for butter might be reduced.

CHAPTER 11

4. a. See the table below.

b. The external cost per tonne is $100 ($20 000/ 200; 40 000/400; and so on).

	Quantity (tonnes)				
Costs	0	200	400	600	800
Total private costs	$0	$100 000	$140 000	$200 000	$280 000
Total external costs	0	20 000	40 000	60 000	80 000
Total social costs	0	120 000	180 000	260 000	360 000
Marginal private costs per tonne	$500		$200	$300	$400
Marginal external costs per tonne	100		100	100	100
Marginal social costs per tonne	600		300	400	500

Note: Costs in this table are expressed in dollars per tonne. The quantities in each column increase by 200 tonnes over the previous column.

c. The privately optimal output level is between 600 t and 800 t — that is, at the quantity where the marginal-private-cost curve intersects the marginal-revenue (demand) curve.

d. The socially optimal level of output is between 400 t and 600 t — that is, at the quantity where the marginal-social-cost curve intersects the marginal-revenue (demand) curve.

CHAPTER 12

16. a. See the table below.

17. a. Firm A is a perfect competitor, and Firm B, an imperfect competitor, in the product market. Firm A's marginal revenue, and therefore its product price, remains constant, while Firm B's decreases as output increases.

b. The marginal-revenue-product curve also serves as the demand curve for factors of production.

c. Both firms should hire between 3 and 4 units of labour. For Firm A, the price of labour equals the marginal revenue product of labour between 3 and 4 units of labour; and for Firm B, the marginal revenue product of labour is greater than the price of labour between 3 and 4 units, but less than the price of labour between 4 and 5 units.

CHAPTER 13

8. If the supply of workers was perfectly elastic, a change in demand would not affect the equilibrium wage rate.

10. a. The supply curve becomes horizontal, or perfectly elastic, at the union's demanded wage and remains horizontal until it reaches the upward-sloping supply curve.

b. The marginal-labour-cost curve becomes horizontal at the union wage and remains so until the supply curve starts to rise. At this point, there is a kink in the marginal-labour-cost curve and it jumps to the original upward-sloping marginal-labour-cost curve.

c. The quantity of workers hired will be determined by the intersection of the marginal-labour-cost curve and the demand curve for labour.

d. The wage paid will be the wage demanded by the union.

e. The union will have maximized the total wages paid but not the number of workers employed. The number of workers employed would be maximized by setting the union wage equal to the wage that would occur at the equilibrium between supply and demand in a labour market where the union and employer had equal bargaining strength.

CHAPTER 14

10. The Lorenz curve depicting the situation after the revolution should be closer to the 45° line than the one depicting the situation before the revolution. The Gini coefficient would be smaller after the revolution.

12. a. $16 000

b. $12 000

CHAPTER 15

7. a. The supply curve for Canadian dollars shifts outward to the right. The Canadian dollar depreciates relative to the U.S. dollar.

Units of Labour	Total Physical Product for Firms A and B	Marginal Physical Product for Firms A and B	Marginal Revenue for Firm A	Marginal Revenue for Firm B	Marginal Revenue Product for Firm A	Marginal Revenue Product for Firm B
0	0					
1	20	20	$10	$30	$200	$600
2	30	10	10	25	100	250
3	35	5	10	20	50	100
4	38	3	10	15	30	45
5	39	1	10	10	10	10

b. The supply curve for Canadian dollars shifts outward to the right. The Canadian dollar depreciates relative to the Mexican peso.

c. The demand curve for Canadian dollars shifts upward to the right. The Canadian dollar appreciates relative to the U.S. dollar.

d. The demand curve for Canadian dollars shifts upward to the right. The Canadian dollar appreciates relative to the U.S. dollar.

9. a. capital account; inflow

b. capital account; outflow

c. current account; outflow

d. current account; the inflow is reduced

CHAPTER 17

12. a. aggregate expenditure = $190 000; aggregate output = $190 000; disequilibrium

b. $50 000

c. $190 000

CHAPTER 18

9. a. Aggregate expenditure = $170 000; aggregate output = $170 000; equilibrium

b. $0; there is no unplanned inventory investment in this economy.

11. GNP = $427.8 million

CHAPTER 19

12. a. $500; $620; $800

b. $500

c. This consumption schedule is a straight line with a constant slope. You can tell because the marginal propensity to consume determines the slope of the consumption schedule, and in this case, the MPC is constant at 0.6.

14. − $500; $415

16. a. aggregate expenditure = $40 + $165 + $210 + $40 = $455

b. slope = 0.8 − 0.1 = 0.7

c. aggregate expenditure = $40 + 0.8 ($1200) + $165 + $210 + $40 − 0.1 ($1200) = $1295

CHAPTER 20

4. a. See the table below.

b. multiplier = $1/(0.15 + 0.10) = 4$

c. $4 \times \$500 = \$2000$

6. a. multiplier = $1/1 − 0.8 (1 − 0.2) = 2.78$

b. Real domestic income would increase by $556 (that is, $200 × 2.78).

8. a. multiplier = $1/1 − 0.85 (1 − 0.1) = 4.26$

b. Real domestic income would decline by $426 (that is, 4.26 × − $100).

CHAPTER 21

13. a. a deflationary gap

b. The multiplier is $1/0.15 + 0.1 = 4$, and the desired change in real domestic income is $300. Therefore, the change in government purchases can be calculated as $300 ÷ 4 = $75.

15. a. The net-tax multiplier is $-0.75/0.25 = -3$. Since the desired change in income is $300, the net change in taxes is $300 ÷ 3 = − $100.

b. The desired change in real domestic income is − $200, so the change in net taxes must be − $200 ÷ − 3 = $67.

CHAPTER 22

6. $M_1 = \$32.6 + \$27.4 = \$60$
$M_2 = M_1 + \$184.6 = \$244.6$
$M_3 = M_2 + \$19.8 = \$22.6 = \$287$

Round	Increase in Aggregate Desired Expenditures MPC = 0.85	Increase in Imports MPM = 0.1	Increase in Aggregate Desired Expenditure on Domestic Goods and Services $MPC_D = 0.75$
1	$500	$ 0	$500
2	375	50	325
3	243.75	32.50	211.25

CHAPTER 23

3. a. money multiplier = 1/0.6 = 16.67; change in money supply = 16.67 × $200 million = $3334 million.

b. The central bank would have bought $200 million of securities on the open market.

5. a. 10 × −$400 million = $4000 million

b. The central bank would have sold $400 million of securities on the open market.

CHAPTER 24

11. a. An increase in the bank rate would attract foreign investors to Canada, causing an increased demand for the Canadian dollar. An increased demand for Canadian currency would increase the value of the Canadian dollar or at least help it maintain its value relative to the U.S. dollar.

b. Higher Canadian interest rates would attract more foreign money to Canada, but would also make it more expensive for Canadians to borrow money for investment or consumption purposes.

13. a. The money demand curve will shift to the left.

b. The interest rate should fall if the money supply curve remains fixed and the money demand curve shifts to the left.

CHAPTER 25

13. The multiplier is 1/(1 − 0.8) = 5. The net change in real domestic income is 5 × $275 million = $1375 million.

15. a. The tax cut is likely to increase the desired consumption portion of aggregate desired expenditure, shifting that schedule upward and increasing real domestic income. An increased domestic income will cause the money demand curve to shift upward to the right. With a fixed money supply, interest rates will rise, causing desired investment to fall. A drop in desired investment will shift the aggregate expenditure curve downward and reduce domestic income, resulting in a total or partial offsetting of the expansionary effects of the tax cut.

b. An increase in the money supply would stop interest rates from rising and avert a decline in desired investment.

CHAPTER 26

3. Net exports must equal −$250 in order to have a balance-of-payments equilibrium, so real domestic income must be $3300, derived as follows:

$$\$80 - 0.1Y = -\$250$$
$$Y = (-\$250 - \$80)/-0.2$$
$$Y = \$3300.$$

5. The tax cut is likely to increase the desired consumption portion of aggregate desired expenditure, shifting that schedule upward and increasing real domestic income. An increased domestic income will cause the money demand curve to shift upward to the right. If the money supply is fixed, interest rates will rise, causing desired investment to fall. A drop in desired investment will shift the aggregate expenditure schedule downward and reduce real domestic income, thereby totally or partially offsetting the expansionary effects of the tax cut. The higher interest rates will, however, increase the net capital inflow in the balance of payments. If the balance of payments was previously in equilibrium, a capital surplus may result (assuming that net exports increase less with the probable slight increase in domestic income than does net capital inflow).

CHAPTER 27

8. a. Yes; the level of real domestic income will change by the full amount of the multiplier effect since input-price increases and diminishing productivity do not occur as output increases.

b. No; when the aggregate supply curve slopes upward, costs are rising because of increased input prices and diminishing marginal productivity as output increases. The diminishing productivity and price increases will result in a decline in aggregate desired expenditure, which means that the level of real domestic income will change by less than the amount of the full multiplier effect as a result of the increase in desired government purchases.

10. a. The aggregate demand curve will shift downward and to the left.

b. Real output will decline.

c. The aggregate supply curve will shift downward, probably as a result of declining input prices.

d. The price level is likely to drop as the recession continues and aggregate supply decreases.

Solutions to Effective-Thinking Problems

Problem 1: Rhino Poaching

I. Define the Situation

Who is involved? Rhinoceroses; poachers; game wardens; black-market buyers and sellers.

What is happening? Poachers are killing rhinos for their horns.

Where does the situation occur? In Africa, where rhinos are present in the wild.

Why are rhino horns being poached? Prices for rhino horns are high on the black market; local incomes are low, so selling rhino horns adds greatly to poachers' incomes.

How serious is the problem? Rhinos are rapidly decreasing in number; if poaching continues at the current rate, the species could be eliminated from the wild entirely within a few years.

II. State the Problem and the Goal

Analysis 1 *What might be the problem(s)?*
- there are too few game wardens to successfully protect rhinos in the wild
- poachers are able to get around protective measures set up by wardens
- given current supply and demand conditions, the black market places a high price on rhinoceros horns
- the supply of rhinos is decreasing rapidly as a result of poaching
- rhinos move around and are therefore hard to protect in the wild

Synthesis 2 *What could be the goal(s) you want to achieve?*
- hire more game wardens to protect rhinos from poachers
- find better ways for wardens to protect rhinos from poachers

- change black-market supply and/or demand conditions for rhino horns
- increase the supply of wild rhinos
- find ways to stop rhinos from moving around in the wild

Evaluation 3 *Of all the possible goals in Step 2, which one(s) should you achieve?*
- change black-market supply and/or demand conditions for rhino horns

III. Generate Ideas for Meeting Your Goal in Step 3

Analysis 4 *What problems might be involved in meeting the goal in Step 3?*
- black-market demand for rhino horns is great because many people believe the horns have special properties
- it might be difficult to change the supply of rhino horns on the black market
- high black-market prices provide a continual incentive for poachers to supply horns
- governments lack the income or ability to spend funds to eliminate black markets

Synthesis 5 *What could be done to solve the goal problems in Step 4?*
- provide locals with enough income to make rhino poaching less attractive as a source of extra funds
- reduce or eliminate the poachers' supply of rhino horns by having game wardens surgically remove the horns, making the rhinos undesirable to poachers
- reduce or eliminate the poachers' supply of horns by rounding up all the rhinos and keeping them in captivity
- institute education programs to reduce the demand for rhino horns

Evaluation 6 *Of all the possible solutions to your goal problems in Step 5, what should be done to solve those problems?*

(Assume that the removal of their horns does not endanger the rhinos' health or their ability to survive in the wild.)

- reduce or eliminate the poachers' supply of rhino horns by having game wardens surgically remove the horns, making the rhinos undesirable to poachers

IV. Define the New Situation

Who is involved? Rhinos; poachers; game wardens; black-market buyers and sellers.

What is happening? Poachers are killing rhinos for their horns, but if horns are removed, rhinos have no poaching value; plans call for dehorning wild rhinos.

Where does the situation occur? In Africa, where rhinos are present in the wild.

Why are rhino horns being poached? Prices for horns are high on the black market; local incomes are low, so selling rhino horns adds greatly to poachers' incomes.

How serious is the problem? Rhinos are rapidly decreasing in number; if poaching continues at the current rate, the species could be eliminated from the wild entirely within a few years.

V. Prepare a Plan

(Assume that the costs of dehorning the rhinoceroses are less than the benefits of saving them.)

Analysis 7 *What might be a problem with the new situation?*

- the need for extra funding to catch and dehorn the rhinos
- the need for veterinary advice on dehorning
- the need to train workers and wardens in capturing and dehorning wild rhinos
- wardens may not be able to find the remaining horned rhinos as fast as the poachers can
- monitoring any health problems of dehorned rhinos

Synthesis 8 *What could be part of a plan to solve the new-situation problems identified in Step 7?*

- ask governments and international wildlife agencies to fund the dehorning of rhinos
- ask for international help to quickly find the remaining rhino population
- ask for international help to monitor any health problems of dehorned rhinos

Evaluation 9 *Which of the possible plans in Step 8 should be used to solve the new-situation problems?*

- ask governments and international wildlife agencies to fund the dehorning of rhinos

VI. Take Action

Analysis 10 *What might be a problem with the plan you selected in Step 9?*

- outrage over rhino dehorning by animal-protection groups
- health problems for dehorned wild rhinos
- increased poaching of other animals once rhinos lose their black-market value

Synthesis 11 *What could be becomes reality as you implement the plan.*

- put the rhino-dehorning plan into operation

Evaluation 12 *What should be the next action, once you see the results of the implemented plan?*

- evaluate the change in rhino poaching and in the number of rhinoceros in the wild after a year of the dehorning program
- evaluate changes in the poaching of other wild animals in areas where rhinos were being poached before
- evaluate changes in supply, demand, and equilibrium prices on the black market for rhino horns

Problem 2: Small Business

I. Define the Situation

Who is involved? A friend; a new designer-chair company operating in an imperfectly competitive market; potential buyers of the chair; other chair companies that produce a similar product.

What is involved? Production of output (that is, designer chairs); pricing of the chairs; costs of production; revenue for the business.

How serious are the consequences? The success of your friend's proposed new business; you gain a share of the profits and must pay a share of the losses.

II. State the Problem and the Goal

Analysis 1 *What might be the problem(s)?*
(Assume a desire to maximize profits and minimize losses.)

- knowing the profit-maximizing or loss-minimizing output of chairs
- knowing costs of production for various levels of output
- knowing revenues for various levels of sales
- knowing profits and/or losses for various levels of sales
- knowing the market demand for your chairs
- knowing about products, prices, etc., of competing firms

Synthesis 2 *What could be the goal(s) you want to achieve?*

- find the profit-maximizing or loss-minimizing output of chairs

- determine costs for various levels of output
- determine revenues for various levels of sales
- determine profits and/or losses for various levels of sales
- determine the market demand for your chairs
- get as much information as possible about products, prices, etc., of competing firms

Evaluation 3 *Of all the possible goals in Step 2, which one(s) should you achieve?*

- find the profit-maximizing or loss-minimizing output of chairs
- determine costs for various levels of output
- determine revenues for various levels of sales
- get as much information as possible about products, prices, etc., of competing firms

III. Generate Ideas for Meeting Your Goals in Step 3

Analysis 4 *What problems might be involved in meeting the goals in Step 3?*

- demand for designer chairs can vary with changes in economic conditions
- output decisions can change between the short run and the long run
- competitors' products may influence demand for your chair in ways you may not expect
- demand and cost conditions may differ between the short run and the long run
- estimates of costs and revenues may prove not to have been accurate

Synthesis 5 *What could be done to solve the goal problems in Step 4?*

(Assume an oligopolistic or monopolistically competitive industry — that is, a structure of imperfect competition — where you are one of a number of sellers. This must be the case, since you sell more chairs as your price decreases — that is, you have a downward-sloping demand curve.)

- calculate costs (for example, total costs, average variable costs, average fixed costs, marginal costs) based on best estimates
- calculate revenues (for example, total revenue, marginal revenue) based on best estimates of the market
- calculate profits from best estimates of cost and revenue figures
- develop short-run plans if average variable costs aren't covered in the short run
- calculate revenues and profits under several demand scenarios
- try to estimate competitors' costs and revenues (for example, in the case of possible oligopolistic interdependence)
- advertise to establish your chair as unique — that is, unlike the products produced by your competitors

Evaluation 6 *Of all the possible solutions to your goal problems in Step 5, what should be done to solve those problems?*

- calculate costs (for example, total costs, average variable costs, average fixed costs, marginal costs) based on best estimates (see the graph and table that follow)
- calculate revenues (for example, total revenue, marginal revenue) based on best estimates of the market (see the accompanying table and graph)
- calculate profits from best estimates of cost and revenue figures
- develop short-run plans if average variable costs aren't covered in the short run
- advertise to establish your chair as unique — that is, unlike the products produced by your competitors

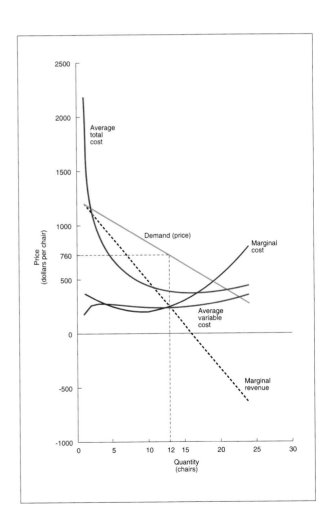

Quantity	Total Variable Cost	Total Fixed Cost	Total Cost	Marginal Cost	Price	Total Revenue	Marginal Revenue	Average Total Cost	Average Variable Cost	Average Fixed Cost	Total Profit
1	$ 180	$2000	$ 2 180		$1200	$1200		$2180.00	$180.00	$2000.00	$ −980
2	520	2000	2 520	$340	1160	2320	$1120	1260.00	260.00	1000.00	−200
3	825	2000	2 825	305	1120	3360	1040	941.67	275.00	666.67	535
4	1100	2000	3 100	275	1080	4320	960	775.00	275.00	500.00	1220
5	1350	2000	3 350	250	1040	5200	880	670.00	270.00	400.00	1850
6	1580	2000	3 580	230	1000	6000	800	596.67	263.33	333.33	2420
7	1795	2000	3 795	215	960	6720	720	542.14	256.43	285.71	2925
8	2000	2000	4 000	205	920	7360	640	500.00	250.00	250.00	3360
9	2200	2000	4 200	200	880	7920	560	466.67	244.44	222.22	3720
10	2405	2000	4 405	205	840	8400	480	440.50	240.50	200.00	3995
11	2620	2000	4 620	215	800	8800	400	420.00	238.18	181.82	4180
12	2850	2000	4 850	230	760	9120	320	404.17	237.50	166.67	4270
13	3100	2000	5 100	250	720	9360	240	392.31	238.46	153.85	4260
14	3375	2000	5 375	275	680	9520	160	383.93	241.07	142.86	4145
15	3680	2000	5 680	305	640	9600	120	378.67	245.33	133.33	3920
16	4020	2000	6 020	340	600	9600	0	376.25	251.25	125.00	3580
17	4400	2000	6 400	380	560	9520	−80	376.47	258.82	117.65	3120
18	4825	2000	6 825	425	520	9360	−160	379.17	268.06	111.11	2535
19	5300	2000	7 300	475	480	9120	−240	384.21	278.95	105.26	1820
20	5830	2000	7 830	530	440	8800	−320	391.50	291.50	100.00	970
21	6420	2000	8 420	590	400	8400	−400	400.95	305.71	95.24	−20
22	7075	2000	9 075	655	360	7920	−480	412.50	321.59	90.91	−1155
23	7800	2000	9 800	725	320	7360	−560	426.09	339.13	86.96	−2440
24	8600	2000	10 600	800	280	6720	−640	441.67	358.33	83.33	−3880

IV. Define the New Situation

Who is involved? A friend; a potential new designer-chair company operating in an imperfectly competitive market; potential buyers of the chair; other chair companies that produce a similar product.

What is involved? Production of output (that is, designer chairs); pricing of the chairs; costs of production; revenue for the business.

How serious are the consequences? The success of your friend's proposed new business; you gain a share of the profits and must pay a share of the losses.

What will be done? Produce twelve chairs to maximize profits based on best estimates of costs, revenues, and the current market for your chair.

V. Prepare a Plan

Analysis 7 *What might be a problem with the new situation?*

- if cost and revenue figures were not accurately estimated, twelve chairs may not be the profit-maximizing or loss-minimizing quantity of output
- it may be difficult to determine price and output information about your competitors in advance

- there may be some oligopolistic interdependence among your firm and competing firms that influences the market in which you operate
- in the short run, you may not cover average total costs or average variable costs; if average variable costs are not covered, you should shut down in the short run to avoid further losses

Synthesis 8 *What could be part of a plan to solve the new-situation problems identified in Step 7?*

- advertise your chair to increase or realize the estimated demand; target the planned ad campaign at likely buyers
- try to determine or anticipate competitors' future price and output decisions
- attempt to establish a shared-monopoly situation in your part of the chair industry

Evaluation 9 *Which of the possible plans in Step 8 should be used to solve the new-situation problems?*

- advertise your chair to increase or realize the estimated demand; target the planned ad campaign at likely buyers
- try to determine or anticipate competitors' future price and output decisions

VI. Take Action

Analysis 10 *What* might *be a problem with the plan you selected in Step 9?*

- your chair may not enjoy the demand you have projected
- you may have to shut down production in the short run if your revenues do not cover average variable costs

Synthesis 11 *What* could be *becomes reality as you implement the plan.*

- start up the chair-manufacturing process to produce twelve chairs, and start the advertising campaign

Evaluation 12 *What* should *be the next action, once you see the results of the implemented plan?*

- reevaluate your cost, revenue, and market-demand estimates every six months
- reevaluate the advertising campaign and the market demand for your chair every six months

Problem 3: Pickled-Cocktail-Onion Firm

I. Define the Situation

Who is involved? A perfectly competitive firm producing cocktail onions (that is, the firm is a price taker); people living near the onion-pickling plant; the government.

What is involved? A short-run situation; production of output; production costs; revenues from production; negative externalities from production for neighbours of the plant.

Where does the situation occur? In and near the onion-pickling plant.

How serious is the problem? Neighbours are suffering discomfort from the chemicals produced in the onion-pickling process and are asking the government to take action.

II. State the Problem and the Goal

Analysis 1 *What* might *be the problem(s)?*

- knowing the profit-maximizing (or loss-minimizing) level of output for the firm
- knowing the firm's costs of production (that is, the firm's private costs)
- knowing the firm's revenues
- knowing the firm's current profits and/or losses
- knowing and assessing the cost of negative externalities of production (that is, identifying total and marginal social costs and total and marginal external costs)
- finding a way to compensate neighbours for the negative externalities of onion production
- knowing the socially optimal level of output for the onion firm

Synthesis 2 *What* could *be the goal(s) you want to achieve?*

- finding the profit-maximizing (or loss-minimizing) level of output for the firm
- determining the firm's costs of production
- determining the firm's revenues
- determining the firm's current profits and/or losses
- determining and assessing the cost of negative externalities of production (that is, identifying total and marginal social costs and total and marginal external costs)
- determining a way to compensate neighbours for the negative externalities of onion production
- determining the socially optimal level of output for the onion firm

Evaluation 3 *Of all the possible goals in Step 2, which one(s) should you achieve?*

- finding the profit-maximizing (or loss-minimizing) level of output for the firm
- determining the firm's costs of production (that is, the firm's private costs)
- determining the firm's revenues
- determining and assessing the cost of negative externalities of production (that is, identifying total and marginal social costs and total and marginal external costs)
- determining the socially optimal level of output for the onion firm

III. Generate Ideas for Meeting Your Goals in Step 3

Analysis 4 *What problems* might *be involved in meeting the goals in Step 3?*

- since the firm is a perfect competitor and therefore a price taker, the market price of $22 may change at any time
- short- and long-run output decisions could differ
- estimates of costs and revenues may prove not to be accurate
- it is difficult to put a monetary value on the discomforts suffered by the plant's neighbours

Synthesis 5 *What* could *be done to solve the goal problems in Step 4?*

- calculate the firm's private costs (for example, total costs, marginal costs, average total costs, average variable costs) based on its estimates of fixed and variable costs
- calculate the firm's revenues (for example, total revenue, marginal revenue) based on data provided
- calculate or estimate the marginal costs to the plant's neighbours who suffer discomforts from the chemicals released in the course of production
- calculate or estimate the marginal and total social costs of the plant's production

Output (cases per week)	Fixed Cost	Variable Cost	Total Cost	Marginal Revenue (price per case)	Total Revenue	Marginal Cost	Total Profit/Loss
30	$1000	$ 240	$1240	$22	$ 660		$ −580
40	1000	360	1360	22	880	$12	−480
50	1000	500	1500	22	1100	14	−400
60	1000	720	1720	22	1320	22	−400
70	1000	1050	2050	22	1540	33	−510
80	1000	1440	2440	22	1760	39	−680
90	1000	1980	2980	22	1980	54	−1000
100	1000	2700	3700	22	2200	72	−1500

Output (cases per week)	Average Total Cost	Average Variable Cost	Total External Cost	Marginal External Cost	Total Social Cost	Marginal Social Cost
30	$41.33	$ 8	$100		$1340	$17
40	34.00	9	150	$5	1510	19
50	30.00	10	200	5	1700	27
60	28.67	12	250	5	1970	38
70	29.29	15	300	5	2350	44
80	30.50	18	350	5	2790	59
90	33.11	22	400	5	3380	77
100	37.00	27	450	5	4150	98

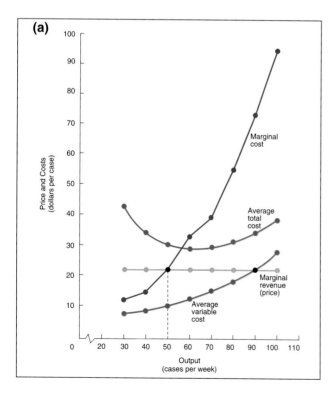

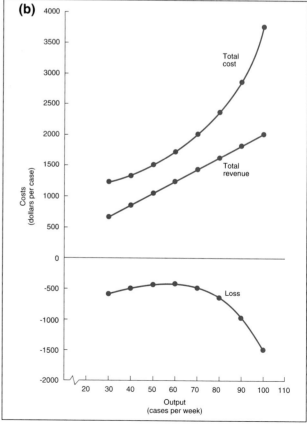

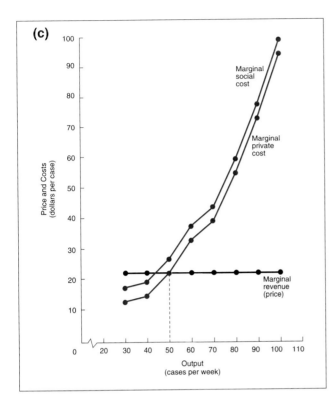

(c)

IV. Define the New Situation

Who is involved? A perfectly competitive firm producing cocktail onions; people living near the onion-pickling plant; the government.

What is involved? A short-run situation; production of output; production costs; revenues from production; negative externalities from production for neighbours of the plant; a loss-minimizing optimal private output of 50 cases per week and a socially optimal output of approximately 44 cases per week.

Where does the situation occur? In and near the onion-pickling plant.

How serious is the problem? Neighbours are suffering discomfort from the chemicals produced in the onion-pickling process and are asking the government to take action.

V. Prepare a Plan

Analysis 7 *What* might *be a problem with the new situation?*

- the firm may not agree to reduce output to the socially optimal level
- neighbours may not agree that the socially optimal level of output is 44 cases per week
- it may be difficult to get the firm and the neighbours to agree on how, if at all, the firm should compensate neighbours for discomforts caused by the plant's production

Synthesis 8 *What* could *be part of a plan to solve the new-situation problems identified in Step 7?*

- get the neighbours and the government to suggest ways the firm could compensate the neighbours if it produces 50 cases per week
- ask the firm for suggestions on how it might compensate the neighbours if it wants to produce 50 cases per week
- have the government require the firm to buy a licence to pollute if it continues to produce output without compensating the neighbours
- tax the firm for the discomfort it causes the neighbours
- move the plant to a new location
- close the plant, since it is taking a loss in the short run

Evaluation 6 *Of all the possible solutions to your goal problems in Step 5, what* should *be done to solve those problems?*

- calculate the firm's private costs (for example, total costs, marginal costs, average total costs, average variable costs) based on its estimates of fixed and variable costs (see the accompanying table and graph [a])
- calculate the firm's current profit or loss based on best estimates of costs and revenues (see the table and graph [b])
- calculate or estimate the marginal costs to the plant's neighbours who suffer discomforts from the chemicals released in the course of production (see the table)
- calculate or estimate the marginal and total social costs of the plant's production (see the table and graph [c])

As the table and graphs illustrate, the firm should produce 50 cases of onions per week to minimize losses. MC = MR at 50 cases, causing a loss of $400, which can be sustained in the short run since total revenue is greater than variable cost. At the current output of 90 cases, the loss is $1000 and MC > MR ($72 > $22). Marginal social costs are calculated by adding marginal private costs and marginal external costs. When marginal social costs are plotted with a price of $22, the optimal output from society's (that is, the neighbours') standpoint is about 44 cases of pickled onions per week.

Evaluation 9 *Which of the possible plans in Step 8* should *be used to solve the new-situation problems?*

- get the neighbours and the government to suggest ways the firm could compensate the neighbours if it produces 50 cases per week
- ask the firm for suggestions on how it might compensate the neighbours if it wants to produce 50 cases per week

- have the government require the firm to buy a licence to pollute if it continues to produce output without compensating the neighbours

VI. Take Action

Analysis 10 *What* might *be a problem with the plan you selected in Step 9?*

- the firm and the neighbours may not reach agreement on the optimal level of output for both
- the government may have trouble determining the appropriate price for the firm's licence to pollute
- some people may still want the plant to close down if it pollutes at all or continues to cause the neighbours discomfort

Synthesis 11 *What* could be *becomes reality as you implement the plan.*

- the firm produces 50 cases of onions per week, having purchased a licence to pollute from the government

Evaluation 12 *What* should *be the next action, once you see the results of the implemented plan?*

- evaluate how the pollution agreement between the firm and the government is working after six months, a year, and so on
- evaluate the firm's profit/loss situation in six months, a year, and so on, since the firm cannot continue to take a loss in the long run

Problem 4: Cost-of-Living Adjustments

I. Define the Situation

Who is involved? A group of northern Manitoba workers; the Winnipeg-based firm that employs them.

What is involved? An appeal for a cost-of-living adjustment for the northern workers; calculation of northern Manitoba cost-of-living increases over a four-year period.

II. State the Problem and the Goal

Analysis 1 *What* might *be the problem(s)?*

- determine the real cost-of-living increases for the northern workers over the four-year period
- determine appropriate price indexes to measure northern Manitoba cost-of-living increases in the area where the workers were employed
- determine whether the cost-of-living adjustments already paid to the northern workers were adequate to compensate them for the northern cost increases
- determine the amount of cost-of-living adjustments paid to other workers in northern Manitoba

Synthesis 2 *What* could *be the goal(s) you want to achieve?*

- estimate the real cost-of-living increases for the northern workers over the four-year period
- estimate appropriate price indexes to measure northern Manitoba cost-of-living increases in the area where the workers were employed
- estimate whether the cost-of-living adjustments already paid to the workers were adequate to compensate them for the northern cost increases
- get records of the cost-of-living adjustments paid to other workers in northern Manitoba during the four-year period

Evaluation 3 *Of all the possible goals in Step 2, which one(s) should you achieve?*

- estimate appropriate price indexes to measure northern Manitoba cost-of-living increases in the area where the workers were employed
- estimate whether the cost-of-living adjustments already paid to the workers were adequate to compensate them for the northern cost increases

III. Generate Ideas for Meeting Your Goals in Step 3

Analysis 4 *What problems* might *be involved in meeting the goals in Step 3?*

- determining a cost-of-living price index that would adequately reflect the price increases experienced by people working in northern Manitoba

Synthesis 5 *What* could *be done to solve the goal problem in Step 4?*

- calculate an exact cost-of-living price index specifically for the area of northern Manitoba where the workers were employed
- use an average of several relevant price indexes to calculate a cost-of-living price index that would approximate price increases in the area of northern Manitoba where the workers were employed

Evaluation 6 *Of the two possible solutions to your goal problems in Step 5, what should be done to solve those goal problems?*

- Use an average of several relevant price indexes to calculate a cost-of-living price index that would approximate price increases in the area of northern Manitoba where the workers were employed

Sample calculations to approximate a cost-of-living index for the northern workers over the four-year period:

Take a simple average of several available indexes. The most likely choices would be the following: (1) the CPI for Winnipeg; (2) the CPI for Yellowknife; and (3) the CPI for Canada. The Canadian Wholesale Price Index and the GDP deflator are not sufficiently relevant to cost-of-living increases in northern Manitoba. It could even be argued that the CPI for Canada as a whole is not sufficiently relevant either, since it reflects so many southern urban areas.

A simple average of the Winnipeg CPI (15 percent inflation over four years) and the Yellowknife CPI (17.8 percent) is 16.4 percent inflation. When the Canadian CPI is added and averaged, the inflation average drops to 16.27 percent for the four years. The workers have already received a 15 percent cost-of-living adjustment, which would mean, according to these calculations, that they have been undercompensated for the cost of northern living by either 1.4 percent or 1.27 percent.

IV. Define the New Situation

Who is involved? A group of northern Manitoba workers; the Winnipeg-based firm that employs them.

What is involved? An appeal for a cost-of-living adjustment for the northern workers; calculation of northern Manitoba cost-of-living increases over a four-year period; a justifiable request by the northern workers for a lump-sum cost-of-living adjustment of 1.4 percent (or 1.27 percent).

V. Prepare a Plan

Analysis 7 *What* might *be a problem with the new situation?*
• the Winnipeg firm does not agree that the price indexes used accurately reflect the northern Manitoba cost-of-living increases over the four-year period
• the Winnipeg firm wants to increase current wages and salaries by 1.4 percent (or 1.27 percent) immediately, without making a lump-sum payment for the past four years
• the Winnipeg firm agrees to provide a lump-sum retroactive payment calculated from different price indexes.

Synthesis 8 *What* could *be part of the plan to solve the new-situation problems identified in Step 7?*
• try to convince the Winnipeg firm that the price indexes used accurately reflect northern Manitoba cost-of-living increases over the four-year period
• calculate the loss or gain to northern workers if the firm increases wages and salaries by 1.4 percent (or 1.27 percent) immediately, without making a lump-sum payment to cover the past four years

Evaluation 9 *Which of the possible plans in Step 8 should* be used to solve the new-situation *problems?*
• try to convince the Winnipeg firm that the price indexes used accurately reflect the northern Manitoba cost-of-living increases over the four-year period

VI. Take Action

Analysis 10 *What* might *be a problem with the plan you selected in Step 9?*
• the firm may not agree to the cost-of-living adjustments and other calculations, so some form of labour action may be necessary

Synthesis 11 *What* could be *becomes reality as you implement the plan.*
• Present the cost-of-living calculations to the workers and the firm

Evaluation 12 *What should* be the next action, once you see the results of the implemented plan?
• evaluate the reaction of the firm to the cost-of-living calculations and be prepared to provide additional information or calculations on behalf of the workers

Problem 5: Target Income

I. Define the Situation

Who or what is involved? Federal Department of Finance policy makers; the entire economy.

What is happening? Unemployment is at an unacceptable level of 15 percent nationally; a higher level of GDP ($560 billion) is predicted to result in acceptable levels of employment.

Where does the situation occur? In the economy as a whole.

How serious is the problem? Unemployment will remain unacceptably high if the economy is not stimulated through fiscal policy.

II. State the Problem and the Goal

Analysis 1 *What* might *be the problem(s)?*
• reducing unemployment to acceptable levels
• reducing unemployment without increasing inflation
• finding the appropriate target level of GDP

Synthesis 2 *What* could *be the goal(s) you want to achieve?*
• stimulate the economy enough to reduce unemployment to acceptable levels
• stimulate the economy to reduce unemployment without increasing inflation
• find the appropriate target level of GDP

Evaluation 3 *Of all the possible goals in Step 2, which one(s) should* you achieve?
• stimulate the economy enough to reduce unemployment to acceptable levels

III. Generate Ideas for Meeting Your Goal in Step 3

(Assume that the target level of GDP that will reduce unemployment to acceptable levels is $560 billion.)

Analysis 4 *What problems* might *be involved in meeting the goal in Step 3?*
- determining the amount of change in government spending needed to reduce unemployment to acceptable levels
- determining the amount of change in taxation needed to reduce unemployment to acceptable levels
- getting unemployment rates down to acceptable levels within a specified period of time
- determining the present equilibrium level of GDP

Synthesis 5 *What could be done to solve the goal problems in Step 4?*
- determine the expenditure multiplier for the economy
- determine the net-tax multiplier for the economy
- calculate the change in government spending needed to reach the target income level of $560 billion, given the expenditure multiplier
- calculate the change in net taxation needed to reach the target income level of $560 billion, given the net-tax multiplier
- calculate the present equilibrium level of GDP

Evaluation 6 *Of all the possible solutions to your goal problems in Step 5, what should be done to solve those problems?*
- determine the expenditure multiplier for the economy
  [First, calculate MPC − MPM = MPC_D (0.75 − 0.25 = 0.5); then, calculate the multiplier: $1/1 − MPC_D = 1/1 − 0.5 = 2$.]
- calculate the change in government spending needed to reach the target income of $560 billion, given the expenditure multiplier
  [Since the change desired is $60 billion (that is, $560 − $500) and the expenditure multiplier is 2, a $30 billion change in desired government spending is required.]
- calculate the present equilibrium level of GDP
  [$500 billion = 440 + 25 + 40 + (40 − 45)$]

IV. Define the New Situation

Who is involved? Federal Department of Finance policy makers; the entire economy.

What is happening? Changes in government spending are being used to stimulate the economy to an equilibrium level of GDP of $560 billion; the expenditure multiplier has been calculated to be 2; and the present equilibrium level of GDP is $500 billion.

Where does the situation occur? In the economy as a whole.

How serious is the problem? Unemployment will remain unacceptably high if the economy is not stimulated through fiscal policy.

V. Prepare a Plan

Analysis 7 *What* might *be a problem with the new situation?*
- getting the fiscal-policy measures in place to stimulate the economy appropriately
- avoiding overshooting the target level of income (stimulating the economy too much could cause inflation to increase)
- avoiding undershooting the target level of income (stimulating the economy too little could result in a failure to lower the unemployment rate to an acceptable level)

Synthesis 8 *What could be part of a plan to solve the new-situation problems identified in Step 7?*
- increase government spending by $30 billion to stimulate the economy by a total of $60 billion
- increase government spending by less than $30 billion to make sure the economy is not stimulated too much
- increase government spending by more than $30 billion to make sure the economy is stimulated by at least $60 billion

Evaluation 9 *Which of the possible plans in Step 8 should be used to solve the new-situation problems?*
- increase government spending by $30 billion to stimulate the economy by a total of $60 billion

VI. Take Action

Analysis 10 *What* might *be a problem with the plan you selected in Step 9?*
- the timing of the increases in government spending might prevent unemployment from being reduced sufficiently within the time period selected
- the economy may be stimulated too much, and inflation may increase
- the economy may be stimulated too little, and unemployment may not fall to an acceptable level

Synthesis 11 *What could* be *becomes reality as you implement the plan.*
- implement 30 billion dollars' worth of desired government-spending programs

Evaluation 12 *What should be the next action, once you see the results of the implemented plan?*
- evaluate the timing and results of the $30 billion government-spending increase

Problem 6: Monetary Policy

I. Define the Situation

Who is involved? The Bank of Canada; the U.S. Federal Reserve; Canadian federal and provincial governments; private investors; the foreign-exchange markets; Canadian consumers.

What happened? Expansionary fiscal policy financed by new debt is causing fears of increased inflation.

How serious are the consequences? Inflation rates may increase, private investment may be crowded out by government borrowing, current- and capital-account positions in the balance of payments may change, the exchange rate for the Canadian dollar may change.

When did this happen? Over the past year.

II. State the Problem and the Goal

Analysis 1 *What might be the problem(s)?*
- inflation rates may increase
- private investment may be crowded out by government borrowing
- the government debt may increase faster than desired
- changes in the value of the Canadian dollar may disrupt foreign trade
- the balance of payments may become unstable, causing major changes in the official-reserves account
- unemployment rates could stop falling or start to rise
- real GDP should continue to grow at a positive rate to allow private investment and employment opportunities

Synthesis 2 *What could be the goal(s) you want to achieve?*
- ensure that inflation rates continue to fall
- stop private investment from being crowded out by government borrowing
- stop the government debt from increasing faster than desired
- ensure that any changes in the value of the Canadian dollar are kept small, in order not to disrupt foreign trade
- ensure that the balance of payments does not become unstable and cause major changes in the official-reserves account
- ensure that unemployment rates remain steady at low rates
- ensure that real GDP continues to grow at a positive rate to allow private investment and employment opportunities

Evaluation 3 *Of all the possible goals in Step 2, which one(s) should you achieve?*
- ensure that inflation rates continue to fall

- ensure that real GDP continues to grow at a positive rate to allow private investment and employment opportunities

III. Generate Ideas for Meeting Your Goals in Step 3

Analysis 4 *What problems might be involved in meeting the goals in Step 3?*
- expansionary fiscal policy by the federal and provincial governments may cause inflation to speed up
- lower inflation rates may cause unemployment to rise
- if it is too rapid, real GDP growth may fuel inflation

Synthesis 5 *What could be done to solve the goal problems in Step 4?*
- employ contractionary monetary policy (involving, for example, the sale of government securities on the open market or draw-downs of federal deposits in chartered banks) to help control rising inflation
- urge the federal and provincial governments to increase spending on job-creation programs
- lower interest rates to stimulate private investment, which might reduce unemployment
- balance monetary policy and expansionary fiscal policy in order to prevent real GDP from growing so fast that it causes increased inflation
- monitor inflation rates in other nations (especially those with which Canada trades heavily) to anticipate needed adjustments in Canadian monetary policy
- monitor interest rates in other nations (especially those with which Canada trades heavily) to anticipate needed adjustments in Canadian monetary policy

Evaluation 6 *Of all possible solutions to your goal problems in Step 5, what should be done to solve those problems?*
- employ contractionary monetary policy to help control rising inflation
- balance monetary policy and expansionary fiscal policy in order to prevent real GDP from growing so fast that it causes increased inflation
- monitor inflation rates in other nations (especially those with which Canada trades heavily) to anticipate needed adjustments in Canadian monetary policy

If graphs are used, they should illustrate the monetary-policy suggestions chosen in Step 6. Ideally, the graphs should reflect the transmission effect of general-equilibrium analysis, showing how changes in the money market (the MS–MD graph) cause changes in interest rates, which in turn affect desired investment and, hence, aggregate desired expenditure and the income level (which, finally, have an impact on money demand).

IV. Define the New Situation

Who is involved? The Bank of Canada; the U.S. Federal Reserve; Canadian federal and provincial governments; private investors; foreign-exchange markets; Canadian consumers.

What happened? Expansionary fiscal policy financed by new debt is causing fears of increased inflation.

How serious are the consequences? Inflation may increase, private investment may be crowded out by government borrowing, current and capital account positions in the balance of payments may change, the exchange rate for the Canadian dollar may change.

When did this happen? Over the past year.

What can be done? Contractionary monetary policy and/or a balancing of monetary and fiscal policy can be implemented to offset the inflationary effects of expansionary fiscal policy.

V. Prepare a Plan

Analysis 7 *What* might *be a problem with the new situation?*

• contractionary monetary policy may slow the economy to the point that the unemployment rate rises
• contractionary monetary policy may not be able to slow the economy enough in the face of expansionary fiscal policy to reduce inflation rates
• inflation rates in other nations with which Canada trades may speed up so much that Canada may not be able to slow its own inflation (in other words, Canada may import inflation from its trading partners)
• interest rates in other nations — especially the United States — may change, forcing Canada to change its interest rates to ensure an adequate capital-account surplus

Synthesis 8 *What* could *be part of the plan to solve the new-situation problems identified in Step 7?*

• monitor the combined effects of contractionary monetary policy and expansionary fiscal policy on inflation and unemployment rates, the balance-of-payments accounts, and the exchange rate

• try to limit trade with nations that have high rates of inflation
• let the exchange rate float to help keep the current account in check (in other words, let exchange rates reflect the difference in buying power and inflation between Canada and its trading partners)

Evaluation 9 *Which of the possible plans in Step 8 should* be used to solve the new-situation problems?

• monitor the combined effects of contractionary monetary policy and expansionary fiscal policy on inflation and unemployment rates, the balance-of-payments accounts, and the exchange rate
• let the exchange rate float to help keep the current account in check (in other words, let exchange rates reflect the difference in buying power and inflation between Canada and its trading partners)

VI. Take Action

Analysis 10 *What* might *be a problem with the plan you selected in Step 9?*

• monetary policy may not be successful in counteracting the expansionary fiscal policy, and inflation may increase
• the Canadian dollar may move so much on foreign-exchange markets that foreign trade is hindered
• contractionary monetary policy may cause domestic interest rates to rise so high that private investment is hindered and unemployment increases

Synthesis 11 *What* could be *becomes reality as you implement the plan.*

• implement contractionary monetary policy

Evaluation 12 *What* should *be the next action, once you see the results of the implemented plan?*

• constantly monitor the effects of contractionary monetary policy on inflation, unemployment, real GDP growth, the balance of payments, and the value of the Canadian dollar in foreign-exchange markets

To the Owner of This Book

We are interested in your reaction to *Economics: Understanding the Canadian Economy*, Fourth Edition, by Roy Vogt, Beverly J. Cameron, and Edwin G. Dolan. With your comments, we can improve this book in future editions. Please help us by completing this questionnaire.

1. Which school do you attend?

2. What was the name of the course in which you used this textbook?

3. How helpful were the effective-thinking problems and skills introduced in the text? Can you suggest any improvements?

4. Did you find the use of colour helpful in learning economics?

5. Were any chapters or sections omitted from your course? If so, which ones?

6. Did you find the book clear and easy to understand?

7. Did you use the Study Guide? If so, please comment on its effectiveness as a learning aid.

8. Are there any improvements you would like to suggest for future editions?

(fold here and tape shut)